Profile from Child Behavior Checklist (CBCL): Syndrome Scales

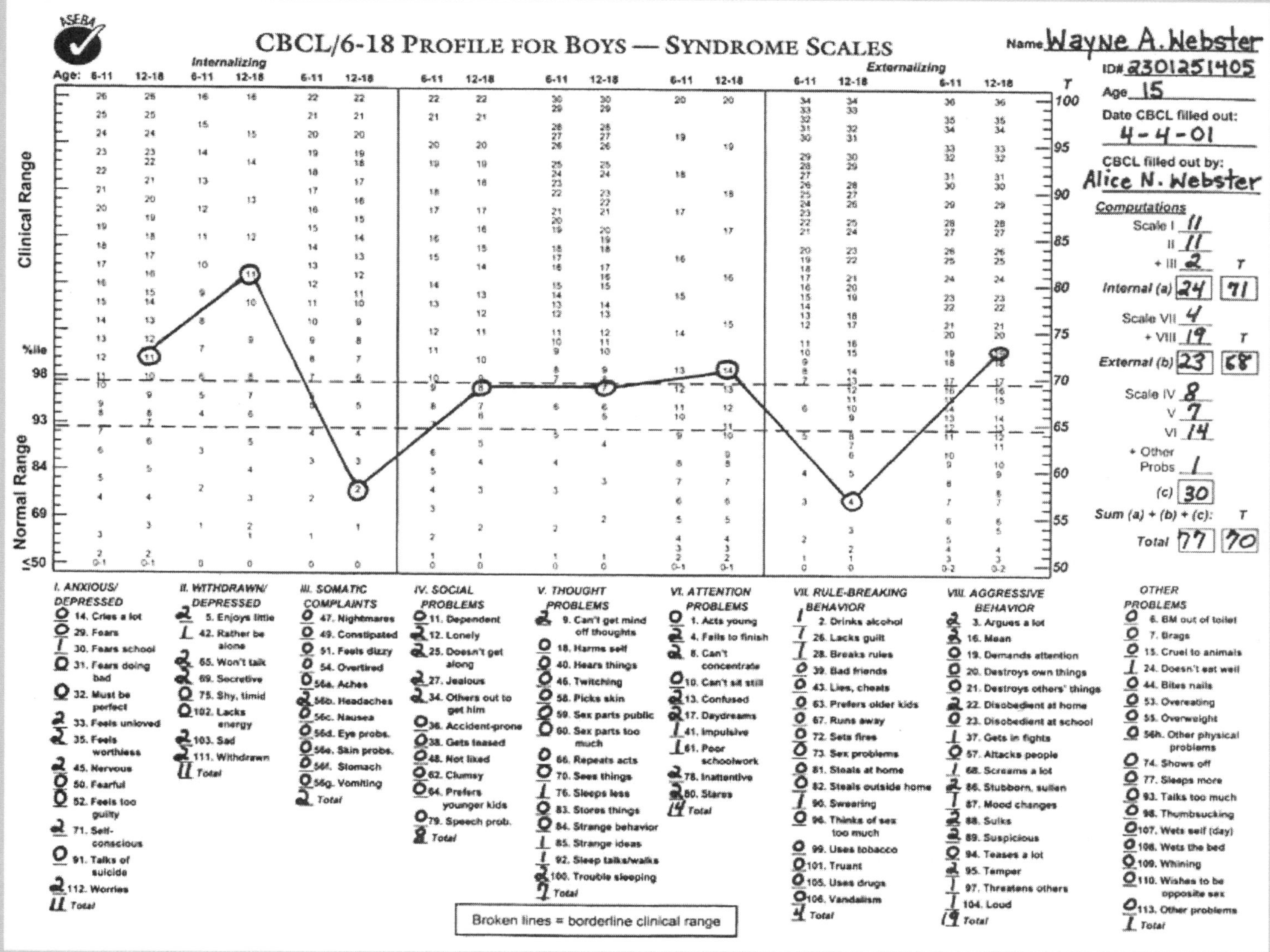

ASEBA

CBCL/6-18 PROFILE FOR BOYS — SYNDROME SCALES

Name Wayne A. Webster
ID# 2301251405
Age 15
Date CBCL filled out: 4-4-01
CBCL filled out by: Alice N. Webster

Computations
Scale I 11
II 11
+ III 2
Internal (a) 24 T 71
Scale VII 4
+ VIII 19
External (b) 23 T 68
Scale IV 8
V 7
VI 14
+ Other Probs 1
(c) 30
Sum (a) + (b) + (c): Total 77 T 70

Internalizing / Externalizing
Clinical Range / Normal Range
%ile: 98, 93, 84, 69, ≤50
T: 100, 95, 90, 85, 80, 75, 70, 65, 60, 55, 50

I. ANXIOUS/DEPRESSED
0 14. Cries a lot
0 29. Fears
1 30. Fears school
0 31. Fears doing bad
0 32. Must be perfect
2 33. Feels unloved
2 35. Feels worthless
2 45. Nervous
0 50. Fearful
0 52. Feels too guilty
2 71. Self-conscious
0 91. Talks of suicide
2 112. Worries
11 Total

II. WITHDRAWN/DEPRESSED
2 5. Enjoys little
1 42. Rather be alone
2 65. Won't talk
2 69. Secretive
0 75. Shy, timid
0 102. Lacks energy
2 103. Sad
2 111. Withdrawn
11 Total

III. SOMATIC COMPLAINTS
0 47. Nightmares
0 49. Constipated
0 51. Feels dizzy
0 54. Overtired
0 56a. Aches
2 56b. Headaches
0 56c. Nausea
0 56d. Eye probs.
0 56e. Skin probs.
0 56f. Stomach
0 56g. Vomiting
2 Total

IV. SOCIAL PROBLEMS
0 11. Dependent
2 12. Lonely
2 25. Doesn't get along
2 27. Jealous
2 34. Others out to get him
0 36. Accident-prone
0 38. Gets teased
0 48. Not liked
0 62. Clumsy
0 64. Prefers younger kids
0 79. Speech prob.
8 Total

V. THOUGHT PROBLEMS
2 9. Can't get mind off thoughts
0 18. Harms self
0 40. Hears things
0 46. Twitching
0 58. Picks skin
0 59. Sex parts public
0 60. Sex parts too much
0 66. Repeats acts
0 70. Sees things
1 76. Sleeps less
0 83. Stores things
0 84. Strange behavior
1 85. Strange ideas
1 92. Sleep talks/walks
2 100. Trouble sleeping
7 Total

VI. ATTENTION PROBLEMS
0 1. Acts young
2 4. Fails to finish
2 8. Can't concentrate
0 10. Can't sit still
2 13. Confused
2 17. Daydreams
1 41. Impulsive
1 61. Poor schoolwork
2 78. Inattentive
2 80. Stares
14 Total

VII. RULE-BREAKING BEHAVIOR
1 2. Drinks alcohol
1 26. Lacks guilt
1 28. Breaks rules
0 39. Bad friends
0 43. Lies, cheats
0 63. Prefers older kids
0 67. Runs away
0 72. Sets fires
0 73. Sex problems
0 81. Steals at home
0 82. Steals outside home
1 90. Swearing
0 96. Thinks of sex too much
0 99. Uses tobacco
0 101. Truant
0 105. Uses drugs
0 106. Vandalism
4 Total

VIII. AGGRESSIVE BEHAVIOR
2 3. Argues a lot
2 16. Mean
0 19. Demands attention
0 20. Destroys own things
0 21. Destroys others' things
2 22. Disobedient at home
0 23. Disobedient at school
1 37. Gets in fights
0 57. Attacks people
1 68. Screams a lot
2 86. Stubborn, sullen
1 87. Mood changes
2 88. Sulks
2 89. Suspicious
0 94. Teases a lot
2 95. Temper
1 97. Threatens others
1 104. Loud
19 Total

OTHER PROBLEMS
0 6. BM out of toilet
0 7. Brags
0 15. Cruel to animals
1 24. Doesn't eat well
0 44. Bites nails
0 53. Overeating
0 55. Overweight
0 56h. Other physical problems
0 74. Shows off
0 77. Sleeps more
0 93. Talks too much
0 98. Thumbsucking
0 107. Wets self (day)
0 108. Wets the bed
0 109. Whining
0 110. Wishes to be opposite sex
0 113. Other problems
1 Total

Broken lines = borderline clinical range

Hand-scored Syndrome Profile from CBCL completed for Wayne Webster by his mother.
From Achenbach, T. M., & Rescorla, L. A. (2001). *Manual for the ASEBA school-age forms & profiles: An integrated system of multi-informant assessment*. Burlington VT: ASEBA, p. 23.

Abnormal Child Psychology

FIFTH EDITION

Eric J. Mash
Oregon Health & Science University
and
University of Calgary

David A. Wolfe
Centre for Addiction and Mental Health
and
University of Toronto

Australia • Brazil • Japan • Korea • Mexico • Singapore • Spain • United Kingdom • United States

Abnormal Child Psychology, Fifth Edition
Eric J. Mash and David A. Wolfe

Publisher: Jon-David Hague

Executive Editor: Jaime Perkins

Associate Development Editor: Nicolas Albert

Assistant Editor: Lauren Moody

Editorial Assistant: Jessica Alderman

Media Editor: Lauren Keyes

Marketing Communications Manager: Laura Localio

Marketing Program Manager: Janay A. Pryor

Content Project Manager: Charlene M. Carpentier

Art Director: Vernon Boes

Manufacturing Planner: Karen Hunt

Rights Acquisitions Specialist: Tom McDonough

Production Services and Composition: S4Carlisle Publishing Services

Photo Researcher: Bill Smith Studio

Text Researcher: Sue Howard

Copy Editor: Mark Kwicinski

Art Editor: Lisa Torri

Illustrator: Precision Graphics

Text Designer: Liz Harasymczuk

Cover Designer: Cheryl Carrington

Cover Image: Masterfile/Royalty Free; Digital Vision

Library of Congress Control Number: 2012933865

Student Edition:
ISBN-13: 978-1-111-83449-4
ISBN-10: 1-111-83449-0

Loose-leaf Edition:
ISBN-13: 978-1-133-59063-7
ISBN-10: 1-133-59063-2

Wadsworth
20 Davis Drive
Belmont, CA 94002-3098
USA

Cengage Learning is a leading provider of customized learning solutions with office locations around the globe, including Singapore, the United Kingdom, Australia, Mexico, Brazil, and Japan. Locate your local office at **www.cengage.com/global.**

Cengage Learning products are represented in Canada by Nelson Education, Ltd.

To learn more about Wadsworth, visit **www.cengage.com/Wadsworth**
Purchase any of our products at your local college store or at our preferred online store **www.CengageBrain.com.**

Printed in the United States of America
2 3 4 5 6 7 16 15 14 13 12

Brief Contents

Contents

PART 3

Emotional Disorders

Cases by Chapter

Chapter 12 Health-Related and Substance Use Disorders

Chapter 13 Eating Disorders and Related Conditions

Chapter 14 Child Maltreatment and Non-Accidental Trauma

Cases by Clinical Aspect

Diagnosis

Causes

Comorbidity

Developmental Pathways

Risk and Protective Factors

Gender

Treatment

Intervention and Prevention

Preface

We are delighted with the momentous success of *Abnormal Child Psychology*, leading to the release of this fifth edition. Over the past 15 years we have become closely connected to the diversity and significance of topics covered by this vibrant and active field, which (in our humble opinion) has established essential core knowledge for students interested in the many diverse areas of psychology that are influenced by normal and abnormal developmental processes. To keep pace with this expanding knowledge base we have reviewed literally thousands of new studies across major and minor areas in this field, resulting in the most up-to-date and comprehensive text on the market.

The positive reception to previous editions of our book and the helpful feedback from students and instructors continues to shape *Abnormal Child Psychology* into a comprehensive yet student-friendly textbook. The fifth edition maintains its focus on the child, not just the disorders, while continuing to keep the text on the cutting edge of scholarly and practical advancements in the field. Because reading textbooks can be demanding, we think you will find that the new full color presentation, graphics, and artwork increase your engagement with and enjoyment of the material from the moment you pick up the book.

This edition continues to expand on important new developments over the past few years such as recent findings on diagnosis, prevalence, causes, subtypes, comorbidity, developmental pathways, risk and protective factors, gender, ethnicity, evidence-based treatments, and early intervention and prevention. Notably, a recent upsurge of research into the role of genes and gene–environment interactions (G × E) as well as new studies of brain structure, functioning, and connectivity have contributed enormously to our understanding of the childhood disorders covered in this book.

At the same time, the fifth edition retains the hallmark features that make it one of the most successful texts in courses on child psychopathology, abnormal child and adolescent psychology, developmental psychopathology, atypical development, and behavior disorders of childhood and adolescence. Among these features are engaging first-person accounts and case histories designed to create powerful links between key topics and the experiences of individual children and their families. The features that follow are also foundational to the text.

Attention to Advances in Abnormal Child and Adolescent Psychology

The past decade has produced extraordinary advances in understanding the special issues pertaining to abnormal child and adolescent psychology. Today, we have a much better ability to distinguish among different disorders of children and adolescents, which has given rise to increased recognition of poorly understood or under-detected problems such as childhood depression and bipolar disorder, teen suicide and substance abuse, eating disorders, disruptive behavior disorders, autism spectrum disorders, learning disorders, and problems stemming from chronic health problems and child maltreatment. Similarly, the field is now more aware of the ways children's and adolescents' psychological disorders are distinguishable from those of adults, and how important it is to maintain a strong developmental perspective in understanding the course of childhood disorders over the lifespan.

In a relatively short time, the study of abnormal child psychology has moved well beyond the individual child and family to consider the roles of community, social, and cultural influences in an integrative and developmentally sensitive manner. Similarly, those of us working in this field are more attuned to the many struggles faced by children and adolescents with psychological disorders and their families, as well as to the demands and costs such problems place on the mental health, education, medical, and juvenile justice systems.

A Focus on the Child, Not Just the Disorders

We believe that one of the best ways to introduce students to a particular problem of childhood or adolescence is to describe a real child. Clinical descriptions, written in an accessible, engaging fashion, help students understand a child's problem in context, and provide a framework from which to explore the complete nature of the disorder. In each chapter, we introduce case examples of children and adolescents with disorders from our own clinical files and from those of colleagues. We then refer to these children when describing the course of the disorder, which provides the student with a well-rounded picture of the child or adolescent in the context of his or her family, peers, community, and culture.

In addition to clinical case material, we use extracts, quotes, and photos throughout each chapter to help the student remain focused on the real challenges faced by children with disorders and their families. First-person accounts and case descriptions enrich the reader's understanding of the daily lives of children and adolescents with problems, and allow for a more realistic portrayal of individual strengths and limitations.

A Comprehensive and Integrative Approach

To reflect the expansion of this field, the causes and effects of various childhood disorders are explained from an integrative perspective that recognizes biological, psychological, social, and emotional influences and their interdependence. This strategy was further guided by a consideration of developmental processes that shape and are shaped by the expression of each disorder. The broader contexts of family, peers, school, community, culture, and society that affect development are also important considerations for understanding child and adolescent disorders, and are a critical feature of this text.

We use both categorical and dimensional approaches in describing disorders, because each method offers unique and important definitions and viewpoints. Each topic area is defined using DSM criteria accompanied by clinical descriptions, examples, and empirically derived dimensions. The clinical features of each disorder are described in a manner that allows students to gain a firm grasp of the basic dimensions and expression of the disorder across its life span. Since children and adolescents referred for psychological services typically show symptoms that overlap into more than one diagnostic category, each chapter discusses common comorbidities and developmental norms that help inform diagnostic decisions.

Attention to Both Developmental Pathways and Adult Outcomes

To provide balance, we approach each disorder from the perspective of the whole child. Diagnostic criteria are accompanied by added emphasis on the strengths of the individual and on the environmental circumstances that influence the developmental course. The developmental course of each disorder is followed from its early beginnings in infancy and childhood through adolescence and into early adulthood, highlighting the special issues pertaining to younger and older age groups and the risk and protective factors affecting developmental pathways. In this manner, we examine developmental continuities and discontinuities and attempt to understand why some children with problems continue to experience difficulties as adolescents and adults, whereas others do not.

Emphasis on Diversity

The importance of recognizing diversity in understanding and helping children with problems and their families is emphasized throughout. New research continues to inform and increase our understanding of the crucial role that factors such socioeconomic status (SES), gender, sexual orientation, race, ethnicity, and culture play in the identification, expression, prevalence, causes, treatments, and outcomes for child and adolescent problems. To sharpen our emphasis on these factors, we were fortunate to receive input from Sumru Erkut, Ph.D., of Wellesley College, an expert in diversity and abnormal child development. As a result of Dr. Erkut's input, we examine differences related to SES, gender, race, ethnicity, and culture for each childhood problem under discussion. In addition, we also recognize the importance of studying distinct groups in their own right as a way of understanding the processes associated with specific problems for each gender, ethnic, or cultural group. While emphasizing new knowledge about diversity issues and childhood disorders, we also caution throughout this text that relatively few studies have examined the attitudes, behaviors, and biological and psychological processes of children and adolescents with mental disorders and problems across different cultures, and we indicate places where this situation is beginning to change.

Coverage of Child Maltreatment and Relationship-Based Disorders

A distinguishing feature of this textbook is its expansion and emphasis on several of the more recent and important areas of developmental psychopathology that do not easily fit into a deficits model or a categorical approach. These problems are sometimes referred to as relationship-based disorders, because they illustrate how some types of childhood problems are a function of their relationships with significant others. Along with recognition of the importance of biological dispositions in guiding development and behavior, we discuss the strong connection between children's behavior patterns and the availability of a suitable child-rearing environment, and how early experience can influence both gene expression and brain development. Students are made aware of how children's overt symptoms can sometimes be adaptive in particular settings or in caregiving relationships that are atypical or abusive, and how traditional diagnostic labels may not be helpful.

Integration of Treatment and Prevention

Treatment and prevention approaches are integral parts of understanding a particular disorder. Applying knowledge of the clinical features and developmental courses of childhood disorders to benefit children with these problems and their families always intrigues students and helps them make greater sense of the material. Therefore, we emphasize current approaches to treatment and prevention in each chapter, where such information can be tailored to the particular childhood problem. Consistent with current health system demands for accountability, we discuss best practice guidelines and emphasize interventions for which there is empirical support.

A Flexible, Even More User-Friendly Text

The book is organized into a logical five-part framework to facilitate understanding of the individual disorders and mastery of the material overall. Following the introductory chapters that comprise Part I, the contents can be readily assigned to students in any order that suits the goals and preferences of the instructor. An overview of the book's five parts follows:

I. Understanding Abnormal Child Psychology (definitions, theories, clinical description, research, assessment, and treatment issues);

II. Behavioral Disorders (attention-deficit/hyperactivity disorders and conduct problems);

III. Emotional Disorders (anxiety and mood disorders);

IV. Developmental and Learning Disorders (intellectual disabilities, autism spectrum disorders, childhood-onset schizophrenia, and communication and learning disorders);

V. Problems Related to Physical and Mental Health (health-related and substance use disorders, eating disorders, and child maltreatment and non-accidental trauma).

The overall length of the text is completely student-centered and manageable without sacrificing academic standards of content and coverage. Dozens of first-person accounts and case histories help students grasp the real-world impact of disorders. Two guides—"Cases by Chapter" and "Cases by Clinical Aspect"—have been provided at the front of the text to help teachers and students navigate the book as easily as possible.

Additionally, chapters are consistently organized to help instructors avoid assigning sections of each chapter (e.g., biological causes) that may not appeal to the level of their students, or that address particular subtopics that fall outside the parameters of a given course (e.g., childhood-onset schizophrenia or pediatric bipolar disorder). For instructors wanting a more detailed presentation of research findings, supplementary readings can be drawn from the many up-to-date citations of original research.

Related but less critical information that enhances each topic appears in "A Closer Look" boxes, so that students can easily recognize that the material is presented to add further insight or examples to the major content areas of the chapter.

Finally, chapters provide many useful pedagogical features to help make students' encounters with and learning of the material an agreeable experience: *key terms* are highlighted and defined where they appear in the text, listed at the chapter's end, and defined in a separate glossary at the back of the book to help students grasp important terminology; DSM-IV-TR tables are provided in addition to general tables to summarize diagnostic criteria; *bullet points* guide students to key concepts throughout the chapters; and interim "Section Summaries" help students consolidate each chapter's key concepts. In addition to the lists of key terms, students will find a listing of "Section Summaries" at the end of each chapter for easy reference while studying.

Summary of Key Features

- "A Closer Look" boxes, previously mentioned, are found throughout the book to draw students into the material and enrich each topic with engaging information. Some examples include: "What Are the Long-Term Criminal Consequences of Child Maltreatment?" "Common Fears in Infancy, Childhood, and Adolescence," and "Did Darwin Have a Panic Disorder?"
- Visual learning aids such as cartoons, tables, and eye-catching chapter- and section-opening quotes, as well as numerous photos and figures, now in full color, illustrate key concepts throughout the text to complement student understanding.
- The authors' in-depth coverage of the role of the normal developmental process in understanding each disorder, as well as their close attention to

important sex differences in the expression, determinants, and outcomes of child and adolescent disorders, promote greater understanding.

- Current findings regarding the reliability and validity of DSM diagnostic criteria for specific disorders are discussed, with inclusion of a website address where students can track the development of DSM-5, which is scheduled to appear in 2013 (http://www.dsm5.org/Pages/Default.aspx).

Notable Content Changes and Updates in the Fifth Edition

Highlights of the content changes and updates to this edition include the following:

- The most current information concerning prevalence, age of onset, and gender distribution for each disorder, including a discussion of issues surrounding the reported increase in prevalence of autistic spectrum disorders.
- Enriched coverage of gender and culture appears in each chapter and includes exciting new findings related to the expression, development, and adolescent outcomes for girls with ADHD, conduct problems, and anxiety and mood disorders, and for children from different ethnic and cultural groups.
- The most recent theories about developmental pathways for different disorders, including the childhood precursors of eating disorders.
- Integrative developmental frameworks for ADHD, conduct problems, anxiety disorders, depression, autism, and child maltreatment.
- Exciting new findings on the interplay between early experience and brain development, including how early stressors, such as abuse, alter the brain systems associated with regulating stress and place the child at risk for developing later problems, such as anxiety or mood disorders.
- Recent genetic discoveries regarding neurodevelopmental disabilities such as autism spectrum disorders, ADHD, and learning and communication disorders.
- Findings from neuroimaging studies of ADHD, autism spectrum disorders, anxiety, and depression that illuminate neurobiological causes.
- New information on family factors in externalizing and internalizing disorders, and in developmental disabilities.
- New findings on subtypes for disorders such as ADHD, oppositional defiant disorder, and conduct disorders.
- Recent findings on the development of precursors of psychopathy.
- Recent findings on patterns of use and misuse of medications for treating ADHD and childhood depression.
- New definitions of intellectual disabilities and adaptive behavior.
- Current findings from neuroimaging studies showing the harmful effects of abuse and neglect and similar forms of trauma on neurocognitive development.
- The most recent follow-up findings from groundbreaking early intervention and prevention programs such as early interventions for children with autism spectrum disorders, Fast Track for conduct disorders, and the Multimodal Treatment Study for Children with ADHD.
- An enhanced focus on evidence-based assessment and treatments including:
  - Behavior therapy, psychopharmacological, and combined treatments for ADHD (Chapter 5)
  - Parent management training, problem-solving skills training, and multi-systemic therapy for oppositional and conduct disorders (Chapter 6)
  - Cognitive behavior therapy, exposure, and modeling for anxiety disorders (Chapter 7)
  - Cognitive behavior therapy and interpersonal therapy for depression (Chapter 8)
  - Advances in early identification and new treatments for autism spectrum disorders (Chapter 10)
  - Treatment for child and adolescence substance abuse problems (Chapter 12)
  - Treatment outcome studies with anorexia and bulimia (Chapter 13)
- Added coverage on important, contemporary topics including:
  - Subtypes of disorders such as the predominantly inattentive subtype of ADHD and new findings on emotional impulsivity (Chapter 5)
  - Temperament and personality disorders (Chapters 2 and 4)
  - Different symptom clusters for oppositional defiant disorder (Chapter 6)
  - Parenting styles (Chapters 2, 6, 7, 8, and 14)
  - The stigma of mental illness (Chapters 1 and 4)
  - The interplay between research findings in abnormal child psychology and public policy implications throughout the book.
- Coverage of many significant reports from the Surgeon General, the World Health Organization, and others that will shape the future of research and practice in children's mental health (Chapters 1 and 2)
- Support organizations for parents and children are now listed in the Instructor's Manual. Detailed

information about the text's instructor and student supplements is provided in the next section of this preface.

- Greatly expanded selection of multimedia and interactive learning resources, foremost among these numerous new video clips—selected by the authors—within PowerLecture. Unique in this market, these current, high-interest videos focus on topics such as ADHD, autism, bullying, life skills, and Down syndrome.

A Comprehensive Teaching and Learning Package

Abnormal Child Psychology, **Fifth Edition**, is accompanied by an array of supplements developed to facilitate both the instructors' and the students' best possible experience, inside as well as outside the classroom. Supplements continuing from the fourth edition have been thoroughly revised and updated; other supplements are new to this edition. Cengage Learning invites you to take full advantage of the teaching and learning tools available to you and has prepared the following descriptions of each.

Instructor's Manual with Test Bank

The Instructor's Manual with Test Bank closely matches the text and consists of lecture outlines and notes, learning objectives, myriad activities and handouts, video and website recommendations, "Warning Signs" transparency masters, and new listings of support organizations for parents and children. In addition to a comprehensive test bank, this resource also includes a set of extras called "Five Minutes More," which comprises additional lecture ideas, transparency/digital slide masters, and activities on selected topics such as the brain, day care, and bilingualism. The Instructor's Manual is available in print and in electronic format on the book's companion website (password-protected).

ABC Video for Abnormal Psychology, Volumes I and II

These ABC videos, available on DVD, feature short, high-interest clips about current studies and research in psychology. Including titles such as Autism Diagnosis in Children and Selective Mutism, these videos are perfect for discussion starters or to enrich lectures.

Psychology CourseMate

Abnormal Child Psychology, fifth edition, includes Psychology CourseMate, a complement to your textbook. Psychology CourseMate includes:

- an interactive eBook
- interactive teaching and learning tools including:
  - Quizzes
  - Flashcards
  - Videos
  - and more
- Engagement Tracker, a first-of-its-kind tool that monitors student engagement in the course.

Go to login.cengage.com to access these resources.

Acknowledgments

One of the most rewarding aspects of this project has been the willingness and commitment on the part of many to share their knowledge and abilities. With great pleasure and appreciation, we wish to acknowledge individuals who have in one way or another contributed to its completion, while recognizing that any shortcomings of this book are our responsibility alone.

In Calgary, Alison and Megan Wiigs, as creative and talented a mother-and-daughter team as there is, have contributed enormously to every phase of this project through five editions. For their devotion to the project, they have our special gratitude. We also thank Carlie Montpetit and Camille Popovich for their perceptive and useful feedback from a student perspective and generous help in locating resource material and references. In Toronto, Anna-Lee Straatman and Debbie Chiodo deserve rich praise for their skilled efforts at locating resource material and checking the manuscript. We are also grateful to colleagues who generously provided us with case materials and other information, including Thomas Achenbach, Ann Marie Albano, Russell Barkley, David Dozois, Scott Henggeler, Giuseppe Iaria, Charlotte Johnston, Alan Kazdin, Philip Kendall, David Kolko, Ivar Lovaas, Margaret McKim, Robert McMahon, Doug Murdoch, Joel Nigg, Gerald Patterson, John Pearce, William Pelham, John Piacentini, Phyl and Rachel Prout, Jerry Sattler, David Shaffer, Rosemary Tannock, and Fred Weizmann. Many thanks again to Sumru Erkut, Ph.D., Associate Director and Senior Research Scientist at Wellesley College's Wellesley Centers for Women, for her expert review of this text's previous edition focusing on diversity. We extend our special thanks to the many students in our courses and those from other universities, who provided us with helpful feedback on this edition.

The production of a textbook involves many behind-the-scenes individuals who deserve special thanks. Rebecca Dashiell gave her support in launching this fifth edition. Jaime Perkins, executive editor, contributed creative ideas, valuable assistance, and friendly reality checks from start to finish. The rest of the devoted and talented staff at and associated with Cengage Learning, including Mary Falcon, freelance development editor; Nic Albert, associate development editor; Charlene Carpentier, content production manager; Vernon Boes, art director; Lauren Keyes, senior media editor; Jessica Alderman, editorial assistant; Lauren K. Moody, assistant editor; Josh Garvin, photo researcher; Bob Kauser, rights acquisition director; Tom McDonough, rights acquisition specialist; Sue Howard, permissions researcher, all deserve our thankful recognition for their contributions toward making the fifth edition of this text top quality.

Once again, we wish to thank our families, whose steadfast support and tolerance for the demands and excesses that go into a project such as this were critically important and exceedingly strong. The preparation of this textbook placed a heavy burden of our time away from them, and we are grateful for their unyielding support and encouragement. Eric Mash thanks Heather Henderson Mash, his wife and soul mate, for her love and support, tolerance of the time that a project like this takes away from family life, and her wise advice on many matters relating to this book. David Wolfe thanks his three children, Amy, Annie, and Alex, who were incredible sources of inspiration, information, humor, and photographs(!). His wife, Barbara Legate, has been a touchstone throughout every edition for her intellectual and emotional support.

Reviewers

A critical part of writing this textbook involved feedback from students, teachers, and experts. We would like to thank several dedicated reviewers and scholars who read most of the chapters for this book and provided us with detailed comments and suggestions that were enormously helpful in shaping the final manuscript of this edition:

Daniel M. Bagner, Florida International University
Paul Bartoli, East Stroudsburg University
Greg Berg, San Jose State University
Mary Ann Coupland, Sinte Gleska University
Casey A. Holtz, Wisconsin Lutheran College
Elizabeth J. Kiel Luebbe, Miami University
Bertha Kondrak, Central TX University
Susan K. Marell, St. Thomas Aquinas College
Lauren Polvere, Clinton Community College
Donald T. Saposnek, UC Santa Cruz

We also wish to again acknowledge and thank the reviewers whose insights helped us in previous editions: Kristin Christodulu, University at Albany, State University of New York; David Day, Ryerson University; Maria Gartstein, Washington State University–Pullman; Claire Novosad, Southern Connecticut State University; Robert Weisskirch, California State University–Monterey Bay; Debora Bell-Dolan, University of Missouri-Columbia; Richard Clements, Indiana University Northwest; Nancy Eldred, San Jose State University; Robert Emery, University of Virginia; Virginia E. Fee, Mississippi State University; Paul Florsheim, University of Utah; Laura Freberg, California Polytechnic State University–San Luis Obispo; Gary Harper, DePaul University; Yo Jackson, University of Kansas; Christopher Kearney, University of Nevada–Las Vegas; Janet Kistner, Florida State University; Marvin Kumler, Bowling Green State University; June Madsen Clausen, University of San Francisco; Patrick McGrath, Dalhousie University; Kay McIntyre, University of Missouri–St. Louis; Clark McKown, University of California–Berkeley; Robert McMahon, University of Washington; Richard Milich, University of Kentucky; Martin Murphy, University of Akron; Jill Norvilitis, Buffalo State College; Narina Nunez, University of Wyoming; Stacy Overstreet, Tulane University; Michael Roberts, University of Kansas; Donald T. Saposnek, Ph.D., University of California, Santa Cruz; Dana Schneider, M.A., MFT, Sonoma State University; Michael Vasey, Ohio State University; Carol K. Whalen, University of California, Irvine; and Eric A. Youngstrom, Ph.D., Case Western Reserve University.

Our thanks also go to Paul Florsheim's students at the University of Utah: Trisha Aberton, Julie Blundell, Josh Brown, Kimbery Downing, Jaime Fletcher, Jeff Ford, Nick Gilson, Regina Hiraoka, Trisha Jorgensen, Michael Lambert, Monica Stauffer, Matthew Warthen, Heather Woodhouse, Kristen Yancey, and Matthew Zollinger.

Finally, we offer a special thanks to Nancy Eldred of San Jose State University for pilot-testing the second edition with her students. The comments were quite helpful in sharpening the student focus of subsequent editions, and we are grateful to her for volunteering for this mission! Thank you Gabriela Beas, Maria Brown, Sara Carriere, Gina Costanza, Gera-Lyne Delfin, Julene Donovan, Brieann Durose, Shelly Gillan, Rochelle Hernandez, Keri Kennedy, Doris Lan, Maggie Lau, Christine McAfee-Ward, Deisy Muñoz, Shirat Negev, Kristi Pimentel, Veronica Rauch, Sandra Ronquillo, Becky Schripsema, Dianalin Stratton, Loyen Yabut, Melissa Zahradnik.

Eric J. Mash
David A. Wolfe

1 Introduction to Normal and Abnormal Behavior in Children and Adolescents

Mankind owes to the child the best it has to give.

—UN Convention on the Rights of the Child (1989)

CHAPTER PREVIEW

AFTER CENTURIES OF SILENCE, misunderstanding, and outright abuse, children's mental health problems and needs now receive greater attention, which corresponds to society's recent concern about children's well-being. Fortunately, today more people like you want to understand and address the needs of children and adolescents. Perhaps you have begun to recognize that children's mental health problems differ in many ways from those of adults, so you have chosen to take a closer look. Maybe you are planning a career in teaching, counseling, medicine, law, rehabilitation, or psychology—all of which rely somewhat on knowledge of children's special needs to shape their focus and practice. Whatever your reason is for reading this book, we are pleased to welcome you to an exciting and active field of study, one that we believe will expose you to concepts and issues that will have a profound and lasting influence. Children's mental health issues are becoming relevant to many of us in our current and future roles as professionals, community members, and parents, and the needs for trained personnel are increasing (McLearn, Knitzer, & Carter, 2007).

Let's begin by considering Georgina's problems, which raise several fundamental questions that guide our current understanding of children's **psychological disorders**. Ask yourself: Does Georgina's behavior seem abnormal, or are aspects of her behavior normal under certain circumstances?

How would you describe Georgina's problem? Is it an emotional problem? A learning problem? A developmental disability? Could something in her environment cause these strange rituals, or is she more likely

GEORGINA

Counting for Safety

At age 10, Georgina's strange symptoms had reached the point where her mother needed answers—and fast. Her behavior first became a concern about 2 years ago, when she started talking about harm befalling herself or her family. Her mother recalled how Georgina would come home from the third grade and complain that "I need to finish stuff but I can't seem to," and "I know I'm gonna forget something so I have to keep thinking about it." Her mother expressed her own frustration and worry: "As early as age 5, I remember Georgina would touch and arrange things a certain way, such as brushing her teeth in a certain sequence. Sometimes I'd notice that she would walk through doorways over and over, and she seemed to need to check and arrange things her way before she could leave a room." Georgina's mother had spoken to their family doctor about it back then and was told, "It's probably a phase she's going through, like stepping on cracks will break your mother's back. Ignore it and it'll stop."

But it didn't stop. Georgina developed more elaborate rituals for counting words and objects, primarily in groups of four. She told her mom, "I need to count things out and group them a certain way—only I know the rules how to do it." When she came to my office, Georgina told me, "When someone says something to me or I read something, I have to count the words in groups of four and then organize these groups into larger and larger groups of four." She looked at the pile of magazines in my office and the books on my shelf and explained, matter-of-factly, that she was counting and grouping these things while we talked! Georgina was constantly terrified of forgetting a passage or objects or being interrupted. She believed that if she could not complete her counting, some horrible tragedy would befall her parents or herself. Nighttime was the worst, she explained, because "I can't go to sleep until my counting is complete, and this can take a long time." (In fact, it took up to several hours, her mother confirmed.) Understandably, her daytime counting rituals had led to decline in her schoolwork and friendships. Her mother showed me her report cards: Georgina's grades had gone from above average to near failing in several subjects. (Based on Piacentini & Graae, 1997)

Even at age 5, Georgina's strange counting ritual was a symptom of her obsessive–compulsive disorder

responding to internal cues we do not know about? Would Georgina's behavior be viewed differently if it occurred in a boy or in a child from an African American or Hispanic background? Will she continue to display these behaviors and, if so, what can we do to help?

When seeking assistance or advice, parents often ask questions similar to these about their child's behavior, and understandably need to know the probable course and outcome. These questions also exemplify the following issues that research studies in abnormal child psychology seek to address:

- Defining what constitutes normal and abnormal behavior for children of different ages, sexes, and ethnic and cultural backgrounds
- Identifying the causes and correlates of abnormal child behavior
- Making predictions about long-term outcomes
- Developing and evaluating methods for treatment and/or prevention

How you choose to describe the problems that children show, and what harm or impairments such problems may lead to, is often the first step toward understanding the nature of their problems. As we discuss in Chapter 7, Georgina's symptoms fit the diagnostic criteria for obsessive–compulsive disorder. This diagnostic label, although far from perfect, tells a great deal about the nature of her disorder, the course it may follow, and the possible treatments.

Georgina's problems also illustrate important features that distinguish most child and adolescent disorders:

- *When adults seek services for children, it often is not clear whose "problem" it is.* Children usually enter the mental health system as a result of concerns raised by adults—parents, pediatricians, teachers, or school counselors—and the children themselves may have little choice in the matter. Children do not refer themselves for treatment. This has important implications for how we detect children's problems and how we respond to them.
- *Many child and adolescent problems involve failure to show expected developmental progress.* The problem may be transitory, like most types of bedwetting, or it may be an initial indication of more severe problems ahead, as we see in Georgina's case. Determining the problem requires familiarity with normal, as well as abnormal, development.
- *Many problem behaviors shown by children and youths are not entirely abnormal.* To some extent, certain problem behaviors are shown by most children and youths. For instance, worrying from time to time about forgetting things or losing track of thoughts is common; Georgina's behavior, however, seems to involve more than these normal concerns. Thus, decisions about what to do also require familiarity with known psychological disorders and troublesome problem behaviors.
- *Interventions for children and adolescents often are intended to promote further development, rather than merely to restore a previous level of functioning.* Unlike interventions for most adult disorders, the goal for many children is to boost their abilities and skills, not only to eliminate distress.

Before we look at today's definitions of abnormal behavior in children and adolescents, it is valuable to discover how society's interests and approaches to these problems during previous generations have improved the quality of life and mental health of children and youths. Many children, especially those with special needs, fared poorly in the past because they were forced to work as coal miners, field hands, or beggars. Concern for children's needs, rights, and care requires a prominent and consistent social sensitivity and awareness that simply did not exist prior to the twentieth century (Aries, 1962). As you read the following historical synopsis, note how the relatively short history of abnormal child psychology has been strongly influenced by philosophical and societal changes in how adults view and treat children in general (Borstelmann, 1983; V. French, 1977).

Historical Views and Breakthroughs

These were feverish, melancholy times; I cannot remember to have raised my head or seen the moon or any of the heavenly bodies; my eyes were turned downward to the broad lamplit streets and to where the trees of the garden rustled together all night in undecipherable blackness;...

—Robert Louis Stevenson, describing memories of childhood illness and depression (quoted in Calder, 1980)

The ability of a society to help children develop normal lives and competencies requires not only medical, educational, and psychological resources but also a social philosophy that recognizes children as persons with a value independent of any other purpose. Although this view of children should seem self-evident to us today, valuing children as persons in their own right has not been a priority of previous societies. Early writings suggest that children were considered servants of the state in the city-states of early Greece. Ancient Greek and Roman societies believed that any person—young or old—with a physical or mental handicap, disability, or deformity was an economic burden and a social embarrassment, and thus was to be scorned, abandoned, or put to death (V. French, 1977).

Prior to the eighteenth century, children's mental health problems—unlike adult disorders—were seldom mentioned in professional or other forms of communication. Some of the earliest historical interest in abnormal child behavior surfaced near the end of the eighteenth century. The Church used its strong influence to attribute children's unusual or disturbing behaviors to their inherently uncivilized and provocative nature (Kanner, 1962). In fact, during this period nonreligious explanations for disordered behavior in children were rarely given serious consideration, because possession by the devil and similar forces of evil was the only explanation anyone needed (Rie, 1971). No one was eager to challenge this view, given that they too could be seen as possessed and dealt with accordingly.

Sadly, during the seventeenth and eighteenth centuries, as many as two-thirds of children died before their fifth birthday, often because there were no antibiotics or similar medications to treat deadly diseases (Zelizer, 1994). Many children were subjected to harsh treatment or indifference by their parents. Cruel acts ranging from extreme parental indifference and neglect to physical and sexual abuse of children went unnoticed or were considered an adult's right for educating or disciplining a child (Radbill, 1968). For many generations, the implied view of society that children are the exclusive property and responsibility of their parents was unchallenged by any countermovement to seek more humane treatment for children. A parent's prerogative to enforce child obedience, for example, was formalized by Massachusetts' Stubborn Child Act of 1654, which permitted parents to put "stubborn" children to death for misbehaving. (Fortunately, no one met this ultimate fate.) Into the mid-1800s, the law allowed children with severe developmental disabilities to be kept in cages and cellars (Donohue, Hersen, & Ammerman, 2000).

The Emergence of Social Conscience

"It is easier to build strong children than to fix broken men."

—attributed to Frederick Douglass

Fortunately, the situation gradually improved for children and youths throughout the nineteenth century and progressed significantly during the latter part of the twentieth century. However, until very recent changes in laws and attitudes, children (along with women, members of minority groups, and persons with special needs) were often the last to benefit from society's prosperity and were the primary victims of its shortcomings. With the acuity of hindsight, we now know that before any real change occurs, it requires a philosophy of humane understanding in how society recognizes and addresses the special needs of some of its members. In addition to humane beliefs, each society must develop ways and means to recognize and protect the rights of individuals, especially children, in the broadest sense (UN Convention on the Rights of the Child, 1989). An overview of some of these major developments provides important background for understanding today's approaches to children's mental health issues.

In Western society, an inkling of the prerequisites for a social conscience first occurred during the seventeenth century, when both a philosophy of humane care and institutions of social protection began to take root. One individual at the forefront of these changes was John Locke (1632–1704), a noted English philosopher and physician who influenced the beginnings of present-day attitudes and practices of childbirth and child rearing. Locke believed in individual rights, and he expressed the novel opinion that children should be raised with thought and care instead of indifference and harsh treatment. Rather than seeing children as uncivilized tyrants, he saw them as emotionally sensitive beings who should be treated with kindness and understanding and given proper educational opportunities (Illick, 1974). In his words, "the only fence [archaic use, meaning 'defense'] against the world is a thorough knowledge of it."

Then, at the turn of the nineteenth century, one of the first documented efforts to work with a special child was undertaken by Jean Marc Itard (1774–1838). Box 1.1 explains how Itard treated Victor (discovered living in the woods outside Paris) for his severe developmental delays rather than sending him to an asylum. Symbolically, this undertaking launched a new era of a helping orientation toward special children, which initially focused on the care, treatment, and training of what were then termed "mental defectives."

As the influence of Locke and others fostered the expansion of universal education throughout Europe and North America during the latter half of the nineteenth century, children unable to handle the demands of school became a visible and troubling group. Psychologists such as Leta Hollingworth (1886–1939) argued that many mentally defective children were actually suffering from emotional and behavioral problems primarily due to inept treatment by adults and lack of appropriate intellectual challenge (Benjamin & Shields, 1990). This view led to an important and basic distinction between persons with mental retardation ("imbeciles") and those with psychiatric or mental disorders ("lunatics"), although this distinction was far from clear at the time. Essentially, local governments needed to know who was responsible for helping children whose cognitive development appeared normal

BOX 1.1 A CLOSER LOOK

Victor of Aveyron

Victor, often referred to as the "wild boy of Aveyron," was discovered in France by hunters when he was about 11 or 12 years old, having lived alone in the woods presumably all of his life. Jean Marc Itard, a young physician at the time, believed the boy was "mentally arrested" because of social and educational neglect, and set about demonstrating whether such retardation could be reversed. Victor—who initially was mute, walked on all fours, drank water while lying flat on the ground, and bit and scratched—became the object of popular attention as rumors spread that he had been raised by animals. He was dirty, nonverbal, incapable of attention, and insensitive to basic sensations of hot and cold. Despite the child's appearance and behavior, Itard believed that environmental stimulation could humanize him. Itard's account of his efforts poignantly reveals the optimism, frustration, anger, hope, and despair that he experienced in working with this special child.

Itard used a variety of methods to bring Victor to an awareness of his sensory experiences: hot baths, massages, tickling, emotional excitement, even electric shocks. After 5 years of training by Dr. Itard, Victor had learned to identify objects, identify letters of the alphabet, comprehend many words, and apply names to objects and parts of objects. Victor also showed a preference for social life over the isolation of the wild. Despite his achievements, Itard felt his efforts had failed, because his goals of socializing the boy to make him normal were never reached. Nevertheless, the case of Victor was a landmark in the effort to assist children with special needs. For the first time an adult had tried to really understand—to feel and know—the mind and emotions of a special child, and had proved that a child with severe impairments could improve through appropriate training. This deep investment on the part of an individual in the needs and feelings of another person's child remains a key aspect of the helping orientation to this day.

© Mary Evans Picture Library/Alamy

Source: From A History of the Care and Study of the Mentally Retarded, by L. Kanner, 1964, p. 15. Courtesy of Charles C. Thomas, Publisher, Springfield, Illinois.

but who showed serious emotional or behavioral problems. The only guidance they had previously had in distinguishing children with intellectual deficits from children with behavioral and emotional problems was derived from religious views of immoral behavior: children who had normal cognitive abilities but who were disturbed were thought to suffer from moral insanity, which implied a disturbance in personality or character (Pritchard, 1837). Benjamin Rush (1745–1813), a pioneer in psychiatry, argued that children were incapable of true adult-like insanity, because the immaturity of their developing brains prevented them from retaining the mental events that caused insanity (Rie, 1971). Consequently, the term *moral insanity* grew in acceptance as a means of accounting for nonintellectual forms of abnormal child behavior.

The implications of this basic distinction created a brief yet significant burst of optimism among professionals. Concern for the plight and welfare of children with mental and behavioral disturbances began to rise in conjunction with two important influences. First, with advances in general medicine, physiology, and neurology, the moral insanity view of psychological disorders was replaced by the organic disease model, which emphasized more humane forms of treatment. This advancement was furthered by advocates such as Dorothea Dix (1802–1887), who in the mid-nineteenth century established 32 humane mental hospitals for the treatment of troubled youths previously relegated to cellars and cages (Achenbach, 1982). Second, the growing influence of the philosophies of Locke and others led to the view that children needed moral guidance and support. With these changing views came an increased concern for moral education, compulsory education, and improved health practices. These early efforts to assist children provided the foundation for evolving views of abnormal child behavior as the result of combinations of biological, environmental, psychological, and cultural influences.

Early Biological Attributions

The successful treatment of infectious diseases during the latter part of the nineteenth century strengthened the emerging belief that illness and disease, including mental illness, were biological problems. However, early attempts at biological explanations for deviant or abnormal behavior were highly biased in favor of locating the cause within the individual child or adult. The public generally distrusted and scorned anyone who appeared "mad" or "possessed by the devil" or similar evil forces. Box 1.2 describes masturbatory insanity, a good illustration of how such thinking can lead to an explanation of abnormal behavior without consideration of objective scientific findings and the base rate of masturbation in the general population. The notion of masturbatory insanity also illustrates how the prevailing political and social climates influence definitions of child psychopathology, which is as true today as it was in the past. Views on masturbation evolved from the moral judgment that it was a sin of the flesh, to the medical opinion that it was harmful to one's physical health, to the psychiatric assertion that sexual overindulgence caused insanity.

In contrast to the public's general ignorance and avoidance of issues concerning persons with mental disorders that continued during the late nineteenth century, the mental hygiene movement provides a benchmark of changing attitudes toward children and adults with mental disorders. In 1909, Clifford Beers, a layperson who had recovered from a severe psychosis, spearheaded efforts to change the plight of others also afflicted. Believing that mental disorders were a form of disease, he criticized society's ignorance and indifference and sought to prevent mental disease by raising the standards of care and disseminating reliable information (M. Levine & Levine, 1992). As a result, detection and intervention methods began to flourish, based on a more tempered—yet still quite frightened and ill-informed—view of afflicted individuals.

Unfortunately, because this paradigm was based on a biological disease model, intervention was limited to persons with the most visible and prominent disorders, such as psychoses or severe mental retardation. Although developmental explanations were a part of this early view of psychopathology, they were quite narrow. The development of the disease was considered progressive and irreversible, tied to the development of the child only in that it manifested itself differently as the child grew, but remained impervious to other influences such as treatment or learning. All one could do was to prevent the most extreme manifestations by strict punishment, and to protect those not affected.

Sadly, this early educational and humane model for assisting persons with mental disorders soon reverted to a custodial model during the early part of the twentieth century. Once again, attitudes toward anyone with

BOX 1.2 A CLOSER LOOK

Masturbatory Insanity

Today, most parents hardly balk at discovering their child engaging in some form of self-stimulation—it is considered a normal part of self-discovery and pleasant-sensation seeking. Such tolerance was not always the case. In fact, children's masturbation is historically significant because it was the first "disorder" unique to children and adolescents (Rie, 1971). Just over a hundred years ago, *masturbatory insanity* was a form of mental illness and, in keeping with the contemporaneous view that such problems resided within the individual, it was believed to be a very worrisome problem (Rie, 1971; Szasz, 1970).

By the eighteenth century, society's objections to masturbation originated from religious views that were augmented by the growing influence of science (Rie, 1971; Szasz, 1970). Moral convictions regarding the wrongfulness of masturbation led to a physiological explanation with severe medical ramifications, based on pseudoscientific papers such as *Onania, or the Heinous Sin of Self-Pollution* (circa 1710) (Szasz, 1970). The medical view of masturbation focused initially on adverse effects on physical health, but by the mid-nineteenth century the dominant thought shifted to a focus on the presumed negative effects on mental health and nervous system functioning. With amazing speed, masturbation became the most frequently mentioned "cause" of psychopathology in children.

Interest in masturbatory insanity gradually waned toward the end of the nineteenth century, but the argument still remained tenable as psychoanalytic theory gained acceptance. Eventually, the notion of masturbatory insanity gave way to the concept of neurosis. It was not until much later in the twentieth century that the misguided and illusory belief in a relationship between masturbation and mental illness was dispelled. Let this example remind us of the importance of scientific skepticism in confirming or disconfirming new theories and explanations for abnormal behavior.

Source: Based on author's case material.

mental or intellectual disabilities turned from cautious optimism to dire pessimism, hostility, and disdain. Particularly children, youths, and adults with mental retardation were blamed for crimes and social ills during the ensuing alarmist period (Achenbach, 1982). Rather than viewing knowledge as a form of protection, as Locke had argued, society returned to the view that mental illness and retardation were diseases that could spread if left unchecked. For the next two decades, many communities chose to prevent the procreation of the insane through eugenics (sterilization) and segregation (institutionalization). We will return to these important developments in our discussion of the history of mental retardation in Chapter 9.

Early Psychological Attributions

Today, many of us take for granted the idea that, in the attempt to conceptualize and understand abnormal child psychology, biological influences must be balanced with important developmental and cultural factors, including the family, peer group, and school. Of course, this perception was not always the case. The long-standing, medically based view that abnormal behavior is a disorder or disease residing within the person unfortunately led to neglect of the essential role of a person's surroundings, context, and relations, and of the interactions among these variables.

The recognition of psychological influences emerged early in the twentieth century, when attention was drawn to the importance of major psychological disorders and to formulating a taxonomy of illnesses. Such recognition allowed researchers to organize and categorize ways of differentiating among various psychological problems, resulting in some semblance of understanding and control. At the same time, there was concern that attempts to recognize the wide range of mental health needs of children and adults could easily backfire and lead to the neglect of persons with more severe disorders. This shift in perspective and increase in knowledge also prompted the development of diagnostic categories and new criminal offenses, the expansion of descriptions of deviant behavior, and the addition of more comprehensive monitoring procedures for identified individuals (Costello & Angold, 2006). Two major theoretical paradigms helped shape these emerging psychological and environmental influences: psychoanalytic theory and behaviorism. We'll limit our discussion here to their historical importance, but additional content concerning their contemporary influence appears in the Chapter 2 discussion of theories and causes.

Psychoanalytic Theory

In Sigmund Freud's day, near the beginning of the twentieth century, many child psychiatrists and psychologists had grown pessimistic about their ability to treat children's mental disorders in a fashion other than custodial or palliative care. Freud was one of the first to reject such pessimism and raise new possibilities for treatment as the roots of these disorders were traced to early childhood (Fonagy, Target, & Gergely, 2006). Although he believed that individuals have inborn drives and predispositions that strongly affect their development, he also believed that experiences play a necessary role in psychopathology. For perhaps the first time, the course of mental disorders was not viewed as inevitable; children and adults could be helped if provided with the proper environment, therapy, or both.

Psychoanalytic theory significantly influenced advances in our ways of thinking about the causes and treatment of mental disorders. Perhaps the most important of these advances from the perspective of abnormal child psychology was that Freud was the first to give meaning to the concept of mental disorder by linking it to childhood experiences (Rilling, 2000). His radical theory incorporated developmental concepts into an understanding of psychopathology at a time when early childhood development was virtually ignored by mainstream child psychiatry and psychology. Rather than focusing on singular, specific causes (a hallmark of the disease model in vogue at the time), psychoanalytic theory emphasized that personality and mental health outcomes had multiple roots. Outcomes depended to a large degree on the interaction of developmental and situational processes that change over time in unique ways (Fonagy et al., 2006). In effect, Freud's writings shifted the view from one of children as innocent or insignificant to one of human beings in turmoil, struggling to achieve control over biological needs and to make themselves acceptable to society through the microcosm of the family (Freud, 1909/1953).

Contributions based on Freud's theory continued to expand throughout the early part of the twentieth century, as clinicians and theorists broke from some of his earlier teachings and brought new insights to the field. His daughter, Anna Freud (1895–1982), was instrumental in expanding his ideas to understanding children, in particular by noting how children's symptoms were related more to developmental stages than were those of adults. Anna Freud's contemporary, Melanie Klein (1882–1960), also took an interest in the meaning of children's play, arguing that all actions could be interpreted in terms of unconscious fantasy. The work of both women made possible the analysis of younger children and the recognition of nonverbal communication for patients of all ages (Mason, 2003).

In recent years, psychoanalytic theory's approach to abnormal child psychology has had less influence on clinical practice and teaching, largely because of the popularity of the phenomenological (descriptive) approach to psychopathology (Costello & Angold, 2006). Nevertheless, it is important to remember that current **nosologies** (the efforts to classify psychiatric disorders into descriptive categories) are essentially nondevelopmental in their approaches. Rather than attempting, as the Freudian approach does, to describe the development of the disease in the context of the development of the individual, nosologies such as those in the Diagnostic and Statistical Manual (DSM-IV-TR [Text Revision]; American Psychiatric Association, 2000) attempt to find common denominators that describe the manifestations of a disorder at every age (Achenbach & Rescorla, 2006). Despite valid criticism and a lack of empirical validation of the content of psychoanalytic theory and its many derivatives, the idea of emphasizing the interconnection between children's normal and abnormal development retains considerable attraction as a model for abnormal child psychology.

Behaviorism

The development of evidence-based treatments for children, youths, and families can be traced to the rise of behaviorism in the early 1900s, as reflected in Pavlov's experimental research that established the foundations for classical conditioning, and in the classic studies on the conditioning and elimination of children's fears (Jones, 1924; J. B. Watson & Rayner, 1920). Initially, John Watson (1878–1958), the "Father of Behaviorism," intended to explain Freud's concepts in more scientific terms, based on the new learning theory of classical conditioning.

Ironically, Watson was perhaps more psychoanalytically inspired by Freud's theories than he intended. As he attempted to explain terms such as *unconscious* and *transference* using the language of conditioned emotional responses (and thereby discredit Freud's theory of emotions), he in fact pioneered the scientific investigation of some of Freud's ideas (Rilling, 2000). Box 1.3 highlights some of Watson's scientific ambitions and his famous study with Little Albert, as well as some of the controversy surrounding his career.

Watson is known for his theory of emotions, which he extrapolated from normal to abnormal behavior. His infamous words exemplify the faith some early researchers—and the public—placed in laboratory-based research on learning and behavior: "Give me a dozen healthy infants . . . and I'll guarantee to take any one at random and train him to become any type of specialist I might select—doctor, lawyer, artist, merchant-chief and, yes, even beggar-man and thief, regardless of his talents, penchants, tendencies, abilities, vocations, and race of his ancestors." (J. B. Watson, 1925, p. 82)

Beyond the work in their lab, the Watson household must have been an interesting place. Consider the following contrasting views and advice on raising children from one of America's first "child experts" and his wife:

> John Watson (1925): Never hug and kiss them, never let them sit in your lap. If you must, kiss them once on the forehead when they say goodnight. Shake hands with them in the morning.

> Rosalie Rayner Watson (1930): I cannot restrain my affection for the children completely. . . . I like being merry and gay and having the giggles. The behaviorists think giggling is a sign of maladjustment, so when the children want to giggle I have to keep a straight face or rush them off to their rooms.

This example and the study of Little Albert illustrate the importance of keeping in perspective any new advances and insights that at first may seem like panaceas for age-old problems. As any soiled veteran of parenting would attest, no child-rearing shortcuts or uniform solutions guide us in dealing with children's problems—raising children is part skill, part wisdom, and part luck. Nonetheless, families, communities, and societal and cultural values play a strong role in determining how successful current child-rearing philosophies are at benefiting children.

Evolving Forms of Treatment

Compared with the times that followed, the period from 1930 to 1950 was a quiet time for research and treatment in abnormal child psychology. A few reports in the 1930s described the behavioral treatment of isolated problems such as bed-wetting (O. H. Mowrer & Mowrer, 1938), stuttering (Dunlap, 1932), and fears (F. B. Holmes, 1936). Other than these reports, psychodynamic approaches were the dominant form of treatment during this period. As a carryover from the 1800s, most children with intellectual or mental disorders were still institutionalized. This practice had come under mounting criticism by the late 1940s, when studies by René Spitz raised serious questions about the harmful impact of institutional life on children's growth and development (R. Spitz, 1945). He discovered that infants raised in institutions without adult physical contact and stimulation developed severe physical and emotional problems. Efforts were undertaken to close institutions and place dependent and difficult children in foster family homes or group homes. Within a 20-year period, from 1945 to 1965, there was a rapid decline in the number of children in institutions, while the number of children in foster family homes and group homes increased.

During the 1950s and early 1960s, behavior therapy emerged as a systematic approach to the treatment of child and family disorders. The therapy was originally based on operant and classical conditioning principles established through laboratory work with animals. In their early form, these laboratory-based techniques to modify undesirable behaviors and shape

BOX 1.3 A CLOSER LOOK

Little Albert, Big Fears, and Sex in Advertising

Most of us are familiar with the story of Little Albert and his fear of white rats and other white furry objects, thanks to the work of John Watson and his graduate assistant (soon to become wife) Rosalie Rayner. However, understanding the times and background of John Watson helps put these pioneering efforts into a broader historical perspective, and highlights the limited concern for ethics in research that existed in his day.

Watson's fascination with and life dedication to the study of fears may have stemmed from his own acknowledged fear of the dark, which afflicted him throughout his adult life. His career break arrived when he was given an opportunity to create a research laboratory at Johns Hopkins University for the study of child development. Instead of conditioning rats, he could now use humans to test his emerging theories of fear conditioning. However, at that time the only source of human subjects was persons whose rights were considered insignificant or who had less than adequate power to protect themselves, such as orphans, mental patients, and prisoners. Just as he had studied rats in their cages, Watson now studied babies in their cribs.

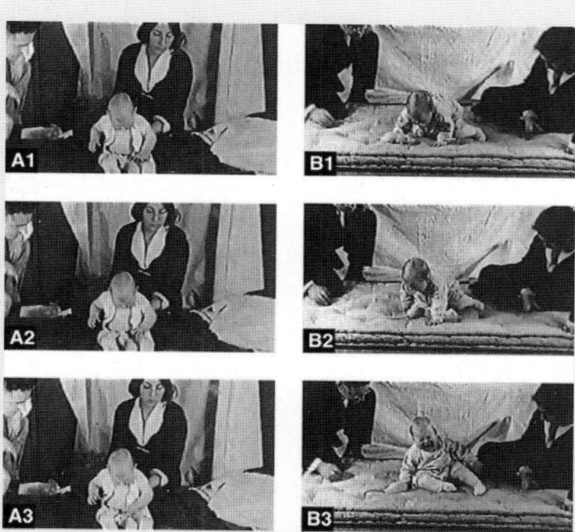

Neurobiology of Pavlovian Fear Conditioning Annual Review of Neuroscience Vol. 24: 897–931, by Stephen Maren; Annual Review of Neuroscience ©2011 Annual Reviews. All rights reserved.

Clearly, his method of obtaining research subjects and experimenting with them would be considered highly unethical today. To demonstrate how fear might be conditioned in a baby, Watson and Rayner set out to condition fear in an 11-month-old orphan baby they named Albert B., who was given a small white rat to touch, toward which he showed no fear. After this warm-up, every time the infant reached to touch the rat, Watson would strike a steel bar with a hammer. After repeated attempts to touch the rat brought on the same shocking sounds, "the infant jumped violently, fell forward and began to whimper." The process was repeated intermittently, enough times that eventually Albert B. would break down and cry, desperately trying to crawl away, whenever he saw the rat. Watson and Rayner had successfully conditioned the child to fear rats. They then conditioned him to fear rabbits, dogs, fur coats, and—believe it or not—Santa Claus masks (Karier, 1986).

It is disconcerting that Albert B. moved away before any deconditioning was attempted, resulting in decades of speculation as to his identity and the strange set of fears he might have suffered. In 2009 a team of psychologists tracked down Little Albert's identity and fate: he was identified as Douglas Merritte, whose mother worked at the campus hospital and was paid $1 for her baby's research participation. Sadly, the team discovered that Douglas died at age 6 of acquired hydrocephalus (Beck, Levinson, & Irons, 2009).

It is ironic, moreover, that Watson went on to develop a career in advertising after he was ousted from the university (presumably as a result of concerns over his extramarital relationship with his graduate student; Benjamin, Whitaker, Ramsey, & Zeve, 2007). His brand of behaviorism, with its emphasis on the prediction and control of human behavior, met with unqualified success on Madison Avenue. As he explained, "No matter what it is, like the good naturalist you are, you must never lose sight of your experimental animal—the consumer." We can thank John B. Watson for advertising's dramatic shift in the 1930s toward creating images around any given product that exploited whenever possible the sexual desires of both men and women.

Source: Based on Karier, 1986.

adaptive abilities stood in stark contrast to the dominant psychoanalytic approaches, which stressed resolution of internal conflicts and unconscious motives. Behavior therapy focused initially on children with mental retardation or severe disturbances. Psychoanalytic practices for these children were perceived as ineffective or inappropriate. Much of this early work took place in institutions or classroom settings that were thought to provide the kind of environmental control needed to change behavior effectively. Since that time, behavior therapy has continued to expand in scope, and has emerged as a prominent form of therapy for a wide range of children's disorders (Ollendick, King, & Chorpita, 2006; Weisz & Kazdin, 2010).

Progressive Legislation

Just how far some countries have advanced in the humane and egalitarian treatment of children and youths is exemplified by the various laws enacted in the past few decades to protect the rights of those with special needs. For example, in the United States the Individuals with Disabilities Education Act (IDEA; Public Law 104-446) mandates free and appropriate public education for any child with special needs in the least restrictive environment for that child. Each child with special needs, regardless of age, must be assessed with culturally appropriate tests. Each of these children must have an individualized education program (IEP) tailored to his or her needs, and must be re-assessed. Similar legislation for protecting the rights of children with disabilities (and ensuring their access to appropriate resources) exists in Canada, the United Kingdom, and many other nations.

In 2007, the United Nations General Assembly adopted a new convention to protect the rights of persons with disabilities around the world. This convention represents an important shift from addressing the "special needs" of children to realizing their rights and removing the physical, linguistic, social, and cultural barriers that remain. Countries that ratify the convention agree to enact laws and other measures to improve disability rights, and also to abolish legislation, customs, and practices that discriminate against persons with disabilities. These efforts signify a paradigm shift in attitudes toward and treatment of people with disabilities—from seeing persons with disabilities as objects of charity to considering them as individuals with human rights. Specific principles addressing the needs of children with disabilities are shown in Box 1.4.

BOX 1.4 A CLOSER LOOK

UN Convention on the Rights of Persons with Disabilities (2007)

[Article 7, pertaining to children's rights]:

1. States Parties shall take all necessary measures to ensure the full enjoyment by children with disabilities of all human rights and fundamental freedoms on an equal basis with other children.
2. In all actions concerning children with disabilities, the best interests of the child shall be a primary consideration.
3. States Parties shall ensure that children with disabilities have the right to express their views freely on all matters affecting them, their views being given due weight in accordance with their age and maturity, on an equal basis with other children, and to be provided with disability and age-appropriate assistance to realize that right.

Source: UN Convention on the Rights of Persons with Disabilities (2007). Office of the United Nations High Commissioner for Human Rights.

SECTION SUMMARY

Historical Views and Breakthroughs

- Early biological explanations for abnormal child behavior favored locating the cause of the problem within the individual, which sometimes led to simplistic or inaccurate beliefs about causes of the behavior.
- Early psychological approaches attempted to integrate basic knowledge of inborn processes with environmental conditions that shape behavior, emotions, and cognitions.
- Greater attention to the problems of children and youths in recent years has improved their quality of life and mental health. This improvement resulted from greater societal recognition of and sensitivity to children's special status and needs since the turn of the twentieth century.

WHAT IS ABNORMAL BEHAVIOR IN CHILDREN AND ADOLESCENTS?

LEE

Early Troubles

I felt sorry for him. I asked him why he didn't go to school: "Oh," he said, "school is just a waste of time. I'm not learning anything there. I got other things to do. Besides, the kids all make fun of me. I wear jeans and they laugh at me. I talk with a Southern drawl and they laugh at me. They don't like me. I don't like them." Although he had hobbies, "most of all, I like to be by myself and do things by myself." And that's what he did a good part of those 18 months in New York. He'd get up at 9 a.m., watch television till 2 or 3 in the afternoon. There was no one else at home. His mother was out working. I asked him what he thought about his mother. He answered: "Well, I've got to live with her, so I guess I love her." But he showed no real relationship to her nor did she to him. (Based on Sites, 1967)

These comments were made by a probation officer reflecting on his involvement with a 13-year-old boy named Lee Harvey Oswald, who was under probation for chronic truancy. Note that the presenting complaint—truancy—was linked to dislike of school, embarrassment by peers, social isolation and alienation, and even his lack of emotional closeness to his mother. This example reveals how a relatively discrete problem can be difficult to classify into its causes, expression, and contributing factors. It also raises several key questions: First, how do we judge what is normal?

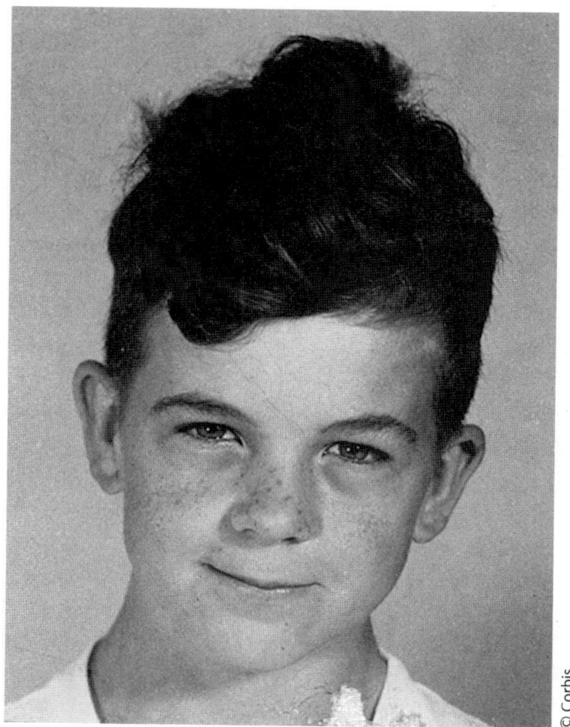

Were there any clues in Lee Harvey Oswald's childhood that might suggest his violent behavior later on?

A lot of kids skip school during adolescence. Second, when does an issue become a problem? In this instance, did anyone sense that Oswald's truancy might lead to or be due to potentially serious social problems? Finally, why are some children's abnormal patterns of behavior relatively continuous from early childhood through adolescence and into adulthood, whereas other children show more variable (discontinuous) patterns of development and adaptation? Was there anything about Oswald's behavior in childhood that indicated that he would assassinate President John F. Kennedy years later?

Although these questions are central to defining and understanding abnormal child behavior and warrant thoughtful consideration, no simple, straightforward answers exist. (This should be familiar ground to those of you who are psychology majors.) More often than not, childhood disorders are accompanied by various layers of abnormal behavior or development, ranging from the more visible and alarming (such as truancy or physical assault), to the more subtle yet critical (such as teasing and peer rejection), to the more hidden and systemic (such as depression or parental rejection).

Moreover, mental health professionals, while attempting to understand children's weaknesses, too often unintentionally overlook their strengths. Yet, many children cope effectively in other areas of their lives, despite the limitations posed by specific psychological disorders. An understanding of children's individual strengths and abilities can lead to ways to assist them in healthy adaptation. Also, some children may show less extreme forms of difficulty or only the early signs of an emerging problem rather than a full-blown disorder. Therefore, to judge what is abnormal, we need to be sensitive to each child's stage of development and consider each child's unique methods of coping and ways of compensating for difficulties (Achenbach, 2010).

Childhood disorders, like adult disorders, have commonly been viewed in terms of deviancies from normal, yet disagreement remains as to what constitutes normal and abnormal. While reading the following discussion, keep in mind that attempting to establish boundaries between abnormal and normal functioning is an arbitrary process at best, and current guidelines are constantly being reviewed for their accuracy, completeness, and usefulness.

Defining Psychological Disorders

The study of abnormal behavior often makes us more sensitive to and wary of the ways used to describe the behavior of others. Whose standard of "normal" do we adopt, and who decides whether this arbitrary standard has been breached? Does abnormal behavior or performance in one area, such as mood, have implications for the whole person?

Although there are no easy answers to these questions, Georgina's real-life problems require an agreement on how to define a psychological (or mental) disorder. A **psychological disorder** traditionally has been defined as a pattern of behavioral, cognitive, emotional, or physical symptoms shown by an individual. Such a pattern is associated with one or more of the following three prominent features:

- The person shows some degree of distress, such as fear or sadness.
- His or her behavior indicates some degree of disability, such as impairment that substantially interferes with or limits activity in one or more important areas of functioning, including physical, emotional, cognitive, and behavioral areas.
- Such distress and disability increase the risk of further suffering or harm, such as death, pain, disability, or an important loss of freedom (American Psychiatric Association [APA], 2000).

To account for the fact that we sometimes show transitory signs of distress, disability, or risk under

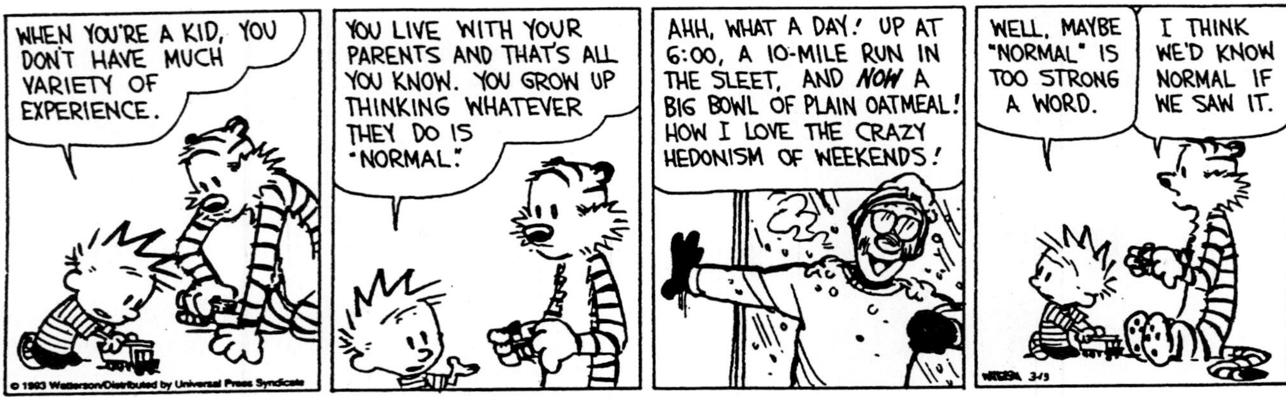

unusual circumstances (such as the loss of a loved one), this definition of a psychological disorder excludes circumstances where such reactions are expected and appropriate as defined by one's cultural background. Furthermore, these three primary features of psychological disorders only describe what a person does or does not do in certain circumstances. The features do not attempt to attribute causes or reasons for abnormal behavior to the individual alone. To the contrary, the understanding of particular impairments should be balanced with recognition of individual and situational circumstances. For example, a child's behavior, thinking, and physical status are all important considerations in determining the degree of success or failure in adapting to the demands of the environment.

Labels Describe Behavior, Not People

It is important to keep in mind that terms used to describe abnormal behavior do not describe people; they only describe patterns of behavior that may or may not occur in certain circumstances. We must be careful to avoid the common mistake of identifying the person with the disorder, as reflected in expressions such as "retarded child" or "autistic child." The field of child and adult mental health is often challenged by **stigma**, which refers to a cluster of negative attitudes and beliefs that motivates fear, rejection, avoidance, and discrimination with respect to people with mental illnesses (Heflinger & Hinshaw, 2010). Stigma leads to prejudice and discrimination against others on the basis of race, ethnicity, disabilities, sexual orientation, body size, biological sex, language, and religious beliefs. Due to stigma, persons with mental disorders may also suffer from low self-esteem, isolation, and hopelessness, and may become so embarrassed or ashamed that they conceal symptoms and fail to seek treatment (Puhl & Latner, 2007). Accordingly, throughout this text we separate the child from the disorder by using language such as "Ramon is a child with mental retardation," rather than "Ramon is mentally retarded." Children like Ramon have many other attributes that should not be overshadowed by global descriptives or negative labels.

In addition, the problems shown by some children may be the result of their attempts to adapt to abnormal or unusual circumstances. Children with chronic health problems must adapt to their medical regimens and to negative reactions from peers; children raised in abusive or neglectful environments must learn how to relate to others adaptively and to regulate emotions that may, at times, be overwhelming. Therefore, the primary purpose of using terms such as *disorder* and *abnormal behavior* for describing the psychological status of children and adolescents is to aid clinicians and researchers in describing, organizing, and expressing the complex features often associated with various patterns of behavior. By no means do the terms imply a common cause, since the causes of abnormal behavior are almost always multifaceted and interactive.

This approach to defining abnormal behavior is similar to the one most often used to classify and diagnose mental disorders, according to the guidelines in the DSM-IV-TR (APA, 2000). We use the approach in guiding the thinking and structure of this book because of its clinical and descriptive utility. Yet, despite advances in defining abnormality and vast improvements in the diagnostic and classification systems, ambiguity remains, especially in defining a particular child's maladaptive dysfunction (Rutter, 2010; Zachar & Kendler, 2007). Boundaries between what constitute normal and abnormal conditions or distinctions among different abnormal conditions are not easily drawn. At present, the DSM-IV-TR approach has achieved some consensus supporting its value in facilitating greater communication and increased standardization of research and clinical knowledge concerning abnormal child psychology. We consider the DSM-IV-TR and current alternatives to classification of childhood disorders in Chapter 4.

Competence

Definitions of abnormal child behavior must take into account the child's **competence**—that is, the ability to successfully adapt in the environment. Developmental competence is reflected in the child's ability to use internal and external resources to achieve a successful adaptation (Masten, 2011). Of course, this begs the question of "what is successful?" Successful adaptation varies across culture and ethnicity, so it is important that the traditions, beliefs, languages, and value systems of a particular culture be taken into account when defining a child's competence. Similarly, some children face greater obstacles than others in their efforts to adapt to their environment. Minority children and families, in particular, must cope with multiple forms of racism, prejudice, discrimination, oppression, and segregation, all of which significantly influence a child's adaptation and development (Children's Defense Fund, 2007).

Judgments of deviancy also require knowledge of a child's performance relative to that of same-age peers, as well as knowledge of the child's course of development and cultural context. In effect, the study of abnormal child psychology considers not only the degree of maladaptive behavior children show but also the extent to which they achieve normal developmental milestones. As with deviancy, the criteria for defining competence can be very specific and narrow in focus, or as plentiful and broad as we wish (Masten & Wright, 2010).

How do we know whether a particular child is doing well, and how do we, as parents, teachers, or professionals, guide our expectations? **Developmental tasks**, which include broad domains of competence such as conduct and academic achievement, tell how children typically progress within each domain as they grow. Knowledge of the developmental tasks provides an important backdrop for considering a child or adolescent's developmental progress and impairments. Examples of several important developmental tasks are shown in Table 1.1.

Conduct is one of the fundamental domains in Table 1.1; it indicates how well a person follows the rules of a particular society. From a young age, children are expected to begin controlling their behavior and to comply with their parents' requests. (This doesn't mean they always do so. . . .) By the time children enter school, they are expected to follow the rules for classroom conduct and to refrain from harming others. Then, by adolescence, they are expected to follow the rules set by school, home, and society without direct supervision. Similar developmental progression occurs in the self domain, where children initially learn to differentiate themselves from the environment, and to gradually develop self-identity and autonomy. In the discussion of disorders in the chapters to follow, we attempt whenever possible to balance the information on abnormal behavior with the growing awareness of children's competencies and strengths.

TABLE 1.1 | Examples of Developmental Tasks

Age Period	Task
Infancy to preschool	Attachment to caregiver(s) Language Differentiation of self from environment Self-control and compliance
Middle childhood 	School adjustment (attendance, appropriate conduct) Academic achievement (e.g., learning to read, do arithmetic) Getting along with peers (acceptance, making friends) Rule-governed conduct (following rules of society for moral behavior and prosocial conduct)
Adolescence 	Successful transition to secondary schooling Academic achievement (learning skills needed for higher education or work) Involvement in extracurricular activities (e.g., athletics, clubs) Forming close friendships within and across gender Forming a cohesive sense of self-identity

Source: From *The Development of Competence in Favorable and Unfavorable Environments: Lessons from Research on Successful Children*, by A. S. Masten and J. D. Coatsworth, 1998, American Psychologist, 53, 205–220. Copyright © 1998 by the American Psychological Association. APA is not responsible for the accuracy of this translation.

Photo Credits (top to bottom): Flashon Studio/Shutterstock.com; Gelpi/Shutterstock.com; OLJ Studio/Shutterstock.com.

Developmental Pathways

Why don't children with similar early experiences have similar problems later in life? Conversely, why do children and adolescents with the same disorder sometimes have very different early experiences or family characteristics? Another aspect of judging deviancy involves deciding when a concern or issue about a child's behavior starts to become a more recognizable pattern, especially since behavior fluctuates and changes considerably as a child develops. Therefore, in addition to distinguishing between normal and abnormal adaptation, we must consider the temporal relationship between emerging concerns in early childhood and the likelihood that they will lead to problems later on.

A **developmental pathway** refers to the sequence and timing of particular behaviors and possible relationships between behaviors over time. The concept allows us to visualize development as an active, dynamic process that can account for very different beginnings and outcomes (Pickles & Hill, 2006). It helps us to understand the course and nature of normal and abnormal development. Two examples of developmental pathways are shown in ● Figure 1.1. The child at the top of the figure has experienced maltreatment at a young age. Maltreatment can significantly alter the child's initial course of development, resulting in diverse and often unpredictable outcomes, such as eating, mood, or conduct disorders. This example illustrates **multifinality**, the concept that various outcomes may stem from similar beginnings (in this case, child maltreatment).

In contrast, other children might set out on their developmental journeys with very different strengths and weaknesses, but later have a similar disorder. As illustrated in the bottom example of Figure 1.1, genetic patterns, familial characteristics, and features of each child's environment represent different pathways leading to a similar outcome (conduct disorder). This example illustrates **equifinality**, the concept that similar outcomes stem from different early experiences and developmental pathways. As we will learn in Chapter 6, children with conduct problems may have very diverse early experiences and risk factors, but later show similar patterns of behavior. By looking at possible developmental pathways, we gain a better understanding of the ways in which children's problems may change or remain the same over time.

In summary, diversity in how children acquire psychological strengths and weaknesses is a hallmark of abnormal child psychology. Because no clear cause-and-effect relationship exists for each child and adolescent disorder, the following assumptions need to be kept firmly in mind (Mash & Dozois, 2003):

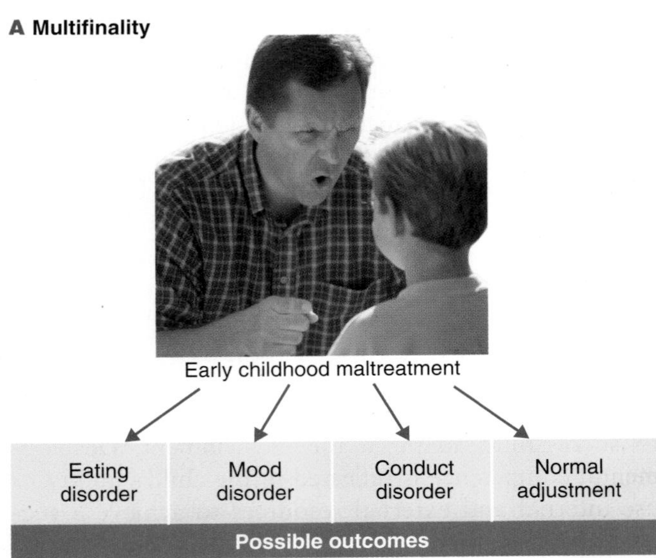

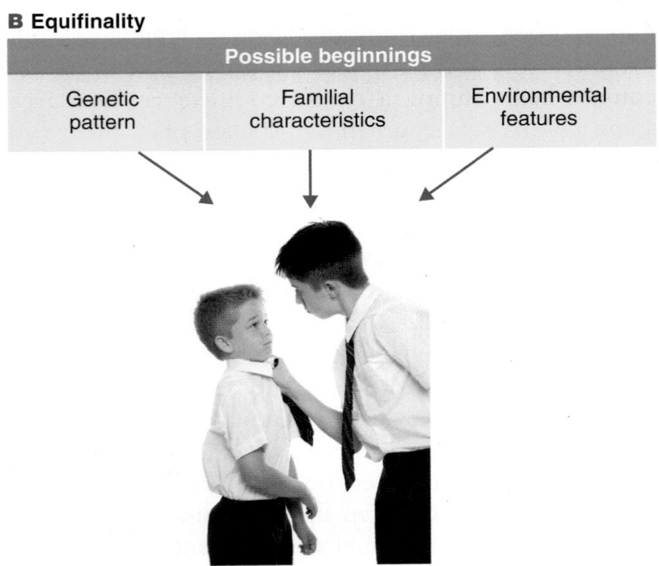

● **FIGURE 1.1** | (a) Multifinality: Similar early experiences lead to different outcomes; (b) Equifinality: Different factors lead to a similar outcome.

Photo Credits: (a) © 2011 SW Productions/Jupiterimages Corporation; (b) © iStockphoto.com/Sarah Salmela.

- There are many contributors to disordered outcomes in each individual.
- Contributors vary among individuals who have the disorder.
- Individuals with the same specific disorder express the features of their disturbance in different ways (e.g., some children with a conduct disorder are aggressive, whereas others may be destructive to property or engage in theft or deceit).

- The pathways leading to any particular disorder are numerous and interactive, as opposed to unidimensional and static.

SECTION SUMMARY

What Is Abnormal Behavior in Children and Adolescents?

- Defining a psychological disorder involves agreement on particular patterns of behavioral, cognitive, and physical symptoms shown by an individual.
- Terms used to describe abnormal behavior are meant to define behavior, not to be used as labels to describe individuals.
- Defining abnormal behavior requires judgment concerning the degree to which a person's behavior is maladaptive or harmful as well as dysfunctional or impaired.
- Diversity in how children acquire psychological strengths and weaknesses is a hallmark of abnormal child psychology. The many contributors to abnormal behavior may vary within and between individuals with similar disorders.
- The study of psychological disorders involves attempts to describe the presenting problems and abilities, to understand contributing causes, and to treat or prevent them.
- Developmental pathways help to describe the course and nature of normal and abnormal development; multifinality means that various outcomes may stem from similar beginnings, whereas equifinality means that similar outcomes stem from different early experiences.

RISK AND RESILIENCE

I am convinced that, except in a few extraordinary cases, one form or another of an unhappy childhood is essential to the formation of exceptional gifts.

—Thornton Wilder (1897–1975)

RAOUL AND JESSE

Why the Differences?

Raoul and Jesse were childhood friends who grew up in the same rundown housing project, in a neighborhood plagued by drugs and crime. By the time they were 10 years old they were both familiar with domestic and community violence, and each lived with his mother and an older sibling after his parents divorced. The boys rarely saw their fathers, and when they did it usually wasn't a pleasant experience. By the time they reached grade 6 they were falling behind at school, and started to get into trouble with the police for staying out too late, hassling kids at school, and breaking into cars. Despite these problems and a struggle to keep up, Raoul finished high school and received 2 years of training in a local trade school. He is now 30 years old, works at a local factory, and lives with his wife and two children. Raoul sums up his life thus far as "dodging bullets to reach where I want to go," but he's happy to be living in a safe neighborhood and to have the hope of sending his children to college.

His friend Jesse never graduated from high school. He dropped out after being expelled for bringing a weapon to school, and has been in and out of prison several times. At age 30, Jesse drinks too much and has a poor record of finding and keeping a job. He has had several short-term relationships and fathered two children, but he rarely visits them and never married either mother. Jesse has lived in several locations over the years, mostly in his old, unchanged neighborhood. (Based on Zimmerman & Arunkumar, 1994)

These brief life histories illustrate two very different developmental paths that started out at the same place. Jesse's troubles might have been predicted based on present knowledge of abnormal development, but it is more difficult to explain how some children, like Raoul, seem to escape harm despite stress and adversity. Perhaps you are familiar with someone—from a novel, movie, or personal friendship—who seems to come out on top despite adversity and limited resources. How do you suppose individuals such as Oprah Winfrey (see Box 1.5) escape the odds and achieve their life goals?

The answer to this complicated question is coming into focus, thanks to studies that look at risk as well as protective factors affecting children's courses of development. A **risk factor** is a variable that precedes a negative outcome of interest and increases the chances that the outcome will occur. In contrast, a **protective factor** is a personal or situational variable that reduces the chances for a child to develop a disorder. As you might suspect, children like Raoul and Jesse, who face many known risk factors such as community violence and parental divorce, are vulnerable to abnormal development. Acute, stressful situations as well as chronic adversity put children's successful development at risk. Chronic poverty, serious caregiving deficits, parental mental illness, the death of a parent, community disasters, homelessness, family breakup, and pregnancy and birth complications are known risk factors that increase children's vulnerability to psychopathology—especially in the absence of compensatory strengths and resources (Kim-Cohen & Gold, 2009).

BOX 1.5 A CLOSER LOOK

Finding One's Strength

Sometimes we can learn a lot from the personal stories of individuals who are famous or well known for their talent or achievements. In some cases, such as that of the popular talk-show host, publisher, actor, and entertainer Oprah Winfrey, the stories reveal early experiences of adversity or loss that these individuals remember as being instrumental in setting them on a life course.

Her grandparents raised Oprah for the first 6 years of her life. Despite living in poverty and being subjected to harsh physical discipline, she was grateful for her grandmother's influence: "I am what I am because of my grandmother. My strength. My sense of reasoning. Everything. All that was set by the time I was six." While moving back and forth between her two parents' homes in her later childhood and adolescent years, Oprah was sexually abused by several people, and as a result gave birth to a stillborn baby at 14 years old. This traumatic experience renewed her resolve to make something of herself. Oprah credits her father and various teachers for helping her navigate those troubled years and giving her the confidence to succeed: "Since my childhood, [my father] has set excellent standards that helped me succeed. For every one of us that succeeds, it's because there's somebody there to show you the way out. The light doesn't necessarily have to be in your family; for me it was teachers and school." Throughout her career, Oprah has channeled these hardships into a driving ambition to succeed, and is currently one of the most successful and influential women in entertainment and popular culture. Oprah's life showcases her resilient adaptation to unfavorable life circumstances, and is a source of her attitude toward life: "I believe that you tend to create your own blessings. You have to prepare yourself so that when opportunity comes, you're ready."

AP Photo/Dima Gavrysh, file

Oprah Winfrey's life exemplifies strength in the face of adversity

Source: Based on Lowe, 1998.

Yet, like Raoul, some vulnerable children do not develop later problems. Instead, they seem resilient despite their stress-filled environments, managing to achieve positive outcomes despite being at significant risk for psychopathology. Children who survive risky environments by using their strong self-confidence, coping skills, and abilities to avoid risk situations may be considered resilient—they seem able to fight off or recover from their misfortune (Luthar, 2006). These children are also most likely to show sustained competence while under stress, or to rebound to a previously healthy level of competence following traumatic or stressful experiences (Kim-Cohen & Gold, 2009). **Resilience** is not a universal, categorical, or fixed attribute of the child. It varies according to the type of stress, its context, and similar factors. Individual children may be resilient with respect to some specific stressors but not others, and resilience may vary over time and across situations. Resilience is seen in children across cultures, despite the extraordinary circumstances that some may face (Kirmayer, Dandeneau, Marshall, Phillips, & Williamson, 2011; Ungar, 2010).

The concept of resilience reminds us that a direct causal pathway rarely leads to a particular outcome. Ongoing interactions exist between protective and risk factors within the child, between the child and his or her surroundings, and among risk factors themselves. Protective factors are personal or situational variables that reduce the chances for a child to develop a disorder. Risk factors do the exact opposite—they increase the child's likelihood of developing a problem. Risk factors and protective factors should be thought of as processes rather than absolutes, since the same event or condition can function as either type of factor, depending on the overall context in which it occurs (Rutter, 2007). For example, placing young children with another family may serve to protect them if they were being severely mistreated. However, for some children out-of-home placement could increase their vulnerability if it creates more stress due to being removed from their mother or father. Throughout each chapter, we offer similar examples of children's vulnerability and resilience in relation to particular circumstances and disorders.

● Figure 1.2 illustrates some of the better-known characteristics of children and adolescents who display resilience, which are sometimes overlooked in attempts to explain abnormal development. These characteristics constitute a protective triad of resources and health-promoting events: the strengths of the individual, the family, and the school and community (Luthar, 2006). Protective factors vary tremendously in magnitude and scope, and not all three resources are necessary. For some children, merely the availability of a supportive grandparent or teacher can effectively change the course and direction of their development. Other children may need additional or different protective factors, such as a better learning environment, community safety, or sufficient family resources.

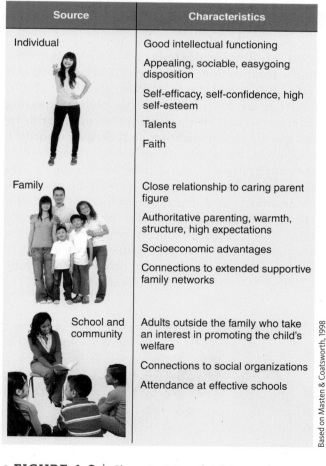

Source	Characteristics
Individual 	Good intellectual functioning Appealing, sociable, easygoing disposition Self-efficacy, self-confidence, high self-esteem Talents Faith
Family 	Close relationship to caring parent figure Authoritative parenting, warmth, structure, high expectations Socioeconomic advantages Connections to extended supportive family networks
School and community 	Adults outside the family who take an interest in promoting the child's welfare Connections to social organizations Attendance at effective schools

Based on Masten & Coatsworth, 1998

● **FIGURE 1.2** | Characteristics of children and adolescents who display resilience in the face of adversity.

Photo Credits (top to bottom): Odua Images/Shutterstock.com; Apollofoto/Shutterstock.com; iofoto/Shutterstock.com.

SECTION SUMMARY

Risk and Resilience

- Children's normal development may be put in jeopardy because of risk factors, which can include acute, stressful situations and chronic adversity.
- Some children seem to be more resilient in the face of risk factors. Resiliency is related to strong self-confidence, coping skills, and the ability to avoid risk situations, as well as the ability to fight off or recover from misfortune.
- Children's resilience is connected to a protective triad of resources and health-promoting events that include individual opportunities, close family ties, and opportunities for individual and family support from community resources.

The Significance of Mental Health Problems Among Children and Youths

It's up to each of us to help create a better world for our children.

—Dr. Benjamin Spock

Until very recently, children's mental health problems were the domain of folklore and unsubstantiated theories in both the popular and scientific literatures. Only a few generations ago, in the mid-nineteenth century, overstimulation in schools was seen as a cause of insanity (Makari, 1993), and only one generation ago, in the mid-twentieth century, autism was believed to be caused by inadequate, uncaring parents (Bettelheim, 1967).

We now recognize that mental health problems of children and adolescents are a frequently occurring and significant societal concern worldwide. For example, by 2020 behavioral health disorders will surpass all physical diseases as a major cause of disability throughout the world (Substance Abuse and Mental Health Services Administration [SAMHSA], 2011; World Health Organization [WHO], 2007). Perhaps most telling of all is the mounting evidence that "*many, if not most, lifetime psychiatric disorders will first appear in childhood or adolescence*" (Costello, Egger, & Angold, 2005, p. 972, italics added; Kessler et al., 2009).

Surveys conducted in North America and elsewhere find that about one child in eight has a mental health problem that significantly impairs functioning (Costello et al., 2005), a finding that extends even to infants and toddlers (Skovgaard et al., 2007). Many other children have emerging problems that place them at risk for later development of a psychological

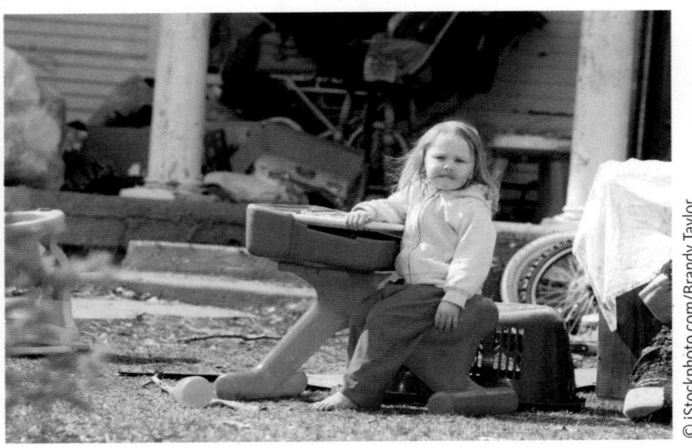

© iStockphoto.com/Brandy Taylor

In the United States, the richest nation on earth, 35.3% of black children, 28.0% of Latino children, and 10.8% of white, non-Latino children live in poverty (Children's Defense Fund, 2007)

disorder. As surprising as it may sound, recent longitudinal studies have found that by their 21st birthday, 3 out of 5 young adults meet criteria for a well-specified psychiatric disorder (Copeland, Shanahan, Costello, & Angold, 2011). Some children have difficulties adapting to school or to family circumstances, so they behave in ways that are developmentally or situationally inappropriate. Others show more pronounced patterns of poor development and maladjustment that suggest one or more specific disorders of childhood or adolescence. The process of deciding which problems merit professional attention and which ones might be outgrown involves a good understanding of both normal and abnormal child development and behavior.

Despite the magnitude of children's mental health needs today, the youngest one-fourth of the population (those under age 18) have very few treatment options, and those options that are available are woefully underfunded (Weisz & Kazdin, 2010). Sadly, the majority of children and youths needing mental health services do not receive them, due largely to poor understanding of mental disorders and limited access to intervention (Mark et al., 2008; McEwan, Waddell, & Barker, 2007). The demand for children's mental health services is expected to double over the next decade because the number of child and adolescent mental health professionals is not expected to increase at the required rate (Health Resources and Services Administration, 2010). A career in children's mental health, anyone?

The chapters that follow explain that a significant proportion of children do not grow out of their childhood difficulties, although the ways in which children express difficulties are likely to change in both form and severity over time. Children's developmental impairments may have a lasting negative impact on later family life, occupations, and social adjustment, even when they no longer have the disorder.

The Changing Picture of Children's Mental Health

If all children and adolescents with known psychological disorders could be captured in a photograph, the current picture would be much clearer than that of only a generation ago. The improved focus and detail are the result of efforts to increase recognition and assessment of children's psychological disorders. In the past, children with various mental health and educational needs were too often described in global terms such as *maladjusted,* because assessment devices were not sensitive to different syndromes and diagnostic clusters of symptoms (Achenbach & Rescorla, 2007). Today, we have a better ability to distinguish among the various disorders. This has given rise to increased and earlier recognition of previously poorly understood or undetected problems—learning disorders, depression, teen suicide, eating disorders, conduct disorders, and problems stemming from chronic health conditions and from abuse and neglect.

Another difference in today's portrait would be the group's composition. Younger children (Skovgaard et al., 2007) and teens (Wolfe & Mash, 2006) would appear more often in the photo, reflecting greater awareness of their unique mental health issues. Specific communication and learning disorders, for example, have only recently been recognized as significant concerns among preschoolers and young school-age children. Similarly, emotional problems, such as anxiety and depression, which increase dramatically during adolescence (Rudolph, Hammen, & Daley, 2006), were previously overlooked because the symptoms are often less visible or disturbing to others than are the symptoms of behavior or learning problems.

© iStockphoto.com/Christopher Futcher

Surveys estimate that about 1 child in 8 has a mental health problem that interferes with his or her development, and 1 in 10 has a specific psychological disorder

What would not have changed in our photo is the proportion of children who are receiving proper services. Fewer than 10% of children with mental health problems receive proper services to address impairments related to personal, family, or situational factors (Costello et al., 2005). Limited and fragmented resources mean that children do not receive appropriate mental health services at the appropriate time. Fortunately, this situation is beginning to change, with greater attention paid to evidence-based prevention and treatment programs for many childhood disorders and calls for more integrated services for children within the school system (Kirby & Keon, 2006; Weisz & Kazdin, 2010).

The children and teens in the picture would not reflect a random cross section of all children, because mental health problems are unevenly distributed. Those disproportionately afflicted with mental health problems are:

- Children from disadvantaged families and neighborhoods (Razza, Martin, & Brooks-Gunn, 2010)
- Children from abusive or neglectful families (Cicchetti, Rogosch, Gunnar, & Toth, 2010; Wekerle, Miller, Wolfe, & Spindel, 2006)
- Children receiving inadequate child care (Pollak et al., 2010)
- Children born with very low birth weight due to maternal smoking, diet, or abuse of alcohol and drugs (D'Onofrio et al., 2010)
- Children born to parents with mental illness or substance abuse problems (Davis, Glynn, Waffarn, & Sandman, 2011; Mellin, 2010)

Also, the children in the picture could not easily be grouped according to these categories, because children often face combinations of environmental stressors and psychosocial deprivations. Such children are especially at risk of having their healthy development compromised to the degree that they are said to show abnormal behavior or to suffer from a mental disorder.

What Affects Rates and Expression of Mental Disorders? A Look at Some Key Factors

New pressures and social changes may place children at increasing risk for the development of disorders at younger ages (Obradovic, Bush, Stamperdahl, Adler, & Boyce, 2010). Many stressors today are quite different from those faced by our parents and grandparents. Some have been around for generations: chronic poverty, inequality, family breakup, single parenting, and so on. Others are now more recent or more visible: homelessness, adjustment problems of children in immigrant families, inadequate child care for working parents, and conditions associated with the impact of prematurity, parental HIV, and cocaine or alcohol abuse on children's growth and development (Chapman, Dube, & Anda, 2007). Even welcome medical advances can have a negative effect. Higher rates of fetal survival have contributed to a greater number of children with behavior and learning difficulties who require specialized services at a younger age.

It is important to remember that the manner in which one's circumstances affect the course (e.g., progression) of a disorder should be distinguished from how they may initially contribute to the problem. That is, environmental stressors, such as poverty, child abuse, or lack of safety, may act as nonspecific stressors that bring about poor adaptation or even the onset of a disorder in some vulnerable children. In contrast, these same environmental influences may affect the course of the disorder in other children by affecting the extent to which the child's problems are attenuated or exacerbated (Williams & Steinberg, 2011). Examples of major factors in the development and expression of child psychopathology are noted next, and resurface throughout our subsequent discussions of each disorder.

Poverty and Socioeconomic Disadvantage

The most dangerous place for a child to try to grow up in America is at the intersection of race and poverty.

—Children's Defense Fund (2007)

If you looked beyond the faces of the children in our hypothetical photo, you would note that in many cases, the background and circumstances of children and youths with mental health problems provide obvious clues to their origins. Some of the most telling clues are the experiences of poverty, disadvantage, and violence faced by many, which can have a cumulative effect on their mental health.

Childhood poverty is a daily reality for about 1 in 5 children in the United States (U.S. Census Bureau, 2011a) and 1 in 7 in Canada (Statistics Canada, 2011), and is especially pronounced among Native American/First Nations and African American children (Spicer & Sarche, 2006). Growing up with poverty has a substantial effect on the well-being of children and adolescents, especially in terms of impairments in learning ability and school achievement. Moreover, low income is tied to many other forms of disadvantage: less education, low-paying jobs, inadequate health care, single-parent

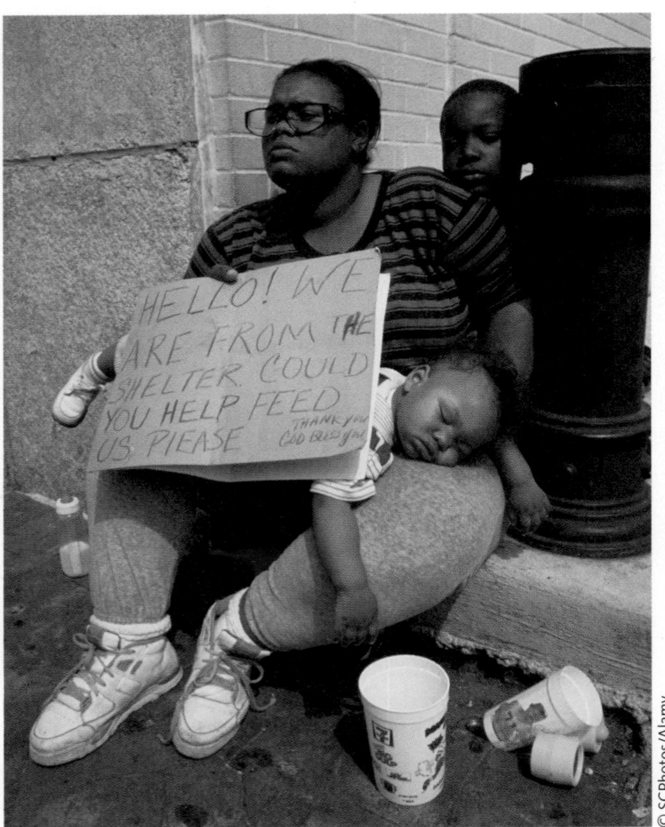

Eighty-eight percent of homeless families in the United States are headed by women

status, limited resources, poor nutrition, and greater exposure to violence. Any one disadvantage can impair children's developmental progress significantly (Razza et al., 2010).

The impact of childhood poverty is telling. Children from poor and disadvantaged families suffer more conduct disorders, chronic illness, school problems, emotional disorders, and cognitive/learning problems than children who are not poor (McMahon & Luthar, 2007). These impairments may be due to the pronounced effect on pre-frontal cortex development stemming from the social inequalities of chronic poverty (Kishiyama, Boyce, Jimenez, Perry, & Knight, 2009). Economic deprivation alone is not responsible for these higher rates, because many children do succeed under harsh circumstances. Nevertheless, the greater the degree of inequality, powerlessness, and lack of control over their lives, the more children's physical and mental health are undermined (Aber, Jones, & Raver, 2007).

Poverty has a significant, yet indirect, effect on children's adjustment, most likely because of its association with negative influences—particularly harsh, inconsistent parenting and elevated exposure to acute and chronic stressors—that define the day-to-day experiences of children in poverty. For example, youths who live in inner-city areas and witness community violence are most likely to develop post-traumatic stress disorder (Kiser, 2007) as well as cognitive delays and impairments that affect both learning and mental health (Farah et al., 2006).

Sex Differences

We have known for some time that boys and girls express their problems in different ways (Zahn-Waxler, Crick, Shirtcliff, & Woods, 2006). For example, hyperactivity, autism, childhood disruptive behavior disorders, and learning and communication disorders are more common in boys than in girls; the opposite is true for most anxiety disorders, adolescent depression, and eating disorders. What we don't understand is whether these differences are caused by definitions, reporting biases (the more "disturbing" problems are most likely to come to the attention of mental health agencies), or differences in the expression of the disorder. For example, aggressive behavior may be expressed more directly by boys (fighting) and more indirectly by girls (spreading rumors). Although mental health problems for girls have been understudied, this situation is changing; therefore, we consider the expression of problems for boys and girls in each chapter.

Sex differences in problem behaviors are negligible in children under the age of 3, but increase with age (Achenbach & Rescorla, 2006). Boys show higher rates of early onset disorders that involve some form of neurodevelopmental impairment, and girls show more emotional disorders, with a peak age of onset in adolescence. For example, boys generally have higher rates of reading disorders, autism spectrum disorders, attention deficit disorder, and early onset persistent conduct problems, whereas girls have higher rates of depression and eating disorders (Copeland et al., 2011; Rutter et al., 2004).

● Figure 1.3 depicts the normal developmental trajectories for girls and boys across the two major dimensions of internalizing and externalizing behaviors. **Internalizing problems** include anxiety, depression, somatic complaints, and withdrawn behavior; **externalizing problems** encompass more acting-out behaviors such as aggression and delinquent behavior. You'll notice from Figure 1.3 (top) that externalizing problems for boys start out higher than for girls in preschool and early elementary years, and that these problems decrease gradually for both boys and girls until the rates almost converge by age 18. The opposite pattern emerges for internalizing problems. Parents report similar rates of internalizing problems for boys and girls in early childhood, but girls outpace boys in these

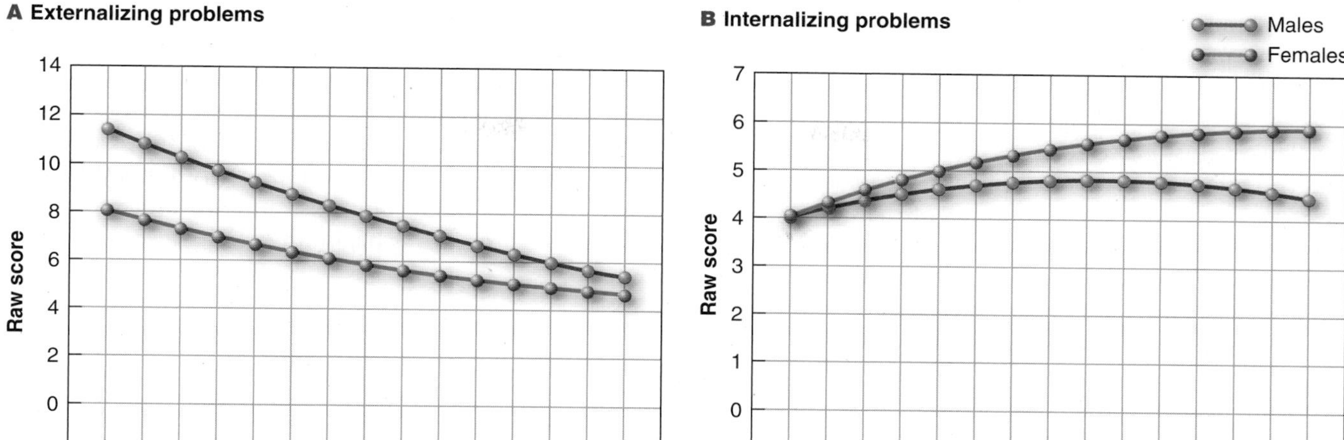

• **FIGURE 1.3** | Normative developmental trajectories of externalizing problems (left graph) and internalizing problems (right graph) from the Child Behavior Checklist. Ages are shown on the *x* axis. The *y* axis represents the raw scores (higher score means more problems).

Adapted from the normative development of child and adolescent problem behaviour., by Bongers, I. L., Koot, H. M., van der Ende, J., & Verhulst, F. C., 2003, Journal of Abnormal Psychology, 112, 179–192. Copyright © 2003 by the American Psychological Association. Reprinted with permission. APA is not responsible for the accuracy of this translation.

problems over time (Bongers, Koot, van der Ende, & Verhulst, 2003). These developmental trajectories of problem behaviors provide a useful basis against which deviations from the normal course can be identified, although these overall trends need to be considered in relation to a number of additional factors that we discuss throughout the text.

Finally, it is interesting to note that the types of child-rearing environments predicting resilience in the face of adversity also differ for boys and girls. Resilience in boys is associated with households in which there is a male role model (such as a father, grandfather, or older brother); structure; rules; and some encouragement of emotional expressiveness. In contrast, girls who display resilience come from households that combine risk taking and independence with support from a female caregiver (such as a mother, grandmother, or older sister; Werner, 2005).

Race and Ethnicity

Physical variations in the human species have no meaning except the social ones that humans put on them.

—The American Anthropological Association, 1998

Racial and ethnic minority persons comprise a substantial and vibrant segment of many countries, enriching each society with many unique strengths, cultural traditions, and important contributions. In the United States the number of minority persons is growing rapidly—by 2050 the nation's population of children is expected to be 62% minority, up from 44% today (U.S. Census Bureau, 2011b).

As reflected in the quote above, the majority of cultural anthropologists today believe that race is a socially constructed concept, not a biological one (Crisp & Turner, 2011; Sternberg, Grigorenko, & Kidd, 2005). This helps explain why very few emotional and behavioral disorders of childhood occur at different rates for different racial groups. Minority children in the United States are overrepresented in rates of some disorders, such as substance abuse, delinquency, and teen suicide (Nguyen, Huang, Arganza, & Liao, 2007). However, once the effects of socioeconomic status (SES), sex, age, and referral status are controlled for (i.e., the unique contributions of these factors are removed or accounted for), few differences in the rate of children's psychological disorders emerge in relation to race or ethnicity (Roberts, Roberts, & Xing, 2006). Some minority groups, in fact, show less psychopathology after controlling for SES (Nguyen et al., 2007; Roberts et al., 2006).

Even though rates of problems are similar, significant barriers remain in access to, and quality and outcomes of, care for minority children (Alegria, Vallas, & Pumariega, 2010). As a result, American Indians, Alaska Natives, African Americans, Asian Americans, Pacific Islanders, and Hispanic Americans bear a disproportionately high burden of disability from mental disorders (Agency for Healthcare Research and Quality, 2011). Specifically, the majority culture has neglected to incorporate respect for or understanding of the histories, traditions, beliefs, languages, and value systems of culturally diverse groups. Misunderstanding and misinterpreting behaviors have led to tragic consequences, including inappropriately placing minorities in the criminal and juvenile justice systems (Pumariega, Rothe, Song, & Lu, 2010).

Minority children and youths face multiple disadvantages, such as poverty and exclusion from society's benefits. This exclusion is often referred to as marginalization, and can result in a sense of alienation, loss of social cohesion, and rejection of the norms of the larger society. Resisting the combined effects of poverty and marginalization takes unusual personal strength and family support. Since there is an overrepresentation of minority-status children in low-SES groups, we must interpret with caution the relationships among SES, ethnicity, and behavior problems that often emerge while discussing childhood disorders. We also have to keep in mind that, despite the growing ethnic diversity of the North American population, ethnic representation in research studies and the study of ethnicity-related issues receive relatively little attention in studies of child psychopathology and treatment (Coll, Akerman, & Cicchetti, 2000; Schwartz, Unger, Zamboanga, & Szapocznik, 2010).

As was the case for SES and sex differences, global comparisons of the prevalence of different types of problems for different ethnic groups are not likely to be very revealing. On the other hand, investigations into the processes affecting the form, associated factors, and outcomes of different disorders for various ethnic groups hold promise for increasing our understanding of the relationship between ethnicity and abnormal child behavior.

Culture

The values, beliefs, and practices that characterize a particular ethnocultural group contribute to the development and expression of children's disorders, and affect how people and institutions react to a child's problem (Rescorla et al., 2011). Because the meaning of children's social behavior is influenced by cultural beliefs and values, it is not surprising that children express their problems somewhat differently across cultures. For example, shyness and oversensitivity in children have been found to be associated with peer rejection and social maladjustment in Western cultures, but to be associated with leadership, school competence, and academic achievement in Chinese children in Shanghai (Chen, Rubin, & Li, 1995; Rubin et al., 2006).

Because of cultural influences, it is important that research on abnormal child behavior not be generalized from one culture to another unless there is support for doing so. Some underlying processes, such as regulating emotion and its relationship to social competence, may be similar across diverse cultures (Eisenberg, Smith, & Spinrad, 2011). Similarly, some disorders, particularly those with a strong neurobiological basis (e.g., ADHD, autistic disorder), may be less susceptible to cultural influences. Nonetheless, social and cultural beliefs and values are likely to influence the meaning given to these behaviors, the ways in which they are responded to, their forms of expression, and their outcomes. We caution throughout this text that few studies have compared the attitudes, behaviors, and biological and psychological processes of children with mental disorders across different cultures, and we indicate places where this situation is beginning to change.

Child Maltreatment and Non-Accidental Trauma

Children and adolescents are being neglected and abused at an alarming rate worldwide (WHO, 2010). Each year nearly 1 million verified cases of child abuse and neglect (a rate of 10 per 1,000 children) occur in the United States (U.S. Department of Health and Human Services, 2010), and more than 80,000 in Canada (Public Health Agency of Canada, 2010). U.S. phone surveys of children and youths between 10 and 16 years old estimate that more than one-third (6 million) of U.S. children in that age bracket experience physical and/or sexual assaults during these ages, not only by family members but also by persons they may know from their communities and schools (Finkelhor, 2011).

These related forms of non-accidental trauma—being the victim of violence at school or being exposed to violent acts in their homes or neighborhoods—lead to significant mental health problems in children and youths.

In a telephone survey of more than 4,000 youths between 12 and 17 years of age, 16% of boys and 19% of girls met the criteria for either post-traumatic stress disorder, major depressive episode, or substance abuse/dependence in relation to acts of violence (Kilpatrick et al., 2003). Tragically, these acts of abuse and trauma are estimated to cost over $100 billion per year in the United States as a result of direct and indirect harm to the lives of these children (Prevent Child Abuse America, 2008). Due to the increasing significance of these acts, more attention is being given to developing ways to prevent, and help youngsters exposed to, maltreatment and trauma. We acknowledge this concern by devoting Chapter 14 to this issue.

Special Issues Concerning Adolescents and Sexual Minority Youths

Early to mid-adolescence is a particularly important transitional period for healthy versus problematic adjustment (Cicchetti & Rogosch, 2002; Wolfe & Mash, 2006). Substance use, risky sexual behavior, violence, accidental injuries, and mental health problems are only a few of the major issues that make adolescence a particularly vulnerable period. Disturbingly, mortality rates more than triple between late childhood and early adulthood, primarily as the result of risk-taking behaviors (Centers for Disease Control and Prevention, 2010).

Late childhood and early adolescence is also a time in which sexual minority youths face multiple challenges that can affect their health and well-being. Growing up in a society that is predominately heterosexual—and largely biased against other sexual identities—makes adolescence a particularly difficult time for lesbian, gay, bisexual, or transgendered (LGBT) youths. According to several large surveys of LGBT youths in middle and high schools, they are more likely to be victimized by their peers as well as by family members, and report more bullying, teasing, harassment, and physical assault than other students (Kosciw, Greytak, & Diaz, 2009). For example, 81% report experiencing verbal abuse related to being LGBT, 38% have been threatened with physical attacks, 22% have had objects thrown at them, 15% have been physically assaulted, and 16% have been sexually assaulted (D'Augelli, 2006). Given the stigma and prejudice that exist in many parts of society, it is not surprising that LGBT youths have higher rates of mental health problems, including depression and suicidal behavior, substance abuse, and risky sexual behavior, compared to their heterosexual counterparts (Coker, Austin, & Schuster, 2010).

In response to mounting concerns, the special needs and problems of adolescents are receiving greater attention, especially because serious consequences are preventable. For example, health promotion efforts to reduce harm from normal risk taking and experimentation in adolescence are being implemented in primary health care settings, schools, and community programs (Beardslee, Chien, & Bell, 2011). Because the problems of adolescents have been neglected relative to those of children, throughout this text we will look at the expression of each disorder in both childhood and adolescence as much as possible.

Lifespan Implications

Over the long term, the impact of children's mental health problems is most severe when the problems continue untreated for months or years. The developmental tasks of childhood are challenging enough without the added burden of emotional or behavioral disturbances that interfere with the progress and course of development. About 20% of the children with the most chronic and serious disorders face sizable difficulties throughout their lives (Costello & Angold, 2006). They are least likely to finish school and most likely to have social problems or psychiatric disorders that affect many aspects of their lives throughout adulthood.

The lifelong consequences associated with child psychopathology are exceedingly costly in terms of economic impact and human suffering. The costs are enormous with respect to demands on community resources such as health, education, mental health, and criminal justice systems; loss in productivity; the need for repeated and long-term interventions; and the human suffering of both the afflicted children and the family and community members they encounter. Fortunately, children and youths can overcome major impediments when circumstances and opportunities promote healthy adaptation and competence.

The growing recognition of the concerns presented in this chapter has led to a number of major initiatives to achieve the goals of prevention and help. These initiatives are summarized in a number of government reports that include recommendations as to how these goals can be achieved. Many of these important reports are available on the Internet (see Box 1.6) and we recommend that you familiarize yourself with these developments.

SECTION SUMMARY

What Affects the Rates and Expression of Mental Disorders? A Look at Some Key Factors

- A clear understanding of both normal and abnormal child development and behavior is needed to decide which problems are likely to continue and which might be outgrown.
- About one child in eight has a mental health problem that significantly impairs functioning.
- A significant proportion of children do not grow out of their childhood difficulties, although the ways in which these difficulties are expressed are likely to change in both form and severity over time.
- Mental health problems are unevenly distributed. Children who experience more social and economic disadvantage or inequality and children exposed to more violent, inadequate, or toxic environments are disproportionately afflicted with mental health problems.
- A child's biological sex, ethnic background, and cultural surroundings are all important contributors to the manner in which his or her behavioral and emotional problems are expressed to and recognized by others.
- Many childhood problems can have lifelong consequences for the child and for society.

Looking Ahead

The significance of children's mental health problems emerges over and over again throughout this text, as we consider the many different individual, family, social, and cultural influences that define abnormal child

BOX 1.6 A CLOSER LOOK

Current Reports on Mental Health Issues Pertaining to Children and Youths

Beginning with the U.S. Surgeon General's Report on Mental Health in 1999, there have been many important national and international initiatives and reports about understanding and helping children and adolescents with mental health problems. The wonders of the information age provide free access to this wealth of information (as if reading your textbook were not enough!). Below is a list of some (by no means all) of the more important documents that are shaping the field. Your Psychology CourseMate provides live links to most of these documents.

Mental Health

United States Public Health Service Office of the Surgeon General. (1999). *Mental health: A report of the Surgeon General.* Rockville, MD: Department of Health and Human Services, U.S. Public Health Service.

Development and Psychopathology

Institute of Medicine. (2000). *From neurons to neighborhoods: The science of early childhood development.* Washington, DC: National Academies Press.

Children's Rights

UNICEF Innocenti Research Centre. (2005). Laying the foundations for children's rights: An independent study of some key legal and institutional aspects of the impact of the Convention on the Rights of the Child. Also see: **http://www.unicef.org/crc/**

Culture, Race, and Ethnicity

United States Public Health Service Office of the Surgeon General. (2001). *Mental health: Culture, race, and ethnicity: A supplement to Mental health: A report of the Surgeon General.* Rockville, MD: Department of Health and Human Services, U.S. Public Health Service.

Children's Mental Health

Report of *Healthy Development: A Summit on Young Children's Mental Health* (2009). Partnering with communication scientists, collaborating across disciplines, and leveraging impact to promote children's mental health. Washington, DC: Society for Research in Child Development. Available online at **www.apa.org/pi/families/summit-report.pdf**

Research on Children's Mental Health

Alberta Mental Health Research Partnership Program. (2009). A report on child and adolescent mental health research. Available online at **http://www.mentalhealthresearch.ca/Publications/prioritythemes/Pages/default.aspx#child%20and%20adolescent%20mental%20health**

Mental Health: International Perspective

World Health Organization. (2007). *The world health report 2007.* Geneva: World Health Organization.

Transforming Mental Health Care

Transforming mental health care in America. Rockville, MD: Substance Abuse and Mental Health Services Administration (SAMHSA). Available online at **http://www.samhsa.gov/federalactionagenda/NFC_TOC.aspx**

Out of the Shadows At Last: Transforming Mental Health, Mental Illness and Addiction Services in Canada. The Standing Senate Committee on Social Affairs, Science and Technology. Available online at **http://www.parl.gc.ca/Content/SEN/Committee/391/soci/rep/rep02may06-e.htm**

Substance Abuse

Substance Abuse and Mental Health Services Administration. (2010). *Results from the 2009 National Survey on Drug Use and Health: Volume I. Summary of National Findings* (Office of Applied Studies, NSDUH Series H-38A, HHS Publication No. SMA 10–4586 Findings).

Rockville, MD. Available online at **http://oas.samhsa.gov/nsduhlatest.htm**

Suicide Prevention

U.S. Department of Health and Human Services. *Suicide Prevention: Resources and Publications.* Substance Abuse and Mental Health Services Administration. Available online at **http://www.samhsa.gov/prevention/suicide.aspx**

Youth Violence

United States Public Health Service Office of the Surgeon General. (2001). *Youth violence: A report of the Surgeon General.* Rockville, MD: Department of Health and Human Services, U.S. Public Health Service. Also see: Centers for Disease Control and Prevention. *Injury Center: Violence prevention.* Available online at **http://www.cdc.gov/ViolencePrevention/youthviolence/index.html**

Reducing Health Risks

World Health Organization. (2008, July). *What are the key health dangers for children?* Available online at **http://www.who.int/features/qa/13/en/index.html**

Violence and Health

World Health Organization. (2002). *World report on violence and health.* Geneva: World Health Organization. Also see: *WHO Violence and Injury Prevention and Disability (VIP): Prevention of Violence.* Available online at **http://www.who.int/violence_injury_prevention/violence/en/**

Sexual Minority Youths

Centers for Disease Control and Prevention. (2011, June). *MMWR: Sexual Identity, Sex of Sexual Contacts, and Health-Risk Behaviors Among Students in Grades 9–12—Youth Risk Behavior Surveillance, Selected Sites, United States, 2001–2009.* Available online at **http://www.cdc.gov/healthyyouth/disparities/smy.htm**

psychology. Because children cannot advocate on their own behalf, and because their mental health needs and developmental issues differ markedly from those of adults, it is important that we keep these concerns in mind. Moreover, children's problems don't come in neat packages. Many disorders discussed in the text overlap with other disorders in terms of symptoms, characteristics, and treatment needs. Once again, the importance of viewing the whole child in relation to his or her difficulties emerges as the best strategy in understanding abnormal child and adolescent psychology, using diagnostic criteria as guideposts rather than as firm rules.

The next three chapters discuss theories, causes, research, and clinical issues. Chapter 2 looks at current ways of viewing child and adolescent disorders. It includes the exciting advances made possible by new discoveries about the brain, and notes how these discoveries have become more integrated with knowledge of the biological and psychological processes affecting children's development and disorders. Chapter 3 reviews research methods with children, youths, and families that help us understand features, causes, course, and treatment methods. Chapter 4 discusses clinical issues pertaining to children's mental health, especially current approaches to assessment, diagnosis, and treatment. Because psychological interventions vary considerably in relation to each disorder, we will describe the most recent and effective treatments for specific disorders in the context of the disorders to which they apply. This allows information on treatments and their effectiveness to be woven into our knowledge about the description and causes of the disorder.

Chapters 5 through 13 examine specific disorders and conditions affecting children and adolescents. We examine four general types of disorders, and the impact of child abuse and neglect:

- *Behavioral disorders.* Chapters 5 and 6 deal with attention-deficit/hyperactivity disorder and oppositional and conduct problems, which are sometimes referred to as externalizing problems because they involve conflicts with the environment.
- *Emotional disorders.* Chapters 7 and 8 discuss anxiety and mood disorders, which are sometimes referred to as internalizing problems because they involve conflicts within the child, which are less visible to others.
- *Developmental and learning disorders.* Chapters 9 through 11 examine a broad range of disorders affecting children's ability to learn or perform normally, including mental retardation, pervasive developmental disorders such as autistic disorder, specific problems related to reading and mathematics, and communication difficulties. Many of these disorders constitute chronic conditions that affect children's ongoing development.
- *Problems related to physical and mental health.* Chapters 12 and 13 discuss child and adolescent disorders stemming from medical or physical conditions that may affect children's overall psychological functioning, and vice versa, such as chronic illness, substance abuse, and eating disorders and related conditions.
- *Child maltreatment and non-accidental trauma.* Chapter 14 is unique because it considers conditions that may be a focus of clinical attention during childhood but are not mental disorders. This chapter, with its particular focus on children at risk, deals with the significance of child abuse and other forms of non-accidental trauma on children's developmental progress and course.

Far greater attention has been devoted to the description and classification of abnormality in children than to healthy child functioning and how children adapt to the challenges of growing up. In light of this imbalance, throughout this text we introduce each disorder with a discussion of normal developmental processes, such as children's normal intellectual development (in relation to mental retardation) and the normal range of misbehavior and acting out (in reference to conduct problems). We also consider children's strengths and adaptive abilities, regardless of the presence of a particular disorder, and factors that are believed to encourage healthy adaptation regardless of other impairments. We then present the core features of each disorder (such as hyperactivity–impulsivity, sad mood, or antisocial behavior), followed by significant associated features (such as problems in self-esteem, peer relations, or substance abuse).

As you begin your journey into the field of abnormal child psychology, keep in mind that the threats facing children today—child poverty, chronic illness, maltreatment, and indifference—are no less significant than those of the past, although they sometimes fail to arouse the indignation of society to the extent that major changes are implemented and maintained. Even countries that have outlawed child labor, child abuse, and many other forms of actual and potential harm have only recently begun to recognize the profound importance of the quality of the early childhood environment for children's health, well-being, and competence. Fortunately, it is unlikely that children and youths will ever again be seen as insignificant, costly burdens on society. As each chapter in this text indicates, efforts aimed at change in policies and programs directed toward children and youths are gaining momentum.

Study Resources

SECTION SUMMARIES

KEY TERMS

COURSEMATE

Access an interactive eBook and chapter-specific interactive learning tools, including flashcards, quizzes, videos, and more in your Psychology CourseMate, accessed through CengageBrain.com.

2

Theories and Causes

> *Everything should be made as simple as possible, but not simpler.*
>
> —Albert Einstein

CHAPTER PREVIEW

AT THE RISK OF sounding vague, we must acknowledge that nearly all child and family disturbances result from multiple, interacting risk factors and processes. Contextual events in the family or school environment exert considerable influence over an individual's course of development (see the Chapter 1 discussion of risk and resilience). Therefore, a given child's problems must be considered in relation to multiple levels of influence—individual, family, community, and culture—rather than be attributed to any one factor. Since the causes of psychological disorders are significant, we devote this chapter to a description of the primary contributions derived from biological and psychological influences.

In this chapter, we consider theories and findings regarding influences that shape the child's ongoing development in many different ways. Some influences (such as biological factors and the effects of environmental factors) are contained within the child, whereas many others (such as family patterns and cultural norms) lie at various distances from the child's immediate surroundings. We will see how examining these various causal influences contribute to a better understanding of abnormal child development, and how they are conceptually related to one another.

Let's begin by considering Jorge's situation and his parents' complaints, which raise important issues. Could Jorge have mild mental retardation that impairs his learning? Is Jorge's mother right about his having a learning disability? Does Jorge have a specific communication or learning problem unrelated to mental retardation that affects his schoolwork? Perhaps his school and family environments have contributed to his learning difficulties and fear of school. Have his parents and teachers expected him to fail? Has he been given much assistance? Has he been abused or neglected at home?

What Is Causing Jorge's Problems?

Suppose you were asked to interview Jorge, his teachers, and his parents to find out why schoolwork is difficult for him. How would you go about this task? What information do you feel would be essential to know, and what plan might you follow to organize and explore the many possible reasons for his problem? Most likely, you would form a working theory in your mind that would assist you in determining what to ask and why. At first, your theory might be very basic and unrefined. Jorge's problem in school might be connected to the negative comments and pressure he is getting from his parents and teacher. As you proceed, your theory about Jorge's problem would likely expand and become more detailed, allowing you to probe with more precise questions.

JORGE

Not Keeping Up

Jorge was almost 14 years old when he was referred to me because of his academic problems. Since grade 4 he had been performing well below average in his classes, had difficulty concentrating, and was considered to be "too quiet and nervous." For the last four summers he had taken extra classes to improve his reading, but was currently reading at the third-grade level. As a result, his parents received a letter from the school saying he likely would not be promoted to the next grade if his work didn't improve. Everyone seemed angry at Jorge for not keeping up.

When I met with Jorge, his version of his school problems was short and to the point: "It's the teachers," he said, as he looked at the floor and squirmed in his seat. "How am I expected to learn anything when they yell at you? When I told my English teacher that I hadn't finished reading my book for class, he said I take too long 'cuz my mind wanders too much. How am I expected to learn when they think I'm dumb?" After further discussion, Jorge summed up his view of the problem in a quiet, sullen voice: "I know I'll never get anywhere with the brain I've got. I can't figure stuff out very fast, and the teachers aren't much help. Just thinking about school makes me jittery. I'm afraid I'll say something stupid in class and everyone will laugh at me."

Jorge's mother and father met with me separately and were quick to add their own opinions about why their son didn't do well in school. They had moved from their Spanish-speaking neighborhood when Jorge was in grade 2, and he struggled to learn English in school because his parents did not speak it at home. His mother admitted that she becomes aggravated and starts to yell when Jorge says he doesn't want to go to school or can't do his schoolwork, but she didn't think this was an issue. She quickly added, "I've read about learning disabilities and I think he's got one. He can't control his mind enough to center on anything. He's scared to go to school, and avoids homework as if his life depended on it." By the end of the interview it was evident that Jorge's parents were angry at him. They felt Jorge blamed his teachers for his own lack of effort, and that he should be in a special classroom and maybe given medications to calm him down so he wouldn't worry so much about school. (Based on authors' case material)

Let's briefly consider possible causes of Jorge's behavior:

1. *Biological influences.* Because we know little about Jorge's early development, we might ask his mother about her prenatal history, including major illnesses, injuries, or perhaps marital problems or undue stresses that might have affected her pregnancy. Jorge's problems also reflect a tendency toward behavioral inhibition; he may approach new or challenging situations with greater apprehension and fear than other children (Gleason et al., 2011).

Children with fears and anxiety—which are affected by levels of stress hormones circulating in the body—are more likely to have parents who had similar problems during childhood (Micco et al., 2009). Jorge may have inherited a tendency to respond to his environment with heightened arousal or sensitivity. Alternatively, his early neurological development and the patterns of connections established within his brain may have been influenced by the child-rearing styles his parents used when he was an infant. These early patterns, in turn, can influence how Jorge approaches new tasks, reacts to criticism, or relates to others (Belsky & de Haan, 2011). Another possibility is that Jorge may have inherited one or more genes that influence his phonological awareness. He may not be able to recognize and process all the phonemes (individual sounds) of his native language and thus suffers from a reading disorder (Scerri & Schulte-Körne, 2010).

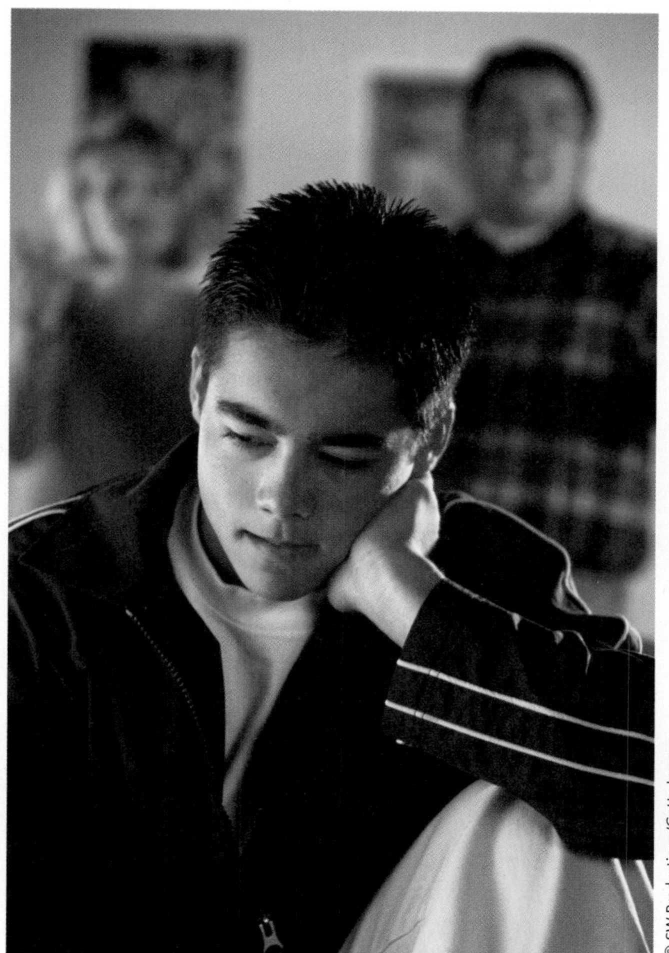

Everyone seemed to be angry with Jorge

2. *Emotional influences.* Children like Jorge not only think and behave in ways that provide clues to their distress, but also show various emotional signals that are not obvious at first. Emotional expression offers another unique window for viewing Jorge's inner world, especially his emotional reactions to challenges such as reading. Consider this possibility: As Jorge approaches his reading assignment or thinks about returning to school the next morning, he is overwhelmed by fear, bordering on panic. His heart races, his breathing quickens, and his thoughts turn to ways to escape from this dreaded situation as quickly as possible. As he is preoccupied by such feelings and worry, his concentration further declines.

Jorge's inability to regulate feelings of arousal, distress, or agitation that may surface without warning is a key element in describing his problem, but we still have not determined how it might have originated. Emotional reactivity and expression are the ways infants and young children first communicate with the world around them, and their ability to regulate these emotions as they adapt is a critical aspect of their early relationships with caregivers (Eisenberg, Smith, & Spinrad, 2011). Emotions can be powerful events, demanding that the child find ways to reduce or regulate their force. The most adaptive way is to seek comfort from a caregiver, which gradually helps the child learn ways of self-regulation. By extension, Jorge's school refusal or phobia could have emerged at a younger age from anxiety about his mother's availability, which grew to a more pronounced and generalized insecurity (Bernstein & Victor, 2010).

3. *Behavioral and cognitive influences.* Jorge has been performing below average in reading for some time. Using our knowledge of learning principles, we might investigate Jorge's current situation from the perspective of events that elicit fear or avoidance, and events that maintain such avoidance by reducing unpleasant reactions. Jorge's lack of progress may be a function of punitive events when he is criticized by his parents or singled out by his teacher.

A behavioral approach to Jorge's problem might be to try to change aspects of his environment—such as the attention he receives from his teacher or parents for his gradual, slow efforts to do his schoolwork—to see what effect this approach has on his school performance and avoidance. We might also consider the teasing or rejection by peers in his school environment that may make him fearful. By observing Jorge at school and narrowing the list of possible events that may contribute to his fears, we can begin to develop hypotheses about Jorge's learning history and, most importantly, possible ways to remedy the problem. One possibility might be to increase the likelihood of reinforcement that is contingent on Jorge's efforts to complete his schoolwork (Little, Akin-Little, & Newman-Eig, 2010).

Cognitive influences, such as a person's interpretation of events, are also important to consider. How does Jorge view the situation, and does his view accurately reflect the situation? Children with fears and worries sometimes develop a belief system that can be self-defeating, leading them to believe that they will fail at anything they try (Beidel & Turner, 2007). Jorge has experienced failure in reading and other events at school, and it is plausible that he anticipates further struggles with schoolwork and other children. His own words are quite clear in this respect: "How am I expected to learn when they think I'm dumb?" "I know I'll never get anywhere with the brain I've got." "Just thinking about school makes me jittery." Such thoughts only tend to make him more anxious and more likely to avoid school as much as possible. In short, his expectations about his performance at school could be heavily laden with fear of failure or ridicule, issues that certainly warrant attention. Children's self-expressions and other cognitions offer a window on their inner world, which may provide clues that we miss when observing their actions.

4. *Family, cultural, and ethnic influences*. An understanding of the possible causes of Jorge's difficulties would be incomplete without consideration of his family and peer relationships, his social setting, and his larger cultural and ethnic identity (Marks, Patton, & Coll, 2011). His early relationship with his parents may have contributed to a lessened ability to regulate his emotions adaptively; his current relationships with his teachers, peers, and family members offer further clues. At the family level, how sensitive are his parents to recognizing his special limitations, and how willing are they to teach him alternative strategies? His mother has high hopes and expectations for her child, as well as a life and problems of her own (including a job). Even though she wants only what's best for Jorge, and her behavior is understandable, it may still be a problem. Her pointed statement, "I've read about learning disabilities and I think he's got one," suggests that she dismisses the problem by labeling it as "his" problem. Neither parent appears to be open to considering other possible explanations. Furthermore, his mother admits to becoming exasperated and yelling at Jorge. What effect might this have on his tenuous self-concept and his attempts to regulate his fear and arousal?

All children, not only those with problems, require a parenting style that is sensitive to their unique needs and abilities and that places appropriate limits on them to help them develop self-control (Morris et al., 2011). Significant adults both within Jorge's family and at school have not been responding to him with sensitivity, so it's not surprising that Jorge's behavior has grown worse over time. Finally, for proper development, children require a basic quality of life that includes a safe community, good schools, proper health and nutrition, access to friends their own age, and opportunities to develop close relationships with extended family and members of their community. These opportunities and necessities are in the background of every child's developmental profile and can emerge as very significant issues for children undergoing parental divorce or living in poverty (Fabricius & Luecken, 2007; Rutter, 2003).

Several important factors that need to be considered in addressing Jorge's problems are shown in ● Figure 2.1. There are many "strikes against Jorge" that need to be considered; clinicians and researchers often attempt to visualize the multiple causes to allow assessment and intervention to address them properly.

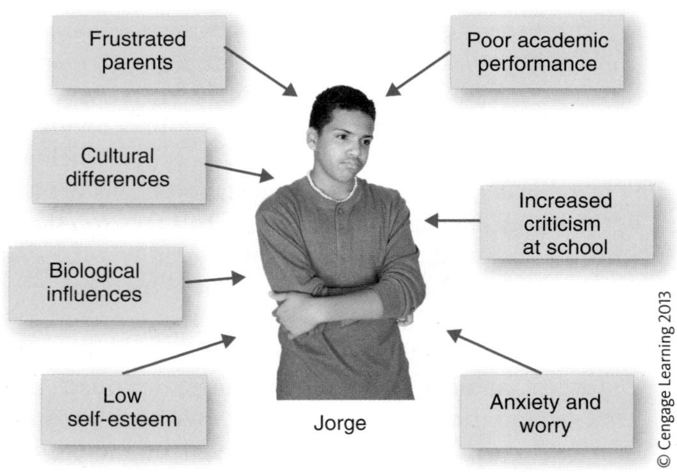

● FIGURE 2.1 | Jorge's concerns: Where do we intervene?

Photo Credit: © 2011 Kin Images/Jupiterimages Corporation.

SECTION SUMMARY

What Is Causing Jorge's Problems?

- Jorge's case exemplifies many interconnected factors that cause or contribute to psychological problems in children.
- The study of causes of abnormal child behavior involves theory and findings on biological, psychological, social, and cultural/ethnic factors.
- Biological factors include genetic and neurobiological contributors, among others.
- Psychological influences include the role of behavioral and cognitive processes, as well as emotional and relationship influences.
- Major social contributors to child problems involve family patterns, peer relations, community factors, and cultural norms.
- Factors in each one of these areas impact and interact with the other areas.

THEORETICAL FOUNDATIONS

Defining what is abnormal within the context of children's ongoing adaptation and development, and sorting out the most probable causes of identified problems, is a complicated process. Very few simple or direct cause-and-effect relationships exist. The study of abnormal child behavior requires an appreciation of developmental processes as well as individual and situational events that can have a major bearing on the course and direction of a particular child's life. Studying normal development informs our theories of abnormal development, and vice versa.

Most clinical and research activity begins with a theoretical formulation for guidance and information. Theory is essentially a language of science that allows us to assemble and communicate existing knowledge more comprehensively. A theory permits us to make educated guesses and predictions about behavior based on samples of knowledge, moving us forward to explore possible explanations. Like a treasure map that provides clues and signposts, a theory offers guidance for our pursuit of causal explanations. Knowledge, skill, and evidence must be added to bring these theoretical clues to life.

The study of the causes of childhood disorders is known as **etiology**, which considers how biological, psychological, and environmental processes interact to produce the outcomes that are observed over time. Research into biological determinants has focused on possible causes such as structural brain damage or dysfunction, neurotransmitter imbalances, and genetic influences. Psychological and environmental models emphasize the role of environmental toxins, early experiences, learning opportunities, disciplinary practices, family systems, and sociocultural contexts. Although these factors are often described as possible "causes," they are in fact primarily risk factors and correlates associated with certain disorders—their causal role is not always clear.

Numerous theoretical models have been proposed to explain and suggest treatment for children's psychological disorders, although many of the theories have not been substantiated or even tested (Weisz & Kazdin, 2010). Until recently, most models focused on single explanations that failed to consider other influences and their interactions. One-dimensional models do not capture the complexities of abnormal child behavior that are increasingly evident from research (Kazdin & Whitley, 2006). The alternative to single-factor explanations is much more complex and informative. It involves consideration of multiple causes that can interact in various ways over time to affect normal and abnormal development. Keeping in mind this central theme of multiple, interactive causes will help you grasp the complexity of each disorder discussed within this text.

Underlying Assumptions

The value of theory lies not only in providing answers but also in raising new questions and looking at familiar problems in different ways. Theory, research, and practice in abnormal child psychology all require an understanding of the assumptions underlying work in this area. Let's look at three prominent assumptions and how they have shaped our approach to abnormal child psychology.

Abnormal Development Is Multiply Determined

Our first underlying assumption is that abnormal child behavior is *multiply determined*. Thus, we have to look beyond the child's current symptoms and consider developmental pathways and interacting events that, over time, contribute to the expression of a particular disorder.

Let's return to Jorge's problems to illustrate this assumption. One way to look at Jorge's problems is to say that he lacks motivation. Although it is a reasonable explanation, this one-dimensional causal model, which attempts to trace the origins of Jorge's reading difficulty to a single underlying cause, is probably too simplistic. Scientific method emphasizes the need to simplify variables to those of most importance, but focusing on one primary explanation rather than identifying and allowing for several possible explanations (for example, genetic factors, reinforcement history, and peer problems) fails to consider the concept

Children's comfort with their environment is shown by their actions

of developmental pathways (discussed in Chapter 1). A particular problem or disorder may stem from a variety of causes, and similar risk factors may lead to very different outcomes.

Another way to view Jorge's difficulties—the way we emphasize here—takes into account multiple influences, including his developmental profile and abilities, his home and school environment, and the ongoing, dynamic interactions among these factors. To address Jorge's reading problem from a multidimensional perspective, we would first assess his current abilities by using multiple sources of data on his ability to function in different settings. Even if we were interested only in his reading ability, we would consider a wide range of characteristics besides those we initially believed to be signs of reading problems. Otherwise, our assumptions about the nature of reading problems might prevent us from considering other explanations. Could criticism and yelling from Jorge's mother affect his concentration or self-esteem? Is Jorge different from other children in terms of his ability to recognize language sounds from written words? These are some of the questions we would want to answer through careful observation and assessment, using a theoretically guided decision-making strategy.

Child and Environment Are Interdependent

Our second assumption extends the influence of multiple causes by stressing how the child and environment are **interdependent**—how they influence each other. This concept departs from the tradition of viewing the environment as acting on the child to cause changes in development, and instead argues that children also influence their own environment. In simple terms, the concept of interdependence appreciates how nature and nurture work together and are, in fact, interconnected (Rutter, 2011). Thus, children elicit different reactions from the same environment; different environments, such as home or school, elicit different reactions from the same child.

The dynamic interaction of child and environment is referred to as a **transaction** (Sameroff, 2010; Sameroff & MacKenzie, 2003). The child and the environment both contribute to the expression of a disorder, and one cannot be separated from the other. A transactional view regards both children and the environment as *active contributors* to adaptive and maladaptive behavior. Most persons who know children best—parents, teachers, child care workers, and others—would probably agree this view makes the most sense: Children act on their environment, and their environment acts on them, as in the example of Jorge. According to this transactional perspective, children's psychological disorders do not reside within the child, nor are they due solely to environmental causes. They most often emerge from a combination of factors, which interact in ways that follow general laws of organized development.

Although a transactional view considers general principles of development that apply to all children, it is also sensitive to individual circumstances—in the child's family or biological makeup—that influence or alter typical outcomes. Learning about such deviations from the norm is what this textbook is all about.

Abnormal Development Involves Continuities and Discontinuities

Think for a moment about how Jorge's various problems might have begun and how they might change or even disappear over time. Might his current problems

"The title of my science project is 'My Little Brother: Nature or Nurture.'"

of avoiding school and homework be connected to his earlier difficulties in reading? Are these qualitatively different problems or different manifestations of the same one? Are his current problems qualitatively different from those he had at a younger age, because his problems today include avoiding school and homework?

Few psychological disorders or impairments suddenly emerge without at least some warning signs or connections to earlier developmental issues. This connection is apparent, for example, in early onset and persistent conduct disorders, where parents and other adults often see troublesome behaviors at a young age that continue in some form into adolescence and adulthood (Reef, van Meurs, Verhulst, & van der Ende, 2010). However, it is critical to note that some forms of abnormal child development may be continuous or discontinuous across childhood, adolescence, and adulthood, in either a consistent or transformed manner (Schulenberg, Sameroff, & Cicchetti, 2006).

Continuity implies that developmental changes are gradual and quantitative (i.e., expressed as amounts that can be measured numerically, such as weight and height changes), and that future behavior patterns can be predicted from earlier patterns. **Discontinuity**, in contrast, implies that developmental changes are abrupt and qualitative (i.e., expressed as qualities that cannot be measured numerically, such as changes in mood or expression), and that future behavior is poorly predicted by earlier patterns.

As an example, consider a preschool child who uses physical aggression with peers. What would you expect that child to be like 10 years later? According to the notion of continuity, he or she would be more likely to engage in antisocial and delinquent behavior as an adolescent and adult. That is, the pattern of problem behavior (in this case, physical aggression) is continuous across developmental periods, although it gradually changes in form and intensity. Pushing a peer may turn into striking someone with a fist or object. Importantly, continuity refers to patterns of behavior, rather than specific symptoms that remain over time. Continuity is well supported for early onset and persistent conduct disorders, which have a significant likelihood of later evolving into serious antisocial acts (Lynam et al., 2009).

Other problem behaviors, such as eating disorders, seem to follow a more discontinuous pattern; they occur more suddenly and without much prior warning. In these cases, there are few good behavioral predictors from early childhood as to why a particular child begins to restrict eating or purge food during early adolescence (see Chapter 13). Sometimes discontinuity can refer to an unexpected or atypical outcome, such as a child who shows normal development until about 18 months of age and then displays loss of language and reduced social engagement (characteristics of autism). In such circumstances, the connection between early and later patterns seems abrupt and discontinuous, which is very baffling to parents.

As we will see throughout our discussion of each disorder, positive factors such as individual competence or social intervention, as well as negative factors such as poverty or discrimination, can influence the continuity or discontinuity of development over time (Rutter, Kim-Cohen, & Maughan, 2006). Returning to Jorge, can you think which of his behavior patterns (if any) were continuous and which seemed to be more discontinuous? Like many problems in abnormal child psychology, Jorge's current behavior pattern involves *both* continuities and discontinuities. Some of his troubles, such as school and homework avoidance, seem qualitatively different (discontinuity) from his reading disorder. His other behaviors, such as slow reading and comprehension, seem to follow (continuity) from his earlier academic problems.

Remember that the concepts of continuity and discontinuity apply to the understanding of abnormal and normal development. However, even with wide fluctuations in the way problems are expressed over time, children show some degree of consistency in organizing their experiences and interacting with their environment, whether that consistency is adaptive or maladaptive (Sroufe, Coffino, & Carlson, 2010). The degree of continuity or discontinuity will vary as a function of changing environmental circumstances and transactions between the child and the environment. These continual changes, in turn, will affect the child's developmental course and direction.

In sum, a central theme of our basic assumptions is that the study of abnormal child psychology must consider abnormality in relation to multiple, interdependent causes and major developmental changes that typically occur across the life cycle. Until recently, developmental aspects of abnormal child behavior were often overlooked in relation to children's behavioral and emotional problems (Cicchetti, 2006). To redress this imbalance, throughout this text we discuss developmental issues pertaining to the nature, symptoms, and course of each disorder.

Changes, Typical and Atypical

● Figure 2.2 presents an overview of developmental periods by age. It gives examples of normal achievements for each period, as well as behavior problems

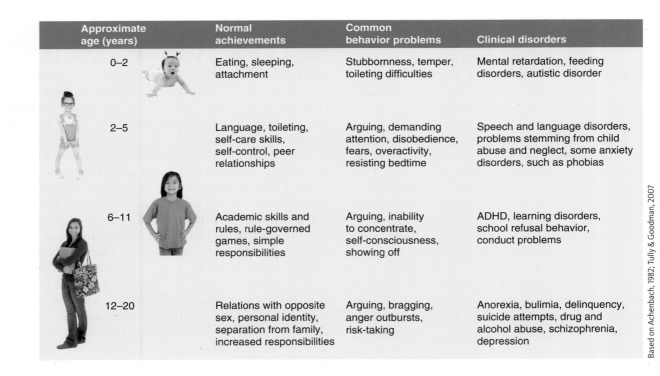

Approximate age (years)	Normal achievements	Common behavior problems	Clinical disorders
0–2	Eating, sleeping, attachment	Stubbornness, temper, toileting difficulties	Mental retardation, feeding disorders, autistic disorder
2–5	Language, toileting, self-care skills, self-control, peer relationships	Arguing, demanding attention, disobedience, fears, overactivity, resisting bedtime	Speech and language disorders, problems stemming from child abuse and neglect, some anxiety disorders, such as phobias
6–11	Academic skills and rules, rule-governed games, simple responsibilities	Arguing, inability to concentrate, self-consciousness, showing off	ADHD, learning disorders, school refusal behavior, conduct problems
12–20	Relations with opposite sex, personal identity, separation from family, increased responsibilities	Arguing, bragging, anger outbursts, risk-taking	Anorexia, bulimia, delinquency, suicide attempts, drug and alcohol abuse, schizophrenia, depression

Based on Achenbach, 1982; Tully & Goodman, 2007

• **FIGURE 2.2** | A developmental overview.

Photo Credits (top to bottom): Michael Pettigrew/Shutterstock.com; YUYI /Shutterstock.com; © iStockphoto.com/Ana Abejon; © iStockphoto.com/Brian McEntire.

most often reported in general population samples and the clinical disorders that typically become evident at each period. Guidelines for the typical sequence of development across several important dimensions are helpful, but we must keep in mind that age in years is an arbitrary way to segment continuous sequences of development. You may find yourself turning back to this table to reorient yourself to children's normal and abnormal development.

An Integrative Approach

How do we attempt to make sense of the many environmental and individual factors that influence child behavior? Since no single theoretical orientation can explain various behaviors or disorders, we must be familiar with many theories and conceptual models—each contributes important insights into normal and abnormal development.

Even models that consider more than one primary cause can be limited by the boundaries of their discipline or orientation. Biological explanations, for instance, emphasize genetic mutations, neuroanatomy, and neurobiological mechanisms as factors contributing to psychopathology. Similarly, psychological explanations emphasize causal factors such as excessive, inadequate, or maladaptive reinforcement and/or learning histories. Biological and psychological models are both multicausal and distinctive in terms of the relative importance each attaches to certain events and processes. Each model is restricted in its ability to explain abnormal behavior to the extent that it fails to incorporate important components of other models. Fortunately, such disciplinary boundaries are gradually diminishing as different perspectives take into account important variables derived from other models. For example, biological influences are often taken into account when explaining how psychological factors, such as behavior or cognition, interact over time and result in a psychological disorder (Cicchetti & Curtis, 2006; Sameroff, 2010).

Over time, major theories of abnormal child psychology have become compatible with one another. Rather than offering contradictory views, each theory contributes one or more pieces of the puzzle of atypical development. As all the available pieces are assembled, the picture of a particular child or adolescent disorder becomes more and more distinct. Psychological theories are merely tools to study human behavior; the more you learn what these tools can and cannot do and which tool to use for which purpose, the more knowledgeable and skilled you will become. Remember that no single integrative theory fully captures the diversity of perspectives and findings represented by current research in abnormal child psychology.

SECTION SUMMARY

Theoretical Foundations

- A theory allows us to make educated guesses and predictions about behavior that are based on existing knowledge, and it allows us to explore these possible explanations empirically.
- A central theme of this text is the importance of considering multiple, interactive causes for abnormal behavior, in conjunction with the major developmental changes that typically occur.
- Three underlying assumptions about abnormal development are stressed: It is multiply determined, the child and the environment are interdependent, and abnormal development involves continuities and discontinuities of behavior patterns over time.
- The complexity of abnormal child behavior requires consideration of the full range of biological, psychological, and sociocultural factors that influence children's development.

Developmental Considerations

Even though children's psychological disorders have very different symptoms and causes, they share common ground: They are an indication of adaptational failure in one or more areas of development (Rutter & Sroufe, 2000). **Adaptational failure** is the failure to master or progress in accomplishing developmental milestones. In other words, at the broadest level, children with psychological disorders differ from children their own age on some aspect of normal development. Again, such failure or deviation is rarely due to a single cause, but typically results from an ongoing interaction between individual development and environmental conditions.

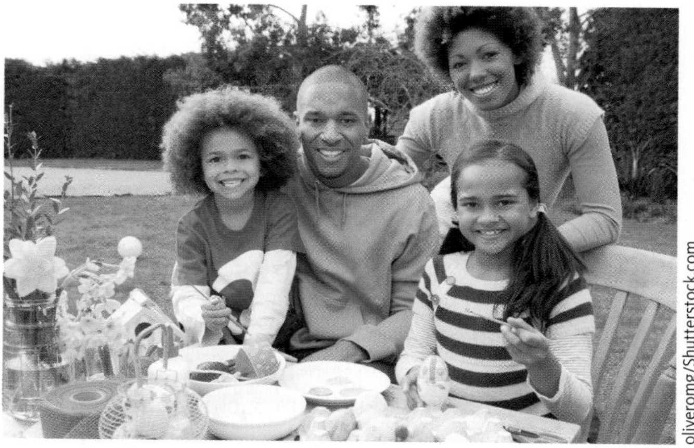
oliveromg/Shutterstock.com

Children's development follows an organized pattern that is nurtured through positive experiences with their caregivers

The causes and outcomes of abnormal child behavior operate in dynamic and interactive ways over time, making them a challenge to disentangle. Designating a specific factor, such as Jorge's reading problem, either as a cause or as an outcome of a particular disorder usually reflects the point at which we take note of the problem. His reading problem, for example, may be viewed as a disorder in its own right (such as a learning disorder in reading), the cause of his other difficulties (such as poor study habits and oppositional behavior), or the outcome of some other condition or disorder (such as a communication disorder). As you read the following chapters and gain a better understanding of the causes of abnormal child behavior, remember that children's behavior and their environment are interconnected.

Organization of Development

Change and reorganization are fundamental aspects of biological and behavioral systems (Sameroff, 2010). An organizational viewpoint looks closely at the psychological processes that may explain how these systems influence each other. In an attempt to understand abnormal development, we may choose to focus on any or all aspects of this organizational process. In the **organization of development** perspective, early patterns of adaptation, such as infant eye contact and speech sounds, evolve with structure over time and transform into higher-order functions such as speech and language. Prior patterns of adaptation are incorporated into successive reorganizations at subsequent periods of development, much as toddlers learn to make certain speech sounds before they develop the ability to use language.

An organizational view of development implies an active, dynamic process of continual change and transformation. As the child's biological abilities unfold during each new stage of development, they interact with environmental factors to direct and redirect the course of development. Because development is organized, sensitive periods play a meaningful role in any discussion of normal and abnormal behavior. **Sensitive periods** are windows of time during which environmental influences on development, both good and bad, are enhanced (Roth & Sweatt, 2011a). Infants, for example, are highly sensitive to emotional cues and proximity to their caregivers, which assists them in developing secure attachments (R. A. Thompson & Meyer, 2007). Toddlers are sensitive to the basic sounds of language, which helps them distinguish sounds and combine them to form words (Shafer & Garrido-Nag, 2007). Sensitive periods can be enhanced opportunities for learning but are not the only opportunities; change can take place at other times. For example, children adopted from orphanages show a number of negative developmental outcomes as a result of their early institutional deprivation. However, their outcome is also affected by later experiences in the post-institutional environment (Reeb, Fox, Nelson, & Zeanah, 2009). Human development is a process of increasing differentiation and integration, more like a network of interconnecting pathways than one straight line.

The attempt to understand the seemingly endless list of possible causes that influence children's normal and abnormal development is made easier by the fact that development generally proceeds in an organized, hierarchical manner (Sameroff, 2010). Simply stated, a child's current abilities or limitations are influenced by prior accomplishments, just as your progress through trigonometry or calculus depends on the command of arithmetic you acquired in elementary school. As children develop greater abilities or show signs of adaptational failure, these changes influence their further developmental success or failure. Studying abnormal child behavior within a developmental psychopathology perspective, as described next, fosters an understanding of the interactive, progressive nature of children's abilities and difficulties.

Developmental Psychopathology Perspective

Developmental psychopathology is an approach to describing and studying disorders of childhood, adolescence, and beyond in a manner that emphasizes the importance of developmental processes and tasks. This approach uses abnormal development to inform normal development, and vice versa (Cicchetti, 2006). It also provides a useful framework for organizing the study of abnormal child psychology around milestones and sequences in physical, cognitive, social-emotional, and educational development. Simply stated, developmental psychopathology emphasizes the role of developmental processes, the importance of context, and the influence of multiple and interacting events in shaping adaptive and maladaptive development. We adopt this perspective as an organizing framework to describe the dynamic, multidimensional process leading to abnormal outcomes in development (Mash & Dozois, 2003).

A central belief of developmental psychopathology is that to understand maladaptive behavior adequately, one must view it in relation to what is normative for a given period of development (Cicchetti, 2006). The main focus is on highlighting developmental processes, such as language and peer relations and how they function, by looking at extremes and variations in developmental outcome. In so doing, this perspective emphasizes the importance and complexity of biological, familial, and sociocultural factors in predicting and understanding developmental changes. It draws on knowledge from several disciplines, including psychology, psychiatry, sociology, and neuroscience, and integrates this knowledge within a developmental framework (Ozonoff, Pennington, & Solomon, 2006).

As we have noted throughout this section, children's behaviors—both adaptive and maladaptive—are interconnected with their environment and influenced by their biological makeup. Recently, the field of developmental psychopathology has taken an interest in developmental cascades to help explain why some problems in childhood go on to become major problems later on, whereas others do not (Masten & Cicchetti, 2010). **Developmental cascades** refer to the process by which a child's previous interactions and experiences may spread across other systems and alter his or her course of development, somewhat like a chain reaction (Masten & Cicchetti, 2010). This concept helps to explain how processes that function at one level or domain of behavior (such as curiosity) can affect how the child adapts to other challenges later on (such as academic performance) (Cox, Mills-Koonce, Propper, & Gariépy, 2010). Throughout this book, the developmental psychopathology perspective adds developmental relevance and richness to categorically based DSM-IV-TR disorders and to early intervention possibilities.

SECTION SUMMARY

Developmental Considerations

- Children's development is organized, which means that early patterns of adaptation evolve over time and transform into higher-order functions in a structured, predictable manner.
- Developmental psychopathology provides a useful framework for organizing the study of abnormal child psychology around milestones and sequences in physical, cognitive, social-emotional, and educational development.

We turn now to three major perspectives on abnormal child development: (1) biological perspectives, which include both genetic and neurobiological factors that are often established (but by no means fixed) at birth or soon thereafter; (2) psychological perspectives, such as emotions, relationships, and thought processes; and (3) familial, social, and cultural influences, which set additional parameters on normal and abnormal development.

Biological Perspectives

Broadly speaking, a neurobiological perspective considers brain and nervous system functions as underlying causes of psychological disorders in children and adults. Biological influences on the very young child's brain development include genetic and constitutional factors, neuroanatomy, and rates of maturation. Regions of the brain are highly influenced by the availability of various biochemicals and neurohormones, which interact differently to affect an individual's psychological experiences (Cicchetti & Cannon, 1999). This process depends on environmental factors that serve to direct or reroute ongoing brain processes. Remember that a neurobiological perspective acknowledges and recognizes the need to incorporate environmental influences in accounting for disorders.

The developing brain has long been a mystery, but its secrets are gradually being revealed. The examination of biological influences begins with the amazing process of neuronal growth and differentiation. During pregnancy, the fetal brain develops from a few all-purpose cells into a complex organ made up of billions of specialized, interconnected neurons (Johnson & de Haan, 2006). The speed and distance these emerging neurons travel is astonishing as they multiply to form various brain structures and functions. The brain stem commands heartbeat and breathing, the cerebellum controls and coordinates sensorimotor integration, and the cortex is where thought and perception originate.

Embryonic development generates an initial overabundance of neurons (Innocenti, 1982). At first these cells are largely undifferentiated, but as they reach their destinations, they become neurons with axons that carry electrical signals to other parts of the brain. These axonal connections, or synapses, form the brain's circuits and lay the foundation for further growth and differentiation. Notably, genes determine the main highways along which axons travel to make their connection; but to reach particular target cells, axons follow chemical cues strewn along their path that tell them the direction to various destinations.

By the fifth month of prenatal development, most axons have reached their general destination, although there are far more axons than the target cells can accommodate. Thus, during early childhood, synapses multiply; then selective *pruning* reduces the number of connections in a way that gradually shapes and differentiates important brain functions (Johnson & de Haan, 2006). The nervous system seems to prepare itself for new growth and demands by sending in reinforcements and then cutting back once the environment has signaled it has everything it needs. Throughout life we undergo cycles that narrow the gap between structure and function. At the level of the nervous system, the microanatomy of the brain is constantly redefined to meet the demands and requirements of an adult world. Like the pruning of a tree, this process fosters healthy growth of different areas of the brain according to individual needs and environmental demands, and eliminates connections that serve to restrict healthy growth.

How permanent are the early connections formed as brain development proceeds in an organized, predictable fashion? This question has provoked different theories and agonized many parents concerned about the significance of their children's early development. For instance, if early brain functions are unlikely to change, this implies that early experiences set the course for lifetime development. Freud's similar contention implied that an individual's core personality is formed from an early age, which sets the pace and boundaries for further personality formation. To the contrary, scientists now believe that brain functions undergo continual changes as they adapt to environmental demands (Fox, Levitt, & Nelson, 2010).

Neural Plasticity and the Role of Experience

Many early neural connections are not stable; some are strengthened and become more established through use, while many others regress or disappear. Thus, the answer to the question about the permanence of early connections is that the brain shows neural plasticity throughout the course of development (Nelson, 2011). **Neural plasticity**, or malleability, means the brain's anatomical differentiation is use-dependent: Nature provides the basic processes, whereas nurture provides the experiences needed to select the most adaptive network of connections, based on the use and function of each. It is truly fascinating how nature and nurture work together to create such highly specific, extremely adaptive central nervous system functions.

Think of the developing brain as a work in progress, one in which the environment plays an essential role as supervisor of this dynamic rewiring project. In fact, environmental experience is now recognized to be critical to the differentiation of brain tissue itself. Although nature has a plan for creating the human brain and central nervous system, environmental opportunities and limitations significantly influence this plan from the beginning. Thus, a transactional model is needed to explain normal and abnormal development. Because the structure of a child's brain remains surprisingly malleable for months and even years after birth, transaction occurs between ongoing brain development and environmental experiences; neither nature nor nurture is sufficient to explain the complexity of the developing brain (Fox et al., 2010).

Experience, of course, comes in all shapes and sizes. The prenatal environment as well as childhood illness and diet count as experience, as do maltreatment and inadequate stimulation. Children's early caregiving experiences play an especially important role in designing the parts of the brain involved in emotion, personality, and behavior (O'Connor, 2006). Normal, healthy methods of childrearing, for instance, may increase children's ability to learn and cope with stress (Belsky & de Haan, 2011). In contrast, abuse and neglect can prime the brain for a lifetime of struggle with handling stress or forming healthy relationships (De Bellis et al., 2002).

The maturation of the brain is an organized, hierarchical process that builds on earlier function, with brain structures restructuring and growing throughout the life span. Primitive areas of the brain mature first, during the first 3 years of life; these brain regions, which govern basic sensory and motor skills, undergo the most dramatic restructuring early in life. Moreover, these perceptual centers, along with instinctive centers such as the limbic system, are strongly affected by early childhood experiences and set the foundation for further development (Nelson, 2011). The prefrontal cortex, which governs planning and decision making, and the cerebellum, a center for motor skills, are not rewired until a person is 5 to 7 years old. Major restructuring of the brain occurs between ages 9 and 11 in relation to pubertal development, and then throughout adolescence the brain once again prunes unnecessary synaptic connections. Thus, the brain certainly does not stop changing after 3 years. For some functions, the windows of influence are only beginning to close at that age, while for others they are only beginning to open. Our brain functions undergo lifelong renovation, with restructuring being a natural by-product of growth.

Because the brain is intrinsically shaped by the effects of early experience, the consequences of inadequate or traumatic experience may be enduring and extremely difficult to change (Glover, 2011). During this evolution of brain growth and differentiation many things can go wrong, thereby altering how neurons form or interconnect. Problems or disruptions occurring at a younger age are typically associated with more severe organic disorders and central nervous system complications. Safeguards such as proper prenatal care, proper nutrition, and avoidance of tobacco or alcohol during pregnancy can go a long way in reducing the risk of such complications and lifelong disabilities.

Genetic Contributions

Genetics explains why you look like your father, and if you don't, why you should.

—Tammy, age 8

To address the important role of genetic influences, we first must understand the nature of genes, bearing in mind that virtually any trait a child possesses results from the interaction of environmental and genetic factors (Rutter, 2011). A review of genetics terminology and function may assist our understanding of some causes of abnormal child behavior.

Each person's unique genome is established at conception and consists of approximately 20,000 to 25,000 genes (International Human Genome Sequencing Consortium, 2004). Genes contain genetic information from each parent, and they are distributed on 22 matched pairs of chromosomes and a single pair of sex chromosomes. In males, the sex chromosome pair consists of an X and a Y chromosome (XY), and in females, the sex chromosome pair consists of two X chromosomes (XX).

Genetic factors are implicated in all of the childhood disorders discussed in this text. Some genetic influences are expressed early in development, such as behavioral inhibition or shyness (Nigg, 2006), whereas others show up years later, such as a depressive cognitive style (Garber & Flynn, 2001). Moreover, the expression of genetic influences is malleable and responsive to the social environment. Positive environmental circumstances can help a child "beat the odds" of developing a significant disorder, despite genetic predisposition (Masten & Wright, 2010).

Many genes have been implicated in childhood disorders, but very rarely is one gene the single cause of a disorder (Rutter & Dodge, 2011). Therefore, rather

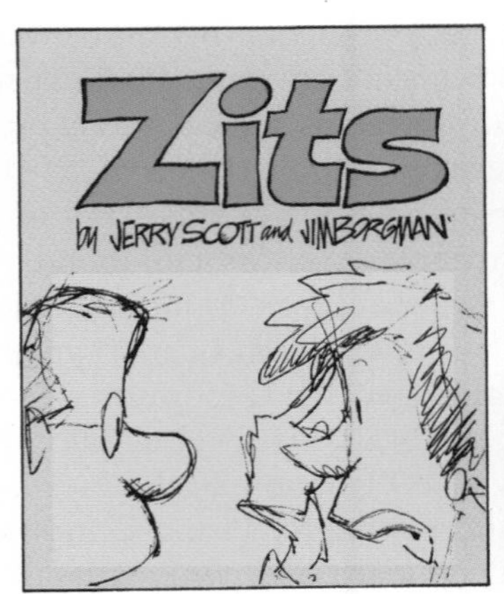

than ask whether a specific disorder is due to genetic makeup or environmental influences, we should be concerned with this question: To what extent are given behaviors due to variations in genetic endowment, the environment, and the interaction between these two factors? An understanding of the nature of genes sheds light on this question.

The Nature of Genes

A gene is basically a stretch of DNA and, by itself, it does not produce a behavior, an emotion, or even a passing thought. Rather, it produces a protein. Although these proteins are vital for the brain to function, very rarely do they cause a behavior to happen. Instead, they produce tendencies to respond to the environment in certain ways (Sapolsky, 1997). Each of us may have genetic vulnerabilities, tendencies, and predispositions, but rarely are the outcomes inevitable. The lesson in all of this is simple, yet important. The false notion that genes determine behavior should be replaced with the more accurate statement: Genes influence how we respond to the environment, and the environment influences our genes. Today, researchers are highly interested in this **gene–environment interaction** (G×E), as discussed in Box 2.1.

BOX 2.1 **A CLOSER LOOK**

Gene-Environment Interactions in Abnormal Child Psychology

Normal and abnormal child development are the result of complex interchanges between nature and nurture, and are affected not only by genetic and environmental influences, but by the timing of when they meet (Lenroot & Giedd, 2011). Researchers refer to this interplay of nature and nurture as *gene–environment interactions,* or G×E. The underlying biological changes to genetic structure result from **epigenetic** mechanisms, which involve changes in gene activity resulting from a variety of environmental factors, such as toxins, diet, stress, and many others; in other words, the environment can turn genes on and off (Roth & Sweatt, 2011b). The growing field of developmental neuroscience has shown that epigenetic changes may play a central role in the long-term impact of early life experiences, as these experiences become biologically embedded in the development of our organ systems, especially the brain (Shonkoff, 2010).

G×E helps explain why some people exhibit disorders and others do not, in the face of similar environmental events. For example, as shown in the top of the diagram below (A), children may be exposed to domestic violence or abuse in their family (a high environmental stressor), but only those who possess a particular genotype may end of showing significant problems later on. Alternatively (B), children who carry a genotype known to increase susceptibility for a particular disorder may only develop that disorder if they are exposed to specific environmental risks (i.e., a toxic prenatal or postnatal environment) (Wermter et al., 2010).

There's more to the story—epigenetic alterations may be reversible through pharmacological and behavioral interventions. Research on gene–environment interactions is opening new windows of opportunity—targeting children with particular risk factors (either genetic, environmental, or both)—that determine the best timing and strategies for early intervention (Bakermans-Kranenburg & Van Ijzendoorn, 2011; Ellis, Boyce, Belsky, Bakermans-Kranenburg, & Van Ijzendoorn, 2011).

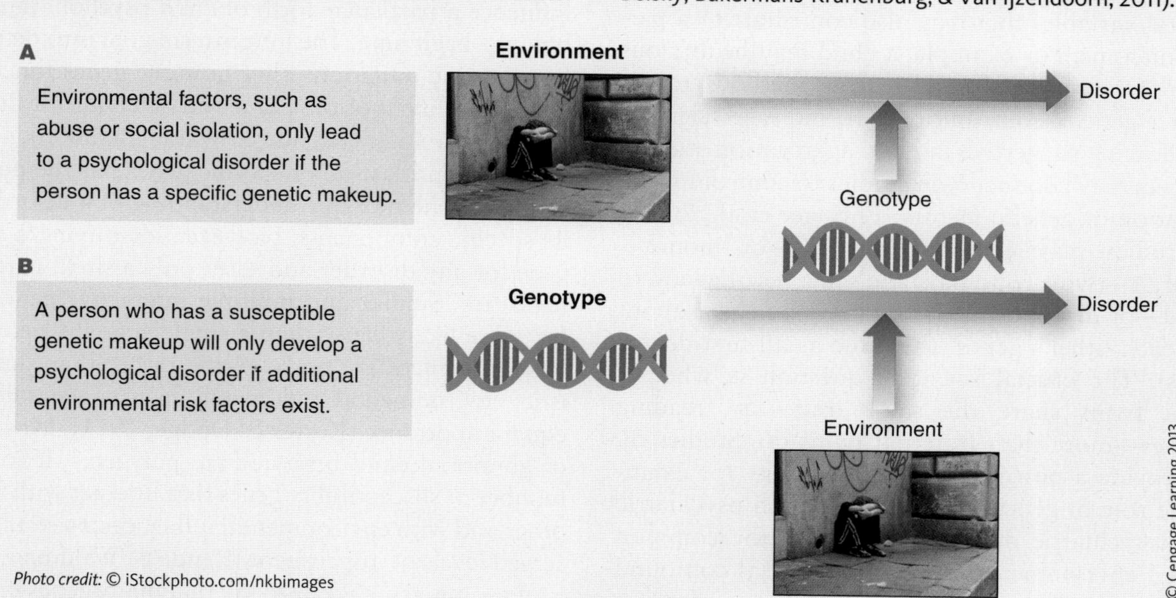

A
Environmental factors, such as abuse or social isolation, only lead to a psychological disorder if the person has a specific genetic makeup.
Environment
Disorder
Genotype
B
A person who has a susceptible genetic makeup will only develop a psychological disorder if additional environmental risk factors exist.
Genotype
Disorder
Environment

Photo credit: © iStockphoto.com/nkbimages

Calvin and Hobbes **by Bill Watterson**

Behavioral Genetics

Sorting out the interactive influences of nature and nurture is the not-so-easy task of **behavioral genetics**, a branch of genetics that investigates possible connections between a genetic predisposition and observed behavior, taking into account environmental and genetic influences. Behavioral genetics researchers often begin their investigations by conducting familial aggregation studies. They look for a nonrandom clustering of disorders or characteristics within a given family and compare these results with the random distribution of the disorders or characteristics in the general population (Rende & Waldman, 2006). For example, parents of children with childhood-onset schizophrenia tend to have higher rates of schizophrenia spectrum disorders relative to normative prevalence rates.

Family aggregation studies cannot control for environmental variables that may also contribute to a particular outcome. For example, a child may be anxious because of his parents' child-rearing methods rather than their genetic contributions. To increase scientific rigor following suggestive familial aggregation studies, researchers may conduct twin studies to control for the contribution of genetic factors (Ehringer et al., 2006). Twin studies may compare identical—or monozygotic (MZ)—twins, who have the same set of genes, to fraternal—or dizygotic (DZ)—twins, who share about half of each other's genes (the same as all first-degree relatives). The crucial scientific question is whether identical twins share the same trait—say, reading difficulties—more than fraternal twins do. Studies on twins provide a powerful research strategy for examining the role of genetic influences in both psychiatric and nonpsychiatric disorders. However, the common or shared environment presents a potential confound in any twin study unless the twins are reared apart (Ehringer et al., 2006).

Molecular Genetics

No twisted thought without a twisted molecule.

—Ralph Waldo Gerard (1900–1974)

In contrast to the methods of behavioral genetics, methods of molecular genetics offer more direct support for genetic influences on child psychopathology. **Molecular genetics** methods directly assess the association between variations in DNA sequences and variations in a particular trait or traits. More than an association, variations in genetic sequences are thought to cause the variations in the trait(s) (Rutter & Dodge, 2011). As we will discuss throughout this book, molecular genetics methods have been used to identify specific genes for many childhood disorders, including autism, attention-deficit/hyperactivity disorder, and learning disability. However, discovering that mutations in one gene or another causally influence a particular form of child psychopathology is only the beginning. The longer-term goal is to determine how genetic mutations alter how the genes function in the development of the brain and behavior for different psychopathologies (Rende & Waldman, 2006).

The identification of specific genes has the potential to greatly enhance our understanding of a disorder and its specific components. However, identifying a specific gene for any disorder addresses only a small part of genetic risk. Similar and multiple interactive genes are a far more likely cause than a single gene. Moreover, genetic influences are probabilistic rather than deterministic; environmental and genetic factors generally have equal importance (Rutter & Dodge, 2011). Most forms of abnormal child behavior are polygenic, involving a number of susceptibility genes that interact with one another and with environmental influences, to result in observed levels of impairment (Rende & Waldman, 2006).

In summary, it is fair to say that many genes influence much of our development and most of our behavior, personality, and even intelligence. However, individual genes cannot account for the major psychological disorders presented in this text. Specific genes are sometimes associated with certain psychological disorders, such as some forms of mental retardation. Genetic contributions to psychological disorders come from many genes, and each makes a relatively small contribution.

Neurobiological Contributions

The study of abnormal child psychology requires a working familiarity with brain structures, as shown in ● Figures 2.3, 2.4, and 2.5. This section provides an overview of major structures mentioned later in the context of specific disorders. Once you are familiar with the various areas and functions of the brain, you will have the basic vocabulary needed to understand the remarkable discoveries being made.

Brain Structure and Function

The brain is often divided into the *brain stem* and the *forebrain* (telencephalon) because of their separate functions. The brain stem (see Figure 2.4), located at the base of the brain, handles most of the autonomic functions necessary to stay alive. The lowest part of the brain stem, called the *hindbrain*, contains the *medulla*, the *pons*, and the *cerebellum*. The hindbrain provides essential regulation of autonomic activities such as breathing, heartbeat, and digestion, and the cerebellum controls motor coordination. The brain stem also contains the *midbrain*, which coordinates movement with sensory input. The midbrain houses the *reticular activating system* (RAS), which contributes to processes of arousal and tension.

At the very top of the brain stem is the *diencephalon*, located just below the forebrain. The diencephalon contains the *thalamus* and *hypothalamus*, which are both essential to the regulation of behavior and emotion. The diencephalon functions primarily as a relay between the forebrain and the lower areas of the brain stem.

Next is the forebrain, which has evolved in humans into highly specialized functions. At the base of the forebrain is an area known as the *limbic*, or border, *system* (see Figure 2.5). It contains a number of structures that are suspected causes of psychopathology, such as the *hippocampus*, *cingulate gyrus*, *septum*, and *amygdala*. These important structures regulate emotional experiences and expressions and play a significant role in learning and impulse control. The limbic system also regulates the basic drives of sex, aggression, hunger, and thirst.

Also at the base of the forebrain lay the *basal ganglia*, which include the *caudate nucleus*. Researchers are

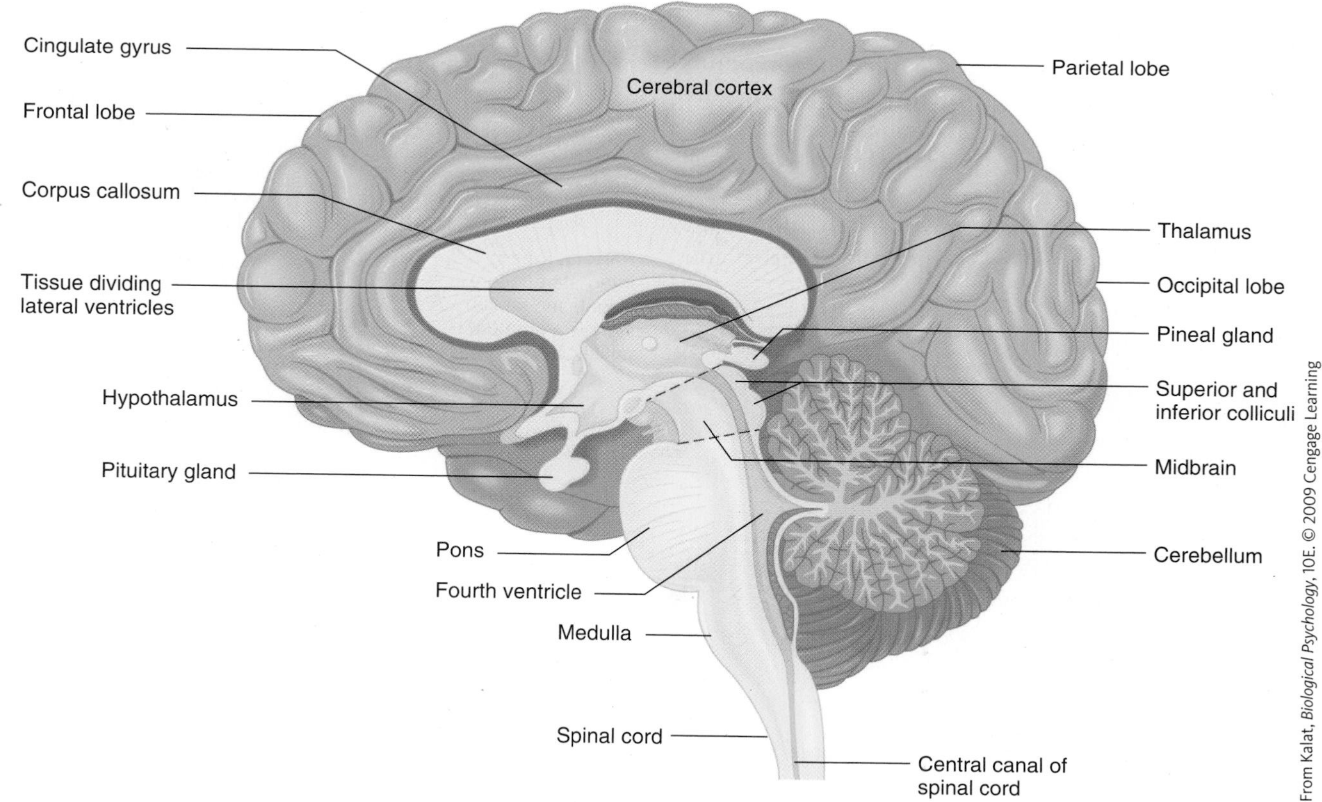

● **FIGURE 2.3** | Structures of the human brain.

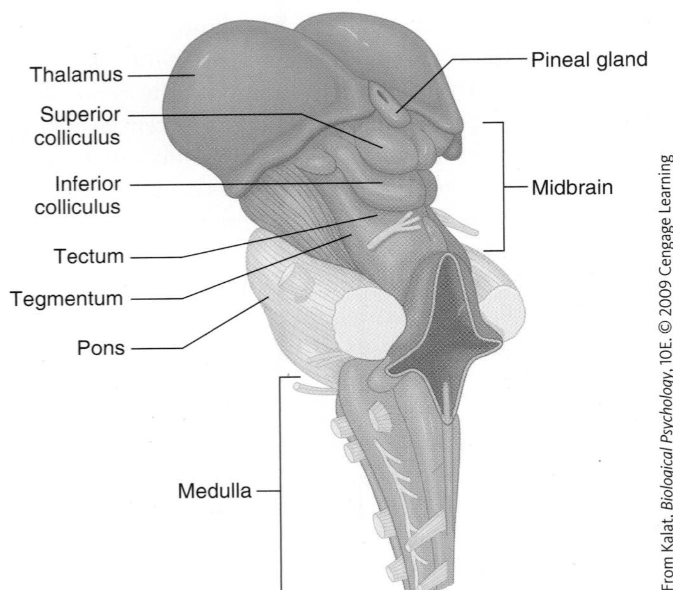

● **FIGURE 2.4** | The brain stem (cerebellum removed to reveal other structures).

discovering that this area regulates, organizes, and filters information related to cognition, emotions, mood, and motor function, and that it has been implicated in attention-deficit/hyperactivity disorder (ADHD, discussed in Chapter 5); disorders affecting motor behavior, such as tics and tremors; and obsessive–compulsive disorder (OCD, discussed in Chapter 7).

The cerebral cortex, the largest part of the forebrain, gives us our distinctly human qualities and allows us to look to the future and plan as well as to reason and to create. The cerebral cortex is divided into two hemispheres that look very much alike, but have different specialties, or functions. The left hemisphere (dominant in right-handed persons) plays a chief role in verbal and other cognitive processes. The right hemisphere (dominant in left-handed persons) is better at social perception and creativity. Researchers believe that each hemisphere plays a different role in certain psychological disorders, such as communication and learning disorders.

Around puberty, the brain develops new brain cells and neural connections, and then once again begins to reorganize and consolidate (Benes, 2006). This new growth and restructuring results in further maturation of the lobes of the brain. ● Figure 2.6 shows the *temporal*, *parietal*, and *frontal lobes* of the brain and their important functions. The **frontal lobes** show up most often in subsequent chapters on disorders and are worth special attention. The frontal lobes contain the functions underlying most of our thinking and reasoning abilities, including memory. These functions enable us to make sense of social relationships and customs and to relate to the world and the people around us, which is why they have considerable relevance in the study of abnormal child psychology. Fortunately, all of these functions continue to mature well into late adolescence and early adulthood. By implication, the brain you had when you reached adolescence is not the one you have now.

Remarkably, these critical brain areas perform their functions in an integrated, harmonious fashion—aided by important regulatory systems and neurotransmitters—that permits the whole to be much larger than the sum of its parts. However, for many disorders defined in this text, one or more of these brain areas are not performing their functions as they should, either as a result of other problems or as a primary cause of the disorder.

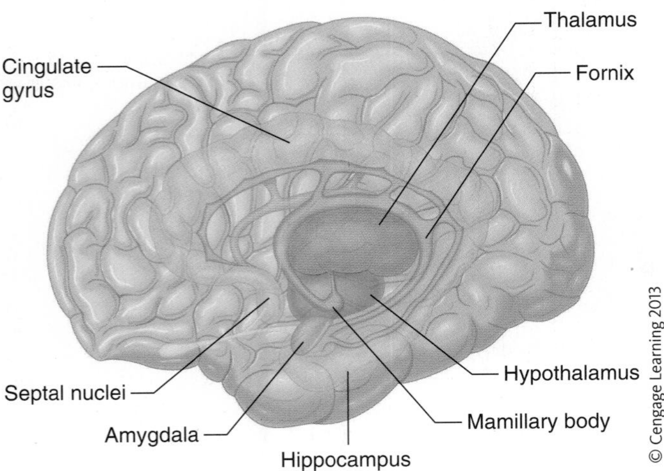

● **FIGURE 2.5** | Structures of the limbic system.

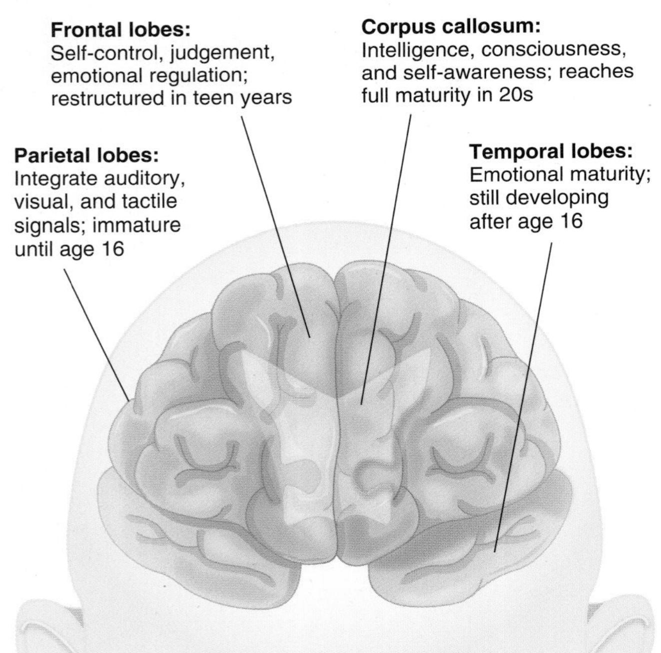

● **FIGURE 2.6** | The lobes of the brain and their functions.

The Endocrine System

The endocrine system is an important regulatory system that has been linked to specific psychological disorders, such as anxiety and mood disorders, in both children and adults. There are several endocrine glands, and each produces a particular hormone that it releases into the bloodstream. The *adrenal* glands (located on top of the kidneys) are most familiar because they produce **epinephrine** (also known as adrenaline) in response to stress. Epinephrine energizes us and prepares our bodies for possible threats or challenges. The *thyroid* gland produces the hormone thyroxine, which is needed for proper energy metabolism and growth and is implicated in certain eating disorders of children and youths (discussed in Chapter 13). Finally, the *pituitary* gland, located deep within the brain, orchestrates the body's functions by regulating a variety of hormones, including estrogen and testosterone. Because the endocrine system is closely related to the immune system, which protects us from disease and many other biological threats, it is not surprising that it is implicated in a variety of disorders, particularly health- and stress-related disorders (discussed in Chapter 12).

One brain connection that is implicated in some psychological disorders involves the hypothalamus and the endocrine system. The hypothalamus carries out the commands it receives from the adjacent pituitary gland and other hormones, such as those regulating hunger and thirst. The pituitary gland in turn stimulates the adrenal glands to produce epinephrine and the stress hormone known as **cortisol**. The hypothalamus control center, coupled with the pituitary and adrenal glands, make up a regulatory system in the brain known as the **hypothalamic–pituitary–adrenal (HPA) axis**. Box 2.2 explains how this axis has been implicated in several psychological disorders, especially those connected to a person's response to stress and ability to regulate emotions, such as anxiety and mood disorders.

Neurotransmitters

Neurotransmitters are similar to biochemical currents in the brain. These currents develop in an organized fashion to make meaningful connections that serve larger functions such as thinking and feeling. Neurons that are more sensitive to one type of neurotransmitter, such as serotonin, tend to cluster together and form **brain circuits**, which are paths from one part of the brain to another (R. R. Dean, Kelsey, Heller, & Ciaranello, 1993). Tens of thousands of these circuits operate in our brains. Their connective pathways and function have been revealed in recent years in ways that were inconceivable only a decade ago.

Brain circuits and neurotransmitters have been tied to particular psychological disorders, but they also offer possible avenues for treatment. Psychoactive drugs work by either increasing or decreasing the flow of

BOX 2.2 A CLOSER LOOK

The HPA Axis and Stress Regulation

The HPA axis is a central component of the brain's neuroendocrine response to stress. The hypothalamus, when stimulated, secretes the corticotropin-releasing hormone (CRH), which stimulates the pituitary gland to secrete the andrenocorticotropic hormone (ACTH) into the bloodstream. ACTH then causes the adrenal glands to release cortisol, the familiar stress hormone that arouses the body to meet a challenging situation. This system, like many others, works on a feedback loop: Cortisol modulates the stress response by acting on the hypothalamus to inhibit the continued release of CRH (Sternberg & Gold, 1997). Researchers are discovering that this important feedback loop, which regulates our level of arousal and apprehension, can be seriously disrupted or damaged by various traumatic and uncontrollable events. These events can cause a child or adolescent to maintain a state of fear or alertness that becomes toxic over prolonged periods of time (Bremner, 2007).

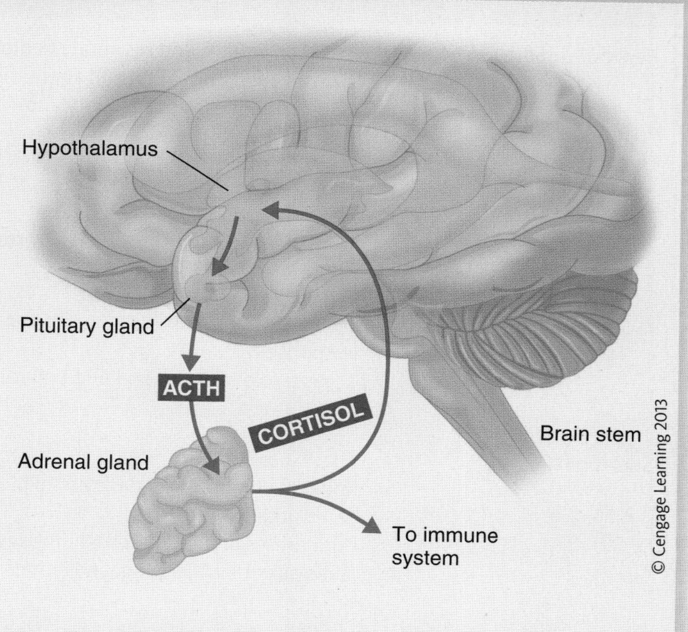

various neurotransmitters—for example, increasing dopamine in the case of stimulant medications for ADHD (Vitiello, 2007). However, like the influence of genetics, changes in neurotransmitter activity may make people *more likely* or *less likely* to exhibit certain kinds of behavior in certain situations, but they do not cause the behavior directly. Table 2.1 summarizes the four neurotransmitter systems most often mentioned in connection with psychological disorders, and is a useful guide to discussions of etiology in later chapters.

SECTION SUMMARY

Biological Perspectives

- Brain functions undergo continual changes, described as neural plasticity, as they adapt to environmental demands.
- Genetic influences depend on the environment. Genetic endowment influences behavior, emotions, and thoughts; environmental events are necessary for this influence to be expressed.
- Gene–environment interactions (G×E) explain how the environment shapes our genotype through a process known as epigenetics.
- Neurobiological contributions to abnormal child behavior include knowledge of brain structures, the endocrine system, and neurotransmitters, all of which perform their functions in an integrated, harmonious fashion.

Psychological Perspectives

Each major psychological perspective described in this section has value in explaining the development of psychopathology. At the same time, each perspective has certain limitations and may be more or less applicable to any particular disorder or situation. Again, bear in mind that abnormal behavior results from transactions between environmental and individual influences. Children's inherited characteristics coupled with the experiences and influences in their environment make them the way they are today. Also, some seemingly maladaptive behaviors, such as excessive fearfulness or watchfulness, may in fact be understandable when considered in the context of the child's environment if it involves parental abuse or school violence.

Our interest in psychological bases for abnormal behavior begins with a focus on the role of emotions in establishing an infant's ability to adapt to her new surroundings. To an infant who has limited means of expression and interpretation, emotions provide the initial filter for organizing so much new information and avoiding potential harm. Similarly, early relationships with one or more caregivers provide structure and regulation to these emotional responses. As the child develops, cognitive processes such as self-efficacy play a larger role in assisting the young child to make sense of

TABLE 2.1 | Major Neurotransmitters and Their Implicated Roles in Psychopathology

Neurotransmitter	Normal Functions	Implicated Role in Psychopathology
Benzodiazepine-GABA	Reduces arousal and moderates emotional responses, such as anger, hostility, and aggression Is linked to feelings of anxiety and discomfort	Anxiety disorder
Dopamine	May act as a *switch* that turns on various brain circuits, allowing other neurotransmitters to inhibit or facilitate emotions or behavior Is involved in exploratory, extroverted, and pleasure-seeking activity	Schizophrenia Mood disorders Attention-deficit/hyperactivity disorder (ADHD)
Norepinephrine	Facilitates or controls emergency reactions and alarm responses Plays a role in emotional and behavioral regulation	Not *directly* involved in specific disorders (acts generally to regulate or modulate behavioral tendencies)
Serotonin	Plays a role in information and motor coordination Inhibits children's tendency to explore their surroundings Moderates and regulates a number of critical behaviors, such as eating, sleeping, and expressing anger	Regulatory problems, such as eating and sleep disorders Obsessive–compulsive disorder Schizophrenia and mood disorders

Source: © Cengage Learning 2013

her world and to reorganize earlier functions that may be unnecessary or even maladaptive as she faces new challenges involving language development, peer interactions, and similar skills. As with brain development, things can go wrong at any point along this continuum of emotional and cognitive development as a function of the child's interaction with her environment.

Emotional Influences

Emotions and affective expression are core elements of human psychological experience. From birth, they are a central feature of infant activity and regulation (Sroufe, 2005). Throughout our lives, emotional reactions assist us in our fight-or-flight response—to alert us to danger and to ensure our safety. From an evolutionary perspective, emotions give special value to events and make particular actions most likely to occur. In effect, emotions tell us what to pay attention to and what to ignore, what to approach and what to avoid. Given their important job, and backed up by powerful stress-regulating hormones such as cortisol, emotions are critical to healthy adaptation.

Interest in emotional processes and their relation to abnormal child behavior has grown considerably in recent years (Arsenio & Lemerise, 2010). Children's emotional experiences, expressions, and regulation affect the quality of their social interactions and relationships, and thus are at the foundation of early personality development. Researchers are discovering a wealth of information demonstrating the influential role of emotion in children's lives. Emotions not only serve as important internal monitoring and guidance systems designed to appraise events as either beneficial or dangerous, but they also provide motivation for action (Hastings, Zahn-Waxler, & Usher, 2007).

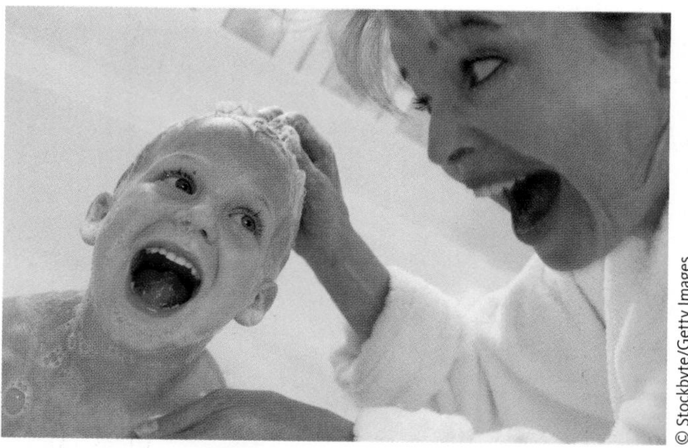

The ability to infer another's emotional state by reading facial, gestural, postural, and vocal cues has an important adaptive function, especially for infants and toddlers

Children have a natural tendency to attend to emotional cues from others, which helps them learn to interpret and regulate their own emotions. They learn, from a very young age, through the emotional expressions of others (Bretherton & Munholland, 2008). Within their first year of life, they learn the importance of emotions for communication and regulation; by their second year, they have some ability to attribute cause to emotional expression. Of particular interest to abnormal child psychology is the finding that children look to the emotional expression and cues of their caregivers to provide them with the information needed to formulate a basic understanding of what's going on. To young children, emotions are a primary form of communication that permits them to explore their world with increasing independence (LaFreniere, 2000).

Emotion Reactivity and Regulation

We can divide emotional processes into two dimensions: emotion reactivity and emotion regulation. **Emotion reactivity** refers to individual differences in the threshold and intensity of emotional experience, which provide clues to an individual's level of distress and sensitivity to the environment. **Emotion regulation**, on the other hand, involves enhancing, maintaining, or inhibiting emotional arousal, which is usually done for a specific purpose or goal (Perlman & Pelphrey, 2011; Southam-Gerow & Kendall, 2002). Jorge, for example, was emotionally reactive to certain academic tasks; he became upset and couldn't concentrate. This emotional reaction could lead to poor regulation, resulting in Jorge becoming distraught and difficult to manage at times. Once again, a transactional process is at work, whereby emotional reactions prompt the need for regulation, which influences further emotional expression.

A further distinction can be made between problems in *regulation* and problems in *dysregulation*. Regulation problems involve weak or absent control structures, such as Jorge's trouble concentrating in class; dysregulation means that existing control structures operate maladaptively (Izard, Youngstrom, Fine, Mostow, & Trentacosta, 2006). For example, a child may be fearful even when there is no reason in the environment to be fearful or anxious.

Children's emotion regulation abilities, as often shown by their emotion reactivity and expression, are important signals of normal and abnormal development. Emotions also help young children learn more about themselves and their surroundings, as part of the process of learning to identify and monitor their feelings and behavior. The child–caregiver relationship plays a critical role in this process because it provides the basic setting for children to express emotions and to experience caring guidance and have limits placed on them. *Authoritative* parents establish limits for the child that are both sensitive to the child's individual development and needs and demanding of the child to foster self-control and healthy regulation (Maccoby & Martin, 1983). Because of its vital role in emotional development, the child–caregiver relationship will surface again and again when we discuss childhood disorders.

Some forms of emotion dysregulation may be adaptive in one environment or at one time but maladaptive in other situations. Children who have been emotionally and sexually abused may show shallow emotions, known as numbing, which is a symptom of a post-traumatic stress reaction that serves to protect the child from overwhelming pain and trauma (described in Chapter 14). If numbing becomes a characteristic way of coping with stressors later in life, however, it may interfere with adaptive functioning and long-term goals.

Temperament and Early Personality Styles

You hear it all the time: "She was an easy baby, right from the first day I brought her home from the hospital," or "Sleep? What's that? Since little Freddy was born, we are up all hours of the night, feeding, changing, and trying to soothe him." Unmistakably, some infants are more placid than others, some are more active, and some are more high-strung, and these differences are often recognizable in the first few days or weeks of life (Thomas & Chess, 1977). What relevance does this have to abnormal development?

The development of emotion regulation or dysregulation is thought to derive from both socialization and innate predispositions, or temperament. **Temperament** refers to the child's organized style of behavior that appears early in development, such as fussiness or fearfulness, which shapes the child's approach to his or her environment, and vice versa (Henderson & Wachs, 2007). Temperament is a subset of the broader domain of personality, so it is often considered an early building block of personality (Stright, Gallagher, & Kelley, 2008). Such constitutional predispositions do not imply a certain destiny leading to a psychological disorder; rather, a particular outcome appears to be based on a series of reciprocal interactions between innate predispositions (debilitative or protective) and situational circumstances, such as a supportive or stressful environment.

Three primary dimensions of temperament have relevance to risk of abnormal child development (Rothbart & Posner, 2006):

1. *Positive affect and approach.* This dimension describes the "easy child," who is generally approachable and adaptive to his or her environment and possesses the ability to regulate basic functions of eating, sleeping, and elimination relatively smoothly.
2. *Fearful or inhibited.* This dimension describes the "slow-to-warm-up child," who is cautious in his or her approach to novel or challenging situations. Such children are more variable in self-regulation and adaptability, and may show distress or negativity toward some situations.
3. *Negative affect or irritability.* This dimension describes the "difficult child," who is predominantly negative or intense in mood, not very adaptable, and arrhythmic. Some children with this temperament show distress when faced with novel or challenging situations, and others are prone to general distress or irritability, including when limitations are placed on them.

These temperament dimensions, or early self-regulatory styles, have been linked to distinct brain activity that underlies a child's cautious versus more eager approach to novel situations, which supports the conclusion that temperament is established during early brain development (Berger & Berger, 2011; Perlman & Pelphrey, 2010). Early infant temperament may be linked to psychopathology or risk conditions in several ways. In some instances, a temperamental style may be highly related to a particular disorder, such as anxiety. In other instances, the condition may develop from the features closely related to temperament, but the condition itself may appear unrelated (Rothbart & Posner, 2006). For example, an infant's extreme sensitivity to emotional stimuli may contribute to a tendency to withdraw from others as a toddler or preschooler; over time, this tendency may transform into an interpersonal style characterized by a self-reported lack of feeling toward others and, consequently, peer rejection or other risk conditions. Also, infant negative affect can contribute to maternal withdrawal or indifference, leading to insecure attachment and its associated risk conditions.

Young children with an irritable temperament may show distress when demands are placed on them

Temperament may influence later development by affecting a child's development of self-control. Notably, fearful or cautious temperament style at a young age is linked to better self-control, presumably because the child is less impulsive and takes his or her time before making choices (Tarullo, Obradovic, & Gunnar, 2009). But like most aspects of child psychology, temperament and self-control have to achieve a reasonable balance—a high degree of self-control is a positive thing for the more exuberant toddlers, but can be problematic for more shy youngsters because others view them as socially withdrawn (White, McDermott, Degnan, Henderson, & Fox, 2011). Thus, a balance between emotional reactivity and self-control, known as *self-regulation*, is the best formula for healthy, normal adjustment.

To recap, emotion reactivity and regulation processes begin at birth and form recognizable patterns of infant temperament and later personality. Emotion regulation involves a variety of increasingly complex developmental tasks aided by the formation of healthy relationships and other environmental resources. The degree of interference with these tasks depends on the fit between the child, her or his environment, and the interaction between the child and the environment. Emotion dysregulation is believed to be the result of interference in the associated developmental processes. The lifelong significance of emotion reactivity and regulation is backed up by strong empirical evidence linking early behavioral styles to adult personality characteristics 30 years later, as described in Box 2.3.

BOX 2.3 **A CLOSER LOOK**

Similarities in Children's Early Behavioral Styles and Adult Personality and Well-Being

Caspi et al. (2003) conducted a landmark study of the connection between early temperament style in children and their later personality traits as adults. These researchers observed more than 1,000 children at age 3 and evaluated their temperament along five dimensions: Undercontrolled, Inhibited, Confident, Reserved, and Well-adjusted. Twenty-three years later they conducted an assessment of these same individuals as adults, and found some interesting consistencies in "personality style" over this length of time.

When observed at age 3, children classified as Undercontrolled (10% of the sample) were rated as irritable, impulsive, and restless. At age 26, these same individuals scored high on personality traits linked to "negative emotionality." They were easily upset and most likely to overreact to minor events, and they reported feeling mistreated, deceived, and betrayed by others. Children classified as Inhibited (8% of the sample) were considered a bit fearful and easily upset, and by age 26 they were described as unassertive and took little pleasure in life. The researchers found that the remaining three temperament groups did not display such dramatic personality profiles as adults, but a considerable amount of continuity in style did occur over time. Confident children (28% of the sample) were seen as friendly and eager to explore, and they were the least conventional and most extroverted as adults. Reserved children (15% of the sample) were described as timid and somewhat uncomfortable, and by adulthood they described themselves as unassertive and were seen by others as being introverted. Finally, the well-adjusted children (40% of the sample), who behaved in an age- and situation-appropriate manner at age 3, showed adult personality traits that closely resembled the average, well-adjusted adult.

The story doesn't end there. The researchers have continued to follow this sample and have determined that their degree of self-control as children predicted their adult health, substance use problems, personal finances, and criminal offenses in their early 30s (Moffitt et al., 2011). These findings provide the strongest evidence to date that children's early behavioral styles forecast how they will typically behave, think, and feel as adults. They also imply that tremendous benefits to individuals and society could result if large-scale programs to teach children self-control skills were offered at an early age.

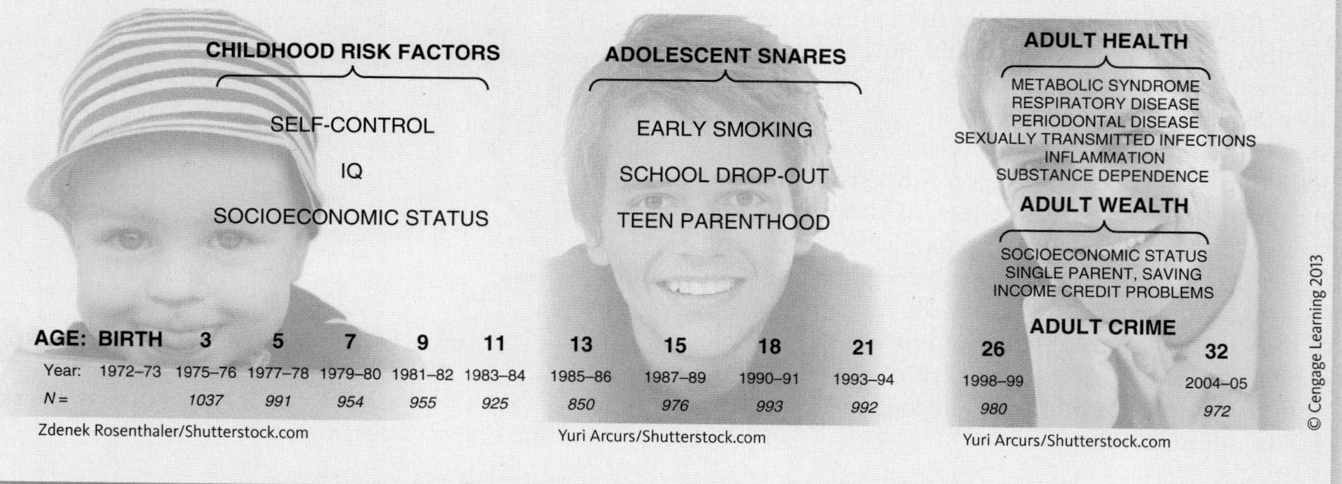

Zdenek Rosenthaler/Shutterstock.com Yuri Arcurs/Shutterstock.com Yuri Arcurs/Shutterstock.com

Behavioral and Cognitive Influences

Behavioral and cognitive explanations for abnormal child behavior emphasize principles of learning and cognition, which shape children's behavior and their interpretation of things around them. Behavioral and cognitive approaches differ essentially in the extent to which they apply cognitive concepts and procedures to the understanding of behavior. Applied behavior analysis, at one end of this continuum, focuses primarily on observable behavior and rejects the notion that cognitive mediation is a necessary consideration for explaining behavior. At the other end is social learning theory, which relies more broadly on cognitive processes and explanations.

Most behavioral explanations assume that the child is best understood and described by behavior in a particular situation rather than in terms of stable traits. Although a child's particular learning history is of interest, behavioral methods focus on the most pragmatic, parsimonious explanation for a particular problem behavior. By the same reasoning, this approach recognizes that success in changing a problem behavior does not imply knowledge about its origin, but rather emphasizes contemporaneous causes, referred to as *controlling variables*. Cognitive theorists, on the other hand, are interested in how certain thought patterns develop over time and how they relate to particular behavioral strategies, such as problem solving. Following is a refresher on some of the major behavioral and cognitive theories.

Applied Behavior Analysis (ABA)

Based on B. F. Skinner's classic studies, ABA examines the relationships between behavior and its antecedents and consequences, which is known as a *functional approach* to behavior. No implicit assumptions are made about underlying needs or motives that contribute to abnormal behavior; ABA describes and tests functional relationships between stimuli, responses, and consequences. ABA is based on four primary operant learning principles, which explain how behaviors are acquired or changed as a result of particular consequences. These four principles are probably familiar to you: *Positive* and *negative reinforcement* are any actions that increase the target response; *extinction* and *punishment* have the effect of decreasing a response. Children are quite accomplished at learning the contingencies between their behavior and its consequences, and have an uncanny ability to apply some of their own! These principles of operant conditioning remain influential across a variety of applied areas—from basic experimental research to clinical treatment (DeGrandpre, 2000).

Classical Conditioning

Based on the extension of Pavlov's famous learning trials and Watson's experiments with Little Albert (see Chapter 1), classical conditioning explains the acquisition of deviant behavior on the basis of paired associations between previously neutral stimuli (such as math problems) and unconditioned stimuli (such as food or criticism). Any neutral event can become a *conditioned stimulus* if it is paired enough times with an event that already elicits a certain response. Paired associations can help explain many adjustment problems in children and adolescents, although we do not typically know what the original association may have been. In addition, more than one learning paradigm may occur at the same time. For this reason, dual learning explanations for undesirable behavior are common (that is, combinations of features of both operant and classical conditioning).

Returning to Jorge's problem, imagine that he associates reading (a neutral event) with humiliation or anxiety (unconditioned stimuli), which prompts him to escape or avoid the activity. His avoidance, in turn, is negatively reinforced by its consequences: His anxiety decreases and he avoids feelings of humiliation. This analysis considers both instrumental (operant) and respondent (classical) conditioning as part of his learning history. Can you think of possible environmental changes or contingencies that might modify Jorge's behavior in a desirable fashion?

Social Learning and Cognition

Social learning explanations consider not only overt behaviors such as Jorge's school problems, but also the role of possible *cognitive mediators* that may influence the behaviors directly or indirectly. According to Albert Bandura's (1977, 1986) social learning explanation, behavior may be learned not only by operant and classical

Children's increasing cognitive abilities play a role in both normal and abnormal development

conditioning, but also indirectly through *observational* (vicarious) learning. Children can learn a new behavior merely by watching another person model the behavior, without apparent reinforcement or practice.

Social learning also incorporates the role of social cognition in acquiring desirable and undesirable behavior. **Social cognition** relates to how children think about themselves and others, resulting in the formation of mental representations of themselves, their relationships, and their social world. These representations are not fixed, but are continually updated on the basis of maturation and social interaction (Herrmann, Call, Hernández-Lloreda, Hare, & Tomasello, 2007). Children's ongoing cognitive development in reasoning, problem solving, and making attributions helps them make sense of who they are and how they relate to their surroundings. Moreover, social learning and social-cognitive viewpoints also consider the role of affect and the importance of contextual variables, such as family and peers, in both the origins and maintenance of problem behaviors (Arsenio & Lemerise, 2010).

Like individual differences in temperament and emotion regulation, crucial differences exist in how children process information and make sense of their social worlds. Like adults, children have a natural desire to evaluate their behavior in various circumstances, especially those involving some element of possible failure, harm, or personal risk. For some children, teens, and adults, these self-appraisals of performance may be based on faulty beliefs or distortions; for others, an attributional bias about their ability or the intentions of others leads them to reinterpret the event in a way that fits their preexisting belief about themselves or others ("I got a good grade in math because the exam was too easy"; "He's a jerk, so who cares if I tease him?") (Lansford, Malone, Dodge, Pettit, & Bates, 2010).

Since the first description of observational learning in the early 1960s, cognitive models have grown in both richness and complexity, and their constructs appear quite often throughout this text. Cognitive distortions, insufficient cognitive mediation, and attributional styles and expectations are important determinants in the development and treatment of behavioral and emotional problems in children and adolescents (Bierman et al., 2010).

SECTION SUMMARY

Psychological Perspectives

- Emotion reactivity and regulation are critical aspects of early and subsequent development, affecting the quality of children's social interactions and relationships throughout their life span.
- Three major approaches to abnormal behavior, based on principles of learning, are applied behavior analysis, principles of classical conditioning, and social learning and social cognition theories. Social learning and social cognition theories place more significance on cognitive processes than overt behavior.

FAMILY, SOCIAL, AND CULTURAL PERSPECTIVES

In addition to biological and psychological influences, children's normal and abnormal development depends on social and environmental contexts. Understanding context requires a consideration of both *proximal* (close-by) and *distal* (further-removed) events, as well as those that impinge directly on the child in a particular situation at a particular time. We consider these wide-ranging environmental conditions and learning experiences in relation to the family and peer context and the social and cultural context.

What exactly do we mean when we refer to a child's environment? Family? Peer groups? Clean air? To appreciate the complex network that constitutes a child's world and contributes to maladjustment, we need to go beyond the traditional view of the environment as being unidimensional or narrowly defined. A child's environment is constantly changing in relation to its many components, much as a lake or stream is affected by a proximal event, such as a rainstorm, as well as more distal events, such as the seasons.

Environmental influences are then further subdivided into shared and nonshared types. **Shared environment** refers to those environmental factors that produce similarities in developmental outcomes among siblings in the same family. For example, if siblings are more similar than expected from only their shared genetics, this implies an effect of the environment they share, such as being exposed to marital conflict or poverty, or being parented in a similar manner. In the example of identical twins, shared environmental influence is estimated indirectly from correlations between twins by subtracting the heritability estimate from the MZ twin correlation. **Nonshared environment**, which refers to environmental factors that produce behavioral differences among siblings, can then be calculated by subtracting the MZ twin correlation from 1.0 (Pike & Kretschmer, 2009; Pike & Plomin, 1996).

Interestingly, it is nonshared environmental factors that create differences among siblings that seem to contribute to a large portion of the variation. Environmental factors that have been postulated as nonshared include differential treatment by parents, peer influences, and school environment (Eley & Lau, 2005).

● Figure 2.7 depicts Bronfenbrenner's (1977) ecological model, which shows the richness and depth of the various layers of a child's environment by portraying it as a series of nested and interconnected structures. Note that the child is at the center of this sphere of influence, which contains various levels interconnected in meaningful ways. The child's immediate environment begins with family members and home surroundings, but it quickly grows more complex as the child enters preschool, visits neighborhood parks, and makes friends.

Social settings also affect the child, even when the child does not directly experience these influences. Parents' friends and jobs, the availability of family support services such as health and welfare programs, and similar community resources and activities that are positive and negative make up the child's larger social framework (Sameroff, 2010). Finally, though far removed from the child's day-to-day activities, cultural ideology or identity governs how children should be treated (the sanctioning of corporal punishment), what they should be taught, and what goals are important to

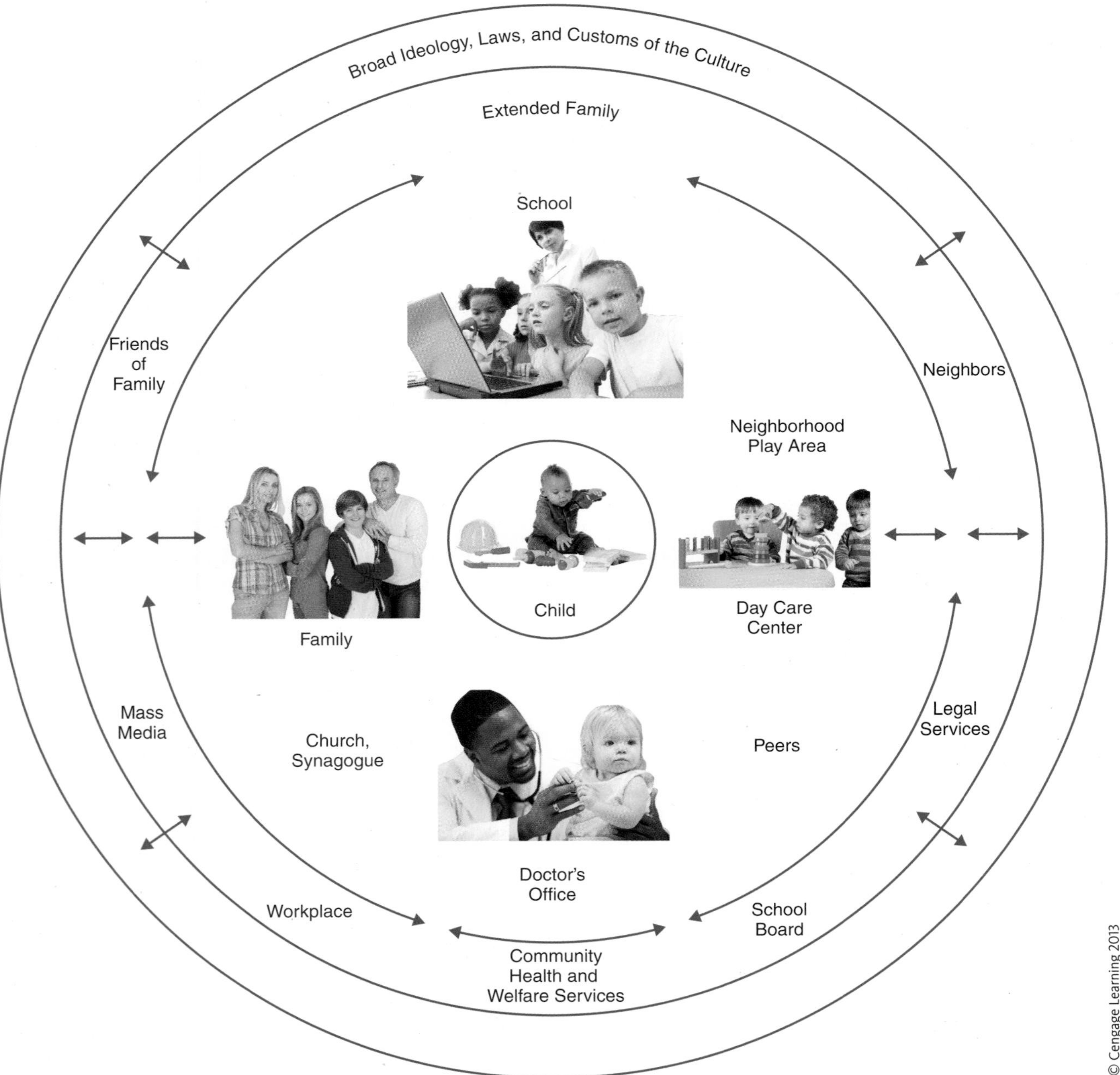

● **FIGURE 2.7** | An ecological model of environmental influences.

Photo Credits (clockwise from center and top): Glenda M. Powers /Shutterstock.com; Dmitriy Shironosov/Shutterstock.com; © iStockphoto.com/jo unruh; © iStockphoto.com/Sean Locke; Goodluz/Shutterstock.com achieve (Achenbach & Rescorla, 2007). These levels of environmental influences and their reciprocal connections (they affect the child, and the child affects them) are key elements in understanding the nature of child abuse and neglect, eating disorders, and many other disorders.

Infant–Caregiver Attachment

The study of abnormal development has profited from extensive work on child–caregiver relationships; this has painted a dramatic picture of the importance of early caregiver attachment to a child's emotional health (Sweeney, 2007). British child psychiatrist John Bowlby (1973, 1988) integrated aspects of evolutionary biology with existing psychodynamic conceptions of early experiences to derive his theory of attachment. **Attachment** refers to the process of establishing and maintaining an emotional bond with parents or other significant individuals. This process is ongoing, typically beginning between 6 and 12 months of age, and provides infants with a secure, consistent base from which to explore and learn about their world (Sroufe, 2005).

In attachment theory, instinctive behaviors are not rigidly predetermined but rather become organized into flexible, goal-oriented systems through learning and goal-corrected feedback. Bowlby reasoned that infants are "preadapted" to engage in relationship-enhancing behaviors such as orienting, smiling, crying, clinging, signaling, and, as they learn to move about, proximity seeking. In order to survive, however, infants must become attached to a specific person (or persons) who is available and responsive to their needs. Adults are similarly equipped with attachment-promoting behaviors to respond to an infant's needs, which are complementary to the needs of the infant—smiling, touching, holding, and rocking.

The evolving infant–caregiver relationship helps the infant regulate her or his behavior and emotions, especially under conditions of threat or stress. Accordingly, attachment serves an important stress-reduction function. The infant is motivated to maintain a balance between the desire to preserve the familiar and the desire to seek and explore new information. Self-reliance develops when the attachment figure provides a secure base for exploration (Bretherton & Munholland, 2008). Moreover, a child's *internal working model* of relationships—what he or she expects from others and how he or she relates to others—emerges from this first crucial relationship and is carried forward into later relationships. The three major organized patterns of attachment (and one disorganized pattern) are summarized in Table 2.2, along with their theoretical and empirical links to various forms of psychopathology.

Keep in mind, however, that attachment features constitute only one aspect of human relationships. Insecure attachments have been implicated in a number of childhood disorders, but no one-to-one correspondence exists between specific patterns of attachment and particular disorders (Sroufe, 2005).

The Family and Peer Context

Child psychopathology research has increasingly focused on the role of the family system, the complex relationships within families, and the reciprocal influences among various family subsystems. There is a need to consider the processes occurring within disturbed families, and the common and unique ways these processes affect both individual family members and subsystems. Within the family, the roles of the mother–child and marital subsystems have received the most research attention, with less attention being given to the role of siblings (Linares, 2006) or fathers (Cassano, Adrian, Veits, & Zeman, 2006; Cowan, Cowan, & Knox, 2010).

Family systems theorists argue that it is difficult to understand or predict the behavior of a particular family member, such as a child, in isolation from other family members (P. A. Cowan & C. P. Cowan, 2006). This view is in line with our earlier discussion of underlying assumptions about children's abnormal development—*relationships*, not individual children or teens, are often the crucial focus. This view, however, is often at odds with mainstream psychological and psychiatric approaches to psychopathology, yet it is compatible with developmental processes.

More and more, the study of individual factors and the study of the child's context are being seen as mutually compatible and beneficial to both theory and intervention. Furthermore, the manner in which the family, as a unit, deals with typical and atypical stress plays an instrumental role in children's adjustment and adaptation. The outcome of stressful events depends in part on the nature and severity of the stress, the level of family functioning prior to the stress, and the family's coping skills and resources. Stress that is positive or tolerable, such as changing schools or a decline in family income, often brings about change, growth, and reorganization of families, and is not usually harmful to children's development (Masten & Wright, 2010; Rutter, 2011). However, some forms of stress are considered "toxic" to child development because they cause strong, frequent, and/or prolonged activation of the child's stress response in the absence of adult protection and support (Shonkoff, 2010). Some of the more influential family-related issues raised in discussions of childhood disorders throughout this book are parental depression, child abuse, parental substance

TABLE 2.2 | Types of Attachment and Their Relation to Disordered Outcomes

Type of Attachment	Description During Strange Situation[1]	Possible Influence on Relationships	Possible Disordered Outcomes
Secure	Infant readily separates from caregiver and likes to explore. When wary of a stranger or distressed by separation, the infant seeks contact and proximity with caregiver; the infant then returns to exploration and play after contact.	Individuals with secure attachment histories tend to seek out and make effective use of supportive relationships.	Although individuals with secure attachments may suffer psychological distress, their relationship strategy serves a protective function against disordered outcomes.
Insecure ***Anxious, avoidant type***	Infant engages in exploration, but with little affective interaction with caregiver. Infant shows little wariness of strangers, and generally is upset only if left alone. As stress increases, avoidance increases.	As children and adults, individuals with an insecure, *avoidant pattern of early* attachment tend to mask emotional expression. They often believe they are invulnerable to hurt, and others are not to be trusted.	Conduct disorders; aggressive behavior; depressive symptoms (usually as a result of failure of self-reliant image).
Insecure ***Anxious, resistant type***	Infant shows disinterest in or resistance to exploration and play, and is wary of novel situations or strangers. Infant has difficulty settling when reunited with caregiver, and may mix active contact-seeking with crying and fussiness.	As children and adults, individuals with an *insecure, resistant* pattern of early attachment have difficulties managing anxiety. They tend to exaggerate emotions and maintain negative beliefs about the self.	Phobias; anxiety; psychosomatic symptoms; depression.
Disorganized, disoriented type (not an organized strategy)	Infant lacks a coherent strategy of attachment. Appears disorganized when faced with a novel situation and has no consistent pattern of regulating emotions.	Individuals with disorganized, disoriented style show an inability to form close attachments to others; may show an indiscriminate friendliness (little selective attachment).	No consensus, but generally a wide range of personality disorders (van Ijzendoorn, Schuengel, & Bakermans-Kranenburg, 1999).

[1]The Strange Situation is a method of assessing infant–caregiver attachment. It involves a series of increasingly stressful separations and reunions that resemble typical daily occurrences, such as meeting strangers and being left alone (Ainsworth, Blehar, Waters, & Wall, 1978).

Note: The relationships between attachment styles and abnormal development are based on both theoretical and empirical findings, summarized in E. A. Carlson and Sroufe (1995). (Sroufe, Carlson, Levy, & Egeland, 1999)

abuse, divorce, marital violence, poverty, and parental criminality.

Although quite distinct, these major family and individual issues share a common thread in terms of their impact on child development: They disrupt, disturb, or interfere with consistent and predictable child care and basic necessities. Such disruption or impairment, in turn, interferes with children's ongoing development to such an extent that their ability to manage stress and form satisfactory relationships with peers, teachers, and other adults cascade into lifelong psychological difficulties (Cox et al., 2010; Obradović, Burt, & Masten, 2010).

Box 2.4 provides a useful summary of the concepts discussed throughout this chapter to assist readers in understanding the major processes affecting normal and abnormal development.

SECTION SUMMARY

Family, Social, and Cultural Perspectives

- Attachment approaches to abnormal child behavior emphasize the evolving infant–caregiver relationship, which helps the infant regulate behavior and emotions, especially under conditions of threat or stress.
- Children's normal and abnormal development depends on a variety of social and environmental settings, including the child's family and peer system and the larger social and cultural context.

BOX 2.4 A CLOSER LOOK

The "Core Story" of Development

For several years a group of neuroscientists, developmental psychologists, pediatricians, and others have been working on a "core story" of child development in an effort to translate complex ideas and findings into actions that reduce social problems and improve children's chances at successful development. We thought a brief list of their core story themes would provide a nice summary of the important issues you have read about in this chapter:

1. Child development is a foundation for community development and economic development, because capable children become the foundation of a prosperous and sustainable society.
2. Brain architecture is constructed through an ongoing process that begins before birth and continues into adulthood. The quality of that architecture establishes either a sturdy or a fragile foundation for all the capabilities and behavior that follow.
3. Skill begets skill as brains are built in a hierarchical fashion, from the bottom up. Increasingly complex circuits and skills build on simpler circuits and skills over time.
4. The interaction of genes and experience shapes the circuitry of the developing brain. Young children serve up frequent invitations to engage with adults, who are either responsive or unresponsive to their needs. This "serve and return" process is fundamental to the wiring of the brain, especially in the early years.
5. Cognitive, emotional, and social capacities are intertwined. Learning, behavior, and both physical and mental health are highly interrelated over the life course. You cannot address one domain without affecting the others.
6. Although manageable levels of stress are normative and growth promoting, toxic stress in the early years (e.g., from severe poverty, serious parental mental health impairment such as maternal depression, child maltreatment, and/or family violence) can damage developing brain architecture and lead to problems in learning and behavior, as well as increased susceptibility to physical and mental illness.
7. Brain plasticity and the ability to change behavior decrease over time. Consequently, getting it right early leads to better outcomes and is less costly, both to society and to individuals, than trying to fix it later.

Source: Based on Shonkoff & Bales, 2011.

Supported by the National Scientific Council on the Developing Child and the FrameWorks Institute (**http://www.frameworksinstitute.org**).

Looking Ahead

Society's understanding of children's healthy, normal development has been gradually evolving toward a more holistic, health-promoting orientation, which is impacting the definitions and services related to children's mental health (Barry, 2009; Lewin-Bizan, Bowers, & Lerner, 2010). This emerging dynamic, interactive view of health recognizes the importance of both individual and environmental factors in achieving positive development. The neuroscience and ecological perspectives on human health and behavior add momentum to this growing view because they consider human adaptation within its normal context.

Children's health and successful adaptation are today seen as worthy and appropriate aspects of the study of abnormal child psychology. Along with an increased emphasis on **health promotion**, today's research and thinking accept the notion that various childhood disorders share many clinical features and causes. Health promotion encourages changes, opportunities, and competence to achieve one's health potential (R. M. Kaplan, 2000; Ungar, 2010). When applied to children, this view recognizes the multicausal and interactive nature of many child and adolescent psychological disorders and the importance of contextual factors. It also speaks to the importance of balancing the abilities of individuals with the challenges and risks of their environments (Kirmayer, Dandeneau, Marshall, Phillips, & Williamson, 2011; Masten & Wright, 2010). Throughout the text we return to the many ways abnormal child psychology can be studied in a developmentally sensitive, systems-oriented manner.

These conceptual shifts are gradually changing the face of mental health and educational services for children and youths, with important implications for pediatrics, psychology, psychiatry, social work, nursing, education, and child development. How individuals think about health, how daily life is organized and experienced, how social policy is developed, how social resources are allocated, and how people are trained to implement these policies have reached their greatest potential in history for achieving major improvements in services to assist younger populations who cannot speak for themselves. Although this tremendous impact on the field of mental health, and on children and youths in particular, has not yet become reality, we are encouraged by how society has progressed in addressing the needs of children.

Study Resources

SECTION SUMMARIES

KEY TERMS

COURSEMATE

Access an interactive eBook and chapter-specific interactive learning tools, including flashcards, quizzes, videos, and more in your Psychology CourseMate, accessed through CengageBrain.com.

Research

3

If we knew what it was we were doing, it would not be called research, would it?

—Albert Einstein (1879–1955)

CHAPTER PREVIEW

IN THIS CHAPTER, WE look at the process of research and the many challenges faced by those who study children with problems and their families. Although people differ on the specifics, **research** is generally viewed as a systematic way of finding answers to questions—a method of inquiry that follows certain rules.

A Scientific Approach

The aim of science is not to open a door to infinite wisdom, but to set a limit to infinite error.

—Brecht, *The Life of Galileo*

In this chapter you will learn ways in which scientific research strategies can be used to understand children with problems and how they can be helped. A scientific approach investigates claims in organized ways that improve on common sense and casual observations. Science requires that a claim be based on theories backed up by data from well-designed studies, and that observations be checked and repeated before conclusions are drawn. A scientific approach is especially important in abnormal child psychology. Although relationships between variables of interest may seem obvious when observed casually—a child consumes too much sugar and becomes hyperactive—these relationships are often not as straightforward as they seem. What we initially may think is a simple connection between cause and effect may be obscured by complex interactions and a combination of variables. Parents and professionals who work with children have a tendency to interpret and relate information according to their own belief systems and experience. These relationships can sometimes become firmly established, independent of whether they are supported by facts. Even when new information comes along, such as studies indicating a lack of correlation between sugar and hyperactivity, one's previous views or understanding can be difficult to change.

Considerable folklore and numerous home remedies and fad treatments ranging from chicken soup to swimming with dolphins characterize the field of abnormal child psychology. Simple explanations, such as "sugar causes hyperactivity," or simple solutions, such as "spare the rod and spoil the child," may appeal to parents or teachers because they promise an easy answer or quick remedy for a complex problem. Folklore and fad treatments, unintentionally or otherwise, play to the vulnerabilities of parents of children with problems, parents who desperately want the best for their children. More often than not, easy answers or quick remedies don't work, and sometimes they bring unfortunate consequences and costs for children with problems and their families.

People have always shown some skepticism about scientific research leading to new knowledge. Consider the following comments:

> After a few more flashes in the pan, we shall hear very little more of Edison and his electric lamp. Every claim he makes has been tested and proved impracticable. (*New York Times*, January 16, 1880)

> Louis Pasteur's theory of germs is ridiculous fiction. (Pachet, professor of physiology [Toulouse, 1872])

Fortunately, the lightbulb, pasteurization, and many other ideas once viewed with skepticism have clearly caught on. Nevertheless, good reasons exist for skepticism toward research in abnormal child psychology. First, experts on childhood problems frequently disagree. Newspapers, magazines, websites, and TV talk shows provide a steady diet of conflicting opinions. The answer we get (e.g., violence on television makes children more aggressive, day care has a harmful effect on children's emotional adjustment) often depends on which "expert" we ask.

Second, research studies that appear in mainstream media are frequently oversimplified, and the way in which findings are presented can make them more or less believable. For example, people are more likely to agree with the findings of a study when the findings are presented with a photo of a brain image, compared to the same findings presented without a brain image or by using a bar graph (McCabe & Castel, 2008). In the absence of information about the limitations of brain imaging procedures, findings can be misrepresented or misunderstood.

Third, research findings in abnormal child psychology are often in conflict with one another. For example, most studies find that elementary-school-age girls are more prone to depression than boys, but some report higher rates of depression in boys, and other studies report no differences. How do we make sense out of inconsistent and sometimes contradictory findings? As we will discuss in this chapter, conflicting findings are often the result of how different studies are conducted—for example, the way depression is defined or how children for the study are selected (e.g., from clinics versus the general population).

A fourth reason for skepticism is that research has led to different recommendations regarding how children with problems should be helped. In some cases the same treatment (e.g., antidepressant medication) has been shown to be helpful, to have no effects, or to be harmful. As one practitioner put it after hearing about an effective new treatment method at a conference, "I'd better hurry home and use it quickly before a new

Recent research in abnormal child psychology has led to important new discoveries

study is published to show that it doesn't work!" Many conclusions from research with children are qualified—rarely are there clear-cut answers. A moderate amount of discipline is good; too little or too much discipline is bad. Certain treatments may work for some children but not for others, for older but not for younger children, or for children with certain cultural backgrounds but not for others.

Finally, even when scientific evidence is relatively clear and produces a consensus, many parents and professionals may dismiss the findings because they have encountered an exception, usually one drawn from personal experience. For example, despite the large amount of research showing that the habitual use of harsh physical punishment by parents can have extremely negative effects on children, a parent may still say, "My father used his belt on me when I was a kid and it sure taught me how to behave properly!"

Because no single study is perfect, it is important to be an informed consumer and to keep in mind that it is the *accumulation* of findings—not one study—that advances the field. Research using a scientific approach in abnormal child psychology has led to exciting new advances in understanding children with problems and how they can best be helped. For example, in Chapter 10, we discuss recent studies that have identified brain abnormalities in children with autism that may tell us why these children have difficulty making social connections with people. Other research—using home videotapes of 12-month-old infants who are later diagnosed with autism at 2 to 3 years of age—has identified early social markers for autism such as the infant "not responding to her name when called" or "rarely making eye contact." Discovery of possible biological and social markers makes it possible to identify children with autism at a younger age than ever before. This is critical because the earlier a child with autism receives help, the better the outcome. In studies of autism and other disorders, findings from study to study do not always agree. Nevertheless, the accumulation of new findings from scientific research into the neurobiology, early social development, and intervention for children with autism has greatly advanced our understanding of this disorder and continues to suggest new ways to help these children.

When Science Is Ignored

The example of *facilitated communication* (FC) illustrates some of the lessons to be learned when scientific methods and evidence are ignored or dismissed. FC is a seemingly well-meant but highly controversial and misused procedure for teaching children with autism and other impairments to communicate. Using this method, a facilitator provides manual assistance by lightly holding a child's hand, wrist, or arm (see photo), while the child supposedly communicates by typing on a keyboard or by pointing to letters on an alphabet board. The alleged purpose of the manual assistance by the facilitator is to help the child press the keys that she or he wants to press—not to influence key selection. However, because the assistance is continued indefinitely, the possibility of direct influence by the facilitator exists.

FC received widespread exposure in the media when it was reported that children who received it showed feats of literacy and intellectual competence far exceeding their presumed abilities (Biklen, 1990). The results were considered remarkable because the typical youngster using FC had a lifelong history of autism, profound mental retardation, or both, and had

Facilitated communication: Who's doing the communicating?

never talked (Jacobson, Mulick, & Schwartz, 1995). Proponents claim that, with this method, children with autism can generate phrases and sentences describing complex memories and feelings and demonstrate other advanced language skills (Biklen & Cardinal, 1997).

However, critics of FC view the method as quackery—no different than a Ouija board. Are the extraordinary outcomes attributed to FC fact, or are they fiction? Scientific research would indicate fiction. Controlled studies have consistently found that the child's supposed communication is being controlled by the facilitator (Mostert, 2001). For example, in one revealing study different questions were delivered through headphones to facilitators and clients (the facilitators and clients were unaware that the questions were different). The resulting answers by the client were found to match the questions given to the facilitator, not the client, indicating that it was the facilitator who was doing the communicating (Wheeler, Jacobson, Paglieri, & Schwartz, 1993).

Unfortunately, FC continues to be used each day with thousands of youngsters with disabilities throughout the world, which illustrates the potentially damaging effects of using practices not based on scientific evidence (Lilienfeld, 2007; Mostert, 2010). As reflected in the following comments by the father of a young boy with autism, parents who want the best for their children are particularly vulnerable to the false promise of questionable interventions:

> Professionals are very quick to dismiss the abilities of autistics. . . . So when facilitated communication proponents say they have found a way around the wall, parents are quick to believe. . . . But . . . the workshops can cost $250. The equipment $800 more. And what do we get for our money? Parents themselves "can't facilitate," they tell us. Our children will require facilitated communication for life, they say, and will never communicate on their own. . . . In short, the price we are asked to pay in an effort to communicate with our children is to allow strangers into our families to mediate our relationships with our own kids and to accept everything the stranger tells us on blind faith. (Mark S. Painter, Sr. [Dillon, 1993])

FC is of special interest to our discussion of a scientific approach to research because it meets many of the criteria of *pseudoscience*: demonstrations of benefit are based on anecdotes or testimonials, the child's baseline abilities and the possibility of spontaneous improvement are ignored, and related scientific procedures are disavowed. The differences between scientific and pseudoscientific claims are not simply whether they are based on evidence or not (Finn, Bothe, & Bramlett, 2005). As we discuss later in this chapter, it is the quality of the evidence, how it was obtained, and how it is presented that are crucial in evaluating whether claims are scientifically believable. Scientists are certainly capable of making incorrect claims. What distinguishes them from pseudoscientists is that they play by the rules of science, are prepared to admit when they are wrong, and are open to change based on new evidence (Lilienfeld, Lynn, & Lohr, 2003). Because a scientific approach to research is diverse and complex, many criteria, methods, and practices are necessary to depict how this approach is applied in abnormal child psychology. This will be our focus in the sections that follow, where we consider the research process in abnormal child psychology, from the questions and topics that researchers who study childhood disorders typically seek to address, to the research process, to the methods and research designs used to study problems in children. In the last section, we discuss important ethical and pragmatic issues. The research that we present throughout this book emphasizes a scientific approach to abnormal child psychology. As we begin this journey, it is also important to keep in mind that science is a social enterprise undertaken by humans, and research is inevitably influenced by scientists' values (Sonuga-Barke, 2011).

SECTION SUMMARY

A Scientific Approach

- A scientific approach to abnormal child psychology is a way of thinking about how best to understand and answer questions of interest, not just an accumulation of specific methods, practices, or procedures.
- Science requires that theories be backed up by evidence from controlled studies and that observations be checked and repeated before conclusions are drawn.
- Facilitated communication (FC) meets many of the criteria of pseudoscience because demonstrations of benefit are based on anecdotes or testimonials, the child's baseline abilities and the possibility of spontaneous improvement are ignored, and typical scientific procedures are disavowed.
- What distinguishes science from pseudoscience is that scientists play by the rules of science, are prepared to admit when they are wrong, and are open to change.

The Research Process

Science is not a collection of facts, any more than opera is a collection of notes. It's a process, a way of thinking, based on a single insight—that the degree to which an idea seems true has nothing to do with whether it is true, and that the way to distinguish factual ideas from false ones is to test them by experiment.

—Ferris (1998)

Research in abnormal child psychology is best characterized as a multistage process involving key decisions at various points. The process typically begins with the researcher(s) developing a hypothesis (research question) on the basis of observation, theory, and previous findings, and deciding on a general approach to research. The next stage involves identifying the sample to be studied, selecting measurement methods, and developing a research design and procedures. The research design and procedures must balance practical considerations with the adequacy of the research to address the hypotheses under investigation. The final stage consists of gathering and analyzing the data and interpreting the results in relation to theory and previous findings in an attempt to resolve the problem that initially led to the research. In this ongoing process, findings and interpretations from the study can then be used to generate future research questions and stimulate further research.

The main stages of the research process are summarized in ● Figure 3.1. Keep in mind that ethical considerations in conducting research with children and families must be considered at every stage of this process. We discuss these ethical considerations in the final section of this chapter, "Ethical and Pragmatic Issues."

Since there is no one "correct" approach to research, most problems in abnormal child psychology are best studied by using multiple methods and strategies. Research is much like any decision-making process. This process requires an understanding of the conceptual, methodological, and practical considerations that permit the researcher to make informed decisions about when certain research methods and strategies are appropriate and when they are not. To study abnormal child psychology, researchers must include research designs and methods of data analysis that can identify direct and indirect effects and different causal pathways for various disorders (Cicchetti & Hinshaw, 2003). We discuss common research questions and topics in abnormal child psychology in the sections that follow, addressing specific issues encountered at different stages of the research process.

Common Research Questions and Topics

Parents typically ask similar questions about their children, and the cases of Whitney (age 14) and Tito (age 7) provide examples. Such questions raise several initial issues for researchers, pointing to areas of inquiry.

WHITNEY

Always Sad

I don't understand why Whitney is so sad all the time. She's continually arguing with her brother, hates school, and has no friends. She's always been a moody child, but became much worse after my husband and I divorced. Is her sadness due to her moody personality, the divorce, or is something at home or at school making her feel this way? (Based on authors' case material)

TITO

Constantly Fighting

Tito is constantly fighting with other kids at school. He never does what we ask him to do. When things don't go his way, he has a full-blown tantrum and throws and breaks things. My husband thinks Tito's just a tough kid, and that all he needs is firm discipline. He uses his belt a lot with Tito, but it doesn't seem to make a difference. I'm really worried. Will Tito outgrow his behavior? Is my husband being too strict? What can I do about it? (Based on authors' case material)

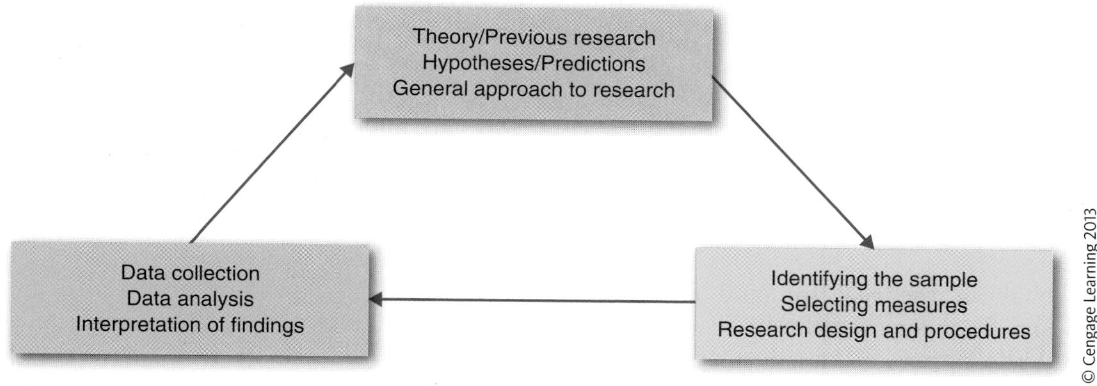

● **FIGURE 3.1** | The research process in abnormal child psychology.

These case examples include typical questions that parents ask about their children's problem behavior and development. They are also questions that spawn research into abnormal child behavior: for example, research on the impact of divorce on children's mood and behavior, as in Whitney's case, or whether fighting and destructive behavior are likely to decrease with age, as in the case of Tito. As we have noted earlier, research typically begins with a hypothesis based on a theory, which predicts certain outcomes or behavior. Research hypotheses guide the researcher's choice of methods and the research designs most appropriate for answering certain questions. Research questions and topics are often based on the theories of atypical development and behavior (discussed in Chapter 2). Some research studies test predictions drawn from a single theory, whereas other studies test predictions based on different theories. When little or no theoretical knowledge is available, investigators may also develop a research question without an explicit prediction. For example, are more children depressed these days than a generation ago? Is child abuse more prevalent in our society than in other parts of the world?

Nature and Distribution of Childhood Disorders

This topic concerns how disorders are defined, diagnosed, and expressed at different ages and in different settings. Related questions are directed at patterns of symptoms, base rates for various child problems and competencies, and natural progressions of problems and competencies over time. Such questions are frequently addressed through **epidemiological research**, which is the study of the incidence, prevalence, and co-occurrence of childhood disorders and competencies in clinic-referred and community samples (Costello, Egger, & Angold, 2005a). **Incidence rates** reflect the extent to which new cases of a disorder appear over a specified period (e.g., the number of youths who develop a depressive disorder during the school year). **Prevalence rates** refer to all cases, whether new or previously existing, observed during a specified period of time (e.g., the number of teens with conduct disorder in the general population during 2007 and 2008). Estimates of incidence and prevalence can be obtained over a short period, such as 6 months, or over a much longer period. For example, *lifetime prevalence* indicates whether children in the sample have had the disorder at any time in their lives.

Knowledge about the risk for, and expression of, an individual disorder over the life course helps us understand the nature of the disorder and use this understanding as the basis for prevention and treatment (Costello & Angold, 2006). For example, studies of teens over time have found depression to be a recurrent disorder with poor long-term outcomes for many youngsters. This knowledge about the course of the disorder has resulted in promising new approaches to preventing and treating depression in young people, which we present in Chapter 8 on mood disorders.

As we noted in Chapter 1, about 10% to 20% of children worldwide have a clinically diagnosable disorder, and many more exhibit specific symptoms or subclinical problems (Belfer, 2008). However, overall rates obscure the enormous variability in reported rates from study to study. It can be very confusing when one study reports a prevalence rate of 1% and another reports a rate of 20% for the same disorder and at roughly the same point in time. Similarly, rates of reported problems in children have been found to vary from 6% to 20% when reported by teachers and from 10% to 40% when reported by parents (Costello & Angold, 2006). Some studies would lead you to conclude that almost every child you encounter has a problem; for others, the problem is so rare you wonder whether it even exists. Which conclusion is accurate?

To answer this question we must know something about epidemiological research and how estimates of the number of cases (e.g., children with a problem or disorder) are made. Cases may be defined in terms of single symptoms, multiple symptoms, or patterns of symptoms with likely causes and associated characteristics. Estimates of prevalence vary widely depending on which definition we use, with estimates based on single symptoms being much higher than those based on patterns of symptoms. It is sobering to learn that lifetime prevalence estimates of mental disorders obtained prospectively (studying the same sample of children over time and assessing them at periodic intervals) are *double* those found in retrospective studies (asking people to remember what occurred at an earlier time), which are subject to recall failure (Moffitt et al., 2010). Case definition in abnormal child psychology is complex because children don't refer themselves for treatment. Therefore, equating illness with seeking treatment can be misleading. The factors that lead to referral sometimes have more to do with the child's parents, teachers, or doctor than with the child's behavior. Therefore, it is important that we study problems in children who are *not* referred to clinics for treatment as well as those who are. Throughout this book you will see many examples of striking differences in prevalence rates and other research findings depending on whether children from clinics or children from community samples are the focus of study.

Prevalence rates also vary depending on whether cases are defined in terms of patterns of symptoms, impairment in functioning (e.g., difficulties at home or at school), or both. Fewer cases are identified when both symptoms and impairment in functioning are used than when definitions are based on either one or the other.

The rate and expression of childhood symptoms and disorders often vary in relation to demographic and situational factors, such as *socioeconomic status* (SES) (e.g., the social, economic, and physical environment in which the child lives as reflected in measures such as family income, education, or occupation); parents' marital status; and the child's age, gender, and cultural background, to name but a few. Consequently, these variables must be assessed and controlled for in most studies. For example, children from one ethnic group may display higher rates of learning problems than those from another ethnic group and may also have a lower SES. If we don't take SES into account we might conclude that differences in learning are related to ethnicity when instead they are a function of factors associated with lower SES such as poor nutrition or fewer learning opportunities. Similarly, although conduct problems are reported to be more frequent in African American than in Caucasian youngsters (McLaughlin, Hilt, & Nolen-Hoeksema, 2007), this finding is likely an artifact related to SES. That is, conduct problems are more prevalent in low-SES families and, since African American children are overrepresented in such families in North America, it is likely that the link between race and conduct problems is accounted for by stressful conditions associated with growing up in a poor family (Bird et al., 2001). In support of this, few differences in conduct problems in African American versus Caucasian youth are reported for primarily middle-class samples (Sameroff, Peck, & Eccles, 2004). The importance of cultural differences is highlighted in Box 3.1, which shows an example of epidemiological research into the types of child behavior problems reported by parents in seven cultures.

Children's cultural differences play an important role in a proper understanding of their behavior and customs

Correlates, Risks, and Causes

Whitney, described at the beginning of this section, displays persistent sadness that seems to be related to several variables: her history of being a moody child, her parents' divorce, her problems at school, and her lack of friends. Do any of these variables, alone or in combination, account for her sadness? If so, in what ways? Three variables of interest in abnormal child psychology are correlates, risk or protective factors, and causes of other variables. Most research in abnormal child psychology is designed to answer questions about the relation between the three general variables and childhood disorders. Because virtually all childhood disorders are the result of multiple variables interacting with one another over time, answers to these questions are rarely straightforward.

Correlates refer to variables that are associated at a particular point in time with no clear proof that one precedes the other. For example, Whitney's having no friends is associated with her sadness. Is she sad because she has no friends, or has her sadness prevented her from making friends? Since we don't know which variable came first, her lack of friends and sadness are correlated variables.

A *risk factor* is a variable that precedes an outcome of interest and increases the chances of a negative outcome (see Chapter 1). For example, Whitney's depressed mood got worse following her parents' divorce. Do you think parental divorce is a risk factor for the development of depression or other problems in children? Remember that a risk factor increases the chances for a certain outcome. It does not mean that it will occur; this will depend on other factors. Obviously, most children of parents who divorce do not become clinically depressed. Divorce is not necessarily a cause of a youngster's depression and low self-esteem, but it can be a risk factor (Hetherington, Bridges, & Insabella, 1998). A *protective factor* is a positive variable that precedes an outcome of interest and decreases the chances that a negative outcome will occur. The close relationship enjoyed by Whitney and her mother may serve as a protective factor against future episodes of depression.

Research into risk and protective factors often requires that large samples of children be studied and that multiple domains of child functioning—physical, cognitive, psychosocial—be assessed over long periods of time. This is necessary because (1) only a small proportion of children at risk for a problem will actually develop the disorder; (2) the areas of child functioning that

BOX 3.1 A CLOSER LOOK

Cross-Cultural Epidemiological Research: Behavior Problems Reported by Parents of Children in Seven Cultures

Widespread movements of refugees and immigrants are placing millions of children into new and unfamiliar environments. Evaluating the mental health of these children can be difficult because of cultural variations in what constitutes abnormal behavior, how to identify such behavior, and what to do about it. Crijnen, Achenbach, and Verhulst (1997) examined the 6-month prevalence rates of child problems as reported by parents or parent surrogates in studies carried out in seven cultures, using the same measurement instrument—the Child Behavior Checklist (CBCL) (Achenbach, 1991a). As shown in the figure, the total problem scores of children in Puerto Rico and China were above the overall mean. In contrast, the total problem scores of children in Germany, Israel, and Australia were below the overall mean. This epidemiological study indicates that parents in different cultures report different rates of problem behavior in their children. However, the findings do not indicate why these differences occur. Other kinds of studies are needed to answer that question—for example, research into cultural variations in child-rearing practices or expectations for child behavior (Achenbach & Rescorla, 2007).

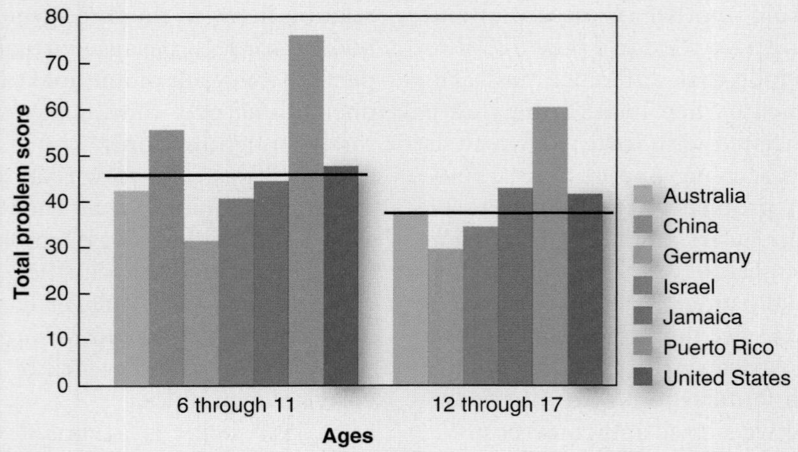

Total problem scores for children in seven different cultures. Overall mean Child Behavior Checklist (CBCL) problem scores and mean CBCL problem scores for each culture at ages 6 through 11 and ages 12 through 17. Overall mean scores across cultures for each age grouping are indicated by *solid horizontal lines*. China did not provide enough 12- through 17-year-olds for analysis.

Source: Adapted from Journal of the American Academy of Child & Adolescent Psychiatry, 36, A.A.M. Crijnen, T.M. Achenbach & F.C. Verhulst, Comparisons of Problems Reported by Parents of Children in 12 Cultures: Total Problems, Externalizing, and Internalizing, 1269-1277, Copyright 1997, with permission from Lippincott Williams & Wilkins.

will be affected, and how they will be affected, are not known in advance; and (3) the ages at which a disorder may occur or reoccur are also not known in advance. Sometimes the effects of exposure to a risk factor during infancy or early childhood may not be visible until adolescence or adulthood. The possibility that delayed, or *sleeper*, effects will occur complicates the study of risk and protective factors, since children must be studied for many years if delayed effects are to be detected.

Finally, other variables are *causes*. They influence, either directly or indirectly through other variables, the occurrence of a behavior or disorder of interest. Tito's father uses severe punishment when his son misbehaves. Is this punishment a cause of Tito's aggressive behavior? Is Tito learning how to be aggressive from his father? Questions about causes are complicated because what qualifies as a cause will vary according to the variables of interest and how far back in time a causal chain can be traced. Because childhood disorders are the result of multiple factors acting in concert, a challenge for researchers is to identify the relative contributions of each factor and—more importantly—to determine how they combine and interact over time to produce specific outcomes (Dodge & Pettit, 2003). When it comes to childhood disorders, "with very few exceptions, there is no such thing as a single basic necessary and sufficient cause" (Rutter, 2007b, p. 378). However, scientific research can help strengthen or weaken certain inferences about the causal role of some variables versus others.

Moderating and Mediating Variables

The key difference between moderating and mediating variables is that moderators have an independent effect on the existing relationship between two variables, whereas mediators account for some or all of the apparent relationship between two variables. **Moderator variables** influence the *direction* or *strength* of the relationship of variables of interest. The association between two variables depends on or differs as a function of moderating variables, such as the child's age, sex, SES, or cultural background. For example, as illustrated in ● Figure 3.2, in a study examining the relation between adolescents' self-reported history of physical abuse and their self-reports of internalizing problems such as anxiety and depression, McGee, Wolfe, and Wilson (1997) found that the correlation between the severity of physical abuse history and internalizing problems was greater for females than males. The child's sex was a moderator variable; that is, the relationship between two of the variables (in this case, abuse and internalizing problems) differed, depending on the third (if the adolescent was a boy or a girl).

Mediator variables refer to the process, mechanism, or means through which a variable produces a particular outcome. Mediators describe what happens at the psychological or neurobiological level to explain how one variable results from another. In one study, Snyder (1991) found that on days when mothers of 4- to 5-year-old children experienced negative moods and frequent hassles, they were most likely to respond negatively to their children's misbehavior and to reinforce their children's coercive tactics during mother–child conflicts. In turn, the use of this maternal discipline was related to an increase in same-day child behavior problems. As shown in ● Figure 3.3, these findings indicate that the relationship between maternal distress and child conduct problems is partly mediated by the disciplinary strategies mothers use on days they feel distressed. Mothers' disciplinary strategies help explain the relationship between maternal distress and child conduct problems.

Outcomes

What are the long-term outcomes for children who experience problems? Many childhood problems decrease or go away as children mature, but we need to know at approximately what age such improvements may be expected. Similarly, will other problems emerge, such as the child developing a low opinion of himself or herself due to trouble with, say, wetting the bed or worrying too much about school? Returning to Tito's oppositional and aggressive behaviors, will we expect his problems to decrease or go away as he gets older, or do they forecast continued conflict with peers, future school problems, and later difficulties in social adjustment? The study of outcomes in abnormal child psychology is perhaps one of the most important research topics in the field today.

Interventions

How effective are our methods for treating or preventing childhood problems? Are some types of treatment more effective than others? Questions about treatment and prevention are concerned with evaluating the short- and long-term effects of psychological, environmental, and biological treatments; comparing the relative effectiveness of differing forms and combinations of treatment; and identifying the reasons that a particular treatment works. The questions also concern identifying factors that influence the referral

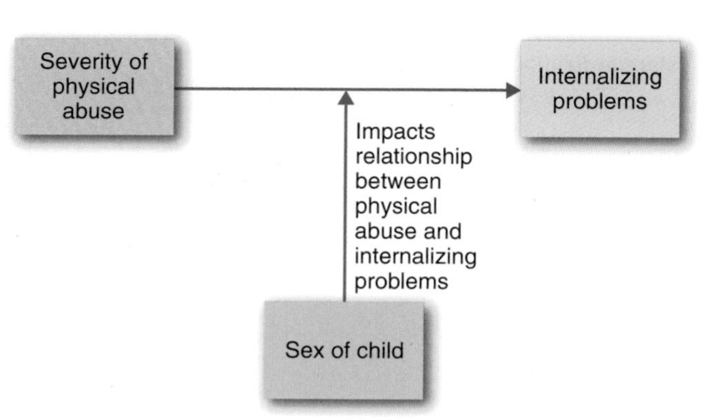

● **FIGURE 3.2** | Example of a moderator variable: Sex of the child moderates the relationship between abuse and internalizing problems.

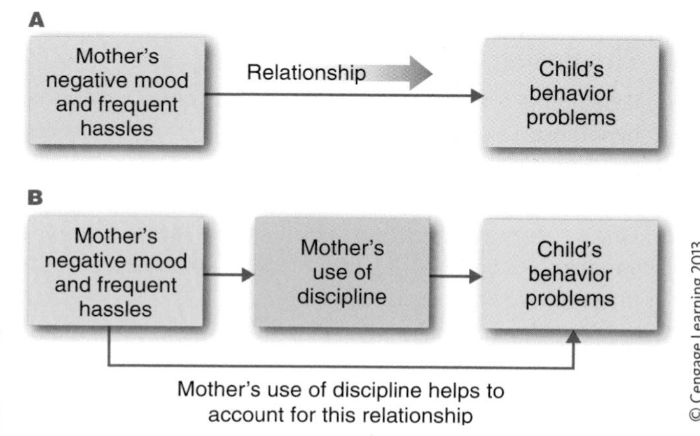

● **FIGURE 3.3** | Mediating variables: The type of discipline used by mothers on days they are feeling distressed mediates the relationship between maternal distress and child behavior problems.

and treatment process; understanding how processes such as the child–therapist relationship contribute to treatment outcomes; and assessing the acceptability of equivalent forms of treatment to children, parents, and teachers.

Many treatments for children and adolescents have not been evaluated, although this situation is steadily improving (Silverman & Hinshaw, 2008). These days, numerous studies evaluate treatment outcomes using **randomized controlled trials (RCTs)**, in which children with a particular problem are randomly assigned to different treatment and control conditions. We discuss the importance of random assignment later in this chapter. Findings from controlled research studies indicate that children who receive treatment are generally better off than children who do not.

However, an important distinction needs to be made between treatment efficacy and treatment effectiveness (Chorpita et al., 2011). **Treatment efficacy** refers to whether the treatment can produce changes under well-controlled conditions. In efficacy research, careful control is exercised over the selection of cases, therapists, and delivery and monitoring of treatment. In contrast, **treatment effectiveness** refers to whether the treatment can be shown to work in clinical practice, not just in well-controlled research settings. In research on effectiveness, treatment is evaluated in clinical settings, clients are usually referred rather than selected, and therapists provide services without many of the rigorous controls used in research. The benefits of treatment for children with problems have generally been found to be greater in controlled research settings (efficacy trials) than in clinical practice (effectiveness trials) (Weiss, Catron, & Harris, 2000).

SECTION SUMMARY

The Research Process

- Research is a multistage process that involves generating hypotheses, devising an overall plan, selecting measures, developing a research design and procedures, gathering and analyzing the data, and interpreting the results.
- One's theory of abnormal child behavior determines the variables studied, the choice of research methods, and the interpretation of research findings.
- Questions about the nature and distribution of childhood problems are addressed through epidemiological research into the incidence and prevalence of childhood disorders and competencies in clinic-referred and community samples.
- Other common research topics in abnormal child psychology focus on correlates, risk and protective factors, causes, moderating and mediating variables, outcomes, and interventions for childhood disorders.

METHODS OF STUDYING BEHAVIOR

The study of children's behavioral and emotional problems requires that the methods we use to measure these problems generate scores that are reliable and valid. This is no easy task. Children's problems must be evaluated based on samples of their behavior in different situations (e.g., home or school) that often reflect differing perspectives of adults. These evaluations are likely affected by the child's age, sex, and cultural background and by the assessors' personal expectations and values. As a result, no single measurement can provide a complete picture of a child's problems, and multiple measures and sources of information are needed.

Standardization, Reliability, and Validity

The methods and measures that we use to study child and family behavior must undergo careful study to determine how well they measure constructs such as depression, anxiety, or intellectual disability. The use of well-standardized, reliable, and valid measures and procedures is essential to scientific research, as depicted in ● Figure 3.4.

Standardization is a process that specifies a set of standards or norms for a method of measurement that are to be used consistently across different assessments of the construct of interest. These standards and norms relate to the procedures that must be followed during administration, scoring, and evaluation of findings—for example, as specified in a manual for an intelligence test. Without standardization, it is nearly impossible to replicate the information obtained using a method of measurement. In addition, results are likely to be unique to the situation in which they are obtained and won't apply to other situations. In some cases, the measure may be applied to many children who vary in age, gender, race, SES, or diagnosis. The scores are then used

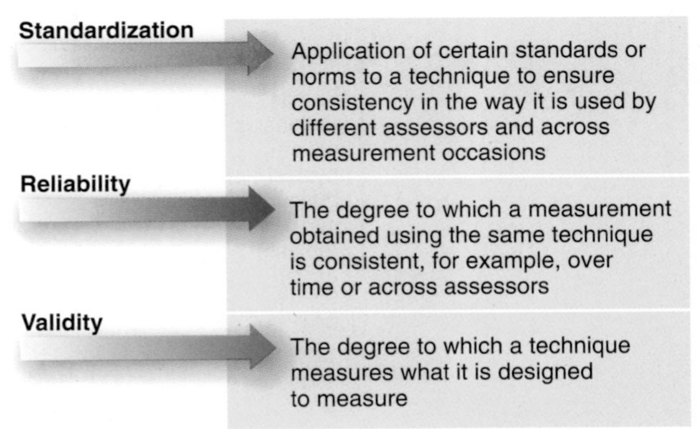

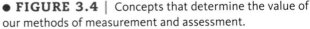

● **FIGURE 3.4** | Concepts that determine the value of our methods of measurement and assessment.

for comparison purposes. However, the test scores of an 8-year-old boy from a low-SES background should be compared with the scores of other children like him, not with the scores of a 16-year-old girl from an upper-SES background.

Reliability refers to the consistency, or repeatability, of results obtained using a specific method of measurement. One type of reliability, *internal consistency*, refers to whether all parts of a method of measurement contribute in a meaningful way to the information obtained. To be reliable, information must also not depend on a single observer or clinician; various people must agree on what they see. This is known as *interrater reliability*. Imagine how you might react if you took your child to see three different psychologists and received three different diagnoses and three different treatment recommendations. How would you know which one was correct? In this case, the diagnoses would not be reliable because two or more of the psychologists did not agree. Similarly, tests or interviews repeated within a short time interval should yield similar results on both occasions. In other words, the results need to be stable over time, which is referred to as *test–retest reliability*.

Reliability alone isn't enough to determine whether a method reflects the investigator's goals—validity must also be demonstrated. The **validity** of a method refers to the extent to which it actually measures the dimension or construct that the researcher sets out to measure. Validity is not all or none but rather a matter of degree, and can be assessed in many ways. First, the measure can be examined for its *face validity*, or the extent to which it appears to assess the construct of interest. A questionnaire that asks if you get nervous before writing an exam would be a face-valid measure of test anxiety, whereas one that asks if you think you are a parrot would not. *Construct validity* refers to whether scores on a measure behave as predicted by theory or past research. For example, a test of intelligence has construct validity if children who obtain high scores on the test also have better grades in school, understanding of concepts, verbal reasoning, recall, and parent ratings of intelligence than do children who obtain low scores on the test. Two components of construct validity are convergent validity and discriminant validity. *Convergent validity* reflects the correlation between measures that are expected to be related—for example, a teen's report of her depression in a screening interview and her scores on a depression questionnaire. It is an indication of the extent to which the two measures assess similar or related constructs, in this case depression. This is in contrast to *discriminant validity*, which refers to the degree of correlation between measures that are not expected to be related to one another. For example, scores on a measure designed to assess depression and another designed to assess intelligence should not correlate.

Finally, *criterion-related validity* refers to how well a measure predicts behavior in settings where we would expect it to do so—at the same time (concurrent validity), or in the future (predictive validity). For example, a child's high scores on a measure of social anxiety should predict that the child displays anxiety or avoidance in current social situations, and will perhaps have difficulties making friends in the future. Criterion-related validity tells whether scores on a measure can be used for their intended purpose.

Measurement Methods

A variety of measurement method options are available to assess important dimensions of children's behavioral, cognitive, emotional, and neurodevelopmental functioning. These methods are explicit plans to observe and assess children and their surroundings in ways that will reveal relatively clear relations among variables of interest.

Among the measurement options in abnormal child psychology are interviews, questionnaires, checklists and rating scales, psychophysiological recordings, brain imaging, performance measures, and direct observations of behavior (Mash & Barkley, 2007). A variety of intellectual, academic, and neuropsychological tests are also used (Sattler, 2008). In this chapter we focus primarily on how these methods are used in research. We talk more about their use in clinical practice and about tests and testing in Chapter 4.

As presented in Table 3.1, a comparison of three of the most commonly used methods of gathering data—interviews, questionnaires, and observations—shows how they differ on important dimensions. Because the information we obtain from children and families often varies as a function of the method used, researchers frequently rely on several methods to define and assess the constructs of interest.

Reporting

Reporting methods assess the perceptions, thoughts, behaviors, feelings, and past experiences of the child, parents, and teachers. These instruments include relatively unstructured clinical interviews, highly structured diagnostic interviews, and questionnaires. An important question regarding reporting methods relates to who is reporting on behavior. For example, with a *self-report measure*, a child or parent will provide information about his or her own behavior, feelings, and thoughts. Alternatively, using an *informant-report measure*, a person who is well acquainted with the child, usually a parent or a teacher, will provide information about a child's behaviors, feelings, or thoughts based on his or her observations of the child.

TABLE 3.1 | Interview, Questionnaire, and Observation

	Interview	Questionnaire	Observation
Structure of situation	Semistructured or structured.	Highly structured.	Structured or unstructured.
Structure of responses	Can probe, expand, and clarify.	Highly structured; no opportunity for probes or clarification.	Can vary from very inclusive observation of all behaviors to highly selective coding of very specific behaviors (e.g., number of "smiles").
Resource requirements	Considerable time needed for interviewing and coding responses and scoring.	Little experimenter time needed for administration.	Extensive time needed for observing and for coding and summarizing observations.
Sources of bias	Relies on participants' perceptions and willingness to report. Responses may be influenced by interviewer characteristics and mannerisms.	Relies on participants' perceptions and willingness to report.	Does not rely on participants' providing specific information, but what is observed may be influenced by the presence of the observer.
Data reduction	Requires analysis or recoding of narrative responses.	Little data reduction needed.	Highly influenced by the complexity of the observation system.

A concern with self- and informant-report methods is how accurately children, parents, or teachers report their own or others' thoughts, feelings, and behaviors. Inaccuracies may occur because of a failure to recall important events, selective recall or bias, and, in some cases, intentional distortions. Some individuals may try to make themselves or others look better or worse than they are. Reporting methods also require a certain level of verbal ability and may not accurately assess individuals who have difficulty expressing themselves. Obviously, young children would fall into this category—children under the age of 7 or 8 are usually not reliable reporters of their own behavior. Individuals from a cultural background different from the one in which a reporting method was developed may have difficulty understanding and responding to certain questions. For this reason it is essential that the reporting method used be sensitive to the language and cultural background of the person being evaluated.

Psychophysiological Methods

Psychophysiological methods assess the relationship between physiological processes and behavior to identify which nervous system structures and processes contribute to children's atypical development and behavior. Among the most common measures are autonomic nervous system activity, such as heart rate, blood pressure, breathing, pupil dilation, and electrical conductance of the skin. Changes in heart rate, for example, may be related to emotional responses. In addition, specific patterns of autonomic arousal may be associated with differences in children's temperament—their degree of shyness with people or responses to novel events (discussed in Chapter 7).

There are many limitations associated with psychophysiological measures, especially with young children. Sometimes findings for these measures are inconsistent from one study to the next, and researchers may have to infer how the child may have processed a particular event or stimulus. Also, a child's physiological response can be influenced easily by other factors, such as the child's reaction to the recording equipment or to hunger, fatigue, or boredom. These extraneous influences must be minimized if conclusions are to be based on psychophysiological measures.

Many studies have used an *electrophysiological measure* of brain functioning, the **electroencephalogram (EEG)**, to link the brain's measurable electrical activity with ongoing thinking, emotion, or states of arousal (Rothenberger, 2009). The EEG records electrical brain activity using electrodes attached to the surface of the child's scalp. Because different EEG waves are related to different states of arousal, differential patterns of EEG activation may suggest sleep disturbances or various emotional states. For example, with respect to emotional states, a greater amount of electrical activity in the right frontal lobe of the brain relative to the left frontal lobe is associated with anxiety and depression (McManis, Kagan, Snidman, & Woodward, 2002).

Neuroimaging Methods

Neuroimaging methods are used to examine the structure and/or function of the living brain (Wong, Grunder, & Brasic, 2007). As we discuss throughout this book, these methods provide new ways of testing neurobiological and other theories for many childhood disorders—for example, by identifying abnormalities in the structure or functioning of specific brain regions, or in how regions of the brain communicate with one another. For example, these brain abnormalities may be associated with problems that children with autism have in recognizing people's facial expressions. *Structural* brain imaging procedures include *magnetic resonance imaging* (MRI) and *coaxial tomographic* (CT) scans. MRI uses radio signals generated in a strong magnetic field and passed through brain tissue to produce fine-grained analyses of brain structures. CT scans also reveal the various structures of the brain. As we will see, findings from CT and MRI studies have led to the hypothesis of abnormal neural maturation in children with ADHD (see Chapter 5).

Structural brain imaging procedures such as MRI and CT study the anatomy of the brain. Brain imaging techniques have also been developed to study how the brain functions. Two types of functional imaging procedures are *functional magnetic resonance imaging* (fMRI) and *positron emission tomography* (PET). fMRI is a form of MRI that registers neural activity in functioning areas of the brain. By doing so it can show which brain areas are active during particular mental operations such as solving a specific type of problem or reacting to a fear-inducing stimulus. PET scans assess cerebral glucose metabolism. Glucose is the brain's main source of energy so measuring how much is used is a good way to determine the brain's activity level. Changes in blood flow within brain tissue in response to specific stimulus events are shown in extremely clear computerized pictures of activated brain areas. Functional imaging procedures provide three-dimensional images of brain activity and supply precise information regarding which regions of the brain are specialized for certain functions or which areas are functioning abnormally in cases of certain disorders.

Diffusion MRI is a magnetic imaging method that produces images showing *connections* between brain regions. This method has become a key technology in the creation of the *human connectome*, which is the structure and organization of connections throughout the central nervous system. As we discuss in Chapter 10, recent studies using diffusion imaging procedures have found that autism cannot be traced to a localized abnormality in one part of the brain but, rather, to a lack of normal connectivity across brain networks.

Neuroimaging studies tell us that children with a particular disorder have structural differences, or abnormal activity in certain areas of the brain, or abnormal brain connectivity, but they do not tell us why. Although remarkable advances have been made in the use of brain-imaging procedures with children during the past two decades, their promise for advancing our understanding or diagnosis of developmental disorders is just beginning (Peterson, 2003). As Dr. Thomas Insel (2010), Director of the National Institute of Mental Health put it: "As exciting as such advances are, brain imaging is still primarily a research tool when it comes to mental disorders . . . The differences in brain structure and activity seen in disorders like schizophrenia or ADHD, for example, are typically only meaningful when comparing group statistics. There is simply too much individual variation in brain structure and function for an individual's scan to be diagnostic or predictive, given the current state of the science."

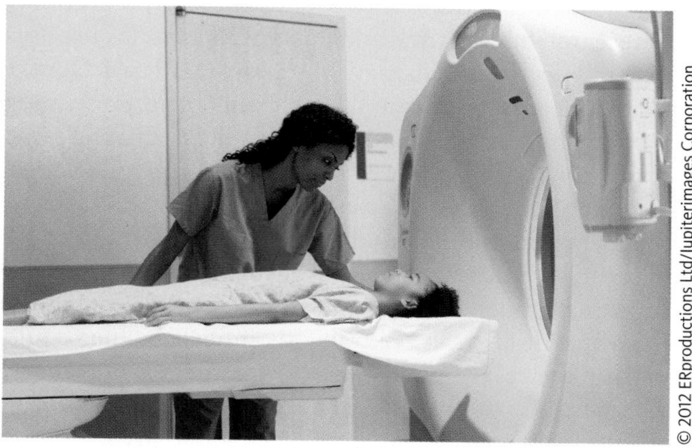

A child about to be evaluated using magnetic resonance imaging (MRI)

Observation Methods

You can observe a lot just by watching.

—Yogi Berra

Using systematic *observational methods*, a researcher can directly observe the behavior of the child and others under conditions that range from unstructured observations in the child's natural environment (referred to as **naturalistic observation**) to highly structured situations involving specific tasks or instructions usually carried out in the clinic or laboratory (referred to as **structured observation**). When using naturalistic observation, the researcher goes into the child's home, classroom, or day care center to observe and record the behaviors of interest of the child and often of parents, teachers, siblings, and peers with whom the child interacts. Alternatively, the researcher may make a video recording of behavior in the natural environment, which can be coded at a later time.

A researcher who uses structured observations in the laboratory or clinic sets up a situation or provides instructions to elicit behaviors of particular interest (Roberts & Hope, 2001). For example, numerous studies of child–caregiver attachment have assessed young children's reactions to increasingly stressful episodes of separation from and reunion with their caregivers in the laboratory using the *Strange Situation* procedure (Ainsworth, Blehar, Waters, & Wall, 1978). By structuring the situation to elicit specific attachment behaviors (e.g., seeking to be close to the mother), the Strange Situation permits researchers to assess the security or insecurity of children's attachment by noting how effectively they can use their caregivers as a source of comfort during times of distress.

Structured laboratory- or clinic-based observations are cost-effective and offer the advantage of focusing observations on the phenomena of interest. The method is especially useful for studying child behaviors that occur infrequently in everyday life. Structured observations give the researcher greater control over the situation than do naturalistic observations, and permit the use of other assessment procedures. For example, when a problem-solving discussion is video-recorded, replays of the interaction can be used to ask family members what they were thinking during the discussion (Sanders & Dadds, 1992). One negative aspect is that questions may arise as to whether observations in the laboratory or clinic provide a representative sample of the behaviors of interest (Mash & Foster, 2001). Being observed through a one-way mirror is a bit like being in a fishbowl; children and parents may not behave in the laboratory as they do in real-life settings. Nevertheless, in general, samples of behavior obtained using observational methods—in the laboratory or in real-world settings—can be very informative. However, they should be regarded as "behavior in the presence of an observer," as the observer's presence is likely to influence the behavior of the children and parents who are being observed.

The behavior of a young girl with social difficulties is observed on the playground as other children play around her

SECTION SUMMARY

Methods of Studying Behavior

- The measures and methods used to study child and family behavior must be standardized, reliable, and valid.
- Self-report and informant-report methods include unstructured clinical interviews, structured diagnostic interviews, and questionnaires.
- Psychophysiological methods are used to assess the relationship between physiological processes and behavior, and include measures of heart rate, blood pressure, breathing, pupil dilation, and electrical conductance of the skin.
- Electrophysiological measurements, such as the EEG, link electrical brain activity with ongoing thinking, emotion, or states of arousal.
- Neuroimaging methods are used to examine the structure and/or function of the brain, and connections between parts of the brain.
- Observational methods are used to directly observe the behavior of the child and others in unstructured settings such as the home, classroom, or playground, and in structured task situations in the laboratory or clinic.

RESEARCH STRATEGIES

The research strategies used to study children with problems ultimately contribute to the overall accuracy of research findings and conclusions. If a researcher uses bias in selecting participants or chooses a research task that does not represent the problem of interest, then the validity of the results may be on shaky ground—the study may not be a fair test of the research question.

Research studies may be examined with respect to their internal and external validity. **Internal validity** reflects how much a particular variable, rather than extraneous influences, accounts for the results, changes, or group differences. Extraneous influences that could explain the results are called *threats to internal validity*. They include maturation, the effects of testing, subject selection biases, and others. For example, let's suppose you found that providing relaxation training over several months to a group of 5-year-old children decreased their nighttime fears. It's possible that the observed decrease may be due to the extraneous influences of *maturation* or *the effects of testing*—the children's fears decrease because they are getting older or are being assessed repeatedly, rather than as a result of the relaxation training.

The reduction in fears could also be due to *subject selection biases*, which are factors that operate in selecting subjects or in the selective loss or retention of subjects during the study. For example, if children with only mild fears are selected for our study, a high likelihood exists that their fears will decrease over time, even in the absence of treatment, relative to children with more severe fears. Also, if children with more severe fears or children who do not benefit from relaxation training dropped out of the study prematurely, the observed decrease in fears may be the result of this selective loss of the most fearful subjects rather than treatment.

External validity refers to the degree to which findings can be generalized, or extended, to people, settings, times, measures, and characteristics other than the ones in a particular study. Threats to external validity may include characteristics of the participants that apply to some people but not others, the reactivity of subjects to participating in the research, the setting in which the research is carried out, or the time when measurements are made. For example, many research studies in abnormal child psychology underrepresent cultural minorities and children from low-SES backgrounds, often because of difficulties in recruiting and retaining participants, or because cultural minorities are less likely to receive mental health services for their problems (Cummings & Druss, 2011). Because of this, it is difficult to generalize the findings from these studies to these other groups. As another example, children or parents may not behave naturally in an unfamiliar laboratory setting. If findings from a study in the laboratory are quite different from what is found in real-life settings, this study too would have low external validity.

As much as possible, potential threats to internal and external validity need to be addressed when designing a research study. As we discuss in the sections that follow, careful attention to how the sample is identified, how variables of interest are defined and measured, how participants are assigned to conditions or groups, and the types of control groups used are just a few of the many research design considerations needed to increase our confidence that our findings are best accounted for by the variable(s) of interest and are not due to extraneous influences.

Identifying the Sample

The validity of any research study in abnormal child psychology depends on the classification systems used to identify the samples of children who participate in the research. First, a careful definition of the sample is critical for comparability of findings across studies and clear communication among researchers. Without such uniform standards, wide differences may result in estimated base rates for various childhood disorders and for many other findings.

In addition to our sample definition, a second issue is the need to consider possible comorbidities within our sample. **Comorbidity** is the simultaneous occurrence of two or more childhood disorders that is far more common than would be predicted from the general population base rates of the individual disorders. It has direct implications for the selection of research participants and for the interpretation of results. Research samples drawn from clinical populations will have a disproportionately high rate of comorbidity because referral for treatment is most likely based on the combined symptoms of all disorders.

A failure to consider comorbidity may result in an interpretation of findings in relation to one disorder, when these findings are more validly attributed to a second disorder or to a combination of disorders. To deal with comorbidity in research samples, some researchers may select only participants with single, or pure, disorders. This strategy may yield small, atypical samples whose findings do not generalize to other populations. Although there is not a single research strategy to address questions about comorbidity, studies that compare children showing single disorders with children showing comorbid disorders are needed to help disentangle the effects of comorbidity. It also needs to be recognized that much of the comorbidity among disorders may be artifactual, related more to the overlap in symptoms used to define and diagnose childhood disorders than to the co-occurrence of distinct conditions (Drabick & Kendall, 2010; Rutter, 2010).

A third issue is that we must be sensitive to the setting and source of referral of children for research. *Random selection* occurs when subjects are drawn from a population in a way that gives each individual in that population an equal chance of being selected for the study. This is rare in studies of child psychopathology. At the other end of the spectrum are studies that use *samples of convenience*, in which subjects are selected for a study merely because of their availability, regardless of whether they provide a suitable test of the questions or conditions of interest. Research samples in abnormal child psychology have been selected from numerous settings, including outpatient psychology and psychiatry clinics, schools, hospitals, day care centers, and the community. Effects related to different settings are often confounded with effects related to different referral sources (e.g., physicians,

Comorbidity: Ten-year-old girl with multiple disabilities including intellectual disability, autism, and epilepsy

teachers, and parents), since referral sources also differ across settings.

General Research Strategies

There are several different, yet complementary, approaches to research design that offer various advantages and disadvantages. The choice of approach frequently depends on the research questions being addressed, the nature of the childhood disorder under investigation, and the availability of resources (Hartmann, Pelzel, & Abbott, 2011).

Nonexperimental and Experimental Research

One goal of scientific research is to simplify and isolate variables in order to study them more closely. This goal is met by varying or manipulating values of the variable(s) of interest while trying to control or hold constant other factors that could influence the results. Doing this makes it possible to study the association between the particular variables of interest. The basic distinction between nonexperimental versus experimental research reflects the degree to which the investigator can manipulate the experimental variable or, alternatively, must rely on examining the natural covariation of several variables of interest. The *independent variable* is manipulated by the researcher. Based on a research hypothesis, the independent variable is anticipated to cause a change in another variable. The variable expected to be influenced by the independent variable is called the *dependent variable*. The greater the degree of control that the researcher has over the independent variable(s), the more the study approximates a true experiment.

In a **true experiment** the researcher has maximum control over the independent variable or conditions of interest and can use random assignment of subjects to groups, include needed control conditions, and control possible sources of bias. Conversely, the less control the researcher has in determining which participants will and will not be exposed to the independent variable(s), the more nonexperimental the research will be. Most variables of interest in child psychopathology cannot be manipulated directly, including the nature or severity of the child's disorder, parenting practices, or genetic influences. As a result, much of the research conducted on children with problems and their families relies on nonexperimental, correlational approaches.

In *correlational studies*, researchers often examine relationships among variables by using a **correlation coefficient**, a number that describes the degree of association between two variables. A correlation coefficient can range from −1.00 to +1.00. The size of the correlation indicates the strength of the association between two variables. A zero correlation indicates no relationship; the closer the value gets to −1.00 or +1.00, the stronger is the relationship. The sign of the correlation coefficient (plus or minus) indicates the direction of the relationship. A positive sign (+) indicates that as one variable increases in value, so does the other, whereas a negative sign (−) indicates that as one variable increases, the other decreases.

For example, a positive correlation of +.70 between symptoms of anxiety and symptoms of depression indicates that children who show many symptoms of anxiety are also likely to display symptoms of depression. Alternatively, children who show few symptoms of anxiety are likely to display few symptoms of depression. However, a negative correlation of −.70 between symptoms of depression and social skills, for example, indicates that children who show many symptoms of depression have fewer social skills.

The primary limitation of correlational studies is that interpretations of causality cannot be made. A correlation between two variables does not entail

Children's symptoms of anxiety and depression are often positively correlated

that one variable causes the other. If we find a relationship between depression in children and depression in their parents, it could mean that being around a child who is depressed may lead to depression in parents, or that parental depression may lead to depression in the child, or that depression in the child and parent may both be due to another, more fundamental variable, such as a shared genetic disposition to depression.

In experimental investigations, researchers must take steps to control for characteristics of participants that could decrease the accuracy of the findings. For example, if two groups of children differ with respect to education, intelligence, SES, or the presence of related disorders, it would be impossible to determine whether the independent variable or the other characteristics led to the results. **Random assignment** of participants to treatment conditions protects against this problem, because the probability of a subject's appearing in any of the groups is the same. By assigning participants to groups on the basis of the flip of a coin, numbers drawn from a hat, or a table of random numbers, the chance is increased that characteristics other than the independent variable will be equally distributed across treatment groups.

As we have noted, many hypotheses in abnormal child psychology cannot be tested by randomly assigning participants to conditions, or by manipulating conditions in the real world. A compromise involves the use of natural experiments, also called *quasi-experimental designs* or *known-group comparisons*. In **natural experiments**, comparisons are made between conditions or treatments that already exist. The experiments may involve children with different disorders, parents with different problems, or different family environments (for example, children who have suffered from neglect versus children who have not). These studies are essentially correlational, but the subjects are selected to ensure that their characteristics are as comparable as possible with the exception of the independent variable. Despite the extreme care exercised by researchers to equate existing groups, natural experiments cannot achieve the same level of precision and rigor as true experimental research. Nevertheless, for many important questions in abnormal child psychology, natural experiments using known-group comparisons are the only option (Rutter, 2007b).

Prospective and Retrospective Research

Research designs that address questions about the causes and long-term outcomes of childhood disorders may differ with respect to the time the sample is identified and the time data are collected. In a **retrospective design**, a sample of people is identified at the current time and asked for information relating to an earlier time. Individuals are identified who already show the outcome of interest, and they are compared with controls who do not show the outcome. Assessments focus on characteristics in the past, and inferences are made about past characteristics and the current outcome. For example, a sample of young adults with a substance use disorder might be asked to provide retrospective ratings and descriptions of their early family experiences.

Although data are immediately available in retrospective studies, they are also highly susceptible to bias and distortion in recall. Parents of teenagers diagnosed with schizophrenia may reinterpret their views of the teen's childhood, distorting their recollection of the teen's prior behavior or friendships. Moreover, retrospective designs fail to identify the individuals who were exposed to certain earlier experiences but did not develop the problem. Young adult females with an eating disorder may report more childhood experiences of sexual abuse. However, this finding could not serve as the basis for a conclusion that childhood sexual abuse is a specific precursor of eating disorders in young adulthood. The retrospective study fails to identify those children who experienced childhood sexual abuse but did not develop an eating disorder as young adults.

In **real-time prospective designs**, the research sample is identified and then followed over time, with data collected at specified time intervals. The same youngsters are followed or assessed over time in order to understand the course of change or differences that may develop over time or during important developmental transitions such as middle-school entry or adolescence. For example, infants who are fearful in response to novel events may be followed over time to determine if they later develop anxiety disorders or other problems to a greater extent than infants who are not fearful.

Prospective designs correct for several of the problems associated with retrospective research. By following a sample over time we can identify those children who develop a disorder as well as those who do not. Since information is collected in real time, problems relating to bias and distortion in recall are minimized. Disadvantages of prospective designs include loss of participants over time and the extended length of time needed to collect data.

Analogue Research

Analogue research evaluates a specific variable of interest under conditions that only resemble or approximate the situation for which one wishes to generalize. Analogue studies focus on a circumscribed research question under well-controlled conditions. Often, the purpose of the research is to illuminate a specific process that would otherwise be difficult to study.

For example, Lang, Pelham, Johnston, and Gelernter (1989) were interested in whether the higher-than-normal rates of alcohol consumption observed in fathers of boys with attention-deficit/hyperactivity disorder (ADHD)/conduct disorder (CD) might be partly due to the distress associated with interacting with their difficult children (these researchers must have been parents, too!). Male and female single college students who were social drinkers were randomly assigned to interact with boys who were trained to perform behaviors characteristic of either typical children (friendly and cooperative) or children with ADHD/CD (overactive and disruptive). Participants also rated their own mood before and after interactions with the child. Following the interaction, participants were given a 20-minute break while they anticipated another interaction with the same child. During the break, beer was freely available for their consumption. Both male and female participants reported comparable levels of elevated distressed mood after interacting with children enacting the ADHD/CD role. However, only the men who had interacted with these children drank enough to increase blood alcohol levels.

The findings suggest that interacting with a child with ADHD/CD may increase alcohol consumption in fathers. However, an analogue study only resembles the conditions of interest—the study participants were single college students, not parents of children with ADHD/CD; the children did not really have ADHD/CD; drinking was confined to an artificial laboratory setting; and only beer was available. Therefore, it is difficult to know if similar effects would occur in real-life circumstances (despite anecdotal reports by some parents that their kids drive them to drink!). These conditions raise the question of external validity, or the generalizability of research findings.

Research Designs

Research designs are the strategies used to examine question(s) of interest. They refer to the ways in which a researcher arranges conditions to draw valid inferences about the variables of interest.

Case Study

The **case study**, which involves an intensive, usually anecdotal, observation and analysis of an individual child, has a long tradition in the study of abnormal development and behavior. Itard's description of Victor, the Wild Boy of Aveyron; Freud's treatment of a phobia in Little Hans; John Watson's conditioning of a phobic reaction in Albert B.; and many other similar case studies have played an influential role in shaping the way we think about children's problems. The case study, especially as used in the clinical context, brings together a wide range of information about an individual child from various sources, including interviews, observations, and test results. The goal is to get as complete a picture as possible of the child's psychological functioning, current environment, and developmental history. Sometimes the goal is to describe the effects of treatment on the child.

Case studies yield narratives that are rich in detail and provide valuable insights into factors associated with a child's disorder. Nevertheless, they also have drawbacks. They are typically viewed as unscientific and flawed because they are characterized by uncontrolled methods and selective biases, by inherent difficulties associated with integrating diverse observations and drawing valid inferences among the variables of interest, and by generalizations from the particular child of interest to other children. Hence, case studies have been viewed primarily as rich sources of descriptive information that provide a basis for subsequent testing of hypotheses in research using larger samples and more controlled methods. They may also provide a source for developing and trying out new treatment methods.

Despite their unscientific nature, there are compelling reasons why systematically conducted case studies are likely to continue to play a useful role in research on childhood disorders. First, some childhood disorders such as childhood-onset schizophrenia are rare, making it difficult to generate large samples of children for research. Second, the analyses of individual cases may contribute to the understanding of many striking symptoms of childhood disorders that either occur infrequently or are hidden and therefore difficult to observe directly. Third, significant childhood disturbances such as post-traumatic stress disorder (see Chapter 7) often develop as the result of natural disaster, severe trauma, or abuse. These extreme events and circumstances are not easily studied using controlled methods.

Single-Case Experimental Designs

Single-case experimental designs have most frequently been used to evaluate the impact of a clinical treatment, such as reinforcement or stimulant medication, on a child's problem (Kazdin, 2011). The central features of single-case experimental designs that distinguish these from uncontrolled case studies include systematic repeated assessment of behavior over time, the replication of treatment effects within the same subject over time, and the participant's serving as his or her own control by experiencing all treatment conditions (Barlow, Nock, & Hersen, 2009). Many single-subject designs exist, the most common being the A-B-A-B (reversal) design and the multiple-baseline design carried out across behaviors, situations, or individuals.

In an **A-B-A-B reversal design**, a baseline of behavior is first taken (A), followed by an intervention phase (B), then a return-to-baseline phase where the intervention is removed (A), and a final phase in which the intervention is reintroduced (B). When changes in behavior occur only during the intervention phases, this provides evidence that changes in behavior are due to the intervention. Findings from a study using a *reversal design* are presented in ● Figure 3.5. In this example, a behavioral intervention was used to reduce self-injurious behavior (SIB) in Ann, a 5-year-old girl with profound mental retardation and multiple handicaps. Ann's SIB consisted of biting her hand and wrists during grooming activities, such as brushing her teeth. These behaviors were getting progressively worse and causing open wounds. During the initial baseline phase, the percentage of intervals in which Ann engaged in SIB during three brief sessions of tooth brushing ranged from 20% to 60%.

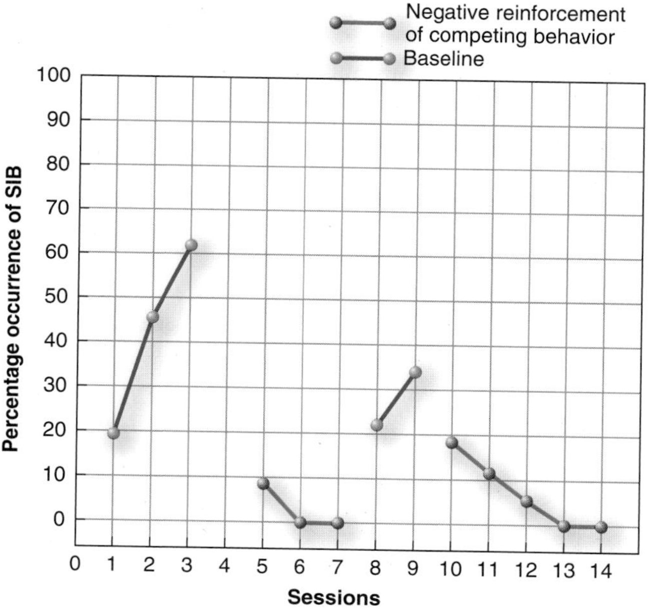

● **FIGURE 3.5** | A-B-A-B (reversal) design: treatment of Ann's self-injurious behavior.

Adapted from *Use of Negative Reinforcement in the Treatment of Self-Injurious Behavior* by M.W. Steege, D.P. Wacker, K.C. Cigrand, W.K. Berg, G.C. Novak, T.M. Reimers, G.M. Sasso & A. DeRaad, 1990, Journal of Applied Behavior Analysis, 23, 459–467. Copyright © 1990 by the Society for the Experimental Analysis of Behavior, Inc.

Intervention consisted of a negative reinforcement procedure in which Ann was permitted to briefly escape from the grooming activity when she performed an appropriate competing behavior (in this case, pushing a button that, when activated, played the message "Stop!"). She was also physically guided by a trainer to brush her teeth whenever she engaged in SIB. When these procedures were implemented during the intervention phase, an immediate reduction of SIB to 10% resulted, with no SIB occurring in the next two sessions. During the reversal, or return-to-baseline, phase, treatment was withdrawn and Ann's SIB increased to previous baseline levels. When treatment was reinstituted, SIB decreased again, with no biting observed during the final two sessions. The finding that Ann's levels of SIB decreased only during the intervention phases, and not during the baseline or return-to-baseline phases, suggests that the reductions in Ann's SIB resulted from the intervention procedures.

Although the reversal design is applicable for use with a wide range of behaviors, there are limitations. One limitation is that if a treatment really works, the behavior may not reverse during the return-to-baseline phase. Do you see any other limitations of this design? Once Ann stopped engaging in SIB following intervention, do you think there was sufficient justification for reinstituting her harmful behavior for experimental purposes? We intentionally selected this example to illustrate a major limitation of the A-B-A-B design, which is the ethical concerns surrounding the return-to-baseline condition following effective treatment for dangerous or even undesirable behaviors. The multiple-baseline design that we describe next gets around this concern, because no reversal is needed once intervention is introduced.

In a **multiple-baseline design** across behaviors, different responses of the same individual are identified and measured over time to provide a baseline against which changes may be evaluated. Each behavior is then successively modified in turn. If each behavior changes only when it is specifically treated, the inference of a cause-and-effect relationship between the treatment and the behavior change is made. Other common varieties of multiple-baseline designs involve successive introductions of treatment for the same behavior in the same individual across different situations, or for the same behavior across several individuals in the same situation. The critical feature of the multiple-baseline approach is that change must occur only when treatment is instituted, and only for the behavior, situation, or individual that is the target of treatment. Simultaneous changes must not occur for untreated behaviors, situations, or individuals until the time that each is, in turn, targeted for treatment.

Findings from a study using a multiple-baseline design across situations are presented in ● Figure 3.6. In this example, the same intervention procedures used with Ann were used to reduce self-injurious behavior (SIB) in Dennis, a 6-year-old boy, also with profound mental retardation and multiple handicaps. Dennis's SIB consisted of biting his hands, wrists, or arms during grooming activities such as tooth brushing, face washing, and hair brushing. His SIB was getting worse and causing open wounds. During the initial baseline phase, the percentage of intervals in which Dennis engaged in SIB averaged 50% or more during tooth brushing, face washing, and hair brushing. When intervention was implemented during tooth brushing, an immediate decrease in Dennis's SIB resulted, with consistently low rates of SIB maintained throughout treatment. Moreover, no changes in Dennis's SIB were observed during face washing or hair brushing until the intervention was introduced during those situations.

Because changes in Dennis's SIB occurred only when intervention was introduced during each of the specific situations, there is support for the hypothesis that intervention led to those changes. A multiple-baseline design avoids the problem associated with the reversal design of having to return to baseline when treating dangerous or unwanted behaviors.

Several advantages and limitations are associated with the use of single-case experimental designs. These designs preserve the personal quality of the case study and offer some degree of control for potential alternative explanations of the findings, such as the effects of maturation and reactivity to observation. Single-case designs also provide an objective evaluation of treatment for individual cases, permit the study of rare disorders, and facilitate the development and evaluation of alternative and combined forms of treatment. The

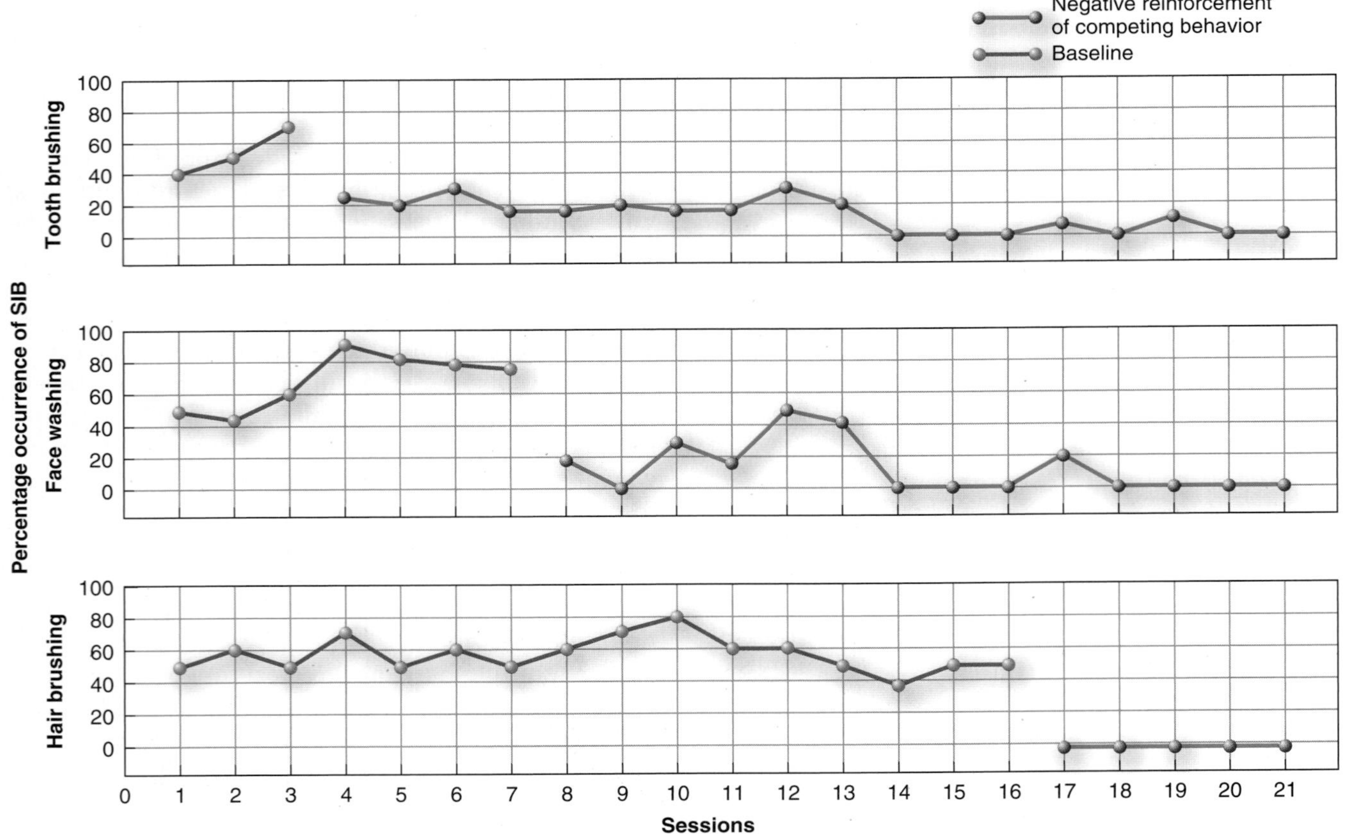

● **FIGURE 3.6** | Multiple-baseline design across situations: treatment of Dennis's self-injurious behavior.

Adapted from *Use of Negative Reinforcement in the Treatment of Self-Injurious Behavior*, by M. W. Steege, D. P. Wacker, K. C. Cigrand, W. K. Berg, G. C. Novak, T. M. Reimers, G. M. Sasso & A. DeRaad, 1990, Journal of Applied Behavior Analysis, 23, 459–467. Copyright © 1990 by the Society for the Experimental Analysis of Behavior, Inc.

negative aspects of the design are the possibilities that specific treatments will interact with unique characteristics of a particular child, the limited generalization of findings to other cases, and the subjectivity involved when visual inspection rather than statistical analysis is used to evaluate the data. The findings for Ann and Dennis were fairly clear-cut. Difficulties in interpretation arise when baseline data or observed changes are highly variable.

Between-Group Comparison Designs

Many research designs are based on comparisons between one group of children assigned to one or more conditions and other groups of children assigned to one or more different conditions. When participants are randomly assigned to groups, and groups are presumed to be equivalent in all other respects, one group typically serves as the *experimental group* and the other serves as the *control group*. Any differences observed between groups are then attributed to the experimental condition.

The choice of an appropriate control or comparison group often depends on what we know prior to the study and the questions we wish to answer. For example, if an established and effective treatment for adolescent depression exists, testing a new approach against a no-treatment control group will likely answer the wrong question, not to mention raising ethical concerns about withholding a proven effective treatment. We don't want to know if the new approach is better than nothing—we want to know if it is better than the best available alternative treatment.

In many cases, assignment of participants to groups may not be possible, particularly when one wishes to make comparisons between known or intact groups, such as children who have been referred to clinics for depression versus those with depression who have not been referred. In these types of known-group comparisons there is no assignment but rather the selection criteria for including or excluding participants from the groups must be carefully specified.

Cross-Sectional and Longitudinal Studies

Researchers interested in developmental psychopathology need information about the ways in which children and adolescents change over time. To obtain this information, researchers extend correlational and experimental approaches to include measurements taken at different ages. Both cross-sectional and longitudinal designs are research strategies in which a comparison of children of different ages serves as the basis for research.

In **cross-sectional research**, different youngsters at different ages or periods of development are studied at the same point in time, whereas in **longitudinal research**, the same children are studied at different ages or periods of development. In cross-sectional studies, researchers don't have to worry about the many problems associated with studying the same group of children over a long period. When participants are measured only once, researchers need not be concerned about selective loss of participants, practice effects, or general changes in the field that would make the findings obsolete by the time the study is complete. Although cross-sectional approaches are efficient, they are limited in the information they generate regarding developmental changes. Evidence about individual change is not available. Rather, comparisons are limited to age-group averages.

Longitudinal designs are conducted prospectively. Data collection occurs at specified points in time from the same individuals initially selected because of their membership in one or more populations of interest. In studies of child psychopathology, the populations of interest often consist of children at risk for developmental problems due to exposure to any one of a number of factors—for example, having a mother with depression or growing up in an abusive family situation.

The prospective longitudinal design allows the researcher to identify patterns that are common to all youngsters and to track differences in developmental paths that children follow. For example, a longitudinal study can tell that certain fears may decrease with age for all children, but that some children may have an anxious disposition and show less of a reduction in specific fears with age. Because data are collected on the same individuals at time 1 and time 2, causal inferences between earlier events and later events and behavior based on temporal ordering can be made. Such inferences of causality cannot be made in cross-sectional designs, where different individuals are assessed at the two time points. Longitudinal designs also allow for identification of individual developmental trends that would be masked by averaging data over individuals. The prepubertal growth spurt exemplifies this, where rapid accelerations in growth occurring at different ages across the population are not reflected in growth measures averaged across adolescents. An example of a longitudinal study is presented in Box 3.2.

Despite their advantages, longitudinal designs have many practical and design difficulties. Practical concerns include obtaining and maintaining research funding and resources over many years and the long wait for meaningful data. Design difficulties relate to aging effects and cohort effects. *Aging effects* are general changes that occur because as participants age there are increases in physical prowess, impulse control, or social opportunity. *Cohort effects* are influences related to being a member of a specific **cohort**, which is a group of individuals who are followed during the same time and experience the same cultural or historical events.

BOX 3.2 **A CLOSER LOOK**

Longitudinal Research: Does Child Maltreatment Lead to More Peer Rejection Over Time?

Dodge, Pettit, and Bates (1994a) assessed a representative sample of 585 boys and girls for physical maltreatment in the first 5 years of life and then followed them for 5 consecutive years, from kindergarten through the fourth grade. Twelve percent of the sample was identified as having experienced maltreatment. The children's peers, teachers, and mothers independently rated the maltreated children as being more disliked, less popular, and more socially withdrawn than the nonmaltreated children in every year of evaluation—and the magnitude of the difference increased over time. As shown in the accompanying figure, by grade 4 more than twice as many maltreated as nonmaltreated children were rejected by their peer group. The results suggest that early maltreatment may disrupt relationships with adults, which in turn impairs a child's ability to form effective relationships with other children.

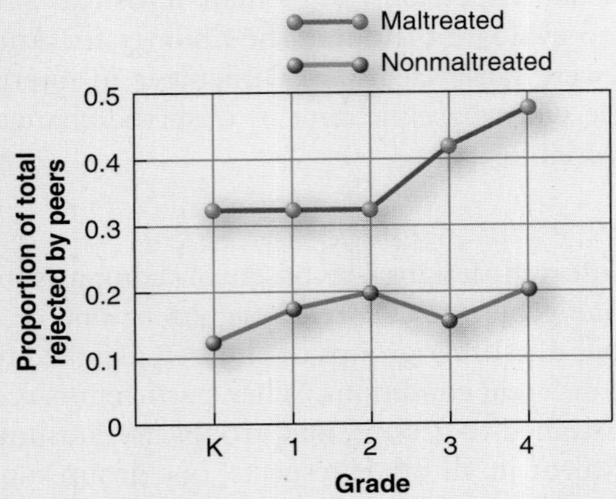

Proportions of maltreated and nonmaltreated children rejected by their peer group.

Source: Adapted from Effects of Physical Maltreatment on the Development of Peer Relations by K.A. Dodge, G.S. Pettit & J.E. Bates, 1994, Development and Psychopathology, 6, 43-55.

For example, the cohort of teens who lived in war-torn Yugoslavia in the early 1990s differ in many respects from North American teenagers living through the technological boom of the early 1990s.

The experience of being repeatedly studied, observed, interviewed, and tested may also threaten the validity of a longitudinal study. Children and adults may become more sensitized to the thoughts, feelings, and behaviors under investigation, thus thinking about them and revising them in ways that have nothing to do with age-related change. Furthermore, with repeated testing, participants may improve as the result of practice effects, including greater familiarity with test items and better test-taking skills. Finally, changes within the field of abnormal child psychology may create problems for longitudinal studies that cover an extended period. Theories and methods are constantly changing, and those that first led to the longitudinal study may become outdated.

Qualitative Research

Qualitative research focuses on narrative accounts, description, interpretation, context, and meaning (Denzin & Lincoln, 2011; Fiese & Bickham, 1998). The purpose of qualitative research is to describe, interpret, and understand the phenomenon of interest in the context in which it is experienced (Patton, 2002). This approach can be contrasted with a quantitative approach, which emphasizes operational definitions, careful control of the subject matter, the attempted isolation of variables of interest, quantification of dimensions of interest, and statistical analysis. Rather than beginning with already developed observational systems or assessment tools, qualitative researchers strive to understand the phenomenon from the participant's perspective. Qualitative data are typically collected through observations or open-ended interviewing and are recorded narratively as case study notes, for example. The observations and narrative accounts obtained are examined to build general categories and patterns.

Proponents of qualitative research believe that it provides an intensive and intimate understanding of a situation that is rarely achieved in quantitative research (Denzin & Lincoln, 2011). Qualitative methods, such as the use of examples or stories, may be particularly engaging to children and enable the discussion of sensitive topics, while allowing the children a sense of control over the research situation (Barter & Renold, 2000). On the other hand, qualitative methods may also be biased by the researcher's values and preferences, and the findings cannot easily be generalized to individuals and situations other than the ones studied. Nonetheless, quantitative and qualitative research methods can be used in complementary ways (Lyons & Coyle, 2007). Qualitative methods can be used to identify important dimensions and theories that can then be tested quantitatively. Alternatively, qualitative

BOX 3.3 A CLOSER LOOK

Qualitative Research: Parents and Professionals Negotiate Bad News

In a study using qualitative research methods, Abrams and Goodman (1998) were interested in what takes place between parents of children with developmental delays and professionals during a diagnostic feedback session. In particular, they wanted to learn more about negotiation—a process that describes the socially constructed nature of encounters in which participants come to a mutual understanding through the natural use of language. Parents were told that the purpose of the study was to examine how professionals communicate information to parents, and signed a release form so that the feedback sessions could be audiotaped. Tapes from 10 feedback sessions with different parents were then transcribed in complete detail, resulting in over 700 pages of transcription. Analysis of the discourse identified negotiation over the diagnostic label in 8 of the 10 cases. As a form of negotiation, some parents engaged in "bargaining," in which they tried to circumscribe the label and limit its impact. Here's an example of bargaining in the case of a child who received a diagnosis of mental retardation:

PROFESSIONAL: This degree of delay means that he's mentally retarded.

FATHER: Is there anything that can be done for him?

PROFESSIONAL: There are always things that can be done. [Mother weeps]

MOTHER: But he's not severely retarded?

PROFESSIONAL: No.

FATHER: More moderate.

PSYCHOLOGIST: Our best guess is that he will continue to be slow and probably in the mildly retarded range—which would mean that he would be—let's call him "educable."

At first, the mother found the diagnosis of mental retardation emotionally difficult to accept. However, after regaining her composure, she actively engaged in a cognitive adjustment of the diagnostic label to make it less overwhelming. By doing this, she was able to locate her son's label in the mildly retarded range and, in so doing, limit her sense of loss. In reality, her son had an IQ score of 54, which placed him on the borderline between moderate and mild retardation. On the basis of their analysis of this and many other samples of discourse, the researchers concluded that interpretations made during a diagnostic feedback session are arrived at through a process of negotiation and are not simply "given" by professionals.

Source: Abrams and Goodman, 1998, p. 94.

case studies may be used to illuminate the meaning of quantitatively derived findings. Additionally, if qualitative data have been reduced to numbers through word counts or frequency counts of themes, the data can be analyzed using quantitative methods.

To get a feel for qualitative research, consider the study described in Box 3.3. This study looks at some ways that parents of children with intellectual disability and child psychology professionals may arrive at a consensus during a diagnostic feedback session.

SECTION SUMMARY

Research Strategies

- Careful attention must be given to the way in which samples are identified for research in abnormal child psychology, including issues such as how the disorder of interest is defined, criteria for inclusion in the study, comorbidity, the setting from which subjects are drawn, and sample size.
- We can distinguish between nonexperimental and experimental research strategies on the basis of the degree to which the investigator can manipulate the experimental variable or, alternatively, must rely on examining the covariation of variables of interest.
- In prospective research, a sample is followed over time, with data collected at specified intervals. In retrospective research, a sample is identified at the current time and the sample members asked for information relating to an earlier time.
- Analogue research evaluates a specific variable under conditions that only resemble the situation for which the researcher wishes to generalize.
- The case study involves an intensive, usually anecdotal, observation and analysis of an individual child.
- Single-case designs involve repeated assessments of the same subject over time, the replication of treatment effects within the same subject, and the subject's serving as his or her own control. Two common examples are the A-B-A-B (reversal) design and multiple-baseline design across behaviors, situations, or individuals.
- Between-group designs compare the behavior of groups of individuals assigned to different conditions, such as an experimental group, or a comparison group and a control group.

(continues)

SECTION SUMMARY *(continued)*

- In cross-sectional research, different individuals at different ages or stages of development are studied at the same point in time. In longitudinal research, the same individuals are studied at different ages or stages of development.
- Qualitative research focuses on narrative accounts, description, interpretation, context, and meaning, and strives to understand the phenomenon from the participant's perspective and in the context in which it is experienced.

Ethical and Pragmatic Issues

The image of overzealous scientists in white lab coats using children as guinea pigs for their experiments is a far cry from current research practices in abnormal child psychology. Researchers have become increasingly sensitive to the possible ethical misuses of research procedures, and are correspondingly more aware of the need for standards to regulate research practices (Hoagwood & Cavaleri, 2010).

Research in abnormal child psychology must meet certain standards that protect children and families from stressful procedures. Any study must undergo careful ethical review before it can be conducted. Current ethical guidelines for research with children are provided through institutional review boards, federal funding agencies, and professional organizations such as the American Psychological Association and the Society for Research in Child Development. Links to these and other related organizations' websites are available in your Psychology CourseMate.

Ethical standards for research with children attempt to strike a balance between supporting freedom of scientific inquiry and protecting the rights of privacy and the overall welfare of the research participants. Finding this balance is not always easy, especially with children. Although researchers are obligated to use nonharmful procedures, exposing the child to mildly stressful conditions such as a brief separation from their parent or exposure to an anxiety-producing stimulus may be necessary in some instances if benefits associated with the research are to be realized. Children are more vulnerable than adults to physical and psychological harm, and their immaturity may make it difficult or impossible for them to evaluate exactly what research participation means. In view of these realities, precautions must be taken to protect children's rights during the course of a study.

Informed Consent and Assent

The individual's fully informed consent to participate, obtained without coercion, serves as the single most protective regulation for research participants. **Informed consent** requires that all participants be fully informed of the nature of the research—as well as the risks, benefits, expected outcomes, and alternatives—before they agree to participate. Informed consent also includes informing participants of the option to withdraw from the study at any time, and of the fact that participation or nonparticipation in the research does not affect eligibility for other services.

Regarding research with children, protection is extended to obtaining both the informed consent of the parents or other legal guardian acting for the child and the assent of the child. **Assent** means that the child shows some form of agreement to participate without necessarily understanding the full significance of the research, which may be beyond younger children's cognitive capabilities. Guidelines for obtaining assent of the child call for doing so when the child is around the age of 7 or older. Researchers must provide school-age children with a complete explanation of the research activities in language they can understand. Factors that require particular attention when seeking children's assent include age, developmental maturity, psychological state, family factors, and the influence of the investigator seeking assent (Meaux & Bell, 2001). In addition to parents and children, consent must be obtained from other individuals who act on behalf of children, such as institutional officials when research is carried out in schools, day care centers, or medical settings.

Voluntary Participation

Participation in research is to be voluntary, yet some individuals may be more susceptible to subtle pressure and coercion than others. Protection for vulnerable populations, including children, has received considerable attention. Families of high-risk infants and children are potentially more vulnerable, owing in part to the families' distress over their children's high-risk status. Although instructed otherwise, parents recruited from social service agencies or medical settings may still feel that their treatment or quality of care will be threatened if they do not participate in the research. Maltreating parents may feel that their failure to participate in research could result in the loss of their child, a jail sentence, or failure to receive services.

The role of the researcher requires balancing successful recruiting with not placing pressure on potential participants. Volunteerism is itself a biasing factor in research. Individuals who agree to participate in research obviously differ from those who are approached but refuse. The question of whether volunteerism significantly biases findings on the variables of interest remains unanswered.

Confidentiality and Anonymity

Information revealed by individuals through participation in research is to be safeguarded. Most institutions require that individuals be informed that any information they disclose will be kept confidential, and that they be advised regarding any exceptions to confidentiality. Adult informants must be told about the limits of confidentiality prior to their participation in research. In research with children, one of the most frequently encountered challenges to confidentiality occurs when the child or parent reveals past abuse or information that would suggest the possibility of future abuse of the child. Procedures for handling this situation vary across studies. They depend on the circumstances of the disclosure (for example, by an adult within the context of therapy) and the reporting requirements of the state or province.

Nonharmful Procedures

No research procedures should be used that may harm the child either physically or psychologically. Whenever possible, the researcher is also obligated to use procedures that are the least stressful to the child and family. In some instances, psychological harm may be difficult to define, but when doubt is present, the researcher has the responsibility to seek consultation from others. If harm seems inevitable, alternative methods must be found or the research must be abandoned. In cases where exposure of the child to stressful conditions may be necessary if therapeutic benefits associated with the research are to be realized, careful deliberation and analysis of the risks and benefits by an institutional review board are needed.

Other Ethical and Pragmatic Concerns

Sensitivity to ethical concerns is especially important when the research involves potentially invasive procedures, deception, the use of punishment, the use of participant payment or other incentives, or possible coercion. In longitudinal research, investigators must be particularly sensitive to the occurrence of unexpected crises, unforeseen consequences of research, and issues surrounding the continuation of the research when findings suggest that another course of action is required to ensure the child's well-being.

Many research problems typically addressed through standardized instructions and procedures are compounded by children's limited experience and understanding of novel research tasks, and the particular characteristics of children with problems and their families. Researchers working with children with mental health problems and/or developmental disorders may face unique research challenges, such as motivating the children; keeping within time limitations; ensuring that instructions are well understood; and coping with possible boredom, distraction, and fatigue. Similarly, the families of children with problems often exhibit characteristics that may compromise their research participation and involvement. These characteristics include high levels of stress, marital discord, parental psychiatric disorders, substance use disorders, restricted resources and/or time for research, and limited verbal abilities.

The final responsibility for the ethical integrity of any research project lies with the investigator. Researchers are advised or—in the case of research funded by government agencies—required to seek advice from colleagues. Special committees exist in hospitals, universities, school systems, and other institutions to evaluate research studies on the basis of risks and benefits. This evaluation involves weighing the costs of the research to participants in terms of inconvenience and possible psychological or physical harm against the value of the study for advancing knowledge and improving the child's life situation. If there are any risks to the safety and welfare of the child or family that the research does not warrant, priority is always given to the participants.

SECTION SUMMARY

Ethical and Pragmatic Issues

- Research in abnormal child psychology must meet certain standards that protect children and families from stressful procedures, including informed consent and assent, voluntary participation, confidentiality and anonymity, and nonharmful procedures.
- To ensure that research meets ethical standards, researchers seek advice from colleagues and have their research evaluated by institutional ethics review committees. The final responsibility for the ethical integrity of any research project is with the investigator.

Study Resources

SECTION SUMMARIES

KEY TERMS

A-B-A-B reversal design 73
analogue research 72
assent 78
case study 72
cohort 75
comorbidity 69
correlation coefficient 70
cross-sectional research 75
electroencephalogram (EEG) 66
epidemiological research 60
external validity 69
incidence rates 60
informed consent 78
internal validity 68
longitudinal research 75
mediator variables 63
moderator variables 63
multiple-baseline design 73
natural experiments 71
naturalistic observation 67
neuroimaging 67
prevalence rates 60
qualitative research 76
random assignment 71
randomized controlled trials (RCTs) 64
real-time prospective designs 71
reliability 65
research 56
research designs 72
retrospective design 71
single-case experimental designs 73
standardization 64
structured observation 67
treatment effectiveness 64
treatment efficacy 64
true experiment 70
validity 65

COURSEMATE

Access an interactive eBook and chapter-specific interactive learning tools, including flashcards, quizzes, videos, and more in your Psychology CourseMate, accessed through CengageBrain.com.

Assessment, Diagnosis, and Treatment

4

If there is anything that we wish to change in the child, we should first examine it and see whether it is not something that could better be changed in ourselves.

—C. G. Jung

CHAPTER PREVIEW

Clinical Issues
The Decision-Making Process
Developmental Considerations
Purposes of Assessment

Assessing Disorders
Clinical Interviews
Behavioral Assessment
Psychological Testing

Classification and Diagnosis
Categories and Dimensions
The Diagnostic and Statistical Manual (DSM)

Treatment
Intervention
Cultural Considerations
Treatment Goals
Ethical and Legal Considerations
General Approaches to Treatment
Treatment Effectiveness
New Directions

MOST CHILDREN AND ADOLESCENTS referred for assessment and treatment have multiple problems. More often than not, the accumulation of these problems over time results in a referral. We have emphasized that most childhood disorders involve breakdowns in normal development. Felicia (see below), for example, is having difficulty coping with the demands of adolescence—gaining autonomy from her parents, getting along with peers, performing well in school, establishing her self-identity, and regulating her emotions. Felicia also experienced the added stress of her mother's hospitalization for pneumonia.

The clinician who sees Felicia will need to evaluate how well she can cope with events in her life in relation to the nature of the events; her appraisal of the events; her physical status, cognitive abilities, and personality; and support from her parents, teachers, or peers. To sort out the importance of these complex and interacting forces, we must devise an effective plan of assessment that leads to diagnostic and treatment decisions. We will be revisiting Felicia's case throughout the chapter to see how we address these issues.

Clinical Issues

In this chapter we emphasize the clinical strategies and methods used to assess children with psychological and behavioral problems, and the various approaches to the classification and diagnosis of childhood disorders. We also provide a brief introduction to treatment—a topic that we will discuss in detail for the individual disorders in the chapters that follow. We begin this important overview of clinical issues with a look at the decision-making process that surrounds assessment, diagnosis, and treatment.

The Decision-Making Process

How do we determine whether Felicia has a psychological disorder that requires professional attention, or whether she will simply outgrow or overcome her problems on her own? Mental health clinicians have to consider many important questions systematically to understand a child's basic problem(s) and to make diagnoses and devise treatment plans. In many ways this process is like good detective work. It requires

FELICIA

Multiple Problems

Jaren Jai Wicklund/Shutterstock.com

Felicia seemed unhappy and withdrawn at home and at school

Felicia, age 13, was referred because of her depression, school refusal, social withdrawal at home and school, and sleep disturbance. Her parents first noticed her recent difficulties about a year ago, just after her mother was hospitalized for pneumonia. Felicia was in a regular eighth-grade class and began to refuse to attend school. She complained of frequent stomach pains before school as a reason not to attend. Her social behavior also got worse at this time. She wanted to be close to her mother at all times and frequently requested her mother's help with homework or chores. Felicia became extremely quiet, appeared sad and unhappy, and withdrew from social activities. Not long afterward, she began to complain of sleep problems and a loss of appetite. At about this time her grades in school dropped from mostly Bs to Cs and Ds. She reported that no one liked her, that she couldn't do anything well, and that her life was hopeless. (Adapted from *Depression,* by D. J. Kolko, 1987. In M. Hersen and V. B. Van Hasselt (Eds.), Behavior Therapy with Children and Adolescents: A Clinical Approach, p. 160. Copyright © 1987 by John Wiley & Sons, Inc. Reprinted by permission of John Wiley & Sons, Inc.)

© Cengage Learning 2013

Clinical assessment is like good detective work

sorting through the many factors that bring a child or adolescent to the attention of professionals, and checking out alternative hypotheses and plans. This ongoing decision-making process is aimed at finding answers to both immediate and long-term questions about the nature and course of the child's disorder and its optimum treatment (Mash, 2006).

The decision-making process typically begins with a clinical assessment. **Clinical assessments** use systematic problem-solving strategies to understand children with disturbances and their family and school environments (Mash & Hunsley, 2007). Strategies typically include an assessment of the child's emotional, behavioral, and cognitive functioning, as well as the role of environmental factors (Sattler & Hoge, 2006). These strategies—which should be based on scientific evidence—form the basis of a flexible and ongoing process of hypothesis testing regarding the nature of the problem, its causes, and the likely outcomes if the problem is treated or left untreated (Haynes, Smith, & Hunsley, 2011).

Clinical assessment is much broader than interviewing or testing alone. The ultimate goal of assessment is to achieve effective solutions to the problems being faced by children and their families, and to promote and enhance their well-being. *Clinical assessments are meaningful to the extent that they result in practical and effective interventions.* In other words, a close and continuing partnership between assessment and intervention is vital; they should not be viewed as separate processes (Mash & Hunsley, 2005).

The focus of clinical assessment is to obtain a detailed understanding of the *individual* child or family as a unique entity (e.g., Felicia and her family), referred to as **idiographic case formulation.** This is in contrast to a **nomothetic formulation,** which emphasizes broad general inferences that apply to large *groups* of individuals (e.g., children with a depressive disorder). A clinician's nomothetic knowledge about general principles of psychological assessment, normal and abnormal child and family development, and specific childhood disorders is likely to result in better hypotheses to test at the idiographic level (Haynes, Mumma, & Pinson, 2009; Kazdin, 2000).

As you can imagine, the process of decision-making is similar to studying for several exams at the same time. You must be familiar with fundamental information in areas such as childhood depression or learning disorders, and then be able to integrate this knowledge in new ways to make it applicable to help solve a particular problem. Like studying for exams, this process at first seems like you are trying to cram everything into a funnel to distill what is most important. Unlike studying for exams, however, working with children and families and applying your training and experience to new situations is often very enjoyable!

Clinicians begin their decision making with an assessment, which can range from a clinical interview with the child and parents to more structured behavioral assessments and psychological testing. Keep in mind that assessment is not something done *to* a child or family—it is instead a collaborative process in which the child, family, and teacher all play active roles. Because adults play a critical role in defining the child's problem and providing information, it is particularly important to establish a rapport with them, and active family and teacher involvement are important for both assessment and intervention (Dowell & Ogles, 2010).

Developmental Considerations

Diversity is the one true thing we all have in common. Celebrate it every day.

—Anonymous

In assessing children and families one needs to be sensitive to the child's age, gender, and cultural background as well as to normative information about both typical and atypical child development. Such knowledge provides the clinician with a context for evaluating and understanding the behavior and circumstances of an individual child and family.

Age, Gender, and Culture

The recognition of diversity in the growing array of children's developmental functions and capacities at various ages is a crucial building block for assessment and treatment. How might Felicia's age, gender, or cultural background influence our approach to assessment, diagnosis, and treatment?

School refusal in a 13-year-old like Felicia is significant because it results in missed academic and social opportunities. In contrast, a 13-year-old's refusal to travel by airplane may be inconvenient or distressing, but in most cases would not have the same serious consequences as missing school. A child's age has implications not only for judgments about deviancy but also for selecting the most appropriate assessment and treatment methods. For example, at what age can a child provide reliable information in an interview? With respect to treatment, how might time-out for misbehavior for a 3-year-old be different from time-out for a school-age child?

Like age, the child's gender also has implications for assessment and treatment. Numerous studies have reported gender differences in the rates and expression of childhood disorders (Bell, Foster, & Mash, 2005). As shown in Table 4.1, some childhood disorders and conditions are more common in males than females, others are more common in females than males, and still others are equally common (Hartung & Widiger, 1998; Rutter, Caspi, & Moffitt, 2003).

As we have emphasized, most childhood disorders are identified and defined by adults, usually because adults find the child's symptoms particularly salient or troublesome. In general, overactivity and aggression are more common in boys than girls, who tend to express their problems in less observable ways (Keenan & Shaw, 1997). In fact, among the symptoms that best distinguish boys who are referred for treatment are "showing off or clowning" (as reported by parents) and "disturbing other pupils" (as reported by teachers) (Achenbach & Rescorla, 2001). Thus, boys may receive an excess of referrals, and girls may be overlooked because of their less visible forms of suffering. Our assessments and interventions must be sensitive to possible referral biases related to gender and gender differences. The difficulty in distinguishing between true gender differences and differences in reporting is illustrated by the finding that the rate of ADHD diagnoses during the early to mid-1990s increased approximately threefold among girls, compared with twofold for boys (Robison, Skaer, Sclar, & Galin, 2002). Could the rate of ADHD in girls possibly increase threefold during one decade? It is more likely that increasing recognition of the disorder and its various forms of expression in girls contributed to the dramatic increase in these ADHD diagnoses (Hinshaw & Blachman, 2005).

TABLE 4.1 | Gender Patterns for Selected Problems of Childhood and Adolescence

More Commonly Reported Among Males	
Attention-deficit/hyperactivity disorder	Autistic disorder
	Language disorder
Childhood conduct disorder	Reading disorder
Intellectual disability	Enuresis
More Commonly Reported Among Females	
Anxiety disorders	Eating disorders
Adolescent depression	Sexual abuse
Equally Reported Among Males and Females	
Adolescent conduct disorder	Feeding disorder
Childhood depression	Physical abuse and neglect

Source: Adapted from Gender Differences in the Diagnosis of Mental Disorders. Conclusions and Controversies of DSM-IV by C. M. Hartung and T. A. Widiger, 1998, Psychological Bulletin, 123, 260–278. Copyright © 1998 by the American Psychological Association. Reprinted with permission. APA is not responsible for the accuracy of this translation.

The study of gender differences has contributed enormously to our understanding and assessment of childhood disorders (Rose & Rudolph, 2006). However, it is also extremely important to study both girls and boys as distinct groups in their own right. An exclusive focus on sex differences could delay careful study of the expression of and underlying processes associated with specific disorders in one group or the other (Hinshaw, 2008). For example, studies into social aggression in girls have found that when angry, girls show aggression indirectly through verbal insults, gossip, ostracism, getting even, or third-party retaliation—referred to as *relational aggression* (Crick & Rose, 2000). As girls move into adolescence, the function of their aggressive behavior increasingly centers on group acceptance and affiliation. When adjustment problems are studied in relation to issues most salient for girls (e.g., relationships, body image), it has been shown that girls experience significant problems during childhood. These problems include relational aggression and also behaviors that are self-serving, directed outward, and intended to physically harm others. This combination of relational and physical aggression is the strongest predictor of future psychological–social adjustment problems in girls (Crick, Ostrov, & Werner, 2006). Interestingly, children who engage in forms of social aggression that are not typical of their sex (overtly aggressive girls and relationally aggressive boys) are significantly more maladjusted than children who engage in gender-normative forms of aggression (Crick, 1997).

Finally, cultural factors must be carefully considered during assessment and treatment of children and their families (Achenbach & Rescorla, 2007; Nikapota, 2009). Cultural patterns reflect learned behaviors and values that are shared among members, are transmitted to group members over time, and distinguish the group members of one group from another. Culture can

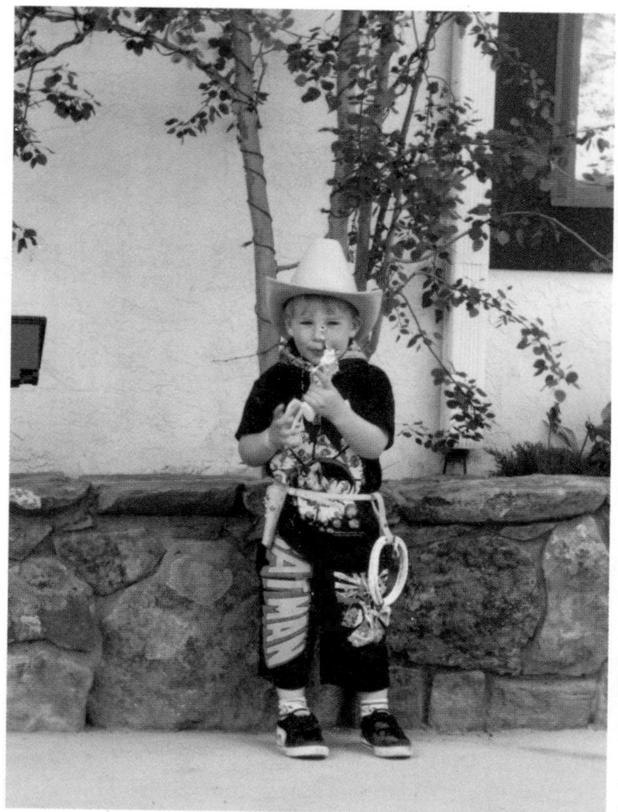

Biology and socialization interact to create different interests and behavior profiles of girls and boys

include ethnicity, language, religious or spiritual beliefs, race, gender, SES, age, sexual orientation, geographic origin, group history, education and upbringing, and life experiences.

Ethnic minority youth may have a greater risk of being misdiagnosed. For example, one study found that psychiatrically hospitalized African American adolescents were more often diagnosed with organic/psychotic disorders and less often diagnosed with mood/anxiety disorders than Caucasian teens (Kilgus, Pumariega, & Cuffe, 1995). In addition, African American and Hispanic children are less likely than white children to receive treatment (Zimmerman, 2005). Culturally competent assessment and treatment practices require that clinicians examine their own belief systems and the culturally based assumptions that guide their clinical practice.

Cultural information is necessary to establish a relationship with the child and family, motivate family members to change, obtain valid information, arrive at an accurate diagnosis, and develop meaningful recommendations for treatment. Thus, a clinical assessment should include a systematic review of the child and family's cultural background, the role of culture in the expression and evaluation of the child's symptoms and dysfunction, and the impact that cultural values may have on the relationship between the child and family and the clinician. Ethnic identity and racial socialization are key factors to consider in the assessment of all children and families, including those from the dominant culture (Dishion & Stormshak, 2007b).

Culture-bound syndromes refer to recurrent patterns of maladaptive behaviors and/or troubling experiences specifically associated with different cultures or localities (American Psychiatric Association, 2000). For example, *mal de ojo* or the "evil eye" is a concept that is widespread throughout Mediterranean cultures and Latino communities elsewhere in the world, a malady to which children are especially vulnerable. Believed to be caused by a hateful look or glance from a malicious person, the evil eye can cause a child to experience fitful sleep, crying without apparent cause, diarrhea, vomiting, and fever. Culture-bound syndromes rarely fit neatly into one Western diagnostic category (Alarcón, 2009). In addition, although the cross-cultural validity of Western diagnostic criteria may vary widely depending on the disorder, data regarding the validity of Western diagnostic criteria across cultures for many childhood disorders is lacking (Canino & Alegria,

2008). Therefore it is important that clinicians assess the extent to which a child's cultural background and context affect the expression of both individual symptoms and clinical disorders.

The way in which a child's adjustment is defined is also embedded in the child's culture, which identifies certain coping styles as acceptable (e.g., not expressing emotion, praying, crying) or certain behaviors as problems (e.g., lying, aggressiveness) (Yasui & Dishion, 2007). Thus, what is considered abnormal may vary from one cultural group to the next (Serafica & Vargas, 2006). For example, a child's shyness and oversensitivity are likely to lead to peer rejection and social maladjustment in Western cultures, but the same qualities may be associated with leadership, school competence, and academic achievement in Chinese children (Chen, Rubin, Li, & Li, 1999). In addition, it may be difficult to engage parents from some cultures if mental health issues are seen as particularly taboo, if intervention into personal family matters by strangers is viewed negatively, or if the causes of the illness in that culture are seen as physical or spiritual.

In negotiating treatment plans with children and families who may not share the clinician's concept of mental illness, a clinician must recognize the diversity that exists across and within racial and ethnic groups in lifestyle and patterns of acculturation (i.e., level of adaptation to dominant culture versus background culture). Generalizations about cultural practices frequently fail to capture these regional, generational, SES, and lifestyle differences. For example, SES level is a major confound in findings of differences in rates of psychopathology between various cultures, because ethnic minority cultures are frequently overrepresented in low SES populations (Glover & Pumariega, 1998). An individual's acculturation level can also significantly impact assessment and subsequent interventions. The lower the level of one's acculturation, the higher one scores on measures of psychopathology, particularly in conjunction with low SES and education level (Cuéllar, 2000). Having an awareness of the cultural customs and values that can affect behaviors, perceptions, and reactions to assessment and treatment, as well as recognizing the major confound of SES with these factors, puts the clinician in a better position to develop a meaningful assessment and intervention strategy.

Culturally competent children's mental health services may be provided in a number of ways. For example, in therapy for Hispanic children and adolescents, cultural competence may be achieved by matching children and families with clinicians of the same ethnicity, by customizing the treatment to Hispanic cultural values, beliefs, and customs (e.g., familism, spiritualism, and *respeto*), or by incorporating ethnic and cultural narratives and role play into therapy (Malgady, 2010). Similarly, understanding the cultural context is essential for identifying treatment goals in relation to what constitutes optimal functioning for children in particular cultural groups. For example, optimal functioning among children of color may reflect cultural values, beliefs, and practices that moderate racial stress and adversity—such as collectivism, racial and ethnic pride, spirituality, religion, and family and community importance, rather than Western-bound goals of "happiness," "hope," "subjective well-being," and "self-determination." In addition, for children of color, overcoming adversity related to racism and oppression may result in important skills related to optimal functioning (Constantine & Sue, 2006).

Recognizing diversity across and within ethnic groups is an important role of the clinician

Normative Information

Felicia's school refusal and sad mood began to occur following her mother's hospitalization. Is Felicia showing a normal reaction to a stressful life event? How common are these symptoms in girls her age after a brief period of separation from a parent? Felicia also withdrew from social contact and experienced sleep disturbances. Adolescence is a time of biological and social upheaval for many youths; therefore, we need to know if Felicia is different from other girls her age with respect to these problems and, if so, when should we become concerned and take action?

Knowledge, experience, and basic information about norms of child development and behavior problems are the crucial beginning to understanding how children's problems or needs come to the attention of professionals. As many parents discover, figuring out what to expect of their children at various ages can be challenging. Parents are faced with determining what difficulties are likely to be chronic versus common and transient, deciding when to seek advice from others, and determining what treatment is best for their child. Immigrant parents can have even more difficulty with these tasks when trying to assess their second-generation child's behavior as the child attempts to navigate at least two different cultures (Falicov, 2003).

Isolated symptoms of behavioral and emotional problems generally show little correspondence with children's overall adjustment. Usually, the *age inappropriateness* and *pattern* of symptoms, rather than individual symptoms, define childhood disorders. As well, the extent to which symptoms result in impairment in the child's functioning is a key consideration. Nevertheless, certain symptoms do occur more frequently in children referred for assessment and treatment.

Examples of parent- and teacher-rated symptoms that best distinguish referred and nonreferred children ages 6 to 18 are shown in Table 4.2. As you can see, these symptoms are relatively common behaviors that occur to some extent in all children—sadness, a lack of concentration, and demands for attention top the list. Primarily, the problems displayed by children referred for treatment are similar to problems that occur in less extreme forms in the general population or young children.

Purposes of Assessment

Assessments of children and families are always carried out in relation to one or more purposes. These purposes guide the assessment process, including decisions regarding the use of particular assessment methods. As described below, three common purposes of assessment are description and diagnosis, prognosis, and treatment planning (Mash & Hunsley, 2007).

TABLE 4.2 | Parent- and Teacher-Rated Problems That Best Discriminate Between Referred and Nonreferred Children

• Unhappy, sad, or depressed	• Poor school work
• Can't concentrate	• Inattentive
• Demands attention	• Stubborn
• Disobedient at school	• Moody
• Doesn't get along	• Sulks
• Impulsive	• Temper
• Nervous	

Source: From Achenbach, T. M. and Rescorla, L. A. (2001), Manual for the ASEBA School-Age Forms & Profiles, ISBN 978-0-938565-73-4. Burlington, VT: University of Vermont, Research Center for Children, Youth, and Families) p. 144. Reprinted by permission.

Description anod Diagnosis

"Diagnosis is not the end but the beginning of practice."

—Fischer (1879–1962)

The first step in understanding a child's problem is to provide a **clinical description**, which summarizes the unique behaviors, thoughts, and feelings that together make up the features of the child's psychological disorder. A clinical description attempts to establish basic information about the child's (and usually the parents') presenting complaints, especially how the child's behavior or emotions are different from or similar to those of other children of the same age, sex, socioeconomic, and cultural background.

If you conducted an evaluation of Felicia, what information would be most important to include in your clinical description? You would start by describing how her behavior differs from normal behavior of girls her age. First, assessing and describing the *intensity*, *frequency*, and *severity* of her problem would communicate a sense of how excessive or deficient her behavior is, under what circumstances it may be a problem, how often it does or does not occur, and how severe the occurrences are. Second, you would need to describe the *age of onset* and *duration* of her difficulties. Some problems are transient and will spontaneously remit, while others persist over time. Like frequency and intensity, age of onset and duration of the problem behavior must be appraised with respect to what is considered normative for a given age. Finally, you would want to convey a full picture of her *different symptoms and their configuration*. Although Felicia needed help because of particular problems at school and with her peers, you need to know the full range, or profile, of her strengths and weaknesses to make informed choices about the likely course, outcome, and treatment of her disorder.

After establishing an initial picture of Felicia's presenting complaints, you would next determine whether this description meets the criteria for diagnosis of one or more psychological disorders. **Diagnosis** means analyzing information and drawing conclusions about the nature or cause of the problem, or assigning a formal diagnosis. Does Felicia meet standard diagnostic criteria for a depressive disorder and, if so, what might be the cause?

Diagnosis has acquired two separate meanings, which can be confusing. The first meaning is *taxonomic diagnosis*, which focuses on the formal assignment of cases to specific categories drawn from a system of classification such as the DSM-IV-TR (APA, 2000) or from empirically derived categories (discussed later in this chapter) (Achenbach & Rescorla, 2001). *Problem-solving analysis*, the second, much broader meaning of diagnosis, is similar to clinical assessment and views diagnosis as a process of gathering information that is used to understand the nature of an individual's problem, its possible causes, treatment options, and outcomes.

Thus, Felicia's assessment will involve a complete diagnostic (problem-solving analysis) to get the most comprehensive picture possible. In addition, Felicia may receive a formal diagnosis of *major depressive disorder* (discussed in Chapter 8), which means that she possesses characteristics that link her to similar youths presumed to have the same disorder (taxonomic diagnosis). A secondary diagnosis of an anxiety disorder, such as separation anxiety disorder or school phobia, may be necessary for Felicia since comorbidity of depression and anxiety is very common among girls her age. Comorbidity exists when certain disorders among children and adolescents are likely to co-occur within the same individual, especially disorders that share many common symptoms (see Chapter 3). Awareness of one disorder alerts us to the increased possibility of another disorder. Some of the more common comorbid disorders are conduct disorder (CD) and attention-deficit/hyperactivity disorder (ADHD), autism and intellectual disability, and childhood depression and anxiety (Drabick & Kendall, 2010).

Prognosis and Treatment Planning

Prognosis is the formulation of predictions about future behavior under specified conditions. If Felicia does not receive help for her problem, what will likely happen to her in the future? Will her problems diminish as she gets older or will they get worse?

"They're trying to figure out whether it's a chemical thing or I'm just a crybaby."

Naturally, parents and others immediately want to know the possible short- and long-term outcomes for their child, and what events might alter such projections. Remember that many childhood concerns, such as fears, worries, and bed-wetting, are common at certain ages, so any decision to treat a child's particular problem must be based on an informed prognosis. Clinicians must weigh the probability that circumstances will remain the same, improve, or deteriorate with or without treatment, as well as what course of treatment should be followed.

In addition, treatments for children and adolescents often focus on enhancing the child's development rather than merely removing symptoms or restoring a previous level of functioning. In Felicia's case, for example, an assessment might reveal that she has poor social skills, so intervention plans might focus on efforts to teach her these skills in a concerted fashion to reduce the chances of continuing social relationship difficulties. A prognosis based on careful assessment can also serve to inform parents and others about the importance of doing something now that may reduce the likelihood of major problems later.

Treatment planning and evaluation means using assessment information to generate a plan to address the child's problem and evaluate its effectiveness. Felicia's mother keeps her daughter home from school when Felicia complains of stomach pains. She also does Felicia's homework. Does this information suggest a possible course of action? Felicia thinks she can't do anything well. Will helping her to change this and other irrational beliefs make a difference in her depression? When action is taken, how can we evaluate whether it is having the desired effect?

Treatment planning and evaluation may involve further specification and measurement of possible contributors to the problem, determination of resources and motivation for change, and recommendations for the treatments likely to be the most feasible, acceptable, and effective for the child and family. For example, are Felicia's parents unintentionally rewarding her physical complaints and school refusal by giving her extra attention when she doesn't go to school? Is Felicia willing to discuss with a therapist why she refuses to go to school? Are her parents willing to set limits on her behavior despite a history of struggle and failure with previous attempts?

SECTION SUMMARY

Clinical Issues

- Clinical assessment is directed at differentiating, defining, and measuring the child's behaviors, cognitions, and emotions of concern, the environmental circumstances that may contribute to these problems, and the child's strengths and competencies.

- Assessments are meaningful to the extent that they result in effective interventions; a close and continuing partnership must exist between assessment and intervention.
- Age, gender, and culture influence how children's symptoms and behavior are expressed and recognized, and have implications for selecting the most appropriate methods of assessment and treatment.
- The age inappropriateness and the pattern of symptoms, rather than individual symptoms, usually define childhood disorders.
- Three purposes of assessment are (1) description and diagnosis that determine the nature and causes of the child's problem, (2) prognosis that predicts future behavior under specified conditions, and (3) treatment planning and evaluation.

Assessing Disorders

If something exists, it exists in some amount. And if it exists in some amount, then it is capable of being measured.

—René Descartes

Not everything important can be measured, and not everything that can be measured is important.

—Albert Einstein

If you were planning to assess Felicia's problems, where would you begin and what might you include in your assessment? Should you interview Felicia, both parents, and her teacher? Do you need to observe Felicia at home? At school? Are there psychological tests or questionnaires to help you pinpoint Felicia's strengths and weaknesses, such as intelligence, emotion, concentration, social skills, and learning ability?

You'll quickly recognize how massive the decision-making process can seem. In view of this complexity, many clinical settings use a multidisciplinary team approach to assessment. Individuals with specific expertise in psychological test administration and interpretation work with others to generate the most complete picture of a child's mental health needs. Multidisciplinary teams may include a psychologist, a physician, an educational specialist, a speech pathologist, and a social worker.

Some children may need to be referred for a medical exam as part of a comprehensive assessment to investigate if a physical problem is related to their disorder. For example, a physiological problem may be causing a particular child's bed-wetting or sleep disorder. A thorough medical assessment by a physician could evaluate Felicia's stomach pains, sleep disturbances, and weight loss and be used to determine whether Felicia's depression was related to drug use or a general medical condition such as hypothyroidism (low levels of thyroid hormones).

Ideally, the clinical assessment of children experiencing difficulties relies on a **multimethod assessment approach**, which emphasizes the importance of obtaining information from different informants in a variety of settings and using a variety of methods that include interviews, observations, questionnaires, and tests. Decisions regarding which available assessment method will be useful in a specific case are based on whether the assessment is for diagnosis, treatment planning, or treatment evaluation; on whether the problem is observable (like aggression), or internal (like anxiety); and on the child's and family's characteristics and abilities. In addition, the methods used need to be reliable, valid, cost-effective, and useful for treatment (Hunsley & Mash, 2008).

Clinical assessment consists of many strategies and procedures designed to help understand the child's thoughts, feelings, and behaviors as they occur in specific situations. Clinical interviews are usually conducted with the parents and child separately or in a family interview, and they help establish a good working relationship with the child and family. They are also extremely useful in obtaining basic information about existing concerns as viewed by the child and family members and in pinpointing directions for further inquiry. Behavioral assessments, checklists and rating scales, and psychological tests are then used in accordance with a decision-making approach. Information is also obtained from teachers and other significant individuals who interact with the child in various settings. The purpose is to obtain the most complete picture possible in order to develop and implement an appropriate treatment plan, within the limits of available resources.

A comprehensive assessment requires that some consideration be given to evaluating the child's strengths and weaknesses in areas ranging from basic language and self-care skills to coping and leadership abilities. If our detective work suggests that a particular area of functioning deserves closer scrutiny, then a more in-depth assessment of that area is warranted. However, if initial assessments indicate that certain areas of functioning are not a problem, then further assessments may not be necessary. For example, for a child performing poorly in school, an assessment of intellectual functioning and academic performance is essential. On the other hand, for a child experiencing difficulties at home but doing fine at school, assessment of intellectual and academic functioning may be unnecessary. Keep in mind that the most comprehensive assessment procedures will have little clinical impact unless they are practical to use in the settings in which youth with mental health problems are typically assessed. Thus, practitioners and policy makers more and more are seeking assessment protocols that are cost-effective and feasible to use within real-world service delivery settings (Ebesutani, Bernstein, Chorpita, & Weisz, 2012).

Clinical Interviews

Children and adolescents don't usually refer themselves for treatment. Typically, they are referred because of the impact of their behavior on others. Thus, they often do not understand why they are seeing someone, and in fact they may not even experience any distress or recognize any cause for concern. (To be fair, some adults are like this too!) The initial clinical interview can be very important not only in obtaining information, but also in setting the stage for collaboration and cooperation among the child, family members, and other concerned parties.

The clinical interview is the assessment procedure most universally used with parents and children. However, based on interviewers' theoretical orientations, styles, and purposes, interviews may vary considerably in terms of the kinds of information obtained and the meaning assigned to that information (Sattler & Mash, 1998). Interviews allow professionals to gather information in a flexible manner over many sessions. The findings can then be integrated with more time-consuming assessments, such as family observations or psychological testing.

Clinical interviews use a flexible, conversational style that helps the child or parent to present the most complete picture possible. Interviewees will be encouraged to tell their stories with minimal guidance, which permits the children and parents to convey their thoughts and feelings in ways that approximate how they think in everyday life. During the clinical interview, the interviewer may observe nonverbal communications by the child and parent, such as facial expressions, body posture, voice, mannerisms, and motor behavior. These informal observations can provide the clinician with additional insights into the parent/child relationship that may be relevant in determining the presenting problem and the direction for treatment planning.

Clinical interviews can provide a large amount of information during a brief period. For example, during an hour-long interview with a parent, much detail about the child's developmental history, likes and dislikes, behavioral strengths and deficits, response to discipline, relationships with others, and school performance can be obtained—far more than would be learned by observing the parent and child interacting for the same amount of time (Sattler, 1998).

Lesley Rigg/Shutterstock.com

Children's initial reactions to seeing a mental health professional are often ones of fear and resistance

Many clinicians develop their own style for engaging school-age children and adolescents in discussing their situation. We often use video games, crafts, and similar enticements to help the child feel more comfortable. When younger children are referred, it may be more appropriate to involve one parent in a joint game or activity. Younger children are more likely to "be themselves" around their parents than a stranger. (For this age group, drawing, coloring, and similar fun activities are almost always successful at initiating a new relationship.) Also, because of their developmental level, younger children or children with intellectual disabilities may be capable of providing only general impressions of their internal states, behavior, and circumstances.

Depending on the child's age, you may want to adopt a child-friendly approach for the interview that fits with the child's developmental status, the nature of the problem, and the interview purpose. The interview typically will attempt to elicit information about the child's self-perceptions and perceptions of others, and to obtain samples of how the child responds in a social situation with an adult. Children's views of why they were brought to the clinic, their expectations for improvement, and their understanding of the assessment situation are all important to consider, along with the manner in which they interpret significant events such as divorce or family violence. Engaging unwilling children can be difficult. Since other people typically seek help on behalf of the child, some children and adolescents may not feel they have a problem and see no need to be interviewed.

What questions would you ask Felicia's parents? Perhaps you want to know how long Felicia's reluctance to separate from her parents has been a concern, and whether prior help has been sought. You might also want to discuss the exact nature of the problems her parents are concerned about and to provide them with some indication of the next steps in the assessment and treatment process.

Developmental and Family History

Initial assessments often include a **developmental history** or **family history**, in which information is obtained from the parents regarding potentially significant developmental milestones and historical events that might have a bearing on the child's current difficulties. This information can be gained using a background questionnaire or interview that typically covers the following areas (Sattler, 1998):

- *The child's birth and related events*, such as pregnancy and birth complications or the mother's use of drugs, alcohol, or cigarettes during pregnancy
- *The child's developmental milestones*, such as age of walking, use of language, bladder and bowel control, and self-help skills
- *The child's medical history*, including injuries, accidents, operations, illnesses, and prescribed medications
- *Family characteristics and family history*, including the age, occupation, cultural background, and marital status of family members and the medical, educational, and mental health history of parents and siblings
- *The child's interpersonal skills*, including relations with adults and other children, and play and social activities
- *The child's educational history*, including schools attended, academic performance, attitudes toward school, relations with teachers and peers, and special services
- *The adolescent's work history and relationships*, including relationships with others of the same sex and the opposite sex
- *A description of the presenting problem*, including a detailed description of the problem and surrounding events, and how parents have attempted to deal with the problem in the past
- *The parents' expectations* for assessment and treatment of their child and themselves

Here is part of the developmental and family history given by Felicia's parents:

FELICIA

History

Her parents reported that Felicia was the result of an unplanned pregnancy following an initial miscarriage, the adoption of a son, and the birth of a sister. The pregnancy and Felicia's early life were described as uncomplicated and generally happy. Felicia reached developmental milestones late, required extra assistance with tasks, was quite reserved and uncommunicative, and experienced speech articulation problems. Her parents said they tended to "baby" Felicia since she was seen as "slow." She was similarly described as developmentally immature by her teachers. As a result, she had repeated the first grade even though her attendance and academic performance were consistently good.

Felicia's adopted brother, age 23, attended a local college and lived at home. Her sister, age 16, also lived at home and attended high school. Felicia's mother had trained to become a registered nurse; her father held a Ph.D. in chemistry and managed the research department of a large company. No significant problems were reported for the other children, with the exception of some difficulty on the part of the brother in establishing independence.

Felicia's mother described experiencing a significant depression after each of her pregnancies and following her own father's death the previous year, a loss that was reported to have been very painful for Felicia also. Felicia's father reported no difficulties and was considered a stable and dependable person. (Adapted from *Depression*, by D. J. Kolko, 1987. In M. Hersen and V. B. Van Hasselt (Eds.), Behavior Therapy with Children and Adolescents: A Clinical Approach, pp. 159–160. Copyright © 1987 by John Wiley & Sons, Inc. Reprinted by permission of John Wiley & Sons, Inc.)

Many events presented in this developmental and family history may be relevant to the assessment of Felicia's current problems and must be explored as the assessment proceeds. For example, the babying described by Felicia's parents may reflect a more general pattern of overdependency on her parents that is contributing to her school refusal. The significant depression experienced by Felicia's mother following her pregnancies may suggest a family risk for depression. The death of Felicia's grandfather a year earlier may have been a triggering event, leading to a mood disturbance in both Felicia and her mother. During the early stages of assessment, these are hypotheses; as evidence accumulates with ongoing detective work, hypotheses can be supported or rejected as indicated by new data.

Semistructured Interviews

Most interviews with children and parents are unstructured. Clinicians use their preferred interview style and format, as well as their knowledge of the disorder, to pursue various questions in an informal and flexible manner. Unstructured clinical interviews provide a rich source of clinical hypotheses. However, their lack of standardization may result in low reliability and selective or biased gathering of information. To address this problem, clinicians sometimes use **semistructured interviews** that include specific questions designed to elicit information in a relatively consistent manner regardless of who is doing the interview. The format of the interview usually ensures that the most important aspects of a particular disorder are covered. An appealing feature of semistructured interviews, especially for older children and youths, is that they can be administered by computer, something many children find entertaining and often less threatening at first than a face-to-face interview. The semistructured format also permits the clinician to follow up on issues of importance that may emerge during the interview.

The consistency and coverage of semistructured interviews may be offset by a loss of spontaneity between the child and clinician, especially if the interview is conducted too rigidly. Under such circumstances, children and adolescents may be reluctant to volunteer important information not directly relevant to the interviewer's questions. With appropriate modifications that make the interview process easier to follow, however, semistructured interviews are reliable and very useful in assessing a wide range of children's symptoms (Edelbrock, Crnic, & Bohnert, 1999). Sample questions from a semistructured interview for young people like Felicia who are experiencing depression are presented in Table 4.3.

TABLE 4.3 | Semistructured Interview Questions for an Older Child or Adolescent with Depression

Depressed Mood/Irritability • Do you feel sad? • Do you get moody?
Loss of Interest • Have you lost interest in doing things, like your hobbies? • Is there anything you look forward to doing?
Self-Deprecatory Ideation • Do you feel that you are worthless? • Have you thought about committing suicide?
Sleep Disturbances • Do you have trouble sleeping lately? • Do you need more sleep than usual lately?
Change in School Performance • Do you have trouble concentrating in school? • Have you ever refused to go to school?
Decreased Socialization • Have there been any changes in your relationships with friends? • Do you feel a need to be alone?
Somatic Complaints • Do you get pains in your stomach? • Do you get muscle pains and aches?
Loss of Usual Energy • Do you feel you have less energy to do things? • Do you often feel tired?
Change in Appetite and/or Weight • Do you have to force yourself to eat? • Has there been a change in your weight?

Source: Adapted from Clinical and Forensic Interviewing of Children and Families: Guidelines for the Mental Health, Education, Pediatric, and Child Maltreatment Fields by J. M. Sattler, pp. 938-940. Copyright © 1998 by Jerome M. Sattler Publisher, Inc. Adapted by permission.

Behavioral Assessment

The clinical interviews described in this chapter are valuable in eliciting information from parents and school-age children. They provide an initial look at how the child and family think, feel, and behave, and an initial suggestion of the factors that might be contributing to the child's problems. However, it is often necessary to obtain a firsthand look at the child's behavior in everyday life situations at home or at school, or to ask someone who sees the child on a regular basis to observe the child's behavior.

Behavioral assessment is a strategy for evaluating the child's thoughts, feelings, and behaviors in specific settings, and then using this information to formulate hypotheses about the nature of the problem and what can be done about it (Haynes & Heiby, 2004). Behavioral assessment frequently involves observing the child's behavior directly, rather than inferring how children think, behave, or feel on the basis of their descriptions of inkblots or the pictures they draw.

Using behavioral assessment, the clinician or another person who sees the child regularly identifies **target behaviors**, which are the primary problems of concern, with the goal of then determining what specific factors may be controlling or influencing these behaviors. Sometimes this is a straightforward task, as with a child who complains of illness every Monday morning and, as a result, is kept out of school for the day (sound familiar?). In other cases, the child displays multiple problems at home or school. Felicia's school refusal appears to be part of a larger pattern of difficulties that includes social withdrawal, depression, and possibly separation anxiety.

Even the seemingly simple task of identifying what is bothering a child can be a challenge. Remember that an adult usually decides that the child has a problem and that the child should be referred for an assessment.

Adults often disagree about the nature of the child's problem, especially when they observe children in different settings (De Los Reyes & Kazdin, 2005). Ratings by various people may be influenced by differences between their culture and that of the child. For example, when teachers rate youths from another cultural background, they are more likely to rate them higher on behavioral and emotional problems than are the teachers of a similar background, the parents, or the children themselves (Skiba, Knesting, & Bush, 2002). Further, a child's presenting problem can often be very different from the one eventually identified as the target for intervention.

A commonly used and simple framework for organizing findings in behavioral assessment has been dubbed the "ABCs of assessment":

A = Antecedents, or the events that immediately precede a behavior

B = Behavior(s) of interest

C = Consequences, or the events that follow a behavior

In Felicia's case we might observe the following sequence: (A) Whenever Felicia's mother asks her to go to school (antecedent), (B) Felicia complains that she has stomach pains and refuses to go (behaviors), and (C) her mother lets Felicia stay home (consequence). This antecedent–behavior–consequence sequence might suggest that Felicia is being reinforced for her physical complaints and school refusal by not having to go to school. In addition, because there are no positive consequences for going to school and no negative ones for staying at home, Felicia might act this way on future school days. The ABCs of assessment can be used to organize information in specific contexts, as just described, or as an overall framework for assessment.

Behavior analysis or **functional analysis of behavior** is the more general approach to organizing and using assessment information in terms of antecedents, behaviors, and consequences across many levels (Hanley, Iwata, & McCord, 2003). As shown in ● Figure 4.1, functional analysis can be used to identify a wide range of antecedents and consequences that might be contributing to Felicia's school refusal and depression. The antecedents and consequences for Felicia's behavior include events in the immediate situation (a reduction in anxiety), more remote occurrences (being teased at school), events in the external environment, and Felicia's inner thoughts and feelings.

The goal of functional analysis is to identify as many factors as possible that could be contributing to a child's problem behaviors, thoughts, and feelings, and to develop hypotheses for the factors that are most important and/or most easily changed. In some cases, hypotheses can be confirmed or rejected by changing the antecedents and consequences to see if the behavior changes. For example, we might teach Felicia to relax when thinking about going to school in order to reduce her anxiety (changing an antecedent) to see if this decreases her school refusal. Or she could be instructed to substitute more positive self-statements ("I can succeed in school") for her negative ones ("I'm no good at anything") to see if this decreases her depressive symptoms and raises her self-esteem. In these examples, you can see a close interplay between assessment and intervention when carrying out a functional analysis.

The process of gathering information about the child's behavior in specific settings takes many different forms. Often it involves either asking the parent, teacher, or child about what goes on in specific situations, or observing the child. Clinicians develop their initial hypotheses based on information provided by the parents and the child during the interview. They pursue the hypotheses further using behavioral assessments, such as behavior checklists and rating scales, and observations of behavior in real life or in role-play simulations. In general, behavioral assessment can be viewed as an approach to organizing assessment information for an individual child and developing hypotheses for treatment (Francis & Chorpita, 2004).

Checklists and Rating Scales

Reports concerning child behavior and adjustment can be obtained using global checklists and problem-focused rating scales. Global behavior checklists ask

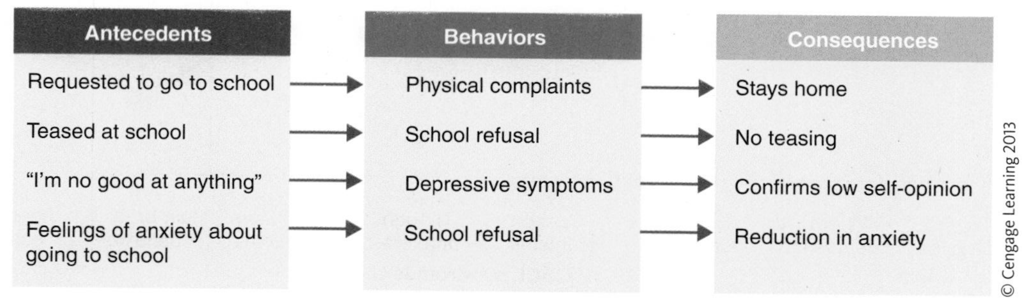

● **FIGURE 4.1** | Functional analysis: antecedents, behaviors, consequences.

parents, teachers, and sometimes the youth themselves to rate the presence or absence of a wide variety of child behaviors, or the frequency and intensity of these behaviors.

Unlike a clinical interview, the use of a well-developed checklist is strengthened by its known degree of standardization and by the opportunities to compare an individual child's score with a known reference group of children of a similar age and the same gender (Fernandez-Ballesteros, 2004). Checklists are also economical to administer and score. They provide a rich source of information about parents' or teachers' reports of children's behavior, including possible differences in the reports of parents in the same family, and differences between parent and teacher reports. Keep in mind, however, that informants may differ in their views of the child's strengths and weaknesses because they interact with the child in different surroundings and circumstances. These discrepancies are not necessarily bad, because they inform the clinician of the possible range of behavior the child engages in, possible circumstances that increase or decrease target behaviors, and possible demands or expectations placed on the child that may be unrealistic. Nevertheless, these discrepancies underscore the importance of obtaining information from multiple observers (Grigorenko, Geiser, Slobodskaya, & Francis, 2010).

The Child Behavior Checklist (CBCL) developed by Thomas Achenbach and his colleagues is a leading checklist for assessing behavioral problems in children and adolescents (Achenbach & Rescorla, 2001). The reliability and validity of the CBCL has been documented in numerous studies, and it is widely used in treatment settings and schools. The parent-completed form of the CBCL is part of a set of scales for children ages 6 to 18 that also includes a teacher and youth self-report, a classroom observation measure, and an interview. A notable feature of the CBCL is that it has been used to assess children in 80 or more cultural groups throughout the world and as such provides a robust measure for evaluating immigrant, refugee, and minority children from diverse backgrounds (Achenbach et al., 2008).

The scales of the CBCL can be used to form a profile that gives the clinician an overall picture of the variety and degree of the child's behavioral problems. A CBCL profile derived from a checklist completed by Felicia's mother is shown in ● Figure 4.2. The profile shows that her major areas of concern about her daughter are with respect to symptoms of *anxious/depressed* (e.g., "fears school," "cries a lot"), *withdrawn/depressed* (e.g., "rather be alone," "enjoys little"), and *somatic complaints* (e.g., "feels dizzy," "aches"). Felicia's scores on these dimensions are extreme, and place her in the upper 5% or higher (clinical or near-clinical range) when compared with girls of a similar age.

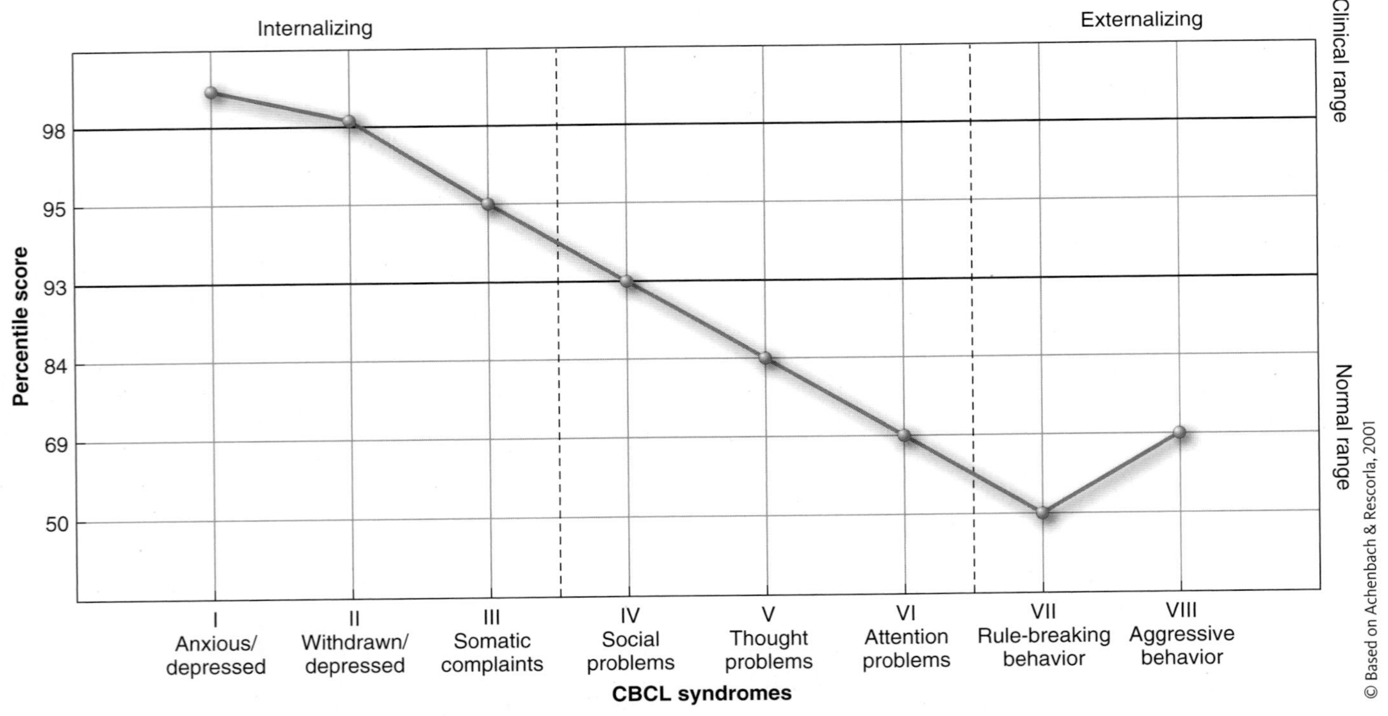

● **FIGURE 4.2** | Child Behavior Checklist (CBCL) profile for Felicia.

Brief problem checklists based on scales such as the CBCL may also be administered to children and caregivers in a brief rating scale or interview format. These checklists provide a practical and cost-effective way to monitor ongoing progress in treatment and to modify treatment as necessary (Achenbach, McConaughy, Ivanova, & Rescorla, 2011; Chorpita et al., 2010). Other checklists monitor progress in relation to a small number of "top problems" identified by the child or parents as important (Weisz et al., 2011).

In addition to checklists such as the CBCL that span a wide range of behavior problems, other rating scales focus mainly on specific disorders—depression, anxiety, autism, ADHD, or conduct problems—or on particular areas of functioning, such as social competence, adaptive behavior, or school performance (Mash & Barkley, 2007). Ratings of the child are usually provided by parents and teachers. Clinicians may opt to administer self-report checklists in an engaging, child-friendly manner that increases the child's interest in the material. We like to administer questionnaires to adolescents by computer, simply because they find this approach more interesting. With younger children, we like to hand them a card showing the range of responses they may have, using happy or sad faces and similar icons that appeal to that age group. Rating scales provide the clinician with a more focused look at specific problems than a global behavior checklist provides. You will see many examples of rating scales used to assess specific problems in the chapters to follow.

Behavioral Observation and Recording

Since some children are not old enough or skilled enough to report on their own behavior, parents, teachers, or clinicians may keep careful records of specific target behaviors. Parents or other observers typically record *baseline* (prior to intervention) data on one or two problems that they wish to change—for example, how often their child complies with their requests or how often he or she throws a temper tantrum (Dishion & Granic, 2004).

Recordings by parents have the advantage of providing ongoing information about behaviors of interest in life settings that might not otherwise be accessible to observation by the clinician. Parental monitoring may also provide secondary benefits that are not directly related to assessment—teaching parents better observation skills, assessing parental motivation, and providing parents with realistic estimates of their child's rate of responding and feedback regarding the effects of treatment. However, many practical problems may arise in asking parents to keep accurate records; for example, children often know when they are being watched and may react differently. Box 4.1 illustrates why observing behavior can be a useful part of any clinical assessment.

The clinician may also set up a *role-play simulation* in the clinic to see how the child and family might behave in daily situations encountered at home or school, or in a problem-solving situation like figuring out how to play a game together (Roberts & Hope, 2001). When observing families who have physically abused their preschool-age child, for example, we choose activities most likely to elicit both parent–child cooperation and conflict: We first ask parents to play with their child so that we can observe their teaching style, and then ask them to have the child put away her or his favorite toys, which often results in noncompliance and conflict (Wolfe, 1991).

In Felicia's case, role-play simulations were used to assess her social skills. The clinician first described the situation to Felicia as follows: "You're sitting in the school cafeteria eating lunch by yourself when Maria, a girl from your math class, comes over to your table and sits across from you." Next, the clinician takes the role of Maria and says, "Hi Felicia. How's your lunch?" Felicia then responds, and the interaction continues, giving the clinician a chance to directly observe Felicia's social skills in a situation that might come up in everyday life.

Remember, direct observation is not foolproof. Clinicians must take into account the informant, the child, the nature of the problem, and the family and cultural context because any of these issues can distort the findings. Despite its limitations, direct observation is a valid and beneficial step in the decision-making process for most families who voluntarily seek assistance and understand what may be required to conduct a thorough assessment and treatment plan, and it can be quite helpful to less motivated families as well.

Psychological Testing

A **test** is a task or set of tasks given under standard conditions with the purpose of assessing some aspect of the child's knowledge, skill, or personality. Most tests are standardized on a clearly defined reference group—for example, children of a certain age, sex, or SES, referred to as a *norm group*. An individual child's scores can then be compared with the scores of a comparable group of children to determine the extent to which that child's scores deviate from the norm. The prevalence and visibility of test use in our culture have led some people to adopt the mistaken view that testing and psychological assessment are one and the same. Although tests play an important role in a child's assessment, they represent only one part of the overall decision-making process.

It is also important to keep in mind that many psychological tests, because they may have been "normed" on narrow and limited samples, may not be appropriate to use with individuals from racial, ethnic, or cultural

BOX 4.1 A CLOSER LOOK

Observing Behavior: Seeing the Whole Picture

Sometimes observations of a child with his or her parent can be extremely illuminating. Recently, the mother of Sammy, a 4-year-old child with severe behavior problems, came to one of our clinics for assistance. During the interview she told the clinician that her son was "impossible to get dressed," and "doesn't listen to a thing I say to him." She had been told by a family member that Sammy seemed "hyperactive," and her family doctor had requested a psychological assessment as a result of her insistence on this diagnosis.

A note from his preschool teacher painted a very different picture of this young boy. His teacher spoke frankly of Sammy's undeveloped skills at following directions or concentrating on a task for any length of time, but pointed out how he settled down much like the other children once he found something to do that he enjoyed. This boy seemed calm during our visit with him at the clinic, so we decided to get a clearer picture of the situation by visiting his home and school.

When we visited the home, the problem stood out within minutes. His home was littered with his toys and games, which his mother let him rummage through and toss around the room freely. Attempts to get her to provide some structure to his play and other activities resulted in an immediate confrontation between the two—he simply turned away and grabbed the toys he wanted, and she became upset and started to chase after him, yelling at him to put his toys away. "See," she said, turning to the observer, "he doesn't do a thing I ask him to do." The boy clutched his toys and quieted down at this point, turned on the TV, and plunked himself in front of it. Similar attempts on Sammy's part to avoid doing what his teacher asked were observed during our school visit, although his teacher was more successful at getting him back to the activity at hand by using praise and other positive rewards.

Obviously, the description this mother gave us of her son's behavior lacked a few of the details that make an accurate diagnosis possible. Her description also failed to mention how upset she got when Sammy "didn't listen," and that the home environment was rather chaotic and unstructured for a child his age. Without this home observation visit, our assessment of the problem and recommendations for treatment might have been quite different if we attributed his misbehavior primarily to hyperactivity, as the mother initially led us to assume. We developed strategies to teach the mother how to structure her home in a child-friendly manner, how to spend time playing with her son, and how to encourage his compliance by starting with simple requests and using the positive rewards of praise, attention, and activities he enjoyed.

Khorkova Olga (aka Mamontenok)/Shutterstock.com

Observing behavior directly assists in obtaining an accurate picture of the child's behavior under certain circumstances

Source: Based on authors' case material.

groups other than those with whom the tests were normed. It has also been argued that many standardized tests, particularly intelligence and achievement tests, are culturally biased, unfairly penalizing those children whose family, SES, and cultural background are different from those of Euro-American middle-class children. These and other valid criticisms have led to improved tests. For example, test developers now select normative groups that are representative of the population, and test items that are as free of cultural bias as possible. In addition, several professional organizations have joined together to develop a Code of Fair Testing Practices, which presents guidelines for professionals for "fulfilling their obligation to provide and use tests that are fair to all test takers regardless of age, gender, disability, race, ethnicity, national origin, religion, sexual orientation, linguistic background, or other personal characteristics" (Joint Committee on Testing Practices, 2004, p. 2). As a result of these efforts, clinicians have become increasingly sensitive to cultural factors in test administration and interpretation (Sattler, 2008).

Clinicians commonly use developmental scales, intelligence and educational tests, projective tests, personality tests, and neuropsychological tests to assess children's disorders of development, learning, and behavior (Sattler & Hoge, 2006). In fact, tests (particularly intelligence tests) are among the most frequently used assessment methods with children (Cashel, 2002). Remember, however, that test scores should always be interpreted in the context of other assessment information. Often, observations of a child's behavior during the test situation can tell us as much or more about the child as his or her test scores.

Developmental Testing

Developmental tests are used to assess infants and young children, and are generally carried out for the purposes of screening, diagnosis, and evaluation of early development. **Screening** refers to the identification of children at risk, who are then referred for a more thorough evaluation. The assessment of infants and young children at risk for developing later problems has increased in frequency as new laws and policies direct public attention and action to the importance of early identification for developing effective strategies for early intervention and prevention (DelCarmen-Wiggins & Carter, 2004; Essex et al., 2009). As we discuss in Chapter 10, much current emphasis is being placed on early screening of children for autism as a key to early intervention. Because screening tests are brief, a more thorough assessment of a young child's development is also needed.

Intelligence Testing

Evaluating a child's intellectual and educational functioning is a key ingredient in clinical assessments for a wide range of childhood disorders (Sattler, 2008). For some children, impairments in thinking and learning may result from their behavioral or emotional problems. The drop in Felicia's grades from Bs to Cs and Ds was likely a function of the impact of her school refusal and depression on her school performance. For other children, particularly those with intellectual disabilities or learning and language disorders, problems in thinking and learning may be part of the disorder itself.

In many other cases, the nature of the relationship between the child's disorder and disturbances in thinking and learning is less clear. For example, children with ADHD score lower on standard tests of intelligence and do more poorly in school than other children. Is this lowered performance related to their inattentiveness in the test situation or classroom, or to some other more basic deficit in how they process information? Intellectual and educational assessments can help answer some of these questions.

How would you define intelligence? Most people think intelligence involves problem-solving ability, verbal ability, and social intelligence. David Wechsler, whose test has come to be the one most frequently used to assess intelligence in children, defined intelligence as "the overall capacity of an individual to understand and cope with the world around him" (Wechsler, 1974, p. 5). This definition is consistent with theories on which commonly used intelligence tests are based. Although debate remains about how "intelligence" should be defined, intelligence tests are used clinically primarily for answering practical questions, such as identifying children who may have difficulty succeeding in a regular classroom, and planning interventions.

Numerous tests for assessing intelligence in children exist, each with its own strengths and weaknesses. The most popular intelligence scale used with children today is the Wechsler Intelligence Scale for Children (WISC-IV) (Wechsler, 2003). It is the most recent version of a test that was introduced over 50 years ago. The WISC-IV is made up of 10 mandatory and 5 supplementary subtests that span the age range of 6 to 16 years. According to Wechsler, these subtests assess the child's global capacity in different ways, but do not represent different types of intelligence. Relative to earlier versions, the WISC-IV places greater emphasis on fluid reasoning abilities, higher-order reasoning, and information processing speed, and less emphasis on possible externally or culturally influenced factors such as arithmetic knowledge (Prifitera, Saklofske, & Weiss, 2005). Other tests assess intelligence in younger children, including the Wechsler Preschool and Primary Scale of Intelligence—III (WPPSI-R) (Wechsler, 2002), Stanford-Binet-5 (SB5) (Roid, 2003), and the Kaufman Assessment Battery for Children (K-ABC-II) (Kaufman & Kaufman, 2004).

Examples of questions and items included on each WISC-IV subtest are shown in Box 4.2. The WISC-IV is individually administered to the child by a highly trained examiner who follows prescribed procedures. The test produces a Full Scale IQ, derived from four indices: Verbal Comprehension Index, Perceptual Reasoning Index, Working Memory Index, and Processing Speed Index. The profile of these four abilities represents key indicators of the cognitive strengths and weaknesses considered important to the assessment of learning disabilities, executive functions, attention disorders, traumatic brain injuries, intellectual disability, lead poisoning, giftedness, and various other medical and neurological concerns (Prifitera et al., 2005). Nevertheless, the best evidence indicates that the overall general intelligence score should be favored over the individual indices when interpreting

BOX 4.2 A CLOSER LOOK

Items Similar to Those Included in WISC-IV

I. Verbal Comprehension Index

Similarities (23 items)

In what way are a pencil and a piece of chalk alike?
In what way are tea and coffee alike?
In what way are an inch and a mile alike?
In what way are binoculars and a microscope alike?

Vocabulary (36 items)

What is a ball?
What does *running* mean?
What is a poem?
What does *obstreperous* mean?

Comprehension (21 items)

Why do we wear shoes?
What is the thing to do if you see someone dropping a package?
In what two ways is a lamp better than a candle?
In the United States, why are we tried by a jury of our peers?

Information (33 items)

How many legs do you have?
What must you do to make water freeze?
Who developed the theory of relativity?
What is the capital of France?

Word Reasoning (24 items)

The task is to identify the common concept being described with a series of clues.
Clue 1: This has a motor . . .
Clue 2: . . . and it is used to cut grass.

II. Perceptual Reasoning Index

Block Design (14 items)

The task is to reproduce stimulus designs using four or nine blocks (see below).

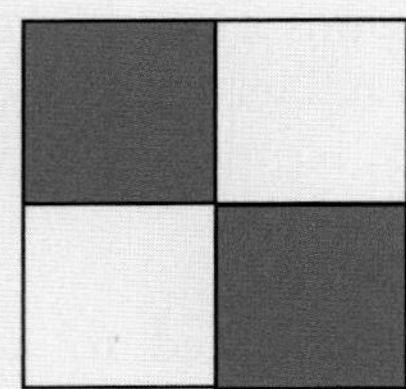

Picture Concepts (28 items)

The task is to choose one picture from each of two or three rows of pictures in such a way that all the pictures selected have a characteristic in common (see below).

Matrix Reasoning (35 items)

The task is to examine an incomplete matrix and select whichever of the five choices best completes the matrix (see below).

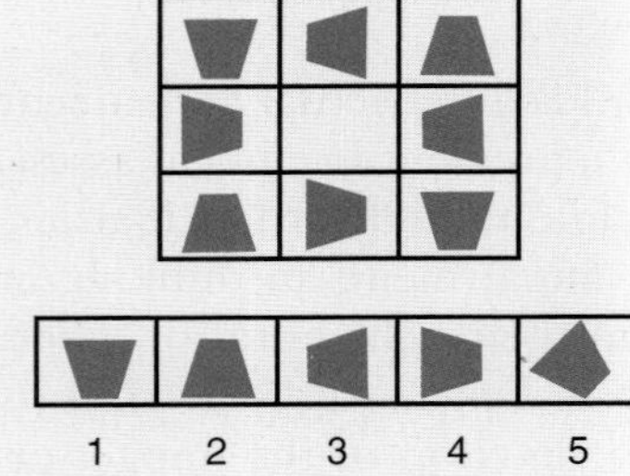

Picture Completion (38 items)

The task is to look at a picture—such as that of a car without a wheel, a scissors without a handle, or a telephone without numbers on the buttons—and identify the essential missing part (see below).

BOX 4.2 A CLOSER LOOK

III. Working Memory Index

Digit Span (16 items; 8 in Digit Span Forward, 8 in Digit Span Backward)

In one part, the task is to repeat in a forward direction a string of from 2 to 9 digits presented by the examiner (example: 1–8). In the other part, it is to repeat in a backward direction a string of from 2 to 8 digits (example: 6–4–9).

Letter–Number Sequencing (10 items, each with 3 trials)

The task is to listen to a string of from 2 to 8 letters and digits (example: 1–b) and repeat it back with the numbers in ascending order followed by the letters in alphabetical order (example: e–6–d–9 would be repeated back as 6–9–d–e).

Arithmetic (34 items)

If I have one piece of candy and get another one, how many pieces will I have?
At 12 cents each, how much will 4 bars of soap cost?
If suits sell for 1/2 of the regular price, what is the cost of a $120 suit?

IV. Processing Speed Index

Coding (59 items in Coding A and 119 items in Coding B)

The task is to copy symbols from a key (see below).

1	2	3	4	5	6
x	o	=	L	/	V

2	4	1	5	6	3	5	2	1	6	4	3

Symbol Search (45 items in Part A and 60 items in Part B)

The task is to decide whether a stimulus figure (a symbol) appears in an array (see below).

⌂	◊	☼	□	◊	±	Δ	=	¤		YES	NO
☼	±	◊	Δ	±	□	=	¤	⌂		YES	NO
=	¤	Δ	⌂	☼	□	±	x	◊		YES	NO

Cancellation (2 items, one Random and one Sequenced)

The task is to scan both a random arrangement and a sequenced arrangement of pictures and mark target pictures (animals) within a specified time limit (see below).

Note. The items resemble those that appear on the WISC–IV but are not actually from the test.

Adapted from Sattler, J. M., Assessment of Children: WISC-IV and WPPSI-III Supplement, Exhibit 9–1 in Assessment of Children: Cognitive Foundations, Sixth Edition, 2008 (pp. 268–269). Copyright 2008 by Jerome M. Sattler Publisher, Inc.

the WISC-IV (Watkins, 2010). True to tradition, IQ scores on the WISC-IV are good predictors of academic achievement.

Felicia obtained a Verbal Comprehension IQ score of 107, a Perceptual Reasoning Index score of 105, a Working Memory Index score of 104, a Processing Speed Index score of 105, and a Full Scale IQ score of 106 on the WISC-IV, which means that her intelligence is in the average range. With this information, the clinician next considers how her test scores relate to each other, and if there is a pattern to the results that might clarify her relative strengths and weaknesses. He or she must also consider any circumstances in the testing situation that might have affected Felicia's performance—anxiety, personality factors, motivation, or medication—and how her scores compare with those of other girls of comparable age, grade, ethnic group, or disability. Finally, and most important, the clinician must consider how the test scores will be used in treatment and educational planning.

Projective Testing

Projective tests present the child with ambiguous stimuli such as inkblots or pictures of people, and the child is then asked to describe what she or he sees. The hypothesis is that the child will "project" his or her own personality—unconscious fears, needs, and inner conflicts—on the ambiguous stimuli of other people and things. Without being aware, the child discloses his or her unconscious thoughts and feelings to the clinician, thus revealing information that would not be shared in response to direct questioning (Leichtman, 2004). Many "junior-sized" versions of projective tests have been developed for younger children, in which the ambiguous stimuli have been made child-friendly by incorporating family scenes or pictures of animals (Levitt & French, 1992).

Projective testing has generated more controversy over the past 50 years than any other clinical assessment method. Most clinicians have strong views about projective testing, either pro or con. You may very well have your own strong opinions about the Rorschach inkblot and similar methods. Some clinicians believe that projective tests provide a rich source of information about the child's coping styles, affect, self-concept, interpersonal functioning, and ways of processing information (Verma, 2000). Other clinicians see them as inadequate with respect to meeting minimum standards for reliability and validity (Lilienfeld, Wood, & Garb, 2006; Wood, Lilienfeld, Garb, & Nezworski, 2000).

Despite the controversy surrounding their use, projective tests continue to be one of the most frequently used clinical assessment methods (Cashel, 2002). Representative of the many projective techniques used with children and adolescents are human figure drawings, the Rorschach inkblot test, and thematic picture tests in which children are asked to tell a story in response to pictures of children in everyday situations with their families, peers, or alone. Clinicians may also attempt to assess the child's inner life through play—for example, through the use of puppets, storytelling, or other material (Chethik, 2000). Although they are not formal projective tests, play and drawings are presumed by some clinicians to function in much the same way as projectives—as a window into the child's unconscious processes.

Personality Testing

Personality is usually considered an enduring trait or pattern of traits that characterize the individual and determine how he or she interacts with the environment (Roberts & DelVecchio, 2000). For example, children who withdraw from social contact may be characterized by their parents as shy; others who are socially busy are characterized as outgoing. In a sense, a child's early temperament (discussed in Chapter 2) provides a foundation on which personality is built. Several dimensions of personality have been identified, including whether a child or adolescent is timid or bold, agreeable or disagreeable, dependable or undependable, tense or relaxed, reflective or unreflective (Shiner, 2007). These central dimensions of personality have been dubbed the "Big 5" factors (Mervielde & Fruyt, 2002). Many of the methods already discussed, such as interviews, projective techniques, and behavioral measures, provide some information about the child's personality. However, many objective inventories focus specifically on personality, using either the child or a parent as informants. Two of the more frequently used personality inventories with children are the Minnesota Multiphasic Personality Inventory—Adolescent (MMPI-A) (Butcher et al., 2006) and the Personality Inventory for Children, Second Edition (PIC-2) (Lachar, 1999). Examples of the content that may be included in personality inventories are shown in Table 4.4.

"You must be Mary's parents. I recognized you from her drawings!"

Neuropsychological Assessment

Put simply, neuropsychology is the study of brain–behavior relations (Pennington, 2009). In the clinical context, **neuropsychological assessment** attempts to link brain functioning with objective measures of behavior known to depend on an intact central nervous system. For example, try closing your eyes and then

TABLE 4.4 | Self-Report of Personality Scale Definitions

Construct	Definition
Anxiety	Feelings of nervousness, worry, and fear; the tendency to be overwhelmed by problems
Attitude to school	Feelings of alienation, hostility, and dissatisfaction regarding school
Attitude to teachers	Feelings of resentment and dislike of teachers; the belief that teachers are unfair, uncaring, or overly demanding
Atypicality	The tendency toward bizarre thoughts, or other thoughts and behaviors considered odd
Depression	Feelings of unhappiness, sadness, and dejection; a belief that nothing goes right
Interpersonal relations	The perception of having good social relationships and friendships with peers
Locus of control	The belief that rewards and punishments are controlled by external events or people
Relations with parents	A positive regard towards parents and a feeling of being esteemed by them
Self-esteem	Feelings of self-esteem, self-respect, and self-acceptance

Source: Behavior Assessment System for Children, Second Edition (BASC-2).

touching the tip of your nose with your ring finger, first with your right hand and then with your left. How do you think you would do on this task if you were sleep-deprived? Even a simple task like this one depends on many psychological functions and an intact nervous system. For children with certain brain injuries or dysfunctions, carrying out this or other tasks may prove difficult.

The premise underlying neuropsychological assessments is that behavioral measures can be used to make inferences about central nervous system dysfunction and, more important, the consequences of this dysfunction for the child. Neuropsychological assessments use this information clinically for determining a diagnosis, planning treatment, documenting the course of recovery, measuring subtle but significant improvements, and following up on children with neurological impairments or learning disorders (Farmer & Muhlenbruck, 2000).

Neuropsychological assessments frequently consist of comprehensive batteries that assess a full range of psychological functions: verbal and nonverbal *cognitive functions* such as language, abstract reasoning, and problem solving; *perceptual functions* including visual, auditory, and tactile–kinesthetic; *motor functions* relating to strength, speed of performance, coordination, and dexterity; and *emotional/executive control* functions such as attention, concentration, frustration tolerance, and emotional functioning.

Although neuropsychological assessments were originally used to identify an underlying brain injury or process, this is no longer their primary purpose. The routine use of neuroimaging procedures (Chapter 3), combined with mixed or inconsistent neuropsychological findings, has led the focus away from diagnosis toward obtaining information about strengths and deficits in functioning. This information can lead to effective intervention for children with a wide range of neurodevelopmental and learning problems (Riccio, Sullivan, & Cohen, 2010).

SECTION SUMMARY

Assessing Disorders

- Clinical assessment relies on a multimethod assessment approach, which emphasizes obtaining information from different informants in a variety of settings, using a variety of methods.
- The clinical interview continues to be the most universally used assessment procedure with parents and children.
- In unstructured interviews, interviewers use their preferred style and format to pursue various questions in an informal and flexible manner. In contrast, semistructured interviews include specific questions designed to elicit information in a relatively consistent manner regardless of who is doing the interview.
- Behavioral assessment evaluates the child's thoughts, feelings, and behaviors in specific settings and uses this information to formulate hypotheses about the nature of the problem and what can be done about it.
- Reports concerning child behavior and adjustment can be obtained using global checklists and problem-focused rating scales. An individual child's scores can be compared with a known reference group of children of similar age and the same gender.
- Tests are tasks given under standard conditions with the purpose of assessing some aspect of the child's knowledge, skill, or personality.
- Evaluating a child's intellectual functioning is a key ingredient in clinical assessments for a wide range of childhood disorders.
- Projective tests present children with ambiguous stimuli to assess their inner thoughts and feelings that reflect aspects of their personality.
- Objective personality tests assess whether a child is timid or bold, agreeable or disagreeable, dependable or undependable, tense or relaxed, reflective or unreflective.
- Neuropsychological assessment attempts to link brain functioning with objective measures of behavior that are known to depend on central nervous system functioning.

Classification and Diagnosis

Over the past two decades, major changes have occurred in the classification of childhood disorders (Mash & Hunsley, 2007). By **classification**, we mean a system for representing the major categories or dimensions of child psychopathology, and the boundaries and relations among them. As you may recall, one definition of diagnosis refers to the assignment of cases to categories of a classification system.

We begin our discussion of this important topic by considering some of the reasons for classification and diagnosis with children and adolescents, and we will go into some detail about current approaches. Because diagnosis is not without criticism, we also raise awareness of the impact of labeling children. Until now, we have looked at Felicia's problems on a very individual basis. We looked at her depression, school refusal, and social skills deficits, and assessed her general intellectual functioning and behavior. This information tells us what is unique about Felicia and how she differs from others her age. Isn't this enough, you might ask? Why do we need to pigeonhole Felicia by tagging her with a diagnostic label such as "major depressive disorder"? Can't we just find a way to help her with her problems based on what we have learned about her unique characteristics?

The limitation of this approach is that if we treated every child as unique, research into the causes and treatment of childhood disorders would be impossible to conduct, and we would have little direction in how to proceed in treating an individual case (Waldman & Lilienfeld, 1995). For this reason, we also need to consider what Felicia has in common with others who present with similar problems or symptoms, and whether there are general principles that apply to many children. In effect, we do this throughout this text, as we learn about the core symptoms of child and adolescent disorders, their prevalence and course, their prognosis, and their treatment. Without such information to use for comparison, making the best decisions concerning Felicia's problem and course of action would be difficult.

As you may recall from our earlier discussion, clinical assessment and diagnosis involve two related strategies for determining the best plan for a given individual. We use an *idiographic* strategy to highlight a child's unique circumstances, personality, cultural background, and other features that pertain to his or her particular situation. Each child who comes in for an assessment has unique strengths and challenges that make his or her problem a little different from the "textbook" case.

In addition, we use a *nomothetic* strategy as part of our assessment in order to benefit from all the information accumulated on a given problem or disorder and to determine the general category of problems to which the presenting problem belongs. That is, we attempt to name or classify the problem using an existing system of diagnosis, such as DSM-IV-TR (APA, 2000). Classifying the problem leads to a foundation of knowledge from which we can draw upon to understand the child and family; helps us to communicate with others; and helps us to select an intervention, preferably one shown by research to be effective for children with similar difficulties.

Although most of us recognize the advantages of classification for medical and psychological problems, developing a classification system that is simple and concise enough to be of practical benefit is not an easy task (Taylor, 2011). In fact, despite years of effort, there is no single, agreed-upon, reliable, and valid worldwide classification system for childhood disorders. DSM-IV-TR has become the standard in North America, but—although it has been used with children across a wide age range—concerns continue to be raised about its limited coverage of childhood disorders and insensitivity to the developmental complexities that characterize these problems (e.g., changes in symptom expression with age), particularly for very young children (Egger & Emde, 2011; Pine et al., 2011).

Categories and Dimensions

The first approach to diagnosing child psychopathology involves the use of categorical classification systems. **Categorical classification** systems are based primarily on informed professional consensus, an approach that has dominated and continues to dominate the field of child (and adult) psychopathology (APA, 2000). A *classical* (or pure) categorical approach assumes that every diagnosis has a clear underlying cause such as an infection or a malfunction of the nervous system, and that each disorder is fundamentally different from other disorders. Therefore, individual cases can be placed into distinctive categories.

We might say, for example, that Felicia meets the criteria for a major depressive disorder but not for separation anxiety disorder. The disadvantage to this approach, of course, is that children's behavior seldom falls neatly into established categories, so a certain degree of confusion remains. Moreover, categories of behavior (as opposed to some medical diseases) do not typically share the same underlying causes; thus, the mental health field has had to modify the classical categorical approach to accommodate the current state of knowledge. Children given the same diagnosis don't necessarily share the same etiology, nor do they respond to the same treatment. It is therefore crucial to understand that current diagnostic categories represent only our current knowledge about how symptoms cluster together.

The second approach to describing abnormal child behavior involves empirically based dimensional classification. **Dimensional classification** approaches assume that many independent dimensions or traits of behavior exist, and that all children possess them to varying degrees. For example, rather than saying that Felicia's symptoms fit the category of major depressive disorder, we might say that she is significantly above average (often referred to as being within the *clinical range*) on the dimensions of depression and anxiety. These and other traits or dimensions are typically derived using statistical methods from samples drawn from both clinically referred and nonreferred child populations to establish ranges along each dimension (Achenbach & Rescorla, 2001).

Although dimensional approaches based on statistical data are more objective and potentially more reliable than clinically derived categorical systems, they too have limitations. First and foremost, the derived dimensions are dependent on sampling, method, and informant characteristics, as well as the age and sex of the child (Mash & Hunsley, 2007). Consequently, integrating information obtained from different methods and various informants, over time or across situations, can be challenging. Dimensional approaches may also be insensitive to contextual influences. For example, suppose you were a parent and were asked to describe whether your child "acts too young" using the scale "never, sometimes, a lot." You might want to clarify the circumstances or context under which she sometimes acts too young ("whenever I take her grocery shopping" or "when she is playing with other children"). Dimensions provide a useful estimate of the degree to which a child displays certain traits and not others, yet they often have to be tailored to the child's unique circumstances and developmental opportunities.

Many dimensions of child psychopathology have been identified through research. These include the *externalizing behavior* and *internalizing behavior* dimensions, which reflect aggressive/rule-breaking behaviors and anxious/withdrawn/depressed behaviors, respectively. Some of the most common dimensions identified in children and adolescents are presented in Table 4.5, along with examples of specific associated problem behaviors.

Although the debate has not been resolved as to which approach is "best," there is a growing consensus that each approach has value in classifying childhood disorders, and that a combined approach may be needed (Pickles & Angold, 2003). Some

TABLE 4.5 | Commonly Identified Dimensions of Child Psychopathology and Examples of Items That Reflect Each Dimension

Anxious/ Depressed	**Withdrawn/ Depressed**	**Social Problems**
Cries a lot Worries Feels worthless Nervous, tense	Would rather be alone Refuses to talk Secretive Shy, timid	Too dependent Doesn't get along with peers Gets teased Not liked
Somatic Complaints	**Thought Problems**	**Aggressive Behavior**
Feels dizzy Overtired Aches, pains Headaches	Hears things Sees things Strange behavior Strange ideas	Argues Mean to others Attacks people Destroys others' things
Attention Problems	**Rule-Breaking Behavior**	
Inattentive Can't concentrate Can't sit still Confused	Lacks guilt Bad companions Lies Runs away from home	

Source: Achenbach, T. M. & Rescorla, L. A. (2001). Manual for the ASEBA School-Age Forms and Profiles. (Burlington, VT: University of Vermont, Research Center for Children, Youth, and Families, 2001. Reprinted with permission.

severe forms of intellectual disability may be best conceptualized as qualitatively distinct conditions (categories), whereas most other childhood disorders, such as depression or anxiety, may be best described as extreme points on one or more continuous dimensions.

Also, depending on whether the purpose is clinical diagnosis or research, one approach may be more useful than the other. A dimensional approach to conceptualizing psychological factors such as behavior, affect, and cognitive abilities among children is compatible with research methods that determine the degree of association between two or more variables. Therefore, a dimensional approach is often preferred by those conducting psychological research. A categorical approach, on the other hand, is often more compatible with clinical purposes, where the objective is to incorporate the whole pattern of the child's behavior into a meaningful diagnosis and treatment plan. In addition, categories are useful for communicating among clinicians (Mead, Hohenshil, & Singh, 1997), and categorical diagnoses are often required for clinical decisions—for example, to determine a child's eligibility for specialized services. In light of the different types of information provided by dimensions and categories, it is important to incorporate dimensions into current diagnostic practices, while also finding feasible ways to reach categorical decisions (Rutter, 2011).

The Diagnostic and Statistical Manual (DSM)

A synopsis of the evolution of current systems is shown in Box 4.3, which provides a perspective on how far we have come in recognizing mental disorders in children and adolescents. The terminology and focus of prior systems reflected the major theoretical views of mental illness at the time; a shift to a more objective, informed approach had occurred by the 1980s.

DSM-IV-TR (the "TR" stands for "text revision") (APA, 2000) includes the same diagnostic criteria as DSM-IV (APA, 1994) and updates the text information and wording to reflect new information and findings about prevalence and associated features since the DSM-IV was originally introduced in 1994. The DSM-IV-TR is a multiaxial system consisting of five axes. A **multiaxial system** is a classification system consisting of several axes (domains) of information about the child or adolescent that may assist a clinician in planning the treatment of a disorder. In other words, the axes serve to add further context and detail to the description of an individual's particular circumstances by organizing and communicating clinical information, capturing the complexity of clinical situations, and describing the diversity of individuals with the same diagnosis. The five axes of the DSM-IV-TR are described in the following paragraphs.

Axis I is where the various *clinical disorders or conditions* are reported, except for intellectual disability and personality disorders that are reported on Axis II, because they are presumed to be stable. Axis I diagnostic categories that apply to infants, children, and adolescents are listed in Table 4.6, and will be discussed in detail in the chapters to follow. The disorders in the first section of Table 4.6 traditionally have been thought of as first occurring in childhood or as exclusive to childhood, so they require operational criteria that differ from those used to define disorders in adults.

The second section in Table 4.6 lists other major disorders that are not listed separately for children in DSM-IV-TR. Under the current DSM-IV-TR guidelines, diagnostic criteria for mood, anxiety, eating, and sleep disorders can apply to children as well as adults, with minor modifications. A child can (and often does) receive more than one Axis I diagnosis, with the principal diagnosis listed first (e.g., ADHD; anxiety disorder). You should not try to memorize all of these terms right now, but simply get a feel for the organization and coverage to follow.

BOX 4.3 A CLOSER LOOK

Classification of Childhood Disorders: The Evolution of Current Classification Systems

The slow process of formal recognition of the prevalence and significance of mental disorders began in 1948, when the sixth edition of the *World Health Organization's International Classification of Diseases* (ICD) added a section on mental disorders (APA, 1994). Because this early attempt by the ICD system to classify mental disorders was felt to be inadequate, the American Psychiatric Association developed its own *Diagnostic and Statistical Manual* (DSM-I) in 1952 (APA, 1952) and revised it in 1968 (DSM-II) (APA, 1968). These first attempts by the APA were not a huge success, but they did launch a sustained effort to improve the classification of mental disorders, an effort that continues today. Unfortunately, children and adolescents were virtually neglected in the early versions of DSM; most childhood disorders were relegated to the adult categories, with the exception of mental retardation (intellectual disability), schizophrenia–childhood type, and transient disturbances in behavior or mood.

As a formal classification system, the DSM-III (APA, 1980) was a significant advance over the earlier versions. Clinical descriptions were replaced by explicit criteria that, in turn, enhanced diagnostic reliability (Achenbach, 1985; APA, 1980). In addition, DSM-III included more child categories, adopted a multiaxial system, and placed a greater emphasis on empirical data (Achenbach, 1985). These changes reflected the beginnings of a conceptual shift in both diagnostic systems and etiological models away from an isolated focus on a disorder as existing within the child alone, toward an increased emphasis on also considering the surrounding context in which the problem occurred.

The DSM-III was revised in 1987 (DSM-III-R) to help clarify the numerous inconsistencies and ambiguities that were noted in its use. The DSM-III-R was also developed to be a *prototypical* classification system by which a child could be diagnosed with a certain subset of symptoms without having to meet all criteria. This was an important change, especially in view of the heterogeneity associated with most childhood disorders (Mash & Hunsley, 2007). On the other hand, it also means that individuals with the same diagnosis can and often do show very different patterns of symptoms. To make this point stick, consider that there were nearly 150 million different ways for an individual to meet the DSM-III-R criteria for an antisocial personality disorder (Widiger, 1993).

Source: Based on authors' case material.

TABLE 4.6 | Categories That Apply to Children

DSM-IV-TR

(1) Disorders Usually First Diagnosed in Infancy, Childhood, or Adolescence

Mental Retardation [*Intellectual Disability*] (mild, moderate, severe, profound)

Learning Disorders (in reading, mathematics, and written expression)

Communication Disorders (expressive, mixed receptive–expressive, phonological, and stuttering)

Pervasive Developmental Disorders (autistic disorder, Asperger's disorder, Rett's Disorder, Childhood Disintegrative Disorder)

Attention Deficit and Disruptive Behavior Disorders (attention-deficit/hyperactivity disorder, conduct disorder, oppositional defiant disorder)

Feeding and Eating Disorders of Infancy or Early Childhood (pica, rumination, feeding disorder of infancy or early childhood)

Elimination Disorders (encopresis, enuresis)

Other Disorders of Infancy, Childhood, or Adolescence (separation anxiety, selective mutism, reactive attachment disorder of infancy or early childhood, stereotypic movement disorder)

(2) Selected Categories for Disorders of Childhood or Adolescence That Are Not Listed Separately for Children in DSM-IV-TR

Mood Disorders (depressive disorders, bipolar disorders)

Anxiety Disorders (specific phobia, social phobia, obsessive–compulsive disorder, post-traumatic stress disorder, acute stress disorder, generalized anxiety disorder, anxiety disorder due to a general medical condition)

Eating Disorders (anorexia nervosa, bulimia nervosa)

Sleep Disorders (dyssomnias, parasomnias)

Source: Reprinted with permission from the Diagnostic and Statistical Manual of Mental Disorders, Fourth Edition, Text Revision, (Copyright ©2000). American Psychiatric Association.

Axis II is used to report *personality disorders and intellectual disability*. The purpose for using a separate axis for these two disorders is to ensure they are given consideration, especially when a more visible or acute Axis I disorder is present. Axis II is often used for diagnosing children with intellectual disability. However, personality disorders are rarely diagnosed until late adolescence or early adulthood, by which time it is evident that the person's pattern of behavior or inner experience is enduring and problematic (Shiner, 2007). However, it is now recognized that although personality and behavior patterns may be less stable in children than adults, this is a matter of degree. As a result, increased attention is being given to personality traits and disorders in younger individuals (Cohen, 2008). Personality disorders include: antisocial, borderline, histrionic, paranoid, schizoid, schizotypal, narcissistic, avoidant, dependent, and obsessive–compulsive.

As described in the DSM-IV-TR (APA, 2000), personality disorders share a common set of criteria:

- An enduring pattern of inner experience and behavior that deviates noticeably from the expectations of the individual's culture. For example, one individual may show very different ways of thinking, feeling, and behaving compared to others in his or her culture.
- This enduring pattern of unusual thinking, feeling, or behaving is inflexible, and pervasive across a wide range of situations, and results in clinically significant distress or impairment in functioning.

In addition to the general diagnostic criteria noted above, the DSM-IV-TR stipulates that additional diagnostic considerations should be used in describing personality disorders among children and adolescents:

- Personality Disorder categories may be applied to children or adolescents in those relatively unusual instances when the individual's particular maladaptive personality traits appear to be pervasive, persistent, and unlikely to be limited to a particular developmental stage or an episode of an Axis I disorder (APA, 2000, p. 687).
- To diagnose a personality disorder in an individual under age 18, the features must have been present for at least 1 year (APA, 2000, p. 687). The one exception to this is Antisocial Personality Disorder, which cannot be diagnosed in individuals under the age of 18 years.

Remember, some personality traits that may be regarded as pathological during adulthood are considered relatively normal during adolescence (such as mood swings and impulsivity!). For this reason, the diagnostic criteria emphasize that a personality trait must *deviate markedly* from cultural expectations to be considered symptomatic of a personality disorder.

Axis III is used to report current *general medical conditions* that may be relevant to the understanding or management of the individual's mental disorder. Because the DSM-IV-TR assumes that mental disorders are closely related to physical and biological factors, the purpose of distinguishing general medical conditions is to encourage thoroughness in evaluation and to enhance communication among health care providers.

General medical conditions can be related to mental disorders in a variety of ways. In some cases, the medical condition may play a direct causal role in the development of behavioral or psychological problems, such as a disruption in sleep due to depression. Most commonly with children, however, an Axis I disorder, such as anxiety, may be a psychological reaction to a medical condition, such as being diagnosed with childhood cancer or diabetes. Clearly, it is important to document the co-occurrence and temporal order of problems to gain an overall understanding and to develop an appropriate treatment plan for an individual.

Axis IV describes any *psychosocial and environmental problems* that may affect the diagnosis, treatment, and prognosis of disorders listed on Axes I and II. Such problems include negative life events, environmental disruptions or deficiencies, family or other interpersonal stress, and lack of social support or personal resources (APA, 2000). Typically, clinicians note only those problems that have been present over the past year unless prior events—for example, an automobile accident—have likely contributed to the mental disorder. Contextual factors, such as child abuse or parental unemployment, are potentially important for understanding an individual's behavior and emotions. We remind you of this important consideration throughout our discussion of various disorders of childhood and adolescence because a child's presenting problem is often better understood if we can see the whole picture.

Finally, Axis V is used to report the clinician's ratings of the individual's *overall level of functioning*, primarily for planning treatment and monitoring its impact. A Global Assessment of Functioning (GAF) rating scale, ranging from 1 to 100, provides a hypothetical continuum of mental health and mental illness with respect to psychological, social, and occupational functioning. A low score indicates greater impairment in social functioning or personal care, whereas a higher score reflects mild or transient symptoms or the absence of symptoms.

Based on our clinical assessment, Felicia was given the following DSM-IV-TR diagnosis and multiaxial evaluation:

Axis I	Major depressive disorder, single episode
Axis II	No diagnosis
Axis III	None
Axis IV	Death of a family member; disruption of family by separation; academic problems
Axis V	GAF 60 (this score indicates moderate symptoms and moderate difficulties in social and school functioning as the highest level of functioning in the past year)

A diagnosis of Major Depressive Disorder (MDD), which is discussed in Chapter 8, was made because Felicia showed symptoms of depressed mood, loss of interest in almost all activities, significant weight loss, insomnia nearly every night, and feelings of worthlessness that persisted for more than 2 weeks and represented a change from her previous functioning. These symptoms were causing significant distress and impairment in Felicia's social and school functioning. Although the loss of her grandfather may have been a factor in Felicia's depression, it did not seem to be the major factor accounting for her symptoms.

Criticisms of DSM-IV-TR

Although DSM-IV-TR includes numerous improvements over previous versions because of its greater emphasis on empirical research and more explicit diagnostic criteria sets, it is not faultless. Because DSM-IV-TR focuses on descriptions of symptoms as the basis for generating categories, it has been criticized for failing to capture the complex adaptations, transactions, and setting influences that we have identified as crucial to understanding and treating psychopathology in children (Mash & Hunsley, 2007). DSM-IV-TR also gives relatively less attention to disorders of infancy and childhood than adulthood, and fails to capture the interrelationships and overlap known to exist among many childhood disorders.

A further difficulty with DSM-IV-TR diagnostic criteria for children is the relative lack of emphasis on the situational and contextual factors surrounding and contributing to various disorders in making a clinical diagnosis (Beauchaine, 2003). This reflects the fact that DSM-IV-TR views mental disorder as individual psychopathology or risk for psychopathology, rather than in terms of problems in psychosocial adjustment or adaptation. However, DSM-IV-TR does consider factors such as culture, age, and gender that are associated with the expression of each disorder, and it has increased its recognition of the importance of family problems and extrafamilial relational difficulties. In all likelihood, this awareness of the context for childhood disorders will increase in sophistication and depth with future revisions of the DSM.

A final criticism deals with how DSM-IV-TR is used rather than with the classification system itself. In some cases, DSM-IV-TR categorical diagnoses can be an impediment to gaining proper services to address children's needs. For example, to qualify for a special education class, a child may be required to meet specific diagnostic criteria for a learning disorder. In the "typical" case such requirements are usually met. However, some children may not have developed problems to the degree that they meet specific diagnostic criteria or their problems may relate to more than one DSM category. These children may not qualify for services that otherwise could prove beneficial. In this context, it would be difficult to access programs to *prevent* future problems from developing in at-risk children.

As we write this book, plans are actively underway for DSM-5, currently scheduled for publication in 2013.

In light of the limitations we have raised regarding DSM-IV, there are many issues to be addressed and choices that will need to be made in DSM-5 in relation to disorders of childhood and adolescence (Regier, Narrow, Kuhl, & Kupfer, 2011). We preview a number of these for specific disorders in the chapters that follow. The American Psychiatric Association has created a website to keep students, the public, and professionals informed about the plans for DSM-5 and to serve as a vehicle for feedback and suggestions. Check out www.dsm5.org for the most recent developments.

Pros and Cons of Diagnostic Labels

What's the use of their having names, the gnat said, "if they won't answer to them?" No use said Alice, "but it's useful to the people that name them, I suppose. If not, why do things have names at all?"

—Lewis Carroll, 1871

Despite every attempt to the contrary, the history of classification of mental disorders has been fraught with disparaging and negative connotations that become attached to the labels used to describe these disorders (Hinshaw & Stier, 2008). The terms "moron," "imbecile," and "idiot," for instance, were originally chosen in the early 1900s as neutral terms to describe lower levels of intellectual functioning, but quickly became an insult when they began to be used in common language. As a result, they gave way to terms such as "mental deficiency," and then "mental retardation," which has now given way to the term "intellectual disability" for much the same reason. Stigma, it would seem, rapidly catches up with changes in terminology.

Much has been written about the positive and negative aspects of assigning diagnostic labels to children. On the positive side, labels help clinicians summarize and order observations. This can facilitate communication among professionals and sometimes aid parents by providing more recognition and understanding of their child's problem. A label that implies that the child's disorder is outside the control of the family or child may also be welcomed. Moreover, descriptive labels are consistent with the natural tendency to think in terms of categories. That is, we tend to talk about ourselves, our friends, and our children as being happy, angry, depressed, or fearful, rather than use a number on a scale that signifies a range of emotion, even if a number might give a more accurate account. Finally, the use of descriptive terms or labels assists clinicians in locating a relevant body of detailed research and clinical data, and facilitates research on the causes, epidemiology, and treatment of specific disorders.

On the negative side are criticisms as to whether current diagnostic labels are effective in achieving any of the aforementioned purposes. There are also concerns about negative effects and stigmatization associated with the assignment of labels to children (Ben-Zeev, Young, & Corrigan, 2010; Hinshaw, 2007a). Public stigma and media messages allow negative attitudes to grow around children who are labeled. Once labeled, others may perceive and react to a child differently ("he's a hyperactive boy—you'll never get him to listen"). Classmates pick up on the use of labels, especially labels associated with visible treatments such as taking medication. A note sent by a classmate to a boy with ADHD reflects this: "Jack was ill, he took his pill, let's hope it makes him sit still." Standing out and being teased by other children may worsen the problem. Equally disturbing is that labels can negatively influence children's views of themselves and their behavior. In general, the reactions of others to persons who seem different or who have been diagnosed with a mental illness reveal a tendency to generalize inappropriately from the labels (Corrigan, 2000).

SECTION SUMMARY

Classification and Diagnosis

- Classification refers to a system for representing the major categories of child psychopathology and the relations among them.
- Diagnosis refers to the assignment of cases to categories of the classification system.
- Childhood disorders have been classified using categories and dimensions.
- Categorical classification systems have been based primarily on informed professional consensus.
- Dimensional classification approaches assume that many independent dimensions or traits of behavior exist and that all children possess these to varying degrees.
- The DSM-IV-TR is a multiaxial system consisting of five axes: clinical disorders, personality disorders and intellectual disability, general medical conditions, psychosocial and environmental problems, and global assessment of functioning.
- The DSM-IV-TR has been criticized for failing to capture the complexity of child psychopathology, for giving less attention to disorders of infancy and childhood than to those of adulthood, and for its relative lack of emphasis on situational and contextual factors.

TREATMENT

I have found the best way to give advice to your children is to find out what they want and then advise them to do it.

—Harry S. Truman

Over the last two decades, effective treatment approaches for children with behavioral and emotional problems have grown tremendously in their sophistication and their breadth (Chorpita et al., 2011; Graeff-Martins et al., 2008). Interventions today are planned by combining the most effective approaches to particular problems in an ongoing developmentally sensitive manner (Mash, 2006). Behavioral reward programs, for example, may be very useful for teaching parents of a young, difficult child ways to encourage desirable behavior. Once the child is a bit older he or she may profit from cognitive–behavioral methods that address how the child thinks about social situations, such as making friends and avoiding conflicts.

A thorough clinical assessment and diagnosis constitute a critical first step in helping Felicia and other children who have psychological problems and their families. However, assessment and diagnosis are only the beginning of an ongoing helping process. We next must ask: "How can we help Felicia reduce her feelings of depression and hopelessness, eliminate her sleep disturbances and other somatic complaints, increase her school attendance and performance, and improve her social skills and relationships with other children and her parents?" This is where intervention comes into play.

How do we determine the best type of intervention for children like Felicia and for those with other problems? We will consider this question in some detail for each disorder discussed in the chapters that follow; thus, our coverage of treatment and prevention in this section is intended to provide only a brief introduction. Our discussion of interventions in later chapters addressing specific problems follows from our general conviction that the most useful treatments are based on what we know about the nature, course, associated characteristics, and potential causes of a particular childhood disorder. However, this is not enough. We also need data to show that our interventions work (Silverman & Hinshaw, 2008). Interventions that zoom in on a specific problem with clear guidelines for treatment appear to be the most effective. Thus, our chapter-by-chapter coverage of treatments will be selective, focusing primarily on interventions that are tailored to what we know about each disorder and that have evidence for their effectiveness in treating youths with this disorder.

In this section, we provide an overview of what we mean by intervention, cultural considerations in treatment, treatment goals, ethical and legal considerations, main approaches to helping children with problems and their families, and what we know about the effectiveness of interventions for children. The overall goal is to introduce you to important foundational issues associated with interventions for youths and their families.

Intervention

Better put a strong fence 'round the top of the cliff than an ambulance in the valley.

—Joseph Malins (1895)

Intervention is a broad concept that encompasses many different theories and practices directed at helping the child and family adapt more effectively to their current and future circumstances. There is no one best single approach to working with children and families—multiple problems require multiple solutions. Clinical assessment and diagnosis are usually followed by efforts to select and implement the most promising approach to intervention (Mash, 2006). Since psychological disorders typically represent failures in adaptation on the part of the child and/or his or her social environment, problem-solving strategies are part of a *spectrum* of activities for treatment, maintenance, and prevention.

● Figure 4.3 illustrates a spectrum of interventions and intervention settings for children and families. As shown, the strengths of youths, their families, communities, and cultures are nourished and maintained by effective interventions across a variety of life settings using a coordinated system of care (AACAP, 2007a). Interventions in the upper portion of the figure range from the most universal (directed at groups not having specific risks, problems, or disorders) on the left, to those that focus specifically on youths with lasting long-term conditions (e.g., autism) on the right (Weisz, Sandler, Durlak, & Anton, 2005).

Note that interventions cover a wide range of actions, from prevention to maintenance. **Prevention** efforts are directed at decreasing the chances that undesired future outcomes will occur (Ialongo et al., 2006). They are based on the premise that it is inherently better to promote health and prevent problems before they occur. **Treatment** refers to corrective actions that will permit successful adaptation by eliminating or reducing the impact of an undesired outcome that has already occurred; **maintenance** refers to efforts to increase adherence to treatment over time to prevent relapse or recurrence of a problem. Prevention, treatment, and maintenance efforts complement one another by focusing on different stages of problem development with youths identified in different ways and in different settings, including those who may never seek help. By targeting both risks *and* existing problems and disorders, the combination of prevention and treatment has enormous potential to reach a diverse range of youths and families across a wide range of settings (Weisz et al., 2005).

Interventions are best depicted as part of the ongoing decision-making approach that we have been emphasizing throughout this chapter. Our assessments should help us answer many questions that are essential for intervention. In Felicia's case, our answers to some

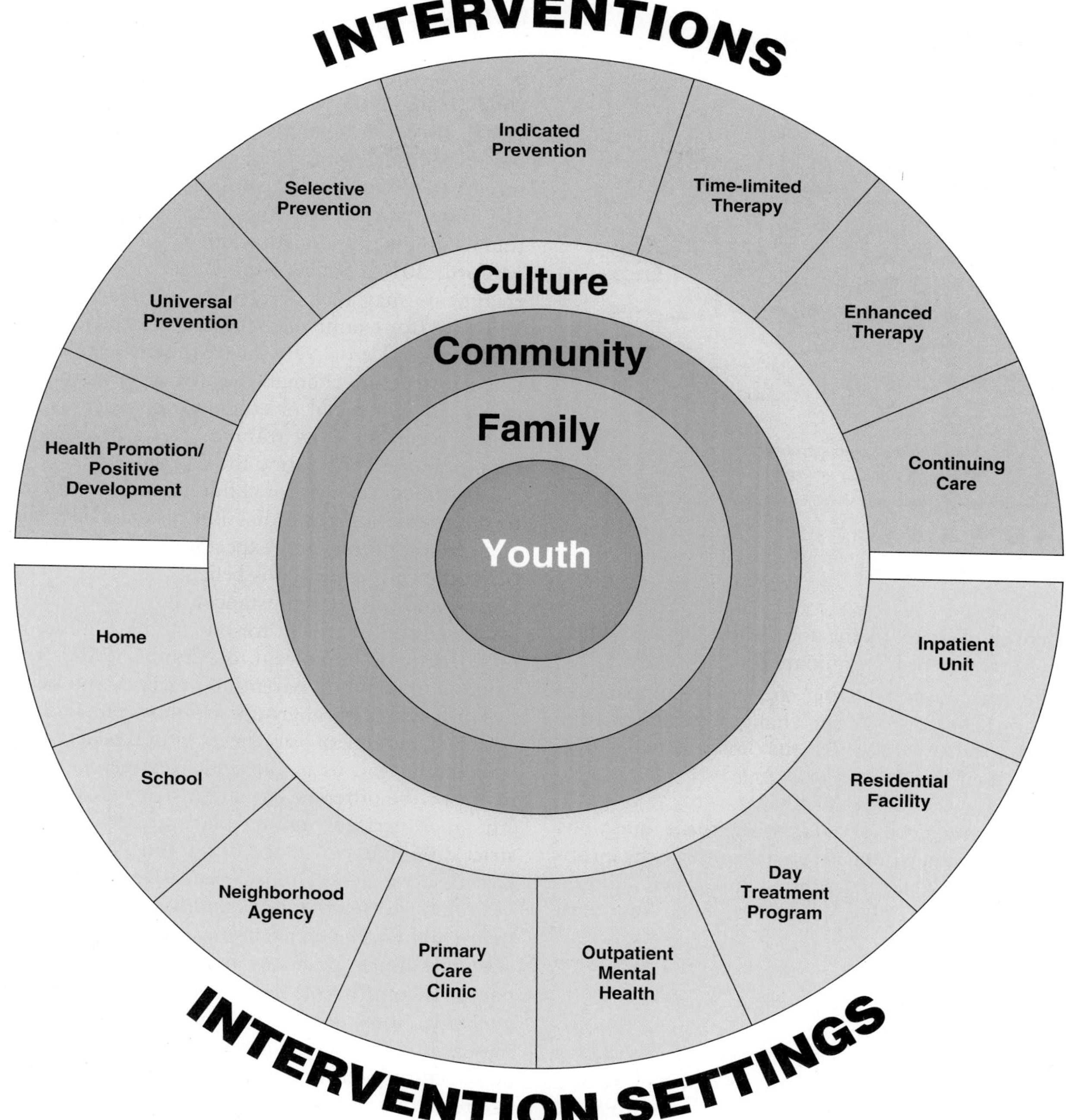

● **FIGURE 4.3** | The intervention spectrum and settings for childhood disorders.

Adapted from Weisz, J. R., Sandler, I. N., Durlak, J. A., and Anton, B. S. (2005). Promoting and protecting youth mental health through evidence-based prevention and treatment. American Psychologist, 60(6), 628–648 and From "Promoting and Protecting Youth Mental Health through Evidence-Based Prevention and Treatment", p. 633, by J. R. Weisz, I. N. Sandler, J. A. Durlak and B. S. Anton. Copyright © 2005 American Psychological Association. Reprinted by permission of the American Psychological Association. APA is not responsible for the accuracy of this translation.

of the following questions will guide us in determining which, if any, of the numerous available treatment options will be used:

- Should Felicia's difficulties be treated? If so, which ones? Depression? School refusal? Social skills deficits? Relations with family members? All of them?
- What are the projected outcomes for Felicia in the absence of treatment?
- Based on the evidence, what treatments are likely to be most effective, efficient, and cost-effective for Felicia's depression, school refusal, and social skills deficits?
- What treatments are likely to be most acceptable to Felicia and to her family?

"I like to think that each generation will need a little less therapy than the generation before."

- When should treatment for Felicia begin? When should treatment be terminated?
- Is the intervention having the desired impact on Felicia's behavior? Are the changes meaningful for Felicia and her family? Do they make a real difference in their lives?

The ultimate goal of addressing these questions should be to achieve effective solutions to the problems faced by Felicia, her family, and other children like her, and then to promote and enhance long-term adjustments.

Cultural Considerations

Most interventions for youths with problems have failed to incorporate the unique experiences of ethnic minority children and families into their treatments (Yasui & Dishion, 2007). However, as evidence-based interventions have developed, so has a growing awareness of the cultural context of children and families receiving psychological interventions (Huey & Polo, 2008; Scott et al., 2010). Parents from different ethnic groups and cultures have different parenting values and use different child-rearing practices. They also have different beliefs about child problems, how mental health services are provided, how they describe their children's problems when they seek help, and the interventions they prefer (Yasui & Dishion, 2007; Yeh et al., 2005). The **cultural compatibility hypothesis** states that treatment is likely to be more effective when compatible with the cultural patterns of the child and family. The importance of cultural sensitivity in treatment is reflected in the finding that for some problems and treatments the ethnic similarity between a child's caregiver and the therapist is associated with better treatment outcomes for the child (Halliday-Boykins, Schoenwald, & Letourneau, 2005). Recently, existing evidence-based treatments have been successfully adapted and implemented to meet the needs of specific cultural groups—as, for example, in the case of a cognitive–behavioral intervention for trauma in American Indian youth (Goodkind, LaNoue, & Milford, 2010). Such cultural adaptations of existing treatments may include changes in treatment surface structure (for example, changes in treatment materials, mode of service delivery, or treatment setting), as well as deep structure changes that focus on factors unique to a particular racial or ethnic group, such as cultural beliefs regarding how trauma affects health and cultural practices for treating these problems.

Treatment services for children must not only attend to the presenting symptoms but also consider the specific values, norms, and expectations within many cultures; the various religious beliefs and practices of each family; and other circumstances that might make what is a successful treatment for one family a failure for another (Schwoeri, Sholevar, & Combs, 2003). Cultural values and common parenting practices and beliefs for five different cultural groups are shown in Table 4.7.

Can you think of how these cultural beliefs and practices might lead us to different treatments? One issue might be the different parenting styles cross-culturally. African American families place greater emphasis on strict discipline, whereas Latino and Native American parents are generally more permissive. In helping families establish effective rules and forms of discipline for their children, the clinician must be aware of these important cultural practices and find methods that each parent is comfortable using. As we emphasized earlier, generalizations about cultural practices and beliefs may fail to capture the diversity that exists within and across cultural groups, so we must be extremely careful not to stereotype individuals of any cultural group.

Treatment Goals

What are the typical goals of treatment? Reducing symptoms (problems), producing more substantial changes that will enhance the child's long-term functioning—or both? Since both are important, treatment goals often focus on building children's skills for adapting to facilitate long-term adjustment, rather than on merely eliminating problem behaviors or briefly reducing subjective distress. Other treatment goals and outcomes are also of crucial importance to the child, family, and society (Jensen, Hoagwood, & Petti, 1996; Kazdin, 1997). These include:

TABLE 4.7 | Cultural Values and Parenting Practices and Beliefs

	African American	Latino American	Asian American	Native American	European American
Cultural Values	Communalism Individualism Kinship relations Unity Creativity Cooperation Authenticity Racial identity	Family loyalty Interpersonal connectedness Mutual respect Self-respect	Self-control Social courtesy Emotional maturity Respect for elders	Centrality of family Sharing Harmony Humility	Independence Autonomy Individualism Initiative Acquisition of skills Self-development Standing up for one's own rights
Parenting Practices and Beliefs	Authoritarian parenting No-nonsense parenting Unilateral parent decision-making Egalitarian family structure Strict discipline Communal parenting	Authoritarian parenting Patriarchal family structure High expression of parental warmth Communal parenting Freedom	Authoritarian parenting Structural and managerial parental involvement Patriarchal family structure Strict discipline Parental control Negotiation of conflict Parent as teacher	Permissive, lax parenting Shame as discipline Patriarchal and matriarchal family structures Communal parenting	Authoritative parenting More egalitarian family structure Parent as manager Demanding

Sources: Adapted from Forehand and Kotchik, 1996; and from Yasui and Dishion, 2007.

- *Outcomes Related to Child Functioning:* Reduction or elimination of symptoms, reduced degree of impairment in functioning, enhanced social competence, improved academic performance
- *Outcomes Related to Family Functioning:* Reduction in family dysfunction, improved marital and sibling relationships, reduction in stress, improvement in quality of life, reduction in burden of care, enhanced family support

Studio 1One/Shutterstock.com

Supri Suharjoto/Shutterstock.com

Cultural background is an important consideration in understanding the child's uniqueness and expectations

- *Outcomes of Societal Importance:* Improvement in the child's participation in school-related activities (increased attendance, reduced truancy, reduction in school dropout rates), decreased involvement in the juvenile justice system, reduced need for special services, reduction in accidental injuries or substance abuse, enhancement of physical and mental health

The interlocking network of physical, behavioral, social, and learning difficulties that characterizes most childhood disorders requires a multidisciplinary approach to attain these treatment and prevention goals. In many instances, children require medication or medical intervention that must be coordinated with psychosocial interventions, such as in connection with ADHD, autism, eating disorders, depression, and chronic medical conditions. Thus, the use of combined treatments is common. In addition, psychological interventions for children and adolescents often require integration with effective teaching strategies, as illustrated in later chapters on learning disorders, communication disorders, and intellectual disability. Finally, some children require the integration of community and social services that aid in their protection and basic needs, which we discuss in Chapter 14 on child abuse and neglect.

Ethical and Legal Considerations

As we have seen, many children referred for assessment and treatment experience multiple disadvantages and arguably need special help and protection. Both ethically and legally, clinicians who work with children and families are required to think about the impact that their actions will have not only on the children they see, but also on the responsibilities, rights, and relationships that connect children and parents (Dishion & Stormshak, 2007a; Prout & Prout, 2007).

The ethical codes of professional organizations, such as the American Academy of Child and Adolescent Psychiatry (1980/1995) and the American Psychological Association (2002/2010), provide minimum ethical standards for practice, including: (a) selecting treatment goals and procedures that are in the best interests of the client; (b) making sure that client participation is active and voluntary; (c) keeping records that document the effectiveness of treatment in achieving its objectives; (d) protecting the confidentiality of the therapeutic relationship; and (e) ensuring the qualifications and competencies of the therapist. There is also an increasing emphasis on involving children, depending on their developmental level, as active partners in decision making regarding their own psychological or medical treatment (McCabe, 1996).

In addition to these general ethical standards there is a growing recognition of the unique challenges and ethical dilemmas associated with mental health interventions with children and families (Belitz & Bailey, 2009). Several core ethical issues for mental health interventions with children and families versus interventions with adults are highlighted in Table 4.8. Ethical issues with children are complex because of ongoing changes in the legal status of children and a trend toward recognition of minors' constitutional rights, including self-determination and privacy (Melton, 2000). However, a more basic issue is determining when a minor is competent to make his or her own decisions, rather than only determining whether he or she has the legal right to do so. Some of the challenging issues faced by clinicians working with children include deciding when a minor can provide informed consent or refuse treatment as well as balancing the rights of the child to confidentiality against those of the parents and the integrity of the family.

In addition to these ethical and legal concerns, much larger ethical questions concern the provision

TABLE 4.8 | Core Ethical Issues in Clinical Work with Children and Families

1. Children are inherently more vulnerable than adults.
2. Children's abilities are more variable and change over time.
3. Children are more reliant upon others and upon their environment.
4. Ethical principles and practices in the treatment of adults must be modified in response to the child's current developmental abilities and legal status.
5. Boundary and role issues are often more prevalent and more complex when caring for children than for adults.
6. Adult practices, and the adult knowledge base, do not transfer reliably to the care of children.
7. Practitioners must develop skills to work with families, agencies, and systems.
8. It is key to monitor one's own actions and motivations.
9. Seeking consultation and advice is helpful in difficult situations.
10. It is essential to maintain an absolute commitment to the safety and well-being of the patient.

Source: Reprinted from Psychiatric Clinics of North America, 32, Belitz, J. & Bailey, R. A., Clinical ethics for the treatment of children and adolescents: A guide for general psychiatrists, 243–257, Copyright 2009, with permission from Elsevier.

of services for children and families. Many interventions currently used to treat children with complex problems are known to be limited in scope—for example, 1 hour per week of therapy—and cannot realistically be expected to have a meaningful or lasting impact on children experiencing severe problems. Furthermore, many currently used interventions are intrusive, expensive, and not supported by data (Kazdin, 2000). A more fundamental and thorny ethical question in some cases is whether we should provide any treatment when we know that the treatment may not make a difference or, even worse, may have harmful effects.

Clinicians who work with children and their parents need to be aware of federal, state, and local laws that affect both the assessment and treatment of children with special needs. Many of these laws apply to children with mental and physical disabilities and handicaps, and are based on the recognition that disability is a natural part of the human experience and that all citizens (children included) are entitled to equal treatment and education. Two laws that have had a profound influence on services for children with disabilities is the Education for All Handicapped Children Act (1975) and its amendment, the Individuals with Disabilities Education Improvement Act (2004). Following are two of the many purposes of these laws:

- To ensure that all children with disabilities have available to them a free, appropriate public education that emphasizes special education and related services designed to meet their unique needs and prepare them for employment and independent living.
- To ensure that the rights of children with disabilities and of the parents of such children are protected.

General Approaches to Treatment

The number and diversity of treatments for children have grown tremendously, to the point where more than 550 treatments are currently in use to help children (Kazdin, 2000)! While we will (thankfully) not attempt to cover them all, in the remainder of this chapter we provide an overview of several of the major approaches. More than 70% of practicing clinicians who work with children and families identify their approach as **eclectic**, which means that they use different approaches for children with different problems and circumstances, and that they see most of these approaches as having value. In light of this practice, the large number of treatments specified above likely represents a vast underestimate of the full range of treatments used with children. Let's now turn to a brief overview of some of the general approaches to treatment and see how they might apply to Felicia.

Psychodynamic Treatments

Psychodynamic approaches view child psychopathology as determined by underlying unconscious and conscious conflicts (Lesser, 1972). Therefore, the focus is on helping the child develop an awareness of unconscious factors that may be contributing to his or her problems (Galatzer-Levy, Bachrach, Skolnikoff, & Waldron, 2000). With younger children, this awareness can occur through play therapy (Chethik, 2000); with older children, it occurs through verbal interactions with the therapist. As underlying conflicts are revealed, the therapist helps the child resolve the conflicts and develop more adaptive ways of coping.

In Felicia's case, a therapist would help her gain insight into her problem through an intensive process of psychotherapy, perhaps lasting months or even years. The therapist might explore her earliest memories of her relationship with her parents by having her recall positive and negative memories and explore how she constructs her childhood memories and relationships. The assumption is that once she resolves the underlying problems, such as insecure attachment to her mother, Felicia's overt symptoms of depression, social withdrawal, school refusal, and physical complaints will be alleviated (Muratori, Picchi, Bruni, Patarnello, & Romagnoli, 2003).

Behavioral Treatments

Behavioral approaches assume that many abnormal child behaviors are learned. Therefore, the focus of treatment is on re-educating the child, using procedures derived from theories of learning or from research. Such procedures include positive reinforcement or time-out, modeling, and systematic desensitization (Morris & Kratochwill, 2007). Behavioral treatments often focus on changing the child's environment by working with parents and teachers.

In Felicia's case, a therapist might try to decrease her school refusal by instructing her parents to not let her stay at home when she protests, and by rewarding her for going to school with praise or a preferred activity. In addition, the therapist might use modeling, role-playing, and practice to help Felicia learn more effective social skills.

Cognitive Treatments

Cognitive approaches view abnormal child behavior as the result of deficits and/or distortions in the child's thinking, including perceptual biases, irrational beliefs, and faulty interpretations (Kendall, 2011b). For example, for an attractive girl who gets A grades but thinks she is ugly and is going to fail in school, the emphasis in treatment is on changing these faulty cognitions. As cognitions change, the child's behaviors and feelings are also expected to change.

In Felicia's case, she may believe that she can't do well in school, or that if she goes to school then harm will befall her mother, or that children at school will think she's stupid. Changing these negative views by challenging them, and by helping Felicia develop more rational and more adaptive forms of thinking, should lead to changes in her behavior.

Cognitive–Behavioral Treatments

Cognitive–behavioral approaches view psychological disturbances as the result of both faulty thought patterns, and faulty learning and environmental experiences. These approaches begin with the basic premise that the way children and parents think about their environment determines how they will react to it (Meichenbaum, 1977). Combining elements of both the behavioral and cognitive models, the cognitive–behavioral approach grew rapidly as behavior therapists began to focus on the important role of cognition in treatment for both the child and family (Kendall, 2011a).

Faulty thought patterns that are the targets of change include distortions in both cognitive content (e.g., erroneous beliefs) and cognitive process (e.g., irrational thinking and faulty problem solving). As you will learn, cognitive distortions and biases have been identified in children with a variety of problems including, for example, depression, conduct disorder, and anxiety disorders.

The major goals of cognitive–behavioral treatment are to identify maladaptive cognitions and replace them with more adaptive ones, to teach the child to use both cognitive and behavioral coping strategies in specific situations, and to help the child learn to regulate his or her own behavior. Treatment may also involve how others respond to the child's maladaptive behavior. Using a cognitive–behavioral approach, a therapist would help Felicia learn to think more positively and use more effective social skills and coping strategies.

Client-Centered Treatments

Client-centered approaches view child psychopathology as the result of social or environmental circumstances that are imposed on the child and interfere with his or her basic capacity for personal growth and adaptive functioning. The interference causes the child to experience a loss or impairment in self-esteem and emotional well-being, resulting in even further problems. The therapist relates to the child in an empathic way, providing unconditional, nonjudgmental, and genuine acceptance of the child as an individual, often through the use of play activities with younger children and verbal interaction with older youths (Axline, 1947). The therapist respects the child's capacity to achieve his or her goals without the therapist's serving as a major adviser or coach—the therapist respects the child's self-directing abilities.

In Felicia's case, being babied by her parents, who viewed her as slow, may have led to interference in her adaptive functioning and to low self-esteem. In treatment, a therapist would comment on what Felicia is saying and feeling to help her understand her feelings, and to increase the congruence between her feelings and behavior. In therapy, Felicia would lead the way as the clinician follows.

Family Treatments

Family models challenge the view of psychopathology as residing only within the individual child and, instead, view child psychopathology as determined by variables operating in the larger family system. Like other approaches, the many varieties of family therapy differ widely in their underlying assumptions and approach to treatment. However, nearly all of the approaches view individual child disorders as manifestations of disturbances in family relations (Rivett, 2008).

Treatment involves a therapist and sometimes a cotherapist who interact with the entire family or a select subset of family members, such as the parents and child or the husband and wife. Therapy typically focuses on the family issues underlying problem behaviors. Depending on the approach, the therapist may focus on family interaction, communication, dynamics, contingencies, boundaries, or alliances. It is also essential to adapt family interventions to the cultural context of the family (Kumpfer, Alvarado, Smith, & Bellamy, 2002).

In Felicia's case, her overall helplessness and physical symptoms may be serving to maintain her role as the baby in the family, or may be serving as the parents' way of avoiding their own marital difficulties by focusing the problem on Felicia. A therapist would assist Felicia and her family in identifying and changing this and other dysfunctional ways in which family members relate to one another.

Biological Treatments

Medical models view child psychopathology as resulting from psychobiological impairment or dysfunction, and rely primarily on pharmacological and other biological approaches to treatment. Examples include the use of stimulant medications for the treatment of ADHD, anti-psychotic medications for the treatment of schizophrenia or serious aggressive and destructive behavior, and selective serotonin reuptake inhibitors (SSRIs) such as fluoxetine (Prozac) for the treatment of depression and other disorders. Table 4.9 provides a convenient summary of medications and their typical uses with children and adolescents, which you may find helpful when reviewing treatment for specific disorders discussed in other chapters.

Other, much more controversial forms of biological intervention include electroconvulsive therapy (ECT) for severe depression, the administration of large doses of vitamins or minerals to children with autism, and the scrupulous elimination of food additives and preservatives from the diets of children with ADHD. In Felicia's case, a psychiatrist might consider using SSRIs or other medications to treat her depressive symptoms. As shown in ● Figure 4.4, the use of medications for children's mental health problems increased significantly from the late 1980s to the mid 1990s, which can be attributed to increasing public acceptance of these medications as part of the treatment of mental health problems among children and youths during that time period (Olfson, Marcus, Weissman, & Jensen, 2002). Growth in the use of medications for children's mental health problems has slowed or leveled off over the last decade, although the percentage of children receiving more than one class of medication has increased (Comer, Olfson, & Mojtabai, 2010). Along with increased use, concerns have been expressed about the frequent use of medications with very young children (Gleason et al., 2007). The prescription of medication also varies in relation to the racial/ethnic status of the child. For example, more than 20% of non-Hispanic white adolescents report using prescription medication for depression versus 4%–9% of Asian, black, and Hispanic youths (Cummings & Druss, 2011).

TABLE 4.9 | Descriptions of Common Medications for Children and Youths[a]

Type of Medication	Treatment Uses	Examples
Stimulant and non-stimulant medications for ADHD	Attention-deficit hyperactivity disorder (ADHD)	*Stimulants*: Dextroamphetamine (*Dexedrine, Adderall*), Methylphenidate (*Ritalin, Metadate, Concerta*) *Non-stimulant*: Atomoxetine (*Strattera*)
Antidepressant medications	Depression, school phobias, panic attacks, and other anxiety disorders, bed-wetting, eating disorders, obsessive–compulsive disorder, personality disorders, post-traumatic stress disorder, and ADHD.	*Selective serotonin reuptake inhibitors (SSRIs):* Fluoxetine (*Prozac*), Sertraline (*Zoloft*), Paroxetine (*Paxil*), Fluvoxamine (*Luvox*), Venlafaxine (*Effexor*), Citalopram (*Celexa*), and Escitalopram (*Lexapro*). *Tricyclic antidepressants (TCAs):* Amitriptyline (*Elavil*), Clomipramine (*Anafranil*), Imipramine (*Tofranil*), and Nortriptyline (*Pamelor*). *Monoamine oxidase inhibitors (MAOIs):* Phenelzine (*Nardil*) and Tranylcypromine (*Parnate*).
Antipsychotic medications	Controlling psychotic symptoms (delusions, hallucinations), disorganized thinking, motor tics, and Tourette's syndrome. They are occasionally used to treat severe anxiety and may help in reducing very aggressive behavior.	*First generation antipsychotics*: Chlorpromazine (*Thorazine*), Thioridazine (*Mellaril*), Fluphenazine (*Prolixin*), Trifluoperazine (*Stelazine*), Thiothixene (*Navane*), and Haloperidol (*Haldol*). *Second generation antipsychotics (also known as atypical or novel):* Clozapine (*Clozaril*), Risperidone (*Risperdal*), Quetiapine (*Seroquel*), Olanzapine (*Zyprexa*), Ziprasidone (*Zeldox*), Ziprasidone (*Geodon*), and Aripiprazole (*Abilify*).
Mood stabilizers and anticonvulsant medications	Bipolar disorder, severe mood swings (manic and depressive), aggressive behavior, impulse control disorders.	Lithium (lithium carbonate, *Eskalith*), Valproic acid (*Depakote, Depakene*), Carbamazepine (*Tegretol*), Gabapentin (*Neurontin*), Lamotrigine (*Lamictil*), and Topiramate (*Topamax*).
Anti-anxiety medications	Severe anxiety.	*Benzodiazepines:* Alprazolam *(Xanax)*, Lorazepam (*Ativan*), Diazepam (*Valium*), and Clonazepam (*Klonopin*). *Antihistamines*: Diphenhydramine (*Benadryl*) and Hydroxyzine (*Vistaril*). *Atypical*: Buspirone (*BuSpar*) and Zolpidem (*Ambien*).

[a]These medications are often used in association with other forms of intervention such as psychotherapy, parent training, etc.

Source: Based on Psychiatric medication for children and adolescents. II: Types of medications, American Academy of Child & Adolescent Psychiatry, 2004.

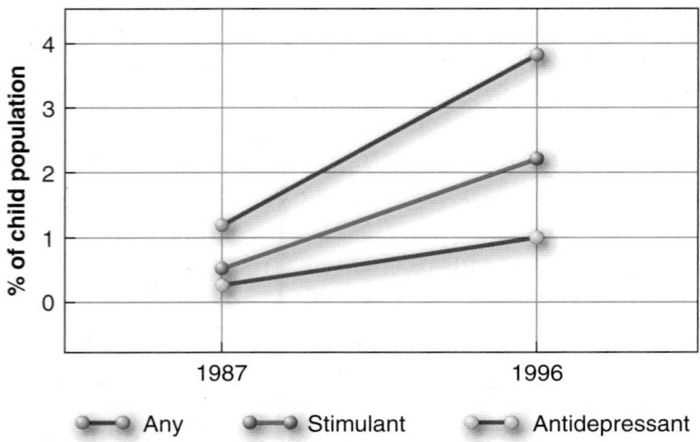

• FIGURE 4.4 | Usage of psychiatric medication by children in the United States between 1987 and 1996.

Adapted from Journal of the American Academy of Child and Adolescent Psychiatry, 41, A Olfson, M., Marcus, S. C., Weissman, M. M., & Jensen, P. S., National trends in the use of psychotropic medications by children, 514–521, Copyright 2002, with permission from Elsevier.

Combined Treatments

Combined treatments refer to the use of two or more interventions, each of which can stand on its own as a treatment strategy (Kazdin, 1996). In some instances, combinations of stand-alone interventions may consist of different conceptual approaches—using cognitive–behavioral and pharmacological treatments for children with ADHD, or using cognitive–behavioral treatment and family therapy in combination. In other instances, combined treatments may be derived from the same overall conceptual approach—using social skills training and cognitive restructuring in a group treatment program for adolescents with a social phobia, or using individual behavior management and family behavior therapy in the treatment of children with oppositional disorders.

More communities are now implementing comprehensive mental health programs for children, often delivered through schools to reach the most children and their families and to integrate mental health intervention and education (Atkins, Hoagwood, Kutash, & Seidman, 2010). In addition, youths who participate in school-based universal social and emotional learning programs have been found to show significantly improved social and emotional skills, attitudes, behavior, and academic performance (Durlak, Weissberg, Dymnicki, Taylor, & Shellinger, 2011). Box 4.4 describes an innovative school-based program that pays particular attention to the cultural diversity of families in their community.

In Felicia's case, we used a combined treatment approach that included cognitive–behavioral treatment for depression, behavioral treatment for school refusal, and social skills training.

BOX 4.4 **A CLOSER LOOK**

Model Comprehensive Mental Health Program: A Culturally Competent School-Based Mental Health Program

Program	Dallas School-Based Youth and Family Centers
Goal	To establish the first comprehensive, culturally competent, school-based program in mental health care in the 12th-largest school system in the nation. The program overcomes stigma and inadequate access to care for underserved minority populations.
Features	Annually serves the physical and mental health care needs of 3,000 low-income children and their families. The mental health component features partnerships with parents and families, treatment (typically six sessions), and follow-up with teachers. The well-qualified staff, who reflect the racial and ethnic composition of the population they serve (more than 70% Latino and African American), train school nurses, counselors, and principals to identify problems and create solutions tailored to meet each child's needs.
Outcomes	Improvements in attendance, discipline referrals, and teacher evaluation of child performance. Preliminary findings reveal improvement in children's standardized test scores in relation to national and local norms.
Biggest challenge	To sustain financial and organizational support of collaborative partners despite resistance to change or jurisdictional barriers. Program's $3.5 million funding comes from the school district and an additional $1.5 million from Parkland Hospital.
How other organizations can adopt	Recognize the importance of mental health for the school success of all children, regardless of race or ethnicity. Rethink how school systems can more efficiently partner with and use state and federal funds to deliver culturally competent school-based mental health services.
Sites	Dallas and Fort Worth, Texas

Source: President's New Freedom Commission on Mental Health, 2003.

FELICIA

Multiple Solutions

Our clinical assessment of Felicia suggested a combined treatment approach to treat three significant problems: school refusal, depression, and social difficulties.

To treat Felicia's school refusal, a behavioral program was implemented that required her to attend class daily. Felicia earned points for her attendance, class participation, and completion of class assignments, which could later be traded in for the opportunity to engage in preferred activities such as going to a movie, or for money that could be used to purchase music apps and other things that Felicia had previously selected.

When Felicia refused to go to school, she lost points and was given a brief period of time-out from positive reinforcement. She had to sit in the kitchen by herself and was not permitted to read or watch TV. This behavioral program resulted in consistent school attendance and much-improved academic performance.

To treat Felicia's depressive symptoms, we used a cognitive–behavioral approach. Felicia learned that depression can occur for many reasons—the loss of her grandfather, thinking lots of negative thoughts, and not having any friends. We next taught Felicia how to relax to give her some immediate relief and provide her with a successful experience. Felicia then learned to monitor and rate her mood daily, and to identify thoughts and events that accompanied both her positive and negative moods. Felicia increased her positive thinking by learning to identify, challenge, and change her negative cognitions. After several weeks of treatment, Felicia began to feel less depressed, as reflected in her positive daily mood ratings and reports by her parents.

Both Felicia's teacher and parents felt that her feelings of depression might be the result of her social interaction difficulties at home and school, and that she might become less depressed if these problems could be decreased. Therefore, a social–cognitive skills training program was also implemented to simultaneously address her depressive symptoms and interpersonal difficulties. This program consisted of three parts. In the first part, Felicia was given behavioral social skills training that consisted of instruction, modeling of appropriate and inappropriate social behaviors, role playing and rehearsal, coaching, feedback, and a final role play. This training focused on those social skills, such as making eye contact and speaking clearly, that our initial assessment identified as lacking. Training was conducted in the situations that Felicia and her therapist identified as being problematic—for example, the role-play simulation we described earlier in which another teen sits at Felicia's table in the school cafeteria.

The second part of the treatment focused on cognitive skills, including general problem-solving skills, self-evaluation, and self-reinforcement. Felicia was taught to use certain cues that would prompt the correct use of her individual social skills in different situations—"What do I want to accomplish?" or "How do I do this now?" She also learned to evaluate the adequacy of her social behavior and whether she had improved on each social skill. To support Felicia's use of these strategies, a third behavioral component was included whereby Felicia could earn points for the accuracy of her judgments and the effectiveness of her social skills during the role plays. The results of the behavioral role-playing social skills intervention for Felicia are shown in ● Figure 4.5.

Following treatment, Felicia began to show increased emotional expressiveness and social responsiveness at home. She smiled more and argued less with her parents. She also began to assert herself more appropriately. Attempts by her teacher to have her speak up in class were met with considerable success. Gradually, she began to engage in more interactions with her peers and to participate in activities. Her mood also began to brighten as she made efforts to initiate conversations and engage in more reciprocal interactions with other children, her teacher, and her parents. At the end of the treatment program Felicia was more interactive and assertive and had learned to be more socially appropriate during interactions. She was less depressed and more animated.

One year following her treatment, Felicia reported no symptoms of depression and few feelings of hopelessness. She was attending school regularly, showed improved academic performance, and was participating in activities and interacting more with other children. In this example, a combined approach of cognitive–behavioral therapy, behavioral social skills training, and cognitive problem-solving training was successful in helping Felicia and her family. (Adapted from *Depression,* by D. J. Kolko, 1987. In M. Hersen and V. B. Van Hasselt (Eds.), Behavior Therapy with Children and Adolescents: A Clinical Approach, pp. 163–164. Copyright © 1987 by John Wiley & Sons, Inc. Reprinted by permission of John Wiley & Sons, Inc.)

Treatment Effectiveness

A growing emphasis on improving outcomes and reducing the costs of health care in general has led to the development of best practice guidelines for treating children and families with psychological problems. **Best practice guidelines** are systematically developed statements to assist practitioners and patients with decisions regarding appropriate treatment(s) for specific clinical conditions. These guidelines are intended to offer recommendations on the most effective and cost-effective treatments for children with particular problems and their families (March et al., 2007).

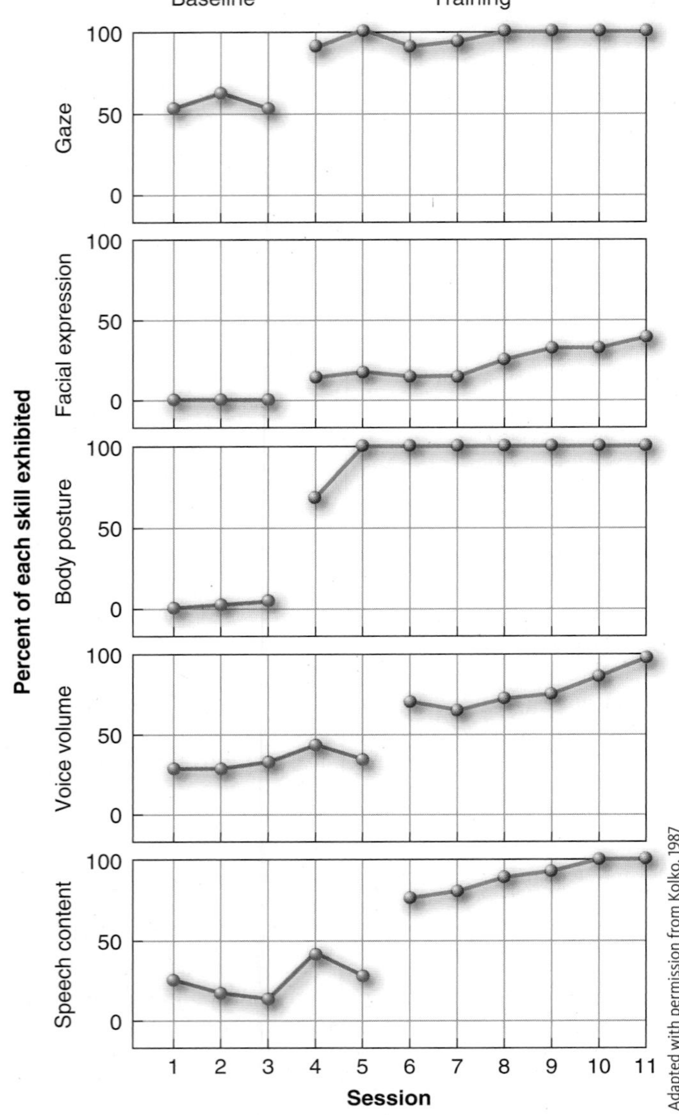

• **FIGURE 4.5** | Results of behavioral role-play intervention.

Adapted from *Depression* by D. J. Kolko, 1987. In M. Hersen and V. B. Van Hasselt (Eds.), "Behavior Therapy with Children and Adolescents: A Clinical Approach", pp. 163–164. Copyright © 1987 by John Wiley & Sons, Inc. Reprinted by permission of John Wiley & Sons, Inc.

Two main approaches have been used to develop best practice guidelines. The *scientific approach* derives guidelines from a comprehensive review of current research findings. The *expert-consensus approach* uses the opinions of experts to fill in the gaps in the scientific literature—for example, when research is inconclusive or when there is a lack of information about multicultural issues. Thus, evidence-based practice is not the blind application of research findings, but rather involves the use of the best available scientific evidence combined with good individual clinical expertise (Sackett, Straus, Richardson, Rosenberg, & Haynes, 2000). A number of professional organizations whose members provide services to children and families have developed excellent best practice guidelines. We will be discussing many of the best practice interventions that are recommended for children with particular problems in the chapters that follow.

Consistent with the growing emphasis on improving outcomes, efforts to evaluate treatments for childhood disorders have intensified (Chorpita et al., 2011; Weisz & Kazdin, 2010). These efforts allow us to take a closer look at the overall effectiveness of commonly used treatment methods.

Let's begin with the good news:

- Changes achieved by children receiving psychotherapy are consistently greater than changes for children not receiving psychotherapy.
- The average child who is treated is better off at the end of therapy than at least 75% of those children who did not receive treatment, particularly with respect to symptom reduction.
- Treatments have been shown to be effective for children with a wide range of problems, including both internalizing and externalizing disorders.
- Treatment effects tend to be lasting, with the effects at follow-up (usually around 6 months after treatment) similar to those found immediately following treatment.
- Effects are about twice as large for problems that are specifically targeted in treatment as they are for changes in nonspecific areas of functioning. This result suggests that treatments are producing focused changes in targeted areas such as anxiety rather than producing nonspecific or global effects such as changes in how the child feels (Weisz, 1998).
- The more outpatient therapy sessions children receive, the more improvement is seen in their symptoms (Angold, Costello, Burns, Erkanli, & Farmer, 2000).

So what's the bad news? Although research findings present a generally positive picture of psychotherapy with children and of behavioral and cognitive–behavioral approaches in particular, there are a number of important limitations.

First, although research generally shows that most treatments are effective in reducing symptoms such as anxiety, depression, and oppositional behavior, fewer than 20% of treatments demonstrate evidence for reducing impairment in life functioning (Becker, Chorpita, & Daleiden, 2011). Thus, greater attention to the development and evaluation of interventions that also result in meaningful changes in the child's overall life functioning is needed. Second, we must be aware of the critical difference between research therapy that is carried out in laboratory-based outcome studies and therapy that is carried out in community-based clinics (Wagner, Swenson, & Henggeler, 2000). Most of the evidence-based treatment outcome studies for specific disorders that we will discuss fall into the category of research therapy. However, compared with research therapy, clinic therapy is typically conducted with more severe cases, directed at a diverse set of problems and children, and carried out in clinic or hospital settings by professional career therapists with large caseloads (Weisz & Weiss, 1993). In general, clinic therapy is less structured and more flexible than research therapy, and uses relatively more nonbehavioral methods, such as psychodynamic and eclectic approaches. In contrast to the findings for research therapy, similar analyses for studies of clinic therapy have resulted in minimal effects (Andrade, Lambert, & Bickman, 2000; Weisz, Donenberg, Han, & Weiss, 1995). These findings suggest that conventional services for children as they are currently carried out may have limited effectiveness. However, few controlled studies exist of child therapy outcomes in settings where it is typically conducted, although this situation is changing. Thus, it is premature to draw any conclusions from the findings from clinic and community studies until more empirical data about therapy in clinical practice are available (Weisz, Jensen-Doss, & Hawley, 2006).

In summary, although the efficacy of treatments for many child and adolescent mental health problems is substantial, testing of the effectiveness and cost-effectiveness of these treatments in real-world settings and dissemination of this information and its use in public settings are key issues that require further attention.

New Directions

Despite the availability of many potentially effective assessment and treatment procedures, as many as 70%–80% of children and families with significant mental health needs do not receive any specialized assessment or treatment services (Merikangas et al., 2011). Service rates are highest for children with ADHD and other behavior disorders, but fewer than one in five youths receive services for their anxiety, eating, or substance use disorders. This situation is even worse for youths from low-income families, ethnic minority youths, and those in the child welfare and juvenile justice systems. This raises the larger issue of whether current evidence-based practices are, by themselves, a viable way to help these large, unrecognized, and underserved groups of children and to reduce the gap between children's mental health needs and the availability and access to effective services (Kazak et al., 2010).

In response to this issue there has been a recent general "call to action" from many family, public, professional, and scientific organizations to address these challenges and actively promote the uptake of evidence-based assessment and treatment practices into public heath and mental health systems. This has led to an increasing number of opportunities for partnerships among the various stakeholders, along with financial incentives at the state and federal levels to support these efforts. The result has been several exciting new initiatives that focus on:

1. Increasing the recognition of children's mental health needs, not only on the part of laypersons, but also among education, welfare, juvenile justice, and health care professionals (Jensen et al., 2011);
2. Developing a much wider range of child mental health service delivery models based on: (a) the use of new technologies (e.g., Internet, smart phones); (b) non-traditional service providers (e.g., parents, health counselors); (c) self-help interventions (e.g., self-help books, recordings, Internet); (d) the media (e.g., education entertainment); and (e) special settings where youth in need of mental health services are typically present (e.g., schools, primary care) (Kazdin & Blase, 2011); and
3. Broadening the framework and delivery systems for children's mental health assessment and intervention services to include multiple systems and disciplines (Kazak et al., 2010).

The goal of these new initiatives is to translate evidence-based practices into real world settings so as to significantly reduce the personal, social, and economic costs of children's mental health problems and related conditions, at both the individual and societal levels.

SECTION SUMMARY

Treatment

- Interventions for childhood disorders cover a wide range of strategies and settings related to prevention, treatment, and maintenance.
- Treatment goals now include outcomes related to child and family functioning as well as those of societal importance.
- Both ethically and legally, clinicians who work with children are required to think not only about the impact that their actions will have on the children they see, but also on the responsibilities, rights, and relationships that connect children to their parents.
- A tremendous number and diversity of treatments for children and families now exist, including psychodynamic, behavioral, cognitive, cognitive–behavioral, client-centered, family, biological, and combined approaches.
- Best practice guidelines are systematically developed statements derived from research findings and clinical

(continues)

SECTION SUMMARY *(continued)*

consensus that assist clinicians and families with decisions regarding appropriate treatment(s) for specific childhood problems.

- Reviews of controlled treatment outcome studies have found that the changes achieved by children receiving therapy are consistently greater than changes for children not receiving therapy. However, these differences are not consistently found in studies of treatment outcomes based on clinic samples.
- The goal of new treatment initiatives is to better serve unrecognized and underserved populations of children with mental health problems and to translate evidence-based practices into real world settings in ways that will significantly reduce the personal, social, and monetary costs associated with these problems.

Study Resources

SECTION SUMMARIES

KEY TERMS

behavior analysis 93
behavioral assessment 92
best practice guidelines 117
categorical classification 102
classification 102
clinical assessments 83
clinical description 87
cultural compatibility hypothesis 110
culture-bound syndromes 85
developmental history 91
developmental tests 97
diagnosis 87
dimensional classification 103
eclectic 113
family history 91
functional analysis of behavior 93
idiographic case formulation 83
intervention 108
maintenance 108
multiaxial system 104
multimethod assessment approach 89
neuropsychological assessment 100
nomothetic formulation 83
prevention 108
prognosis 88
projective tests 100
screening 97
semistructured interviews 92
target behaviors 92
test 95
treatment 108
treatment planning and evaluation 88

COURSEMATE

Access an interactive eBook and chapter-specific interactive learning tools, including flashcards, quizzes, videos, and more in your Psychology CourseMate, accessed through CengageBrain.com.

5

Attention-Deficit/ Hyperactivity Disorder (ADHD)

> *ADHD is not a problem with knowing what to do; it is a problem with doing what you know.*
>
> —Russell A. Barkley (2006a)

CHAPTER PREVIEW

DESCRIPTION AND HISTORY
Description
History

CORE CHARACTERISTICS
Inattention (IA)
Hyperactivity—Impulsivity (HI)
Subtypes
Additional DSM Criteria
What DSM Criteria Don't Tell Us

ASSOCIATED CHARACTERISTICS
Cognitive Deficits
Speech and Language Impairments
Developmental Coordination and Tic Disorders
Medical and Physical Concerns
Social Problems

ACCOMPANYING PSYCHOLOGICAL DISORDERS AND SYMPTOMS
Oppositional Defiant Disorder and Conduct Disorder
Anxiety Disorders
Mood Disorders

PREVALENCE AND COURSE
Gender
Socioeconomic Status and Culture
Course and Outcome

THEORIES AND CAUSES
Genetic Influences
Pregnancy, Birth, and Early Development
Neurobiological Factors
Diet, Allergy, and Lead
Family Influences

TREATMENT
Medication
Parent Management Training (PMT)
Educational Intervention
Intensive Interventions
Additional Interventions
A Comment on Controversial Treatments
Keeping Things in Perspective

Description and History

We begin our discussion of attention-deficit/hyperactivity disorder (ADHD) with a description of the primary symptoms and behaviors of children with this disorder. We then consider the different views of ADHD that have been presented since the disorder was first described more than 100 years ago.

JOHN

Inattentive, Hyperactive, Impulsive

John is a 7-year-old whose mother is desperate for help. "He walked at 10 months and has kept me running ever since. As a child he was always bouncing around the house and crashing into things. He's in constant motion, impulsive, and never listens. When I ask him to put his shirt in the hamper, I find him playing, his shirt still on the floor. John has no routines and seldom sleeps. Discipline doesn't work, nor do the techniques that work for my other boys. He's oblivious to his behavior. He never finishes anything, and except for sitting down to play a video game, rarely watches TV except on the run."

John's teacher says his main problems in school are staying on task and keeping track of what's happening. "He blurts things out in class and is constantly fidgeting or out of his chair," she says. Although John can complete his assignments, he forgets to bring home the book he needs to do his homework. When he does complete his homework, he forgets to put it in his backpack or to hand it in. John has great difficulty waiting his turn or following rules with other children. Other kids think he's weird and don't want to play with him. John's parents are demoralized and don't know what to do. (From The Hyperactive Child Book, by Patricia Kennedy, Leif Terdal, and Lydia Fusetti, pp. 8–9. St. Martin's Press, Inc.)

Description

Attention-deficit/hyperactivity disorder, or **ADHD,** describes children who, like John, display persistent age-inappropriate symptoms of inattention, hyperactivity, and impulsivity that are sufficient to cause impairment in major life activities (APA, 2000).

The term ADHD may be new, but children who display overactive and unrestrained behaviors have been around for some time. In 1845, Heinrich Hoffmann, a German neurologist, wrote in a child's storybook one of the first known accounts of hyperactivity. His humorous poem described the mealtime antics of a child aptly named "Fidgety Phil," who "won't sit still; / He wriggles, / And jiggles," and "Swings backwards and forwards, / And tilts up his chair." When his chair falls, Philip screams and grabs the tablecloth, and "Down upon the ground they fall, / Glasses, plates, knives, forks, and all" (Hoffmann, 1845).

Fidgety Phil, 1845, Blackie & Son, Ltd., Glasgow

Jose Azel/Getty Images

Fidgety Phil, 1845, and Dusty N., 1994: Mealtimes are an especially trying time for children with ADHD and their parents

More recently, a compelling article about ADHD titled "Life in Overdrive" described the behavior of 7-year old Dusty N.:

> Dusty awoke at 5:00 one recent morning in his Chicago home. Every muscle in his 50-pound body flew in furious motion as he headed downstairs for breakfast. After pulling a box of cereal from the cupboard, Dusty started grabbing cereal with his hands and kicking the box, scattering the cereal across the room. Next he began peeling the decorative paper covering off the TV table. Then he started stomping the spilled cereal to bits. After dismantling the plastic dustpan he had gotten to clean up the cereal, he moved on to his next project: grabbing three rolls of toilet paper from the bathroom and unraveling them around the house. (Adapted from *Time*, July 18, 1994, p. 43)

Although the accounts of Phil and Dusty N. are separated by almost 150 years, the mealtime behaviors of both boys typify the primary symptoms of ADHD. The boys are **inattentive,** not focusing on mealtime demands and behaving carelessly; **hyperactive,** constantly in motion; and **impulsive,** acting without thinking.

ADHD has no distinct physical symptoms that can be seen in an X-ray or a lab test. It can only be identified by characteristic behaviors that vary considerably from child to child. As we shall discuss, ADHD has become a blanket term used to describe several different patterns of behavior that likely have different causes.

The behavior of children with ADHD is puzzling and full of contradictions. Rash and disorganized behaviors are a constant source of stress for the child and for parents, siblings, teachers, and classmates. Why can't he sit still? Why can't she ever get anything done? Why does he make so many careless mistakes? However, at certain times or in some situations, the child with ADHD seems fine. Such inconsistencies may cause others to think the child could do better if only she tried harder or if her parents or teachers would set firmer limits. However, increased effort and stricter rules usually don't help, because most children with ADHD are already trying hard. They want to do well but are constantly thwarted by their limited self-control. As a result, they experience the hurt, confusion, and sadness of being blamed for not paying attention or being called names like "space cadet." They may be scolded, put down, or even spanked for failing to complete homework or chores. Unfortunately, they may not know why things went wrong or how they might have done things differently.

Feelings of frustration, being different, not fitting in, and hopelessness may overwhelm a child with ADHD (Young, Bramham, Gray, & Rose, 2008). For example, David says: "I got no friends cause I don't play good and when they call me Dope Freak and David Dopey I cry, I just can't help it" (Ross & Ross, 1982). Such comments leave little doubt that ADHD can severely disrupt a child's life, consume vast amounts of energy, produce emotional pain, damage self-esteem, and seriously disrupt relationships. In addition to the child's personal suffering, societal costs of ADHD are also high, with an estimated cost of about $32 billion a year in the U.S. (about $11,000 per child in 2005 dollars) (Pelham, Foster, & Robb, 2007).

History

Over the years, there have been numerous explanations for the troublesome behaviors of ADHD (Eisenberg, 2007). In 1798, a Scottish-born physician, Sir Alexander Crichton, was one of the first to describe a syndrome similar to ADHD that included early onset, restlessness, inattention, and poor school performance. These individuals described themselves as having "the fidgets," and displayed a severe problem attending no matter how hard they tried (Palmer & Finger, 2001). Symptoms of overactivity and inattention were described as a disorder in 1902 by the English physician George Still (what a coincidence!), who believed that the symptoms arose out of poor "inhibitory volition" and "defective moral control" (see ● Figure 5.1). In the early 1900s, the onset of widespread compulsory education demanded self-controlled behavior in a group setting, which further focused attention on children with the symptoms of ADHD.

Another view of ADHD arose from the worldwide influenza epidemic from 1917 to 1926. A number of children who had developed encephalitis (brain inflammation) and survived experienced multiple behavior problems, including irritability, impaired attention, and

THE LANCET, April 19, 1902.

The Goulstonian Lectures

ON

SOME ABNORMAL PSYCHICAL CONDITIONS IN CHILDREN.

Delivered before the Royal College of Physicians of London on March 4th, 6th, and 11th, 1902,

BY GEORGE F. STILL, M.A., M.D. CANTAB., F.R.C.P. LOND.,

ASSISTANT PHYSICIAN FOR DISEASES OF CHILDREN, KING'S COLLEGE HOSPITAL; ASSISTANT PHYSICIAN TO THE HOSPITAL FOR SICK CHILDREN, GREAT ORMOND-STREET.

LECTURE II.

Delivered on March 6th.

MR. PRESIDENT AND GENTLEMEN,—In my first lecture I drew your attention to some points in the psychology and development of moral control in the normal child and then considered the occurrence of defective moral control in association with general impairment of intellect; before going further it may be well to review briefly the points which have been raised. Moral control, we saw, is dependent upon three psychical factors, a cognitive relation to environment, moral consciousness, and volition, which in this connexion might be regarded as inhibitory volition. Moral control, therefore, is not present at birth, but under normal psychical conditions is gradually developed as the child grows older. The variation in the degree of moral control which is shown by different children at the same age and under apparently similar conditions of training and environment suggested that the innate capacity for the development of such control might also vary in different individuals.

● **FIGURE 5.1** | English physician George Still was one of the first to describe the symptoms of ADHD.

hyperactivity. These children and others who had suffered birth trauma, head injury, or exposure to toxins displayed behavior problems that were labeled *brain-injured child syndrome*, which was associated with mental retardation. In the 1940s and 1950s, this label was then erroneously applied to children displaying similar behaviors, but with no evidence of brain damage or mental retardation, and led to the terms *minimal brain damage* and *minimal brain dysfunction (MBD)* (Strauss & Lehtinen, 1947). These terms provided a convenient way to attribute behavior problems to a physical cause. Although certain head injuries can explain some cases of ADHD, the brain damage theory was eventually rejected because it did not explain the majority of cases (Rie, 1980).

In the late 1950s, ADHD was referred to as *hyperkinesis*, which was attributed to the poor filtering of stimuli entering the brain (Laufer, Denhoff, & Solomons, 1957). This view led to the definition of the *hyperactive child syndrome*, in which motor overactivity was considered the main feature of ADHD (Chess, 1960). However, it was soon realized that hyperactivity was not the only problem; there was also the child's failure to regulate motor activity in relation to situational demands.

In the 1970s, it was argued that in addition to hyperactivity, deficits in attention and impulse control were also primary symptoms of ADHD (Douglas, 1972). This view was widely accepted and has had a lasting impact on the DSM criteria for defining ADHD. In the 1980s, interest in children with ADHD increased dramatically, and the sharp rise in the use of stimulants generated controversy that continues to this day (Mayes & Rafalovich, 2007). More recently, the problems of poor self-regulation, difficulty in inhibiting behavior, and motivational deficits have been emphasized as central impairments of the disorder (Nigg, Hinshaw, & Huang-Pollack, 2006). Although there is growing agreement about the nature of ADHD, views continue to evolve as a result of new findings and discoveries.

SECTION SUMMARY

Description and History

- Attention-deficit/hyperactivity disorder (ADHD) describes children who display persistent age-inappropriate symptoms of inattention, hyperactivity, and impulsivity that cause impairment in major life activities.
- ADHD can only be identified by characteristic patterns of behavior, which vary quite a bit from child to child.
- The behavior of children with ADHD is a constant source of stress and frustration for the child and for parents, siblings, teachers, and classmates, and also has high costs to society.
- The disorder that we now call ADHD has had many different names, primary symptoms, and presumed causes, and views of the disorder are still evolving.

Core Characteristics

Experts developed the DSM-IV-TR criteria for ADHD after reviewing research and conducting field trials with children throughout North America (APA, 2000). Table 5.1 shows two lists of key symptoms that were identified for defining ADHD and distinguishing it from related problems. The first list includes symptoms of *inattention*; the second list includes symptoms of *hyperactivity-impulsivity*. These two dimensions have now been well documented in research across various ethnic and cultural groups in North America and throughout the world (Bauermeister, Canino, Polanczyk, & Rohde, 2010). However, to define the two dimensions of ADHD as inattention and hyperactivity–impulsivity oversimplifies the disorder. First, each dimension includes many distinct processes that have been defined and measured in various ways. Second, although we discuss attention and impulse control separately, the two are closely connected developmentally—attention helps the child regulate his behavior, emotions, and impulses (Nigg et al., 2006).

Inattention (IA)

LISA

Just Can't Focus

At age 17, Lisa struggles to pay attention and act appropriately. But this has always been hard for her. She still gets embarrassed thinking about the time that her parents took her to a restaurant to celebrate her 10th birthday. She was so distracted by the waitress's bright red hair that her father had to call her name three times before she remembered to order. Then, before she could stop herself, she blurted, "Your hair dye looks awful!"

In school, Lisa was quiet and cooperative but often seemed to be daydreaming. She was smart, yet couldn't improve her grades no matter how hard she tried. Several times she failed exams. She knew the answers, but couldn't keep her mind on the test. Her parents responded to her low grades by taking away privileges and scolding her, "You're just lazy, Lisa. You could get better grades if you only tried."

Lisa found it agonizing to do homework. Often, she forgot to plan ahead by writing down the assignment or bringing home the right books. And when trying to work, every few minutes she found her mind drifting to something else. As a result, she rarely finished and her work was full of errors. One day, after Lisa had failed yet another exam, her teacher found her sobbing, "What's wrong with me?" (Adapted from National Institute of Mental Health [NIMH], 1994)

TABLE 5.1 | Diagnostic Criteria for Attention-Deficit/Hyperactivity Disorder

DSM-IV-TR

A. Either (1) or (2):

(1) Six (or more) of the following symptoms of **inattention** have persisted for at least 6 months to a degree that is maladaptive and inconsistent with developmental level:

Inattention

(a) Often fails to give close attention to details or makes careless mistakes in schoolwork, work, or other activities

(b) Often has difficulty sustaining attention in tasks or play activities

(c) Often does not seem to listen when spoken to directly

(d) Often does not follow through on instructions and fails to finish schoolwork, chores, or duties in the workplace (not due to oppositional behavior or failure to understand instructions)

(e) Often has difficulty organizing tasks and activities

(f) Often avoids, dislikes, or is reluctant to engage in tasks that require sustained mental effort (e.g., schoolwork or homework)

(g) Often loses things necessary for tasks or activities (e.g., toys, school assignments, pencils, books, or tools)

(h) Is often easily distracted by extraneous stimuli

(i) Is often forgetful in daily activities

(2) Six (or more) of the following symptoms of **hyperactivity—impulsivity** have persisted for at least 6 months to a degree that is maladaptive and inconsistent with developmental level:

Hyperactivity

(a) Often fidgets with hands or feet or squirms in seat

(b) Often leaves seat in classroom or in other situations in which remaining seated is expected

(c) Often runs about or climbs excessively in situations in which it is inappropriate (in adolescents or adults, may be limited to subjective feelings of restlessness)

(d) Often has difficulty playing or engaging in leisure activities quietly

(e) Is often "on the go" or often acts as if "driven by a motor"

(f) Often talks excessively

Impulsivity

(g) Often blurts out answers before questions have been completed

(h) Often has difficulty awaiting turn

(i) Often interrupts or intrudes on others (e.g., butts into conversations or games)

B. Some hyperactive-impulse or inattentive symptoms that caused impairment were present before age 7 years.

C. Some impairment from the symptoms is present in two or more settings (e.g., at school [or work] and at home).

D. There must be clear evidence of clinically significant impairment in social, academic, or occupational functioning.

E. The symptoms do not occur exclusively during the course of a Pervasive Developmental Disorder, Schizophrenia, or other Psychotic Disorder and are not better accounted for by another mental disorder (e.g. Mood Disorder, Anxiety Disorder, Dissociative Disorder, or a Personality Disorder).

Code based on type:

314.01 Attention-Deficit/Hyperactivity Disorder, Combined Type: if both Criteria A1 and A2 are met for the past 6 months

314.00 Attention-Deficit/Hyperactivity Disorder, Predominantly Inattentive Type: if Criterion A1 is met but Criterion A2 is not met for the past 6 months.

314.01 Attention-Deficit/Hyperactivity Disorder, Predominantly Hperactive-Impulsive Type: if Criterion A2 is met but Criterion A1 is not met for the past 6 months.

Coding note: For individual (especially adolescents and adults) who currently have symptoms that no longer meet full criteria, "In Partial Remission" should be specified.

Source: Reprinted with permission from the Diagnostic and Statistical Manual of Mental Disorders, Fourth Edition, Text Revision, (Copyright ©2000). American Psychiatric Association.

Children who are inattentive find it difficult, during work or play, to focus on one task or follow through on requests or instructions. While playing soccer, as the rest of the team heads downfield with the ball, the child with ADHD may get sidetracked by playing in a mud puddle. The child may attend automatically to enjoyable things, but have great difficulty focusing on new or less enjoyable tasks. Common complaints about inattention are that the child doesn't or won't listen, follow instructions, or finish chores or assignments. It is not sufficient to say that a child has an attention deficit when there are so many different types of attention. The child could have a deficit in only one type or in more than one type (Barkley, 2006a).

Attentional capacity is the amount of information we can remember and attend to for a short time. When someone gives you directions or a phone number, how much information can you attend to and remember briefly? Children with ADHD do not have a deficit in their attentional capacity. They can remember the same amount of information for a short time as other children (Taylor, 1995).

Selective attention is the ability to concentrate on relevant stimuli and not be distracted by task-irrelevant stimuli in the environment. When you're studying for a test (relevant stimuli), how easily are you distracted by voices in another room?

Distractibility is a common term for a deficit in selective attention. Distractions can be disruptive to all children, including those with ADHD. However, children with ADHD are much more likely than others to be distracted by stimuli that are *highly salient and appealing* (Milich & Lorch, 1994).

Sustained attention or vigilance is the ability to maintain a persistent focus over time or when fatigued. When you're tired and have to study for a test, can you still pay attention until you've reviewed all the required material? A primary attention deficit in ADHD seems to be sustained attention. When children with ADHD are assigned an uninteresting or repetitive task, their performance is poor compared to other children. Although no one likes to work on uninteresting tasks, most of us will when we have to. Children with ADHD may not be able to persist at such tasks even when they want to. They work best on self-paced tasks they themselves have chosen—playing a computer game or building a model airplane—and on tasks they find especially interesting that do not require them to sustain their attention. Most tasks, though, require sustained attention for successful performance, and many tasks are not particularly interesting.

Deficits in sustained attention are one of the core features of ADHD. However, children with ADHD may show performance deficits from the very beginning of a task or response, not just a decrement over time. This suggests that their attentional problems may be in alerting and preparing for the task from the outset, and not only in sustaining attention that has already occurred. **Alerting** refers to an initial reaction to a stimulus, and involves the ability to prepare for what is about to happen. It helps the child achieve and maintain an optimally alert attentional state. A child with an alerting deficit (such as the lack of alertness you may experience when you are very tired) may respond too quickly in situations requiring a slow and careful approach and too slowly in situations requiring a quick response. This pattern of responding is often seen in children with ADHD. Thus, their deficits in sustaining attention may be partly related to their difficulty in alerting (Mullane, Corkum, Klein, McLaughlin, & Lawrence, 2011).

"I need you to line up by attention span."

Hyperactivity–Impulsivity (HI)

MARK

Junior Wild Man

Mark, age 14, has more energy than most boys his age. But then, he's always been overactive. At age 3 he was a human tornado, dashing around and disrupting everything in his path. At home, he darted from one activity to the next, leaving a trail of toys behind him. At meals, he upset dishes and talked non-stop. He was reckless and impulsive, running into the street despite oncoming cars, no matter how often his mother explained the danger or scolded him. At the playground, his tendency to overreact—like socking playmates simply for bumping into him—had already gotten him into trouble several times. His parents didn't know what to do. Mark's doting grandparents reassured them, "Boys will be boys. Don't worry, he'll grow out of it." But he didn't. (Adapted from NIMH, 1994)

Although the symptoms of hyperactivity and impulsivity are distinct in DSM, when children display one symptom they usually display the other as well. These symptoms are best viewed as a single dimension of behavior called *hyperactivity—impulsivity* (Barkley, 1997a). The strong link between hyperactivity and impulsivity suggests that both are part of a fundamental deficit in regulating behavior. There are different reasons for hyperactivity–impulsivity. For example, a child may be constantly out of his seat in the classroom because he wants to look outdoors, because he is anxious about completing an assigned task, or because he can't control his motor behavior. The main problem in ADHD seems to be one of controlling motor behavior (Barkley, 2006a).

© Britt Erlanson/Getty Images

Sitting through a class lesson is hard for a child with ADHD

Hyperactivity

The image of a motor-driven ball of speed is the stereotype of a child with ADHD. Sitting still through a class lesson can be impossible for children with ADHD. They may fidget, squirm, climb, run about the room aimlessly, touch everything in sight, or noisily tap a pencil. Parents and teachers describe them as "always on the go" and "talking incessantly." The activity is excessively energetic, intense, inappropriate, and not goal directed. The children are extremely active, but unlike other children with a high energy level, they accomplish very little. Recordings of body movements indicate that even when they sleep, children with ADHD display more motor activity than other children (Teicher, Ito, Glod, & Barber, 1996). However, the largest differences are found in situations requiring the child to inhibit motor activity—to slow down or sit still in response to the structured task demands of the classroom.

Impulsivity

Children who are impulsive seem unable to bridle their immediate reactions or think before they act. They may take apart an expensive clock with little thought about how to put it back together. It's very hard for them to stop an ongoing behavior or to regulate their behavior in accordance with the demands of the situation or the wishes of others. As a result, they may blurt out inappropriate comments or give quick, incorrect answers to questions that are not yet completed. Because it is difficult to wait or take turns, they interrupt conversations, intrude on others' activities, and lash out in frustration when upset. They also experience difficulty resisting immediate temptations and delaying gratification (Sonuga-Barke, Sergeant, Nigg, & Willcutt, 2008). Minor mishaps are common, such as spilling drinks or knocking things over, but more serious accidents and injuries can result from reckless behavior, such as running into the street without looking (Brehaut, Miller, Raina, & McGrail, 2003).

Impulsivity may take different but overlapping forms (Winstanley, Eagle, & Robbins, 2006). *Cognitive impulsivity* is reflected in disorganization, hurried thinking, and the need for supervision. Remember John not handing in his homework even though it was done? *Behavioral impulsivity* includes impulsively calling out in class or acting without considering the consequences. Children who are behaviorally impulsive have difficulty inhibiting their response when the situation requires it. A child may touch a stove to see if it is hot even when she is old enough to know better. Cognitive and behavioral impulsivity (and inattention) predict problems with academic achievement, particularly in reading (Rabiner, Coie, & The Conduct Problems Prevention Research Group, 2000). However, only behavioral impulsivity predicts rule-breaking behavior and thus may be a specific sign of increased risk for conduct problems (Willoughby, Curran, Costello, & Angold, 2000). *Emotional impulsivity* is reflected in impatience, low frustration tolerance, hot temper, quickness to anger, and irritability. Although less studied than other types of impulsivity, recent findings suggest that emotional impulsivity may be an important component of ADHD that contributes to poor educational, occupational, and other adult outcomes beyond those associated with inattention and hyperactivity–impulsivity (Barkley & Fischer, 2010).

In summary, the core features of ADHD—IA and HI are made up of many processes. Children with ADHD display a unique constellation and severity of symptoms but may not differ from comparison children on all types and measures of IA and HI. The primary attention deficit in ADHD is an inability to engage and sustain attention and to follow through on directions or rules while resisting salient distractions. The primary impairment in HI is an inability to voluntarily inhibit dominant or ongoing behavior in order to meet ongoing situational demands.

Subtypes

Since children with ADHD differ in many ways, investigators have become increasingly interested in identifying subtypes (Milich, Balentine, & Lynam, 2001). A **subtype** is a group of individuals with something in common—symptoms, etiology, problem severity, or likely outcome—that makes them distinct from other groupings. DSM specifies three subtypes of ADHD based on primary symptoms:

- **Predominantly inattentive type (ADHD-PI)** describes children who primarily have symptoms of inattention.
- **Predominantly hyperactive—impulsive type (ADHD-HI)** describes children who have primarily symptoms of hyperactivity-impulsivity.

- **Combined type (ADHD-C)** describes children who have symptoms of *both* inattention and hyperactivity-impulsivity.

Children with ADHD-PI are described as inattentive and drowsy, daydreamy, spacey, in a fog, or easily confused. (Interestingly, the same 1845 storybook that described the hyperactive behavior of "Fidgety Phil" also described an inattentive young boy named "Hans Look-in-the-Air.") They may have a learning disability, process information slowly, find it hard to remember things, and display low academic achievement (Massetti et al., 2008). They are often rated as anxious and apprehensive, socially withdrawn, and may display mood disorders (Maedgen & Carlson, 2000).

Children with the ADHD-HI and ADHD-C subtypes are more likely to display problems in inhibiting behavior and in behavioral persistence (Solanto et al., 2007). They are also more likely to be aggressive, defiant, rejected by peers, and suspended from school or placed in special education classes (Short, Fairchild, Findling, & Manos, 2007). Children with ADHD-C are the ones most often referred for treatment. The ADHD-HI subtype is the rarest group. This subtype primarily includes preschoolers and may have limited validity for older children. Since this group is usually younger than children with ADHD-C, it is not yet known whether they are actually two distinct subtypes, or the same children at different ages (Barkley, 2006a).

Although differences among children with the various DSM subtypes have been identified, findings are not always consistent (Nigg, Tannock, & Rohde, 2010). Subtypes may also be unstable over time—a child described as ADHD-PI at one time may be categorized as ADHD-HI or ADHD-C at another point in time, and vice versa (Lahey & Willcutt, 2010). Valo and Tannock (2010) found that 50% of ADHD cases were reclassified from one subtype to another depending on the number of people reporting on the child's symptoms, the methods used to assess symptoms, and how information across reporters and methods was combined.

Thus, although the heterogeneity of ADHD symptoms is widely acknowledged, issues remain regarding the reliability and validity of the discrete subtypes specified in DSM-IV-TR and their symptom criteria. It is not yet known whether these inconsistencies will be addressed in DSM-5 and, if so, how. Several alternatives have been proposed, including not having any subtypes; using groupings based on personality traits such as introversion, extraversion, or poor control (Martel, Goth-Owens, Martinez-Torteya, & Nigg, 2010); or using a two-step procedure in which the ADHD diagnosis is first confirmed overall, then followed by quantification of the severity of inattention and hyperactivity–impulsivity based on the respective numbers of symptoms (Lahey & Willcutt, 2010).

Our knowledge of ADHD subtypes is still "under construction." Some researchers have suggested that current subtypes are not different types of ADHD but rather separate disorders with different cognitive and behavioral profiles, different co-occurring problems, different responses to medications, and different underlying causes (Grizenko, Paci, & Joober, 2010). Most previous research has studied mixed groups of children with ADHD, not broken out by subtype. It is important to keep this in mind, since inconsistencies in the literature may reflect findings that mix together samples of children with different subtypes.

Additional DSM Criteria

Not every child who displays inattention and/or hyperactive–impulsive behavior has ADHD. Most children blurt out things they didn't mean to say, jump from one activity to another, make careless mistakes, or become forgetful and disorganized at times. This doesn't mean they will have a lifelong disorder. To diagnose ADHD using DSM, the behaviors must also:

- appear before age 7;
- occur more often and with greater severity than in other children of the same age and sex;
- continue for more than 6 months;
- occur across several settings (e.g., home and school); and
- produce significant impairments in the child's social or academic performance.

Illnesses, accidents, middle ear infections, mild seizures, chronic abuse, or stressful life events such as a major move can result in behaviors that mimic the symptoms of ADHD. A normally agreeable 9-year-old boy who becomes inattentive or argumentative immediately after the separation of his parents is likely having an adjustment reaction, not experiencing ADHD. The disruptive behaviors of children with mild intellectual disabilities, learning disorders, or conduct problems may be mistaken for ADHD, as can the inattentive or restless behaviors of children with anxiety disorders. Therefore, it is important to investigate other possible reasons for the child's symptoms (Smith, Barkley, & Shapiro, 2007).

An overreliance on individual symptoms or rating scales to diagnose ADHD can be unreliable and misleading (Solanto & Alvir, 2009). Before a diagnosis of ADHD is made, it is essential to carry out a thorough assessment that includes a developmental history, parent and teacher reports, normed assessment instruments, and behavioral observations (Johnston & Mah, 2008). Importantly, since there is only a modest relationship between ADHD symptoms and impairment in childhood, a child can display ADHD symptoms without necessarily displaying significant impairment. Conversely, a child may display remitted or subclinical levels of ADHD symptoms but still suffer significant maladjustment (Mick et al., 2011). Thus, in evaluating ADHD, it is important to assess both the child's symptoms and impairment in functioning (Gathje, Lewandowski, & Gordon, 2008).

What DSM Criteria Don't Tell Us

The current DSM criteria for ADHD have a number of limitations (Bell, 2011; Rohde, 2008):

- *Developmentally insensitive*. Although DSM states that clinical judgment may be used to assess whether symptoms are "inconsistent with developmental level," it applies the same symptoms to individuals of all ages, even though some symptoms, particularly for HI behaviors (running and climbing), apply more to young children (Pine et al., 2011). Similarly, the number of symptoms needed to make a diagnosis is not adjusted for age or level of maturity, even though many children with HI symptoms show a general decline in these symptoms with age.
- *Categorical view of ADHD*. According to DSM, ADHD is a disorder that a child either has or doesn't have. However, because the number and severity of symptoms are also calculated on a scale, children who fall just below the cutoff for ADHD are not necessarily different from children just above the cutoff. In fact, over time, some children may move in and out of the DSM category as a result of fluctuations in their behavior. Both statistical and neurobiological research support the idea that ADHD is a dimensional rather than a categorical disorder, representing an extreme or delay in normal traits that all children possess to a degree (Marcus & Barry, 2011; Shaw et al., 2011). However, it may still be useful to talk about categories even when a disorder is of a continuous or changing nature. For example, there is no magic cutoff for defining high blood pressure, but most of us would agree that people with high blood pressure are at greater risk for certain negative outcomes.
- *Requirement of an onset of symptoms before age 7 is arbitrary and overly restrictive*. There seems to be little difference between children with an onset of ADHD before or after age 7 (Barkley & Biederman, 1997), and about one-half of children with ADHD-PI are not identified until well after age 7 (Applegate et al., 1997). Moreover, extending the requirement from age 7 to age 12 does not significantly change the overall prevalence of ADHD (Polanczyk et al., 2010). As a result of these findings, the age of onset requirement may be extended to age 12 or later in DSM-5 (Barkley, 2010; Kieling et al., 2010).

These limitations highlight the fact that DSM criteria are designed for specific purposes—classification and diagnosis. They help shape our understanding of ADHD but are also shaped by—and in some instances lag behind—new research findings.

SECTION SUMMARY

Core Characteristics

- DSM-IV-TR uses two lists of symptoms to define ADHD. The first list includes symptoms of inattention, poor concentration, and disorganization. The second list includes symptoms of hyperactivity-impulsivity.
- Children who are inattentive find it difficult to sustain mental effort during work or play, and find it difficult to resist salient distractions while doing so.
- Children with ADHD are extremely active, but unlike other children with a high energy level, they accomplish very little.
- Children with ADHD are impulsive, which means they seem unable to bridle their immediate reactions or they may fail to think before they act.
- DSM specifies three subtypes of ADHD based on primary symptoms of inattention, hyperactivity-impulsivity, or a combination of both.
- A diagnosis of ADHD requires the appearance of symptoms before age 7, a greater frequency and severity of symptoms than in other children of the same age and gender, persistence of symptoms, occurrence of symptoms in several settings, and impairments in functioning.
- Although useful, the DSM criteria have several limitations; an important one is developmental insensitivity.

Associated Characteristics

In addition to their primary difficulties, children with ADHD often display other problems. For example, Lisa was failing in school and Mark was getting into fights. In the sections that follow, we consider the characteristics and problems commonly associated with ADHD, including cognitive deficits, speech and language impairments, medical and physical concerns, and social problems.

Cognitive Deficits

Children and adolescents with ADHD display a variety of cognitive deficits, including deficits in executive functions, intellectual deficits, impairments in academic functioning, learning disorders, and distorted self-perceptions. These are discussed in the sections that follow.

Executive Functions

Executive functions are cognitive processes in the brain that activate, integrate, and manage other brain functions (Pennington & Ozonoff, 1996). They underlie the child's capacity for self-regulation functions such as self-awareness, planning, self-monitoring, and self-evaluation. Like a symphony conductor whose artistic direction enables an orchestra to produce complex music, executive functions allow the brain to perform both routine and complex tasks (Brown, 2000). Executive functions are varied and include:

- *Cognitive processes*, such as working memory (holding facts in mind while manipulating information), mental computation, planning and anticipation, flexibility of thinking, and the use of organizational strategies.
- *Language processes*, such as verbal fluency and the use of self-directed speech.
- *Motor processes*, such as allocation of effort, following prohibitive instructions, response inhibition, and motor coordination and sequencing.
- *Emotional processes*, such as self-regulation of arousal level and tolerating frustration.

For most children, these different processes work in concert, enabling them to exercise deliberate control of their attention and impulses and to maintain problem-solving behaviors in order to attain a future goal. Many executive functions reflect abilities that emerge and develop rapidly in preschool children, continue to mature in older children and adolescents, and peak in young adults (Best & Miller, 2010). However, as a group, children with ADHD consistently show deficits in one or more executive functions, especially response inhibition, vigilance, working memory, and planning (Holmes et al., 2010). In fact, as shown in Table 5.2, many symptoms of IA and HI reflect impairments in executive functions.

In light of their close connection with symptoms of ADHD, impairments in executive functioning have come to be viewed as a key deficit in ADHD. However, executive functioning deficits are not *uniquely* associated with ADHD but also occur in children with other disorders such as autism and conduct disorder (Banaschewski et al., 2005). In addition, executive functioning deficits occur in only about half of children with ADHD (Lambek et al., 2011), suggesting they are one important component of ADHD but that other deficits also need to be examined. One study of children with ADHD with and without executive functioning deficits found the two groups were comparable in ADHD symptoms and school functioning. However, those with executive functioning deficits had lower IQ scores and displayed greater response variability. In contrast, those with ADHD without executive functioning deficits showed more aversion to delay of reward. If confirmed, these and other findings suggest multiple pathways for ADHD (Lambek et al., 2010), a point we return to in a later section on causes.

TABLE 5.2 | Impaired Executive Functions in ADHD and Examples of Resulting Impairments

Impaired Executive Function	Resulting Impairment
1. Organize, prioritize, and activate	Trouble getting started Difficulty organizing work Misunderstand directions
2. Focus, shift, and sustain attention	Lose focus when trying to listen Forget what has been read and need to re-read Easily distracted
3. Regulate alertness, effort, and processing speed	Excessive daytime drowsiness Difficulty completing a task on time Slow processing speed
4. Manage frustration and modulate emotion	Very easily irritated Feelings hurt easily Overly sensitive to criticism
5. Working memory and accessing recall	Forget to do a planned task Difficulty following sequential directions Quickly lose thoughts that were put on hold
6. Monitor and regulate action	Find it hard to sit still or be quiet Rush things, slap-dash Often interrupt, blurt things out

Source: Based on Brown, 2000.

Intellectual Deficits

Most children with ADHD are of at least normal overall intelligence, and many are quite bright (Antshel et al., 2008). Their difficulty is not in a lack of intelligence, but rather in applying their intelligence to everyday life situations (Barkley, 2006a). As a result, the children never quite live up to their potential. They do score about 5 to 9 points lower on IQ tests than both control children and their own siblings (remember, most still have total IQ scores within the average or above-average range). Since IQ tests such as the WISC-IV include subtests related to specific deficits of children with ADHD (e.g., working memory) their lower test scores are not surprising (Frazier, Demaree, & Youngstrom, 2004). In addition, lower IQ scores can be the direct result of the effects of ADHD symptoms on test-taking behavior. For example, a child who scores lower on an IQ test because he or she is not paying attention to instructions is not necessarily less intelligent. On average, inattention has been estimated to account for about a 2 to 5 point lowering of overall IQ-test scores in children with ADHD (Jepsen, Fagerlund, & Mortensen, 2009).

Impaired Academic Functioning

Most children with ADHD experience severe difficulties in school, even more so for those with co-occurring disorders (Bernard-Brak, Sulak, & Fearon, 2010). They frequently have lower productivity, grades, and scores on achievement tests. They may also fail to advance in grade or may be placed more frequently in special education classes. Finally, they may be expelled or fail to finish high school (Loe & Feldman, 2007). Particularly disturbing are findings that the academic skills of children with ADHD are impaired before they enter the first grade (Barkley, Shelton et al., 2002).

Learning Disorders

Many children with ADHD have a specific learning disorder (see Chapter 11); that is, they have trouble with language or certain academic skills, typically reading, spelling, and math (Willcutt et al., 2007). When learning disorders are broadly defined as performance below expected grade level, nearly 80% of children with ADHD qualify for a learning disorder by late childhood. However, when defined more narrowly as a significant delay in reading, arithmetic, or spelling that is relative to the child's general intellectual functioning, or defined as extremely low achievement in a specific academic subject(s), the number drops to around 25% (Barkley, 2006a). Children with ADHD and those with learning problems show distinct patterns of cognitive deficits, which may be present in combination in those with both disorders (Gooch, Snowling, & Hulme, 2011).

Different pathways may underlie the association between ADHD and learning disorders (Taylor, 2011). For example, the child's cognitive and intellectual deficits may directly lead to learning problems. ADHD may also predispose the child to conduct problems (to be discussed in Chapter 6) in school that may in turn result in poor academic performance. The association could also be due to common neuropsychological deficits (McGrath et al., 2011) or a common genetic link, although findings suggest that the two disorders are transmitted independently within families (Del'Homme, Kim, Loo, Yang, & Smalley, 2007).

Distorted Self-Perceptions

The many failures experienced by children with ADHD have led to the common belief that these children must suffer from low self-esteem—and there is some support for this (Treuting & Hinshaw, 2001). However, many children with ADHD report a higher self-esteem than is warranted by their behavior (Owens, Goldfine, Evangelista, Hoza, & Kaiser, 2007). For example, they may perceive their relationships with their parents no differently than do control children, even though their parents see things in a more negative light (Gerdes, Hoza, & Pelham, 2003). This exaggeration of one's competence is referred to as a **positive illusory bias.** Recent findings suggest that self-esteem in children with ADHD may vary with the subtype of

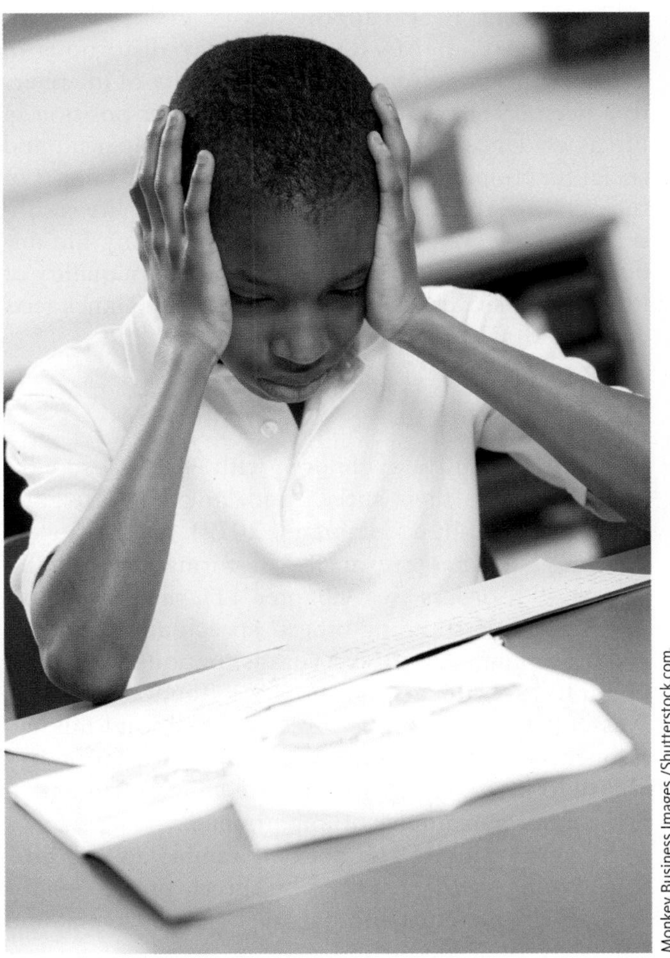
Monkey Business Images /Shutterstock.com

The structured demands of a classroom can be painful for a child with ADHD

ADHD, the accompanying disorders, and the area of performance being assessed (e.g., conduct, scholastic achievement). Children with ADHD who display inattentive and depressive/anxious symptoms tend to report lower self-esteem, whereas children with symptoms of hyperactivity–impulsivity and conduct problems appear to exaggerate their self-worth (Owens et al., 2007). The bias in the latter group is most dramatic in the areas of performance in which the child is most severely impaired. Increases in positively biased self-perceptions of behavior in children with ADHD have also been found to predict greater aggression over time (Hoza et al., 2010).

Several explanations for the positive illusory bias in children with hyperactivity–impulsivity have been proposed—it serves a self-protective function that allows the child to cope every day despite frequent failures; it reflects a diminished self-awareness as a result of impairments in executive functions; or it is a result of not knowing what constitutes successful or unsuccessful performance (Ohan & Johnston, 2002). To date, there is some support for the self-protective function of positive bias (Hoza et al., 2010), although other explanations may also apply.

Children with ADHD also display distortions in their perceptions of quality of life. **Quality of life** refers to a person's subjective perception of their position in life as evidenced by their physical, psychological, and social functioning. According to parents, the impact of their child's ADHD on the child's quality of life is substantial. However, despite experiencing many life difficulties, children with ADHD rate their own quality of life more positively than others rate them (Danckaerts et al., 2010).

Speech and Language Impairments

About 30% to 60% of children with ADHD also have impairments in their speech and language (Helland, Biringer, Helland, & Heimann, 2012). In addition to showing a higher prevalence of formal speech and language disorders (see Chapter 11), they may have difficulty understanding others' speech and using appropriate language in everyday situations (McInnes, Humphries, Hogg-Johnson, & Tannock, 2003; Wassenberg et al., 2010). Excessive and loud talking, frequent shifts and interruptions in conversation, inability to listen, and inappropriate conversation are a few common examples of impairments.

Children with ADHD not only ramble on, but their conversation is characterized by speech production errors, fewer pronouns and conjunctions, tangential and unrelated comments, abandoned utterances, and unclear links (Mathers, 2006; McGrath et al., 2008). Can you understand the following statement by a boy with ADHD?

> And all of a sudden the soldiers—and all of a sudden he gets faint and you know when he says "Good doctors, I want to talk with you" and all of a sudden he goes in the door and inside they come off it from the thing. So he puts—I think this something on the doorknob. (Tannock, Fine, Heintz, & Schachar, 1995)

When speech is unclear, as in this example, it is difficult for the listener to understand who and what the child is talking about. Unfortunately, miscommunication is all too common in children with ADHD.

Developmental Coordination and Tic Disorders

As many as 30% to 50% of children with ADHD display motor coordination difficulties, such as clumsiness, poor performance in sports, or poor handwriting, especially when they attempt to execute complex motor sequences (Fliers et al., 2010). An overlap exists between ADHD and **developmental coordination disorder (DCD)**, a condition characterized by marked motor incoordination and delays in achieving motor milestones (Pearsall-Jones, Piek, & Levy, 2010). About 20% of children with ADHD also have **tic disorders**—sudden, repetitive, nonrhythmic motor movements or sounds such as eye blinking, facial grimacing, throat clearing, and grunting (Simpson, Jung, & Murphy, 2011). These children experience more behavioral, social, and academic difficulties than those with ADHD alone. When present, tic disorders decline to low rates by adolescence and do not significantly affect later psychosocial functioning (Peterson, Pine, Cohen, & Brook, 2001).

Medical and Physical Concerns

In addition to the difficulties we have discussed, children and adolescents with ADHD also experience a number of medical and physical concerns, including health-related problems, accident proneness, and risk-taking behaviors.

Health-Related Problems

In terms of specific problems, studies have reported higher rates of asthma (Fasmer et al., 2011) and bedwetting (Duel, Steinberg-Epstein, Hill, & Lerner, 2003), although findings are not consistent. Sleep disturbances are common in children with ADHD (Gruber, Sadeh, & Raviv, 2000). Resistance to going to bed, difficulty in falling asleep, fewer total hours asleep, and involuntary sleep movements such as teeth grinding or restless sleep may be the most significant disturbances (Spruyt &

Gozal, 2011). Some of the sleep problems in children with ADHD may be related to their use of stimulant medications, and/or co-occurring conduct or anxiety disorders, rather than to only their ADHD (Mick, Biederman, Jetton, & Faraone, 2000).

Accident-Proneness and Risk Taking

Given their problems with impulsivity, motor inhibition, and lack of planning and forethought, it is not surprising that over 50% of parents of children with ADHD describe their child as accident-prone. These children are about three times more likely to experience serious accidental injuries, such as broken bones, lacerations, severe bruises, burns, poisonings, or head injuries (Barkley, 2006a; Brehaut et al., 2003). Young adult drivers with ADHD are at higher risk than others for traffic accidents (Cox, Madaan, & Cox, 2011).

ADHD is a significant risk factor for the early initiation of cigarette smoking, substance use disorders, and risky sexual behaviors such as multiple partners and unprotected sex (Barkley, Murphy, & Fischer, 2008; Lee, Humphreys, Flory, Liu, & Glass, 2011). The substance use disorders of young people with ADHD are also more frequent, severe, and persistent than substance use disorders of those without ADHD (Charach, Yeung, Climans, & Lillie, 2011). These findings suggest a progression of hyperactive–impulsive behaviors during childhood to a pattern of irresponsible and risky adult behavior. There are a number of possible reasons that ADHD may lead to substance use problems, a notable one being co-occurring conduct problems (Wilens, 2011).

One longitudinal study spanning over a half century found that impulsive behavior was the most significant childhood characteristic that predicted reduced life expectancy (an average of 8 years less) (Friedman et al., 1995). A lifelong pattern of accident-proneness, auto accidents, and risk taking, combined with a reduced concern for health-promoting behaviors, such as exercise, proper diet, safe sex, and moderate use of tobacco, alcohol, and caffeine, may very well predict a reduced life expectancy for individuals with ADHD (Barkley, 2006a).

The need for further research into health-related problems in children and adolescents with ADHD is accentuated by findings that show they have significantly higher rates of inpatient and outpatient hospitalizations and emergency room visits. Average medical costs for children with ADHD are more than double the costs for those without ADHD (Leibson, Katusic, Barbaresi, Ransom, & O'Brien, 2001) and at least comparable to the costs for children with asthma (Chan, Zhan, & Homer, 2002).

Social Problems

DENNIS

Nothing Sticks

With my other children, I could tell them one time, "Don't do that," and they would stop. But Dennis, my child with ADHD, I could tell him a hundred times, "Dennis, don't carve soap with my potato peeler," "Don't paint the house with used motor oil," or "Don't walk on Grandma's white sofa in your muddy shoes," but he still does it. It's like every day is a brand new day and yesterday's rules are long forgotten. . . . I just cannot stay one step ahead of him. He does things my other kids never thought of. (From The Hyperactive Child Book, by Patricia Kennedy, Leif Terdal, and Lydia Fusetti, pp. 8–9. St. Martin's Press, Inc.)

Social problems in family life and at school are common in children with ADHD. Those who experience the most severe social disability are at greatest risk for poor adolescent outcomes and other disorders such as depression and conduct disorder (Greene et al., 1996). Children with ADHD don't listen, and are often hostile, argumentative, unpredictable, and explosive. As a result, they are in frequent conflict with adults and other children. It is common for children with ADHD to be removed from swimming lessons because of disruptive behavior, or to be kicked out of gymnastics. For one child with ADHD taking dance lessons, the teachers offered to buy back her shoes if only her parents would take her out!

To get along with others, you must follow social rules and respect conventions. Children with ADHD do not play by the same rules as others and don't seem to learn from past mistakes, despite their awareness of expected social behaviors and a desire to conform to them. Many social blunders by children with ADHD appear more thoughtless than intentional. Even with good intentions, their behaviors have an annoying quality that is a source of great distress for their parents, siblings, teachers, and classmates. In the words of one mother: "*Our grade one parent interview was highly traumatic; her teacher cried!*"

Family Problems

Families of children with ADHD experience many difficulties, including interactions characterized by negativity, child noncompliance, excessive parental control, and sibling conflict (Mash & Johnston, 2005; Mikami & Pfiffner, 2008). Parents may experience high levels of distress and related problems—most commonly depression in mothers and antisocial behavior, such as substance abuse, in fathers. Further stress on family life stems from the fact that parents of children with ADHD may themselves have ADHD and other associated conditions (Chen & Johnston, 2007). This can also be a barrier to effective treatment for the child (Sonuga-Barke, Daley, & Thompson, 2002).

Families of children with ADHD also report less parenting competence, fewer contacts with extended family members, greater caregiver strain, less instrumental support, and slightly higher rates of marital conflict, separation, and divorce (Bussing et al., 2003; Johnston & Mash, 2001). They report generally higher levels of parenting stress that may fluctuate over the course of the day in relation to the child's ADHD-related behaviors (Whalen, Odgers, Reed, & Henker, 2011). Parents of these children also show increased alcohol consumption that in some instances could be a direct result of stressful interactions with their children (Pelham & Lang, 1999). When interviewed, siblings of children with ADHD report that they feel victimized by their ADHD sibling, and that this experience is often minimized or overlooked (Kendall, 1999).

It is important to note that the links between ADHD and high levels of family conflict, parental psychopathology, and marital discord in many cases are due to the child's co-occurring conduct problems rather than to ADHD symptoms alone (Johnston & Mash, 2001).

> Things I've learned from my ADHD child (honest and no kidding):
>
> If you hook a dog leash over a ceiling fan, the motor is not strong enough to rotate a 42-pound boy wearing Batman underwear and a Superman cape. It is strong enough, however, if tied to a paint can, to spread paint on all four walls of a 20 × 20 foot room. (An anonymous mother in Austin, Texas)

Peer Problems

Peer problems in both boys and girls with ADHD are apparent at an early age and are quickly evident when the child enters a new social situation. These children display little of the give-and-take that characterizes other children (Hoza, 2007). Children with ADHD can be bothersome, stubborn, socially awkward, and socially insensitive. Others describe them as socially conspicuous, loud, intense, and quick to react. They are socially active but usually "off the mark" with respect to the style, content, or timing of their behavior, which often has an annoying quality that brings out the worst in other children (Whalen & Henker, 1992). Children with ADHD seem to get into trouble even when trying to be helpful, and although their behavior seems thoughtless, it is often unintentional. They often see their own behavior more favorably than it is perceived by others, and may be puzzled by others' negative reactions (Nijmeijer et al., 2008).

In light of their social difficulties, it is not surprising that children with ADHD are disliked and uniformly rejected by peers, have few friends, and report receiving low social support from peers (Hoza et al., 2005). Their lack of skill in correctly recognizing emotions in others, in regulating their own emotions and behavior (Kats-Gold, Besser, & Priel, 2007), and the aggressiveness that frequently accompanies ADHD often lead to social conflict and a negative reputation (Erhardt & Hinshaw, 1994). The social problems of these children may increase their risk of later disorders other than ADHD and spill over into other areas of development (Murray-Close et al., 2010). Once labeled "ADHD" by peers, a negative process begins whereby the child suffers more negative treatment and rejection by peers, leading to a cascading of negative effects over time.

Children with ADHD are not deficient in social reasoning or understanding (Whalen & Henker, 1992). They simply don't use what they know during social exchanges, and may continue to be dominant or assertive even when the situation changes and requires accommodation, negotiation, or submission (Landau & Milich, 1988). Their social agenda may also differ from the agenda of their peers, especially when ADHD is accompanied by aggression. They may actually value and prefer troublemaking, sensation seeking, and having fun at the expense of following rules and getting along with others (Melnick & Hinshaw, 1996).

Despite their many social problems with peers, some adolescents with ADHD may meet their social needs by maintaining one or two positive close friendships (Glass, Flory, & Hankin, 2010). The social premise for such relationships may differ from other teens, possibly with a mutual focus on "having fun" rather than seeking emotional support. Positive friendships may buffer the negative outcomes of peer rejection commonly seen in children with ADHD. Since most research on ADHD has examined peer relationships in general, further research into close friendships is needed to determine their nature and function during adolescence.

SECTION SUMMARY

Associated Characteristics

- Besides their primary difficulties, children with ADHD display other problems such as cognitive and learning deficits, speech and language impairments, motor incoordination, medical and physical concerns, and social problems.

- Children with ADHD display deficits in executive functions, the higher-order mental processes that underlie the child's capacity for planning and self-regulation.
- Children with ADHD score slightly lower on IQ tests, but most are of normal intelligence. Their difficulty is in applying their intelligence to everyday life situations.
- Children with ADHD experience school performance difficulties, including lower grades, a failure to advance in grade, and more frequent placements in special education classes.
- Many children with ADHD have a specific learning disorder, typically in reading, spelling, or math.
- Some children with ADHD report a higher self-esteem than is warranted by their behavior, referred to as a positive illusory bias.
- They often have speech and language impairments, and have difficulty using language in everyday situations.
- Children with ADHD may display motor coordination difficulties and tic disorders.
- They may experience health-related problems, especially sleep disturbances, and are accident-prone.
- They experience numerous social problems with family members, teachers, and peers.

Accompanying Psychological Disorders and Symptoms

Children with ADHD typically present a mixed bag of symptoms and impairments, with ADHD being only one, albeit a significant one. Nearly two-thirds of parents report behaviors other than the core symptoms of ADHD as most concerning, typically aggression and defiance (Findling, Conner, Wigal, Eagan, & Onafrey, 2009). One reason that ADHD is so challenging is that as many as 80% of children with ADHD have a co-occurring psychological disorder, such as oppositional and conduct disorders, anxiety, and mood disorders (Pliszka, 2000). As we noted previously, learning disorders and motor coordination problems are also quite common, as are substance use disorders in adolescence (see Chapter 12). Some children with ADHD display symptoms of autism spectrum disorders (to be discussed in Chapter 10), possibly originating from similar familial/genetic factors (Rommelse, Guerts, Franke, Buitelaar, & Hartman, 2011).

Oppositional Defiant Disorder and Conduct Disorder

SHAWN

Bad Boy

Shawn, now an energetic and talkative young adult, recalls his childhood with ADHD as a total disaster: "I did really bad in school. My parents and teachers were always on my back. They bugged me about being too loud, too defiant, too explosive, and too aggressive. Then I began to use drugs: marijuana, and later, cocaine. I barely managed to squeak through high school. I couldn't concentrate at all. I'd study for hours and then forget everything I'd read. I had to cheat my way through high school." (Based on authors' case material)

About one-half of all children with ADHD—mostly boys, like Shawn—meet criteria for oppositional defiant disorder (ODD) by age 7 or later (Kutcher et al., 2004). Children with ODD overreact by lashing out at adults and other kids. They are stubborn, short-tempered, argumentative, and defiant. About 30% to 50% of children with ADHD eventually develop conduct disorder (CD) (Beauchaine, Hinshaw, & Pang, 2010), a condition that is more severe than ODD. Children with CD violate societal rules and are at high risk for getting into serious trouble at school or with the police. They may fight, cheat, steal, set fires, or destroy property. CD is also associated with the use of illegal

"Sam, neither your father nor I consider your response appropriate."

drugs, which may explain why children with ADHD have a higher risk for developing substance abuse problems in adolescence (Szobot & Bukstein, 2008). Early occurring ADHD, particularly when severe symptoms of hyperactivity–impulsivity are present, is one of the most reliable predictors of ODD and CD. Longitudinal studies have found that ADHD leads to ODD and CD rather than vice versa (Thapar, van den Bree, Fowler, Langley, & Whittinger, 2006). Interestingly, persistent and severe ODD and CD outcomes among children with ADHD are related to variations in a specific gene (*COMT* gene) known to be associated with the regulation of neurotransmitters in the areas of the brain implicated in ADHD. These findings suggest a sub-group of children with ADHD who are at biological risk for developing later conduct problems (Caspi et al., 2008).

ADHD, ODD, and CD run together in families, which suggests a common predisposing cause. In support of this, there is a substantial common genetic contribution for the three disorders, especially between ADHD and ODD (Coolidge, Thede, & Young, 2000). There is also evidence for a contribution from a shared environment, perhaps related to family adversity and deficits in parenting (Burt, Krueger, McGue, & Iacono, 2001). We discuss both ODD and CD in greater detail in Chapter 6.

Anxiety Disorders

T. J.

Overactive and Anxious

T. J. was first referred for help at age 6. He had been very active and impulsive since he was a toddler. His parents reported that he had trouble sleeping and would wake up several times each night. They also said that he showed great anxiety during even brief separations from them and seemed to be worrying about something the whole time. T. J. confirmed that he had "terrible bad dreams" and felt that no one liked him. (Based on Tannock, 2000)

About 25% of children with ADHD experience excessive anxiety (Manassis, 2007). These children worry about being separated from their parents, trying something new, taking tests, making social contacts, or visiting the doctor. They may feel tense or uneasy and constantly seek reassurance that they are safe and protected. Because these anxieties are unrealistic, more frequent, and more intense than normal, they have a negative impact on the child's thinking and behavior. Findings regarding whether or not co-occurring anxiety worsens the symptoms or severity of ADHD are inconsistent (Hammerness et al., 2010). However, those children with co-occurring ADHD and anxiety display social and academic difficulties and experience greater long-term impairment and mental health problems than those with either condition alone (Manassis, Tannock, Young, & Francis, 2007).

Mood Disorders

ADHD at 4 to 6 years of age is a risk factor for future depression and suicidal behavior in adolescence, particularly for girls (Chronis-Tuscano, Molina, et al., 2010). As many as 20% to 30% of young people with ADHD experience depression (Spencer, Wilens, Biederman, Wozniak, & Harding-Crawford, 2000), and even more will develop depression or another mood disorder by early adulthood (Fischer, Barkley, Smallish, & Fletcher, 2002). These youths feel so sad, hopeless, and overwhelmed that they are unable to cope with everyday life. Depression lowers self-esteem; reduces interest or pleasure in favorite activities; increases irritability; and disrupts sleep, appetite, and the ability to think (Mick, Santangelo, Wypij, & Biederman, 2000). The association between ADHD and depression may be a function of family risk for one disorder increasing the risk for the other. This suggests that depression in a child with ADHD is not due solely to the child's demoralization as a result of their ADHD symptoms (Biederman, Mick, & Faraone, 1998).

Controversy abounds regarding the association between ADHD and pediatric bipolar (manic–depressive) mood disorder (BP) (to be discussed in Chapter 8). In part, this is due to the difficulty in distinguishing between symptoms of ADHD and the unregulated high energy level, poor judgment, and over-talkativeness of children with BP, as well as to possible shared underlying mechanisms (Youngstrom, Arnold, & Fraser, 2010). The relationship between the two disorders seems to go mainly in one direction—a diagnosis of childhood BP sharply increases the child's risk for previous or co-occurring ADHD, but a diagnosis of ADHD does not appear to increase the child's risk for BP (Hassan, Agha, Langley, & Thapar, 2011).

SECTION SUMMARY

Accompanying Psychological Disorders and Symptoms

- A factor that makes ADHD so challenging is that children with the disorder have much higher than expected rates of other psychiatric disorders, particularly conduct problems, anxiety, and mood disorders.

- As many as 50% of children with ADHD also meet criteria for oppositional defiant disorder or conduct disorder.
- About 25% of children with ADHD experience excessive anxiety. The presence of co-occurring anxiety is associated with more social and academic difficulties, and greater long-term impairment and mental health problems.
- As many as 20% to 30% children with ADHD experience depression or another mood disorder. Although depression may be partly related to their demoralization as a result of their symptoms, it also can result from an elevated risk for depression in families of children with ADHD.
- The relation between ADHD and bipolar disorder is controversial. A diagnosis of childhood bipolar disorder appears to sharply increase the child's risk for previous or co-occurring ADHD, but a diagnosis of ADHD does not appear to elevate the child's risk for bipolar disorder.

Prevalence and Course

"When we began our studies in the 1960's no one believed such children existed; while now people find them under every rock."

—Dr. Leon Eisenberg, child psychiatrist and ADHD pioneer (1922–2009)

The striking increase in ADHD alluded to in the above quote likely reflects an epidemic in diagnostic practices rather than in ADHD. This increase is based partly on growing knowledge about ADHD, pressures from parents seeking treatment for children, and adults identifying their own ADHD (Taylor, 2009). The growing recognition of ADHD has established that it affects millions of children throughout the world and across all socioeconomic levels. Although rates vary widely with sampling methods, the best estimate is that about 6% to 7% of all school-age children and adolescents in North America and just over 5% worldwide have ADHD (Boyle et al., 2011; Merikangas et al., 2010; Polanczyk, Silva de Lima, Lessa Horta, Biederman, & Rohde, 2007). As many as one-half of all children referred to clinics display ADHD symptoms either alone or in combination with other disorders, making ADHD one of the most common referral problems (Barkley, 2006a).

Reports of parents, teachers, and doctors are all used to identify children with ADHD. However, these people don't always agree, because the child's behavior may differ from setting to setting. Also, different adults may emphasize different symptoms when making a judgment. Teachers, for example, are most likely to rate a child as inattentive when oppositional symptoms are also present (Abikoff, Courtney, Pelham, & Koplewicz, 1993). Prevalence rates and patterns of comorbidity also differ when teacher's reports are compared with parent's reports (Gadow & Nolan, 2002). Since adults may disagree, prevalence estimates of ADHD are much higher when based on one person's opinion rather than based on a consensus.

Gender

ADHD occurs more frequently in boys than in girls, with estimates ranging from 2% to 4% for girls and 6% to 9% for boys age 6 to 12 years (Polanczyk & Jensen, 2008). In adolescence, overall rates of ADHD decrease slightly for both sexes, but boys still outnumber girls by the same ratio of about 2.5:1, a ratio that declines by adulthood to about 1.6:1 (Kessler et al., 2005; Merikangas et al., 2010). This ratio is even higher in clinic samples, where boys outnumber girls by 6:1 or more—most likely because boys are referred more frequently due to their overt defiance and aggression or because parents and teachers may think that learning assistance is less effective for girls than boys with ADHD (Ohan & Visser, 2009). Interestingly, when girls with ADHD also display defiance and aggression, they are referred at a younger age than boys, a finding that implies lower tolerance by adults or a greater concern for these behaviors when they occur in girls (Silverthorn, Frick, Kuper, & Ott, 1996).

ADHD in girls may go unrecognized and unreported because teachers fail to recognize and report inattentive behavior unless it is accompanied by the disruptive symptoms normally associated with boys. In addition, the symptoms used to diagnose ADHD may also contribute to the sex difference in prevalence. DSM criteria were developed and tested mostly with boys with ADHD, and many of the symptoms, such as excessive running around, climbing, and blurting out answers in class, are generally more common in boys than girls. Thus, the specified cutoffs and symptoms may be more appropriate to boys than girls, because girls with ADHD may have to display not only extreme behavior but also uncharacteristic behavior from their same-sex peers before they will be referred (Hinshaw & Blachman, 2005). Girls with ADHD may be more likely than boys to display inattentive/disorganized symptoms characteristic of a sluggish cognitive tempo including: forgetfulness, lethargic behavior, mental confusion, drowsiness, tendency to daydream (McBurnett, Pfiffner, & Frick, 2001), anxiety, depression (Rucklidge & Tannock, 2001), and hyperverbal rather than hyperactive motor behavior (Nadeau, Littman, & Quinn, 1999). Thus, current DSM criteria may be insensitive to the problems that are especially relevant to girls (Ohan & Johnston, 2005). Although it may be premature to expand the current symptom lists for ADHD to include additional items appropriate to girls, it is clear that sampling, referral, and definition biases may all contribute to reports of the prevalence of ADHD as higher in boys than girls.

In the past, girls with ADHD were a highly understudied group (Hinshaw & Blachman, 2005). However, recent studies show that among clinic-referred school age children with ADHD, boys and girls are quite similar with respect to their expression and severity of symptoms, brain abnormalities, deficits in response inhibition and executive functions, level of impairment, family correlates, response to treatment, and outcomes (Biederman et al., 2006; Hinshaw, Owens, Sami, & Fargeon, 2006; Rucklidge, 2008). Follow-up studies of girls with ADHD indicate clear evidence of major problems through adolescence and young adulthood. These include anxiety; depression; romantic relationship difficulties; conflict with mothers; significant peer rejection and conduct problems; large deficits in academic achievement; continuing deficits in attention, executive functions, and language; and high rates of service utilization (Babinski et al., 2010; Biederman et al., 2010; Hinshaw, Carte, Fan, Jassy, & Owens, 2007; Hinshaw et al., 2006; Mick et al., 2011). Noteworthy is that girls with ADHD who display impulsive–hyperactive behaviors are more likely to develop eating disorder symptoms (bingeing–purging behaviors, body dissatisfaction) than girls with ADHD who display only symptoms of inattention or non-ADHD girls (Mikami, Hinshaw, Patterson, & Lee, 2008). This finding supports the need to consider behaviors and outcomes for girls with ADHD that reflect female-relevant domains of impairment.

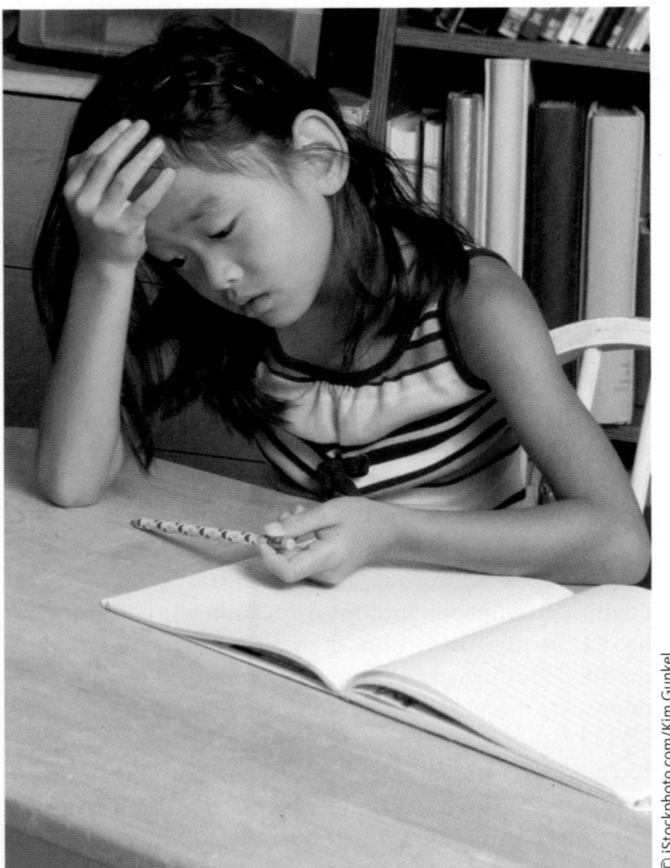

Girls with ADHD may be described by their teachers as "spacey" or "in a fog." Without hyperactivity and disruptive behavior, ADHD in girls may go unrecognized or be ignored.

In summary, ADHD in girls is a significant disorder with the same developmental course and many of the same features seen in boys with ADHD, including poor outcomes such as antisocial behavior, major depression, and other mental health problems (Monuteaux, Mick, Faraone, & Biederman, 2010).

Socioeconomic Status and Culture

ADHD affects children from all social classes, although there are slightly more children with ADHD in lower than higher socioeconomic status (SES) groups (Peterson et al., 2001). Such differences are best accounted for by co-occurring conduct problems in children with ADHD, since conduct problems are related to conditions that accompany low SES such as family adversity and stress (Szatmari, Offord, & Boyle, 1989). Findings regarding the relationships among ADHD, race, and ethnicity have been inconsistent, and it remains unclear whether current tools for assessing ADHD adequately capture the expression of ADHD in minority groups. Higher rates of teacher-rated ADHD and observed rates of ADHD behavior in the classroom have been found for African American versus European American children, which are not explained by rater bias or SES (Miller, Nigg, & Miller, 2009). Slightly lower rates of ADHD have been reported for Hispanic, Asian, American Indian, and Pacific Islander children (Cuffe, Moore, & McKeown, 2005). Knowledge about ADHD and access to treatment seem to be greater among Caucasian, non-Hispanic, and higher-educated families (McLeod, Fettes, Jensen, Pescosolido, & Martin, 2007; Miller et al., 2009). However, recent research suggests that when families from different ethnic groups do receive treatment, they do not differ in the benefits derived (Jones et al., 2010).

ADHD has been identified in every country around the world where it has been studied. Estimates vary across countries and cultures, with the highest rates found in South America and Africa (8%–12%) and the lowest rates in Japan and China (2%–5%). European and North American rates are in-between (4%–6%). These variations are mainly the result of differences in source of information (e.g., parents, teachers) and the way ADHD is diagnosed across studies done in different parts of the world. When a uniform diagnostic method is used, the rates of ADHD are highly similar worldwide (Buitelaar et al., 2006).

Differences across cultures may also reflect varying cultural norms and tolerance for the symptoms of ADHD (Weisz, Weiss, Suwanlert, & Chaiyasit, 2006). In cultures that value reserved and inhibited patterns of child behavior, such as Thailand, symptoms of ADHD are less common than in the United States. Moreover, when ADHD symptoms do occur, teachers in Thailand view them as more problematic—likely due to their culture-linked values and expectations (Weisz, Chayaisit, Weiss, Eastman, & Jackson, 1995). Thus, becoming an identified child with ADHD is partly a function of the discrepancy between a child's behavior and cultural expectations about how children ought to behave (Moffitt & Melchior, 2007).

In summary, ADHD is a universal phenomenon that is diagnosed more often in boys than girls in all cultures and whose expression, associated features, impairments, and outcomes are quite similar wherever it occurs (Faraone, Sergeant, Gillberg, & Biederman, 2003).

Course and Outcome

In the sections that follow, we describe how symptoms of ADHD change with development. These changes over the life span are illustrated with Alan, now age 35, diagnosed with ADHD in grade 1.

Infancy

ALAN

Off and Running

Our baby-sitter swears I was sitting up watching TV by 4 months. Then from a crawling position I ran, and we were off . . . I was all over the house, into everything, and Mom soon realized I could not be left alone. Darting here, there, and anywhere, I didn't like playing with my toys, preferring to explore on my own. (From a chapter by R. A. Barkley and L. J. Pfinffner in "Taking Charge of ADHD: The Complete, Authorized Guide for Parents" by R. A. Barkley, 1995, p. 208. Copyright © 1995 by Guilford Publications.)

It is likely that signs of ADHD are present at birth (one mother reported her child was so overactive in the womb that the kicking nearly knocked her over!). Assessments of activity levels in the home (using motion detectors) are related to mothers' ratings of ADHD in infants as young as 2 years of age (Ilott, Saudino, Wood, & Asherson, 2010). However, reliable identification of ADHD is difficult prior to age 3. When parents of an older child with ADHD describe what their child was like as a baby, they often say their baby had a difficult temperament—extremely active, unpredictable, over- or under-sensitive to stimulation, and irritable with erratic sleep patterns or feeding difficulties. Although these reports suggest the early presence of ADHD, there are two problems with the interpretation. First, parents' recollections may be colored by their child's later difficulties. Second, most infants with a difficult temperament do not develop ADHD. Although a difficult temperament in infancy may indicate something amiss in development, and in some cases may be a risk factor for later ADHD, it cannot by itself be taken as an early sign of ADHD. For example, one study reported an association between persistent crying during infancy and a ten-fold higher risk for hyperactivity at 8 to 10 years of age (Wolke, Rizzo, & Woods, 2002). However, most infants who cry persistently do not go on to develop ADHD.

Preschool

ALAN

Preschool Outcast

I often wondered why I wasn't in group-time in preschool. The teacher sent me in the corner to play with a toy by myself. Because of being singled out I didn't have many friends. I was different, but I didn't know why or what it was. (From a chapter by R. A. Barkley and L. J. Pfinffner in "Taking Charge of ADHD: The Complete, Authorized Guide for Parents" by R. A. Barkley, 1995, p. 208. Copyright © 1995 by Guilford Publications.)

With the growing number of hyperactive–impulsive symptoms at 3 to 4 years of age, ADHD becomes an increasingly visible and significant problem (Greenhill, Posner, Vaughan, & Kratochvil, 2008). Preschoolers with ADHD act suddenly and without thinking, dashing from activity to activity, grabbing at immediate rewards; they are easily bored and react strongly and negatively to routine activities (Campbell, 2002). Parents find it very difficult to manage the hyperactivity and noncompliance of their child, who may also be defiant and aggressive. Preschoolers with ADHD often roam about the classroom or daycare, talking excessively and disrupting other children's activities. Those who display a persistent pattern of hyperactive–impulsive and oppositional behavior for at least 1 year are likely to continue on to difficulties into middle childhood and adolescence (Olson, Bates, Sandy, & Lanthier, 2000). Difficulties in resisting temptation, delaying gratification, and inhibiting behavior during the pre-school years have also been found to predict ADHD symptoms in third grade (Campbell & von Stauffenberg, 2009). At this age the combination of severe ADHD-related symptoms and disruptions in the parent–child relationship is especially predictive of continuing ADHD behavior patterns (Campbell, Shaw, & Gilliom, 2000).

Elementary School

ALAN

I Couldn't Do Anything Right

Toward the middle half of first grade, the teacher called my Mom in for a conference. She was telling my Mom, "I'm always having to call on Alan. 'Alan, be still. Please. Yes, you can sharpen your pencil for the third time. You have to go to the bathroom again?'?" By the time I got to third grade things were getting off track. I felt like nothing I did was right. I would try to do good work. My teacher would write on my papers, "Needs to concentrate more on answers," "Needs to turn in all work," "Needs to follow directions." I really didn't think my teacher liked me. She was very stern, never seemed to smile, and was always watching me. (From a chapter by R. A. Barkley and L. J. Pfinffner in "Taking Charge of ADHD: The Complete, Authorized Guide for Parents" by R. A. Barkley, 1995, p. 208. Copyright © 1995 by Guilford Publications.)

Symptoms of inattention become especially evident when the child starts school. Classroom demands for sustained attention and goal-directed persistence are formidable challenges for these children (Kofler, Rapport, & Alderson, 2008). Not surprisingly, this is when they are usually identified as having ADHD and referred for special assistance. Symptoms of inattention continue through grade school, resulting in low academic productivity, distractibility, poor organization, trouble meeting deadlines, and an inability to follow through on social promises or commitments to peers. The hyperactive–impulsive behaviors that were present in preschool continue, with some decline, from 6 to 12 years of age (Barkley, 2006a).

During elementary school, oppositional defiant behaviors may increase or develop. By 8 to 12 years of age, defiance and hostility may take the form of serious problems, such as lying or aggression. During the school years, ADHD increasingly takes its toll as children experience problems with self-care, personal responsibility, chores, trustworthiness, independence, social relationships, and academic performance (Stein, Szumoski, Blondis, & Roizen, 1995).

Adolescence

ALAN

A Parent's Viewpoint

It wasn't until Alan was 13 that I understood that ADHD was a lifelong condition. His inability to block out the high level of activity in junior high caused him to become a frequent visitor to the principal's office. And he began to do poorly in math, the subject he had always done well at, because he couldn't concentrate on all the steps involved. I had him thoroughly evaluated for ADHD again and discovered he wasn't outgrowing it. In fact, it was causing him more trouble, not less. It was then that I realized how ADHD shapes personality, torments the victims, and fragments relationships. (From a chapter by R. A. Barkley and L. J. Pfinffner in "Taking Charge of ADHD: The Complete, Authorized Guide for Parents" by R. A. Barkley, 1995, p. 208. Copyright © 1995 by Guilford Publications.)

Many children with ADHD do not outgrow their problems when they reach adolescence, and sometimes their problems can get much worse. Although hyperactive–impulsive behaviors decline significantly by adolescence, they still occur at a level higher than in 95% of same-age peers who don't have ADHD. The disorder continues into adolescence for at least 50% or more of clinic-referred elementary school children (Spencer, Biederman, & Mick, 2007). In addition, most teens continue to display significant impairments in their emotional, behavioral, and social functioning (Barkley, 2006b; Lee, Lahey, Owens, & Hinshaw, 2008). Childhood symptoms of hyperactivity–impulsivity (more so than those of inattention) are generally related to poor adolescent outcomes (Barkley, 2006b).

Adulthood

ALAN

Adult Challenges

Alan is now 35 years old. He frequently feels restless, cannot sit at a desk for more than a few minutes, cannot get organized, does not follow through on plans because he forgets them, loses his keys and wallet, and fails to achieve up to his potential at work. During conversations, his mind wanders and he interrupts others, blurting out whatever comes to mind without considering the consequences. He often gets into arguments. His mood swings and periodic outbursts make life difficult for those around him. Now his marriage is in trouble. He feels helpless and frustrated. (Based on authors' case material)

Although difficult to confirm, many well-known and highly successful adults, including inventor Thomas Edison, comedian Robin Williams, and 8-time Olympic gold medal winner in swimming Michael Phelps may have had ADHD as children. Some children with ADHD either outgrow their disorder or learn to cope with it, particularly those with mild ADHD and without conduct or oppositional problems. Better outcomes are more likely for those children whose symptoms are less severe and who receive good care, supervision, and support from their parents and teachers, and who have access to economic and community resources, including educational, health, and mental health services (Kessler et al., 2005).

Unfortunately, like Alan, most children with ADHD will continue to experience problems, leading to a lifelong pattern of suffering and disappointment (Barkley et al., 2008). Once thought of primarily as a disorder of childhood, ADHD is now well established as an adult disorder. Adults with ADHD are restless, easily bored, and constantly seeking novelty and excitement; they may experience work difficulties, impaired social relations, and suffer from depression, low self-concept, substance abuse, and personality disorder (Antshel & Barkley, 2009). Although the situation is now changing, many adults with ADHD have never been diagnosed, particularly those without accompanying behavior problems. As a result they may feel that something is wrong with them, but they don't know what it is. Since many adults with ADHD are bright and creative individuals, they often feel frustrated about not living up to potential. Alan has had to contend with a number of significant problems as he continues to adapt to adult responsibilities of marriage, finances, and work. The help he has received for his ADHD helps him cope, but it is an ongoing challenge.

A few words of caution are in order regarding the developmental course and outcomes for ADHD. First, age of onset, course, and outcomes may differ depending on the samples, measures used, accompanying disorders, and the subtype of ADHD (Faraone, Biederman, & Mick, 2006). For example, negative outcomes are much greater in clinic versus community samples and for those children with accompanying conduct problems. Little information is currently available regarding long-term outcomes for children with the inattentive subtype. Interestingly, ADHD symptoms and impairments in adulthood are more severe when reported by other adults than by the person with ADHD (Barkley, Fischer, Smallish, & Fletcher, 2002). Thus, the developmental course and outcomes we have presented describe an overall pattern, but additional follow-up studies are needed to fill in important details.

SECTION SUMMARY

Prevalence and Course

- The best estimate is that ADHD affects about 6% to 7% of all school-age children.
- The diagnosis of ADHD is about 2 to 3 times more common in boys than girls.
- Girls with ADHD have a significant disorder; girls with ADHD in community samples appear to be less impaired than boys with ADHD; clinic-referred girls with ADHD display many of the same features and outcomes as boys with ADHD.
- ADHD occurs across all socioeconomic levels and has been identified in every country where it has been studied.
- Symptoms of ADHD change with development. A difficult infant temperament may be followed by hyperactive-impulsive symptoms at 3 to 4 years of age, which are followed, in turn, by the increasing visibility of symptoms of inattention around the time that the child begins school.
- Although some symptoms of ADHD may decline in prevalence and intensity as children grow older, for many individuals ADHD is a lifelong and painful disorder.

THEORIES AND CAUSES

The word cause is an altar to an unknown god.

—William James (1842–1910)

Many explanations for ADHD have been advanced, and some are highly controversial. For example, it has been argued (without much support) that ADHD is a trait left over from our evolutionary past as hunters (Hartmann, 1993). Others contend that ADHD is a myth, a disorder that has been fabricated because as a society we need it (Baughman, 2006; Breggin, 2001).

Despite much attention to the nature and causes of ADHD, clear answers have been elusive because diagnostic practices are not standardized and research is challenging. Nevertheless, research into the basic nature of ADHD leads to fascinating theories about possible mechanisms and causes (Coghill, Nigg, Rothenberger, Sonuga-Barke, & Tannock, 2005; Martel, 2009). As summarized in Box 5.1, interrelated theories have emphasized deficits in cognitive functioning, reward and motivation, arousal level, and self-regulation. No single theory can explain the many difficulties associated with ADHD. However, identifying the influences of the processes emphasized by each theory helps to increase our understanding of ADHD and develop more integrative models (Shiels & Hawk, 2010).

Numerous causes for ADHD have been proposed. However, many have not been adequately tested or have fallen by the wayside in the face of weak, inconsistent, or nonexistent support. Among these are that ADHD is caused by too much sugar intake, yeast, fluorescent

BOX 5.1 A CLOSER LOOK

Interrelated Theories of ADHD

Cognitive Functioning Deficits

Children with ADHD display specific cognitive deficits in sustained attention, response inhibition (i.e., inability to delay initial reactions to events or to stop behavior once it gets going), working memory, or executive functions. These in turn may lead to other cognitive, language, and motor difficulties. Cognitive deficits are important for understanding ADHD. However, since more than 50% of children with ADHD do not show major impairment on any specific cognitive task, the evidence does not support a *single* cognitive deficit as the cause of ADHD (Nigg, 2005).

Reward/Motivation Deficits

Children with ADHD display an abnormal sensitivity to rewards (i.e., higher reward threshold) and usually a heightened sensitivity or an aversion to delay (Sonuga-Barke et al., 2008). As a result, they have difficulties in motivating themselves and performing well when rewards are unavailable or delayed (Aase & Sagvolden, 2006). In support of this theory, recent research has connected ADHD with disruptions in the dopamine reward pathways of the brain (Volkow et al., 2009).

Arousal Level Deficits

Children with ADHD have an abnormal level of arousal—either too high or, more commonly, too low. Hyperactivity–impulsivity reflects an underaroused child's effort to maintain an optimal level of arousal by excessive self-stimulation (Zentall, 1985). Although this theory has received some support (Antrop, Roeyers, Van Oost, & Buysse, 2000), it has not yet been presented as a comprehensive model to account for the full range of problems found in children with ADHD.

Self-Regulation Deficits

Children with ADHD have a higher-order deficit in their ability to self-regulate—to use thought and language to direct their behavior. Deficiencies in self-regulation and effortful control lead to impulsivity, poor maintenance of effort, poor modulation of arousal level, emotion dysregulation, and attraction to immediate rewards. Self-regulatory theories examine the interplay among cognitive, arousal, and reward/motivational processes to understand how individuals with ADHD regulate their behavior in specific contexts (Douglas, 1999; Martel, 2009)

lighting, motion sickness, bad parenting, poor school environment, urban living, or too much TV.

While many factors may lead to ADHD, current research strongly suggests that ADHD is a neurodevelopmental disorder for which genetic and neurobiological factors play a central role (Kieling, Gonclaves, Tannock, & Castellanos, 2008; Mick & Faraone, 2008). However, biological and environmental risk factors together shape the development of behavioral and emotional regulation and the expression of ADHD symptoms over time, following several different pathways (Froehlich et al., 2011; Nigg et al., 2006; Sonuga-Barke, Auerbach, Campbell, Daley, & Thompson, 2005). Since ADHD is a complex and chronic disorder involving genetic, neural, cognitive, and behavioral mechanisms, any explanation that focuses on just one cause is likely to be inadequate (Banerjee, Middleton, & Faraone, 2007; Coghill et al., 2005). Although data do not yet permit a comprehensive causal model, ● Figure 5.2 shows a possible developmental pathway for ADHD that highlights several known causal influences and outcomes. We discuss each of these causal influences in the sections that follow.

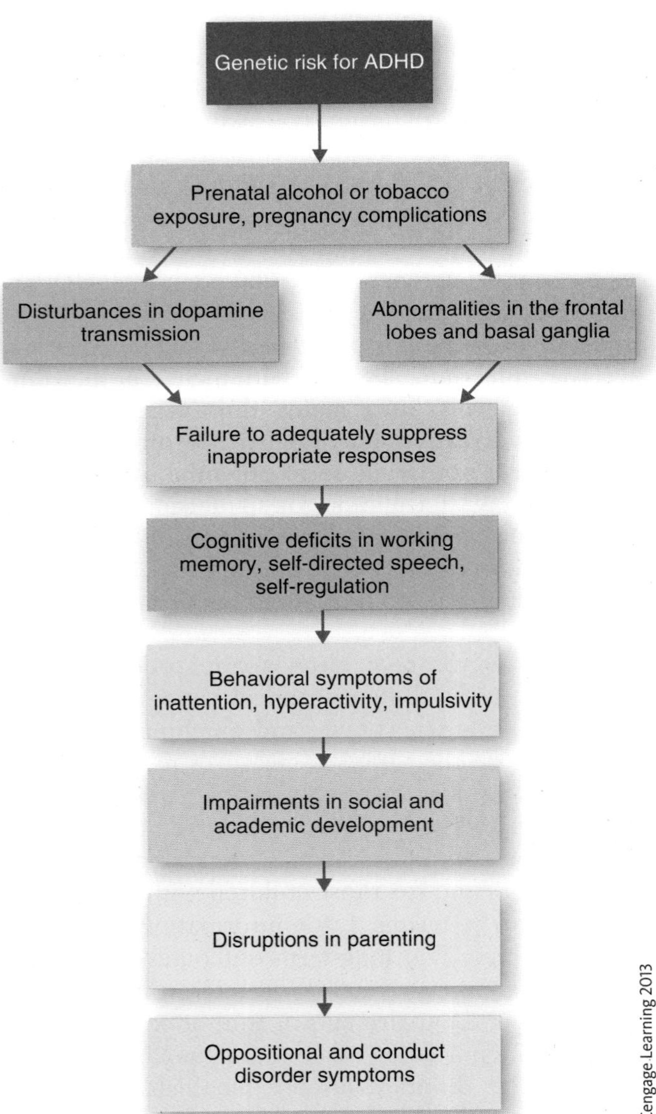

● **FIGURE 5.2** | A possible developmental pathway for ADHD.

Genetic Influences

Several lines of evidence point to genetic influences as key causal factors in ADHD (Faraone & Mick, 2010).

- *ADHD runs in families*. About one-third of the biological relatives of children with ADHD also have the disorder (Smalley et al., 2000). Remarkably, if a parent has ADHD, the risk to their child is nearly 60% (Biederman et al., 1995).
- *Adoption studies*. Rates of ADHD are nearly three times higher in biological versus adoptive parents of children with ADHD (Sprich, Biederman, Crawford, Mundy, & Faraone, 2000).
- *Twin studies*. Twin studies report extraordinarily high heritability estimates for ADHD, averaging about 75% for hyperactive–impulsive and inattentive behaviors, making ADHD among the most heritable of childhood disorders (Nikolas & Burt, 2010). Further, ADHD concordance rates for identical twins average 65%, about twice that of fraternal twins (Levy & Hay, 2001).
- *Specific gene studies*. Molecular genetic analysis suggests that specific genes may contribute to the expression of ADHD (Banaschewski, Becker, Scherag, Franke, & Coghill, 2010). The focus has been on genes involved in dopamine regulation, for three primary reasons. First, dopamine is a neurotransmitter used by the brain with a central role in psychomotor activity and reward seeking. Second, brain structures implicated in ADHD (see below) are rich with dopamine innervation, and neuroimaging studies have found evidence for dopamine dysregulation in these brain structures (Spencer et al., 2007). Third, primary medications that reduce ADHD symptoms act primarily by blocking the dopamine transporter (DAT1), a receptor on the presynaptic neuron involved in the re-uptake of dopamine, thereby increasing the availability of dopamine in the synapse. Findings for the association between variants in the dopamine transporter (DAT1) and ADHD have been mixed (Li, Sham, Owen, & He, 2006). However, this may be related to a G × E interaction. For example, children with this genetic risk who are also exposed to environmental risks such as psychosocial adversity or maternal smoking during pregnancy may develop a greater number of ADHD symptoms than those who are not exposed to the environmental risk (Laucht et al., 2007).

Consistent support has been found for the association between ADHD and a variant of one of the dopamine receptor genes, DRD4 (seven-repeat form). Interestingly, this gene has previously been linked to the personality trait of sensation seeking (high levels of thrill-seeking, impulsive, exploratory, and excitable behavior) (Ebstein et al., 1996); it affects responsiveness to medication; and it impacts parts of the brain associated with executive functions and attention. In addition to the association between ADHD and the DRD4 dopamine receptor gene, several other genes related to the regulation of dopamine, as well as noradrenaline, have recently been identified (Faraone & Mick, 2010; Nikolas, Friderici, Waldman, Jernigan, & Nigg, 2010).

Findings that implicate specific genes within the dopamine system in ADHD are intriguing, and are consistent with a model suggesting that reduced dopaminergic activity may be related to the behavioral symptoms of ADHD. For example, preliminary findings indicate that brain activity related to inhibitory control of behavior in children with ADHD may differ as a function of variations in specific genes within the dopamine system (Bédard et al., 2010). Keep in mind, however, that the effects of individual gene variants are very small and—in the vast majority of cases—the heritable components of ADHD are likely to be the result of multiple genes interacting on several different chromosomes (Neale et al., 2010). For example, associations have also been found between ADHD and genes within the serotonin system (Guimarães et al., 2009), and gene mutations that impair maternal serotonin production during pregnancy may increase the risk of ADHD-related symptoms in offspring (Halmøy et al., 2010). Recent work has also implicated genes associated with serotonin function in aversion to reward delay, suggesting that different genes may regulate different ADHD behaviors (Sonuga-Barke et al., 2011). Thus, it is highly unlikely that ADHD is caused by only one gene. As Kates (2007) noted, "Finding a gene mutation that transmits risk for ADHD is like looking for a needle in a haystack of the 3 billion base pairs of DNA that constitute the human genome" (p. 547). Nevertheless, taken together, the findings from family, adoption, twin, and specific gene studies strongly indicate that the risk for ADHD is inherited, although the precise mechanisms are not yet known (Mick et al., 2010). Findings from genome-wide association studies are just beginning to reveal the specific neurodevelopmental networks that may be involved in ADHD (Poelman, Pauls, Buitelaar, & Franke, 2011).

Pregnancy, Birth, and Early Development

Many factors that can compromise the development of the nervous system before and after birth may be related to ADHD symptoms, including: pregnancy and birth complications, maternal exposure to severe stress during pregnancy, low birth weight, malnutrition, early neurological insult or trauma, and diseases of infancy (Lindström, Lindblad, & Hjern, 2011; Linnet et al., 2003; Martel, Lucia, Nigg, & Breslau, 2007). Although these early factors predict later symptoms of ADHD, they may not be specific to ADHD; they may elevate the risk of developing many later problems, not only ADHD. Also, keep in mind that exposure to these risk factors is not randomly assigned and therefore could be related to ADHD in either the parent or child.

A mother's use of cigarettes, alcohol, or other drugs during pregnancy can have damaging effects on her unborn child. One study found that mothers of children with ADHD reported higher rates of heavy smoking (10 cigarettes per day) and more psychosocial stress during pregnancy compared to mothers of unaffected control children (Motlagh et al., 2010). Consistent support has been found for an association between maternal cigarette smoking during pregnancy and ADHD, particularly for female offspring, and for children who carry a specific genetic risk for ADHD (Braun, Kahn, Froehlich, Auinger, & Lanphear, 2006; Neuman et al., 2007). Whether this association is causal or due to other unmeasured environmental or genetic factors is unclear at this time (Obel et al., 2011; Thapar et al., 2009). Exposure to alcohol before birth may also lead to symptoms of inattention, hyperactivity, impulsivity, and associated impairments in learning and behavior (Mick, Biederman, Faraone, Sayer, & Kleinman, 2002).

Evidence suggests that mothers of children with ADHD use more alcohol, tobacco, and drugs than do control parents, even when they are not pregnant (Mick, Biederman, Faraone, et al., 2002). Since parental substance use is often associated with a chaotic home environment both before and after birth, it is difficult to disentangle the influence of substance abuse and other factors that occur prior to birth from the cumulative impact of a negative family environment that occurs during later development. Other substances used during pregnancy, such as cocaine, can adversely affect the normal development of the brain and lead to higher than normal rates of ADHD and other psychiatric disorders (Weissman et al., 1999). To summarize, although pregnancy and birth complications and substance use during pregnancy are not the cause of most cases of ADHD, they may be important contributing factors for some children.

Neurobiological Factors

ADHD is far from well understood, but there is substantial support for neurobiological causal factors (Krain & Castellanos, 2006). Evidence comes from research showing differences between children with and without ADHD on measures of brain function (Barkley, 2006a; Kieling et al., 2008), including:

- Differences on psychophysiological measures (e.g., EEG, galvanic skin response, and heart rate deceleration), suggesting diminished arousal or arousability (Beauchaine, Katkin, Strassberg, & Snarr, 2001; Monastra, Lubar, & Linden, 2001).
- Differences on measures of brain activity during vigilance tests, suggesting under-responsiveness to stimuli and deficits in response inhibition (Pliszka, Liotti, & Woldorff, 2000).
- Differences in blood flow to the prefrontal regions of the brain and the pathways connecting these regions to the limbic system, suggesting decreased blood flow to these regions (Hendren, De Backer, & Pandina, 2000).

Brain Abnormalities

Brain imaging studies make it possible to test hypotheses about the location of brain dysfunction in ADHD and to provide assessments of brain structure and function (Kelly, Margulies, & Castellanos, 2007; Liston, Cohen, Teslovich, Levenson, & Casey, 2011). Findings from these studies suggest abnormalities primarily in the **frontostriatal circuitry of the brain.** This region consists of the prefrontal cortex and inter-connected areas of gray matter located deep below the cerebral cortex, collectively known as the *basal ganglia* (basement structures). These areas of the brain are associated with attention, executive functions, delayed responding, and response organization. Lesions in this region result in symptoms similar to those of ADHD. Children with ADHD have a smaller right prefrontal cortex than children without ADHD (Filipek et al., 1997) and show structural abnormalities in several regions of the basal ganglia (Sobel et al., 2010). Interestingly, in identical twins discordant for ADHD, it is only the twin with ADHD who displays abnormalities in these brain structures (Castellanos et al., 2003).

Brain differences may not be restricted exclusively to the prefrontal cortex and parts of the basal ganglia. Recent findings indicate that children with ADHD have smaller total and right cerebral volumes (by 3–4%) and a smaller cerebellum. These data provide support for the growing notion that the deficits associated with ADHD may involve a cerebellar–prefrontal–striatal network (Mackie et al., 2007; Valera, Faraone, Murray, & Seidman, 2007). Recent work also suggests that specific regions of the thalamus may also be involved in the brain circuitry of ADHD, with different thalamic sub-circuits associated with differing ADHD symptoms (Ivanov et al., 2010).

In addition to identifying brain abnormalities, brain scan studies now focus on how brain connections and networks are wired during development. Newer studies suggest that circuits may develop differently or later in ADHD (Fair et al., 2010; Shaw et al., 2007). For example, one study (see Box 5.2) identified a delay in brain maturation in children with ADHD, particularly in the prefrontal regions (Shaw et al., 2007).

In summary, brain scan studies indicate the importance of the frontostriatal region of the brain in ADHD and the pathways connecting this region with the limbic system (via the striatum) and the cerebellum and thalamus. However, further research is required to reliably

BOX 5.2 A CLOSER LOOK

Does the Brain Develop Abnormally in Children with ADHD, or Is It Just Delayed?

Findings from brain-imaging studies suggest the latter. Dr. Philip Shaw and his colleagues at the National Institute of Mental Health studied a large group of children with ADHD and a comparison group of typically developing children at different ages. Using magnetic resonance imaging (MRI), the researchers tracked changes in the cortical thickness of the children's brains. Typically, the cortex reaches a peak thickness at around age 7 or 8. However, as shown to the right, in children with ADHD, there was about a 2 to 3 year delay in reaching this peak thickness, relative to typically developing controls. The greatest delay (about 5 years) was in the pre-frontal cortex that regulates self-control.

The overall pattern of brain development was the same for both groups, suggesting a developmental delay and not abnormal development in children with ADHD. The brains of children with ADHD did reach one developmental milestone earlier than those of typically developing children—maturation of the motor cortex that plans and controls movements. The researchers proposed that the delay in the development of areas of the cortex related to self-control, combined with the earlier development of the motor cortex, may account for the fidgety, restless, and uncontrolled hyperactive behavior of children with ADHD.

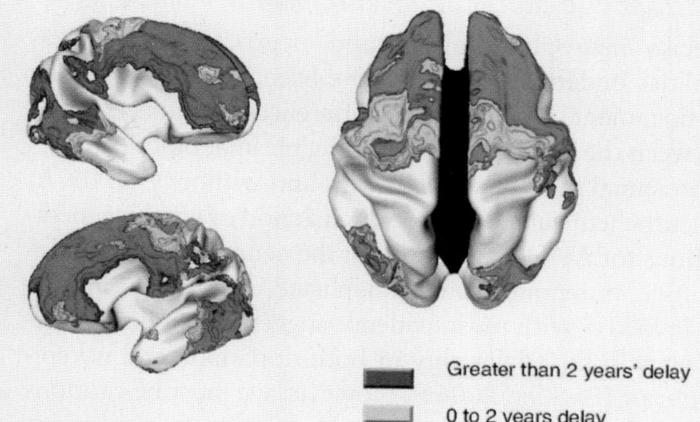

Regions where the ADHD group had delayed cortical maturation, as indicated by an older age of attaining peak cortical thickness

Interestingly, other brain image studies have found that delayed cortical maturation in the prefrontal cortex is associated with a greater number of symptoms of hyperactivity-impulsivity, even in typically developing children who have not been diagnosed with ADHD (Shaw et al., 2011).

Although these brain scan findings are captivating, they raise other important questions. First, the cause of the maturational delay in children with ADHD is not known at this time, although recent work suggests that delayed or decreased myelination may be a factor (Nagel et al., 2011). Second, if ADHD is just a delay in development, why do so many children continue to display ADHD as adults? Delay alone may not fully characterize all children with ADHD. In addition, even when brain maturation "catches up," the expression of behavior may still be different, since the timing of brain maturation may be as important as its end-point (Fair et al., 2010). Answers to these questions await further research. The hope is that brain imaging studies will increase our understanding of how ADHD develops and in doing so may one day help to tailor treatments for children with ADHD.

Source: Based on authors' case material.

identify more localized abnormalities. Furthermore, although neuroimaging studies can tell us that children with ADHD have a structural difference or less activity in certain regions of the brain, they don't tell us why.

A few additional words of caution are needed when evaluating the neurobiological evidence for ADHD. First, samples have been defined differently across studies and sample sizes are generally small. This gives rise to inconsistent findings and presents problems with interpretation and generalization. Second, ADHD includes a complex set of symptoms, making the search for a single neurobiological cause too simplistic. Third, the differences in brain structure and activity seen in ADHD (and other disorders) are usually only meaningful when comparing group statistics. The amount of variation in brain structure or function from one brain to the next is simply too great to be diagnostic or predictive for an individual, given what we currently know (Insel, 2010). Thus, although research using brain imaging has greatly

"Young man, go to your room and stay there until your cerebral cortex matures."

increased our understanding of ADHD, much research remains to be done before neuroimaging procedures can be integrated into clinical practice (Bush, 2008).

Neurophysiological and Neurochemical Findings

Precise neurophysiological and neurochemical abnormalities underlying ADHD have been extremely difficult to document. No consistent differences have been found between the biochemistry of urine, plasma, blood, and cerebrospinal fluid of children with and without ADHD. At a neurochemical level, the known action of effective medications for ADHD suggests that the neurotransmitters dopamine, norepinephrine, epinephrine, and serotonin may be involved, with most evidence suggesting a selective deficiency in the availability of both dopamine and norepinephrine (Barkley, 2006a). However, we must be cautious in drawing conclusions from the effects of medications alone. Using medication for effective treatment of ADHD symptoms does not prove that deficits in the chemical or its action are the cause of the symptoms, any more than the elimination of a headache by aspirin implies that the headache was caused by aspirin deficiency. Medications may operate at levels of neuroanatomy and neurochemistry that are far removed from primary causal influences.

Diet, Allergy, and Lead

The relationship of sugar to hyperactivity achieved epic significance when "What is sugar?" was the correct response to "The major cause of hyperactivity in North America" on the popular TV show *Jeopardy* (Barkley, 1995). However, study after study has conclusively shown that sugar is not the cause of hyperactivity (Milich, Wolraich, & Lindgren, 1986). So why do nearly one-half of the parents and teachers who are asked think that children are sugar sensitive? It may be the power of suggestion.

In one study, mothers who believed their children were sugar sensitive were told their children would be given a drink of Kool-Aid™ containing either sugar or, as a placebo, the sugar substitute aspartame. After the children drank their Kool-Aid, they and their mothers spent time playing and working together. In fact, none of the children was given sugar—they all received Kool-Aid with aspartame. But the mothers who thought their children had received sugar rated them as more hyperactive than the mothers who believed their children had received aspartame. Perhaps even more telling was that during play and task interactions, mothers who thought their children had received sugar were more critical of them, hovered more, and talked to them more frequently (Hoover & Milich, 1994). These findings suggest that what parents believe about the causes of their children's ADHD can affect their views of their children and how they treat them (Johnston & Leung, 2001). Such beliefs may be fueled by media portrayals—for example, when Bobby Hill, the son on the TV show "King of the Hill," is diagnosed with ADHD after eating at least four bowls of "Cookie Crunch" cereal (the last with extra sugar!). His mother, Peggy, "a hot shot substitute teacher," wonders if she should stay at home more often so she can give Bobby more attention, a notion reinforced by Bobby's father Hank who comments, "Well, it is called attention *deficit* disorder" (Kennedy, 2008).

There has been a long-time controversy about the possibility that allergic reactions and diet are causes of ADHD. A popular view in the 1970s and 1980s was that food additives caused children to be hyperactive and inattentive, and parents were encouraged to withhold foods containing artificial flavorings, colorings, preservatives, and sugars. By the 1990s food additives appeared to have been discarded as an explanation for ADHD (McGee, Stanton, & Sears, 1993). However, recent studies have revived this idea, focusing on the moderating role of genetic factors to explain why food additives may affect the behavior of some children more than others (McCann et al., 2007; Stevenson, 2010; Stevenson et al., 2010). In a close vote (8 to 6), a U.S. Food and Drug Administration Advisory Panel (March 31, 2011) concluded that foods that contain artificial dyes used to enhance colors do not need warning labels, but this issue continues to be debated. Other insights into micronutrients have changed the focus of dietary research on ADHD, with much interest currently in essential fatty acids, which are commonly lacking in the diet of North American children, as well as in other nutrients such as zinc and iron, which may be metabolized abnormally in some children (Arnold & DiSilvestro, 2005; Howard et al., 2011; Stevens et al., 2003).

Exposure to low levels of lead that are found in dust, water, soil, and flaking paint in areas where leaded gasoline and paint were once used may be associated with ADHD symptoms in the classroom (Fergusson, Horwood, & Lynskey, 1993). Although most children with ADHD do not have significantly elevated lead levels in their teeth or blood (Kahn, Kelly, & Walker, 1995), recent work persistently links ADHD to slight, subclinical elevations in lead exposure (Braun et al., 2006). All children have a little lead in their blood, and those with ADHD have a little more. In addition, lead exposure in combination with other risk factors such as nicotine during pregnancy may further increase a child's risk for ADHD (Froehlich et al., 2009). These findings suggest a possible role of lead exposure that requires further follow up using causally informative prospective studies (Nigg, Nikolas, Knottnerus, Cavanagh, & Frederici, 2010).

Family Influences

Twin studies find that psychosocial factors in the family account for only a small amount of the variance in ADHD symptoms (Nikolas & Burt, 2010), and explanations of ADHD based exclusively on negative family influences have received little support (Barkley, 2006a). Nevertheless, family influences are important in understanding ADHD for several reasons (Mash & Johnston, 2005).

- *Family influences may lead to ADHD symptoms or to a greater severity of symptoms.* In some cases, ADHD symptoms may be the result of interfering and insensitive early care-giving practices (Carlson, Jacobvitz, & Sroufe, 1995), especially in children with a specific genetic risk for ADHD (Martel et al., 2011). In addition, for children at risk for ADHD, family conflict may raise the severity of their hyperactive–impulsive symptoms to a clinical level (Barkley, 2003). Especially important is the **goodness of fit,** or the match between the child's early temperament and the parent's style of interaction (Chess & Thomas, 1984). An overactive child with an over-stimulating parent is a seemingly poor fit. As we have seen, many parents of children with ADHD also have the disorder, which means that the parents' ADHD symptoms may disrupt early parent–child interactions (Murray & Johnston, 2006). For example, mothers with higher levels of ADHD symptoms have been found to show less involvement, less positive parenting, and more inconsistent discipline with their children than mothers with lower levels of ADHD symptoms (Chronis-Tuscano et al., 2008). Finally, a recent study found that mothers with variants in the dopamine transporter gene (DAT1) were more like to display negative and controlling behaviors when interacting with their children, particularly when their children were highly disruptive (Lee et al., 2010). Although preliminary, these findings are fascinating, in that they suggest the possible importance of a parent-gene × child-gene interaction in families of children with ADHD, with the effects mediated by the child-rearing environment.
- *Family problems may result from interacting with a child who is impulsive and difficult to manage* (Mash & Johnston, 1990). The clearest support for this child-to-parent direction of effect comes from double-blind placebo control drug studies in which children's ADHD symptoms were decreased using stimulant medications. Decreases in children's ADHD symptoms produced a corresponding reduction in the negative and controlling behaviors that parents had previously displayed when their children were not medicated (Barkley, 1988). Somewhat surprisingly, preliminary findings suggest that stimulant medications that have dramatic effects on mothers' ADHD symptoms may have no effect on either observed parenting or child behavior (Chronis-Tuscano, Rooney, Seymour, Lavin, & Pian, 2010).
- *Family conflict is likely related to the presence, persistence, or later emergence of associated oppositional and conduct disorder symptoms.* In children with an inherited biological risk for ADHD, family conflict may heighten the emergence of early ODD and later comorbid ADHD and CD (Beauchaine et al., 2010). Many interventions for ADHD try to change patterns of family interaction to head off an escalating cycle of oppositional behavior and conflict. Family influences may play a major role in determining the outcome of ADHD and its associated problems, even if the influences are not the primary cause of ADHD (Johnston, Hommersen, & Seipp, 2009; Kaiser, Burnett, & Pfiffner, 2011).

In sum, ADHD has a strong biological basis and is an inherited condition for many children. It is likely that ADHD is a heterogeneous disorder, particularly at the level of neurobiology. Although evidence is converging on specific brain areas, findings are correlational, and we do not yet know the specific causes of the disorder. ADHD is likely the result of a complex pattern of interacting influences, perhaps giving rise to the disorder through a final common pathway in the nervous system. We are just beginning to understand the complex ways in which biological risk factors, brain development, family relationships, and broader system influences interact to shape the development and outcome of ADHD.

SECTION SUMMARY

Theories and Causes

- Theories about possible mechanisms and causes for ADHD have emphasized deficits in cognitive functioning, reward/motivation, arousal level, and self-regulation.
- There is strong evidence that ADHD is a neurodevelopmental disorder; however, biological and environmental risk factors together shape its expression.
- Findings from family, adoption, twin, and specific gene studies suggest that ADHD is inherited, although the precise mechanisms are not yet known.
- Many factors that compromise the development of the nervous system before and after birth may be related to ADHD symptoms, such as pregnancy and birth complications, maternal smoking during pregnancy, low birth weight, malnutrition, maternal alcohol or drug use, early neurological insult or trauma, and diseases of infancy.
- ADHD appears to be related to abnormalities and developmental delays in the frontostriatal circuitry of the brain and the pathways connecting this region with the limbic system, the cerebellum, and the thalamus.
- Neuroimaging studies tell us that in children with ADHD there is a structural difference or less activity in certain regions of the brain, but they don't tell us why.
- The known action of effective medications for ADHD suggests that several neurotransmitters are involved, with

(continues)

SECTION SUMMARY *(continued)*

most evidence suggesting a selective deficiency in the availability of both dopamine and norepinephrine.

- Psychosocial factors in the family do not typically cause ADHD, although they are important in understanding the disorder. Family problems may lead to a greater severity of symptoms and relate to the emergence of co-occurring conduct problems.

TREATMENT

MARK

Medication and Behavior Therapy

In third grade, Mark's teacher threw up her hands and said, "Enough!" In one morning, Mark had jumped out of his seat six times to sharpen his pencil, each time accidentally charging into other children's desks and toppling books and papers. He was finally sent to the principal's office when he began kicking a desk he had overturned. In sheer frustration, his teacher called a meeting with his parents and the school psychologist.

But even after they developed a plan for managing his behavior in class, Mark showed little improvement. Finally, after an extensive assessment, they found that he had ADHD with symptoms of both inattention and hyperactivity–impulsivity. He was put on Ritalin™, a stimulant medication, to control the hyperactivity during school hours. With a psychologist's help, his parents learned to reward desirable behaviors and to have Mark take time out when he became too disruptive. Soon Mark was able to sit still and focus on learning. (Adapted from NIMH, 1994)

LISA

Behavior Therapy and Counseling

Because Lisa wasn't disruptive in class, it took a long time for teachers to notice her problem. Lisa was first referred to the school evaluation team when her teacher realized that she was a bright girl with failing grades. The team ruled out a learning disability but determined that she had the inattentive subtype of ADHD. The school psychologist recognized that Lisa was also dealing with depression.

Lisa's teachers and the school psychologist developed a treatment plan that included a program to increase her attention and develop her social skills. They also recommended that Lisa receive counseling and cognitive behavior therapy to help her recognize her strengths and overcome her depression. (Adapted from NIMH, 1994)

More and more children are receiving help for their ADHD, with rates of outpatient treatment for ADHD more than tripling from 1987 to 1997, from 0.9 to 3.4 per 100 children (Olfson, Gameroff, Marcus, & Jensen, 2003). However, it is still the case that less than half of children with ADHD, particularly those in greatest clinical need, actually receive specialty services (Zima et al., 2010). Of those who do receive services, many do not continue their treatment for any length of time (Hechtman, 2006). Although there is no known cure for ADHD, a variety of treatments can be used to help children like Mark and Lisa cope with their symptoms and any secondary problems that may arise (Antshel & Barkley, 2008; Pelham & Fabiano, 2008). An overview of these treatments is presented in Table 5.3.

TABLE 5.3 | Treatments for Children with ADHD

Primary Treatments	Focus of Treatment
Stimulant medication	Managing ADHD symptoms at school and home
Parent management training	Managing disruptive child behavior at home, reducing parent–child conflict, and promoting prosocial and self-regulating behaviors
Educational intervention	Managing disruptive classroom behavior, improving academic performance, teaching prosocial and self-regulating behaviors
Intensive Treatment	**Focus of Treatment**
Summer treatment programs	Enhancing present adjustment at home and future success at school by combining many of the primary and additional treatments in an intensive summer treatment program
Additional Treatments	**Focus of Treatment**
Family counseling	Coping with individual and family stresses associated with ADHD, including mood disturbance and marital strain
Support groups	Connecting adults with other parents of children with ADHD, sharing information and experiences about common concerns, and providing emotional support
Individual counseling	Providing a supportive relationship in which the youth can discuss personal concerns and feelings

Source: © Cengage Learning 2013.

The primary treatment approach (recommended by *Consumer Reports* and the U.S. Surgeon General) combines stimulant medication, parent management training, and educational intervention (AACAP, 2007; Chronis, Jones, & Raggi, 2006; Kaiser & Pfiffner, 2011). Interventions that use elements of all approaches have also been provided in intensive summer treatment programs. Additional treatments, for which there is far less evidence, include family counseling and support groups, and child-focused treatments, such as social skills training and individual counseling (Smith, Barkley, & Shapiro, 2006). Other treatments, such as neurofeedback/biofeedback (Lofthouse, McBurnett, Arnold, & Hurt, 2011) and complementary and alternative biomedical treatments, such as diet and vitamin/mineral supplements (Hurt, Arnold, & Lofthouse, 2011) are used, despite limited or inconsistent supporting evidence (Tomlinson, Wilkinson, & Wilkinson, 2009). A rationale and procedures for early detection and early intervention for ADHD is now beginning to emerge (Sonuga-Barke, Koerting, Smith, McCann, & Thompson, 2011) as are focused interventions for specific ADHD deficits—for example, working memory (Beck, Hanson, Puffenberger, Benninger, & Benninger, 2010) and inattention (Rabiner, Murray, Skinner, & Malone, 2010).

Although somewhat similar treatments are used for children and adolescents with ADHD, research with teens has been extremely limited (Barkley, 2006b). Similarly, only a few studies have looked at treatment efficacy for specific ADHD subtypes, such as children who are predominantly inattentive (e.g., Pfiffner et al., 2007). Therefore, although recognizing that children with different ADHD symptoms may have different treatment needs (Solanto, Pope-Boyd, Tryon, & Stepak, 2009), most of our discussion centers on treatments for school-age children with ADHD who show symptoms of both inattention and hyperactivity-impulsivity.

Medication

When I'm not medicated . . . my muscles just don't want to relax. They don't want to settle down. I just feel very "go-go-go." I can't be still. My body tries to keep up with my mind but it can't just do it fast enough.

— Angelique (Waite & Ramsey, 2010, p. 429)

The use of stimulants and other medications to treat the symptoms of ADHD in children has been the subject of considerable debate. Most of you likely have opinions about stimulants for ADHD—perhaps that they are overprescribed, used as a quick fix, do not let kids be kids, and lead to over-diagnosis. Let's look at the role of stimulant medications and the controversy that surrounds them.

Stimulants

Stimulant medications have been used to treat the symptoms of ADHD since the chance discovery of their effectiveness in the 1930s (see Box 5.3). Several other types of medications have also been used, including noradrenergic drugs, anti-depressants, and anti-hypertensives (Daughton & Kratochvil, 2009). We focus our discussion on stimulants because they are the most studied, most effective, and most commonly used treatment for the management of symptoms of ADHD and its associated impairments. Nevertheless, it is important to keep in mind that many other potentially effective medication options are available for children with ADHD, including the non-stimulant drug atomoxetine (Strattera™) and a patch which releases medication directly through the skin into the bloodstream, eliminating the need to take medication orally (Pelham et al., 2011).

Stimulants come in several types, including both short- and long-acting forms. The two most effective stimulants in treating children with ADHD are dextroamphetamine (Dexedrine or Dextrostat™) and **methylphenidate** (Ritalin™), the most commonly used drug by far (Faraone & Buitelaar, 2010). These medications alter activity in the frontostriatal region of the brain by affecting neurotransmitters (dopamine) important to this region. Interestingly, preliminary findings from brain scan studies of individuals with ADHD suggest that stimulants may also help to normalize structural abnormalities and functional connections within this region (Sheridan, Hinshaw, & D'Esposito, 2010; Sobel et al., 2010).

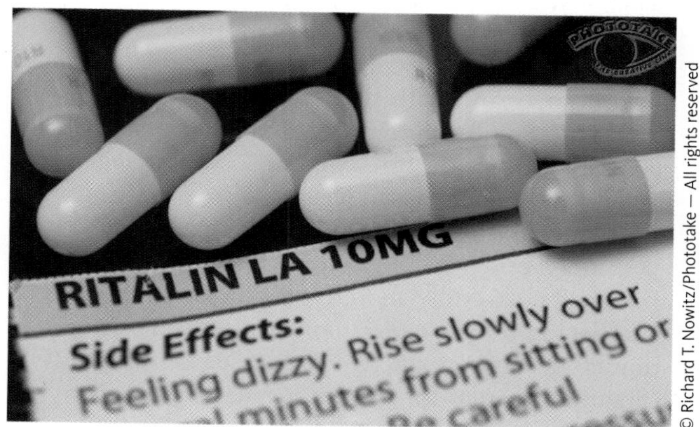

Stimulant medications are commonly used to treat children with ADHD

BOX 5.3 A CLOSER LOOK

The "Accidental" Discovery of Math Pills

The use of stimulant medication for children with learning and behavior problems was first reported in 1937 by Charles Bradley, the medical director of a small hospital for children with major difficulties in learning or behavior. Dr. Bradley described dramatic improvements in some of the children he treated with Benzedrine. Why did Dr. Bradley decide to use stimulants to treat these problems in the first place?

Dr. Bradley was a very conscientious physician, and all patients were given careful workups. These workups included a spinal tap, which naturally led to headaches afterward that frequently were lasting, severe, or both, and were presumed to be due to the loss of spinal fluid. Dr. Bradley speculated that if he could stimulate the choroid plexus to secrete spinal fluid at a faster rate, the headaches would be relieved more quickly. He decided to proceed along these lines and chose the most potent stimulant available at the time, Benzedrine. (*Note*: This type of powerful stimulant is no longer used.) The effect on the headaches was negligible, but to his astonishment, the teachers reported major improvements in learning and behavior in many children that lasted until the Benzedrine regimen was withdrawn. The children themselves noted the greater ease of learning and called the medication "math pills," presumably because mathematics was the hardest subject for them, and their improved ability to learn was most noticeable in that subject.

Source: Based on Gross, 1995.

For about 80% of children with ADHD, stimulants produce dramatic increases in sustained attention, impulse control, and persistence of work effort, and decreases in task-irrelevant activity and noisy and disruptive behaviors. Stimulants may also improve the child's academic productivity; cooperation and social interactions with parents, teachers, and peers; and, occasionally, physical coordination such as handwriting or sports ability (Barkley, 2006a; Swanson, McBurnett, Christian, & Wigal, 1995). Stimulant medications used appropriately and with proper supervision are usually quite safe. Some children may experience side effects such as reduced appetite, weight loss, slowing of expected gains in height and weight, increase in heart rate and blood pressure, or problems falling asleep. However, most potential side effects are typically benign and can be carefully monitored and often eliminated by reducing the dose (Graham et al., 2011). Although stimulants can be addictive if misused or abused (one recreational name for Ritalin is Vitamin R!), they are not addictive for most children who take them, nor do they lead to an increased risk for later substance abuse (Looby, 2008). Stimulants seldom make children "high," nervous, or jumpy, or turn them into non-feeling zombies. Qualitative findings suggest that young people on medication are generally positive about taking it and report that it reduces their disruptive behavior and improves their relationships with peers (Singh et al., 2010).

The short-term benefits of medication are well documented (Spencer, Biederman, & Wilens, 2000). Unfortunately, follow-up studies raise questions about their long-term benefits (Jensen et al., 2007). The effects of stimulants are temporary and occur only while the child is taking medication. In this sense, the use of stimulants is similar to other important treatments for chronic conditions, such as insulin used for diabetes; however, they are not a cure. Many young people receiving stimulants for severe behavior problems remain impaired, despite many years of medication treatment. The limited long-term benefits of stimulants raise important issues about their clinical use that are yet to be resolved (Swanson & Volkow, 2009).

Controversy: The Ritalin Wars

There is no pharmacologic free lunch. The key question is always this: Is the gain to public health from proper use of an agent . . . greater than the danger of wide-scale misuse or the social cost of the regulatory machinery itself?

—Leon Eisenberg (2007)

Public awareness of and controversy about the potential misuse of medication is evidenced by efforts (ultimately unsuccessful) to introduce legislation in the U.S. Congress with the express purpose "to protect children and their parents from being coerced into administering a controlled substance in order to attend school, and for other purposes" (Child Medication Safety Act of 2007). Why the concern? Community and physician surveys, increased production of Ritalin, and pharmacy audits all indicate that stimulant consumption has more than tripled since 1990 in North America (Scheffler, Hinshaw, Modrek, & Levine, 2007). The co-prescription of stimulants with other medications, most commonly anti-depressants, has also increased during this period (Comer, Olfson, & Mojtabai, 2010). It is estimated that more than 2 million school-age children in the U.S. regularly take stimulants (Zuvekas, Vitiello, & Norquist, 2006). Across ages, use is estimated to be 0.6% in children less than 4 years of age, 4.5% in 5- to 9-year-olds, 8.5% in 10- to 15-year-olds, and 4.8% in 15- to 19-year-olds (Swanson & Volkow, 2009). Moreover, the use of Ritalin is at least 5 times higher in North America than in the rest of the world, although use worldwide is also increasing. This increase may stem from a widening of the diagnostic criteria for ADHD, greater use of stimulants among girls and older individuals, widespread third-party medication coverage, and direct marketing efforts by drug companies. Also, as changes in public policy and laws increase eligibility for special education and other services for individuals with ADHD, more individuals may receive this diagnosis and subsequently be placed on medication (DuPaul & Stoner, 2003). Recent findings indicate that although stimulant use in children ages 15 and younger in the U.S has leveled off over the past decade, it continues to increase in older adolescents and young adults. This increase is related to the growing recognition of ADHD in adults, but has also raised concerns about a possible diversion of stimulants from medical to non-medical use in older individuals (Swanson & Volkow, 2009).

Given the astronomic increase in the use of stimulants to treat ADHD in North America, despite the similarities of prevalence across different parts of the world, we need to ask if ADHD is overdiagnosed and if stimulants are overprescribed (Eisenberg, 2007). Because of the wide variability in diagnostic practices, treatment decisions, and rates of stimulant use in various schools, communities, geographic regions, and populations, it is not surprising that research findings concerning diagnosis and medication use are inconsistent (Angold, Erkanli, Egger, & Costello, 2000; Jensen et al., 1999). Perhaps the best overall conclusion to be drawn from the research is that in many cases stimulants are currently being used inappropriately: underprescribed in some cases and overprescribed in others. We need a better understanding of the factors leading to the diagnosis of ADHD and stimulant use so that further steps can be taken to increase appropriate use—for example, improved screening and diagnosis, and better education of service providers (Jensen, 2000). Consider the following comments by the parents of a child with ADHD:

> When all is said and done, we stand in the middle on the issue of medication—not dramatically opposed, but not wildly enthusiastic either. Ideally, stimulants should be prescribed, monitored carefully, and there should be ongoing communication with parents and school personnel. However, the world being what it is, a lot of people seem to be falling short of the ideal a lot of the time. (McCluskey & McCluskey, 2000, p. 11)

Despite their limitations, stimulants—when properly used—remain among the most effective treatments for managing symptoms of ADHD. Nevertheless, since stimulants do not address many of the associated individual, family, academic, and peer problems of children with ADHD, additional primary interventions such as parent management training and educational interventions are needed.

Parent Management Training (PMT)

Being the parent of a child who is overactive, disorganized, irritable, and does not listen or follow directions is difficult and exhausting. Usual discipline tactics like reasoning, warning, or scolding often don't work. Thus, parents may feel powerless and at a loss as to what to do. Out of frustration, they may spank, ridicule, or yell at their child, even though they know it is not effective. These reactions leave everyone in the family feeling more upset than ever. **Parent management training (PMT)** provides parents with a variety of skills to help them:

- manage their child's oppositional and noncompliant behaviors;
- cope with the emotional demands of raising a child with ADHD;
- contain the problem so that it does not worsen; and
- keep the problem from adversely affecting other family members.

Parents are first taught about ADHD so that they understand the biological basis of the disorder. This helps to remove the burden of guilt from parents who may think they have caused the problem. Parents are also given a set of guiding principles for raising a child with ADHD, such as using more immediate, frequent, and powerful consequences; striving for consistency; planning ahead; not personalizing the child's problems; and practicing forgiveness (Barkley, 2000).

Parents are next taught behavior management principles and techniques, such as identifying behaviors they wish to encourage or discourage, using rewards and sanctions to achieve specified goals, establishing a home token program, noticing what their child does well, and praising their child's strengths and accomplishments. For disruptive behavior, parents also learn to use penalties such as loss of privileges or time-out as well as how to manage noncompliance in public places. Parents may also learn to use a school–home-based reward program where teachers evaluate the child on a daily report card. This card serves as a means for rewards or punishments (usually tokens) that will be administered at home for classroom conduct. Parents also learn how to manage future misconduct and are given follow-up sessions (Smith et al., 2006).

Parents are encouraged to spend time each day sharing an enjoyable activity with their child. They learn to structure situations in ways that will maximize the child's success and minimize failures. For example, if the child has difficulty completing tasks, it may be necessary to break the task into smaller steps and then praise the completion of each step. In PMT, parents also learn to reduce their own levels of arousal through relaxation, meditation, or exercise. Reduced arousal or anger allows parents to respond more calmly to their child's behavior.

Numerous studies support the effectiveness of PMT and other behavioral interventions in treating children with ADHD (Fabiano et al., 2009; Webster-Stratton, Reid, & Beauchaine, 2011); however, the relative advantages and long-term benefits of PMT when used on its own to treat ADHD are still being debated. As we will discuss, the effects of stimulants appear to be as strong as or stronger than the effects of PMT in treating the primary symptoms of ADHD. PMT may produce additional therapeutic benefits by treating the associated problems, improving family functioning, and increasing consumer satisfaction (Chronis et al., 2004a). To date, PMT has focused mainly on teaching parents to manage the overt disruptive behaviors that accompany their child's ADHD, rather than on changing the deficits underlying the child's ADHD. New approaches that combine PMT with therapy that is directed at the parent–child processes that mediate the development of attention and self-regulatory skills may provide incremental benefits for children with ADHD (Sonuga-Barke et al., 2006).

Educational Intervention

ALAN

Boxed in at School

My teacher wanted to make me concentrate better, so one day she put my desk in the far corner, separated from the rest of the class. A few days had passed. I still wasn't finishing my work on time, but I was trying. My teacher didn't care; it wasn't finished. She then put a refrigerator box around my desk so I couldn't see anyone. I could hear as other kids in class would make fun of me. It really hurt; I was ashamed of myself and mad at my teacher. I couldn't tell my Mom because I might get into trouble. I hated school, didn't like my teacher, and started not liking myself. . . . It was hard to face the next day. A week had passed, and I poked holes in the cardboard so I could see who was making fun of me. I started peeping through the holes, making the other kids laugh. The teacher would get so annoyed. So I became the class clown. I was expelled for two days. When my Mom found out what was going on, boy, did she get angry; she was mad that the teacher would do this and mad that the principal allowed it and no one could see what this was doing to me. (From a chapter by R. A. Barkley and L. J. Pfinffner in "Taking Charge of ADHD: The Complete, Authorized Guide for Parents" by R. A. Barkley, 1995, p. 209. Copyright © 1995 Guilford Publications.)

Classroom requirements to sit still, pay attention, listen to instructions, wait your turn, complete assignments, and get along with classmates are not easily met by children with ADHD. Their inattention and hyperactivity–impulsivity make learning very difficult, at times even painful. Although some children with ADHD are placed in a special education class for all or part of the day, most remain in the regular classroom. Whenever possible, it is preferable to keep children with ADHD in class with their peers.

Educational interventions focus on managing inattentive and hyperactive–impulsive behaviors that interfere with learning, and providing a classroom environment that capitalizes on the child's strengths (DuPaul & Stoner, 2003). Techniques for managing classroom behavior are similar to those recommended to parents. The teacher and child set realistic goals and objectives, set up a mutually agreed-upon reward system, carefully monitor performance, and reward the child for meeting goals. Disruptive or off-task classroom behaviors may be punished with **response-cost procedures** that involve the loss of privileges, activities, points, or tokens following inappropriate behavior, or with brief periods of time-out. These procedures have proved to be effective in reducing disruptive classroom behavior and enhancing academic productivity (Pfiffner, Barkley, & DuPaul, 2006).

Many strategies for instructing children with ADHD are simply good teaching methods. Letting children know what is expected of them, using visual aids, providing cues for expected behavior, and giving written as well as oral instructions all help children focus their attention and remember important points. In addition, children with ADHD may require other accommodations to help them learn. For example, the teacher may seat the child near his or her own desk, provide a designated area in which the child can move about, establish a clearly posted system of rules, and give the child frequent cues for expected behaviors. A card or a picture on the child's desk can provide a visual reminder for acceptable behavior such as raising a hand instead of shouting out. Repeating instructions, providing extra time, writing assignments on the board, and listing all of the books and materials needed for a task may increase the likelihood that children with ADHD will complete their work (Pfiffner et al., 2006).

School-based interventions for ADHD have received considerable support (DuPaul, 2007). An integrative review found that contingency management procedures aimed at improving behavior and interventions directed at increasing academic performance both had substantial positive effects (DuPaul & Eckert, 1997). Recent efforts have focused on a variety of school-based interventions for ADHD, including those for individual students in regular and special education classes, combined home and school interventions, and schoolwide interventions that incorporate both universal and targeted treatments (Waschbusch, Pelham, & Massetti, 2005).

Intensive Interventions

There are no quick cures for ADHD. More intensive (and ongoing) treatments than previously used may be required to produce meaningful changes in long-term outcomes. As described below, the Summer Treatment Program and the Multimodal Treatment Study for Children with ADHD are two examples of programs that have provided intensive treatment to children with ADHD and their families.

Summer Treatment Program

Over the past 25 years, Dr. William Pelham and his colleagues have developed and disseminated an exemplary intensive summer treatment program (Pelham et al., 2010). In this program, treatment is provided to children with ADHD ages 5 to 15 in a camp-like setting where they engage in classroom and recreational activities with other children. Summer treatment has two major advantages over other interventions: It maximizes opportunities to build effective peer relations in normal settings, and it provides continuity to academic work to ensure gains made during the school year are not lost. These programs are coordinated with stimulant medication trials, parent management training, social skills training, and educational interventions in an all-out treatment effort.

The Summer Treatment Program packs 360 hours of day-treatment into a period of 8 weeks, the equivalent of 7 years of weekly therapy. Ratings by parents and counselors suggest that children who participate show overall improvements in behavior, decreases in problem severity, and improvements in social skills and academic performance. Children also rate themselves as doing better, and parents report higher levels of self-efficacy. Dropout rates are low and consumer satisfaction is high. The program is also cost-effective compared to more traditional treatments. Preliminary findings from controlled studies of outcomes are promising (Chronis et al., 2004b; Pelham et al., 2000); however, although growing, these programs are not yet widely available and it's still too early to tell whether this kind of intensive program will make a long-term difference for these children.

Courtesy of William E. Pelham

Courtesy of William E. Pelham

Children with ADHD participating in a Summer Treatment Program

The MTA Study

The Multimodal Treatment Study of Children with ADHD (MTA Study) is a landmark multisite study sponsored by the U.S. National Institute of Mental Health (NIMH) and the Department of Education. It represents the first large, randomized clinical trial for children with ADHD. The study sought to answer three questions: How do long-term medication and behavioral treatments compare with one another? Are there additional benefits when they are used together? What is the effectiveness of systematic carefully delivered treatments versus routine community care? (MTA Cooperative Group, 1999a).

Carefully diagnosed children ages 7 to 9 years with ADHD were randomly assigned to one of four treatment groups, followed by major assessments at periodic intervals during and after treatment.

- *Medication Management*: This group received stimulant medication 7 days a week;
- *Behavioral treatment*: This group received 35 sessions of parent management training, up to 10 teacher and school visits per year, and participation in an intensive 8-week summer treatment program, which taught academic and social skills and had a classroom aide who continued to reinforce strategies learned in the summer treatment program in the child's actual classroom for half a day, 5 days per week, for 12 weeks;
- *Combined behavioral treatment and medication*: This group received both medication and behavioral treatment; or

- *Routine community treatment*: This group received treatment as it was routinely delivered in community care. In fact, 66% of children in this group received stimulant medication.

The major finding from the MTA Study after 14 months of active treatment was that all groups showed reductions in ADHD symptoms over time, but there were significant variations in the amount of change. First, stimulant medication was superior to behavioral treatment and to routine community care in treating the symptoms of ADHD. Second, combining behavioral treatments with medication resulted in no additional benefits for the core symptoms of ADHD over medication alone, but did provide modest benefits for non-ADHD symptoms and other outcomes related to positive functioning (MTA Cooperative Group, 1999a). Composite outcome measures showed that combined treatment was best, followed by medication, then behavior therapy, and, finally, community treatment (Conners et al., 2001; Swanson et al., 2001).

The benefits of combined treatment were also found at a 24-month follow up (MTA Cooperative Group, 2004a, 2004b). However, by 36 months there were no significant treatment group differences, with all groups showing equal benefits for ADHD symptoms (Jensen et al., 2007). Consistent with this result, findings from the MTA Study at 6 and 8 years following enrollment in the program indicate that the effects of both medication and behavioral treatments either decline or cease entirely when the treatment stops (Molina et al., 2009). Thus, the efficacy of treatment for children with ADHD will require that these treatments continue to be provided in a comprehensive, carefully monitored, and ongoing fashion. The interventions in the MTA study were more intensive and monitored more closely than is typically the case in real world clinical practice. Further research will be needed to determine the intensity of intervention and frequency of monitoring needed to maintain treatment gains and optimal functioning over time and across contexts in light of available treatment resources (Abikoff, 2009).

Other questions from the MTA Study that continue to be addressed concern which treatments work best for which children, for which outcomes, and why? (Hinshaw, 2007). For example, children with ADHD and comorbid anxiety and children from families on social assistance may benefit more from behavioral treatments than those without these difficulties (MTA Cooperative Group, 1999b), and behavioral treatments may be associated with less substance use at a later age (Molina, et al., 2007). In general, the long-term findings from the MTA study indicate that the initial clinical presentation in childhood (e.g., severity, co-occurring conduct problems, social disadvantage) and the strength of ADHD symptom response to *any* treatment are better predictors of adolescent outcomes than the type of treatment received in childhood (Molina et al., 2009).

The MTA study findings can be interpreted in different ways and are likely to be debated for some time to come. It seems that for children who have uncomplicated ADHD with no co-occurring disorders, adequate social functioning, and good academic performance, medication management may be the best treatment option. However, for those who have ADHD complicated by oppositional symptoms, poor social functioning, and ineffective parenting, combining medication and behavioral treatment may be the best option. In both cases, ongoing interventions will likely be needed. Whatever the final verdict, findings from the MTA study continue to raise numerous questions of clinical importance for children with ADHD and their families.

Additional Interventions

Other interventions have been used to provide support to children with ADHD and their families. Among these interventions are family counseling and support groups and individual counseling for the child. (A brief overview of these interventions can be found in Table 5.3.)

Family Counseling and Support Groups

Many families of children with ADHD experience frustration, blame, and anger for some time. As we have discussed, siblings may feel neglected or resent the time their parents spend with the child with ADHD. Family members may require special assistance not only in managing behavior but also in dealing with their own thoughts and feelings. Counseling the family helps everyone develop new skills, attitudes, and an ability to relate more effectively.

Support groups for people who are coping with ADHD in various ways can be very helpful to members. There are many local and national support groups for parents of children with ADHD. Members share information, emotional support, personal frustrations and successes, referrals to qualified professionals, discoveries about what works, and their aspirations for their children and themselves. There are also online bulletin boards and discussion groups. Sharing experiences with others that have similar concerns helps parents feel that they are not alone.

Individual Counseling

Life can be very hard for children with ADHD. They have few successes on which to build their sense of self-competence. Perhaps as a result, even when they succeed, they may attribute their success to uncontrollable factors such as task ease or luck (Hoza, Waschbusch,

BOX 5.4 A CLOSER LOOK

Questions Asked by Children and Adolescents with ADHD

Children (Ages 4 to 10)

I just found out I have ADHD. How can I keep this secret from my brother?

I heard ADHD means you're weird. Is that right?

Is it true that if you have ADHD you can think faster than other people?

Will the medicine make me smarter?

Adolescents (Ages 11 to 17)

How do you know the medicine isn't dangerous?

Any advice on how to deal with the fact that I feel like a reject because I have ADHD?

How long am I going to have ADHD?

How can I convince [my teacher] that ADHD exists and that it affects my performance?

Source: Based on Hallowell and Ratey, 1994.

Pelham, Molina, & Milich, 2000). Being punished or told they are stupid or bad is often their main form of attention. They have few friends and are constantly in trouble. The cumulative impact can leave them feeling isolated and believing that they are abnormal, stupid, or doomed to failure. Individual counseling attempts to address these concerns, although evidence for its effectiveness in treating children with ADHD is limited. Children usually come into counseling with many questions about ADHD and treatment that are addressed at the outset and in later sessions (see Box 5.4).

A Comment on Controversial Treatments

Understandably, parents want to explore all possible ways to help their children with ADHD. Over the years, many treatments that sound plausible have been proposed. Some are enthusiastically endorsed by professionals, and individual patient reports claim dramatic success; others are pure charlatanism. Treatments proposed for children with ADHD that have not been scientifically substantiated include: restricted diets, allergy treatments, medication to correct inner ear problems, vestibular stimulation, running, walks in the park, treatment for yeast infection, megavitamins, sensory integration training, chiropractic adjustment, eye training, special colored glasses, and metronome therapy. Fad treatments may prove to be expensive, provide false hope for a quick cure, and delay the use of evidence-based treatments that are known to be of some benefit (Waschbusch & Hill, 2003).

Keeping Things in Perspective

MARK

Good Support System

Through my years so far, I've been through a lot. My Mom says I have a good heart; I care about those in need. I'm not dumb. You can't always measure smartness by tests. I feel I'm doing better now. It helps to talk to people who understand. What I'm trying to say is: no matter what comes my way, I can survive. I have those who really care, and from that I draw my strength. (From R. A. Barkley and L. J. Pfinffner in "Taking Charge of ADHD: The Complete, Authorized Guide for Parents" by R. A. Barkley, 1995, p. 211. Copyright © 1995 by Guilford Publications. Reprinted by permission.)

Young people with ADHD have problems that should not be minimized, especially if doing so prevents children and adolescents with ADHD and their families from receiving help. However, as Mark's comments illustrate, in helping those with ADHD and their families, it is important not to lose sight of the fact that each child is unique and has assets and resources that need to be recognized and supported. These assets can serve as a buffer in reducing the child's behavior problems and referral concerns (Short et al., 2007).

In closing, many of our current treatments for ADHD developed prior to advances in our theory and knowledge about the possible causes of ADHD. One day soon, it may be possible to design more effective treatments that are sensitive to the different types of ADHD and to specific cognitive and behavioral deficits of individual children (Casey, Nigg, & Durston, 2007).

SECTION SUMMARY

Treatment

- There is no cure for ADHD, but a variety of treatments can be used to help children cope with their symptoms and any secondary problems that may arise over the years.
- The primary approach to treatment combines stimulant medication, parent management training, and educational intervention.
- Stimulants are the most effective treatment for managing symptoms of ADHD; however, their limited long-term benefit raises important issues about their clinical use that are yet to be resolved.

(*continues*)

SECTION SUMMARY (*continued*)

- Parent management training (PMT) provides parents with a variety of skills to help them manage their child's oppositional and defiant behaviors and cope with the difficulties of raising a child with ADHD.
- Educational interventions focus on managing inattentive and hyperactive–impulsive behaviors that interfere with learning, and on providing a classroom environment that capitalizes on the child's strengths.
- Findings from the MTA Study, a landmark controlled comparison of intensive treatments for ADHD, suggest that for children with uncomplicated ADHD, medication may be the best treatment option; however, for those with ADHD and oppositional symptoms, poor social functioning and ineffective parenting, combining medication and behavioral treatment may be the best option.
- Additional interventions for ADHD include family counseling and support groups, and individual counseling for the child.

Study Resources

SECTION SUMMARIES

KEY TERMS

COURSEMATE

Access an interactive eBook and chapter-specific interactive learning tools, including flashcards, quizzes, videos, and more in your Psychology CourseMate, accessed through CengageBrain.com.

Conduct Problems

6

Our youth now love luxury. They have bad manners, contempt for authority and disrespect for their elders. Children nowadays are tyrants.

—Socrates, 470–399 B.C.

CHAPTER PREVIEW

CHILDREN'S CONDUCT PROBLEMS HAVE long been a societal concern and considered to be forerunners of juvenile delinquency and adult criminality. However, despite enormous public, scientific, and professional attention, substantial numbers of youths continue to display antisocial, destructive, and violent behaviors, many of which are hidden from public view. Many types of adolescent conduct problems have increased substantially over the past 25 years, a change that has affected males and females, all social classes, and all family types (Collishaw, Maughan, Goodman, & Pickles, 2004). Although the most lethal forms of youth violence in the United States have been steadily decreasing since 1994, the prevalence of other forms of antisocial behavior (e.g., aggravated assault) remains alarmingly high, and the proportion of females involved in violent crimes has increased (Zahn et al., 2008). A nationally representative survey of U.S. high school students in 2009 found that about 32% had been in a physical fight in the past year, 18% reported carrying a weapon in the last month, and 8% reported being threatened or injured with a weapon on school property (Eaton et al., 2010; Robers, Zhang, & Truman, 2010). Tragically, there are many victims of youth violence. In the United States in 2004, nearly 3,000 children and teens died from gunshot wounds, about one every three hours, which is more than the number of American military deaths between 2003 and 2006 in Iraq and Afghanistan (Children's Defense Fund, 2007).

The high prevalence of youths with conduct problems and the harm inflicted on their victims create an urgent need for understanding and assistance. Tragic school shootings by youths, such as the mass murder–suicide at Virginia Tech in 2007 that resulted in 33 deaths, provide stark reminders of the societal impact of youth violence. These youths often have a background that suggests a history of social isolation and rejection, unusual social behavior, and a fascination with violent themes. As such, these incidents raise important questions about factors that contribute to violence and other antisocial behavior by young people in our society (McNamara & Findling, 2008).

Unfortunately, school shootings and media portrayals of extreme antisocial acts may also fuel popular beliefs that aggression is inherent in humans, that some children are born bad, or that youth violence is symptomatic of a decaying society. In fact, although it is an ongoing and extremely serious problem, much recent progress has been made in understanding, reducing, and preventing youth violence as well as less harmful but still serious forms of antisocial conduct (Moffitt et al., 2008).

© Masterfile

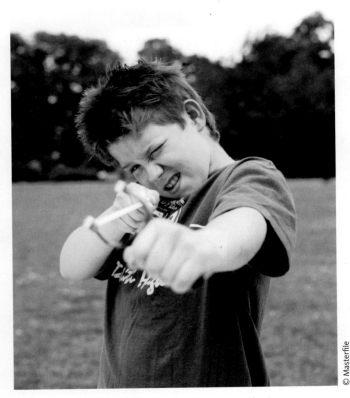

Early conduct problems may be forerunners of delinquency and adult criminal behavior

Description of Conduct Problems

"... those who violate social and criminal codes do so for very many reasons, ... before studying our cases we must do our best to group them into different sorts ..."

—John Bowlby (1907–1990)

ANDY

Young Rage

"Andy threw his booster seat in my face and hit my jaw. He thought it was funny. He was acting up, and I think he had already had one time-out for yelling and screaming and interrupting us at the table. And I said, "Fine, you are not having dessert." He flew into a rage. He picked up a metal fork and threw it at me with all his force, and hit me—barely missed my eye. There was blood on my forehead. I was hysterical. I was terrified to see that type of rage in a 4-year-old." (Adapted from *Troubled Families—Problem Children: Working with Parents: A Collaborative Process* by C. Webster-Stratton and M. Herbert, 1994, pp. 44–45. Copyright © 1994 by John Wiley & Sons, Ltd. Reprinted by permission of John Wiley & Sons, Ltd.)

MARVELLE

Defiant

"She just drives me up the wall. She's irritable all the time and never does anything I ask her to do. When she doesn't get her way she throws a full-blown tantrum. Her behavior is also a problem at school. Her teacher can't get her to do schoolwork—she simply refuses. She's also defiant, won't stay in her seat, and talks constantly. She's disrupting the entire class. I'm worried that she's headed for serious problems if she doesn't shape up soon." (Based on authors' case material)

NICK

Not Like Other Kids

Outwardly, Nick is a normal 10-year-old. He loves sports, especially football. He has a talent for drawing and an aptitude for math . . . but Nick isn't like other kids. At age 2, he put a can of cat food on the stove, and lit the burner—it exploded. In one 5-day period last March, he threw a rock at a girl at the YMCA, hitting her in the head and drawing blood; set fire to his room; pushed his sister down the stairs; whipped the family dog with a chain; and stole $20 from his mother's wallet. (Adapted from Colapinto, 1993, p. 122)

Conduct problem(s) and **antisocial behavior(s)** are terms used to describe a wide range of age-inappropriate actions and attitudes of a child that violate family expectations, societal norms, and the personal or property rights of others (McMahon, Wells, & Kotler, 2006). Like the children in our examples, youths with conduct problems display a variety of disruptive and rule-violating behaviors ranging from annoying but relatively minor behaviors such as whining, swearing, and temper tantrums to more serious forms of antisocial behavior such as vandalism, theft, and assault. Given such diversity, we need to consider many types, pathways, causes, and outcomes of conduct problems.

Although we may be shocked by their actions, children with severe conduct problems frequently (not always) grow up in extremely unfortunate family and neighborhood circumstances where they experience physical abuse, neglect, poverty, or exposure to criminal activity (Lahey, Miller, Gordon, & Riley, 1999). Thus, in many cases, aggressive behaviors are an adaptation to home and neighborhood violence and neglect. These circumstances do not excuse the behaviors but rather provide an important backdrop for understanding and preventing these problems. Consider the case of Steve.

STEVE

Not Without Cause

Twelve-year-old Steve was referred because he stabbed his father in the leg and stole a car. He had a history of lying, fighting at school, and theft, and was in constant trouble with school personnel and police. He readily admitted stabbing his father in the leg, but his story included some interesting details that hadn't come up previously. He and his two brothers were in their parents' bedroom while the father was raping the mother. She was screaming for help and panicked. Steve went and got a knife from the kitchen; his brothers tried to restrain him but could do so only partially. He stabbed his father in the calf, deeply and with a long cut. After the stabbing, Steve felt he was going to get beaten, because his father had a long history of physically abusing the boys. He fled to his grandfather's house, took the car keys without permission, drove off, and crashed the car in a field. The police brought Steve to us. By all accounts, he had stabbed his father. And indeed he stole a car. (Based on Kazdin, A. E. (1995). Conduct disorders in childhood and adolescence (2nd ed). Thousand Oaks, CA: Sage)

Steve's tragic family situation may evoke sympathy and concern. Children with severe conduct problems are often seriously disturbed and need help. At the same time, the callousness of their deeds often evokes outrage, concern for innocent victims, and a desire to severely punish or confine them. This creates an inconsistency between society's concern for children who experience early adversity or abuse and the tendency to criminalize and demonize youths who display violent behaviors. As they grow older, these children walk a fine line between pleas from the mental health and juvenile justice systems for understanding and rehabilitation, and demands from the general public and the criminal justice system to punish the offenders and protect the victims (Steinberg, 2009). Most people have opinions about the nature of youth violence and what can be done about it. To examine some of your own views, consider the statements in Box 6.1.

BOX 6.1 A CLOSER LOOK

Beliefs About Youth Violence: True or False?

Most future offenders can be identified during early childhood.	T	F
Child abuse and neglect inevitably lead to violent behavior later in life.	T	F
African American and Hispanic youths are more likely to become involved in violence than other racial or ethnic groups.	T	F
Getting tough with juvenile offenders by trying them in adult criminal courts reduces the likelihood that they will commit more crimes.	T	F
Most violent youths will end up being arrested for a violent crime.	T	F
Nothing works with respect to treating or preventing violent behavior.	T	F

Note: All of the above statements are false. Such false ideas can be harmful when they fail to recognize the true nature of a problem or when they lead to inappropriate policies or practices.

Source: Adapted from Youth Violence: A Report of the Surgeon General (Department of Health and Human Services, 2001).

SECTION SUMMARY

Description of Conduct Problems

- Conduct problems or antisocial behavior(s) are age-inappropriate actions and attitudes of a child that violate family expectations, societal norms, and the personal or property rights of others.
- The nature, causes, and outcomes of conduct problems in children are wide-ranging, requiring that we consider several different types and pathways.
- Many children with severe conduct problems grow up in extremely unfortunate family and neighborhood circumstances.

CONTEXT, COSTS, AND PERSPECTIVES

"... the extent to which any of us conform with the social and criminal codes is a matter of degree ..."

—John Bowlby (1950)

To understand antisocial behavior in young people and its impact on society, we next consider its expression in the context of normal development, its societal costs, and the different ways in which such behavior has been viewed by the juvenile justice, mental health, and public health systems.

Context

Most young people break the rules from time to time. Did you ever defy authority, lie, spread rumors, fight, skip school, run away, break curfew, destroy property, steal, text while driving, or drive under the influence of alcohol? If so, welcome to the club—many young people admit to these antisocial acts. In 2009, about 72% of high school students in the U.S. had consumed alcohol, 46% had smoked cigarettes, and 37% had smoked marijuana (Eaton et al., 2010). Very few adolescents (about 6%) refrain from antisocial behavior entirely, and those who do describe themselves as excessively conventional, anxious, and socially inhibited—not well adjusted at all during adolescence (Moffitt, Caspi, Harrington, & Milne, 2002).

Antisocial behaviors appear and then decline during normal development (Tremblay, 2003). Most toddlers hit, kick, intentionally break things, tell lies, and resist adult authority, but most also learn to control these behaviors by the time they enter school. About 50% of parents report that their preschoolers steal, lie, disobey, or destroy property, in contrast to 10% of parents who report the same about young adolescents (Achenbach, 1991a). This decline partially reflects the parents' lack of awareness of the trouble their teens may be getting into. However, teens also report that their antisocial behaviors decrease with age (Achenbach, 1991b). Frequencies of three common antisocial behaviors for clinic-referred and non-referred boys and girls of different ages, as reported by their parents, are shown in ● Figure 6.1.

The graphs in Figure 6.1 illustrate several important features of antisocial behaviors in the context of normal development:

- Antisocial behaviors vary in severity, from minor disobedience to fighting.

Policies and practices that place youths with conduct problems together can increase their antisocial and delinquent behavior

- Some antisocial behaviors decrease with age (e.g., disobeying at home), whereas others increase with age and opportunity (e.g., hanging around kids who get into trouble).
- Antisocial behaviors are more common in boys than girls during childhood, but this difference narrows in adolescence.

Even though many antisocial behaviors decrease with age, children who are the most physically aggressive in early childhood maintain their relative standing over time (Broidy et al., 2003). Longitudinal studies find aggressive acts such as persistent physical fighting to be highly stable, with an average correlation of about 0.70 for measures of these behaviors taken at different times (Loeber, Green, Lahey, & Kalb, 2000). This makes aggressive behavior about as stable as IQ scores!

Social and Economic Costs

The staggering costs borne by the educational, health, criminal justice, social service, and mental health systems that deal with youths with conduct problems make it the most costly mental health problem in North America (Welsh et al., 2008). Although antisocial acts are universal in young people, an early, persistent, and extreme pattern of antisocial behavior occurs in only about 5% of children (Hinshaw & Lee, 2003). These children cause considerable and disproportionate amounts of harm, accounting for over 50% of all crime in the United States, and about 30% to 50% of clinic referrals (Loeber, Burke, Lahey, Winters, & Zera, 2000).

More teenagers in the United States die from firearm injuries than from all diseases combined, and they are more than twice as likely as adults to be victims of violence, most often committed by other teens (Snyder & Sickmund, 2006). The costs of antisocial behavior can be understood not only in terms of lives but also in dollars. As much as 20% of all mental health expenditures in the United States are attributable to crime (National Institute of Justice, 1996). The additional public costs per child with conduct problems across the healthcare, juvenile justice, and educational systems are enormous, at least $10,000 or more a year (Foster, Jones, & The Conduct Problems Prevention Research Group, 2005). The lifetime costs to society for one youth to leave high school for a life of crime and substance abuse has been estimated to be at least two million dollars (Cohen, 2005).

Perspectives

Conduct problems have been viewed from several perspectives, each using different terms and definitions to

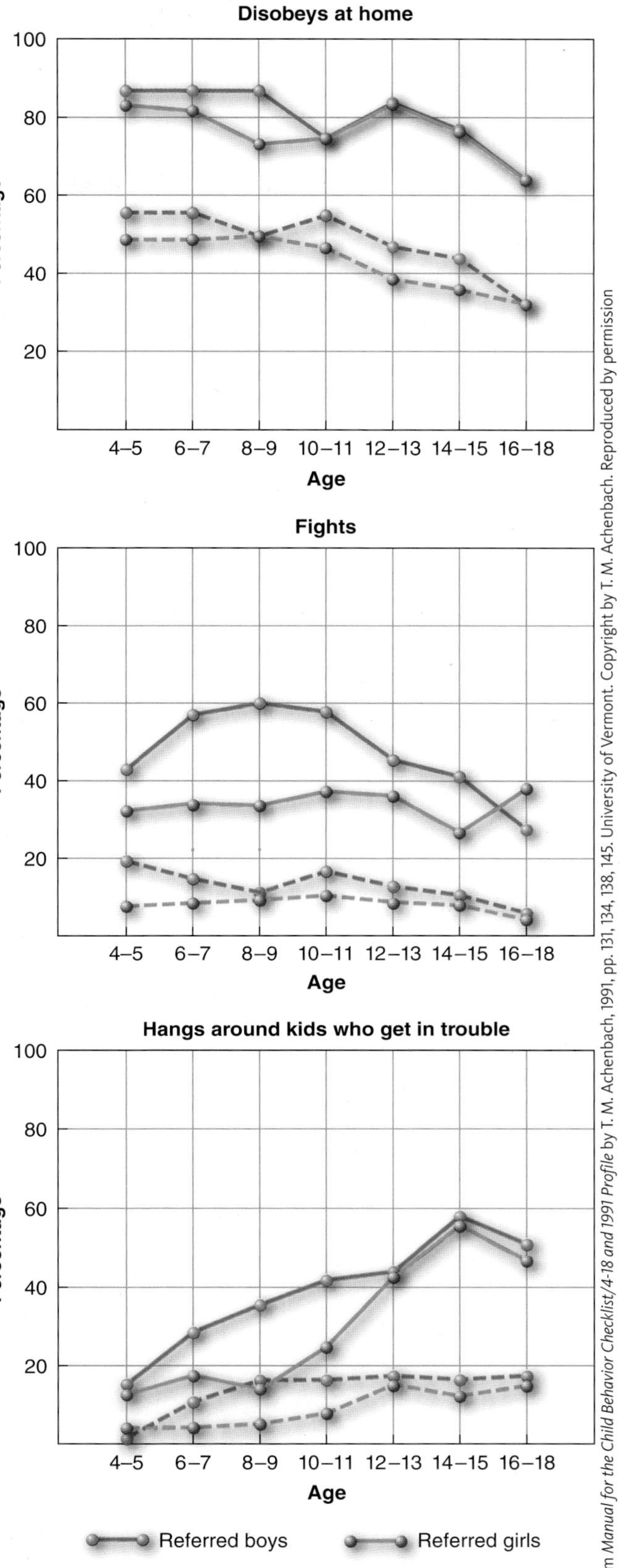

● **FIGURE 6.1** | Parent-reported frequencies for common antisocial behaviors in clinic and nonreferred boys and girls ages 4 to 18.

describe similar patterns of behavior. These include the legal, psychological, psychiatric, and public health perspectives (Loeber, Burke, & Pardini, 2009a).

Legal

Legally, conduct problems are defined as delinquent or criminal acts. The broad term **juvenile delinquency** describes children who have broken a law, ranging from sneaking into a movie without paying to homicide. Delinquent acts include property crimes (e.g., vandalism, theft, breaking and entering) and violent crimes (e.g., robbery, aggravated assault, homicide). Legal definitions depend on laws that change over time or differ across locations. Since the labeling of an act as delinquent results from apprehension and court contact, legal definitions exclude the antisocial behaviors of very young children that usually occur at home or school. It is also important to distinguish official records of delinquency from self-reported delinquency. Youths who display antisocial behavior and are apprehended by police may differ from youths who display the same patterns but are not apprehended because of their intelligence or resourcefulness. Debate is ongoing about the age at which children should be held responsible for their delinquent behavior. The minimum age of criminal responsibility is 12 in most states and provinces, but this has fluctuated over the years in relation to society's tolerance or intolerance of antisocial behavior in youth.

Given the large numbers of youths involved in criminal activities, we must ask whether these behaviors are understandable (albeit objectionable) adaptations to a hostile environment—the most common reason that youths give for carrying a weapon is self-defense (Simon, Dent, & Sussman, 1997). Unfortunately, no clear boundaries exist between delinquent acts that are a reaction to environmental conditions, such as a high-crime neighborhood, and those that result from factors within the child, such as impulsivity. Some criminal behaviors, such as arson and truancy, are arbitrarily included in current mental health definitions, whereas selling drugs and prostitution are not. A legal definition of delinquency may result from one or two isolated acts, whereas a mental health definition usually requires the child to display a persistent pattern of antisocial behavior. Thus, only a subgroup of children who meet a legal definition of delinquency will also meet the definition for a mental disorder (Hinshaw & Lee, 2003).

Psychological

From a psychological perspective, conduct problems fall along a continuous dimension of **externalizing behavior**, which includes a mixture of impulsive, overactive, aggressive, and rule-breaking acts (Burns et al., 1997). Children at the upper extreme, usually one or more standard deviations above the mean, are considered to have conduct problems. The externalizing dimension itself consists of two related but independent sub-dimensions labeled "rule-breaking behavior" and "aggressive behavior" (Achenbach & Rescorla, 2001). Rule-breaking behaviors include running away, setting fires, stealing, skipping school, using alcohol and drugs, and committing acts of vandalism. Aggressive behaviors include fighting, destructiveness, disobedience, showing off, being defiant, threatening others, and being disruptive at school.

Two additional independent dimensions of antisocial behavior have been identified: overt–covert and destructive–nondestructive (Frick et al., 1993). The **overt–covert dimension** ranges from overt visible acts such as fighting to covert hidden acts such as lying or stealing. Children who display overt antisocial behavior tend to be negative, irritable, and resentful in their reactions to hostile situations and to experience higher levels of family conflict (Kazdin, 1992). In contrast, those displaying covert antisocial behavior are less social, more anxious and more suspicious of

Two sides of the externalizing dimension: overt (left) and covert (right)

others, and come from homes that provide little family support. Most children with conduct problems display both overt and covert behaviors. These children are in frequent conflict with authority, show the most severe family dysfunction, and have the poorest long-term outcomes (Loeber, Lahey, & Thomas, 1991). The **destructive–nondestructive dimension** ranges from acts such as cruelty to animals or physical assault to nondestructive behaviors such as arguing or irritability.

As shown in ● Figure 6.2, crossing the overt–covert with the destructive–nondestructive dimension results in four categories of conduct problems: (A) covert–destructive, or property violations; (B) overt–destructive, or aggression; (C) covert–nondestructive, or status violations; and (D) overt–nondestructive, or oppositional behavior. Children who display overt–destructive behaviors, particularly persistent physical fighting, are at especially high risk for later psychiatric problems and impairment in functioning (Broidy et al., 2003).

Psychiatric

From a psychiatric perspective, conduct problems are defined as distinct mental disorders based on DSM symptoms (APA, 2000). In DSM-IV-TR, **disruptive behavior disorders** are persistent patterns of antisocial behavior, represented by the categories of oppositional

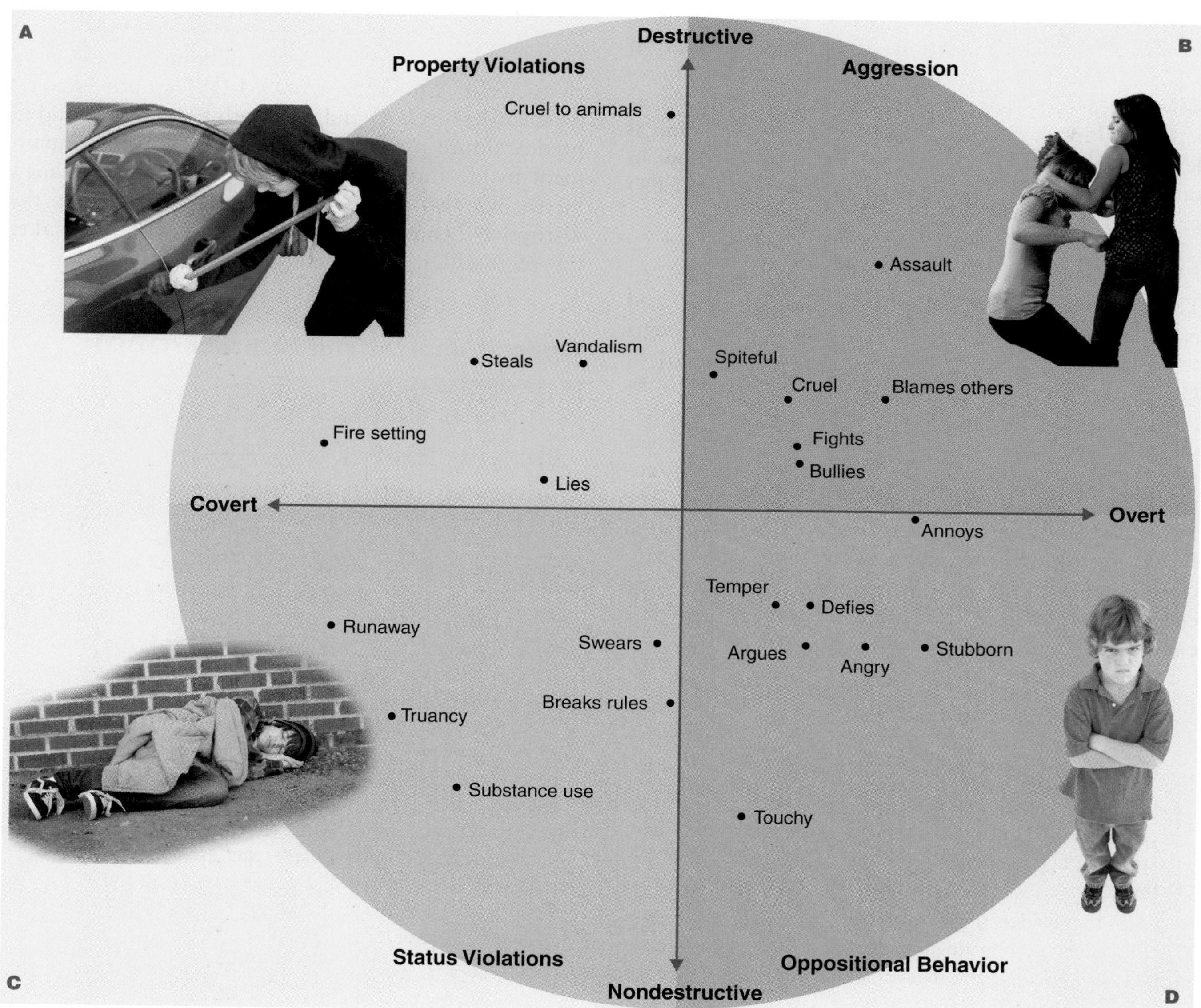

FIGURE 6.2 | Four categories of conduct problems.

Adapted from "Oppositional Defiant Disorder and Conduct Disorder: A Meata-Analytic Review of Factor Analyses and Cross-Validation in a Clinic Sample," by P. J. Frick, Y. Van Horn, B. B. Lahey, M.3A. G. Christ, R. Loeber, E. A. Hart, L. Tannenbaum & K. Hanson, Clinical Psychology Review, 13, 319–340. Copyright © 1993 Elsevier Science, Ltd. Reprinted with permission from Elsevier Science.
Photo Credits: (a) © 2011 Paul Bradbury/Jupiterimages Corporation; (b) © 2011 Weston Colton/Jupiterimages Corporation; (c) © iStockphoto.com/Patrick Herrera; (d) © Monkey Business Images/Dreamstime.com

defiant disorder (ODD) and conduct disorder (CD). Also relevant to understanding childhood conduct problems and their adult outcomes is the diagnosis of antisocial personality disorder (APD). In the next section of this chapter, on features of the DSM, we define each of these disorders.

Note: Both categorical (psychiatric) and dimensional (psychological) perspectives have proven validity for the classification of conduct problems in youth. Categories such as CD or ODD are associated with different patterns of behaviors and outcomes. On the other hand, dimensional measures of externalizing behavior in adolescence may be better predictors of adult outcomes than categorical measures (Fergusson, Boden, & Horwood, 2010). In other words, each perspective provides useful information. Therefore, in addition to categories, DSM-5 will likely also include dimensional measures that are sensitive to both the *severity* of children's conduct problems and to **subclinical levels of symptoms** (troubling symptoms too few in number to qualify for a categorical diagnosis of CD or ODD).

Public Health

This perspective blends the legal, psychological, and psychiatric perspectives with public health concepts of prevention and intervention (U.S. Department of Health and Human Services, 2001). The goal is to reduce the number of injuries and deaths, personal suffering, and economic costs associated with youth violence, in the same way that other health concerns such as automobile accidents or tobacco use are addressed. The public health approach cuts across disciplines and brings together policy makers, scientists, professionals, communities, families, and individuals to understand conduct problems in youths and determine how they can be treated and prevented (Dodge, 2011).

SECTION SUMMARY

Context, Costs, and Perspectives

- For most children, antisocial behaviors appear and then decline during normal development, although children who are most aggressive maintain their relative standing over time.
- Costs to the educational, health, social service, criminal justice, and mental health systems that deal with youth make conduct problems the most costly mental health problem in North America.
- From a legal perspective, conduct problems are defined as criminal acts that result in apprehension and court contact and are referred to as delinquency.
- From a psychological perspective, conduct problems fall along a continuous dimension of externalizing behavior, which includes a mix of impulsive, overactive, aggressive, and rule-breaking acts.
- From a psychiatric perspective, conduct problems are viewed as distinct categories of mental disorder based on DSM symptoms. These are called disruptive behavior disorders, and include oppositional defiant disorder (ODD) and conduct disorder (CD).
- A public health perspective cuts across disciplines and blends the legal, psychological, and psychiatric perspectives with public health concepts of prevention and intervention.

DSM-IV-TR: Defining Features

In this section we discuss the defining features and characteristics for the two DSM-IV disruptive behavior disorders—ODD and CD. Both have been found to predict future psychopathology and enduring impairment in life functioning (Burke, Waldman, & Lahey, 2010). We also consider the relationship between the disruptive behavior disorders, antisocial personality disorder (APD), and psychopathic symptoms.

Oppositional Defiant Disorder (ODD)

GORDON

Enjoying His Power

He just digs his heels in, "That's it, I am not wearing these socks! Forget it, I'm not going!" And he is right. He's gone to school in his pajamas, without lunch, in the pouring rain without a coat . . . He will explain to me, "Mom, we are done with this discussion." . . . He doesn't have an easy-going bone in his body. He is not ever going to say, "Okay, I'll put that turtleneck on." It's going to be, "I will do something but only on my terms . . . I will do nothing that you want me to do and furthermore I'll throw such a tantrum and throw this cereal bowl all over the wall, so you will be late, and mad at me when you clean it up." . . . He enjoys that power. (Adapted from *Troubled Families—Problem Children: Working with Parents: A Collaborative Process* by C. Webster-Stratton and M. Herbert, 1994, p. 47. Copyright © 1994 by John Wiley & Sons, Ltd. Reprinted by permission of John Wiley & Sons, Ltd.)

Gordon's frequent arguing and active defiance of his mother are consistent with a diagnosis of **oppositional defiant disorder (ODD)**. These children display an age-inappropriate recurrent pattern of stubborn, hostile, disobedient, and defiant behaviors (see Table 6.1 for DSM diagnostic criteria). ODD usually appears by age 8, and was included in the DSM to capture early displays of antisocial and aggressive behavior by preschool and school-age children (Keenan, 2011). Many of these behaviors, such as temper tantrums or arguing, are extremely common in young children. However, severe and age-inappropriate ODD behaviors can have extremely negative effects on parent–child interactions (Greene & Doyle, 1999). Children with ODD also have a substantial risk of developing secondary mood, anxiety, and impulse-control disorders (Nock, Kazdin, Hiripi, & Kessler, 2007).

Interestingly, recent findings suggest that symptoms of ODD can be grouped into those of *negative affect* (e.g., angry/irritable mood) and those of *defiance* (e.g., defiant/headstrong behavior), which differentially predict later emotional and behavioral disorders in early adulthood (Burke, Hipwell, & Loeber, 2010; Stringaris, Maughan, & Goodman, 2010). For example, in one study, only negative affect predicted later depression, whereas defiance predicted later behavior disorders (Stringaris & Goodman, 2009).

TABLE 6.1 | **Diagnostic Criteria for Oppositional Defiant Disorder**

DSM-IV-TR

A. A pattern of negativistic, hostile, and defiant behavior lasting at least 6 months, during which four (or more) of the following are present:

(1) often loses temper
(2) often argues with adults
(3) often actively defies or refuses to comply with adults' requests or rules
(4) often deliberately annoys people
(5) often blames others for his or her mistakes or misbehavior
(6) is often touchy or easily annoyed by others
(7) is often angry and resentful
(8) is often spiteful or vindictive

Note: Consider a criterion met only if the behavior occurs more frequently than is typically observed in individuals of comparable age and developmental level.

B. The disturbance in behavior causes clinically significant impairment in social, academic, or occupational functioning.

C. The behaviors do not occur exclusively during the course of a Psychotic or Mood Disorder.

D. Criteria are not met for Conduct Disorder, and, if the individual is age 18 years or older, criteria are not met for Antisocial Personality Disorder.

Note: ODD is not diagnosed when criteria for conduct disorder (CD) are met.

Source: Reprinted with permission from the Diagnostic and Statistical Manual of Mental Disorders, Fourth Edition, Text Revision, (Copyright © 2000). American Psychiatric Association.

Conduct Disorder (CD)

GREG

Dangerous Distress

Greg, age 10, was referred because of his excessive fighting, hyperactivity, temper tantrums, and disruptive behavior at home and at school. At home, Greg argued with his mother, started fights with his siblings, stole from his parents, and constantly threatened to set fires when disciplined. On three separate occasions, he actually had set fires to rugs, bedspreads, and trash in his home. One fire led to several thousand dollars in damages. Greg also lied frequently; at school his lying got others into trouble, precipitating frequent fights with peers and denials of any wrongdoing.

Greg was brought to the clinic because his parents felt that he was becoming totally unmanageable. A few incidents were mentioned as unusually dangerous—for example, Greg's attempt to suffocate his 2-year-old brother by holding a pillow over his face. Also, Greg had recently wandered the streets at night and had broken windows of parked cars.

Greg's parents occasionally resorted to severe punishment, using paddles and belts, or locking him in his room for 2 to 3 days. His father has been employed only sporadically for the last 2 years, and spent much of his time at home sleeping or watching TV. The loss of income led to increased stress. Greg said that he could not stand to be with his dad because his dad got mad all the time over little things. Greg's mother worked full time and was not at home very much. She had a history of depression, with two suicide attempts in the last 3 years. She was hospitalized on each occasion for approximately 2 months. Greg's behavior became even worse during these periods.

Although Greg's intelligence was within the normal range, his academic performance was behind grade level, and he was in a special class because of his overactive and disruptive behavior. His parents were told that unless they got help, Greg could not return to the school the next year. His parents did not know where to turn. They talked about giving Greg up or putting him in a special boarding school where more discipline might make him "shape up." (Adapted from *Conduct Disorders in Childhood and Adolescence* by A. E. Kazdin, pp. 2–3. Copyright © 1995 by Sage Publications.)

Greg's chronic and unmanageable behavior qualifies for a diagnosis of **conduct disorder (CD)**. Children with conduct disorder display a repetitive and persistent pattern of severe aggressive and antisocial acts that involve inflicting pain on others or interfering with rights of others through physical and verbal aggression, stealing, or committing acts of vandalism (see Table 6.2 for DSM diagnostic criteria).

TABLE 6.2 | **Diagnostic Criteria for Conduct Disorder**

DSM-IV-TR

A. A repetitive and persistent pattern of behavior in which the basic rights of others or major age-appropriate societal norms or rules are violated, as manifested by the presence of three (or more) of the following criteria in the past 12 months, with at least one criterion present in the past 6 months:

Aggression to People and Animals

(1) Often bullies, threatens, or intimidates others
(2) Often initiates physical fights
(3) Has used a weapon that can cause serious physical harm to others (e.g., a bat, brick, broken bottle, knife, gun)
(4) Has been physically cruel to people
(5) Has been physically cruel to animals
(6) Has stolen while confronting a victim (e.g., mugging, purse snatching, extortion, armed robbery)
(7) Has forced someone into sexual activity

Destruction of Property

(8) Has deliberately engaged in fire setting, with the intention of causing serious damage
(9) Has deliberately destroyed others' property (other than by fire setting)

Deceitfulness or Theft

(10) Has broken into someone else's house, building, or car
(11) Often lies to obtain goods or favors or to avoid obligations (i.e., "cons" others)
(12) Has stolen items of nontrivial value without confronting a victim (e.g., shoplifting, but without breaking and entering; forgery)

Serious Violations of Rules

(13) Often stays out at night despite parental prohibitions, beginning before age 13 years
(14) Has run away from home overnight at least twice while living in parental or parental surrogate home (or once without returning for a lengthy period)
(15) Is often truant from school, beginning before age 13 years

B. The disturbance or behavior causes clinically significant impairment in social, academic, or occupational functioning.

C. If the individual is 18 years or older, criteria are not met for Antisocial Personality Disorder

Code based on age at onset:

312.81 Conduct Disorder, Childhood-Onset Type: onset of at least one criterion characteristic of Conduct Disorder prior to age 10 years

312.82 Conduct Disorder, Adolescent-Onset Type: absence of any criteria characteristic of Conduct Disorder prior to age 10 years

312.89 Conduct Disorder, Unspecified Onset: age at onset is not known

Specify severity:

Mild: few if any conduct problems in excess of those required to make the diagnosis and conduct problems cause only minor harm to others

Moderate: number of conduct problems and effect on others intermediate between "mild" and "severe"

Severe: many conduct problems in excess of those required to make the diagnosis **or** conduct problems cause considerable harm to others.

Greg's case illustrates several key features of CD (Kazdin, 1995):

- Children with CD engage in severe antisocial behaviors. Greg set fires and tried to suffocate his 2-year-old brother. He also displayed less severe problems, such as noncompliance and temper tantrums, but these weren't the main reasons for referral.
- They often have co-occurring problems such as ADHD, academic deficiencies, and poor relations with peers.
- Their families often use child-rearing practices, such as harsh punishment, that contribute to the problem and often have their own problems and stresses, such as marital discord, psychiatric problems, and unemployment. Greg's mother had a history of depression and his father was frequently unemployed.
- Their parents feel these children are out of control, and they feel helpless to do anything about it. Greg's parents want to give him up or put him in a boarding school.

CD and Age of Onset

Should we attach any special significance to the age at which symptoms of CD first occur? DSM makes the distinction between youths with an early or late onset of CD. Those with **childhood-onset conduct disorder** display at least one symptom of the disorder before age 10, whereas those with **adolescent-onset conduct disorder** do not. Increasing evidence points to the importance of age of onset in diagnosing and treating children with CD (Lahey & Waldman, 2003). Children diagnosed with childhood-onset CD are more likely to be boys, show more aggressive symptoms, account for a disproportionate amount of illegal activity, and persist in their antisocial behavior over time (Lahey, Goodman, et al., 1999). In contrast, youths diagnosed with adolescent-onset CD are as likely to be girls as boys and do not display the severity or psychopathology that characterizes the childhood-onset group. They are also less likely to commit violent offenses or to persist in their antisocial behavior as they get older. Age of onset does make a difference.

CD and ODD

There is much overlap between the symptoms of CD and ODD (Nottelman & Jensen, 1995). This raises the question of whether ODD is a separate disorder from CD; a milder, earlier version; or a reflection of the same underlying temperament and deficits (Lahey, 2008). Symptoms of ODD typically emerge 2 to 3 years before CD symptoms, at about age 6 years for ODD versus age 9 years for CD (Nock et al., 2007). Since ODD symptoms emerge first, it is possible that they are precursors of CD for some children. However, nearly half of all children with CD have no prior ODD diagnosis (Rowe, Costello, Angold, Copeland, & Maughan, 2010), and most children who display ODD do not progress to more severe CD—at least 50% maintain their ODD diagnosis without progressing, and another 25% cease to display ODD problems entirely (Burke et al., 2010). Thus for most children, ODD is an extreme developmental variation and a strong risk factor for later ODD and other problems, but not one that necessarily signals an escalation to more serious conduct problems (Keenan et al., 2011).

Antisocial Personality Disorder (APD) and Psychopathic Features

Persistent aggressive behavior and CD in childhood may be a precursor of adult **antisocial personality disorder (APD)** (also referred to as *dyssocial personality disorder*), a pervasive pattern of disregard for, and violation of, the rights of others, as well as involvement in multiple illegal behaviors (APA, 2000). As many as 40% of children with CD develop APD as young adults (Lahey, Loeber, Burke, & Applegate, 2005). In addition to their early CD, adolescents with APD may also display **psychopathic features,** which are defined as a pattern of callous, manipulative, deceitful, and remorseless behavior—the more menacing side of human nature (Blair, Peschardt, Budhani, Mitchell, & Pine, 2006). Consider these chilling comments by Jason.

JASON

No Conscience

Jason, age 13, had been involved in serious crime—including breaking and entering, thefts, and assaults on younger children—by age 6. Listening to Jason talk was frightening. Asked why he committed crimes, this product of a stable, professional family replied, "I like it. My f_____ parents really freak out when I get in trouble, but I don't give a sh__ as long as I'm having a good time. Yeah, I've always been wild." About other people, including his victims, Jason had this to say: "You want the truth? They'd screw me if they could, only I get my shots in first." He liked to rob homeless people, especially "f_gots," "bag ladies," and street kids, because, "They're used to it. They don't whine to the police . . . One guy I got into a fight with pulled a knife and I took it and rammed it in his eye. He ran around screaming like a baby. What a jerk!" (Adapted from Hare, 1993, p. 162)

Like Jason, youths who display psychopathic features appear to be aware that their aggressive behavior will cause others to suffer—but they don't care when it does. Rather, their goals in conflict situations involve revenge, dominance, and forced respect (Pardini, 2011). Far less is known about psychopathic features in children than in adults. However, signs of a lack of conscience occur in some children as young as 3 to 5 years (Kochanska, De Vet, Goldman, Murray, & Putnam, 1994). Other children, like Jason, began committing brutal acts of violence at age 6 with little remorse. A subgroup of preschoolers with behavior problems show a worrisome increase in their lack of concern for others as they begin to enter middle childhood (Hastings, Zahn-Waxler, Robinson, Usher, & Bridges, 2000). Finally, adolescents with CD are less likely than peers to show affective empathy or embarrassment, which suggests a failure to inhibit emotions and actions in accordance with social conventions (Lovett & Sheffield, 2007).

These and many other findings point to a subgroup of children with CD whose lack of concern for others may place them at especially high risk for extreme antisocial and aggressive acts and for poor long-term outcomes. They display a **callous and unemotional (CU) interpersonal style** characterized by traits such as lacking in guilt, not showing empathy, not showing emotions, and related traits of narcissism and impulsivity (Frick & White, 2008).

The behaviors and related characteristics making up these traits are shown in Table 6.3. Children who display CU traits also display a lack of *behavioral inhibition* as reflected in their preference for novel and perilous activities and a diminished sensitivity to cues for danger and punishment when seeking rewards (Frick et al., 2003). Of the traits shown in Table 6.3, it is the callous–unemotional and interpersonal/narcissistic features of psychopathy that can be most reliably distinguished from behaviors consistent with ODD, CD, and ADHD. Features associated with impulsivity are more similar to behaviors of children with ADHD (Loeber, Burke, & Pardini, 2009b).

Children with CU traits display a greater number and variety of conduct problems, and they have more frequent contact with police and a stronger parental history of APD than other children with conduct problems (Christian, Frick, Hill, Tyler, & Frazer, 1997). Research with adolescents has found that CU interpersonal and affective traits predict persistent delinquency, future recidivism, and symptoms of APD in early adulthood (McMahon, Witkiewitz, Kotler, and The Conduct Prevention Research Group, 2010; Pardini & Loeber, 2008). In addition, different developmental processes may underlie the behavioral and emotional problems seen in children with CD who also display CU traits versus those who do not (Blair et al., 2006; Frick et al., 2003). CU symptoms in childhood are about as stable as ODD and CD symptoms over time, but developmental changes have also been noted, suggesting that these are not unchanging characteristics of the child. For example, some children display stable high levels of CU traits, others show increasing or decreasing levels, and others show stable low levels (Fontaine, McCrory, Boivin, Moffitt, & Viding, 2011). CU traits in childhood and early adolescence are likely precursors of adult forms of psychopathy although further research is needed to confirm this (Lynam, Caspi, Moffitt, Loeber, & Stouthamer-Loeber, 2007). Given the evidence supporting the use of CU traits in identifying an important sub-group of children with conduct problems, strong consideration is being given to including a specifier in DSM-5 to indicate when CU traits accompany a diagnosis of CD (Frick & Moffitt, 2010; Scheepers, Buitelaar, & Matthys, 2011).

At this point you might want to look at Box 6.2 to sharpen your knowledge of DSM criteria by considering whether or not TV cartoon personality Bart Simpson qualifies for a diagnosis of ODD or CD.

TABLE 6.3 | Callous–Unemotional Traits and Related Dimensions in Children

Callous–Unemotional Traits	Narcissistic/Interpersonal Traits	Impulsivity
Is unconcerned about the feelings of others	Thinks he or she is more important than others	Acts without thinking of the consequences
Does not feel bad or guilty over misdeeds	Brags excessively about abilities, accomplishments, or possessions	Does not plan ahead or leaves things until the last minute
Is unconcerned about how well he/she does at school or work	Uses or "cons" others to get what he/she wants	Engages in risky and dangerous activities
Is not good at keeping promises	Can be charming at times, but in ways that seem insincere or superficial	Blames others for mistakes
Does not show feelings or emotions	Teases or makes fun of others	Gets bored easily
Does not keep the same friends	Becomes angry when corrected or punished	

Source: Reprinted from Cognitive and Behavioral Practice, Vol. 7, Paul J. Frick, A Comprehensive and Individualized Treatment Approach for Children and Adolescents with Conduct Disorders, PP 30–37, Copyright © 2000, with permission from Elsevier.

BOX 6.2 A CLOSER LOOK

Bart Simpson: ODD or CD?

Sharpen your knowledge of DSM-IV-TR criteria for ODD and CD by considering whether TV cartoon personality Bart Simpson qualifies for a diagnosis of one of these disorders. Here is a list of antisocial acts displayed by Bart:

- Flushes a cherry bomb down the toilet
- Rearranges party snacks to say "Boy our party sucks"
- Loosens the top on Milhouse's salt shaker
- Lights Homer's tie on fire
- Tricks Flanders kids into giving cookies away
- Pretends to be Timmy (trapped in a well)
- Pulls carpet up, writes "Bart" on carpet
- Plays with and later breaks grandpa Abe's false teeth
- Flushes Homer's wallet and keys down toilet
- Cuts all of baby Maggie's hair off
- Paints extra lines on parking lot
- Leaves box factory tour
- Pops heads off Mr. Burns's statues/floods his car
- Smashes Mr. Burns's windows
- Recounts throwing mail in sewer with Milhouse
- Phones 911 to get babysitter into trouble

Comment: Based on Bart's symptoms of aggression, destruction of property, deceitfulness, and serious violation of rules, he easily qualifies for a DSM diagnosis of CD. Like most children with CD, Bart also displays behaviors of ODD, but this diagnosis is not currently made when criteria for CD are met.

Source: Based on authors' case material.

SECTION SUMMARY

DSM-IV-TR: Defining Features

- Children with oppositional defiant disorder (ODD) display an age-inappropriate pattern of stubborn, hostile, and defiant behaviors that reflect symptoms of emotionality and temperamental activity.
- Conduct disorder (CD) describes children who display severe aggressive and antisocial acts involving inflicting pain upon others or interfering with rights of others through physical and verbal aggression, stealing, or committing acts of vandalism.
- Children who display childhood-onset CD (before age 10) are more likely to be boys, show more aggressive symptoms, account for a disproportionate amount of illegal activity, and persist in their antisocial behavior over time.
- Children with adolescent-onset CD are as likely to be girls as boys and do not display the severity or psychopathology that characterizes the childhood-onset group.
- There is much overlap between CD and ODD. However, most children who display ODD do not progress to more severe CD.
- Persistent aggressive behavior and conduct problems in childhood may be a precursor of adult antisocial personality disorder (APD), a pervasive pattern of disregard for, and violation of, the rights of others, as well as involvement in multiple illegal behaviors.
- A subgroup of children with conduct problems display psychopathic features including callous–unemotional (CU) traits such as lacking in guilt, not showing empathy, and not displaying feelings or emotions. These children also display a preference for novel and perilous activities and a diminished sensitivity to cues for danger and punishment when seeking rewards.

ASSOCIATED CHARACTERISTICS

Many child, family, peer, school, and community factors are associated with conduct problems in youths. Some factors co-occur with conduct problems, others increase their likelihood, and still others are the result of these problems. To fully understand conduct problems, we must examine these various factors and how they interact over time.

Cognitive and Verbal Deficits

Although most children with conduct problems have normal intelligence, they score nearly 8 points lower than their peers on IQ tests (Pajer et al., 2008). This IQ deficit may be greater (more than 15 points) for children with childhood-onset CD, and cannot be accounted for solely by socioeconomic disadvantage, race, or detection by the police (Lynam, Moffitt, & Stouthamer-Loeber, 1993). Lower IQ scores in children with CD may be related to the co-occurrence of ADHD (Waschbusch, 2002). When ADHD is also present, the association between a lower IQ and an increased risk for CD is clear. It is less clear how a lower IQ mediates this risk (Rutter, 2003b).

Verbal IQ is consistently lower than performance IQ in children with CD, suggesting a specific and pervasive deficit in language (Zadeh, Im-Bolter, & Cohen, 2007). This deficit may affect the child's receptive listening, reading, problem solving, expressive speech and writing, and memory for verbal material (Brennan, Hall, Bor, Najman, & Williams, 2003; Jaffee & D'Zurilla, 2003). It has been suggested that verbal and language deficits may contribute to conduct problems by interfering with the development of self-control, emotion regulation, or the labeling of emotions in others, which may lead to a lack of empathy (Hastings et al., 2000).

Verbal deficits are present early in a child's development, long before the emergence of conduct problems. However, their presence alone does not predict future aggression—family factors are also important. Children with both verbal deficits and family adversity display 4 times as much aggressive behavior as children with only one factor (Moffitt, 1990). Thus, verbal deficits may increase the child's vulnerability to the effects of a hostile family environment. How this occurs is not known, but one possibility is that a child's verbal deficits may make it more difficult for parents to understand their child's needs, which leads to parents' frustration, fewer positive interactions, more punishment, and greater difficulties in teaching social skills (Patterson, 1996). Verbal deficits, such as poor receptive language skills, may also lead to rejection by mainstream peers, adding to the development of conduct problems (Menting, van Lier, & Koot, 2011).

It is important to keep in mind that the relationship between different cognitive/verbal deficits and antisocial behavior may vary for specific types of antisocial behaviors. For example, one study found that verbal abilities were negatively related to physical aggression, but positively associated with theft, and that inductive reasoning was negatively associated with increases in theft across adolescence (Barker et al., 2011). These findings highlight the importance of studying specific types of conduct problem behaviors in order to better understand their possible underlying mechanisms.

Children with conduct problems rarely consider the future consequences of their behavior or its impact on others. They fail to inhibit their impulsive behavior, keep social values or future rewards in mind, or adapt their actions to changing circumstances. This pattern suggests deficits in executive functions similar to those of

"How am I supposed to think about consequences before they happen?"

children with ADHD (Raine et al., 2005). Because ODD/CD and ADHD frequently co-occur, the observed deficits in executive functions in these children could be due to the presence of co-occurring ADHD (Pennington & Ozonoff, 1996).

It is also possible that the types of executive functioning deficits experienced by children with ODD and CD may differ from those experienced by children with ADHD (Nigg et al., 2006). For example, Rubia (2010) has made the distinction between *cool* (as in temperature, not as in Lady Gaga) cognitive executive functions, such as attention, working memory, planning, and inhibition, and *hot* executive functions that involve incentives and motivation. Both cool and hot executive functions are associated with distinct but interconnected brain networks. Cool executive function deficits are thought to be more characteristic of children with ADHD, whereas hot executive function deficits are more characteristic of children with conduct problems. Children with both ADHD and conduct problems, which is common, likely display a combination of both types of executive function deficits.

School and Learning Problems

Every time you stop a school, you will have to build a jail.

—Mark Twain (November 23, 1900)

Children with conduct problems display many school difficulties, including academic underachievement, grade retention, special education placement, dropout, suspension, and expulsion (Roeser & Eccles, 2000). Although the frustration and demoralization associated with school failure can lead to antisocial behavior in some children (Maughan, Gray, & Rutter, 1985), there is little evidence that academic failure is the primary cause of conduct problems, particularly in early childhood. Since many young children display patterns of disruptive behavior long before they enter school, it is more likely that a common factor, such as a neuropsychological or language deficit, lack of self-control, or socioeconomic disadvantage, underlies both conduct problems and school difficulties (Lahey & Waldman, 2003).

Underachievement and conduct problems are also likely to influence one another over time. Subtle early language deficits may lead to reading and communication difficulties, which in turn may heighten conduct problems in elementary school. Children with poor academic skills are increasingly likely to lose interest in school and to associate with delinquent peers. By adolescence, the relationship between conduct problems and underachievement is firmly established, which, in one pathway, may lead to anxiety or depression in young adulthood (Masten et al., 2005)

Self-Esteem Deficits

Although many children with conduct problems have low self-esteem, there is little support for the view that low self-esteem is the primary cause of conduct problems. Rather, these problems seem to be related to an inflated, unstable, and/or tentative view of self (Baumeister, Bushman, & Campbell, 2000). For example, aggressive children may overestimate their social competence and acceptance by other children (David & Kistner, 2000). Any perceived threat to their biased view of self (e.g., rejection) may lead to aggressive behavior, which provides a way to avoid a lowering of self-concept (Orobio de Castro, Brendgen, Van Boxtel, Vitaro, & Schaepers, 2007). Consistent with this view, self-esteem among youth gang members seems to conform to a pattern in which any increment in self-esteem—from increased status, respect, or prestige—for one group member takes away from what is available for others (Anderson, 1994). Thus, youths with conduct problems may experience high self-esteem that over time permits them to rationalize their antisocial conduct (Menon et al., 2007).

Peer Problems

He is so aggressive around other children. We can't really trust him not to walk up and wallop the smaller ones. He pokes them in the eyes or pushes them down . . . It's almost like he seeks out other children to hurt them.

—Webster-Stratton and Herbert (1994)

Young children with conduct problems display verbal and physical aggression toward other children and poor social skills (Miller & Olson, 2000). Preschoolers who show poor self-regulation have difficulty taking the perspective of others, experience corporal punishment from their parents, and display higher levels of peer aggressiveness during the transition to grade school (Olson, Lopez-Duran, Lunkenheimer, Chang, & Sameroff, 2011). As they grow older, most children with conduct problems are rejected by their peers, although some may remain quite popular (Rodkin, Farmer, Van Acker, & Van Acker, 2000). Peer rejection in elementary school is a strong risk factor for adolescent conduct problems. For example, children rejected for a period of 2 or 3 years by grade 2 are about 5 times more likely than others to display conduct problems later in adolescence (Laird et al., 2001). As they enter school, some of these children become bullies, a particularly offensive pattern associated with continuing conduct problems into adolescence and adulthood (see Box 6.3).

Children with conduct problems are able to make friends. Unfortunately, their friendships are often based on a mutual attraction of like-minded antisocial individuals (Button et al., 2007). Notably, the combination of early antisocial behavior and associating with deviant peers is a powerful predictor of conduct problems during adolescence (Laird, Pettit, Dodge, & Bates, 2005). Involvement with antisocial peers becomes increasingly stable during childhood and supports the transition to adolescent criminal acts such as stealing, truancy, or substance abuse (Patterson, 1996). In fact, about two-thirds of all recorded youth offenses are committed in the company of two to three peers (Snyder & Sickmund, 2006). Involvement with deviant peers is also one of the strongest predictors of accelerated autonomy and early sexual activity in adolescence (French & Dishion, 2003).

TOM AND MATTHEW

Murderous Meeting of Minds

On February 16, 1995, in the small Minnesota town of Delano, 14-year-old Tom and his best friend Matthew ambushed and killed Tom's mother . . . These boys spent much time together. They admitted to planning the ambush (one saying they had planned it for weeks, the other, for a few hours). They were armed and waiting when Tom's mother came home from work. One conclusion seems relatively certain: This murder was an unlikely event until these antisocial friends reached consensus about doing it. (Adapted from Hartup, 1996, p. 1)

Friendships between antisocial boys are abrasive, unstable, of short duration, and not very productive (Dishion & Patterson, 2006). Positive exchanges, when they do occur, are compromised by the bossy and coercive behaviors that accompany them. Antisocial friends may engage in "deviant talk," selectively rewarding one another for discussions of rule breaking, but having little to say about prosocial behavior. As a result of this differential reinforcement, they may become more alike in their antisocial tendencies over time, leading to a further escalation in the frequency and variety of their antisocial activities (Piehler & Dishion, 2007).

The fact that deviant peer involvement is an especially strong predictor of substance use, delinquent behavior, and violence makes intervention in this area a high priority. Unfortunately, many well-intentioned programs such as group therapy, summer programs, or boot camps tend to create groups for youth with conduct problems—the very situation that may produce the most damage (Dishion, Bullock, & Granic, 2002).

Aggressive children also show distortions in how they think about social situations. They underestimate their own aggressiveness and its negative impact, and they overestimate the amount of aggression directed at them. Subgroups of aggressive children may think about social situations in different ways. For example, *reactive–aggressive* children (those showing an angry, defensive response to frustration or provocation) display a **hostile attributional bias**, which means they are more likely to attribute hostile and mean-spirited intent to other children, especially when the intentions of others are unclear (e.g., when another child accidentally bumps into a reactive–aggressive child, they are likely to think the other child did it on purpose). In contrast, *proactive–aggressive* children (those who use aggressive behavior deliberately to obtain a desired goal) are more likely to view their aggressive actions as positive and to value social goals of dominance and revenge rather than affiliation (Crick & Dodge, 1996). Aggressive children display a lack of concern for others, and their solutions to social problems are few in number, mostly aggressive, and inappropriate (Hastings et al., 2000; Dodge & Pettit, 2003).

It is important to keep in mind that many children with conduct problems live in highly aggressive and threatening circumstances. In some cases, their bias toward seeing threat and aggression in others may be an accurate reflection of the realities of living in a hostile social world, and their aggressive style of responding may be an adaptive reaction to that world.

Family Problems

He is so violent with his sister. He split her lip a couple of times. And he almost knocked her out once when he hit her over the head with a 5-pound brass pitcher. He's put plastic bags over her head.

—Webster-Stratton and Herbert (1994)

Family problems are among the strongest and most consistent correlates of conduct problems (Dishion & Patterson, 2006). Two types of family disturbances are related to these problems in children. *General family*

BOX 6.3 **A CLOSER LOOK**

Bullies and Their Victims

For 2 years, Johnny, a quiet 13-year-old, was a human plaything for some of his classmates. The teenagers badgered Johnny for money, forced him to swallow weeds and drink milk mixed with detergent, beat him up in the restroom, and tied a string around his neck, leading him around as a "pet" (Olweus, 1995, p. 196).

© Masterfile/Radius Images

Bullying among school children is a very old, familiar, and particularly offensive form of antisocial behavior. **Bullying** occurs when one or more children intentionally and repeatedly expose another child who cannot readily defend himself or herself to negative actions. Such actions may take the form of physical contact, offensive words, making faces or dirty gestures, and intentional exclusion from a group. Bullying usually involves an imbalance of power so that the victim has difficulty defending herself or himself (Guerra, Williams, & Sadek, 2011). The scope of this problem is large. In 2007, about 32% of students age 12–18 reported having been bullied at school, most commonly by being made fun of; being the subject of rumors; or being pushed shoved, tripped, or spit on (Robers et al., 2010). Boys are much more likely than girls to bully other children, and are also somewhat more likely to be the victims of bullying. Victims are typically perceived as vulnerable, weak, or different. The following comments by high school students capture the diverse factors related to victimization and being seen as different (Guerra et al., 2011):

> "You can get bullied because you are weak or annoying or because you are different. Kids with big ears get bullied. Dorks get bullied. You can also get bullied because you think too much of yourself and try to show off. Teacher's pet gets bullied. If you say the right answer too many times in class you can get bullied. . . . If you do not want to get bullied you have to stay under the radar, but then you might feel sad because no one pays attention to you." (p. 306)

No youth who is seen as different is exempt. For example, at a 2011 White House Conference on the Prevention of Bullying, President Barack Obama admitted that as a youth he was a victim of bullying: "I have to say, with big ears and the name that I have, I wasn't immune. I didn't emerge unscathed" (Brown, 2011). Although victimization by a bully is strongly associated with emotional problems, some children are resilient. Interestingly, in one study, youths with a particular genotype (involving the serotonin transporter 5-HTT gene) were found to be less likely to suffer adverse effects following bullying victimization—another example of G × E interaction (Sugden et al., 2010).

Unfortunately, widespread access to the Internet and cell phones has led to new forms of bullying by youths who use electronics to taunt, insult, threaten, harass, or intimidate a peer. Electronic/Internet or cyber-bullies may use text messaging, e-mails, defaming websites, and online "slam books" to aggress against peers by circulating rumors, secrets, insults, and threats to harass, manipulate, and harm their victims. Cyber-bullying may even be more common than face-to-face bullying, with as many as 50% of youths reporting being victims and 20% reporting being bullies. There is also a huge overlap between traditional and cyber-bullying. About 90% of traditional bullies are also cyber-bullies and about 90% of victims of traditional bullies are also victims of cyber-bullies (Raskauskas & Stoltz, 2007).

A child's status as a victim or a bully is likely to be stable over time, and victims and bullies display certain typical characteristics. Typical victims are characterized by anxious and submissive patterns of behavior, low self-esteem, and, in the case of boys, by physical weakness. These children send a signal to others that if they are attacked or insulted, they won't retaliate. Typical bullies are distinguished by their aggressiveness toward both peers and adults. They are often impulsive, need to dominate other people, are stronger than other boys, show little empathy for their victims, and derive satisfaction and, often, material gain from inflicting injury and suffering on their victims. One study found that nearly 40% of boys who were bullies in school were later convicted of three or more criminal offenses by the time they were 24 years old (Olweus, 1995). Thus, bullying in school appears to be part of a more general pattern of antisocial behavior.

The high prevalence of bullying and its impact on victims (sadly, some may commit suicide) make it a significant social problem. To combat this problem, websites (e.g., http://stopbullyingnow.hrsa.gov) and school-wide interventions and policies that increase awareness of the problem, develop clear rules against bullying, and provide support and protection for victims have been developed and successfully used in countries throughout the world (Karna et al., 2011).

Source: Based on authors' case material.

disturbances include parental mental health problems, a family history of antisocial behavior, marital discord, family instability, limited resources, and antisocial family values. *Specific disturbances in parenting practices and family functioning* include excessive use of harsh discipline, lack of supervision, lack of emotional support and involvement, and parental disagreement about discipline.

The two types are interrelated, since general family disturbances such as maternal depression often lead to poor parenting practices that can lead to antisocial behavior and feelings of parental incompetence that may lead to increased maternal depression, which completes the circle.

High levels of conflict are common in families of children with conduct problems. So too are poor parenting practices such as ineffective discipline, negative control, inappropriate use of punishment and rewards, failure to follow through on commands, and a lack of involvement in child rearing (Larsson, Viding, Rijsdijk, & Plomin, 2008; Trentacosta & Shaw, 2008). Parents may also exhibit social–cognitive deficits similar to those of their children, which suggests that the tendency of antisocial children to infer hostile intent may mirror the social perceptions of their parents (MacBrayer, Milich, & Hundley, 2003). Finally, there is often a lack of family cohesion, which is reflected in emotional detachment, poor communication and problem solving, low support, and family disorganization (Henggeler, Melton, & Smith, 1992). Household chaos—characterized by high noise levels, crowding, people coming and going all the time—and a lack of predictability and family routines is also associated with child conduct problems (Deater-Deckard et al., 2009).

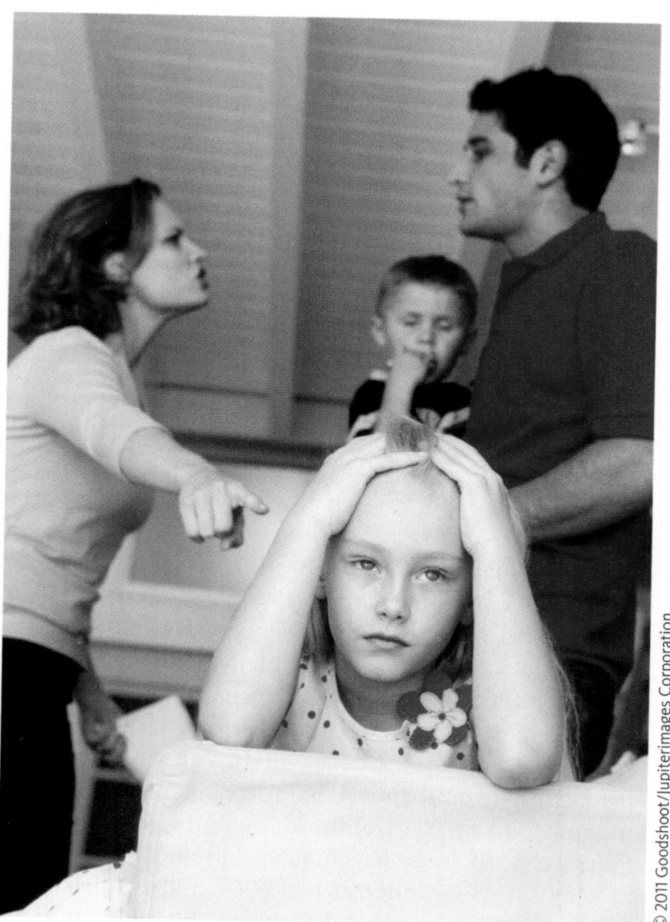

Conflict in families of children with conduct problems is common

From Cain and Abel to TV's Bart and Lisa Simpson, conflict between siblings has generated much attention (Johnston & Freeman, 1998). Conflict is especially high between children with conduct problems and their siblings. Non-referred siblings sometimes display as much negative behavior as their referred siblings, even when their sibling with conduct problems is not present (Dishion & Patterson, 2006). This suggests that their difficulties are not simply immediate reactions to the annoying behaviors of their antisocial brother or sister. There are many possible reasons for the similarities in the problem behaviors of siblings, including poor parenting practices, the effects of modeling, direct influence of the other sibling, marital discord, parent mental health problems, and shared hereditary influences. Whatever the reasons, the collaboration of siblings in one another's deviant behavior can be as powerful as deviant peer relationships in heightening the risk for later conduct problems, and may also contribute to later aggression towards peers (Ensor, Marks, Jacobs, & Hughes, 2010).

In this section we have described many common problems in families of children with conduct problems. Later in this chapter, we consider how these family problems might combine with other factors to cause additional difficulties.

Health-Related Problems

Young people with persistent conduct problems engage in many behaviors that place them at high risk for personal injuries, illnesses, overdoses from drug abuse, sexually transmitted diseases, substance abuse, and physical problems as adults (Odgers et al., 2007a). Rates of premature death (before age 30) due to various causes (e.g., homicide, suicide, accidental poisoning, traffic accident, or drug overdose) are 3 to 4 times higher in boys with conduct problems than in boys without these problems (contrary to popular belief, it's not only the good that die young!) (Kratzer & Hodgins, 1997). Antisocial behavior in childhood predicts an early onset and persistence of sexual activity and sexual risk-taking by age 21 (Ramrakha et al., 2007). This exposes young people to more years at risk for contracting sexually transmitted diseases through contact with multiple partners and a failure to use contraceptives.

Substance use disorders and adolescent antisocial behavior are strongly associated (Conner & Lochman, 2010). For example, youths who have used or sold drugs are more likely than nonusers to carry a handgun, belong to a gang, use alcohol, or engage in a host of other antisocial behaviors (Snyder & Sickmund, 2006). Adolescent substance abuse is related to the imminent dangers of accidents, violence, school dropout, family difficulties, and risky sexual behavior (Gilvarry, 2000). Early conduct problems are a known risk factor for adolescent substance use (Fergusson, Horwood, & Ridder, 2007). The prevalence of delinquent behavior varies with substance use severity, with about 10% of adolescent multiple drug users committing more than 50% of all felony assaults, felony thefts, and various other reported crimes (Johnston, O'Malley, Bachman, & Schulenberg, 2008). One distinguishing feature of adult criminal offenders is their use of tobacco, alcohol, and marijuana prior to age 15 (Farrington, 1991). Thus, the evidence indicates that conduct problems during childhood are a risk factor for adolescent and adult substance abuse, and this relationship is mediated by drug use and delinquency during early and late adolescence (Fergusson et al., 2007). We talk more about substance use problems in Chapter 12, when we discuss health-related disorders.

SECTION SUMMARY

Associated Characteristics

- Many children with conduct problems show verbal and language deficits despite their normal intelligence.
- These children experience a variety of school difficulties, including academic underachievement in language and reading, which may result from co-occurring ADHD.
- Antisocial behavior may be related to an inflated, unstable, and/or tentative view of self.
- Children with conduct problems have interpersonal difficulties with peers, including rejection and bullying. Their friendships are often with other antisocial children.
- General family disturbances, and disturbances in parenting practices and family functioning, are among the strongest and most consistent correlates of conduct problems.
- Youths with conduct problems engage in many behaviors that place them at high risk for health-related problems, including personal injuries, illnesses, sexually transmitted diseases, and substance abuse.

Accompanying Disorders and Symptoms

Most children with conduct problems suffer from one or more additional disorders, most commonly ADHD, depression, and anxiety (Lahey, 2008).

Attention-Deficit/Hyperactivity Disorder (ADHD)

More than 50% of children with CD also have ADHD. There are several possible reasons for this overlap (Beauchaine, Hinshaw, & Pang, 2010; Rhee, Wilcutt, Hartman, Pennington, & DeFries, 2008):

- A shared predisposing vulnerability such as impulsivity, poor self-regulation, or temperament may lead to both ADHD and CD.
- ADHD may be a catalyst for CD by contributing to its persistence and escalation to more severe forms, particularly when shaped by ineffective parenting emotional reactions and behaviors.
- ADHD may lead to childhood onset of CD, which is a strong predictor of continuing problems.

Despite the large overlap, two lines of research suggest that CD and ADHD are distinct disorders. First, a model that includes both CD and ADHD consistently provides a better fit to the data than a model based on only a single disorder (Waschbusch, 2002). Second, CD is less likely than ADHD to be associated with cognitive impairments, neurodevelopmental abnormalities, inattentiveness in the classroom, and higher rates of accidental injuries (Hinshaw & Lee, 2003).

Depression and Anxiety

About 50% of youths with conduct problems also receive a diagnosis of depression or anxiety (Wolff & Ollendick, 2006). Recent evidence suggests that it is ODD and not CD that best accounts for the connection between conduct problems and depression, and that this relationship is driven by the symptoms of negative affect of ODD rather than its behavioral symptoms (Burke & Loeber, 2010). Boys with combined conduct and internalizing problems have poor outcomes in early adulthood, including having the highest risk of later psychiatric disorders and criminal offenses (Sourander et al., 2007). Most girls with CD develop a depressive or anxiety disorder by early adulthood, and for both sexes, an increasing severity of antisocial behavior is associated with an increasing severity of depression and anxiety (Zoccolillo, Pickles, Quinton, & Rutter, 1992). Adolescent CD is also a risk factor for completed suicide in young people with a family history of depression (Renaud, Brent, Birmaher, Chiappetta & Bridge, 1999).

Findings regarding the relation between anxiety disorders and antisocial outcomes for children with conduct problems are puzzling but quite interesting (Drabick, Ollendick, & Bubier, 2010). In some studies, co-occurring anxiety has been identified as a protective factor that inhibits aggressive behavior (Pine, Cohen, Cohen, & Brook, 2000). However, other studies have found that anxiety increases the risk for later antisocial behavior (Rutter, Giller, & Hagell, 1998). In support of anxiety as a protective factor, boys with CD and anxiety disorder show a higher level of salivary cortisol associated with a greater degree of behavioral inhibition (McBurnett et al., 1991). In boys with CD only, lower levels of salivary cortisol are directly associated with more aggressive and disruptive behaviors (McBurnett, Lahey, Rathouz, & Loeber, 2000). It has been hypothesized that the relation between anxiety and antisocial outcomes may depend on the type of anxiety. In this formulation, anxiety related to shyness, inhibition, and fear may protect against conduct problems, whereas anxiety associated with negative emotionality and social avoidance/withdrawal based on a lack of caring about others may increase the child's risk for conduct problems (Lahey & Waldman, 2003). Consistent with this view, children with callous–unemotional traits show less anxiety than other children with conduct problems (Frick, Lilienfeld, Ellis, Loney, & Silverthorn, 1999). It has been proposed that different pathways underlie the relationship between conduct problems and anxiety such that anxiety may serve as a buffer or facilitator of conduct problems, depending on the underlying conditions (Drabick et al., 2010).

SECTION SUMMARY

Accompanying Disorders and Symptoms

- About 50% of children with CD also have ADHD. Despite the overlap, CD and ADHD appear to be distinct disorders.
- About 50% of children with conduct problems are diagnosed with depression or a co-occurring anxiety disorder. Symptoms of negative affect associated with ODD best account for the relationship between conduct problems and depression.
- Anxiety related to shyness, inhibition, and fear may protect against conduct problems, whereas anxiety associated with negative emotionality and social avoidance/withdrawal based on a lack of caring about others may increase the child's risk for conduct problems.

PREVALENCE, GENDER, AND COURSE

In the sections that follow we consider the prevalence of conduct problems, the important role that gender plays in the expression of antisocial behavior, and the different ways that conduct problems emerge over the course of development.

Prevalence

ODD is more prevalent than CD during childhood, but by adolescence the prevalence is about equal. Lifetime prevalence estimates are 12% for ODD (13% for males, and 11% for females), and 8% for CD (9% for males and 6% for females) (Merikangas et al., 2010). The reason overall lifetime prevalence rates are comparable is that ODD either declines or stays constant from early childhood to adolescence whereas CD increases over the same time period. Prevalence estimates for CD and ODD across cultures are similar, although most comparisons to date have been made between Western countries rather than between Western and non-Western countries (Canino, Polanczyk, Bauermeister, Rohde, & Frick, 2010).

Gender

In all of the recorded history of the more than ten million animal species, including four thousand mammals which populate the planet, only two species have been documented to engage in warfare.... male chimpanzees and male humans.

—From Eme (2007)

ANN

Runaway

Until recently, Ann, age 13, lived with her mother, stepfather, and younger brother. For the last 6 months, she has been living in a youth shelter under the custody of the courts, because of repeatedly running away from home. Ann was described by her parents as defiant and argumentative, and frequently lied and stole. She often stole clothes and jewelry from the homes of relatives and friends, as well as from her parents.... Over the past 3 years, Ann had run away from home on four occasions. Each time, the police had to be called. Running away was precipitated by being grounded for stealing or smoking cigarettes.... One time, Ann was gone for 3 nights. The police found her wandering the streets late at night on the other side of town (about 10 miles from her home). Ann would not tell them who she was or where she lived... (Adapted from *Conduct Disorders in Childhood and Adolescence* by A. E. Kazdin, pp. 3–5. Copyright © 1995 by Sage Publications.)

Clear gender differences in the frequency and severity of antisocial behavior are evident by 2 to 3 years of age (Dodge, Coie, & Lynam, 2006). During childhood, rates of conduct problems are about 2 to 4 times higher for boys than girls, with boys showing an earlier age of onset and greater persistence (Eme, 2007; Lahey et al., 2006). This gender difference does not imply that girls do not display severe conduct problems, including physically aggressive behavior, just that they do so much less often than boys.

The gender disparity in conduct problems increases through middle childhood, narrows greatly in early adolescence—due mainly to a rise in covert nonaggressive antisocial behavior in girls (McDermott, 1996)—and then increases again in late adolescence when males are at the peak of their delinquent behavior (Lahey et al., 2006). Ann steals, lies, and runs away from home, but she is not physically aggressive. In contrast to boys, whose early symptoms of CD are aggression and theft, early symptoms for girls are usually sexual misbehaviors (Offord, Alder, & Boyle, 1986). Antisocial girls are more likely than others to develop relationships with antisocial boys, then become pregnant at an earlier age and display a wide spectrum of later problems including anxiety, depression, and poor parenting (Foster, 2005).

Although gender differences in the overall amount of antisocial behavior decrease in early adolescence, boys remain more violence-prone than girls throughout their life span, and are more likely to engage in repeated acts of physical violence (Odgers & Moretti, 2002). For conduct problems that are chronic from early childhood to adulthood, the male-to-female ratio is marked, about 10:1. In contrast, more transient forms of antisocial behavior in adolescence show a male-to-female ratio of about 2:1 (Moffitt, Caspi, Rutter, & Silva, 2001).

© Photofusion Picture Library/Alamy

Girls will be girls

In addition, physical aggression by girls during childhood, when it does occur, does not seem to forecast continued physical violence and other forms of delinquency in adolescence, as it does for boys (Broidy et al., 2003). This does not mean that girls are nonviolent—about 45% of girls commit at least one violent act (compared with 65% of boys). Interestingly, the sex difference in antisocial behavior has decreased by more than 50% over the past 50 years, suggesting that females may be more susceptible to or affected by contemporary risk factors, such as family discord or media influences, and/or a growing recognition of these problems in girls (Rutter et al., 1998). Unfortunately, antisocial behavior is increasingly becoming an equal opportunity affliction—conduct problems are one of the most common mental disorders in adolescent girls.

Explaining Gender Differences

The precise reasons for gender differences in antisocial behavior are not known, although genetic, neurobiological, and environmental risk factors have all been implicated (Eme, 2007; Messer, Goodman, Rowe, Meltzer, & Maughan, 2006). Genetic and environmental risk factors for antisocial behavior in childhood may also be qualitatively different for males and females (Meier, Slutske, Heath, & Martin, 2011). Gender differences may be partly related to definitions of conduct problems that place a strong emphasis on physical aggression, and minimal emphasis on the less physically aggressive forms of antisocial behaviors that characterize girls (Crick, Bigbee, & Howes, 1996). When girls are angry they are more likely to use indirect and relational forms of aggression (see Box 6.4), such as verbal insults, gossip, tattling, ostracism, threatening to withdraw one's friendship, getting even, or third-party retaliation (Cote, Vaillancourt, Barker, Nagin, & Tremblay, 2007; Crick & Nelson, 2002). (See also Chapter 4.) In addition, girls are more likely than boys to become emotionally upset by aggressive social exchanges (Crick, 1995). As girls move into adolescence, the function of their aggressive behavior increasingly revolves around group acceptance and affiliation, whereas for boys, aggression remains confrontational (Crick & Rose, 2000).

Fewer differences in antisocial behaviors exist between boys and girls referred for treatment than for children in community samples. Although clinically referred boys and girls with conduct problems display comparable amounts of externalizing behavior (Dishion & Andrews, 1995), referred girls are more deviant than boys in relation to their same-age, same-sex peers (Webster-Stratton, 1996; Zoccolillo, 1993). Girls' behavior is considered more covert because boys typically engage in more rough and tumble

BOX 6.4 **A CLOSER LOOK**

Social Aggression in Girls: "I Hurt Her Through the Grapevine"[1]

Over the course of a school day, Rachel Simmons (2002) met with eight groups of 9th grade girls and began each meeting with the same question:

Dusaleev Viatcheslav/Shutterstock.com

Girls are more likely than boys to use indirect forms of social aggression, such as gossiping and spreading rumors

"What are some of the differences between the ways guys and gals are mean?"

From periods one through eight she heard the same responses: "Girls can turn on you for anything." "Girls whisper." "They glare at you." "They destroy you from the inside." "Girls are manipulative." "There's an aspect of evil in girls that there isn't in boys." "Girls target you when they know you're weakest." "Girls do a lot behind each other's backs." "Girls plan and premeditate."

"In bold, matter-of-fact voices, girls described themselves . . . as disloyal, untrustworthy, and sneaky. They claimed girls use intimacy to manipulate and overpower others. They said girls are fake, using each other to move up the social hierarchy. They described girls as unforgiving and crafty, lying in wait for a moment of revenge that will catch the unwitting victim off guard, and with an almost savage eye-for-an-eye mentality."

[1] Crick et al. (2001, p. 15)

Source: Adapted from Simmons, 2002, pp. 15–16.

play, bullying, fighting, and noncompliance than girls. With overt antisocial behavior more common in boys, their symptoms are more noticeable at a younger age, which could account for the reported earlier age of onset of conduct problems in boys. Recent longitudinal research has found that nearly 90% of girls with CD had an age of onset prior to age 10 (Keenan, Wroblewski, Hipwell, Loeber, & Stouthamer-Loeber, 2010). In light of these data, it has become clear that changes in diagnostic criteria are needed to detect girls with CD at a younger age. Although the precise nature of such changes is yet to be determined, research suggests that further study of relational aggression and callous-unemotional features in girls may prove useful (Keenan et al., 2010; Kroneman, Hipwell, Loeber, Koot, & Pardini, 2011).

Some girls have an early menarche, which may indirectly heighten their conduct problems by increasing their involvement with deviant peers (Burt, McGue, DeMarte, Krueger, & Iacono, et al., 2006). Interestingly, an early onset of menarche predicts increased delinquency primarily for girls who attend mixed-gender schools rather than all-girl schools. In mixed-gender schools, girls' exposure to boys who model antisocial behavior and pressure girls for early sexual relations may interact with early physical maturation. Such exposure may lead to antisocial behavior in these girls, who are more likely to find rewards and opportunities for antisocial activities in the company of boys than girls (Moffitt, Caspi, Belsky, & Silva, 1992). In contrast to earlier findings, a recent study found that girls reaching menarche at an early age had a greater risk of early pregnancy and sexually transmitted infection by age 18, but little evidence to indicate that age of menarche was related to later antisocial or criminal behavior (Boden, Fergusson, & Horwood, 2011). Although the reason for these discrepant findings is not known, they do suggest that early age of menarche plays a role in determining sexual behavior outcomes but not necessarily in determining longer-term outcomes in other areas of adjustment, such as antisocial behavior.

Another recent study found that *both* early maturing girls and early maturing boys were at risk for being exposed to peers who may draw them into delinquent behavior (Negriff, Ji, & Trickett, 2011). However, for early maturing children who had been maltreated, exposure to abuse had a greater effect on the development of delinquency than did exposure to delinquent peers. These findings suggest that different mechanisms may underlie the relationship between early maturation and delinquency for different groups of children. Most likely both early maturing girls and boys are vulnerable to an interaction between genetic and environmental risks for delinquent behavior (Harden & Mendle, 2012).

Developmental Course and Pathways

Longitudinal studies have greatly advanced our understanding of antisocial patterns by revealing both a general developmental progression and important variations on this theme (Frick & Viding, 2009).

General Progression

An approximate ordering of the different forms of disruptive behavior and antisocial behavior from early childhood through adolescence is shown in ● Figure 6.3.

Although there are isolated reports, such as that of a 9-month-old infant being expelled from day care for punching other children, early signs of conduct problems are usually not so obvious (Kazdin, 1995, p. 27). The earliest indications of conduct problems may be a *difficult temperament* in the first few years of life, expressed as fussiness, irritability, irregular sleeping and eating patterns, or fearfulness in response to novel events. Interestingly, fussiness in the first year of life was a stronger predictor of later conduct problems in boys, whereas fearfulness was a stronger predictor of later conduct problems in girls (Lahey et al., 2008). As was the case for ADHD, although difficult temperament often precedes later conduct problems, it may not be specific to them. The evidence regarding early temperament and later conduct problems suggests a general link, but has not yet identified specific aspects of temperament that predict distinct types of maladjustment (Loeber et al., 2009a).

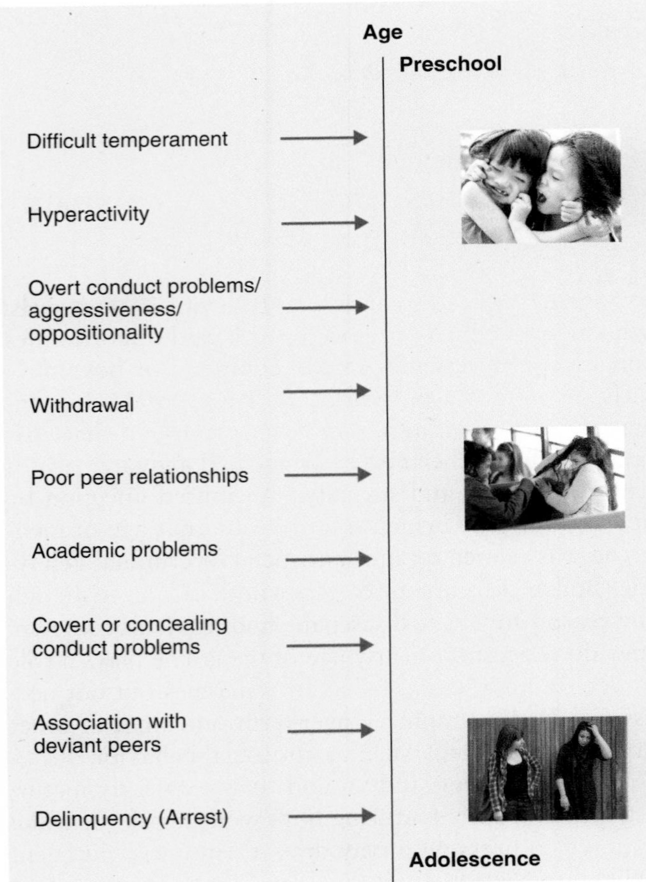

● **FIGURE 6.3** | Approximate ordering of the different forms of disruptive and antisocial behavior from childhood through adolescence.

From *Development and Risk Factors of Juvenile Antisocial Behavior and Delinquency* by R. Loeber, 1990, 'Clinical Psychology Review', 10, 1–41. Copyright © 1990 Elsevier Science, Ltd. Reprinted with permission of Elsevier Science.
Photo Credits (top to bottom): © Andrewblue/Dreamstime.com; © iStockphoto.com/Christopher Futcher; Elena Rostunova/Shutterstock.com

During the preschool and early school years, the child with a difficult temperament displays an increase in hyperactivity and impulsivity with growing mobility, weak emotion regulation skills, and a heightened risk for simple forms of oppositional and aggressive behaviors that peak during the preschool years (Tremblay, 2000). Preschoolers with ODD display stubbornness, temper tantrums, irritability, and spitefulness—problems that remain stable from 2 to 5 years of age. Discipline problems and poor self-control and emotion regulation during early childhood, especially when accompanied by harsh parenting and high levels of stress, are strong indicators that the child will continue to experience persistent behavior problems and negative outcomes across nearly every area of life functioning in adolescence and adulthood (Calkins & Keane, 2009; Campbell et al., 2010; Moffitt et al., 2011).

Most children with conduct problems show *diversification*—they add new forms of antisocial behavior over time rather than simply replacing old behaviors. Poor social skills and social–cognitive deficits often accompany early oppositional and aggressive behaviors, predisposing the child to poor peer relationships, rejection by peers, and social isolation and withdrawal. When the child enters school, impulsivity and attention problems may result in reading difficulties and academic failure. Covert conduct problems, such as truancy or substance use, also begin to appear during the elementary school years and increase into early adolescence. From ages 8 to 12, behaviors such as fighting, bullying, fire setting, vandalism, cruelty to animals and people, and stealing begin to emerge.

In this progression, we see a snowballing negative cycle over time where one deficit or problem behavior produces direct and indirect changes in others. For example, peer rejection leads to social–cognitive deficits and aggression; social–cognitive deficits lead to peer rejection and aggression; aggression leads to peer rejection (Lansford, Malone, Dodge, Pettit, & Bates, 2010). Conversely better social–cognitive skills may increase peer acceptance and lower aggressiveness. These cascading effects highlight the importance of looking at the progression of antisocial behavior over time as a dynamic developmental process involving relationships among neurobiological dispositions, social environments, cognitions, and behavior (Lansford et al., 2010).

Across cultures, major conduct problems become more frequent during adolescence. Delinquent behavior shows a dramatic rise in middle adolescence that peaks around the age of 17, followed by an equally dramatic drop in late adolescence and young adulthood (Hirschi & Gottfredson, 1983). Adolescence is characterized by a growing association with deviant peers and by increasing rates of arrest, re-arrest, and conviction as the age of criminal responsibility is met. From ages 12 to 14, property destruction, running away from home, truancy, mugging, breaking and entering, use of a weapon, and forced sex occur with increasing frequency (Lahey & Waldman, 2003). By age 18, many children with conduct problems display antisocial personality development and behaviors that forecast an antisocial future, including substance dependence, unsafe sex, dangerous driving habits, delinquent friends, and unemployment (Moffitt, Caspi, Dickson, Silva, & Stanton, 1996).

Does this developmental progression mean that every young child with conduct problems goes on to become a delinquent adolescent? Definitely not. The sequence in Figure 6.3 shows a maximum progression that begins early in life and persists through adolescence. Although some children display this maximum progression, others will desist from their antisocial behavior at a young age. About 50% of children with early conduct problems do improve. Those who do so tend to display less extreme levels of early conduct problems, have higher intelligence and SES, fewer delinquent friends, mothers that are not teenagers, and parents with more social skills and fewer mental health problems (Lahey, Loeber, Burke, & Rathouz, 2002; Nagin & Tremblay, 2001). It is important to note, however, that even among children who display antisocial behavior and then desist at a young age, other problems may emerge in young adulthood, suggesting that their recovery is far from complete (Moffitt et al., 2002). Some children may not display problems until adolescence, and not all children display the full range of difficulties described. Still others may display a chronic low-level of persistent antisocial behavior from childhood or adolescence through adulthood (Fergusson & Horwood, 2002). These differences lead us to consider important variations on the general progression.

Pathways

There are likely as many unique pathways to the development of antisocial behavior as there are children who display these problems. Although a number of different pathways have been identified (Hoeve et al., 2008), evidence across cultures and countries supports two common pathways—the life-course–persistent (LCP) path and the adolescent-limited (AL) path (Moffitt, 2006). As shown in ● Figure 6.4, a small number of children with conduct problems (less than 10%) show a persistent pattern of antisocial behavior throughout their lives, whereas the majority display antisocial behavior that occurs mainly during adolescence. From the outset, we ask you to keep in mind that, although the designation of two pathways is a useful way to think about how conduct problems develop in different ways, it is likely that children display a range of levels of severity and continuity over time, and that many do not fit neatly on one pathway or the other (Lahey, 2008). For example, other pathways that have been identified include the low-level chronic offense path, and the adult-onset antisocial behavior path (Loeber et al., 2009a).

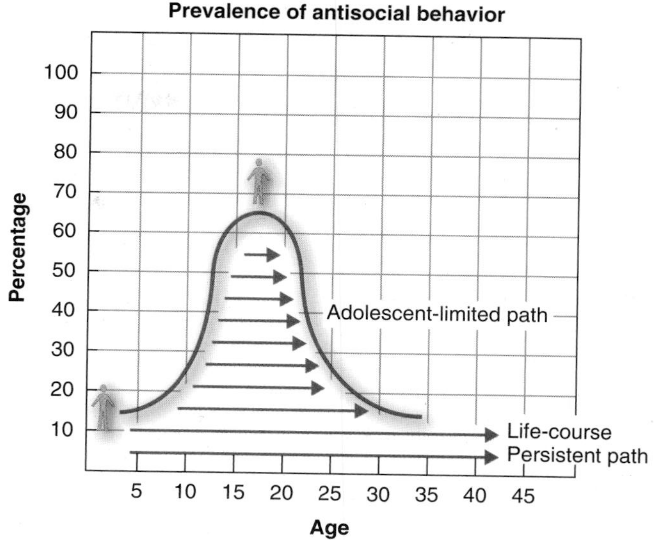

● **FIGURE 6.4** | The changing prevalence of participation in antisocial behavior across the life span.

From *Adolescence-Limited and Life-Course-Persistent Antisocial Behavior: A Developmental Taxonomy* by T. E. Moffitt, 1993, 'Psychological Review', 100, 674–701. Copyright © 1993 by the American Psychological Association. Reprinted with permission. APA is not responsible for the accuracy of this translation

The **life-course persistent (LCP) path** describes children who engage in aggression and antisocial behavior at an early age and continue to do so into adulthood (Moffitt et al., 1996). They may display "biting and hitting at age 4, shoplifting and truancy at age 10, selling drugs and stealing cars at age 16, robbery and rape at age 22, and fraud and child abuse at age 30" (Moffitt, 1993, p. 679). Their underlying disposition remains, but the way it is expressed changes with new "opportunities" at different points in development. For these children, antisocial behavior begins early because of subtle neuropsychological deficits that may interfere with their development of language, memory, and self-control, resulting in cognitive deficits and a difficult temperament by age 3 or younger. These deficits heighten the child's vulnerability to antisocial elements in the social environment, such as abuse or poor parenting, which in turn lead to oppositional and conduct problems (Lansford et al., 2011; Moffitt, 1993). These children experience greater social adversity (e.g., maternal insensitivity, single parenting, low income) than their peers from infancy through mid-adolescence (Roisman et al., 2010).

About one-half of the children who display high levels of childhood-onset antisocial behavior continue on the LCP path by engaging in less serious nonaggressive antisocial behaviors (e.g., stealing and truancy) during middle childhood, followed by affiliation with delinquent peers and more serious delinquent activities during adolescence (Brame, Nagin, & Tremblay, 2001; Dandreaux & Frick, 2009). They are the subgroup of teens most likely to commit violent crimes and to drop out of school. LCP youths display consistency in their behavior across situations—for example, by lying at home, stealing from stores, and cheating at school. As young adults, they have difficulty forming lasting relationships and may display a hostile mistrust of others, aggressive dominance, impulsivity, and psychopathic features. Complete spontaneous recovery is rare after adolescence. The LCP path is associated with a family history of externalizing disorders and is often perpetuated by the progressive accumulation of its own consequences (Odgers et al., 2007b). For example, poor self-control and diminished verbal intellect may lead to irreversible decisions, such as dropping out of school or abusing drugs, which further limit opportunities for recovery.

The **adolescent-limited (AL) path** describes youths whose antisocial behavior begins around puberty and continues into adolescence, but who later desist from these behaviors during young adulthood (Farrington, 1986). This path includes most juvenile offenders whose antisocial behavior is limited primarily to their teen years (Hamalainen & Pulkkinen, 1996). Teens on the AL path display less extreme antisocial behavior than those on the LCP path, are less likely to drop out of school, and have stronger family ties. Their delinquent activity is often related to temporary situational factors, especially peer influences. The behavior of AL youths is not consistent across situations; they may use drugs or shoplift with their friends while continuing to follow rules and to do well in school. Although these children do not display antisocial behavior in childhood, they do experience, like youngsters on the LCP path, greater social adversity and personal risk during childhood relative to other youths, suggesting that the AL pathway is not simply part of normal adolescent development (Roisman et al., 2010).

MARCUS

Call of the Wild

"I grew up in a real poor family. My mom was on welfare all my life—we never had much. As soon as I got to the age of 11, I was interested in other kids who were breaking the rules. I used to see what they used to do—and what they had."

Marcus joined a gang when he turned 13. Two years later, after a number of arrests and four detentions in a juvenile facility, he became disillusioned with gang life and managed to turn his life around. He is now 17 and works as a youth minister for a church dedicated to helping other young people like himself. (Adapted from Goldentyer, 1994)

The attraction of still-forbidden adult privileges, such as drinking alcohol, driving a car, and having sex, may motivate some youths with few previous risk signs to engage in antisocial behavior as they enter adolescence. These youths may observe their LCP peers obtaining desired adult privileges via illicit means and mimic their delinquent activities. Eventually, when access to adult privileges becomes available, AL youths cease their law-breaking, relying instead on the more adaptive and prosocial behaviors and values they learned prior to adolescence (Moffitt, Lynam, & Silva, 1994).

Contrary to expectations, some youths on the adolescent-limited path continue to display antisocial behavior well into their twenties before they eventually stop. Others do not desist in their twenties at all but continue to display higher than normal levels of impulsivity, substance abuse and dependence, property crimes, and mental health problems (Moffitt et al., 2002). Persistence in early adulthood is often the result of *snares*, or outcomes of antisocial behavior that close the door to getting a good job, pursuing higher education, or attracting a supportive partner. Common snares include: unplanned parenthood, dropping out of school, addiction to drugs or alcohol, disabling injuries, unemployment or erratic work history, severed family connections, imprisonment, bad reputation, and a delinquent self-image (Moffitt et al., 1994). Thus, despite their potential, some individuals with no history of childhood antisocial behavior who initiate delinquent activity in adolescence continue to experience problems well into adulthood (Moffitt et al., 2002). Therefore, referring to these individuals as "adolescent-limited" is somewhat misleading.

The identification of the LCP and AL pathways (and their variations) helps us understand why adult antisocial behavior is almost always preceded by antisocial behavior during childhood and adolescence (Brame et al., 2001). Nevertheless, most antisocial adolescents do not go on to become antisocial adults. At the crossroads of early adulthood, LCP and most AL teens go different ways. Antisocial behavior is stable for youths on the LCP path, who continue on the same road, but unstable for those on the AL path.

Adult Outcomes

By their early twenties, the number of active offenders decreases by about 50%, and by their late twenties, almost 85% of former delinquents desist from offending. This general relationship between age and crime applies to males and females, for most types of crimes, and in numerous Western nations (Caspi & Moffitt, 1995). Clearly, looking forward, most children with conduct problems do not grow up to be antisocial adults (Maughan & Rutter, 2001). However, adult outcomes depend not only on the type and variety of conduct problems developed during childhood and adolescence, but also on the number and combination of risk and promotive factors in the child, family, and community (Kokko & Pulkkinen, 2000). Also, even when antisocial behavior decreases in adulthood, coercive interpersonal styles may sometimes persist, along with family, health, and work difficulties.

A significant number of children with conduct problems, particularly those on the LCP path, do go on as adults to display criminal behavior, psychiatric problems, social maladjustment, health problems, lost productivity, and poor parenting of their own children (Fergusson, Horwood, & Ridder, 2005). As adults, they are more likely to be downwardly socially mobile and to display an erratic work history, perhaps due to lower skill attainment and difficulties in getting along with co-workers and supervisors. They also have more violent marriages and cohabitations, higher rates of divorce, and are more likely than others to select partners with similar antisocial characteristics, providing the next generation with a double dose of both genetic and environmental risk (Moffitt et al., 2002). One follow-up study of adult women who were arrested for severe conduct problems in adolescence found that most continued to display these problems. A majority had depressive and anxiety disorders, 6% died a violent death, many had dropped out of school, one-third were pregnant before the age of 17 years, one-half were rearrested, and many had suffered traumatic physical injuries (Zoccolillo & Rogers, 1991, 1992). Thus, males and females experience different but poor adult outcomes. Males are at higher risk for criminal behavior, work problems, and substance abuse, whereas females are more likely to experience depression, suicidal behavior, and health problems (Moffitt et al., 2001).

SECTION SUMMARY

Prevalence, Gender, and Course

- ODD is more prevalent than CD during childhood, but by adolescence the prevalence is about equal. The lifetime prevalence rates for ODD and CD are about 12% and 8%, respectively.
- During childhood, conduct problems are about 2 to 4 times more common in boys than girls. This difference narrows greatly in early adolescence, due mainly to a rise in covert nonaggressive antisocial behavior in girls, and then increases again in late adolescence and beyond.
- Girls are more likely than boys to use indirect and relational forms of aggression—for example, verbal insults, gossip, or third-party retaliation.
- There is a general progression of antisocial behavior from difficult early temperament and hyperactivity, to oppositional and aggressive behavior, to social difficulties, to school problems, to delinquent behavior in adolescence, to antisocial personality development, to criminal behavior in adulthood.
- The life-course–persistent (LCP) path describes children who display antisocial behavior at an early age and who continue to do so into adulthood.
- The adolescent-limited (AL) path describes teens whose antisocial behavior begins around puberty and continues into adolescence, and who later desist from these behaviors in young adulthood.
- A significant number of children with conduct problems continue to experience difficulties as adults, including criminal behavior, psychiatric problems, social maladjustment, health and employment problems, and poor parenting of their own children.

"We won't know till they're older which one is the evil twin."

CAUSES

When it comes to conduct problems, there are no simple or single causes. Consider two brothers—one, John Edgar, is an award-winning author (*Brothers and Keepers*), while his brother Robbie is in prison for murder. How do we account for such striking differences between brothers raised in the same family? Are they due to differences in genetic makeup, neurobiological functioning, birth complications, temperament, intelligence, family experiences, peer influences, difficulties in school, or some combination of these factors?

Historically, conduct problems were viewed as either the result of an inborn characteristic or learned through poor socialization practices. Early theories focused mainly on the child's aggression and invoked one primary cause, such as an aggressive drive, frustration, poor role models, or reinforcement. However, most of these "smoking gun" explanations can be challenged on one point or another. For example, not all children behave aggressively as would be predicted by the aggressive-drive theory, and frustration sometimes leads to cooperation rather than aggression. Although each single-cause theory highlights a potentially important determinant, no single theory can explain all forms of antisocial behavior.

We next consider several proposed causes of conduct problems. Although we examine them separately, conduct problems are best accounted for by the interplay among predisposing child, family, community, and cultural factors that operate in a transactional fashion over time (Granic & Patterson, 2006). These factors are summarized in Table 6.4.

TABLE 6.4 | Summary of Causal Influences for Antisocial Behavior

Child
Genetic risk, prenatal and birth complications, exposure to lead, low arousal and reactivity, functional and structural deficits in prefrontal cortex, difficult temperament, attention-deficit/hyperactivity (ADHD), insecure attachments, childhood-onset of aggression, social avoidance and withdrawal, social–cognitive deficits, lowered verbal intelligence and verbal deficits
Family
Antisocial family values, parental antisocial or criminal behavior, paternal antisocial personality disorder, maternal depression, parental substance abuse, marital discord, teen motherhood, single parenthood, chaotic household, large family, low socio-economic status, low education of mother, family carelessness in permitting access to weapons
Ineffective Parenting
Poor supervision and monitoring, inconsistent discipline, avoidance of discipline due to concerns about the child's reaction, harsh discipline and maltreatment, discordant parent–child interactions, poor communication and problem solving, parental neglect, low parental warmth
Peers
Early peer aggression, rejection by peers, association with deviant siblings, association with deviant peers
School
Poor academic performance, weak bonding to school, low educational aspirations, low school motivation, poorly organized and functioning schools
Neighborhood and Community
Neighborhood disadvantage and poverty, disorganized neighborhoods, gang membership, availability of weapons
Sociocultural
Media portrayal of violence, cultural attitudes encouraging use of aggression, socialization of children for aggression

Source: Adapted from Loeber and Farrington, 2000, p. 749.

Genetic Influences

Heredity is something a man believes in until his own son begins behaving like a delinquent.

—Author unknown

The universality of aggressive behavior and antisocial behavior in humans, and the fact that such behaviors run in families within and across generations, highlight the importance of genetic influences. Adoption and twin studies indicate that 50% or more of the variance in antisocial behavior is attributable to heredity for both males and females (Baker, Jacobson, Raine, Lozano, & Bezdjian, 2007). Research indicates that parents pass on a general liability for externalizing disorders to their children that may be expressed in different ways, including inattention, hyperactivity, or oppositional and conduct problems (Bornovalova, Hicks, Iacono, & McGue, 2010). The heritability of conduct problems also varies by age, age of onset, and other factors (Burt & Neiderhiser, 2009). For example, the strength of the genetic contribution is higher for children who display the LCP versus AL pattern and also higher for those with callous–unemotional traits (Viding, Jones, Frick, Moffitt, & Plomin, 2008). Overall, adoption and twin studies suggest that genetic and environmental factors contribute to antisocial behavior across development. The studies do not, however, specify the mechanisms by which the factors operate.

It is likely that genetic risks for antisocial behavior operate via several pathways (Rutter, 2003b). First, genetic factors may be related to a difficult temperament, lack of response to distress in others, impulsivity, a tendency to seek rewards, or an insensitivity to punishment that combine to create an antisocial "propensity" or "personality" (Waldman et al., 2011). Second, genetic factors may increase the likelihood that a child will be exposed to environmental risk factors, such as parental divorce, maltreatment, or other negative life events that are associated with an increased risk of antisocial behavior. Third, children's genotype and neurobiology may moderate their susceptibility to these environmental insults in determining whether they develop later antisocial behavior (Ellis & Boyce, 2011). These and other pathways will need to be addressed if the causes of antisocial behavior are to be understood (Rutter, 2006a).

Exciting new studies into gene variants have identified possible gene–environment (G × E) interactions in the development of conduct problems (Dodge, 2009). A variant of the gene that encodes the neurotransmitter metabolizing enzyme monoamine oxidase-A (MAOA) has been of particular interest because this gene is related to neural systems involved in aggression. When threatened or provoked humans naturally feel rage and an impulse to react aggressively. Activation of the MAOA enzyme helps us inhibit that response, thus playing a key role in regulating behavior following threatening events. Research has found that maltreated children with a low-active MAOA genotype are much more likely to develop antisocial behavior than maltreated children who do not have this genotype (Kim-Cohen et al., 2006). An interaction between the low-active MAOA genotype and physical discipline before age 5 has also been related to adolescent delinquent behavior (Edwards et al., 2010). Brain imaging studies have also found that individuals with the low-active MAOA genotype show patterns of arousal in areas of the brain that are associated with aggression in response to emotion-provoking stimuli (Buckholtz & Meyer-Lindenberg, 2008).

In addition to MAOA, other genes and G × E interactions have been implicated in the association between negative parenting and childhood conduct problems (Albaugh et al., 2010; Lahey et al., 2011). Findings to date suggest that some of these genes may not be specific to any one type of externalizing disorder but will predispose individuals to a broad spectrum of conduct problems (Dick, 2007). G × E interaction effects in conduct disorders are fascinating. However, research into these effects is just beginning and replication studies are needed (Hebebrand, Scherag, Schimmelmann, & Hinney, 2010). Similarly, research into how G × E interaction effects develop *over time* is still in its infancy (Dodge, 2009).

Prenatal Factors and Birth Complications

A number of pregnancy and birth factors (e.g., low birth weight) are related to the development of serious conduct problems (Brennan, Grekin, & Mednick, 2003). Malnutrition during pregnancy is associated with later antisocial behavior, which may be mediated by protein deficiency (Raine, 2002). Exposure to lead before and after birth and the mother's use of nicotine, marijuana, and other substances during pregnancy may also be associated with later conduct problems (Carpenter & Nevin, 2010; Murray, Irving, Farrington, Colman, & Bloxsom, 2010; Nigg & Breslau, 2007). There is also support for maternal alcohol use during pregnancy playing a role in conduct problems—the greater the amount of alcohol consumed, the greater the risk of child conduct problems (D'Onofrio et al., 2007; Larkby, Goldschmidt, Hanusa, & Day, 2011). Although pregnancy and birth factors are correlated with conduct problems, strong evidence of direct biological causation is lacking (Hodgins, Kratzer, & McNeil, 2001). For example, it is likely that the relation between mothers' smoking during pregnancy and adolescent conduct problems and criminality is best accounted for by the transmission of an underlying antisocial tendency from mother to child and other family background variables, rather than exposure to cigarette byproducts during pregnancy (D'Onofrio et al., 2008, 2010; Gatzke-Kopp & Beauchaine, 2007).

Neurobiological Factors

Gray (1987) proposed that people's behavioral patterns are related to two subsystems of the brain, each having distinct neuroanatomical regions and neurotransmitter pathways. The **behavioral activation system (BAS)** stimulates behavior in response to signals of reward or nonpunishment. In contrast, the **behavioral inhibition system (BIS)** produces anxiety and inhibits ongoing behavior in the presence of novel events, innate fear stimuli, and signals of nonreward or punishment. Other behavioral patterns may result from the relative balance or imbalance of activity in these two neural systems. Think of the BAS as similar to the gas pedal and the BIS as similar to the brakes—some individuals ride one more heavily than the other.

It has been proposed that antisocial patterns of behavior result from an overactive BAS *and* an underactive BIS—a pattern determined primarily by genetic predisposition. Consistent with an overactive BAS, children with conduct problems show a heightened sensitivity to rewards (Frick et al., 2003). In addition, they fail to respond to punishment and continue to respond under conditions of no reward—patterns that are consistent with an underactive BIS (Fowles, 2001). Strikingly, a lack of fear of socializing punishment at age 3 has been found to predict criminal offending 20 years later (Gao, Raine, Venables, Dawson, & Mednick, 2010).

Individual differences in antisocial behavior have been related to variations in stress regulating

BOX 6.5 A CLOSER LOOK

Do the Brains of Children with Early-Onset Conduct Disorders Differ From Those of Children with Adolescent-Onset Conduct Disorders?

Despite the many differences between children with early-onset versus adolescent-onset CD, recent brain-imaging findings suggest that both groups may display similar brain abnormalities compared to children without CD. Using magnetic resonance imaging (MRI), neuroscientists in England measured the size of specific brain regions of 65 teenage boys with CD and 27 teenage boys without CD (Fairchild et al., 2011). They found that the amygdala, a region of the brain involved in reading others' emotions, empathy, and recognizing when others are distressed, was markedly smaller in teens with CD than in the healthy comparison group. However, no differences were found between teens with early-onset versus adolescent-onset conduct disorders. The image to the right, shows the amygdala (for each side of the brain), the region of the brain for which the reduction in volume was largest for teens with CD versus healthy comparison children.

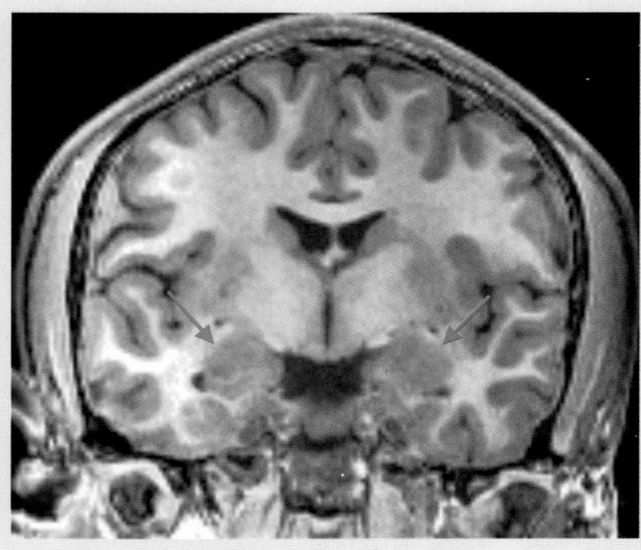

Image courtesy of Dr. Giuseppe Iaria, Department of Psychology, University of Calgary (www.neurolab.ca)

These preliminary findings are important, since it has been argued that early-onset CD is a neurodevelopmental condition, whereas adolescent-onset CD is mostly the result of teens associating with and mimicking other teens who are getting into trouble. However, this study shows that abnormalities in brain structures underlying social-information processing may contribute to the emergence of both adolescent-onset as well as early-onset CD (Fairchild et al., 2011).

mechanisms, including the hypothalamic–pituitary adrenal (HPA) axis and autonomic nervous system (ANS), serotonergic functioning, and structural and functional deficits in the prefrontal cortex of the brain (van Goozen, Fairchild, Snoek, & Harold, 2007). Children with CD who show an early onset of aggressive symptoms display low psychophysiological/cortical arousal and low reactivity of the autonomic nervous system (e.g., a lower resting heart rate) (Lorber, 2004; Raine, 2002). Low arousal and autonomic reactivity may lead to diminished avoidance learning in response to warnings or reprimands, a poor response to punishment, and a fearless, stimulus-seeking temperament. In turn, this may lead to antisocial behavior, a failure to develop the anticipatory fear needed to avoid such behavior, and a lack of conscience. Most children respond to discipline and punishment by reducing their antisocial behavior. Often, the opposite occurs with children with conduct problems—when disciplined or punished they may increase their antisocial behavior and become even more defiant.

Neuroimaging studies have identified structural and functional brain abnormalities in several brain regions in youths with conduct disorders, including in those with high levels of psychopathic features. These brain regions include the amygdala, prefrontal cortex, anterior cingulate, and insula, as well as interconnected regions. Imaging studies also show reduced activation in some of these areas (e.g., the amygdala) when viewing emotional stimuli such as angry or sad faces, or during tasks that require learning not to respond to punishing stimuli (Finger et al., 2011; Huebner et al., 2008; Passamonti et al., 2010). These brain regions are involved in processing social and emotional information. Therefore abnormalities in these regions likely underlie the socio-cognitive and emotional deficits that characterize children with conduct problems. Interestingly, as described in Box 6.5, similar brain abnormalities may be present both in youths with early- and adolescent-onset conduct disorders (Fairchild et al., 2011).

Although much additional work is needed, early findings from neuroimaging and other studies suggest three neural systems underlying cognitive, social, and emotional differences across different types of conduct problems. The first includes subcortical neural systems that lead to aggressive behavior. In this context, dysfunction in the integrated functioning of brain circuits involving the amygdala has been implicated (Blair, 2011). The second neural circuit involves prefrontal cortex decision-making circuits and socioemotional information-processing circuits that assess social cues and evaluate the consequences of aggressing or not aggressing, and the third neural circuit involves frontoparietal regions involved in regulating emotions and impulsive motivational urges (Coccaro, Sripada, Yanowitch, & Phan, 2011, p. 1153). In the future, further research into these neural circuits may help to reveal mechanisms through which inborn dispositions may place a child at risk for later conduct problems (Viding & Jones, 2008).

Social–Cognitive Factors

Social–cognitive abilities refer to the skills involved in attending to, interpreting, and responding to social cues. There is a strong relationship between social–cognitive deficits and antisocial behavior across all types of conduct problem trajectories (e.g., childhood limited, adolescent-onset, early-onset persistent), especially for children showing early-onset persistent conduct problems. As many as 40% of boys and 25% of girls with persistent conduct problems display significant social–cognitive impairments (Oliver, Barker, Mandy, Skuse, & Maughan, 2011). The connection between children's thinking in social situations and their aggressive behavior has been looked at in several ways. Some approaches focus on immature forms of thinking, such as egocentrism, a lack of social perspective taking, theory of mind deficits, or deficits in moral reasoning (Blair, 2010; Olson et al., 2011). Others emphasize cognitive deficiencies, such as a child's failure to use verbal mediators to regulate his or her behavior (Meichenbaum, 1977), or cognitive distortions, such as interpreting a neutral event as an intentionally hostile act (Crick & Dodge, 1994). Other approaches focus more broadly on the social–cognitive processes involved in antisocial decision-making (Fontaine et al., 2010). Recent research has also found deficits in facial expression recognition and eye contact in children with conduct problems, which may further contribute to their antisocial behavior and social difficulties (Dadds, Jambrak, Passalich, Hawes, & Brennan, 2011; Fairchild, Van Goozen, Calder, Stollery, & Goodyer, 2009).

Dodge and Pettit (2003) have presented a comprehensive social–cognitive framework to account for aggressive behavior and antisocial behavior in children. In this model, cognitive and emotional processes play a central mediating role. Children are presumed to develop social knowledge about their world based on a unique set of predispositions, life experiences, and sociocultural contexts. In specific social situations, children then use this social knowledge to guide their processing of social information in ways that lead directly to certain behaviors. For example, when teased in the schoolyard by peers, does the child laugh with the crowd, walk away, or strike back aggressively? A set of emotional and thought processes are presumed to occur between the social stimulus of being teased and the child's reaction. The thinking and behavior of antisocial/aggressive children in social situations are often characterized by deficits in one or more of these steps, as outlined in Table 6.5.

TABLE 6.5 | Steps in the Thinking and Behavior of Aggressive Children in Social Situations

Step 1: Encoding Socially aggressive children use fewer cues before making a decision. When defining and resolving an interpersonal situation, they seek less information about the event before acting.
Step 2: Interpretation Socially aggressive children attribute hostile intentions to ambiguous events.
Step 3: Response Search Socially aggressive children generate fewer and more aggressive responses and have less knowledge about social problem solving.
Step 4: Response Decision Socially aggressive children are more likely to choose aggressive solutions.
Step 5: Enactment Socially aggressive children use poor verbal communication and strike out physically.

Source: From *A Review and Reformulation of Social information Processing Mechanism in Children's Social Adjustment* by N. R. Crick and K. A. Dodge, 1994, Psychological Bulletin', 115, 74–101.

Family Factors

I am convinced that increasing rates of delinquency are due to parents who are either too careless or too busy with their own pleasure to give sufficient time, companionship, and interest to their children.

—Former FBI director J. Edgar Hoover, *The New York Times*, December 6, 1947

Many family factors have been implicated as possible causes of children's antisocial behavior—early maternal age at childbearing, poor disciplinary practices, harsh discipline, a lack of parental supervision, a lack of affection, marital conflict, family isolation, and violence in the home (D'Onofrio et al., 2009; Hoeve et al., 2008; Lansford et al., 2011). For children who are at genetic risk for antisocial behavior, positive parenting practices may reduce the influence of the child's genotype on later antisocial behavior, whereas negative parenting practices can have the opposite effect (Feinberg, Button, Neiderhiser, & Hetherington, 2007). Although the association between family factors and conduct problems is well established, the nature of this association and the possible causal role of family factors continue to be debated.

Family difficulties are related to the development of both ODD and CD, with a stronger association for children on the LCP versus the AL path (Lahey, Loeber, Quay, Frick, & Grimm, 1992). A combination of individual child risk factors (e.g., difficult temperament) and extreme deficits in family management skills most likely accounts for the more persistent and severe forms of antisocial behavior (Caspi & Moffitt, 1995).

Family factors are related to children's antisocial behavior in complex ways. For example, physical abuse is a strong risk factor for later aggressive behavior. One reason for this link between factors appears to be deficits in the child's social information processing that result from the physical abuse (Dodge & Pettit, 2003). As we have seen, the child's genotype can also moderate the link between maltreatment and later antisocial behavior, a possible reason that not all children who have been abused grow up to victimize others (Caspi et al., 2002).

The effect of marital conflict on children's aggressive behavior may be affected by several factors, including the parents' unavailability, the use of inconsistent or harsh discipline, lax monitoring, and how the child interprets conflict between parents (Cummings & Davies, 2002). Other conditions associated with marital conflict or divorce such as stress, depression, loss of contact with one parent, financial hardship, and greater responsibility at home may also contribute to antisocial behavior (Emery, 1999). Interestingly, contact with an absent father following marital break-up can be either a risk or a protective factor for antisocial behavior, depending on whether the father is antisocial (Jaffee, Moffitt, Caspi, & Taylor, 2003).

Nick's mother says:

> Nick hit a neighborhood kid on the head with a two-by-four; the injured child required 16 stitches. Then he killed another kitten by jumping on it from his bunk bed. I lost control. I told him I hated him, I grabbed him by the cheek, I pinched it a little too hard. I didn't know what to do. (Colapinto, 1993, p. 150)

Cruel and aggressive child behaviors can evoke strong reactions, like the anger and overly harsh response by Nick's mother. An important concept for understanding family influences on antisocial behavior is **reciprocal influence**, which means that the child's behavior is both influenced by and influences the behavior of others. Negative parenting practices and parent-child conflict may lead to antisocial behavior, but they may also be a reaction to the oppositional and aggressive behaviors of their children (Klahr, McGue, Iacono, & Burt, 2011).

For example, in an interesting study of reciprocal influence, mothers of boys with and without CD were asked to interact with three boys—their own son, a boy with CD, and a boy without CD (Anderson, Lytton, & Romney, 1986). All mothers were more demanding and negative when interacting with a child with CD, which supports a child-to-parent effect. However, mothers of

© Bob Kalman/The Image Works

Physical abuse is a strong risk factor for later aggressive behavior

© Masterfile

A child's oppositional behavior may also lead to negative parenting behavior boys with CD responded most negatively to their own sons, suggesting that previous negative interactions with their child also had an effect. Reciprocal influence is a useful way to think of the interplay between family influences and antisocial behavior over the course of development. However, it is also possible that some aspects of the family environment are related to antisocial behavior as a result of a shared genetic predisposition that leads both parent and child to display similar behavior patterns.

Recent studies generally support the view that child behaviors exert greater influence on parenting behaviors than the reverse, perhaps more so for mothers than fathers (Narusyte et al., 2011). This suggests that the inborn level of emotional dysregulation that children bring to their interactions with parents may have a greater influence on outcomes than ineffective parenting behaviors (Loeber et al., 2009a). Nevertheless, as we will discuss, interventions directed at changing ineffective parenting behaviors are among the most effective methods for reducing children's conduct problems.

Coercion Theory

Gerald Patterson's **coercion theory** contends that parent–child interactions provide a training ground for the development of antisocial behavior (Patterson, Reid, & Dishion, 1992). This occurs through a four-step, escape-conditioning sequence in which the child learns to use increasingly intense forms of noxious behavior to escape and avoid unwanted parental demands. The *coercive parent–child interaction* described in Box 6.6 begins when a mother finds her son Paul, who is failing in school, watching TV rather than doing his homework. Coercive parent–child interactions are made up of well-practiced actions and reactions, which may occur with little awareness. This process is called a "reinforcement trap" because, over time, all family members become trapped by the consequences of their own behaviors. For example, mothers of antisocial children are eight times *less* likely to enforce demands than are mothers of nonproblem children (Patterson et al., 1992).

The relationship between parenting and conduct problems also appears to be affected by a child's callous–unemotional traits. In one report, ineffective parenting was related to conduct problems, but only in children low on CU traits (Wootton, Frick, Shelton, & Silverthorn, 1997). Children with CU traits displayed significant conduct problems regardless of the quality of parenting they received. The relationship between parental discipline and conduct problems may also be affected by the amount of discipline—too much or too little can both have adverse effects. The relationship between parental discipline and antisocial behavior may also vary with the family's cultural background, the emotional climate in which discipline is used, and the gender of the parent–child pair. For example, discipline may be most effective in same-gender parent–child pairs: discipline of daughters by mothers and sons by fathers (Deater-Deckard & Dodge, 1997).

BOX 6.6 A CLOSER LOOK

Coercive Parent–Child Interaction: Four-Step Escape Conditioning Sequence

Step 1

Raising her voice, Paul's mother scolds, "Why are you sitting in front of the TV when you should be doing your homework?"

Step 2

Paul snaps back, "School is boring, my teachers are stupid, and I don't have any homework to do." Paul's arguing has the immediate effect of punishing his mother for her scolding and, over time, may reduce her efforts to do something about his homework and school problems.

Step 3

Paul's mother withdraws her demand for him to complete his homework, allowing herself to be satisfied that he does not have any homework to do. She lowers her voice and says, "Does Mrs. Smith still put everyone to sleep in her English class?" The mother's withdrawal of her demand for homework reinforces Paul's arguing and increases the chances that the next time she makes an issue of homework, he will argue with her. Over time, Paul may also turn up the volume of his negative reactions by shouting or throwing things.

Step 4

As soon as Paul's mother withdraws her demand, Paul stops arguing and engages in neutral or even positive behavior. He says "You're sure right about Mrs. Smith, Mom. It's tough to keep your eyes open in her class." Paul, by ceasing his noxious behavior, reinforces his mother for giving in and increases the likelihood that she will do so again in response to his arguing and protests.

From *Antisocial Boys* by G. R. Patterson, J. B. Reid, and T. J. Dishion, 1992, p. 41.

Attachment Theories

Attachment theories emphasize that the quality of children's attachment to parents will determine their eventual identification with parental values, beliefs, and standards. Secure bonds with parents promote a sense of closeness, shared values, and identification with the social world. Attachment theories contend that children refrain from antisocial behavior because they have a stake in conformity.

Children with conduct problems often show little internalization of parent and societal standards. Even when they comply with parental requests, they may do so because of perceived threats to their freedom or physical safety (Shaw & Bell, 1993). When these threats are not present, such as when the child is unsupervised, antisocial behavior is likely to occur. Weak bonds with parents may lead the child to associate with deviant peers, which in turn may lead to delinquency and substance abuse (Elliott, Huizinga, & Menard, 1989).

Research findings support a relationship between insecure attachments, particularly for children with disorganized attachments, and the development of antisocial behavior during childhood and adolescence (Pasco Fearon, Bakersmans-Kranenburg, van IJzendoorn, Lapsley, & Roisman, 2010). However, it is unclear whether attachment quality by itself can predict current or future variation in the severity of conduct problems. It is likely that the relationship between attachment and antisocial behavior is affected by many factors, including the child's gender, clinical status, temperament, and family management practices (Pasco Fearon et al., 2010).

Other Family Problems

In addition to the negative parenting practices and attachment problems that we have discussed, other family factors such as family instability and stress, and parental criminality and psychopathology may also contribute to children's conduct problems.

JAKE AND REGGIE

All Odds Against Them

Linda M., single mother of 2-year-old Jake and 4-year-old Reggie, sought treatment because Reggie was engaging in severe and uncontrollable aggressive behaviors, including hitting, kicking, and biting Jake. She was depressed and at risk for suicide. Her boyfriend Hank is the father of the two children. He lives nearby and demands that she come over so he can see the children. During these visits, he engages her in what she refers to as "forced sex" (i.e., rape), and he demands that Jake and Reggie remain with them and watch. In principle, Linda could have refused the visits. However, Hank threatened that if she did not comply, he would stop paying child support, take Jake and Reggie away in a custody battle, kill himself, or come over to the house and kill her and the two boys. These threats of violence were to be taken seriously because Hank had a prior arrest record for assault and brandished a gun. (Adapted from *Conduct Disorders in Childhood and Adolescence* by A. E. Kazdin, p. 17. Copyright © 1995 by Sage Publications.)

Family Instability and Stress

Families of children with conduct problems are often characterized by an unstable family structure with frequent transitions, including changes in parents and changes in residence (Dishion & Patterson, 2006). Family instability is related to a child's heightened risk for antisocial behavior, academic problems, anxiety and depression, association with deviant peers, and criminal conviction (Kasen, Cohen, Brook, & Hartmark, 1996). In most cases, the impact of divorce on a child's antisocial behavior is related to the family disruption and conflict that accompany it (Emery, 1999). In some cases, a child's antisocial behavior may contribute to family instability by increasing the chances of divorce (Block, Block, & Gjerde, 1986).

High family stress is associated with negative child behavior in the home, and may be both a cause and an outcome of antisocial behavior. Unemployment, low SES, and multiple family transitions are all related to childhood conduct problems. Among family stressors, poverty is one of the strongest predictors of CD and high rates of crime (Pagani, Boulerice, Vitaro, & Tremblay, 1999). But what constitutes the "active ingredient" in the link between poverty and antisocial behavior? In this regard, instability, residential mobility, and disruptions in parenting practices have all been found to be important (Dodge, Pettit, & Bates, 1994b). The **amplifier hypothesis** states that stress amplifies the maladaptive predispositions of parents (e.g., poor mental health), thereby disrupting family management practices and compromising parents' ability to be supportive of their children (Conger, Ge, Elder, Lorenz, & Simons, 1994).

Parental Criminality and Psychopathology

Aggressive and antisocial tendencies run in families, within and across generations (Blazei, Iacono, & Krueger, 2006; D'Onofrio et al., 2007). In fact, children's aggression is correlated with their parents' childhood aggression at the same age (Huesmann, Eron, Lefkowitz, & Walder, 1984). Parents of antisocial children have higher rates of arrests, motor vehicle violations, license suspensions, and substance abuse (Dishion & Patterson, 2006). Antisocial individuals are likely to be ineffective parents, especially during discipline confrontations when they display an irritable, explosive style of interaction. Certain types of parental psychopathology, such as APD, are strongly and specifically related to CD in their children (Herndon & Iacono, 2005). This relationship is particularly clear for fathers, as is the link between paternal criminal behavior and substance abuse and child antisocial patterns (Lahey, 2008). The strong association between paternal APD and child antisocial behavior is independent of whether the father lives in the home, or of the degree of contact between father and child (Tapscott, Frick, Wootton, & Kruh, 1996). For mothers, antisociality, histrionic personality (excessive emotionality and attention seeking), and depression are related to children's antisocial behavior (Dishion & Patterson, 2006).

Societal Factors

Causes of antisocial behavior at the level of the individual and family tell only part of the story, since they interact with the larger societal and cultural context in determining conduct problems (Sampson, 1992). There is little doubt that poverty, neighborhood crime, family disruption, and residential mobility are related to crime and delinquency in young people (Schonberg & Shaw, 2007). However, the specific mechanisms by which these conditions lead to crime and delinquency are not known.

Theories of social disorganization propose that community structures impact the family processes that then affect the child's adjustment (Sampson & Laub, 1994). Adverse contextual factors (e.g., low SES) are associated with poor parenting, particularly coercive and inconsistent discipline and poor parental monitoring (Lahey, Van Hulle, D'Onofrio, Rodgers, & Waldman, 2008). In turn, these factors are associated with an early onset of antisocial behavior, early arrest, and chronic offending during adolescence (Capaldi & Patterson, 1994). A vicious cycle of adaptational failure and added stress places downward pressure on both the parent and the child. The antisocial individual is more vulnerable and at greater risk of entering a class of divorced, unemployed, and disadvantaged people (Dishion & Patterson, 2006). For example, social disadvantage, increased mobility, divorce, early sexual activity, and working-mother status may lead to an increase in mothers who are at greater risk for antisocial parenting practices. Also, less skilled antisocial mothers may drift into areas of large cities that isolate them from family and neighbors and lead them to function in an atmosphere of mistrust and minimal communication. When these women become pregnant again, they may have reduced access to public health services. Poor diet and drugs may result in a higher incidence of low birth weight, prematurity, and birth defects in their offspring, which in turn make their infants and toddlers more difficult to parent. The combination of a difficult infant and an unskilled parent increases the likelihood of antisocial behavior and subsequent onset of arrest. In this way, the generation of conduct problems cycles again and again.

Neighborhood and School

Antisocial behavior in youth is disproportionately concentrated in poor neighborhoods characterized by a criminal subculture that supports drug dealing and prostitution, peer group violence, delinquent

© Bob Daemmrich/Alamy

Weapons signs, such as this one in the Austin, Texas area, are routinely posted outside schools

gang membership, frequent transitions and mobility, and low social support from neighbors or religious groups (Leventhal & Brooks-Gunn, 2000). In addition, antisocial people tend to select neighborhoods with other people like them (Harden et al., 2009). The **social selection hypothesis** states that people who move into different neighborhoods differ from one another before they arrive, and those who remain differ from those who leave. For individuals with antisocial traits, this creates a community organization that minimizes productive social relations and effective social norms, and the antisocial behavior becomes stabilized (Sampson, Raudenbush, & Earls, 1997). The effects of community characteristics on crime and delinquency are likely to be reinforced by neighborhood social disorganization characterized by few local friendship and acquaintance networks, low participation in local community organizations, and an inability to supervise and control teenage peer groups (Sampson & Groves, 1989). In fact, the main influence of effective parents in high-risk neighborhoods seems to be in countering gang membership (Tolan, Gorman-Smith, & Henry, 2003).

In high-risk neighborhoods, enrollment in a poor school is associated with antisocial and delinquent behavior, whereas a positive school experience can be a protective factor for the development of these behaviors (Rutter, 1989). A good school environment characterized by clear requirements for homework completion, high academic expectations, clear and consistent discipline policies, and incentives for appropriate school behavior and achievement may partially compensate for poor family circumstances. Systematic interventions to promote these school characteristics have resulted in school-wide reductions in children's conduct problems (Gottfredson, Gottfredson, & Hybel, 1993).

Media

I believe that this kind of vicarious adventure, escape, excitement, even blood and thunder is necessary and important to most children as outlets for their own emotions, particularly their feelings of aggression.

—Josette Frank, Media Consultant

Programs interestingly depicting antisocial conduct, crime, and murder, influence children to antisocial attitudes and lead to aggression.

—Judge Jacob Panken, New York City Children's Court

These contrasting expert opinions were presented 65 years ago (*The New York Times*, April 14, 1946), in reference to the influence of *radio* on children. The controversy regarding media influences on aggression in young people rages on today. Parents, teachers, policymakers, and the press have expressed concerns about the possible adverse impact of violence in movies, TV, video games, text messages, and the Internet on children's social development and aggressive behavior. In considering media influences on children's antisocial behavior, we discuss the relation between TV violence and children's aggressive behavior because most of the research has been conducted in this area. Research into the new media is increasing at a rapid pace (Varnhagen, 2006). The findings from studies of TV violence and children's aggressive behavior should help us in answering questions about children's use of the Internet, their exposure to unwanted or undesirable information, and how they are affected by this exposure.

At one extreme, some researchers claim that TV violence verges on child maltreatment and that we can reduce murders by unplugging the TV; others argue that there is little evidence for a causal relation between TV violence and aggressive behavior. By the time a child in the United States reaches grade 6, he or she has witnessed 8,000 or more murders on TV and well over 100,000 other acts of violence (Leland, 1995). The concern is that this steady diet of violence leads children to think violence is normal, to become desensitized to the suffering of real people, or to become aroused by images they see and want to mimic these violent acts. For example, one 5-year-old boy, after watching his favorite cartoon characters pull one of their famous arson stunts, set his house ablaze. His younger sister was killed in the fire. Thus, exposure to media violence can be both: (1) a short term *precipitating* factor for aggressive and violent behavior that results from priming, excitation, or imitation of specific behaviors, and (2) a long-term *predisposing* factor for aggressive behavior acquired via desensitization to violence and observational learning of an aggression-supporting belief system (i.e., "the world is a hostile place," "aggression is acceptable," "aggression can be used to solve social problems") (Huesmann, Moise-Titus, Podolski, & Eron, 2003).

Exposure to media violence may reinforce preexisting antisocial tendencies in some children. For example, in a series of studies spanning more than a decade, children with conduct problems were found to view relatively large amounts of violent material, prefer aggressive characters, and believe fictional content to be true (Gadow & Sprafkin, 1993). However, it is not only children with preexisting violent tendencies who are likely to be affected. Long-term studies have found that childhood exposure to media violence between ages 6 and 9, identification with aggressive TV characters, and perceived realism of TV violence predict serious aggressive and criminal behavior 15 years later (Huesmann et al., 2003).

Calvin and Hobbes **by Bill Watterson**

GRAPHIC VIOLENCE IN THE MEDIA.

DOES IT GLAMORIZE VIOLENCE? SURE. DOES IT DESENSITIZE US TO VIOLENCE? OF COURSE. DOES IT HELP US TOLERATE VIOLENCE? YOU BET. DOES IT STUNT OUR EMPATHY FOR OUR FELLOW BEINGS? HECK YES.

The correlation between TV violence and aggression is indisputable—but does TV violence cause aggression, and if so, how? Although research suggests a causal relation (Anderson & Bushman, 2002; Johnson, Cohen, Smailes, Kasen, & Brook, 2002), answers to these questions remain elusive despite decades of research and a pressing urge to act on research findings through social policies to filter violent content and inform users. It is unlikely that media influences alone (TV or other forms) can account for the substantial amount of antisocial behavior in young people (Rutter & Smith, 1995). Like other risk factors, media influences interact with child, family, community, and cultural factors in contributing to conduct problems. But clearly they are an important and unique contributing factor. Exposure to media violence won't turn an otherwise well-adjusted child into a violent criminal. However, "just as every cigarette one smokes increases a little bit the likelihood of a lung tumor some day . . . every violent TV show increases a little bit the likelihood of a child growing up to behave more aggressively in some situation" (Huesmann et al., 2003, p. 218).

Cultural Factors

Cultural differences in the expression of aggressive behavior are dramatic. Across cultures, socialization of children for aggression has been found to be one of the strongest predictors of aggressive acts such as homicide and assault. As the following examples of contrasting socialization practices illustrate, aggression may be an inadvertent consequence of a culture's emphasis on training "warriors":

The Kapauku of Western New Guinea:

> At about 7 years of age, a Kapauku boy begins to be under the father's control, gradually sleeping and eating only with the men and away from his mother . . . His training [to be a brave warrior] begins when the father engages his son in mock stick fights. Gradually the fights become more serious and possibly lethal when the father and son shoot real war arrows at each other. Groups of boys play at target shooting; they also play at hitting each other over the head with sticks. (Ember & Ember, 1994, p. 639–640)

The homicide rate among the Kapauku from 1953 to 1954 was estimated at 200 per 100,000, approximately 4 times the current murder rates in the United States.

The Lepcha of the Indian Himalayas:

> The Lepcha are very clear about what they expect from their children. "Good children help out with the work, tell the truth, listen to teaching from elders, help old people, and are peaceable. Bad children quarrel with and insult people, tell lies, draw their knives in anger when reprimanded, and do not do their share of the work." (Ember & Ember, 1994, p. 641)

Interviews with the Lepcha people revealed that the only authenticated murder in their culture had occurred about 200 years ago (Ember & Ember, 1994).

Rates of antisocial behavior vary widely across and within cultures, and not necessarily in relation to technological gains, material wealth, or population density. For example, some third world countries that value interdependence are characterized by high rates of prosocial behavior, and some places with high population density have very low rates of violence. The United States is by far the most violent of all industrialized nations, with homicide rates that are many times the rates in Europe.

Minority status is related to antisocial behavior in the United States, with elevated rates of antisocial behavior in African American, Hispanic American, and Native American youths (Elliott, Huizinga, & Ageton, 1985). However, studies of national samples have reported either no or very small differences in antisocial behavior related to race or ethnicity when SES, gender, age, and referral status are controlled for (Lahey et al., 1995). Thus, although externalizing problems are reported to be more frequent among minority-status youth, this finding is likely related to disparities including economic hardship, limited employment opportunities, residence in high-risk urban neighborhoods, and membership in antisocial gangs, which is on the rise (Children's Defense Fund, 2007; Egley & O'Donnell, 2009).

SECTION SUMMARY

Causes

- Conduct problems in children are best accounted for by multiple causes or risk and protective factors that operate in a transactional fashion over time.
- Adoption and twin studies indicate that genetic influences account for about 50% of the variance in antisocial behavior.
- Genetic contributions to overt forms of antisocial behavior, such as aggression, are stronger than for covert acts, such as stealing or lying.
- Antisocial behavior may result from an overactive behavioral activation system (BAS) and an underactive behavioral inhibition system (BIS). Low levels of cortical arousal and autonomic reactivity and deficits in the amygdala, prefrontal cortex, and other brain regions play an important role, particularly for childhood-onset/persistent CD.
- Many family factors have been implicated as possible causes of children's antisocial behavior, including marital conflict, family isolation, violence in the home, poor disciplinary practices, a lack of parental supervision, and insecure attachments.

(continues)

SECTION SUMMARY *(continued)*

- Family instability and stress, parental criminality and antisocial personality, and antisocial family values are risk factors for conduct problems.
- The structural characteristics of the community provide a backdrop for the emergence of conduct problems by giving rise to community conditions that interfere with the adoption of social norms and the development of productive social relations.
- School, neighborhood, and media influences are all potential risk factors for antisocial behavior, as are cultural factors, such as minority group status and ethnicity.

Treatment and Prevention

SCOTT

Salvageable?

Scott, age 10, was referred after setting a fire in the schoolyard. While his therapist saw Scott as "potentially salvageable," his parents were not willing to pursue therapy. As a result, Scott was placed in a boarding school for "troubled boys" . . . After 3 weeks at this school, he was expelled for burning down the dorm . . . Charges were pressed and he was sent to a group home for delinquent boys. He remained there for 3 months before he and two older boys ran away. They were caught a few days later when they attacked a homeless man, stealing his money ($4.85) and beating him. As a result of this crime, Scott was sent to a detention facility until he turned 18. His therapist heard nothing further. (Based on Morgan, 1999)

Many forms of treatment will be tried throughout the life of a child with severe conduct problems. Treatment may begin during the preschool years or, more typically, as was the case with Scott, when severe antisocial behavior at school leads to referral. Ongoing contacts with the educational, mental health, and judicial systems may result in referral for one or more of a wide range of treatments. The most promising treatments use a combination of approaches that are applied across individual, family, school, and community settings (Kazdin, 2007; Lochman, Powell, Boxmeyer, & Jimenez-Camargo, 2011). In addition, treatment frequently requires that related family problems, such as maternal depression, marital discord, abuse, and other stressors be addressed if gains are to be generalized and maintained (McMahon et al., 2006).

Most people understand that family dysfunction, abuse, school expulsion, association with drug-using peers, residence in a high-crime area, and minimal parental supervision contribute to serious conduct problems (Henggeler, 1996). However, despite this recognition, typical and often court-mandated treatments such as psychotherapy, group therapy, tutoring, punishment, wilderness programs, or boot camps fail to meaningfully address these determinants, and thus are among the least effective approaches (Lipsey, 1995). Despite their lack of effectiveness in treating serious antisocial behavior, office-based individual counseling and family therapy are often provided because they can be relatively inexpensive (Tate, Reppucci, & Mulvey, 1995). Group treatments that bring together antisocial youth may only make the problem worse, since associating with like-minded individuals often encourages antisocial behavior (Dishion & Dodge, 2005).

As we saw for Scott, restrictive approaches such as residential treatment, inpatient psychiatric hospitalization, and incarceration also show little effectiveness and have the additional disadvantage of being extremely expensive (Henggeler & Santos, 1997). Unfortunately, a significant proportion of mental health dollars for youths continues to be spent on restrictive out-of-home placements that may cause more harm than good (Sondheimer, Schoenwald, & Rowland, 1994). Incarceration may not even serve a community protection function, since youths who are incarcerated and then released often commit more crimes than youths kept at home and given treatment (Henggeler, 1996).

Since children's conduct problems are known to show a developmental progression, diversification, and escalation over time, treatments must be sensitive to where a child is in this trajectory. Treatment methods and goals will differ for preschoolers, school-age children, and adolescents, and differ according to the type and severity of the child's conduct problems. In general, the further along a child is in the progression of antisocial behavior, the greater is the need for intensive interventions and, unfortunately, for children like Scott, the poorer is the prognosis. In fact, if early-onset antisocial behavior is not changed by the end of grade 3, it might best be treated as a chronic condition much like diabetes, which cannot be cured but can be managed or contained through ongoing interventions and supports (Kazdin, 1995). This troubling situation of high treatment effort and cost with less return for older children has led to a reevaluation of priorities and a growing emphasis on early intervention and prevention (Powell, Lochman, & Boxmeyer, 2007). A comprehensive, two-pronged approach to the treatment of conduct problems is needed that includes (Frick, 2000):

- *Early intervention/prevention* programs for young children just starting to display problem behaviors
- *Ongoing interventions* to help older youths and their families cope with the many associated social, emotional, and academic problems

TABLE 6.6 | Effective Treatments for Children with Conduct Problems

Treatment	Overview
Parent Management Training (PMT)	Teaches parents to change their child's behavior in the home and in other settings using contingency management techniques. The focus is on improving parent–child interactions and enhancing other parenting skills (e.g., parent–child communication, monitoring, and supervision).
Problem-Solving Skills Training (PSST)	Identifies the child's cognitive deficiencies and distortions in social situations and provides instruction, practice, and feedback to teach new ways of handling social situations. The child learns to appraise the situation, change his or her attributions about other children's motivations, be more sensitive to how other children feel, and generate alternative and more appropriate solutions.
Multisystemic Therapy (MST)	An intensive approach that draws on other techniques such as PMT, PSST, and marital therapy, as well as specialized interventions such as special education, and referral to substance abuse treatment programs or legal services.

To illustrate the many treatments for children and adolescents with conduct problems, we next highlight three representative treatment approaches with some proven success (Eyberg, Nelson, & Boggs, 2008)—parent management training (PMT), problem-solving skills training (PSST), and multisystemic therapy (MST) (see Table 6.6). We also discuss promising new preventive interventions for young children. Almost all forms of treatment provide corrective interpersonal experiences with parents, siblings, and peers, because most antisocial acts, including violence, occur between the child and family members or peers. In addition, given the pervasiveness of conduct problems across settings, nearly all treatments include components designed to change the child's behavior at home, at school, and in the community.

Parent Management Training (PMT)

Parent management training (PMT) teaches parents to change their child's behavior at home and in other settings (Brinkmeyer & Eyberg, 2003; McMahon & Forehand, 2003). Its underlying assumption is that maladaptive parent–child interactions are at least partly responsible for producing and sustaining the child's antisocial behavior. Changing the way parents interact with their child will lead to improvements in the child's behavior. Although negative parent–child exchanges are seen as the joint outcome of parent and child behavior, the easiest and most desirable point of entry in modifying these interactions is by changing parent behavior. The goal of PMT is for the parent to learn specific new skills (Kazdin, 2005). To achieve this goal, many of the same procedures that we have discussed for working with children with ADHD and their families are used (see Chapter 5, pp. 151–152). These include teaching parents to monitor their children's behavior, to present clear commands and rules, and to systematically provide rewards and minor forms of punishment such as time out from positive reinforcement. Many variations of PMT can be individual versus group training, training in the clinic versus in the home, or the use of live versus videotaped training materials.

PMT has a number of strengths and some limitations (McMahon et al., 2006). Many excellent treatment manuals and training materials have been developed that facilitate its widespread use (e.g., Barkley, 1997b; McMahon & Forehand, 2003). In addition, PMT has been evaluated more than any other treatment for conduct problems (Eyberg et al., 2008). These evaluations have repeatedly demonstrated short-term effectiveness in producing changes in parent and child behavior. The average child whose parents participate in PMT shows better adjustment after treatment than 80% of referred children whose parents do not participate (Serketich & Dumas, 1996). In addition to changes in the referred child, PMT has also been associated with reductions in the problem behaviors of siblings and reduced stress and depression in the parents.

PMT has been most effective with parents of children younger than 12 years of age and less so with adolescents (Dishion & Patterson, 1992). In light of this, promising adaptations of these interventions have also been developed for working with older adolescents and their families (Dishion & Kavanagh, 2003). Although PMT can produce short-term gains, its long-term effectiveness is less clear (McMahon et al., 2006). In addition, PMT makes numerous demands on parents to master and implement procedures in the home, attend meetings, and maintain phone contacts with the therapist. For families under stress with few resources, these demands may be too great to allow the family to continue in treatment (Lundahl, Risser, & Lovejoy, 2006).

The application of PMT is rarely straightforward. The need to change their own parenting practices may not be recognized by parents who believe that difficulties occur because their child is stubborn, their marriage is bad, work is interfering with the time they spend together, or school personnel are unfair. In fact, parents of children with conduct problems frequently believe they use good parenting practices but their child fails to respond. It is important to address these parental beliefs and concerns if treatment is to be successful (Morrisey-Kane & Prinz, 1999). In addition, PMT practitioners have increasingly come to recognize the importance of marital and social support, therapy style and engagement, and ethnic and cultural factors in treatment (Scott, O'Connor, Matias, Price, & Doolan, 2010; Yasui & Dishion, 2007).

Problem-Solving Skills Training (PSST)

Problem-solving skills training (**PSST**) focuses on the cognitive deficiencies and distortions displayed by children and adolescents with conduct problems in interpersonal situations (Kazdin, 2010). PSST is used both alone and in combination with PMT, as required by the family's circumstances. The underlying assumption of PSST is that the child's perceptions and appraisals of environmental events will trigger aggressive and antisocial responses, and that correcting faulty thinking will lead to changes in behavior. As described in Box 6.7, the child is taught to use five problem-solving steps to identify thoughts, feelings, and behaviors in problem social situations.

During PSST, the therapist uses instruction, practice, and feedback to help the child discover different ways to handle social situations. To accomplish this, children learn to appraise the situation, identify self-statements and reactions, and alter their attributions about other children's motivations. They also learn to be more sensitive to how other children feel, to anticipate others' reactions, and to generate appropriate solutions to social problems.

PSST is effective with children and youths who are clinically referred for conduct problems, with benefits extending to parent and family functioning (Kazdin, 2010). Research supports the emphasis on the relationship between maladaptive cognitions and aggressive behavior on which PSST is based, and PSST procedures are carefully specified in treatment manuals. However, it is not yet clear whether changes in maladaptive cognitions are responsible for behavioral improvements. Indeed, the alteration of cognitive processes may not necessarily lead to changes in behavior. Finally, although most children improve as a result of PSST, some may continue to display more problems than their nondeviant peers. Thus, more enduring PSST interventions are being developed to meet the needs of families of children with conduct problems whose problems are particularly severe.

BOX 6.7 A CLOSER LOOK

Cognitive Problem-Solving Steps

Problem Situation

Jason, one of the kids in your class, has taken your Nintendo game. You want to get it back. What do you do?

Step 1: What Am I Supposed to Do?

I want to get my Nintendo game back from Jason.

Step 2: I Have to Look at All My Possibilities

I can beat him up and take it back, ask him to give it back, or tell my teacher.

Step 3: I Had Better Concentrate and Focus

If I beat him up, I would get into trouble. If I asked him, he might give it back.

Step 4: I Need to Make a Choice

I'll try asking him, and if that doesn't work, I will tell my teacher.

Step 5: I Did a Good Job or I Made a Mistake

I made a good choice. I won't get into trouble. Jason and I can still be friends if he returns my Nintendo game. If not, I did my best to get it back before asking my teacher for help. I did a good job!

Source: From Kazdin, A. E. (1996). Problem solving and parent management training in treating aggressive and antisocial behavior. In E. D. Hibbs & P. S. Jensen (Eds.), Psychosocial treatments for child and adolescent disorders (pp. 377–408). Washington, DC: American Psychological Association. Reprinted with permission. APA is not responsible for the accuracy of this translation.

Multisystemic Therapy (MST)

Multisystemic Therapy (**MST**) is an intensive empirically-supported family and community-based treatment for adolescents with severe conduct problems that place them at high risk for out-of-home placements (Henggeler & Schaeffer, 2010). MST views the adolescent with conduct problems as functioning within interconnected social systems, including the family, school, neighborhood, and court and juvenile services (Henggeler, Schoenwald, Borduin, Rowland, & Cunningham, 2009). Antisocial behavior results from, or can be maintained by, transactions within or between any of those systems. MST seeks to empower caregivers to improve youth and family functioning (Cunningham, Henggeler, Brondino, & Pickrel, 1999). Thus, treatment is carried out with all family members, school personnel, peers, juvenile justice staff, and other individuals in the child's life. MST is an intensive approach that also draws on PMT, PSST, and marital therapy, as well as specialized interventions such as special education and referral to substance abuse treatment programs or legal services. In effect, MST attempts to address the many determinants of severe antisocial behavior (Wells, Adhyaru, Cannon, Lamond, & Baruch, 2010). The guiding principles of MST are outlined in Table 6.7.

TABLE 6.7 | The Nine Principles of Multisystemic Therapy (MST)

1. **Finding the fit** The primary purpose of assessment is to understand the "fit" between the identified problems and their broader systemic context.
2. **Positive and strength focused** Therapeutic contacts emphasize the positive and use systemic strengths as levers for change.
3. **Increasing responsibility** Interventions are designed to promote responsible behavior and decrease irresponsible behavior among family members.
4. **Present focused, action oriented, and well defined** Interventions are present-focused and action-oriented, targeting specific and well-defined problems.
5. **Targeting sequences** Interventions target sequences of behavior within and between multiple systems that maintain identified problems.
6. **Developmentally appropriate** Interventions are developmentally appropriate and fit the developmental needs of the youth.
7. **Continuous effort** Interventions are designed to require daily or weekly effort by family members.
8. **Evaluation and accountability** Intervention efficacy is evaluated continuously from multiple perspectives, with providers assuming accountability for overcoming barriers to successful outcomes.
9. **Generalization** Interventions are designed to promote treatment generalization and long-term maintenance of therapeutic change by empowering caregivers to address family members' needs across multiple systemic contexts.

Source: Adapted from Table 2.1 in Multisystemic therapy for antisocial behavior in children and adolescents (2nd ed.) by S. W. Henggeler, S. K. Schoenwald, C. M. Borduin, M. D. Rowland, & P. B. Cunningham. New York: Guilford Press. Reprinted by permission.

Outcome studies of MST with extremely antisocial and violent youths have found this approach to be superior to usual services, individual counseling, community services, and psychiatric hospitalization. In addition, studies have found decreases in delinquency and aggression with peers, improved family relations, and reductions in out-of-home placements. Importantly, MST has been found to reduce long-term rates of criminal behavior for periods as long as 5 years after treatment. MST is also cost-effective, with costs that are 10 times less than conventional interventions and estimated savings over the years of about \$10 to \$20 for each dollar spent on MST (Klietz, Borduin, & Schaeffer, 2010).

Since studies of MST have not yet differentiated between adolescents who show life-course–persistent and those with adolescence-limited patterns of antisocial behavior, it is difficult to know whether successful outcomes reported for this approach apply equally to both groups. It is possible that part of the success of MST may be in helping adolescent-limited youths decrease their association with deviant peers and, by doing so, lowering the age at which they desist from delinquent behavior.

Preventive Interventions

Until recently, treatments for older children with conduct problems were given far greater attention than programs of early intervention and prevention. Fortunately, this situation is changing, with a growing recognition of the need for intensive home- and school-based interventions that can compete with the child's negative developmental history, poor family and community environment, and deviant peer associations (Prinz & Sanders, 2007; Wilson & Lipsey, 2007). The main assumptions of preventive interventions are (Webster-Stratton, 1996):

- Conduct problems can be treated more easily and more effectively in younger than older children.
- By counteracting risk factors and strengthening promotive factors at a young age, it is possible to limit or prevent the escalating developmental trajectory of increased aggression, peer rejection, self-esteem deficits, conduct disorder, and academic failure that is commonly observed in children with childhood-onset conduct problems.
- In the long run, preventive interventions will reduce the substantial costs to the educational, criminal justice, health, and mental health systems that are associated with conduct problems.

Carolyn Webster-Stratton has developed an intensive and multifaceted early-intervention program for parents and teachers of 2- to 10-year-old children with or at risk for conduct problems (*Incredible Years*; Webster-Stratton & Reid, 2010). This program uses interactive videotapes as a foundation for training, which permits widespread use at a relatively low cost. In addition to teaching child management skills, the program also addresses the associated individual, family, and school difficulties that accompany conduct problems. Parents are taught personal self-control strategies for managing anger, depression, and blame. As a result, they learn effective communication skills, strategies for coping with conflict at home and at work, and ways to strengthen social supports. Teachers are taught ways to strengthen positive relationships with students, effective classroom discipline, strategies for teaching social skills, anger management, problem solving skills, and how to increase collaboration with parents. In addition to the parent and teacher training programs, there is also an Incredible Years Child Training program for 3- to 8-year-olds who meet with a therapist in small groups of 6 children for 2 hours a week. Children view videotapes of conflict situations at school and home that illustrate problem-solving and social skills. Following this, children discuss feelings, generate ideas for more effective responses, and role-play alternative behaviors.

A number of studies have provided support for the effectiveness of these early interventions in reducing later conduct problems and maintaining positive outcomes in adolescence for two-thirds or more of children whose parents are involved (Webster-Stratton, Reid, & Hammond, 2004; Webster-Stratton, Rinaldi, & Reid, 2010). This early intervention/prevention program is now more frequently based in schools, with a growing emphasis on matching the type, timing, and amount of intervention to the level of risk and specific needs of the child and family (Webster-Stratton & Reid, 2010).

An innovative program designed to prevent the development of serious chronic antisocial behavior in high-risk children is *Fast Track* (Conduct Problems Prevention Research Group, 2007). Fast Track is a multisite, collaborative research project that exemplifies the comprehensive effort needed to treat children at risk for serious conduct problems. The program was directed at high-risk kindergarten children who were identified in terms of their disruptive behavior and poor peer relations. The intervention began in grade 1 and continued through grade 10. It was divided into an elementary school phase and a transition to middle and high schools phase, with each phase including goals and interventions relevant to successful adjustment during each of these developmental periods.

The goals were to reduce disruptive and aggressive behaviors at home and school and to improve the quality of the child's relationships with parents, teachers, and peers. Children were taught the social–cognitive skills needed for effective interpersonal problem solving and emotion regulation. Other important goals were to strengthen academic skills, especially reading, and to improve the quality of the relationship between family members and school personnel. During the transition to adolescence, issues related to peer affiliation and peer influence, academic achievement and orientation, social cognition and identity development, and parent and family relations were addressed.

Five integrated treatment components were used to achieve these goals: (1) parent management training; (2) home visiting/case management; (3) social–cognitive skills training; (4) academic tutoring; and (5) teacher-based classroom intervention. Fast Track interventions were implemented with close collaboration among parents, teachers, and project staff. The strengths of the program were that they targeted the deficits and determinants that research has shown to be important in youth with conduct problems and that they used treatment procedures for which there is already some empirical support (Eyberg et al., 2008).

The findings from the Fast Track intervention are complex, since multiple behaviors and attitudes were assessed over a wide age range, and outcomes for various behaviors and areas of functioning differed over time. In general, the overall results indicate that the intervention had a significant impact, particularly with respect to reducing conduct problems and enhancing the child's social competence and family relations. However, interventions were less successful in reducing disruptive behavior in the classroom or improving academic performance. Importantly, by grade 9, for children who initially had the highest risk for conduct problems (top 3%), the intervention prevented 75% of CD cases. In contrast, the intervention had little impact on children who were initially at only moderate levels of risk (Slough, McMahon, & The Conduct Problems Prevention Research Group, 2008). Taken together, the findings support the efficacy of the Fast Track intervention for children at highest initial risk for conduct problems. For these children, Fast Track was effective in preventing diagnoses of CD, ODD, and ADHD, highlighting the importance of interventions that target children with the highest risk at a young age (Conduct Problems Prevention Research Group, 2011). Only time will tell whether this all-out effort will result in changes in public policy and will achieve its intended long-term goal to prevent serious chronic antisocial behavior and to enhance psychosocial outcomes into late adolescence and young adulthood (Dodge & McCourt, 2010).

Although tremendous advances have been made in the treatment and prevention of conduct problems, much work remains to be done. The main conclusion to be drawn from intervention and prevention efforts over the past 100 years is that *the degree of success or failure in treating antisocial behavior depends on the type and severity of the child's conduct problem and related risk and protective factors* (Kazdin & Wassell, 1999). Children who come from mostly middle-class healthy families and who have mild conduct problems are likely to benefit from individual, parent, family, and school-based interventions; those who come from highly dysfunctional homes and poor neighborhoods and who display severe and persistent problems are likely to benefit very little, if at all, *unless* early, much more intensive, and long-term interventions are used. If interventions are to succeed, it will also be necessary to find cost-effective interventions and ways to help families persevere with interventions that could prove to have real benefits (Rutter, 2003b). Although significant short-term gains for children with severe conduct problems have been achieved using intensive interventions, the degree of normalization and long-term impact of these approaches is yet to be determined.

SECTION SUMMARY

Treatment and Prevention

- Considerable efforts to help children and adolescents with conduct problems have led to several approaches with some proven success.
- The focus of parent management training (PMT) is on teaching parents to change their child's behavior in the home.
- The underlying assumption of problem-solving skills training (PSST) is that faulty perceptions and appraisals of interpersonal events trigger antisocial responses. The focus is on changing behavior by changing the way the child thinks in social situations.
- Multisystemic therapy (MST) is an intensive approach that is carried out with all family members, school personnel, peers, juvenile justice staff, and other individuals in the adolescent's life.
- Recent efforts have focused on trying to prevent conduct problems through intensive programs of early intervention/prevention.
- The degree of success or failure in treating antisocial behavior depends on the type and severity of the child's conduct problem and related risk and protective factors.

Study Resources

SECTION SUMMARIES

KEY TERMS

COURSEMATE

Access an interactive eBook and chapter-specific interactive learning tools, including flashcards, quizzes, videos, and more in your Psychology CourseMate, accessed through CengageBrain.com.

7 Anxiety Disorders

It is hard to be brave, when you're only a very small animal.

—Piglet (Pooh's Little Instruction Book, 1995)

CHAPTER PREVIEW

Separation Anxiety: Brad is terrified of being separated from his mother. He follows her around the house constantly, always needing to know where she is.

Generalized Anxiety: Jared "worries about everything"—how he is doing in school, events in the news, and family finances.

Social Anxiety: Li-Ming is very preoccupied with what others think of her. She doesn't interact with anyone at school, and feels completely isolated.

Obsessive–Compulsive Disorder: Georgina can't stop thinking about not being able to sleep. Every night before bedtime she goes through the same routine of counting and grouping all the clothes and shoes in her bedroom closet and opening and closing the closet door.

Panic Attack: Claudia describes her sudden attack of overwhelming anxiety. "My heart started pumping so fast I thought it would explode. I thought I was going to die."

ALL CHILDREN EXPERIENCE FEAR, worry, or anxiety as a normal part of growing up, but each child in our examples suffers from an anxiety disorder that is excessive and debilitating. An anxiety disorder is one of the most common mental health problems in young people, with lifetime prevalence estimates between 8% and 30% (Merikangas et al., 2010). Estimates vary widely with the child's age, type of anxiety disorder, and whether impaired functioning is part of the diagnosis. Conservatively, at least one child in every elementary school classroom is likely to have an anxiety disorder (Cartwright-Hatton, McNicol, & Doubleday, 2006). Despite their early onset, high frequency, and associated problems, anxiety disorders in children often go unnoticed and untreated (Gregory et al., 2007). This may be due to the frequent occurrence of fears and anxiety during normal development, the invisible nature of many symptoms (e.g., a knot in the stomach), and the fact that anxiety is not nearly as damaging to other people or property as are conduct problems (Albano, Chorpita, & Barlow, 2003).

For a long time, anxiety in children was thought to be a mild and transitory disturbance that would fade over time with normal life experiences. However, we now know that many children who experience anxiety will continue to display anxiety and other problems into adolescence and adulthood (Bittner et al., 2007). Although isolated symptoms of fear and anxiety are usually short lived, anxiety disorders have a more chronic and stable course (Carballo et al., 2010). In fact, nearly one-half of those affected have an illness duration of 8 years or longer (Keller et al., 1992), and parents' reports of their child's anxiety symptoms predict anxiety disorders 24 years later (Reef, van Meurs, Verhulst, & van der Ende, 2010). The societal costs for clinically anxious youngsters are also substantial, with estimated costs about 20 times higher for families with an anxious child compared to those from the general population (Bodden, Dirksen, & Bögels, 2008). Thus, anxiety disorders in children are common, distressing, long-lasting, and costly problems (Rapee, Schneiring, & Hudson, 2009).

Description of Anxiety Disorders

Anxiety is a mood state characterized by strong negative emotion and bodily symptoms of tension in which the child apprehensively anticipates future danger or misfortune (Barlow, 2002). This definition captures two key features of anxiety—strong negative emotion and an element of fear. Children who experience excessive and debilitating anxieties are said to have **anxiety disorders**. These disorders occur in many forms. Some children, like Brad, feel anxious whenever they are separated from their mother or are away from home. Others, like Jared, worry about almost everything and feel anxious most of the time for no apparent reason. Some children feel anxious only in certain situations, such as when they have to travel by airplane or, like Li-Ming, when they have to give a talk in class. Others, like Georgina (whose counting compulsion is described in Chapter 1), experience repeated, intrusive, and unwanted thoughts that produce anxiety, and they spend hours in ritualized behavior in an effort to alleviate that anxiety. Some children, like Claudia, have unpredictable bouts of such sudden and intense anxiety that they become terrified and immobilized. Still others have persistent and frightening thoughts after a traumatic event, such as a hurricane, sexual abuse, or exposure to war.

Many youngsters with anxiety disorders suffer from more than one type, either simultaneously or at separate times during their development (Costello, Egger, & Angold, 2005b). In view of the substantial overlap among these disorders, we begin this chapter by discussing the general features and mechanisms of anxiety that apply across all types. The common occurrence of fears and anxieties in childhood and adolescence requires that we also consider the role of these emotions in normal development. We then examine each anxiety disorder and what makes it unique.

Experiencing Anxiety

> When Isabella saw a dog running loose in front of her house, she became pale, sweaty, cold, and trembly. Her thoughts raced so fast that she couldn't think. She froze. Her heart pounded, she felt tense, and she found it difficult to breathe.

Isabella is experiencing anxiety in response to an event she sees as potentially threatening or dangerous. As humans, we are programmed to detect and react to signs of anxiety in ourselves and in others. In fact, anxiety is both expected and normal at certain ages and in certain situations. One-year-old infants become distressed when separated from their mothers, and almost all young children have short-lived specific fears—of the dark, for example. The child's world can be a strange and menacing place, full of unknown dangers—some real, others imagined. Although no one likes to feel anxious, the alternative of not feeling anxious when the situation calls for it is far worse.

Youngsters with anxiety experience strong negative emotion and physical tension, and anticipate future danger

Anxiety often hits us when we do something important, and in moderate doses it helps us think and act more effectively. You will probably be better prepared for your next exam if you're just a little bit nervous about taking it. Similarly, some anxiety may help a child prepare harder for an upcoming oral report or athletic event. In this sense, anxiety is an adaptive emotion that readies children both physically and psychologically for coping with people, objects, or events that could be dangerous to their safety or well-being.

Although some anxiety is good, too much is not. Excessive, uncontrollable anxiety can be debilitating. A child may fail a test because she spends too much time thinking about how awful it would be to fail, making it nearly impossible to think about anything else (e.g., how to solve a math problem). In children with anxiety disorders, this normally useful emotion works against them.

When children experience fears beyond a certain age, in situations that pose no real threat or danger, to an extent that seriously interferes with daily activities, anxiety is a serious problem. Even if the child knows there is little to be afraid of, he or she is still terrified and does everything possible to escape or avoid the situation. This pattern of self-defeating behavior, known as the **neurotic paradox** (Mowrer, 1950), can become self-perpetuating—much like Sisyphus repeatedly pushing the rock up the hill, only to have it roll back down each time.

First and foremost, anxiety involves an immediate reaction to *perceived* danger or threat—a reaction known as the **fight/flight response**. All of its effects are aimed at escaping potential harm, either by confronting the source of danger (fight) or by evading it (flight). If you look up to see a grand piano about to fall in your direction and experience no anxiety whatsoever, you will pay serious consequences. To avoid such a fate, your fight/flight response would kick into overdrive and you would jump out of harm's way.

Think of a recent situation that made you anxious. What was it about the situation that made you anxious? What physical symptoms did you notice? What were you thinking? What did you do? Describing what it's like to be anxious isn't easy, because anxiety is a complex reaction with many symptoms, as shown in Table 7.1. How many of these symptoms did you experience? What do these many symptoms have in common?

The symptoms of anxiety are expressed through three interrelated response systems: the *physical system*, the *cognitive system*, and the *behavioral*

TABLE 7.1 | The Many Symptoms of Anxiety

Physical		
Increased heart rate	Dizziness	Blushing
Fatigue	Blurred vision	Vomiting
Increased respiration	Dry mouth	Numbness
Nausea	Muscle tension	Sweating
Stomach upset	Heart palpitation	
Cognitive		
Thoughts of being scared or hurt	Thoughts of incompetence or inadequacy	Thoughts of bodily injury
Thoughts or images of monsters or wild animals	Difficulty concentrating	Images of harm to loved ones
Self-deprecatory or self-critical thoughts	Blanking out or forgetfulness	Thoughts of going crazy
	Thoughts of appearing foolish	Thoughts of contamination
Behavioral		
Avoidance	Trembling lip	Avoidance of eye contact
Crying or screaming	Swallowing	Physical proximity
Nail biting	Immobility	Clenched jaw
Trembling voice	Twitching	Fidgeting
Stuttering	Thumb sucking	

Source: Adapted from *Fears and Anxieties*, by B. A. Barrios and D. P. Hartmann, 1997, p. 235. In E. J. Mash and L. G. Terdal (Eds.), Assessment of Childhood Disorders, 3rd ed. Copyright © 1997 by Guilford Publications. Reprinted by permission.

system. It is essential to know how the three sets of symptoms work, since more than one may be evident in different children with the same anxiety disorder. Also, as we will discuss, different response systems are more dominant in certain anxiety disorders. Let's take a closer look at how each response system works.

Physical System

When a person perceives or anticipates danger, the brain sends messages to the sympathetic nervous system, which produces the fight/flight response. The activation of this system produces many important chemical and physical effects that mobilize the body for action:

- *Chemical effects*. Adrenaline and noradrenaline are released from the adrenal glands.
- *Cardiovascular effects*. Heart rate and strength of the heart beat increase, readying the body for action by speeding up blood flow and improving delivery of oxygen to the tissues.
- *Respiratory effects*. Speed and depth of breathing increase, which brings oxygen to the tissues and removes waste. This may produce feelings of breathlessness, choking or smothering, or chest pains.
- *Sweat gland effects*. Sweating increases, which cools the body and makes the skin slippery.
- *Other physical effects*. The pupils widen to let in more light, which may lead to blurred vision or spots in front of the eyes. Salivation decreases, resulting in a dry mouth. Decreased activity in the digestive system may lead to nausea and a heavy feeling in the stomach. Muscles tense in readiness for fight or flight, leading to subjective feelings of tension, aches and pains, and trembling.

These physical symptoms are familiar signs of anxiety. Overall, the fight/flight response produces general activation of the entire metabolism. As a result, the individual may feel hot and flushed and, because this activation takes a lot of energy, he or she feels tired and drained afterward.

Cognitive System

Since the main purpose of the fight/flight system is to signal possible danger, its activation produces an immediate search for potential threat. For children with anxiety disorders, it is difficult to focus on everyday tasks because their attention is consumed by a constant search for threat or danger. When these children can't find proof of danger, they may turn their search inward: "If nothing is out there to make me feel anxious, then something must be wrong with me." Or they may distort the situation: "Even though I can't find it, I know there's something to be afraid of." Or they may do both. Children with anxiety disorders will invent explanations for their anxiety: "I must be a real jerk." "Everyone will think I'm a dummy if I say something." "Even though I can't see them, there are germs all over the place." Activation of the cognitive system often leads to subjective feelings of apprehension, nervousness, difficulty concentrating, and panic.

Behavioral System

The overwhelming urges that accompany the fight/flight response are aggression and a desire to escape the threatening situation, but social constraints may prevent fulfilling either impulse. For example, just before a final exam you may feel like attacking your professor or not showing up at all, but fortunately for your professor and your need to pass the course, you are likely to inhibit these urges! However, they may show up as foot tapping, fidgeting, or irritability (consider the number of teeth marks in pencils), or as escape or avoidance by getting a doctor's note, requesting a deferral, or even faking illness. Unfortunately, avoidance is the very thing that perpetuates anxiety, despite the temporary feeling of relief. Avoidance behaviors are negatively reinforced; that is, they are strengthened when they are followed by a rapid reduction in anxiety. As a result, each time a child is confronted with an anxiety-producing situation, the faster she or he tries to get out of it, the faster the anxiety drops off— so the more the child avoids such situations. As children with anxiety disorders engage in more and more avoidance, carrying out everyday activities becomes exceedingly difficult.

CHANTELLE

The Terror of Being Home Alone

When Chantelle, age 14, realized she was at home alone, she was terrified. Her thoughts raced so fast it was impossible to think clearly. She forgot all the right things to do. Her heart pounded and she tensed up. She felt like she couldn't breathe, and she began to sob. She wanted to run but felt completely immobilized. (Based on authors' case material)

Chantelle's reactions show how the three response systems of anxiety interact and feed off one another. Physically, Chantelle's heart pounded, she tensed, and she had difficulty breathing. Cognitively, she could not think clearly. Behaviorally, she was completely immobilized.

Anxiety Versus Fear and Panic

It is important to distinguish anxiety from two closely related emotions—fear and panic. **Fear** is an immediate alarm reaction to current danger or life-threatening emergencies. Although fear and anxiety have much in common, the fear reaction differs both psychologically and biologically from the emotion of anxiety. Fear is a *present-oriented* emotional reaction to current danger marked by a strong escape tendency and an all-out surge in the sympathetic nervous system. The overriding message is alarm: "If I don't do something right now, I might not make it at all." In contrast, anxiety is a *future-oriented* emotion characterized by feelings of apprehension and lack of control over upcoming events that might be threatening. Fear and anxiety both warn of danger or distress. However, only anxiety is frequently felt when no danger is actually present (Barlow, 2002).

Panic is a group of physical symptoms of the fight/flight response that unexpectedly occur in the absence of any obvious threat or danger. With no explanation for physical symptoms such as a pounding heart, the child may invent one: "I'm dying." The sensations themselves can feel threatening and may trigger further fear, apprehension, anxiety, and panic (Barlow, 2002).

Normal Fears, Anxieties, Worries, and Rituals

Since fear and anxiety in moderate doses are adaptive, it is not surprising that emotions and rituals that increase feelings of control are common during childhood and adolescence. It is only when the emotions and rituals become excessive, or occur in a developmentally inappropriate context, that they are of concern.

Normal Fears

Since children and their environments constantly change, fears that are normal at one age can be debilitating a few years later. For example, fear of strangers may serve a protective function for infants and young children, but when it persists beyond a certain age it can seriously interfere with the development of peer relations. Whether or not a specific fear is normal also depends on its effect on the child and how long it lasts. If a fear has little impact on the child's daily life or lasts only a few weeks, it is likely a part of normal development.

The number and types of common childhood fears change over time, with a general age-related decline in number (Gullone, 1999). Even so, specific fears are common in older children, and many teens report that their fears cause them considerable distress and significantly interfere with daily activities (Ollendick & King, 1994). Girls tend to have more fears than boys at almost every age; they also rate themselves as more fearful and report fears that are more intense and disabling than do boys. Although fears show a general

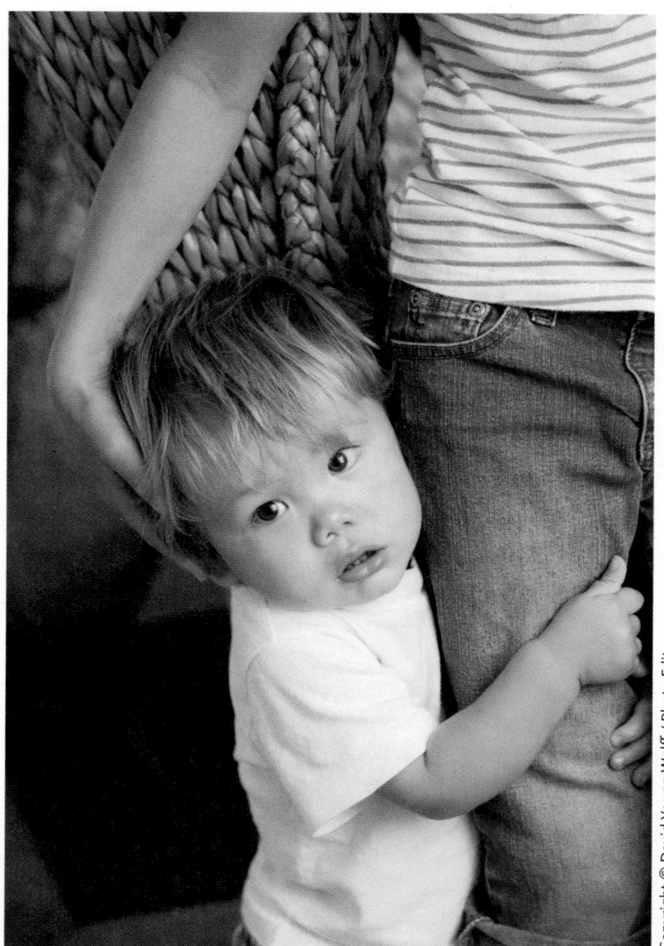

Copyright © David Young-Wolff / Photo Edit

All children experience some fear, anxiety, and worry as a normal part of growing up

decline with age, some, such as school-related fears, remain stable; others, such as social fears, may increase (Muris, 2007). Common fears and anxieties of infants, children, and adolescents are shown in Table 7.2. Also shown are possible relevant symptoms and corresponding DSM-IV-TR anxiety disorder diagnoses that may develop in relation to these symptoms.

Normal Anxieties

Like fears, anxieties are very common during childhood and adolescence. Various types of anxiety are evident by age 4 (Eley, Lichenstein, & Moffitt, 2003), and about 25% of parents report that their child is too nervous, fearful, or anxious (Achenbach, 1991a). The most frequent symptoms of anxiety in normal samples are separation anxiety, test anxiety, overconcern about competence, excessive need for reassurance, and anxiety about harm to a parent (Barrios & Hartmann, 1997).

Younger children generally experience more anxiety symptoms than do older children, primarily about separation from parents (Bell-Dolan, Last, & Strauss, 1990). Girls display more anxiety than boys, but generally experience similar types of symptoms. Although some specific anxieties decrease with age, such as separation anxiety and anxiety about school, nervous and anxious symptoms may not show the age-related decline observed for many specific fears (Hale, Raaijmakers, Muris, van Hoof, & Meeus, 2008). Anxious symptoms may reflect a stable trait that predisposes children to develop excessive fears related to their stage of development. Thus, the disposition to be anxious may remain stable over time, even though the objects of children's fears change.

Normal Worries

If worrying about the future is so unproductive, why do we do so much of it? Part of the reason seems to be that the process of worry—thinking about all possible negative outcomes—serves an extremely useful function in normal development. In moderate doses, worry can help children prepare for the future—for example, by checking their homework before they hand it in or by rehearsing for an upcoming class play. Worry is a central feature of anxiety, and anxiety is related to the number of children's worries and to their intensity (Silverman, La Greca, & Wasserstein, 1995). Children of all ages worry, but the forms and expressions change. Older children report a greater variety and complexity of worries, and are better able to describe them than are younger children (Chorpita, Tracey, Brown, Collica, & Barlow, 1997).

Children with anxiety disorders do not necessarily worry more than other children, but they seem to worry more intensely (Weems, Silverman, & La Greca, 2000). Intense worries about being around strangers, going to school, or having bad things happen to the child or parents occur frequently in children with anxiety disorders and rarely in other children. Other intense worries—over personal safety, doing a good job, and being embarrassed—occur in both groups, but more often in children with anxiety disorders. Still other intense worries about schoolwork, aches and pains, or performance in sports are equally common in all children.

Normal Rituals and Repetitive Behavior

Ritualistic, repetitive activity is extremely common in young children (Peleg-Popko & Dar, 2003). A familiar example is the bedtime ritual of saying good night—addressing people in a certain order or giving a certain

TABLE 7.2 | **Common Fears and Anxieties of Infancy, Childhood, and Adolescence; Possible Symptoms; and Corresponding DSM-IV-TR Diagnoses**

Developmental Period	Age	Common Fears and Anxieties	Possible Symptoms	Corresponding DSM-IV-TR Anxiety Disorder
Early infancy	Within first weeks	Loss of physical support, loss of physical contact with caregiver	–	–
	0–6 months	Intense sensory stimuli (loud noises)	–	–
Late infancy	6–8 months	Shyness/anxiety with stranger, sudden, unexpected, or looming objects	–	Separation anxiety disorder
Toddlerhood	12–18 months	Separation from parent, injury, toilet, strangers	Sleep disturbances, nocturnal panic attacks, oppositional defiant behavior	Separation anxiety disorder, panic attacks
	2–3 years	Fears of thunder and lightning, fire, water, darkness, nightmares	Crying, clinging, withdrawal, freezing, avoidance of salient stimuli (e.g., turning the light on), night terrors, enuresis	Specific phobias (natural environment subtype), panic disorder
		Fears of animals	–	Specific phobias (animal subtype)
Early childhood	4–5 years	Separation from parents, fear of death or dead people	Excessive need for reassurance	Separation anxiety disorder, generalized anxiety disorder, panic attacks
Primary/elementary school age	5–7 years	Fear of specific objects (animals, monsters, ghosts)	–	Specific phobias
		Fear of germs or getting a serious illness	–	Obsessive-compulsive disorder (OCD)
		Fear of natural disasters, fear of traumatic events (e.g., getting burned, being hit by a car or truck)	–	Specific phobias (natural environment subtype), acute stress disorder, posttraumatic stress disorder, generalized anxiety disorder
Primary/elementary school age	5–11 years	School anxiety, performance anxiety, physical appearance, social concerns	Withdrawal, timidity, extreme shyness with unfamiliar adults and peers, feelings of shame	Social phobia (social anxiety disorder)
Adolescence	12–18 years	Personal relations, rejection from peers, personal appearance, future, natural disasters, safety	Fear of negative evaluation	Social phobia (social anxiety disorder)

Source: Based on Beesdo, Knappe, & Pine, 2009.

number of hugs and kisses. Normal ritualistic behaviors in young children include preferences for sameness in the environment (e.g., watching the same DVD over and over again), rigid likes and dislikes, preferences for symmetry (e.g., carrying a toy in each hand), awareness of minute details or imperfections in toys or clothes (e.g., being bothered by a minuscule thread on a jacket sleeve), and arranging things so they are "just right" (e.g., insisting that different foods not touch each other on the plate). Rituals help young children gain control and mastery over their social and physical environments, and make their world more predictable and safer (Evans et al., 1997). Any parent who has violated these rituals and paid the price can appreciate how important they are to the young child.

Many common routines of young children fall into two distinct categories: repetitive behaviors and doing things "just right." These categories are strikingly similar to those found for older individuals with obsessive—compulsive disorder (OCD), which we discuss in detail later in the chapter. However, it is not known whether OCD is an extreme point on a continuum of normal developmental rituals or an entirely different problem (Evans, Gray, & Leckman, 1999). Recent findings suggest that the neuropsychological mechanisms underlying compulsive, ritualistic behavior in normal development and those in OCD may be similar (Pietrefesa & Evans, 2007).

Anxiety Disorders According to DSM-IV-TR

Anxiety disorders in DSM-IV-TR are divided into nine categories that closely define the types of reaction and avoidance. To give you an overall picture, these nine categories are described briefly in Box 7.1. Keep in mind that significant associations exist between nearly all anxiety disorders, and that the number of children with multiple anxiety disorders increases with age. In the following sections, we discuss the characteristic features of each anxiety disorder, including its prevalence, comorbidity, and developmental course. Then we examine the associated characteristics and causes of anxiety disorders, and the treatments used to help children with these problems.

BOX 7.1 A CLOSER LOOK

Main Features of Nine DSM-IV-TR Anxiety Disorders

Separation Anxiety Disorder (SAD)

Characterized by excessive worry regarding separation from home or parents. Youths may show signs of distress and physical complaints on separation, experience unrealistic worries about harm to self or others when separated, and display an unwillingness to be alone.

Generalized Anxiety Disorder (GAD)

Characterized by ongoing and excessive worry about many events and activities. Youth may worry about their grades in school, their relations with peers, and their own or others' safety. They may constantly seek comfort or approval from others to help reduce their worry.

Specific Phobia

Characterized by severe and unreasonable fears of a specific object or situation, for example, dogs, spiders, darkness, or riding on a bus.

Social Phobia (Social Anxiety Disorder)

Characterized by a severe and unreasonable fear of being embarrassed or humiliated when doing something in front of peers or adults.

Obsessive—Compulsive Disorder (OCD)

Characterized by recurrent and severe thoughts and behaviors that are distressing, time consuming, and intrusive. Common obsessions include thoughts about contamination, ongoing doubts, and aggressive or upsetting impulses. Common compulsions include repetitive washing, checking, or touching.

Panic Disorder (PD)

Characterized by recurrent, unexpected and severe attacks of anxiety. These attacks may consist of shortness of breath, sweating, upset stomach, dizziness, or fear of dying.

Panic Disorder with Agoraphobia

Youth with panic disorder may also experience anxiety and avoid situations in which attacks have occurred, for example, shopping malls, or movie theaters.

Posttraumatic Stress Disorder (PTSD)

Following exposure to a traumatic life threatening event or injury youths may display agitated and disorganized behavior, experience intense fear, anger, sadness, and avoid places or situations that remind them of the traumatic event. In addition, they may become depressed, withdrawn and unresponsive, and emotionally detached.

Acute Stress Disorder

Following exposure to a traumatic event youths may display short-term symptoms of PTSD lasting for less than a month.

SECTION SUMMARY

Description of Anxiety Disorders

- Anxiety disorders are among the most common mental health problems in children and adolescents, but they often go unnoticed and untreated.
- Anxiety is an adaptive emotion that prepares youngsters to cope with potentially threatening people, objects, or events. Strong negative emotions, physical tension, and apprehensive anticipation of future danger or misfortune characterize it.
- The symptoms of anxiety are expressed through three interrelated response systems: physical, cognitive, and behavioral.
- Fear is a present-oriented emotional reaction to current danger. In contrast, anxiety is a future-oriented emotion characterized by feelings of apprehension and a lack of control over upcoming events that might be threatening.
- Fears, anxieties, worries, and rituals in children are common, change with age, and follow a predictable developmental pattern with respect to type.
- DSM-IV-TR specifies nine anxiety disorders based on types of reaction and avoidance.

SEPARATION ANXIETY DISORDER

BRAD

"Don't Leave Me!"

Brad, age 9, is unable to enter any situation that requires separation from his parents—playing in the backyard, going to other children's homes, or staying with a babysitter. When forcibly separated from his parents, Brad cries or throws a full-blown tantrum. When his mother plans to leave the house, he runs through all the horrible things that might happen to her, in an endless series of what-if questions. When she becomes frustrated and angry, Brad becomes even more anxious. The more anxious he gets, the more he argues with his mother, and the angrier she gets. Brad has also threatened to hurt himself if forced to go to school.

Brad's separation problems began about a year ago, when his father was drinking too much and was frequently absent for long periods. Brad's problem gradually worsened over the course of the year, until he completely refused to go to school. Help was sought, but Brad continued to get worse. He developed significant depressive symptoms, including sadness, guilt about his problems, and occasional wishes to die. (Adapted from Last, 1988)

Separation anxiety is important for the young child's survival and is normal at certain ages. From about age 7 months through the preschool years, almost all children fuss when they are separated from their parents or others to whom they are close. In fact, a lack of separation anxiety at this age may suggest insecure attachment or other problems. Unfortunately, like Brad, some children continue to display such anxiety long after the age when it is typical or expected. When anxiety persists for at least 4 weeks and is severe enough to interfere with normal daily routines such as going to school or participating in recreational activities, the child may have a separation anxiety disorder. The DSM-IV-TR criteria are presented in Table 7.3.

Children with **separation anxiety disorder (SAD)** display age-inappropriate, excessive, and disabling anxiety about being apart from their parents or away from home. Young children with SAD may have vague feelings of anxiety or repeated nightmares about being kidnapped or killed, or about the death of a parent. They frequently display excessive demands for parental attention by clinging to their parents and shadowing their every move, trying to climb into their parents' bed at night, or sleeping on the floor just outside their parents' bedroom door. Older children with SAD may have difficulty being alone in a room during the day, sleeping alone even at home, running errands, going to school, or going to camp. They may also have specific fantasies of illness, accidents, kidnapping, or physical harm.

Children with SAD fear new situations and may display physical complaints. To avoid separation, they may fuss, cry, scream, or threaten suicide if their parent leaves (although serious suicide attempts are rare); physical complaints may include rapid heartbeat, dizziness, headaches, stomachaches, and nausea. Not surprisingly, parents, especially mothers, become highly distressed. Over time, as we saw with Brad, children with SAD may become increasingly withdrawn, apathetic, and depressed, and are at risk for developing a variety of other anxiety disorders during adolescence (Aschenbrand, Kendall, Webb, Safford, & Flannery-Schroeder, 2003).

Prevalence and Comorbidity

SAD is one of the two most common anxiety disorders to occur during childhood (the other is specific phobia), and is found in about 4% to 10% of all children. It is common in both boys and girls although more prevalent in girls. More than two-thirds of children with SAD have another anxiety disorder, and about half develop a depressive disorder following the onset of SAD. They may also display specific fears of getting

TABLE 7.3 | Diagnostic Criteria for Separation Anxiety Disorder (SAD)

DSM-IV-TR

A. Developmentally inappropriate and excessive anxiety concerning separation from home or from those to whom the individual is attached, as evidenced by three (or more) of the following:

(1) Recurrent excessive distress when separation from home or major attachment figures occurs or is anticipated

(2) Persistent and excessive worry about losing, or possible harm befalling, major attachment figures

(3) Persistent and excessive worry that an untoward event will lead to separation from a major attachment figure (e.g., getting lost or being kidnapped)

(4) Persistent reluctance or refusal to go to school or elsewhere because of fear of separation

(5) Persistently and excessively fearful or reluctant to be alone or without major attachment figures at home or without significant adults in other settings

(6) Persistent reluctance or refusal to go to sleep without being near a major attachment figure or to sleep away from home

(7) Repeated nightmares involving the theme of separation

(8) Repeated complaints of physical symptoms (such as headaches, stomachaches, nausea, or vomiting) when separation from major attachment figures occurs or is anticipated

B. The duration of the disturbance is at least 4 weeks.

C. The onset is before age 18 years.

D. The disturbance causes clinically significant distress or impairment in social, academic (occupational), or other important areas of functioning.

E. The disturbance does not occur exclusively during the course of a Pervasive Developmental Disorder, Schizophrenia, or other Psychotic Disorder and, in adolescents and adults, is not better accounted for by Panic Disorder with Agoraphobia.

Specify if:

Early Onset: if onset occurs before age 6 years

Source: Reprinted with permission from the Diagnostic and Statistical Manual of Mental Disorders, Fourth Edition, Text Revision, (Copyright © 2000). American Psychiatric Association.

lost, or of the dark. School reluctance or refusal is also quite common in older children with SAD (Albano et al., 2003).

Onset, Course, and Outcome

Of children referred for anxiety disorders, SAD has the earliest reported age of onset (7 to 8 years) and youngest age of referral (Shear et al., 2006). SAD generally progresses from mild to severe. It may begin with harmless requests or with complaints such as restless sleep or nightmares, which progress to the child sleeping nightly in his or her parents' bed. Similarly, school mornings may evoke physical complaints and an occasional absence from school, which escalates into daily tantrums about leaving for school and outright refusal. The child may become increasingly concerned about the parents' daily routine and whereabouts (Albano et al., 2003).

Often, SAD occurs after a child has experienced major stress, such as moving to a new neighborhood, entering a new school, death or illness in the family, or an extended vacation. Brad's SAD emerged after his father developed a problem with alcohol and subsequently left home. The symptoms of SAD may also fluctuate over the years as a function of stress and transitions in the child's life. Although they may lose friends as a result of their repeated refusal to participate in activities away from home, children with SAD are reasonably socially skilled and get along with others. However, their school performance may suffer as a result of frequent school absences. The child may require special assignments just to keep up, and in extreme cases may have to repeat the school year (Albano et al., 2003).

SAD persists into adulthood for more than one third of children and adolescents. As adults, these individuals are more likely than others to experience relationship difficulties (e.g., never marry or become separated or divorced), other anxiety disorders and mental health problems (particularly panic disorder and depression), and functional impairment in their social and personal lives (Lewinsohn, Holm-Denoma, Small, Seeley, & Joiner, 2008; Shear, Jin, Ruscio, Walters, & Kessler, 2006).

Since school reluctance and refusal are quite common in youngsters with SAD, this is an opportune time to consider these problems.

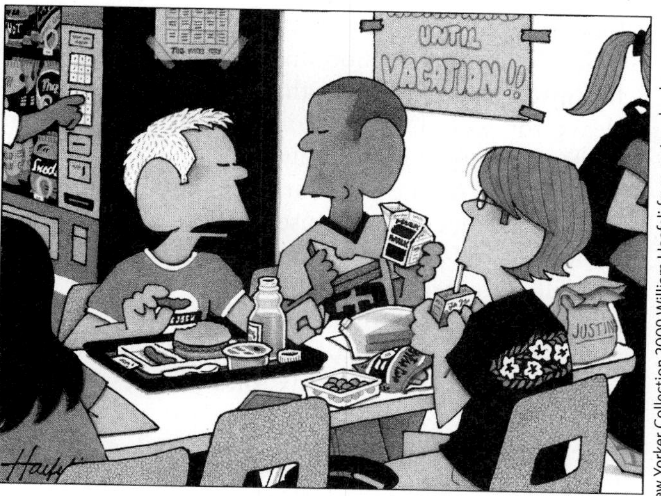

"When you head off to camp, your parents will want to see some separation anxiety."

School Reluctance and Refusal

ERIC

Won't Go to School

Eric, age 12, was referred by a school psychologist and his parents for his intense school refusal behavior. On entering seventh grade and a new school, he began to experience a variety of negative symptoms, such as hyperventilation, anxiety, sad mood, and somatic complaints. Although attendance was not a problem at first, by mid-September Eric began to report severe headaches on school mornings. School attendance then became intermittent. By late September, his aversion to school had worsened and he was staying at home on most days. (Adapted from Kearney, 1995)

Although starting school is exciting and enjoyable for most children, many are reluctant to go to school and—for a few—school may create so much fear and anxiety that they will not go. These children can become literally sick with worry, let minor physical complaints keep them at home, or pretend to be ill. **School refusal behavior** is defined as the refusal to attend classes or difficulty remaining in school for an entire day. It includes youngsters who resist going to school in the morning but eventually attend, those who go to school but leave at some point during the day, those who attend with great dread that leads to future pleas for nonattendance, and those who miss the entire day (Kearney, 2007).

School refusal is equally common in boys and girls, and it occurs most often between the ages of 5 and 11 years. Excessive and unreasonable fears of school usually first occur during preschool, kindergarten, or first grade, and peak during the second grade. However, school refusal can occur at any time and may have a sudden onset at a later age, as happened with Eric. Children who refuse school may complain of a headache, upset stomach, or sore throat just before it's time to leave for school, then begin to "feel better" when permitted to stay at home, only to feel "sick" again the next morning. As the time for school draws near, the child may plead, cry, and refuse to leave the house, and even have a full-blown panic reaction. School refusal often follows a period at home during which the child has spent more time than usual with a parent (e.g., brief illness, holiday break, or summer vacation). At other times, school refusal may follow a stressful event such as a change of schools (as happened with Eric), an accident, or the death of a relative or family pet.

For many children, fear of school is really a fear of leaving their parents—separation anxiety. However, school reluctance and refusal can occur for many reasons (Kearney & Albano, 2004). Most children who refuse to go to school have average or above-average intelligence, suggesting it is not a difficulty with academics that leads to this problem. A fear of school may be associated with submitting for the first time to authority and rules outside the home, being compared with unfamiliar children, and experiencing the threat of failure. Some children fear school because they are afraid of being ridiculed, teased, or bullied by other children, or being criticized or disciplined by their teachers. In other cases, the child's fear may result from an excessive or irrational fear of being socially evaluated or embarrassed when having to recite in class or undress in front of unfamiliar people in a gym class. Eric was extremely anxious about meeting new people, being late for class, moving from class to class, taking classes involving public speaking, and participating in gym class. He refused to attend school mainly to escape being socially evaluated and, to a lesser extent, to gain attention from his parents (Kearney & Silverman, 1996).

The possible long-term consequences are serious for a child who displays a persistent pattern of school refusal

School reluctance and refusal are common problems related to anxiety

behavior and does not receive help. Academic or social problems may develop as a result of missed instruction and peer interaction. Treatment usually emphasizes an immediate return to school and other routines, and must take into account the specific functions being served by school refusal behaviors (Kearney & Albano, 2007).

SECTION SUMMARY

Separation Anxiety Disorder

- Children with separation anxiety disorder (SAD) display age-inappropriate, excessive, and disabling anxiety about being apart from parents or away from home.
- SAD is one of the most common anxiety disorders of childhood, with the earliest reported age of onset and the youngest age of referral.
- School refusal behavior is defined as the refusal to attend classes or difficulty remaining in school for an entire day.

GENERALIZED ANXIETY DISORDER

JARED

Perpetual Worrywart

Jared, age 13, was referred because of his excessive anxiety, worry, and somatic complaints—his mother describes him as overly concerned about everything. Jared says he worries about most things, but especially about not being good enough for his parents, being teased by other kids, not doing well at school, making mistakes, and being in an accident in which he or his parents are injured. Jared ruminates for days about things that have already occurred, such as what he said in class the previous day or how he did on last week's test. Once he begins to worry, he says, "I just can't stop, no matter how hard I try." Jared reports that when he is worrying about the past or anticipating an upcoming event he has headaches, stomachaches, and a rapid heartbeat. His mother (who also worries a lot, but not nearly as much as Jared) says that Jared is extremely self-critical and needs constant reassurance. (Based on authors' case material)

TABLE 7.4 | Diagnostic Criteria for Generalized Anxiety Disorder (GAD)

DSM-IV-TR

A. Excessive anxiety and worry (apprehensive expectation) occurring more days than not for at least 6 months, about a number of events or activities (such as work or school performance).

B. The person finds it difficult to control the worry.

C. The anxiety and worry are associated with three (or more) of the following six symptoms (with at least some symptoms present for more days than not for the past 6 months).

Note: Only one item is required for children.

(1) Restlessness or feeling keyed up or on edge
(2) Being easily fatigued
(3) Difficulty concentrating or mind going blank
(4) Irritability
(5) Muscle tension
(6) Sleep disturbance (difficulty falling or staying asleep, or restless unsatisfying sleep)

D. The focus of the anxiety and worry is not confined to features of an Axis I disorder, e.g., the anxiety or worry is not about having a Panic Attack (as in Panic Disorder), being embarrassed in public (as in Social Phobia), being contaminated (as in Obsessive-Compulsive Disorder), being away from home or close relatives (as in Separation Anxiety Disorder), gaining weight (as in Anorexia Nervosa), having multiple physical complaints (as in Somatization Disorder), or having a serious illness (as in Hypochondriasis), and the anxiety and worry do not occur exclusively during Posttraumatic Stress Disorder.

E. The anxiety, worry, or physical symptoms cause clinically significant distress or impairment in social, occupational, or other important areas of functioning.

F. The disturbance is not due to the general physiological effects of a substance (e.g., a drug of abuse, a medication) or a general medical condition (e.g., hyperthyroidism) and does not occur exclusively during a Mood Disorder, a Psychotic Disorder, or a Pervasive Developmental Disorder.

Source: Reprinted with permission from the Diagnostic and Statistical Manual of Mental Disorders, Fourth Edition, Text Revision, (Copyright © 2000). American Psychiatric Association.

Some worrying is a part of normal development. However, children like Jared with a **generalized anxiety disorder (GAD)** experience excessive and uncontrollable anxiety and worry about many events or activities on most days. They worry when there's nothing obvious to provoke the worry. For children with GAD, worrying can be episodic or almost continuous. Often the worrier is unable to relax and has physical symptoms such as muscle tension, headaches, or nausea. Other symptoms may include irritability, a lack of energy, difficulty falling asleep, and restless sleep. The DSM criteria for GAD are presented in Table 7.4.

In other anxiety disorders, anxiety converges on specific situations or objects, such as separation, social performance, animals or insects, or bodily sensations. In contrast, the anxiety experienced by children with GAD is widespread and focuses on a variety of everyday life events. It was once thought that children who were generally anxious did not focus their anxiety on one specific thing, which is referred to as "free-floating anxiety." However, these children do in fact focus their anxiety, but on many different things. Hence, the term "generalized anxiety" is more accurate. Since excessive worry is a hallmark feature of GAD, some have proposed that it be called a "generalized worry disorder" in DSM-5 (Andrews et al., 2010).

Children with GAD are likely to pick up on every frightening event in a movie, on the Internet, or on TV and relate it to themselves. If they see a news report on TV about a car accident, they may begin to worry about being in a car accident themselves. They always expect the worst possible outcome and underestimate their ability to cope with situations or events that are less than ideal. They don't seem to realize that the events they worry about have an extremely low likelihood of actually happening. Thus, their thinking often consists of what-if statements: "What if the school bus breaks down?" "What if I get hit by lightning?" Children with GAD do not restrict their worries to frightening or catastrophic events; they also worry excessively about minor everyday occurrences, such as what to wear or what to watch on TV. This generalized worry about minor events distinguishes children with GAD from those with other anxiety disorders (Albano et al., 2003).

Like Jared, children with GAD are often self-conscious, self-doubting, and worried about meeting others' expectations. Their worry may lead to significant interpersonal problems, especially those involving a tendency to be overly nurturing to others. Children with GAD seek constant approval and reassurance from adults and fear people whom they perceive as unpleasant, critical, or unfair. They tend to set extremely high standards for their own performance and are highly self-critical when they fall short. Moreover, they continue to worry even when evidence contradicts their concern. For example, a child with GAD who received a grade of A on every previous class assignment may worry about failing on the next assignment (Silverman & Ginsburg, 1995). Children with GAD also show an intolerance of uncertainty, which may result in impaired decision-making under conditions of uncertainty (Krain et al., 2006).

Children with GAD can't seem to stop worrying even when they recognize how unhappy they are making themselves and others. This characteristic is what makes their anxiety abnormal. A normal child who is worried about an upcoming sport competition can still concentrate on other tasks and will stop worrying once the competition is over. However, for children with GAD one "crisis" is followed by another in a never-ending cycle. The uncontrollable nature of the worry is an important clinical feature of GAD (Chorpita et al., 1997).

A diagnosis of GAD in children requires at least one somatic symptom. In fact, GAD is frequently identified by a doctor as a result of a child's physical complaints that involve muscle tension and agitation, rather than the heart rate increases and sweating that characterize other anxiety disorders. Headaches, stomachaches, muscle tension, and trembling are among the most commonly reported symptoms (Eisen & Engler, 1995).

© Masterfile

Youngsters with a generalized anxiety disorder worry about almost everything

For children with GAD, chronic worry may function as a type of cognitive avoidance that inhibits emotional processing (Borkovec, Ray, & Stoeber, 1998). Because they are so busy thinking about upcoming problems, they may not produce images of threats that elicit intense negative emotion and autonomic activity. Although they don't experience most of the unpleasantness that accompanies negative imagery, they never have a chance to confront their problems and find solutions. For children with GAD, chronic worry may serve the same dysfunctional purpose as behavioral avoidance does in children with specific phobias (Borkovec, 1994).

Prevalence and Comorbidity

GAD is found in 3% to 6% of all children (Albano et al., 2003). In general, the disorder is equally common in boys and girls, with a slightly higher prevalence in older adolescent females. Children with GAD have a high rate of other anxiety disorders and depression. For younger children, co-occurring SAD and ADHD are most common; older children with GAD tend to have specific phobias, panic disorder, and major depression, as well as impaired social adjustment, low self-esteem, and an increased risk for suicide (Keller et al., 1992).

Onset, Course, and Outcome

The average age of onset for GAD is around 10 to 14 years (Beesdo, Pine, Lieb, & Wittchen, 2010). Older children present with a higher total number of symptoms and report higher levels of anxiety and depression than younger children, but these symptoms may diminish with age (Strauss, Lease, Last, & Francis, 1988). In a community sample of adolescents with GAD, the likelihood of their having GAD at follow-up was higher if symptoms at the time of initial assessment were severe (Cohen, Cohen, & Brook, 1993). Nearly one-half of severe cases were re-diagnosed after 2 years, suggesting that severe generalized anxiety symptoms persist over time, even in youngsters who have not been referred for treatment.

SECTION SUMMARY

Generalized Anxiety Disorder

- Youngsters with a generalized anxiety disorder (GAD) experience chronic or exaggerated worry and tension, often accompanied by physical symptoms.
- For children with GAD, worry may serve the same dysfunctional purpose as behavioral avoidance does in children with specific phobias.
- GAD is one of the most common anxiety disorders that occur during childhood, found in 3% to 6% of all children, with an onset in late childhood or early adolescence.

SPECIFIC PHOBIA

CHARLOTTE

Arachnophobia

For 2 years, Charlotte, age 8, has complained of an intense fear of spiders. "Spiders are disgusting," she says. "I'm scared to death that one will crawl on me, especially when I'm sleeping. When I see a spider, even a little one, my heart pounds, my hands feel cold and sweaty, and I start to shake." Charlotte's mother says that her daughter goes completely pale when she sees a spider, even at a distance, and tries to avoid any situation where she thinks there might be one. Charlotte's fear is beginning to interfere with her daily activities. For example, she won't play in the backyard and refuses to go on class or family outings where she might encounter a spider. She is afraid to go to sleep at night because she thinks a spider might crawl on her. (Based on authors' case material)

As we have seen, many children have specific fears that are mildly troubling, come and go rapidly until about age 10, and rarely require special attention. However, if the child's fear occurs at an inappropriate age, persists, is irrational or exaggerated, leads to avoidance of the object or event, and causes impairment in normal routines, it is called a **specific phobia**. Like Charlotte, children with a specific phobia display a marked fear of clearly discernible objects or situations for at least 6 months. The DSM-IV-TR criteria for specific phobia are shown in Table 7.5.

Children with a specific phobia show an extreme and disabling fear of objects or situations that in reality pose little or no danger or threat, and children go to great lengths to avoid them. They experience extreme fear or dread, physiological arousal to the feared stimulus, and fearful anticipation and avoidance when confronted with the object of their fear. Their thinking usually focuses on threats to their personal safety, such as being stung by a bee or struck by lightning. Anticipatory anxiety is also common. For example, a child with a phobia of dogs may think: "What if a big dog is running loose on my way to school and I get attacked and bitten in the face?" These worries cause distress severe enough to disrupt everyday activities. The children are constantly on the lookout for the feared stimulus and, as we saw with Charlotte, go to great lengths to avoid contact.

Children's beliefs regarding the danger of the feared stimulus are likely to persist despite evidence no danger exists or efforts to reason with them. Unlike most adults with a specific phobia, children often do not recognize that their fears are extreme and unreasonable. If the feared object is rarely encountered, the phobia may not lead to serious impairment. However, if it is encountered regularly or if the fear seriously interferes with important life events, the child's phobia can become a serious problem (Albano et al., 2003).

The phobias that can develop in children and adolescents seem limitless, and include fears of telephones, water, menstruation, newspapers, mathematics, haircuts, and bowel movements, to name just a few. Although it is possible to develop a phobia of almost any object, situation, or event—ranging from A (apiphobia, a fear of bees) to Z (zemmiphobia, a fear of the great mole rat)—children are much more likely to develop certain fears than others.

TABLE 7.5 | Diagnostic Criteria for Specific Phobia

DSM-IV-TR

A. Marked and persistent fear that is excessive or unreasonable, cued by the presence or anticipation of a specific object or situation (e.g., flying, heights, animals, receiving an injection, seeing blood).

B. Exposure to the phobic stimulus almost invariably provokes an immediate anxiety response, which may take the form of a situationally bound or situationally predisposed panic attack.

Note: In children, the anxiety may be expressed by crying, tantrums, freezing, or clinging.

C. The person recognizes that the fear is excessive or unreasonable.

Note: In children, this feature may be absent.

D. The phobic situation(s) is avoided or else is endured with intense anxiety or distress.

E. The avoidance, anxious anticipation, or distress in the feared situation(s) interferes significantly with the person's normal routine, occupational (or academic) functioning, or social activities or relationships, or there is marked distress about having the phobia.

F. In individuals under age 18 years, the duration is at least 6 months.

G. The anxiety, Panic Attacks, or phobic avoidance associated with the specific object or situation are not better accounted for by another mental disorder, such as Obsessive-Compulsive Disorder (e.g., fear of dirt in someone with an obsession about contamination), Posttraumatic Stress Disorder (e.g., avoidance of stimuli associated with a sever stressor), Separation Anxiety Disorder (e.g., avoidance of school), Social Phobia (e.g., avoidance of social situations because of fear of embarrassment), Panic Disorder With Agoraphobia, or Agoraphobia Without History of Panic Disorder.

Specify type:

Animal Type

Natural Environment Type (e.g., heights, storms, water)

Blood-Injection-Injury Type

Situational Type (e.g., airplanes, elevators, enclosed places)

Other Type (e.g., fear of choking, vomiting, or contracting an illness; in children, fear of loud sounds or costumed characters)

Source: Reprinted with permission from the Diagnostic and Statistical Manual of Mental Disorders, Fourth Edition, Text Revision, (Copyright © 2000). American Psychiatric Association.

"I'm not a scaredy-cat—I'm phobic."

According to evolutionary theory, human infants are biologically predisposed as a result of natural selection to learn certain fears (Seligman, 1971). The sources of most children's phobias can be traced to the natural dangers encountered during human evolution—snakes, the dark, predators, heights, blood, loud noises, and unfamiliar places. These fears are adaptive in an evolutionary sense because they alert the individual to possible sources of danger, thereby increasing the likelihood of survival. It's not only by chance that the most common and most heritable specific phobia in children is a fear of animals, particularly dogs, snakes, insects, and mice (Essau, Conradt, & Petermann, 2000). Although evolutionary theory explains a readiness to acquire specific types of fears, it doesn't explain why children differ in their fearfulness or why some children develop pathological anxiety.

Common types of specific phobias in young people include fears of animals or insects (e.g., dogs or spiders); fears of natural events (e.g., heights or thunderstorms); fears of blood, injuries, or medical procedures (e.g., seeing blood or receiving an injection); and fears of specific situations (e.g., flying in airplanes, riding the bus).

Prevalence and Comorbidity

About 4% to 10% of all children experience specific phobias at some time in their lives, and those with this disorder tend to have multiple phobias (Bolton et al., 2006). However, very few of these children are referred for treatment, suggesting that most parents do not view specific phobias as significantly harmful. There does seem to be a family vulnerability for particular types of phobias—children are at increased risk mainly for the phobic disorder exhibited by their parent (LeBeau et al., 2010). Family risk can be attributed to both genetic and environmental factors. Specific phobias, particularly blood phobia, are more common in girls than boys (Essau et al., 1999). The most common co-occurring disorder for children with a specific phobia is another anxiety disorder. Although comorbidity is frequent for children with specific phobias, it tends to be lower than for other anxiety disorders (LeBeau et al., 2010).

Onset, Course, and Outcome

Phobias involving animals, darkness, insects, blood, and injury typically have their onset at 7 to 9 years of age, which is similar to normal development. However, even though fears and phobias decline with age, clinical phobias are more likely to persist over time than are normal fears. Specific phobias can occur at any age but seem to peak between 10 and 13 years of age (LeBeau et al., 2010).

SECTION SUMMARY

Specific Phobia

- Children with a specific phobia exhibit an extreme and disabling fear of particular objects or situations that in reality pose little or no danger.
- Evolutionary theory contends that human infants are biologically predisposed to learn certain fears that alert them to possible sources of danger. This may explain why the most common specific phobia in children is a fear of animals such as dogs, snakes, and insects.
- DSM categorizes specific phobias into five subtypes based on the focus of the phobic reaction and avoidance: animal, natural environment, blood–injection–injury, situational, and other.
- About 4% to 10% of children experience specific phobias, but only a very few are referred for treatment. Specific phobias can occur at any age, but seem to peak between 10 and 13 years of age.

Social Phobia (Social Anxiety Disorder)

To understand the world one must not be worrying about one's self.

—Albert Einstein (1879–1955)

- Kaylie is terrified to use the phone because, she says, she doesn't know how to have a conversation and would be embarrassed by the long periods of silence.
- Eugene is too embarrassed to use a public restroom.
- Li-Ming is terrified of speaking in front of her class—she's afraid of being humiliated.

Each of these youngsters has a **social phobia** or **social anxiety disorder**—a marked and persistent fear of social or performance requirements that expose them to scrutiny and possible embarrassment (Knappe, Beesdo-Baum, & Wittchen, 2010). They go to great lengths to avoid these situations, or they may face the challenge with great effort, wearing a mask of fearlessness. Long after the age at which a fear of strangers is considered normal, children with social phobias continue to shrink from people they don't know. When in the presence of other children or adults, they may blush, fall silent, cling to their parents, or try to hide. The DSM criteria for social phobia are shown in Table 7.6.

In addition to their extreme anxiety in social situations that make many people anxious, youngsters with social phobias may feel anxious about the most mundane activities—handing out papers in class, buttoning their coat in front of others, or ordering a Big Mac and fries at McDonalds. Their most common fear is doing something in front of other people. They fear that if they speak in public, they may stumble over their

TABLE 7.6 | Diagnostic Criteria for Social Phobia

DSM-IV-TR

A. A marked and persistent fear of one or more social or performance situations in which the person is exposed to unfamiliar people or to possible scrutiny by others. The individual fears that he or she will act in a way (or show anxiety symptoms) that will be humiliating or embarrassing.

Note: In children, there must be evidence of the capacity for age-appropriate social relationships with familiar people, and the anxiety must occur in peer settings, not only in interactions with adults.

B. Exposure to the feared social situation almost invariably provokes anxiety, which may take the form of a situationally bound or situationally predisposed panic attack.

Note: In children, the anxiety may be expressed by crying, tantrums, freezing, or shrinking from social situations with unfamiliar people.

C. The person recognizes that the fear is excessive or unreasonable.

Note: In children, this feature may be absent.

D. The feared social or performance situations are avoided or else are endured with intense anxiety or distress.

E. The avoidance, anxious anticipation, or distress in the feared social or performance situation(s) interferes significantly with the person's normal routine, occupational (academic) functioning, or social activities or relationships, or there is marked distress about having the phobia.

F. In individuals under age 18 years, the duration is at least 6 months.

G. The fear or avoidance is not due to the direct physiological effects of a substance (e.g., a drug of abuse, a medication) or a general medical condition and is not better accounted for by another mental disorder (e.g., Panic Disorder With or Without Agoraphobia, Separation Anxiety Disorder, Body Dysmorphic Disorder, a Pervasive Developmental Disorder, or Schizoid Personality Disorder).

H. If a general medical condition or another mental disorder is present, the fear in Criterion A is unrelated to it, e.g., the fear is not of Stuttering, trembling in Parkinson's disease, or exhibiting abnormal eating behavior in Anorexia Nervosa or Bulimia Nervosa.

Specify if:

Generalized: if the fears include most social situations (also consider the additional diagnosis of Avoidant Personality Disorder)

Source: Reprinted with permission from the Diagnostic and Statistical Manual of Mental Disorders, Fourth Edition, Text Revision, (Copyright © 2000). American Psychiatric Association.

words; if they ask a question, they may sound stupid; if they enter a room, they may trip and look awkward. One teenage girl was so fearful of being the focus of attention during meals that she spent every lunch period during her first year in high school sitting in a bathroom stall (Albano et al., 2003, p. 287).

Youngsters with social phobias are more likely than other children to be highly emotional, socially fearful, and inhibited, sad, and lonely. They frequently experience socially distressing events with which they are unable to cope effectively, in part related to a lack of social skills (Beidel, Turner, & Morris, 1999). These children want to be liked by other people. However, their fear of acting in a way that may invite humiliation is so intense and pervasive that it often leads to loneliness and suffering because they cannot form the relationships they desire (La Greca & Lopez, 1998). If other people attempt to push them into social situations they may cry, have a tantrum, freeze, or withdraw even further. In the most severe cases, children develop a **generalized social phobia.** They fear most social situations, are afraid to meet or talk with new people, avoid contact with anyone outside their family, and find it extremely difficult to attend school, participate in recreational activities, or socialize (Hofmann et al., 1999). Current evidence supports the view of social anxiety disorder as existing on a continuum of severity from lesser to greater as a function of the number of social situations that are feared and/or avoided—not as a categorically defined "generalized" subtype (Bögels et al., 2010).

The anxiety associated with social phobia can be so severe that it produces stammering, sweating, upset stomach, rapid heartbeat, or a full-scale panic attack. Adolescents with a social phobia frequently believe that their visible physical reactions will expose their hidden feelings of inadequacy, which makes them more anxious. In a repeating cycle, children with a social phobia anticipate their awkwardness and poor performance, which triggers further anxiety as they approach the feared situation, and further increases their nervousness and physical symptoms. As a result, they avoid social activities such as calling a classmate for missed homework, asking the teacher to explain something, answering the telephone, or dating (Albano, 1995).

Social phobias encompass a variety of social fears, including fear of performance situations, such as speaking in front of others, and fear of interaction situations, such as talking to others at a party. Recent research suggests that interaction- and performance-related social fears may differ from one another in their risk factors and clinical characteristics, and that sub-grouping children with different types of social phobias may help to further our understanding of this disorder (Knappe et al., 2011).

Prevalence, Comorbidity, and Course

Social phobia is common, with a lifetime prevalence of 6%–12%, and affecting nearly twice as many girls as boys (Knappe et al., 2010). Girls may experience more social anxiety because they are more concerned with social competence than are boys and attach greater importance to interpersonal relationships and evaluation by peers (Inderbitzen-Nolan & Walters, 2000). Some support for this hypothesis comes from an fMRI brain imaging study

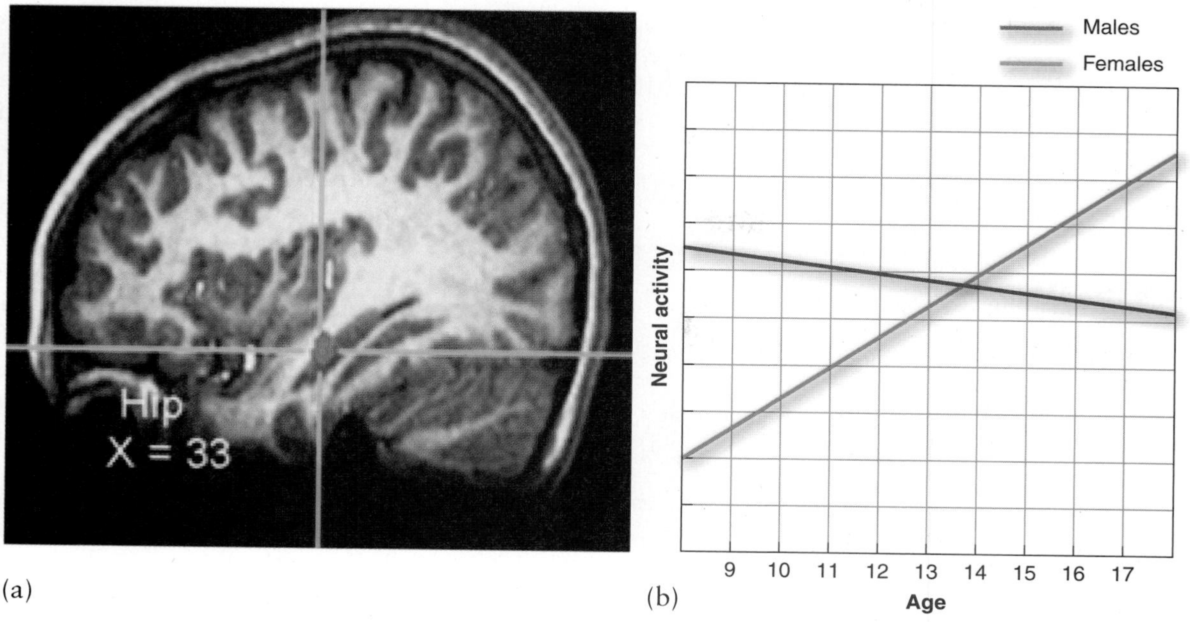

● **FIGURE 7.1** | The figure (a) shows increased neural activity as detected in the hippocampus while participants appraised how they thought preferred peers would evaluate them. (b) As age increased, neural activity in the hippocampus increased in females but did not change in males.

into the neural correlates of anticipated evaluation by peers in 9- to 17-year-old male and female adolescents (Guyer, McClure-Tone, Shiffrin, Pine, & Nelson, 2009). Females who thought that a peer they wished to interact with was evaluating them showed age-related increases in activation of brain regions (e.g., hippocampus) associated with processing emotional information. These increases did not occur in males. Representative findings from this study are shown in ● Figure 7.1 and suggest that, relative to males, adolescent females may have an increasing biological sensitivity to being evaluated by peers, which may, over time, increase their vulnerability to developing social anxiety disorders.

Among children referred for treatment for anxiety disorders, as many as 20% have social phobia as their primary diagnosis. It is also the most common secondary diagnosis for children referred for other anxiety disorders (Albano et al., 2003). Even so, many cases of social phobia are overlooked because shyness is common in our society and because these children are not likely to call attention to their problem even when they are severely distressed (Essau, Conradt, & Petermann, 1999).

Two thirds of children and adolescents with a social phobia have another anxiety disorder—most commonly, a specific phobia or panic disorder (Beidel et al., 1999). About 20% of adolescents with a social phobia also suffer from major depression. They may also use alcohol and other drugs as a form of self-medication to reduce their anxiety in social situations (Albano et al., 2003).

Social phobias are extremely rare in children under the age of 10, and generally develop after puberty, with the most common age of onset in early- to mid-adolescence (Wittchen, Stein, & Kessler, 1999). Early pubertal timing is linked to higher anxiety symptoms in girls (Reardon, Leen-Feldner, & Hayward, 2009). However, it is unclear whether early puberty leads to anxiety or if anxiety influences pubertal timing. In either case, this is a time when teens experience heightened self-consciousness, doubts, and worries about their appearance, social prowess, and what others may think of them. How to walk, what to say, and how to dress are ever present in the minds of most teens, a fact often exploited by advertisers. Common sources of anxiety at this age include consolidation of identity, sexuality, social acceptance, and conflict about independence; the symptoms of anxiety they most frequently report include fears of public speaking, blushing, excessive worry about past behavior, and self-consciousness (Bell-Dolan et al., 1990). The prevalence of social phobia appears to increase with age, although more information is needed to determine the natural course of the disorder and its long-term outcome (Neal & Edelmann, 2003). One characteristic in early adolescence that predicts symptoms of social anxiety several years later is the youngster's perception of not being accepted by peers (Teachman & Allen, 2007). The average duration of symptoms of social anxiety is about 20 to 25 years—thus, it is not a short-lived condition of adolescence and young adulthood. In the absence of effective treatment, the likelihood of a complete and long-lasting remission for social phobia, especially the generalized subtype, is the lowest for all anxiety disorders (Knappe et al., 2010).

Selective Mutism

KEISHA

Mum's the Word

Keisha, age 6, doesn't speak at kindergarten to teachers or peers and did not do so during her 2 years in preschool. Two years ago she had difficulties being left at preschool and it took about 2 months before she could be left without crying. Although she doesn't talk to other children, she interacts with them and participates in school activities. Keisha speaks openly to all family members at home but does not speak to them in public if others might hear her. She says that she does not know why she doesn't talk, but has told her mother that she feels scared. Her mother says Keisha is shy and is a worrier. (Adapted from Leonard & Dow, 1995)

Children with **selective mutism** fail to talk in specific social situations, even though they may speak loudly and frequently at home or in other settings (Viana, Beidel, & Rabian, 2009). This disorder is rare, estimated to occur in about 0.5% of all children (Bergman, Piacentini, & McKracken, 2002). Average age of onset is about 3 to 4 years. However, there is often a considerable lag between age of onset and referral, possibly because the child's mutism may not occur at home. Although not included as an anxiety disorder in DSM-IV-TR, selective mutism has many factors in common with the anxiety disorders (Leonard & Dow, 1995). For example, about 45% to 75% of children with selective mutism meet diagnostic criteria for a social phobia in ways other than their reluctance to speak (Viana et al., 2009), and nearly 40% of their parents have also been diagnosed with a social phobia during their lifetime (Chavira, Shipon-Blum, Hitchcock, Cohan, & Stein 2007).

Based on these similarities, it has been suggested that selective mutism may be an extreme type of social phobia rather than a unique disorder (Dummit et al., 1997). However, there are also differences between the two disorders—for example, oppositional features and nonverbal social engagement occur in selective mutism, but less so in social phobia (Yaganeh, Beidel, & Turner, 2006). Relatedly, one study identified three subgroups of children with selective mutism: anxious—mildly oppositional; (2) anxious—communication delayed; and (3) exclusively anxious (Cohan & Chavira, 2008). Some children with selective mutism also display developmental delay, language impairments, or auditory processing deficits. One hypothesis is that because of their auditory processing deficits, some children fail to get used to their own vocalizations and are therefore over-stimulated by them, making speaking aversive (Bar-Haim et al., 2004). Anecdotal accounts from adults who suffered from selective mutism as children also suggest that in some cases trauma played a role and not talking was a self-protective response (Omdal, 2007). For example, Dr. Maya Angelou, a celebrated African-American poet and writer who captivates audiences with her words, was mute for nearly 5 years after suffering the trauma of being raped as an 8-year-old child.

In summary, most children with selective mutism fail to talk in some settings because they are socially anxious, but there may be other reasons as well. Thus, it would be premature to conclude that selective mutism and social phobia are the same disorder. Behavioral and cognitive behavioral interventions have been used to help children with selective mutism, although controlled studies are needed to evaluate their effectiveness (Cohan, Chavira, & Stein, 2006).

SECTION SUMMARY

Social Phobia (Social Anxiety Disorder)

- Children with social phobia fear being the focus of attention or scrutiny, or of doing something in public that will be intensely humiliating.
- Social phobias are common, with a lifetime prevalence of 6% to 12%, and affecting nearly twice as many girls as boys.
- They generally develop after puberty, at a time when most teens experience heightened self-consciousness and worries about what others think of them.
- Children with selective mutism fail to talk in specific social situations, even though they may speak loudly and frequently at home or in other settings.

Obsessive—Compulsive Disorder

Insanity: doing the same thing over and over again and expecting different results.

—Attributed to Albert Einstein

PAUL

Counting and Cleaning

Paul, age 16, is continually distracted by powerful and peculiar thoughts, such as counting how many times he blinks and how many steps it takes to get to the kitchen. He avoids stepping on any floor tiles with dirt on them because he doesn't want to get germs on his feet. He is obsessed with germs on door handles and feels compelled to avoid touching them unless he first uses a cloth (which he always has with him) to clean the handle off. On those rare occasions that he misplaces or forgets to bring a clean cloth with him, he gets extremely anxious, freezes, and feels sick to his stomach. (Based on authors' case material)

Paul has an **obsessive—compulsive disorder (OCD)**, which is an unusual disorder of ritual and doubt. Youngsters with OCD experience recurrent, time-consuming (taking more than 1 hour a day), and disturbing obsessions and compulsions (Evans & Leckman, 2006). **Obsessions** are persistent and intrusive thoughts, ideas, impulses, or images. Most children describe their obsessions as very similar to worries. However, obsessions are much more than heightened worries about everyday problems, such as homework or popularity. They are excessive and irrational, and are focused on improbable or unrealistic events, or on greatly exaggerated real-life events. Children with OCD may complain about being unable to stop "hearing" recurring rhymes or songs, or may experience fears of having a serious disease such as cancer or of being attacked by an intruder. In children, the most common obsessions focus on contamination, fears of harm to self or others, or concerns with symmetry and exactness, while in adolescence, sexual, somatic, and religious preoccupations also become more common (Geller et al., 1998). Since these and other obsessions create considerable anxiety and distress, children with OCD go to great lengths to try to neutralize them with another action, known as a compulsion.

Compulsions are repetitive, purposeful, and intentional behaviors (e.g., hand washing) or mental acts (e.g., repeating words silently) that are performed in response to an obsession. For example, as a result of an obsession with germs, a child with OCD may feel compelled to clean door handles, check for dirt, or engage in some other ritual as a way of decreasing anxiety. One 7-year-old boy was so obsessed with germs that he felt compelled to wash his homework! Multiple compulsions are the norm, the most common being excessive washing and bathing (occurring in about 85% of cases), repeating, checking, touching, counting, hoarding, and ordering or arranging (Geller et al., 1998). The DSM criteria for OCD are shown in Table 7.7.

TABLE 7.7 | Diagnostic Criteria for Obsessive—Compulsive Disorder

DSM-IV-TR

A. Either obsessions or compulsions:

Obsessions as defined by (1), (2), (3), and (4):

(1) Recurrent and persistent thoughts, impulses, or images that are experienced, at some time during the disturbance, as intrusive and inappropriate and that cause marked anxiety or distress

(2) The thoughts, impulses, or images are not simply excessive worries about real-life problems

(3) The person attempts to ignore or suppress such thoughts, impulses, or images, or to neutralize them with some other thought or action

(4) The person recognizes that the obsessional thoughts, impulses, or images are a product of his or her own mind (not imposed from without as in thought insertion)

Compulsions as defined by (1) and (2):

(1) Repetitive behaviors (e.g., hand washing, ordering, checking) or mental acts (e.g., praying, counting, repeating words silently) that the person feels driven to perform in response to an obsession, or according to rules that must be applied rigidly

(2) The behaviors or mental acts are aimed at preventing or reducing distress or preventing some dreaded event or situation; however, these behaviors or mental acts either are not connected in a realistic way with what they are designed to neutralize or prevent or they are clearly excessive

B. At some point during the course of the disorder, the person has recognized that the obsessions or compulsions are excessive or unreasonable.

Note: This does not apply to children.

C. The obsessions or compulsions cause marked distress, are time consuming (take more than 1 hour a day), or significantly interfere with the person's normal routine, occupational (or academic) functioning, or usual social activities or relationships.

D. If another Axis I disorder is present, the content of the obsessions of compulsions is not restricted to it (e.g., preoccupation with food in the presence of an Eating Disorder; hair pulling in the presence of Trichotillomania; concern with appearance in the presence of Body Dysmorphic Disorder; preoccupation with having a serious illness in the presence of Hypochondriasis; preoccupation with sexual urges or fantasies in the presence of a Paraphilia; or guilty ruminations in the presence of Major Depressive Disorder).

E. The disturbance is not due to the direct physiological effects of a substance (e.g., a drug of abuse, a medication) or a general medical condition

Specify if:

With Poor Insight: if, for most of the time during the current episode, the person does not recognize that the obsession and compulsions are excessive or unreasonable.

Source: Reprinted with permission from the Diagnostic and Statistical Manual of Mental Disorders, Fourth Edition, Text Revision, (Copyright ©2000). American Psychiatric Association.

Most children with OCD have multiple obsessions and compulsions, and certain compulsions are commonly associated with specific obsessions. For example, washing and cleaning rituals are likely to be associated with contamination obsessions, such as a concern with dirt or germs, a concern or disgust with body wastes or secretions (e.g., urine, feces, saliva), or an excessive concern about chemical or environmental contamination. Compulsions involving counting over and over to a certain number are frequently related to a concern about harm—that something terrible might happen, such as the death of a parent or a fire. Obsessions with symmetry, exactness, or order are often associated with compulsions for arranging and ordering, such as repeatedly packing and unpacking a suitcase or rearranging drawers (Piacentini, 1997). Interestingly, in adults, each symptom dimension of OCD (e.g., contamination-related, symmetry-related) may be mediated by a distinct but partially overlapping neural system; however, this not the case for children. This suggests important developmental differences in the neural mechanisms of OCD symptoms in children versus adults (Gilbert et al., 2009).

How can children with OCD be so reasonable about some things yet so disturbed with respect to their obsessions and compulsions? Most children over age 8 persist in their obsessions or compulsions even though they recognize them as excessive and unreasonable (children ordinarily use the words *dumb* or *stupid*). However, OCD is extremely resistant to reason, even when the child recognizes the "silliness" of the routines. For example, one of 10-year-old Emilio's obsessive thoughts is that a long, flexible, pipe-like structure protrudes from his chest. He knows this is not so, but he must behave as if the pipe is there and move in such a way that no person or object comes too close in front of him (Despert, 1955).

Children with OCD often involve family members in their rituals; for example, demanding that their clothes be washed 2 or 3 times a day, not allowing others to eat certain foods for fear of illness or contamination, or having a parent get up at 5 a.m. to assist them in dressing rituals that may take hours to complete (Piacentini, 1997; Waters & Barrett, 2000). Some children with OCD insist that certain phrases be repeated or that questions be answered in a certain way. Consider this exchange between Heather, age 11, and her mother:

HEATHER: You said before that we were having dessert. Now you say we're having ice cream. Which one is it?

MOTHER: Ice cream is dessert.

HEATHER: But which one is right?

MOTHER: Both.

HEATHER: But are we having ice cream or dessert?

MOTHER: We're having ice cream.

HEATHER: So why did you say we were having dessert?

Heather became so argumentative, insistent, and persistent that her mother thought she had a severe behavior problem. However, with further assessment, it became clear that Heather's oppositional behavior was an expression of OCD. When interviewed about her problem, Heather said: "I can't help it. When I'm with my mother, I have to make her say things 'just right' or I feel terrible."

Compulsions are intended to neutralize or reduce the anxiety and tension of the obsessions, or to prevent some dreaded event or situation from happening. Although rituals may provide temporary relief from anxiety, in the long run they fail to achieve their intended purpose. As a result, children with OCD increasingly become trapped in a time-consuming and never-ending cycle of obsessions and compulsions. Many hours each day are dominated by disabling, alarming, and sometimes ridiculous thoughts, and by repeated compulsive behaviors. The child's preoccupation with obsessions and rituals makes it extremely difficult, if not impossible, to focus on anything else. As we saw with Paul, even a simple activity like opening a door may become an insurmountable problem.

As a result of such excessive preoccupations, normal activities of children with OCD are reduced, and health, social and family relations, and school functioning can be severely disrupted (Evans & Leckman, 2006). Cleaning or washing rituals may lead to health problems, such as skin irritation of the hands and forearms as a result of prolonged washing, or gum lesions as a result of prolonged tooth brushing. Dressing or washing rituals may result in chronic lateness. Counting and checking rituals and intrusive thoughts may prevent concentration at school and interfere with schoolwork. These rituals may require the child to check and recheck every answer on a test so often that he or she is unable to finish it. Homework may become a daily struggle, as the child spends hours repeatedly checking and correcting the work. Bedtime rituals may preclude inviting friends to sleep over and cause repeated refusals to accept similar invitations from friends. Contamination fears may interfere with school attendance and social activities such as going to the movies or participating in sports (Piacentini, 1997).

Because of the odd and senseless nature of OCD symptoms, many children try to mask or hide their rituals, especially in social situations or at school

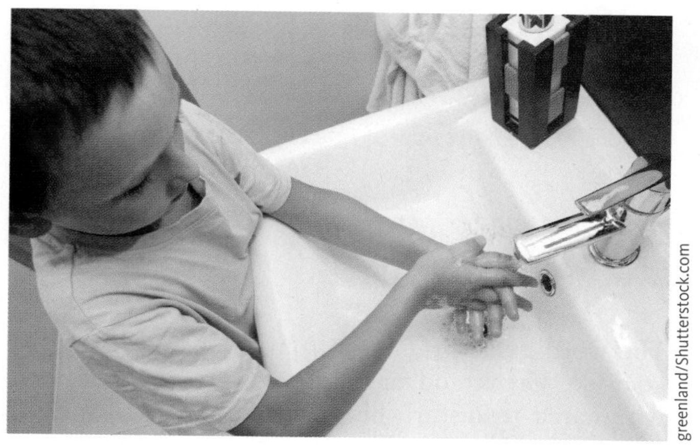

(Rapoport et al., 2000). In less severe cases, teachers, friends, and family members may be unaware of the child's OCD for months or even years. However, as the rituals become more elaborate and time-consuming, they become increasingly difficult to conceal. With considerable effort, children with OCD may muster the energy to suppress their symptoms for brief periods. However, suppression commonly has a rebound effect, with increased symptoms once the child is in a safe place. As the child becomes too overwhelmed by anxiety to cope, or when websites, magazine articles, or TV shows about OCD bring the problem into focus, others become more and more aware of its seriousness (Piacentini, 1997).

Prevalence and Comorbidity

The lifetime prevalence of OCD in children and adolescents is 1% to 3%, suggesting that it occurs about as often in young people as in adults (Zohar, 1999). Clinic-based studies of younger children suggest that OCD is about twice as common in boys than in girls. However, this gender difference has not been observed in community samples of adolescents, which may be a function of age differences, referral bias, or both (Albano et al., 2003). The most common comorbidities are other anxiety disorders, depressive disorders (especially in older children with OCD), and disruptive behavior disorders. Substance-use disorders, learning disorders, and eating disorders are also overrepresented in children with OCD, as are vocal and motor tics (Piacentini & Graae, 1997).

Onset, Course, and Outcome

The mean age of onset of OCD is 9 to 12 years with two peaks, one in early childhood and another in early adolescence (Hanna, 1995). Children with an early onset of OCD (age 6–10) are more likely to be boys and more likely to have a family history of OCD than children with a later onset, suggesting a greater role of genetic influences in such cases (Walitza et al., 2010). These children have a high rate of co-occurring chronic tic disorders, *trichotillomania* (hair loss from compulsive pulling or twisting of hair), and ADHD (Leckman et al., 2010). They may also have prominent motor patterns, engaging in compulsions without obsessions and displaying odd behaviors, such as finger licking or compulsively walking in geometric designs.

The developmental course of OCD in young children indicates that they typically have obsessions that are more vague than those of older children,

Haunted by their habits: washing, checking, and exactness

and are less likely to feel that their obsessions are abnormal. Young children with OCD often ask their parents endless questions related to their obsessions and make no effort to hide their discomfort. Most children over age 8 are aware that their obsessions are abnormal, and they are usually uncomfortable talking about them. They may try to hide or minimize them or deny they have them, which frustrates parents who know that something is wrong and want to help.

One half to two thirds of children with OCD continue to meet the criteria for the disorder 2 to 14 years later. Although most children, including those treated with medication, show some improvement in symptoms, fewer than 10% show complete remission, and many experience interpersonal problems, work difficulties, and lower quality of life as adults (Palermo et al., 2011). Predictors of a poorer outcome include a poor initial response to treatment, hoarding symptoms in childhood, a lifetime history of tic disorder, and parental psychopathology at the time of referral. Thus, OCD remains a serious and chronic disorder for a significant number of children (Evans & Leckman, 2006).

SECTION SUMMARY

Obsessive—Compulsive Disorder

- Youngsters with obsessive—compulsive disorder (OCD) experience repeated, intrusive, and unwanted thoughts or obsessions that cause anxiety, often accompanied by ritualized behaviors or compulsions to relieve the anxiety.
- Among the most common obsessions in children are contamination and fears of harm to self and others. Among the most common compulsions are washing and bathing, and repeating, checking, and arranging.
- OCD has a mean age of onset of 9 to 12 years and affects about 1% to 3% of all children. Children with an early onset are more likely to be boys and are more likely to have a family history of the disorder than are those with a later onset.
- OCD is a serious and chronic disorder, with as many as two-thirds of children continuing to have the disorder 2 to 14 years after being diagnosed.

Panic

In this section we consider youngsters who experience symptoms of panic that are characterized by a sudden and overwhelming period of intense fear or discomfort.

Panic Attacks

"When my heart starts pounding, I feel like I'm going to die."

"No one really knows how terrified I am when I have these attacks."

"I can't help being so frightened. My dad says I should snap out of it. I wish I could."

—Author's files

The word *panic* originates from the name "Pan," the goat-like Greek god of nature. Pan terrified travelers who dared to disturb his roadside nap by surprising them with a bloodcurdling scream. So intense was this scream that it sometimes scared the intruders to death. An unexpected and devastating feeling of terror came to be known as panic.

A **panic attack** is a sudden and overwhelming period of intense fear or discomfort that is accompanied by four or more physical and cognitive symptoms characteristic of the fight/flight response (see Table 7.8). Usually, a panic attack is short, with symptoms reaching maximal intensity in 10 minutes or less and then diminishing slowly over the next 30 minutes or the next few hours. Panic attacks are accompanied by an overwhelming sense of imminent danger or impending doom, and by an urge to escape. Although they are brief, they can occur several times a week or month. It is important to remember that although the symptoms are dramatic, they are not physically harmful or dangerous.

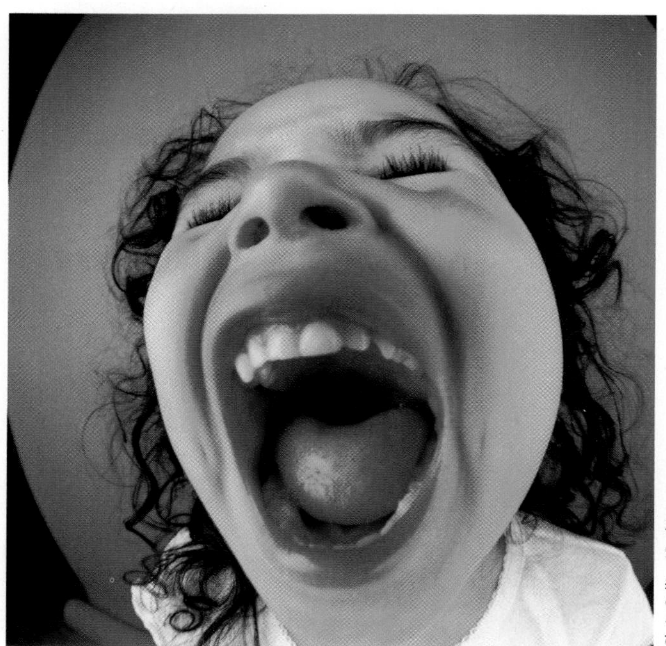

Chris Collins/Corbis

Panic

TABLE 7.8 | Diagnostic Criteria for a Panic Attack

DSM-IV-TR

Note: A Panic Attack is not a codable disorder. Code the specific diagnosis in which the Panic Attack occurs (e.g., Panic Disorder With Agoraphobia).

A discrete period of intense fear or discomfort, in which four or more of the following symptoms developed abruptly and reached a peak within 10 minutes:

(1) Palpitations, pounding heart, or accelerated heart rate
(2) Sweating
(3) Trembling or shaking
(4) Sensations of shortness of breath
(5) Feeling of choking
(6) Chest pain or discomfort
(7) Nausea or abdominal distress
(8) Feeling dizzy, unsteady, lightheaded, or faint
(9) Derealization (feelings of unreality) or depersonalization (being detached from oneself)
(10) Fear of losing control or going crazy
(11) Fear of dying
(12) Paresthesias (numbness or tightening sensations)
(13) Chills or hot flashes

Source: Reprinted with permission from the Diagnostic and Statistical Manual of Mental Disorders, Fourth Edition, Text Revision, (Copyright © 2000). American Psychiatric Association.

Panic attacks are easily identified in adults, but some controversy exists over how often they occur in children and adolescents. Although panic attacks are extremely rare in young children, they are common in adolescents (Mattis & Ollendick, 2002). One explanation is that young children lack the cognitive ability to make the catastrophic misinterpretations (e.g., "my heart is beating rapidly and I'm sitting here watching TV like I always do—I must be going crazy") that usually accompany panic attacks (Nelles & Barlow, 1988). However, research suggests that young children may in fact be capable of such misinterpretations (Mattis & Ollendick, 1997).

If limited cognitive capacity is not the primary reason that panic attacks are so rare in young children, what is? In a revealing study, the relationship between the occurrence of panic attacks and pubertal stage was assessed in 754 girls in the sixth and seventh grades. Importantly, increasing rates of panic were related to pubertal development, not to increasing age (Hayward et al., 1992). The significance of pubertal development and anxiety disorders in females is more generally supported by findings that sixth- to eighth-grade females who developed internalizing symptoms were on average 5 months earlier in their pubertal development than females who did not develop symptoms (Hayward, Killen, Wilson, & Hammer, 1997). Given that spontaneous panic attacks are rare before puberty and are related to pubertal stage, and that adolescence is the peak time for the onset of the disorder, the physical changes that take place around puberty seem critical to the occurrence of panic.

Why do the physical symptoms of the fight/flight response occur if an adolescent is not initially frightened? One possibility is that things other than fear can produce these symptoms. A youngster may be distressed for a particular reason, and stress can increase production of adrenaline and other chemicals that may produce physical symptoms of panic. Increased adrenaline may be chemically maintained in the body even after the stress is no longer present. Another possibility is that the youngster may breathe a little too fast (subtle hyperventilation), which also can produce symptoms. Because the over-breathing is very slight, the child gets used to it and doesn't realize that he or she is hyperventilating. A third possibility is that some youngsters are experiencing normal bodily changes but, because they are constantly monitoring their bodies (as adolescents are prone to do), they notice these sensations far more readily (Barlow, 2002).

Panic Disorder

CLAUDIA

An Attack Out of Nowhere

Claudia, age 16, was watching TV after a noneventful day at school. She suddenly felt overwhelmed by an intense feeling of lightheadedness and a smothering sensation, as if she couldn't get any air to breathe. Her heart started to pound rapidly, as if it would explode. The attack came on so fast and was so intense that Claudia panicked and thought she was having a heart attack that would kill her. She began to sweat and tremble, and she felt the room was spinning. These feelings reached a peak within 2 minutes . . . but this was the seventh attack that Claudia had experienced this month. She frantically ran to her mother and pleaded to be taken to the hospital emergency room—again. (Based on authors' case material)

Some adolescents who experience repeated severe panic attacks have no other symptoms. Others, like Claudia, have a progression of distressing symptoms and develop a panic disorder (see Box 7.2). Adolescents with **panic disorder (PD)** display recurrent unexpected attacks followed by at least 1 month of persistent concern about having another attack, constant worry about the consequences, or a significant change in their behavior related to the attacks. This type of worry is referred to as *anticipatory anxiety*. Those who suffer many panic attacks develop considerable secondary anxiety and may feel anxious most of the time.

Adolescents with PD may avoid locations where they've had a previous panic attack, or situations or activities in which they fear an attack might occur, or situations in which help may not be available. An adolescent with PD like Claudia might think: "It would be bad enough to have an attack at all, but it would be really dangerous if I had one while riding my bike to school. I'd be totally preoccupied with the attack and would have an accident. I'd probably destroy my bike and wind up seriously hurting myself or someone else in the process!" Claudia's avoidance of riding a bike to school could be misinterpreted as a fear of bike riding, when it is actually a fear of having a panic attack while riding the bike.

If not recognized and treated, PD and its complications can seriously interfere with relationships at home and at school, and with school performance. Some adolescents with PD may be reluctant to go to school or be separated from their parents. In severe cases, the tendency to avoid everyday life circumstances may increase and generalize, to the point that the older adolescent with PD becomes terrified to leave the house at all. This pattern, characterized by a fear of being alone in and avoiding certain places or situations, is called **agoraphobia**. Agoraphobia, which usually doesn't develop until age 18 or older, is related to a fear of having a panic attack in situations (e.g., stores, restaurants, or crowds) where escape would be difficult or help is unavailable in the event of incapacitation (Wittchen, Gloster, Beesdo-Baum, Fava, & Craske, 2010). An older adolescent with agoraphobia who dares to venture into a feared situation does so only with great distress, or when accompanied by a family member or a friend.

Prevalence and Comorbidity

Whereas panic attacks are common among adolescents, affecting about 3% to 4% of teens, PD is less common, affecting about 1% of teens (Goodwin & Gotlib, 2004). Adolescent females are more likely than adolescent males to experience panic attacks, and a fairly consistent association has been found between panic attacks and stressful life events (King, Ollendick, & Mattis, 1994). Most referred adolescents with PD

BOX 7.2 **A CLOSER LOOK**

Did Darwin Have a Panic Disorder?

Charles Darwin (1809–1882) was a gregarious and daring traveler and outdoorsman in his college days. However, in his late twenties—just a year after returning to England after a 5-year voyage to South America and the Pacific aboard HMS *Beagle*—he started to complain of an "uncomfortable palpitation of the heart." The symptoms arose shortly after he began keeping a secret notebook that, 22 years later, would become his book-length elaboration of the theory of evolution, *On the Origin of Species*. Over the years, his affliction was described as a case of bad nerves, a tropical disease, intellectual exhaustion, arsenic poisoning, suppressed gout, and a host of other complaints. However, in his journal Darwin described his malady as a "sensation of fear . . . accompanied by troubled beating of the heart, sweat, trembling of muscles."

Source: Desmond & Moore, 1991.

have one or more other disorders, most commonly an additional anxiety disorder or depression (Doerfler, Connor, Volungis, & Toscano, 2007). After months or years of unrelenting panic attacks and the restricted lifestyle that results from avoidance behavior, adolescents and young adults with PD may develop severe depression and may be at risk for suicidal behavior. Others may begin to use alcohol or drugs as a way of alleviating their anxiety.

Onset, Course, and Outcome

The average age of onset for a first panic attack in adolescents with PD is 15 to 19 years, and 95% of adolescents with the disorder are postpubertal (Bernstein, Borchardt, & Perwien, 1996). PD occurs in otherwise emotionally healthy youngsters about half the time. The most frequent prior disturbance, if one exists, is a depressive disorder (Last & Strauss, 1989). Unfortunately, youngsters with PD have the lowest rate of remission for any of the anxiety disorders (Last, Perrin, Hersen, & Kazdin, 1996).

SECTION SUMMARY

Panic

- A panic attack is a sudden and overwhelming period of intense fear or discomfort accompanied by physical and cognitive symptoms.
- Adolescents who experience repeated panic attacks and persistently worry about the possible implications and consequences of having another attack have a panic disorder (PD).
- Many postpubertal adolescents experience panic attacks, but PD is much less common.

Posttraumatic and Acute Stress Disorders

Children with **posttraumatic stress disorder (PTSD)** display persistent anxiety following an overwhelming traumatic event that occurs outside the range of usual human experience (Fletcher, 2007). When the diagnosis of PTSD was first introduced, the reference points were catastrophic events, such as war, torture, rape, natural disasters (e.g., earthquakes and hurricanes), and disasters of human origin (e.g., fires and automobile accidents). A distinction is made between these types of trauma and other lower-magnitude but very stressful life events, such as illness or family breakup. The traumatic experiences associated with PTSD are likely to exceed and overwhelm the coping abilities of most humans. Nevertheless, because low-magnitude stressors occur far more frequently than extreme stressors, many children who display PTSD symptoms may experience only a low-magnitude stressor (Copeland, Keeler, Angold, & Costello, 2010).

The experiences associated with PTSD involve actual or threatened death or injury, or a threat to one's physical integrity. PTSD is most common among children exposed to major accidents, natural disasters, kidnapping, brutal physical assaults, war and violence, or sexual abuse (see Chapter 14) (Davis & Siegel, 2000). Among the specific traumatic events associated with the onset of PTSD in children are the Oklahoma City bombing, the school shootings in Littleton, Colorado, the terrorist attacks on the United States on September 11, 2001, the ravaging impact of Hurricane Katrina on New Orleans and the U.S. Gulf Coast, and the 2004 great Indian Ocean earthquake and tsunamis (Comer & Kendall, 2007; Dean et al., 2008).

As a result of exposure to war in recent decades more than 2 million children worldwide have been killed, approximately 6 million have been injured or permanently disabled, 1 million have been orphaned, and 20 million have been displaced (Barenbaum, Ruchkin, & Schwab-Stone, 2004). Many others have been injured by land mines or targeted for ethnic cleansing and genocide. Millions of other children have been exposed to bombing, shelling, sniper fire, and terrorist attacks resulting in untold loss of family, friends, and community support (Bellamy, 2002; Machel, 2001). The tragedy of these events underscores the need to understand how they affect children's mental health, and, more importantly, to find effective ways of helping the child victims of such atrocities (Ehntholt & Yule, 2006).

As illustrated in the following case example of Marcie, the three core DSM-IV features of PTSD are persistent (for more than 1 month):

- Reexperiencing of the traumatic event
- Avoidance of trauma-associated stimuli and numbing of general responsiveness
- Symptoms of extreme arousal

Symptoms of PTSD are both conspicuous and complex. They include intense fear, helplessness, and horror, which in children may be expressed as agitated behavior and disorganization. Children with PTSD show many of the same symptoms as combat soldiers exposed to the horrors of war. They may experience physiological symptoms, nightmares, fears, and panic attacks both in the short term and for many years (Kirsch, Wilhelm, & Goldbeck, 2011). They may regress developmentally and display age-inappropriate behaviors, such as a

MARCIE

Not the Only Victim

While accompanying her mother to a neighbor's house, Marcie, age 6, was viciously mauled in the face by a large German shepherd. Her brother Jeff, age 7, and her two younger sisters observed the incident. Although the mother warned the children to keep away from the dog, Marcie and Jeff let it approach and Jeff was able to pet the dog. Marcie then bent toward the dog to pet it, and the dog attacked. The mother immediately applied pressure to the bleeding wound, as the two youngest children clung to their mother's legs. The dog's owner (who had followed the dog down the driveway) panicked and ran to the children's home to get their father, leaving the dog unleashed and barking at the frightened family for about 20 minutes. The father took the family home, cleaned Marcie's wound, and then took her for emergency medical treatment. Marcie received stitches in her face while she was strapped down and in extreme distress.

Following the incident, all the children displayed some fear and reverted to behaviors displayed at a younger age, such as bed-wetting and finger sucking. They also displayed irritability and developed varying degrees of sleep disturbances and nightmares. Moreover, Marcie developed an intense fear of medical procedures or any situation that reminded her of a medical procedure. Thus, intense fear and panic reactions accompanied follow-up visits to the plastic surgeon. Excessive distress was shown in everyday first-aid situations such as caring for a minor scratch or scrape. (Adapted from *Behavioral Assessment and Treatment of PTSD in Prepubertal Children: Attention to Developmental Factors and Innovative Strategies in the Case Study of a Family* by A. M. Albano, P. P. Miller, R. Zarate, G. Cote, D. H. Barlow, 1997, pp. 245–262, 'Cognitive and Behavioral Practice', Vol. 2, Copyright © 1997 by the Association for Advancement of Behavior Therapy. Reprinted by permission.)

fear of strangers. Children with PTSD avoid situations that could remind them of the traumatic event or they may reenact the event in play. They may feel pessimistic, vulnerable, or numb, and have problems in school (Anthony, Lonigan, & Hecht, 1999).

Some key symptoms of PTSD are expressed differently in children than in adults. For example, instead of flashbacks and waking recall of the traumatic event, young children are likely to re-experience trauma in nightmares. Initially, the nightmares reflect the traumatic event, but over time they may become nonspecific. Similarly, daytime recall may be expressed in play or through reenactment of the event or related themes. Trauma reactions of preschool children may include repetitive drawing and play focused on trauma-related themes, regressive behavior, antisocial or aggressive behavior, and destructive behavior (Perrin, Smith, & Yule, 2000). Given these differences, concerns have been raised regarding whether DSM-IV-TR criteria are sufficiently sensitive to age-related symptoms of PTSD or are able to detect the presence of PTSD in very young children. To address these concerns, it has been proposed that additional age-related manifestations be included in DSM-5, and that an age-related subtype ("PTSD in Preschool Children") be added which lowers the number of symptoms of "avoiding trauma stimuli" and "numbing of general responsiveness" required for the diagnosis (Pynoos et al., 2009; Scheeringa, Zeanah, & Cohen, 2010).

Acute stress disorder is characterized by the development during or within 1 month after exposure to an extreme traumatic stressor of at least three of the following dissociative symptoms: an absence of emotional responsiveness, derealization, a reduced awareness of surroundings, depersonalization, or dissociative amnesia. The traumatic event is persistently re-experienced, and the child displays marked avoidance of stimuli that arouse memories of it. These disturbances last for at least 2 days, but do not persist longer than a month (APA, 2000). Acute stress disorder is short-lived and emphasizes acute dissociative reactions to the trauma, whereas PTSD has long-lasting effects. Acute stress disorder occurs following trauma in about 10% to 20% of children and, although short-lived, is still a problem for a significant number of youth who are exposed to trauma (Meiser-Stedman, Dalgleish, Smith, Yule, & Glucksman 2007).

Prevalence and Comorbidity

About 14% of children age 2 to 17 in the United States report lifetime exposure to natural disaster and about two-thirds experience one or more potentially traumatic events by age 16 (Becker-Blease, Turner, & Finkelhor, 2010; Copeland, Keeler, Angold, & Costello, 2007). Most do not develop PTSD, except following several traumas or a history of anxiety. Nevertheless, a small but significant number of children who are exposed to trauma develop PTSD, and many others experience some PTSD symptoms as well as other emotional disturbances (Briggs-Gowan et al., 2010; McLaughlin et al., 2010). In a large national sample of over 4,000 adolescents ages 12 to 17 in the United States, the 6-month prevalence of PTSD was 3.7% for boys and 6.3% for girls. In addition, nearly 75% of these youngsters displayed a comorbid diagnosis of depression and/or substance abuse (Kilpatrick et al., 2003). Thus, PTSD is a significant problem, and rates may be increasing (Perrin et al., 2000).

The prevalence of PTSD symptoms is appreciably greater in children who are exposed to life-threatening events than children who are not (Furr, Comer,

Edmunds, & Kendall, 2010). For example, nearly 40% of children exposed to the Buffalo Creek dam collapse in 1972 showed probable PTSD symptoms 2 years after the disaster (Fletcher, 2003). PTSD in children is also strongly correlated with degree of exposure. In children exposed to a schoolyard sniper attack, proximity to the attack was directly related to the risk of developing PTSD symptoms (Pynoos et al., 1987). Traumatized children frequently exhibit symptoms of disorders other than PTSD (e.g., depression), and children with other disorders may have PTSD as a comorbid diagnosis (Famularo, Fenton, Kinscherff, & Augustyn, 1996). The PTSD that occurs in children traumatized by fires, hurricanes, or chronic maltreatment may worsen or lead to disruptive behavior disorders (Amaya-Jackson & March, 1995).

Onset, Course, and Outcome

PTSD can strike at any time during childhood. Its course depends on the age of the child when the trauma occurred and the nature of the trauma. Since the traumatic experience is filtered cognitively and emotionally before it can be appraised as an extreme threat, how trauma is experienced depends on a number of factors. These include the child's developmental level and pre-disaster characteristics, such as level of anxiety and stress; cognitive appraisal of the threat, and coping style; characteristics of the disaster experience; and other factors (Furr et al., 2010; Weems et al., 2007). In one study of children age 6 years or younger with PTSD, it was found that their symptoms continued after 2 years even with treatment (Scheeringa, Zeanah, Myers, & Putnam, 2005). This finding raises the troubling possibility that very young children who are vulnerable to developing PTSD following trauma may have an increased vulnerability to a more chronic course of the disorder, perhaps related to the impact of trauma on the developing brain (Bremner, 2007). Despite these differences related to age and timing, exposure to horrific events is traumatic to nearly all children.

Longitudinal findings suggest that PTSD can become a chronic psychiatric disorder for some children, persisting for decades and in some cases for a lifetime (Fletcher, 2003). Children with chronic PTSD may display a developmental course marked by remissions and relapses. In a much less common delayed variant (Andrews, Brewin, Philpot, & Stewart, 2007), children exposed to a traumatic event may not exhibit symptoms until months or years later when a situation that resembles the original trauma triggers the onset of PTSD. For example, sexual violence during adulthood may trigger PTSD in a survivor of childhood sexual abuse.

Efforts to help children cope with their feelings and reactions following a disaster focus on helping the child acknowledge the experience and their reactions, and addressing pre- and post-disaster factors that are known to affect the child's adjustment. These include developmental level, general anxiety, coping style, and social support (La Greca, Silverman, Vernberg, & Roberts, 2002). Cognitive–behavior treatment involving imagined or real-life exposure to feared stimuli has been shown to be effective treatment in helping children with PTSD (AACAP, 2010; Silverman, Ortiz, et al., 2008).

SECTION SUMMARY

Posttraumatic and Acute Stress Disorders

- Youngsters with posttraumatic stress disorder (PTSD) display persistent frightening thoughts following overwhelming traumatic events such as threatened death or injury, natural disasters, or sexual abuse.
- Children with PTSD re-experience the traumatic event, avoid associated stimuli, and display symptoms of extreme arousal.
- An acute distress disorder is short-lived and emphasizes acute dissociative reactions, whereas PTSD has long-lasting effects.
- Several factors appear to be important in children's course of recovery from PTSD, including the nature of the traumatic event, preexisting child characteristics, and social support.

Associated Characteristics

Children with anxiety disorders display a number of associated characteristics, including cognitive disturbances, physical symptoms, social and emotional deficits, and depression.

Cognitive Disturbances

For most children, the development of cognitive maturity is associated with a reduction in fears. However, children with anxiety disorders continue to evaluate nonthreatening events as threatening, which suggests a disturbance in how they perceive and process information (Hadwin, Garner, & Perez-Olivas, 2006).

Intelligence and Academic Achievement

Children with anxiety disorders typically have normal intelligence, and there is little evidence of a strong relationship between anxiety and IQ. However, excessive anxiety may be related to deficits in specific areas of cognitive functioning, such as memory, attention, and speech or language. High levels of anxiety can interfere with academic performance. One study found that anxiety in the first grade predicted anxiety in the fifth grade and significantly influenced fifth-grade achievement (Ialongo, Edelsohn, Werthamer-Larsson, Crockett, & Kellam, 1995). The specific mechanisms involved could include anything from frequent absences to direct interference on cognitive tasks such as taking a test or solving a math problem. Youngsters with anxiety disorders, particularly generalized social anxiety, may also fail to reach their academic potential because they drop out of school prematurely (Van Ameringen, Mancini, & Farvolden, 2003).

Threat-Related Attentional Biases

Children with anxiety disorders selectively attend to information that may be potentially threatening or dangerous (e.g., an angry-looking face)—a tendency referred to as anxious vigilance or hypervigilance (Bar-Haim, Lamy, Pergamin, Bakersman-Kranenburg, & van IJzendoorn, 2007). The more severe the children's anxiety, the stronger is their attention to potentially threatening stimuli (Waters, Henry, Mogg, Bradley, & Pine, 2010). Anxious vigilance permits the child to avoid potentially threatening events by early detection, with minimal anxiety and effort. Although this may benefit the child in the short term, it has the unfortunate long-term effect of maintaining and heightening anxiety by interfering with the information-processing and coping responses needed to learn that many potentially threatening events are not so dangerous after all (Lonigan, Vasey, Phillips, & Hazen, 2004).

Cognitive Errors and Biases

When faced with a clear threat, both non-anxious and anxious children use rules to confirm information about danger (e.g., seeing a large dog approaching who is growling with bared teeth), and minimize information about safety (e.g., that the dog is on a leash). However, highly anxious children often do this in the face of less obvious threats, suggesting that their perceptions of threats activate danger-confirming thoughts (Muris, Rapee, Meesters, Schouten, & Geers, 2003). Children with conduct problems (see Chapter 6) also put a negative spin on ambiguous events. The main difference is that children with conduct problems select aggressive solutions in response to perceived threat, whereas anxious children choose avoidant solutions that emphasize personal safety (Chorpita, Albano, & Barlow, 1996). Children with anxiety disorders employ more maladaptive and less adaptive cognitive coping strategies in response to stressful life events than non-anxious children. Their cognitive coping strategies rely more on catastrophizing (e.g., thinking that something is far worse than it actually is) and rumination and less on positive reappraisal and planning (Legerstee, Garnefski, Jellesma, Verhulst, & Utens, 2010).

Although threat-related attentional and cognitive errors and biases are associated with anxiety in children, the precise nature of these errors and their role in causing anxiety has not yet been established (Alfano, Beidel, & Turner, 2002). One possibility is that the child's temperament may heighten attentional biases to threat and behavioral avoidance and by doing so promote the acquisition of fears (Field, 2006). In general, children with anxiety disorders see themselves as having less control over anxiety-related events than do other children. However, different types and degrees of cognitive errors may occur in children with different anxiety disorders—for example, inflated responsibility and overestimation of threat in those with OCD (Taylor & Jang, 2011).

Physical Symptoms

As we have seen, many children with anxiety disorders have somatic symptoms, such as stomachaches or headaches. These complaints are more common in youngsters with GAD, PD, and SAD than in youngsters with a specific phobia. Somatic complaints are also more frequent in adolescents than in younger children, and in children who display school refusal. One study found that 90% of youngsters with anxiety disorders experience at least one sleep-related problem, most commonly insomnia, nightmares, and reluctance/refusal to sleep alone (Alfano, Ginsburg, & Kingery, 2007). Some may experience *nocturnal panic*, an abrupt waking in a state of extreme anxiety that is similar to a daytime panic attack. Nocturnal panic attacks usually occur in adolescents who suffer from PD. They prevent a return to sleep and are vividly recalled the next day (Craske & Rowe, 1997).

It is of interest to note that higher levels of anxiety in adolescence are associated with reduced accidents and accidental death in early adulthood, but higher rates of non-accidental death in later life. High levels of anxiety in adolescence may reduce risky behaviors and by doing so lead to short-term survival benefits, but anxiety takes its toll over time by increasing the long-term risk of serious health problems (Lee, Wadsworth, & Hotopf, 2006).

Social and Emotional Deficits

Since many anxious children expect danger in social situations, it's not surprising that they experience interaction difficulties with other children, including siblings (Fox, Barrett, & Shortt, 2002). In fact, they display low social performance and high social anxiety, and their parents, teachers, and peers are likely to view them as anxious and socially maladjusted (Chansky & Kendall, 1997; Krain & Kendall, 2000). These children, particularly those with a social phobia, may also be less popular with their peers (Verduin & Kendall, 2008). Compared to their peers, children with anxiety disorders are more likely to see themselves as shy and socially withdrawn, and to report low self-esteem, loneliness, and difficulties in starting and maintaining friendships.

Some difficulties with peers and siblings may be related to specific deficits in understanding emotion, particularly in hiding and changing emotions (Southam-Gerow & Kendall, 2000) and in differentiating between thoughts and feelings (Alfano et al., 2002). Findings regarding how children with anxiety disorders are viewed by other children are mixed (Kendall, Panichelli-Mindel, Sugarman, & Callahan, 1997). Childhood anxiety disorders are most likely associated with diminished peer popularity when they coexist with depression.

Anxiety and Depression

We have already discussed co-occurring disorders in relation to each anxiety disorder, and it is important to keep in mind that a child's risk for accompanying disorders will vary with the type of anxiety disorder. GAD, SAD, and social phobia are more commonly associated with depression than is specific phobia (Watson, 2009). Depression is also diagnosed more often in children with multiple anxiety disorders and in children who show severe impairments in their everyday functioning (Woodward & Fergusson, 2001).

The strong and undeniable relationship between anxiety and depression in children and adolescents merits further discussion (Garber & Weersing, 2010). Does anxiety lead to depression? Are anxiety and depression the same disorder with different clinical features? Are they on a continuum of severity? Are they distinct disorders with different causes but some overlapping features?

Children with anxiety and depression are older at age of presentation than children with only anxiety, and in most cases symptoms of anxiety both precede and predict symptoms of depression (Avenevoli, Knight, Kessler, & Merikangas, 2008). Symptoms of anxiety and depression may form a single indistinguishable dimension in younger children, but are increasingly distinct in older children and children with at least one diagnosable disorder (Cole, Truglio, & Peeke, 1997).

The concept of negative affectivity is useful in understanding the nature of the link between anxiety and depression (Anderson & Hope, 2008). **Negative affectivity** is a persistent negative mood, as reflected in nervousness, sadness, anger, and guilt. In contrast, **positive affectivity** refers to a persistent positive mood that includes states such as joy, enthusiasm, and energy. Negative affectivity is related to both anxiety and depression, whereas positive affectivity is negatively correlated with depression but is independent of anxiety symptoms and diagnoses (Lonigan, Phillips, & Hooe, 2003). In general, children with anxiety do not differ from children with depression in their negative affect, which suggests that a general underlying dimension of negative affectivity is common to both anxiety and depression (Chorpita, 2002). Rather, the difference between children who are anxious and children who are depressed may be the lower positive affectivity in those who are depressed. It has also been proposed that a third construct, *physiological hyperarousal* (e.g., somatic tension, shortness of breath, dizziness) may be unique to children who are anxious. Although this hypothesis has received some support, particularly with respect to panic disorder, fewer studies have investigated this construct and findings have been inconsistent (Anderson & Hope, 2008).

Consistent with the idea of anxiety and depression as distinct dimensions with different developmental pathways are findings that some of the predictors and environmental influences associated with anxiety are different from those of depression. In terms of predictors, social and externalizing problems predict later anxiety disorders, whereas internalizing symptoms are generally better predictors of mood disorders (Roza, Hofstra, van der Ende, & Verhulst, 2003). In terms of environmental influences, threatening life events such as physical jeopardy or the risk of losing a parent are related to symptoms of anxiety but not depression. In contrast, life events involving actual loss and stress, such as the death of a family member or family stress, are associated with depression but not anxiety (Eley & Stevenson, 2000).

SECTION SUMMARY

Associated Characteristics

- Children with anxiety disorders display deficits in specific areas of cognitive functioning, such as memory, attention, and speech and language.
- They selectively attend to information that may be potentially threatening, a tendency referred to as anxious vigilance.
- These children often have somatic symptoms, such as stomachaches or headaches, and may experience sleep disturbances.
- Children with anxiety disorders report being socially withdrawn and lonely, and may be viewed by others as socially maladjusted.
- There is a strong and undeniable relationship between anxiety and depression in children and adolescents. The difference between children who are anxious and those who are depressed may be the greater positive affectivity in those who are anxious.

Gender, Ethnicity, and Culture

Studies across ethnicities and cultures have found a preponderance of anxiety disorders in girls during childhood and adolescence (Anderson & Mayes, 2010; McLean & Anderson, 2009). By age 6, twice as many girls as boys have experienced symptoms of anxiety, and this discrepancy persists through childhood, adolescence, and young adulthood (Roza et al., 2003; see ● Figure 7.2). The fact that girls are more likely than boys to report anxiety may contribute to this variation, although how much is not known (Wren et al., 2007). For adolescents with anxiety, the differences between genders cannot be accounted for solely by psychosocial factors such as stress, self-perceived social competence, or emotional reliance. This suggests that female vulnerability to anxiety may also be related to genetic influences and related neurobiological differences, as well as to varying social roles and experiences (Lewinsohn, Gotlib, Lewinsohn, Seeley, & Allen, 1998).

One study of gender role orientation in boys and girls with anxiety disorders found that self-reported masculinity was related to lower overall levels of fearfulness and fewer specific fears of failure and criticism, medical fears, and fears of the unknown (Ginsburg & Silverman, 2000). In contrast, no relation was found between self-reported femininity and fearfulness. This suggests that gender role orientation, especially masculinity, may play a role in the development and persistence of fearfulness in children.

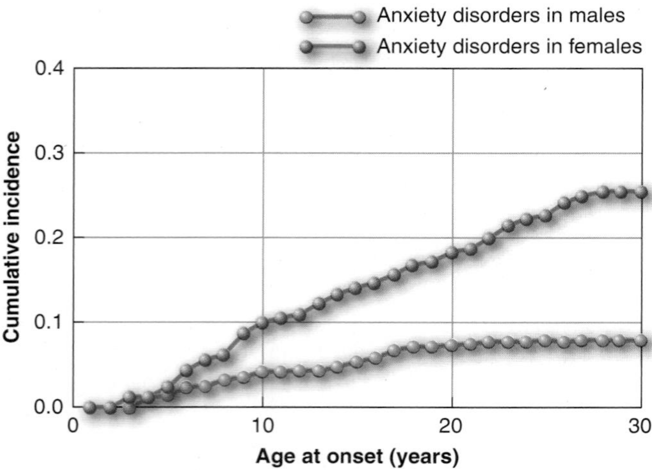

● **FIGURE 7.2** | Cumulative incidence of anxiety disorders in females and males.

Figure 1 from Stable Prediction of Mood and Anxiety Disorders Based on Behavioral and Emotional Problems in Childhood: A 14-Year Follow-Up During Childhood, Adolescence, and Young Adulthood Sabine J. Roza, M.Sc.; Marijke B. Hofstra, M.D.; Jan van der Ende, M.S.; Frank C. Verhulst, M.D. Am J Psychiatry 2003;160:2116–2121. Adapted with permission from the American Journal of Psychiatry, (Copyright © 2003). American Psychiatric Association.

There is general support for a higher prevalence of anxiety in ethnic minority groups in the United States. However, symptom expression, biological factors, and family processes may differ somewhat by ethnic group (Anderson & Mayes, 2010). Studies comparing the number and nature of fears in both African American and white youngsters have found the two groups to be quite similar (Ginsburg & Silverman, 1996). However, African American children generally report more symptoms of anxiety than do white children (Cole, Martin, Peeke, Henderson, & Harwell, 1998), although white children report more symptoms of social phobia and fewer symptoms of separation anxiety than do African American children (Compton, Nelson, & March, 2000). It has been found that symptoms of anxiety are higher in children of parents with fewer years of formal education, suggesting that variations in child anxiety across racial/ethnic groups may also be accounted for by group differences in parental education (Wren et al., 2007).

Among children who are referred for anxiety disorders, whites are more likely to present with school refusal and higher severity ratings, while African Americans are more likely to have a history of PTSD (Last & Perrin, 1993). Although anxiety may be similar in the two groups, patterns of referral, help-seeking behaviors, diagnoses, and treatment processes are likely to differ. For example, African American parents who need help with their child's OCD symptoms may be more likely to turn to members of their informal social network, such as clergy or medical personnel, than to mental health professionals (Hatch, Friedman, & Paradis, 1996). Their family members are also less likely to be drawn into the child's OCD symptoms. Although ethnicity is not related to outcomes in the treatment of anxiety disorders, it may be related to premature termination of treatment (Kendall & Flannery-Schroeder, 1998).

Research comparing phobic and anxiety disorders in Hispanic and white children has found marked similarities in age at intake, gender, primary diagnosis, proportion of school refusal, and proportion with more than one diagnosis. Hispanic children are more likely to have a primary diagnosis of SAD. Hispanic parents also rate their children as more fearful than do white parents (Ginsburg & Silverman, 1996). Few studies have examined anxiety disorders in Native American children. Prevalence estimates from one study of Native American youth in Appalachia (mostly Cherokee) indicate rates of anxiety disorders similar to those for white youth, with the most common disorder for both groups being SAD. Rates of SAD were slightly higher for Native American youth, especially girls (Costello, Farmer, Angold, Burns, & Erkanli, 1997).

The experience of anxiety is pervasive across cultures. Although cross-cultural research into anxiety disorders in children is limited (Lewis-Fernández et al., 2010), specific fears in children have been studied and documented in virtually every culture. Developmental fears (e.g., a fear of loud noises or of separation from the primary caregiver) occur in children of all cultures at about the same age. The details may vary from culture to culture, but the number of fears in children tends to be highly similar across cultures, as does the presence of gender differences in pattern and content.

Nevertheless, the expression, developmental course, and interpretation of symptoms of anxiety are affected by culture (Ingman, Ollendick, & Akande, 1999). For example, in relation to panic-like symptoms, higher rates are found for paresthesias (feeling of tingling or numbing of the skin) among African Americans, trembling among Caribbean Latinos, dizziness among several East Asian Groups, and fear of dying among Arabs and African Americans (Craske et al., 2010). Native Hawaiian adolescents display rates of OCD that are twice as high as other ethnic groups (Guerrero et al., 2003). When attempting to explain such differences, it is important to keep in mind that genetic and/or environmental risk factors may play a role.

Cultural differences in traditions, beliefs, and practices about children can affect the occurrence of anxiety and related symptoms, and how they are perceived by others and experienced by the child (Wang & Ollendick, 2001). For example, James, a 16-year-old Chinese American boy, had been to multiple doctors throughout his life for treatment for stomach cramps, nausea, and hot flushes in the morning before going to school and also in anticipation of social interactions. James had a social phobia but both he and his family felt his problem was physical and wanted to focus only on his physical symptoms in therapy and not his subjective feelings of anxiety.

Increased levels of fear in children are found in cultures that favor inhibition, compliance, and obedience (Ollendick, Yang, King, Dong, & Akande, 1996). Chinese cultural values such as human malleability and self-cultivation may heighten levels of general distress and specific fears (e.g., social evaluative) (Dong, Yang, & Ollendick, 1994). In addition, Chinese adolescents report higher levels of social anxiety than American youth, including anxiety about humiliation and rejection and public performance fears (Yao et al., 2007). This is likely related to their collectivistic versus individualistic value orientation. Children in Thailand display more symptoms of anxiety, such as shyness and somatic complaints, than children in the United States (Weisz, Weiss, Suwanlert, & Chaiyasit, 2003). Perhaps the most accurate way to analyze cultural differences in anxiety is using Weisz and colleagues' (2003, p. 384) **behavior lens principle**, which states that child psychopathology reflects a mix of actual child behavior and the lens through which it is viewed by others in a child's culture.

SECTION SUMMARY

Gender, Ethnicity, and Culture

- About twice as many girls as boys experience symptoms of anxiety, and this difference is present in children as young as 6 years of age.
- Children's ethnicity and culture may affect the expression and developmental course of fear and anxiety, how anxiety is perceived by others, and expectations for treatment.

THEORIES AND CAUSES

Over the years, numerous theories and causes have been proposed to explain the origins of fear and anxiety in children, including brain disease, mental strain, parenting practices, conditioning, and instinct (Treffers & Silverman, 2001). The recent study of fear and anxiety in children dates back to Freud's (1909/1953) classic account of the case of Little Hans; Watson and Rayner's (1920) conditioning of a fear in Little Albert; and Bowlby's (1973) monumental works on early attachment and loss. Although each early theory has been debated since it was introduced, all have had a lasting impact on how we think about anxiety in children.

Early Theories

Classical psychoanalytic theory views anxieties and phobias as defenses against unconscious conflicts rooted in the child's early upbringing. Certain drives, memories, and feelings are so painful that they must be repressed and displaced onto an external object, or symbolically associated with the real source of anxiety. Thus, anxiety and phobias will protect the child against unconscious wishes and drives. Freud's most famous case of a phobia was Little Hans, a 5-year-old who feared horses. According to Freud, Little Hans unconsciously felt that he was in competition with his father for his mother's love and feared his father's revenge (the Oedipus complex). Hans's fear was repressed and displaced onto horses, a symbol of his castrating father. Having something specific to fear was less stressful for Hans than suffering from anxiety without apparent cause.

Behavioral and learning theories held that fears and anxieties were learned through classical conditioning. In the case of Little Albert, Watson and Rayner (1920) created what looked very much like a rat phobia (see Chapter 1, Box 1.3), and claimed that fears were learned by association. Operant conditioning has been cited in explaining why fears persist once they are established. The principle is that behavior will continue if it is reinforced or rewarded. Once something has become frightening, there is the automatic reward of instant relief whenever the child avoids the feared object or situation. Thus, through negative reinforcement, avoidance of a feared stimulus becomes a learned response, which serves to maintain the child's fear even when not exposed to it. The combination of classical and operant conditioning in the learning and maintenance of fears is called the **two-factor theory** (Mowrer, 1947). Social learning theories also showed that children could learn fears through observation of others, without experiencing the feared stimulus directly (Bandura & Walters, 1963).

Bowlby's *theory of attachment* (1973) presents a very different explanation for children's fears. According to attachment theory, fearfulness in children is biologically rooted in the emotional attachment needed for survival. Infants must be close to their caregivers if their physical and emotional needs are to be met. Attachment behaviors, such as crying, fear of strangers, and distress, represent active efforts by the infant to maintain or restore proximity to the caregiver. Separation gradually becomes more tolerable as the child gets older. However, children who are separated from their mothers too early, who are treated harshly, or who fail to have their needs met consistently, show atypical reactions to separation and reunion. Early insecure attachments become internalized and determine how children see the world and other people. Children who view the environment as undependable, unavailable, hostile, or threatening may later develop anxiety and avoidance behavior.

No single theory is sufficient to explain the various anxiety disorders in children, the differences among children in the expression of these disorders, or the variations in outcomes over time. It is important to recognize that different anxiety disorders may require different causal models. In contrast to early theories, current models of anxiety emphasize the importance of interacting biological and environmental influences (Gregory & Eley, 2007; McClure & Pine, 2006). This approach takes into account brain development and psychopathology and integrates this knowledge with research on genetic variation and environmental effects (Monk, 2008). Genetic vulnerability reflects a disposition toward broad anxiety-related traits, whereas early environmental risk may influence developing neural circuitry as well as the specific types of anxieties that emerge. In the sections that follow, we consider the role of temperament, genetic and family risk, neurobiological factors, and family influences.

Temperament

> Once I visited with a group of preschool children from the campus day care center when I noticed a little Caucasian boy slowly sneaking up behind a little Chinese girl who was walking in front of him. The boy came to within 2 feet of the girl, his presence still undetected, stopped, and then screamed at the top of his lungs, "BOO!!" Even though I saw it coming, the intensity of the boy's scream startled me a bit. However, much to my surprise, the intended victim showed hardly any reaction. Instead, this pint-sized version of Wonder Woman paused for a moment, slowly turned, looked at the boy (who appeared dumbfounded by this unexpected display of fearlessness), and with a relaxed smile on her face, calmly said, "I'm used to that sort of thing." She then turned and continued on her way, with the little boy trailing behind like a puppy dog (I think he was in love).

The lesson of this story is that children (like adults) differ markedly in their psychological and physical reactions to novel or unexpected events, perhaps because of their wiring, gender, cultural background, prior experience (in this example, perhaps with a pesky little brother?), or a combination of factors. How would you react if someone snuck up behind you and yelled "BOO!!"? Readiness to react to unfamiliar or discrepant events is one distinguishing feature of all mammals. Orienting, attending, vigilance, wariness, and motor readiness in response to the unfamiliar are important mechanisms for survival. From an evolutionary perspective, abnormal fears and anxieties reflect variation among infants in their initial behavioral reactions to novelty (Kagan, 2008).

This variation is partly the result of inherited differences in the neurochemistry of brain structures thought to play an important role in detecting discrepant events. These brain structures include the amygdala, which has a primary function to react to unfamiliar or unexpected events (Fitzgerald, Angstadt, Jelsone, Nathan, & Phan, 2006), and its projections to the motor system, the anterior cingulate and frontal cortex, the hypothalamus, and the sympathetic nervous system. Children with a high threshold to novelty, such as the little Chinese girl in the story, are presumed to be at low risk for developing anxiety disorders. Other children (about 15% to 20%) are born with a low threshold to becoming overexcited and to withdrawing in response to novel stimulation as infants, a tendency to be fearful and anxious as toddlers, and a tendency to be unusually shy or withdrawn in novel or unfamiliar situations as young children. This type of temperament is called **behavioral inhibition (BI)**, an enduring trait for some and a predisposing factor for the development of later anxiety disorders, particularly social anxiety disorder (Chronis-Tuscano et al., 2009; Kagan, 2008). In a recent study, adolescents who were behaviorally inhibited as toddlers and young children showed social withdrawal in adolescence, and this relationship was moderated by a heightened attention bias to threat (Perez-Edgar et al., 2010).

However, the road from BI during infancy and childhood to a later anxiety disorder is neither direct nor straightforward. Different risk factors and pathways to adolescent social anxiety disorders have been identified—one, for example, based on gender and early BI, and another based on exposure to early maternal stress (Essex, Klein, Slattery, Goldsmith, & Kalin, 2010). Although BI may contribute to later anxiety disorders, this is not an inevitable outcome (Prior, Smart, Sanson, & Oberklaid, 2000). Such an outcome may depend on whether the inhibited child grows up in an environment that fosters this tendency (Kagan, Snidman, & Arcus, 1992). For example, a parent's use of firm limits that teaches children how to cope with stress may reduce their risk for anxiety. In contrast, it is possible that well-meaning but overprotective parents who shield their sensitive child from stressful events may inadvertently cause timidity to persist by preventing the child from confronting fears. By not confronting them, they cannot eliminate them. Such tendencies in the parents of inhibited children may be common. Thus, inhibited children may be at high risk not only because of their inborn temperament, but also because of their elevated risk of exposure to anxious, overprotective parenting.

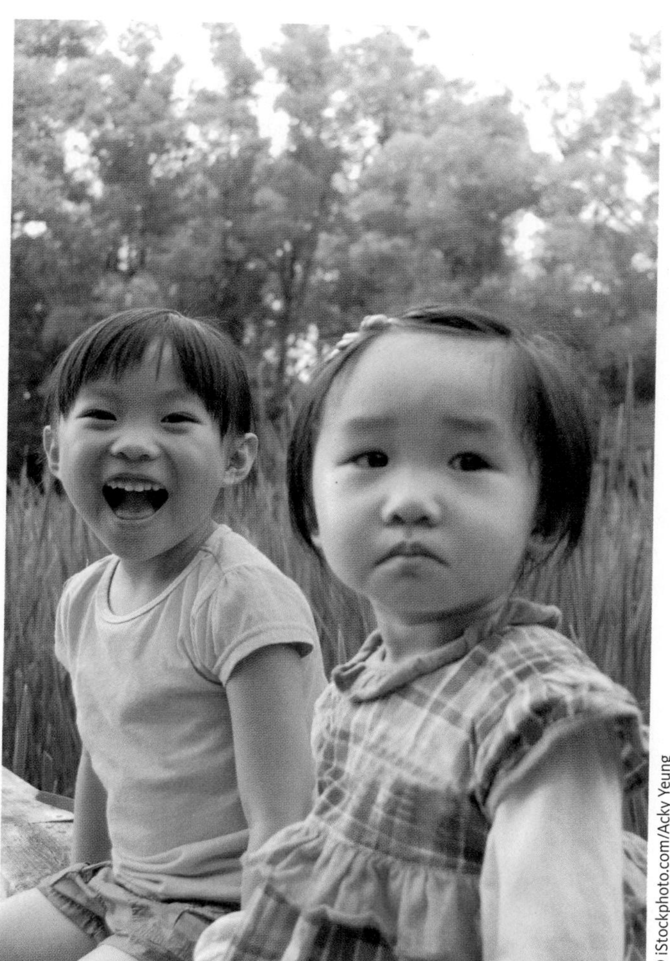

© iStockphoto.com/Acky Yeung

Early differences in temperament may predispose some children to develop anxiety disorders

Family and Genetic Risk

I was always considered shy . . . Now I see my daughter is just like I was. Did I do something to cause this?

—From Beidel and Turner (1998)

Family and twin studies suggest that children's general tendencies to be inhibited, tense, or fearful are inherited (Gregory & Eley, 2007). In addition, both shared and non-shared environmental influences have been shown to play a substantial role. Two lines of evidence suggest that anxiety disorders run in families. First, parents of children with anxiety disorders have increased rates of current and past anxiety disorders (Cooper, Fearn, Willets, Seabrook, & Parkinson, 2006). Second, children of parents with anxiety disorders have an increased risk for anxiety disorders (Merikangas, Avenevoli, Dierker, & Grillon, 1999). In general, family studies consistently show a relationship between an anxiety disorder in the child and anxiety disorders in first-degree relatives. Children of parents with anxiety disorders are about 5 times more likely to have anxiety disorders than are children of parents without anxiety disorders (Beidel & Turner, 1997). However, they are not necessarily the same disorders (Mancini, van Ameringen, Szatmari, Fugere, & Boyle, 1996). Nearly 70% of children of parents with agoraphobia meet diagnostic criteria for disorders such as anxiety and depression, and report more fear and anxiety and less control over various risks than do children of comparison parents. However, the fears of parents with agoraphobia and the fears of their children are no more closely aligned than those of non-anxious parents and their children, once again supporting the view that for most anxiety disorders it may be a general predisposition for anxiety that is perpetuated in families (Capps, Sigman, Sena, & Henker, 1996).

Twin studies suggest that about one-third of the variance in childhood anxiety symptoms is accounted for by genetic influences (Eley, 1999). However, identical twin pairs do not typically have the same types of anxiety disorders. This is consistent with the view that a disposition to become anxious is inherited, with the form of the disorder shaped by environmental influences. The amount of genetic influence is highest for obsessive—compulsive behaviors and shyness/inhibition (Taylor, Jang, & Asmundson, 2010). Although moderate genetic influence has also been reported for specific fears and separation anxiety in young children (Bolton et al., 2006), environmental factors such as maternal psychiatric problems, ineffective parenting, or poverty seem to play a relatively stronger role (Muris & Merckelbach, 2001).

Specific gene studies have focused on variants in genes related to the serotonin system (Lau et al., 2009). These variants have been associated with behavioral inhibition, particularly among those who are also exposed to environmental risk (Lau & Pine, 2008). They are of interest because serotonin has been implicated in anxiety and is the site of action for widely used antianxiety and antidepressant medications (Lesch et al., 1996). In addition to serotonin markers, other candidate genes that have received attention are those involved in the dopamine system and in mediating the response to stress through brain systems implicated in anxious and avoidant behavior (Smoller et al., 2003). The most consistent findings thus far have linked genes to broad anxiety-related traits such as behavioral inhibition. Little research currently exists to support a strong direct link between specific genetic markers and *specific* types of anxiety disorders. Rather, it appears that small contributions from multiple genes seem related to anxiety when certain psychological and social factors are also present. Further studies into G × E interactions for anxiety are needed (Gregory & Eley, 2007). Future research examining the ways in which multiple genetic factors interact with multiple sources of environmental adversity, may help to overcome the unreliability of findings in studies that attempt to identify interactions between a single gene and a single measure of environmental adversity (Fergusson, Horwood, Miller, & Kennedy, 2011).

Neurobiological Factors

No single structure or neurotransmitter controls the entire anxiety response system. Rather, several interrelated systems operate together in complex ways to produce anxiety. The parts of the brain most often connected with anxiety involve neural circuits related to potential threat and fear conditioning—the hypothalamic—pituitary–adrenal (HPA) axis; the limbic system (amygdala, hippocampus), which acts as a mediator between the brain stem and the cortex; the ventrolateral prefrontal cortex; and other cortical and subcortical structures (Monk, 2008; Pine, 2007). Potential danger signals are monitored and sensed by the more primitive brain stem, which then relays the signals to the higher cortical centers through the limbic system. As we discussed in Chapter 6, this brain system is referred to as the behavioral inhibition system and is believed to be overactive in children with anxiety disorders. As we have discussed, anxious individuals display threat biases at multiple levels of information processing (e.g., attention to threat, fear learning). It has been proposed that abnormalities in learning safety cues in childhood may establish threat-related appraisal biases early in development, which may then lead to chronic anxiety disorders in adulthood (Britton, Lissek, Grillon, Norcross, & Pine, 2011). Consistent with this, healthy teens have greater difficulty distinguishing between threat and safety cues than adults, relying more on areas of the brain involved in basic fear responses (hippocampus, right amygdala) than those areas involved in more reasoned judgment about what is safe or not (pre-frontal cortex) (Lau et al., 2011). This may be one reason why teens (and youth with anxiety disorders) generally report more pervasive worries and are more vulnerable to stress-related problems.

Particularly noteworthy are findings that the regulation of the brain circuits underlying threat and fear conditioning can be shaped by early life stress, thus providing a possible biological basis for an increased vulnerability to later stress and the development of fearfulness and anxiety disorders (Heim, Shugart, Craighead, & Nemeroff, 2010). As we discussed in Chapter 2 (Box 2.2), activation of the HPA axis is closely related to the regulation of stress and fear and involves the release of cortisol needed to meet a challenging situation. Pathological anxiety has been related to elevations of cortisol secretion, reflected in an exaggeration of normal HPA reactions or a failure of the HPA axis response to habituate to repeated exposure to the same stressor (van der Vegt, van der Ende, Huizink, Verhulst, & Tiemeier, 2010). Prolonged exposure to elevated levels of cortisol as a result of early stress or trauma may have neurotoxic effects on the developing brain—for example, reduced cerebral volume or changes in the volume of the hippocampus (Weems & Silverman, 2008). Early life stress may also produce lasting hyper-reactivity of corticotrophin-releasing factor (CRF) systems, which are closely related to the HPA axis, as well as alterations in other neurotransmitter systems that create a heightened response to stress (Pine, 2003).

Brain scans of children with GAD and PTSD suggest abnormalities (larger volume) in brain regions associated with social information processing and fear conditioning (amygdala and superior temporal gyrus) (De Bellis, Keshavan, Frustaci, et al., 2002; De Bellis, Keshavan, Shifflett, et al., 2002). These studies also report more pronounced right—left hemisphere brain asymmetries in children with GAD and PTSD, which have also been reported in children who are behaviorally inhibited or anxious/depressed (Kagan & Snidman, 1999). As we have discussed, an over-excitable amygdala has been strongly implicated in children who are behaviorally inhibited and youngsters with anxiety disorders (McClure et al., 2007b; Schwartz, Wright, Shin, Kagan, & Rauch, 2003). The amygdala detects and organizes reactions to natural dangers by quickly scanning incoming stimuli that are novel and/or potentially threatening. Interestingly, children with anxiety disorders who have higher levels of pretreatment amygdala activation in response to emotional information show a better response to both cognitive behavior therapy and drug treatment (McClure et al., 2007a). In addition to the brain regions we have discussed, neuroimaging studies have also suggested the importance of other brain regions for specific anxiety disorders such as OCD (Friedlander & Desrocher, 2006; Hajcak, Franklin, Foa, & Simons, 2008).

The neurotransmitter system that has been implicated most often in anxiety disorders is the γ-aminobutyric acid—ergic (GABA-ergic) system. Neuropeptides are generally viewed as anticipatory stress modulators whose abnormal regulation may play a role in anxiety disorders (Sallee & Greenawald, 1995). A group of neurons known as the locus ceruleus ("deep blue place") is a major brain source for norepinephrine, an inhibitory neurotransmitter. Overactivation of this region is presumed to lead to a fear response, and underactivity to inattention, impulsivity, and risk-taking. Abnormalities of these systems may be related to anxiety states in children (Sallee & Greenawald, 1995).

New findings using brain scans have increased our understanding of the neurobiological mechanisms in anxiety disorders. Although the situation is rapidly changing, research using neuroimaging with children is limited and difficult to conduct. Nevertheless, the brain regions we have described have been consistently implicated in fear and anxiety. While acknowledging that pathways are likely to be complex, the plasticity of these neural systems during early development makes research into possible mechanisms a priority for both understanding and preventing future anxiety disorders in children.

Family Factors

As we have discussed, anxiety runs in families, and the relationship between family factors and childhood anxiety disorders has generated considerable attention (Knappe et al., 2010). Among the many family factors of interest are specific parenting practices, including the parent's use of discipline and modeling of anxious behaviors; broader family dimensions such as family functioning as a whole, parenting stress, and the marital relationship; the parent—child attachment relationship; and the beliefs that parents hold about their child's anxious behavior (Bögels & Brechman-Toussaint, 2006).

Parenting practices such as rejection, overcontrol, overprotection, and modeling of anxious behaviors have all been identified as contributors to childhood anxiety symptoms and disorders (Edwards, Rapee, & Kennedy, 2010; McLeod, Wood, & Weisz, 2007). Although most research has focused on mothers, fathers also play a role, and both parents may contribute to their child's anxiety in ways that are specific to their different parenting roles (Bögels & Phares, 2008). Parents of anxious children are often described as overinvolved, intrusive, or limiting of their child's independence.

Observations of interactions between 9- to 12-year-old children with anxiety disorders and their parents found that parents of children with anxiety disorders were rated as granting less autonomy to their children than other parents; the children rated their mothers and fathers as being less accepting (Siqueland, Kendall, & Steinberg, 1996). Other studies have found that mothers of children previously identified as behaviorally inhibited or anxious are more likely to be critical and to be less positive when interacting with their children (Whaley, Pinto, & Sigman, 1999). Emotional overinvolvement by parents is also associated with an increased occurrence of SAD in their children (Hirshfeld, Biederman, & Rosenbaum, 1997). These findings generally support the association between excessive parental control and anxiety disorders in children, although the strength of this association appears to be small and the causal mechanisms and directionality of effect are not yet known (McLeod et al., 2007). A recent study found a relationship between mothers' use of extreme control and higher levels of child anxiety. However, the overlap between high child anxiety and maternal control was mainly due to shared genetic factors. This suggests that mothers not only influence their children's anxiety, but also that children with high levels of anxiety may elicit extreme maternal control (Eley, Napolitano, Lau, & Gregory, 2010).

Another study looked at the broader relationship between *family functioning* and child anxiety (Pagani, Japel, Vaillancourt, Côté, & Tremblay, 2008). The dimensions of family functioning that were of interest included problem solving, communication, family roles, affective involvement, and emotional responsiveness. It was found that prolonged exposure to high doses of family dysfunction was associated with the most extreme trajectories of anxious behavior during middle childhood. This association was found to exist over and above the influence of other aspects of family dysfunction such as marital transitions, SES, family size, and parent's depressive symptoms. In general, findings in support of an association between family functioning and anxiety disorders are suggestive, but it is unclear whether family dysfunction relates specifically to anxiety disorders (Bögels & Brechman-Toussaint, 2006).

Not only are parents of children with anxiety disorders more controlling than other parents, they also have different expectations. For example, when they thought the child was being asked to give a videotaped speech, mothers of children with anxiety disorders expected their children to become upset and had low expectations for their children's coping (Kortlander, Kendall, & Panichelli-Mindel, 1997). It is likely that parental attitudes shape—and are shaped by—interactions with the child, during which parent and child revise their expectations and behavior as a result of feedback from each other (Barrett, Rapee, Dadds, & Ryan, 1996). This process may impact not only on the child's behavior, but may also play a role in the development of information processing biases in the child (Hadwin et al., 2006).

Parental anxiety disorder alone may not lead to an elevated risk of anxiety disorders in children of high- or middle-SES parents, but may increase risk in children of low-SES parents (Beidel & Turner, 1997). These findings are consistent with the idea that some children have a genetic vulnerability to anxiety, which may be actualized in the context of specific life circumstances, such as the stressful conditions that are often present in low-SES families. Children with an initial disposition to develop high levels of fear may be especially vulnerable to the type of power-assertive parenting often used by low-SES parents. These children may be particularly sensitive to punishment and, when exposed to physical discipline, may become hypervigilant to hostile cues, and develop a tendency to react defensively or aggressively (Colder, Lochman, & Wells, 1997).

Insecure attachments may be a risk factor for the development of later anxiety disorders (Brumariu & Kerns, 2010; Dadds, 2002), and are associated with anxiety disorder symptoms in early adolescence (Muris & Meesters, 2002). Mothers with anxiety disorders have been found to have insecure attachments themselves, and 80% of their children are also insecurely attached (Manassis, Bradley, Goldberg, Hood, & Swinson, 1994). Infants who are ambivalently attached have more anxiety diagnoses during childhood and adolescence than infants who are securely attached (Bernstein et al., 1996), although a clear link between specific types of insecure attachments and specific anxiety disorders has not been established. Although it is a risk factor, insecure attachment may be a nonspecific factor because many infants with insecure attachments develop disorders other than anxiety (e.g., depression, disruptive behavior disorder), and many do not develop disorders.

Clearly articulated causal models for anxiety disorders in children are just beginning to emerge (Muris, 2007). In the absence of an integrative model, we present the possible developmental pathway shown in ● Figure 7.3. Children with an inborn predisposition to be anxious or fearful who sense that the world is not a safe place may develop a psychological vulnerability to anxiety. Once anxiety occurs, it feeds on itself. The anxiety and avoidance continue long after the stressors that provoked them are gone. Keep in mind that many children with anxiety disorders do not continue to experience problems as adults. Therefore, it will be important to identify risk and protective factors that would explain these differences in outcomes (Pine & Grun, 1999). In addition, this illustration is an oversimplification, since different developmental pathways are likely for children with different anxiety disorders, or even for those with the same disorder.

SECTION SUMMARY

Theories and Causes

- No single theory can explain the many different forms of anxiety disorder in children.
- Early theories viewed anxiety as a defense against unconscious conflicts, a learned response, or an adaptive mechanism needed for survival.
- Some children are born with a tendency to become overexcited and to withdraw in response to novel stimulation (behavioral inhibition)—an enduring trait for some, and a possible risk factor for later anxiety disorders.
- Family and twin studies suggest a moderate biological vulnerability to anxiety disorders.
- Anxiety is associated with specific neurobiological processes. The potential underlying vulnerability of children at risk for anxiety is most likely localized to brain circuits involving the brain stem, the limbic system, the HPA axis, and the frontal cortex.
- Anxiety is associated with a number of family factors including specific parenting practices, family functioning, the parent—child attachment, and parents' beliefs about their children's anxious behavior.
- Children with anxiety disorders will likely display features that are shared across the various disorders, as well as other features that are unique to their particular disorder.

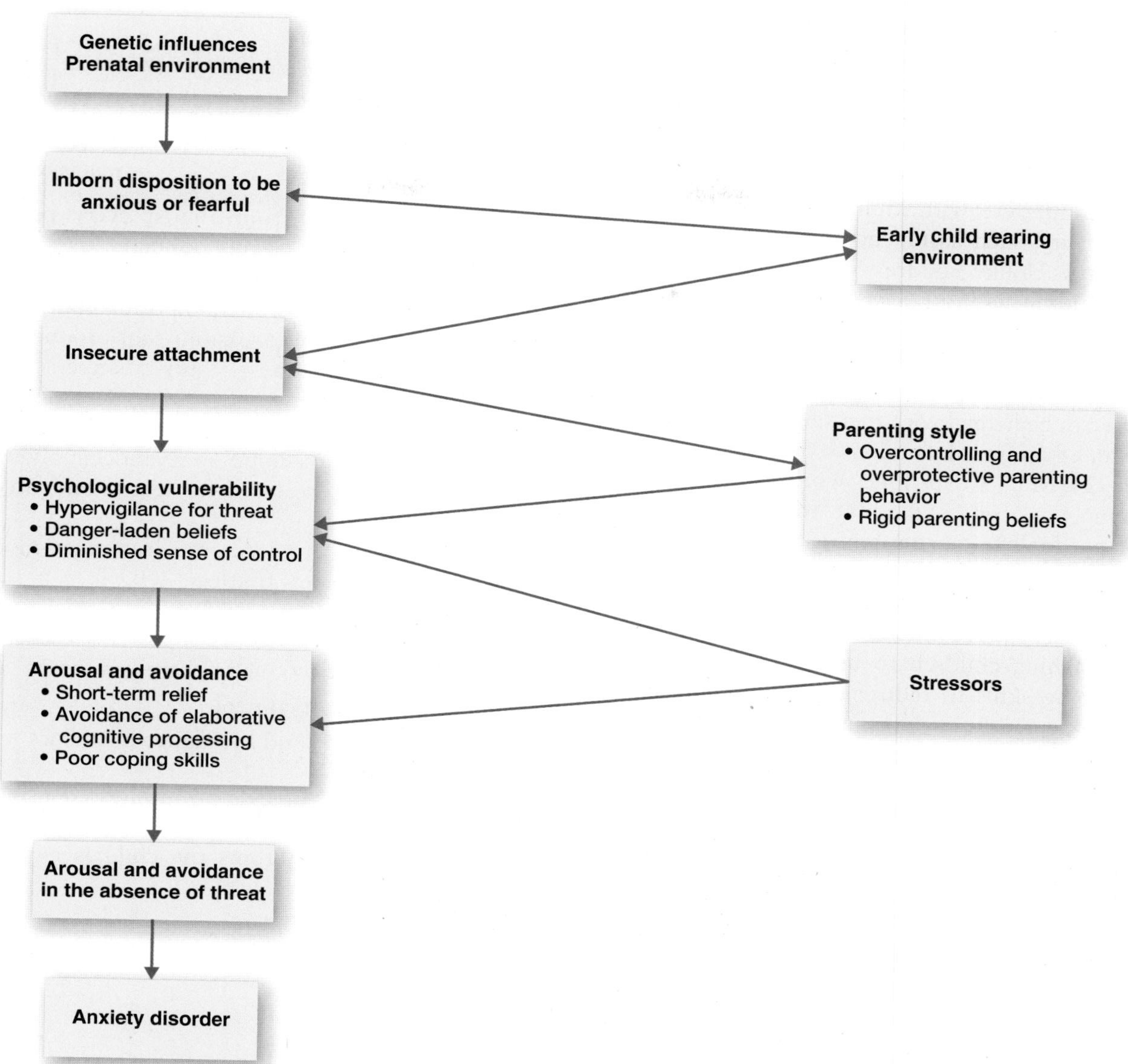

● **FIGURE 7.3** | A possible developmental pathway for anxiety disorders.

Treatment and Prevention

CANDY

Afraid to Swallow

Candy, age 11, was hospitalized for dehydration. Her voice trembled and her eyes widened with fear as she described being rushed to the emergency room in an ambulance after she fainted. She was embarrassed that something as simple as eating was so hard for her, but it terrified her to even think about trying. Candy detested being thin, and desperately wanted to be "just like other kids." After talking with Candy, it was clear that she dreaded eating because she was afraid of vomiting in public. Her fear began when she couldn't eat in front of other kids in the school cafeteria, but advanced quickly to her not being able to eat at all. Candy doesn't have an eating disorder—she has a severe social phobia. (Based on authors' case material)

Since most fears and anxieties are not associated with serious disturbances, deciding whether a child's anxiety is serious enough to warrant treatment is seldom easy. Although anxiety disorders are extremely disabling for the child and family, they are rarely life threatening. Children with anxiety disorders can be exceedingly quiet, shy, compliant, eager to please, or secretive, and their distress may go unnoticed. Sometimes a severe disruption to a normal routine may be needed before a parent seeks help. If a child is so afraid of spiders or dogs that she is terror-stricken when going outside regardless of whether a spider or dog is nearby, then treatment may be needed. Treatment may also be required when parents repeatedly make important decisions that interfere with family life to accommodate a child's fears, such as not going camping or driving on holidays. Unlike children who provoke or offend others, children with anxiety disorders typically don't cause trouble, and as a result they receive far less professional attention than children with conduct problems. This situation is unfortunate, because many of these children can be helped with treatment (AACAP, 2007b; Shin-ichi, Okajima, Matsuoka, & Sakano, 2007).

In 1924, Mary Cover Jones worked with 3-year-old Peter, who was afraid of a rabbit. She eliminated Peter's fear by gradually exposing him to the rabbit when he was relaxed, by having him watch other children play with a rabbit, and by rewarding him for approaching the rabbit. These treatment techniques are still used today. Teaching children to use behavioral and cognitive coping skills to reduce anxious avoidance also increases the child's options and opportunities. In this regard, in addition to reducing or preventing symptoms of anxiety, early intervention may prevent future problems, such as loss of friends, failure to reach social and academic potential, low self-esteem, and depression (Rapee, 2002).

Overview

Timidity will always diminish if the occasions that produce it be skillfully repeated, until they cease to cause surprize, for the timid apprehend the unexpected.

—Yoritomo-Tashi (1916)

Decades of research from almost every perspective imaginable corroborate the popular adage that the best way to defeat your fears is to face them. Although specific procedures may vary, exposing children to the situations, objects, and occasions that produce anxiety is the main line of attack in any treatment for anxiety disorders (Chorpita & Southam-Gerow, 2006). As described in Box 7.3, when former three-time world heavyweight boxing champion Evander Holyfield was only 17 years old, he faced his fears—and was never afraid again.

Treatments for anxiety are directed at modifying four primary problems (Barlow, 2002):

- Distorted information processing
- Physiological reactions to perceived threat
- Sense of a lack of control
- Excessive escape and avoidance behaviors

These central problems are addressed using a variety of treatment strategies that are matched to the types of anxiety symptoms the child is experiencing

BOX 7.3 A CLOSER LOOK

Evander Holyfield: The Best Way to Defeat Fear Is to Face It

Evander Holyfield, a former three-time world heavyweight boxing champion, has the reputation of having no fear of failure or injury. In fact, Holyfield is amazed by his courage, since he used to be paralyzed by fear. From age 8, when he began boxing, until he was 17, he knew nothing but the constant anxiety of being bullied. "I was scared at everything I did, but especially boxing," he says. "I don't know how I ever got started, but I was scared. I don't know why I stayed. But I won a lot of fights, never got hurt, and as much torment as I was living in, I just assumed I would quit before I got to, say, 18. From watching the older kids box, I knew there came a time when you could get hurt, your nose would be bloody, your eye cut. I'd quit before that happened to me."

However, at 17, he suddenly found himself looking at a left hook from nowhere. Holyfield, then a slim 147 pounds of quivering nerves, was knocked unconscious, more or less, but he rose from the deck and charged his opponent. It was quite a little amateur fight.

The fight came back to him in a dream that night, after his head had cleared. He had been knocked down, yes, but he had gotten up and fought, after a fashion. Amazingly, he remembered nothing from the experience except numbness; it hadn't hurt at all. "I was never afraid again" he says.

Stefan Wermuth/Reuters /Lando

Source: Adapted from "Lovestruck" by Richard Hoffer, Sports Illustrated, June 30, 1997.

(Muris, 2007). In the following sections, we describe the most commonly used treatments for anxiety disorders, including behavior therapy, cognitive–behavior therapy (CBT), family interventions, and medications. Typically, combined forms of treatment that involve multiple components and target multiple symptoms are used (Chorpita, 2007; Hannesdottir & Ollendick, 2007). It is also important that treatments for children with anxiety disorders are sensitive to the ethnic and cultural factors that we discussed earlier in the chapter (Harmon, Langley, & Ginsburg, 2006). We conclude by highlighting recent efforts directed at the prevention of anxiety.

Behavior Therapy

The main technique of behavior therapy for phobias and anxiety disorders is **exposure**, causing children to face what frightens them, while providing ways of coping other than escape and avoidance. Exposure procedures have been used successfully with boys and girls of all ages from a variety of ethnic backgrounds. About 75% of children with anxiety disorders are helped by this treatment (Chorpita & Southam-Gerow, 2006).

Usually the process is gradual, and referred to as **graded exposure**. The child and therapist make a list of feared situations, from least to most anxiety producing, and the child is asked to rate the distress caused by each situation on a scale from 1 to 10; this is called a Subjective Units of Distress Scale (SUDS) or fear thermometer. The child is then exposed to each situation, beginning with the least distressing and moving up the hierarchy as the level of anxiety permits.

For Wayman, an 8-year-old-boy with OCD, leaving his bedroom closet door open was an anxiety-provoking situation with a SUDS rating of 8. Exposure was achieved by asking him to imagine being in this bedtime situation:

THERAPIST: It is nighttime. Your parents have tucked you in and have gone to bed themselves. You reach over to shut off the light on the nightstand, and you notice that your bedroom closet door is open just a bit, just enough for something to crawl out and into your room. It's dark in that corner and you think you see something. You shut off the light and lie down. You hear a strange, scratching noise coming from the closet. It sounds like something is moving. What's your SUDS rating?

WAYMAN: (Points to fear thermometer.) It's a seven.

THERAPIST: Stay with it. Tell me about what happens next.

WAYMAN: The closet door creaks open a bit more, and now I know that something is there. It can come get me. It's a monster.

THERAPIST: You begin to sweat. You want so badly to go and shut that door, but you stay in bed. You close your eyes, but the sound doesn't stop. It seems to be getting closer. You look over and see a horrible face, with red eyes staring at you. You want to scream, but you know you can't. What's your SUDS rating now?

WAYMAN: Eight. This is the worst part.

THERAPIST: Okay, good, stay with the image. Stay with it. What's your SUDS rating now?

WAYMAN: Five.

With repeated exposure to the fear, Wayman's SUDS ratings continued to decrease, and he was able to leave his bedroom closet door open without feeling anxious. (Adapted from Albano, Knox, & Barlow, 1995)

A second behavior therapy technique for treating children's fears and anxiety is **systematic desensitization**, which consists of three steps: teaching the child to relax; constructing an anxiety hierarchy; and presenting the anxiety-provoking stimuli sequentially while the child remains relaxed. With repeated presentation, the child feels relaxed in the presence of stimuli that previously provoked anxiety.

In a third technique known as **flooding**, exposure is carried out in prolonged and repeated doses. Throughout the process, the child remains in the anxiety-provoking situation and provides anxiety ratings until the levels diminish. Flooding is typically used in combination with **response prevention**, which prevents the child from engaging in escape or avoidance behaviors. More than other approaches, flooding may create distress, especially during the early stages of treatment. This procedure must be used carefully, especially with young children who may not understand the rationale.

In exposure-based therapies, the feared object can be confronted many ways, including real-life, role-playing, and imagining, or by observing others in contact with the feared object or situation (modeling). There is also evidence that exposure through virtual reality can be effective (Krijn, Emmelkamp, Olafsson, & Biemond, 2004).

One of the most effective procedures for treating specific phobias involves participant modeling and reinforced practice. Using this procedure, the therapist models the desired behavior (e.g., approaching the feared object), encourages and guides the child in practicing this behavior, and reinforces the child's efforts. Although all exposure procedures are effective, real-life, or *in vivo exposure,* works best—but it is not always easy to implement. Once the child faces her fear in a real-life situation with no adverse consequences, she is more confident of doing it again.

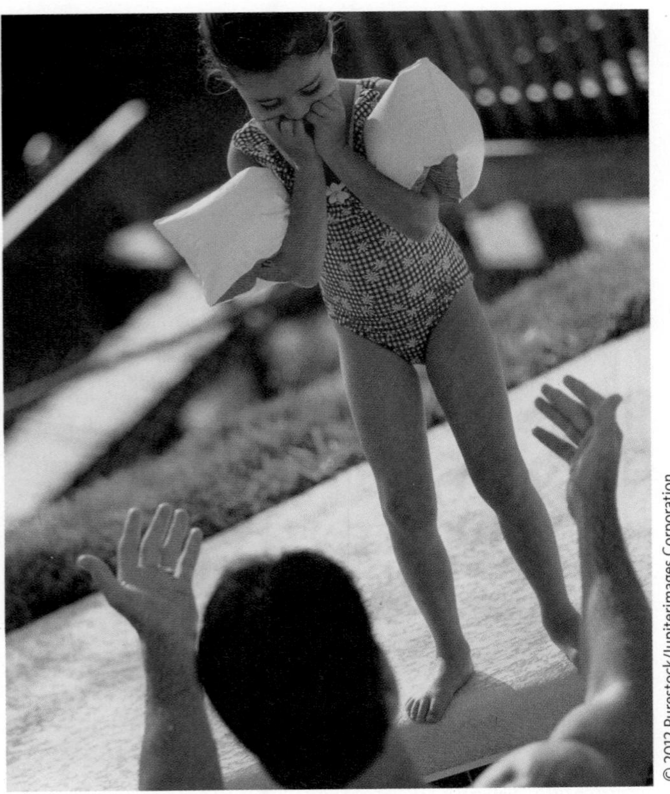

© 2012 Purestock/Jupiterimages Corporation

Five-year-old girl with a fear of water being encouraged and guided to enter the pool

Other useful behavior therapies are directed at reducing the physical symptoms of anxiety. These include muscle relaxation and special breathing exercises. Children who are anxious often take rapid shallow breaths (hyperventilation) that can produce increased heartbeat, dizziness, and other symptoms. Relaxation procedures are often used with gradual exposure.

Cognitive–Behavior Therapy (CBT)

The most effective procedure for treating most anxiety disorders is cognitive–behavior therapy (CBT) (Chorpita et al., 2011; Silverman, Pina, & Viswesvaran, 2008). In addition to using behavior therapy procedures, CBT teaches children to understand how thinking contributes to anxiety, and how to modify their maladaptive thoughts to decrease their symptoms (Kendall & Suveg, 2006). For example, as part of a comprehensive CBT for panic disorder, a teen who becomes lightheaded during a panic attack and fears she is going to die may be helped by a clinical strategy in which the therapist asks her to spin in a circle until she becomes dizzy. When she becomes alarmed and thinks, "I'm gonna die," she learns to replace this thought with one that is more appropriate; for example, "It's just a little dizziness—I can handle it" (Hoffman & Mattis, 2000). Making the youngster aware of thought patterns and ways to change them complements exposure and other behavior therapy procedures, such as positive reinforcement and relaxation. CBT and exposure-based treatments are almost always used in combination. An example of a combined approach for treating adolescents with social phobia is presented in Box 7.4 (Albano & DiBartolo, 2007). Similar programs for treating teens with social anxiety in the school setting have also proven effective (Warner, Fisher, Shrout, Rathor, & Klein, 2007).

The CBT treatment program *Coping Cat*, developed by Philip Kendall and his colleagues, is one of the most carefully evaluated treatments for youngsters 7 to 13 years old with GAD, SAD, and social phobia (Kendall, Furr, & Podell, 2010). A teen version is available, as is an Australian adaptation (*Coping Koala*). This approach emphasizes learning processes and the influence of contingencies and models, as well as the pivotal role of information processing. Treatment is directed at decreasing negative thinking, increasing active problem solving, and providing the child with a functional coping outlook. The intervention creates behavioral experiences with emotional involvement, while simultaneously addressing thought processes (Kendall et al., 2010).

Skills training and exposure are used to combat the problematic thinking that contributes to anxious distress and the behavioral avoidance that serves to maintain it. A variety of effective techniques are used including modeling, role-play, exposure, and relaxation training. Therapists use social reinforcement to encourage and reward the children, who are also taught to reward themselves for successful coping. Children first learn to use the following four steps of a "FEAR" plan:

- F = Feeling frightened? (recognizing physical symptoms of anxiety)
- E = Expecting bad things to happen? (recognizing anxious cognitions)
- A = Attitudes and actions that will help (coping self-talk and behavior to use when anxious)
- R = Results and rewards (evaluating performance and administering self-reward for effort)

After children learn the FEAR plan, the second part of the program is devoted to exposure and practice. Children attend 16 to 20 sessions over a period of 8 weeks. To enhance the skills learned in therapy, they must practice using them in anxiety-producing situations at home and school. Controlled evaluations of this approach have found it to be extremely effective in the short term. Most children show reductions in anxiety, with 71% of children freed of their primary diagnosis at the end of treatment and 54% not meeting criteria for any anxiety disorder. For many children, these gains have been maintained for 7 years following treatment

BOX 7.4 **A CLOSER LOOK**

Cognitive–Behavior Therapy for Adolescent Social Phobia

Ann Marie Albano and her colleagues have developed a comprehensive group CBT treatment program for adolescents with a social phobia (Albano, 2003). Treatment is carried out in small groups of four to six teens and involves sixteen 90-minute sessions. The treatment includes a number of important elements (Albano, Detweiler, & Logsdon-Conradsen, 1999).

Psychoeducational

In this phase, teens are informed about the nature of anxiety. A model emphasizing the cognitive, physiological, and behavioral symptoms increases their awareness and understanding of what provokes and maintains their symptoms. They are taught self-monitoring to help them identify anxiety triggers and reactions. To help the teens identify their symptoms, they are placed in anxiety-provoking situations, such as entering a classroom late, and asked to describe their physical, cognitive, and behavioral reactions:

THERAPIST: What would you be feeling? (physical)

TEEN: Butterflies, dizziness, shortness of breath.

THERAPIST: What would you be thinking? (cognitive)

TEEN: Everyone will be looking at me. What if the teacher yells at me? My face will be all red; they'll see it.

THERAPIST: What would you do? (behavioral)

TEEN: Skip the class. Not look up at anyone. Go to the nurse's office instead.

(Adapted from Marten, Albano, & Holt, 1991. Used by permission of the author.)

Skill Building

In this phase, teens learn cognitive restructuring, social skills, and problem-solving skills. Adolescents are taught to identify cognitive distortions—errors in thinking that perpetuate anxiety. Systematic rational responses are developed to replace these cognitions. Modeling, role-playing, and systematic exposure exercises are used.

Specific social skills for interpersonal interactions, maintenance of relationships, and assertiveness are identified and taught. Adolescents first identify behaviors that negatively influence social interactions, such as not smiling, making nervous gestures, not showing interest, speaking too softly, or criticizing or ignoring others. They then practice better forms of social interaction (Marten et al., 1991).

Problem Solving

In this phase, a model for identifying problems and developing realistic goals is presented and rehearsed. The teen is taught how to cope by using a proactive approach rather than avoidance. Two therapists role-play in a situation that produces social anxiety. They verbalize their automatic thoughts and rational coping responses to model stages of cognitive restructuring. One therapist (T1) verbalizes the automatic thoughts, and the other therapist (T2) acts as the "rational responder," as illustrated in the following example:

Scene: You Have Been Called on to Give a Brief Talk in Front of Your Class

T1: "Oh no, I can't do this!"

T2: "Okay, calm down, stay cool. Don't think so negatively."

T1: "Everyone will be looking at me. I'll mess up."

T2: "They have to do this too. We're all a little nervous."

T1: "What will I say? I can't think!"

T2: "Okay, I can say things clearly, I know this stuff."

T1: "My heart is beating so fast, I'm gonna be sick."

T2: "I feel nervous, but it will pass. I'll be fine."

T1: "Boy, I'm glad that's over, I'll never do this again."

T2: "Alright! I did it! That was okay. I made it!" (Adapted from Marten et al., 1991)

Therapists then discuss the role-play with the group, drawing on the members' experiences in similar situations.

Exposure

In this phase, teens develop a fear and avoidance hierarchy of social situations, which serves as the focus of in-session exposures. Group members and therapists simulate the situations. Exposures target the behavioral avoidance and cognitive component of anxiety, showing that anxiety will dissipate with habituation.

Generalization and Maintenance

To enhance generalization and maintenance of treatment effects, the prosocial and coping behaviors that the teen learns in the group are modeled and practiced during snack-time sessions. In addition, to increase generalization to the home setting, the program also includes a component for active parent participation (Marten et al., 1991).

When asked how she had changed following treatment for her social phobia, here's what one girl said:

> "Well, my friends told me that when they used to ask my opinion about something, I would always say, 'I don't care' or 'I don't know.' Now when they ask me, I give them my opinion. They said they like me much better now because I say what I think." (Beidel & Turner, 1998, p. 223)

Source: Used by permission of Ann Marie Albano.

(Kendall, Safford, Flannery-Schroder, & Webb, 2004). Replication studies using CBT have found maintenance of gains for 8 to 13 years after treatment (Saavedra, Silverman, Morgan-Lopez, & Kurtines, 2010). In general, children who are younger, have fewer internalizing symptoms, and whose mothers do not display depressive symptoms generally show more favorable outcomes (Southam-Gerow, Kendall, & Weersing, 2001).

Recently, computer-based, computer-assisted, and online CBT have also been shown to be effective in treating anxiety disorders in children and adolescents (Khanna & Kendall, 2010; Spence et al., 2011). These approaches have the added benefit of using less therapist time and/or providing greater access for families who have difficulty accessing clinic-based treatment, making it a viable and cost-effective option for many youngsters with anxiety disorders. Although CBT is effective in a variety of formats in treating childhood anxiety disorders, studies have not tested whether its effectiveness is by changes in the hypothesized key components—child's cognitions and coping skills. Thus, CBT in a variety of formats works, but we don't yet know why.

Family Interventions

Anxiety disorders often occur in a context of parental anxiety and problematic family relationships, which may influence the effectiveness of any of the treatment approaches. In some cases, child-focused treatment may have spillover effects into the family. For example, as children come to view themselves as more competent and less avoidant, parents' perceptions about what their child can and can't do change as well. As a result, parents may begin to respond differently to their child, and their own feelings and functioning are improved (Kendall & Flannery-Schroeder, 1998). Greater parental involvement in modeling and reinforcing coping techniques, inclusion of parental anxiety management strategies, and inclusion of parent skills training may be especially important in treating younger children with anxiety. Recent studies have found these types of modified CBT approaches for younger children and their families to be effective in reducing anxiety and improving coping skills in children in the 4 to 9 year age range, with comparable outcomes to treatments for CBT with older children (Cartwright-Hatton et al., 2011; Hirshfeld-Becker et al., 2010).

Addressing children's anxiety disorders in a family context may result in more dramatic and lasting effects than only focusing on the child, particularly for children of anxious parents (Creswell & Cartwright-Hatton, 2007; Suveg et al., 2006). In one study it was found that nearly 70% of the children with anxiety disorders who completed individual or family treatment did not meet criteria for any anxiety disorder at posttreatment. The addition of a family component that focused on interactions, managing emotion, communication, and problem solving significantly enhanced short-term outcome and long-term maintenance (Barrett, Dadds, & Rapee, 1996).

Given the important role of the family in childhood OCD, treatments for OCD have increasingly emphasized family involvement (Waters & Barrett, 2000). The primary treatment for children with OCD involves CBT that helps them learn to confront their worst fears gradually (graded exposure) while being prevented from engaging in their rituals (response prevention) (Freeman et al., 2008; March & Mulle, 1998). Family treatment for OCD provides education about the disorder and helps families cope with their feelings such as helplessness in not being able to relieve the child's pain, frustration that the child cannot "just stop," jealousy from siblings, and disappointment that the child is not "normal" (Piacentini, Jacobs, & Maidment, 1997). Both individual child CBT and family-based interventions have proven to be effective in treating children with OCD, although further controlled research is needed (Barrett, Farrell, Pina, Peris, & Piacentini, 2008). Generally, CBT has been found to be effective for less severe cases of OCD displaying lower symptom severity, less impairment, greater insight, and fewer externalizing symptoms (Garcia et al., 2010).

Medications

A variety of medications have been used to treat the symptoms of anxiety in children and adolescents, the most common and effective ones being selective serotonin reuptake inhibitors (SSRIs) (Reinblatt & Riddle, 2007). Although used to treat all of types of anxiety disorders, the strongest evidence for their effectiveness is for OCD (Garcia et al., 2010). Findings regarding the effectiveness of medications for treating anxiety disorders other than OCD have been less consistent (Huemer, Erhart, & Steiner, 2010). However, some studies suggest the potential use of medications in managing the symptoms of anxiety for youngsters with social phobia, SAD, and GAD (Reinblatt & Riddle, 2007).

Given the lack of controlled studies and possible adverse side effects associated with the use of SSRIs for children with anxiety disorders, CBT is generally considered the first line of treatment, with medication for those with severe symptoms, comorbid disorders, or when CBT is not available or proves unsuccessful (AACAP, 2007b). Some children who are severely anxious may require medication before they are able to participate in CBT. To date, there have been relatively few studies of the effectiveness of medications for the treatment of anxiety disorders in children, particularly for specific phobias and PTSD; however, clinical trials and a growing number of controlled studies provide some knowledge about the use of these compounds (Reinblatt & Riddle, 2007).

Prevention

Given their frequency, early onset, chronicity, and the personal suffering and public health costs associated with anxiety disorders, early identification and prevention efforts need to be a priority. In an innovative prevention study, researchers first identified very young children (a mean age of less than 4 years) who were at-risk for later anxiety disorders (Rapee, Kennedy, Ingram, Edwards, & Sweeney, 2010). As described in the case of Jack (see Box 7.5), children were selected based on both a high *withdrawal* score on a temperament questionnaire and high scores on a laboratory test of *behavioral inhibition*. A relatively brief intervention consisting of six 90-minute group sessions with parents was then carried out. The sessions provided an overview of the developmental aspects of anxiety, principles of parenting techniques (particularly the role that parental overprotection plays as a risk factor for anxiety), cognitive restructuring for parental worries about their child, and—for the children as they matured—the use of exposure hierarchies for the child, and the importance of ongoing use of these techniques, especially during high risk periods such as school entry. A no treatment control group was simply monitored in the clinic at 12-month intervals, on the same schedule as the parents who received intervention.

As shown in ● Figure 7.4, the overall number and the severity of diagnosed anxiety disorders decreased for both groups following the start of the study. Importantly, like Jack, children in the intervention group showed significantly fewer anxiety disorders and lower symptom severity at the last two follow-ups relative to controls. Mothers also reported that their children showed lower levels of anxiety 3 years following treatment, with a similar trend for children's reports of their own anxiety at the 3-year follow-up. Particularly interesting was that the intervention effects were modest at 1 year but stronger at 2 and 3 years. Also, the

BOX 7.5 **A CLOSER LOOK**

Early Intervention and Prevention of Anxiety Disorders

Jack

"Participating with Confidence"

Background

"Jack," age 3 years 11 months, was referred by his parents, who were concerned about his difficulty interacting with people outside the immediate family and participating in new activities. Despite attending the same preschool for 6 months, Jack was unable to initiate or reciprocate play with other children and spoke only to his main teacher. He tended to watch rather than participate in group activities. Jack's parents had withdrawn him from group swimming classes because he cried if he thought anyone was looking at him. His parents also avoided most social engagements because Jack constantly clung to them and demanded to go home. Both parents described themselves as having been very shy as children and were keen for Jack to avoid this experience.

Behavioral Inhibition Assessment

When Jack arrived at the laboratory for the behavioral inhibition assessment, he hid behind his mother when greeted and sat on his mother's lap rather than at the table with the assessor. He did not respond verbally to the assessor for over 30 minutes, and when he did, his speech was soft and monosyllabic and he avoided eye contact. He reacted fearfully in the cloaked stranger interaction and returned to his mother's lap. Jack did not approach the novel toy or interact with the other child in the peer interaction component. Jack's assessment showed that he met all criteria for behavioral inhibition, and he also met DSM-IV criteria for social phobia.

Intervention

His parents were randomly allocated to the 6-week parent education program. In the program, Jack's parents were encouraged to reduce their overprotective parenting style by not allowing Jack to avoid situations that made him anxious, such as attending parties and new activities. They were also encouraged to give Jack the opportunity to speak for himself rather than answering for him. Jack's parents were assisted in developing a graded exposure hierarchy to previously feared situations. They began with reinforcing Jack's efforts to reply when familiar people greeted him and gradually worked up to helping him to join in small group activities.

Outcome

At his final follow-up assessment, at age 6 years 10 months, Jack no longer met criteria for social phobia and was no longer as strongly inhibited. Jack's mother reported that he was still reserved when he first met unfamiliar people and that she would still describe him as "shy." However, he was participating with confidence in most school and extracurricular activities and he had a small group of close friends.

Source: Excerpt from Altering the Trajectory of Anxiety in At-Risk Young Children. Ronald M. Rapee, Ph.D.; Susan J. Kennedy, Ph.D.; Michelle Ingram, M.Clin.Psych.; Susan L. Edwards, Ph.D.; Lynne Sweeney, Ph.D. From the Centre for Emotional Health, Department of Psychology, Macquarie University. Am J Psychiatry 2010;167:1518–1525. Adapted with permission from the American Journal of Psychiatry, (Copyright © 2010). American Psychiatric Association.

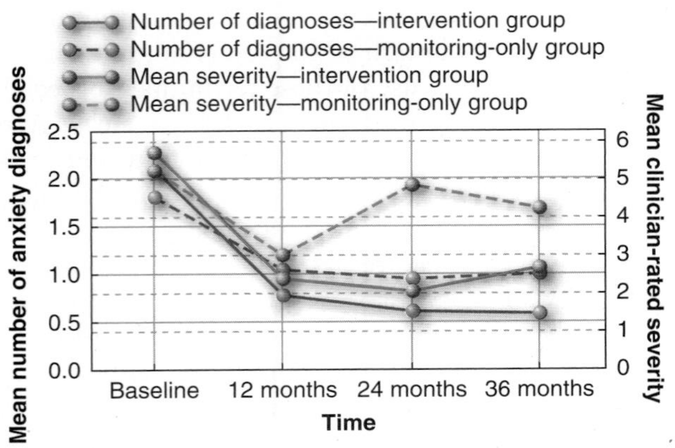

• **FIGURE 7.4** | Number and severity of diagnosed anxiety disorders over 3 years in children whose parents received an intervention or who received only monitoring.

severity differences between treated and untreated children seem to be mainly due to an increase in symptoms for the control group, suggesting that untreated children may be on a worsening developmental trajectory (Cuthbert, 2010). Follow-up studies are needed to explore possible reasons for these outcomes. Universal programs of primary prevention have also proven to be a promising approach to preventing anxiety in older children (Barrett, Farrell, Ollendick, & Dadds, 2006). With further research, these and other innovative programs of early intervention and prevention offer hope for the many children and families who suffer from anxiety disorders.

SECTION SUMMARY

Treatment and Prevention

- Exposing youngsters to the situations, objects, and occasions that produce their anxiety is the main line of attack in treating fears and anxieties.
- The most effective procedures for treating specific phobias involve participant modeling and reinforced practice.
- Cognitive–behavior therapy (CBT) teaches children to understand how their thinking contributes to anxiety, how to change maladaptive thoughts to decrease their symptoms, and how to cope with their fears and anxieties other than by escape and avoidance.
- Medications such as SSRIs are effective in treating children with OCD. However, findings for the effectiveness of medications used to treat other anxiety disorders have been inconsistent.
- Family interventions for anxiety disorders may result in more dramatic and lasting effects than focusing only on the child.
- Prevention programs have had some success in decreasing symptoms of anxiety, although further research is needed to evaluate their long-term benefits.

Study Resources

SECTION SUMMARIES

KEY TERMS

Study Resources *(continued)*

panic disorder (PD) 222
positive affectivity 227
posttraumatic stress disorder (PTSD) 223
response prevention 237
school refusal behavior 208
selective mutism 216
separation anxiety disorder (SAD) 206
social anxiety disorder 213
social phobia 213
specific phobia 211
systematic desensitization 237
two-factor theory 230

COURSEMATE

Access an interactive eBook and chapter-specific interactive learning tools, including flashcards, quizzes, videos, and more in your Psychology CourseMate, accessed through CengageBrain.com.

8 Mood Disorders

> *This is my depressed stance. When you're depressed, it makes a lot of difference how you stand. The worst thing you can do is straighten up and hold your head high because then you'll start to feel better. If you're going to get any joy out of being depressed, you've got to stand like this.*
>
> —Charlie Brown (Charles M. Schulz, 1922–2000)

CHAPTER PREVIEW

DONNA

Desperate Despair

Donna, age 12, says, "Sometimes I feel like jumping off the roof or finding some other way to hurt myself." Over the past 3 months, Donna has become more and more withdrawn, and her feelings of sadness, worthlessness, and self-hatred scare her. Her teacher describes Donna as "a loner who seems very troubled and unhappy." She's always been a good student, but she is now having difficulty concentrating, is failing tests, and feels totally unmotivated. At home, Donna is having trouble sleeping, has no appetite, and frequently complains of headaches. Most days she stays in her room and does nothing. When her mother asks her to do something, Donna becomes extremely upset. Her mother says Donna is "moody and irritable most of the time." (Based on authors' case material)

MICK

Up and Down

Mick, age 16, is moody all of the time. Sometimes he is sad, sullen, and apathetic. At other times he is full of life and energy, or intensely angry. When full of energy, he can go with little or no sleep for days without feeling tired. He moves constantly, talks incessantly, and cannot be interrupted. These extreme changes in mood make Mick feel out of control, and sometimes he thinks about hurting himself. He is frightened by his thoughts and drinks or uses drugs when they are available to reduce the pain. (Based on authors' case material)

PERHAPS YOU KNOW A child or teen who seems constantly unhappy, shows little enthusiasm for anything, is moody, or—at worst—thinks life just isn't worth living. This child may have a **mood disorder** (also called an *affective disorder*), in which a disturbance in mood is the central feature. Mood is broadly defined as a feeling or emotion—for example, sadness, happiness, anger, elation, or crankiness. Children with mood disorders suffer from extreme, persistent, or poorly regulated emotional states, such as excessive unhappiness or swings in mood from deep sadness to high elation. Mood disorders are one of the most common, chronic, and disabling illnesses in young people (Goodyer, 2008).

Overview of Mood Disorders

Mood disorders come in several brands. At one end of the spectrum are children who experience severe depression. Like Donna, these children suffer from **dysphoria**, a state of prolonged bouts of sadness. They feel little joy in anything they do and lose interest in nearly all activities, a state known as **anhedonia**. In the words of one depressed teen:

> Depression makes you lose interest in all the stuff you used to think was fun. You might quit playing guitar or drop out of yearbook, and claim that you just don't have the energy or desire to pursue extracurricular activities—or curricular activities, for that matter. (Reprinted with permission from Solin, 1995)

Many young people with depression express these combined feelings of sadness and loss of interest. However, some never report feeling sad. Rather, they express their depression through their irritable mood. **Irritability** refers to easy annoyance and touchiness, characterized by an angry mood and temper outbursts (Stringaris, 2011). Others may describe these children as cranky, grouchy, moody, short-fused, or easily upset. Being around them is difficult because any little thing can set them off. Irritability is one of the most common symptoms of depression, occurring in about 80% of clinic-referred children with depression (Goodyer & Cooper, 1993). Irritability in adolescence has also been found to predict self-reports of depressive and anxiety disorders up to 20 years later (Stringaris, Cohen, Pine, & Leibenluft, 2009).

At the opposite end of the mood spectrum are a smaller number of youths, those like Mick, who also experience episodes of **mania**, an abnormally elevated or expansive mood, and feelings of **euphoria**, which is an exaggerated sense of well-being. They suffer from an ongoing combination of extreme highs and extreme lows, a condition known as **bipolar disorder (BP)** or *manic–depressive illness*. Their highs may alternate with lows, or they may feel both extremes at about the same time.

DSM-IV-TR divides mood disorders into two general categories, depressive disorders and bipolar disorder (APA, 2000). We will discuss each of these primary mood disorders in the sections that follow.

SECTION SUMMARY

Overview of Mood Disorders

- Children with mood disorders suffer from extreme, persistent, or poorly regulated emotional states—for example, excessive unhappiness or swings in mood from deep sadness to high elation.

(*continues*)

SECTION SUMMARY (continued)

- Mood disorders are common and are among the most persistent and disabling illnesses in young people.
- There are two major types of mood disorders: depressive disorders and bipolar disorder.

DEPRESSION

"And how are you?" said Winnie-the-Pooh.
Eeyore shook his head from side to side.
"Not very how," he said. "I don't seem to have felt at all how for a long time."

—A. A. Milne, *Winnie-the-Pooh* (1926)

Depression refers to a pervasive unhappy mood, the kind of gloomy feeling displayed by Eeyore, the sad and indecisive old gray donkey in *Winnie-the-Pooh*. The symptoms of depression are so universal that depression is sometimes called "the common cold of psychopathology." Everyone feels sad, blue, out of sorts, or "down in the dumps" at times. (Even reading or writing about depression can be a real downer—can anyone think of a way to put a positive spin on feelings of dejection, hopelessness, worry, loneliness, or self-blame?) Sometimes our sadness is a normal reaction to an unfortunate event in our lives like losing a friend or a job. At other times, we may feel depressed without really knowing why. These feelings soon pass, however, and we resume our normal activities. Clinical depression, in contrast, is more severe than the occasional blues or mood swings that everyone gets from time to time.

Childhood is usually thought of as a happy and carefree time, a period unfettered by the worries, burdens, and responsibilities of adulthood. We tend to think of young people as positive and upbeat, not depressed. In fact, a common reaction to hearing that a child is depressed is "What does she have to be depressed about?" Even when children experience disappointment, disapproval, or other inevitable negative events in their lives, their sadness, frustration, and anger are expected to be short-lived. When children become sad, irritable, or upset, parents often attribute the negative moods to temporary factors, such as a lack of sleep or not feeling well, and expect the moods to pass. Thus, for a long time it was thought that children didn't get depressed, and when they did, it would be short-lived. We now know this is not true. Over 800,000 teens in the United States suffer from depression each year, and more than 500,000 make a suicide attempt that requires medical attention (NIMH, 2003).

Unlike most children who bounce back quickly when they are sad, children who are depressed can't

© Bubbles Photolibrary/Alamy

Depression in children goes well beyond normal mood swings

seem to shake their sadness, and it begins to interfere with their daily routines, social relationships, school performance, and overall functioning. Depressed youths often have accompanying problems such as anxiety or conduct disorders. Although clinical depression may resemble the normal emotional dips of childhood, for many young people it is pervasive, disabling, long lasting, and life threatening (Abela & Hankin, 2008b). Unfortunately, depression often goes unrecognized and untreated because parents and, in some cases, teachers may not recognize the child's underlying subjective negative mood.

History

As discussed above, not long ago, people doubted the existence of depression in children. This mistaken belief was rooted in traditional psychoanalytic theories, which viewed depression as a result of hostility or anger turned inward, usually caused by actual or perceived loss. Because children lacked sufficient superego development to permit aggression to be directed against the self, it was believed that they were incapable of experiencing depression (Rochlin, 1959). In another mistaken view, symptoms of depression were considered normal and passing expressions of certain stages of development, a belief that also has proved false. Depression in young people is a recurrent problem, as it is for adults.

As depression in children was acknowledged, a popular view emerged that children express depression much differently than adults, in ways that are often indirect and hidden. This idea came to be known as *masked depression*. It was thought that any known clinical symptom in children, including hyperactivity, learning problems, aggression, bed-wetting, separation anxiety, sleep problems, and running away, could be a sign of an underlying but masked depression (Cytryn & McKnew, 1974). Because this concept is too encompassing to be useful, the once popular notion of masked depression has been rejected. Depression in children isn't masked, but may simply be overlooked because it frequently co-occurs with more visible disorders, such as conduct problems.

Depression in Young People

Almost all young people experience some symptoms of depression, and as many as 5% of children and 10% to 20% of adolescents experience significant depression at some time (Avenevoli, Knight, Kessler, & Merikangas, 2008). These youngsters display lasting depressed mood while facing real or perceived distress and experience disturbances in their thinking, physical functioning, and social behavior. Suicidal behavior among teens, which is frequently associated with depression, is also a very serious concern (Goldston & Compton, 2007).

Even when children recover from their depression, they are likely to experience recurrent bouts and continued impairments—as many as 90% show significant impairment in their daily functions (Simonoff et al., 1997). The long-lasting emotional suffering, problems in everyday living, and heightened risk of these youths for suicide, substance abuse, bipolar disorder, poorer health outcomes, and higher health care costs make depression in young people a significant concern (Fombonne, Wostear, Cooper, Harrington, & Rutter, 2001a; Keenan-Miller, Hammen, & Brennan, 2007).

Depression and Development

Children express and experience depression differently at different ages (Weiss & Garber, 2003). An infant may show sadness by being passive and unresponsive; a preschooler may appear withdrawn and inhibited; a school-age child may be argumentative and combative or complain of feeling sick; a teenager may express feelings of guilt and hopelessness, sulk, or feel misunderstood. These examples are not various types of depressions; they likely represent different stages in the developmental course of the same process.

No one pattern fits all children within a particular age group or developmental period, and depression is not clearly recognizable as a clinical disorder using DSM criteria until children are older. Depression in children under the age of 7 is diffuse and less easily identified. However, recent studies suggest that age-modified diagnostic criteria may be used to identify and treat depression in children as young as 3 to 5 years (Lenze, Pautsch, & Luby, 2011; Luby, Belden, Sullivan, & Spitznagel, 2007). It is important to recognize depressive symptoms in preschool children since their symptoms can persist or reoccur and develop into depressive disorders during late childhood or early adolescence (Luby, Si, Belden, Tandon, & Spitznagel, 2009).

We know the least about depression in infants (Guedeney, 2007). In the 1940s, American psychoanalyst René Spitz described a condition he called *anaclitic depression*, in which infants raised in a clean but emotionally cold institutional environment displayed reactions that resembled depression (Spitz & Wolf, 1946). These infants displayed weeping, withdrawal, apathy, weight loss, and sleep disturbance. They also showed an overall decline in development, and in some cases, death. Although Spitz attributed this depression to an absence of mothering and the lack of opportunity to form an attachment, other factors, such as physical illness and sensory deprivation, may also have played a role.

It also became clear that similar symptoms could occur even in noninstitutionalized infants raised in

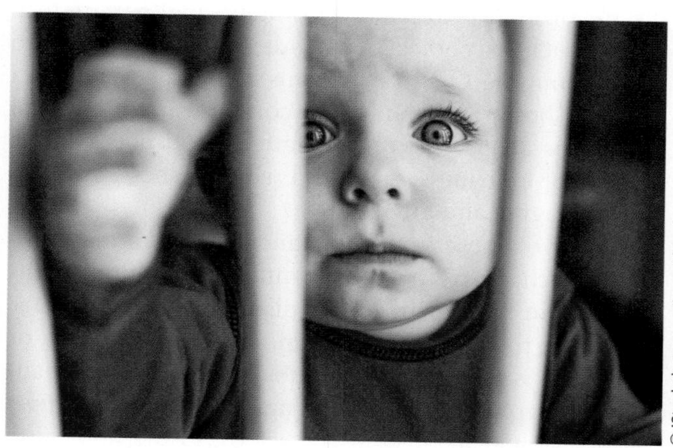

Depression in institutionalized infants: A physical appearance that in an adult might be described as depression

severely disturbed families in which their mother was depressed, psychologically unavailable, or physically abusive. These infants may experience sleep disturbances, loss of appetite, increased clinging, apprehension, social withdrawal, crying, and sadness (Goodman & Brand, 2009).

Preschool children who are depressed may appear extremely somber and tearful. They generally lack the exuberance, bounce, and enthusiasm in their play that characterize most preschoolers. They may display excessive clinging and whiny behavior around their mothers, as well as fears of separation or abandonment. In addition to getting upset when things don't go their way, many are irritable for no apparent reason. Negative and self-destructive verbalizations may occur, and physical complaints such as stomachaches are common (Luby et al., 2003).

School-age children with depression display many of the symptoms of preschoolers in addition to increasing irritability, disruptive behavior, temper tantrums, and combativeness. A parent may say, "Nothing ever pleases my child—she hates herself and everything around her." School-age children may look sad, but are often unwilling to talk about their sad feelings. Physical complaints may include weight loss, headaches, and sleep disturbances. Academic difficulties and peer problems are also common, and may include frequent fighting and complaints of not having friends or being picked on. Suicide threats may also begin to occur at this age.

Preteens with depression display many of the symptoms of younger children, in addition to increasing self-blame and expressions of low self-esteem, persistent sadness, and social inhibition. A child may say, "I'm stupid" or "Nobody likes me." Feelings of isolation from family are also common. The preteen may also experience an inability to sleep or may sleep excessively. Disturbances in eating are also common. Teens show increased irritability, loss of feelings of pleasure or interest, and worsening school performance. Angry discussions with parents regarding normal parent–teen issues, such as choice of friends or curfew, are also more common. Other symptoms at this age include a negative body image and self-consciousness, physical symptoms such as excessive fatigue and energy loss, feelings of loneliness, guilt, and worthlessness, and suicidal thoughts and attempts.

Many of these symptoms and behaviors may also occur in children and teens who are developing normally or in those with other disorders or conditions. Therefore, the presence of sad mood, loss of interest, or irritability is essential for diagnosing depression. In addition, regardless of the child's age, the symptoms must reflect a change in behavior, persist over time, and cause significant impairment in functioning (Rudolph & Lambert, 2007).

Anatomy of Depression

The term *depression* has been used in various ways. It is important to distinguish between depression as a symptom, depression as a syndrome, and depression as a disorder (Cantwell, 1990).

As a *symptom*, depression refers to feeling sad or miserable. Depressive symptoms often occur without the existence of a serious problem, and are relatively common at all ages. For most children, symptoms of depression are temporary, related to events in the environment, and not part of any disorder.

As a *syndrome*, depression is more than a sad mood. A syndrome refers to a group of symptoms that occur together more often than by chance. Along with sadness, the child may display a reduced interest in activities, cognitive and motivational changes, and somatic and psychomotor changes. The occurrence of depression as a syndrome is far less common than isolated depressive symptoms, and often includes mixed symptoms of anxiety and depression, which tend to cluster on a single dimension of *negative affect* (Ollendick, Seligman, Goza, Byrd, & Singh, 2003). At times, a depressive syndrome may occur following certain life events—for example, as a normal grief reaction following the loss of a loved one. However, bereavement is regarded as a clinical syndrome only if the symptoms persist or reoccur beyond a reasonable adjustment period (Kaplow, Saunders, Angold, & Costello, 2010).

As a *disorder*, depression comes in two types. The first, **major depressive disorder (MDD)** has a minimum duration of 2 weeks and is associated with depressed mood, loss of interest, other symptoms (e.g., sleep disturbances, negative self-esteem, hopelessness), and significant impairment in functioning. The second, **dysthymic disorder (DD)**, is associated with depressed mood, generally less severe but longer lasting symptoms (a year or more), and significant impairment in functioning. Depressive disorders may be associated with common causes, associated features, and a characteristic course, outcome, and response to treatment. As we discuss next, these disorders are defined using DSM criteria.

SECTION SUMMARY

Depression

- Depression in young people involves numerous and persistent symptoms, including impairments in mood, behavior, attitudes, thinking, and physical functioning.
- For a long time it was mistakenly believed that depression didn't exist in children in a form comparable to depression in adults.
- It is now known that depression in young people is prevalent, disabling, and often under-referred.

- The way in which children express and experience depression changes with age.
- It is important to distinguish between depression as a symptom, syndrome, and disorder.
- Depressive disorders come in two types, major depressive disorder and dysthymic disorder.

Major Depressive Disorder (MDD)

JOEY

Feeling Worthless and Hopeless

Ten-year-old Joey's mother and teacher are concerned about his irritability and temper tantrums at home and at school. With little provocation, he bursts into tears, yells, and throws objects. In class he seems to have difficulty concentrating and seems easily distracted. Increasingly shunned by his peers, he plays by himself at recess, and at home spends most of his time in his room watching TV. His mother notes that he has been sleeping poorly and has gained 10 pounds over the past couple of months from constant snacking. The school psychologist has ruled out learning disabilities or ADHD; instead, she says Joey is a deeply unhappy child who expresses feelings of worthlessness and hopelessness, and even a wish that he would die. These feelings began about 6 months ago when Joey's father, divorced from his mother for several years, remarried and moved to another town, and now spends far less time with Joey. (Adapted from Hammen & Rudolph, 2003)

ALISON

"I Couldn't Take It Any More"

Alison, age 17, gets high grades, is a talented musician, and is attractive. However, for the past 3 years, she has been fighting to stay alive. "There are times when I was in school and I would start to cry—I had no idea why. My friends would say, 'What have you got to be depressed about, Alison? You're smart, talented, and can have any boy you want.' When my closest friend moved away 3 years ago, I was really lonely," says Alison. "I'd write notes about suicide and talk about killing myself. I couldn't eat and was tired most of the time. Even the smallest decision was overwhelming. Some days I'd never get out of bed I was so depressed. I couldn't stand school and hated everyone." Alison's feelings of hopelessness lasted for days, then weeks, then months. Finally, "I couldn't take it anymore," says Alison. "I wanted to die—so I tried to kill myself." (Based on authors' case material)

Although Joey and Alison differ in age and symptoms, both display the key features of major depressive disorder (MDD): sadness, loss of interest or pleasure in nearly all activities, irritability, plus a number of additional specific symptoms that are present for at least 2 weeks. These symptoms must also represent a change from previous functioning. DSM criteria for a major depressive episode are presented in Table 8.1.

A diagnosis of MDD depends on the presence of a major depressive episode plus the exclusion of other conditions, such as the prior occurrence of a manic episode. (In this case, a diagnosis of bipolar disorder would be made.) It also requires ruling out physical factors that may have caused or prolonged the depression, a depression that is part of normal bereavement, and underlying thought disorders.

The cases of Joey and Alison highlight three important points about the diagnosis of MDD in children and adolescents (Hammen & Rudolph, 2003):

- The same DSM criteria for diagnosing adults can be used to diagnose school-age children and adolescents.
- Because children's disruptive behaviors attract more attention, or are more easily observed compared with internal, subjective suffering, depression in children can be easily overlooked.
- Some features of depression are likely more common in children and adolescents than in adults—notably, irritable mood.

Children and adolescents with MDD frequently display similar symptoms and have comparable rates of comorbidity and recurrence as adults (Birmaher et al., 2004). However, relative to adults, clinic-referred youths with major depression have almost exclusively first-episode depressions, will recover somewhat faster from their depressive episodes, and are at greater risk for developing bipolar disorder. Children who develop major depression suffer from their disorder for many years longer than adults, making early-onset of this disorder a particularly severe form of affective illness (Kovacs, 1996).

Prevalence

Between 2% and 8% of all children aged 4 to 18 experience MDD (Costello, Erkanli, & Angold, 2006). Depression is relatively rare (about 1%–2%) among preschool and school-age children (Egger & Angold, 2006), but increases two- to threefold by adolescence (NIMH, 2003). Since depression comes and goes, prevalence estimates vary with the time frame in which symptoms are assessed. For example, in 13- to

TABLE 8.1 | **Diagnostic Criteria for** Major Depressive Episode

DSM-IV-TR

A. Five (or more) of the following symptoms are present during the same 2-week period and represent a change from previous functioning; at least one symptom is either (1) depressed mood or (2) loss of interest or pleasure.
Note: Do not include symptoms that are clearly due to a general medical condition, or mood-incongruent delusions or hallucinations.

(1) Depressed mood most of the day, nearly every day, as indicated by subjective account (e.g., feels sad or empty) or observations by others (e.g., appears tearful)
Note: In children and adolescents, can be irritable mood.

(2) Markedly diminished interest or pleasure in all, or almost all, activities most of the day, nearly every day (as indicated by subjective account or observations by others)

(3) Significant weight loss when not dieting or weight gain (e.g., a change of more than 5% of body weight in a month), or decrease or increase in appetite nearly every day
Note: In children, consider failure to make expected weight gains.

(4) Insomnia or hypersomnia nearly every day

(5) Psychomotor agitation or retardation nearly every day (observable by others, not merely subjective feelings of restlessness or being slowed down)

(6) Fatigue or loss of energy nearly every day

(7) Feelings of worthlessness or excessive or inappropriate guilt (which may be delusional) nearly every day (not merely self-reproach or guilt about being sick)

(8) Diminished ability to think or concentrate, or indecisiveness, nearly every day (either by subjective account or as observed by others)

(9) Recurrent thoughts of death (not just fear of dying), recurrent suicidal ideation without a specific plan, or a suicide attempt or a specific plan for committing suicide

B. The symptoms do not meet criteria for a Mixed Episode (see p. 365).

C. The symptoms cause clinically significant distress or impairment in social, occupational, or other important areas of functioning.

D. The symptoms are not due to the direct physiological effects of a substance (e.g., a drug of abuse, a medication) or a general medical condition (e.g., hypothyroidism).

E. The symptoms are not better accounted for by Bereavement, i.e., after the loss of a loved one, the symptoms persist for longer than 2 months or are characterized by marked functional impairment, morbid preoccupation with worthlessness, suicidal ideation, psychotic symptoms, or psychomotor retardation.

Source: Reprinted with permission from the Diagnostic and Statistical Manual of Mental Disorders, Fourth Edition, Text Revision, (Copyright ©2000). American Psychiatric Association.

18-year-olds, the prevalence of depression is about 3% when taken at a single point in time and about 8% when taken over a 1-year period. However, lifetime prevalence estimates—whether a child has ever been depressed—range from about 10% to 14% (Avenevoli et al., 2008; Merikangas et al., 2010).

Despite being so high, these rates may underestimate the problem. First, the estimates using a DSM diagnosis of MDD might be lower than the self-reported symptoms of depression. Second, many children who just barely fail to meet diagnostic criteria for MDD still show significant impairments in their social competence, cognitive attributions, coping skills, family relations, and experience of stress. They are also at greater risk than other youths for developing future depression and other disorders, such as substance abuse (Gotlib, Lewinsohn, & Seeley, 1995).

The modest increase in depression from preschool to elementary school is likely not biologically based, but rather is a reflection of the school-age child's growing self-awareness and cognitive capacity, verbal ability to report symptoms, and increased performance and social pressures. In contrast, the sharp increase in depression in adolescence appears to be the result of biological maturation at puberty interacting with important developmental changes that occur during this tumultuous time period. This hypothesis is supported by the emergence of large sex differences in depression after puberty, the emergence of bipolar disorder, and the relative stability in rates of depression through adolescence (Birmaher et al., 1996).

Comorbidity

RAYMOND

Depressed and Enraged

Raymond, age 16, lives alone with his single mother. For the past few months he has been persistently sad and unhappy, overcome with feelings of worthlessness. He is socially withdrawn, and spends most of his time alone at home or avoiding contact with peers on those days when he manages to attend school. He is constantly tired but still finds it difficult to sleep, lying awake at night for hours and then struggling to drag himself from bed in the morning. Both he and his mother are concerned about his weight, which has increased substantially due to his inability to control his appetite for chips, candy, and soda. Even if he makes it to school, he finds he is unable to concentrate on his work.

Raymond's listlessness and withdrawal are countered, however, by his defiance and repeated outbursts of anger and aggression. He frequently lashes out in rage at his mother, recently punching his fist through a wall and a door at home. He also has been in several fights with other students at school as a result of being teased by his peers. He rarely complies with rules and limits at home or at school, leading to frequent conflicts with his mother and with school authorities. The event that precipitated Raymond's current referral was his arrest for shoplifting at a local store. (Adapted from Compas & Hammen, 1994)

Like Raymond, who has MDD and a co-occurring conduct disorder, as many as 90% of young people with depression have one or more other disorders, and 50% have two or more (Simonoff et al., 1997). The most frequent co-occurring disorders in *clinic-referred* youngsters with MDD are anxiety disorders, particularly generalized anxiety disorders; specific phobias; and separation anxiety disorders. Depression and anxiety become more visible as separate but co-occurring disorders as the severity of the child's problem increases and as the child gets older (Gurley, Cohen, Pine, & Brook, 1996). Dysthymia, conduct problems, ADHD, and substance use disorder are also common in clinic-referred youngsters with depression (Birmaher et al., 1996). Further, about 60% of adolescents with MDD have a comorbid personality disorder, which is most commonly borderline personality disorder—characterized by instability of interpersonal relationships, self-image, and affects, and marked impulsivity (Muehlenkamp, Ertelt, Miller, & Claes, 2011).

Many co-occurring disorders are present before depression and are likely to persist after the child is no longer depressed. However, pathways to comorbid conditions and adult outcomes may differ by disorder and sex (Diamantopoulou, Verhulst, & van der Ende, 2011). For example, with regard to anxiety, adolescent girls have been found to display high levels of depression regardless of prior anxiety, whereas for adolescent boys, prior anxiety has been found to increase their risk for depression (Gallerani, Garber, & Martin, 2010). In another example, girls who display early conduct problems have a high risk of developing later depressive symptoms, especially if they have been maltreated (Brensilver, Negriff, Mennen, & Trickett, 2011). Generally, externalizing problems are better predictors of internalizing problems than vice versa (Kessler et al., 2011). However, a recent study found that depression in early adolescence also predicted later delinquency in females (Kofler et al., 2011). Thus, the presence of a co-occurring disorder is significant because it can increase the risk for recurrent depression, increase the duration and severity of depressive episodes, and increase the risk for suicide attempts, all of which may in turn increase the co-occurring problems. The presence of another disorder also decreases a depressed youth's response to treatment and is related to less effective outcomes (Birmaher et al., 1996).

Onset, Course, and Outcome

The onset of depression in adolescence may be gradual or sudden. Either way, a youth typically has a history of milder episodes of depression that do not meet DSM diagnostic criteria (Gotlib & Hammen, 1992). Most adults with depression recall having their first depressive episode between the ages of 15 and 19 (Kessler, Merikangas, & Wang, 2007). However, prospective studies of children and adolescents usually find earlier ages of onset, most commonly between the ages of 13 and 15 (Merikangas et al., 2010).

The average episode of MDD in clinically referred children and adolescents lasts about 8 months, with longer episodes if a parent has a history of depression (Kaminski & Garber, 2002). Although almost all young people eventually recover from their initial depressive episode, their disorder itself, unfortunately, does not go away (Birmaher, Arbelaez, & Brent, 2002). MDD is a recurrent condition with a chance of recurrence of about 25% within 1 year, 40% within 2 years, and 70% within 5 years. Thus, a significant number of children develop a chronic, relapsing disorder that persists into young adulthood (Fombonne et al., 2001a).

Those with an onset of depression prior to age 15 and a recurrent episode prior to age 20 display more severe, chronic, suicidal depressions; greater co-occurring anxiety and worse social functioning at age 15; and poorer psychosocial outcomes at age 20 (Hammen, Brennan, Keenan-Miller, & Kerr, 2008). For those hospitalized for depression, nearly one-half will be rehospitalized within 2 years following remission.

In addition, about one-third of adolescents with MDD will develop a bipolar disorder within 5 years after the onset of their depression, known as a *bipolar switch* (DelBello et al., 2003; McCauley et al., 1993). Thus, depression is a condition that endures over the course of development, creating a long-term social, emotional, and economic burden for the youth and the family.

Why do depressive episodes reoccur, and why does the length of time between episodes get progressively shorter? One possible explanation is that the first episode may sensitize the child to future episodes (Rudolph & Flynn, 2007). According to this idea, the first episode may be linked to a specific stressor and is accompanied by lasting changes in biological processes that heighten future reactivity to stress (Post et al., 1996). The initial externally produced changes in the brain can be conditioned so that following the first depressive episode, individuals are increasingly vulnerable to stress, and even nonsevere stress or minor events that resemble loss or stress experiences may result in depression (Stroud, Davila, Hammen, & Vrshek-Schallhorn, 2011). This process is known as *stress sensitization* (Post & Weiss, 1998).

Even after recovery from their depressive episode, many youths continue to show milder symptoms of depression and experience adjustment and health problems and chronic stress (Lewinsohn & Essau, 2002). This is a significant concern because these problems are risk factors for future depressive episodes (Daley, Hammen, & Rao, 2000).

In addition to their recurring bouts of depression, the immediate and long-term prospects for children with MDD include many other negative outcomes (Fergusson, Boden, & Horwood, 2007). For example, adolescents who are depressed have a greater than normal risk for delinquency, arrest, and conviction; dropping out of school; and unemployment (Lewinsohn et al., 1994). A history of depression during the school years also increases the risk for later tobacco use, substance use disorder, suicidal behavior, impairment, a poor work record, marital problems, and health service use (Gotlib, Lewinsohn, & Seeley, 1998; Rice, Lifford, Thomas, & Thapar, 2007).

The overall outcome for young people with depression is not optimistic. Although almost all will recover from their depression, they continue to be at high risk for later episodes of mood and other disorders and for impaired social and academic functioning. One mother of a depressed teen paints a realistic picture of the long-term outcome for a child who suffers from depression:

> Depression in kids, when it hits them in their teens, leaves a hole in their lives. When they're young and just starting out in life, they're supposed to become independent. But that doesn't happen with depressed kids. They're out of synch and get left behind. And they never really catch up. That leaves a permanent scar. (Adapted from Owen, 1993, p. C1)

As they become adults, children and adolescents with MDD continue to experience many negative long-term outcomes that include a high rate of suicide and suicide attempts, adult depression and other psychiatric disturbances, high rates of psychiatric and medical hospitalizations, alcohol abuse/dependence, psychosocial impairments, lower educational achievement, and employment problems (Fombonne, Wostear, Cooper, Harrington, & Rutter, 2001b; Jaycox et al., 2009).

Gender, Ethnicity, and Culture

In what has been called depression's double standard, females are twice as likely as males to suffer from depression, are more susceptible to milder mood disorders, and are more likely to experience recurrent

Teenage girls are particularly vulnerable to depression and related problems

episodes (Zahn-Waxler, Race, & Duggal, 2005). This sex difference is not present among children ages 6 to 11, where depression is equally common in boys and girls (Speier, Sherak, Hirsch, & Cantwell, 1995). However, sex differences in emotional reactivity are present in children who are depressed or at-risk for depression as early as the preschool period, with boys displaying more anger and girls more sadness (Luby et al., 2009). In addition, sex differences in specific symptoms that forecast later depression (e.g., fearfulness, feelings of inadequacy, negative self-evaluation, and negative affect) may in fact be present prior to 10 years of age, with girls reporting significantly more of these symptoms than boys (Rudolph, Hammen, & Daley, 2006).

Sex differences in diagnosable depression begin between ages 13 and 15, when the rate rises for girls (Wade, Cairney, & Pevalin, 2002). As shown in ● Figure 8.1, rates of depression as well as gender differences in rates increase dramatically between ages 15 and 18 (Hankin, Wetter, & Cheely, 2008). The ratio of girls to boys is about 2:1 to 3:1 after puberty, a pattern that continues throughout adolescence and adulthood.

Although depression occurs more frequently in girls than boys, symptom presentation is generally quite similar for both sexes. (Slightly more girls than boys report symptoms related to weight and appetite disturbances and worthlessness/guilt [Lewinsohn, Pettit, Joiner, & Seeley, 2003].) However, the correlates of depression may differ for the sexes. For example, depression is more highly related to school-related stress in boys than in girls (Sund, Larsson, & Wichstrom, 2003).

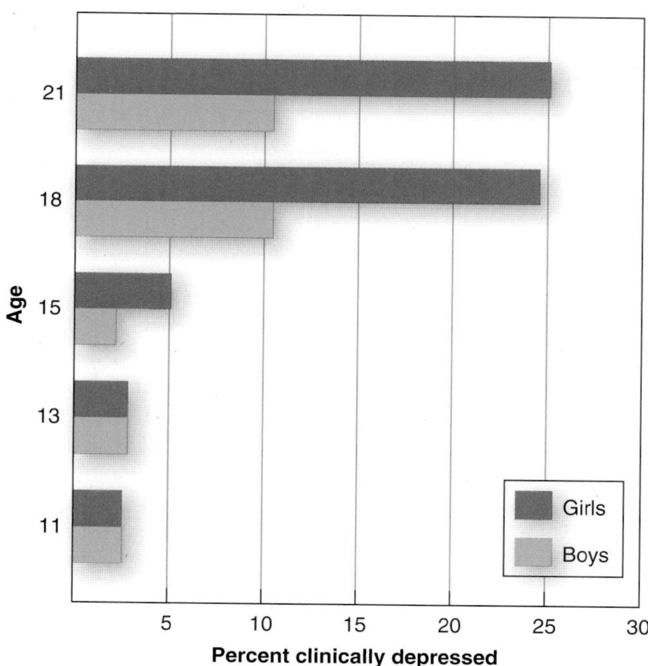

● **FIGURE 8.1** | The overall rate of depression and the proportion of females with depression increase dramatically during adolescence.

Adapted from "Development of Depression from Preadolescence to Young Adulthood: Emerging Gender Differences in a 10-year-Longitudinal Study" by B. L. Hankin, L. Y. Abramson, T. E. Moffitt, P. A. Silva, R. McGee & K. E. Andell, 1998, 'Journal of Abnormal Psychology', 107, 128–140. Copyright © 1998 by the American Psychological Association. Reprinted with permission. APA is not responsible for the accuracy of this translation.

The increase in depression during adolescence and the emergence of sex differences in depression at this time have led to a special interest in this developmental period (Rudolph et al., 2006). Many physical, psychological, and social changes during adolescence may heighten the risk for depression in girls. Hormonal changes in estrogen and testosterone may affect brain function, increasing sexual maturity may affect social roles, interpersonal changes and expectations may result in heightened exposure to stressful life events, and non-normative changes such as early maturation may lead to isolation from one's peer group (Hankin et al., 2008).

These changes may diminish self-worth, lead to depressed mood, and evoke self-focused attention. It is also thought that females may be at higher risk than males because they have a greater orientation toward cooperation and sociality. They also use ruminative coping styles to deal with stress—especially stress involving interpersonal loss and disruptions. These two characteristics may put girls at a disadvantage during adolescence, when they face somewhat greater biological and stressful role-related challenges than boys (Zahn-Waxler et al., 2005). Interpersonal stress and a lack of social support are particularly salient aspects of depression for adolescent girls (Rudolph & Flynn, 2007).

Low birth weight has been found to predict depression in adolescent girls but not boys, and girls with low birth weight are especially vulnerable to adversity after puberty (Costello, Worthman, Erkanli, & Angold, 2007; Van Lieshout & Boylan, 2010). This suggests that low birth weight may be a marker for poor intrauterine conditions that lead to adjustments in fetal development, which in turn have long-term consequences for females' response to stress in adolescence. Research also suggests that increased levels of testosterone and estrogen at puberty, particularly when they occur in combination with social stress, increase the risk for depression in girls (Angold, Worthman, & Costello, 2003). Hormones and sleep cycles, which can alter mood, differ dramatically between males and females. One study of blood flow in regions of the brain during periods of sadness in men and in women found that although men and women considered themselves to be equally sad, their brain activity differed. When asked to feel sad, both sexes activated regions of the prefrontal cortex, but women showed a much wider activation of the limbic system. These findings with adults suggest that sex differences in depression may be partly rooted in biological differences in the brain processes that regulate emotions (George, Ketter, Parekh, Herscovitch, & Post, 1996).

The incidence of depression has been found to vary across regions worldwide (Culbertson, 1997); however, few studies have examined ethnic, racial, or cultural differences in clinically depressed youths and findings have been inconsistent (Anderson & Mayes, 2009). One study compared the prevalence of major depression across nine ethnic groups in a large community sample of children in grades 6 to 8 (Roberts, Roberts, & Chen, 1997). Of these groups, African American and Hispanic youths both had significantly higher rates of depression. However, only Hispanic youths with depression showed an elevated risk for impaired functioning. In another study, pubertal status was found to be a better predictor of depressive symptoms than chronological age in Caucasian girls, but not in African American or Hispanic girls (Hayward, Gotlib, Schraedley, & Litt, 1999). Similarly, 6th grade obesity was found to be associated with a greater likelihood of depressed mood in the 8th grade for Caucasian girls, but not for African American or Hispanic girls (Anderson et al., 2011).

A large community study of high school students found that non-white (African American, Hispanic, and Asian) adolescents reported more symptoms of depression than white adolescents (Rushton, Forcier, & Schectman, 2002). However, these differences likely reflect differences in SES, since depression and lower SES are related. Race and ethnicity are known sources of varying levels of exposure to stress and availability of resources. As a result, low SES may increase vulnerability to stress and by doing so increase the likelihood of depression. In a longitudinal study of 4 race–ethnic groups (whites, African Americans, Hispanics, and Asians) during the transition from adolescence to young adulthood, it was found that race and ethnicity were important in understanding depressive symptoms during this transition (Brown, Meadows, & Elder, 2007). In females, initial rates of depressive symptoms were highest for Hispanic and Asian teens and lowest for whites, with African American youths falling in between. As expected, males displayed lower levels of symptoms, but the findings for race–ethnic group differences were similar to those for females. Within gender, all groups showed decreases in symptoms over time; however, whites continued to display fewer depressive symptoms than the other three groups, particularly relative to African Americans. This lasting race–ethnic inequality in depressive symptoms creates a risk for emotional and physical health in later life, as stress may accumulate in the context of a lack of resources.

SECTION SUMMARY

Major Depressive Disorder (MDD)

- The key features of MDD are sadness, loss of interest or pleasure in nearly all activities, and irritability, plus many specific symptoms that are present for a duration of at least 2 weeks.
- The overall prevalence of MDD for youths ages 4 to 18 is between 2% and 8%, with rates that are low during childhood but increase dramatically during adolescence.
- The most frequent accompanying disorders in young people with depression are anxiety disorders, dysthymia, conduct problems, ADHD, and substance use disorder.
- Almost all young people recover from their initial depressive episode, but about 70% have another episode within 5 years and many develop bipolar disorder.
- Depression in preadolescent children is equally common in boys and girls, but the ratio of girls to boys is about 2:1 to 3:1 after puberty.
- The relationship between depression and race/ethnicity during childhood and adolescence is an understudied area.

In the next section, we discuss dysthymic disorder, a milder but more chronic form of depression, about which we know relatively little compared to MDD. Many children with dysthymia eventually develop MDD; therefore, the two disorders are related.

Dysthymic Disorder (Dysthymia)

DEBORAH

A Childhood Without Laughter

A few months ago, my mother unearthed some pictures of me as a baby that I had never seen before. One showed me at about 9 months old, crawling on the grass of Golden Gate Park. I was looking directly at the camera, my tongue sticking out of the corner of my mouth, and I was laughing happily. My face was lit from within, and looked more than a little mischievous. I was absolutely transfixed by that photo for days. I would continually take it out of my wallet and stare at it, torn between laughter and tears. For a while I couldn't figure out what it was about the picture that drew me. Finally it hit me; this was the only picture of myself as a child that I had seen that showed me laughing. All the photos I had ever seen depicted a child staring solemnly or smiling diffidently, but never laughing. I looked at the Golden Gate Park picture and wished that I had remained that happy, and that depression had not taken away my childhood. When I first was diagnosed with depression at age 24, I discussed my childhood with my doctor. Although it is hard to diagnose a child from 20 years in the past, it seemed clear to both of us that I had suffered from dysthymia (mild, long-term depression) probably from the time I was a small child. (*A Childhood Without Laughter* by D. M. Deren. Copyright © 1996, 1997 by Deborah M. Deren, Revised June 8, 1997. Reproduced by permission.)

Like Deborah, young people who suffer from dysthymic disorder (DD) or **dysthymia** experience symptoms of depressed mood that occur on most days and that persist for at least 1 year. They are unhappy or irritable most of the time. (The sad and gloomy life of Eeyore the donkey in the 100 Acre Wood likely qualifies for a diagnosis of dysthymia.) Combined with their chronic depressed mood, these children also display at least two somatic (e.g., eating problems, sleep disturbances, low energy) or cognitive symptoms (e.g., lack of concentration, low self-esteem). Although the symptoms of dysthymia are chronic, they are less severe than those for children with MDD.

Children with dysthymia are characterized by poor emotion regulation, which includes constant feelings of sadness, feelings of being unloved and forlorn, self-deprecation, low self-esteem, anxiety, irritability, anger, and temper tantrums (Masi et al., 2003). Some may experience **double depression**, where a major depressive episode is superimposed on the child's previous dysthymia, causing the child to present with both disorders.

The chronic nature of dysthymia raises the issue of whether it is a mood disorder or a general personality style (Daley et al., 1999). For example, we all know people we would describe as "sad sacks"—nothing ever seems to make them happy. However, dysthymia seems to follow a chronic course that is typical of mood disorders, and the similarities between dysthymia and MDD in young people suggest that it is a mood disorder, not a personality style (Renouf & Kovacs, 1995). One study found that children with either MDD or dysthymia alone did not differ in their clinical features, demographics, or associated characteristics, leading to unanswered questions about the validity of this distinction. However, those with both disorders were more severely impaired than children with just one of the disorders (Goodman, Schwab-Stone, Lahey, Shaffer, & Jensen, 2000).

Note that the lack of differences between youth with a dysthymic disorder and those with a chronic type of major depression has led to the proposal that the term *chronic depressive disorder* be used to describe both conditions in DSM-5. In comparison to non-chronic major depression, chronic forms of depression, whether referred to as dysthymia or chronic major depression, are associated with a poorer response to treatment, greater long-term morbidity at follow-up, and greater familial loading for affective disorders (McCullough et al., 2003).

Prevalence and Comorbidity

Rates of dysthymia are lower than those of MDD, with approximately 1% of children and 5% of adolescents displaying the disorder (Birmaher et al., 1996). The most prevalent co-occurring diagnosis with dysthymia is MDD. During the course of their dysthymia, as many as 70% of children may have an episode of major depression (Renouf & Kovacs, 1995). About one-half of the children with dysthymic disorder also have one or more co-occurring nonaffective disorders that preceded the dysthymia, including anxiety disorders, conduct disorder, and ADHD (Kovacs, Akiskal, Gatsonis, & Parrone, 1994).

Onset, Course, and Outcome

Dysthymic disorder develops about 3 years earlier than MDD, most commonly around 11 to 12 years of age (Kovacs, Obrosky, Gatsonis, & Richards, 1997). Since dysthymia frequently precedes MDD, it could be a precursor to its development (Lewinsohn, Hops, Roberts, Seeley, & Andrews, 1993). Childhood-onset dysthymia has a prolonged duration, with an average episode length of 2 to 5 years.

Almost all children eventually recover from dysthymic disorder. On the other hand, they also have an extremely high risk of developing other disorders, especially MDD, anxiety disorders (separation anxiety disorder and generalized anxiety disorder are the most common), and conduct disorder (Masi et al., 2003). They are also at increased risk for the subsequent development of bipolar and substance use disorders (Kovacs et al., 1994).

Adolescents with a history of dysthymic disorder report receiving less social support from friends. This finding appears to be unique to children with dysthymia when compared to children with MDD (Klein, Lewinsohn, & Seeley, 1997). Those who recover from their dysthymia have the same family relationships, cognitive styles, and school functioning as other children. The only area that continues to be affected is psychosocial functioning (Klein et al., 1997). However, it is not known whether deficits in psychosocial functioning precede or follow dysthymia. They may be a predisposing factor for the development of dysthymic disorder, or a lasting scar of the illness (Renouf & Kovacs, 1995).

The early onset and extended duration of dysthymia make it a serious problem. Children who develop the disorder at age 9 then recover 4 years later will have spent more than 30% of their entire lives and over 50% of their school-age years being depressed. Since depression is associated with many other academic, cognitive, family, and social problems, these long-lasting episodes of dysthymia can have extremely harmful effects on development (Renouf & Kovacs, 1995). Since early-onset dysthymic disorder is almost always followed by MDD and sometimes by a bipolar disorder, its early diagnosis may help to identify children at risk for later mood disorders and has important implications for prevention.

SECTION SUMMARY

Dysthymic Disorder

- Children with dysthymic disorder display depressive symptoms on most days for at least 1 year.
- About 5% of children and adolescents have an episode of dysthymia by the end of adolescence.
- The most common accompanying disorders with dysthymia are superimposed MDD, anxiety disorders, conduct disorder, and ADHD.
- The most common age of onset for dysthymic disorder is between 11 and 12 years, with an average episode length of between 2 and 5 years.
- Almost all young people eventually recover from their dysthymia, but many will develop MDD.
- Children who recover from their dysthymic disorder differ mainly from other children on measures of psychosocial functioning.

Now that we have a good understanding of MDD and dysthymic disorder, we next consider their associated characteristics and possible causes.

Associated Characteristics of Depressive Disorders

Young people with depressive disorders experience deficits in intellectual performance and academic achievement, and disturbances in self-perceptions, self-esteem, social problem solving, interpersonal behavior, and life stressors (Garber & Kaminsky, 2000). Since depression often occurs with anxiety and other disorders, we don't know whether these associated deficits and disturbances are specific to depression or related to the presence of psychopathology in general. In addition, it is often difficult to know whether cognitive and psychosocial deficits are an outcome or a cause of depression.

Intellectual and Academic Functioning

Certain depressive symptoms—difficulty concentrating, loss of interest, and slowness of thought and movement—are likely to have a harmful effect on a child's intellectual and academic functioning. However, the overall intellectual potential of depressed youths is comparable to the potential of those who are not depressed. The association between severity of depression and children's overall intelligence is weak, suggesting that the effects of depression on cognitive functions may be selective. For example, depression may be associated with impairments on nonverbal tasks that require attention, coordination, speed, or recall of emotionally coded information, such as facial expressions (Guyer, Choate, Grimm, Pine, & Keenan, 2011), but not necessarily on tasks that require verbal skills or overall intelligence (Wilkinson & Goodyer, 2006).

Children with depression perform more poorly than others in school. They score lower on standard achievement tests, are rated by their teachers as achieving less academically, and have lower levels of grade attainment (Cole, 1990). Poor concentration and thinking ability, slowed movement or agitation, fatigue, insomnia, and somatic complaints may lead to repeating a grade, being late or skipping school, failure to complete homework, and dissatisfaction with or refusal of school. Jenn, a 15-year-old girl with MDD, and her mother had this to say about school:

> "School is a big waste of time," says Jenn. "I don't want to be there. I don't have the energy or motivation for school. I just say I'm sick so I can stay at home in bed and sleep all day." Jenn's mother says, "We used to fight about school so much that eventually I'd let her stay home—just to avoid having another fight."

It is difficult to determine whether depression is a cause or outcome of learning difficulties. Most likely it is both. For example, learning difficulties in adolescents, particularly girls, has been found to lead to feelings of inadequacy as a student, which prospectively predict depressive symptoms (Kiuru, Leskinen, Nurmi, & Salmela-Aro, 2011). It is unclear whether depression has an enduring effect on school performance. Some studies find that school difficulties do not occur following the child's recovery from depression, while others report that academic problems continue even after recovery (Kovacs & Goldston, 1991). In general, the association between depression and school difficulties is not as strong as the association between depression and social dysfunction (Lewinsohn, Gotlib, & Seeley, 1997).

Cognitive Biases and Distortions

"Good morning, Pooh Bear," said Eeyore gloomily. "If it is a good morning," he said. "Which I doubt."

—A. A. Milne, *Winnie-the-Pooh* (1926)

ELLIE

Life's Hardly Worth It

"... like everything's worthless, like it's just not worth it to even be.... It's—it seems like it's a silly thing to even go through life and exist. And from one day to the next you're always wondering if you're going to make it to the next day if it's—if you can stand it, if it's worth trying to get to tomorrow.... It's just—just, I feel like—I feel mostly like I'm worthless, like there's something wrong with me. It's really not a pleasant feeling to know that you're a total failure, a complete nothing, and I get the feeling that I never do nothing right or worthwhile or anything." (Adapted from McKnew, Cytryn, & Yahraes, 1983)

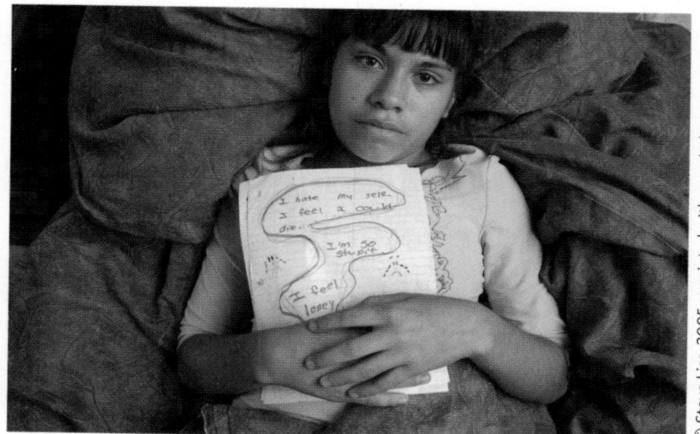

Depression in young people is associated with negative thoughts and feelings of worthlessness

Many children with depression experience biases, deficits, and distortions in their thinking (Lakdawalla, Hankin, & Mermelstein, 2007). Selective attention to depression-relevant cues such as sad facial expressions, along with selective inattention to positive cues such as happy facial expressions are common (Ehrmantrout, Allen, Leve, Davis, & Sheeber, 2011; Hankin, Gibb, Abela, & Flory, 2010). Given the importance of accurately reading emotional cues for successful social relationships, these selective attentional biases can contribute to adverse relationships with family members and peers.

Some cognitive disturbances, such as Ellie's painful feelings of worthlessness, are part of the diagnosis of depression. Negative beliefs ("I never do nothing right") and attributions of failure ("I'm a total failure") are not part of the diagnosis but typically accompany the disorder. Negative thoughts that are self-critical and automatic, such as "I'm a real loser," "I'm ugly," or "I'm gonna fail," are common. Unfortunately, these thoughts can't simply be swept aside by suggesting to a depressed youth that she or he "look at the bright side."

Depressed children often devalue their own performance by not acknowledging their accomplishments. They dismiss praise when it is given and frequently make inaccurate interpretations of their experiences (Fichman, Koestner, & Zuroff, 1996). To focus narrowly on negative events for long periods is referred to as a **depressive ruminative style** (Nolen-Hoeksema, Girgus, & Seligman, 1992). These youngsters view themselves as ineffective in most areas of their lives, and make self-directed disparaging comments when faced with further failure or rejection (e.g., "It must be my fault"). They misread situations, feel slighted by otherwise harmless remarks, and are easily frustrated—small setbacks are seen as major catastrophes. Negative thinking and faulty conclusions are generalized across situations, so the depressed youth sees no hope of gaining any pleasure or satisfaction.

It is not unusual for young people with depression to think that no one can help them out of their misery. Many report hopelessness or negative expectations about the future that are related to diminished self-esteem and to suicide ideation and attempts (Marciano & Kazdin, 1994). Since feelings of hopelessness dominate their lives, they experience a vicious downward cycle in which self-defeating negative thoughts become pervasive and impair performance at school and home. As performance deteriorates they perceive more failure, and receive—and even seek—further negative feedback. These outcomes maintain their low self-opinion and view of an inability to change, which lead to further impairments in functioning.

Their pessimistic outlook also places them at greater risk for depressive symptoms, especially in response to stressful life events. Since their pessimism may continue after remission of depressive symptoms, they remain at risk for future depressive episodes. We will return to the role of cognitive disturbances in depression later, in the section on cognitive theories.

Negative Self-Esteem

Eeyore, the old grey Donkey, stood by the side of the stream and looked at himself in the water. "Pathetic," he said. "That's what it is. Pathetic."

—A. A. Milne, *Winnie-the-Pooh* (1926)

FARAH

Never Good Enough

Fifteen-year-old Farah's mother says that Farah is a "model daughter" who is near the top of her class, active in school activities, and extremely popular. Her mother is concerned about "how hard Farah is on herself, thinking that she has to be perfect." If Farah doesn't get the highest grade on a test, she won't allow herself to see her friends for a week, and spends most of the time in her room studying. Farah acknowledges that she sets very high standards for herself and if she fails to meet these standards becomes extremely self-critical and self-punitive. She has even slapped herself in the face after what she saw as academic "failure" (getting an A-minus rather than an A). Farah's accomplishments bring her little satisfaction, and any perceived failure leads to immediate self-condemnation. Farah's overall self-worth is low and her sense of self, which is based on competency in academic achievement, is highly vulnerable. (Based on authors' case material)

Almost all young people with depression experience negative self-esteem. In fact, low self-esteem is the symptom that seems most specifically related to depression in adolescents (Lewinsohn et al., 1997). Self-esteem in children with depression is also highly reactive to daily life events, and such daily fluctuations in self-esteem appear to be related to depression following exposure to major life stresses (Roberts & Gotlib, 1997). Thus, both low self-esteem and unstable self-esteem seem to play an important role in depression.

Since physical appearance and approval from peers are especially important as sources of self-esteem for most adolescents, perceived incompetence in these areas may heighten the risk for depression. The fact that self-esteem problems in adolescent girls are often related to a negative body image may partly contribute to their higher risk for depression (Hankin & Abramson, 2001).

An interesting developmental model of self-esteem and depression hypothesizes that children seek and receive feedback from others about their competence or incompetence in several domains: academics, social relations, sports, conduct, and physical appearance (Jordan & Cole, 1996). Self-views are constructed from this feedback, and the outcome may be a varied and positive self-view leading to optimism, energy, and enthusiasm. Or, it may be a narrow and negative self-view leading to pessimism, a sense of helplessness, and possibly, depression (Seroczynski, Cole, & Maxwell, 1997). Children whose self-views are negative and narrowly focused in one domain—for example, in academics—may show instability in their self-esteem because they lack alternative compensatory areas of functioning, such as sports or social relations. This may make them vulnerable to developing depression when faced with stress in their primary domain.

Social and Peer Problems

Young people who are depressed experience significant disruptions in their relationships. They have few friends or close relationships, feel lonely and isolated, feel that others do not like them (which, unfortunately, often becomes a reality), and display extensive impairments in their social skills (Rudolph, Flynn, & Abaied, 2008). Chronic peer-related loneliness during childhood has been found to predict depressive symptoms in early adolescence (Qualter, Brown, Munn, & Rotenberg, 2010). In addition, children with depression who report poor friendships at the time of referral have a reduced likelihood of recovery from depression (Goodyer, Herbert, Tamplin, Secher, & Pearson, 1997). Even when children recover from their depression, they continue to experience some social impairment.

Social withdrawal is common in youngsters with depression. They often spend significant amounts of time alone, show little interest in seeing friends, and engage in few activities. Their social withdrawal may reflect an inability to maintain social interactions, which is possibly related to negative, irritable, and aggressive behavior toward others, and deficits in initiating conversations or making friends (Rockhill et al., 2007). These factors can seriously interfere with social development, depriving youngsters with depression of the social exchanges that lead to healthy interpersonal relationships.

Youngsters who are depressed use ineffective styles of coping in social situations. For example, they use less active and problem-focused coping, and more passive, avoidant, ruminative, or emotion-focused coping (Hammen & Rudolph, 2003). A strong risk factor for the onset of depression in adolescent females is **co-rumination**, a negative form of self-disclosure and discussion between peers focused narrowly on problems or emotions to the exclusion of other activities or dialogue (Stone, Hankin, Gibb, & Abela, 2011). Co-rumination seems to be one mechanism underlying adolescent females' heightened risk for depression. Ironically, co-rumination between peers is associated with higher ratings of friendship quality and closeness, which in turn, have been found to predict increases in co-rumination. Thus, what appear to be socially rewarding and supportive relationships with peers not only fail to protect female teens from distress, but also may increase their risk for depression when based on maladaptive styles of interaction (Stone et al., 2011).

Depressed teens may also make poor choices in dealing with social problems, such as turning to alcohol or drugs in response to a break-up with a boy or girlfriend. In the words of Page, age 17:

> I was so unhappy that I didn't care about myself—even about being safe. I was out drinking a lot, doing a lot of pot. Sometimes I would just black out and not know what was happening. One night I think a bunch of guys had sex with me when I passed out, I don't know. I never remembered anything, it was all hearsay the next day. I made some really bad boyfriend choices. I would date guys who reinforced my view of myself as ugly, stupid, and uncool. I dropped my preppy boyfriend and started dating a 20-year-old guy who was living in his own apartment and playing in a band. He had tattoos on his arms and stomach. I would date guys just so I could get a ride, even though I didn't like them. I would pick boyfriends who were depressed or ones that my parents really didn't like. (From "I Did Not Want to Live," by Sabrina Solin Weill, 1995. *Seventeen*, April 1, 1995, pp. 154–156, 176.)

Interestingly, the basic understanding required for appropriate social relations appears to be relatively intact in youngsters with depression. They are generally capable of providing cognitive solutions to interpersonal problems (Kovacs & Goldston, 1991). However, as with Page, their deficits in social behavior are in sharp contrast to their social understanding.

Family Problems

Youngsters with depression experience less supportive and more conflictual relationships with their mothers, fathers, and siblings. They report feeling socially isolated from their families and prefer to be alone rather than with them. In family situations, the child's social isolation may not be a social skill deficit, but rather a reflection of the child's desire to avoid conflict. Family relationship difficulties have been found to persist even when children are no longer clinically depressed (Sheeber, Davis, Leve, Hops, & Tildesley, 2007).

During interactions, these children may be quite negative toward their parents, and their parents in turn may respond in a negative, dismissing, or harsh manner (Coyne, Downey, & Boergers, 1992). When repeated over time, these interactions may adversely affect the family relationships. Children with depression who are irritable, unresponsive, and unaffectionate provide little positive reinforcement for their parents, and frustrate their parent's desire for satisfaction in the parenting role (Kovacs, 1997).

"It's my youth, and I don't have to enjoy it if I don't want to."

Depression and Suicide

CARLA

"It Became Too Much"

Carla, age 12, was admitted to the intensive care unit unconscious and unstable after ingesting eight of her mother's 50-mg Elavil™ tablets, an unknown quantity of antidepressants, and approximately 20 tablets of Tylenol 3™. This suicide attempt, her first, came after arguing with her father over chores and restrictions imposed because her grades were so bad. Carla said she went to the medicine cabinet and ingested everything she could find because "it became too much" and she "did not want to live." For the previous month, she had displayed a noticeable change of mood, behaving with more instability and depression, feeling worthless and hopeless. In this period she had lost her appetite and had dropped two dress sizes. She increasingly had isolated herself, staying alone in her room. Her school performance, for which her father had restricted her, had declined from B's the previous term to D's. (From *Adolescent Suicide: Assessment and Intervention* by A. L. Berman and D. A. Jobes, 1991, p. 144. Copyright © 1991 by the American Psychological Association. Reprinted with permission. APA is not responsible for the accuracy of this translation)

Carla's case illustrates the profound feelings of hopelessness, helplessness, and despair that often lead a youngster with depression to attempt suicide. Most youngsters with depression report suicidal thinking, and as many as one-third who think about killing themselves actually attempt it (Goldston, Daniel, & Arnold, 2006). Drug overdose and wrist cutting are the most common methods for adolescents who attempt suicide. For children who complete suicide, the most common methods are firearms (57%), hanging or suffocation (28.4%), and poisoning or overdose (7.6%) (CDC, 2002).

The link between depression, suicidal behavior, and completed suicide is undeniable, strong, and sobering (Dervic, Brent, & Oquendo, 2008). Although rates of suicidal behavior vary across countries, the two strongest risk factors for suicidal behavior are consistent worldwide—having a mood disorder and being a young female (Nock et al., 2008). Suicidal ideation (e.g., thinking about killing oneself) is common across many different types of psychological disorders, but actual suicide attempts are much more common during depression (see Box 8.1). In one 7- to 9-year follow-up of children with psychiatric disorders, 84% of all suicide attempts were found to occur for depressive disorders (Shaffer et al., 1996).

BOX 8.1 A CLOSER LOOK

Depressive Disorder Is Associated with Suicide Thoughts and Suicide Attempts

What's the use?
I look ~~arou~~ around here and all
I see,
Is a school and a world
that could do without me.
I've gotten here but only by
fate.
My death, I'm sure, will not come
late.
I try each day to see the use
of being here.
There is none.
I try to find a meaning,
But the wars have been fought,
my battle is yet to come.
When I close my eyes the pain
goes.
When I open them again the
pain. shows.
I try to not cry aloud,
Wouldn't matter anyway I'm lost
in this crowd.
You can pretend I don't live,
But I'll keep living 'till my
life gives.

Teri's note

Teri: What's the Use?

Teri, age 15, had been depressed since her father died when she was 11. According to her mother, over the past 14 months her behavior had gone from moody to sullen. She had disobeyed restrictions imposed as punishments, and had run away from home on several occasions. She labeled herself as "stupid," spoke and wrote often of death and suicide (see accompanying note). On three occasions she had cut her wrists, albeit only superficially. Her school performance had declined and she spoke now of hating school. Her peer associations were almost exclusively with other alienated teens, described by her as "punks and other anarchists."

Source: Adolescent Suicide: Assessment and Intervention by A. L. Berman and D. A. Jobes, 1991, p. 144. Copyright © 1991 by the American Psychological Association. Reprinted with permission. APA is not responsible for the accuracy of this translation.

About 60% of youngsters who are clinically depressed report having thoughts about suicide, and 30% actually attempt suicide by 17 years of age, with most attempts coming within the first year following the onset of suicidal thoughts. Unfortunately, about one-half of them eventually make further attempts (American Academy of Child and Adolescent Psychiatry [AACAP], 2001). The suicide attempts of youngsters with depression almost never occur during times when they are symptom-free—90% or more have depressive features at the time of their suicidal episode. Finally, among youngsters who kill themselves, the odds of having major depression are 27 times higher than among controls (Brent et al., 1993; Shaffer et al., 1996).

In general, young females with depression show more suicidal ideation and attempt suicide much more often than young males. The risk factors for non-fatal suicide attempts are similar for males and females (Thompson & Light, 2010). However, since girls typically don't use guns, they are usually less successful in completing suicide than boys (Goldston et al., 2006). Ages 13 and 14 are peak periods for a first suicide attempt by youngsters with depression. Suicide prior to puberty is rare, most likely because depression and substance abuse before puberty are also rare. In adolescents with depression, suicide attempts double during the teen years but show an abrupt decline after age 17 or 18. It is possible that as young people mature, they are better able to tolerate their negative mood states and acquire more resources for coping, thus making it less likely that they will attempt suicide during periods of sadness (Borowsky, Ireland, & Resnick, 2001).

In light of the strong connection between symptoms of depression and suicidal ideation and behavior, a primary strategy for reducing suicide in young people is to increase the availability of effective treatments for depression (Brown et al., 2007). We discuss these treatments later in the chapter. Since racial and ethnic groups are known to differ in rates of suicidal behaviors and the circumstances under which they occur (e.g., precipitants, risk and protective factors, and patterns of help seeking), it is also important that suicide prevention and treatment programs are sensitive to these cultural differences (Goldston et al., 2008).

SECTION SUMMARY

Associated Characteristics of Depressive Disorders

- Youngsters with depression have normal intelligence, although certain symptoms such as difficulty concentrating, loss of interest, and slowness of thought may negatively affect intellectual functioning.
- They perform more poorly than others in school, score lower on standard achievement tests, and have lower levels of grade attainment.
- They often experience deficits and distortions in their thinking, including negative beliefs, attributions of failure, and self-critical automatic negative thoughts.
- Almost all youngsters with depression experience low or unstable self-esteem.
- Youngsters with depression have few friends and close relationships, feel lonely and isolated, and feel that others do not like them.
- They experience poor relations and conflict with their parents and siblings, who in turn may respond in a negative, dismissing, or harsh manner.
- Most youngsters with depression report suicidal thinking, and about 30% who think about killing themselves actually attempt it.

THEORIES OF DEPRESSION

Many theories have been proposed to explain the onset and course of depression. Until recently, however, most were developed to explain depression in adults, then directly applied to children with minimal regard for developmental differences (Garber & Horowitz, 2002). In the sections that follow, we consider several of these theories. Keep in mind, however, that depression is likely a final, common pathway for interacting influences that predispose a child to develop the disorder (Hammen & Rudolph, 2003). No one theory can explain all forms of depressive disorder and differences in symptoms and severity within the same disorder. An overview of the primary theories of depression is presented in Table 8.2.

Psychodynamic

Early psychodynamic theories viewed depression as the conversion of aggressive instinct into depressive affect. Depression is presumed to result from the loss of a love object that is loved ambivalently. This loss can be actual, as in the case of the death of a parent, or symbolic, as a result of emotional deprivation, rejection, or inadequate parenting. The individual's subsequent rage toward the love object is then turned against the self. Since children and adolescents were believed to have inadequate development of the superego or conscience, the hostility directed against internalized love objects that have disappointed or abandoned them does not produce guilt, so they do not become depressed (Bemporad, 1994; Poznanski, 1979). However, recent studies have found that high levels of maladaptive guilt and shame are related to the onset of depression in children as young as 3 to 5 years (Luby et al., 2009). Furthermore, the fact that depression does occur in many youngsters who do not experience loss or rejection—and doesn't occur in many children who do—casts

TABLE 8.2 | Overview of Theories of Depression

Psychodynamic	Introjection of the lost object; anger turned inward; excessive severity of the superego; loss of self-esteem
Attachment	Insecure early attachments; distorted internal working models of self and others
Behavioral	Lack or loss of reinforcement or quality of reinforcement; deficits in skills needed to obtain reinforcement
Cognitive	Depressive mindset; distorted or maladaptive cognitive structures, processes, and products; negative view of self, world, and future; poor problem-solving ability; hopelessness
Self-Control	Problems in organizing behavior toward long-term goals; deficits in self-monitoring, self-evaluation, and self-reinforcement
Interpersonal	Impaired interpersonal functioning related to grief over loss; role dispute and conflict; role transition; interpersonal deficit; single parenting; social withdrawal; interaction between mood and interpersonal events
Socio-environmental	Stressful life circumstances and daily hassles as vulnerability factors; social support, coping, and appraisal as protective factors
Neurobiological	Neurochemical and receptor abnormalities; neurophysiological abnormalities; neuroendocrine abnormalities; genetic variants

Source: Adapted from *A Developmental Cognitive Model of Unipolar Major Depression*, by D. J. A. Dozois, unpublished manuscript. Adapted by permission of the author.

doubt on the psychodynamic model. Contrary to this theory, many children do experience clinical depression.

Attachment

Attachment theory focuses on parental separation and disruption of an attachment bond as predisposing factors for depression. John Bowlby hypothesized that a child confronted with unresponsive and emotionally unavailable caregiving goes through a typical sequence involving protest, despair, and detachment (Bowlby, 1961). A parent's consistent failure to meet the child's needs is associated with the development of an insecure attachment, a view of self as unworthy and unloved, and a view of others as threatening or undependable. These factors may place the child at risk for later depression, particularly in the context of stressful interpersonal relationships (Rudolph, Hammen, & Burge, 1997). Attachment relationships also serve to regulate biological and behavioral systems related to emotion. For example, a secure attachment may help reduce distress, whereas an insecure attachment may lead to difficulties in regulating emotion, which in turn may become a risk factor for later depression. In support of this theory, children with insecure attachments are more likely than children with secure attachments to display symptoms of depression (e.g., Toth & Cicchetti, 1996). In addition, children and adolescents with depression are more likely to experience disturbances in attachment than children without depression (Stein et al., 2000). In a recent study, only 8% of adolescents with depression were securely attached versus 52% of controls, and 40% of them had an insecure attachment that was unresolved with regard to loss or abuse (Ivarsson, Granqvist, Gillberg, & Broberg, 2010).

Behavioral

Behavioral views emphasize the importance of learning, environmental consequences, and skills and deficits during the onset and maintenance of depression. Depression is related to *a lack of response-contingent positive reinforcement* (Lewinsohn, 1974). This lack of positive reinforcement may occur for three reasons. First, a youngster may be unable to experience available reinforcement, often due to interfering anxiety. Second, changes in the environment, such as the loss of a significant person in the child's life, may result in a lack of availability of rewards. Finally, a youngster may lack the skills needed to have rewarding and satisfying social relationships.

Children may also receive sympathy for their sadness, which produces the desired attention and concern. However, this sympathy is usually short-lived because even people who care about the youngster begin to avoid him or her. This reduction in attention may then lead to withdrawal, impairment in functioning, and heightened feelings of depression. Few studies have tested specific behavioral hypotheses with children, and this model seems incomplete in the light of what is known about other factors that may lead to a vulnerability to depression. Nevertheless, the behavioral model highlights the importance of learning processes in the emergence, expression, and outcome of depression in young people.

Cognitive

Cognitive theories focus on the relation between negative thinking and mood (Abela & Hankin, 2008a). The underlying assumptions are that how young people view themselves and their world will influence their mood and behavior, and that cognitive vulnerabilities interact with negative events to increase depressive symptoms. A variety of negative cognitions, attributions, misperceptions, and deficiencies in cognitive problem-solving skills are related to depression in young people (Lakdawalla et al., 2007). Cognitive theories emphasize **depressogenic cognitions**, which are the negative perceptual and attributional styles and beliefs associated with depressive symptoms.

For example, **hopelessness theory** proposes that depression-prone individuals tend to make internal, stable, and global attributions to explain the causes of negative events. In other words, when something bad happens, they think they are responsible (internal attribution), the reason they are to blame won't change over time (stable attribution), and the reason that something bad happened applies to most things they do and in most situations (global attribution) (Abramson, Seligman, & Teasdale, 1978). In contrast, they attribute positive events to something outside themselves (external), which is not likely to happen again (unstable), and is seen as unique to this event (specific). A *negative attributional style* results in the individual's taking personal blame for negative events in his or her life and leads to helplessness and avoidance of these events in the future. Helplessness may in turn lead to hopelessness about the future, which promotes further depression (Abramson, Metalsky, & Alloy, 1989).

The cognitive model developed by Aaron Beck (1967) proposes that depressed individuals make negative interpretations about life events because they use biased and negative beliefs as interpretive filters for understanding these events. Depressed individuals show cognitive problems in three areas.

First, they display *information-processing biases*, or errors in their thinking in specific situations, called *negative automatic thoughts*. These often include thoughts of physical and social threat, personal failure, and hostility (Schniering & Rapee, 2004). They may selectively attend to negative information, assume blame for negative events, maximize and exaggerate negative events, and minimize positive events. They also assign negative labels to events, and then react emotionally to the label rather than the event. For example:

- EVENT: Child didn't receive an invitation to Ashley's party.
- LABEL: "I didn't receive an invitation because Ashley doesn't like me. *Nobody likes me*."
- EMOTIONAL REACTION: Unhappiness and depression.

Second, depression is believed to be associated with a negative outlook in the following three areas, referred to as the **negative cognitive triad** (see ● Figure 8.2):

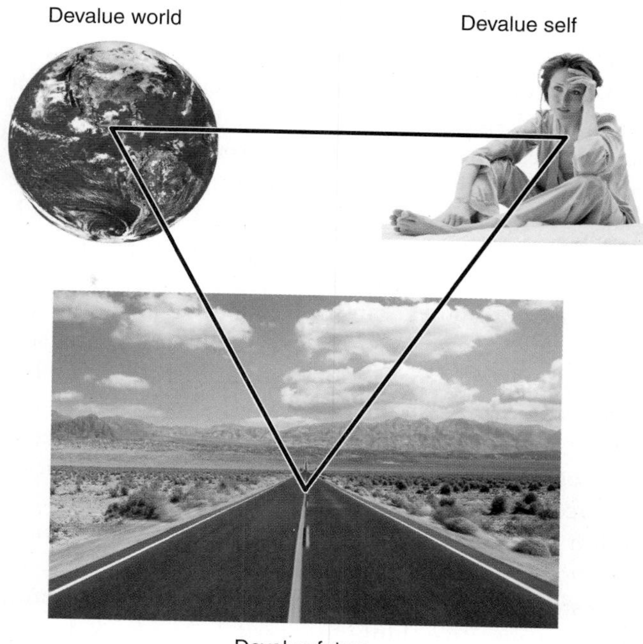

● **FIGURE 8.2** | The Negative Cognitive Triad: Depression is related to a devaluation of self, the world, and the future.

Photo credits: © 2012 Tom Merton/Jupiterimages Corporation; thumb/Shutterstock.com; kavram/Shutterstock.com

- Negative views about *oneself* (e.g., "I'm no good," "I'm boring")
- Negative views about the *world* (day-to-day experiences) (e.g., "They're no good," "It's too hard")
- Negative views about the *future* (e.g., "It's always going to be this bad," "I'll never graduate")

These negative views become increasingly more stable with age, maintain feelings of helplessness, undermine the youngster's mood and energy level, and are related to the child's severity of depression (LaGrange et al., 2008; Stark, Schmidt, & Joiner, 1996).

Third, depressed youngsters have **negative cognitive schemata**, which are stable structures in memory that guide information processing, including self-critical beliefs and attitudes. These schemata are rigid and resistant to change even in the face of contradictory evidence, and may heighten the youngster's sensitivity to depression, especially when activated by stress.

Applying cognitive theories to depression in young people raises questions about the cognitive capacities of children at various stages of development, and the development and stability of cognitive structures that may be involved in their depressive thinking (Abela & Hankin, 2008a). A well-developed sense of self and a time perspective for the future are needed to experience depression; these cognitive processes are still developing in children. In addition, many of the cognitive errors and distortions discussed so far, such as illogical thinking or faulty attributions, are normal ways of thinking in young children!

Although higher rates of negative thinking are found in youngsters with depression, there are still many unanswered questions about the relation between cognition and depression (Lakdawalla et al., 2007). More information is needed about how negative cognitions develop. Are the negative cognitions that accompany depression the result of parental rejection and negative parenting practices? Is there a relation between maternal and child cognitions, as suggested by the relationship between mothers' and children's negative thinking (Stark, Schmidt, & Joiner, 1996)? How and when does a cognitive vulnerability for depression interact with stress to result in depression (Cole et al., 2008)? At this time, there is support for a cognitive vulnerability–stress interaction in adolescents, but less so for younger children (Lakdawalla et al., 2007). Longitudinal studies are needed to answer these and other questions concerning the role of cognition in the development of depression in young people.

Other Theories

Self-control theories view youngsters with depression as having difficulty organizing their behavior in relation to long-term goals and displaying deficits in self-monitoring, self-evaluation, and self-reinforcement. As a result, they selectively attend to negative events and to the immediate consequences of their behavior. These youngsters set excessively high standards for performance, make negative causal attributions, administer insufficient self-rewards, and use excessive self-punishment. Research suggests that children with depression display a number of these deficits (Rehm & Sharp, 1996).

Interpersonal models view disruptions in interpersonal relationships, especially with family and peers, as the basis for the onset and maintenance of depression (Hammen, 1999). Depressive symptoms in adolescence are associated with increases in the negative quality and decreases in the positive quality of relationships over time (Oppenheimer & Hankin, 2011). The behaviors of a depressed youngster are unpleasant to others, leading family members and others to become annoyed and frustrated. As the youngster becomes more aware of how others are reacting, he or she feels even more needy, and then unthinkingly and annoyingly seeks excessive reassurance, which in turn leads to further interpersonal rejection (Joiner, 1999). Interpersonal models also propose that the child's depression may serve a function in the family—for example, to reduce conflict between parents.

Socioenvironmental models emphasize the relationship between stressful life events and depression. Adolescents with depression experience significantly more psychosocial adversity than controls or adolescents with other psychiatric disorders (Ivarsson et al., 2010). Some life events related to the onset of depression are social disadvantage, unemployment, single-parent status, large family, personal loss, abuse, and poor social support. Stressful life events may be linked to depression in several ways. First, depression can be a direct reaction to the occurrence of stressful life events, such as the loss of a parent. Second, the impact of stress may be moderated by individual risk factors, such as genetic risk. This is referred to as the **diathesis–stress model of depression** because the occurrence of depression depends on the interaction between the youngster's personal vulnerability (diathesis) and life stress. Third, negative environmental events may be internalized as negative cognitive styles (e.g., rumination), which then predispose the child to develop depression (Abela & Hankin, 2011). Finally, depression may result in behaviors and impairments in functioning that generate stressful life circumstances that in turn lead to depressive reactions (Hammen, Brennan, & Le Brocque, 2011). Stress generation following depression may also be heightened by early developmental risk factors such as child abuse and neglect (Harkness, Lumley, & Truss, 2008).

Neurobiological models of depression in young people focus on genetic vulnerabilities and neurobiological processes. Several neurobiological abnormalities have been identified, although findings are far less consistent for children than for adults (NIMH, 2003). We consider possible biologic and other factors in the next section on causes.

SECTION SUMMARY

Theories of Depression

- Psychodynamic theories presume that depression results from the actual or symbolic loss of a love object, and view depression as the conversion of aggressive instinct into depressive affect.
- Behavioral views emphasize the importance of learning, environmental consequences (particularly a lack of

response-contingent reinforcement), and skills deficits during the onset and maintenance of depression.

- Cognitive theories of depression focus on the relation between negative thinking and mood, with the underlying assumption that how young people view themselves and their world will influence their mood and behavior.
- Other theories of depression have emphasized the role of deficits in self-control, interpersonal disturbances, stressful life events, and genetic and neurobiological processes.

Causes of Depression

In light of the many vulnerability, risk, and protective factors that have been implicated, an integrative framework is necessary to account for depression in young people and for its nonoccurrence in the presence of risk (Hammen & Rudolph, 2003; Miller, 2007). The framework presented in ● Figure 8.3 highlights possible causes of depression in young people and the interplay among genetic, neurobiological, family, cognitive, emotional, interpersonal, and environmental factors. Given these many interacting influences, multiple pathways to depression are likely (Eaves, Silberg, & Erkanli, 2003).

Within this framework, genetic risk influences neurobiological processes, and is reflected in an early temperament characterized by oversensitivity to negative stimuli, high negative emotionality, and a disposition to feeling negative affect. These early dispositions increase exposure to and are shaped by negative experiences within the family, and continue to exert influence throughout development. Core beliefs about self and others develop as a result of experiences within the family. Parenting that is insensitive, disengaged, or rejecting may lead to an insecure attachment and a view of self as incompetent, other people as threatening or unresponsive, and relationships as negative and unpredictable. Negative family experiences may also create an inconsistent emotional and social environment, which makes it difficult for the child to effectively regulate emotions and interpersonal behavior and to cope with stress (Compas, Connor-Smith, Saltzman, Thomsen, & Wadsworth, 2001).

Cognitive, emotional, and interpersonal problems may lead directly to depression. Or, they may elicit conflict, rejection by others, and social isolation, which will eventually lead to depression. In other instances, negative beliefs, poor social relationships, and difficulty in regulating emotions may create a *vulnerability* to develop depression when confronted with life stress. In any of these scenarios, the child's depression may then interfere with future development by further disrupting interpersonal relationships, damaging existing competencies, producing further difficulties in regulating emotions, creating additional stress, and confirming the child's already negative views about self and others (Hammen & Rudolph, 2003).

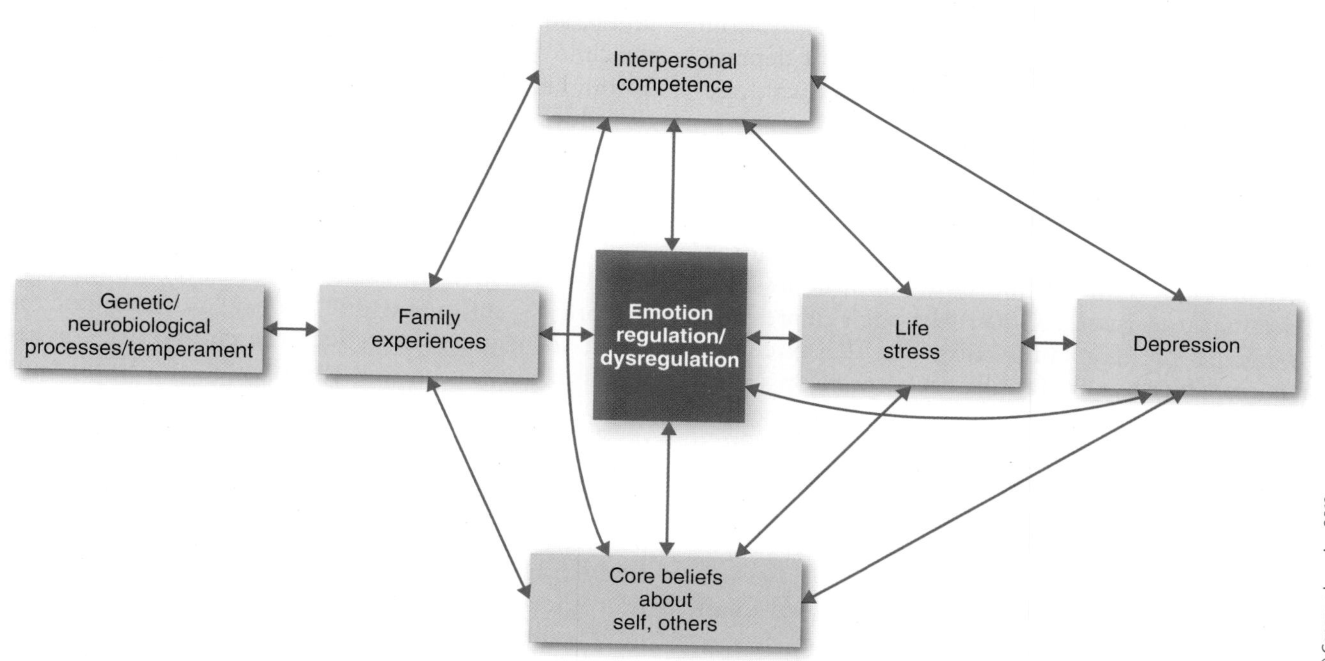

● **FIGURE 8.3** | A developmental framework for depression in young people.

In the sections that follow, we examine several of these possible interacting causal influences for depression.

Genetic and Family Risk

Twin and other genetic studies suggest a moderate genetic influence on depression in children and adolescents, with heritability estimates ranging from 30% to 45% across studies (Franic, Middeldorp, Dolan, Ligthart, & Boomsa, 2010; Lemery & Doelger, 2005). There is consistent evidence that MDD in young people runs in families across generations. In fact, the single best predictor of a child's risk for MDD is a high family loading for this disorder (Weissman et al., 2005). Children with a parent who suffered from depression as a child are 14 times more likely than controls to become depressed themselves *before the age of 13* (Weissman, Warner, Wickramaratne, & Prusoff, 1988).

Children of parents with depression have about 3 times the risk of having depression compared with children of parents having no psychiatric disorders (Weissman et al., 2006). The child's risk for depression is even higher when both parents have a mood disorder. Children of depressed parents also have an earlier age of onset for their depression (by about 3 years), and are more likely to show an onset before puberty than children of nondepressed parents (Weissman, Warner, Wickramaratne, Moreau, & Olfson, 1997). This is a significant factor, because a family history of depression is most likely associated with recurrence of depression and a continuation of depression into adulthood for children with an onset of depression before puberty (Wickramaratne, Greenwald, & Weissman, 2000).

The lifetime prevalence of depression in mothers of children with depression is also high, about 50% to 75% (Kovacs, 1997). A family history of depression is also greater in first-degree relatives of children with depression than in children without depression (Wickramaratne et al., 2000). Although depression in young people is a family disorder, the extent to which transmission in families is genetic, psychosocial, or both is not yet known. Causal influences may also differ with development, with support for a greater role for shared environmental influences for depression during childhood in contrast to a greater genetic influence during adolescence (Scourfield et al., 2003).

Studies into possible genetic markers for early-onset depressive disorders have implicated regions on several chromosomes. However, findings generally suggest that no specific region makes a large contribution to the risk of MDD, and that multiple regions are involved (Holmans et al., 2007). Studies of specific genes have focused primarily on those involved in the synthesis, release, and reuptake of the neurotransmitter serotonin and to a lesser extent on other genes, such as brain-derived neurotrophic factor (BDNF), that have been implicated in brain plasticity and response to stress (Levinson, 2006).

In general, family and twin studies and specific gene studies suggest that a vulnerability to negative affect may be inherited, and that certain environmental stressors may be required for these vulnerabilities to result in depression (Eley & Stevenson, 2000; Rice, Harold, & Thapar, 2003). Support for G × E interactions comes from several studies. One 3-year longitudinal study found that the effects of family conflict on depressive symptoms were greater for children and adolescents at genetic risk for depression (Rice, Harold, Shelton, & Thapar, 2006). A second study found that individuals with variants in the serotonin transporter gene displayed more depressive symptoms, diagnosable depression, and suicidality in relation to stressful life events than those who did not (Caspi et al., 2003). A recent study found that youths with variants in the serotonin transporter gene who experienced more stressors relative to their typical level displayed increases in depressive but not anxious symptoms over time, suggesting a G × E interaction specific to depression (Hankin, Jenness, Abela, & Smolen, 2011). Another study found a higher risk for depression in children who were maltreated, but only in children with variants in both the BDNF and serotonin transporter genes. Importantly, social support was also found to ameliorate the child's genetic risk for depression (Kaufman et al., 2006). Finally, other genes (COMT) have been found to reduce the risk for depressive symptoms in children exposed to severe psychosocial deprivation as a result of being raised in an institution from a young age (Drury et al., 2010).

The findings that specific genes may increase or decrease sensitivity to stress through their impact on the brain's emotional and arousal systems, and by doing so heighten or reduce the child's risk for depression are fascinating (Bradley et al., 2008; Gatt et al., 2010). However, it is important to note that there have been few studies with children and results have been inconsistent (e.g., Karg, Burmeister, Shedden, & Sen, 2011; Risch et al., 2009). Thus, findings in this area, particularly those for the serotonin transporter gene, must be viewed cautiously until they can be confirmed in studies that consider how multiple genes interact with multiple sources of environmental adversity in youngsters with and without depression (Fergusson, Horwood, Miller, & Kennedy, 2011).

Neurobiological Influences

Although we can't point to one part of the brain that causes a young person to become depressed, abnormalities in the structure and function of several brain regions have been implicated. Most studies of young people with depression have focused on neural systems that regulate emotional functions such as neuroendocrine stress responses, autonomic activity, and reward sensitivity. Brain scan studies have identified multiple abnormalities in the structure and function of the amygdala, cingulate and prefrontal cortex, and related limbic and striatal brain areas (Miller, 2007). For example, smaller volumes of the amygdala, hippocampus, and thalamus have been identified in adolescents and adults with depressive disorders. Interestingly, smaller volumes of several of these brain structures in infants as young 6 weeks of age have been associated with higher internalizing behaviors at 18 and 36 months of age (Herba et al., 2010). This suggests a possible biological vulnerability for the development of internalizing problems that may be present early in life. Recent studies have also identified cortical thinning in the right hemisphere of children and adults with or at risk for depression based on family history (Falluca et al., 2011; Peterson et al., 2009). Cortical thinning in the right hemisphere might produce disturbances in arousal, attention, and memory for social stimuli that predispose the individual to developing a depressive disorder.

In general, brain activity has been found to be less active in regions of the brain associated with attention and sensory processes, but more active than normal in regions involved in recognizing and regulating emotions, mediating stress responses, and learning and recalling emotion-arousing memories (Yurgelon-Todd, Sava, & Dahlgren, 2007). For example, the amygdala may overstimulate brain structures involved in forming certain types of memories, perhaps accounting for the tendency of depressed youngsters to ruminate on past negative life events. Overactivity of the amygdala may also affect the recognition and consolidation of social stimuli (e.g., faces, tone of voice) from a very early age so that ordinary interpersonal events are seen or recalled as aversive or emotionally arousing (Gaffrey et al., 2011; Lau et al., 2009; Monk et al., 2008). Neuroimaging studies of youngsters with MDD have also identified disruptions in neural activity in areas of the brain associated with decision making about future rewards and responses to rewarding outcomes (Forbes et al., 2006).

The hippocampus, one of the brain's memory centers, has also been implicated in depression. Parts of the hippocampus are involved in recognizing the environmental contexts for reward or danger including sensitivity to stress. Brain scan studies have found that individual variations in hippocampal volume interact with family stress to prospectively predict differences in depressive symptoms in adolescent girls over a period of 2.5 years (Whittle et al., 2011). Because of variants in the hippocampus, individuals with depression may experience a constant state of anxiety and have difficulty recognizing situations that are safe (Davidson, Pizzagalli, & Nitschke, 2002). Studies of other brain regions have found that healthy adolescents who respond to peer rejection with greater activation of the anterior cingulate cortex are more likely to show an increase in depressive symptoms over the following year (Masten et al., 2011). These findings suggest that activity in brain regions involved in affective processing of socio-emotional stimuli may provide a possible neurobiological marker for predicting healthy youngsters' future risk for depression.

Other studies into the neurobiological correlates of depression in young people have focused on HPA-axis dysregulation; sleep abnormalities suggestive of reduced neuroplasticity; variants in brain-derived neurotrophic factor (BDNF), which is involved in nerve growth and development; and the brain neurotransmitters serotonin, dopamine, and norepinephrine, which are widely spread throughout brain circuits thought to underlie mood disorders (Miller, 2007). Although findings related to these neurobiological correlates are suggestive, it is important to note that studies of children are few in number, and the findings are far less consistent than for adults (Kaufman, Martin, King, & Charney, 2001).

HPA-axis dysregulation is evidenced by abnormal cortisol responses in children and adolescents with depression, including higher baseline levels and atypical or overactive responses to stressors (Lopez-Duran, Kovacs, & George, 2009). HPA-axis and other neurobiological findings have led to a strong interest in the impact of early exposure to stress on later negative moods. As we discussed in Chapter 7, mounting evidence suggests that early adversity (e.g., prenatal stress, harsh or neglectful parenting) may produce HPA-axis abnormalities (e.g., alterations in corticotrophin-releasing hormone [CRH] circuits), which sensitize the child to later stress, thus increasing the risk for developing depression (Heim & Nemeroff, 2001; Huizink, Mulder, & Buitelaar, 2004).

Infants of depressed mothers show higher levels of salivary cortisol (the stress hormone) and less relative left frontal lobe electrical activity than infants of mothers without depression (Dawson, Frey, Panagiotides, Osterling, & Hessl, 1997). Like higher levels of cortisol, decreased relative left frontal lobe activity may be a vulnerability factor for negative emotional states and later onset of depression (Nusslock et al., 2011; Forbes et al., 2008), although not all studies support this finding (e.g., Shankman et al., 2011). Nevertheless, research suggests that interactions between depressed mothers and their infants may produce biochemical and neurological changes that form and perpetuate a lasting basis for depressive disorder (Cytryn & McKnew, 1996; Post et al., 1996).

In summary, findings from studies of neurobiological correlates suggest that youngsters with depression may have a heightened sensitivity to stress. Repeated neuroendocrine activation related to stress might increase youngsters' susceptibility to chronic depressive symptoms, which in turn may lead to further extreme biological activation and psychosocial stress. Neurobiological findings are suggestive, but additional research will be needed to clarify the specific neural circuits underlying depression in young people. The characteristics, course, and outcome of a depressive episode may depend on the extent to which different neural circuits and processes are involved in response to environment demands, and when during development these networks are formed (Goodyer, 2008).

Family Influences

"I was always able to explain away my daughter's symptoms," says the mother of a 12-year-old. "When she was 10 and fought with me about everything, I just wrote it off as preadolescent hissy fits. When she dropped out of gymnastics—which had been her raison d'être—and started losing weight, I told myself she was just searching for a new identity. But when her best friend came to me and told me that my daughter was talking about suicide, I was forced to face the truth. I keep blaming myself. What did I do to cause this depression? What could I have done to prevent it?"

—From "Childhood Depression," by K. Levine, pp. 42–45, 'Parents', October 1995. Reprinted by permission of the author

Family influences play an important role in the development, maintenance, and course of depression in young people (Restifo & Bögels, 2009). One approach to examining these influences looks at families of children and adolescents with depression; the second approach considers families in which parents are depressed.

When Children Are Depressed

Families of children with depression display more critical and punitive behavior toward their depressed child than toward other children in the family. Compared to families of youngsters without depression, these families display more anger and conflict, greater use of control, poorer communication, more overinvolvement, and less warmth and support (Sheeber et al., 2007; Stein et al., 2000). They often experience high levels of stress, disorganization, marital discord, and a lack of social support (Messer & Gross, 1995; Slavin & Rainer, 1990). Youngsters with depression describe their families as less cohesive and more disengaged than do youngsters without depression (Kashani, Allan, Dahlmeier, Rezvani, & Reid, 1995).

Research points strongly to the link between childhood depression and family dysfunction. One longitudinal study found that less support and more conflict in the family were associated with more depressive symptoms in adolescents both concurrently and prospectively over a 1-year period. In contrast, more depressive symptoms did not predict a worsening of family relationships over the same time period. Thus, family problems precede and may be directly related to the development of depressive symptoms (Sheeber et al., 1997).

When Parents Are Depressed

To mother appropriately requires the action of systems that regulate sensation, perception, affect, reward, executive function, motor output and learning. When a mother is at risk to engage in less than optimal mothering, such as when she is depressed . . . the function of many or all of maternal and related systems may be affected.

—Barrett & Fleming, 2011, p. 368

MRS. D.

Not Up to Mothering

Mrs. D. is depressed and has been helpless and needy for most of her 5-year-old daughter Maria's life. She moves ever so slowly to prepare breakfast for Maria and herself. Wringing her hands, she pays little attention to events around her. Maria has been tugging at her mother for some time, apparently wanting food. Mrs. D. mumbles something, sobs continuously, and wipes tears from her cheek as she moves between the cupboard and kitchen table. Maria persists in trying to gain her mother's attention, and finally Mrs. D. hugs her and strokes her hair. At first Maria pulls back; then she snuggles against her mother's legs. Finally, Mrs. D. fills a bowl with cereal, and she and Maria sit down to eat in total silence, during which Mrs. D. looks sadly at her daughter. Deep bouts of depression periodically incapacitate Mrs. D., and any problem that Maria has sends her to bed. Mostly, Maria is left on her own to handle problems. (Adapted from Radke-Yarrow & Zahn-Waxler, 1990)

Depression interferes with the parent's ability to meet the basic physical and emotional needs of the child, including feeding, bedtime routines, medical care, and safety practices. Mothers who suffer from depression like Mrs. D. also create a child-rearing environment teeming with negative mood, irritability, helplessness, less emotional flexibility, and unpredictable displays of affection. When their children display negative emotions and distress, mothers with a history of depression are less likely to respond supportively with comfort, empathy, or assistance, and more likely to disapprove, dismiss, punish, or ignore their child's negative emotions (Silk et al., 2011). Depressed mothers also display less energy in stimulating play, less consistent discipline, less involvement, poor communication, lack of affection, and more criticism and resentment of their children than well mothers (Goodman, 2007). High levels of marital conflict, family discord, and stress may also be present in the home when a parent is depressed (Hammen, 2002). Critically, this type of negative family environment in combination with child genetic predispositions can adversely affect the development of stress regulatory systems and predispose the child to a lifetime of depressive illness and other negative health outcomes (Taylor, Way, & Seeman, 2011).

The first year of a child's life seems to be a particularly sensitive period for the effects of maternal depression on the child's later behavior and other adverse outcomes (Bagner, Pettit, Lewinsohn, & Seeley, 2011). For example, maternal depressions prior to or during pregnancy are not as good a predictor of later child problems as maternal depression during the child's first year. Depressed mothers also differ from one another in their styles of interaction; some are more intrusive and others are more withdrawn. These differences are important because they may be associated with different child outcomes. For example, as early as infancy, children of depressed mothers display atypical patterns of jealousy, with avoidance and "tuning out" associated with an intrusive maternal style, and heightened sociability toward strangers associated with a withdrawn maternal style (Hart, Jones, & Field, 2003). Thus, the offspring of mothers with depression attempt to cope with the unpredictability of their environment in different ways, which are often maladaptive and show reactions ranging from aggressive behavior to withdrawal, failure to thrive, school refusal, depression, even suicidal behavior (Goodman & Tully, 2008). Like Maria, they must take care of themselves and learn how to handle their own problems.

© Chris Rout/Alamy

Maternal depression interferes with the mother's ability to meet the needs of her children

It is not surprising that children of depressed mothers show cognitive deficits, emotional delays, separation difficulties, insecure attachments, and less positive affect across development (Olino et al., 2011). These children also display early signs of a cognitive vulnerability to depression. They tend to be self-critical, display a negative attributional style, and have a lower self-concept. They also have difficulties regulating their emotions and experience decreased social acceptance as young as age 5 (Dagne & Snyder, 2011; Maughan, Cicchetti, Toth, & Rogosch, 2007). As a result of these disturbances in emotion regulation, the children are ill equipped to cope effectively with stressful events, which subsequently places them at risk for higher levels of depression, lower functioning across multiple domains, and lower perceived competence (Garber & Cole, 2010; Goodman et al., 2011). Given the emotion-regulation disturbances seen in both depressed mothers and their children, it is not surprising that by adolescence or earlier, maternal depression is associated with greater *mutual* engagement in negative affect during parent-child interactions, rather than solely reflecting the mothers' own negativity (Connell, Hughes-Scalise, Klosterman, & Azem, 2011).

Follow-up studies of these children confirm the risks associated with growing up in a family with a depressed parent. Over a 10-year period, children of depressed parents not only had increased rates of depression, particularly before puberty, but also higher rates of phobias, panic disorder, and alcohol dependence (Weissman et al., 1997). Relative to controls, offspring of depressed parents received more outpatient treatment over 10 years, and had poorer overall functioning in work, family, and marital relationships. In terms of health care use, children of depressed parents have a higher rate of medically attended physical injuries in the home, emergency and sick visits, and inpatient and specialty service use, and a lower rate of well-child care visits (Phalen, Khoury, Atherton, & Kahn, 2008; Sills, Shetterly, Xu, Magid, & Kempe, 2007). The findings from follow-up studies are sobering in documenting the serious long-term negative outcomes and impairments in the children whose parents suffer from depression (Weissman et al., 2006).

Several issues regarding the relationship between child depression, maternal depression, and family factors need to be considered. First, the kinds of family difficulties we have described are related to many other child disorders, and may not be specific to depression. Second, it is difficult to know whether family problems are the result of a co-occurring condition, such as child conduct problems or maternal anxiety disorder, rather than depression. Third, most studies are correlational, making it impossible to determine the direction of influence. An adverse family environment can lead to child depression, but child depression may also evoke negative and critical reactions from family members and produce distress in others. Fourth, another factor, such as genetic risk, may account for both depression and family disturbances. Some support exists for all these mechanisms of family influence in child depression. Finally, a shortcoming of existing research has been the relative lack of attention to fathers with depression. A steadily growing number of studies indicate that paternal depression has significant but small effects on parenting, with depressed fathers showing less positive and more negative parenting behaviors than those who are not depressed (Wilson & Durbin, 2010). However, few studies have examined paternal behavior in relation to child outcomes. Although internalizing and externalizing problems in children are more strongly associated with depression in mothers relative to depression in fathers, depression in fathers still may play an important moderating role—for example, through its impact on the marital relationship (Connell & Goodman, 2002; Kane & Garber, 2004).

The high frequency of maternal depression combined with the numerous associated developmental, health, and behavioral problems in children of depressed mothers creates a pressing need for effective treatments for depressed mothers and their children (Wachs, Black, & Engle, 2009). Importantly, recent studies have found that reductions in parents' depressive symptoms with treatment can lead to both immediate and longer-term decreases in their children's problem behaviors and symptoms, and to favorable changes in their child's global functioning (Wickramaratne et al., 2011).

Stressful Life Events

CARLINE

How Depression Acts

I don't feel depressed all the time. It comes and goes. Usually it takes something to set it off. It could be something big, like when we moved, but anything, no matter how small, can really get to me, and then I start feeling bad and can't do anything. So today things are OK and I don't feel so bad. But tomorrow, or the next day, something might happen, no matter how minor, and I just might not want to get out of bed, or do anything. (Based on authors' case material)

Depression is associated with both severe and nonsevere stressful life events (Rudolph et al., 2006). Severely stressful events may include a move to a new neighborhood, a change of schools, a serious accident or family illness, an extreme lack of family resources, a violent family environment, or parental conflict or divorce (Gilman, Kawachi, Fitzmaurice, & Buka, 2003; Goodyer et al., 1997). At times, nonsevere stressful events, or "daily hassles," such as a poor grade on a test, an argument with a parent, criticism from a teacher, a fight with a boyfriend, or a broken date, may also result in depression. Relative to nondepressed youngsters, those who become depressed experience significantly more severe and nonsevere stressful life events in the year preceding their depression—especially events related to romantic relationships, education, relationships with friends or parents, work, and health (Birmaher et al., 1996).

Triggers for depression often involve interpersonal stress or actual or perceived personal losses, such as the death of a loved one, abandonment, rejection, or a threat to one's self-esteem (Eley & Stevenson, 2000; Goodyer, 1999). For example, a recent relationship break-up seems to be an especially significant predictor for first versus later episodes of major depression during adolescence (Monroe, Rohde, Seeley, & Lewinsohn, 1999). Sadness and depression following loss are common. In children ages 6 to 17 who had recently suffered the most horrible loss possible—the loss of a parent—all experienced sadness, grief, and other symptoms (Cerel, Fristad, Verducci, Weller, & Weller, 2006). Thirty percent of adolescents who had lost a friend or peer through suicide developed a depressive disorder within 6 months following the loss (Brent et al., 1992). Yet depressive disorder is not an inevitable outcome to personal losses—most children who experience the loss of a parent or friend show far fewer depressive symptoms than children who are clinically depressed, and they do not develop major depression (Cerel et al., 2006).

Emotion Regulation

Emotion regulation refers to the processes by which emotional arousal is redirected, controlled, or modified to facilitate adaptive functioning, and to the balance maintained among positive, negative, and neutral mood states (Cole & Hall, 2008). Youngsters demonstrate wide differences in regulating their emotions and managing their negative mood states (Keenan, 2000). For example, if a favorite playmate cannot be found, one child may cry and cannot be comforted; another may cry for a short time, then find someone else to play with; and another child may look to an adult for comfort. Children's strategies for self-regulation play a crucial role in overcoming, maintaining, or preventing negative emotional states. As we have discussed, young children who experience prolonged periods of emotional distress and sadness, or who are exposed to maternal negative moods, may have problems regulating negative emotional states and may be prone to the development of depression (Dagne & Snyder, 2011; Durbin & Shafir, 2008).

A variety of skills are necessary to manage one's own emotions. These include recognizing changes in emotion, accurately interpreting the conditions that led to mood change, setting goals to change one's mood, and implementing effective coping responses. Youngsters with depression may show deficits in one or more of these regulatory skills and, as a result, have difficulty overcoming their negative moods (Sheeber, Allen, Davis, & Sorensen, 2000; Yap et al., 2011). They may use avoidance or negative behavior to regulate their distress, rather than more problem-focused and adaptive coping strategies. Since emotion regulation encompasses neurobiological regulatory processes, acquired behavioral and cognitive strategies, and external resources for coping, depression may result from difficulties in any one or more of these areas (Cole & Hall, 2008).

SECTION SUMMARY

Causes of Depression

- Depression is likely a final common pathway for interacting influences that predispose a child to develop the disorder.
- Family and twin studies and specific gene studies suggest that what may be inherited is a vulnerability to depression and anxiety, and that certain environmental stressors may be required to express these disorders.
- Youngsters with depression may experience heightened reactions to stress that increase their vulnerability to depression. Studies of neurobiological correlates have focused on limbic and prefrontal neural circuits; the HPA axis; sleep abnormalities; growth hormone; variants in brain-derived neurotrophic factor (BDNF), which is involved in nerve growth and development; and the brain neurotransmitters serotonin, dopamine, and norepinephrine.
- Families of children with depression display anger and conflict, greater use of control, less effective communication, more overinvolvement, and less warmth and support than families of children who are not depressed.
- Children of depressed parents experience increased rates of depression before puberty; higher rates of phobias, panic disorder, and alcohol dependence as adolescents and adults; and other negative health outcomes.
- Depression is associated with both severe stressful life events, such as a move to a new neighborhood, and less-severe stressful events or daily hassles, such as criticism from a teacher or an argument with a boyfriend.
- Young children who experience prolonged periods of emotional distress and sadness may have problems in regulating their negative emotional states and may be prone to the development of depression.

TREATMENT OF DEPRESSION

LEETA

Feeling Better

Leeta, age 16, sat slumped in her chair. Disheveled and distracted, she answered questions in a vague and unfocused manner. She was admitted to the hospital after she slit her wrists with a knife; she had become despondent, irritable, and out of control at home. Leeta's thoughts and reasoning were distorted. She expressed a pervasive sense of hopelessness and was certain that she would remain in hospitals for the rest of her life.

Fortunately, this was not the case. She became involved in cognitive–behavioral therapy that focused on accurate reasoning, a more positive self-image, and ways to lessen family turmoil, and was also treated with antidepressant medication. One year later, Leeta entered our office for a follow-up interview with energy and excitement. "I never thought that I would feel like hanging out with friends and doing things again. It's not that I don't get sad once in a while, but it doesn't take over my whole life." (Adapted from Oster & Montgomery, 1995)

Many potentially effective psychosocial and psychopharmacological treatments are available to treat youngsters with depression (Brent, Poling, & Goldstein, 2011; David-Ferdon & Kaslow, 2008). Despite this availability, less than half of children with depression receive help for their problem (Olfson, Gameroff, Marcus, & Waslick, 2003). Rates of treatment vary by racial/ethnic background, being highest for non-Hispanic white youth (40%) and lowest for Asian youth (19%). About one third of African American and Hispanic youth receive treatment for their depression (Cummings & Druss, 2011). In one study of adolescents who killed themselves, most of whom had a depressive disorder, only 7% had been in treatment prior to their suicide (Brent et al., 1988). The high comorbidity, associated deficits, and recurrence of depression in young people require a combination of treatments, with an emphasis on eliminating depressive symptoms, maintaining positive outcomes, and preventing relapse (AACAP, 2007d).

Cognitive–behavioral therapy (CBT), the treatment used with Leeta, has shown the most success in treating children and adolescents with depression (Watanabe, Hunot, Omori, Churchill, & Furukawa, 2007). In addition, Interpersonal Psychotherapy for Adolescent Depression (IPT-A), which focuses on improving interpersonal functioning by enhancing communication skills in significant relationships, has also proven to be an effective treatment (Mufson et al., 2004). CBT and IPT-A are also more efficacious for treating depression than other forms of therapy (e.g., family therapy or nondirective supportive therapy) (David-Ferdon & Kaslow, 2008).

With regard to psychopharmacological treatment, tricyclic antidepressants have not proven to be nearly as effective for depressed young people as for depressed adults (Papanikolaou, Richardson, Pehlivanidis, & Papadopoulou-Daifoti, 2006). In contrast, new-generation antidepressants, especially the selective serotonin reuptake inhibitors (SSRIs), have demonstrated moderate efficacy in controlled studies with young people (Fombonne & Zinck, 2008). However, concerns have been raised about their effectiveness, overuse, and possible side effects, which we discuss later in this section. In addition to CBT, IPT-A, and medications, many variations in these treatments (e.g., individual versus group format, increasing amounts of parental involvement, combined treatments, computer-based treatments, and online treatments) are available. Other treatments that emphasize self-control, cognitive and social problem solving, social support, family relationships, and increasing social and academic functioning, have also been used with varying degrees of success (David-Ferdon & Kaslow, 2008).

An early onset of depression places youngsters at greater risk for experiencing multiple episodes of major depression throughout their lives. Therefore, it is critical that treatment begin as soon as possible; very early and aggressive intervention is warranted to reduce the length of a depressive episode, reduce the likelihood of future episodes, minimize associated impairments in functioning, and reduce the risk of suicide. An overview of the main treatments for youngsters with depression is presented in Table 8.3.

Psychosocial Interventions

Most psychosocial interventions for depression in young people use an integrated approach derived from two traditions—behavior therapy and cognitive therapy. These two approaches for depression were originally developed with adults, but have since been adapted and applied with children and adolescents.

Behavior therapy maintains that depression results from and is sustained by a lack of reinforcement due to a restricted range of potential reinforcers, few available reinforcers, or inadequate skills for obtaining rewards (Lewinsohn, 1974). The treatment focuses on increasing pleasurable activities and events, and provides the

TABLE 8.3 | Treatments for Youngsters with Depression

Behavior Therapy	Aims to increase behaviors that elicit positive reinforcement and to reduce punishment from the environment. May involve teaching social and other coping skills, and using anxiety management and relaxation training.
Cognitive Therapy	Focuses on helping the youngster with depression become more aware of pessimistic and negative thoughts, depressogenic beliefs and biases, and causal attributions of self-blame for failure. Once these self-defeating thought patterns are recognized, the child is taught to change from a negative, pessimistic view to a more positive, optimistic one.
Cognitive–Behavioral Therapy (CBT)	The most common form of psychosocial intervention. Combines elements of behavioral and cognitive therapies in an integrated approach. Attribution retraining may also be used to challenge the youngster's pessimistic beliefs.
Interpersonal Psychotherapy for Adolescent Depression (ITP-A)	Explores family and interpersonal interactions that maintain depression. Family sessions are supplemented with individual sessions in which youngsters with depression are encouraged to understand their own negative cognitive style and the effects of their depression on others, and to increase pleasant activities with family members and peers (Mufson, Dorta, Moreau, & Weissman, 2004).
Medication	Treats mood disturbances and other symptoms of depression using antidepressants, especially selective serotonin reuptake inhibitors (SSRIs).

youngster with the skills needed to obtain more reinforcement. Interventions such as social skills training teach children assertiveness, communication, how to accept and give feedback, social problem solving, and conflict resolution skills in order to increase positive social interactions. Strategies such as daily monitoring, structuring activities, and scheduling activities are used to help youngsters with depression become more active, engage in rewarding experiences, and solve problems (McCauley, Schloredt, Gudmundsen, Martell, & Dimidjian, 2011).

Cognitive therapy teaches youngsters with depression to identify, challenge, and modify negative thought processes such as misattributions, negative self-monitoring, short-term focus, excessively high performance standards, and a failure to self-reinforce. They are taught to identify and eliminate negative thoughts, such as "It's my fault," or "What's the point?" and taught to replace them with positive thoughts, such as "She really likes me," or "I'm an interesting person." A child who has been rejected by a friend might be encouraged to think, "She was in a bad mood," rather than "She hates me." When youngsters are presented with specific situations and examples of irrational negative thinking, they are taught to substitute alternative logical explanations that are more positive. For example:

- SITUATION: Two girls, Diana and Colleen, both ask friends to get together with them after school. Both girls' friends say they can't because they have too much homework to do.
- IRRATIONAL THINKING: Diana feels rejected and thinks, "Because my friend won't get together with me, she doesn't like me, and she'll never want to do anything with me again."
- RATIONAL THINKING: In contrast, Colleen thinks, "Well, my friend is busy today, but we can get together some other time. She's still my best friend."

In practice, behavior therapy and cognitive therapy are integrated into a unified cognitive behavior therapy (CBT) approach in which more adaptive cognitions are hypothesized to lead to more adaptive behavior and vice versa (Stark et al., 2006). Examples of these integrated CBT approaches for children and adolescents follow.

Primary and Secondary Control Enhancement Training (PASCET)

John Weisz and his colleagues (Weisz, Southam-Gerow, Gordis, & Connor-Smith, 2003) have developed a 15-session, individualized CBT-based program for youngsters ages 8 to 15 with depression. In treatment sessions and in take-home assignments, youngsters learn and practice two types of coping skills:

- *Primary control skills* (ACT skills) for changing objective events in their lives (e.g., changing the activities they engage in, learning to relax) to conform with their wishes.
- *Secondary control skills* (THINK skills) for altering the subjective impact of stressful life events (e.g., altering their negative thoughts and feelings).

The focus of the PASCET program is to help the child change conditions that are changeable, and to change the subjective impact of those that are not. Parents are also involved in the program and encouraged to support their children in using these coping skills. PASCET is an excellent example of a program that has evolved since its initial use in the schools to reduce depressive symptoms. It is now being implemented and evaluated in community mental health clinics with youngsters who have been referred for depression (Bearman & Weisz, 2009).

The ACTION Program

Kevin Stark and his colleagues have developed a comprehensive CBT approach for children with depression (Stark et al., 2006). The primary components of this treatment are appropriate for children and adolescents, and for boys and girls. However, the current format is designed to be gender sensitive, with treatment activities, skills emphasized, and a focus on interpersonal relationships specific to girls within the 9- to 13-year age range (Stark et al., 2008). Like the PASCET program, ACTION uses a holistic approach that involves both child and parents. The ACTION acronym is used to nourish the idea that youngsters can have an impact on their moods, and it is presented to them as follows (Stark & Kendall, 1996, p. 14):

A = Always find something to do to feel better.
C = Catch the positive.
T = Think about it as a problem to be solved.
I = Inspect the situation.
O = Open yourself to the positive.
N = Never get stuck in the negative muck.

Multiple treatment procedures are used to reduce the child's mood disturbances, behavioral deficits, and cognitive symptoms:

- *Dysphoria*, *anger*, *anhedonia*, and *excessive anxiety* are treated by educating the child about the relation between mood, thinking, and behavior, and by using anger management procedures, scheduling pleasant activities, and relaxation training.
- *Interpersonal deficits* are treated using social skills training.

- *Cognitive distortions* and *negative and self-critical thinking* are addressed by using cognitive-restructuring procedures and training in effective problem-solving and self-control procedures.

Interventions can be carried out in both individual and group formats, and they make use of a workbook that includes a variety of exercises such as this one:

- SITUATION: You accidentally drop your books . . . a group of classmates are talking and laughing at the other side of the room.
- NEGATIVE THINKING: Now look at what I've done. They must think I'm a complete idiot.
- COPING RESPONSE: No, they're probably laughing at something else. Besides, I know them. They're not like that. It's not like I'm the first person ever to drop her books. It's really no big deal.

Interventions with parents are used to facilitate the child's use of effective coping strategies outside of treatment, and to change events that may contribute to and prolong the child's problems. Since negative parent–child interactions may result in negative thinking, changing maladaptive patterns within the family is an important feature of the ACTION program. Several methods are used to change parental and family cognitions and behavior, including teaching parents effective forms of discipline, ways to manage anger, and ways to change negative thinking. Interventions with the entire family teach negotiation and conflict resolution skills, recreational planning, and effective problem solving and family communication (Stark et al., 2006). ACTION is a promising intervention built on a sound theoretical and research base. The program is currently being evaluated as a comprehensive treatment package for depression (Stark, Streusand, Krumholz, & Patel, 2010).

Adolescent Coping with Depression Program (CWD-A)

One of the most well-established and comprehensive CBT programs for the treatment of depression in adolescents is the Adolescent Coping with Depression Program (CWD-A) (Clarke, Lewinsohn, & Hops, 2001). CWD-A is a nonstigmatizing psychoeducational approach that emphasizes skills training to promote adolescents' control over their moods and enhancement of their ability to cope with problematic situations. Treatment is provided in 16 two-hour sessions over an 8-week period for groups of up to 10 adolescents ages 13 to 18. Adolescents use a workbook that includes brief readings, short quizzes, structured learning tasks, and forms for homework assignments for each session. The core treatment sessions with adolescents involve group activities and role playing. In addition, complementary therapy with the youngsters' parents is carried out to accelerate and support the learning of new skills, and to assist in applying the skills learned in the group to everyday life situations. Periodic "booster sessions" help to maintain the skills taught during treatment (Clarke & DeBar, 2010).

Initially, adolescents learn that depression can result from many causes, including inherited tendencies, stress, and excessive negative thinking. Relaxation training is then used to quickly provide a successful experience and some immediate relief. Subsequent sessions include the following components (Clarke & DeBar, 2010):

- Self-change skills are taught, such as self-monitoring of mood and behavior, and ways to establish realistic goals.
- Pleasurable activities and opportunities for reinforcement are increased.
- Positive thinking is increased by identifying, challenging, and changing negative cognitions.
- Training in social, communication, and problem-solving skills is integrated throughout the program.
- Specific skills are taught, such as conversational skills, ways to plan social activities, and ways to make friends.
- Goal setting is used to identify short and long-term life goals, and potential barriers.
- Final sessions emphasize integrating the skills learned and making plans for the future.

The CWD-A program and modified versions have demonstrated beneficial, albeit moderate, treatment and prevention effects in many controlled studies by its developers and others (Cuijpers, Muñoz, Clarke, & Lewinsohn, 2010; Stice, Rohde, Gau, & Wade, 2010). However, as with the other treatments we have discussed, there is a need for further evaluation by independent investigators, extending its use to a wider variety of depressed youngsters, longer-term follow up studies, and comparisons with other treatments for depression, particularly medication (Clarke & DeBar, 2010).

Interpersonal Psychotherapy for Adolescent Depression (IPT-A)

IPT-A is based on the idea that adolescent depression affects relationships, which in turn affect mood. Thus, treatment focuses on the adolescent's depressive symptoms and the social context in which these symptoms occur (Young & Mufson, 2008). The emphasis in IPT-A is on increasing adolescents' independence and negotiating their interdependence on others by addressing relevant developmental issues such as romantic relationships, separation from parents, and peer relationships. The adolescent takes an active role in identifying a specific problem area (e.g., loss and grief, interpersonal disputes, role transitions, interpersonal deficits), discussing communication and problem-solving techniques for that area, practicing these skills in session, and applying them outside sessions in the context of significant relationships. The treatment is structured around addressing the identified problem areas, and both the therapist and adolescent are expected to play an active role (Mufson, Dorta, Moreau, & Weissman, 2004).

IPT-A is designed as a once weekly, 12-session outpatient treatment. Treatment is divided into three phases. The *initial phase* (4 sessions) addresses the diagnosis of depression, educates the adolescent and family about depression, introduces the principles of IPT-A and the structure of treatment, identifies an interpersonal problem area, and makes a treatment contract. The *middle phase* (5 sessions) further clarifies the problem, identifies strategies for effectively targeting the problem, and implements interventions to resolve the problem. A number of techniques are used. For example, if an adolescent reports a fight with her boyfriend, she would be asked how this made her feel and whether or not this affected her depressive symptoms. This helps to educate the adolescent about the link between interpersonal events and mood, and makes her feel more comfortable and skilled at identifying and communicating feelings. Other techniques in this phase focus on helping the adolescent to recognize the impact of her communication on others, the feelings generated, and how modifying the communication may impact the outcome of the interaction and the adolescent's associated feelings. Additional techniques involve problem solving around interpersonal situations, role playing both communication and problem solving skills, and the use of homework to practice these skills between sessions (Young & Mufson, 2008).

The *termination phase* (3 sessions) reviews progress in the identified problem area, links changes in interpersonal functioning and relationships to improved mood and decreased depressive symptoms, and identifies strategies that have been most helpful. It also addresses the importance of continuing to use the learned strategies following treatment, highlights areas that still need improvement, and considers what to do if symptoms of depression return.

IPT-A has been shown to be an effective treatment for adolescent depression in a number of controlled studies in clinic, school, and community settings, using both individual and group formats (Mufson, 2010). In an effort to reach more youngsters, IPT-A is also being developed as a preventive intervention ("Teen Talk") for adolescents in grades 7 to 10 who display elevated levels of depressive symptoms. Preliminary findings suggest that Teen Talk may be a useful approach to preventing more severe forms of depression (Young, Mufson, & Davies, 2006).

In concluding our discussion of psychosocial treatments, the good news is that a wide variety of treatments for young people with depression have been shown to be effective for most youths who receive them (March & Vitiello, 2009; TADS Team, 2009). However, nearly half of those who recover, especially girls, show depression relapse (Curry et al., 2011), and effect sizes have been moderate and smaller than those reported for adults (Weisz, McCarty, & Valeri, 2006). Hence, there is a need to explore more effective treatments that build on our growing understanding of childhood depression; reduce the rate of depression relapse or deterioration; and personalize treatment to meet the child's cognitive, emotional, and developmental profile (Brent & Maalouf, 2009). There is also a need to study treatments of longer duration and the use of booster sessions following treatment, and to evaluate outcomes over longer follow-up periods.

Medications

"I kept hearing about Prozac in the news," says one father, "and when we finally brought my 9-year-old to a psychiatrist, I thought he could just give her this pill and change our lives. After a year, I can say that things are a bit better. But it took lots of trials with lots of different pills."

—From "Childhood Depression," by K. Levine, pp. 42–45, 'Parents', October 1995. Reprinted by permission of the author

Antidepressant medications are commonly used to treat youngsters with depression. An estimated 1.4 million youngsters in the United States received antidepressant medication in 2002 (Vitiello, Zuvekas, & Norquist, 2006), with nearly 60% of those treated in outpatient settings filling prescriptions for these drugs (Olfson et al., 2003). For many youngsters, antidepressant medications can shorten a depressive episode and return them to the important developmental tasks of childhood and adolescence. As we have noted, although tricyclic antidepressants are effective with adults, they have consistently failed to demonstrate any advantage over placebo in treating depression in young people, and may have some potentially serious cardiovascular side effects (Fombonne & Zinck, 2008). As a result they are no longer regarded as primary drugs for the management of depressive symptoms in young people.

SSRIs have clearly become the first line of antidepressant medication treatment for youngsters with depression, with one national survey reporting that over 90% of prescriptions written for these youngsters were for SSRIs (Olfson et al., 2003). Among the most commonly used SSRIs are fluoxetine (Prozac™), sertraline (Zoloft™), and citalopram (Celexa™). SSRIs achieve their antidepressant effects by blocking the reuptake of serotonin, thereby increasing its availability in the synapse and stimulating the post-synaptic neuron. At present, the only SSRI that is approved by the Food and Drug Administration (FDA) for use with children and adolescents with MDD is fluoxetine.

A number of controlled investigations have demonstrated that some SSRIs are moderately effective in reducing symptoms of depression in children and adolescents. One meta-analysis found that 40% to 60% of children responded to Prozac versus 20% to 35% of those on placebo (Hetrick, McKenzie, & Merry, 2010). Support for the effectiveness of other SSRIs was limited. There was also little evidence that children and adolescents who took SSRIs showed improvement in their school performance, interpersonal relations, or social functioning on a day-to-day basis (Hetrick et al., 2010). Others have argued that research supports the use of SSRIs, that combined treatments using medication and CBT in combination are likely to be the most effective, and that greater treatment effects are obtained for children with more severe depressions (March, 2010).

After they were first marketed in the late 1980s, the use of Prozac and other SSRIs increased dramatically. For example, nearly three-quarters of a million prescriptions for SSRIs for children ages 6 to 18 were written in 1996—an 80% increase in only 2 years (*APA Monitor*, December 1997). However, despite some support for their efficacy, both professional and public concerns have been voiced about their use with children and adolescents. The main concerns are possible serious side effects such as suicidal thoughts and self-harm, and a lack of information about the long-term effects of these medications on the developing brain. Related to these concerns and recent warnings by the FDA, the use of SSRIs with young people has decreased by about 20% in recent years (Gibbons et al., 2007; Libby et al., 2007). Links to the FDA and other organizations' websites are available on your Psychology CourseMate. In 2004, the FDA asked all manufacturers of antidepressant medications to include in their labeling a boxed warning (black box) and Patient Education Guide to alert consumers about the increased risk of suicidal thinking and behavior in youngsters treated with these medications. A summary of the main points included in these black box warnings is presented in Box 8.2.

The FDA warnings were based on a pooling of findings from 24 short-term placebo-controlled studies of antidepressant trials with more than 4,400 youngsters with MDD and other disorders. The overall findings indicated an increased risk of suicidal thinking or behavior in youngsters with depression (4% on active medication versus 2% on placebo (Hammad, Laughren, & Racoosin, 2006). Not evaluated were the risk for untreated youth with depression, the long-term effects of medication, or the combination of medication and psychosocial interventions, and there were no completed suicides in any of the studies. In addition, findings regarding increases in suicidality from other recent studies have been inconsistent (Gibbons et al., 2012). Also inconsistent are findings regarding the use of medications either alone or in combination with psychosocial interventions. Some studies have found a benefit of combined treatment versus medication alone, with an enhancement of the safety of medications when used in combination with CBT (e.g., TADS Team, 2004, 2007), whereas others have not (e.g., Goodyer et al., 2007). Thus, despite much research, the risks, long-term safety, and benefits associated with the use of antidepressant medications with young people remain uncertain (Moreno, Arango, Parellada, Shaffer, & Bird, 2007a). In light of the potential effectiveness of the psychosocial treatments for depression in youth that we have discussed, careful consideration must be given to determining which youngsters are most or least likely to benefit from antidepressant medication (AACAP, 2007d).

Notwithstanding these concerns, untreated depression has profound long-term consequences, including a high risk for suicide, and there is some evidence that a higher use of antidepressant medications across counties

BOX 8.2 A CLOSER LOOK

Summary of Food and Drug Administration (FDA) Black Box Warnings for the Use of Antidepressants with Children and Adolescents

- Youth with MDD are at an increased risk for suicidal thinking or behavior.
- When considering an antidepressant for a child or adolescent, it is important to weigh the increased risk of suicidality with the possible benefits of the medication.
- In starting young people on antidepressants, they must be very closely monitored for worsening of symptoms, suicidality, or unusual changes in behavior.
- Family members must closely observe the youngster for increases in symptoms or worsening of functioning, and immediately communicate any such observations to their provider.
- A statement needs to be included regarding whether the medication is approved for use with children and adolescents.

Source: © Cengage Learning 2013.

off the mark
by Mark Parisi
THAT'S THE WAY, UH, HUH UH, HUH...
I LIKE IT!
UH, HUH UH, HUH...
www.offthemark.com
ATLANTIC FEATURE © 1996 MARK PARISI
EEYORE WHEN HE REMEMBERS HIS PROZAC
Atlantic Feature © 1996 Mark Parisi

in the United States is associated with lower rates of suicide in young people (Gibbons, Hur, Bhaumik, & Mann, 2006). Thus, there may be possible risks that go along with not using medications, especially when numerous research and clinical studies indicate that many young people benefit from drug treatment relative to the risks from suicidal ideation and suicide attempts (Bridge et al., 2007).

In the absence of better data regarding drug effects, side effects, and long-term safety of medication use with depressed children, there are currently no easy answers to this dilemma. Some say it is unethical to treat depressed children using medications in light of the potential dangers. Others say that the risks associated with drug treatment are no greater than risks for other treatments and that it is unethical to withhold treatment in light of the known benefits. Given the many social, political, and economic implications surrounding the use of medications to treat depression in young people, we may hear a lot more about this issue for some time to come (e.g., Riddle, 2004).

In concluding our discussion of the treatment of depression, we note that controlled studies of psychological treatments and medication have found that up to 60% of youngsters with depression respond to placebo (Bridge et al., 2007) and about 15% to 30% respond to brief treatment (Goodyer et al., 2007). Thus, in youngsters with mild or brief depression, an absence of suicidality, and minor impairment in functioning, the use of education, support, and case management related to school and family stressors may be effective. However, for those who are more severely depressed, display suicidal ideation and behavior, and show significant impairment in functioning, the specific types of psychological and pharmacological treatments that we have discussed will likely be needed (AACAP, 2007d; Cheung et al., 2007).

Prevention

In view of the recurring nature of depression, successful efforts during childhood and adolescence to prevent the onset of depression may reduce a lifelong risk of illness and reduce the use and costs of health care resources (Horowitz & Garber, 2006; Stice, Shaw, Bohon, Marti, & Rohde, 2009).

Early studies of prevention with grade school and high school students with subclinical symptoms of depression found CBT/problem-solving approaches to be effective in reducing depressive symptoms and lowering risk for developing depression up to 2 years after treatment (Gillham & Reivich, 1999; Shochet et al., 2001). However, not all programs have reported benefits. For example, in a recent controlled study, a comprehensive school-based program for adolescents attempted to develop individual resiliency skills and enhance protective factors in the environment. The program failed to produce significant changes in levels of depressive symptoms or risk or protective factors in participating adolescents over the three years of the study (Sawyer et al., 2010). These negative results, despite extensive efforts to use evidence-based interventions, highlight some of the challenges in implementing school-based, universal prevention programs. Among these challenges are the need for effective teacher training over a large and diverse geographical area so that programs are implemented as prescribed, the difficulty in engaging young adolescents in prevention programs, and the amount of time required to implement policy and practice changes at "whole school" levels (Sawyer et al., 2010).

Other large-scale prevention efforts (e.g., *Columbia Teen Screen*) have been directed at the early detection of high school students at risk for depression and suicide to ensure these students receive help (Shaffer et al., 2004). The importance of school-based screening is highlighted by the finding that although 90% of parents report that they are confident in their ability to tell if their child is thinking about suicide, only about one-third of teens with mental health problems are known to their parents. School-based screening for suicide has had moderate success in identifying students who are at high risk for suicide and other mental health problems, but concerns have been raised regarding the number of youngsters who are falsely identified as being at risk (Scott et al., 2010).

Recent prevention efforts have also focused on providing family group cognitive-behavioral interventions to 9- to 15-year-old children of parents with a history of MDD (Compas et al., 2011). Depressed parents and their children are taught a wide array of problem solving and coping skills, including teaching children ways of coping with their parent's depression. The goals of the program are to educate families about depression, increase awareness of the impact of stress and depression on functioning, help families recognize and monitor stress, facilitate the use of effective ways of coping with stress, and improve parenting skills. In a randomized controlled study, children who participated in the preventive intervention were compared to those in a written-information comparison group. Those who received the intervention showed significantly lower rates of MDD over a 2-year period, significantly lower rates of internalizing and externalizing symptoms at 18 months, and significantly lower rates of externalizing symptoms at 24 months. Marginal effects were found for reductions in parents' symptoms of depression at 18 and 24 months but not for episodes of MDD (Compas et al., 2011). Preventive interventions like this have the potential to protect unaffected children of depressed parents from developing the disorder and to improve outcomes of children with depression who are currently receiving treatment.

A high priority must be given to the development and continued refinement of identification, early intervention, and prevention efforts for youngsters at risk for depressive disorders (Barrera, Torres, & Munoz, 2007; Farrell & Barrett, 2007). The development of programs for preschool children with depression (Lenze et al., 2011) and online and computer-based interactive programs for use in primary care, school, and other settings are examples of promising new prevention approaches (Spence et al., 2011; Van Voorhees et al., 2009).

SECTION SUMMARY

Treatment of Depression

- Cognitive–behavioral therapy and interpersonal psychotherapy have had the most success in treating depression in young people.
- SSRIs have been recommended as the first line of drug treatment for children with depression, but concerns have recently been raised about their use.
- A high priority needs to be given to programs aimed at preventing depression in young people.

Bipolar Disorder (BP)

In a sense, depression is a view of the world through a dark glass, and mania is that seen through a kaleidoscope—often brilliant but fractured.

—K. R. Jamison (1997)

BEN

Extreme Mood Swings

Ben, age 14, was living in a residential treatment center. He had a history of moodiness, hyped-up activity, sleeplessness, and a sexual preoccupation with the girls in his class—he had even approached his teacher with offers of sexual intimacy. Ben's thoughts raced, his speech was rapid and fragmented, and he had wide mood swings. At the high extreme, Ben rarely slept, and he yelled, sang, and disturbed everyone—charging about the residence day and night with a seemingly endless supply of energy. He felt "absolutely terrific" at these times and thought he could fly. The low extreme found Ben curled up in a ball beneath a stack of blankets, a withdrawn and hopeless young man who expressed feelings of worthlessness and thoughts of suicide. (Based on authors' case material)

Ben displays the essential features of bipolar disorder (BP): a striking period of unusually and persistently elevated, expansive, or irritable mood, alternating with or accompanied by one or more major depressive episodes. The two mood states associated with the manic phase of BP are elation and a profound sense of well-being (euphoria). However, these feelings can quickly change to anger and hostility if the youngster's behavior is interfered with. Since many youngsters with BP have simultaneous feelings of depression, they are easily reduced to tears. It is at once remarkable and almost inconceivable how a young person with this disorder such as Ben can be so manic, elated, and wild at one moment; so depressed and immobile the next; and at other times seemingly so normal (Geller & Luby, 1997).

Symptoms of BP in young people were recognized as early as 150 A.D., when the physician Aretaeus of Cappadocia described manic behavior in young men in puberty (Kotsopoulos, 1986). In modern times, BP was generally considered an adult illness, receiving very little attention in children and adolescents (Geller & DelBello, 2003). More recently, there has been as upsurge of professional and public interest children and adolescents with BP as reflected in increasing rates of diagnosis, treatment, and media coverage (Carmichael,

2008; Danner et al., 2009). For example, since 1994 the estimated number of youth outpatient office visits for BP has increased at least 40-fold, with about 90% of the youngsters receiving psychotropic medication during these visits (Moreno et al., 2007b). As we will discuss, along with the increased interest has come considerable controversy—BP in young people is difficult to identify because it occurs infrequently, shows extreme variability of clinical presentation within and across episodes, and overlaps in symptoms with more common childhood disorders such as ADHD (Staton, Volness, & Beatty, 2008; Youngstrom, 2007). Debate continues as to the appropriate diagnostic criteria for BP in children and adolescents (Carlson, 2011), and attempts are under way to more clearly define the boundaries of BP across the developmental spectrum in DSM-5 (American Psychiatric Association, 2010).

At the center of the storm is whether BP can be diagnosed in prepubertal children. Some clinicians avoid the use of this label entirely, and instead label emotionally labile children with the less stigmatizing categories of depression or ADHD. Others use the label of BP liberally in young children, often based solely on the presence of mood swings, irritability, and aggression. Thus, clinicians presented with *identical* diagnostic information vary widely in their assessment of BP, from 0% risk to 100% risk (Jenkins, Youngstrom, Washburn, & Youngstrom, 2010). A focal point of the debate is whether BP looks the same in young children as in adults. If it does, then euphoria, grandiosity, and classic manic symptoms are needed for the diagnosis. If not, then irritability and mood fluctuations would be sufficient to make the diagnosis. How the BP label is used with young children has important implications for treatment, given the few available medications for stabilizing mood in children and their greater risks in children than adults (Ghaemi & Martin, 2007).

Young people with BP display significant impairment in functioning, including previous hospitalization, MDD, medication treatment, and co-occurring disruptive behavior and anxiety disorders. A history of psychotic symptoms and suicidal ideation and attempts are also common (Axelson et al., 2006). Youngsters with BP show severe and cyclical mood changes and outbursts. Mania typically occurs in episodes, with an onset and offset. Thus, in its fully developed state it is clearly different from a child's usual condition (Carlson, 2002). During a manic episode, youths with BP may display intense symptoms such as irritability and rage. Or they may show silly, giddy, overexcited, overtalkative behavior coupled with expansive, grandiose beliefs (e.g., a teen who feels she has a special connection to God). It is normal for children to pretend to have special powers or abilities, but a youngster with BP, during a manic episode, will actually believe he is X-Man Wolverine and that he is indestructible and all-powerful. He might believe he can walk on water, control traffic, or jump off buildings without hurting himself—and kill himself in the process.

Restlessness, agitation, and sleeplessness are also typical of youngsters with BP. Sexual disinhibition (like Ben's propositioning his teacher) may also occur when the youth becomes uncharacteristically preoccupied with sexual themes, sexually touching others, or "talking dirty." Youths with BP may experience unrealistic elevations in self-esteem (believing they are "the chosen one") and vast surges of energy; they may go with little or no sleep for days without feeling tired. They may be able to concentrate for hours on one activity that interests them, such as drawing or becoming engrossed in a mentally demanding fantasy game. At the same time, however, they may be highly distractible, constantly jumping from one thing to another (Geller & Luby, 1997).

The elated mood of youths with mania may (erroneously) give them the appearance of being happy and cheerful. Like Ben, they may say, "I feel absolutely terrific." It is difficult to recognize that a laughing, happy youngster also has a history of misery and distress. For this reason, evaluating a youth's current mood in relation to his or her developmental history is essential, particularly when there is an inconsistency between the child's elated mood and his or her history of trouble at home or school (Youngstrom, 2007).

Current research suggests that BP with an onset prior to age 18 is essentially the same disorder that occurs in adults, although possible differences in long-term outcomes and associated characteristics are not known (Carlson, Pine, Nottelmann, & Leibenluft, 2004). Although not without problems, with age-related adjustments the diagnosis of BP in young people can be made using the DSM criteria used for adults. There are three subtypes of BP: bipolar I disorder; bipolar II disorder; and cyclothymic disorder. These subtypes are related to whether the youngster displays a manic, mixed, or hypomanic episode. A *manic episode*, which is the hallmark feature of BP, involves a discrete period of a week or more during which the youngster displays an ongoing, pervasive, and unusually elevated or irritable mood. This episode is accompanied by the types of symptoms we have been describing such as an exaggerated self-esteem, a reduced need for sleep, racing thoughts, rapid and frenzied speech, attention to irrelevant details, increased activity, or over-involvement in pleasurable but often reckless and risky behaviors. In addition, the youngster does not meet criteria for a depressive episode during the period of mood disturbance; the mood disturbance is not due to substance use or abuse or to a medical condition; and the disturbance causes significant impairment in usual activities or requires hospitalization in order to prevent the child or others from harm. A *mixed episode* refers to cases where the child experiences both a manic episode and a major depressive episode for a week or more. Finally, a *hypomanic episode* has features that resemble a manic episode but the mood disturbance and symptoms are less severe, of shorter duration, and produce less impairment in functioning than a manic episode.

A diagnosis of *bipolar I disorder* requires evidence for a manic or mixed episode, and one or more major depressive episodes; a *bipolar II disorder* requires a hypomanic episode in combination with one or more major depressive episodes; and a *cyclothymic disorder* describes children or adolescents who display numerous and persistent hypomanic and depressive symptoms for a year or more that cause considerable distress and impairment in functioning, but do not meet criteria for a manic or mixed episode or for a major depressive disorder.

A difficulty in using DSM criteria for BP to diagnose youngsters with mania is that they often present with atypical symptoms (Youngstrom, 2007). Changes in mood, psychomotor agitation, and mental excitation are often volatile and erratic rather than persistent. Irritability, belligerence, and mixed manic–depressive features occur more frequently than euphoria. Unlike for adults, developmental limitations and the social environment place constraints on children's reckless behaviors, which typically involve school failure, fighting, dangerous play, and inappropriate sexual conduct. Thus, classic manic symptoms of grandiosity, psychomotor agitation, and reckless behavior must be differentiated from manic symptoms of common childhood disorders, such as ADHD, and from typical childhood behaviors, such as bragging, imaginary play, overactivity, and youthful blunders (American Academy of Child and Adolescent Psychiatry [AACAP], 2007c; Danner et al., 2009).

How are some of the more notable symptoms of mania expressed in youngsters with BP? When in a manic state, youngsters show great conviction about the correctness or importance of their ideas. Adolescents with BP may show grand delusions—illogical and strong beliefs that lead to poor judgment and impulsive behavior (Jamison, 1997). For example, they may badger their teachers about how to teach. This badgering may become so intense that teachers contact the parents, pleading with them to ask their children to cease. Youngsters with BP may intentionally fail subjects, acting on their illogical belief that children can choose what to pass or fail, because they believe they are not being taught correctly. They may steal expensive items, and be unresponsive to efforts by police or parents to explain that their actions are wrong and illegal. Although these youngsters know that stealing is illegal for others, they believe they are above the law. They may believe that they will achieve great fame, for example, as a brain surgeon, even though they are failing all of their classes at school. Similarly, a youngster with BP who is short, clumsy, and lacks any athletic ability may practice basketball with great fervor and strongly believe that he will become the next LeBron James. Another child may feel she has the ability to change the weather at will.

In contrast to youngsters with depression who can't fall asleep and may lie in bed for hours fretting and brooding, those with mania show high levels of activity at bedtime, spend very little time in bed, and require very little sleep. A child with mania might spend several hours at bedtime rearranging clothes in a dresser or closet, or an adolescent may wait until his or her parents are asleep and then sneak out of the house to a party.

For children with mania, their words, thoughts, and actions occur in fast motion. Increased verbal production with puns, word plays, and incessant speech are common. At all ages, children with mania show *pressured speech*—they talk too much and too fast, change topics too quickly, and cannot be interrupted. They also have *racing thoughts* that they may describe in concrete terms—for example, by saying they can't do their schoolwork because their thoughts keep interrupting. In the words of one teen, "I wish I had a switch on my forehead so I could turn off my racing thoughts" (Geller & Luby, 1997). Like an adult with BP, a child with the disorder also shows a *flight of ideas*, which is an illogical jump from one idea to another. For example, in reply to the question, "Do you live in Los Angeles?" the child may reply, "Some people like to swim in the ocean. Do you have a dog?"

For manic children of all ages, even slight changes in their surroundings can lead to significant distractibility. Heightened psychomotor agitation and goal-directed actions resemble normal activities carried out in excess, with a seemingly endless supply of energy. During a brief period of time, a manic youngster might draw several pictures, read a book, work on the computer, prepare a snack, make multiple phone calls, write a letter, and vacuum the house.

Accepting dares is common for youngsters with BP. In older adolescents, this may appear as a pattern of reckless driving that results in multiple tickets for speeding or driving under the influence. In preadolescents, it may be expressed as grandiose delusions of being able to jump out the window because they believe they can fly. They also may push the limits on usual childhood climbing on things, based on the strong belief that they are above the possibility of danger (Geller & Luby, 1997). In extreme cases, they may experience violent agitation with delusional thinking as well as visual and auditory hallucinations.

Prevalence

Although the prevalence of BP in young people has yet to be adequately established, lifetime prevalence estimates range from 0.4% to 2.9% (Costello et al., 2002; Lewinsohn, Seeley, Buckley, & Klein, 2002; Merikangas et al., 2010). However, because of the complicated presentation of symptoms and the difficulties in making an accurate diagnosis, it is possible that BP in young people is more common and occurs at a younger age than previously thought (Luby & Belden, 2006; Youngstrom, 2007). The duration of manic symptoms in young people often does not meet the 1-week duration requirement of DSM to be a manic episode. In a recent epidemiological study of 8 to 19 year olds, it was that found recurrent episodes of mania or hypomania that met the DSM criteria for episode duration were extremely rare (< 0.3%), and restricted to 16 to 19 year olds (Stringaris, Santosh, Leibenluft, & Goodman, 2010). In light of this finding, the most common diagnoses are the milder bipolar II disorder and cyclothymic disorder, rather than bipolar I disorder (Lewinsohn, Klein, & Seeley, 1995). Children are also likely to present with rapid cycling episodes (at least 4 mood episodes of a mood disturbance over a 1-year period), with about 80% of children showing this course (Geller et al., 1995).

Despite accounts of the onset of mania in children as young as 5 or 6 years old, the incidence of BP prior to puberty is extremely rare, but it increases during adolescence and is as nearly high as it is for adults (Lewinsohn, Klein, & Seeley, 2000). In sharp contrast to the effects of depression, BP affects boys and girls equally. However, symptoms may be expressed differently, with boys showing more manic mood and girls more depressed mood (Duax, Youngstrom, Calabrese, & Findling, 2007). In studies of youngsters with early-onset BP, boys seem to be affected more often than girls, especially when the age of onset is younger than 13 years. Rates of BP have not been found to differ by ethnicity or culture, but few studies have investigated this issue in children and adolescents (AACAP, 2007c).

Comorbidity

High rates of co-occurring disorders are extremely common in children with BP, with the most typical being separation anxiety disorders, generalized anxiety disorders, ADHD, and conduct problems (Sala et al., 2010). Co-occurring substance use disorders are also common, as are suicidal thoughts and ideation (Kim & Miklowitz, 2002; Youngstrom, 2007). In addition, medical problems such as cardiovascular and metabolic disorders, epilepsy, and migraine headaches are also common in youngsters with BP, which further complicates how it is managed (Sheffer & Linden, 2007).

Many youngsters with BP display co-occurring symptoms of ADHD, such as poor judgment, distractibility, inattention, irritability, hyperactivity, anger, poor impulse control, demanding behaviors, and the tendency to jump from one topic or activity to another. For youngsters first seen because of symptoms of BP, about 60% to 90% of prepubertal children and 30% of adolescents also have ADHD (Geller & Luby, 1997).

Oppositional and conduct disorders occur in as many as 80% of children and adolescents with BP (Leibenluft & Rich, 2008). Symptoms of grandiosity, mania, and poor judgment in BP may be confused with symptoms of conduct problems. For example, one 11-year-old boy with BP, who believed he would be a famous rock star, stole several hundred dollars' worth of music and was totally unaffected when questioned by the police. Conduct disorder overlaps with BP on symptoms such as running away, driving under the influence, substance abuse, sexual promiscuity, and stealing. Similarly, the flight of ideas and or pressured speech associated with mania may be mistaken for a language disorder (Carlson, 2002; Geller & Luby, 1997).

In trying to differentiate the symptoms of BP from those of comorbid conditions, if symptoms occur or worsen only during a mood episode, they may indicate mania. However, if they are chronic, occur between episodes, and represent the child's typical level of behavior, the presentation would be more consistent with ODD, ADHD, or anxiety disorder (Leibenluft & Rich, 2008).

Onset, Course, and Outcome

About 60% of all patients with BP experience their first episode prior to age 19 years, with a peak age of onset between 15 and 19 years old (Merikangas et al., 2007; Post et al., 2008). Although BP in preschool children may be identified using age-adjusted mania symptoms (Luby, Tandon, & Belden, 2009), onset prior to age 10 is extremely rare. Youngsters with BP may first present with either depressive or manic episodes, although most report that their first mood episode was major depression. This is consistent with the reported high rates of switching from depression to mania (Geller & Luby, 1997).

Risk factors for eventual mania include a major depressive episode (characterized by rapid onset, psychomotor retardation, and psychotic features) and a family history of mood disorders, especially BP (AACAP, 2007c). When a young person presents with a first episode of obvious mania, it's very likely that further manic episodes will follow. Bipolar episodes are generally shorter than major depressive episodes, lasting from 4 to 6 months if left untreated. About 70% of adolescents recover from their initial episode within 6 months, but 50% will have at least one recurrent episode (Birmaher et al., 2006).

Adolescents with mania often have complex presentations that include psychotic symptoms such as hallucinations, paranoia, and thought disorder. They also have unstable moods with mixed manic and depressive features, and severe deterioration in behavior. These diverse forms of presentation may result in an underdiagnosis of BP in teens and may be misdiagnosed as schizophrenia.

Because of the difficulty in recognizing symptoms of BP in young people, it is common for the symptoms to be noticed well before a youngster is treated or hospitalized, but not labeled as BP (Youngstrom, Findling, Youngstrom, & Calabrese, 2005). A look back at the histories of adults with BP symptoms often shows that mood swings began around puberty; however, there is frequently a 5- to 10-year lag between the onset of symptoms and display of the disorder serious enough to be recognized and treated (Carlson, 1994).

An early onset and course of BP is chronic and resistant to treatment, with a poor long-term prognosis similar to that in adults (AACAP, 2007c). In a 5-year prospective follow-up study of adolescents with BP, nearly 50% of all patients had a relapsing course or never achieved complete remission (Strober et al., 1995). Compared with adults, adolescents with BP may have a more prolonged early course and a poorer response to treatment. However, long-term prognosis appears to be similar to that for adults, with most patients continuing to experience significant symptoms and functional impairment (DelBello, Hanseman, Adler, Fleck, & Strakowski, 2007).

Causes

JESSI

Runs in the Family

"Jessi's father had been an alcoholic and a manic depressive," says her mother, "probably since he was an adolescent. He died of dehydration that occurred during a manic episode. His illness had been a mystery to us. Growing up, Jessi knew her father was ill, and when she was older, she began to worry about what his sickness might mean for her. I worried too," says Jessi's mother. "By the time Jessi was in her early twenties, something was clearly wrong. At first, I noticed only that she had become less reliable—forgetting things, arriving late, and occasionally missing appointments with me. Frequently, she complained of fatigue, a cold, flu, or a stomachache. Increasingly, her responses were brief, perfunctory. Though we didn't know it then, Jessi was experiencing a huge mood shift that was taking months to complete itself. Jessi had MDD, without the manic swings of the bipolar disorder her father had suffered from." (Adapted from Dowling, 1992)

Few studies have examined the causes of BP in young people, although research with adults indicates that BP is one of the most heritable forms of mental disorder (McInnes, Humphries, Hogg-Johnson, & Tannock, 2003). Findings from family and gene studies with adults indicate that BP is the result of a genetic vulnerability combined with environmental factors, such as life stress or a negative family climate. When an identical twin has BP, there is only a 65% chance that the other twin will have it too, suggesting that in addition to genes, other factors are important. Although BP can affect anyone, it has definitely been shown to run in families (Geller et al., 2006). If one or both parents have BP, the chances are about 5 times greater that their children will also develop BP or, like Jessi, often another mood disorder (Hodgins, Faucher, Zarac, & Ellenbogen, 2002).

Besides mood disorder, children at risk for BP by virtue of having parents with the disorder also display a wide range of psychopathology, particularly conduct problems and ADHD, as well as social and academic difficulties (Singh et al., 2007). Relatives of youngsters with BP also have a higher incidence of the disorder. Family incidence and risk for a broad range of psychiatric problems are highest in cases of early-onset BP, with lifetime prevalence rates of about 15% in first-degree relatives (AACAP, 2007c; Rende et al., 2007). This rate is 15 times greater than the prevalence of the disorder in the general population.

Increasing evidence suggests that BP arises from multiple genes, and recent studies have identified several chromosomal regions and susceptibility genes (Alsabban, Rivera, & McGuffin, 2011; McInnis et al., 2003). There is likely a complex mode of inheritance rather than a single dominant gene. Individuals with a genetic predisposition do not necessarily develop BP, since environmental factors play an important role in determining how genes are expressed (Geller & Luby, 1997). The ways in which environmental factors play a role are not well understood. However, one study suggests that parental bipolar disorder creates a negative family climate, including problem-solving and communication deficits, which predict family conflict, which in turn predicts child BP (Du Rocher Schudlich, Youngstrom, Calabrese, & Findling, 2008).

Brain scans of children identified as being at risk for BP that were taken before and after the onset of a manic episode have shown changes in the brain that reflect a pattern of emotion dysregulation in general, rather than one that is specific to BP onset (Gogtay et al., 2007). Generally, mood fluctuations in BP have been related to abnormalities in the structure and function of the amygdala, prefrontal and anterior cingulate cortex, hippocampus, thalamus, and basal ganglia, but findings have not always been consistent with respect to the types of abnormalities (Garrett & Chang, 2008; Gogtay et al., 2007). Such inconsistencies may be related to ongoing brain changes that are occurring in young people and the point in development at which brain structure and function are assessed.

Some studies have found that BP in adolescents is related to reduced volumes of the amygdala and hippocampus (Beardon et al., 2007; Blumberg et al., 2003). As you may recall, we discussed the importance of the amygdala for recognizing and regulating emotions in relation to depression. Research has found that youth with BP misread neutral facial expressions as hostile and in doing so show heightened activation of the amygdala and its connectivity to parts of the brain involved in processing face information (Rich et al., 2008). These and other findings suggest that youths at risk for and with BP display unique neural correlates and deficits in face emotion processing (Brotman et al., 2010). Such deficits may be related to the poor social skills, aggression, and irritability that characterize youngsters with BP.

Treatment

Treatment of BP in children and adolescents is receiving increasing attention. Although there is no cure for BP, in most cases treatment can stabilize mood and allow for management and control of symptoms. Treatment of BP generally requires a multimodal plan that includes close monitoring of symptoms, education of the patient and the family about the illness, matching treatments to individuals, medications such as lithium, and psychotherapeutic interventions to address the youngster's symptoms and related psychosocial impairments (AACAP, 2007c; Kowatch et al., 2005). The general goals of treatment are to decrease the child's symptoms and to prevent relapse, while also reducing long-term illness and enhancing the youngster's normal health and development (Geller & Delbello, 2008). Youngsters with BP have been given multiple medications. The FDA has approved lithium for use down to 12 years of age. However, there are currently no drugs that are FDA approved for the treatment of BP in children younger than this age (AACAP, 2007c). Medications are typically used to address manic or mixed symptoms and depressive symptoms, or to prevent relapse. Although clinical trials of medication have had some success, at this time, controlled studies of medication treatment for children and adolescents with BP are limited to nonexistent (Smarty & Findling, 2007). The current recommended treatments are based on findings with adults; however, as we saw with tricyclic antidepressants, such an extrapolation may not be warranted (Geller et al., 1998). Hence, mood-stabilizing medication needs to be used with caution and conservatively with young people with BP, particularly those who do not fit the classic presentation of symptoms as seen in adults (Horst, 2009).

In general, lithium is the first agent of choice in the treatment of BP, although other medications have been used, including valproate and/or atypical antipsychotics, as well as adjunctive medications to treat secondary symptoms (AACAP, 2007c; Sanchez & Soares, 2011). Lithium is a common salt that is widely present in the natural environment—for example, in drinking water—usually in amounts too small to have any effects. However, the side effects of therapeutic doses of lithium can be serious, especially when used in combination with other medications, and may include toxicity (poisoning), renal and thyroid problems, and substantial weight gain (Gracious et al., 2004). It can be given to young people when used with the same safety precautions and similar careful monitoring used for adults. However, lithium cannot be given to children in chaotic families or to children who are unable to keep the multiple appointments needed for monitoring potentially dangerous side effects (Carlson, 1994; Geller & Luby, 1997). In addition, one study found that only 35% of adolescents with BP reported full adherence with medication (DelBello et al., 2007).

Medications may decrease symptoms of BP but do not help with the associated functional impairments or pre-existing or co-occurring substance use disorders, learning and behavior problems, and family- and peer-related issues. Nonadherence to medication regimens has been shown to be a major contributor to relapse. Thus, the family must be educated about the negative effects of nonadherence and to recognize possible symptoms of relapse. Psychosocial interventions focus on providing information to the child and family about the disorder, symptoms and course, possible impact on family functioning, and heritability of the disorder (Fristad & Goldberg Arnold, 2004; Geller & Luby, 1997). Controlled research on psychosocial treatments for youngsters with BP is beginning to appear (Fristad, Verducci, Walters, & Young, 2009; Goldstein, Axelson, Birmaher, & Brent, 2007; Miklowitz et al., 2011). This has resulted in several promising new approaches using CBT, family-focused therapy, and individual treatments that have been used to enhance the effects of medication in reducing symptoms of BP (Miklowitz, 2011). Ongoing efforts to identify young children at risk for developing BP may one day provide opportunities for both psychopharmacological and psychosocial preventative interventions (Howes & Falkenberg, 2011; Luby & Navsaria, 2010).

SECTION SUMMARY

Bipolar Disorder

- A recent surge in interest in the diagnosis of bipolar disorder (BP) in children and adolescents has generated considerable controversy surrounding difficulties in identifying the disorder in young people.
- Youngsters with BP show periods of abnormally and persistently elevated, expansive, and/or irritable mood.
- They may display symptoms such as an inflated self-esteem, decreased need for sleep, pressured speech, flight of ideas, distractibility, and reckless behavior.
- BP is far less common than MDD in young people, with prevalence estimates of 1% or lower.
- BP has a peak age of onset in late adolescence and affects males and females about equally.
- The most common accompanying disorders are ADHD, anxiety disorders, disruptive behavior disorders, and substance abuse.
- Very few studies have examined the causes of BP in children and adolescents. Family and gene studies with adults indicate that BP is the result of a genetic vulnerability in combination with environmental factors, such as life stress or disturbances in the family.
- Brain imaging studies of youngsters with BP point to abnormalities in regions of the brain involved in emotion regulation, including the amygdala and anterior cingulate cortex.
- BP in young people requires a multimodal treatment plan with education of the patient and the family about the illness, medication, and psychotherapeutic interventions to address the youngster's symptoms and related psychosocial impairments.

Study Resources

SECTION SUMMARIES

KEY TERMS

COURSEMATE

Access an interactive eBook and chapter-specific interactive learning tools, including flashcards, quizzes, videos, and more in your Psychology CourseMate, accessed through CengageBrain.com.

Intellectual Disability (Mental Retardation)

9

The scientific history of idiocy has yet to be produced; its data are scarce, and the study has not many charms.

—P. M. Duncan & W. Millard (1866)

CHAPTER PREVIEW

INTELLIGENCE AND INTELLECTUAL DISABILITY

The Eugenics Scare

Defining and Measuring Children's Intelligence and Adaptive Behavior

The Controversial IQ

FEATURES OF INTELLECTUAL DISABILITIES

Clinical Description

Degrees of Impairment

Level of Needed Supports

Race, Sex, and SES Prevalence

DEVELOPMENTAL COURSE AND ADULT OUTCOMES

Motivation

Changes in Abilities

Language and Social Behavior

Emotional and Behavioral Problems

Other Disabilities

CAUSES

Inheritance and the Role of the Environment

Genetic and Constitutional Factors

Neurobiological Influences

Social and Psychological Dimensions

PREVENTION, EDUCATION, AND TREATMENT

Prenatal Education and Screening

Psychosocial Treatments

UNTIL THE MID-19TH CENTURY, children and adults who today would be diagnosed as having mental retardation were labeled "idiots" and often were lumped together with persons suffering from mental disorders or medical conditions. They typically were ignored or feared, even by the medical profession, because their differences in appearance and ability were so little understood.

Although age-old fears, resentment, and scorn continue to overshadow many important discoveries about subnormal intelligence, the field of intellectual disability has experienced monumental gains over the past century in determining causes and providing services. Advances in understanding the development of children with mental retardation, along with research in genetics, psychopathology, and other areas, have dramatically changed the face of this field.

We use the terms *intellectual disability* and *mental retardation* interchangeably throughout this chapter because both terms remain in common use. Intellectual disability (ID) is characterized by significant limitations in both intellectual functioning and adaptive behavior that begin before age 18 (American Association on Intellectual and Developmental Disabilities [AAIDD], 2010; formerly the American Association on Mental Retardation). It is not a mental disorder (in the sense of abnormal emotions, cognitions, or behaviors) or a medical disorder; rather, it is a disorder pertaining to limitations in intellectual functioning (typically measured by an IQ score) and adaptive behavior (typically expressed as *conceptual, social, and practical* adaptive skills). Mental retardation appears on Axis II in the DSM-IV-TR because it is considered a stable condition rather than a clinical disorder.

Importantly, modern definitions of intellectual disability take into account a person's intellectual functioning within the context of what is typical for that individual's peers and culture. Cultural and linguistic diversity, as well as differences in communication, sensory, motor, and behavioral factors, must be carefully considered in determining a deficit or disability (AAIDD, 2010). An appreciation of the rapid improvements in knowledge and treatment of intellectual disability, as well as an understanding of the prejudice and ignorance that had to be overcome, can be gained by looking at how the disorder has been viewed over the years.

Intelligence and Intellectual Disability

Throughout recorded history, persons with intellectual and other disabilities have suffered scorn and rejection from fellow townspeople, largely due to fear and ignorance. The prevailing misunderstanding and mistreatment of children with intellectual disabilities changed very little until the end of the 18th century, fueled by the discovery of feral children such as Victor, the "wild boy of Aveyron" (discussed in Chapter 1), and by the expansion of humanitarian efforts to assist other oppressed or neglected groups, such as slaves, prisoners, the mentally ill, and persons with physical disabilities.

Ignorance resulted in the segregation of children with intellectual disabilities, who were subjected to inhumane treatment. Today, most children with ID are integrated into regular classrooms.

By the mid-19th century, the concept of mental retardation had spread from France and Switzerland to much of Europe and North America. During the same period, Dr. Samuel G. Howe convinced his contemporaries that training and educating the "feeble-minded" was a public responsibility, and he opened the first humanitarian institution in North America for persons with mental retardation—the Massachusetts School for Idiotic and Feeble-Minded Youth.

Parents of children with ID can be credited with advancing a perspective and response to the need for long-term care that was completely different from that of the prevailing public and professional opinions. By the 1940s, parents began to meet in groups and began to create local diagnostic and guidance centers to increase the availability of humane care. These groups organized in 1950 to form the National Association for Retarded Children, which quickly established a scientific board made up of representatives from every specialty possible to assist in the study, prevention, and care of persons with mental retardation (Kanner, 1964). These efforts gained momentum when President John F. Kennedy, who had a sister with mental retardation, formed the President's Panel on Mental Retardation in 1962 and called for a national program to combat mental retardation. Soon thereafter, exposés in the media of the use of solitary confinement and restraints increased public awareness of and outrage at the treatment of persons with mental retardation.

The Eugenics Scare

Three generations of imbeciles are enough.

—Justice Oliver Wendell Holmes Jr., commenting on the Supreme Court's 1927 decision to uphold eugenics sterilization laws

Evolutionary degeneracy theory, a pervasive 19th-century phenomenon, attributed the intellectual and social problems of children with mental retardation to regression to an earlier period in human evolution (Bowler, 1989). In fact, mental deficiency experts in the 19th century believed they had found the "missing link" between humans and lower species (Gelb, 1995). J. Langdon H. Down, best known for the clinical description of the genetic syndrome that bears his name, interpreted the "strange anomalies" among his medical sample of persons with mental retardation as an evolutionary throwback to the Mongol race (Down, 1866). Down believed that parents in one racial group might give birth to a child with mental retardation who was a "retrogression" to another group. While grounded in speculation and misinformed conclusions, evolutionary degeneracy theory and its notion of inferiority received growing support by the late-19th century as an explanation for insanity, mental deficiency, and social deviance. Box 9.1 depicts how this popular theory was conveniently used to explain undesirable human characteristics.

By 1910, the eugenics movement was gaining momentum. **Eugenics** was first defined by Sir Francis Galton (Charles Darwin's cousin) in 1883 as "the science which deals with all influences that improve the inborn qualities of a race" (cited in Kanner, 1964, p. 128). Public and professional emphasis shifted away from the needs of persons with mental retardation toward a consideration of the needs of society; society was to be protected from the presumable harm done by the presence of these persons in the community.

Consequently, persons with intellectual disability often were blamed for the social ills of the time, which is a powerful example of how labeling a problem can quickly become an explanation for it. Box 9.2, in fact, shows a 1912 *New York Times* article reflecting this public sentiment. The appearance, ability, and behavior of persons with mental retardation were considered evidence of their lack of moral fiber, a belief that led to the diagnostic term *moral imbecile*, or *moron*, used to describe and explain their differences. This concept became a straightforward explanation for acts of deviance, and justified wide-ranging attempts to identify and control such individuals. Morons, considered the least intellectually impaired (roughly comparable to mild mental retardation today) were seen as a threat to society because, unlike the insane, they could easily pass for normal (Gelb, 1995). The intellectually impaired and other "undesirables" were once again seen as a public menace, to be feared and ostracized.

Meanwhile, early developmental psychologists proposed that children between the ages of 8 and 12 pass through an "ancestral stage," during which moral reasoning emerges. As G. Stanley Hall, a prominent psychologist who was instrumental in the development of educational psychology, described it, children of this age were "mature savages" who required strong social forces to ensure that they advanced beyond this stage and became fit for civilized life (Gelb, 1995). Persons with different abilities or less social status—especially members of minority groups, women, children, and the physically and mentally challenged—were considered less capable of judgment or reasoning, which of course provided further justification for restricting their rights and opportunities for advancement.

BOX 9.1 A CLOSER LOOK

The Infamous Kallikaks

Psychologist Henry Goddard, who began one of the largest training schools for mental retardation in the early 20th century, was also a proponent of the popular degeneracy theory and eugenics movement. In his book *The Kallikak Family: A Study in the Heredity of Feeble-Mindedness* (1912), Goddard traced two lines of descendants from a Revolutionary War soldier, Martin Kallikak, who fathered a child by a "feebleminded barmaid" during the war, which began the first line, and then fathered other children by a "respectable girl" he married after the war. The name "Kallikak" was invented by Goddard from a combination of two Greek words: *kalos*, meaning "attractive, pleasing," and *kakos*, meaning "bad, evil."

Goddard reported that many descendants of the first union were feebleminded, delinquent, poor, and alcoholic, whereas those of the second union were of good reputation. He claimed this outcome was evidence for the inheritance of intelligence, although he overlooked the two families' obvious environmental differences (Achenbach, 1982). A closer look at the disclaimer from the preface to the book is telling: "It is true that we have made rather dogmatic statements and have drawn conclusions that do not seem scientifically warranted by the data."

Source: Based on authors' case material.

BOX 9.2 A CLOSER LOOK

Early 20th Century Perspectives on Mental Retardation

WEAK-MINDED FILL RANKS OF CRIMINALS
DR. HENRY GODDARD SAYS SOCIAL PROBLEMS
CAN BE SOLVED BY SEGREGATING THEM

WOULD NOT LET THEM MARRY

THIS POLICY WOULD IN TIME LARGELY
REDUCE CRIMES, DISEASE, AND DRUNKENNESS,
HE BELIEVES

From the army of 300,000 feeble-minded persons in the United States come the recruits that swell the ranks of the drunkards, criminals, paupers, and other social outcasts. Twenty-five per cent of the girls and boys in our reformatories are lacking in mental fibre and are unable to discern the difference between right and wrong or are too weak in character to do right whenever there is any inducement to do wrong. Sixty-five per cent of the children have a mother or a father, or both, who are feeble-minded. This country has so far taken no steps to segregate these irresponsible persons, so the number of them is constantly increasing. . . .

This army furnishes the ranks of the criminals, paupers, drunkards, the ne'er-do-wells, and others who are social misfits. Their incapacity would be a priori cause of believing that they eventually will become public charges in one form or another, and investigation, in fact, proves that the groups of criminals, paupers, etc., actually do contain large percentages of people mentally irresponsible.

Source: The New York Times, *March 10, 1912.*

Defining and Measuring Children's Intelligence and Adaptive Behavior

Around 1900, the pioneering work of two French educators, Alfred Binet and Theophile Simon, led to some of the first major advancements in the field of children's intellectual functioning. Binet and Simon were asked to develop a way to identify schoolchildren who might need special help in school. They approached this monumental task by developing the first intelligence tests to measure judgment and reasoning, which they believed were basic processes of higher thought. These early test questions asked children to manipulate unfamiliar objects such as blocks or figures, and to solve puzzles and match familiar parts of objects. The test later became the Stanford–Binet scale, which remains one of the most widely used intelligence tests.

From these beginnings in intellectual testing, **general intellectual functioning** is now defined by an intelligence quotient (IQ or equivalent) that is based on assessment with one or more of the standardized, individually administered intelligence tests, such as the Wechsler Intelligence Scales for Children (WISC-IV), the Stanford–Binet (SB5), and the Kaufman Assessment Battery for Children (KABC-II). These tests assess various verbal and visual–spatial skills in the child (such as knowledge of the world, reasoning, and similarities and differences) and mathematical concepts, which together are presumed to constitute the general construct known as intelligence.

By convention, intelligence quotient scores (with a mean of 100 and standard deviation of 15) are derived from a standardized table based on a person's age and test score. Because intelligence is defined along a normal distribution, approximately 95% of the population has scores within 2 standard deviations of the mean (i.e., between 70 and 130). Subaverage intellectual functioning is defined, accordingly, as an IQ of about 70 or below (approximately 2 standard deviations below the mean).

As we will discuss later in this chapter, the definition of mental retardation includes not only subaverage intellectual functioning, but also a subaverage level of adaptive functioning. **Adaptive functioning** refers to how effectively individuals cope with ordinary life demands, and how capable they are of living independently and abiding by community standards (Hodapp, Thornton-Wells, & Dykens, 2009). Note that some children and adolescents may learn to adapt quite well to their environment despite their lowered intelligence as measured by an IQ test; therefore, they would not be considered to have mental retardation. Table 9.1 gives examples of the three major categories of adaptive behavior (conceptual, social, and practical adaptive skills).

The Controversial IQ

If a person's intelligence is relatively stable over time, it would be tempting to conclude that it is largely innate and fixed. On the other hand, if intellectual and cognitive development is significantly shaped by environment, perhaps cognitive growth can be stimulated at an early age and the level of mental retardation decreased.

Because intelligence is measured in relation to agemates, IQ generally is stable from childhood through adulthood (Carr, 2005; Whitaker, 2008). One exception to this general rule is IQ that is measured during early infancy, when considerable fluctuation can still occur. For typically developing children, IQ measured prior to the first birthday has virtually no correlation with the IQ score achieved at age 12; however, by the time children are 4 years old, the correlation with IQ 12 years later is high (r = .77) (Neisser et al., 1996).

TABLE 9.1 | Specific Examples of Adaptive Behavior Skills

Specific Examples of Adaptive Behavior Skills
Conceptual Skills
Receptive and expressive language
Reading and writing
Money concepts
Self-directions
Social Skills
Interpersonal
Responsibility
Self-esteem
Gullibility (likelihood of being tricked or manipulated)
Naiveté
Follows rules
Obeys laws
Avoids victimization
Practical Skills
Personal activities of daily living such as eating, dressing, mobility, and toileting
Instrumental activities of daily living such as preparing meals, taking medication, using the telephone, managing money, using transportation and doing housekeeping activities
Occupational Skills
Maintaining a safe environment

Source: From the American Association on Intellectual and Developmental Disabilities (AAIDD).

The picture is dramatically different, however, for infants and children with developmental delays or mental retardation. At the lower IQ levels (say, below 50), even the youngest infants show IQ stability over time, with correlations between infant and childhood test scores ranging from .50 to .97 (Sattler, 2006). Researchers have discovered a similar pattern of IQ stability from middle childhood to young adulthood among children with mild to moderate intellectual delays (Mortensen, Andresen, Kruuse, Sanders, & Reinisch, 2003; Toth & King, 2010).

Even though the IQ of cognitively delayed infants and young children is unlikely to change, proper environmental circumstances will help children reach their fullest potential. Since the early 1960s, researchers in child development and retardation have been investigating ways to provide early stimulation programs that will help children with developmental delays and environmental disadvantages build on their existing strengths. Despite its strong genetic component, mental ability is always modified by experience. Not surprisingly, infancy through early childhood offer the most significant opportunity for influencing intellectual ability, due to the young child's rapid brain development and response to environmental stimulation (Campbell & Ramey, 2010; Pungello et al., 2010).

The importance of genetic makeup notwithstanding, IQ can and does change for some individuals by 10 to 20 points between childhood and adolescence (Simonoff, Bolton, & Rutter, 1996). Differences in outcome vary widely in relation to opportunities for each child to learn and develop. Children who live in healthy environments, where caregivers provide appropriate levels of stimulation and help them manage ambient levels of stress, are most likely to reach their full potential. Moreover, tests can sample only a limited spectrum of intellectual ability, and are incapable of accounting for each individual's unique learning history (Sattler, 2006).

Are We Really Getting Smarter?

Scores have risen sharply since the beginning of IQ testing, ranging from a 5- to a 25-point increase in a single generation (Kanaya, Scullin, & Ceci, 2003). When James Flynn brought this phenomenon of rising IQ scores to the attention of scientists in 1987, it became known as the "Flynn effect." The gain has averaged about 3 IQ points per decade, adding up to more than a full standard deviation since the 1940s. Once a test is re-normed (about every 15 to 20 years) the mean is reset to 100, resulting in a brief reversal of this gain in IQ scores.

In attempting to explain the Flynn effect, scientists have considered the rising standards of living, better schooling, better nutrition, medical advances, more stimulating environments, even the influence of computer games and complex toys (Flynn, 2007). IQ tests themselves have once again come under scrutiny, as have children's exposure to problems similar to those on the tests—like the mazes and puzzles they see on their cereal boxes and fast-food bags. Yet the consistent IQ gains are too large to be the result simply of increased familiarity with testing methods.

Although the exact cause of the effect remains unknown, experts on children's intelligence suspect the gains reflect a meaningful aspect of intellectual growth and development. A relatively permissive and child-focused parenting style has emerged during recent decades, which may have given children greater facility with language and stronger overall cognitive capacity. Moreover, there are unprecedented cultural differences between successive generations, as daily life and occupational experiences are far more complex today. There is a possible downside to the Flynn effect, however. Test scores drop an average of 5.6 points among persons with borderline and mild mental retardation after a test is re-normed, which can have a significant impact on a child's eligibility for proper educational placement and other related services (Kanaya et al., 2003).

Are IQ Tests Biased or Unfair?

Concern has been expressed over the relatively lower mean of the distribution of intelligence test scores of African Americans, typically about 1 standard deviation (about 15 IQ points) below that of whites (Jencks & Phillips, 1998). Although recent estimates suggest that African Americans have gained 4 to 7 IQ points on non-Hispanic whites since 1972 (Dickens & Flynn, 2006), considerable concern remains as to why differences in test results exist at all.

The controversy in IQ score differences is fueled by researchers who argue that IQ is 80% heritable and therefore largely genetically determined (Rushton & Jensen, 2006). Other researchers argue that economic and social inequality—not test bias or racial differences—are the simplest explanations for existing group differences in test performance between African Americans and whites (Brooks-Gunn, Klebanov, Smith, Duncan, & Lee, 2003). For example, when personal and family background characteristics are statistically controlled, African American and white children achieve similar test scores. However, once these students enter school, the gap between white and African American children grows, which researchers believe may be due to lower-quality schools in lower-income neighborhoods (Levitt & Fryer, 2004; Nisbett, 2009). A much higher proportion of African Americans and other ethnic minority groups in the United States as well as in other countries are poor and have fewer opportunities for advancement relative to whites. Poverty and inequality are linked to poor nutrition, inadequate prenatal care, fewer intellectual resources, and similar realities that can have negative effects on children's developing intelligence (Sternberg, 2010; Turkheimer, Haley, Waldron, D'Onofrio, & Gottesman, 2003).

SECTION SUMMARY

Intelligence and Intellectual Disability

- The early history of mental retardation was plagued by ignorance and blame.
- By the mid-20th century, progress toward understanding mental retardation moved more rapidly, as parents, researchers, politicians, and the public sought better answers regarding its causes and better ways to assist both children and adults with ID.
- Mental retardation refers to limitations in both intelligence and adaptive behavior. However, many persons with this disorder are capable of learning and of living fulfilling lives.
- Despite its drawbacks, the IQ has become a principal standard for diagnosing mental retardation, combined with other skills and abilities of the child.

FEATURES OF INTELLECTUAL DISABILITIES

MATTHEW

Gaining at His Own Pace

Matthew was almost 6 years old when he was referred for a psychological assessment. His brief school record described him as "developmentally delayed," and the school was concerned that his speech and social skills were very limited. He also had temper tantrums at home, and his new first-grade teacher had expressed concerns about his aggressive behavior toward children in his class.

I first met with Matt in his home. "Show me some of your favorite toys or games," I suggested, unsure of how comfortable he was with a stranger at his home. He was a thin boy, with curly hair and a cautious, reserved expression. He looked me over for what must have been several minutes while I spoke with his mother and father. Although he said "OK," I wasn't sure he meant it—he stayed put and seemed uninterested in my request. Matt had turned 6 a few months ago, but I noticed that his clothes, games, and vocabulary were closer to those of my 3-year-old daughter. "I don't want to talk about school stuff!" he exclaimed, quite loudly, when I asked about his favorite subjects. "I only like recess and lunchtime—the stuff they won't let you do till the bell rings!" There was a certain degree of truth, and humor, to his statement, although I don't think he intended it as such. . . .

Matt became a bit more interested when I brought out some testing materials. He completed with ease a puzzle designed for toddlers, and was able to make the sounds of animals in the puzzle. But his emotional expression remained subdued, with little spontaneous laughter or joy. He seemed watchful and cautious. "Tell me about this story," I said to Matt, holding up a card showing some animals arguing over a ball. "What do you think is going on in this picture, and what are the characters, like the elephant and the zebra, thinking and feeling?" Matt started right in: "He's mad 'cuz the zebra grabbed the ball and ran away with it into the woods. That's all I see." My attempts to elicit more detail were met with only an inquisitive look.

After a few minutes of this, we took a break and brought out his toys. "Do you like *Harry Potter?*" he asked. We found some common ground among the characters in the book, and under these "ideal" conditions, Matt's communication became more at ease and spontaneous. He expressed a wide range of emotion throughout the interview, and settled in to his own comfortable level of relating. Gradually, his language production increased as we continued with the more relaxed play sessions.

In private, Matt's mother told me about his behavior problems around other children, such as hitting, biting, throwing objects, and demanding attention. I saw a brief episode of it myself, when his 3-year-old sister came into the room: "Get out! This man is here to play with me!" Overall, Matt behaved like a much younger child—for example, by shouting or pushing when he couldn't get his way immediately. When we met for the second time, in my office, Matt's WISC-IV full-scale IQ was assessed at 64, and his adaptive abilities score was 68, based on his mother's report on the Vineland Adaptive Behavior Scales. Despite his mild mental retardation, however, Matt has been gaining over the past year in school, and he is showing a healthy gain in his developmental milestones as well. (Based on authors' case material)

You judge a person by how they look or how they talk or what the tests show, but you can never really tell what is inside the person.

—Ed, 27 years old, who was labeled mentally retarded and placed in a state institution at age 15 (Bogdan & Taylor, 1982)

Intellectual disabilities encompass perhaps the widest variation in cognitive and behavioral abilities of any childhood disorder. Some of these children function quite well in school and the community, whereas others, those with significant physical and cognitive impairments, require daily supervision and assistance. The situations of Matthew, age 6, and Vanessa, age 8, illustrate some of the unique challenges children with ID face every day.

Matthew was diagnosed as having mild mental retardation. Although delayed in his speech and language development, he was developing effective verbal skills and was capable of attending a regular classroom. Establishing friendships with children at school was sometimes problematic because he was often slow at understanding the rules of games and was teased by some children because of his slowness.

VANESSA

Gaining at Home

Vanessa is an 8-year-old girl with moderate mental retardation (IQ = 52) and limited communication skills. She was diagnosed prior to her fourth birthday, after medical and psychological examinations were undertaken to determine why she was not making many speech sounds or learning basic self-help skills. Vanessa's mother told us about how her daughter's special needs were poorly met while she was a resident in a special school for children with intellectual disabilities, and how this led to her parents' decision to raise Vanessa at home with the help of their community:

> When our family moved here we were told that we would receive $75 per month to care for her at home, or she could live at the Children's Training Center. Vanessa had been diagnosed with moderate mental retardation prior to her fourth birthday, and we knew that we could not care for her daily needs at home with the limited assistance being offered. So we made the difficult decision to place her at the training center. But, even though Vanessa came home every weekend, we felt there was something missing from her life; something beyond staff care and attention was needed to foster her growth.
>
> About 2 years later, things changed dramatically. Vanessa was injured by another resident, and we decided that she should return home once and for all. We made every effort to find services she needed for her training and education in our own community. She now attends an integrated classroom at the same school as her older brother, and her teachers have noticed strong gains in her behavior and language. She participates in recreational programs, and has become an accomplished swimmer and basketball player. (Based on authors' case material)

Vanessa was diagnosed as having moderate mental retardation. She could feed and dress herself with minimum assistance, and she communicated in short sentences, although her speech was not always discernible to people outside her family. Vanessa required more daily assistance to complete her routines, but she too was able to attend a local school during part of the day. As these cases show, the special needs of both children were sometimes overshadowed by economic and educational limitations, which required creativity and coordinated assistance on the part of parents, teachers, and other professionals.

Clinical Description

When the psychiatrist interviewed me he had my records in front of him—so he already knew I was mentally retarded. It's the same with everyone. If you are considered mentally retarded there is no way you can win. There is no way they give you a favorable report.

—Ed, describing part of his intake interview at the state institution (Bogdan & Taylor, 1982)

Children with ID show a considerable range of abilities and interpersonal qualities. With proper assistance, children with mild intellectual impairments, such as Matthew, can carry out their daily routine much like other children. They can attend a regular classroom, adjust to the demands of physical and intellectual challenges, and develop meaningful and lasting relationships with peers and adults. Many show normal physical development and can learn the physical coordination required to ride a bike. Others, like Vanessa, who have more severe impairments, will require greater daily supervision and care throughout their childhood and sometimes into early adulthood, at which time they may have developed the necessary skills to live more independently.

Both Matthew and Vanessa, however, experience limitations that involve most areas of daily living. Their most obvious difficulties are learning to communicate effectively, due to their limited speech and language skills. Although Matthew eventually learned effective verbal communication, for several years Vanessa had to rely on sign language and nonverbal expressions or gestures to express her needs. Both children had problems developing friendships with other children because of their limited ability to comprehend what other children were expressing, especially during games and social activities that require stamina and formal rules. Many cognitive abilities such as language and problem solving are affected; therefore, most children have difficulty with some aspect of learning. The degree of difficulty depends on the extent of cognitive impairment, which is the primary reason current definitions of mental retardation emphasize this aspect.

Table 9.2 summarizes the DSM-IV-TR diagnostic criteria for mental retardation. These criteria consist of three core features that describe this disorder in both children and adults. First, such individuals must have "significantly subaverage intellectual functioning," determined by formal intelligence testing or clinical judgment (in the case of an infant or an untestable subject). An individual must have an IQ score of approximately 70 or below to meet this first criterion, which falls 2 standard deviations below the average IQ score of 100 and thereby includes roughly 2% to 3% of the population.

The second criterion for diagnosing mental retardation requires "concurrent deficits or impairments in adaptive functioning," which refers to the ability to perform daily activities. In effect, an IQ score of 70 or below is not sufficient to receive a diagnosis of mental retardation. A person also must show significant limitations in at least two areas of adaptive behavior, such as communication, self-care, social/interpersonal skills, or functional academic or work skills (Lancioni, Singh, O'Reilly, & Sigafoos, 2009). This aspect of the definition is important because it specifically excludes persons who may function well in their own surroundings, yet for various reasons may not perform well on standard IQ tests. Importantly, whether a child or adolescent exhibits these various adaptive skills is related not only to ability, but also to experience and opportunity. Using public transportation, walking to a neighborhood store, and making simple purchases all can be affected by the individual's place of residence (urban versus rural, for example), or their concerns about neighborhood safety. Clinicians and educators must make educated guesses regarding a person's potential for performing a certain task if the person has not had experience with a particular skill on the test.

TABLE 9.2 | Diagnostic Criteria for Mental Retardation

DSM-IV-TR

(1) Significantly subaverage intellectual functioning with an IQ of approximately 70 or below on an individually administered IQ test (for infants, a clinical judgment of significantly subaverage intellectual functioning)

(2) Concurrent deficits or impairments in present adaptive functioning (i.e., the person's effectiveness in meeting the standards expected for his or her age by his or her cultural group) in at least two of the following areas: communication, self-care, home living, social/interpersonal skills, use of community resources, self-direction, functional academic skills, work, leisure, health, and safety

(3) The onset is before age 18 years.

Code based on degree of severity reflecting level of intellectual impairment:

317	Mild Mental Retardation: IQ level 50–55 to approximately 70
318.0	Moderate Mental Retardation: IQ level 35–40 to 50–55
318.1	Severe Mental Retardation: IQ level 20–25 to 35–40
318.2	Profound Mental Retardation: IQ level below 20 or 25
319	Mental Retardation, Severity Unspecified: when there is strong presumption of Mental Retardation but the person's intelligence is untestable by standard tests

Source: Reprinted with permission from the Diagnostic and Statistical Manual of Mental Disorders, Fourth Edition, Text Revision, (Copyright ©2000). American Psychiatric Association.

The final criterion for mental retardation stipulates that the child's below-average intellectual and adaptive abilities must be evident prior to age 18. The purpose of establishing this upper limit for the age of onset is twofold. First, it acknowledges that mental retardation is a developmental disorder that is evident during childhood and adolescence. Problems in learning and comprehension are most likely to occur during this time of rapid brain development. Second, this age criterion rules out persons who may show mental deficiencies caused by adult-onset degenerative diseases, such as Alzheimer's disease, or by head trauma.

The definition of mental retardation continues to be somewhat inaccurate and arbitrary, largely because it is based on a statistical concept—a cutoff IQ score—rather than on the nature or qualities of the person (Toth & King, 2010). Those with more severe cognitive impairments are more likely to be correctly diagnosed; however, the majority of persons diagnosed with ID fall into the mild range. The ramifications of diagnosing someone with ID can be serious. As Ed described so well, a careful balance must be struck between identifying the special needs of persons with intellectual disabilities and labeling them as having mental retardation on the basis of somewhat arbitrary criteria (Schalock et al., 2007).

Additionally, the definition and identification of intellectual disability depend somewhat on our social institutions. When children enter the school system, it is a significant point at which their abilities are compared and deficiencies are most likely to be detected. If children are placed in a poorly matched learning environment, their developmental progress can be disrupted. Following their school years, persons with mild mental retardation often blend back into the larger population, and their "diagnosis" no longer has as much meaning to either their education or training (Hodapp & Burack, 2006).

Degrees of Impairment

Children with ID vary widely in their degree of disability. Some show cognitive impairments from early infancy, such as limited vocalizations or poor self-regulation, whereas other impairments may go relatively unnoticed throughout the elementary school years. Because of the wide variation in cognitive functioning and impairment, classification systems for mental retardation have always attempted to delineate various degrees of cognitive impairment. The DSM-IV-TR has continued the tradition by designating retardation as mild, moderate, severe, or profound; these designations are based primarily on IQ scores. The American Association on Intellectual and Developmental Disabilities (AAIDD, 2010), in contrast, has restructured its description of varying degrees of mental retardation, choosing to base its categories on the level of support or assistance the person needs, rather than on IQ.

According to the DSM-IV-TR definition (APA, 2000), persons with **mild mental retardation** (IQ level of 55–70) constitute the largest group, estimated to be as many as 85% of persons with the disorder. Children with mild mental retardation often show small delays in development during the preschool years, but typically are not identified until academic or behavior problems emerge during the early elementary years. This category also has an overrepresentation of minority group members, most likely due to the social and economic disparities noted previously.

As a group, children with mild mental retardation typically develop social and communication skills during the preschool years (ages 0–5 years), perhaps with modest delays in expressive language. They usually have minimal or no sensorimotor impairment, and engage with peers readily. Like Matthew, however, some may find school and peer relationships to be challenging. By their late teens, these children can acquire academic skills up to approximately the sixth-grade level. During their adult years, they usually achieve social and vocational skills adequate for minimum self-support, but may need supervision, guidance, and assistance, especially when under unusual social or economic stress. With appropriate supports, individuals with mild mental retardation usually live successfully in the community, either independently or in supervised settings.

Persons with **moderate mental retardation** (IQ level of 40–54) constitute about 10% of those with ID. Individuals at this level of impairment are more intellectually and adaptively impaired than someone with mild mental retardation, and usually are identified during the preschool years when they show delays in reaching early developmental milestones. By the time they enter school, they may communicate through a combination of single words and gestures, and show self-care and motor skills similar to an average 2- to 3-year-old. Many persons with Down syndrome function at the moderate level of retardation. Some of these individuals may require only a few supportive services to function on a daily basis, but others may continue to require some help throughout life.

Like Vanessa, most individuals with this level of mental retardation acquire limited communication skills during their early years, and by age 12 may be using practical communication skills. They benefit from vocational training and, with moderate supervision, can attend to their personal care. They also can benefit from training in social and occupational skills, but are unlikely to progress beyond the second-grade level in academic subjects. Adolescents with moderate mental retardation often have difficulty recognizing social conventions such as appropriate dress or humor, which interferes with peer relationships. By adulthood, persons with moderate mental retardation typically adapt well to living in the community, and can perform unskilled or semiskilled work under supervision in sheltered workshops (specialized manufacturing facilities that train and supervise persons with ID) or in the general workforce.

Those with **severe mental retardation** (IQ level of 25–39) constitute approximately 3% to 4% of persons with ID. Most of these individuals suffer one or more organic causes of retardation, such as genetic defects, and are identified at a very young age because they have substantial delays in development and visible physical features or anomalies. Milestones such as standing, walking, and toilet training may be markedly delayed, and basic self-care skills are usually acquired by about age 9. In addition to intellectual impairment, they may have problems with physical mobility or other health-related problems, such as respiratory, heart, or physical complications.

Most persons functioning at this severe level of mental retardation require some special assistance throughout their lives. During early childhood they acquire little or no communicative speech; by age 12, they may use some two to three-word phrases. Between 13 and 15 years of age, their academic and adaptive abilities are similar to those of an average 4- to 6-year-old. They profit to a limited extent from instruction in pre-academic subjects, such as familiarity with the alphabet and simple counting, and can master skills such as sight reading "survival" words such as "hot," "danger," and "stop." During their adult years, they may be able to perform simple tasks in closely supervised settings. Most adapt well to life in the community, in group homes or with their families, unless they have an associated disability that requires specialized nursing or other care (Toth & King, 2010).

Persons with **profound mental retardation** (IQ level below 20 or 25) constitute approximately 1% to 2% of those with ID. Such individuals typically are identified in infancy because of marked delays in development and biological anomalies such as asymmetrical facial features. During early childhood they show considerable impairments in sensorimotor functioning; by the age of 4 years, for example, their responsiveness is similar to that of a typical 1-year-old. They are able to learn only the rudiments of communication skills, and they require intensive training to learn basic eating, grooming, toileting, and dressing behaviors.

Persons with profound mental retardation require lifelong care and assistance. Almost all of these individuals show organic causes for their retardation, and many have severe co-occurring medical conditions, such as congenital heart defect or epilepsy, that sometimes lead to death during childhood or early adulthood. Most of these individuals live in supervised group homes or small, specialized facilities. Optimal development may occur in a highly structured environment with constant aid and supervision and an individualized relationship with a caregiver. Motor development, as well as self-care and communication skills, may improve if appropriate training is provided. For example, persons with profound mental retardation usually can perform simple tasks, such as washing their hands and changing their clothes, provided they have close supervision.

Level of Needed Supports

The DSM-IV-TR categories have been criticized as potentially stigmatizing and limiting because they emphasize the degree of impairment. This criticism provided the major impetus for the AAIDD focus on levels of needed support and assistance (AAIDD, 2010). Rather than use the traditional IQ-based levels of impairment, the AAIDD emphasizes resources and strategies necessary to promote the overall adjustment and well-being of a person with intellectual disability. Specific needs of the individual are evaluated and strategies and services are developed to optimize individual functioning. Table 9.3 defines these AAIDD categories.

TABLE 9.3 | Examples of Support Areas and Support Activities

Teaching and Education Activities
• Interacting with trainers and teachers and fellow trainees and students • Learning and using problem-solving strategies • Using technology for learning • Learning and using functional academics (reading signs, counting change, etc.)
Home Living Activities
• Preparing and eating food • Housekeeping and cleaning • Dressing • Bathing and taking care of personal hygiene and grooming needs
Community Living Activities
• Using transportation • Participating in recreation and leisure activities • Going to visit friends and family • Shopping and purchasing goods
Employment Activities
• Learning and using specific job skills • Interacting with co-workers • Completing work-related tasks with speed and quality • Accessing and obtaining crisis intervention and assistance
Health and Safety Activities
• Accessing and obtaining therapy services • Avoiding health and safety hazards • Accessing emergency services • Maintaining mental health/emotional well-being
Behavioral Activities
• Learning and making appropriate decisions • Incorporating personal preferences into daily activities • Maintaining socially appropriate behavior in public • Controlling anger and aggression
Social Activities
• Participating in recreation and leisure activities • Making appropriate sexual decisions • Making and keeping friends • Engaging in loving and intimate relationships
Protection and Advocacy Activities
• Managing money and personal finances • Protecting self from exploitation • Exercising legal rights and responsibilities • Using banks and cashing checks

Source: Frequently Asked Questions on Intellectual Disability and the AAIDD Definition. by American Association on Intellectual and Developmental Disabilities (AAIDD), 2010. Reprinted with permission.

Although similarities do exist between these levels of support and the DSM-IV levels of impairment, the major difference concerns the AAIDD emphasis on the interaction between the person and the environment in determining his or her level of functioning. Defined in this manner, mental retardation is determined not so much by the ability of the person alone (as in the DSM-IV-TR definition), but by the level of support the person needs to function adaptively in the community (Hodapp & Burack, 2006).

The AAIDD approach underscores the areas of assistance the child needs, which can be translated into specific training goals. Instead of a diagnosis of moderate mental retardation, Vanessa might receive the following AAIDD diagnosis: "Vanessa is a child with ID who needs limited supports in home living, academic skills, and development of self-help skills." Matthew's diagnosis might state: "Matt is a child with mental retardation who requires support on an as-needed basis, especially during stressful or demanding times—for example, during the transition to school, when making new friends, and when faced with new academic challenges." Like the DSM-IV-TR's degrees of impairment, the AAIDD's list of support areas and activities has value in describing persons with intellectual disabilities and faces similar challenges in surmounting the unfortunate pressures of stigmatization.

Race, Sex, and SES Prevalence

Based on available evidence and estimates, the total number of children and adults with ID most likely falls between 1% and 3% of the entire population (Bebko & Weiss, 2006; Maulik, Mascarenhas, Mathers, Dua, & Saxena, 2011). Recall that the number of persons diagnosed with ID depends on the point at which the line is drawn for cutoff scores for IQ and adaptive behavior. Even with a stable IQ criterion of 70 and below, however, the number of persons with ID is open to debate. Each person applies his or her own cognitive abilities in unique ways that may be more or less adaptive in her or his own environment.

There are about twice as many males as females among those with mild mental retardation, with this sex ratio decreasing to 1.5:1.0 among those with more severe forms of the disorder (Handen, 2007). Similar to racial differences in the diagnosis of mental retardation, however, this gender difference may be an artifact of identification and referral patterns rather than true differences in prevalence (Einfeld et al., 2010). If a true male excess of mental retardation does exist, researchers suspect this may be due to the occurrence of X-linked genetic disorders such as fragile-X syndrome (discussed later in the chapter), which affect males more prominently than females (Handen, 2007).

It is a well-established finding that mental retardation is more prevalent among children of lower socioeconomic status (SES) and children from minority groups. This link is found primarily among children in the mild mental retardation range; children with more severe levels are identified almost equally in different racial and economic groups. Whether or not signs of organic etiology are present, diagnoses of mild mental retardation increase sharply from near zero among children from higher SES to about 2.5% in the lowest SES category (APA, 2000). These figures indicate that SES factors play a suspected role both in the cause of mental retardation and in the identification and labeling of persons with ID (Maulik et al., 2011).

The overrepresentation of minority and low-SES children in the group with mild mental retardation is a complicated and unresolved issue. As we noted, average IQ levels for the African American population are lower than IQ levels found in the white population, resulting in more African American children among samples of mild mental retardation. What specific environmental circumstances might create such an imbalance in IQ findings? To answer this question, Brooks-Gunn et al. (2003), tested the theory that the differences can be partially explained based on social and economic disadvantage. They accounted for initial African American versus white child IQ differences of over 17 points by the independent effects of economic deprivation, home environment, and maternal characteristics. As shown in ● Figure 9.1, initial IQ differences were almost 18 points between a sample of African American and white children at 5 years of age, controlling for gender and birth weight. However, these differences were reduced by about 71% after adjusting for differences in poverty and home environment.

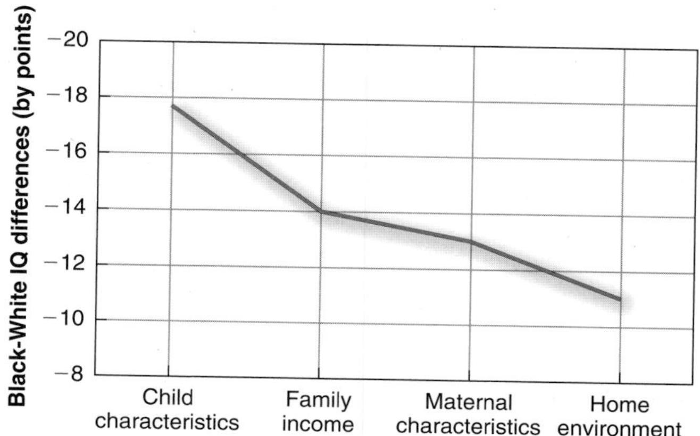

● **FIGURE 9.1** | Factors accounting for differences in IQ scores between white and African American children.

Based on data from Brooks-Gunn, J., Klebanov, P. K., Smith, J., Duncan, G. J., & Lee, K. (2003). The Black-White test score gap in young children: Contributions of test and family characteristics. Applied Developmental Science, 7(4), pp. 239–252

SECTION SUMMARY

Features of Intellectual Disabilities

- The DSM-IV-TR criteria for mental retardation consist of subaverage intellectual functioning (defined as an IQ of 70 or below), deficits or impairments in adaptive functioning, and onset before age 18.
- Children with ID vary widely in their degree of disability or level of functioning.
- The DSM-IV-TR describes a person's level of functioning in terms of degrees of impairment—mild, moderate, severe, or profound—based on ranges in IQ scores.
- The American Association on Intellectual and Developmental Disabilities (AAIDD) describes a person's level of functioning in terms of needed support or assistance rather than IQ.
- Mental retardation occurs in an estimated 1% to 3% of the population, more often among males than females.
- Mental retardation occurs more often among children from lower socioeconomic and minority groups. Economic disadvantage and discrimination practices often account for the latter findings.

DEVELOPMENTAL COURSE AND ADULT OUTCOMES

To appreciate the manner in and extent to which children with intellectual disabilities achieve various developmental milestones, consider how typically developing children express themselves. An infant exploring his or her world relies on primitive sensorimotor functions—touching, tasting, and manipulating objects—to learn about the environment. At this stage of development everything is new, and the brain is establishing literally millions of new connections each day.

Then, between 18 and 24 months, the toddler begins to acquire language and to draw on memories of past experience to aid in understanding the present. For an intellectually normal child, it is during this stage that the child's environmental conditions and opportunities are known to play a crucial role in fostering enthusiasm for learning and in establishing the roots of intellectual sophistication. Although the majority of children with ID progress through each developmental milestone in roughly the same manner as other children, important differences in their developmental accomplishments are evident.

Much of the knowledge about other issues involved in the developmental course and adult outcomes for children with ID is derived from studies of children with Down syndrome. Chromosome abnormalities are the single most common cause of moderate to severe mental retardation. **Down syndrome** is the most common disorder resulting from these abnormalities. These children, along with their parents, have frequently participated in studies comparing their development with that of their normally developing peers.

DAN

With His Brother's Help

When I was almost 3 and my sister was 5, we had a baby brother. I helped feed him and take care of him until he was almost 3. I was 5 by then, and could do most of the things he could do, but about that time he caught up to me. I could still do some things he couldn't, but not many. He could do some things I had trouble with. We became good friends. Every time he learned a new skill, I would either learn it with him, or he would teach me later. I was really little for my age, so we were pretty close in size. We shared a bunk bed, toys, and clothes. We learned to do a lot of things together. When he learned to ride a bike, and I wasn't ready to learn yet, mom and dad got me a Powerwheel motorized bike so I could ride, too. When he learned to read, he taught me how, too. When he played baseball and football, he took me with him.

In those days, I still went to school in another district, so most of my friends were his friends. Now that we go to the same school it is sometimes hard for him to remember that I have my own friends, too. I have to tell him I am the big brother. He sometimes gets teased at school because he is my brother, but he is learning to explain instead of fight. Mostly, the kids are all nice to us. (Based on authors' case material)

Dan, a 15-year-old with Down syndrome, describes how his early development was similar to, but much slower than, that of his younger brother.

Dan, with moderate mental retardation, is describing how his younger brother Brian, with normal intelligence, caught up with him by the time Brian was 2 years old, and progressed through developmental milestones at a faster pace. Does Dan's development follow the same organized sequence as Brian's? Will his development show specific deficits in certain intellectual abilities such as language, or will he eventually catch up? This case illustrates the developmental-versus-difference controversy (Weiss, Weisz, & Bromfield, 1986), an issue that has intrigued those in the field of child development and mental retardation for some time. Simply stated, the **developmental-versus-difference controversy** is this: Do all children—regardless of intellectual impairments—progress through the same developmental milestones in a similar sequence, but at different rates? Or does the development of children with ID proceed in a different, less sequential, and less organized fashion?

The developmental position, which applies primarily to individuals not suffering from organic impairment, consists of two primary hypotheses: First, the *similar sequence hypothesis* argues that all children, with or without mental retardation, pass through stages of cognitive development in an identical (invariant) order; they differ only in their rate and upper limit of development (Bennett-Gates & Zigler, 1998). Second, the *similar structure hypothesis* suggests that children with ID demonstrate the same behaviors and underlying processes as typically developing children at the same level of cognitive functioning (such as Dan and his younger brother were at ages 5 and 2). That is, if children with ID are matched to typically developing children by their mental age, then the children with ID will show equivalent performance on cognitive tasks, such as problem solving, spelling, and moral reasoning. The developmental position rejects the notion of a specific deficit or difference among children with ID, and instead emphasizes how these children traverse the stages more slowly and attain a lower developmental ceiling than typically developing children (Bennett-Gates & Zigler, 1998).

In contrast, the **difference viewpoint** argues that cognitive development of children with ID differs from that of children without mental retardation in more than a developmental rate and upper limit. According to this position, even when his mental age is matched to his younger brother's, Dan will show qualitatively different reasoning and problem-solving strategies, and he may never be able to accomplish some tasks beyond a certain level.

Although this issue has not been resolved, ample evidence supports the developmental hypothesis for children with familial, as opposed to organic, types of retardation (both are discussed in the section on causes). Specifically, children with familial mental retardation generally follow developmental stages in an invariant order, the same as children with normal intellectual abilities, with the possible exception of some children with co-occurring brain abnormalities or autism (Bennett-Gates & Zigler, 1998). The similar structure hypothesis has also been supported for children with familial mental retardation, with some exceptions. Children with familial mental retardation show slight deficits in memory and information processing when compared with mental age-matched children without ID (Schuchardt, Gebhardt, & Mäehler, 2010), which may be due to the children's difficulty in staying motivated to perform repetitive, boring tasks (Weisz, 1999).

The picture for children with organically based mental retardation (such as Dan, who has Down syndrome) is more straightforward. They often have one or more specific deficit areas that cause them to perform more poorly than mental-age–matched children without mental retardation. Thus, Dan is likely to show some differences in his performance in certain areas of development, including his expressive language. Nevertheless, he will likely pass through the same developmental sequences as his younger brother, but at a slower pace.

Motivation

Many children who fall within the mild range of mental retardation are bright enough to learn and to attend regular schools and classrooms. However, they are more susceptible to a sense of helplessness and frustration, which places additional burdens on their social and cognitive development. As a consequence, they begin to expect failure, even for tasks they can master; in the absence of proper instruction, their motivation to tackle new demands decreases (Harris, 2006).

Ed, describing his memory of comments made by his teacher in elementary school, expresses this phenomenon well:

> Her negative picture of me stood out like a sore thumb. That's the problem with people like me—the schools and teachers find out we have problems, they notice them, and then we are abandoned. That one teacher was very annoyed that I was in her class. She had to put up with me. (Bogdan & Taylor, 1982)

Consequently, compared with typically developing children of their same mental age, children with ID expect little success, set lower goals for themselves, and settle for minimal success when they are able to do better (Weisz, 1999). This learned helplessness may be unwittingly condoned by adults. When they are told a child is "retarded," adults are less likely to urge that child to persist following failure than to urge a normal child at the same level of cognitive development. On the other hand, young children with mild mental

© Denys Kuvaiev|Dreamstime.com

"Acknowledge our children's differences but respect their uniqueness." —Parent of a child with Down syndrome retardation improve in their ability to remain on task and develop goal-directed behavior when provided with stimulating environments and caregiver support (Wilkins & Matson, 2009).

Changes in Abilities

Intellectual disability is not necessarily a lifelong disorder. Although it is a relatively stable condition from childhood into adulthood, any individual's IQ score can fluctuate in relation to level of impairment and type of retardation. Children such as Matthew who have mild mental retardation may develop, with appropriate training and opportunities, good adaptive skills in other domains, and may no longer have the level of impairment required for a diagnosis of mental retardation (APA, 2000).

The major cause of a child's mental retardation certainly affects the degree to which his or her IQ and adaptive abilities may change. Children with Down syndrome, who are not representative of the course of mental retardation in general, may plateau during the middle childhood years, and then decrease in IQ over time. For example, from 1 to 6 years of age, children with Down syndrome often show significant age-related gains in adaptive functioning, but as they grow older, their pace of development levels off or even declines (Margallo-Lana et al., 2007). Similarly, as they grow older, a deceleration is often seen in their rate of social development (Hazlett, Hammer, Hooper, & Kamphaus, 2011). This observation has been termed the *slowing and stability hypothesis* (Hodapp et al., 2009), and affirms that children with Down syndrome may alternate between periods of gain in functioning and periods of little or no advance. Although these children continue to develop in intelligence, they do so at progressively slower rates throughout the childhood years.

Language and Social Behavior

Research on language development and social functioning among children and adolescents with Down syndrome suggests that their development follows a largely predictable and organized course (Roberts, Price, & Malkin, 2007). Because their cognitive development, play, self-knowledge, and knowledge of others are interrelated in organized and meaningful ways, the underlying symbolic abilities in children with Down syndrome are believed to be largely intact.

However, important differences in language development exist between children with Down syndrome and their typically developing age-mates. Perhaps the most striking difference for children with Down syndrome is the considerable delay in expressive language development, which is necessary to establish independent living skills. Their expressive language is often much weaker than their receptive language, especially as they attain communication abilities beyond the 24-month level (Roberts et al., 2007).

In addition to the development of symbolic and language skills, a major milestone during infancy and early childhood development concerns the ability to form a secure attachment relationship with one's primary caregivers. Although slower than normal, many children with Down syndrome form secure attachment relationships with their caregivers by 12 to 24 months of developmental age (Dykens, Hodapp, & Evans, 2006). Still, a significant number may have problems in developing a secure attachment because they express less emotion than other children. In one study, children with Down syndrome were not picked up and held by either the mother or the stranger in the strange situation to the same extent as non-delayed children. (See Chapter 2, Table 2.2 for a description of the "strange situation" method of assessing child–caregiver attachment.) Even when these children made approaches with appropriate signals for contact, mothers and strangers rarely completed the contact, presumably because the children did not show the distress signals of crying, reaching, or holding on that typically tell the parent "I want to be picked up!" (Vaughn, Contreras, & Seifer, 1994). This finding has important implications for parents of young children with Down syndrome: Even though they may show few signals of distress or desire for contact, these infants and toddlers need to be held and nurtured just as others do.

Following the attachment period, the next important developmental milestones relate to the emergence of a sense of self, which establishes the early foundations of personality. Like other children, toddlers with Down syndrome begin to delight at recognizing themselves in mirrors and photos, although this milestone is often delayed. The experience of self-recognition in most infants is immediately met by smiles and laughter, a finding that is repeated among toddlers with Down syndrome as well (Mans, Cicchetti, & Sroufe, 1978). This positive affect accompanying their visual self-recognition suggests that these children feel good about themselves. However, as toddlers and preschoolers, children with Down syndrome show delayed and aberrant functioning in their *internal state language*, the language that reflects the emergent sense of self and others (through the use of words such as "mad" and "happy"). Because internal state language is critical to regulating social interaction and providing a foundation for early self–other understanding, these children may be at increased risk for subsequent problems in the development of the self-system (Gerenser & Forman, 2007; Huck, Kemp, & Carter, 2010).

Children with ID, especially those with moderate to mild impairments, learn symbolic play—games, puppets, and sports—in much the same manner as other children. Nevertheless, they often fail to gain their peers' acceptance in regular education settings, because they may have deficits in social skills and social–cognitive ability (Cook & Oliver, 2011). Concerns about the social development of children with ID are increasing as a result of the movement to include children with different levels of ability in regular classrooms and schools, rather than only placing them in institutions or specialized facilities. Typically developing children seem to prefer playing with other typically developing children, and as a result, children with ID are more socially isolated from other children their age (Guralnick, Neville, Hammond, & Connor, 2008). Despite their limited social skills, these integrated classrooms allow children with intellectual disabilities to interact with typically developing peers, which in turn has a positive impact on their social status (Leffert, Siperstein, & Widaman, 2010; Siperstein, Glick, & Parker, 2009).

Emotional and Behavioral Problems

PATTIE

Disturbed or Disturbing?

Pattie was labeled mentally retarded and lived in over 20 homes and institutions before being committed to a state school at age 10. At the age of 20, she discussed some of her experiences and feelings: "I guess I was very disturbed. I call it disturbed, but it was when I was very upset. A lot of people at (the institution) . . . told me I was disturbed—that I was disturbed and that I was retarded—so I figure that all through my life I was disturbed. Looking at the things I done, I must have been disturbed. . . . Upset and disturbed are the same in my mind. Crazy to me is something else. It is somebody that is really gone. I mean really out. Just deliberately kill somebody just to do it. That is what I call crazy. I guess what I was was emotionally disturbed—yeah. Emotionally disturbed is a time when too many things are bothering me. They just build up till I get too nervous or upset. My mind just goes through all these changes and different things. So many things inside that were bothering me." (Based on Bogdan & Taylor, 1982)

Pattie's description of her feelings while living in various institutions illuminates how "disturbing" her behavior could be. But are her feelings a function of her environment and personal limitations? Many children and adolescents with ID have to face many obstacles related to their intellectual, physical, and social impairments, and often they have little control over their own lives.

In the early 1970s, a major study was conducted to gain some understanding of the extent of psychiatric disorders among children and adults with and without mental retardation (Rutter, Tizard, Yule, Graham, & Whitmore, 1976). Ratings by parents and teachers each revealed that about one-third of the children with mild mental retardation and one-half of the children with more severe forms of mental retardation showed major signs of emotional disturbance, suggesting these problems are common. Since then, research has estimated the rate of emotional and behavioral disturbances among children with intellectual disabilities is three to seven times greater than among typically developing children (Emerson, 2003; Emerson, Einfeld, & Stancliffe, 2010). These problems are due largely to limited communication skills, additional stressors, and more neurological deficits faced by these children and youth (Adams & Oliver, 2011; de Ruiter, Dekker, Verhulst, & Koot, 2007).

The general sense is that the nature and course of psychiatric disorders in children and adolescents with and without intellectual disabilities is very similar. Youths with mild as well as moderate disabilities show similar levels of stability and persistence for most problem behaviors over the course of their development (Einfeld et al., 2006; de Ruiter, Dekker, Douma, Verhulst, & Koot, 2008). The most common psychiatric diagnoses given to children with ID involve impulse control disorders, anxiety disorders, and mood disorders (Bouras & Holt, 2007). Although these problems are sometimes severe and often require intervention, they are considered part of the spectrum of problems that coexist with ID, not indicators of other psychiatric illnesses (Hodopp, Kazemi, Rosner, & Dykens, 2006). By early adulthood, persons with intellectual disabilities continue to show a greater risk for psychopathology than the general population, although problems in attention and aggression show a significant decline from childhood rates (de Ruiter et al., 2007; Mueller & Prout, 2009).

Adjustments usually are needed in how DSM-IV-TR diagnostic criteria for other mental disorders are applied, however. The frequency of temper tantrums, hyperactivity, and mood disorders among these children requires consideration of what is normal or typical for other children with similar levels of retardation. For example, the diagnosis of ADHD (see Chapter 5) requires behavioral disturbance that is inappropriate for an individual's developmental level. Among individuals with profound mental retardation, their attention spans, distractibility, and on-task behaviors vary considerably. An individual with profound mental retardation must be compared to other children with profound mental retardation for the purpose of diagnosing any other psychiatric disturbance (Bouras & Holt, 2007).

Internalizing Problems

Adolescence is a developmental period of increased risk for mood disorders and other internalizing symptoms, which is especially true for those with ID

(Hodapp & Dykens, 2009). Like their normally developing peers, adolescents with Down syndrome and other forms of mental retardation may show a decline in their previously sociable and cheerful behaviors, and in some cases suffer from significant symptoms of depression and social withdrawal.

ADHD-Related Symptoms

Teachers and parents of children with ID commonly report ADHD-related symptoms that require adjustments in instruction and child management strategies (Antshel, Phillips, Gordon, Barkley, & Faraone, 2006). When a teacher is present to prompt the appropriate behavior and participate in the activity, children with ID with and without ADHD generally will remain on task. However, when instructed to work on their own without teacher assistance, differences between those with and without ADHD emerge during these independent tasks (Handen, McAuliffe, Janosky, Feldman, & Breaux, 1998). When children with ID and ADHD are placed on stimulant medication, they are able to remain on task for longer periods and their accuracy on cognitive tasks improves, although their responses are more varied than responses of normal-IQ children (Di Nuovo & Buono, 2007).

Other Symptoms

Children and adults with ID may show additional symptoms that can be particularly troublesome. Pica (discussed in Chapter 13), which can result in the ingestion of caustic and dangerous substances, is seen in its more serious forms among children and adults with ID. **Self-injurious behavior (SIB)** is a serious and sometimes life-threatening problem that affects about 8% of persons across all ages and levels of retardation (Bodfish, 2007). Some common forms of SIB include head banging, eye gouging, severe scratching, rumination, some types of pica, and inserting objects under the skin. The long-term prognoses for pica and SIBs are not favorable. Emotional withdrawal, stereotypies (frequent repetition of the same posture, movement, or form of speech, e.g., head banging, hand or body movements), and avoidance of eye contact are often still evident more than 20 years later among persons with more severe forms of mental retardation (Taylor, Oliver, & Murphy, 2011; Thompson & Reid, 2002).

Thus, children with ID may show emotional and behavioral problems that require special recognition and learning strategies. In general, these problems do not constitute major psychiatric disorders, but they do reflect the greater challenges these children may have in learning to express their needs and in adapting to their surroundings. A 7-year-old girl with mild mental retardation, for instance, may be at a developmental level comparable to a typically developing 4-year-old. In the classroom, therefore, she may have difficulty sitting in her seat and remaining on task. She may not always control her emotions or her behavior as well as other 7-year-olds in the class, leading to occasional outbursts of laughter or anger. It is important to keep these problems within a developmental perspective. We would not expect a 4-year-old to behave as well in the classroom as an older child, and expectations and teaching methods have to be adjusted accordingly. As expressed so well by Ed and Pattie, labeling a child with a diagnostic term that implies pathology or inability is often ill-conceived and counterproductive. Such terms must be used sparingly—only in instances, such as self-injurious behaviors, where special attention is warranted.

Other Disabilities

Children with intellectual disabilities may also suffer other physical and developmental disabilities that can affect their health and development in pervasive ways. Such disabilities are usually related to the degree of intellectual impairment. Based on a meta-analysis of 31 studies, the prevalence of chronic health conditions in this population is much higher than in the general population (Oeseburg, Dijkstra, Groothoff, Reijneveld, & Jansen, 2011). ● Figure 9.2 shows some of the more common developmental disabilities found among children with intellectual disabilities.

Despite major co-occurring physical and intellectual disabilities, children and adults with Down syndrome now have a life expectancy approaching 60 years. About two-thirds of adults with Down syndrome survive beyond 30 years of age, largely as a result of better medical treatments for respiratory infections and congenital heart disorders. However, most individuals

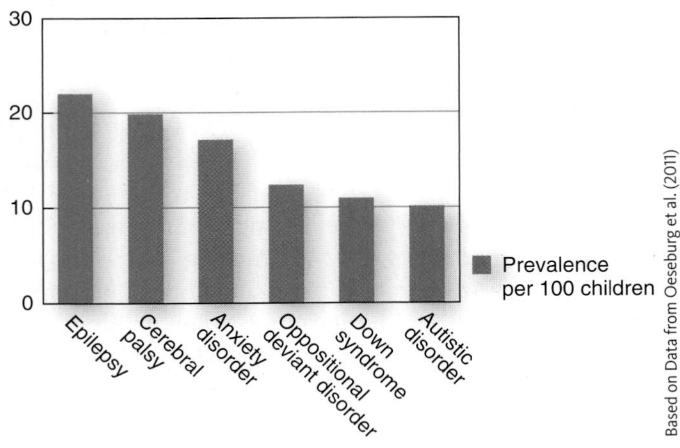

● **FIGURE 9.2** | Chronic health conditions among children with intellectual disabilities.

with Down syndrome who live beyond the age of 40 demonstrate cognitive decline (much like Alzheimer's disease) due to gene damage on chromosome 21 (Torr, Strydom, Patti, & Jokinen, 2010). Moreover, increased life expectancy is more dramatic for whites than for minorities across various countries, due to fewer minority financial and social supports and less access to quality health care (McDermott, Durkin, Schupf, & Stein, 2007; Tyrer, Smith, & McGrother, 2007).

SECTION SUMMARY

Developmental Course and Adult Outcomes

- Children with intellectual disability follow developmental stages in the same order as typically developing children. However, their goals and motivation are reduced over time because of feelings of frustration, which often lead to expectations of failure.
- Adaptive skills and level of impairment may improve over time, especially for children with mild mental retardation, if appropriate training and opportunities are provided.
- Developmental disabilities, such as speech and language problems and behavioral disturbances, are common. Emotional and behavioral problems are considered part of the spectrum of problems coexisting with intellectual disability, rather than indicators of mental disorder.
- Children with intellectual disability have a greater chance of having other physical and developmental disabilities, such as cerebral palsy, epilepsy, and emotional and behavioral disorders that can affect their health and development in pervasive ways.

CAUSES

It is astounding to consider that there are over 1,000 genetic disorders associated with ID, in addition to other organic causes (Hodapp & Dykens, 2009). Yet, despite the number of known causes, scientists cannot account for mental retardation in the majority of cases, especially the milder forms. A genetic or environmental cause is known for almost two-thirds of individuals with moderate to profound mental retardation, whereas the causes are known for only about one-quarter of the individuals with mild mental retardation (McDermott et al., 2007). Some causes happen before birth (prenatal), as is the case with all genetic disorders and accidents in the womb. Other causes are birth-related (perinatal) insults, such as prematurity or a lack of oxygen (anoxia) at birth. Still other causes are an inflammation of the brain lining (meningitis), head trauma, and other factors that occur after birth (postnatal).

Historically, causes of intellectual disabilities were divided into two fairly distinct groups—an organic group and the cultural–familial group (Hodapp & Dykens, 2003). The causes in the **organic group** have a clear biological basis and are usually associated with severe and profound mental retardation, whereas causes in the **cultural–familial group** have no clear organic basis and are usually associated with mild mental retardation (Hodapp et al., 2006).

Recently, the AAIDD has identified four major categories of risk factors that contribute to intellectual disabilities: biomedical, social, behavioral, and educational. These four risk factors interact across time and even across generations from parent to child, and provide a more comprehensive explanation of the interacting causes of problems associated with intellectual impairments (AAIDD, 2010; Chapman, Scott, & Stanton-Chapman, 2008). The definitions, characteristics, and causes of mental retardation on the basis of these four risk factors are summed up in Table 9.4.

Although a distinction between organic and nonorganic risk factors does help to understand the underlying causes of intellectual disability, keep in mind that the distinctions are less clear in milder forms of intellectual disability than they are in more severe forms. For example, the large majority of persons at more severe levels of intellectual impairment (96%) show a clear etiology for the disorder, whereas a sizeable percentage (32%) of those with mild impairments does not (Simonoff et al., 1996).

Considerable knowledge exists about organic mental retardation due to the strong biological factors involved. As well, the increased ability to diagnose organic problems has led to increased estimates of this type of intellectual disability relative to cultural–familial causes—about one-third to one-half of all persons with ID show a clear organic cause (Hodapp et al., 2006). In stark contrast, the cultural–familial group remains somewhat of a mystery, although it comprises one-half to two-thirds of all persons with ID (Hodapp & Dykens, 2003). As noted in Table 9.4, the prime suspects are environmental and situational factors such as poverty, inadequate childcare, poor nutrition, and parental psychopathology, which mostly affect the psychological (not biological) development of the child. However, more specific cause-and-effect relationships have not been determined. Accordingly, both genetic and environmental factors are implicated in milder forms of mental retardation, but in a manner as yet to be determined (Toth & King, 2010).

The relative importance of the environment also stands out in the two-group distinction. The socioeconomic background of the organic group is about the same as for the general population, which fits with the notion that severe forms of mental retardation can affect anyone, regardless of SES. The familial group is overrepresented by those of lower SES and social

TABLE 9.4 | Risk Factors for Intellectual Disability

Timing	Biomedical	Social	Behavioral	Educational
Prenatal	1. Chromosomal disorders 2. Single-gene disorders 3. Syndromes 4. Metabolic disorders 5. Cerebral dysgenesis 6. Maternal illness 7. Parental age	1. Poverty 2. Maternal malnutrition 3. Domestic violence 4. Lack of access to prenatal care	1. Parental drug use 2. Parental alcohol use 3. Parental smoking 4. Parental immaturity	1. Parental cognitive disability without supports 2. Lack of preparation for parenthood
Perinatal	1. Prematurity 2. Birth injury 3. Neonatal disorders	1. Lack of access to prenatal care	1. Parental rejection of caretaking 2. Parental abandonment of child	1. Lack of medical referral for intervention services at discharge
Postnatal	1. Traumatic brain injury 2. Malnutrition 3. Meningoencephalitis 4. Seizure disorders 5. Degenerative disorders	1. Impaired child-caregiver interaction 2. Lack of adequate stimulation 3. Family poverty 4. Chronic illness in the family 5. Institutionalization	1. Child abuse and neglect 2. Domestic violence 3. Inadequate safety measures 4. Social deprivation 5. Difficult child behaviors	1. Impaired parenting 2. Delayed diagnosis 3. Inadequate early intervention services 4. Inadequate special education services 5. Inadequate family support

disadvantage, and is significantly related to a family history of mental retardation. This fits with the assertion that an impoverished social environment can influence intellectual growth and ability in subtle, yet crucial, ways.

In most cases, the risk factors for intellectual disabilities have been supported empirically, with some adjustments as noted earlier in terms of non-organic risk factors. First, the percentage of individuals with a clear organic cause has increased over the last few decades due to the greater knowledge of genetic and organic causes. As well, the original assumption that mild mental retardation is not due to biomedical (organic) causes had to be tempered by findings that epilepsy, cerebral palsy, and other organic disorders are found more often among persons with mild mental retardation than among those without intellectual disabilities (Hodapp & Burack, 2006).

Inheritance and the Role of the Environment

The study of human intelligence has received the lion's share of attention in terms of the underlying processes involved in genetic makeup, and the environmental factors that influence genetic expression. Still, the long-standing debate concerning the relative contributions of genes and environment is far from being fully resolved (McDermott et al., 2007). Conceivably, genetic influences on development are potentially modifiable by environmental input, although the practicality of the modifications is another matter. Similarly, environmental influences on development involve the genes or structures to which the genes have contributed (Neisser et al., 1996). Simply stated, children do not inherit an IQ—they inherit a **genotype**, which is a collection of genes that pertain to intelligence. The expression of the genotype in the environment—the gene–environment interaction—is referred to as the **phenotype**. The **heritability** of a trait describes the proportion of the variation of a trait attributable to genetic influences in the population (Neisser et al., 1996). Heritability of any given trait, therefore, can range from none (0%) to 100% genetically determined.

Is it possible to estimate the heritability of intelligence and, by implication, the heritability of mental retardation? This intriguing question can now be answered with some degree of confidence, but little fanfare. The overwhelming evidence points to a heritability of intelligence of approximately 50%; that is, both

genetic and nongenetic factors play a powerful role in the makeup and expression of intelligence (Davis, Arden, & Plomin, 2008).

There are so many specific genetic causes of mental retardation that some skepticism about the importance of environmental effects still remains. The difficulty of identifying, pinpointing, and measuring specific, nongenetic variables certainly adds to this dilemma. However, considerable evidence has demonstrated that major environmental variations do affect cognitive performance and social adjustment in children from disadvantaged backgrounds (Ramey, Ramey, & Lanzi, 2007). For example, children born to socially disadvantaged parents and then adopted into more privileged homes have higher IQ scores and stronger self-esteem than siblings reared by their disadvantaged, biological parents (Juffer & van IJzendoorn, 2007; van IJzendoorn & Juffer, 2005).

The prenatal environment may influence IQ to a greater extent than previously appreciated. A review of studies of twins and non-twin siblings revealed that a shared prenatal environment (i.e., all children shared the same mother) accounted for 20% of IQ similarity in twins but only 5% among non-twin siblings (Devlin, Daniels, & Roeder, 1997). These findings imply that prenatal influences such as nutrition, hormone levels, and toxic substances may be misidentified as genetic when in fact they are environmental (Rutter, 2011). The practical benefits of this research are important to consider: If early environmental (prenatal) influences have a significant impact on intellectual functioning, then expanding public health initiatives aimed at improving maternal nutrition and reducing prenatal exposure to toxins may not only improve maternal prenatal care, but may unexpectedly improve children's intellectual and cognitive functioning as well.

Genetic and Constitutional Factors

Despite the rapid expansion of knowledge regarding the genetic mechanisms underlying conditions associated with ID, the actual biological mechanisms that cause impaired intellect are poorly understood (Hodapp & Burack, 2006). Identification of abnormal genes, or genes involving an increased risk for particular disorders, is invaluable for genetic screening and counseling, but the identification does not specify a more effective treatment mode for mental retardation.

Because so many conditions cause mental retardation, the focus in this section will be on several different disorders or classes of disorder including: Down syndrome, fragile-X syndrome, Prader-Willi and Angelman syndromes, and single-gene conditions. Each disorder illustrates different aspects of genetic mechanisms. The various ways in which genes may interact with environmental influences also are highlighted.

Chromosome Abnormalities

The most common disorder that results from chromosome abnormalities is Down syndrome. These abnormalities also can occur in the number of sex chromosomes, resulting in mental retardation syndromes such as Klinefelter's (XXY, a disorder in which males have an extra X chromosome) and Turner's (XO, a disorder in which women are missing a second X chromosome). These latter disorders are somewhat common—about 1 in 400 live births—but they are generally less devastating than genetic irregularities in their effects on intellectual functioning (Simonoff et al., 1996).

The number of children with Down syndrome has gradually decreased from 1 in 700 births to 1 in 1,000 births over the last two decades, due to increased prenatal screening and terminated pregnancies diagnosed with Down syndrome (Hazlett et al., 2011; Roizen & Patterson, 2003). The syndrome produces several distinguishing physical features including: a small skull; a large tongue protruding from a small mouth; almond-shaped eyes with sloping eyebrows; a flat nasal bridge; a short, crooked fifth finger; and broad, square hands with a simian (monkeylike) crease across the palm. These physical features are sometimes inconspicuous, and can appear to varying degrees.

In most Down syndrome cases, the extra chromosome results from **nondisjunction**, which is the failure of the 21st pair of the mother's chromosomes to separate during meiosis. When the mother's two chromosomes join with the single 21st chromosome from the father, the result is three number 21 chromosomes instead of the normal two (known as trisomy 21). Because nondisjunction is strongly related to maternal age, the incidence of Down syndrome increases from about 1 per 1,000 live births for mothers less than 35 years old to about 20 per 1,000 when the mother is 45 years of age or older (Morris, Wald, Mutton, & Alberman, 2003).

Although the chromosomal basis of Down syndrome is well understood, the specific cause of mental retardation in these children is not known. Based on recent gene mapping of chromosome 21, it is believed that some genes may have localized effects on brain development (Roizen, 2007). Testing this theory from a functional perspective, researchers pinpointed differences in hippocampal function among young children with and without Down syndrome based on neuropsychological testing (Pennington, Moon, Edgin, Stedron, & Nadel, 2003). Because the hippocampus plays an important role in long-term memory, these findings help to explain some of the underlying processes that affect the ability of children with Down syndrome to acquire normal language skills (a fundamental aspect of IQ).

Fragile-X syndrome is the most common cause of inherited mental retardation (Down syndrome occurs more frequently but is rarely inherited). This disorder affects about 1 in 4,000 males and 1 in 8,000 females (Hagerman, 2011). Physical features are more subtle than in Down syndrome, and may include a large forehead, a prominent jaw, and low, protruding ears. Mental retardation is generally in the mild to moderate range, although some children are profoundly handicapped and others have normal intelligence (Cornish, Levitas, & Sudhalter, 2007). Fragile-X syndrome has a more detrimental effect on males, causing mental retardation in most male cases, compared to about half of females (Reiss & Hall, 2007).

Although the gene for fragile-X syndrome, known as the FMR-1 gene, is located on the X chromosome, this syndrome does not follow a traditional X-linked inheritance pattern. About one-third to one-half of the females who carry and transmit the disorder are themselves affected with a variant of the syndrome and show a slight degree of cognitive or emotional impairment. Further, about 20% of males with the FMR-1 gene transmit the disorder but are not affected themselves (Fatemi & Folsom, 2011).

The behavioral characteristics of fragile-X syndrome are often subtle but distinctive. The majority of affected males have unusual social and communication patterns marked by shyness and poor eye contact, as well as significant delays in cognitive and communication development (Einfeld, 2005). Social anxiety and avoidance are also common in girls with this disorder, even if unaccompanied by mental retardation (Gerenser & Forman, 2007). Notably, most males and about one-third of females with fragile-X syndrome show some autism-like behaviors, such as flapping hands, biting themselves, repetitious actions, and walking on toes, and about 33% of children with fragile-X syndrome receive a formal diagnosis of autism (Hagerman, 2011).

Prader-Willi syndrome is a complex genetic disorder that includes short stature, mental retardation or learning disabilities, incomplete sexual development, low muscle

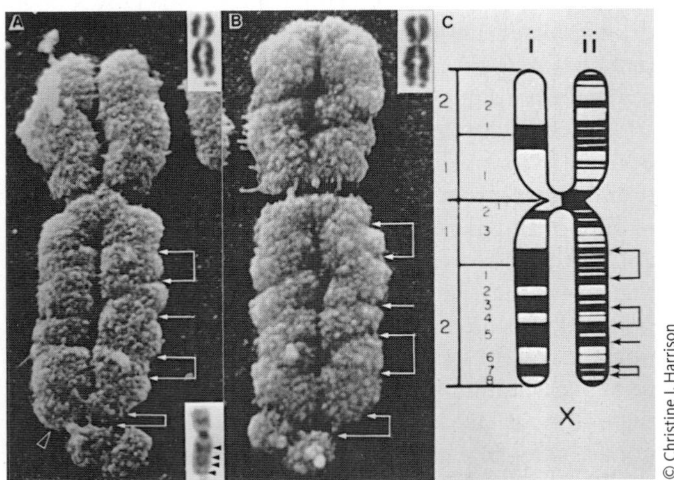

Micrograph showing the "pinched chromosome" found in fragile-X syndrome

Children and adolescents with fragile-X syndrome

tone, and an involuntary urge to eat constantly. The syndrome is rare and estimated to affect only about 5 to 10 per 100,000 births (Dykens, Cassidy, & DeVries, 2011). Between ages 2 and 6, children with this syndrome develop extreme overeating, foraging, and hoarding. They need fewer calories than normal to maintain an appropriate weight because they are small, and they invariably become obese (Hinton, Isles, Williams, & Parkinson, 2010; Theodora, Talebizadeh, & Butler, 2006).

Angelman syndrome is associated with mental retardation that is usually moderate to severe. The behavior of children with this disorder is characterized by ataxia (awkward gait), jerky movements, hand flapping, seizures, and the absence of speech. Distinctive facial features include a large jaw and an open-mouthed expression (Didden et al., 2009).

Both Prader-Willi and Angelman syndromes are associated with an abnormality of chromosome 15, but they are not considered inherited conditions. Rather, these syndromes are believed to be spontaneous genetic birth defects that occur at or near the time of conception. For reasons that are still not well understood, genes in the affected region on the mother's chromosome 15 are not expressed (functional). This lack of a gene or genes that are very close to each other appears to be the cause of the related syndromes. The origin—whether maternal or paternal—of the absent genetic material is the likely cause of the marked phenotypic differences.

Much is being discovered about the genetic influences on intelligence and adaptive abilities. Because these influences are by no means uniform or exact, a challenge remains in accounting for the mechanisms that cause these effects on intelligence and the variations in phenotypic expression. Even with Down syndrome, for example, the range in IQ extends into mild mental retardation, and some individuals have an IQ within the normal range. Molecular genetic and biological techniques are beginning to make it possible to understand why such variation occurs, although knowledge to date is extremely limited (Handen, 2007).

© Chico Sanchez/Alamy

ZUMA Press/Newscom

An 8-year-old boy suffering from Pradi-Willi syndrome (photo on left). Nineteen-year-old Danna has Angelman Syndrome and is part of the inclusion program at her school, allowing her to be with students from the general population (photo on right)

Single-Gene Conditions

Other syndromes affecting intelligence and cognitive functioning can result from genetically based metabolic defects, known as inborn errors of metabolism. Such defects cause excesses or shortages of certain chemicals that are necessary during particular stages of development. Inborn errors of metabolism account for 3% to 7% of cases of severe mental retardation (Antshel & Arnold, 2007).

One of the best understood examples of a single-gene condition is *phenylketonuria* (PKU), a rare disorder occurring in approximately 1 in 15,000 individuals (Waisbren, 2011). Unlike chromosomal abnormalities that cause Down syndrome, the cause of PKU is a recessive gene transmitted by typical Mendelian mechanisms. Children receive the gene from both parents—neither of whom need have PKU—which results in a lack of liver enzymes necessary for converting the amino acid phenylalanine into tyrosine, another essential amino acid. Tyrosine is normally converted into other chemicals needed for physical development. Because the individual is unable to metabolize phenylalanine, which is found in many foods, it accumulates in the body and is converted to phenylpyruvic acid, another abnormal metabolite. This metabolite, in turn, causes brain damage, mental retardation, musty body odor, hyperactivity, seizures, and dry, bleached skin and hair.

PKU is a good example of a genetic disorder that can be treated successfully by environmental changes. All infants are now screened at birth for the presence of this defect in most countries around the world, and immediately placed on a restricted diet if necessary. However, now that affected individuals have received early treatment, young women with PKU have begun to reproduce, resulting in high rates of birth defects and subsequent mental retardation in their offspring. Severe dietary restriction, begun prior to conception, is currently the best precaution for these problems (Waisbren, 2011).

Neurobiological Influences

Fetal and infant development also can be affected by adverse biological conditions such as malnutrition, exposure to toxic substances, and various prenatal and perinatal stressors. These conditions directly or indirectly cause lowered intelligence and mental retardation in some, but by no means all, circumstances. The effects often depend on the degree of insult to the fetus and the time of fetal development (the first trimester being the period of greatest susceptibility). Pregnancy and delivery are times of greatest susceptibility to trauma, infections, or other complications that account for about 10% of mental retardation overall (APA, 2000). Other general medical conditions acquired during infancy or childhood, such as infections, traumas, and accidental poisonings, account for about 5% or so of suspected or known causes of mental retardation (APA, 2000).

Prenatal exposure to alcohol due to maternal alcohol consumption during pregnancy is the most widely recognized preventable cause of mental retardation. *Fetal Alcohol Spectrum Disorder* (FASD) is an umbrella term that covers the range of outcomes associated with all levels of prenatal alcohol exposure (Riley, Infante, & Warren, 2011). Even small amounts of prenatal alcohol may have negative effects on growth and intellectual abilities. For example, significant deficits in physical development were found among adolescents with prenatal alcohol exposure when mothers had less than one drink per day (Day et al., 2002).

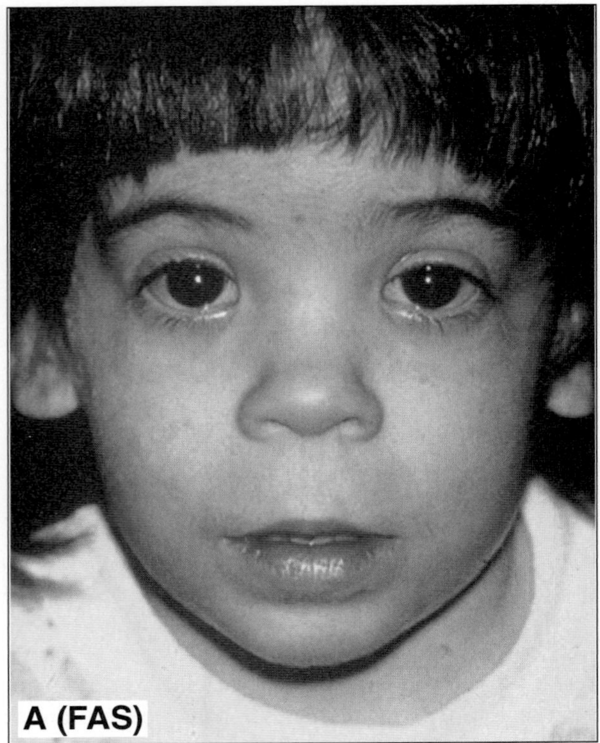

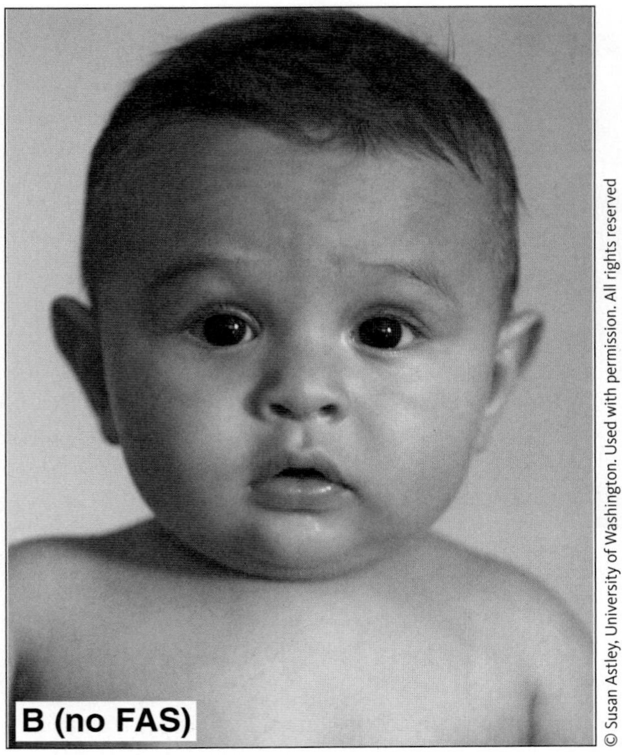

Characteristics of children with fetal alcohol spectrum disorders (photo on left) compared to child without evidence of the disorder (photo on right). Children with FASD show features such as skin folds at the corner of the eye, low nasal bridge, short nose, smooth area between nose and upper lip, small head circumference, small eye opening, small midface, and thin upper lip. These facial features are consistent in children with fetal alcohol spectrum disorders across geographic locations and from different ethnic backgrounds

The most extreme form of FASD is **fetal alcohol syndrome**, considered to be a leading known cause of mental retardation because of its clear link to intellectual impairment. Fetal alcohol syndrome is estimated to occur in 0.5 to 2.0 per 1,000 live births (Centers for Disease Control and Prevention, 2011), although it is considered grossly under-diagnosed and may be considerably more common. Alarmingly, the incidence of this disorder is about 4 times higher among African Americans and 16 times higher for Native Americans when compared with majority populations (MMWR, 2002). Despite over two decades of public health warnings about abstaining from alcohol immediately before and during pregnancy, fetal alcohol spectrum disorders have not declined, most likely because women at greatest risk are not heeding such warnings (Watson, Finkelstein, Gurewich, & Morse, 2011).

Fetal alcohol syndrome is characterized by central nervous system (CNS) dysfunction, abnormalities in facial features, and growth retardation below the 10th percentile. The mechanism that causes the abnormalities is not clear but is believed to involve the *teratogenic* (damage to fetal development) effects of alcohol on the development of the central nervous system, and

Lip-Philtrum (space between the nose and upper lip) Guide

1 2 3 4 5

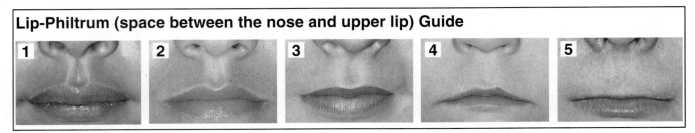

The series of photos above provides a more detailed look at degrees of philtrum groove smoothness. In Photo 1, you see a normal lip-philtrum groove. As your eye moves to the right, you see philtrums that are progressively smoother. In Photo 5, you see the smoothness characteristic of FAS

the related damage from metabolic and nutritional problems associated with alcoholism (Niccols, 2007). On average, for children and youths with this disorder, their IQ is in the mild range of mental retardation (Streissguth, 2007). In addition to intellectual deficits, they often have long-term difficulties that resemble ADHD, including attention deficits, poor impulse control, and serious behavior problems, which often persist into adulthood and carry high treatment costs (Amendah, Grosse, & Bertrand, 2011; Manning & Hoyme, 2007).

Several teratogens other than alcohol are known to increase the risk of mental retardation because of their effect on central nervous system development. Viral infections, such as rubella (German measles), contracted by the mother during the first 3 months of pregnancy can cause severe defects in the fetus. However, immunization has virtually eliminated this cause of retardation in most developed countries. Syphilis, scarlet fever, tuberculosis of the nervous system, degenerative diseases of the nerves, and sometimes measles and mumps can lead to mental retardation. It also can be caused by X-rays, certain drugs taken by the mother during pregnancy, mechanical pressure on the child's head during birth, lack of oxygen due to delays in breathing at birth, poisons such as lead and carbon monoxide, and tumors and cysts in the head (Hodapp & Dykens, 2003). In essence, any biochemical or infectious substance that cannot be destroyed or regulated by the mother's immune system or regulatory system can pose a risk to fetal development and, in turn, intellectual ability.

Social and Psychological Dimensions

The final group of factors that cause mental retardation, or occur in association with it, is perhaps the least understood and most diverse. Broadly defined, these factors include many environmental influences, such as deprived physical and emotional care and stimulation of the infant, and other mental disorders that are often accompanied by mental retardation, such as autistic disorder. Together these factors account for about 15% to 20% of mental retardation (APA, 2000). Although quite broad in scope, these influences are largely indirect and unproven because they often are embedded in different layers and degrees of individual and family circumstances. In this section, we focus on the role of the caregivers and the family in supporting the development of a child with ID, as well as the stress and challenges that may interfere with this role. Parental deviance, such as abuse or neglect, and how it can affect intellectual and behavioral development is discussed in greater detail in Chapter 14.

Parents not only provide their children with their genes, but also provide the child-rearing environment and atmosphere that serve to direct and shape the child's psychological development right from the beginning. Consider the comments by the father of a young child with Down syndrome, who had to learn how to ask for proper assistance and to connect with other families of Down syndrome children:

> I will never forget when the nurse told us how much these children can achieve. Her advice to contact a local association for children with Down syndrome was an important beginning. Other parents at the association helped me understand that Down syndrome was a chromosomal aberration and not a disease, and [gave advice on] how to look for help. My son was hardly a month old when he began physiotherapy to help him learn and interact with others. Jake is 3 years old now and he is full of life. He walks, repeats several words, and understands directions. (Adapted from Martin, 1995)

How do families who have a child with ID contribute to the child's healthy development or, alternatively, to his or her decline? The field of intellectual disabilities in recent years has shown a major change in how this question is addressed. Rather than focusing only on the family's negative influence, researchers are interested in learning more about the successful ways some families cope with the additional stress and demands of raising a child with ID. As is the case when dealing with other stressors, individual members and the family unit can be affected negatively as well as positively, such as when a couple or siblings are brought closer together by caring for a child with special needs (Hodapp, 2007; Lobato et al., 2011; Neece, Blacher, & Baker, 2010).

One way in which parents adapt successfully to having a child with special needs is to use social supports and community resources, although individual preferences regarding type of support may vary, and supports that help mothers may not help fathers. Mothers often are concerned about how raising a child with ID may affect their personal relationships with their husbands, and about the restrictions the child's care may place on their role in the family, whereas fathers worry about not feeling close to the child. Thus, mothers and fathers differ in how they understand and relate to the child with ID, the aspects of raising the child they see as stressful, and the factors that best alleviate stress (Gerstein, Crnic, Blacher, & Baker, 2009).

An understanding of the social and independent functioning of young people with Down syndrome has helped us understand the factors that affect their adjustment to community living. Not surprisingly, early cognitive development is a strong predictor of developmental progress and self-sufficiency among such children, as shown in areas such as language (Roberts et al., 2007). However, family factors are also important, particularly mothers' strategies for coping with their children's problems, and their families' levels of social support (Gray et al., 2011).

SECTION SUMMARY

Causes

- The two-group approach emphasizes the important etiological differences between organic and cultural–familial causes of mental retardation.
- Organic causes include genetic and constitutional factors, such as chromosome abnormalities, single gene conditions, and neurobiological influences.
- Suspected cultural–familial, or non-organic, causes of intellectual disability include diverse social, behavioral, and educational risk factors.
- Some of the established risk factors for ID include alcohol, lead, and other toxins or injuries that affect prenatal and postnatal development. Other risk factors affect the quality of physical and emotional care and stimulation of the infant and small child, such as poverty and inadequate family supports.

PREVENTION, EDUCATION, AND TREATMENT

We plead for those who cannot plead for themselves.

—Motto of Highgate, the first public institution for persons with mental retardation, established in London, England, October 1847

As we turn our discussion toward treatment methods for children with ID, consider for a moment how you would apply your knowledge of psychological and educational treatments to best assist a child such as Vanessa or Matthew. Would you start with Matthew's behavior problems and try to get them under control first, and then teach him other skills? Would Vanessa likely benefit from individualized treatment that emphasizes gradual speech training and self-help skills?

As is true for several other disorders we have discussed, such as ADHD and some types of conduct disorders, the primary presenting problems—in this case, intellectual retardation and limited adaptive abilities—are chronic conditions that pose limitations across many important areas of development. Consequently, programs often must be designed to fit the educational and developmental levels of each individual child even more so than, say, treatment programs for children with behavior or anxiety problems. It is useful to begin this task with an overview of major environmental and individual characteristics that may increase the risk of adjustment problems, or serve to protect the child from such problems.

A child's overall adjustment is a function of parental participation, family resources, and social supports (on the environmental side), combined with his or her level of intellectual functioning, basic temperament, and other specific deficits (on the individual side). Treatment can be designed to build on the child's existing resources and strengths in an effort to bolster particular skill areas or learning abilities. In other words, it is not necessary to focus attention primarily on what the child lacks, but rather on how best to match teaching and therapeutic methods to the child's own levels and abilities to accomplish realistic, practical goals. Thus, treatment and education for children with ID involves a multicomponent, integrated strategy that considers children's needs within the context of their individual development, their family or institutional setting, and their community (Wilkins & Matson, 2009).

The severity of mental retardation can be prevented or reduced in some instances by taking proper precautions. Therefore, we begin this section by discussing current health care practices involving parental education and prenatal screening. These procedures, implemented in many communities, are designed to inform parents of proper prenatal care and risks, and to detect abnormal fetal development. We then turn to psychosocial treatments for children with ID and their families, which have become a common part of many treatment and education plans. In short, treatment focuses on teaching the child necessary skills and abilities, such as language, personal care and hygiene, and social skills, as well as on teaching skills and providing supports to parents and other caregivers.

Psychopharmacological interventions for children and adults with intellectual disabilities have been hindered by both professional and public perceptions that psychotropic drugs are used to control behavior—a view based on unfortunate and inappropriate use in the past and on the drugs' major side effects. Although many newer classes of compounds that reduce unpleasant side effects have become available over the past decade, these compounds have not been systematically studied in treating people with ID. Nevertheless, drug treatment is beneficial in some cases. As with other childhood disorders, drug treatment can be targeted at desirable changes in specific behaviors or dimensions, such as compulsions, aggression, or self-injury, rather than at treating the underlying disorder itself (Golombek & King, 2010; Ghuman et al., 2009).

Prenatal Education and Screening

One of the best opportunities to promote healthy child outcomes occurs during prenatal development (Hodapp & Burack, 2006). Although not all forms of mental retardation can be prevented prenatally, many debilitating forms related to fetal alcohol syndrome, lead poisoning, or rubella easily can be prevented if proper precautions are taken. A much larger number of children are positively affected by prenatal education and health care if one includes not only the prevention of specific risks, but also the promotion of proper child care, especially during the child's first 2 years.

Not too long ago, a pregnant woman would have seen her doctor for several visits prior to childbirth, and may have gained additional knowledge through reading and from family members. At that time, the focus was largely on the medical needs of the pregnancy, with little opportunity to consider what it means to raise a child and to prepare for the added stress and complexity that child care involves.

Today, almost all communities have prenatal programs for parents, and fathers have taken on a much larger role as well. Parents are provided with information about the different periods of fetal development, and are cautioned about the use of alcohol, tobacco, nonprescribed drugs, and caffeine during pregnancy. These programs, often run by public health nurses, community colleges, churches, and other community organizations, have filled much of the gap in services between basic medical care and basic child care that parents need prior to the birth of a baby. The stresses of childbirth and postnatal adjustment are described, with opportunities for parents to consider the additional supports they may need and the changes they may need to make to ensure the child's health and safety. Many programs also include discussion of children with special needs, so that parents are not left feeling confused and alone (Ramey et al., 2007).

In providing these important prenatal services, there is an increasing multicultural focus that sensitively and appropriately considers the cultural background of therecipients (Nisbett, 2009; Pumariega, Rothe, Song, &Lu, 2010). We now recognize that family members make choices based on cultural influences. To be of most help, prenatal and postnatal services must be culturally diverse and culturally sensitive. Meeting this goal involves working with informal support and assistance networks, such as churches, community and spiritual leaders, and community organizations, in ways that extend self-determination. Prenatal programs are increasingly breaking away from a set curriculum and are being modified to establish a better fit with each cultural group or community—for example, by providing information on ways to access health care and family services for persons with limited transportation, limited income, and so forth.

Prenatal screening constitutes a particular form of genetic screening that is used to determine whether a fetus has a genetic abnormality, such as Down syndrome, that would lead to a seriously handicapping condition. Ultrasound scanning can detect many conditions associated with physical defects, and testing of amniotic fluid during fetal development assists the prenatal diagnosis of chromosomal abnormalities and genetic diseases identifiable at the DNA level (Roizen & Patterson, 2003). The next decade probably will see substantial advances in genetic screening that will allow for much greater precision in genetic counseling. For example, there is hope new molecular genetic techniques will replace invasive techniques such as amniocentesis, and will allow for quicker diagnosis of a broad range of genetic disorders (Twisk et al., 2007). Ethical and practical guidelines first must be developed, however, because there is a fundamental difference between using genetic information to prevent an illness or disease and altering genetic material to promote desired (or get rid of undesired) personal characteristics.

Psychosocial Treatments

The first psychosocial treatment we consider involves intensive, broad-ranging, early-intervention services for families with young children that are designed to reduce risk factors and promote healthy child development. Although expensive to deliver, these services are proving to be of considerable benefit to children and families over the long term, and they accomplish a great deal more than merely reducing intellectual deficits. We then take a close look at the existing educational and therapeutic methods that have successfully benefited children with various levels of mental retardation. We discuss the application of behavioral, cognitive–behavioral, and family-oriented interventions, with an emphasis on the task of integrating known treatments that best match the different needs of these children.

As a prelude to the discussion of psychosocial treatments, we acknowledge the importance of community-based activities that offer people with disabilities a choice of ways to develop their interpersonal and practical skills and self-confidence. Studies find that athletes who participate in Special Olympics score higher on measures of social competence and have more positive self-perceptions than non-athlete comparisons (Special Olympics, 2011).

Early Intervention

For over 25 years, the involvement of caregivers and other adults in intensive, child-focused activities from an early point in time has been one of the most promising methods for enhancing the intellectual and social skills of young children with developmental disabilities, including children with intellectual disability, learning disabilities, and lack of environmental stimulation (Wilkins & Matson, 2009). Many of these children would be described as disadvantaged or high-risk, synonymous terms referring to family circumstances such as low income, insufficient health care, and poor housing; child characteristics such as low IQ, poor adaptive abilities, and physical or health disabilities; or a combination of both. Early educational intervention consists of systematic efforts to provide high-risk children with supplemental educational experiences before they enter school, and the intervention frequently includes other family and child services.

One of the more successful examples of an early educational intervention is the Carolina Abecedarian Project (Campbell & Ramey, 2010). The intervention was offered to children of poor families, who were provided with enriched environments from early infancy through pre-school years. In follow-up studies of over 100 children, results showed that by age 2 test scores of children in the enrichment group were already higher than test scores of children in control groups, and they remained some 5 points higher at age 15, 10 years after the end of the program. At age 15, members of the treated group were less likely to score in the mentally retarded or low-normal range of intellectual functioning. The enrichment group also outperformed the control groups in academic achievement through 10 years in school for both reading and mathematics, and there were fewer instances of grade retention or special education classes (Ramey et al., 1999, 2000). By young adulthood, those who received the intervention had better educational attainment, skilled employment, and fewer problem behaviors (Campbell, Ramey, Pungello, Sparling, & Miller-Johnson, 2002; Pungello et al., 2010).

Based on these and related findings, the optimal timing for intervention appears to be during the preschool years (Hodapp & Burack, 2006). Early education programs such as the Abecedarian project are highly relevant to the issue of environmental effects in mental retardation, because they involve children from socially disadvantaged backgrounds, who have a much higher risk of retardation. Although the programs clearly are effective, the lasting benefits depend on the stability and continuation of environmental changes that foster healthy child development. Box 9.3 offers a set of practical recommendations for enhancing children's lives through early intervention.

Dan's mother added some additional ideas, based on her own experiences:

> Be creative. He learns by repetition, so the more closely you follow the "house" system and coordinate all the topics of all the classes, the easier he and the other students can learn. He can learn spelling words of items he touches in science lab. He can learn history related to his library book of the week. Combine the lesson plans to touch all phases of the subject.

BOX 9.3 A CLOSER LOOK

Practical Recommendations for Enhancing Children's Lives Through Early Intervention

- *Encouragement of exploration.* Children are encouraged by adults to explore and gather information about their environments.
- *Mentoring in basic skills.* A trusted, familiar adult teaches children basic cognitive skills such as labeling, sorting, sequencing, and comparing.
- *Celebration of developmental advances.* Family and others who know the child celebrate and reinforce each of the child's accomplishments.
- *Guided rehearsal and extension of new skills.* Responsible others assist the child in rehearsing and extending newly acquired skills.
- *Protection from harmful displays of disapproval, teasing, or punishment.* Constructive criticism and negative consequences for unacceptable behaviors are used.
- *A rich and responsive language environment.* Adults provide a predictable and understandable environment for communication. Spoken and written language are used to convey information, provide social awards, and encourage the learning of new material and skills.

Source: C. T. Ramey and S. L. Ramey, 1992.

Behavioral Treatments

As noted earlier, for many years the mode for dealing with problems faced by persons with ID was to isolate them from society by placing them in institutions or separate schools, a practice that curtailed their ability to interact with typically developing peers. Behavioral interventions first emerged in the context of these restricted settings, and were initially seen primarily as a means to control or redirect negative behaviors, such as aggression or self-injurious behavior.

Through the efforts of concerned behavior therapists, important principles were established concerning the implementation of behavioral methods with children and other persons who are unable to provide fully informed consent. The Association for Behavior Analysis (ABA) Task Force stipulated that each individual has the right to the least-restrictive effective treatment, as well as a right to treatment that results in safe and meaningful behavior change (Van Houten et al., 1988). These efforts, coupled with continued input from parents and educators, led to a greater emphasis on positive methods for teaching basic academic and social skills in both schools and communities to help children and adolescents with ID adapt in the most normal fashion.

Vanessa's treatment plan typifies how several important behavioral methods are successfully applied. Language training often is considered a fundamental starting point for teaching more advanced skills to children with ID, and behavioral methods are well suited for this purpose (Matson, Matson, & Rivet, 2007; van der Schuit, Segers, van Balkom, & Verhoeven, 2011). The plan developed for Vanessa offers a useful example of how these methods are applied. Vanessa participated in one-to-one therapy sessions during which she was reinforced (by edibles and praise) for emitting sounds that imitated the therapist's sounds. The speech therapist used a *shaping* procedure that began by forming a list of responses (such as "ge," "ga," "oh") that were progressively more similar to the target response (in this case, the word go). After Vanessa mastered the first sound, she was reinforced only for attempts at the next sound on the list, and so on, until the desired sound or word was gradually shaped.

To encourage her speech sounds and simple words to become functional speech and language, the therapist taught Vanessa to imitate the names of pictures shown to her. If she said the name of the picture, such as "dog," within a few seconds, she received social rewards and, if necessary, tangible rewards such as candy. As Vanessa became more adept at naming the pictures, the therapist began to use some of the trained words in response to questions he would pose, such as "What is this?" Gradually, Vanessa's mother and father were brought into the sessions with the therapist to begin asking her similar questions and promoting her use of functional speech. As her speech grew, new words and short sentences were introduced—ones that would be of most use to Vanessa on a daily basis at home, at the cafeteria, and when asking to use the bathroom.

Vanessa's behavior during mealtimes also presented considerable problems for her parents. She had difficulty getting food onto her fork or spoon, so her parents were taught to use simple methods of *modeling* and *graduated guidance* to assist. After demonstrating how to hold a spoon, they would show her how to pick up her food and bring it to her mouth. They carefully demonstrated each step involved, from dipping the spoon to placing it in the mouth, each time praising her for her attempts. As required, they would guide her hand to show her how each step was done.

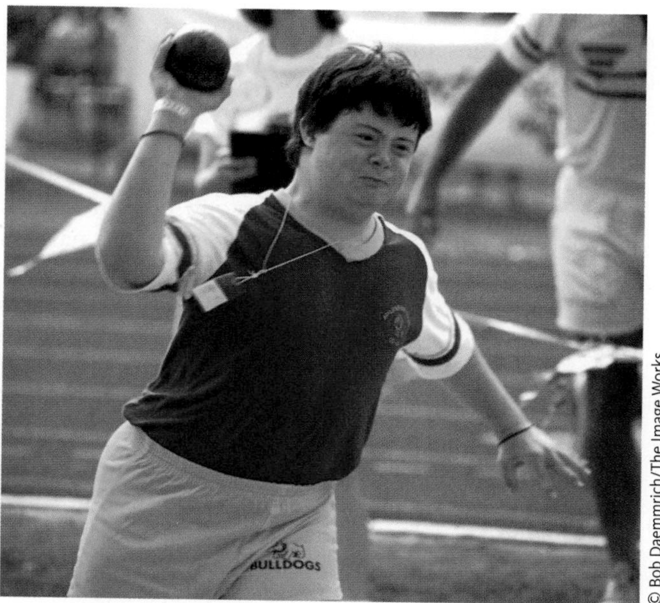

© Bob Daemmrich/The Image Works

Social and sports events are an important way of fostering independence, social competence, and self-esteem in persons with ID

Unfortunately, without much warning, Vanessa would sometimes throw or spit her food, so her parents were also taught how to respond to such outbursts. Their first attempt to stop this problem was to remove her food for half a minute or so. If this tactic did not settle the behavior, or if she became more aggressive, they used time-out from reinforcement. They provided a short reprimand ("Don't throw food!") and told her why she was in timeout. Without ceremony, they turned her chair into the corner for about a minute. At the first sign of settling her behavior, they turned Vanessa around in her chair to face them and returned to a positive, guided method of helping her to learn to feed herself.

In addition to their training in basic skills to promote language and readiness to learn, many older children and adolescents with ID benefit from training in specific social skills to promote their integration into regular classrooms and other activities. As mentioned previously, individuals with ID have various degrees of difficulty in communication, self-control, anger management, correct recognition and labeling of affect in others, social problem-solving, and a host of other interpersonal limitations (Matson et al., 2007).

Tailored to each student's individual needs, social skills training uses positive reinforcement strategies to teach and reward important interpersonal skills such as smiling, sharing, asking for help, attending, taking turns, following directions, and solving problems (Kemp & Carter, 2002). Nondisabled peers also can be taught effective ways to increase opportunities for social interaction of children with mental retardation, a method known as social inclusion. This method is successful in increasing the quantity and quality of interactions between children with disabilities and their nondisabled peers, and it promotes the development of friendships (Siperstein et al., 2009).

Cognitive–Behavioral Therapy

The same theories that led to the development of cognitive therapy techniques for children with other types of learning and behavior problems generally apply to children with ID as well. These methods are most effective for children with some receptive and expressive language skills, like the skills Vanessa acquired after careful and prolonged training through the use of visual and physical prompts. Once children are able to follow adult verbal directives and to verbally describe their own actions, they are in a position to benefit from verbal self-regulation training programs (Cobb, Sample, Alwell, & Johns, 2006). Self-instructional training is most beneficial for children who have developed some language proficiency but still have difficulty understanding and following directions. **Self-instructional training** teaches children to use verbal cues, initially taught by the therapist or teacher, to process information, to keep themselves on task ("I'm not gonna look. I'm gonna keep working."), and to remind themselves of how to approach a new task ("What do I have to do here? First, I have to . . .").

Education of children with ID has been plagued by the fact that specific cognitive skills can be taught, yet children often lack the higher-order (meta-cognitive) capabilities to apply these skills in new situations. Children with intellectual disabilities use fewer, simpler, and more passive cognitive strategies in memory and learning task situations than do children without such disabilities (Gardner, Graeber-Whalen, & Ford, 2001). Therefore, instructional methods developed to assist the average or above-average learner are often ineffective. Coupled with this concern is the continued reliance on verbal instruction to teach behavioral and cognitive skills to normal and exceptional children.

Language problems may require verbal instructional techniques to be replaced by methods that capitalize on a particular child's strongest learning channels. These methods often rely less on verbal, symbolic representation and more on perceptual, visually oriented techniques such as modeling and picture cuing.

Specific learning techniques also can be used to improve memory and learning. For example, in addition to being taught various basic math skills, students learn to identify the type of math problem they confront, and then to choose the appropriate strategy for solving the problem. The first goal of this training is to teach the child to be *strategical*—to use cognitive strategies—and then to be *metastrategical*—to make discriminations regarding how to apply different strategies in different situations. This method has been successful in teaching children with learning difficulties a range of adaptive skills, such as math and language (Hay, Elias, Fielding-Barnsley, Homel, & Freiberg, 2007).

Family-Oriented Strategies

The presence in the family of a child with ID is a challenge but not an insurmountable problem. Families are central to the development of any child, but for families of a child with ID, child care involves an expanded commitment of time, energy, and skills. The needs of the child often dictate that family members participate in various community services and educational systems with which they may be quite unfamiliar. In the end, the majority of parents of children with ID come to see their child as a positive contributor to their family and quality of life, although the family experiences a higher-than-average level of stress and parental depressive symptoms (Gerstein et al., 2009; Hodapp, 2007). This view of the child as a positive contributor is reassuring, given the finding that individual services provided for the child are usually more effective when family members are active participants (AAIDD, 2010).

What exactly do the parents of a child with ID need to be most effective? Family members need support and guidance, access to necessary services, opportunities for a short caregiving break such as a weekend, and the availability of goal-oriented counseling to cope with the practical difficulties of demanding caregiving tasks, sleep disruption, marital discord, and restricted leisure and social opportunities. Short-term, problem-focused behavior therapy for the parents is one of the most successful approaches (Bagner & Eyberg, 2007). Each family's treatment goals are developed individually; then parents are provided with solutions matched to their needs. For example, parents may be taught assertiveness skills or behavior management techniques (discussed in the next section). In some instances, the solutions involve obtaining new resources from teachers or day-care staff or from neighbors and extended family.

Parent training has been widely used to assist parents of children with ID. As opposed to the focus of many other applications of parent training, when the child has mental retardation the primary focus on behavior change is skill acquisition rather than behavior problem reduction (Bagner & Eyberg, 2007). The parents' roles as primary teachers often continue well past the normal childhood years, so parent training often entails a relevant focus on development to prepare the family to tackle each new challenge.

There are three critical, but not exclusive, periods during the family life cycle in which parent training and family counseling are most beneficial. The first occurs during the child's infancy and toddlerhood, when parents are coming to terms with the child's disability and may need assistance in learning ways to provide adequate stimulation of early language formation and similar developmental skills. A second critical time is during the preschool and school years, when parents often want to know more about the best way to teach their child basic academic and social skills. Intensive programs, which demand a considerable amount of the parents' time, are usually best suited for the preschool years when the family is most focused on child developmental issues (Brown et al., 2008). Finally, parental concerns reemerge during the child's emergence into young adulthood. At this age, the child is no longer eligible for funded schooling, and new issues of housing, employment, relationships, and financial planning associated with independent living become concerns.

Some children and adolescents with ID benefit from **residential care**, or out-of-home placement, which also carries with it unique responsibilities of family members.

Residential care services are seldom a full replacement for the love and attention of the family, yet they may be necessary and beneficial under some circumstances, such as aggressive behavior of the child or the need for specialized language or social skills training that cannot be provided adequately in the home or regular school setting. Residential care may range from part-time care, when the child returns home each evening or weekend, to full-time care, when home visits are less frequent. Some residential programs may serve only a few children at a time, much like a group home; others may be large, multidisciplinary tertiary care facilities serving persons of all ages with various disabilities.

Whether the child or adolescent with ID lives at home or in a community residential setting, he or she is likely to attend a regular school, at least for a part of each day. The **inclusion movement** calls for integration of individuals with disabilities in regular classroom settings, regardless of the severity of the disability. The school curriculum must be adaptable to meet the individual needs and abilities of children with ID. For example, because children with Down syndrome often have strong visual short-term memories, a visually based approach to teach them how to read has been determined more effective than traditional phonetic approaches (Hazlett, Hammer, Hooper, & Kamphaus, 2011). Furthermore, this movement has raised anew the issue of how persons with disabilities are perceived and treated by professionals and peers.

Regardless of the structure of the residential program, research has determined that family involvement plays a critical role in children's adaptation to and benefit from such settings. Facilities that offer ways to promote family involvement, such as weekend visits and participation in classroom activities, strengthen the important attachment between children with ID and their families (Grant, Ramcharan, & Flynn, 2007). Because one goal of residential care is often to enable the child to live at home or in a family-like community setting, efforts to maintain family involvement are invaluable.

SECTION SUMMARY

Prevention, Education, and Treatment

- Intervention efforts are most successful when offered at the earliest point in time, especially through the preschool years.
- Interventions for children with ID are matched to the child's individual needs and abilities, and are integrated with the family, school, and community.
- Successful interventions often include behaviorally based training and educational components that teach specific skills and reduce undesired behavior.

Study Resources

SECTION SUMMARIES

KEY TERMS

COURSEMATE

Access an interactive eBook and chapter-specific interactive learning tools, including flashcards, quizzes, videos, and more in your Psychology CourseMate, accessed through CengageBrain.com.

10

Autism Spectrum Disorders and Childhood-Onset Schizophrenia

It wasn't just that she didn't understand language. She didn't seem to be aware of her surroundings. She wasn't figuring out how her world worked, learning about keys that fit into doors, lamps that turned off because you pressed a switch, milk that lived in the refrigerator . . . If she was focusing on anything, it was on minute particles of dust or hair that she now picked up from the rug, to study with intense concentration. Worse, she didn't seem to be picking up anyone's feelings.

—From Maurice (1993a)

CHAPTER PREVIEW

Autism Spectrum Disorders (ASD)

The compelling description that begins this chapter, from a mother talking about her 2-year-old daughter, offers a first glimpse into the mystery of autism, perhaps the most captivating and telling of all childhood disorders. **Autism**, or what is now more commonly referred to as **autism spectrum disorder** (**ASD**), is a complex neurodevelopmental disorder characterized by abnormalities in social behavior, language and communication skills, and unusual behaviors and interests. ASD touches every aspect of the child's interaction with his or her world, involves many parts of the brain, and undermines the traits that make us human—our social responsiveness, ability to communicate, and feelings for other people.

Description and History

Imagine yourself the parent of an infant or toddler who won't cuddle, look into your eyes, or respond to your affection or touching. Unlike other children who are social beings from the start, your child doesn't seem to form a loving relationship with you as you interact with him. In fact, he seems incapable of forming a normal relationship or communicating with anyone. As he grows older, he rarely speaks. When he does speak, he talks in unusual ways, for example, by parroting what you say to him or blurting out seemingly meaningless phrases, such as "dinosaurs don't cry." Your child doesn't use facial expressions or gestures to communicate his needs or to tell you how he feels—no smiles, no nods, no head shakes, no holding up toys for you to look at. Nor does he seem to understand the smiling faces that you and others make as you try to engage him socially. Your child shows little interest in sharing pride or pleasure with you or anyone else. Over the first few years of life, he becomes more and more isolated, caught up in his own little world of rituals and interests that, when interrupted, cause him to become extremely upset. Something is seriously wrong. Naturally, you are concerned and have many questions. In this chapter we address a number of critical questions asked by families of children with ASD (Interagency Autism Coordinating Committee [IACC], 2011). These include: When should I be concerned? How can I understand what is happening? What caused this to happen? Which treatments will help? Where can I turn for services? What does the future hold for my child as a teenager and adult? You might want to keep these questions in mind as you read the chapter, and consider how you would respond to them as you learn more about ASD.

The term ASD refers to three DSM-IV-TR **pervasive developmental disorders** (**PDDs**), all characterized by significant impairments in social and communication skills and by stereotyped patterns of interests and behaviors (Johnson, Myers, and the Council on Children with Disabilities, 2007). They are: Autistic Disorder, Asperger's Disorder, and Pervasive Developmental Disorder, Not Otherwise Specified (PDD-NOS). As we shall see, ASD is not one particular thing. Children with these disorders vary widely in the form, pervasiveness, and severity of their symptoms and abilities, and there is much overlap among disorders on the autism spectrum. Following our discussion of ASD, two rare disorders, Childhood Disintegrative Disorder and Rett's disorder, both currently included under the DSM-IV-TR category of PDD, will also be discussed.

Children with ASD behave in unusual and frequently puzzling ways

Although *childhood-onset schizophrenia* (COS) is not on the autism spectrum in DSM-IV-TR, we conclude the chapter with a separate section about this disorder. Historically, autism and COS were thought of as a single condition. Subsequently, they came to be viewed as distinct disorders, with different family histories, outcomes, and associated features (R. Asarnow & Kernan, 2008). However, findings from recent studies using newer research methods suggest that there may be more overlap between autism and COS than thought, and the possibility that the two are linked may need to be re-examined (King & Lord, 2011).

Most everyone has seen or heard the frequent media messages about ASD. Although interest in ASD is at an all-time high, ancient myths suggest that children with this disorder have been around for centuries. For example, stories of elfin children, left in the place of real human babies who were stolen away by the "little people," describe these "changelings" as strange and remote, much like a child with ASD (Wing & Potter, 2002). The factual history of autism begins in 1943, when psychiatrist Dr. Leo Kanner described 11 children who, in the first few years of life, displayed more attention to objects than to people, avoided eye contact, lacked social awareness, had limited or no language, and displayed stereotyped motor activities. They also exhibited **preservation of sameness**, which is an anxious and obsessive insistence on the maintenance of sameness in daily routines and activities, which no one but the child may disrupt. Their parents described them as "acting as if people weren't there" and "oblivious to everything around him" (Kanner, 1943, p. 242). Around the same time, Dr. Hans Asperger, an Austrian doctor, described a milder form of this disorder that became known as *Asperger's disorder* (Asperger, 1944). Because of the intense interests of the children he studied and their lengthy descriptions of these interests, he compared them to "absent-minded professors." Interestingly, Dr. Asperger's own preoccupations, interests, and social aloofness suggest that he himself may have been on the autism spectrum (Lyons & Fitzgerald, 2007).

Kanner (1943, 1944) used the term *early infantile autism* (autism literally means "within oneself") to describe these children. There is, said Kanner (1943), "an extreme autistic aloneness that, whenever possible, disregards, ignores, shuts out anything that comes to the child from outside" (p. 242). He described the parents of the children he observed as highly intelligent and obsessive people who were cold, mechanical, and detached in their relationships—called the "refrigerator parent" (who, according to Kanner, just happened to "defrost enough to produce a child"). Although he clearly saw autism as an inborn deficit, he also planted the seeds for the psychoanalytic view that "the precipitating factor in infantile autism is the parent's wish that his child should not exist" (Bettelheim, 1967, p. 125). This early view that autism resulted from a child's defensive withdrawal from an intellectual, coldhearted, and hostile parent has found no support (Rutter, 1999). Children with autism have not withdrawn from reality because of a mental disorder—rather, they have failed to enter reality because of widespread and serious disturbances in their development. Autism is now recognized as a strongly biologically based lifelong neurodevelopmental disability that is present in the first few years of life (Rutter, 2000).

Children with ASD behave in unusual and frequently puzzling ways. They may squeal with excitement at the sight or sound of a wheel spinning on a toy car, yet ignore or have a full-blown tantrum if someone attempts to play with them. At times they may look through you as if you are a pane of glass, but other times stare directly into your face or tug on your arm to lead you to something they want. When you speak to a child with ASD, she may act as if she is deaf, but then quickly turn in the direction of the faint crinkling sound of a candy wrapper in another room.

Some children with ASD display extreme fear or avoidance of noisy or moving objects such as running water, swings, elevators, battery-operated toys, or even the wind. One child was so afraid of a vacuum cleaner that he would not go anywhere near the closet where it was kept. When someone used it in the house, he ran to the garage and covered his ears with his hands. Yet the same child was oblivious to the sounds of traffic roaring by him on a dangerous freeway. Although children with ASD fear many things, they are also attracted to and preoccupied with other objects and activities—for example, a rotating fan or a flickering light. These children often develop unusual attachments or reactions to odd objects, such as a rubber band, a piece of sandpaper, or a string.

Other children with ASD may have extraordinary perceptual abilities—for example, identifying the brand of a vacuum cleaner by its sound alone. These perceptual abilities may result in distress in response to minor changes in the environment—shown, for instance, by screaming, kicking, and lashing out at others if a chair is moved from its usual location. They may spend hour after hour playing in a corner of their room, engaged in stereotyped or repetitive motor activities, such as rocking, lining up objects, or repeatedly flapping their hands and fingers as they flip through pages of a magazine. Rather than seeing the big picture, children with ASD are much more likely to fixate on a minuscule object or event in their world, such as a tiny spot on their shirt. Whereas most of us see the hugeness of trees in the forest, a child with autism is more likely to fixate on one pine needle.

SECTION SUMMARY

Autism Spectrum Disorders

- The term ASD includes three pervasive developmental disorders (PDDs): autistic disorder, Asperger's disorder, and PDD-NOS, all characterized by severe and widespread impairments in social interaction and communication skills and by stereotyped patterns of behaviors, interests, and activities.
- Historically, autism and childhood-onset schizophrenia (COS) were lumped together as a single condition; now recognized as separate disorders, recent research suggests that there may be more overlap of the two disorders than was previously thought.
- ASD has increasingly come to be recognized as a biologically based lifelong neurodevelopmental disability that is present in the first few years of life.
- Children with ASD behave in unusual and frequently puzzling ways.
- They may spend hours engaging in stereotyped or repetitive motor activities, or focus on minuscule details of their world rather than their entire environment.

DSM-IV-TR: Defining Features of Autism

The DSM-IV-TR criteria for **autistic disorder** are presented in Table 10.1. In addition to the core symptoms of the disorder, the child must also show delays or abnormal functioning in social interaction, in language, or in imaginative play prior to age 3 years.

TABLE 10.1 | Diagnostic Criteria for Autistic Disorder

DSM-IV-TR

A. A total of six (or more) items from (1), (2), and (3), with at least two from (1), and one each from (2) and (3).

(1) Qualitative impairment in social interaction, as manifested by at least two of the following:

(a) Marked impairment in the use of multiple nonverbal behaviors such as eye-to-eye gaze, facial expressions, body postures, and gestures to regulate social interaction

(b) Failure to develop peer relationships appropriate to developmental level

(c) A lack of spontaneous seeking to share enjoyment, interests, or achievements with other people (e.g., by a lack of showing, bringing, or pointing out objects of interest)

(d) Lack of social or emotional reciprocity

(2) Qualitative impairments in communication as manifested by at least one of the following:

(a) Delay in, or total lack of, the development of spoken language (not accompanied by an attempt to compensate through alternative modes of communication such as gesture or mime)

(b) In individuals with adequate speech, marked impairment in the ability to initiate or sustain a conversation with others

(c) Stereotyped and repetitive use of language or idiosyncratic language

(d) Lack of varied, spontaneous make-believe play or social imitative play appropriate to developmental level

(3) Restricted repetitive and stereotyped patterns of behavior, interests, and activities, as manifested by at least one of the following:

(a) Encompassing preoccupation with one or more stereotyped and restricted patterns of interest that is abnormal either in intensity or focus

(b) Apparently inflexible adherence to specific, nonfunctional routines or rituals

(c) Stereotyped and repetitive motor mannerisms (e.g., hand or finger flapping or twisting, or complex whole-body movements)

(d) Persistent preoccupation with parts or objects

B. Delays of abnormal functioning in at least one of the following areas, with onset prior to age 3 years: (1) social interaction, (2) language as used in social communication, or (3) symbolic or imaginative play.

C. The disturbance is not better accounted for by Rett's Disorder or Childhood Disintegrative Disorder.

Source: Reprinted with permission from the Diagnostic and Statistical Manual of Mental Disorders, Fourth Edition, Text Revision, (Copyright © 2000). American Psychiatric Association.

Autism Across the Spectrum

When we hear the term ASD, we may think of Temple Grandin in the highly acclaimed HBO film of the same name (2010), a high-functioning and insightful woman with ASD who has become a Professor of Animal Sciences, one of the top scientists and consultants in the humane livestock handling industry, and a leading advocate for persons with ASD. Although some individuals with ASD display the abilities and special talents that are often portrayed in the movies, most do not.

Autism is defined as a **spectrum disorder**, because its symptoms, abilities, and characteristics are expressed in many different combinations and in any degree of severity (Lord, Cook, Leventhal, & Amaral, 2000). Thus, ASD is not an "all or nothing" phenomenon. At one end of the spectrum we may find a mute child, crouched in a corner of his room, spinning a paper clip over and over again for hours; at the other end of the spectrum is a researcher who is also able to hold a corporate job—as long as it doesn't require interacting with customers. Although children with ASD vary widely in IQ, age, SES, gender, and race, the majority of them display most of the core features of the disorder (Mayes & Calhoun, 2011). Nevertheless, despite the similarities in their core profile, they show enormous variability in the expression and severity of their symptoms. This variability among children with ASD applies widely across their social, communicative, and behavioral impairments (Jones & Klin, 2009).

Children with ASD not only vary widely in their social abilities, language, and behaviors, but they may also, in varying degrees, display features not specific to ASD—most commonly, intellectual disability and epilepsy. Thus, children with the same diagnosis of ASD can be vastly different from one another in their intellectual ability, severity of language problem, and degree of progress. To illustrate this point, let's compare and contrast two children, Lucy and John, both diagnosed with autism.

HBO/The Kobal Collection/Redin, Van

Dr. Temple Grandin (left) with award-winning actress Clare Danes, who portrayed her in the highly acclaimed film *Temple Grandin*

LUCY

ASD with Intellectual Disability

Lucy's parents watched her development right from the start, because there had been so many difficulties during pregnancy and delivery. Labor began 3 weeks early, and lasted 23 hours, so that forceps were needed to assist the delivery. She had to have oxygen to revive her, spent 4 days in the special-care unit, and received treatment for jaundice.

Indeed, it seemed that everything in Lucy's development was troubling. For example, she was always too distressed to feed or she fed so ravenously and quickly that she vomited. Nights were no better—she took hours to settle, and always woke early. By her first birthday she had only just started to sit up, and was still not crawling. Their family physician said that she was indeed delayed in her development. At 14 months she began to crawl (6 months is typical), and at 19 months she pulled herself up on the furniture (most children do this around 12 months); she made little progress in other areas.

At 2 years Lucy still did not use any words, and was unresponsive to her parents' attempts to engage her in simple games like peek-a-boo. At 30 months she started to walk (most children walk by 14 months). However, her main sounds were a strange clicking noise made with the back of her tongue, and a variety of screams. She still seemed oblivious to people around her (including her parents) unless they had something she wanted. A pediatrician thought the delay in her development might be due to the difficulties with her delivery and suggested that Lucy be checked every 12 months.

She loved to play with a particular blue and red rattle that she would shake or spin for hours. Once she had the rattle she did not look at anyone, and if someone tried to take it from her she screamed and banged her head on the floor. Understandably, this devastated her parents. Lucy took great interest in odors, sniffing food, toys, clothes, and (to her parents' embarrassment) people. She also liked to feel things, and often tried to stroke stockings on women's legs, even of complete strangers. If they tried to stop her, she had a tantrum.

When Lucy was 4 years old, her pediatrician suspected she suffered from ASD, and referred her to a psychologist for a detailed assessment. The diagnosis was confirmed, and her parents were told that Lucy was generally delayed in her development. They were heartbroken, but they felt that finally Lucy would get the help she desperately needed. (*Autism: The Facts*, by Baron-Cohen and Bolton, (1993) pp. 1–8. By permission of Oxford University Press)

JOHN

ASD with Average Intelligence

John was born after a normal pregnancy and delivery. As an infant, he was easy to feed and slept well. He seemed happy and content to lie in his crib for hours. He sat unsupported at 6 months (which is in the normal range), and soon after, he crawled. His parents saw him as independent and willful. However, his grandmother thought John lacked interest in people.

John walked on his first birthday (in sharp contrast to Lucy, who did not walk until 30 months); yet during his second year he did not progress as well as expected. Although he made sounds, he did not use words. Indeed, his ability to communicate was so limited that even when he was 3 years old, his mother still found herself trying to guess what he wanted (as if he were a much younger child). Occasionally he would grab hold of her wrist and drag her over to the sink, yet he never said anything like "drink."

At this time his parents also became concerned about John's extreme independence. Even when he fell down and hurt himself, he would not come to his parents for help. He never became upset when his mother had to go out and leave him with a neighbor or relative. In fact, he seemed to be more interested in his toy bricks than in people. He spent hours lining the bricks up in exactly the same way and in precisely the same sequence of colors.

After his third birthday his parents became increasingly concerned, despite reassurances from their doctor. John used no words and showed no interest in other children. He did not wave bye-bye or show any real joy when they tried to play peek-a-boo. John always wriggled away from his mother's cuddles, and only seemed to like rough-and-tumble play with his father. His mother worried that she had done something wrong, and felt depressed, rejected, and guilty.

When John was 3.5 years old, he was referred to a child psychiatrist who told his parents that John had ASD, but added that his abilities in spatial tasks (such as jigsaw puzzles) suggested normal intelligence in these areas. Although it was still too early to tell how John would progress, there were indications he would do better than most children with ASD. John received speech therapy, and a psychologist helped his parents plan ways of encouraging communication and reducing temper tantrums.

At age 4, John suddenly began to speak in complete sentences. However, his speech was quite unusual. For example, he often repeated back word for word whatever his parents had said. If they asked him "Do you want a drink?" he would say "you want a drink" in reply. At other times, John made rather surprising remarks. For instance, he would say "You really tickle me" in a tone of voice exactly similar to that of a family friend who had first used the expression some days before. However, his use of this phrase, and most of his speech, was usually inappropriate to the setting, and lacked any clear meaning. (*Autism: The Facts*, by Baron-Cohen and Bolton, (1993) pp. 1–8. By permission of Oxford University Press)

Lucy and John both display the defining features of ASD. They failed to develop normal two-way social relationships and communication in the first few years of life, and displayed repetitive interests and preoccupations. When Lucy was young, her parents described her as "living in a glass bubble." Extreme social unresponsiveness is typical of many children with ASD. John is more socially outgoing and talkative when he approaches others; however, his efforts at social contact are repetitive and unnatural. His abnormalities in communication are less obvious than his social deficits, and consist of speaking in one-sided and stereotyped phrases. In contrast, Lucy is seriously lacking in her ability to communicate and is silent most of the time (Baron-Cohen & Bolton, 1993).

In addition to their abnormalities in social and language development, John and Lucy both display ritualistic behavior. Lucy checks the location of little pieces of thread that she has tied on all the chairs in her house, and John insists on taking exactly the same route to school each day. John and Lucy also have repetitive interests: John likes nothing better than counting lampposts, while Lucy, if allowed to do so, watches the same video over and over again. Both children can spend hours absorbed in nothing but these narrow interests, and these obsessions may lead to other problems. For example, John or Lucy may scream intensely if even a minor change occurs in one of their daily routines (Baron-Cohen & Bolton, 1993).

Despite the many similarities shown by John and Lucy, their stories also show how children with ASD can be quite different from one another. Three critical factors contribute to these differences:

- *Level of intellectual ability*: Intellectual ability ranges from profound disability to above-average intelligence. John is of average intelligence, whereas Lucy has a severe intellectual disability. Because of her intellectual disability, Lucy was slow to develop in all areas. As a result of Lucy's limited overall level of functioning, she shows a much narrower range of interests and activities than John shows.
- *Severity of their language problems*: John speaks quite a lot, whereas Lucy is mute. Children with ASD can fall anywhere between these two extremes.

- *Behavior changes with age*: Some children make little progress, whereas others develop speech or become more outgoing. When significant gains are made, they are usually made by children like John, who have average or above-average intelligence and acquire speech at a young age.

SECTION SUMMARY

DSM-IV-TR: Defining Features of Autism

- In DSM-IV-TR, autism or ASD is a severe disorder with an onset before age 3 years, which is characterized by abnormalities in social functioning, language, and communication, and by unusual interests and behaviors.
- Autism is a spectrum disorder, which means that its symptoms and characteristics are expressed in many different combinations and in any degree of severity.

Core Deficits of ASD

Despite nearly 70 years of research, considerable debate continues today about the core deficits of ASD. Most likely, ASD consists of several deficits, not one primary deficit, that affect the child's social–emotional, language, and cognitive development (Dawson & Toth, 2006). As we discuss each core deficit of ASD, keep in mind that these aspects of development are interconnected—they do not develop in isolation. For example, children with ASD may display a decreased ability to regulate levels of alertness, which in turn is related to increased deficits in social communication (Keehn, Lincoln, Muller, & Townsend, 2010).

Social Impairments

Children with ASD experience profound difficulties in relating to other people, even when they have average or above-average intelligence (Pelphrey, Shultz, Hudac, & Vander Wyk, 2011). From a young age, they show deficits in many skills that are crucial for early social development: a lack of monitoring of the social activities of others; a lack of social and emotional reciprocity; unusual nonverbal behaviors such as using atypical facial expressions, eye-to-eye gaze, body postures, and gestures to regulate social interaction; lack of interest and/or difficulty relating to others, especially other children; and a failure to share enjoyment and interests with others (e.g., Landa, Holman, O'Neill, & Stuart, 2011; Shic, Bradshaw, Klin, Scassellati, & Chawarska, 2011). They may also display difficulties in imitating others' social behavior, sharing a focus of attention with others, and engaging in make-believe play (Ozonoff & South, 2001).

Social expressiveness and sensitivity to social cues are limited, recognition of complex emotions and mental states in everyday life is impaired, and little sharing of experiences or emotions with other people takes place. These children have great difficulty integrating the social, communicative, and emotional behaviors that are required when greeting a familiar person. Their lack of understanding of people as social partners may lead to their treating people as objects, or to directing their actions at the body parts of other people, as when the child attacks a restraining hand rather than the person (Phillips, Gomez, Baron-Cohen, Laa, & Riviere, 1995).

Children with ASD display atypical processing of faces and facial expressions (Dawson, Webb, & McPartland, 2005; Simmons et al., 2009). In processing information about the human face, they may overemphasize one part of the face, such as the mouth, rather than attending to its overall shape or focusing on the eyes as most children do (Joseph & Tanaka, 2003). The child's focus on the mouth rather than the eyes may reflect a tendency to attend to stimuli in which sound and motion co-occur (Klin, Lin, Gorrindo, Ramsay, & Jones, 2009). They also display deficits in recognizing facial expressions of emotion, particularly in detecting fear. This may be because the identification of fear relies more heavily on the eye region than other emotions, and individuals with ASD do not look at the eyes as often as others when viewing faces (Boraston, Corden, Miles, Skuse, & Blakemore, 2008; Dalton et al., 2005).

Children with ASD display impairments in **joint attention**, which is the ability to coordinate attention to a social partner and an object or event of mutual interest (Mundy & Newell, 2007). Joint attention, which typically emerges between 9 and 14 months of age, involves making a social connection with another person by directing that person's attention to objects or people by pointing, showing, and looking, and by communicating shared interest. Although children with ASD may bring an object to a person, or point to an object when they want something done for them, they show little desire to share interest and attention with another person for the sheer pleasure of interaction. Poor quality of eye contact and smiling during parent–infant interactions in the first year of life may be related to deficits in joint attention in the second year of life in children later diagnosed with ASD (Clifford & Dissanayake, 2008). In turn, deficits in joint attention have been found to impede language development in infants with ASD at 20 months, and to predict greater problems in language, communication, and social behavior at age 42 months (Charman, 2003; Luyster, Kadlec, Carter, & Tager-Flusberg, 2008).

Although it was once thought that these children failed to form a social bond with their parents, or that they could not tell the difference between their parents and other adults, research has proved this wrong (Dissanayake & Sigman, 2000). Most children with ASD are more responsive to their caregivers than to unfamiliar adults, directing more social behavior and seeking to be closer to them than to strangers after a brief separation (Sigman & Mundy, 1989). In addition, once the children's disoriented and disorganized repetitive motor behaviors are taken into account, children with ASD display slightly lower—but comparable—rates of secure attachment to their mothers than normal controls. When lower rates of secure attachment are found, it is usually in children with greater ASD severity (Naber et al., 2008). They show a preference for their mother over a stranger, use their mother as a secure base for exploration, and are comforted by their mother when distressed. Importantly, the quality of infant–mother attachment in young children with ASD contributes substantially to the development of the child's play behavior, which is important for the development of social skills (Naber et al., 2007).

It is not a global deficit in their ability to form attachments that children with ASD suffer from. Rather, the deficit seems to be in their ability to understand and respond to social information (Rogers, Ozonoff, & Maslin-Cole, 1993). As shown in Box 10.1, a child with ASD will likely notice when his mother leaves the room and will look for her, both signs of attachment. However, unlike a normal child, he may have little understanding of the event or how to respond in order to change the situation, making it seem as if he has no attachment. Thus, although children with ASD are attached to their parents, the way they express attachment is unusual and difficult to "read." As a result, parents may feel that their child is not attached at all, and may feel disheartened by the child's lack of the cuddling, reaching, and responsiveness that typically accompany attachment behavior.

It is important to note that traditional assessments of attachment using the Strange Situation conceptualize deficits in social functioning in relation to the concept of security/insecurity, which may not be relevant to understanding the deficits in social functioning that characterize most children with ASD. As a result, questions have been raised regarding whether the Strange Situation is a useful way to evaluate the unusual qualities

BOX 10.1 **A CLOSER LOOK**

Attachment in Children with ASD

This young boy with ASD notices that his mother has left the room. He wanders around the room looking for her, but there's essentially no change in his expression. He doesn't seem to know what to do to change the event.

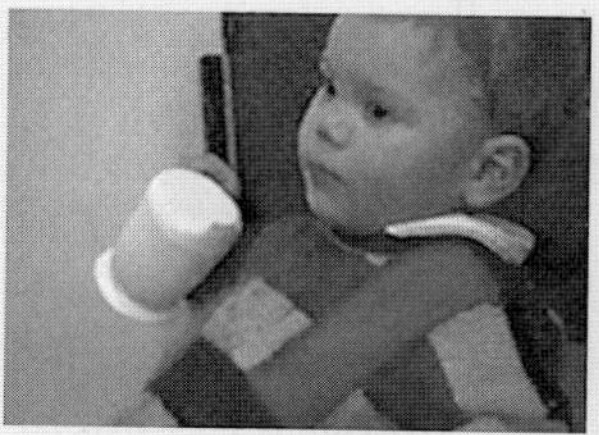

A child his age without ASD is likely to react like this:

This child's facial expression changes in 10 seconds from "Oh no, she's not really leaving me" to "You gotta be kidding" to "Oh my god, she's gone." He's crying, but as soon as his mother returns, he's comforted and he's fine.

Source: Behavior Disorders of Childhood, produced by Alvin H. Perlmutter, Inc. in association with Toby Levine Communications. Reproduced with permission.

of social relationships associated with ASD (Rutter, Kreppner, & Sonuga-Barke, 2009).

In addition to their social difficulties, children with ASD have difficulty processing emotional information contained in body language, gestures, facial expressions, or the voice. Preschool-age children with ASD do not look for or attend to the emotional cues provided by other people. In contrast to other children of the same mental age, they may sort pictures of people according to the type of hat these people are wearing rather than by their emotional expressions (Weeks & Hobson, 1987).

Children with ASD also have difficulties in understanding emotional information, and their own bodily expressions of emotion—often characterized by limited spontaneous use of expressive gestures, and bizarre, rigid, or mechanical facial expressions—are very different from those of typical children (Loveland et al., 1994). They also have difficulties in recognizing emotions from body movements of others (Atkinson, 2009). Thus, children with ASD both process and express emotional information in unusual ways.

Communication Impairments

For two years the mother of a young man with autism would correct her son by saying, "Don't do that. It doesn't look normal." The son would stop the inappropriate behavior. Then she would add, "You want to look normal, don't you?" The son would say, "Yes." Then one day it occurred to the mother to ask her son, "Do you know what normal means?" "Yes," he said, and the mother was impressed. She pushed for his definition. He said, "It's the second button from the left on the washing machine."

—From Our Old Ways Just Aren't Working: Donnellan by Karin Melberg Schwier, p. 8, Saskatchewan Association for Community Living, Dialect, February 1988

Most children have passed predictable milestones on the path to learning language by age 3; one of the earliest is babbling. By the first birthday, a typical toddler says words, turns when he hears his name, points when he wants a toy, and when offered something he does not like, makes it clear that the answer is "no." In contrast, children with ASD display serious abnormalities in communication and language that appear early in their development and persist (Mitchell et al., 2006). Atypical early vocalizations are a sensitive indicator of a heightened risk for later ASD symptoms in infants with a family history of ASD (Paul, Fuerst, Ramsay, Chawarska, & Klin, 2011). Even before children learn to talk, they have at their disposal a rich array of facial expressions, vocalizations, and gestures to communicate their needs, interests, and feelings. One of the first signs of language impairment is the inconsistent use of these early preverbal communications. For example, a typical child with ASD may point to a stuffed animal she wants that is out of reach. By doing this, she is demonstrating the ability to use **protoimperative gestures**—gestures or vocalizations that are used to express needs. However, this child will fail to use **protodeclarative gestures**—gestures or vocalizations that direct the visual attention of other people to objects of shared interest.

The primary purpose of protodeclarative gestures is to engage other people in interaction; for example, a toddler excitedly points to a dog to direct her mother's attention to this fascinating creature that she sees. The use of protodeclarative gestures requires shared social attention and an implicit understanding of what other people are thinking—abilities that are lacking in children with ASD. They are also missing other declarative gestures, for example, the *showing gesture*, which young children without ASD use to show someone else something of interest, such as a newly discovered object (or a handful of shaving cream; see Box 10.2).

As many as one-half of all children with ASD do not develop useful language; this includes some children who begin to speak and then regress in their speech development, usually between 12 and 30 months of age. Children with ASD with no speech or only limited speech do not use gestures to communicate, because motor skills underlie both spoken and "non-verbal" communication (Gernsbacher, Sauer, Geye, Schweigert, & Goldsmith, 2008). Instead, they rely on primitive forms of communication, such as pulling their mother's hand in a desired direction or bringing her a box to be opened. Children with autism may use *instrumental gestures* to get someone else to do something for them immediately, but they fail to use *expressive gestures* to convey feelings (Frith, 2003). These two types of gestures are illustrated in ● Figure 10.1.

Children with ASD who develop language usually do so before age 5. Although almost all children with ASD show delays in their language development, it is their lack of spontaneity and their use of qualitatively deviant forms of communication that is most striking (Chiang & Carter, 2008). The rhythm and intonation of their speech is often unusual (Peppe, McCann, Gibbon, O'Hare, & Rutherford, 2007), but most noticeable is their lack of social chatter—their failure to use language for social communication. Parents and teachers of children with ASD describe their communications as nonsensical, silly, incoherent, and irrelevant, having little meaningful connection with the situation in which they occur. This is illustrated in the following interview with Jerry, a 5-year-old boy with ASD who has a great deal of expressive language (Bemporad, 1979, pp. 183–184):

BOX 10.2 A CLOSER LOOK

Early Communication in ASD

When a dab of shaving cream is put in the hand of this child with ASD, he pays attention to the shaving cream, and that's all he pays attention to. He is oblivious to the fact that his father is a foot away and his mother is close by. He shows no signs of wanting to share his experience with others.

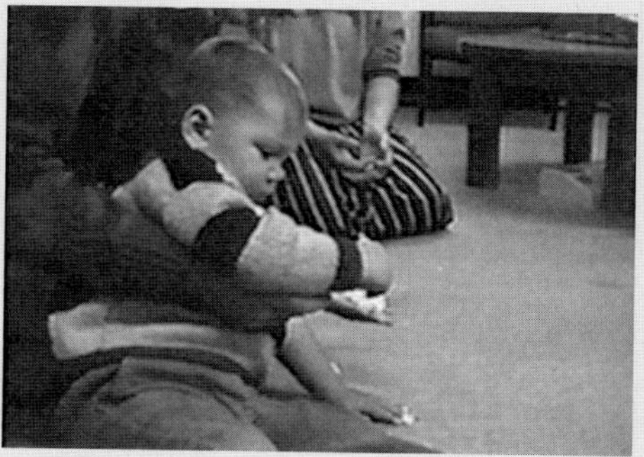

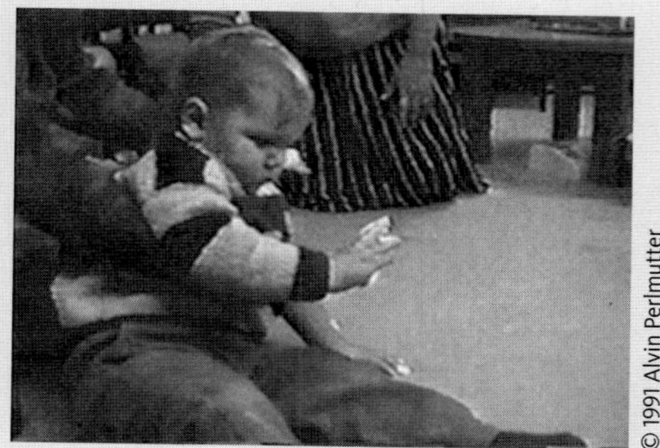

This normally developing child is delighted with the shaving cream, and immediately incorporates everyone into his experience by showing his mother what he has in his hand. He has something to communicate and wants to let everyone in on it.

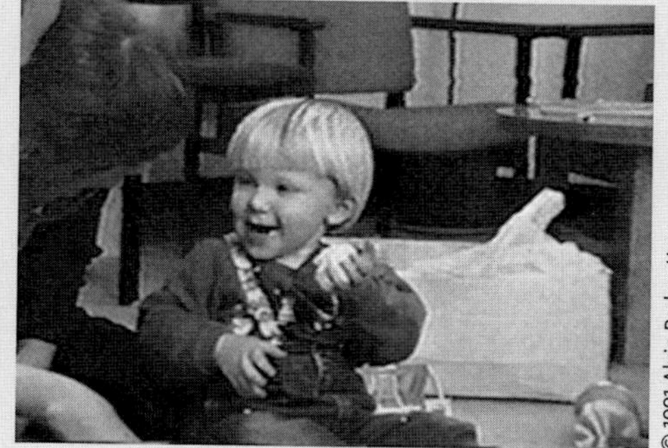

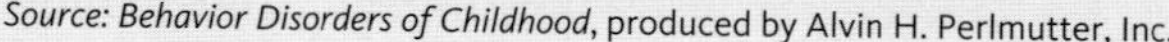

Source: Behavior Disorders of Childhood, produced by Alvin H. Perlmutter, Inc.

INTERVIEWER: "Would you draw a man or a woman?"

JERRY: "A man was business to a lady."

INTERVIEWER: "What does that mean?"

JERRY: "No, a man is present to a lady, yes, yes, yes. A radio. Lady gives the pedal. Great big handkerchief and napkin, all tucked in. So see, there it is. We'll paint the picture and put it in a frame."

Other common qualitative language impairments in children with ASD include pronoun reversals and echolalia. **Pronoun reversals** occur when the child repeats personal pronouns exactly as heard, without changing them to suit the situation. For example, a child named Tim when asked, "What's your name?" answered, "Your name is Tim," rather than "My name is Tim." **Echolalia** can be either immediate or delayed and is the child's parrot-like repetition of words or word combinations that she or he has heard. A child who is asked the question "Do you want a cookie?" responds by repeating, "Do you want a cookie?" Although echolalia was once thought to be pathological, it may actually be a critical first step in language acquisition for many children with ASD. Echolalia and other unconventional verbal behavior, such as *perseverative speech*—incessant talking about one topic and incessant questioning—may serve a variety of communicative and developmental functions for children with ASD. These behaviors may reflect the child's desire to communicate, although in a very primitive way (Prizant, 1996; Prizant & Wetherby, 1989).

Language impairments in children with ASD occur at multiple levels of analysis (Stefanatos & Baron, 2011). However, their primary problem is not so much with the computational (sounds, words, and grammar)

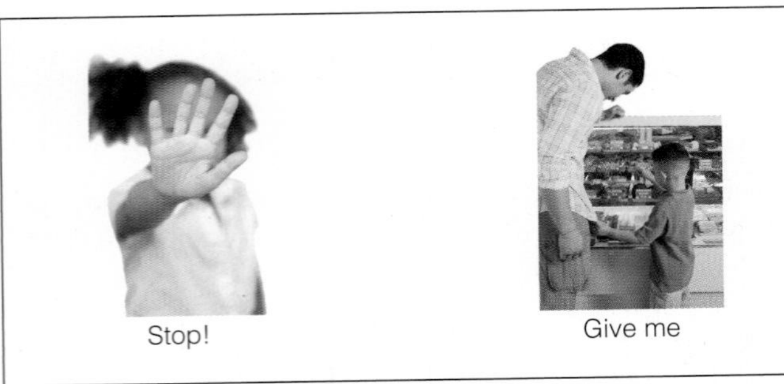

Instrumental Gestures

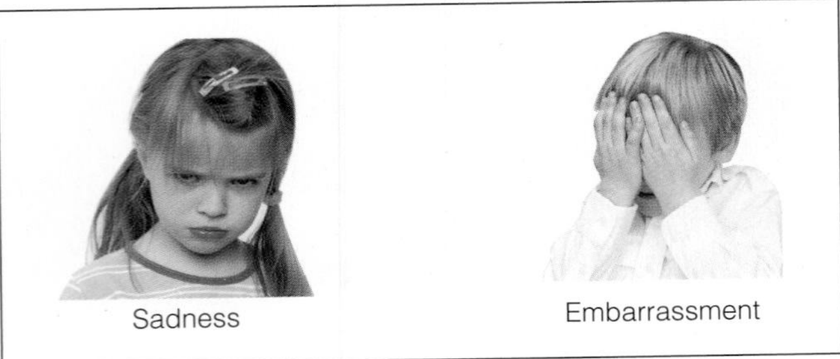

Expressive Gestures

● **FIGURE 10.1** | Instrumental and expressive gestures. Children with ASD may use gestures to get others to do things for them but not to convey feelings.

Photo Credits: (a) © 2012 Karin Dreyer Photography/Jupiterimages Corporation; (b) © 2012 Image Source/Jupiterimages Corporation; (c) © 2012 Michaela Begsteiger/ Jupiterimages Corporation; (d) © 2012 Digital Vision/Jupiterimages Corporation.

or the semantic (meaning) use of language. Rather, these children display profound impairments in **pragmatics**, which is the appropriate use of language in social and communicative contexts. An example of pragmatics (or, in this case the lack of it) is shown in ● Figure 10.2. The point of the question "Can you look at me?" is to request that an action be taken, not to request information about the child's ability to look at his mother. To understand this, a child must know more than what words mean—a child must "read" the context in which words are used. Lacking in pragmatic competence, children with ASD often have difficulty understanding nonliteral statements or adjusting their language to fit the situation (Dawson, 1996; Tager-Flusberg, 1993).

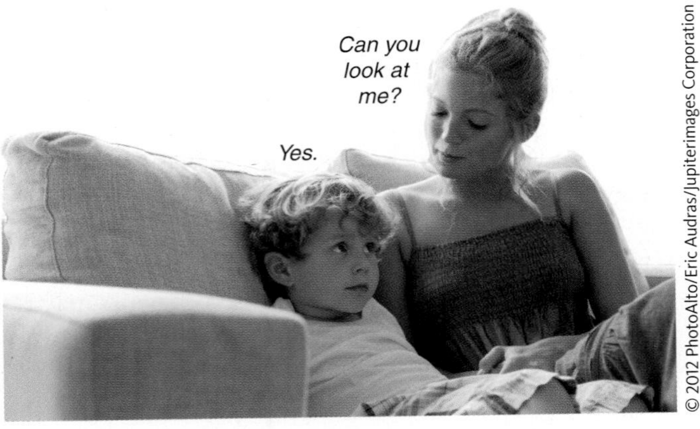

© 2012 PhotoAlto/Eric Audras/Jupiterimages Corporation

● **FIGURE 10.2** | Children with ASD have difficulty with the pragmatic use of language.

High-functioning children with ASD who have mastered word order and have large vocabularies may continue to display impairments in pragmatics. In addition, they continue to show both nonverbal and verbal deficits that reflect a basic failure to recognize the thoughts, feelings, and intentions of other people. At a nonverbal level, their monotone voice and lack of gestures suggest difficulty in communicating emotions. At a verbal level, they display problems with narrative discourse, including impoverished stories and difficulty providing sufficient information to others. As they get older, children with ASD make little use of language for social convention, for example, to greet others or to be polite. It has been suggested that the common element underlying all the communication deficits in ASD is a general failure to understand that language can be used to inform and influence other people (Tager-Flusberg, Paul, & Lord, 2005).

Restricted and Repetitive Behaviors and Interests

Children with ASD frequently display restricted and repetitive behaviors and narrow patterns of interests such as a fascination with arithmetic (Honey, McConachie, Randle, Shearer, & Le Couteur, 2008; Leekam, Prior, & Uljarevic, 2011). These behaviors are characterized by their high frequency, repetition in a fixed manner, and desire for sameness in the environment. Some children may perform stereotyped body movements, such as rocking or flapping their hands and arms, with such intensity that they begin to perspire; others may react explosively to a minor change in their routine. They may show stereotyped and repetitive behaviors at times when they are not explicitly directed to engage in another activity, suggesting a possible deficit in their ability to initiate activities on their own. Other stereotyped behaviors occur in unpredictable or demanding situations, and may provide the child with a sense of control over the environment and a way to cope with changes that are not understood (Klinger, Dawson, & Renner, 2003). Recent research has identified two dimensions of restricted repetitive behaviors in children with ASD: "repetitive sensory and motor behaviors" and "insistence on sameness behaviors." The frequency of the former remains relatively high over time, whereas the latter starts low and increases or worsens over time (Richler, Huerta, Bishop, & Lord, 2010).

Self-stimulatory behaviors are stereotyped as well as repetitive body movements or movements of objects,

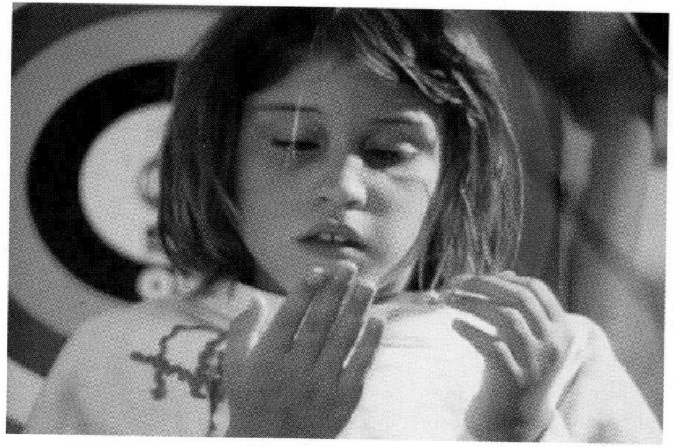
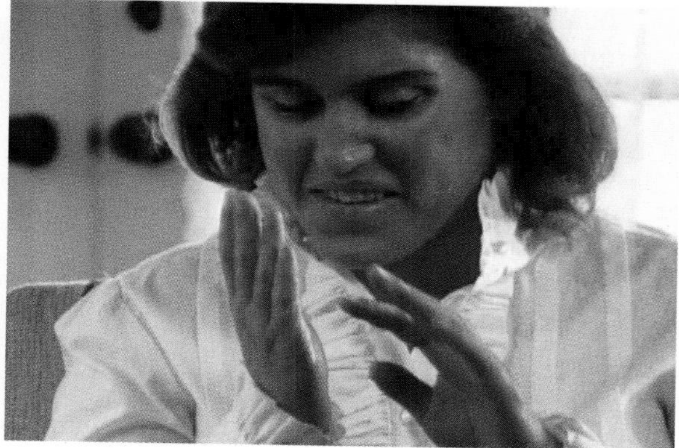

Pamela engaging in self-stimulation as a 7-year-old child and 20 years later as an adult

for example, hand flapping or pencil spinning. Although self-stimulatory and repetitive behaviors also occur in children with other forms of developmental disability, they are especially common and persistent in children with ASD. A particular behavior, such as moving the fingers in front of the eyes, may persist from childhood through adulthood. In the accompanying photos of Pamela, taken 20 years apart, her self-stimulatory behavior looks amazingly similar. Self-stimulation may involve one or more of the senses, for example, staring at lights, rocking, or smelling objects.

The exact reasons that children with ASD engage in self-stimulatory and other repetitive behaviors are not known, although many theories have been advanced (Turner, 1999). One theory is that these children crave stimulation, and self-stimulation serves to excite their nervous system. Another theory is their environment may be too stimulating, and they engage in repetitive self-stimulation as a way of blocking out and controlling unwanted stimulation. Other theories maintain that self-stimulation is maintained by the reinforcement it provides. In the case of an individual child, any one of these reasons may apply (Leekam et al., 2011).

SECTION SUMMARY

Core Deficits of ASD

- Children with ASD experience profound difficulties in relating to other people, including deficits in orienting to social stimuli, imitating others, sharing a focus of attention with others, and noticing and understanding other people's feelings.
- They display serious abnormalities in communication and language, including deficits in the use of preverbal vocalizations and gestures, language oddities such as pronoun reversal and echolalia, and difficulties with the appropriate use of language in social contexts.
- They display stereotyped and repetitive patterns of behaviors, interests, and activities that include obsessive routines and rituals, abnormal preoccupations, insistence on sameness, or stereotyped body movements.

Associated Characteristics of ASD

In addition to their core deficits, children with ASD display a number of associated characteristics. These include intellectual deficits and strengths, sensory and perceptual impairments, cognitive and motivational deficits, and medical conditions and physical characteristics.

Intellectual Deficits and Strengths

The intelligence of children with ASD varies widely, from profound intellectual disability to superior ability. Those with superior abilities often capture media attention yet, in reality, about 70% of children with autism have co-occurring intellectual impairment. Approximately 40% have severe to profound impairments with IQs less than 50, and 30% have mild to moderate impairments with IQs between 50 and 70. The remaining 30% have average intelligence or above (Fombonne, 2003).

Intelligence in children with ASD has typically been assessed using the WISC-IV (Mayes & Calhoun, 2008). Most children with intellectual disability without ASD show a general delay across all areas of intellectual functioning on this test. In contrast, the performance of children with autism tends to be uneven across different WISC subtests. One common pattern is a relatively low score on verbal subtests such as comprehension, and relatively high scores on nonverbal subtests involving short-term memory for strings of numbers, or arranging blocks to form a specific pattern (Happé, 1994b). Studies have found that children with ASD score higher on other tests of intellectual functioning than they do on the commonly used WISC-IV, raising the possibility that intelligence in this population may be higher than previously estimated (Dawson, Soulieres, Gernsbacher, & Mottron, 2007).

Low intellectual ability in children with ASD, particularly low verbal IQ, is generally associated with more severe symptoms and poorer long-term outcomes (Bolton et al., 1994). Only those children with average intelligence or above have the potential to achieve relatively independent living status as adults. IQ scores of children with ASD are typically stable over time and are good predictors of their level of educational attainment.

Despite their intellectual deficits, a small but significant number of children with ASD develop *splinter skills*, or *islets of ability*. Their special talents may be in spelling, reading, mathematics, music, or drawing. As many as 25% of children with ASD display a special cognitive skill that is above average for the general population and well above their own general level of intellect (Howlin et al., 2004).

In addition, about 5% of children with ASD develop an isolated and often remarkable talent that far exceeds normally developing children of the same age. These children, referred to as *autistic savants*, display supernormal abilities in calculation, memory, jigsaw puzzles, music, or drawing. One boy with ASD had an IQ of 60 but could recite the daily lottery numbers for the past 5 years. Another boy learned to play the piano by reproducing any tune he heard on the radio, from Brahms to Bacharach. Psychologists who studied this boy estimated that he had more than 2,000 tunes in his head (Gzowski, 1993, p. 91). Nadia, a girl with ASD, was obsessed with horses; she drew hundreds of pictures of them with incredible vividness and accuracy when she was only 3 years old. One of Nadia's drawings at age 5 is reproduced in ● Figure 10.3. After seeing a picture of a horse in a story, Nadia could generate endless images of what this horse would look like in any pose (Baron-Cohen & Bolton, 1993).

It is not clear whether the special abilities of a few children with ASD reflect intact abilities or indicate a cognitive deficit. However, superior performance by children with ASD has typically been viewed as a side effect of abnormal brain functioning, rather than a reflection of genuine intelligence. One idea is that autistic savants tend to segment information into parts rather than looking at the whole, which leads to exceptional performance in certain domains (Pring, Hermelin, & Heavey, 1995). Another explanation is that children with ASD think in images rather than abstract ideas, which allows them to remember material like a camera or a recorder (Hurlbert, Happé, & Frith, 1994). Unfortunately, despite the fascination and appeal of the skills of autistic savants or the more common splinter skills, in most cases the skills are not used constructively to enhance everyday living.

(Age 5)

● **FIGURE 10.3** | Drawing of a horse by Nadia at age 5.

Nadia: A Case of Extraordinary Drawing Ability, 978-0126357509, 1977, Selfe, 1 figure only. Copyright Elsevier 1977.

Sensory and Perceptual Impairments

Many sights, sounds, smells, or textures that most children find normal can be confusing or even painful to children with ASD. A child with ASD may perceive and react to a specific person's voice as to a loud shriek, to a gentle stroke on the arm as to a sharp pain. These sensory abnormalities are both common and persistent in children with ASD, with 90% or more having problems in two or three sensory domains that continue well into adulthood (Klintwall et al., 2011; Leekam, Nieto, Libby, Wing, & Gould, 2007). These include oversensitivities or undersensitivities to certain stimuli (e.g., unusual reactions to auditory stimulation), overselective and impaired shifting of attention to sensory input, and impairments in mixing across sensory modalities—for example, an inability to simultaneously see the movement and hear the sound of a person's clapping (Reynolds & Lane, 2008; Rogers & Ozonoff, 2005).

Children with ASD may display sensory–perceptual deficits such as sensory dominance and stimulus overselectivity. *Sensory dominance* is the tendency to focus on certain types of sensory input over others—for example, a preference for sights over sounds. *Stimulus overselectivity* is the tendency to focus on one feature of an object or event in the environment while ignoring other equally important features. A selective focus on one narrow part of the environment while ignoring other important features gives children with ASD the appearance of having tunnel vision or tunnel hearing, and makes it very difficult for them to learn about their world (Klinger et al., 2003).

Cognitive and Motivational Deficits

Two types of cognitive limitations proposed to underlie ASD are: (1) specific cognitive deficits in processing social–emotional information, and (2) more general cognitive deficits in information processing, planning, and attention.

Deficits in Processing Social–Emotional Information

The social and communication deficits of children with ASD have generated much interest in how they process social–emotional information, such as emotional expressions, voice and facial cues, and internal mental states. As we have discussed, their unusual social behavior suggests a significant impairment in their social sensitivities. Social interaction is not entirely absent or impaired, but rather they have great difficulty in situations that require social understanding.

At around 12 months, most normally developing infants can tell when they and another person are attending to the same thing. They begin to recognize that people's actions are driven by desires and directed at goals. This ability contributes to the emergence of pretend, or "as if," play. Young children with ASD, however, don't understand pretense, nor do they engage in pretend play (Stanley & Konstantareas, 2007). For example, a normally developing child may give a doll a drink of water from an empty cup while making the appropriate slurping sounds, whereas a child with ASD may simply spin the cup repetitively. The deficits in spontaneous pretend play in young children with ASD led to the hypothesis that these children would also display impairments in their understanding of beliefs and desires or other mental states in themselves or others that cannot be seen directly. The development of such an awareness of mental states in themselves and others is referred to as **mentalization** or **theory of mind (ToM)** (Baron-Cohen, Tager-Flusberg, & Cohen, 2000). By age 4, most children can comprehend what others might know, think, and believe, something that even older individuals with ASD have great difficulty doing. The ToM hypothesis of ASD begins with the premise that the ability to read the intentions, beliefs, feelings, and desires of others from their external behavior has adaptive significance in human evolution. ToM proposes that all humans are, by nature, mind readers. We spend our waking lives reading subtle cues that enable us to fill in the blanks about other people's beliefs and intentions. We do this automatically and with little conscious effort.

Suppose, for example, that a student walked into your class about 10 minutes after it began, looked around the room, and then left. How would you explain the student's behavior? As a mind reader, you may have thought: "Maybe she was *trying* to find a book she lost, and she *thought* she left it in this classroom," or "Maybe she *wanted* to find a friend who was taking this class, but *realized* that her friend was not in class that day." No doubt you can come up with many explanations for this student's behavior, and most will be based on her mental states (the words in italics). You may not be 100% certain of the reason, but chances are you can easily generate many possibilities.

It has been proposed that the primary problems of individuals with ASD stem from a deficit in their ToM mechanism. In other words, children with ASD suffer in varying degrees from "mindblindness"; that is, "they fail to develop the capacity to mindread in the normal way" (Baron-Cohen, 1995, p. 5). Interestingly, when asked what brains do, most 5-year-olds say that brains are for thinking, dreaming, keeping secrets, and so on. But when children with ASD are asked this question, they may say that the brain is what makes people move—expressing nothing about mental activity (Baron-Cohen, 1995). A child with ToM deficits may be able to learn, remember, and know things about the social world but has little understanding of their meaning.

The original test used to determine children's ability to detect mental states of others was called the Sally–Anne Test. A similar test is described in Box 10.3. This test, which is extremely simple, illustrates what it means to have an everyday ToM.

A small but significant number of children with ASD (estimates range widely, from 15% to 60%) demonstrate some knowledge of ToM—they pass the Sally–Anne Test or tests like it (Happé, 1995a). In contrast to the children with ASD who do not pass false-belief tests, those children with ASD who pass the tests display insightful and interactive behavior and have better verbal and communication abilities (Frith & Happé, 1994). They also display far more verbal ability than other children of the same chronological age, suggesting that they may work out ToM tasks in a conscious and logical way (Happé, 1995a, 1995b). All children

BOX 10.3 A CLOSER LOOK

The Sally–Anne Test: What It Means to Have a Theory of Mind

Two dolls, Sally and Anne, are used as props. Sally has a basket; Anne has a box. Sally puts a marble in her basket and covers it, then leaves the room. Anne takes the marble from the basket and hides it in her own box. Next, Sally comes back from her walk and wants to play with her marble. The critical question is: Where will Sally look for her marble?

Most 4-year-olds can answer this question reliably. Sally will look for her marble in her basket where she put it. Even children with intellectual disabilities realize that Sally will think that the marble is where she had left it. They also indicate that Sally did not know what Anne did because she was out of the room when Anne moved the marble.

This understanding demonstrates that young children have attributed a mental state to another person. They grasp that someone can have a false belief about a situation. The false belief is a mental state, not a physical state, and it can very helpfully explain and predict behavior—for instance, that Sally will look for her marble in her basket. Understanding false belief naturally implies an understanding of true belief, of knowledge and ignorance, and of intentions and feelings. This is a theory of mind (ToM).

Most children with ASD, even of a mental age far in excess of 4 years, find the simple Sally–Anne test a great puzzle and tend to get it wrong. They say that Sally will look for the marble in Anne's box (where it really is)—even though they remember correctly that Sally had put the marble into her basket, and was not present when Anne transferred it to her box. Despite remembering the simple sequence of events, they cannot make sense of them by inferring that Sally has a false belief—so they do not take into account at all what Sally thinks; they miss the important change (her previously correct belief is now false). Thus, they cannot predict Sally's behavior. Their lack of understanding of false belief reflects a lack of understanding of others' mental states; hence the claim that individuals with ASD do not have a theory of mind (ToM).

Source: Adapted from *Autism* By Uta Frith, From *Scientific American*, June 1993.

who succeed at ToM tasks, including children with ASD, usually understand metaphors, irony, and a range of speaker emotions, such as the intention to lie or tell a joke. However, youngsters with ASD who understand a false belief give laborious explanations for their insights, suggesting the use of conscious and deliberate strategies to discern mental states. In contrast, understanding a false belief may be so natural, automatic, and unconscious for most children that they may have difficulty explaining how they come up with their answer (Happé, 1995a). Even youngsters with ASD who pass ToM tests tend to show impairments on complex tests that use more real-life situations (Happé, 1994a).

Brain scan studies suggest that the ability to mentalize is associated with a specific region of the brain that is connected to a widespread network of brain regions involved in social cognition (Gallagher & Frith, 2003). Regarding the difficulties displayed by children with ASD, these findings may have implications for understanding the neural basis of ASD, which we will return to in a later section. Although specific socio-emotional cognitive deficits, as in ToM, are very common in children with ASD, the fact that they do not occur in all of these children suggests that mechanisms other than ToM are needed to explain the cognitive deficits in autism.

General Deficits

It has been suggested that children with ASD display a general deficit in higher-order planning and regulatory behaviors (Russell, 1997). These processes, called *executive functions* (see Chapter 5), permit us to maintain effective problem solving by inhibiting inappropriate behaviors, engaging in thoughtful actions, sustaining task performance and self-monitoring, using feedback, and flexibly shifting from one task to another. This presence of a general deficit in executive functioning is suggested by their difficulties in cognitive functions such as planning and organizing, changing to a new cognitive set, disengaging from salient stimuli, processing information in novel and unpredictable environments, and generalizing previously learned information to new situations (O'Hearn, Asato, Ordaz, & Luna, 2008). There are many types of executive functions, so it will be important to identify which deficits in executive function are specific to individuals with ASD (Russo et al., 2007). For example, children with ASD display executive functioning deficits that are more generalized and profound than those with ADHD, showing some deficits that are the same as children with ADHD (e.g., vigilance, inhibitory) and others that are different (e.g., cognitive flexibility/switching) (Corbett, Constantine, Hendren, Rocke, & Ozonoff, 2009).

Another general cognitive deficit hypothesized to underlie ASD is a weak drive for **central coherence**, which refers to the strong tendency of humans to interpret stimuli in a relatively global way that takes the broader context into account (Frith, 1993). By doing this, we can extract meaning from complex sets of information and remember the main points rather than the precise details. It has been proposed that individuals with ASD have a weak tendency for central coherence and tend to process information in bits and pieces rather than looking at the big picture (Frith & Happé, 1994). Understanding other peoples' words, gestures, or feelings can be extremely difficult for someone lacking in central coherence, as reflected in this statement by Donna Williams, an adult with ASD who has written extensively about what it is like to have this disorder:

> It is hard to care or be interested in what a person feels when you perceive a body and then a hand and an eye and a nose and other bits all moving but not perceived in any connected way, with no perception of the context. (Nemeth, 1994, p. 49)

Consistent with a general deficit in central coherence, individuals with ASD perform surprisingly well on tasks in which a focus on parts of a stimulus, rather than the overall pattern, serves to facilitate performance. One such task, the Embedded Figures Test (Jolliffe & Baron-Cohen, 1997) is shown in ● Figure 10.4. The advantage for individuals with ASD on this task may be caused by their spontaneous mental segmentation of the figures into unconnected and meaningless units. This segmentation happens to facilitate the identification of the figure embedded in the whole pattern, resulting in higher scores on this task.

A deficit in ToM and weak central coherence may also affect the child's generalized knowledge of what happens at everyday real-life events such as going on a field trip (Loth, Gomez, & Happé, 2008). These types of mental scripts are important tools in structuring the child's social experiences while accounting for the variability that surrounds real-life events, and may be impaired in children with autism.

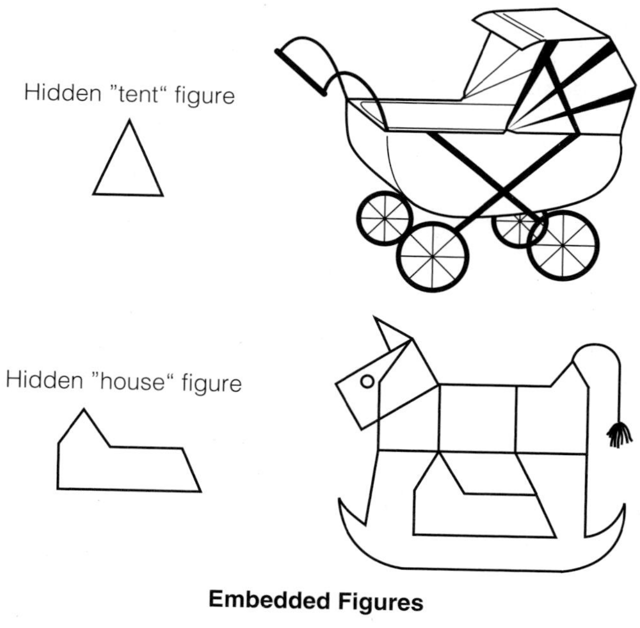

Hidden "tent" figure

Hidden "house" figure

Embedded Figures

● FIGURE 10.4 | Embedded Figures Test: Children with autism perform relatively well on tasks that require attention to details of a figure rather than the overall pattern.

From *A Manual for the Embedded Figures Test* by H. A. Witkin, P. K. Oltman, E. Raskin, and S. A. Karp, pp. 21–26. Consulting Psychologists Press, Inc. Copyright © 1971 by Stephen Karp. Reprinted by permission of S. A. Karp.

Are These Cognitive Deficits Specific to ASD?

Of the cognitive deficits that we have described, lack of ToM seems to be the one most specific to children with ASD compared to children with intellectual disability or specific language deficits. However, studies of ToM across a variety of other disorders including ADHD and conduct disorder suggest that these children also have difficulties in accurately interpreting other people's intentions (Sprung, 2010). Deficits in processing socio–emotional information appear to be less specific to ASD than ToM deficits; they occur in many other conditions, including schizophrenia and intellectual disability. There is even less diagnostic specificity for executive functioning deficits, which occur in many other clinical groups of children, including those with ADHD and conduct disorder (Griffith, Pennington, Wehner, & Rogers, 1999). Further work is needed to determine whether the kinds of deficits in executive functioning in children with ASD differ from those in children with other problems (Hill, 2004).

Are These Cognitive Deficits Found in All Individuals with ASD?

As we have noted, some individuals with ASD pass ToM tests. However, it is not yet clear whether normal-IQ individuals with ASD have actually developed a ToM. The fact that many of these individuals still display severe social impairments in everyday life suggests that they have not developed a ToM, but instead may have learned to use an alternative strategy to solve ToM tasks.

It seems unlikely that a single cognitive abnormality can explain all the deficits present in children with ASD (Tager-Flusberg, 2007). The presence of multiple cognitive deficits, some specific and some general, may help us explain why ASD exists in so many forms and levels of severity. Finally, although we have discussed the general and specific deficits in cognitive functioning in ASD individually, they are related to one another. For example, there is likely a link between the development of certain executive functions and the emergence of children's ToM.

In addition to the cognitive deficits previously discussed, another view is that children with ASD have an underlying impairment in social motivation—that is, they fail to find social stimuli intrinsically rewarding (Dawson et al., 2002). For example, most infants find the mutual exchange of positive emotions during social interactions involving eye-to-eye contact rewarding, and it motivates them to notice and attend to social and emotional cues. In contrast, children with ASD may fail to find eye-to-eye contact rewarding and thus are less motivated and less likely to attend to social cues, extract meaning from others' emotional expressions, and participate in social exchanges. As a result, they have fewer opportunities to engage in behaviors essential for the development of social communication and language (Garcia-Perez, Hobson, & Lee, 2008; Hobson, 2002/2004). As one adolescent with ASD put it, "I still have to remind myself that there are people." Motivational theories remind us that the poor perspective-taking skills of children with ASD are not only manifestations of a cognitive deficit in their ToM abilities, but may also reflect less inclination to shift their perspective.

Medical Conditions and Physical Characteristics

A small percentage of children with ASD, no more than about 10%, have a coexisting medical condition that may play a causal role in their disorder (Challman, Barbaresi, Katusic, & Weaver, 2003; Fombonne, 2003). These include motor and sensory impairments, seizures, immunological and metabolic abnormalities, sleep problems, and gastrointestinal symptoms (IACC, 2011). About 25% or more of individuals with ASD also experience seizures (Mouridsen, Rich, & Isager, 2011). Compared with individuals with intellectual disability who typically display seizures at a young age, those with ASD are more likely to have an onset of seizures in late adolescence or early adulthood (Bailey, Phillips, & Rutter, 1996). Sleep disturbances are also common, occurring in about 65% of children with ASD, and are typically related to the sleep–wake rhythm and problems with sleep onset and maintenance (Dawson, 2010; Hollway & Aman, 2011). So too are gastrointestinal symptoms, occurring in about 50% of children with ASD (Dawson, 2010). These may be related to food selectivity and unusual eating habits and obsessions ranging from minor problems in eating, to disruptive mealtime behaviors, to clinically significant feeding problems (Seiverling, Williams, & Sturmey, 2010).

Children with ASD are usually described as having a normal or attractive physical appearance, and they do not display the visible physical deviations that often accompany severe intellectual disability that is not associated with ASD. They may have subtle but distinctive minor physical anomalies such as facial asymmetries, which suggest the influence of genetic or other prenatal factors (Ozgen, Hop, Hox, Beemer, & van Engeland, 2010).

As many as 90% of individuals with ASD have a head size that is above average. About 20% have a significantly larger-than-normal head size that places them in the upper 3% of the general population (Redcay & Courchesne, 2005). This characteristic is more common in higher-functioning individuals and distinguishes them from individuals with intellectual disability, language disorder, and ADHD (Gillberg & de Souza, 2002). Interestingly, infants with ASD tend to have a smaller than average head size at birth, but then show an excessive increase in growth from 6 to 12 months, leading to the larger-than-normal head size observed at a later age, which is then followed by head growth deceleration (Courchesne, Carper, & Akshoomoff, 2003; Dawson et al., 2007). The cause of this rapid growth during the first year of life is not known, but one implication is that the overproduction of brain connections too quickly makes it difficult for developing children with ASD to adapt to and make sense out of their experiences (Lewis & Elman, 2008). It is not yet clear whether accelerated growth in head size is specific to ASD, or whether it also occurs in children with other psychiatric disorders (Rommelse et al., 2011).

Accompanying Disorders and Symptoms

The two disorders that most often accompany ASD are intellectual disability and epilepsy (Fombonne, 2003). Additional behavioral and psychiatric symptoms may include ADHD and conduct problems (Guttmann-Steinmetz, Gadow, & DeVincent, 2009), anxieties and fears (White, Oswald, Ollendick, & Scahill, 2009), and mood problems (Magnuson & Constantino, 2011). Some children with ASD also engage in extreme and sometimes potentially life-threatening *self-injurious behavior* (SIB)—any self-inflicted behavior that can cause tissue damage to the child's own body (see Chapter 9). The most common forms of SIB are head banging, hand or arm biting, and excessive scratching and rubbing. Head banging, if not prevented, can be severe enough to produce bleeding or even brain injury. SIB may occur for a variety of reasons—self-stimulation, to gain attention, or to eliminate unwanted demands—or, it may occur for no apparent reason (Carr, 1977). Whatever the reasons, rates of emergency/hospital treatment for self-inflicted injuries in children with ASD are 7 times greater than for typically developing children (McDermott, Zhou, & Mann, 2008). However, SIB may not occur more frequently in young children with ASD than in those with other forms of developmental delay (Richler, Bishop, Kleinke, & Lord, 2007).

SECTION SUMMARY

Associated Characteristics of ASD

- About 70% of children with ASD also have intellectual disabilities; about 40% have IQs less than 50, and 30% have IQs between 50 and 70. The remaining 30% have average intelligence or above.

- Sensory–perceptual abnormalities and deficits are common in children with ASD and include oversensitivities or undersensitivities to certain stimuli, and a tendency to focus on one feature of a stimulus while ignoring others.
- Children with ASD display a deficit in theory of mind (ToM)—the ability to understand other people's and one's own mental states, including beliefs, intentions, feelings, and desires.
- Children with ASD display a general deficit in higher-order planning and regulatory behaviors (e.g., executive functions).
- They may display co-occurring medical conditions and physical features such as seizures, sleep problems, gastrointestinal symptoms, or an accelerated growth in head size.
- Children with ASD may display co-occurring symptoms of ADHD, conduct problems, anxieties and fears, and mood problems.

Prevalence and Course of ASD

For decades, ASD was thought to be a rare disorder, affecting about 4 children per 10,000 (Tanguay, 2000). However, recent findings worldwide indicate a much higher prevalence rate—as high as 1%, or 100 children per 10,000, for all forms of ASD (Centers for Disease Control and Prevention, 2009, 2010). The estimated prevalence for the subtypes of ASD are approximately 22 of 10,000 for autistic disorder; 33 of 10,000 for PDD-NOS; and 10 of 10,000 for Asperger's disorder (Fombonne, Zakarian, Bennett, Meng, & McLean-Heywood, 2006). Approximately 1 million or more individuals in the United States are affected, with an estimated annual cost of $35 billion to $90 billion, the higher estimate being comparable to Alzheimer's disease (Ganz, 2007; Knapp, Romeo, & Beechum, 2009). Given the growing emphasis on early identification and intervention for children with ASD, it is likely that these costs will continue to rise.

Many causes for the apparent dramatic increase in ASD have been proposed—vaccines, mercury, diet, caffeine, antibiotics, allergies, environmental pollutants, and electromagnetic radiation—but none have been scientifically substantiated to date (Wing & Potter, 2002). It seems likely that most, if not all, of the rise in prevalence is caused by a greater awareness among parents and professionals; a broadening of the concept and its definition over the years; greater recognition of milder forms of ASD; changes in diagnostic criteria and categories; diagnostic substitution (i.e., the number of children receiving special education under other diagnostic categories, primarily intellectual disability, speech impairment, and learning disabilities, has decreased as those diagnosed with ASD have increased); and better case-finding methods (King & Bearman, 2009; Wazana, Besnahan, & Kline, 2007). However, whether there is also a real increase in prevalence due to an unidentified cause remains an open question. Interestingly, in contrast to scientific opinion that the increase in ASD prevalence is mainly due to changes in diagnostic practices, many lay people believe that the increase is due to increased exposure to new environmental, medical, and technological hazards (e.g., vaccinations, cell phone towers) (Russell, Kelly, & Golding, 2009).

ASD is found in all social classes and has been identified worldwide. It is about 3 to 4 times more common in boys than in girls, a ratio that has remained fairly constant over the years, even with increasing prevalence estimates (Fombonne, 2003). The sex difference is most apparent among children with IQs in the average or above range, perhaps being as high as 10:1 in higher-functioning individuals. However, among children with ASD and profound intellectual disability, the numbers of boys and girls are similar. Thus, although girls are less often affected by ASD than are boys, when they are affected, they tend to have more severe intellectual impairments (Koenig & Tsatsanis, 2005). Girls with ASD who do not have an intellectual impairment are more likely to be formally diagnosed at a later age than boys (Giarelli et al., 2010). In general, the clinical manifestations of ASD are quite similar for boys and girls, although there may be some differences in their cognitive profile (Carter et al., 2007). For example, it has been found that girls with ASD show more pretend play than boys, suggesting that pretense may be less of an impairment for girls (Knickmeyer, Wheelwright, & Baron-Cohen, 2008).

In considering the high ratio of males to females with ASD, Simon Baron-Cohen (2002) proposed the *extreme male brain theory of ASD*. Those with ASD are presumed to fall at the extreme high end of a continuum of cognitive abilities associated with systemizing (understanding the inanimate world), and at the extreme low end of abilities associated with empathizing (understanding our social world). Both abilities are present in all males and females, but males are presumed to show relatively more systemizing and females show more empathizing. Frequent interests and behaviors that occur among individuals with ASD (e.g., attention to detail, collecting, and interest in mathematics, mechanical knowledge, and scientific and technical information) are presumed to reflect an extreme on the systemizing dimension of the male brain, and a relative absence of empathizing (e.g., mindreading, empathy, eye contact, and communication) (Baron-Cohen, Richler, Bisarya, Gurunathan, & Wheelright, 2003). The extreme male brain theory is intriguing but somewhat controversial. Further research into the neurocognitive aspects of these dimensions in individuals with ASD will be needed before we can infer that they are "from Mars and not Venus."

Rates of ASD are comparable across different racial and ethnic groups. Where differences have been found, prevalence is higher among Caucasian children than African American children. African American and white children do not differ on core symptoms of ASD (Cuccaro et al., 2007). However, African American children are nearly three times more likely than Caucasian children to receive another diagnosis such as ADHD or adjustment disorder before being diagnosed with ASD, and nearly three times more likely to experience delays in receiving intervention (Mandell, Ittenbach, Levy, & Pinto-Martin, 2007). Prevalence estimates are lower for Hispanic children than for Caucasian and African American children (Centers for Disease Control and Prevention, 2007). Societies differ in how they integrate ASD into their cultural frameworks. For example, in contrast to viewing ASD as a disorder, some cultures view children with ASD as having special skills or being more in touch with the spirit world. Cultural views range from the Navajo, who embrace their children with ASD as blessed (Kapp, 2011), to the South Koreans, who may hide their children with ASD to protect siblings from being considered tainted and unmarriageable (Grinker, 2007).

Age of Onset

ANNE-MARIE

First Birthday

We were celebrating Anne-Marie's first birthday and had just paraded in, bearing the cake with much fanfare. Daniel, her big brother, almost two and a half years old, and greatly excited, joined us in singing. Anne-Marie, in her high-chair, gazed solemnly at the cake, her baby body still, her mouth unsmiling. . . . I couldn't help once again making a silent comparison to her brother, who at his first birthday party had squealed with delight. . . . Who knows, really, what the first sign was, at what point Anne-Marie began to slip away from us? Was it around that first celebration, or after or before? (Based on Maurice, 1993b)

The *diagnosis* of ASD is usually made in the preschool period or later. However, most parents of children with ASD become seriously concerned a year or more before a diagnosis is made, typically during the months preceding their child's second birthday (McConkey, Truesdale-Kennedy, & Cassidy, 2009) At this time, their child's lack of progress in language, imaginative play, and social relations stands in sharp contrast to rapid developments in these areas by other children of the same age. Although deficits of ASD become increasingly noticeable around age 2, elements are probably present and noticed earlier, as reflected in Anne-Marie's solemn reaction to her first birthday party (Yirmiya & Charman, 2010).

At present, the period from 12 to 18 months seems to be the earliest point in development that ASD can be reliably detected. For example, an interesting study found that children with ASD generally did not show signs of the disorder at 6 months of age, but between 6 and 12 months they failed to gain new social skills or showed a loss of previously acquired ones (Ozonoff et al., 2010). Most children with ASD showed a subtle and gradual loss of specific social skills between 6 and 18 months that went unnoticed by parents. These findings suggest that traditional views that symptoms of ASD are present at birth, or that the child shows dramatic regression at a later age, may not accurately depict how ASD develops. Instead, the onset of symptoms may be more accurately represented as being on a continuum based on the amount and timing of loss of previously acquired skills (Ozonoff et al., 2009).

Currently, diagnoses of ASD that are made around age 2 to 3 years are stable for most children (Bryson, Rogers, & Fombonne, 2003; Kleinman et al., 2008). However, with increasing research into key early indicators, systematic screening and direct observation of infants at risk for ASD (e.g., those with older siblings with the disorder), and universal screening of young infants, it is likely that ASD can and will be reliably detected at an earlier age, particularly for those with low IQ (Bryson, Zwaigenbaum, McDermott, Rombough, & Brian, 2008; Oosterling et al., 2010; Pierce et al., 2011; Swinkels et al., 2006). Possible early indicators of ASD may include: "uses few gestures to express social interest," "doesn't respond when name is called," "rarely makes eyes contact when interacting," "limited babbling, particularly in a social context," and "displays odd or repetitive ways of moving hands and/or fingers" (Zwaigenbaum et al., 2009). Children with ASD have been found to differ from typically developing children on most of these indicators between the ages of 12 and 24 months. However, in one study, only early communicative gestures were found to distinguish children with ASD from those with developmental delay or language impairment (Vaness et al., 2011). As part of its campaign to raise awareness about the importance of early identification for intervention, the American Academy of Pediatrics (AAP) has recommended that all children be screened for ASD at 18 months and 24 months (Hampton, 2007). The organization Autism Speaks has a link on its website where you can view fascinating video clips that show some of the early red flags for ASD. Links to this and other organizations' websites are available on your Psychology CourseMate.

Course and Outcome

Children with ASD develop along different pathways. Some show abnormal behavior soon after birth; some, 25% or more, show seemingly normal development for the first year or longer followed by *regression* (the loss of previously acquired language and social skills, with an onset of ASD) (Baird et al., 2008); while others appear to later improve significantly. The symptoms of children with ASD change over time. Most symptoms show a gradual improvement with age, even though children continue to experience many problems. During adolescence, some symptoms, such as hyperactivity, self-injury, and compulsivity, may worsen (Spector & Volkmar, 2006). During later adolescence and adulthood, abnormalities such as stereotyped motor movements, anxiety, and socially inappropriate behaviors are common, even in high-functioning individuals, who also often experience loneliness, social problems, and work difficulties. Complex obsessive–compulsive rituals may develop, and talking may be characterized by idiosyncratic and perseverative speech, monotonous tone, and self-talk (Newsom & Hovanitz, 2006).

Findings from early studies of children with ASD who received limited help indicated that an overwhelming majority (70% or more) showed poor outcomes with limited progress and continuing handicaps that did not permit them to lead an independent existence (Lotter, 1978). More recent follow-up studies report slightly better, but quite similar, outcomes (Eaves & Ho, 2008; Howlin, Goode, Hutton, & Rutter, 2004). Very few adults with ASD achieve high levels of independence. Most remain quite dependent on their family and other support services, with no permanent job and few friends. They continue to display problems in communication, stereotyped behaviors and interests, and poor reading and spelling abilities. Overall, children with better language skills and IQ scores above 70 show better outcomes, but outcomes can be variable even for high-functioning individuals (Bennett et al., 2008).

SECTION SUMMARY

Prevalence and Course of ASD

- ASD is a disorder that affects 1% of children. It is 3 to 4 times more common in boys than girls. ASD is found across all social classes and has been identified in every country in which it has been studied.
- ASD is most often identified around age 2 years or older, although elements are probably present at a much earlier age.
- Children with ASD may develop along different pathways. Some show abnormal behavior soon after birth; others show seemingly normal development for the first year or longer followed by regression; while others appear to later improve significantly.
- Most children with ASD show gradual improvement of their symptoms with age, although they continue to display social impairments that make them different from other people throughout their lives.
- The two strongest predictors of adult outcomes in children with ASD are IQ and language development.

Causes of ASD

No single abnormality can account for all the impairments associated with ASD, or for the many forms of the disorder, ranging from mild to severe. Although the precise causes of ASD are still not known, our understanding of possible mechanisms has increased dramatically (Dawson & Faja, 2008). These advances are evident when we consider that, not long ago, autism was being attributed to cold and unloving parents.

It is now generally accepted that autism is a biologically based neurodevelopmental disorder with multiple causes (Dawson, 2008). This does not rule out environmental risk factors, particularly physical events that occur during prenatal development (e.g., antiseizure medication taken during pregnancy). To understand ASD, we must consider problems in early development, genetic influences, and neuropsychological and neurobiological findings.

Problems in Early Development

Children with ASD experience more health problems during pregnancy, at birth, or immediately following birth than other children. Although not proven as independent risk factors, prenatal and neonatal complications such as preterm birth, bleeding during pregnancy, toxemia (blood poisoning), viral infection or exposure, a lack of vigor after birth, and others have been identified in a small percentage of children with ASD (Gardener, Spiegelman & Buka, 2009; Ronald, Happé, Dworzynski, Bolton, & Plomin, 2010). A recent study found that very preterm birth (gestational age of <26 weeks) was associated with a much higher rate of developing ASD, with a prevalence of 8% diagnosed by age 11 (Johnson et al., 2010). Other risk factors that affect the prenatal environment may place the fetus at increased risk for ASD. These include parental age, in vitro fertilization, maternal use of prescription and non-prescription drugs, toxic chemicals in the environment during pregnancy, and maternal illnesses during pregnancy such as diabetes or infections (Szatmari, 2011). For example, with regard to parental age, a study of over 7 million children in California found that older fathers and mothers were more likely to have a child with ASD than were younger parents (Grether, Anderson, Croen, Smith, & Windham, 2009). It was found that a 10-year increase in maternal or paternal age was associated with a 38% and 22% greater risk of ASD, respectively. Exposure to antidepressant medication (SSRIs) during the first trimester of pregnancy has also been found to increase the risk of ASD (Croen, Grether, Yoshida, Odouli, & Hendrick, 2011). Although problems during pregnancy and birth may not be the primary cause of ASD, they do suggest that fetal or neonatal development has been compromised (Szatmari, 2011).

A controversial proposal is that some cases of ASD in children who speak only a few words and have other social–communicative behaviors that disappear in the second year of life may be linked to vaccinations. Two hypotheses have attracted the most attention. The first incriminated the measles components of combination vaccines for measles–mumps–rubella (MMR) (Wakefield et al., 1998; retracted February, 2010). The second lay blame on exposure to ethyl mercury (thimerosal), a preservative used in other vaccines (Ball, Ball, & Pratt, 2001). Both hypotheses claimed that the apparent ASD "epidemic" coincided with the introduction of MMR and/or increased exposure to thimerosal as a result of the increased number of recommended childhood vaccinations in the first 3 years of life. However, current scientific evidence does not support an association between MMR vaccines or thimerosal and ASD (Fombonne, 2008; Institute of Medicine, 2004; see also The Editors of The Lancet, 2010). Nevertheless, as many as 50% of parents of children with ASD believe that their child's disorder was caused by vaccinations (Harrington, Rosen, Garneco, & Patrick, 2006).

Genetic Influences

Studies of specific chromosomal anomalies and gene disorders, findings from family and twin studies, and specific gene studies indicate a substantial role for genetic factors in ASD (Rutter, 2005). However, despite strong evidence for a genetic contribution and some noteworthy findings emerging from tests of more than 100 genes, the rate of progress in gene discovery has been slow, and the genetic architecture of ASD remains largely unknown (El-Fishawy & State, 2010). In addition, as we discuss later, recent preliminary findings suggest that environmental factors may play a larger role in ASD susceptibility than previously thought.

Chromosomal and Gene Disorders

The discovery of the fragile-X anomaly (see Chapter 9) in about 2% to 3% of children with ASD led to increased attention to this and other chromosomal defects that might be related to ASD (Turk & Graham, 1997). In general, individuals with ASD have an elevated risk of about 5% for chromosomal anomalies (Barton & Volkmar, 1998; Dykens & Volkmar, 1997). However, these anomalies alone do not indicate the specific gene sites underlying the disorder, because ASD has been associated with anomalies involving several chromosomes (Freitag, Staal, Klauck, Duketis, & Waltes, 2010).

ASD is also associated with *tuberous sclerosis*, a rare single-gene disorder. The manifestations of this disorder can vary widely from mild to severe, and may include neural deficits, seizures, and learning disabilities. Most cases are derived from new mutations with no family history of the disorder (Bailey et al., 1996). About 25% or more of children with tuberous sclerosis also have ASD. This makes the association between ASD and tuberous sclerosis greater than that for any other genetically based condition.

Family and Twin Studies

Recent studies have found that as many as 15% to 20% of siblings of individuals with ASD also have the disorder, a number nearly twice that of earlier reports (Ozonoff et al., 2011). In addition, family members of children with ASD also display higher than normal rates of social and language deficits, and unusual personality features that are very similar to those found in ASD, but less severe (Constantino, Zhang, Frazier, Abbacchi, & Law, 2010; Spiker, Lotspeich, Dimiceli, Myers, & Rische, 2002). Referred to as the *broader autism phenotype*, these deficits include social oddities such as aloofness, lack of tact, and rigidity; pragmatic language problems such as over- or under-communicativeness; and poor verbal comprehension. Family members with the broader phenotype do not, however, display the atypical language (e.g., echolalia), extreme stereotyped repetitive behavior, or intellectual disability and epilepsy often associated with a formal diagnosis of ASD (Rutter, 2000). These findings are consistent with a general family risk for ASD that is genetically mediated (Piven, 1999). In addition, a growing number of studies have reported similar neurophysiological correlates (e.g., atypical brain activation, reduced white matter) for children with ASD *and* their "unaffected siblings," suggesting a family susceptibility to ASD involving a wide array of brain regions and networks (Barnea-Goraly, Lotspeich, & Reiss, 2010; Belmonte, Gomot, Baron-Cohen, 2010).

Twin studies have reported concordance rates for ASD in identical twins ranging from 70% to 90%, in contrast to near zero rates for fraternal twins (Rutter, 2005). These findings indicate that the heritability of an underlying liability for ASD may be as high as 90%, and suggest that almost all the variance in the expression of ASD can be attributed to inherited genetic factors

(Freitag et al., 2010; Lichtenstein, Carlström, Råstam, Gillberg, & Anckarsäter, 2010). However, more recent findings suggest that the impact of genetic factors may have been overestimated in earlier studies, and that of environmental experiences seriously underestimated. Hallmayer et al. (2011) found that a large proportion of the variance in susceptibility to ASD could be explained by *shared environmental experiences* (58%), with heritability accounting for a smaller amount (38%). If replicated, these findings suggest that susceptibility to ASD may have a moderate genetic heritability component and a substantial shared twin environmental component. To date, the major focus of research on ASD has been on genetic influences with minimal attention to environmental factors. The finding that shared environmental experiences have a significant influence on ASD susceptibility suggests that environmental factors occurring prior to or by the end of the first year of life may play a particularly important role. Thus, further research into problems in early development of the type we discussed previously, such as low birth weight, multiple births, maternal infections during pregnancy, and parental age, may help to advance our understanding of ASD (Hallmayer et al., 2011).

Molecular Genetics

New research using molecular genetics has pointed to particular areas on many different chromosomes as possible locations for *susceptibility genes* for ASD (Dawson & Faja, 2008). Susceptibility genes are causally implicated in the susceptibility to ASD but do not cause it directly on their own. Although several searches for major ASD genes have been undertaken, they have not yielded consistent results (Freitag et al., 2010). No single gene has been found to be relevant for most cases of ASD. Inconsistent findings in gene studies may be due to the considerable etiologic heterogeneity within ASD and the diverse ways in which it appears. Rather than a single gene, rare mutations of larger effect and a few common variants of small effect in several genes seem to be causal for many cases of ASD (Freitag et al., 2010). Thus, ASD is likely to be a complex genetic disorder resulting from simultaneous genetic variations in multiple genes (El-Fishawy & State, 2010). Moreover, the expression of ASD gene(s) may be influenced by environmental factors (e.g., exposure to drugs, maternal illness)—"a second hit" occurring primarily during fetal brain development.

Finally, there are a number of situations in which epigenetic dysregulation (changes in gene expression caused by mechanisms other than changes in the underlying DNA sequence) may be associated with the development of ASD as, for example, in the case of comorbid genetic conditions such as Fragile X syndrome or genes or genomic regions exhibiting abnormal epigenetic regulation (Grafodatskaya, Chung, Szatmari, & Weksberg, 2010). Thus, in searching for genetic alterations responsible for ASD, it may also be necessary to look beyond variations in specific genes into epigenetic regulation of gene function.

Brain Abnormalities

Although there is no known biological marker for ASD, impressive advances have been made in documenting the neurobiological basis of the disorder (Neuhaus, Beauchaine, & Bernier, 2010; Pelphrey, Shultz, Hudac, & Vander Wyk, 2011). Current research suggests that the behavioral features of ASD may result from abnormalities in brain structure and functioning that are consistent with early disturbances in neural development (Minshew, Johnson, & Luna, 2000). Importantly, although many brain regions are implicated, the disorder does not seems to lie in an abnormality localized in one part of the brain but, rather, in a lack of normal connectivity across brain networks that underlie the core features of ASD (Stigler, McDonald, Anand, Saykin, & McDougle, 2011).

Neuropsychological impairments in ASD occur in many domains, including verbal intelligence, orienting and selective attention, memory, pragmatic language, and executive functions (Dawson et al., 2002). The widespread nature of these deficits suggests multiple regions of the brain are involved at both the cortical and subcortical levels (Happé & Frith, 1996). The types of neuropsychological deficits also vary as a function of the severity of the child's disorder. For example, low-functioning children with ASD may show impairments in basic memory functions, such as visual recognition memory, which are mediated by the brain's medial temporal lobe (Barth, Fein, & Waterhouse, 1995). In contrast, high-functioning children may have more subtle deficits in working memory or in encoding complex verbal material, suggesting the involvement of higher cortical functions (Dawson, 1996).

Biological Findings

Brain imaging studies have looked for structural and functional abnormalities in brain development, or consistently localized brain lesions associated with the symptoms of ASD (Williams & Minshew, 2007). In terms of abnormal brain development, a recent longitudinal study examined brain growth at multiple points in time from ages 1.5 to 5 years in normal toddlers and toddlers who received a confirmed diagnosis of ASD at around 4 years of age (Schumann et al., 2010). The toddlers with ASD showed evidence of cerebral gray and white matter overgrowth in all regions by age 2.5 years, around the time that their clinical symptoms began to appear. Almost all brain regions were found to develop at an abnormal rate, and this finding was more pronounced in girls.

In terms of localized brain abnormalities, studies have consistently identified structural abnormalities in the cerebellum and in the medial temporal lobe and related limbic system structures (Bauman & Kemper, 2005; Courchesne et al., 2007). The *cerebellum*, a relatively large part of the brain located near the brain stem, is most frequently associated with motor movement. However, it is also partially involved in modulating emotion, language, executive function, learning, thought, and attention (Hodge et al., 2010). Specific areas of the cerebellum are found to be significantly smaller than normal in youngsters with ASD, particularly in those with a higher level of functioning (Scott, Schumann, Goodlin-Jones, & Amaral, 2009). It has been proposed that cerebellar abnormalities may underlie the problem that children with ASD have in rapidly shifting their attention from one stimulus to another (Courchesne et al., 2007).

A second localized brain abnormality is in the medial temporal lobe and connected limbic system structures such as the amygdala and hippocampus (Groen, Teluij, Buitelaar, & Tendolkar, 2010; Schumann & Amaral, 2009). These areas of the brain are associated with functions that are often disturbed in children with ASD—for example, emotion regulation, learning, and memory. The amygdala plays an especially important role in recognizing the emotional significance of stimuli; in orienting toward social stimuli; in the perception of eye gaze direction; and, with the hippocampus, in long-term memory (Schulkin, 2007). Findings from brain scan studies suggest both structural and functional abnormalities in the amygdala of those with ASD (although not in all cases) (Monk, 2008). For example, amygdala enlargement in toddlers with ASD is correlated with the severity of their social and communication impairments (Schumann, Barnes, Lord, & Corchesne, 2009).

Studies of brain metabolism in individuals with autism suggest decreased blood flow in the frontal and temporal lobes. Studies have also found a decrease in the functional connections between cortical and subcortical regions, and a delay in the maturation of the frontal cortex, as indicated by reduced cerebral blood flow in the frontal brain regions of preschool-age children with autism (Zilbovicius et al., 1995).

In relation to connections among specific brain regions and tracts (parts of the brain that carry signals from one brain region to another and allow communication between the two hemispheres), abnormalities in the corpus callosum, frontal lobe cortex, and other brain tracts have been found in youngsters with ASD (Kumar et al., 2010; Shukla, Keehn, & Muller, 2011) and in their unaffected siblings (e.g., Barnea-Goraly et al., 2010). In support of the role of abnormalities in connectivity, reductions in the area of the corpus callosum (the main fiber tract connecting the hemispheres) have been found in children with ASD (Frazier & Hardan, 2009). A recent study also found significantly reduced interhemispheric connectivity specific to brain regions with functional relevance to ASD (Anderson et al., 2011). Postmortem studies of single axons in prefrontal regions of the brain have revealed a disconnection of long-distance brain pathways, excessive connections between adjacent areas, and inefficiency in pathways for emotion, which may account for why individuals with ASD have with difficulty in shifting attention, engage in repetitive behavior, and avoid social interactions (Zikopoulos & Barbas, 2010).

Atypical patterns of connectivity in the *default mode network* (DMN) have also been found in children with ASD. The DMN is a network of brain regions that are active when the individual is not focused on the external world and the brain is at wakeful rest—focusing on internal tasks such as daydreaming, thinking about the future, retrieving autobiographical memories, and assessing others' perspectives. This finding is important since the DMN includes brain regions (e.g., medial prefrontal cortex, medial temporal lobe) hypothesized to be involved in the higher-order social cognitive processes that are impaired in children with ASD—for example, memory, theory of mind, and integration of information (Stigler et al., 2011).

ASD as a Disorder of Risk and Adaptation

Based on the causal factors we have discussed, a model of risk and adaptation is needed to understand how ASD develops. Genetic and environmental factors lead to abnormalities in brain development, which in turn lead to generalized disturbances in how the child processes information and interacts with his or her environment (Dawson, 2008). These disturbances are likely to disrupt critical input affecting brain development during early periods of sensitivity (Dawson et al., 2002). Therefore, the relationship between the child's early risk for ASD and later outcomes will be mediated by alterations in how the child interacts with and adapts to his or her environment. Depending on the interaction between early risk factors and the environment in which the child develops, different children will follow different developmental pathways. Although pathways may change at any point in development, the longer the child is on a maladaptive pathway, the more difficult it is for change to occur. Thus, as we discuss in the next section on treatment, the earlier the risk for ASD can be identified and the sooner intervention begins, the greater the likelihood that the child will have a better outcome (Sigman, Spence, & Wang, 2006).

SECTION SUMMARY

Causes of ASD

- ASD is a biologically based neurodevelopmental disorder that may result from multiple causes.
- ASD is a genetic condition, although the specific genes have yet to be identified, and shared environmental experiences are also involved.
- Nonautistic relatives of individuals with ASD display higher than normal rates of social, language, and cognitive deficits that are similar in quality to those found in autism, but are less severe and are not associated with intellectual deficits or epilepsy.
- Neuropsychological impairments occur in many areas of functioning, including intelligence, attention, memory, language, and executive functions.
- Structural abnormalities in the cerebellum and the medial temporal lobe, prefrontal cortex, and related limbic system structures have been found.
- The disorder is not represented by a localized abnormality in one part of the brain but rather by a lack of normal connectivity and communication among brain networks that underlie the core features of ASD.
- The relationship between the child's early risk for ASD and later outcomes will be mediated by how the child interacts with and adapts to his or her environment.

TREATMENT OF ASD

I have not counted the trials of medication, the diets, . . . the behavioral programs. If they total five hundred, there are five hundred fewer to try. . . . I'm a believer. . . . I believe my son can get well.

—From Swackhamer (1993)

Autistic people suffer from a biological defect. Although they cannot be cured, much can be done to improve their lives.

—U. Frith (1997)

These two sentiments, the first by the mother of a child with ASD, the second by an ASD expert, underscore the promise, pain, and uncertainty that surround efforts to help children with ASD and their families. Parents of children with ASD report having tried, on average, between seven and nine different therapies for their child, and are currently using between four and six (Goin-Kochel, Myers, & Mackintosh, 2007). It has been estimated that about *400 different treatments* are being used by individuals with ASD (Interactive Autism Network, 2011). The fact that no one treatment has been successful in eliminating the symptoms of ASD makes many parents vulnerable to new claims of dramatic improvements. This is especially true for a dizzying array of widely publicized treatments such as vitamins, nutritional supplements, special diets (e.g., gluten-casein free diets), medications (e.g., antipsychotics, stimulants, antidepressants), hyperbaric oxygen therapy (sealing the child in a pressurized oxygen chamber), chelation therapy (removal of heavy metals from the body), weighted vests (to provide "calming" stimulation), secretin (a hormone that controls digestion), immunotherapy (use of substances that target a variety of hypothesized but as yet unproven immune system abnormalities), auditory training, music therapy, dance/movement therapy, repetitive transcranial magnetic stimulation (stimulating key motor cortical sites to improve motor activity), sensory integration, facilitated communication, horseback riding, use of trained service dogs, and even swimming with dolphins. Unfortunately, most of these treatments have not lived up to their claims under close scientific scrutiny and may have harmful effects (Stigler, Sweeten, Posey, & McDougle, 2009; Umbarger, 2007).

Although behavioral, educational, and medical treatments may improve learning and behavior, and may permit a few children to achieve near-normal functioning, there is no known cure for ASD. The goals for most treatments are to minimize the core problems of ASD, maximize the child's independence and quality of life, and help the child and family cope more effectively with the disorder (Myers, Johnson, and the Council on Children with Disabilities, 2007). These goals can be facilitated by treatments designed to enhance development and learning, to reduce associated maladaptive behaviors, and to educate and support parents in meeting these goals. Understanding parents' beliefs about the causes of their child's ASD may also be important for treatment (Dardennes et al., 2011).

Promising new programs of early intervention, community-based education, and community living options are all reasons for optimism about improving outcomes for children with ASD (Newsom & Hovanitz, 2006). The most benefit is likely to come from developmentally oriented, early behavioral interventions that involve parents and which are used along with special educational methods (Rutter, 2006b). Most children treated using these newer evidence-based methods show significant gains in language, communication, and measured IQ, and a modest reduction in the severity of the core symptoms of autism (Virués-Ortega, 2010; Young, Corea, Kimani, & Mandell, 2010). However, questions remain concerning how intensive the interventions need to be (e.g., 20 vs. 40 hours per week), how much change can be achieved, and the extent to which changes can be directly attributed to the intervention. Additional controlled studies are needed before long-term outcomes can be fully assessed (Charman, 2011; Vismara & Rogers, 2010).

© Daily Mail/Rex/Alamy

A mother and her two young sons with autism: The demands of parenting a child with autism are considerable

Overview

EMILIE

A Full-Time Job

When Emilie was 2 she was diagnosed with autism, Emilie's mother recalled, her eyes brimming with tears. "We've been relying on ourselves ever since." Emilie's mother and father have read about children with autism who became accomplished scientists and musicians—but progress for Emilie, now age 4, has been slow. Two months ago they hired a specialist to teach them a new one-on-one approach for getting through to Emilie with a reward system. Pictures of food are taped to hallway walls. On the fridge is a cut-out of a glass of milk. After years of shrieking and kicking for what she wants, Emilie is learning to express her needs. When she points to what she wants, she gets a reward—a potato chip or an activity she likes. Every afternoon mother and daughter spend 2 hours on the floor, face to face, their legs interlocked. "Listen to maman, Emilie. Look at me. Look at me. Say 'yes.' Say 'yes.' Do you like chips, Emilie? You can have one if you just say the word, 'yes.'"

Emilie's mother coaxes patiently, firmly, holding out a bowl of chips. But Emilie runs to the radiator and climbs it, teetering there. When her mother pulls her down Emilie shrieks, kicks, and falls to the floor crying. In a minute the episode is over, and the lesson begins again. This time Emilie looks at her mother, says "yes," and holds out her hand for a chip. "Bravo, sweetheart. You did it. I knew you could," her mother beams. Emilie's mother has used the reward system to build Emilie's vocabulary to 22 words. That, to her parents, has been a monumental breakthrough.

"We have to motivate her," says her mother, whose only respite is an evening out once or twice a month with her husband. "If we let her be, she'd just climb or hide under the cover all day long. That's my nightmare, that she'll end up in a psychiatric hospital, withdrawn from the world. I can see that we are slowly beginning to get through to her," Emilie's mother says with a deep sigh. "She didn't pay any attention to us at all before. She never showed any affection or made eye contact. But now she looks at me and says 'maman.' Sometimes she hugs me. It doesn't happen every day. But it grabs my heart when it does." (From Susan Semenak, *The Gazette*, November 21, 1996, pp. A1 and A15. Reprinted by permission)

Emilie's case captures the demands, frustrations, aspirations, and hopes of a family trying to do the best possible for their child with ASD. A number of treatments are available for helping children with ASD, such as Emilie, and their families. These treatments focus on the specific social, communication, cognitive, and behavioral deficits of ASD that we have discussed throughout this chapter. They include strategies for: engaging children in treatment; decreasing disruptive behaviors; teaching appropriate social behavior, including joint attention, imitation, and reciprocal interaction; increasing functional, spontaneous communication; promoting cognitive skills such as symbolic play and perspective taking; and teaching adaptive skills that prepare the child for increased responsibility and independence. Family interventions enable parents to participate fully in their child's treatment and to cope with the substantial demands associated with raising a child with ASD. In addition, educational interventions and speech and language therapy are commonly used. Also, for some children antipsychotic medications (e.g., risperidone) may help to decrease interfering and challenging symptoms such as irritability, aggression, and repetitive behaviors (McDougle et al., 2005), particularly when they are combined with intensive behavioral intervention (Frazier et al., 2010). However, the effectiveness of these medications must be balanced against known adverse effects such as weight gain or liability to develop metabolic disorders (McPheeters et al., 2011).

Because children with ASD have great difficulty making changes and generalizing previously learned skills to new environments, these areas must be directly addressed in treatment. It is also critical that treatment be tailored to meet the needs of the individual child and the family, thus making it possible for each child to meet his or her full potential. In the following paragraphs we highlight how several of the treatment components mentioned previously are implemented.

Initial Stages

Initially, treatment focuses on building rapport and teaching the child learning-readiness skills. Various procedures help the child feel comfortable being physically close to the therapist and to identify rewards to strengthen the child's social behavior, affection, and play. Imitating the child's use of toys may increase eye contact, touching, and vocalizations directed toward the therapist. Prompting the child to engage in play with a preferred toy may decrease social avoidance.

Children with ASD must learn to sit in a chair, come when called, and attend to their teacher if they are to progress. These readiness skills are taught using two approaches. The first is a step-by-step approach to presenting a stimulus and requiring a specific response, referred to as **discrete trial training**. The second attempts to strengthen behavior by capitalizing on naturally occurring opportunities, referred to as **incidental training**. Most interventions use a combination of these approaches (Ghezzi, 2007).

© Nir Alon/Alamy

The mother of Max, a 4-year-old boy with autism, spends hours each day teaching communication skills to her son

Reducing Disruptive Behavior

Young children with ASD display many disruptive and interfering behaviors, such as tantrums or throwing objects, as well as self-stimulation, aggression, and self-injury. These behaviors are common reactions to demands on the child that are made early in treatment, and must be eliminated if the child is to learn more adaptive forms of social interaction and communication. Many procedures are effective in eliminating disruptive behavior, including rewarding competing behaviors, ignoring, and mild forms of punishment.

Teaching Appropriate Social Behavior

Teaching appropriate social behavior is a high treatment priority (White, Keonig, & Scahill, 2007). The salience of social cues may be increased by pairing people with whom the child has contact, with actions, activities, and events that the child finds pleasant or useful. Younger children are also taught ways to express affection through smiling, hugging, tickling, or kissing—behaviors that enable them to return the affection they receive from others. Other ways to enhance social interaction include teaching social toy play, social pretend play, and specific social skills such as initiating and maintaining interactions, taking turns and sharing, and including others in activities. Parent-assisted Children's Friendship Training programs for school-age children with ASD target conversational skills, peer entry skills, developing friendship networks, good sportsmanship, good host behavior during play dates, and handling teasing (Frankel et al. 2010). Group social skills interventions have also been shown to improve social behaviors in children with high-functioning ASD (Derosier, Swick, Davis, McMillen, & Matthews, 2010).

One strategy for teaching appropriate social behavior to children with ASD involves teaching normal or mildly handicapped peers to interact with them. Peers are taught to initiate age-appropriate social behaviors such as playing with toys, commenting about activities, or acknowledging their partner's responses. Teachers may signal and reward the peers' social initiations with the child with ASD. Other strategies use prompts and rewards for teaching the child with ASD to initiate interactions, and in some cases to involve siblings as trainers (Kohler, Strain, & Goldstein, 2005).

Teaching Appropriate Communication Skills

Several strategies are used to help children with ASD communicate more appropriately. **Operant speech training** is a step-by-step approach that first increases the child's vocalizations, and then teaches imitation of sounds and words, the meanings of words, labeling objects, making verbal requests, and expressing desires. The emphasis is on teaching the child to use language more spontaneously and more functionally in everyday life situations to influence others and to communicate better (Newsom & Hovanitz, 2006).

Early Intervention

As methods to identify ASD at a very young age are developed, possibilities for effective early intervention with infants and toddlers increase dramatically (Wallace & Rogers, 2010). The promise of early intervention derives, in part, from the plasticity of neural systems early in development (Mundy & Neal, 2001), and the fascinating but yet-to-be tested hypothesis that providing very young children with ASD with intensive and highly structured experiences may alter their developing brains in ways that permit outcomes that are not otherwise possible (Dawson, 2008). Nowadays, whenever possible, intensive interventions for children with ASD begin before the age of 3—the earlier the intervention, the better the outcome is likely to be.

The treatments for ASD that we have described are often implemented in the context of comprehensive programs of early intervention (Harris, Handleman, & Jennett, 2005). A variety of early intervention programs are available, some based on a learning/behavioral model (e.g., Applied Behavior Analysis; Lovaas & Smith, 2003), others based on a structured teaching model (e.g., TEACCH; Mesibov, Shea, & Schopler, 2005), and others based on developmental (e.g., Early Start Denver Model; Dawson et al., 2010) or relationship-focused (DIR or Floor Time; Greenspan & Wieder, 2006) approaches. Although these and other programs may differ in philosophy and emphasis, they share many common goals and features. There is a growing consensus that the most effective interventions for children with ASD include the following features (Johnson et al., 2007):

- Early: Begin intervention as soon as an ASD diagnosis is seriously considered.
- Intensive: Active engagement of the child at least 25 hours a week, 12 months a year, in systematically planned, developmentally appropriate educational activities with specific objectives.
- Low Student–Teacher Ratio: Allow sufficient one-on-one time and small-group instruction to meet specific individualized goals.
- High Structure: Use predictable routines, visual activity schedules, and clear physical boundaries to minimize distractions.
- Family Inclusion: Include a family component with parent training as indicated.
- Peer Interactions: Promote opportunities for interactions with typically developing peers.
- Generalization: Teach child to apply learned skills in new settings and situations and to maintain the use of these skills.
- Ongoing Assessment: Monitor child's progress and make adjustments in treatment as needed.

The average age of children with ASD entering early intervention programs has been 3 to 4 years or younger. These children have an average IQ in the mid-50s, although many are not testable at the time of their intake for treatment. Early intervention provides direct one-to-one work with the child for 15 to 40 hours per week and active involvement of the family. In effect, these programs become a way of life for the family—24 hours a day, 7 days a week. Programs are carried out at home and in the preschool, and efforts are made to include the child in interactions with normal peers, especially later in treatment.

Comprehensive reviews of outcomes for children with ASD completing early intervention programs find that many of them are able to function in regular educational placements, although the type of setting and amount of support services needed varied considerably. Most children also show developmental gains, as reflected in improvements in their behavior, IQ scores, scores on developmental tests, and classroom observations (Eikeseth, Smith, Jahr, & Eldevik, 2007; Howard, Sparkman, Cohen, Green, & Stanislaw, 2005).

The UCLA Young Autism Project

The UCLA Young Autism Project began nearly 50 years ago under the direction of Dr. Ivar Lovaas (1927–2010). Now referred to as the Applied Behavior Analysis (ABA) or Early Intensive Behavioral Intervention (EIBI) approach, it is the most detailed and labor intensive of the early intervention programs and begins the earliest. It is one of the only programs that currently qualifies as an evidence-based treatment for ASD based on outcomes evaluated against control groups of similar-age children receiving less intensive intervention (Rogers & Vismara, 2008; Virués-Ortega, 2010). For these reasons, we focus on this approach, while recognizing that other potentially useful approaches that have yet to be evaluated, and a few others that have, are also available.

The program includes many of the key elements of early intervention and is based on principles of applied behavior analysis, including the use of rewards and punishment, and shaping by successive approximation (Lovaas, 2003). Parents are taught to act as the primary therapists for their children, with direction and help from therapists who work with them in the home.

Early intervention is essential for children with autism spectrum disorders

The average age of children entering the program is 32 months.

In a landmark research investigation, children with ASD were assigned to one of three groups. Although this assignment was not carried out randomly, the groups were found to be comparable with respect to age, language, intellectual functioning, and other measures prior to intervention. The experimental group of 19 children received 40 hours per week of intensive intervention. Control group 1 consisted of 19 children who attended special education classes and received 10 hours per week of one-to-one instruction. Control group 2 consisted of 21 children from a larger study who also attended special education classes but did not receive one-to-one instruction.

For children in the experimental condition, the first year of the program emphasized reducing disruptive behaviors and teaching appropriate behaviors such as compliance, imitation, and appropriate toy play. The second year emphasized expressive and abstract language and interactive play. Children were also taught how to function in a preschool group and, if possible, were enrolled in regular education preschool. The third year of the program emphasized the appropriate expression of emotions, pre-academic tasks, assertiveness, and observational learning.

The first outcome data were obtained when the children were 7 years old. Remarkably, 47% of the children in the experimental group were found to be functioning educationally and intellectually at a normal level. They successfully completed a regular first-grade class without support, were recommended for promotion by their teachers to a regular second-grade class, and scored at or above average on standardized IQ tests. On average, IQ scores of these children increased by 37 points, from 70 to 107; overall, the experimental group children showed an increase in mean IQ from 53 to 83. Children in the two control conditions did not fare nearly as well, resulting in only 1 of 40 children placed in a regular first-grade class; overall, these children showed only minimal increases in IQ scores. The experimental group children were assessed again when their average age was 13 years, with similar results. The nine children who were placed in regular classrooms were virtually indistinguishable from same-age normal peers.

Nearly all children with ASD benefit from early intervention, but uncertainty remains as to (1) how much the rate of progress depends on the severity of the child's ASD, the child's IQ and language ability, and the area of functioning being targeted (i.e., cognitive performance, language skills, adaptive behavior), and (2) what the long-term outcomes will be (Institute of Education Sciences, 2010; Reichow & Wolery, 2009; Warren et al., 2011). Additional studies have supported the effectiveness of the ABA approach in comparisons with other treatments and when used in community settings (Rogers & Vismara, 2008; Magiati, Charman, & Howlin, 2007). Claims have been made that some children with ASD can achieve normal functioning if given intensive intervention before age 3. However, earlier reports of "recovery" have not been replicated, and the question of whether they can achieve full recovery is a matter of some debate (Gresham & MacMillan, 1997; Smith & Lovaas, 1997).

Medications

Many children with ASD receive psychotropic medication, most commonly antidepressants, stimulants, and tranquilizers/antipsychotics (Mandell et al., 2008). As with many of the other childhood disorders we have discussed, medication use for children with ASD has also increased, and many of these children receive multiple medications (Oswald & Sonenklar, 2007). Although certain medications may help in the alleviation of specific behavioral symptoms (Froehlich, 2011), their benefits are limited, variable from child to child, and do not alter the core deficits of children with ASD (Rutter, 2006b). Given the limited evidence of the effectiveness of medications, particularly for very young children, it is crucial that their risks, benefits, and costs be carefully evaluated (McPheeters et al., 2011).

SECTION SUMMARY

Treatment of ASD

- Treatments for ASD are directed at maximizing the child's potential and helping the child and family cope more effectively with the disorder.
- Treatments for ASD focus on the specific social, communication, cognitive, and behavioral deficits displayed by children with this disorder.
- The most effective treatments use highly structured skills-oriented strategies that are tailored to the individual child and provide education and supportive counseling for the family.
- Nearly all children with ASD benefit from early intervention; however, controlled studies are needed to evaluate long-term outcomes.
- Medications may be of help in alleviating some symptoms. However, their benefits are limited, variable from child to child, and do not change the core deficits of children with ASD.

© Paul Doyle/Alamy

A teenage boy with mild autism and his parents: Active family involvement is a key ingredient for successful treatment outcomes

Other Pervasive Developmental Disorders (PDD)

In addition to autistic disorder, DSM-IV-TR specifies four other PDDs. As we have noted, two of these, Asperger's disorder and PDD-NOS, are commonly included with autistic disorder under the ASD label that we have been using. Although all PDDs have some clinical features in common, how they are related is not yet known. We briefly describe each of the other PDDs below.

Asperger's Disorder (AD)

Asperger's disorder (AD) is characterized by major difficulties in social interaction and unusual patterns of interest and behavior in children with relatively intact cognitive and communication skills (Klin, Volkmar, & Sparrow, 2000). They display the same social impairments and the restricted, stereotyped interests as children with autism but not the same general delays in language, cognitive development, development of age-appropriate self-help skills, adaptive behavior (other than social interaction), or curiosity about the environment. Children with AD have a higher verbal mental age, less language delay, and greater interest in social contact than children with autism; however, for the most part few qualitative differences between the two groups have been found (Macintosh & Dissanayake, 2004).

Generally, individuals with AD tend to be egocentric, socially inept, and preoccupied with abstract, narrow interests that cause them to appear eccentric. Their preoccupations may include topics such as the weather, facts about TV stations, or maps, which are learned in rote fashion and reflect poor understanding. Other common clinical features of AD include clumsy and ill-coordinated movements and an odd posture. These youngsters lack empathy, engage in inappropriate, one-sided social interaction, show little ability to form friendships, and are socially isolated. They display poor nonverbal communication, pedantic and flat speech, and may ramble on about topics that have little interest to anyone but themselves. Older children and adults with AD display marked difficulties with conversational skills and other pragmatic abilities, even when other aspects of language are intact (Volkmar et al., 1996). Also common in children and adults with AD are anxiety disorders, particularly social phobias and obsessive–compulsive symptoms (Kuusikko et al., 2008; Soderstrom, Rastam, & Gillberg, 2002). Sleep difficulties are also quite frequent in children with AD, particularly short sleep duration and sleep onset problems (Paavonen et al., 2008).

Our knowledge of AD is limited but increasing (Gillberg, 2002). Boys are more likely affected than girls, although the precise ratio of boys to girls is unknown. We also know little about the possible genetic links that increase the likelihood of finding similar conditions in other family members, which may be stronger for AD than for autism (Volkmar, Klin, & Pauls, 1998). The higher intellectual functioning in children with AD suggests a better long-term outcome than is typically seen in autism. One study found that 27% of those with AD had good adult outcomes, and 26% had restricted or poor outcomes—with a very restricted life, no occupation, and no friends. Adult outcomes for those with autism were significantly worse with the vast majority (76%) having poor or very poor outcomes (Cederlund, Hagberg, Billstedt, Gillberg, & Gillberg, 2008).

Findings for Asperger's disorder suggest that brain abnormalities in the cerebellum and limbic system are similar to those for autism, but less severe (Bauman, 1996; Stanley-Cary, Rinehart, Tonge, White, & Fielding, 2011). This selective involvement may underlie the prominent social and pragmatic language difficulties of individuals with AD, despite their strong cognitive skills. Some findings suggest that the neurobiology of the two disorders may be partially distinct (McAlonan et al., 2008). However, findings in this area are inconsistent with other studies reporting no differences (Via, Radua, Cardoner, Happé, & Mataix-Cols, 2011).

Is AD a separate disorder or is it simply a variant of autism occurring in higher-functioning individuals? The two groups may show distinct patterns of social impairment, with those with AD being rated mostly as "socially active but odd," and those with autism rated mostly as "aloof and passive" (Ghaziuddin, 2008). Nevertheless, the bulk of evidence would indicate that AD is a variant of autism and not a separate disorder (Frith, 2004). Most research suggests that individuals with AD and those with high functioning autism are more alike than different and become more so with age (Kamp-Becker et al., 2010; Via et al., 2011; Witwer & Lecavalier, 2008).

Pervasive Developmental Disorder, Not Otherwise Specified (PDD-NOS)

Pervasive Developmental Disorder, Not Otherwise Specified (PDD-NOS) describes children who display the social, communication, and behavioral impairments associated with PDD but do not meet criteria for other PDDs, schizophrenia, or other disorders (Volkmar, Shaffer, & First, 2000). PDD-NOS might better be called *atypical autism*, since the category is often used to diagnose children who fail to meet criteria for autistic disorder because of their late age of onset, atypical symptoms, subthreshold symptoms, or a combination of these factors. PDD-NOS is the most frequently diagnosed disorder on the autism spectrum, suggesting that this category as currently defined in DSM may be too broad (Volkmar et al., 2000).

Childhood Disintegrative Disorder

Childhood disintegrative disorder describes children who evidence prior to age 10 a significant loss of previously acquired skills. This regression follows a period of apparently normal development in verbal and nonverbal communication, social relationships, play, and adaptive behavior for the first 2 years of life. Children with childhood disintegrative disorder show losses in at least two of the following areas: expressive or receptive language, social skills or adaptive behavior, bowel or bladder control, play, or motor skills (Mouridsen, 2003). In addition, autism-like abnormalities in social interaction, communication, and restricted, repetitive, and stereotyped behaviors are also present (see Table 10.1).

Childhood disintegrative disorder is a very rare condition, mostly affecting boys, with a prevalence rate of about 1 in 50,000 children (Fombonne, Simmons, Ford, Meltzer, & Goodman, 2003). For this diagnosis to be made, the disturbances cannot be better accounted for by another specific PDD or by schizophrenia. The symptoms, degree of impairment, and outcomes for those with childhood disintegrative disorder appear similar to those for most children with ASD, with the exception of age of onset and a period of normal development, typically for the first 2 to 4 years of life (Hendry, 2000; Malhotra & Gupta, 1999). After the loss of previously acquired skills and symptom onset, this disorder presents very much like ASD (Palomo et al., 2008).

Rett's Disorder

Rett's disorder is a severe and disabling neurological developmental disorder that predominantly affects females (Matsuishi, Yamashita, Takahashi, & Nagamitsu, 2011). The disorder was discovered by Andreas Rett (1966) in his clinic in Vienna, Austria, when he observed two girls in his waiting room making identical stereotyped hand-washing movements. Only female cases have been reported to date, although variants of the disorder have been reported in a few males (Leonard et al., 2001). After examining these girls, Rett noted a remarkably similar pattern of early development and symptoms which now constitute the diagnostic criteria for Rett's disorder (see Table 10.2).

In effect, the girl's mental and social development regresses—she no longer responds to her parents and withdraws from any social contact (although often social interaction develops later). If she has been talking, she stops; she cannot control her feet; she wrings her hands. Rett's disorder is rare, affecting about 1 in 10,000 to 1 in 22,000 females (Ghidoni, 2007). It is a severe neurodevelopmental disorder caused by specific X-linked gene mutations (MECP2 gene) found in up to 95% of those affected (Marchetto et al., 2010). These mutations are usually lethal to the male fetus; therefore, Rett's occurs almost exclusively in females (Ghidoni, 2007). The most

TABLE 10.2 | Diagnostic Criteria for Rett's Disorder

DSM-IV-TR

A. All of the following:
   (1) apparently normal prenatal and perinatal development
   (2) apparently normal psychomotor development through the first 5 months after birth
   (3) normal head circumference at birth

B. Onset of all of the following after the period of normal development:
   (1) Deceleration of head growth between ages 5 and 48 months
   (2) Loss of previously acquired purposeful hand skills between ages 5 and 30 months with the subsequent development of stereotyped hand movements (e.g., hand-wringing or hand washing)
   (3) Loss of social engagement early in the course (although often social interaction develops later)
   (4) Appearance of poorly coordinated gait or trunk movements
   (5) Severely impaired expressive and receptive language development with severe psychomotor retardation

Source: Reprinted with permission from the Diagnostic and Statistical Manual of Mental Disorders, Fourth Edition, Text Revision, (Copyright © 2000). American Psychiatric Association.

dramatic effects of these mutations occur between 8 and 18 months, but more subtle effects may occur earlier in development than previously thought and are present at birth (Huppke, Held, Laccone, & Hanefeld, 2003). Although the presentation of Rett's disorder can vary, ranging from extremely severe with almost no development to mild mental handicap, most of those affected experience a variety of serious problems, including severe or profound intellectual disability, epileptic seizures, motor handicaps, and difficulties with communication (Hagberg, 1995; Huppke et al., 2003). *Apraxia*, the inability to execute desired movements, is common in girls with Rett's; 25% of the girls may never walk, and about 50% of those who do walk will lose the ability. Most girls with Rett's disorder are severely impaired and are likely to need assistance with all activities of daily living, including feeding, dressing, and toileting. The inclusion of childhood disintegrative disorder and Rett's disorder with the other PDDs has been questioned, because the former are neurodegenerative diseases with seemingly different causes and courses than autistic disorder, Asperger's disorder, and PDD-NOS (Malhotra & Gupta, 2002).

In concluding our discussion of the PDDs, we note that distinctions among the different PDDs have been found to be inconsistent over time, variable across diagnostic settings, and often associated with severity, language level, or intellectual ability rather than the features of the disorder per se. For these reasons, a proposed change for DSM-5 is to create a single overarching diagnostic category of ASD that includes autistic disorder, Asperger's disorder, childhood disintegrative disorder, and PDD-NOS. The ASD diagnosis would be adapted to the child's clinical presentation by including specifiers (e.g., severity, verbal ability) and associated features (e.g., genetic disorders, epilepsy, intellectual disability) (American Psychiatric Association, 2010). If this proposal is approved, the single ASD category would replace the current DSM-IV-TR PDD designation and its subtypes. There is some consensus that a single spectrum disorder better represents the current state of knowledge about pathology and clinical presentation, although concerns have been raised about dropping the subtypes (Wing, Gould, & Gillberg, 2011). Since children with Rett's disorder often have symptoms of autism for only a brief period during early childhood, after which social interaction develops, its inclusion in the autism spectrum may not be appropriate for most individuals. Thus, it has been recommended that Rett's disorder not be included in the DSM-5 ASD category. Whatever form DSM-5 takes, the term Autism Spectrum Disorders (ASD), as described at the outset of this chapter to include autistic disorder, Asperger's disorder, and PDD-NOS, is now commonly used in research and clinical practice.

SECTION SUMMARY

Other Pervasive Developmental Disorders (PDD)

- Asperger's disorder is characterized by major difficulties in social interaction and by unusual patterns of interest and behavior in children with relatively intact cognitive and communication skills.
- Children with pervasive developmental disorder, not otherwise specified (PDD-NOS) display the social, communication, and behavioral impairments associated with PDD but do not meet criteria for other PDDs, schizophrenia, or other disorders.
- Children with childhood disintegrative disorder show a significant loss of previously acquired language, social skills, and adaptive behavior prior to age 10 that follows a period of apparently normal development.
- Rett's Disorder is a severe neurological developmental disorder in girls, the result of a specific gene mutation.
- A proposed change for DSM-5 is to create a single ASD category that includes autistic disorder, Asperger's disorder, childhood disintegrative disorder, and PDD-NOS (but not Rett's disorder). Specifiers (e.g., severity, verbal ability) and associated features (e.g., genetic disorders, epilepsy, intellectual disability) would be used to describe the child's clinical presentation.

Childhood-Onset Schizophrenia (COS)

I have a special power in my nose and I can control what's on TV and what people say or do.

—From "Schizophrenia: Hidden Torment," by M. Nichols, *Maclean's*, January 30, 1995

This statement by a young girl with schizophrenia highlights the seriousness of this disorder. **Schizophrenia** is a neurodevelopmental disorder of the brain that is expressed in abnormal mental functions and disturbed behavior (White & Hilgetag, 2011). It is characterized by severe psychotic symptoms, including: bizarre delusions (false beliefs), hallucinations (false perceptions), thought disturbances, grossly disorganized behavior or catatonic behavior (motor dysfunctions ranging from wild agitation to immobility), extremely inappropriate or flat affect, and significant deterioration or impairment in functioning (McDonnell & McClellan, 2007).

The term *childhood schizophrenia* was previously applied to a highly diverse mix of children with little in common other than their experience of a profound and chronic disturbance during early childhood (Rutter, 1972). The label was often given to children who displayed borderline or no psychotic symptoms and who by today's standards would likely be diagnosed with ASD or another PDD. Clinically, several factors distinguish children with schizophrenia from children with ASD. They include: a later age of onset of their problem, less intellectual impairment, less severe social and language deficits, hallucinations and delusions as the child gets older, and periods of remission and relapse (J. R. Asarnow & Asarnow, 2003).

Earlier approaches to diagnosis attempted to construct a category for childhood schizophrenia distinct from the category of schizophrenia in adults. However, current thinking is that the criteria used to diagnose schizophrenia in adults can also be used to diagnose this disorder in children (Asarnow, Tompson, & McGrath, 2004). Early- or **childhood-onset schizophrenia (COS)** is a progressive neurodevelopmental disorder (Rapoport & Gogtay, 2011). Rather than being a distinct form of schizophrenia, COS is a rare and possibly more severe form of schizophrenia that has an onset prior to age 18 and worse long-term outcomes (Kyriakopoulos & Frangou, 2007; Remschmidt et al., 2007).

In the initial stages of COS, the afflicted youngster may have difficulty concentrating, sleeping, or doing schoolwork, and may start to avoid friends. As the illness progresses, she or he may begin to speak incoherently and see or hear things that no one else does. Periods of improvement may be followed by terrifying relapses that are characterized by disordered thinking, in which the youngster leaps illogically from one idea to another. The youngster may experience hallucinations, paranoia, and delusions. During their psychotic phases, youngsters with schizophrenia may be convinced that they have godlike powers or that people are spying on them. When in the grip of a psychosis, they may behave unpredictably and may become violent and suicidal.

Several of the clinical features of COS are illustrated in the case of Mary, a girl who first began to display symptoms of the disorder when she was about 10 years old.

MARY

Depressed, Disorderly, Doomed

Mary had always been a very shy child. At times she would become mute, she had severe difficulty making friends, was frequently oppositional, and occasionally wet the bed. By age 10, Mary had problems in school in addition to her continuing social isolation. She became depressed, felt that the devil was trying to make her do bad things, believed that her teacher was trying to hurt her, and became preoccupied with germs. Her behavior became increasingly disorganized; she talked of killing herself, appeared disheveled, and ran in front of a moving car in an apparent suicide attempt.

This episode precipitated an inpatient psychiatric evaluation, where Mary continued to show bizarre behavior. She lapsed into periods of intense anxiety and had one episode of uncontrolled screaming. At times she would stare blankly into space and was frequently mute. Although Mary's functioning improved during hospitalization and she returned to her family, throughout her childhood and adolescence she was tormented by fears, hallucinations, the belief that others were out to get her, and occasional bouts of depression, often accompanied by suicide attempts. She continued to be socially isolated and withdrawn and to perform poorly at school. At age 17, after several brief inpatient hospitalizations, Mary was admitted to a state hospital where she remained until the age of 19. During this period her affect was increasingly flat, and her psychotic symptoms persisted. One week after discharge from the hospital, Mary went into her room, locked the door, and overdosed on her medications. She was found dead the next morning. (Based on J. R. Asarnow & Asarnow, 2003)

Mary's tragic story illustrates several key features of COS.

- Although most cases have their onset during late adolescence or early adulthood, schizophrenia does occur during childhood (Nicolson & Rapoport, 1999).
- COS has a gradual rather than sudden onset in childhood, with the child displaying a wide range of impairments that precede his or her psychotic symptoms (Nicolson et al., 2000).
- When the disorder is present in childhood, the symptoms likely will persist into adolescence and adulthood.
- COS has a profound negative impact on the child's developing social and academic competence.

Mary's futile 10-year struggle with schizophrenia underscores the tremendous pain and personal suffering experienced by youngsters with this illness.

DSM-IV-TR: Defining Features of Schizophrenia

DSM-IV-TR criteria for schizophrenia are presented in Table 10.3. In addition to the presence of hallmark symptoms such as delusions, hallucinations, grossly disorganized speech and behavior, and negative symptoms such as flat affect, continuous signs of

TABLE 10.3 | **Diagnostic Criteria for Schizophrenia**

DSM-IV-TR

A. Characteristic symptoms: At least two or more of the following symptoms are present for a significant portion of time during a 1-month period.

(1) Delusions

(2) Hallucinations

(3) Disorganized speech (e.g., frequent derailment or incoherence)

(4) Grossly disorganized or catatonic behavior

(5) Negative symptoms (e.g., affective flattening, alogia, or avolition)

Note: Only one Criterion A symptom is required if delusions are bizarre or hallucinations consist of a voice keeping up a running commentary on the person's behavior or thoughts, or two or more voices conversing with each other.

B. *Social/occupational dysfunction:* For a significant portion of the time since the onset of the disturbance, one or more major areas of functioning such as work, interpersonal relations, or self-care are markedly below the level achieved prior to the onset (or when the onset is in childhood or adolescence, failure to achieve expected level of interpersonal, academic, or occupational achievement).

C. *Duration:* Continuous signs of the disturbance persist for at least 6 months. This 6-month period must include at least 1 month of symptoms (or less if successfully treated) that meet Criterion A (i.e., active-phase symptoms) and may include periods of prodromal or residual symptoms. During these prodromal or residual periods, the signs of the disturbance may be manifested by only negative symptoms or two or more symptoms listed in Criterion A present in an attenuated form (e.g., odd beliefs, unusual perceptual experience).

D. *Schizoaffective and Mood Disorder exclusion:* Schizoaffective Disorder and Mood Disorder With Psychotic Features have been ruled out because either (1) no Major Depressive, Manic, or Mixed Episodes have occurred concurrently with the active-phase symptoms; or (2) if mood episodes have occurred during active-phase symptoms, their total duration has been brief relative to the duration of the active and residual periods.

E. *Substance/general medical condition exclusion:* The disturbance is not due to the direct physiological effects of a substance (e.g., a drug of abuse, a medication) or a general medical condition.

F. *Relationship to a Pervasive Developmental Disorder:* If there is a history of Autistic Disorder or another Pervasive Developmental Disorder, the additional diagnosis of Schizophrenia is made only if prominent delusions or hallucinations are also present for at least a month (or less if successfully treated).

Classification of longitudinal course (can be applied only after at least 1 year has elapsed since the initial onset of active-phase symptoms):

Episodic With Interepisode Residual Symptoms (episodes are defined by the reemergence of prominent psychotic symptoms); *also specify if:* **With Prominent Negative Symptoms**

Episodic With No Interepisode Residual Symptoms

Continuous (prominent psychotic symptoms are present throughout the period of observation); *also specify if:* **With Prominent Negative Symptoms**

Single Episode In Partial Remission; *also speficy if:* **With Prominent Negative Symptoms**

Other or Unspecified Pattern.

Source: Reprinted with permission from the Diagnostic and Statistical Manual of Mental Disorders, Fourth Edition, Text Revision, (Copyright © 2000). American Psychiatric Association.

disturbance must persist for at least 6 months. In addition, the individual must show a significant decrement in one or more areas of functioning or, in the case of children and adolescents, a failure to achieve expected levels of interpersonal, academic, or occupational achievement.

The use of the same diagnostic criteria for children and adults facilitates comparisons between cases of childhood-onset and adult-onset schizophrenia and the identification of continuities in the disorder during the course of development. However, schizophrenia may be expressed differently at different ages. For example, hallucinations, delusions, and formal thought disturbances are extremely rare and difficult to diagnose before the age of 7; when they do occur, they may be less complex and reflect childhood themes (Caplan, 1994). A failure to adjust diagnostic criteria for developmental changes, such as social withdrawal or peer problems, may overlook children who show early signs of schizophrenia but may not develop the full-blown adult type until a later age (McClellan, Breiger, McCurry, & Hlastala, 2003).

Other developmental considerations may also come into play in making a diagnosis. For example, it is sometimes difficult to distinguish between pathological symptoms, such as delusions, and the rich imaginative fantasies typical of many young children. Also, because cognitive and language processes are developing during childhood, it is extremely difficult to diagnose the symptom of disorganized speech (e.g., switching topics mid-sentence, incoherent or tangential speech). One difference between children and adults with schizophrenia is that young children may not experience their psychotic symptoms as distressing or disorganizing. Thus, when psychotic symptoms appear early in development, children may have difficulty distinguishing them from normal experience (Russell, 1994).

Symptoms of schizophrenia fall into two categories. The first, positive symptoms (also called psychotic or active symptoms), involve excesses or disturbances in normal functioning such as delusions or hallucinations. The second, negative symptoms, involve a loss in normal functioning, for example, disturbances in sleep patterns.

Positive Symptoms

Youngsters with COS may display psychotic symptoms such as delusions and hallucinations (Polanczyk et al., 2010). **Delusions** are disturbances in thinking involving disordered thought content and strong beliefs that are misrepresentations of reality. **Hallucinations** are disturbances in perception in which things are seen, heard, or otherwise sensed even though they are not real or present. The most common presenting symptom for children with schizophrenia is auditory hallucinations (e.g., hearing voices that other people cannot hear), which occur in about 80% of cases with an onset prior to age 11. About 40% to 60% of children with schizophrenia also experience visual hallucinations, delusions, and thought disorder (Caplan, Guthrie, Tang, Komo, & Asarnow, 2000). Examples of psychotic symptoms reported by children with schizophrenia are presented in Box 10.4.

Negative Symptoms

Negative symptoms of schizophrenia may include a slowing of thinking, speech, and movement, and indifference to social contact. These symptoms generally reflect a loss of motivation, and can range from minor to severe. Although these symptoms are much less dramatic than the positive symptoms, they can be very persistent and difficult to treat. They also may be difficult to recognize in young people, because some of these changes are behaviors that might be expected to occur to some degree during adolescence.

BOX 10.4 A CLOSER LOOK

Psychotic Symptoms in Children with Schizophrenia

Hallucinations

An 8-year-old boy stated: "I once heard a noise coming from the south and the east; one told me to jump off the roof and one told me to smash my mom."

A 12-year-old boy saw a ghost (man) with a red, burned, scarred, and cut face on multiple occasions and in different locations. He had been seeing this since age 5.

Delusions

A 9-year-old boy was convinced he was a dog (his parents were German Shepherds) and was growing fur, and on one occasion, refused to leave a veterinarian's office unless he received a shot.

An 11-year-old boy described "waste" produced when the good and bad voices fought with each other; the "waste" came out of his feet when he swam in chlorinated pools.

Thought Disorder

"I used to have a Mexican dream. I was watching TV in the family room. I disappeared outside of this world and then I was in a closet. Sounds like a vacuum dream. It's a Mexican dream. When I was close to that dream earth, I was turning upside down. I don't like to turn upside down. Sometimes I have Mexican dreams and vacuum dreams. It's real hard to scream in dreams."

Source: From A. T. Russell, The Clinical Presentation of Childhood-Onset-Schizophrenia, *Schizophrenia Bulletin*, 1994, volume, 20, 631–646. Copyright © 1994, by permission of Oxford University Press.

SECTION SUMMARY

DSM-IV-TR: Defining Features of Schizophrenia

- Schizophrenia is a neurodevelopmental disorder of the brain that is expressed in abnormal mental functions and disturbed behavior.
- Unlike children with ASD, children with COS have a later age of onset, show less intellectual impairment, display less severe social and language deficits, develop hallucinations and delusions as they get older, and experience periods of remission and relapse.
- COS is a more severe form of adult-onset schizophrenia rather than a different disorder.
- Youngsters with COS may display psychotic symptoms such as delusions and hallucinations, and negative symptoms such as a slowing of thinking, speech, and movement, and indifference to social contact.

Precursors and Comorbidities

For a majority of children with COS, the onset of their disorder is gradual rather than sudden, with nearly 95% showing a clear history of behavioral, social, and psychiatric disturbances before the onset of psychosis (Russell, 1994). For example, Mary was oppositional and had difficulty making friends well before she began to display her psychotic symptoms. Developmental precursors for the onset of schizophrenia include speech and language problems, static cognitive impairments and maturational delays, problems in motor development, movement abnormalities (e.g., facial tics, grimaces), higher levels of social impairment, unusual thought content, suspicion/paranoia, substance abuse, and a genetic risk for schizophrenia with a recent deterioration in functioning (Cannon et al., 2008; Mittal & Walker, 2007; Reichenberg et al., 2010).

Children with COS often display other symptoms and disorders, such as anxiety and depression, ADHD, conduct problems, movement abnormalities, and suicidal tendencies. About 70% of the children meet criteria for another diagnosis, most commonly mood disorder or oppositional/conduct disorder (Russell, Bott, & Sammons, 1989). Returning to the question of whether ASD and COS are related, one study found that COS is preceded by ASD in 30%–50% of cases (Rapoport, Chavez, Greenstein, Addington, & Gogtay, 2009). Additionally, epidemiological and family studies have found associations between the two disorders, and both show theory of mind deficits and mirror neuron (neurons that fire both when an individual acts and when they see the same action performed by another) impairments. Both disorders also show signs of accelerated brain development at ages near disorder onset, and brain imaging studies also suggest similar abnormalities in neural connectivity. Similar risk genes and rare small chromosomal variants have also been found (King & Lord, 2011; Rapoport et al., 2009). Taken together, these findings suggest that the possibility that COS and ASD are linked may need to be re-visited.

Prevalence

Schizophrenia is extremely rare in children under 12 years of age. It begins to increase dramatically in frequency in adolescence, with a modal onset around 22 years of age (Abel, Drake, & Goldstein, 2010):

- Estimates of COS indicate a prevalence rate of less than 1 child in 10,000 (J. R. Asarnow & Asarnow, 2003).
- These estimates suggest that schizophrenia occurs at least 100 times more often in adults than in children (Bromet & Fennig, 1999).
- COS has an earlier age of onset (by 2–4 years) in boys (Häfner et al., 1998), and an onset prior to 12 years of age is about twice as common in boys as in girls. However, this sex difference disappears in adolescence (Frazier et al., 1997).

The reasons that more males have COS are not known; a greater general biological vulnerability of males for neurodevelopmental disorders and different causes have both been suggested as possibilities. For adults, the rates of schizophrenia are higher in lower socioeconomic groups. However, there is little information regarding the relationship between social class and COS. In a related vein, the incidence rates and pattern of symptoms in adults with schizophrenia are similar across cultures, countries, and racial groups (Myers, 2011), but little information regarding cross-cultural patterns is available for COS (J. R. Asarnow & Asarnow, 1994).

Section Summary

Precursors and Comorbidities

- For a majority of children with COS, the onset of their disorder is gradual rather than sudden, with nearly 95% showing a clear history of behavioral, social, and psychiatric disturbances before the onset of psychosis.
- Developmental precursors for the onset of schizophrenia include speech and language problems, cognitive impairments and delays, problems in motor development, social impairment, unusual thought content, substance abuse, and a genetic risk for schizophrenia with a recent deterioration in functioning.
- Children with COS often display other symptoms and disorders, such as anxiety and depression, ADHD, conduct problems, movement abnormalities, and suicidal tendencies.
- Recent findings suggest that the possibility that COS and ASD are linked may need to be re-visited.

Prevalence

- Schizophrenia is extremely rare in children under 12 years of age, occurring much less often than in adolescents and adults.
- COS has an earlier age of onset in boys, and an onset prior to 12 years of age is about twice as common in boys as in girls. This sex difference disappears in adolescence.

Causes and Treatment of COS

We are just beginning to understand the possible causes of COS and ways of helping these children and their families. In the following sections, we discuss preliminary work into biological and family factors that have been implicated thus far as well as recent treatments for this disorder.

Causes

A key issue in understanding schizophrenia is why a genetically based, neurobiological disorder is not expressed clinically until 15 to 20 years after birth, at which time it progressively disables its victims. In understanding this issue, investigators have proposed a **neurodevelopmental model of schizophrenia** in which a genetic vulnerability and early neurodevelopmental insults result in impaired connections between many brain regions including the cerebral cortex, white matter, hippocampus, cerebellum, and parts of the limbic system (Rapoport, Addington, & Frangou, 2005; Walker, Shapiro, Esterberg, & Trotman, 2010). This defective neural circuitry is then vulnerable to dysfunction until revealed by developmental processes and events during puberty (e.g., synaptic and hormonal changes) and by exposure to stress (Lewis & Lieberman, 2000). The neurodevelopmental model provides a useful framework for understanding how a condition like schizophrenia that first presents as a disorder in adolescence or early adulthood can be partly understood as a function of events occurring much earlier in development (Owen, O'Donovan, Thapar, & Craddock, 2011). A model of early-occurring neural pathology in schizophrenia is consistent with the findings that infants and children who later develop COS often display developmental impairments well before the onset of their psychotic symptoms, including deficits in motor, language, cognitive, and social functioning (Marenco & Weinberger, 2000).

Biological Factors

Evidence suggests a strong genetic contribution to schizophrenia in childhood, with heritability estimates around 80% (R. F. Asarnow et al., 2001; Gejman, Sanders, & Duan, 2010). For example, the rate of schizophrenia among relatives of children with COS is about double the rate for family members of adults with schizophrenia. One landmark twin study found concordance rates of 88% and 23%, respectively, for identical versus fraternal twins with schizophrenia with an onset prior to 15 years of age (Kallman & Roth, 1956). Molecular genetic studies have identified a number of potential susceptibility genes for COS, many of which have been previously linked with schizophrenia in adults (Kyriakopoulos & Frangou, 2007). Several common gene variants with small effects have been implicated along with some extremely rare gene variants with potentially large effects (Pogue-Geile & Yokley, 2010). However, specific gene findings account for a very small amount of the variance, and most of the genetic influences on susceptibility to schizophrenia have yet to be identified. Given the large number of weak genetic (and environmental) risk factors, it is likely that COS is best represented by a continuum of risk involving many G × E interactions (Rapoport & Gogtay, 2011). For example, a recent study found a 9-fold increased risk of schizophrenia in cases where the presence of a parent with psychosis was combined with maternal depression during pregnancy (Maki et al., 2010).

The occurrence of central nervous system dysfunction among individuals with schizophrenia, and the dramatic improvements associated with medication, suggest that schizophrenia is a disorder of the brain (Lewis & Lieberman, 2000). Brain scan studies of youngsters with COS have found enlarged ventricles and a shrinkage in brain gray matter that spreads across the brain during adolescence, beginning in the rear brain structures involved in attention and perception, and spreading to the frontal parts of the brain involved in executive functions such as planning and organization (Vidal et al., 2006). The progressive loss of gray matter was accompanied by delayed/disrupted white matter growth, hippocampal volume loss, and a progressive decline in cerebellar volume. Interestingly, most of these changes were also found in the non-psychotic siblings of the children with COS. However, siblings showed later normalization of the earlier gray matter abnormalities, suggesting the role of restorative/protective factors. In contrast, the static hippocampal volume loss across age in children with COS was not shared by their siblings, and thus appears to be specific to schizophrenia (Rapoport & Gogtay, 2011). A recent study found that atypical neural activity in a network of language-associated brain regions during discourse processing was associated with subsequent thought disorder severity and social outcome in youth at risk for psychosis (Sabb et al., 2010). Findings like this are important in identifying potential biomarkers for COS that may suggest strategies for intervention and prevention.

No single brain lesion has been identified in all cases of COS, and the lesions that have been found in some cases are not specific to schizophrenia (Kyriakopoulos & Frangou, 2007). Additionally, atypical developmental patterns of brain development over time are often more prominent than anatomic brain differences at any one time point (Rapoport & Gogtay, 2011). In general, brain research on COS points to a widespread developmental disruption of neural connectivity that likely involves susceptibility genes that impact on developmental processes involved in establishing connectivity within and between brain regions (Karlsgodt et al., 2008).

Environmental Factors

COS is a familial disorder, but the less than 100% concordance rates for identical twins suggest that nongenetic influences contribute to the likelihood for a child to develop schizophrenia. Nongenetic factors, including exposure to infectious, toxic, or traumatic insults, and stress during prenatal or postnatal development, may play a role in schizophrenia through their interaction with a genetic susceptibility for schizophrenia (Arseneault, Cannon, Fisher, Polanczyk, & Moffitt, 2011; Lahti et al., 2009; Rapoport et al., 2005). Several nongenetic factors occurring during pregnancy and birth are associated with an increased risk for later schizophrenia, including: maternal diabetes, low birth weight, older paternal age, winter birth, and prenatal maternal stress (King, St-Hilaire, & Heidkamp, 2010). Each of these factors alone is associated with a slight increase in risk, which multiplies when they are combined with each other and/or with other risk factors. In considering other nongenetic influences, the elevated likelihood of psychiatric illness in parents of children with schizophrenia will likely have a negative effect on parental role functioning.

Parents of children with schizophrenia score higher than parents of children with depression on **communication deviance**, which is a measure of interpersonal signs of attentional and thought disturbance. Children from families with high communication deviance display the most severe impairment and the poorest attentional functioning. These findings suggest that communication deviance may be associated with a severe form of schizophrenia, or that family interaction may worsen the severity of dysfunction (J. R. Asarnow, Goldstein, & Ben-Meir, 1988). Parents of children with schizophrenia are more likely to use harsh criticism of their children than are parents of depressed children or normal controls.

Support for the role of the family environment comes from studies showing that exposure to a poor family environment and certain patterns of communication may interact with a genetic risk for schizophrenia to further increase a child's risk for developing a schizophrenia-spectrum disorder. For example, in a longitudinal study of children of biological mothers with schizophrenia-spectrum disorders who were adopted at an early age, poor child-rearing environments and communication deviance of the adoptive parents predicted which adoptees developed a schizophrenia-spectrum disorder (Wahlberg, Wynne, Hakko, Laksy, & Moring, 2004; Wynne et al., 2006). Those children with a dysfunctional child-rearing environment and adoptive parents who displayed high rates of communication deviance were significantly more likely to develop schizophrenia-spectrum disorder than those raised in more positive family environments. For children with a low genetic risk for schizophrenia, a poor family environment and deviant parent communication patterns did not increase the risk for the later development of a schizophrenia-spectrum disorder.

Family findings highlight the stress, distress, and personal tragedy often experienced by families of children with schizophrenia (J. R. Asarnow & Asarnow, 2003). In the words of June Beeby, the mother of 17-year-old Matthew, who was diagnosed with schizophrenia and believed that God wanted his mother and his sister to die:

> "It's quite horrendous. First of all, you've got somebody that you love, a child that you've raised. And then suddenly, the child becomes a crazy person" (M. Nichols, 1995, p. 70). On a dark and cold winter day, June Beeby arrived home to find her son dead in a pool of blood. "He had taken two ordinary dinner knives . . . and plunged them into his eyes until they pierced his brain" (p. 70). In a diary entry that he had made 2 years before he took his life, Matthew had described an encounter with God: "He used his power and he controlled my brain for nine months. . . . God wanted me to feel that I would die, in order for individuals to live forever in heaven" (p. 74).

Treatment

As a parent you feel you have a tremendous responsibility to keep a son or daughter safe. . . . But when your child is schizophrenic you can't do that, because the person doesn't want help.

—From "Schizophrenia: Hidden Torment," by M. Nichols, *Maclean's*, January 30, 1995

COS is a chronic disorder with a poor long-term outcome for most sufferers, although some youngsters may display more positive outcomes (Röpcke & Eggers, 2005). In either case, outcomes for most afflicted individuals are vastly improved over what they once were. Current treatments emphasize the use of antipsychotic medications (e.g., clozapine, risperidone) combined with psychotherapeutic and social and educational support programs (Armenteros & Davies, 2006; Shaw & Rapoport, 2006; AACAP, 2001). Although we know far less about the use of antipsychotic medications with children than with adults, they are widely used to treat children with schizophrenia, and a majority of youngsters with schizophrenia will spend much of their life on some medication (J. R. Asarnow et al., 2004; McClellan et al., 2007). Medications help control psychotic symptoms in children with schizophrenia by blocking dopamine transmission at the D2 dopamine receptor. However, adverse effects with antipsychotic treatment are prevalent and associated with reduced adherence to treatment. Depending on the type of medication, these side effects can be serious and may include increased levels of prolactin, motor dysfunction (e.g., tremor), weight gain, sedation, or dysregulation of glucose. Thus, it is extremely important that these side effects be carefully monitored and managed with changes in dose or type of medication as needed (Tiffin, 2007). There is also a need for psychosocial treatments, such as family intervention, social skills training, and cognitive behavior therapy (Addington, Piskulic, & Marshall, 2010). The need for educational support is also widely recognized in clinical practice (McDonnell & Dyck, 2004; Tiffin, 2007). Although findings from psychosocial treatments are promising, more controlled studies with children are needed.

SECTION SUMMARY

Causes and Treatment of COS

- Current views regarding the causes of COS are based on a neurodevelopmental model in which a genetic vulnerability and early neurodevelopmental insults result in impaired connections between many brain regions. This impaired neural circuitry may increase the child's vulnerability to stress.
- COS is a disorder that involves multiple genes and is associated with environmental and developmental vulnerability factors.
- Brain studies in COS suggest a shrinkage in brain gray matter that spreads across the brain during adolescence, beginning in the rear brain structures involved in attention and perception, and spreading to the frontal parts of the brain involved in executive functions such as planning and organization.
- Although medications may help control psychotic symptoms in children with schizophrenia, psychosocial treatments such as social skills training, family intervention, cognitive behavior therapy, and educational support are also needed.

Study Resources

SECTION SUMMARIES

KEY TERMS

COURSEMATE

Access an interactive eBook and chapter-specific interactive learning tools, including flashcards, quizzes, videos, and more in your Psychology CourseMate, accessed through CengageBrain.com.

Communication and Learning Disorders

> *If you can read this, thank a teacher.*
>
> —Anonymous

CHAPTER PREVIEW

Definitions and History

Language Development

Phonological Awareness

Communication Disorders

Expressive Language Disorder

Stuttering

Learning Disorders

Reading Disorder

Mathematics Disorder

Writing Disorder

EVERYONE HAS IMPORTANT NEEDS and ideas. Imagine not being able to get them across. Sights and sounds surround you, but you cannot focus your attention long enough to make sense of them. When you are shown how to read or add, you find that the letters and numbers look and sound too much alike. Although these difficulties vary from person to person, they are common daily experiences of many children and adolescents with communication and learning disorders. Everyday tasks can be confusing and frustrating, and sometimes result in a cycle of academic failure and lowered self-esteem.

JAMES

Smart But Can't Read

James, age 9, was a growing concern for his teacher: "James is obviously a very bright boy, and he wants to do well. I've noticed that he likes art, and is always wanting to draw. But he gets really upset when I ask him to do some work in class.

He looks like he dreads coming to school. And he complains that some words he tries to read don't make sense to him. I'm worried that his increasing frustration is going to cause other problems in school or with friends. Sometimes he gets mad at something and he has trouble calming down. If he is trying to create something that doesn't turn out the way he envisioned it, he explodes and slams his fist against the wall."

What James's mother heard was all too familiar. She knew that her son would get involved in something only if he could do it his own way. Her mind wandered briefly to when he was a toddler and sometimes got so anxious and worried about something that he had trouble sleeping or felt sick. She shared with his teacher her frustration at trying to find out what the problem was: "Getting him to read at home is like pulling teeth. He won't read at all on his own because he knows he can't read many of the words." (Based on authors' case material)

FRANCINE

Shunned and Falling Behind

Francine, age 7, was entering a new school for the second time in 2 years. The first school was too challenging, and the other kids teased her because she "doesn't know what 2 plus 2 is." She is content to play for hours by herself and is not interested in the things that other kids her age are doing. "Most of the time," her mother explained, "Francine seems sad and in a bit of a fog." Although school performance was a major concern, her mother was also quite worried about Francine's lack of friends and the way other children treated her.

Her mother and father proudly shared their daughter's early childhood history and developmental milestones with me during our first interview. "Francine walked before she was a year old, and was a very talkative baby and toddler, who picked up new words quite quickly. She was a healthy and normal baby—we can't figure out why she seems so uninterested in school and other kids." They went on to explain: "When she entered preschool and kindergarten, she seemed uninterested in making friends. The other kids basically ignored her, even though she didn't do anything to bother them. My husband and I didn't think much of it at first. In fact, we bragged about how she took an early interest in reading and would spend a lot of her time alone with a book or magazine, even when she was 4 or 5, although she didn't usually understand what she read. But we grew more concerned around age 5 because she paid little attention to popular movies, toys, and things other kids her age played with. When she was a preschooler, we also noticed that she had trouble with numbers and understanding concepts like "more," "less," or "bigger." She knows what these words mean now, but she is still confused when we ask her to count something.

Yesterday I gave her her allowance and just for the heck of it, I used pennies, nickels, and dimes to see if she could add them up. No matter how hard we tried, she became confused, switching from one coin to the other, and she thought she had a bigger allowance if I stacked the pennies up! And if you ask her to arrange something, like setting the table for dinner, you never know what you'll end up with!" (Based on authors' case material)

Children with communication or learning disorders can learn, and they are as intelligent as anyone else. Their disorders usually affect only certain limited aspects of learning, and rarely are they severe enough to impair the pursuit of a normal life—but they can be very stressful. Consider the experiences of James and Francine: James and Francine have different learning problems. James's are with language and reading. His ability to distinguish the different sounds (phonemes) of language is underdeveloped, which is the primary reason for his poor word recognition and writing ability. Francine's problems are mostly with nonverbal learning, such as math. She can read quite well, but she has difficulty understanding some of the subtleties of others' facial expressions and gestures. She also confuses terms and instructions that describe numerical or spatial relationships, such as "larger than" or "sit beside the couch."

The field of learning and communication disorders, broadly referred to as "learning disabilities," has changed dramatically during the last 30 years. For many years, learning problems were attributed to poor motivation or poor instruction. Fortunately, breakthroughs in neuroimaging techniques led to increased recognition of differences in the neurological makeup and development of children with problems in language and related cognitive tasks. With recent advances in detection and intervention aimed at early language development, signs of communication problems are detected at an early age, and children are provided with alternative teaching methods that build on their developmental strengths.

In this chapter, we emphasize the relationship between language development and the subsequent appearance of a learning problem once the child enters school. We put these problems in a developmental context by showing how communication disorders (diagnosed primarily in early childhood) and learning disorders (identified most often during early school years) have interconnected features and underlying causes. As a case in point, preschoolers with communication disorders are more likely to develop a learning disability by middle childhood or early adolescence (Johnson & Beitchman, 2006).

Slowly but surely, most children learn the letters of the alphabet and how to use them to read and write words. For children with certain learning disabilities, however, the shapes and sounds of different letters continue to be confusing.

Definitions and History

Learning disability is the general term for learning problems that occur in the absence of other obvious conditions, such as mental retardation or brain damage. The term has been replaced in the DSM-IV-TR by two more specific terms, *learning disorders* and *communication disorders*, but the common use of the term requires that it be clarified and defined.

A learning disability affects how individuals with normal or above-average intelligence take in, retain, or express information. Incoming or outgoing information can be scrambled as it passes between the senses and the brain. Unlike most physical disabilities, a learning disability is a hidden handicap and is often undetected in young children (Lyon, Fletcher, Fuchs, & Chhabra, 2006). Thus, children with learning disabilities often must cope not only with their limitations in reading, writing, or math but also with the frustration of convincing others that their problems are as legitimate as visible disabilities.

Learning difficulties often show up in schoolwork and can impede a child's ability to learn to read or write or do math, but they also can affect many other parts of life, including work, daily routines, family life, and friendships. Some learning problems are specific and affect a narrow range of ability, whereas others may affect many different tasks and social situations. Each type of learning disability, whether it is related to reading, writing, math, or language, is characterized by distinct definitions and diagnoses. Knowledge of communication and learning disorders is growing rapidly as a result of increased scientific interest and research support. We now recognize that a learning disability, though challenging, does not have to be a handicap. Many well-known people with learning problems used their talents in exceptional ways, including Albert Einstein, Winston Churchill, and Thomas Edison.

For all intents and purposes, the terms *learning disorders* and *learning disabilities* are used interchangeably. Simply stated, the main characteristic shared by all children with learning disabilities is not performing up to their expected level in school. Otherwise, symptoms vary tremendously (Rice, 2007). The recognition of learning disorders has brought needed attention to many children and adults who are unable to acquire academic skills at a normal rate.

Children with learning disabilities constitute the majority of children in North America who receive special education services (Gerenser & Forman, 2007). Yet, experts still struggle to adequately define learning disabilities because of their many forms and overlapping symptoms, which you will note in the following lengthy definition:

Learning disabilities is a general term that refers to significant problems in mastering one or more of the following skills: listening, speaking, reading, writing, reasoning, and mathematics. Learning disabilities do not include problems primarily attributed to visual, hearing, or motor handicaps; mental retardation; emotional disturbance; or environmental disadvantage. Emotional and social disturbances and other adaptive deficiencies may occur with learning problems, but they do not by themselves constitute a learning disability (Individuals with Disabilities Education Improvement Act [IDEA], 2004).

In Chapter 9, we describe intelligence as involving basic cognitive abilities that include problem solving,

Bettmann/Corbis

Few realize that Albert Einstein had early speech and language difficulties, given his monumental contributions to society

BOX 11.1 A CLOSER LOOK

Aspects of Multiple Intelligence

- *Linguistic*: A sensitivity to the meaning, function, and grammatical rules of words, as in writing an essay.
- *Musical*: A sensitivity and creativity in hearing and manipulating tones, rhythms, musical patterns, pitch, and timbre, as in composing a symphony.
- *Logical/mathematic*: The ability to solve problems and see abstract relationships, as in calculus or engineering.
- *Spatial*: A sensitivity to the perception, manipulation, and creation of different forms and contexts, as in painting.
- *Bodily/kinesthetic*: The ability to use the body and the relevant part of the brain to coordinate movements in special and highly coordinated ways, as in dance and athletics.
- *Intrapersonal*: The ability to recognize, define, and pursue inner feelings and thoughts, as in poetry and self-knowledge.
- *Interpersonal*: The ability to sense the moods, feelings, and actions of other people, as in teaching, parenting, and politics.

Source: Based on Gardner, 2006.

verbal skills, and mental reasoning. The term *multiple intelligence*, described in Box 11.1, implies there are diverse forms of intelligence, and suggests that each type is as important as the others but for different reasons. Broadening the concept of intelligence to include more than logical, mathematical, or language abilities helps focus attention on individual strengths. For example, we are all stronger in some areas of learning and performance than others (we enjoy writing and reading, but don't ask us to fix your car). Similarly, children with learning disorders, who have normal intelligence, show a pattern of relative strengths and weaknesses that can make some learning tasks much more difficult. This pattern is noteworthy mostly because it is so extreme and unexpected for a child who otherwise shows normal cognitive and physical development.

Communication disorders is a diagnostic term that refers to difficulty in

- producing speech sounds (phonological disorder),
- speech fluency (stuttering),
- using spoken language to communicate (expressive language disorder),
- understanding what other people say (mixed expressive—receptive language disorder)

These disorders are developmentally connected to the later onset of learning disorders.

Learning disorders is a diagnostic term that refers to specific problems in

- reading (often referred to as **dyslexia**, meaning difficulty in processing language)
- math
- writing ability

These disorders are determined by achievement test results that are substantially below what is expected for the child's age, schooling, and intellectual ability.

An unexpected pattern of strengths and weaknesses in learning was first noted and studied during the late 19th century by physicians who were treating patients with medical injuries (Hammill, 1993). Franz Joseph Gall, a pioneer of language disorders, was struck by what he observed among some of his brain-injured patients: They had lost the capacity to express their feelings and ideas clearly through speech, yet they did not seem to suffer any intellectual impairments. One of his patients could not speak, but had no problem writing his thoughts on paper. Because he knew that this patient had normal speech before the head injury, Gall reasoned that the problem must have resulted from brain damage that had disrupted the neurological processes related to speech. For the first time, scientists began to pinpoint areas in the brain that control the ability to express and receive language processes.

These early observations, based on known medical injuries, raised the possibility that people with learning disabilities differ from people with mental retardation in terms of relative strengths and deficits. People with learning disabilities have normal intellectual processes in most areas but are relatively weaker in others, which is known as having an **unexpected discrepancy** between measured ability and actual performance. This premise remains at the foundation of today's definition of learning disorders. However, debate now focuses on whether the discrepancy is necessary for distinguishing learning disabilities (Maehler & Schuchardt, 2011), a point we will return to later in the chapter.

The links between intellectual disability, organic brain damage, and learning problems fascinated scientists, who had a firmer understanding of brain—behavior relationships by the 1940s. During that time, the question still remained as to why some children who did not fit the definition of mental retardation based on IQ had significant problems in learning. Could mental retardation be restricted to certain intellectual abilities but not others? Were academic problems the same as those assessed by measures of general intelligence?

A. A. Strauss and H. Werner (1943) shed light on this issue by pointing out that children learn in individual ways, challenging the concept that learning is a relatively uniform, predictable process in children without intellectual disabilities. Three important concepts from this period continue to influence the field to this day (Lyon et al., 2003, 2006):

1. Children approach learning in different ways, so each child's individual learning style and uniqueness should be recognized and used to full advantage.
2. Educational methods should be tailored to an individual child's pattern of strengths and weaknesses; one method should not be imposed on everyone.
3. Children with learning problems might be helped by teaching methods that strengthen existing abilities rather than emphasize weak areas.

By the early 1960s, the modern learning disabilities movement had begun. Parents and educators were dissatisfied with the fact that children often had to be diagnosed with mental retardation to receive special education services. A category was needed to describe learning problems that could not be explained on the basis of mental retardation, lack of learning opportunities, psychopathology, or sensory deficits (Lyon et al., 2003).

Thus, the emerging concept of learning disabilities made intuitive sense to many who were familiar with the varied needs of children, and was welcomed as states and provinces began to support special education programs and services. The domination of physicians and psychologists in the field gave way to greater input from educators, parents, and clinicians. Teacher training expanded to include new ways to teach youngsters who could not respond to typical classroom methods. Professionals trained in speech and language pathology became an important part of school-based services.

As the focus of the learning disabilities movement shifted from the clinic to the classroom, parents and educators assumed a major role in programming and placement. They were encouraged by the fact that the term *learning disabled* did not stigmatize children, but rather brought them needed services (Hammill, 1993). The fact that these children had normal intelligence gave parents and teachers hope that difficulties in reading, writing, and math could be overcome if only the right set of instructional conditions and settings could be identified (Lyon et al., 2003). Thus, with the collaborative leadership of parents, educators, and specially trained professionals, the field of learning disabilities grew from its beginning in the 1960s to the major component of educational services it is today.

SECTION SUMMARY

Definitions and History

- *Learning disabilities* is a general term for communication and learning problems that occur in the absence of other obvious conditions such as mental retardation or brain damage.
- Children and adults with learning disabilities show specific deficits in using spoken or written language, often referred to as relative strengths and weaknesses.
- Parents and educators assumed a major role in bringing recognition and services to children with learning disabilities.

Language Development

From birth, infants selectively attend to parental speech sounds and soon learn to communicate with basic gestures and sounds of their own. Usually, by their first birthday they can recognize several words and use a few of their own to express their needs and emotions. Over the next 2 years, their language development proceeds at an exponential pace, and their ability to formulate complex ideas and express new concepts is a constant source of amazement and amusement for parents. Adults play an important role in encouraging language development by providing clear examples of language and enjoying the child's expressions.

Language consists of **phonemes**, which are the basic sounds (such as sharp *ba*'s and *da*'s and drawn-out *ee*'s and *ss*'s) that make up language. When a child

Monkey Business Images/Shutterstock.com

From an early age, children love to express themselves

hears a phoneme over and over, receptors in the ear stimulate the formation of dedicated connections to the brain's auditory cortex. A perceptual map forms that represents similarities among sounds and helps the infant learn to discriminate different phonemes. These maps form quickly; 6-month-old children of English-speaking parents already have auditory maps different from infants in non-English speaking homes, as measured by neuron activity in response to different sounds (Kuhl et al., 2006). By their first birthday, the maps are complete, and infants have less ability to discriminate sounds that are not important in their own language.

Rapid development of a perceptual map is why learning a second language after—rather than with—the first language is difficult; brain connections are already wired for English, and the remaining neurons are less able to form basic new connections for, say, Swedish. Once the basic circuitry is established, infants can turn sounds into words, and the more words they hear, the faster they learn language. The sounds of words serve to strengthen and expand neural connections that can then process more words. Similar cortical maps are formed for other highly refined skills, such as musical ability (Huss, Verney, Fosker, Mead, & Goswami, 2011). A young child who learns to play a musical instrument may strengthen the neural circuits that underlie not only music, but verbal memory as well (Ho, Cheung, & Chan, 2003).

Phonological Awareness

Not all children progress normally through the milestones of language development. Some are noticeably delayed, continuing to use gestures or sounds rather than speech. Others progress normally in some areas, such as following spoken directions and attending to commands, but have trouble finding the words to express themselves clearly.

Although the development of language is one of the best predictors of school performance and overall intelligence (Sattler, 2008), delays or differences in development are not a definitive sign of intellectual retardation or cognitive disorder. Rather, such deviations from normal may be just that—deviations—and may be accompanied by superior abilities in other areas of cognitive functioning. Albert Einstein, who is considered an intellectual genius, began speaking late and infrequently, causing his parents to worry that he was "subnormal." According to family members, when his father asked his son's headmaster what profession his son should adopt, the answer was simply, "It doesn't matter, he'll never make a success of anything" (R. W. Clark, 1971, p. 10).

Since language development is an indicator of general mental development, children who fail to develop language or who show severe delay in acquiring language are considered at risk of having a language-based learning disability. Albert Einstein notwithstanding, early language problems are considered highly predictive of subsequent communication and learning disorders (Heim & Benasich, 2006; Williams, 2010).

Phonology is the ability to learn and store phonemes as well as the rules for combining the sounds into meaningful units or words. Deficits in phonology are a chief reason that most children and adults with communication and learning disorders have problems in language-based activities such as learning to read and spell (Larkin & Snowling, 2008; Nation, Snowling, & Clark, 2007).

A young child is required to recognize that speech is segmented into phonemes (the English language contains about 42, such as *ba, ga, at*, and *tr*). The difficulty of this task for many children is the fact that speech does not consist of separate phonemes produced one after another. Instead, sounds are *co-articulated* (overlapped with one another) to permit rapid communication, rather than pronounced sound by sound (Liberman & Shankweiler, 1991). About 80% of children can segment words and syllables into their proper phonemes by the time they are 7 years old. The other 20% cannot, and it is these children who struggle hardest to read (S. E. Shaywitz & Shaywitz, 2008; Vellutino, Fletcher, Snowling, & Scanlon, 2004).

Generally, early language problems surface as learning problems when children enter school, because now children are taught to connect spoken and written language. Those who do not easily learn to read and write often have difficulty learning the alphabetic system—the relationship of sounds to letters. They also cannot manipulate sounds within syllables in words, which is called a lack of phonological awareness and is a precursor to reading problems (Rvachew, 2007).

Phonological awareness is a broad construct that includes recognition of the relationship that exists between sounds and letters, detection of rhyme and alliteration, and awareness that sounds can be manipulated within syllables in words. Primary-grade teachers detect phonological awareness as they ask children to rhyme words and manipulate sounds. For example, the teacher can say "hat" and ask the child to say the word without the *h* sound, or say "trip" and have the child say the word without the *p*. To assess the child's ability to blend sounds, teachers can say the three sounds *t*, *i*, and *n*, for example, and see if the child can pull the sounds together to say "tin."

In addition to serving as a prerequisite for basic reading skills, phonological awareness and processing also appear highly related to expressive language development (Boada & Pennington, 2006). Readers with core deficits in phonological processing problems have difficulty segmenting and categorizing phonemes, retrieving the names of common objects and letters, storing phonological codes in short-term memory, and producing some speech sounds. Reading and comprehension depend on the rapid and automatic ability to decode single words. Children who are slow and inaccurate at decoding have the most difficulties in reading comprehension (Lyon et al., 2006).

SECTION SUMMARY

Language Development

- Language development is based on innate ability and environmental opportunities to learn, store, and express important sounds in the language, and it proceeds very rapidly during infancy.
- Deficits in phonological awareness—the ability to distinguish the sounds of language—have been identified as a major cause of both disorders in communication and disorders in learning.

Communication Disorders

Children with communication disorders (formerly known as developmental speech and language disorders) have difficulty in producing speech sounds, using spoken language to communicate, or understanding what other people say. In DSM-IV-TR, communication disorders include the diagnostic subcategories of *expressive language disorder, phonological disorder, mixed receptive—expressive disorder*, and *stuttering*. These subcategories are distinguished by the exact nature of the child's impairment.

Recall that during development phonological problems appear before problems in language reception or expression, yet they have strong similarities. The following discussion focuses on expressive language disorder in an effort to highlight early childhood problems that represent the fundamental features of communication disorders. (Stuttering has a unique clinical feature and developmental course, so it is discussed separately.)

Consider Jackie's communication problems at age 3 years:

JACKIE

Screaming, Not Talking

Jackie's mother explained with no hesitation why she asked for help: "My 3-year-old daughter is a growing concern. Since she was a baby, she has been plagued by ear infections and sleep problems. Some nights she screams for hours on end, usually because of the ear infections. She has violent temper outbursts and refuses to do simple things that I ask her to do, like get dressed or put on her coat."

The child, waiting in the playroom, could be heard screaming over her mother's voice. Jackie was asking my assistant for something, but she could not make out what Jackie was saying. It was pretty obvious how frustrated both the child and her mother must feel on occasion. Her mother explained how she and Jackie's father had divorced when Jackie was less than 2 years old, and that after weekend exchanges it sometimes took a few days for Jackie's routine to return to some degree of normalcy.

I opened the letter she had brought from Jackie's preschool teacher, someone who I knew had a great deal of experience with children of this age. "Jackie is a bright and energetic child," the letter began, "but she is having a great deal of difficulty expressing herself with words. When she gets frustrated, she starts to give up or becomes angry—she won't eat her meals or she fights with staff at nap time, even if she is hungry or tired. If a new teacher at day care is introduced, it takes Jackie a long time to get used to the new person. Jackie seems to understand what she is being asked, but can't find the words to express herself, which understandably leads to an emotional reaction on her part." (Based on authors' case material)

Expressive Language Disorder

Jackie's problems met the criteria for an **expressive language disorder**, which is a communication disorder characterized by deficits in expression despite normal comprehension of speech. As a result of these deficits, Jackie showed her frustration loudly and inappropriately. These deficits are often referred to as Specific Language Impairment (SLI), which occurs when a child's language matures at least 12 months behind their chronological age and is not associated with another known disorder such as intellectual disability (American Speech-Language-Hearing Association [ASHA], 2008).

Children's language development follows specific steps, although each child may proceed through the steps at a different pace. Normal variations can make it difficult to predict that a given child's early communication problems will become major problems in learning later on. A common example is the child who points to different objects and makes grunting or squealing noises that the parent quickly recognizes as "more milk" or "no peas." Prior to age 3 or so, many children communicate this way unless parents actively encourage using words and discourage nonverbal communications. Nevertheless, despite plenty of verbal examples and proper language stimulation, some children fail to develop in some areas of speech and language, and later have problems in school. This developmental connection makes the study of communication disorders highly pertinent to the understanding and treatment of subsequent learning problems.

Children with an expressive language disorder, such as Jackie, do not suffer from mental retardation or from one of the pervasive developmental disorders that affect speech and language (see Chapters 9 and 10). A defining characteristic of expressive language disorder is the discrepancy between what children understand (receptive language) and what they are able to say (expressive language). For example, when asked by her parents to go upstairs, find her socks, and put them on, Jackie was quite capable of complying. When asked by her mother to describe what she has just done, however, she might respond simply, "find socks." Table 11.1 shows the major features of the DSM-IV-TR diagnostic criteria for expressive language disorder.

The linguistic abilities of children with expressive language disorders vary significantly, based on the severity of the disorder and the age of the child. Most often these children begin speaking late and progress slowly in their speech development. Their vocabulary often is limited and is marked by short sentences and simple grammatical structure, as in Jackie's response. To fit the diagnostic criteria, these problems must be so severe that they interfere with pre-academic or academic achievement or the ability to communicate in everyday social situations.

Two closely related types of communication disorders deserve clarification: mixed receptive–expressive language disorder and phonological disorder. A **mixed receptive–expressive language disorder** may be present if speaking problems are coupled with the difficulty in understanding some aspects of speech. Although their hearing is normal, children with this disorder cannot make sense of certain sounds, words, or sentences. They may have difficulty understanding particular types of words or statements, such as complex if–then sentences. In severe cases, the child's ability to understand basic vocabulary or simple sentences may be impaired, and there may be deficits in auditory processing of sounds and symbols and in their storage, recall, and sequencing (APA, 2000). Understandably, these problems make the child seem inattentive or noncompliant, and the disorder can be easily misdiagnosed. Imagine how it would feel to be in Greece visiting an English-speaking host and her Greek husband. Unless your host is present, trying to engage in friendly conversation can be frustrating and uncomfortable. Even if both you and the husband can each understand a few words the other is saying, you probably cannot actually converse. If you have ever faced a similar communication barrier, you probably have a greater appreciation of the frustration and discomfort that accompany an expressive language disorder.

When the developmental language problem involves articulation or sound production rather than word knowledge, a **phonological disorder** may be an appropriate diagnosis. Children with this disorder have trouble controlling their rate of speech, or lag behind playmates in learning to articulate certain sounds. The most frequently misarticulated sounds,

TABLE 11.1 | Diagnostic Criteria for Expressive Language Disorder

DSM-IV-TR

A. The scores obtained from standardized individually administered measures of expressive language development are substantially below those obtained from standardized measures of both nonverbal intellectual capacity and receptive language development. The disturbance may be manifest clinically by symptoms that include having a markedly limited vocabulary, making errors in tense, or having difficulty recalling words or producing sentences with developmentally appropriate length or complexity.

B. The difficulties with expressive language interfere with academic or occupational achievement or with social communication.

C. Criteria are not met for Mixed Receptive-Expressive Language Disorder or a Pervasive Developmental Disorder.

D. If Mental Retardation, a speech-motor or sensory deficit, or environmental deprivation is present, the language difficulties are in excess of those usually associated with these problems.

Coding Note: If a speech-motor or sensory deficit or a neurological condition is present, code the condition on Axis III.

Source: Reprinted with permission from the Diagnostic and Statistical Manual of Mental Disorders, Fourth Edition, Text Revision, (Copyright © 2000). American Psychiatric Association.

such as *l, r, s, z, th,* and *ch,* are acquired later in the developmental sequence (APA, 2000). Depending on the severity of the disorder, the speech quality of these children may be unusual, even unintelligible. For example, at age 6, James still said "wabbit" instead of "rabbit" and "we-wind" for "rewind." Preschoolers, of course, often mispronounce words or confuse the sounds that they hear, which is a normal part of learning to speak. When these problems persist beyond the normal developmental range or interfere with academic and social activities, they deserve separate attention.

Prevalence and Course

Children usually reveal problems in speech articulation and expression as they attempt to tackle new sounds and express their own concepts. Even though prevalence estimates account for normal variation in language development and are based on individuals who meet specific diagnostic criteria, the degree of severity can vary considerably. For example, in early childhood, milder forms of phonological disorder are relatively common, affecting close to 10% of preschoolers. However, many of these children outgrow their earlier difficulties, so by the time they are 6 or 7 years old, only 2% to 3% meet the criteria for phonological disorder. Similarly, expressive language disorder (affecting 2% to 3%) and mixed expressive–receptive disorder (affecting less than 3%) are both common among younger school-age children (APA, 2000; Heim & Benasich, 2006).

Communication disorders are identified almost twice as often in boys than girls (Pinborough-Zimmerman et al., 2007). However, because boys show more behavior problems accompanying their language difficulties, they are referred and diagnosed with communication learning disorders more often than girls (Vellutino et al., 2004). Fortunately, by mid-to-late adolescence, most children with a developmental communication disorder have acquired normal language (APA, 2000). About 50% fully outgrow their problems, whereas the other 50% may show considerable improvement but still have some degree of impairment until late adolescence. In contrast, the course and prognosis for children with an acquired type of communication disorder (caused by some event unrelated to development, such as brain lesions, head trauma, or stroke) depend highly on the severity and location of the injury, the child's age, and extent of language development at the time of the event (APA, 2000).

Even though language problems usually disappear or diminish with time, children with communication disorders often have higher than normal rates of negative behaviors that began at an early age (van Daal, Verhoeven, & van Balkom, 2007). Associated behavior problems, such as ADHD and social skill limitations, can add to communication problems and further alter the course of development in terms of how they relate to peers or keep up with educational demands (Durkin & Conti-Ramsden, 2010). To give children with special needs the opportunity to interact with typically developing children, school systems have begun to include these children with different needs into regular, rather than segregated, classrooms. **Inclusion** education strategies are based on the premise that the abilities of children with special needs will improve from associating with normally developing peers, and that by doing so these children will be spared the effects of labeling and special placements.

Causes

Notable findings that support the role of genetics, brain function, and environmental risk factors associated with higher incidence of learning disorders are discussed in the following sections.

Genetics

Language processes appear to be heritable to a significant degree, although the specific genetic underpinnings are difficult to pinpoint. About 50% to 75% of all children with specific language disorders show a positive family history of some type of learning disability (ASHA, 2008; Heim & Benasich, 2006). Twin studies and adoption studies also suggest a genetic connection (McGrath et al., 2007; Plomin, Haworth, & Davis, 2010; Whitehouse, Bishop, Ang, Pennell, & Fisher, 2011).

Scientists are zeroing in on specific deficits in brain functioning that lead to communication disorders and may be heritable. Studies comparing language-impaired children with and without an affected parent suggest that *temporal processing deficits* occur significantly more often in children with a positive family history for a language-based learning disability (Caylak, 2011; Flax et al., 2003). That is, affected children have more difficulty deciphering certain speech sounds because of subtle but important differences in the way neurons fire in response to various sounds. In a twin study, D. V. M. Bishop et al. (1999) found that the variation in temporal processing was due to environmental factors and not genetics because twin—twin correlations were similar for Monozygotic (MZ) and Dizygotic (DZ) twins. However, what does appear to be genetic is a deficit in phonological short-term memory.

The Brain

Language functions develop rapidly and are housed primarily in the left temporal lobe of the brain (see ● Figure 11.1). A circular feedback loop helps strengthen the developmental process of language reception and expression. The better children comprehend spoken language, the better they will be able to express themselves. Feedback from their own vocalizations, in turn, helps shape their subsequent expression. Lack of comprehension and absence of feedback reduces verbal output, and thus interferes with the development of articulation skills (Vellutino, Tunmer, Jaccard, & Chen, 2007).

Anatomical and neuroimaging studies show that deficits in phonological awareness and segmentation are related to problems in the functional connections between brain areas, not to a specific dysfunction of any single area of the brain (Lyon et al., 2006; Richlan, Kronbichler, & Wimmer, 2009). Recent brain imaging studies indicate that poor performance on tasks demanding phonological awareness is associated with less brain activity in the left temporal region, suggesting that phonological problems may stem from neurological deficits or deviations in posterior left-hemisphere systems that control the ability to process phonemes (Richlan et al., 2011; S. E. Shaywitz, Gruen, Mody, & Shaywitz, 2009). We return to these findings on brain function later on in our discussion of reading disorders.

Ear Infections

Another biological cause of expressive language impairment may be recurrent otitis media (middle ear infection) in the first year of life, because hearing loss accompanies frequent or long bouts of infections. Otitis media that occurs during a critical period may cause early language problems that improve relatively quickly, whereas in the absence of such a history, the causes are likely to be more neurological and long lasting. Children with chronic otitis media, however, still face some delays in their social development as they

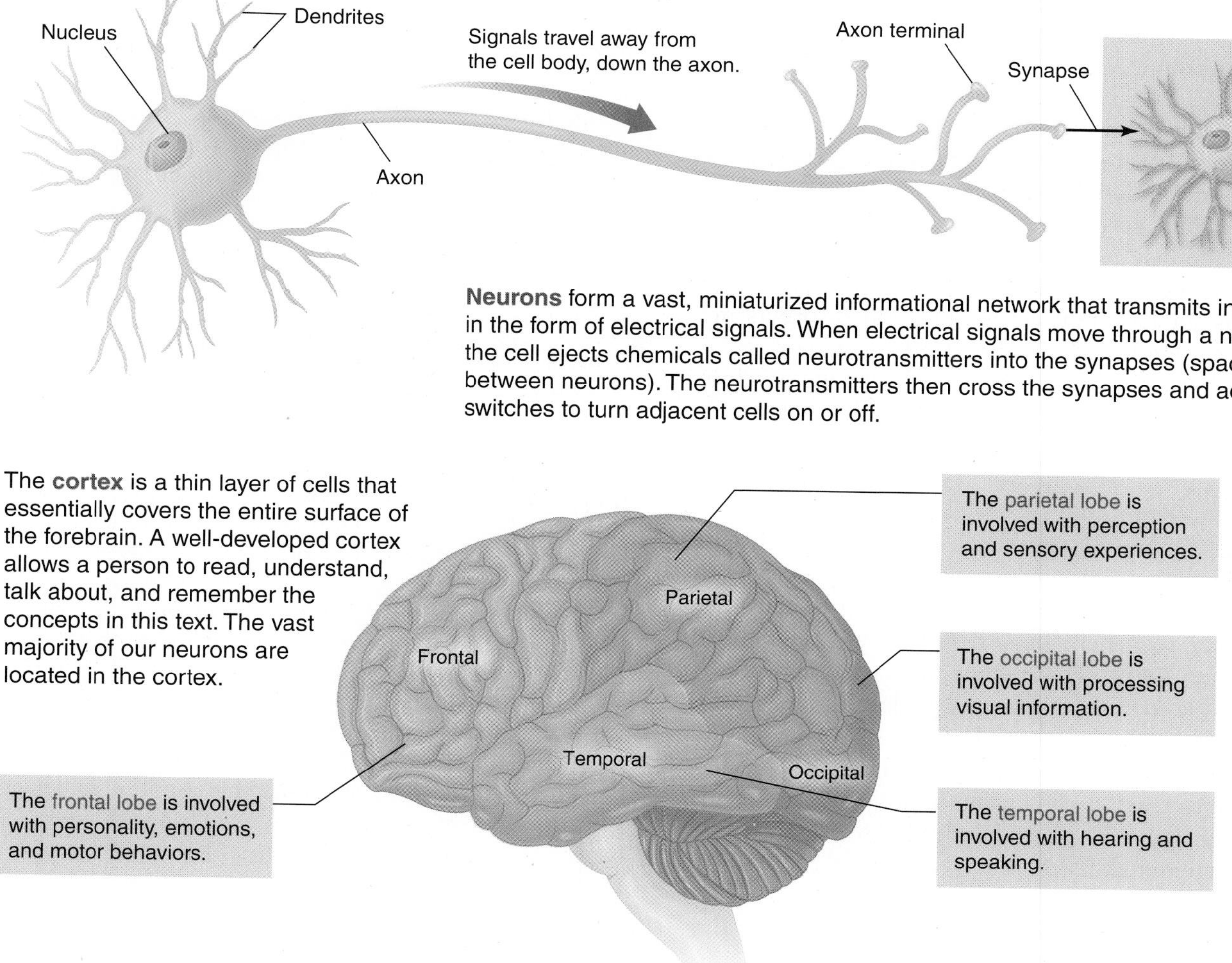
Nucleus
Dendrites
Signals travel away from the cell body, down the axon.
Axon terminal
Synapse
Axon
Neurons form a vast, miniaturized informational network that transmits information in the form of electrical signals. When electrical signals move through a neuron, the cell ejects chemicals called neurotransmitters into the synapses (spaces between neurons). The neurotransmitters then cross the synapses and act like switches to turn adjacent cells on or off.
The **cortex** is a thin layer of cells that essentially covers the entire surface of the forebrain. A well-developed cortex allows a person to read, understand, talk about, and remember the concepts in this text. The vast majority of our neurons are located in the cortex.
The parietal lobe is involved with perception and sensory experiences.
Parietal
Frontal
The occipital lobe is involved with processing visual information.
Temporal
Occipital
The frontal lobe is involved with personality, emotions, and motor behaviors.
The temporal lobe is involved with hearing and speaking.

FIGURE 11.1 | Areas of the brain involved in language functions.

From Plotnik/Kouyoumdjian. Introduction to Psychology, 9E. © 2011 Wadsworth, a part of Cengage Learning, Inc. Reproduced by permission. www.cengage.com/permissions.

attempt to catch up to their peers in learning appropriate forms of verbal communication (Winskel, 2006).

In summary, although biological findings point to abnormal brain functioning, how this abnormality originates is still unclear. The best guess is that communication disorders result from an interaction of genetic influences, slowness or abnormalities of brain maturation, and, possibly, minor brain lesions that escape clinical detection (S. E. Shaywitz, Morris, & Shaywitz, 2008).

Home Environment

How much does the home environment contribute to communication disorders? Do some parents fail to provide adequate examples to stimulate their children's language? Because of the important role parents play in children's development, psychologists have studied this issue carefully.

We noticed when we first visited Jackie at home that her stepfather was a very quiet man who often communicated nonverbally—a gesture, a frown, a short phrase. Her mother used very simple speech when talking to Jackie but not when talking to Jackie's 6-year-old sister. These observations match those of researchers (St. James-Roberts & Alston, 2006; Whitehurst & Lonigan, 1998), who compared verbal interactions of families with and without a child who had an expressive language disorder. They found that parents changed the way they spoke to their children, depending on their children's abilities. When the child spoke in simple, two- or three-word sentences, the parents adjusted their speech accordingly. Note that, except in extreme cases of child neglect or abuse, it is unlikely that communication disorders are caused by parents. Parental speech and language stimulation may affect the pace and range of language development, but not the specific impairments that characterize the disorders (Flax et al., 2003; McGrath et al., 2007).

Treatment

Fortunately, expressive language disorder and similar communication disorders usually self-correct by the age of 6 and may not require intervention. Even so, parents may seek help in understanding their child's speech delays and to ensure that they are doing everything possible to stimulate language development. Specialized preschools, for example, have had good results using a combination of computer- and teacher-assisted instruction to teach early academic skills to young children, which helps to pace the child's practice of new skills (Hatcher et al., 2006; Law, Garrett, & Nye, 2004; Loo, Bamiou, Campbell, & Luxon, 2010).

For Jackie, we designed ways that her parents and day-care teachers could build on her existing strengths. Her day-care teacher had an excellent idea: Because Jackie loved to draw and to talk about her artwork, why not use her interest in drawing to increase her enthusiasm for speaking? When I visited her class, she ran up to show me her drawing, exclaiming, "I draw picture of mom, dad, kitty, and lake." We agreed that her behavior problems could be managed by simple forms of ignoring and distracting and the occasional time-out. Jackie became attached to computer graphics and images, and soon was able to identify letters and small words and to move shapes around the screen. All the while, her expressive language improved, and by age 5 she could pronounce all the letters of the alphabet and was eager to start kindergarten.

Stuttering

Stuttering is the repeated and prolonged pronunciation of certain syllables that interferes with communication. It is quite normal for children who are still learning to speak to go through a period of nonfluency, or unclear speech, as part of their development. It takes practice and patience for a child to develop the coordination for the tongue, lips, and brain to work in unison to produce unfamiliar or difficult combinations of sounds. For most children, this period of speech development passes without notice, and for most parents it is full of wonder and amusement as their children wrestle with new words. Some children, however, progress slowly through this stage, repeating *(wa-wa-wa)* or prolonging *(n-ah-ah-ah-o)* sounds; they struggle to continue or develop ways to avoid or compensate for certain sounds or words. Four-year-old Sayad has speech problems that typify the pattern of stuttering:

SAYAD

Family Legacy

Sayad's parents had received a lot of informal advice from friends and relatives about their son's speech problems, but most of what they said was worrisome. "He'll struggle with this for most of his life," his grandmother had warned. "If something isn't done right away, he'll become a stutterer, and be so self-conscious that he won't be able to keep up in school or with his friends."

Sayad started repeating and prolonging some of his words when he was about 2, but by now his problem had grown more noticeable. As he spoke, he pursed his lips, closed his eyes, and shortened his breathing, seeming to tense up his face. Yet his interactions with me were friendly and at ease. "M-m-m-m-y words get stuck in m-m-m-m-y m-m-mouth," he explained, "and I-I-I-I talk t-t-t-t-too fast. Wh-wh-wh-why can't I talk right?" I soon discovered why his grandmother was so concerned: The child's great-grandfather and great-uncle both stuttered, and Sayad's father had been a stutterer until he was a teenager.

Sayad's mother had been trying to ignore the problem and not draw attention to it, but she was growing more aware that Sayad's peers tease and imitate him. She explained why she came for an assessment: "We were on the way to the store when Sayad kept saying 'where' over and over. After I stopped the car and unfastened his seatbelt, he finished his question—'is daddy?' After that, I gave up on my 'leave it alone' notion and began trying ways to slow Sayad down a bit." (Based on authors' case material)

Prevalence and Course

Stuttering has a gradual onset between the ages of 2 and 7 years, usually peaking at age 5 (APA, 2000; ASHA, 2008). A large population-based study estimated the incidence of stuttering to be about 3% in children, with males affected about 3 times more often than females (ASHA, 2008; Craig, Hancock, Tran, Craig, & Peters, 2002). However, few children actually receive this diagnosis because most children recover from stuttering. This developmental course is important for treatment considerations, because almost 80% of children who stutter before age 5 will no longer stutter once they attend school for a year or so (Packman, Code, & Onslow, 2007).

Causes and Treatment

Many myths and falsehoods surround stuttering. The widely held view that stuttering is caused by an unresolved emotional problem or by anxiety is countered by the lack of supportive evidence (Packman et al., 2007). Because the problem runs in families, researchers have focused on family characteristics as the major causes. However, it is not likely this behavior is acquired primarily as a function of the child's linguistic environment. Sayad's grandmother and mother would be relieved to know that the communicative behavior of mothers does not significantly contribute to the development of stuttering (Howell & Davis, 2011).

Genetic factors play a strong role in the etiology of stuttering, accounting for approximately 70% of the variance in the causes of stuttering (Dworzynski, Remington, Rijsdijk, Howell, & Plomin, 2007). Environmental factors, such as premature birth or parental mental illness, account for the remaining causal influences (Ajdacic-Gross et al., 2010). Genetic factors most likely influence speech by causing an abnormal development in the location of the most prominent speech centers in the brain, which are usually in the left hemisphere. This biological source for stuttering explains many of its clinical features, including the loss of spontaneity and occasional problems in self-esteem (Howell, 2007; Kell et al., 2009).

Since most children outgrow stuttering, one of the most frustrating problems for parents and therapists is to decide whether therapy would be intervention or interference. Therapy is usually recommended if sound and syllable repetitions are frequent, if the parent or child is concerned about the problem, or if the child shows, like Sayad, facial or vocal tension. A common psychological treatment for children who stutter is to teach parents how to speak to their children slowly and use short and simple sentences, consequently removing the pressure the child may feel about speaking (Howell, 2011; Rousseau, Packman, Onslow, Harrison, & Jones, 2007). Other beneficial treatments for stuttering include contingency management, which uses positive consequences for fluency and negative consequences for stuttering (Bothe, Davidow, Bramlett, & Ingham, 2006; Murphy, Yaruss, & Quesal, 2007), and habit reversal procedures, such as learning to regulate breathing (Bate, Malouff, Thorsteinsson, & Bhullar, 2011).

SECTION SUMMARY

Communication Disorders

- Speech and language problems that emerge during early childhood include difficulty producing speech sounds, demonstrating speech fluency, using spoken language to communicate, or understanding what other people say.
- Even though most children with communication disorders acquire normal language by mid-to-late adolescence, early communication disorders are developmentally connected to the later onset of learning disorders.
- Expressive language disorder is a communication disorder defined as a discrepancy between receptive language and expressive language.
- Causes of communication disorders include genetic influences and slow or abnormal brain maturation. Early ear infections may play a causal role in some cases.
- Treatment of children with communication disorders is often unnecessary, since many of these problems are self-correcting soon after children begin attending school.
- Stuttering, or speech dysfluency, occurs mostly in younger children, peaking around age 5. Recovery usually occurs once the child enters school.

Learning Disorders

People do not understand what it costs in time and suffering to learn how to read. I have been working at it for eighty years, and I still can't say that I've succeeded.

—Goethe (1749–1832)

Whether we are studying Roman history or calculus, applying ourselves to the task of learning requires exertion and concentration. Like physical activities, some learning activities are more difficult than others, especially for younger children who have not developed a foundation of good study habits and successful learning experiences. Parents and teachers may notice that a child is struggling unusually hard to master a particular skill, such as reading, and wonder why. The problem may be formally assessed by an IQ test and various standardized tests that assess abilities in specific academic areas.

When achievement in reading, math, or writing is substantially below expectations for the child's age, schooling, and intellectual ability, he or she may be diagnosed with a learning disorder. In practice, *substantially below* is defined as a discrepancy of more than 2 standard deviations between the IQ findings and the actual achievement test findings. In other words, a child with a learning disorder is bright enough to learn the subject material, but does not appear able to do so. However, as we note in the following example, there is some debate as to the validity of using a discrepancy formula to define learning disorders (Lipka & Siegel, 2006).

JAMES

Strong Points Shine

The look on the 9-year-old's face said it all—he did not want to be here. "I'm tired of talking to people" was his terse greeting. I wondered for a moment whether he would talk to me at all, but as soon as he saw my computer, he brightened a bit. To allow time for him to feel more comfortable, I invited James to play a quick game or two. His skill at the action games told me a lot about his basic energy and problem-solving ability—he was a whiz at figuring out the rules of each game and getting a high score. We spoke casually during the warm-up, but it was clear to me that he preferred to concentrate on the game.

A half hour passed, with little more than a few sentences exchanged. A quick trip to the snack bar gave us the common ground we needed to open up and talk a bit. "Why does my teacher want me to come here?" he reasonably asked. As he listened and replied to my explanation, his language problems stood out. His sentences were short, simple, and rapid. Here is an example:

"James, tell me something about your favorite story or a recent movie you've seen."
"I like the movie. Lots of dogs."
"What movie is that, James?"
"Dog movie."

During testing, James often tried to start before I had finished telling him what to do. He was eager to do what I asked, but he stopped abruptly as soon as he had trouble. James could focus on only one sound at a time, so if he missed early cues or initial instructions, he would become disoriented, frustrated, and uncooperative. James wanted to do well, but I could see he was struggling. He completed the WISC-IV in less than an hour, hurrying almost as if to escape his own mistakes. His measured general intelligence was within the normal range, but his performance abilities (performance IQ 109) were much stronger than his verbal abilities (verbal IQ 78). It was obvious as well that the test underestimated his true ability, as a result of his eagerness to finish and his difficulty with understanding some of the instructions.

To my surprise, James was ready to continue on to the next test after only a short computer game break. He explained why this was so: "I put things together, like puzzles. I make cars and planes at my house." As long as I gave him small breaks on the computer, he was willing to tackle the material on the tests. Some of his spelling errors stood out immediately, such as *skr* for *square*, and *srke* for *circle*. When asked to write the sentence "he shouted a warning," he wrote "he shtd a woin." He read "see the black dog" as "see the black pond," and "she wants a ride to the store" as "she was rid of the store." He seemed to use a "best guess" strategy in tackling reading, based on the sounds that he knew: When asked to write the word bigger, he wrote just her. But I noticed that James's enthusiasm picked up a bit as he began telling stories from pictures he was shown, and he marveled at his own ability to rotate shapes on the computer to complete a picture. He left my office more animated and talkative than when he arrived, which showed how nice it must have felt for him to experience success. (Based on authors' case material)

Let's return to James, the 9-year-old with reading problems, and compare James's reading problems with those of Tim, a 7-year-old who has a great deal of trouble with math and drawing. Tim's problems are in the areas of spatial orientation and mathematical reasoning, and further achievement testing confirmed that they fit the diagnostic criteria for a learning disorder in mathematics. However, his academic problems were almost masked by his frustration and low self-esteem. Emotional problems are often seen in children who are bright enough to recognize that their performance is below that of others.

TIM

Warming with Interest

When I first saw Tim, he seemed aloof and disinterested. His eyes stayed focused on the floor, and his body remained expressionless, as if to say, "Leave me alone, and let me outta here." As I searched for something to say, I asked Tim to tell me a little about his family: "Do you have any brothers or sisters? Does your family like to do anything special together?" His tired response, "I have two brothers, my father works all day, mom plays piano. We want a boat," sent me a clear message as to his mood and interest in this activity. My usual ploy of turning on the computer games fell flat—"I hate computers" was Tim's preemptive response. I wondered, "Is he depressed, angry, hurt, frustrated? Just what is going on here?"

Having looked at his school record, I knew he was struggling, especially in math and physical sciences, but his speech and affect expressed more than only academic problems. His school records flashed the news that Tim had a learning disorder, as evidenced by his WISC-IV performance score of 79 that fell in the borderline- to low-average range, and his verbal score of 108 that fell in the average range. The test administrator had politely described Tim's test-taking approach as "reluctant." Notes by teachers indicated that he commonly had problems on tasks involving drawing, particularly if they required memory, and his math and social skills were far below those of others in his class.

I pulled out my *Where's Waldo?* book and we began looking at it together. In addition to being fun, looking for Waldo and his friends (small figures amidst millions of figures and colors) required Tim to be patient. At first he balked, but I noticed that he improved if he used his own verbally mediated strategy to solve the problem. Tim talked to himself as he thought aloud: "Look around the edges first, then start to look closer and closer to the middle of the page. Look for Waldo's red and white shirt—look closely at each section!" The more interested he was, the more he would talk. Once he warmed up, his smile appeared, along with his admission that "this sure beats math lesson." (Based on authors' case material)

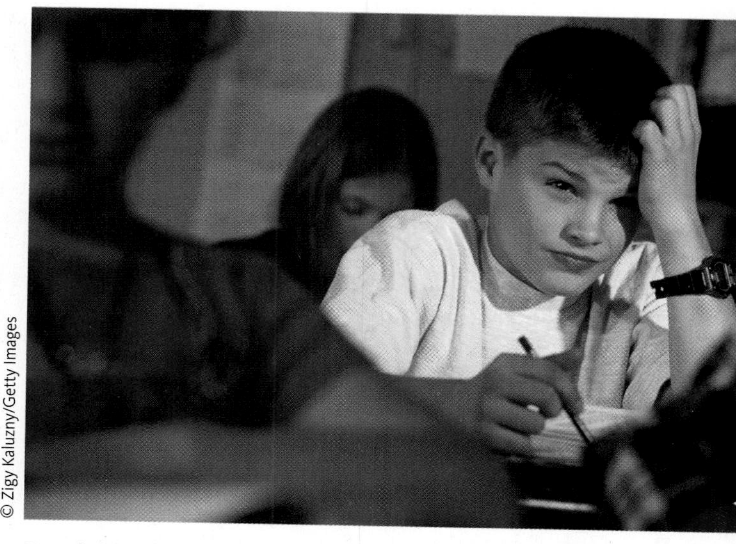

For children with learning disorders, following simple instructions can be confusing and frustrating

James's pattern of strengths and weaknesses shows that although he has reading problems, other strengths compensate for this disability. He has strong talents for figuring out how things work and for drawing ideas on paper. Tim has several strengths, too, especially in linguistic skills such as word recognition, sentence structure, and reading. In contrast to James, Tim has problems primarily in the visual, spatial, and organizational spheres, which show up as difficulties with tactile (touch) perception, psychomotor activity (e.g., throwing and catching), and nonverbal problem solving (e.g., figuring out math problems and assembling things). The limitations of both children can affect every aspect of their formal education as well as their interpersonal abilities, and therefore require comprehensive and ongoing treatment plans.

To better understand the nature of learning disorders, picture yourself asking for directions at a gas station in an unfamiliar town. The attendant says: "Go out the driveway and turn right. Go till you reach the second light, turn left, and look for the sign to Amityville. It's about 3 miles down the road. You'll pass a cemetery and a red schoolhouse, and go under a railroad trestle before you get to Highway 18. When you see the sign, turn right." We all have some difficulty processing such information and recalling it accurately; we drive away repeating to ourselves, "Stop light, go left, cemetery, highway, turn at schoolhouse?" Our driving companions, who heard the same instructions, may recall a different route.

This situation demonstrates that even simple verbal instructions can easily be jumbled. Children and adults with learning disorders experience similar confusion in the everyday situations of processing new information or understanding what they are reading. These learning problems can be difficult to recognize because, for most of us, the material in question is straightforward and simple. The child may be blamed for not listening, not paying attention, or for being "slow," which further disguises the true nature of the learning problems.

The main diagnostic feature of Learning Disorders, including disorders in Reading, Mathematics, and Written Expression, is that the child's performance in one of these areas is substantially below what it should be for their age and intellectual ability. To be classified as a disability, the performance problems must significantly interfere with academic achievement or daily living. (Some children and adults have found ways to compensate for their learning problems and therefore do not display a disability, despite their test findings of poor achievement.) Finally, the disability cannot be related to a sensory problem, such as impaired hearing or sight, unless it goes well beyond what children typically experience.

Because many aspects of speaking, listening, reading, writing, and arithmetic overlap and build on the same functions of the brain, it is not surprising that a child or adult can have more than one form of learning disorder. Recall that phonological awareness facilitates the ability to speak and, later on, to read and write. A single gap in the brain's functioning can disrupt many types of cognitive activity. These disruptions, in turn, can interfere with the development of important fundamental skills and compound the learning difficulties in a short time. Moreover, as we saw with both James and Tim, numerous secondary problems can emerge, such as temper outbursts and withdrawal from social situations, as a result of frustration and lack of success.

Reading Disorder

He has only half learned the art of reading who has not added to it the more refined art of skipping and skimming.

—Arthur James Balfour

Children are naturally attracted to reading, and its importance in our society is unequaled by any other academic accomplishment. We are surrounded by written signs and messages and, by about age 5 or so, most children want to know what they mean. (Capitalizing on this natural curiosity, advertisers have become expert in pairing recognizable symbols with the names of their product or establishment so that children can "read" more quickly.) By the first grade, natural interest and developmental readiness are channeled into formally learning how to read. For many children this process is difficult and tedious; for a sizeable minority, however, it can be confusing and upsetting. The role of parents in this process is critical, because children need positive feedback and need to feel satisfied with their performance, regardless of their speed and accuracy.

When you consider everything involved in learning the basics of reading, such as associating shapes of letters (graphemes) with sounds (phonemes), it is not surprising that some children have difficulty and can quickly fall behind. Read the following sentence: "I believe that abnormal child psychology is one of the most fascinating and valuable courses I have taken." As you read the sentence, did you notice that you had to simultaneously:

- Focus attention on the printed marks and control your eye movements across the page?
- Recognize the sounds associated with letters?
- Understand words and grammar?
- Build ideas and images?
- Compare new ideas with what you already know?
- Store ideas in memory?

Most of us have forgotten all the effort that goes into reading, especially in the beginning. Not surprisingly, children's initial attempts are laborious and monotonous as they wrestle with the sounds and complexities of combined letters. Such mental processing requires a complex intact network of nerve cells that connect our vision, language, and memory centers (Grigorenko, 2007). A small problem in any area can cause reading difficulties. The most common underlying feature of reading disorder, however, is an inability to distinguish or to separate the sounds in spoken words. Phonological skills are fundamental to learning to read, and therefore this deficit is critical.

To assess a child's need for additional practice in mastering phonemes and words, it is important to understand that there are two systems that operate when one reads words, which are essential in the development of reading. The first system operates on individual units (phonemes) and is relatively slow; the second system operates on whole words more quickly. In normal readers, whole words are learned through the development of phonologically based word analysis. However, persistently poor readers seem to rely on rote memory for recognizing words (S. E. Shaywitz & Shaywitz, 2008).

Many clinical signs of reading disorders are first evident only to a trained eye. Some testing methods developed by teachers and school psychologists show how children with reading disorders function in the classroom. They often have trouble learning basic sight words, especially those that are phonetically irregular and must be memorized, such as *the, who, what, where, was, laugh, said*, and so forth. These children have developed their own unique and peculiar reading patterns, which signal the need for different teaching methods. Typical errors include *reversals (b/d; p/q), transpositions* (sequential errors such as *was/saw, scared/sacred*), *inversions (m/w; u/n)*, and *omissions* (reading *place* for *palace* or *section* for *selection*). However, these errors are common in many younger children who are just learning to read and write, and do not necessarily imply a reading disorder.

To assess a child's need for additional practice in certain areas, teachers may log the types of errors the child makes while reading out loud. In addition to decoding words, reading comprehension is assessed by having the student retell a story or suggest the next episode. Average readers rely heavily on auditory and visual modalities for gathering new information, but children with reading disorders may prefer a mode of touch or manipulation to assist them in learning. These various patterns of strengths and weaknesses, if adequately assessed, can then be used to the child's advantage in planning additional teaching methods such as computer-based learning (S. E. Shaywitz et al., 2008).

The core deficits in reading disorders are in **decoding**—breaking a word into parts rapidly enough to read the whole word—coupled with difficulty reading single, small words (Vellutino et al., 2007). When a child cannot detect the phonological structure of language and automatically recognize simple words, reading development will very likely be impaired (Peterson & Pennington, 2010). The slow and labored decoding of single words requires substantial effort and detracts from the child's ability to retain the meaning of a sentence, much less a paragraph or page. The child with a reading disorder lacks the critical language skills required for basic reading, reading comprehension, spelling, and written expression.

Mathematics Disorder

During their preschool years, children are not as naturally drawn to mathematical concepts as they are to reading. This changes rapidly as they discover that they need to count and add to know how much money it takes to buy something or how many days remain until vacation. As in reading, the need to know propels children to learn new and difficult concepts, and little by little their new skills help them understand the world better.

For some children, like Francine and Tim, this curiosity about numbers is compromised by their inability to grasp the abstract concepts inherent in many forms of numerical and cognitive problem solving. Francine's difficulty with numbers and concepts began to show up well before she attended school, which is typically the case. When she encountered math concepts in second grade that required some abstract reasoning, she fell further and further behind.

Many skills are involved in arithmetic: recognizing numbers and symbols, memorizing facts (the multiplication table), aligning numbers, and understanding abstract concepts such as place value and fractions. Any or all may be difficult for children with a mathematics disorder (Vukovic & Siegel, 2010). The DSM-IV-TR criteria for mathematics disorder, like the criteria for learning disorders, are based on assumptions of normal or above-average intelligence as assessed by IQ, normal sensory function, adequate educational opportunity, and the absence of developmental disorders and emotional disturbance. Children and adults with this disorder may have difficulty not only in math, but also in comprehending abstract concepts or in visual—spatial ability. Historically, these characteristics were termed *developmental dyscalculia*, which is defined as the failure to develop arithmetic competence, but the term is seldom used today. Examples of calculation errors typical of children with a mathematics disorder are shown in ● Figure 11.2, an example that points out errors that suggest spatial difficulties and directional confusion.

```
 5 111                1
$62.04               75
 -5.30              + 8
 5634               163
```


FIGURE 11.2 | Errors in math computation by a 10-year-old girl with a mathematics disorder.

From *Learning Disabilities* by H. G. Taylor, 1988, p. 422. In E. J. Mash and L. G. Terdal (Eds.) *Behavioral Assessment of Childhood Disorders*, 2nd ed. Copyright © 1988 The Guilford Press. Reprinted by permission.

Children with mathematics disorders typically have core deficits in arithmetic calculation and/or mathematics reasoning abilities, which include naming amounts or numbers; enumerating, comparing, and manipulating objects; reading and writing mathematical symbols; understanding concepts and performing calculations mentally; and performing computational operations (Andersson, 2010; Lyon et al., 2006). These deficits imply that the neuropsychological processes underlying mathematical reasoning and calculation are underdeveloped or impaired.

Writing Disorder

CARLOS

Slowly Taking Shape

Carlos, age 7, was about to finish second grade when his teacher and parents met to discuss his handwriting problems. The year had gone generally well, but his parents were bracing for bad news. Smiling and pulling out some workbooks, Carlos's teacher lined up examples of how he had gradually become able to print some letters over the course of the year. But what his parents saw was self-explanatory: His shapes were very poor and looked more like those of his 3-year-old sister. Sensing both parents' apprehension, his teacher clarified: "Carlos is having a few problems in his fine motor coordination, in activities such as artwork, putting puzzles together, and similar tasks. He goes too fast when trying to do these tasks, and he forgets to be careful or to follow the pattern. He makes a half-hearted attempt on his writing assignments and then starts talking to his classmates. I'd like him to be seen by a psychologist for testing, and hopefully next fall his new teacher can strengthen his writing and fine motor skills with some additional exercises."

During the initial interview, Carlos took an immediate interest in my computer games, exclaiming how easy it was to use the mouse to draw figures. When asked to use a pencil and paper, however, Carlos balked. I asked him to copy by hand some of the figures he drew on the computer, after first printing them for him on paper. In doing so, he switched to his preferred hand

(*continues*)

(continued)

in the middle of the task. He also showed several letter reversals (b/d; p/q), and pushed down very hard on the pencil in an attempt to trace or draw the figures. Throughout these tasks he talked freely and asked a lot of questions, making me wonder at times who was assessing whom.

Carlos showed evidence on neuropsychological testing of finger *agnosia* (he could not tell which finger I touched when his hand was behind his back), especially with his left hand. He also had considerable difficulty copying a triangle, a circle, and a square based on examples shown to him (see ● Figure 11.3). On the WISC-IV he obtained a performance score of 91, in the low-average range, and a verbal IQ score of 117, in the high-average range. On performance subtests he had particular problems with block design and puzzles, such as object assembly. He had more difficulty with verbal IQ subtests that involved concentration and attention, such as math and digit-span tasks. Throughout the testing, I found Carlos to be impulsive and sometimes quite defiant: If he didn't want to do something, he simply would not do it. These observations were consistent with his parents' frustration at his immature behavior and defiance at home.

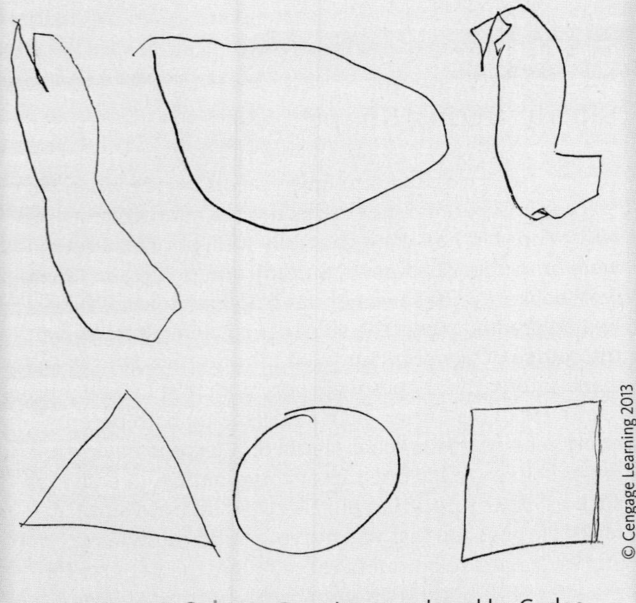

FIGURE 11.3 | *Top*: Drawings produced by Carlos when asked to copy a triangle, a circle, and a square. *Bottom*: Examples of a triangle, circle, and square from a typically developing 7-year-old boy.

(Based on authors' case material)

Carlos has a learning disorder related to written expression. He has strong language and reasoning abilities, as well as normal problem-solving skills for his age, yet he is considerably weaker in his visual–motor abilities, as shown by his writing, figure copying, and figure rotation. Like reading and math, writing derives from several interconnected brain areas that produce vocabulary, grammar, hand movement, and memory.

Children with writing disorders often have problems with tasks that require eye/hand coordination, despite their normal gross motor development. Teachers notice that, compared with children who have normal writing skills, children with writing disorders produce shorter, less interesting, and poorly organized essays, and are less likely to review spelling, punctuation, and grammar to increase clarity (Hooper et al., 2011; Wakely, Hooper, de Kruif, & Swartz, 2006). However, spelling errors or poor handwriting that do not significantly interfere in daily activities or academic pursuits do not qualify a child for this diagnosis. In addition, problems in written expression signal the possibility of other learning disorders, because of shared metacognitive processes: planning, self-monitoring, self-evaluation, and self-modification (Heim & Benasich, 2006). Writing disorders are less understood than other learning disorders, and are found often in combination with learning disorders in reading or mathematics, which also have underlying core deficits in language and neuropsychological development.

Prevalence and Course

Current estimates of the prevalence of all types of learning disorders range from 2% to 10% of the entire population, depending on how the problems are defined and measured (APA, 2000). However, several researchers suggest that due to underreporting, these estimates should be much higher. The prevalence of dyslexia (reading disorder) is estimated to range from 5% to 17% of school-aged children (Lyon et al., 2003; S. E. Shaywitz, 1998).

Reading difficulties may be part of a continuum of reading abilities rather than a discrete, all-or-none phenomenon, which would mean that children with reading disorders are essentially those who fall at the lower end of the continuum (Snowling, 2008). This consideration is useful and important because, clearly, there are strong readers and weak readers, and no definitive cutoff point easily distinguishes the two (Lyon et al., 2006). If prevalence estimates are based on a continuum of reading problems rather than a diagnostic category, reading disabilities are estimated to affect 1 in 5, or at least 10 million children in the United States (S. E. Shaywitz, Escobar, Shaywitz, Fletcher, & Makuch, 1992).

Current estimates of the prevalence of disorders related to mathematics and written expression are highly discrepant due to a lack of epidemiologic studies. Clinical studies put the prevalence of mathematics disorder at about 20% of all children with learning disorders, which means that about 1% of school-age children receive this diagnosis (APA, 2000). If prevalence is estimated on the basis of test scores, however, about 5% to 6% of school-age children would be included (Shalev, 2007). Like reading disorder, mathematics disorder usually becomes apparent during second or third grade, once formal mathematics instruction begins. Therefore, prevalence estimates based solely on diagnoses may be unduly conservative.

Finally, disorder of written expression is considered to be rare when not associated with other learning disorders (APA, 2000). However, given the high rate of developmental language disorders in the general population (8% to 15%) and the significantly high rate of disorders in reading skills previously noted, written language disorders probably affect at least 10% of the school-age population (Lyon et al., 2003, 2006). Because of their high comorbidity, disorders in math and written expression may best be construed as related features of a generalized problem in learning, rather than selective impairments (Landerl & Moll, 2010).

Cultural, Class, and Gender Variations

Social and cultural factors are less relevant to learning disorders than other types of cognitive and behavioral problems; in fact, the diagnostic criteria state that they cannot be attributed to these factors. Nevertheless, some cultural and ethnic factors may affect how children with learning disorders are identified and treated (Johansson, 2006).

As emphasized throughout this text, many childhood disorders reflect an interaction between the child's inherent abilities and resources and the opportunities that exist in the child's local environment. In the case of learning to read, some teaching approaches do not explicitly emphasize specific sound—symbol relationships that are inherent in the dialect of children from diverse ethnic backgrounds. For example, Wood, Felton, Flowers, & Naylor (1991) did an interesting study to illustrate the point that deficits in phonological awareness occur more frequently among populations that use nonstandard English. They followed a random sample of 485 Caucasian (55%) and African American (45%) children from first grade through third grade, and found that although African American youngsters read at the same grade level as Caucasian children at the beginning of the first grade, they show marked declines in reading by the third grade and severe declines by the fifth grade. These findings suggest that greater attention to differences in dialect can lead to better learning opportunities.

Whereas attention to cultural and ethnic issues pertaining to learning disorders is a recent addition to research, sex differences have a long and contentious history. Males are more often diagnosed with learning disorders than females, accounting for 60% to 80% of all children diagnosed (APA, 2000). As with communication disorders, reasons for referral can distort the fact that boys and girls actually have very similar rates of reading problems. It comes as no surprise that schools refer about 4 times as many boys as girls, largely because boys are more likely to show behavior problems. Girls with learning problems often are quiet and withdrawn rather than loud and attention-seeking, and may be overlooked unless educators and parents are well informed. When male–female ratios are derived from epidemiological estimates rather than referrals, boys and girls are represented equally among children with learning disorders in reading, as long as attention-related disorders are taken into account (Hawke, Olson, Willcut, Wadsworth, & DeFries, 2009; Pinborough-Zimmerman et al., 2007).

Development

Children with learning disorders often do not know how or why they are different, but they do know how it feels to be unable to keep up with others in the classroom. Hearing themselves described as "slow," "different," or "behind," they may identify more with their disabilities rather than with their strengths. These daily experiences may cause some children to act out by either withdrawing or becoming angry and noncompliant. Like James, they may stop trying to learn. Like Francine, they may become isolated and limit their participation in activities that their peers enjoy.

What can be expected of Francine, James, Tim, and Carlos during their school years? Proper planning and goal setting are the cornerstone of helping strategies at home and at school. Learning disorders are not easily outgrown, but there is reason for optimism. First and foremost, about three-fourths of the children diagnosed with reading disorder in elementary school still have major reading problems in high school and young adulthood (Young et al., 2002; Johnson, Beitchman, & Brownlie, 2010). Therefore, developmental expectations and educational planning must be ongoing (Lipka & Siegel, 2006).

Do problems continue as a direct and unchangeable result of the disability, or as a result of a failure to identify the learning problem in time to affect its course? The required discrepancy between IQ and performance may hamper early identification, because the assessment often is not done until the child has attempted and failed at reading, usually by the third grade. By that time, the child's achievement may be slow enough to demonstrate the discrepancy, but the child has failed in reading for 2 to 3 years and may have developed other learning problems as a result (Lyon et al., 2003). Furthermore, the discrepancy requirement for the diagnosis of a learning disorder may not be necessary or meaningful. Researchers are now finding very few differences between discrepant and nondiscrepant readers in many factors such as information processing, genetic variables, neurophysiological response, and so forth (Maehler & Schuchardt, 2011; Vellutino et al., 2007). The limitations of this approach should be kept in mind when it is necessary to meet local regulations for determining a child's eligibility for special services.

Children and adolescents with learning disorders are more likely than their peers to show internalizing problems such as anxiety (Nelson & Harwood, 2011) and mood disorders (Maughan, Rowe, Loeber, & Stouthamer-Loeber, 2003), as well as externalizing behaviors such as ADHD (Goldston et al., 2007). The range and type of problems are generally similar for both younger and older age groups. Accordingly, issues pertaining to both younger and older children and adolescents with learning disorders are considered jointly unless particular developmental differences warrant attention. Many of these issues are common to all types of learning disorders unless otherwise noted.

Psychological and Social Adjustment

Students with reading disorders feel less supported by their parents, teachers, and peers than do normal readers, and are more likely to express poor academic or scholastic self-concepts (Heim & Benasich, 2006). As a case in point, the school dropout rate for adolescents with learning disorders is nearly 40%, or approximately 1.5 times the average (APA, 2000).

The connection between learning disorders and behavioral or emotional disorders has generated considerable interest but only cautious conclusions. Common sense suggests that children with learning disorders are faced with considerable challenges that are likely to take a toll on self-esteem and, in time, their social relationships. However, children's self-concepts in sports and appearance are usually less affected (Lyon et al., 2006).

Parents and teachers describe children with learning disorders as being more difficult to manage than typical children, beginning at an early age. Although overall reports of behavior problems increase considerably for all children between early and middle childhood, behavior problems among children with learning disorders are about 3 times higher than the norm by 8 years of age (Benasich, Curtiss, & Tallal, 1993) (see ● Figure 11.4). Most of these problems are not specific to learning disorders, but cover a broad range of problems that overlap 10% to 25% with features of conduct disorder (CD), oppositional defiant disorder (ODD), attention-deficit/-hyperactivity disorder (ADHD), and major depressive disorder across all ages (APA, 2000).

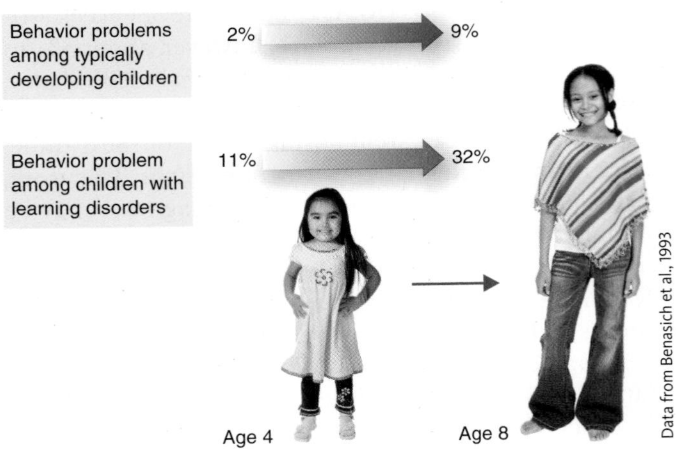

FIGURE 11.4 | Percentage of clinically significant behavior problems among children with and without learning disorders, at 4 years and 8 years of age.

Photo credits: © iStockphoto.com/Rhienna Cutler; © iStockphoto.com/Jack Hollingsworth

These co-occurring problems are often interpreted as individual reactions and coping styles in response to failure, frustration, and, in some instances, punishment and negative attention. In terms of development, however, it is hard to say which comes first: Behavior problems may precede learning problems, may follow them, or occur at the same time (Hinshaw, 1992). One explanation for the higher rate of behavior problems in children with learning disorders as they enter school is their impeded intellectual development, which creates additional academic and social pressure (Tallal & Benasich, 2002). Whereas many of these behavioral and emotional problems gradually decrease from childhood to adolescence, adolescence with learning disorders continue to face challenges in their social relationships (St Clair, Pickles, Durkin, & Conti-Ramsden, 2011).

Based on a review of over 150 studies (Kavale & Forness, 1996), about 3 of every 4 students with learning disorders have significant deficits in social skills. As a group, they are more isolated and less popular among peers than other children, and they tend to make negative impressions on others (Durkin & Conti-Ramsden, 2010). Like Francine, who was described by her mother as "humorless and in a bit of a fog," most children with learning disorders have difficulty grasping the nuances of social interaction and may not know how to greet others, make friends, or join in playground games. Subtle cues of social interaction may be missed or ignored. They may not always interpret correctly or respond appropriately to the frequent nonverbal—but very expressive—communication of other children, such as rolling the eyes to show dislike or disinterest. When children with learning disorders misunderstand the situation and act inappropriately, other children turn away.

A child with a learning disorder also can be an emotional burden for family members. Parents may experience a wide range of emotions, including denial, guilt, blame, frustration, anger, and despair. Brothers and sisters often feel annoyed, embarrassed, or jealous of the attention their sibling receives. Because behavioral problems are usually so disruptive, a child's distress and emotional needs may easily be overlooked.

Adult Outcomes

Unfortunately, the social and emotional difficulties connected to communication and learning disorders may continue into adulthood, largely because of inadequate recognition and services (Johnson et al., 2010). Adults may find ways to disguise their problems, such as watching television news rather than reading newspapers. On the other hand, many excel in nonacademic subjects such as art, music, dance, or athletics. Still others may become outstanding architects and engineers, or they may have extraordinary interpersonal skills (Lyon et al., 2006). Each child and adolescent has many strengths that can be developed to compensate for his or her known deficits. Thus, despite their earlier risk for academic failure and psychosocial problems, many adults with learning disorders lead successful and productive lives (Werner, 1993).

Men with reading disorders do not differ from their peers regarding feelings of global self-worth; symptoms of depression; feelings of competency and satisfaction with jobs, marriages, and other relationships; or frequency of antisocial behavior (Boetsch, Green, & Pennington, 1996). However, men still perceive lower levels of social support from parents and relatives—the only people still in their lives who knew of their problems as children—which confirms the indelible impressions left by early experiences.

One adult describes his own way of compensating for learning problems:

> I faked my way through school because I was very bright. I resent most that no one picked up my weaknesses. Essentially I judge myself on my failures. . . . [I] have always had low self-esteem. . . . A blow to my self-esteem when I was in school was that I could not write a poem or a story. . . . I could not write with a pen or pencil. The computer has changed my life. I do everything on my computer. It acts as my memory. I use it to structure my life and for all of my writing since my handwriting and written expression has always been so poor. (Polloway, Schewel, & Patton, 1992, p. 521)

Whereas the long-term outlook for men with learning disorders is generally positive, the troublesome issue of sexism arises when considering how adult women with learning disorders fare over time. As a group, women with learning disorders have more adjustment problems than men as they leave school and face the demands of adult life. Similar to other adults with disabilities, they also face greater risk of sexual assault and related forms of abuse (Brownlie, Jabbar, Beitchman, Vida, & Atkinson, 2007). Problems and breakdowns in relationships are common, which may reflect the lack of opportunity available to these women to achieve in areas that capitalize on their strengths.

Reading problems often cause poorly qualified graduates to take relatively undemanding and unrewarding jobs. Women who lack competitive skills and strong career options due to school failure tend to get involved at an early age in intimate relationships that are generally unsupportive (Fairchild, 2002). Young men, in contrast, have more wide-ranging options once they leave school, which facilitates more positive social functioning in adulthood. Thus, if they are able to select their own environments in adulthood (and women have more obstacles in this regard than men), both men and women with learning disorders can build on their existing strengths, skills, and talents (Hatch, Harvey, & Maughan, 2010).

It is safe to say that even though learning disorders may remain, people who are given proper educational experiences have a remarkable ability to learn throughout their life spans (Gregg, 2011). Box 11.2 describes some of these important opportunities that increase resilience. Adults can learn to read, although it is difficult because brain development slows down after puberty.

BOX 11.2 A CLOSER LOOK

Factors That Increase Resilience and Adaptation

Several personal characteristics and circumstances aid those with learning disorders in their successful adaptation from childhood, through adolescence, to young adulthood. As part of a longitudinal study of all children born in 1955 on the island of Kauai, Hawaii, E. E. Werner (1993) followed 22 children with learning disabilities and 22 matched controls. She found that most children with learning disabilities adapted successfully to adult life. Those who showed the greatest resilience and flexibility over time had (1) a basic temperament that elicited positive responses from others; (2) a well-developed sense of efficacy, preparedness, and self-esteem that guided their lives; (3) competent care-givers and supportive adults; and (4) opportunities for a second chance if they made mistakes or got into trouble with the law. Although some of these characteristics are present from birth (e.g., temperament), many of the other supportive factors can be increased through the efforts of family members, schools, and communities.

Source: Based on authors' case material.

Current gains in knowledge of the causes and early signs of learning disorders are likely to have a positive impact on early recognition and proper instruction. Nonintrusive electrophysiological measurements of brain reactivity may permit an early diagnosis based on underlying deficits in phonological processing rather than on performance alone. Thus, early identification and intervention may be the key to preventing the long-term consequences of these disorders (Gaysina, Maughan, & Richards, 2010).

Causes

Most learning disorders do not stem from problems in a single area of the brain, but from difficulties in bringing information from various brain regions together so that information can be integrated and understood (Damasio, Tranel, Grabowskia, Adolphs, & Damasio, 2004; Meyer & Damasio, 2009). Minute disturbances may underlie phonological processing deficits. Emerging evidence points to the conclusion that, in many cases, these subtle disturbances begin very early during development, perhaps prenatally (McGrath et al., 2007; Raschle, Chang, & Gaab, 2011).

Recent findings suggest two distinguishable types of reading disorder—those children who are persistently poor readers and those who are accuracy-improved (i.e., they learn ways to compensate for their reading difficulties and improve over time) (S. E. Shaywitz, Mody, & Shaywitz, 2006). Persistently poor readers and accuracy-improved readers have comparable reading skills and SES when they begin school, but by the time they are young adults, the accuracy-improved readers show better cognitive ability. The presence of compensatory factors, such as stronger cognitive ability, may allow the accuracy-improved individuals to minimize the consequences of their phonological defect over time (Ferrer, Shaywitz, Holahan, Marchione, & Shaywitz, 2010). These compensatory factors may be genetically-based, and thus the child's ability improves with maturity, whereas the persistent group may face greater environmental challenges, often associated with poverty and inequality, that reduce reading opportunities.

"Here is my report card. For reference here is your report card, I found in the attic, when you were in the same grade."

Genetic and Constitutional Factors

Children who lack some of the skills needed for reading, such as hearing the separate sounds of words, are more likely to have a parent with a related problem. Around the turn of the 20th century this problem was studied largely by physicians, who considered reading disorders to be an inherited condition called *congenital word blindness* (W. P. Morgan, 1896). Today, estimates based on behavioral genetic studies indicate that heritability accounts for over 60% of the variance in reading disorders (V. M. Bishop, 2006; Plomin et al., 2010), although the exact mode of transmission remains undetermined.

Most attention paid to heritability is aimed at genetic transmission of critical brain processes underlying phonetic processing (Scerri & Schulte-Körne, 2010; Vellutino et al., 2004). Because a parent's learning disorder may take a slightly different form in the child—the father may have a writing disorder and his child an expressive language disorder—it seems unlikely that specific types of learning disorders are inherited directly. More likely, what is inherited is a subtle brain dysfunction that, in turn, can lead to a learning disorder (Newbury et al., 2011; Richlan et al., 2011; Scerri & Schulte-Körne, 2010). For example, an area has been identified on chromosome 6 that predisposes children to reading disorder (Grigorenko, 2007). Genetic transmission provides a plausible explanation for the high rate of 35% to 45% among family members for learning disorders in reading as well as math (Shalev, 2007), which are considerably higher than the estimated base rate of 5% to 10% in the population (Snowling, Gallagher, & Frith 2003).

Neurobiological Factors

Our understanding of learning disorders, particularly reading-based and language-based problems, took an important new direction in the mid-1980s with the discovery that the brains of people with these problems were characterized by cellular abnormalities in the left hemisphere, which contains important language centers (Galaburda, Sherman, Rosen, & Geschwind, 1985). The fact that these cellular abnormalities could occur only during the fifth to seventh month of fetal development strengthened the view that learning disorders evolve from subtle brain deficits present at birth (Lyon et al., 2003). Initial autopsy findings were confirmed by sophisticated brain imaging technology that reveals the brain directly at work and makes it possible to detect subtle malfunctions that never could be seen before.

The suspected deficits, which likely are genetically based, involve specific discrimination tasks, such as detecting visual and auditory stimuli, as well as more pervasive visual—organizational deficits associated with reasoning and mathematical ability (Benassi, Simonelli, Giovagnoli, & Bolzani, 2010; Pennington, 2006). A probable location of these deficits is a structure called the *planum temporale*, a language-related area in both sides of the brain. In a normal brain, the left side of the planum temporale is usually larger than the right side; however, in the brain of an individual with a reading disorder, both sides are equal size (Tallal, 2003).

B. A. Shaywitz, Shaywitz, et al. (2002) found lower activation in numerous sites—primarily the left hemisphere of the brains of dyslexic children compared to nonimpaired children—including the inferior frontal, parieto–temporal, and occipito–temporal gyri. These three areas of the brain respectively are responsible for understanding phonemes, analyzing words, and automatically detecting words. Once a word is learned, this three-part center recognizes it automatically, without first having to decipher it phonetically (S. E. Shaywitz et al., 2006).

From a cognitive standpoint, these neurological findings suggest that children with learning disorders are distinctively disadvantaged compared with average readers in terms of the processing underlying their short-term and working memory. Impairments in short-term memory affect the recall of phonemes and numbers; similarly, impairments in working memory affect how such information is processed and stored so that it can be rapidly accessed. Considerable support now exists concerning how memory deficits explain the performance difficulties of children with a learning disorder (Carretti, Borella, Cornoldi, & De Beni, 2009; Maehler & Schuchardt, 2011; Swanson, Zheng, & Jerman, 2009).

We have stressed that most children with reading and writing disorders have difficulty distinguishing phonemes that occur rapidly in speech. But why is this so? Consider what is involved, as shown in ● Figure 11.5.

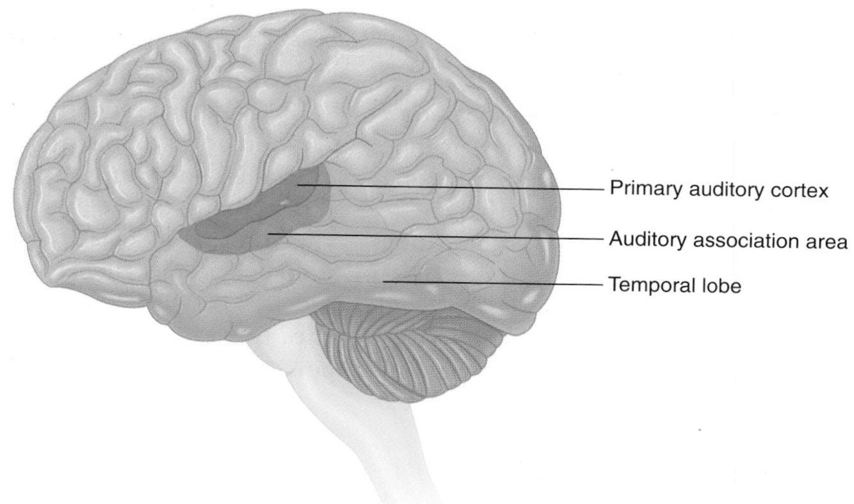

How the brain processes speech

1 The primary auditory cortex (shown in red), which is located on the top edge of each temporal lobe, receives electrical signals from receptors in the ears and transforms these signals into meaningless sound sensations, such as vowels and the consonants in ***ba*** and ***ga***.

2 The meaningless sound sensations are sent from the primary auditory cortex to another area in the temporal lobe, called the auditory association area.

3 The auditory association area (shown in blue), which is located directly below the primary auditory cortex, transforms basic sensory information, such as noises or sounds, into recognizable auditory information, such as words or music. Here, sounds are matched with existing patterns that have been previously formed and stored.

FIGURE 11.5 | How the brain processes speech.

The sound must be processed by various brain areas as it is carried by nerve impulses from the ear to the thalamus to the nerve cells within the auditory cortex, where it is matched to existing patterns, or phonic bins, that have been previously formed and stored.

Compare this process to listening to music. When you first hear a new song, do you recognize aspects that resemble other recordings by that group or another group? Can you distinguish the music of one group from another? As we listen, we tend to cluster sounds into various categories, acquiring our taste for music as we store more collections and melodies into memory. Each time we hear new music, we match it to what we already know and appreciate. Young people are particularly adept at assimilating new sounds, thereby broadening their tastes. In contrast, people who have already formed specific musical tastes tend to stick to what they know, rejecting unrecognizable sounds. This gap in music appreciation is analogous to the gap researchers describe in the phonic abilities of children with learning disorders—they lack certain auditory sites that allow certain sounds to be recognized, so their appreciation of certain words is compromised.

Each neuron in the language processing areas of the brain has immense specificity. Some neurons fire when you silently name an object but not when you read the object's name out loud, and vice versa. Certain neurons are activated when bilingual people speak one language, but not when they speak the other (Ojemann, 1991). Someone can have an expressive language problem despite full comprehension, because the same neurons that are active when a person hears a word are not active when that person speaks it.

In the visual system, different aspects of what you see, such as form, color, and motion, are routed to different regions of the visual cortex. When something moves in your visual field, the region of the cortex that responds to visual motion is activated. Eden et al. (1996) first discovered that adults with reading disorders show no activation in visual motion when asked to view randomly moving dots. A specific defect in perception of visual motion may interfere with many different brain functions, and has been noted among children with autism as well as learning disorders (Benassi et al., 2010; Skottun & Skoyles, 2008). To detect differences between consonant sounds—such as *b* or *t*—we must be able to distinguish between very rapid changes in sound frequency. A subtle neurological deficit in sensitivity could prohibit this distinction, which would then show up clinically as problems in reading and phonological processing (Raschle et al., 2011).

Thus, two major findings implicate specific biological underpinnings of reading disorders: (1) the language difficulties for people with reading disorders are specifically associated with the neurological processing of phonology and storage of such information into memory; and (2) behavioral and physiological abnormalities are found in the processing of visual information. It is not surprising, therefore, that phonological and visual processing problems often coexist among people with reading disorders (Skottun & Skoyles, 2008).

Studies of the causes of learning disorders mostly involve children with reading disorders, but the findings apply to disorders in written expression and mathematics as well. Many—but not all—disabled writers show deficits in reading (Lyon et al., 2003), and some mathematical concepts require reading and writing as well as mathematics skills. In contrast to these language-based disorders, however, are various nonverbal learning disabilities (Drummond, Ahmad, & Rourke, 2005). **Nonverbal learning disabilities (NLD)** are deficits related to right-hemisphere brain functioning, and are characteristic of children who perform considerably worse at math than reading. These deficits involve social skills, spatial orientation, problem solving, and the recognition of nonverbal cues such as body language. In addition to math deficiencies, nonverbal learning disorders may be accompanied by neuropsychological problems such as poor coordination, poor judgment, and difficulties adapting to novel and complex situations (Lyon et al., 2003; Semrud-Clikeman, Walkowiak, Wilkinson, & Minne, 2010).

Recall that Francine had well-developed word recognition and spelling abilities, but significantly worse mechanical–arithmetic skills. Mathematics disorder, and perhaps that of written expression as well, are known to be associated with brain deficits that differ from deficits described for language-based learning disorders. These deficits are largely found in areas not related to verbal ability, which has led to use of the term nonverbal learning disorders.

The search for suspected causes for this nonverbal pattern of learning disabilities focuses on neurological diseases of childhood and developmental disabilities that impair brain functioning. Fetal alcohol syndrome, insulin-dependent diabetes, autism, irradiation (for treatment of various forms of cancer), and several other fetal and early childhood diseases and trauma have been linked to nonverbal learning disorders (Collins & Rourke, 2003). The common element among these various diseases and traumas—the final common pathway leading to the nonverbal learning disorder syndrome—is that they impair development and functioning of the brain, especially in terms of deficits in social cognition (Galway & Metsala, 2011).

Social and Psychological Factors

Emotional disturbances and other signs of poor adaptive ability often accompany learning disorders, perhaps because the underlying causes are the same. The overlap between dyslexia and ADHD, for example, ranges from 30% to 70% depending on how ADHD is defined (Del'Homme, Kim, Loo, Yang, & Smalley, 2007; Fletcher, Shaywitz, & Shaywitz, 1999). Although this degree of overlap suggests that behavioral and learning problems have certain common aspects, they are still distinct and separate disorders (Lyon et al., 2006). Reading disorder is commonly associated with deficits in phonological awareness, whereas ADHD has more variable effects on cognitive functioning, especially in areas of rote verbal learning and memory (Jakobson & Kikas, 2007). ADHD, moreover, is relatively unrelated to phonological awareness tasks. However, some children with learning disorders show symptoms similar to ADHD, including inattention, restlessness, and hyperactivity (Del'Homme et al., 2007).

Prevention and Treatment

Although learning disorders have strong biological underpinnings, intervention methods rely primarily on educational and psychosocial methods. Psychosocial treatments for James, Francine, Carlos, and Tim must be comprehensive and ongoing, with each new task broken down into manageable steps, including examples, practice, and ample feedback. Combined with proper teaching strategies, children and their families may benefit from counseling aimed at helping the children develop greater self-control and a more positive attitude toward their own abilities. Support groups for parents also can fill an important gap between the school and the home by providing information, practical suggestions, and mutual understanding.

Someday, breakthroughs in brain research may lead to new medical interventions, but at present no biological treatments exist for speech, language, and academic disabilities. Where significant problems coexist in concentration and attention, some children respond favorably to stimulant medications that may temporarily improve attention, concentration, and the ability to control their impulsivity (see Chapter 5), albeit with little or no improvement in learning. Typically, the medication schedule ensures that the drug is active during peak school hours, when reading and math are taught.

FRANCINE

Slowly but Surely Improving

To reduce Francine's difficulties with math and, especially, with peer relationships, we considered several factors. First, we decided that teaching should be primarily verbal, with an understanding that she would have the most difficulty in math and science. Her teachers favored allowing Francine to use a calculator and a computer to assist her in learning new concepts. An emphasis on physical education was also planned, to help her with her visual—motor coordination. Her math teacher agreed that using graph paper might help her visualize numerical relationships, which led to noticeable improvements in her schoolwork.

Francine's problems in making friends were a major concern to everyone, and we believed that they were directly linked to her learning disability.
A cognitive—behavioral intervention plan was developed in conjunction with her educational program. Because of Francine's strong verbal skills, we taught her to problem solve through role playing, and encouraged her mother to invite one child at a time for her to play with so that she could practice her skills. Francine had drifted into being a loner and seemed disinterested in looking after herself, so we also discussed ways to develop better self-care at home by giving her an allowance for completing household chores. We spent considerable time explaining the nature of her problems to her parents, and this guidance led to relief and understanding.

We saw the family once again one year later; although some of Francine's problems still existed, her social abilities had improved. She still had difficulties in developing friendships and tended to prefer being alone, but the problem had clearly lessened from the previous year. (Based on authors' case material)

Consider the coordinated planning and effort that went into the treatment programs for Francine: Francine was able to get help because her problems were detected; recall, however, that by the time she was referred, she had already begun to fail at formal schooling. The first step in solving any problem is to realize that it exists. The nature of learning disorders makes this difficult for many children and parents. Although numerous signs of language-based learning disorders are present from early childhood, sophisticated means of assessing problems are not yet available before children are old enough to be formally tested.

Issues of identification are important because a brief window of opportunity may exist for successful treatment. If a problem is detected in early childhood—say, by kindergarten—then language-based deficits can often be remediated successfully. If the problem is not detected until age 8 or so, response to treatment is much lower (Hatcher et al., 2006). This is why prevention of reading difficulties is a hot topic: Training children in phonological awareness activities at an early age may prevent subsequent reading problems among children at risk (Duff & Clarke, 2011; Haager, Klingner, & Vaughn, 2007). These activities consist of games that involve listening, rhyming, identifying sentences and words, and analyzing syllables and phonemes. For example, the child might analyze *sand* as *s-and* and then synthesize it into *sand*, or colored alphabet blocks might be used to break the word into separate phonetic sounds (*s-a-n-d*).

Knowledge of communication and learning disorders has played leapfrog with the philosophy and practice of classroom instruction during the last decade. Discoveries in neurosciences, as noted above, challenged some prevailing educational practices, leading to more systematic ways of assisting children with learning disorders, as explored in the following sections.

The Inclusion Movement

Integrating children with special needs into the regular classroom began as the *inclusion movement* during the 1950s, based on studies showing that segregated classes for students with disabilities were ineffective and possibly harmful (Baldwin, 1958). Resource rooms and specially trained teachers replaced the special classes that had been in vogue, a change that had the further advantage of removing the need to label and categorize children. The Education for All Handicapped Children Act of 1975 in the United States (currently known as Individuals with Disabilities Education Improvement Act [IDEA], 2004) and the provincial Education Acts in Canada mandated that children with special needs must be afforded access to all educational services, regardless of their handicaps. Today, children with special educational needs in North America and many other countries are placed in regular classrooms whenever possible.

In 2002, the *No Child Left Behind* act was signed into law in the U.S. This Act allowed for more intensified efforts by each state to improve the academic achievement of public school students considered at risk for school failure. Today, almost 14% (about 6.6 million) school-age children in the United States from all walks of life receive some level of support through special education, and students with specific learning disabilities account for close to half (45.5%) of these students (National Center for Learning Disabilities [NCLD], 2007; U. S. Dept. of Special Education Programs, 2010).

Response to Intervention Models

The IDEA Act provides for the use of Response to Intervention (RTI) models to identify and assess children. RTI consists of tiered instruction where children who have difficulty learning to read using typical methods of instruction are provided with small-group, intensive instruction. Those who need additional intervention may receive one-on-one special education. This approach seeks to provide each child with the appropriate level of instruction required for his or her individual needs (Kavale & Flanagan, 2007; National Institutes of Health, 2007).

Initiatives to allow children with special needs to receive services without being diagnosed or labeled as mentally retarded, learning disabled, and so forth have become widely available and hold considerable promise. However, implementation and teacher training, as well as the question of whether such initiatives succeed in meeting the special needs of students, continue to be unresolved (Batsche, Kavale, & Kovaleski, 2006; Hunt & McDonnell, 2007; NCLD, 2007).

Instructional Methods

Although controversy remains over the practical aspects of including all children in regular classrooms, most educators today favor direct instruction for children with learning disorders. **Direct instruction** is a straightforward approach to teaching based on the premise that to improve a skill, the instructional activities must approximate those of the skill being taught (see example in Box 11.3) (Hammill, Mather, Allen, & Roberts, 2002). Direct instruction in word structure is necessary because of the child's phonological deficits. Direct instruction in reading emphasizes the specific learning of word structure and word reading until the skill is learned, without concern for the full context of the sentence or story. This method is based on the premise that a child's ability to decode and recognize words accurately and rapidly must be acquired before reading comprehension can occur (Hammill, Mather, Allen, & Roberts, 2002; Haager et al., 2007).

To prevent dyslexia, it is important to provide early interventions that teach both phonologic and verbal abilities. Children must be able to learn the sounds of words to decode them, but they must also understand the meaning of the word to understand the message of the text (Shaywitz et al., 2008). The techniques that have been demonstrated to work are practicing manipulating phonemes, building vocabulary, increasing comprehension, and improving fluency, which helps strengthen the brain's ability to link letters to sounds (Nation et al., 2007).

In brief, the components of effective reading instruction are the same whether the focus is prevention or intervention—phonemic awareness and phonemic decoding skills, fluency in word recognition, construction of meaning, vocabulary, spelling, and writing. Evidence-based evaluations show dramatic reductions in the incidence of reading failure when direct and explicit instruction in these components is provided by the classroom teacher (Duff & Clarke, 2011; Haager et al., 2007; Schuele & Boudreau, 2008). Empirical support for teaching phonics from an early age also is emerging from recent brain imaging studies, as described in ● Figure 11.6 (Eden & Moats, 2002; Davis et al., 2011). For example, instruction in phonemic awareness, phonics, and other reading skills produces more activation in the automatic recognition process, noted previously (see Causes). After undergoing such training, brain scans of people who were once

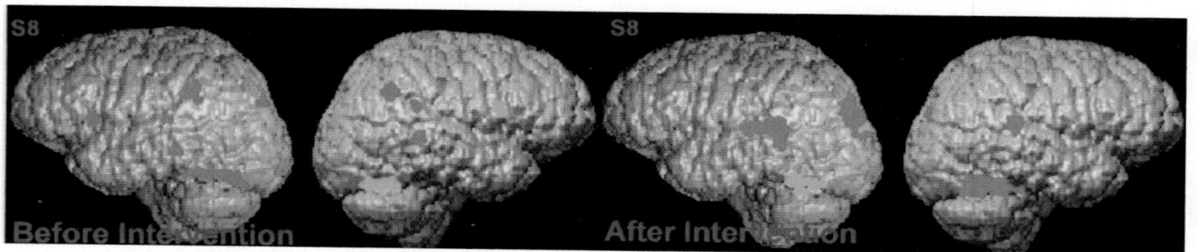

FIGURE 11.6 | Brain activation maps from a child with severe dyslexia before and after an 8-week intense intervention in which word reading skills moved into the average range. The left panel shows the typical brain activation map from magnetic source imaging studies of dyslexia, with predominant activity in temporal and parietal areas of the right hemisphere, but little activation in homologous areas of the left hemisphere. In the right panel there is a significant increase in the activation of these left tempoparietal areas associated with the significant improvement in word reading accuracy that parallels the patterns observed in proficient readers.

Neurology April 23, 2002 vol. 58 no. 8 1203–1213 "Dyslexia-specific brain activation profile becomes normal following successful remedial training" by P. G. Simos, PhD, J. M. Fletcher, PhD, E. Bergman, MD, J. I. Breier, PhD, B. R. Foorman, PhD, E. M. Castillo, PhD, R. N. Davis, MA, M. Fitzgerald, BA and A. C. Papanicolaou, PhD, Neurology © 2012 by AAN Enterprises, Inc.

poor readers begin to resemble those of good readers (National Institutes of Health, 2007).

We now turn to some practical examples of how reading, writing, and math can be taught by applying well-established principles of learning. Behavioral and cognitive–behavioral strategies have been highly beneficial in remediating the problems of children and adolescents with communication and learning disorders (Lyon et al., 2003, 2006). In addition, new methods based on the use of technology offer some children additional ways to acquire basic and advanced academic skills.

Behavioral Strategies

Many problems that children with communication and learning disorders have stem from the fact that the material is simply presented too fast for them (Tallal & Benasich, 2002). Thus, a strategy to provide children with a set of verbal rules that can be written out and reapplied may be more beneficial than one that relies on memory, or on grasping the concept all at once. Tried and true behavioral principles of learning are well suited to this task of teaching systematically.

In addition to academic concepts, some of the associated problems with peers can be addressed in the same fashion, as we saw with Francine. A simple, gradual approach is more beneficial than an approach that tries to solve the problem all at once. Children also need help learning to generalize new information to different situations. An individualized, skills-based approach does not have to be boring or routine; in fact, speech and language therapists are skilled at providing a stimulating but structured environment for hearing and practicing language patterns. During an engaging activity with a younger child, the therapist may talk about toys, and then encourage the child to use the same sounds or words. The child may watch the therapist make the sound, feel the vibration in the therapist's throat, and then practice making the sounds before a mirror.

Behavioral methods often are used in conjunction with a complete program of direct instruction, which typically proceeds in a cumulative, highly structured manner (Wright & Jacobs, 2003), as shown in Box 11.3. Because this method places a strong emphasis on the behavior of the teacher in terms of explicit correction, reinforcement, and practice opportunities, it is sometimes referred to as "faultless instruction": Each concept should be so clearly presented that only one interpretation is possible. Each lesson is structured according to field-tested scripts. Teachers work with one small group of students at a time, and shoot questions at them at a rate as high as 10 to 12 per minute.

This highly structured, repetitive method is clearly effective. Students who receive direct behavioral instruction typically outperform students who receive standard classroom instruction by almost 1 standard deviation on various learning measures (Lyon et al., 2003).

Cognitive–Behavioral Interventions

Cognitive–behavioral interventions are also highly suited for children with learning disorders. Like behavioral methods, these procedures actively involve students in learning, particularly in monitoring their own thought processes. Considerable emphasis is placed on self-control by using strategies such as self-monitoring, self-assessment, self-recording, self-management of reinforcement, and so on (Alwell & Cobb, 2009; Cobb, Sample, Alwell, & Johns, 2006). Essentially, children are taught to ask themselves several questions as they progress, to make themselves

BOX 11.3 A CLOSER LOOK

Steps in Direct Behavioral Instruction

1. Review the child's existing abilities.
2. Develop a short statement of goals at the beginning of each lesson.
3. Present new concepts and material in small steps, each followed by student practice.
4. Provide clear and detailed instructions and explanations.
5. Provide considerable practice for all students.
6. Check student understanding of concepts continually, in response to teacher questions.
7. Provide explicit guidance for each student during initial practice.
8. Provide systematic feedback and corrections.
9. Provide explicit instruction and practice for exercises completed by students at their desks.

Source: From *Treatment of Learning Disabilities* by G. R. Lyons and L. Cutting, 1998. In E. J. Mash and L. C. Terdal (Eds.), *Treatment of Childhood Disorders.*

The following example illustrates how the steps in direct behavioral instruction are applied.

Example: Direct Instruction Lesson

A typical DI lesson includes explicit and carefully sequenced instruction provided by the teacher (model) along with frequent opportunities for students to practice their skills (independent practice) over time (review). For example, if the sound /m/ appeared for the first time, the teacher might say, "You're going to learn a new sound. My turn to say it. When I move under the letter, I'll say the sound. I'll keep on saying it as long as I touch under it. Get ready. mmm" (model). "My turn again. Get ready. mmm" (model). "Your turn. When I move under the letter, you say the sound. Keep on saying it as long as I touch under it. Get ready." (independent practice). "Again. Get ready." (independent practice). If an error occurs during instruction, the teacher would model the sound ("My turn. mmm"), use guided practice ("Say it with me. Get ready. mmm"), and have students practice independently ("Your turn. Get ready"). A "starting over" would be conducted based on this error; this might include starting over at the top of a column or row of sounds so that students get increased practice on the /m/ sound. The /m/ would appear throughout the lesson and in subsequent lessons to ensure skill mastery (firm responding) over time.

Source: Marchand-Martella, Martella, & Ausdemore (2005). An Overview of Direct Instruction.

more aware of the material. Try it yourself: "Why am I reading this? What's the main idea the authors are trying to get across? Where can I find the answer to this question? How does this follow from what I learned a minute ago?"

CARLOS

Plans

In third grade, Carlos's treatment plan was to integrate a cognitive–behavioral approach into regular teaching methods. Rather than using one-to-one instruction, I discussed with his teacher ways of blending some behavioral methods into the classroom. For example, his strengths are in the areas of thinking and speaking, so I discussed using computers and tape recorders to help him learn the materials. He seemed to like these methods, and they helped him bypass some aspects of his writing disability. I discussed practice strategies for visual–motor integration, such as drawing and tracing, and gradually made the task more complex. Because cursive writing is often easier for children than printing, I suggested that Carlos bypass learning to print. A continuous pattern of output is easier for Carlos to plan and produce than a discrete form of output, such as printing.

To help Carlos write a paper, I adopted a basic planning strategy from Graham, MacArthur, Schwatz, and Voth (1992), which helped him structure the tasks into related subproblems. The acronym PLANS helps him to remember to:

Pick goals (related to length, structure, and purpose of the paper)
List ways to meet goals
And
make **N**otes
Sequence notes

This mnemonic was used in a three-step writing strategy to assist Carlos to (1) do PLANS, (2) write and say more, and (3) evaluate whether he is successful in achieving his goals. (Based on authors' case material)

Carlos's treatment program shows how some of these procedures were applied to his particular writing problems:

Computer-Assisted Learning

Studies have shown that a similar level of efficacy in phonetic ability can be achieved by teachers as well as clinicians (Duff & Clarke, 2011), which has led to a growing number of computer and Internet training programs. One problem in reading instruction is maintaining a balance between the basic, but dull, word decoding and the complex, but engaging, text comprehension. Not all the issues have been resolved, but computer-assisted methods for spelling, reading, and math provide more academic engagement and achievement than traditional pencil-and-paper methods.

New research raises cautious hope that computer games and exercises can help children with learning disabilities develop key mental skills

Computers have been used as simple instructional tools to deliver questions and answers since the 1970s. Since discovering phonological awareness and timing problems in the brain, researchers are now testing whether computers can remedy some basic auditory problems. Some children with communication and learning disorders are unable to process information that flashes by too quickly, such as the consonant sounds *ba* and *da*, and this deficit interferes with vital speech processes. Computer programs are able to slow down these grammatical sounds, allowing young children to process them more slowly and carefully (Loo et al., 2010; Gaab, Gabrieli, Deutsch, Tallal, & Temple, 2007; Palmer, Enderby, & Hawley, 2007).

Whether taught by computers, teachers, or both, studies of interventions for learning disorders indicate that successful approaches typically include explicit instruction in phonemic awareness and phonemic decoding. These interventions also provide students with practice reading text and comprehending what they read, with ample assistance and almost daily sessions (Torgesen, Wagner, Rashotte, Herron, & Lindamood, 2010).

In summary, treatment methods for communication and learning disorders are varied and beneficial. Box 11.4 reviews some of the basic elements of a successful beginning reading program, elements that apply to other disabilities as well. For children with reading disorders to learn how to read, they must receive a balanced intervention program composed of direct and explicit instruction in phonemic awareness, a systematic way to generalize this learning to the learning of sound–symbol relationships (phonics), and many opportunities to practice these coding skills by reading meaningful, interesting, and controlled texts. The sooner this intervention occurs in schools, the better (Haager et al., 2007).

BOX 11.4 A CLOSER LOOK

Critical Elements for a Successful Beginning Reading Program

1. *Provide direct instruction in language analysis.* Identify at-risk children early in their school careers—preferably in kindergarten—and teach phonological awareness skills directly.
2. *Provide direct teaching of the alphabetic code.* Code instruction should be structured and systematic, in a sequence that goes from simple to more complex. Teach the regularities of the English language before introducing the irregularities. Nothing should be left to guesswork—be as explicit as possible. Teach a child who is overly reliant on letter-by-letter decoding to process larger and larger chunks of words.
3. *Teach reading and spelling in coordination.* Children should learn to spell correctly the words they are reading.
4. *Provide intensive reading instruction.* Children may need 3 or more years of direct instruction in basic reading skills to ensure competency. As they progress, they should practice more and more reading that is contextualized. Reading materials should have controlled vocabularies that contain mostly words the children can decode. As children develop a core sight vocabulary, introduce only those irregular words that can be read with high accuracy. Guessing is counterproductive.
5. *Teach for automaticity.* Once basic decoding is mastered, children must be exposed to words often enough that they become automatically accessible. This usually requires a great deal of practice, which should be as pleasant and rewarding as possible.

Source: From Rebecca H. Felton, Effects of Instruction on the Decoding Skills of Children with Phonological-Processing Problems, *Journal of Learning Disabilities*, 26, 583–589, copyright © 1993. Reprinted by Permission of SAGE Publications.

SECTION SUMMARY

Learning Disorders

- Learning disorders consist of specific problems in reading, mathematics, or writing ability, with reading disorders as the most common. Mathematics and writing disorders overlap considerably with reading disorders.
- Although learning disorders overlap with behavioral disorders, they are distinct problems. Opportunities to develop and use particular strengths lead to more successful adult outcomes.
- Learning disorders in reading may be caused by phonological problems that arise from physiological abnormalities in the processing of visual information in the brain. These deficits are believed to be largely inherited.
- Treatments for children with communication and learning disorders involve educational strategies that capitalize on existing strengths, and behavioral strategies involving direct instruction.
- Cognitive—behavioral techniques and computer-assisted instruction are also used successfully.

Study Resources

SECTION SUMMARIES

KEY TERMS

communication disorders 355
decoding 367
direct instruction 376
dyslexia 355
expressive language disorder 358
inclusion 360
learning disabilities 354
learning disorders 355
mixed receptive–expressive language disorder 359
nonverbal learning disabilities (NLD) 374
phonemes 356
phonological awareness 357
phonological disorder 359
phonology 357
unexpected discrepancy 356

COURSEMATE

Access an interactive eBook and chapter-specific interactive learning tools, including flashcards, quizzes, videos, and more in your Psychology CourseMate, accessed through CengageBrain.com.

Health-Related and Substance Use Disorders

12

> *How I hate this world. I would like to tear it apart with my own two hands if I could. I would like to dismantle the universe star by star, like a treeful of rotten fruit.*
>
> —Author Peter De Vries, after his daughter died of leukemia

CHAPTER PREVIEW

JEREMIAH

Breath Is Life

Jeremiah Jager, age four, loves blue. He drinks blue soda pop, picks the blue marshmallows out of his Magic Stars cereal, and grabs the blue crayon. But when he got croupy and turned his favorite color this past winter—lips, cheeks, nose—his mother panicked. It was Jeremiah's eighth visit to the ER. And the scariest. "When he turned blue, I said 'I want some answers,'" says Cathy, who figured that—like relatives on both sides of his family—Jeremiah was developing asthma. She called the 800 number for Lung Line at the National Jewish Medical and Research Center in Denver. "This is going to cost twice as much as our car," says Cathy. "But why give birth to them if you're not going to do all you can for them?" Within a week, the Jagers left Alliance, Nebraska, for the long drive to Denver. They had to find out what was wrong with their child. (From *An Epidemic of Sneezing and Wheezing* by C. G. Dowling and A. Hollister, *Life Magazine*, May 1997, p. 79. Copyright 1997. The Picture Collection Inc. Used with permission. All rights reserved.)

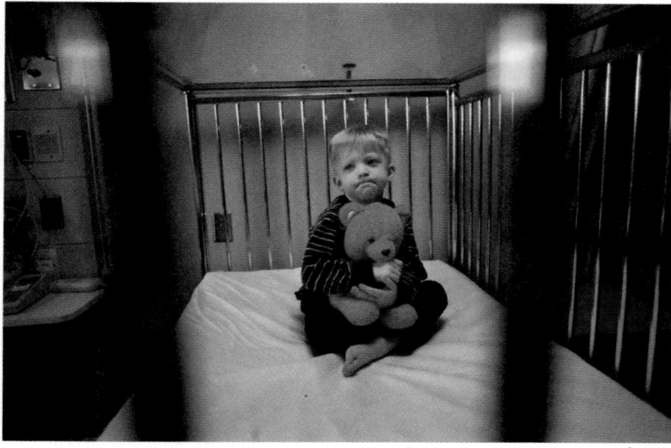

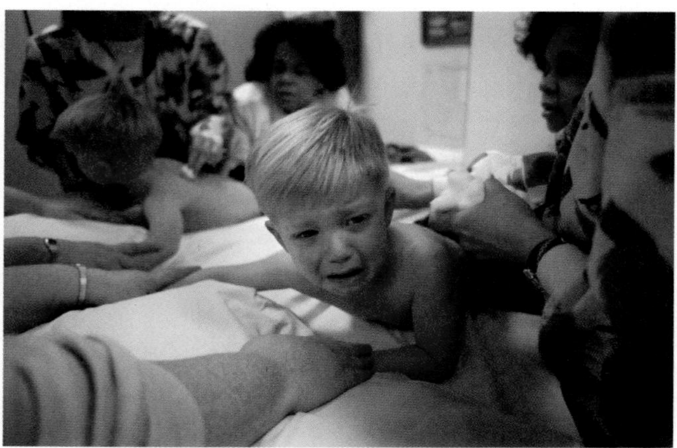

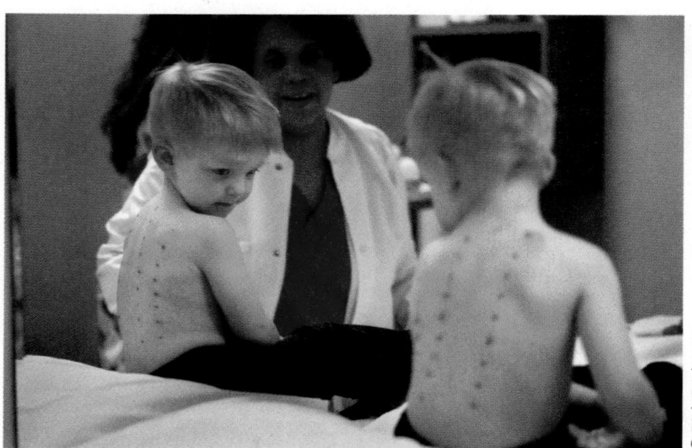

© Rich Frishman

Jeremiah waiting to be tested for allergies. The tests all came up negative.

FREDDIE

Too Worried to Sleep

Freddie, age 12, had considerable difficulty falling asleep. Each night it would take him an hour or two to fall asleep, which made it very difficult for him to get up for school at 6:00 a.m. the next morning. His typical nighttime routine was to watch television downstairs until 9:00 p.m. and then get ready for bed. Once in bed, he read for a while before turning out the lights. He explains: "I start to get sleepy when I'm reading, but as soon as I turn off the lights I'm wide awake. I can't stop from thinking about things, especially stuff that bothers me at school, like homework and making friends. My dad told me I would get sick because I don't sleep enough, and now I'm afraid I'll catch 'mono' like a friend of mine has at school. No matter what I do, I can't seem to just fall asleep like I used to." (Adapted from Bootzin & Chambers, 1990)

WHAT DO JEREMIAH AND Freddie have in common? To varying degrees, these children must face situations that affect their health and well-being; as a result, they and their family members are continually distressed and worried. Jeremiah's parents want answers for his breathing problems, which seem to occur without warning. Because doctors are unable to explain his episodes, Jeremiah's parents secretly wonder whether his breathing problems may be due to psychological causes. Similarly, Freddie's sleep problems are intermingled with worries brought on by his father's comments about him failing to get enough sleep. What role, if any, do psychological factors play in Jeremiah's and Freddie's development and adaptation to their health-related problems?

© Robert Karpa/Masterfile

Sleep problems occur across a number of behavioral and emotional problems in children and adolescents

Children, parents, and other family members are all deeply affected by children's health-related problems, which is why they have considerable psychological importance. The problems discussed in this chapter are not typically viewed as mental health disorders, but rather as health-related problems and medical stressors. Some stressors are mild, such as Freddie's problems falling asleep and sleeping through the night, but problems such as Jeremiah's asthma can be life-threatening and highly disruptive, and may involve complicated and intrusive medical interventions.

Pediatric health-related disorders are a distinct area of specialization, but cover a wide range of concerns, from relatively minor, such as enuresis (bed-wetting) and encopresis (soiling), to chronic illnesses such as cancer and diabetes (Jackson, Alberts, & Roberts, 2010; Prinstein & Roberts, 2006). Health-related disorders are different from other mental disorders largely because children's adjustment problems are more directly connected to the impact of the physical illness. Moreover, the field of pediatric psychology stresses the interaction between physical and mental health, because the various disorders and developmental problems all share medical, psychological, and psychosocial components (Peterson, Reach, & Grube, 2003). The involvement of psychologists and other mental health professionals in children's health-related problems has led to many highly successful ways to assist children and family members in coping with and adapting to their circumstances.

History

Although psychological approaches to aiding children with health-related problems have gained considerable momentum over the past two decades, a long history preceded these developments. Ever since Greek philosophers first suggested that pain and disease were caused by an imbalance in the body's basic elements of fire, air, water, and earth, various cultures have been fascinated and perplexed by the interrelationship between the mind and the body. During the medieval period, these early philosophies were overshadowed by the belief that mental and physical illnesses were caused by demonic possession, requiring a quick and gruesome dispatch of the afflicted person.

Scientific interest in the relationship between emotional and physical well-being remained largely dormant until the late 19th century, when Charcot and Freud brought forth their theories on the nature of hysteria and conversion disorders. Psychodynamic theory and the emerging discoveries of modern medicine often clashed during the early years of the 20th century, however, as debates emerged over the relative importance of the mind–body dichotomy (Siegel, Smith, & Wood, 1991).

Partially as a result of these developments, an early distinction emerged between disorders caused by physical factors and those caused by emotional or psychological factors (Peterson et al., 2003). Physical disorders that stem from, or are affected by, psychological and social factors were referred to as *psychosomatic* and later, *psychophysiological*, which meant that psychological factors affected somatic (physical) function. These terms are no longer used, however, because they wrongly implied that a person's physical symptoms were caused solely by mental problems.

Until 50 years ago, attention was rightfully placed on the acute, infectious diseases such as smallpox, tuberculosis, diphtheria, and typhus that claimed the lives of 1 in 4 children before their ninth birthday (Pollock, 1987). This statistic—simple, unemotional, impartial—belies the emotional toll this high infant and child mortality rate must have had on our ancestors. In fact, some historians argue that prior to the mid-19th century, children's highly unpredictable lifespans contributed to a diminished emotional investment in children among parents and society (Garrison & McQuiston, 1989). Today in Western society it is difficult to conceive of these circumstances, even though high child mortality rates still exist in other countries around the world.

The health-related problems addressed in this chapter—sleep disorders, elimination disorders, chronic illness, and substance use disorders—are good examples of how poorly understood physical symptoms can be misattributed primarily to psychological causes. Moreover, diverse childhood experiences underscore how reliance on fashionable cures and untested folk wisdom, rather than on scientific findings, can be viewed by subsequent generations as unwise and sometimes harmful.

Consider children's sleep and elimination disorders. For centuries, these relatively common afflictions were unfairly attributed to children's inherent stubbornness and laziness. Societal attitudes varied from severe to lenient and were similar to the responses elicited by mental retardation. By the turn of the 20th century, according to professional and public opinion, enuresis, like childhood masturbation, was a potential sign of emotional and behavioral disturbance. Early psychodynamic theory was gaining in popularity and proposed that toileting difficulties reflected unconscious conflicts that, if unresolved, could turn into troublesome personality styles. The sources of the underlying conflict were numerous: lack of parental love, the guilt value of feces, separation anxiety, pregnancy wishes, response to family problems, and traumatic separation from mother between the oral and anal stages of psychosexual development (Fielding & Doleys, 1988).

By the 1920s, the *Infant Care Bulletin*, the official publication of the U.S. Children's Bureau, reflected the harsh stance of society toward children's developmental problems. It advised parents to force their children to have bowel movements on a strict, regular schedule, and to complete toilet training by 8 months of age at the latest! If the baby did not go along with this plan, elimination was induced by inserting a stick of soap into the rectum (Achenbach, 1982).

Fortunately, by the 1940s this advice mellowed toward more natural, developmentally sensitive approaches that allowed children's maturity to dictate when parents could shift from diapers to toileting, which occurred between 12 and 30 months of age. Toilet training issues once again emerged during the rebellious 1960s, when renowned pediatrician Benjamin Spock was blamed for many social problems in North America because his advice on toileting and early childhood discipline from the 1940s on was considered too lenient. Spock had made it clear, though, that "the child supplies the power but the parents have to do the steering" (1945).

The Society of Pediatric Psychology was organized in 1968 to connect psychology and pediatrics, and it established the *Journal of Pediatric Psychology* in 1976. These two landmark events broadened the research and theory on physical outcomes of child health disorders to encompass the psychosocial effects of illness and the interplay between the two (M. C. Roberts & Steele, 2009).

How children adapt to the many situational, developmental, and chronic stressors affecting their health and well-being is a primary interest of pediatric health psychology. We begin by discussing sleep disorders, pausing to consider how important sleep is to our psychological and physical development, and its regulation from birth onward. From there we discuss elimination disorders and chronic illness in children and adolescents, areas in which monumental gains have been made in recent years in helping children overcome or adapt to these challenges. How health-related problems interact with children's and adolescents' psychological well-being, and how they and their families adapt in response, are central themes throughout this chapter.

SECTION SUMMARY

History

- For centuries, poorly understood physical symptoms have been misattributed to psychological causes.
- Today, pediatric health psychologists study how children's health-related problems interact with their psychological well-being, and how they and their families adapt in response.

Sleep Disorders

People who say they sleep like a baby usually don't have one.

—Leo J. Burke

We all have problems sleeping at one time or another. Usually, the problems are not serious and do not interfere with the next day's activities, but sometimes sleep problems can seriously affect our physical and psychological health and well-being. As any parent, sibling, or roommate can attest, these problems can have a major impact on them as well. In fact, problems such as resistance at bedtime, difficulty settling at bedtime, night waking, difficulty waking up, and fatigue are among the most common complaints or concerns expressed by parents of young children (Meltzer & Mindell, 2007).

Arguably, sleep is the *primary* activity of the brain during the early years of development. Consider this: By 2 years of age the average child has spent almost 10,000 hours (nearly 14 months) asleep, and approximately 7500 hours (about 10 months) in waking activities (Anders, Goodlin-Jones, & Sadeh, 2000). During those 2 years, the brain has reached 90% of adult size, and the child has attained remarkable complexity in cognitive skills, language, concept of self, socioemotional development, and physical skills (Dahl, 2007; Dahl & El-Sheikh, 2007). Yet, during most of the time these maturational advances were occurring, the child was asleep.

Gradually, by age 5 or so, a more even balance emerges between sleep and wakefulness. Still, by the time they begin school, children have spent more time asleep than in social interactions, exploration of the environment, eating, or any other single waking activity. Why has evolution favored sleep over these important activities? Wouldn't it be to our advantage to have more waking time to learn language, acquire knowledge, and develop similar adaptive skills? Apparently, sleep serves a fundamental role in brain development and regulation (Dahl, 2007). This role explains why sleep disturbances can affect overall physical and mental health and well-being, and why sleep disorders are important to abnormal child psychology.

Perhaps you have noticed how sleep problems co-occur with many different disorders, including ADHD, depression, anxiety, conduct problems, and developmental disorders (Chorney, Detweiler, Morris, & Kuhn, 2008; Cortese, Faraone, Konofal, & Lecendreux, 2009; Forbes et al., 2008; Ireland & Culpin, 2006). This connection raises an important consideration: Do sleep problems cause or result from other disorders? The answer to this question requires an understanding of how sleep problems interact with a person's psychological well-being. Because our own experience has been that sleep problems commonly arise from particular stressors—an upcoming exam or a relationship problem—we tend to think that sleep difficulties are secondary symptoms of a more primary problem. However, the relationship between sleep problems and psychological adjustment is bidirectional.

Sleep problems may themselves cause emotional and behavioral problems among children and adolescents, and they can be caused directly by a psychological disorder. In some circumstances, sleep problems might result from some underlying factor that is common to both sleep problems and other disorders. Problems in the brain's arousal and regulatory systems can cause increased anxiety (see Chapter 7). Stress-related events, especially those that affect the child's safety—such as war, disaster, and family conflict—both increase arousal and interfere with normal sleep patterns (Alfano, Beidel, Turner, & Lewin, 2006; El-Sheikh & Erath, 2011; Kelly & El-Sheikh, 2011). Simply stated, sleep disorders can cause other psychological problems, or they can result from other disorders or conditions. Sleep disorders have considerable importance to abnormal child psychology because they mimic or worsen many of the symptoms of major disorders (Dahl, 2006; Goldstein, Bridge, & Brent, 2008).

The Regulatory Functions of Sleep

We tend to think that sleep is a time when not much is happening—the "lights are on but nobody's home." This lack of activity and nearly complete loss of awareness during sleep gives us the impression that sleep regulation has little to do with psychological processes such as attention, arousal, emotions, and behavior. So why does the brain—particularly, the developing brain—require long periods of relative inactivity?

Children's sleep patterns help regulate their mood and behavior

Opposing the popular image of sleep as simply rest is the growing awareness that sleep, arousal, affect, and attention are all closely intertwined in a dynamic regulatory system (Dahl, 1996). When the central nervous system (CNS) must increase arousal in response to possible danger, the system must recover soon thereafter and restore the balance between sleep and arousal. It is fascinating how the system changes with development: During infancy the balance is skewed in favor of more sleep, because safety and other needs are provided for by the child's caregivers. As children mature, they start looking after their own needs, becoming more alert and attentive to danger. Gradually, the cycle between sleep and arousal becomes skewed more in favor of arousal, which by then is adaptive and necessary, and the dynamic patterns of sleep help restore the balance.

Most college students suffer sleep loss or disruption as a result of all-night study sessions or late-night partying, so you are probably familiar with sleep's important role in regulating states of emotional arousal and restoration. The giddiness, silliness, and impulsive behaviors children and adults show if sleep-deprived signify impairment in the prefrontal cortex functions. The prefrontal cortex is an important *executive control* center in the brain—it's in charge of processing emotional signals and making critical decisions for response—so impairment results in signs of decreased concentration and diminished ability to inhibit, or control, basic drives, impulses, and emotions (Talbot, McGlinchey, Kaplan, Dahl, & Harvey, 2010).

The prefrontal cortex is uniquely situated in the brain where it can integrate thoughts (higher cortical functions) with emotions (basic CNS functions). If a person is sleep-deprived or otherwise impaired, the first functions

affected are the more complex, demanding tasks that require integrating cognitive, emotional, and social input rapidly and accurately (Dahl, 1996). Ask any parent or teacher and they can tell you: Children with disrupted or inadequate sleep show less executive control the next day; they are more cranky, impulsive, distractible, and emotionally labile, meaning they switch abruptly from, say, laughing to crying. These symptoms are easily confused with those of ADHD, although sleep-related problems usually self-correct within a day or two (Gruber, 2009).

The physiology of sleep also has a fascinating connection to developmental problems that occur during childhood, and it further underscores the crucial role of sleep in restoring balance (Gregory, Van der Ende, Willis, & Verhulst, 2008). Specific stages of sleep are believed to produce an active *uncoupling*, or disconnection, of neurobehavioral systems (Dahl, 1996). In effect, separate aspects of the central nervous system take a break from their constant duty. Think about how your nervous system must continuously maintain an active, close connection while you are awake, which is achieved through electrical signals. These signals require that our neurobehavioral systems maintain precise timing and frequency. (See our discussion of learning disorders in Chapter 11.)

Sleep researcher R. E. Dahl describes the uncoupling process by comparing sleep's role to that of tuning instruments in a large orchestra: Tuning cannot be accomplished while the instrument is continuously playing, or "coupling," with the other instruments in the orchestra. Likewise, retuning or recalibration of the components of the CNS may require temporary uncoupling, or disconnection from other systems. Further, the uncoupling may be particularly critical for children. As children mature, regions of the brain rapidly differentiate and establish specific functions and patterns of interconnection within the CNS (Dahl, 1996, 2007), which requires considerable recalibration or retuning. In Dahl's music analogy, a new instrument must be retuned more often than one that has been broken in.

Maturational Changes

Our sleep patterns and needs change dramatically during the first few years of life, then gradually settle into a stable pattern as we reach adulthood. Newborns sleep about 16 to 17 hours each day, and 1-year-olds sleep about 13 hours a day, including daytime naps that range from 1 to over 2 hours (Acebo et al., 2005; Anders & Eiben, 1997). These maturational changes partially explain why infants and children have sleep problems different from those of older children, adolescents, and adults. Infants and toddlers have more night-waking problems, preschoolers have more falling-asleep problems, and younger school-age children have more going-to-bed problems. In contrast, sleep problems among adolescents and adults typically involve difficulty going to or staying asleep (insomnia), or not having enough time to sleep (R. E. Roberts, Roberts, & Xing, 2011).

Paradoxically, adolescents have an increased physiological need for sleep, but many get significantly less sleep than during early childhood. This results in many teens being chronically sleep-deprived, with daytime symptoms of fatigue, irritability, emotional lability, difficulty concentrating, and falling asleep in class (R. E. Roberts et al., 2011). The bottom line? Let sleeping teens lie—they need to catch up on their sleep!

Features of Sleep Disorders

Primary sleep disorders are presumed to be a result of abnormalities in the body's ability to regulate sleep–wake mechanisms and the timing of sleep, as opposed to sleep problems related to a medical disorder, a mental disorder, or the use of medications. The DSM-IV-TR divides primary sleep disorders into two major categories: dyssomnias and parasomnias (APA, 2000). **Dyssomnias** are disorders of initiating or maintaining sleep, characterized by difficulty getting enough sleep, not sleeping when you want to, not feeling refreshed from sleeping, and so forth. **Parasomnias**, in contrast, are sleep disorders in which behavioral or physiological events intrude on ongoing sleep. Whereas dyssomnias involve disruptions in the sleep process, parasomnias involve physiological or cognitive arousal at inappropriate times during the sleep–wake cycle, which can result in sleepwalking or in nightmares that jolt someone from sleep. Persons suffering from parasomnia sleep disorders often complain of unusual behaviors while asleep, rather than sleepiness or insomnia.

Dyssomnias

Dyssomnias, many of which are common during certain times of development, are disturbances in the amount, timing, or quality of sleep. Freddie, for example, suffered from a common form of childhood insomnia in which he had difficulty getting to sleep. Fortunately, many sleep problems resolve themselves as the child matures, especially if parents are given basic information and guidance, such as to refrain from yelling at the child to go to sleep, and instead to adhere to a bedtime routine (U.S. Department of Health and Human Services, 2011).

Table 12.1 provides a descriptive overview of childhood dyssomnias. For the most part, dyssomnias are common childhood afflictions with the exception of narcolepsy, which is uncommon but may be underdiagnosed in children (Nevsimalova, 2009). Breathing-related sleep disorders are somewhat less common and can affect children of various ages as a result of allergies, asthma, or swollen tonsils and adenoids. Although relatively common, dyssomnias can sometimes have a significant impact on children's behavior and emotional state, much like they impact adult behavior (Reid, Huntley, & Lewin, 2009).

Parasomnias

Parasomnias are somewhat common afflictions during early to mid-childhood and, we might add, are a bit easier to understand because of their more familiar terms and our own experiences. They include **nightmares** (repeated awakenings, with frightening dreams that you usually remember), **sleep terrors** (abrupt awakening, accompanied by autonomic arousal but no recall), and **sleepwalking** (getting out of bed and walking around, but with no recall the next day). Nightmares are referred to as *REM parasomnias* because they occur during REM (dream) sleep, usually during the second half of the sleep period. Although girls and boys report similar rates of nightmares in childhood, by adolescence girls report more nightmares than boys, a pattern that continues into adulthood (Schredl & Reinhard, 2011). Sleep terrors and sleepwalking, in contrast, are referred to as *arousal parasomnias* because they occur during deep sleep in the first third of the sleep cycle, when the person is so soundly asleep that he or she is difficult to arouse and has no recall of the episode the next morning (Dahl, 1996; Reid et al., 2009). Fortunately, as with the dyssomnias, children typically grow out of parasomnias or recover from sleep disruption or sleep loss and do not develop a chronic condition that interferes with daily activities. Characteristics of parasomnia sleep disorders are shown in Table 12.2.

DSM-IV-TR criteria for sleep disorders typically are not met in full by younger children because of the

TABLE 12.1 | Dyssomnias

Sleep Disorder	Description	Prevalence and Age	Treatment
Protodyssomnia	Difficulty initiating or maintaining sleep, or sleep that is not restorative; in infants, repetitive night waking and inability to fall asleep.	25% to 50% of 1- to 3-year-olds.	Behavioral treatment, family guidance.
Hypersomnia	Complaint of excessive sleepiness that is displayed as either prolonged sleep episodes or daytime sleep episodes.	Common among young children.	Behavioral treatment, family guidance.
Narcolepsy	Irresistible attacks of refreshing sleep occurring daily, accompanied by brief episodes of loss of muscle tone (cataplexy).	<1% of children and adolescents.	Structure, support, psychostimulants, antidepressants.
Breathing-related sleep disorder	Sleep disruption leading to excessive sleepiness or insomnia that is caused by sleep-related breathing difficulties.	1% to 2% of children; preschool, elementary ages.	Removal of tonsils and adenoids.
Circadian rhythm sleep disorder	Persistent or recurrent sleep disruption leading to excessive sleepiness or insomnia due to a mismatch between the sleep–wake schedule required by a person's environment and his or her internal sleep cycle (circadian rhythm); late sleep onset (after midnight), difficulty awakening in morning, sleeping in on weekends, resistance to change.	Unknown; possibly 7% of adolescents.	Behavioral treatment, chronotherapy.

Source: Based on authors' case material.

TABLE 12.2 | Parasomnias

Sleep Disorder	Description	Prevalence and Age	Treatment
REM Parasomnia			
Nightmare disorder	Repeated awakenings with detailed recall of extended and extremely frightening dreams, usually involving threats to survival, security, or self-esteem; generally occurs during the second half of the sleep period.	Common between ages 3 and 8.	Provide comfort, reduce stress.
Arousal Parasomnias			
Sleep terror disorder	Recurrent episodes of abrupt awakening from sleep, usually occurring during the first third of the major sleep episode and beginning with a panicky scream; accompanied by autonomic discharge, racing heart, sweating, vocalized distress, glassy-eyed staring; difficult to arouse, inconsolable, disoriented; no memory of episodes in morning.	3% of children; ages 18 months to 6 years.	Reduce stress and fatigue; add late afternoon nap.
Sleepwalking disorder	Repeated episodes of arising from bed during sleep and walking for periods of 5 seconds to 30 minutes, usually during the first third of the major sleep episode; poorly coordinated, difficult to arouse, disoriented; no memory in morning.	15% of children have one attack; 1% to 6% have one to four attacks per week; age 4 to 12 years, rare in adolescence.	Take safety precautions, reduce stress and fatigue, add late afternoon nap.

Source: Based on authors' case material.

transitory nature of their sleep problems (Goodlin-Jones et al., 2009). Refer to Tables 12.1 and 12.2, in lieu of the specific criteria for children, to aid in understanding the major features and differences of the various sleep disorders. Also, note two considerations concerning diagnostic criteria: In addition to the symptoms pertaining to each sleep disorder, as listed in Tables 12.1 and 12.2, DSM diagnostic criteria for all sleep-related disorders emphasize (1) the presence of clinically significant distress or impairment in social, occupational, or other important areas of functioning; and (2) the requirement that the sleep disturbance cannot be better accounted for by another mental disorder, the direct physiological effects of a substance, or a general medical condition (other than a breathing-related disorder) (APA, 2000). These considerations apply to all the disorders discussed in this chapter.

Treatment

Sleeping difficulties in infants and toddlers often subside on their own, but any parent who has been awakened night after night by a screaming child can attest that "waiting for them to grow out of it" seems like forever. If going to sleep or staying asleep becomes difficult, the goal of behavioral interventions is to teach parents to attend to the child's need for comfort and reassurance, but to gradually withdraw more quickly from the child's room after saying goodnight. (This is an example of *extinction*, since parental attention is being removed.)

Parents also can be taught to establish good sleep hygiene appropriate to their child's developmental stage and the family's cultural values. Once established, positive reinforcement methods, such as praise or star charts, can be used to reward the child for efforts to follow the bedtime routine. Sleep hygiene may involve identifying suspected causes of disrupted sleep and involving other family members in maintaining a chosen routine. For example, individualized bedtime rituals, such as reading, singing, or playing a quiet game, establish a positive transition to bedtime, and regular bedtimes and waking times establish a consistent routine (Reid et al., 2009).

Treatment of circadian rhythm sleep disorders requires a highly motivated adolescent and a supportive family because there are no shortcuts or medications that can easily restore a disrupted sleep–wake cycle. The goal of behavioral intervention is twofold: to eliminate the sleep deprivation and to restore a more normal sleep and wake routine. The adolescent is asked to keep a sleep–wake and daily activity log, with regular bedtimes and rise times. If begun early in the disorder, such supportive behavioral methods are often effective. In addition to behavioral methods, melatonin (a natural hormone) supplements have shown effectiveness with children and adolescents in advancing the sleep-wake rhythm and restoring the sleep cycle (van Geijlswijk, Korzilius, & Smits, 2010).

In contrast to treatment for some dyssomnias, prolonged treatment of child and adolescent parasomnias is usually not necessary, particularly if the episodes of sleep intrusion occur infrequently (Owens, Palermo, & Rosen, 2002). Treatment of nightmares consists of providing comfort at the time of occurrence and making every attempt to reduce daytime stressors. If nightmares or sleep terrors are intense and persistent, daytime stresses at school, family conflicts, or emotional disturbance may be implicated (Chorney et al., 2008; Simard, Nielsen, Tremblay, Boivin, & Montplaisir, 2008). If sleepwalking is suspected, parents usually are asked to record episodes at home using a camcorder. If sleepwalking is confirmed, parents must take precautions to reduce the chance of injury to a child who may fall or bump into objects. Because of the possibility of fire or other emergencies, children should never be locked in their rooms. Excessive fatigue or unusual stresses during the daytime often precipitate sleepwalking. Therefore, brief afternoon naps can be beneficial.

SECTION SUMMARY

Sleep Disorders

- Sleep disorders are important to abnormal child psychology because they mimic or worsen many symptoms of the major disorders.
- Sleep disorders can cause psychological problems, result from other disorders, or be a symptom of trauma or stress in the child's life.
- Dyssomnias are disorders of initiating or maintaining sleep, and include hypersomnia, narcolepsy, breathing-related sleep disorders, and circadian rhythm disorder.
- Parasomnias are sleep disorders in which behavioral or physiological events intrude on ongoing sleep, arousing the sleeper. They include nightmares, sleep terrors, and sleepwalking.
- Although most dyssomnias and parasomnias of childhood are common and often disappear with maturity, they still may have a negative impact on the child's daily activity and adjustment. Effective psychological treatments for most childhood sleep disorders involve the establishment and regulation of bedtime routines.

Elimination Disorders

"Step 1: Before you begin, remove all stubbornness from the child." These instructions were provided by a popular toilet training manual years ago, apparently without a hint of irony. For generations, parents have half-jokingly referred to the bathroom, and toilet training in particular, as the "combat zone," where parental right meets child's might. Teaching toddlers how to use the toilet is one of the more significant challenges of parenting, but whether it truly deserved the disproportionate amount of attention it received in the early abnormal child psychology literature is unlikely.

Thanks to a better understanding of the biological and psychological underpinnings of elimination disorders, attention has been directed away from the child's personality or emotional trauma. However, for a significant minority of children, the problems associated with toileting continue well past the age when most children have achieved freedom and independence. Elimination problems can turn into distressing and chronic difficulties, and can affect participation in educational and social activities, camps, sleepovers, and so forth. In extreme cases, toileting accidents can precipitate physical child abuse (R. C. Herrenkohl, Herrenkohl, & Egolf, 1983).

Two elimination problems that occur during childhood and adolescence are **enuresis**, the involuntary discharge of urine during the day or night, and **encopresis**, the passage of feces into inappropriate places, such as clothing or the floor. Child psychologists have studied and treated these elimination problems among children because they can have strong implications on the development of self-competence and self-esteem. Even though most children eventually outgrow problems of enuresis or encopresis by age 10 or so, they may have suffered years of embarrassment and peer rejection that remain troublesome. Fortunately, in most instances the problems can be alleviated through education and retraining efforts involving both parents and children. These disorders are one of the few areas of abnormal child psychology in which early referral and treatment can virtually eliminate long-term consequences.

Enuresis

As many as 7 million children in the United States and Canada go through the same routine each night: turn off the lights, go to sleep, wet the bed. Most of the time the child cannot control the discharge, but on occasion it may be intentional. Although the problem is relatively common, it is stressful for parents and children.

Concerns about correcting children's bed-wetting have perplexed professionals and parents for generations. Here is how Thomas Phaer, "the father of English pediatrics," explained the early cure to physicians under the heading "Of Pyssying in the Bedde" in his *Boke of Children* (1544):

> Many times for debility of vertus retentive of the reines or blader, as wel olde men as children are oftentimes annoyed, whan their urine issueth out either in theyre slepe or waking against theyr wylles, having no power to reteine it whan it cometh, therfore yf they will be holpen, fyrst they must avoid al fat meates, til ye vertue be restored againe, and to use this pouder in their meates and drynkes. (Cited in Glicklich, 1951, p. 862)

The "pouder" was derived from the trachea of a cock or the "stones of a hedge-hogge." This remedy seems tame in view of more "enlightened" mechanical and surgical approaches to enuresis that emerged by the 18th century—yokes made of iron (mercifully covered with velvet) that prevented urination and steel spikes placed on the child's back to prevent lying on the back, the position believed to stimulate bladder function during sleep. If you didn't want your child to be outfitted for one of these devices, other forms of treatment were available. Medicinals such as strychnine, belladonna, sacral plasters, and chloral hydrate were used presumably to stimulate the bladder (regardless of poisonous side effects), or the orifice of the urethra was cauterized (partially closed) with silver nitrate to make it more tender and responsive to passage of urine (Glicklich, 1951). Throughout history, the treatment of childhood bed-wetting reflects society's generally poor understanding and sensitivity to children's needs and problems at the time.

Most children have bed-wetting accidents until age 5 or so, therefore DSM-IV-TR has narrowed the criteria to reflect the developmental nature of this disorder. The criteria stipulate that the problem be frequent (at least twice a week for 3 consecutive months), or accompanied by significant distress or impairment in social, academic, or other important areas of functioning. A chronological age of 5 years, or the equivalent developmental level, was arbitrarily chosen as a developmental benchmark for the point at which most children achieve urinary continence. Finally, the voiding of urine into bed or clothes must not be due exclusively to a general medical condition, or the result of a diuretic, which is a drug that reduces water retention.

DSM-IV-TR distinguishes between three subtypes of enuresis (APA, 2000). *Nocturnal only* is the most common subtype, in which wetting occurs only during sleep at night, typically during the first third of the night. Nocturnal enuresis is significantly more common among boys than girls (Su et al., 2011). Sometimes the child is dreaming of urinating, which indicates that the voiding took place during REM sleep. *Diurnal only* is defined as the passage of urine during waking hours, most often during the early afternoon on school days (APA, 2000). Diurnal enuresis is more common in females than males and is uncommon after age 9. Because of these features, suspected causes of diurnal enuresis often indicate a child's reluctance to use the toilet because of social anxiety or a preoccupation with a school event. Finally, *nocturnal* and *diurnal* can exist in combination.

Prevalence and Course

Although it is not uncommon for young children to wet the bed occasionally, it is not considered to be a clinical problem unless it occurs more than once a month (Brown et al., 2008). Using one or more episodes a month as a cutoff, the incidence of nocturnal enuresis varies from about 4% to 13% of children age 10 or younger (Su et al., 2011). The prevalence of enuresis declines rapidly as children mature: By age 10, only 3% of males and 2% of females are affected, and this evens out to 1% of males and less than 1% of females by late adolescence (Mellon & Houts, 2006). Diurnal enuresis is much less common, and is estimated to affect 3% of 6-year-olds (Peterson et al., 2003). However, prevalence of both forms of enuresis is higher among less educated, lower socioeconomic groups as well as institutionalized children, perhaps due to less structure in their daily routines and added environmental stressors (APA, 2000).

Approximately 85% of children with enuresis have *primary enuresis*, because they have never attained at least 6 months of continuous nighttime control. By definition, primary enuresis starts at age 5. In contrast, *secondary enuresis* is less common and refers to children who have previously established urinary continence but then relapse, usually between the ages of 5 and 6 years (APA, 2000). Children with secondary enuresis often take a longer time establishing initial nighttime continence, or face a higher dose of stressful life events (Mellon & Houts, 2006). Most children do eventually stop bed-wetting, but for those who do not remit on their own, treatment is particularly beneficial in preventing a lengthy and disruptive problem.

You can imagine how younger children are treated when peers discover that they have wet themselves in class or while sleeping over. Teasing, name calling, and social stigmatization are common peer reactions to this unfortunate problem. Although enuresis is a physical condition, it is often accompanied by some degree of psychological distress (Joinson, Heron, Emond, & Butler, 2007; Van Hoecke, De Fruyt, De Clercq, Hoebeke, & Walle, 2006). The impact of this distress often depends on three features related to the nature of the enuresis: (1) limitations imposed on social activities, such as sleeping away from home; (2) effects on self-esteem, including the degree of social ostracism imposed by peers; and (3) parental reactions, such as anger, punishment, and rejection (Christophersen & Friman, 2010;

Waking up to a wet bed is upsetting, and can affect a young child's self-confidence if poorly managed

Houts, 2010). Parents are often poorly informed about the nature of enuresis and may respond by punishing or humiliating the child who suffers from it. Fortunately, these consequences are not inevitable or long-lasting. Many children with enuresis are able to establish their self-esteem and peer relationships despite their occasional embarrassment or anxiety. For others, treatment for bed-wetting usually has a positive impact on their self-concept and peer relations (Brown, Pope, & Brown, 2011; Fritz, Rockney, & the Work Group on Quality Issues, 2004).

Causes and Treatment

For most children with enuresis, one specific etiology cannot be identified (Fritz et al., 2004). Children with nocturnal enuresis need to urinate at night, but they don't wake up when they need to urinate. By age 5 or so, most children have made the transition from urinating around the clock, as they did in infancy, to urinating only during waking hours.

Children who continue to need to urinate at night may have a deficiency during sleep of an important hormone known as *antidiuretic hormone (ADH)*. ADH helps concentrate urine during sleep hours, meaning that the urine contains less water and has therefore decreased volume. For normal children, this decreased volume usually means that their bladders do not overfill while they are asleep, unless they drank excessive fluids before bed. Children with enuresis, however, do not show the usual increase in ADH during sleep (Norgaard, Pederson, & Djurhuus, 1985). They continue to produce more urine during the hours of sleep than their bladders can hold, and if they fail to wake up, bed-wetting results.

The reason children with enuresis fail to wake up when they need to urinate can also be explained by developmental and biological factors. Older children and adolescents are able to sense a full bladder at night, which activates a nerve impulse from the bladder to the brain. This signal may initiate dreams about water or going to the toilet, which usually wakes them up. This signaling mechanism matures during early childhood, so infants understandably have very little ability to detect the need to urinate. Some children with primary enuresis, however, lack normal development of this signal processing in the brain (Ornitz et al., 1999).

Primary enuresis, the most common type, is decidedly not due to stress or child obstinacy. To the contrary, this trait appears to be inherited. If both parents were enuretic, 77% of their children are too; if only one parent was enuretic, then 44% of their offspring are also. If neither parent had this problem, only about 15% of their children develop enuresis. Concordance rates of enuresis for monozygotic (68%) and dizygotic (36%) twins also verify this connection (Bakwin, 1973; Sethi, Bhargava, & Phil, 2005).

Treatments for children with nocturnal enuresis have perhaps the most comprehensive evaluation track record of any psychological intervention for childhood problems (Mellon & Houts, 2006). Dozens of promising behavioral methods have been investigated by hundreds of studies over several decades; they are joined by many other studies of pharmacological agents. Fortunately, these efforts have led to some strong conclusions as to what works best. (This example provides a good lesson in how long it often takes to verify successful treatment methods for psychological disorders.)

The standard behavioral intervention, based on classical conditioning principles, is using an alarm that sounds at the first detection of urine. Bed-wetting alarms have been around since O. H. Mowrer and W. M. Mowrer (1938) first invented the "bell and pad" (a battery-operated device that produced a loud sound as soon as a drop of urine closed the electrical circuit), and they are among the safest and most effective treatments. Modern alarms have a simple moisture sensor that snaps into a child's pajamas, with a small speaker attached to the shoulder to awaken the child. A single drop of urine completes the electronic circuit, setting off a piercing alarm that causes the child to tense and reflexively stop urinating. The one drawback to this method is the alarm's unpopularity with other household members. For the alarm to be effective, an adult must wake the child up, which usually isn't easy; walk him to the bathroom; get him to finish urinating in the toilet; and then reset the alarm. If this ritual is carefully followed, the alarm will begin to wake the child directly within 4 to 6 weeks, and by 12 weeks he will likely master nighttime bladder control and no longer need the alarm. The modern urine alarm, when used in conjunction with other behavioral activities (e.g., monitoring and intermittent reinforcement), has been recommended by the *American Academy of Child and Adolescent Psychiatry* as a minimal standard in the treatment of enuresis (i.e., should apply in at least 95% of enuresis cases) (Fritz et al., 2004).

Another behavioral method, based on operant conditioning principles, involves variations of *dry-bed training*. Children, like adults, wake up more easily when the day holds promise and excitement. Reward systems, such as star charts or other tokens, capitalize on this anticipation. Dry-bed training was originally developed as a brief but intensive intervention in response to parents' frustration over the more intrusive and drawn-out urine alarm. During a single office visit, parents are instructed in bladder retention control training by having their child drink more and more fluids during the day, and then delay urination for longer periods (in an effort to strengthen bladder control); hourly wakings for trips to the toilet; a cleanup routine for accidents (overcorrection, or having the child clean more than just the sheets); and positive reinforcement contingent on dry nights. This routine is practiced nightly for 1 or 2 weeks.

Dry-bed training methods combined with an alarm (referred to today as *full-spectrum home training*) are still commonly used, resulting in a success rate of about 3 in 4 children, and a relapse rate of 10% after 1 year (Brown et al., 2011; Friman, 2008). In less severe or prolonged cases of primary enuresis, a simple incentive such as earning stars or similar tokens for dry nights is often enough to make children responsive to nighttime bladder fullness. Other children, however, may require the alarm treatment to get the message firmly implanted, coupled with close professional monitoring to help parents adhere to the training methods.

In the mid-1980s, desmopressin, a synthetic ADH and simple nasal spray administered before bedtime, became available as a treatment for enuresis. Within a few days, about 70% of children using desmopressin can avoid bed-wetting, with another 10% or so showing significant improvement in the number of dry nights (Brown et al., 2011; Rappaport, 1993). Although desmopressin works very well while children are on the medicine, the difficulty comes in keeping them dry when they stop the medication: the relapse rate can be as high as 80% (Fritz et al., 2004). Unlike alarm systems, which have most children cured of bed-wetting within 12 weeks, treatment with medication often requires some additional behavioral treatment before children are able to stop taking the medicine.

Psychological treatments for enuresis, especially the urine alarm, have been more effective overall than pharmacological treatments (Campbell, Cox, & Borowitz, 2009; Houts, 2010). In particular, urine alarm treatment was found to be superior to any other type of intervention. At the end of treatment, which generally lasts 12 weeks, children treated with a urine alarm or with desmopressin are equally likely to have ceased bed-wetting; however, at their 3-month follow-up, children treated with a urine alarm are almost twice as likely to have ceased bed-wetting as children who received other treatments, including desmopressin. On average, almost one-half of all children treated with alarms remain dry at follow-up, compared with about one-third treated with other behavior therapies and one-quarter treated with tricyclic medications (Mellon & Houts, 2006). Treatment of enuresis is one of the few treatments in which psychological interventions are clearly superior to drug therapies, and should be used instead of waiting for the child to grow out of the problem because of the distress it causes the child and family.

Encopresis

Encopresis refers to the passage of feces into inappropriate places, such as clothing or the floor. Like enuresis, this act is usually involuntary, but may occasionally be done intentionally. The diagnostic criteria stipulate that this event must occur at least once per month for at least 3 months, and that the child must be 4 years old or older (if the child is developmentally delayed, a mental age of at least 4 years is used). Fecal incontinence must not be due to an organic or general medical condition.

Two subtypes of encopresis are described in DSM-IV-TR: with or without constipation and overflow incontinence. Essentially, encopresis results from constipation that produces fecal impaction. Liquid stool above the impaction gradually develops sufficient pressure to leak around the impaction, thereby producing overflow incontinence in most cases (Christophersen & Friman, 2010).

Prevalence and Course

An estimated 1.5% to 3% of children have encopresis. Again, this disorder is 5 to 6 times more common in boys than in girls (Brown et al., 2008), and it decreases rapidly with age. Like enuresis, encopresis can be categorized as primary or secondary. Children with primary encopresis have reached age 4 without establishing fecal continence, whereas children with secondary encopresis have established a period of continence before the current episode of encopresis began.

As many as 1 in 5 children with encopresis show significant psychological problems, but these problems more likely result from, rather than initially cause, the encopresis (Mikkelsen, 2010; Peterson et al., 2003). Understandably, they may feel ashamed and try to avoid situations such as camp or school that might lead to embarrassment. As with enuresis, the degree of children's impairment and associated psychological distress is partially a function of social ostracism by peers, as well as anger, punishment, and rejection on the part of caregivers.

Causes and Treatment

Overly aggressive or early toilet training, family disturbance and stress, and child psychopathology have all been thought to cause encopresis at one time or another (Burket et al., 2006; Peterson et al., 2003). However, like enuresis, encopresis is a physical disorder that can lead to, but seldom results from, psychological factors alone. The sooner it is diagnosed and treated, the less likely the child will suffer any lasting emotional scars or disruptions in social relationships. Exceptions, of course, are children with oppositional defiant and conduct disorders (discussed in Chapter 6), in which encopresis and enuresis may occur as secondary symptoms of broader behavior patterns.

Understanding the etiology of encopresis leads to a discussion of toilet training, where children first learn to control bowel movements. Children must learn how to recognize signals from the muscles and nerves that tell them when it is time for a bowel movement. Sometimes they try to avoid or suppress these signals, especially if something more enjoyable is going on. Some children attempt to suppress their feces to avoid having an accident; this allows feces to build up in the colon over a period of time, causing *megacolon*. If uncleared, the feces that stay in the bowel become large, hard, and dry, which causes further bowel movements to be painful. Over time, the stretched muscles and nerves give fewer and fewer signals to the child about the need to have a bowel movement. This decrease in signals results in stool accidents, and the colon and rectum often do not empty as they should.

About one-half of all children who develop this pattern of avoidance also have abnormal *defecation dynamics*; that is, they contract rather than relax the external sphincter when they attempt to defecate (Campbell et al., 2009). Combined with avoidance tactics, an increased risk of chronic constipation and encopresis develops. In case you're wondering how such dynamics develop, consider how some children (and adults) avoid using a bathroom if they are in a strange place, or if they have been told that public toilets should be avoided because they are germ-infested. Anxiety about defecating in a particular place, or because their toileting experiences were stressful and harsh, can cause chronic constipation. Without reversing this pattern of retention, the child becomes less able to perform the many skills required for successful toileting, including recognizing body cues, undressing, going into the bathroom, sitting on the toilet chair, and relaxing the appropriate muscles (Peterson et al., 2003).

Optimal treatment of encopresis involves both medical and behavioral interventions to help the child learn to empty the colon to allow it to return to normal size and function (Brown et al., 2008). To get the process moving, fiber, enemas, laxatives, or lubricants may be given to disimpact the rectum (Kuhl et al., 2010). Then, to establish a better routine and healthy pattern of elimination, behavioral methods are used in combination with laxatives or similar agents. Laxatives alone do not address the underlying behavioral mechanisms. Children who have large and impacted stools will find defecation frightening and painful, which further encourages them to ignore early rectal distention cues (the urge to defecate) and avoid going to the toilet.

Behavioral methods involve teaching a toilet-training procedure that encourages detection of and response to rectal distention cues, parental efforts to praise the child's clean pants and toilet use, and regularly scheduled toilet times after meals. During these times, children practice tensing and relaxing their external anal sphincter for several minutes; the practice time often is followed by fun time of reading or playing games to desensitize children to sitting on the toilet. Then they are taught to strain and attempt to have a bowel movement. With a combination of laxatives and behavioral treatment, most children improve significantly within the first 2 weeks of treatment, and over 75% maintain these improvements (Campbell et al., 2009; Houts, 2010). Whether the intervention is medical or behavioral in nature, positive reinforcement adds incremental benefits.

SECTION SUMMARY

Elimination Disorders

- Enuresis is the involuntary discharge of urine during the day or night.
- Encopresis is the passage of feces into inappropriate places, such as clothing or the floor.
- Primary enuresis has a strong genetic component, whereas encopresis results from children's efforts to avoid defecation, resulting in chronic constipation.
- Combined pharmacological and psychological treatments of elimination problems are often very successful.

CHRONIC ILLNESS

Who has not feared that the very worst could somehow single out a family member? Who does not worry as a toddler wanders toward the curb, or as a preschooler climbs a playground ladder, or as a teenager suddenly begins having severe headaches and dizziness? Chronic illnesses and medical conditions affect over 12 million children and adolescents in North America, so it is likely that we frequently will hear about these sad events. Here is one mother's reflection:

> When does the pain go away? I don't think ever. It is a lifetime mourning for what could have been. It has nothing to do with lack of acceptance or understanding and everything to do with things we hold close in our hearts; the celebrations never realized. Sharing in the joy of watching others trying out for sports, having a first date, graduate, get accepted at university, or watch a beloved daughter walk down the aisle to be married, will never be experienced. Different experiences are ours. Instead of reflecting on what could have been, look for what's right with your child, not what's wrong. Be proud of all accomplishments. Different joys are ours. Celebrate each achievement, each milestone. They are great motivators for yourself, your child, and others. *Source:* Reprinted with permission from Greey, 1995.

A **chronic illness** is one that persists longer than 3 months in a given year, or that requires a period of continuous hospitalization of more than 1 month. Chronic medical conditions—the wide range of complications relating to physical growth, function, and development, such as a visual or hearing impairment—are part of this picture as well. About 10% to 20% of youths under the age of 18 years will experience one or more chronic health conditions, with approximately 5% of these children suffering from a disease so severe that it regularly interferes with their daily activities, such as forming friendships, attending school, and simply pursuing a normal quality of life (Brown, Daly, & Rickel, 2007).

Children and adolescents whose health and functional ability are compromised by a chronic medical condition face numerous challenges to their development and adjustment. Each day, children with insulin-dependent diabetes must monitor their blood glucose level and diet, and administer insulin through injections. Children with asthma cautiously navigate new situations, on the alert for an attack that can literally leave them breathless, and children with cancer must cope with the stares or comments from peers who have little understanding or compassion for why another child looks different or seems frail. Like other developmental disorders, these conditions impact not only the child but peers and family members as well. This impact, in turn, affects the child's ability to adapt to the condition (Havermans et al., 2011; Sharpe & Rossiter, 2002).

The DSM-IV-TR addresses the mental health issues pertaining to health-related disorders in children and adults indiscriminately, relying mainly on two quite distinct categories: somatoform disorders and psychological factors affecting physical condition. We briefly discuss these DSM categories to provide an understanding of their meaning and limited applicability to pediatric populations.

Somatoform disorders are a group of related problems involving physical symptoms that resemble or suggest a medical condition, but lack organic or physiological evidence (APA, 2000). Somatization (i.e., expression of feelings through physical symptoms), hypochondriasis (i.e., preoccupation with real or fancied ailments), and pain disorders (e.g., recurring stomach pains) are examples of somatoform disorders (Eminson, 2007). The diagnostic criteria involve a clustering of complaints with pain and gastrointestinal, sexual, and pseudoneurological symptoms that exist at any time during the course of the disturbance.

Chronic illness and medical conditions affect over 12 million children and adolescents in North America

These symptoms are not intentionally produced or feigned, and they are real enough to cause significant distress or impairment to the individual. For some somatoform disorders, a strong presumption of a psychological component to the symptom is required for the diagnosis.

Somatoform disorders have been studied largely with adult populations, especially because they imply a chronic, established pattern that is often not detected until young adulthood (Abramowitz & Braddock, 2011). Thus, their diagnostic applicability in reference to children and adolescents is questionable and seldom used (Eminson, 2007). Nonetheless, we raise this topic primarily because the multiple somatic complaints from children, especially recurrent abdominal pain, may be developmental precursors to adult somatoform disorders (Essau, 2007).

The second category, **psychological factors affecting physical condition**, refers to disorders in which psychological factors are presumed to cause or exacerbate a physical condition. DSM criteria primarily address situations in which a person's medical condition is adversely affected by psychological factors, such as a person with diabetes who is depressed and refuses to monitor and regulate her glucose level. However, this diagnostic category does not apply to most children with chronic health conditions, because it is the medical condition and its limitations that affect their psychological adjustment, not the other way around. Psychological symptoms develop in response to the stress of having or being diagnosed with a general medical condition. Rather than depression affecting the course of diabetes, as in the previous example, it is more likely that diabetes causes adjustment difficulties, which sometimes (but by no means always) include clinical disorders, such as depression. Thus, some children and adolescents with chronic illness accompanied by significant adjustment or behavioral problems may receive a diagnosis of *adjustment disorder*, which better accounts for the nature of the stressor (APA, 2000).

Progress in the development of effective medical treatments and cures for children with chronic illness has been spectacular over the past three decades, greatly prolonging the lives of many who previously would have died during infancy or childhood. Remarkably, the survival rate for certain types of cancer, such as acute lymphoblastic leukemia, has increased from about 1 in 5 children in the 1950s to 4 in 5 children today (Brown et al., 2007). At the same time, however, these advances and improved survival rates have led to greater child and adult morbidity. **Morbidity** refers to the various forms of physical and functional consequences and limitations that result from an illness. Increased morbidity implies that more children and adolescents are adapting to the challenges of a chronic illness. For these children, illness has become a chronic life situation and stressor, and can have repercussions well into adulthood. For example, survivors of childhood cancer have a greater risk of developing a physical or mental illness as adults compared to their siblings; approximately 50% will develop a major illness in adulthood, most often chronic anxiety or infertility problems (Cantrell, 2011; Kirchhoff et al., 2010).

As children's survival has improved and life-threatening illnesses are better controlled, attention has moved away from the acute, infectious diseases to a broader emphasis on promoting children's health and development, and assisting in the care of children with chronic illness or handicapping conditions (Prinstein & Roberts, 2006). Pediatric health psychologists are particularly active in helping children with chronic health disorders successfully adapt and attain an optimal quality of life.

To increase our awareness of the ways children with chronic disease learn to cope and adapt to physical and social challenges, we take a look at how children normally think of and express health concerns. This awareness provides a developmentally sensitive context for distinguishing between adaptive and maladaptive coping reactions among children with chronic illness.

Normal Variations in Children's Health

We now recognize that children can communicate about their pain and discomfort about as well as adults, but this was not always true. It was thought that infants did not experience pain at all, and that children were far less sensitive to pain than adults. Because children seemed less able to communicate about their pain, it was wrongly concluded that they had higher pain thresholds than adults. However, children do have a good concept of what pain is, and how to express it (McAlpine & McGrath, 1999). Their concepts of pain and its causes, their descriptions of pain, and their specific pain experiences seem remarkably well formed by an early age, both for boys and girls. Consider this comment:

> It [stomachache] was like bees in your stomach—stinging your stomach, yellow jackets going ping, pong, bop inside—like something just chopped down your stomach. [6-year-old boy]. It [earache] felt like something is inside your ear like a sticker from a rose bush poking deep inside your ear, like way harder than just pricking. [9-year-old boy] (D. M. Ross & Ross, 1984, p. 184)

It is unlikely that children simply pick up pain descriptions from their parents or others. Consider the childlike imagery used by a 7-year-old boy in describing a headache:

> Like there's this big monster in there, see, and he's growing like crazy and there's no room and he's pulling the two sides of my head apart he's getting so big. (D. M. Ross & Ross, 1984, p. 189).

Now picture this common scene: Since age 6, Jackie has informed her parents from time to time that she was "too sick" to go to school. She then would carefully provide them with a list of her symptoms: "My tummy hurts; I feel hot, my throat hurts; I can't feel my toes." Careful questioning would usually result in a further list of symptoms—in fact, most were suggested by one of her parents: "Does your leg hurt too?" [yes]; "How does your head feel?" [achy]; "What does your skin feel like?" [stingy]. The astute reader might note that these symptoms emerged at about the time Jackie was entering the first grade. Would you consider this situation to be typical of how children learn about physical symptoms and their connection to life's responsibilities?

Are somatic complaints in children (such as those expressed by Jackie) normal and commonplace? To no one's surprise, about a third of typical school-aged children report using pain for secondary gains, such as increased parental and peer attention, and avoidance of school and athletic activities. Undeniably, one of the most common ways children express their fears, dislikes, and avoidance is to complain of aches and pains, often of uncertain or dubious origin.

Girls and boys show interesting differences in this respect. When they are asked, girls report more symptoms of pain and anxiety than do boys (Kröner-Herwig, Gassmann, van Gessel, & Vath, 2011). Under stressful circumstances, girls are more likely to cry, cling, and seek emotional support, and boys are more likely to be uncooperative, avoidant, and stoic. Similarly, excessive somatic complaints are associated with emotional disorders in girls and disruptive behavior disorders in boys (Egger, Costello, Erkanli, & Angold, 1999; Jellesma, 2008; Jellesma, Rieffe, & Terwogt, 2008). Does this imply that girls are somehow more sensitive to pain or less able to manage their fear and anxiety than boys? Yes and no. These gender differences stem from socialization expectations as well as biological differences. We are all familiar with the ways boys are encouraged to adopt stoic attitudes about pain, whereas girls are reinforced for passive, affective expression. Both boys and girls are reactive to distress, but they express it according to how they have been taught and what they wish to receive. Therefore, these complaints are within the normal developmental range and do not merit a psychiatric label.

Some children may be more likely than others to experience recurrent pain and physical symptoms because of their family influences (Jellesma, Rieffe, Terwogt, & Westenberg, 2008). For example, children with functional abdominal pain and similar forms of recurrent unexplained pain are more likely to identify someone in their family who often expresses pain than are children whose pain is due to known organic causes (Marshall, Jones, Ramchandani, Stein, & Bass, 2007). In addition, children of mothers with a somatic disorder are 4 times more likely to express physical symptoms when emotionally upset (Craig, Cox, & Klein, 2002; Guite, Lobato, Shalon, Plante, & Kao, 2007). These unexplained, recurrent pain symptoms among children, therefore, seem to originate primarily from family *pain models* (Peterson et al., 2003). Children also learn healthy adaptational patterns at home and elsewhere. Children with well-developed social and academic competence, for instance, are less likely to respond to negative life events, such as divorce or hospitalizations, with amplified stress and pain reactions (Walker, Smith, Garber, & Claar, 2007).

Let's turn our attention now to those children who have chronic health problems or conditions. Each chronic illness has unique challenges. Children with diabetes face daily medical routines, but they have a relatively predictable prognosis; children with cancer experience unpleasant side effects of treatment and must also cope with the uncertain prognosis of their illness.

The one important thing that all chronic illnesses and medical conditions have in common is that they constitute a major stressor that challenges and absorbs both the child's and the family's available coping resources. Viewing chronic illness in this way—as a form of major stress requiring adaptation—has allowed researchers to identify factors that promote successful adaptation to chronic illness. This view also has advanced new ways to assist children in coping with these challenges, as we will see.

Ten to twenty percent of the child population of North America is estimated to suffer some form of chronic health-related disorder or condition (including obesity, diabetes, asthma, and others), and the rate has been rising dramatically in recent years (Brown et al., 2007; Van Cleave, Gortmaker, & Perrin, 2010). Of these children, about two-thirds have mild conditions; the remainder have conditions that result in moderate to severe activity restrictions and bothersome treatment regimens (Peterson et al., 2003). Asthma is the most common chronic illness in childhood, followed by neurological and developmental disabilities and behavioral disorders. Fortunately, severe forms of chronic illnesses—those that pose major physical and intellectual limitations that interfere with children's daily lives—are relatively rare, but their combined rates are sizeable.

TABLE 12.3 Incidence Rates of Selected Chronic Illnesses in Children and Adolescents, Ages 0 to 19 (United States Statistics)

Illness	Incidence (per population annually)
Asthma	9.6% of child population[a]
Cancers and tumors	16/100,000 children diagnosed each year[b]
Diabetes mellitus	24/100,000 children diagnosed each year[c]
Sickle-cell anemia	1/500 African American newborns[d]

Sources: [a]Prevalence of the total child/youth population; Akinbami, Moorman, & Liu (2011); [b]Bloom, Cohen, & Freeman (2011); [c]Centers for Disease Control and Prevention (CDC), (2011); [d]Amendah, Mvundura, Kavanagh, Sprinz, & Grosse, 2010)

Table 12.3 shows the incidence rates (i.e., number of new cases occurring in a specified population during a year) of selected chronic childhood diseases and medical conditions. Survival rates for many of these illnesses have greatly improved (Jemal et al., 2009); therefore, these rates reflect a large proportion of children who have survived these childhood illnesses until age 20 or longer. The impact of living with HIV and AIDS, currently the sixth leading cause of death among 15- to 24-year-olds in the United States, likely will be a major health issue in the years to come (Garvie, Lawford, Banet, & West, 2009; Howland et al., 2007).

Most chronic childhood illnesses do not discriminate in terms of social class and ethnicity—they can affect children from all walks of life. However, there are certain exceptions to how illnesses affect children, such as the specific conditions genetically determined by racial or ethnic descent. For example, cystic fibrosis affects primarily whites, and sickle-cell disease affects primarily persons of African descent (Thompson & Gustafson, 1996). African American children are about 3 times more likely to be hospitalized for asthma than are their white peers, which may be linked to conditions associated with low income and disadvantage (Brown et al., 2007).

As well, a troubling connection exists between socioeconomic status (SES), ethnicity, and survival rates among children and adults with cancer in particular (Wich et al., 2011). Despite attempts to achieve more equitable health care delivery, residents of poorer communities still may receive inferior quality of care, even in universal health care systems like those in Canada (Booth, Li, Jina Zhang-Salomons, & Mackillop, 2010), Korea (Son, Kim, Oh, & Kawachi, 2011), and the U.K. (Stringhini et al., 2010). In addition, the poor may have other ailments that make cancer survival more difficult, or parents may be less inclined to seek medical attention if they have other major life stressors or if they are not aware of critical symptoms. In general, children in poor families are five times as likely to be in fair or poor health as children in families that are not poor (Bloom et al., 2011; CDC, 2007). People with adequate means generally have more options and control over their lives, which translates into greater opportunities for proper medical care for their children. Later in this chapter, we consider some ways to empower families and achieve a greater balance in their roles and available resources.

We now take a closer look at two specific illnesses—diabetes mellitus and childhood cancer—that are representative of the course and patterns of adaptation faced by children with chronic illness.

Diabetes Mellitus

AMANDA

Daily Struggle with Diabetes

Amanda, age 14, was diagnosed with insulin-dependent diabetes mellitus about a year ago. Like most teenagers, she leads an active life, and eating the proper foods is difficult enough without the added burden of daily glucose monitoring and insulin injections. She shared with us some of the ways this disease has affected her life, and how she copes with its demands and limitations:

> Becoming diabetic has completely changed my life. My best friend is the insulin I take and the machine. I use the machine to test my blood sugar four times a day by poking my finger and putting blood on a test strip.
>
> From the reading I am able to adjust my insulin and what I must eat. I am forced to eat a healthy balanced meal regularly about six times every day. I try not to have a negative attitude because I now realize just how lucky I am. I do not know what I would do if I did not have my machine or all of the sugar-free foods that are now available. Not only did diabetes change my physical life, but it altered my mental life as well. It helped me look at my life and realize what was important to me. My close friend, Germaine, helped me get through the first year at school, when some of the other kids wondered why I had to use needles and couldn't eat the same things they do. My parents have been great, and even my younger brother lays off me when he knows I'm having a particularly bad day. In a way, I'm more aware of how important health is to us than most kids at school, and I don't take things for granted the way I used to. (Based on authors' case material)

Amanda suffers from **insulin-dependent diabetes mellitus**, a lifelong metabolic disorder in which the body is unable to metabolize carbohydrates as a result of inadequate pancreatic release of insulin. This lack of insulin has a domino effect on the body's ability to regulate appetite, metabolize carbohydrates into necessary energy, and maintain a balance of blood chemistry. The lack of insulin prohibits glucose from entering the cells, which forces glucose to accumulate in the bloodstream and cause *hyperglycemia*. Glucose also tells the regulatory cells of the hypothalamus when a person is hungry or full, so without this information, the person tends to eat constantly but does not gain weight (Thompson & Gustafson, 1996). A treatment regimen consisting of insulin injections, diet, and exercise is necessary to approximate a normal metabolic state. Although current treatment regimens have greatly improved the health status of people with diabetes, the condition is still associated with significant morbidity and mortality.

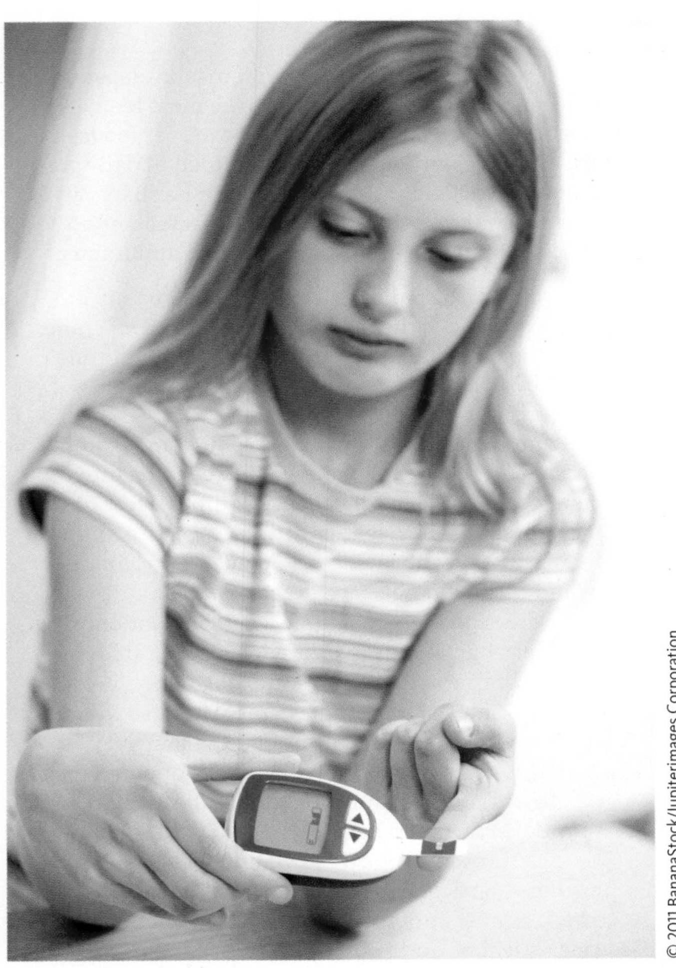

Adolescents with chronic illness, such as diabetes, must adhere carefully to a daily treatment regimen

Diabetes affects boys and girls equally, and is on the increase: a child born in North America in 2000 stands a one in three chance of being diagnosed with diabetes in his or her lifetime (Canadian Diabetes Association, 2008). Initial symptoms often include fatigue, thirst, hunger, frequent urination, and weight loss despite excessive eating. It is a progressive disease, with the more chronic complications that occur during young adulthood or beyond, including circulatory problems that can lead to blindness, kidney failure, and accelerated cardiovascular disease (Siegel, 2008). Individuals with diabetes have an increased risk of illness and death, including double the risk of cardiovascular disease (Franco, Steyerberg, Hu, Mackenbach, & Nusselder, 2007). Given the seriousness of the illness and the longstanding, intrusive treatment requirements, it is understandable that children with diabetes and their families have an increased risk for conflict and adjustment problems (Ellis et al., 2007).

Children with diabetes face daily treatment tasks to maintain their metabolic control, such as blood glucose monitoring, dietary restraints, insulin injections, and learning how to balance energy demands and insulin needs (Peterson et al., 2003). **Metabolic control** is the degree to which the patient's glucose levels are maintained within the normal range. Children and adolescents must carefully monitor their insulin levels—too little insulin can result in a diabetic coma, too much insulin can result in an insulin reaction called *hypoglycemia*. Hypoglycemic episodes are extremely unpleasant and can include irritability, headaches, and shakiness. Adding to the complexity is the fact that illness and stress can upset the relationship between glucose and required insulin levels (Schwartz, Axelrad, Cline, & Anderson, 2011).

Children and teens must carefully follow the instructions given to them by their physician; that is, they must practice careful *regimen adherence*. Good regimen adherence and metabolic control are linked to the individuals' correct knowledge about their disease and its treatment, their belief that adherence is important, and adequate problem-solving skills (Lewandowski & Drotar, 2007; Rasmussen, Ward, Jenkins, King, & Dunning, 2011). As we saw with Amanda, adolescence is a particularly difficult period because of the impact that the illness can have on self-esteem and social and educational experiences—adolescence is difficult enough without the added burden of these daily treatment tasks. Therefore, psychologists have become active in developing ways to promote regimen adherence and metabolic control by helping family members adapt favorably to the demands of the condition (Schwartz et al., 2011). Behavioral strategies have been quite successful in this regard, especially with methods that reinforce symptom reduction or medication use, and self-control methods that teach patients to regulate dosage and monitor their symptoms, blood glucose, and medications (Drotar, 2006; Elkin & Stoppelbein, 2008; Jaser & White, 2011).

Childhood Cancer

CHEN

A Determined Boy Fighting Leukemia

Chen, age 9, explains his feelings about childhood leukemia and its impact on his family and peer relations:

> I've had cancer now for three years. They're still trying to fight it with the right medicine but nothing has worked yet. My friends come visit me—they're pretty OK with everything. But sometimes if you try and tell other kids about it they don't understand because they don't have it. To them we're normal. They don't have any kind of problems that hold them back from doing things. They don't have to worry about being in the hospital, checkups and things, to see how you're doing. You can tell your friends why you have to stop and rest awhile, but they don't really understand—they don't really want to—they want to keep on going. I've got lots of family who care about me and I worry for them. I guess I'm used to all the doctors and medicines I take. Not that I like them but I know it's the only thing that might help. But I liked having the ability to do anything with my friends (or even my parents). I want to be able to get up and go. I'd tell someone else going through this to stay strong and keep the faith. And speak up when you need something!

Chen's mother explains the ordeal he and his family have undergone since his diagnosis:

> Chen received a bone marrow transplant from his brother over a year ago and, thankfully, his leukemia went into remission. But when we went back one year later for a checkup, we were told Chen had suffered a relapse—the cancer had overtaken the bone marrow, and his prognosis is poor. Now our family focuses on enjoying our time together and doing things with Chen. We are fortunate—my employer has gone out of his way to help me stay at home with Chen. Their support over the past year has been incredible. In fact, our whole community has shown tremendous support to our family. But his turn for the worse has made it difficult for us to do the things we have done over the past few weeks. We are angry, hopeful, depressed, joyous, saddened all the time. It is the worst roller coaster that we have ever ridden. Yet, Chen's medical condition has made us more determined to do more than we had ever hoped for, and the kindness shown toward our family has been overwhelming. (Based on authors' case material)

It is difficult for most of us to imagine what Chen and his family have experienced. Their words acknowledge the importance of their strength and determination and their human kindness when faced with a serious childhood illness, which in this case was terminal. Cancer can strike children very suddenly, more so than with adults, and children are often at a more advanced stage of cancer when they are first diagnosed (Brown et al., 2007). White children suffer the highest rates of cancer compared to other ethnic groups, but reasons for this disparity are not known (Bloom et al., 2011). Incidence rates for Hispanic and Asian/Pacific Islander children fall between those for African Americans and whites, while rates for American Indians are much lower than for any other group (National Childhood Cancer Foundation, 2008).

The most common form of childhood cancer is acute lymphoblastic leukemia (ALL), which accounts for close to one-half of all forms of childhood cancer (CDC, 2007). ALL is actually a group of heterogeneous diseases in which there is a malignancy of the bone marrow that produces blood cells. The bone marrow produces malignant cells called lymphoblasts that progressively replace normal bone marrow with fewer red blood cells and more white blood cells, causing anemia, infection, and easy bruising or excessive bleeding (Friedman, Latham, & Dahlquist, 1998). Childhood cancer used to be fatal, but advances in medical treatment have resulted in dramatic improvements in survival rates. Still, long-term complications such as recurrent malignancy, growth retardation, neuropsychological deficits, cataracts, and infertility pose a risk to survival and quality of life.

Like those with diabetes, children with cancer undergo complicated medical treatment regimens, especially during the first 2 to 3 years. In addition, they face school absences, significant treatment side effects, and an uncertain prognosis. Chemotherapy and radiation therapy can cause hair loss and weight changes, as well as nausea, vomiting, increased fatigue, endocrine and growth retardation, and a depressed immune system (Friedman et al., 1998). Children with cancer also must cope with painful medical procedures, such as venipuncture, bone marrow aspirations, and lumbar punctures. Treatment requires children to be away from friends and some family members, which hinders their psychosocial development. Therefore, the psychosocial aspects of pediatric cancer have focused on management of distress related to the multiple diagnostic and treatment procedures these children face.

Although approximately 80% of pediatric cancer patients survive, about half of the survivors will have a serious physical or mental illness as adults (Krull et al., 2010; Zebrack et al., 2002). The most commonly occurring illnesses include infertility, chronic anxiety, and recurrent cancers (Cantrell, 2011; Stuber et al., 2011). Many patients require long-term care into adulthood after never learning the life-skills necessary for self-care.

Development and Course

Children with chronic illnesses are more likely than their healthy peers to suffer emotional and behavioral adjustment problems stemming from the burden of their disease and its treatment, especially children with chronic illness accompanied by disability (Cadman, Boyle, Szatmari, & Offord, 1987; Hysing, Elgen, Gillberg, & Lundervold, 2009). Understandably, children whose normal functional abilities are limited face the greatest challenges in everyday activities, which in turn increases behavioral, social, and school adjustment difficulties. These problems are most often expressed as internalizing symptoms, such as anxiety, depression, or post-traumatic stress disorder, or a combination of both internalizing and externalizing problems (Pao & Bosk, 2011; Pinquart & Shen, 2011; Schwartz & Drotar, 2006).

To keep these symptoms in perspective, one must recognize that adjustment of children with chronic illness typically is better than that of children referred to mental health clinics for non-health-related problems (Eiser, 2007). For the most part, these children are exhibiting stress-related symptoms; the incidence of DSM-IV-TR–type disorders among children with chronic illness is actually low. For example, a meta-analysis of 340 studies revealed that symptoms of depression among children with various chronic health conditions are only slightly higher than those of their healthy peers, an encouraging indication of successful adaptation among the vast majority of these children (Pinquart & Shen, 2011). Moreover, children with diabetes and children with cancer on average report symptoms of anxiety, depression, and low self-esteem within the normal range for their age and gender (Brown et al., 2007; Eiser, 2007).

Although chronically ill populations of children have increased risk of initial adjustment difficulties, it is difficult to say what causes particular symptoms, or why some children adapt more successfully than others. When one considers how these children must cope with unpredictable events and challenges almost every day, it is understandable that they would show an increase in stress-related symptoms. It is especially encouraging to know that most can adapt successfully to the course and consequences of their illness. Symptoms of anxiety, depression, and anger can be thought of as normal responses to stressful experiences associated with the long-term illness and treatment regimens, rather than psychiatric disorders (Eiser, 2007). This is similar to the adjustment problems faced by children with intellectual disabilities and children who have been abused or neglected. Most children with chronic illness show considerable resilience in the face of stressful experiences associated with their condition, and we should exercise caution in applying psychiatric labels or descriptors that fail to capture the context and nature of their circumstances.

Effect on Family Members

The field of pediatric health psychology has clearly adopted a focus on the important role of family functioning in the adjustment of children with chronic illness. The child's circumstances may result in family cohesion and support, as we saw in Amanda's and Chen's families, or result in family disruption and crisis. As parents try to understand and cope with the news of their child's diagnosis, they must at the same time start to accept that their child might always be different from other children. How they react and accept these realities determines, to a large extent, how their child and other siblings will react and adapt. Parents who fail to resolve this crisis are more likely to have problems with attachment and child-rearing, which further complicates the stressful nature of the child's illness (Mullins et al., 2007).

Learning that a child has a life-threatening disease causes trauma and stress to all family members and, in fact, qualifies as a traumatic event that can precipitate post-traumatic stress disorder (PTSD) (Stoppelbein & Greening, 2007). A mother of an infant born with a chronic disability describes her initial reaction:

> I felt like I was bouncing around on a raft in the middle of a terrible storm. I didn't know where I was, where I was going, or what wave was going to break over my head next. Most of the time, I just hung on. Hanging on, I discovered, is the key to survival. (Medvescek, 1997, p. 67)

Many parents of children with chronic illness report that their fears resurface and memories return whenever their child has only a common illness, like a cold or flu (Pai et al., 2007). About 10% of mothers and fathers suffer symptoms of PTSD, a rate that is comparable to other types of traumatic stress exposure (Kazak et al., 2004; Kazak & Bart, 2007). Fortunately, the children themselves do not typically suffer PTSD-related symptoms connected to learning of their disorder, probably because they are very young at the time of diagnosis. However, children's memories of stressful procedures play a role in their experience of distress, and some survivors of childhood cancer recall disturbing memories of the medical procedures many years later (Stuber & Shemesh, 2006).

Families exert a significant impact on the behavior of children with chronic health problems, as they do with healthy children. No one type of chronic illness poses a significantly greater risk of adjustment than any other. Thus, factors associated with children's situations—such as family stress and resources—may be more critical to their adaptation than the challenges posed by the illness alone (Peterson & Drotar, 2006). Regarding older children, the degree to which parents can assist their children in developing more autonomy and control over their treatment regimens in a non-conflictual manner predicts the likelihood that the teen will adhere to the treatment regimen. The normal conflict observed in parent–teenager relationships is heightened in families where the teen is trying to incorporate a treatment regimen into a changing lifestyle. For example, drinking alcohol is a significant risk for teens with diabetes; therefore, conversations and parental expectations regarding experimentation with substance use often are heightened because alcohol use is more deleterious (Jaser & White, 2011).

It is not the amount of concordance between parent and teen perceptions of who is making decisions about treatment that predicts adherence to treatments; it is rather the degree of conflict in the parent–teen relationship (Lewandowski & Drotar, 2007). Thus, parents who can help their teen maintain adherence in a nonconfrontational manner (regardless of whether they agree with their child about who is in fact making treatment decisions) will increase their teen's health and adaptation. In general, the following stress factors that parents face are quite similar across all types of pediatric chronic illness: financial and physical burdens, changes in parenting roles, sibling resentment, child adjustment problems, social isolation, frequent hospitalizations, and grief (Alriksson-Schmidt, Wallander, & Biasini, 2007). It comes as no surprise, therefore, that couples with chronically ill children report more marital conflict, poor communication, role incongruity, and a lack of intimacy and positive affect (Rodrigues & Patterson, 2007).

The point is worth repeating: Despite these psychological and tangible repercussions, many children with chronic illness adapt favorably to these challenges, as do their families (Long & Marsland, 2011). Perceived social support and parental adaptation are key components aiding their adaptation, since primary caregivers play an important role in their children's stress and coping abilities. Specifically, mothers who perceive lower levels of illness-related stress, use more adaptive and active ways to cope with stress and problems, and perceive their families as more supportive than conflictual are more likely to show normal adjustment levels themselves (Thompson & Gustafson, 1996). Regardless of the circumstances, we often see this connection: When maternal abilities remain intact, child and family functioning is less impaired. This illustrates the reciprocal relationship between children's adjustment and parental stress and distress—healthy parental adjustment is related to healthy child adjustment, and vice versa. (Most research has considered only the role of mothers on child adjustment, but the specific influence of fathers on children's coping and adaptation to chronic illness is being recognized [Ware & Raval, 2007].) Thus, parental adjustment is one of the important correlates of children's adjustment to chronic illness.

Siblings of children with a chronic illness also experience heightened social and mental health problems. They tend to have more internalizing symptoms, such as depression and anxiety, lower cognitive scores, and fewer peer activities (Bellin & Kovacs, 2006). These outcomes are worse for chronic illnesses that require daily treatment regimens, which suggests the increased caregiving demands faced by parents and subsequent decreased amounts of parental attention for siblings contribute to their maladjustment. Despite these problems, many children with a chronic illness benefit from sibling relationships and vice versa, due to the positive bond that is often formed between them (Havermans et al., 2011; Long & Marsland, 2011).

Social Adjustment and School Performance

Children's adjustment to chronic illness is reflected not only in terms of psychological distress, but also through developmental accomplishments in social adjustment, peer relationships, and school performance. Because chronic illness results in lifestyle interruptions that interfere with opportunities for social interaction, children with more severe, disruptive illnesses tend to suffer primarily in social adjustment (La Greca, Bearman, & Moore, 2002). This maladjustment often is expressed by children displaying more submissive behavior with their peers, and engaging in fewer social activities overall (Meijer, Sinnema, Bijstra, Mellenbergh, & Wolters, 2002).

Consider child cancer patients' peer relationships. Chen explained how the other children did not understand why he could not join in or behave the same as they did—to them he looked normal, so he must be okay. Negative or ill-informed reactions from peers and others are, unfortunately, a fact of life for some children with chronic illness. In a longitudinal study of children with cancer, adolescents were perceived by their teachers as less sociable, less prone toward leadership, and more socially isolated and withdrawn than their peers (Noll, LeRoy, Bukowski, Rogosch, & Kulkarni, 1991). Similar problems in social adjustment are evident among those children with illnesses that affect primarily the central nervous system—cerebral palsy, spina bifida, and brain tumors—because of the impact of these disorders on cognitive abilities such as social judgment (Hysing et al., 2009).

School adjustment and performance is another domain in which children and adolescents with chronic illness are at increased risk for adjustment difficulties. Risk may stem from two sources: primary effects of the illness or its treatment, and secondary consequences of the illness, such as fatigue, absenteeism, or psychological stress (Witt, Riley, & Coiro, 2003). Primary effects of the illness on school performance are especially evident among children with brain-related illnesses. They must undergo aggressive treatment regimens that put a heavy toll on the central nervous system, especially younger children (Brown et al., 2007). The most common neurocognitive effects appear in nonverbal abilities and attention or concentration functions (Mulhern, Merchant, Gajjar, Reddick, & Kun, 2004; Reeves et al., 2006). Short-term memory, speed of processing, visuomotor coordination, and sequencing ability also frequently are affected (Reeves et al., 2006). Thus, about one-half of the children with brain-related illnesses are placed in special education settings or do not attend school. In contrast, children with physical, non-brain-related illnesses tend to have normal educational placements; however, they continue to have problems in reading, which may be one indirect effect of chronic illness and school absence (Witt et al., 2003).

Family support plays a crucial role in helping children cope with chronic illness

How Children Adapt: A Biopsychosocial Model

We described the adjustment difficulties of children with chronic illness in general terms, but we know that each child's illness and family situation is different. Some children, like Amanda and Chen, have supportive families with adequate resources, but others may not. Countless events can influence children's adaptation to chronic illness; no single factor explains why some children adjust more readily than others.

How do we make sense of the numerous factors influencing children's adjustment? When a single-factor theory is not a sufficient explanation, researchers often develop multifactorial theories that link the most important variables in conceptual and meaningful ways. The *transactional stress and coping model* explains how children's adaptation to chronic illness is influenced not only by the nature of the illness itself, but also by personal and family resources (Gustafson, Bonner, Hardy, & Thompson, 2006; Thompson, Gustafson, George, & Spock, 1994). This model helps make sense of the complicated processes that shape children's outcomes.

The transactional stress and coping model emphasizes the stressful nature of chronic illness, which compels the child and family members to adapt. How they accomplish the adaptation is a key factor in children's outcomes.

Illness parameters encompass the type of illness and the severity of the illness, including visible disfigurement and functional impairment. *Demographic parameters* include the gender, age, and SES of the child, which also can affect the impact of the illness. The model then proposes that important child and family processes mediate the illness–outcome relationship, beyond the illness and demographic factors. Important psychological mediators involve parental adjustment, child adjustment, and their interrelationship, as described next.

Illness Parameters

One would expect that children's psychosocial adjustment varies as a function of their medical condition. Some illnesses have an uncertain course and others have dire effects on everyday activities, adding stress along the way. Different chronic illnesses have many features in common, though, so it often makes sense to study children's adjustment in relation to illness-related dimensions, or parameters, rather than specific illnesses. The common dimensions that vary among different illnesses include things such as the extent to which the illness:

- Is visible to others, or involves physical deformity
- Is severe and life-threatening
- Has a worsening or fatal prognosis versus a stable or improving prognosis
- Requires intrusive or painful procedures
- Affects the child's functional status, such as physical or cognitive impairments that affect performance of everyday tasks (Thompson & Gustafson, 1996)

Children with chronic illness face different challenges along each of these dimensions, so naturally their adjustment may be affected accordingly. Across all medical conditions, the illness parameters that play the most significant role in children's adjustment are *severity, prognosis*, and *functional status* (Lavigne & Faier-Routman, 1993). Functional status seems to be especially important in terms of cognitive impairments, such as conditions that involve the brain and central nervous system.

Personal Characteristics

Chronic medical conditions require both children and family members to accept and cope with considerable stress and uncertainty. What child characteristics and resources might favor successful adaptation? A child's sex is one consideration: Boys with chronic illness show more adjustment problems overall than girls. However, this sex difference depends on the dimension of adjustment and who is reporting the information. Boys are described by parents and teachers as having more behavior problems than girls; however, girls are more likely than boys to self-report anxiety, depression, and negative perceptions of physical appearance (Miller & La Greca, 2005).

Although children's overall adjustment seldom differs as a function of current age or age at the onset of the illness, economic and health disparities that exist among ethnic minority children and their families play a contributing role. These disparities not only affect the course and treatment of chronic illnesses, but also have a pronounced effect on quality of life and risk of disease and disability. Being poor is a risk factor for many stressful life events, but being poor and having a health problem greatly increases distress and adjustment problems (Greenberg, Raymond, & Leeder, 2011). Similarly, treatment studies on chronic illness in children and adolescents have not addressed important cultural issues that affect treatment outcome, especially compliance with the treatment regime (Clay, Mordhorst, & Lend, 2002; Elkin & Stoppelbein, 2008).

Not surprisingly, children with greater intellectual ability and acquired strengths in their self-concept and coping skills also show more positive psychological adjustment, regardless of medical condition. Specifically, children's accurate appraisal of perceived stress—how they interpret and react to daily events and hassles associated with illness management—leads to a better sense of well-being and fewer symptoms of distress and maladjustment (Pai, Drotar, Zebracki, Moore, & Youngstrom, 2006). Chen states this well:

> I now realize that life is full of a series of tests. You never know what is around the corner, but you have to take it as it comes. A positive attitude, and remembering that I have friends and family for support, helps me get through some of the rough days.

Family Adaptation and Functioning

If chronic illness is considered a stressor affecting all family members to some extent, then child adjustment depends in part on the degree of stress and symptoms experienced by other family members, especially the primary caregiver. Undeniably, the family environment assumes greater importance in the lives of children with a chronic illness, in part because a closer parent–child interaction often is necessary to manage the disease.

The transactional model considers parental adaptation to be a key mediator of the relationship between child illness and adjustment for both child and parent. How does a parent "adapt" in a way that favors healthy outcomes? According to the model, parental adaptation is a function of three major processes: (1) how they manage daily stress and view their self-efficacy, as seen with Chen's mother; (2) whether they use active, solution-focused coping; and (3) family functioning and perceived support. Successful parental adaptation, in turn, leads to better parental adjustment and healthier family communication and conflict resolution skills (Wysocki et al., 2008). Ultimately, of course, parents' positive adjustment greatly increases the likelihood of more positive child outcomes. Parent perceptions of illness are one aspect of parental adaptation that plays a key role in promoting their child's health. Perceptions of child vulnerability are related to increased social anxiety in their children and more school absences (Long & Marsland, 2011).

Family functioning often is defined in terms of the availability of two types of primary family resources: *utilitarian* and *psychological*. Utilitarian family resources relate to the practical demands of caring for a child with a disability, such as financial resources and parental education, which influence their ability to understand the illness and seek beneficial assistance for their child. Psychological resources are less tangible but often are considered far more important—how family members support one another, relate to each other and to persons outside the family, and resolve conflicts. Together these two types of family resources account for considerable variance in the behavioral and social adjustment of chronically ill children (Robinson, Gerhardt, Vannatta, & Noll, 2007).

Intervention

The psychological impact of chronic illness occurs through the disruption of normal processes of child development and family functioning. Fortunately, this impact can be lessened and adaptation can be strengthened by the use of psychosocial interventions that reduce stress, enhance social problem-solving skills, and promote effective child-rearing methods. These various methods often entail stress management and skill-building components to assist children and family members in their continuous process of adaptation.

The basic goal of intervention is to enhance the quality of life for the children and their families. Ways to achieve this goal have taken a dramatic shift over the past three decades, given the strong interest of pediatric and health psychologists. Prior to the mid-1970s, intervention efforts primarily were based on a child-centered, medically based model. The health professional was the expert, the child was the patient, and parents were passive observers. Today, parents are expected to participate in the decision-making process and their child's educational planning, which has led to family-centered interventions. In effect, families are now recognized as important resources, and seen as part of the solution; they are kept in the forefront of children's intervention needs, not in the background.

Empowering Families

This underlying philosophy of family empowerment reduces stress and dependency, and enables families to obtain the necessary information to make informed decisions and take competent actions. Chen's family members, for example, took an active role in enhancing his quality of life and were not frightened away or uninformed about his needs and their opportunities. His mother explains:

> Physiotherapy has helped Chen be less dependent on mom and dad. The goal is for him to think ahead and be prepared to do things on his own. An example is at bedtime getting his clothes out and onto the bed for the following morning. Then in the morning he can get himself dressed and transferred into his chair by himself.

Support groups and educational programs of various types offered considerable benefits to children and other family members. Helping families connect with one another and share their common experiences and concerns generates both personal power and important resources for change (Drotar, 2006; Ellis et al., 2007). Participation is the active agent in empowerment, and a cooperative health professional–family model encourages individuals to support one another while providing a venue for modeling positive attitudes and values. Similarly, educational programs that provide information and skills training to family members often are beneficial. The most beneficial promote knowledge and self-management of the illness, reintegration of children into the school setting, and support and coordination of care among parents of children with chronic illness (Drotar & Bonner, 2009). Gaining more knowledge about their child's disease promotes greater parental understanding of the child and the overall effect of the disease on the family.

In short, treatment-related activities for children with chronic illness often are based on the needs of the entire family. However, these efforts must fit the degree to which parents want to be—and realistically can be—involved in their child's overall care. Intervention methods that favor these adaptive processes adhere to medical regimens and psychologically based approaches to help children cope with the pain that is associated with invasive medical procedures and illness, as described in the next section.

Helping Children Cope

Throughout our discussion of children with chronic illness, we have seen how they must cope with numerous stressful circumstances, ranging from painful medical procedures to peer rejection and functional limitations. For this reason, considerable effort has been placed on ways to enhance their successful coping through support groups (see Box 12.1) and recreational activities (see Box 12.2). Much of this work focuses on coping with painful medical procedures, yet these methods also apply to other settings and circumstances, including at school or during home routines. Parent involvement and maternal adaptation are, once again, key components in children's coping; to effectively assist their children, parents must maximize their sense of control over the outcome and progress of their children's health (Robinson et al., 2007).

Enhancing adaptation and quality of life of children with chronic illness similarly requires that children comply as much as possible with medical regimens, both inside and outside the doctor's office. Since children often don't comply with even simpler tasks—like following directions, eating what they should, or getting ready for school—how can we expect them to comply with the unpleasant demands of medical procedures? The significance of these procedures has caused the emphasis in pediatric health psychology to shift to helping children and their parents cope with necessary protocols, rather than developing ways to make them comply.

Evidence suggests that most children and adults do best if a stressful medical procedure is explained first and they are given an opportunity to see what is going to happen. Accordingly, interventions for reducing

BOX 12.1 A CLOSER LOOK

Virtual Support Groups

In her private room at New York City's Mount Sinai Medical Center, 12-year-old Lauren peers intently into the colorful screen of a computer monitor. Lauren was diagnosed with a malignant tumor in her right wrist; 9 months of chemotherapy followed, and the radius bone in her right forearm was replaced with a metal rod. But today her mischievous brown eyes and smile light up the room as she plays. Finally tiring of the game, she clicks her way out and uses the computer to place a video call to one of her friends. "I've had bothersome moments," Lauren says after completing the call. "Like when I was in intensive care, and I wasn't allowed to do anything or see anyone. But this system lets me talk to kids from other hospitals who have the same thing as I do. I realized I'm not alone, and that made me feel better."

The system that cheers Lauren and children like her is an interactive network called STARBRIGHT World (SBW). For some of the children, SBW helps speed their recovery; for those less fortunate, it helps provide a measure of pleasure, comfort, diversion, and solace in their last months and weeks. SBW is a safe and secure online community where kids and teens living with serious illnesses can connect with each other. Kids on SBW can chat, read and post to bulletin boards, email, search for friends with similar illnesses, participate in fun events and contests, surf pre-screened Web sites, and play games.

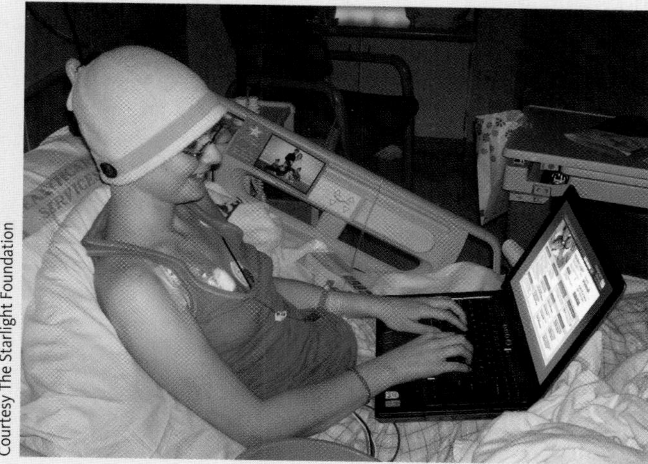

Courtesy The Starlight Foundation

Child with chronic illness speaking to others via Web technology

Source: The Starbright Foundation.

stress and managing pain during pediatric procedures have applied behavioral and cognitive approaches that emphasize *coping and stress management* (Hermann, 2011). Children who actively seek information about impending painful events show improved adjustment and less distress (Williams, Blount, & Walker, 2011). In addition, maternal and family functioning, effective child-rearing strategies to reinforce desired behaviors, and a positive doctor–patient relationship all contribute to children's improved adherence to the requirements of monitoring and treating their illness (Drotar, 2006).

In general, there are two main psychological approaches to helping children cope with stressful medical procedures and chronic and recurrent pain: providing information and training them in coping skills (Thompson & Gustafson, 1996). *Information strategies* offer verbal explanations and demonstrations as well as modeling the procedure, which reduce distress because the medical procedure is more predictable (Jaaniste, Hayes, & von Baeyer, 2007). Coping strategies involve teaching the various coping skills of deep breathing, attention distraction, muscle relaxation, relaxing imagery, emotive imagery, and behavioral rehearsal. For example, children may be asked to imagine themselves as superheroes undergoing a test of their powers (Dahlquist, 1999). Children are encouraged to identify specific stressors associated with their illness (e.g., giving themselves an injection), and to learn ways to handle those stressors and prevent distress or failure. Amanda, for instance, coped with her injections by thinking of positive things in her life.

Parents can serve as coaches during the stress and coping procedures and help their children rehearse coping skills both at home and in the clinic (Walker et al., 2007). Not only does using these coping skills lead to the reduction of pain and physical symptoms, but also it leads to a wide range of benefits that include fewer health care contacts and school absences, and less interference with family functioning (Bromberg, Gil, & Schanberg, 2011; Gil, Anthony, & Carson, 2001). To help children cope with invasive medical procedures, parents are encouraged to use distraction, contingent praise, and active directives ("take a deep breath now"), but they should avoid explanations, vague commands, or criticism (Dahlquist & Nagel, 2009; Hermann, 2011). Because of its demonstrated benefit, cognitive–behavioral therapy for children with chronic medical conditions that require painful medical procedures has become routine (Elkin & Stoppelbein, 2008).

BOX 12.2 A CLOSER LOOK

A Summer Retreat

Promoting social adjustment among children with a chronic illness can be difficult, but enrolling them in summer camps for children with similar illnesses is one way of encouraging social interaction with peers. Camp Oochigeas, the first residential camp for pediatric cancer patients in Canada, is an example of a place where children with similar medical issues can come together and share their experiences. Campers come for a free 2-week stay and participate in a number of camping activities with rest hours and medical regimens built in to their schedule.

Going away to summer camp provides these children with a chance to interact with their peers and be accepted, and to realize they are not the only ones coping with a chronic illness. It boosts their confidence and self-esteem and provides them with a social network that is often missing due to being out of school or feeling different from everyone else. "At a camp like Oochigeas, no one really pays attention to the fact that you have cancer because everyone does." It also gives their families a much needed break from the responsibility of caring for a child with a chronic illness, and it encourages the child to develop some independence and self-care skills. Often, the developmental task of gaining self-care skills and autonomy from parents is delayed for these children due to the nature of their illness. Camp is a way for both the child and parents to have a positive separation experience (in contrast to hospital visits), and to recognize the need for appropriate levels of independence.

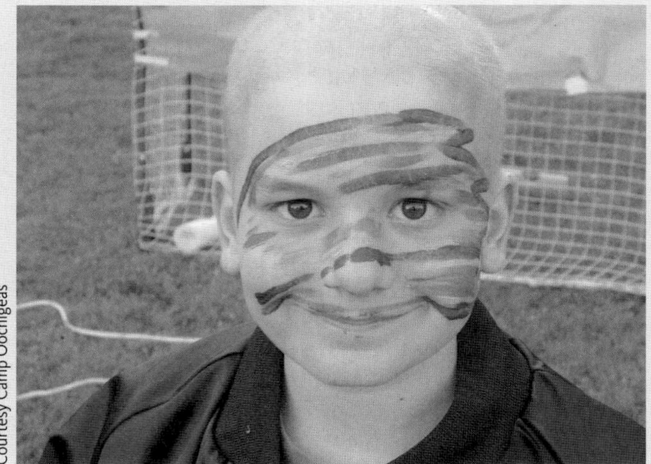
Courtesy Camp Oochigeas

Child with chronic illness attending summer camp

Source: Camp OOCHIGEAS (2006).

SECTION SUMMARY

Chronic Illness

- Children with chronic illness are at increased risk for psychosocial problems, which generally reflect their attempts to cope with stress.
- Children respond to the stress of chronic conditions in many different ways, and adjustment problems are more likely among children with increased disability. Adjustment problems may appear in the form of behavioral and emotional distress symptoms, such as low self-esteem, lack of social competence, poor school performance, and, sometimes, psychiatric disorders.
- Many children and their families adapt favorably to the challenges associated with chronic illness. Perceived social support and maternal adaptation are key components aiding their adaptation.
- Recent shifts to greater family empowerment and parental involvement have resulted in innovative ways to help children cope with the challenges of chronic illness. Psychosocial interventions assist children's adaptation to chronic illness by enhancing their social problem-solving skills and coping skills, and by reinforcing effective child-rearing methods.

Adolescent Substance Use Disorders

Let's begin this section with a short quiz. Many of us believe we have a good understanding of the nature and extent of substance use in our peer culture, so please look at Box 12.3 before reading this section to see if you know the facts! As you probably will discover, many myths remain about substance use that merit greater education and awareness, especially among the most vulnerable youth. Although most adolescents experiment with substances ranging from cigarettes to street drugs without experiencing adverse effects, the risks include increased mortality and morbidity related to impaired driving, unsafe sexual practices, aggression, and similar concerns (Earleywine, 2009; Williams, Holmbeck, & Greenley, 2002). Frequent and prolonged consumption not only increases their risk of developing a substance use disorder, but interferes with the development of important psychosocial skills in young adulthood (Haller, Handley, Chassin, & Bountress, 2010).

BOX 12.3 A CLOSER LOOK

Test Your Knowledge on Substance Use

1. Which age group has the highest percentage of drug abusers?

   a. 10–17, b. 18–25, c. 26–35, d. 36–60, e. 61 and over
2. Which is the most commonly used drug in the United States?

   a. marijuana, b. alcohol, c. cocaine, d. heroin
3. Which of the following poses the greatest health hazard to most people in the United States?

   a. cigarettes, b. heroin, c. codeine, d. LSD, e. caffeine
4. Which of the following drugs does not cause physical dependence?

   a. alcohol, b. morphine, c. peyote, d. codeine
5. Which of the following poses the highest immediate risk?

   a. inhalants, b. marijuana, c. nicotine, d. LSD
6. Overall, why is intravenous injection the most dangerous method of using illicit drugs?

   a. Because the drugs enter the system so rapidly

   b. Because nonsterile equipment and solutions can cause serious complications

   c. Because users usually get a larger amount of the drug by this method

   d. (a) and (c) only

   e. (a), (b), and (c)

Answers

1. (b)
2. (b)
3. (a) Approximately 300,000 deaths annually from coronary disease, other heart disease, lung cancer, respiratory disease, and other types of cancer have been linked to smoking.
4. (c) Physical dependence on mescaline (the active ingredient of the peyote cactus) or other hallucinogens has not been verified.
5. (a) Inhalants. Sniffing aerosols or other volatile substances can result in immediate death.
6. (e) The danger of contracting AIDS, hepatitis, or other infections is often overlooked by drug users who inject with nonsterile equipment.

Source: Brazoria County Sheriff's Department, Narcotic Division.

The use and abuse of substances (e.g., nicotine, alcohol, marijuana, and other drugs) is an increasing area of concern, particularly in adolescents. The abuse of such substances has physical implications for the developing child or adolescent, and may produce symptoms that mimic other psychopathological behaviors. Substance abuse is also related to a wide variety of psychological disorders.

Substance use disorders (SUDs) during adolescence include substance dependence and substance abuse, which result from the self-administration of any substance that alters mood, perception, or brain functioning (Brown & Abrantes, 2006). Whereas almost all abused substances can lead to psychological dependence, some also extend to physical dependence. Psychological dependence refers to the subjective feeling of needing the substance to adequately function. Physical dependence occurs when the body adapts to the substance's constant presence, and tolerance refers to requiring more of the substance to experience an effect once obtained at a lower dose. Another aspect of physical dependence is the experience of withdrawal, an adverse physiological symptom that occurs when consumption of an abused substance is ended abruptly and is thus removed from the body.

Diagnostic criteria for the two types of SUDs (abuse and dependence) are shown in Tables 12.4 and 12.5, based on the DSM-IV-TR (APA, 2000). To receive a diagnosis of **substance dependence**, an adolescent (or adult) must show a maladaptive pattern of substance use for at least 12 months, accompanied by three or more significant clinical signs of distress—tolerance (the need for increased amounts to achieve intoxication), withdrawal (cognitive and physiological changes upon discontinuation of the drug), and other indices of compulsive use. Substance dependence also is characterized as with or without physiological dependence (i.e., with or without evidence of tolerance or withdrawal). Criteria for **substance abuse**, in contrast, involve one or more harmful and repeated negative consequences of substance use over the last 12 months. Because substance dependence is the more serious of the two, a diagnosis of substance abuse would not be given if an individual met criteria for substance dependence.

As with other disorders described in this textbook, these criteria do not adequately consider important developmental differences between adults and adolescents. Whereas substance-abusing adolescents experience withdrawal symptoms, their physiological dependence and symptoms are less common than the same among adults. Adolescents are more likely to show cognitive and affective features associated with substance abuse and/or withdrawal, such as disorientation or mood swings (Brown & Abrantes, 2006).

SUDs among youths also differ from those of adults in terms of their pattern of use, which is likely a function of the restrictions on availability. For example, adolescents tend to drink less often, but drink larger amounts at any one time than adults drink (i.e., binge drinking),

TABLE 12.4 | Diagnostic Criteria for Substance Dependence

DSM-IV-TR

A. A maladaptive pattern of substance use, leading to clinically significant impairment or distress, as manifested by three (or more) of the following, occurring at any time in the same 12-month period:

(1) tolerance, as defined by either of the following:
- **a.** a need for markedly increased amounts of the substance to achieve intoxication or desired effect
- **b.** markedly diminished effect with continued use of the same amount of the substance

(2) withdrawal, as manifested by either of the following:
- **a.** the characteristic withdrawal syndrome for the substance
- **b.** the same (or a closely related) substance is taken to relieve or avoid withdrawal symptoms

(3) the substance is often taken in larger amounts or over a longer period than was intended

(4) there is a persistent desire or unsuccessful efforts to cut down or control substance use

(5) a great deal of time is spent in activities necessary to obtain the substance (e.g., visiting multiple doctors or driving long distances), use the substance (e.g., chain-smoking), or recover from its effects

(6) important social, occupational, or recreational activities are given up or reduced because of substance use

(7) the substance is continued despite knowledge of having a persistent or recurrent physical or psychological problem that is likely to have been caused or exacerbated by the substance (e.g., current cocaine use despite recognition of cocaine-induced depression, or continued drinking despite recognition that an ulcer was made worse by alcohol consumption)

Specify if:

With Physiological Dependence: evidence of tolerance or withdrawal (i.e., either Item 1 or 2 is present)

Without Physiological Dependence: no evidence of tolerance or withdrawal (i.e., neither Item 1 nor 2 is present)

Course specifiers (see text for definitions):

Early Full Remission
Early Partial Remission
Sustained Full Remission
Sustained Partial Remission
On Agonist Therapy
In a Controlled Environment

Source: Reprinted with permission from the Diagnostic and Statistical Manual of Mental Disorders, Fourth Edition, Text Revision, (Copyright ©2000). American Psychiatric Association.

TABLE 12.5 | Diagnostic Criteria for Substance Abuse

DSM-IV-TR

A. A maladaptive pattern of substance use leading to clinically significant impairment or distress, as manifested by one (or more) of the following, occurring within a 12-month period:

(1) recurrent substance use resulting in a failure to fulfill major role obligations at work, school, or home (e.g., repeated absences or poor work performance related to substance use; substance-related absences, suspensions, or expulsions from school; neglect of children or household)

(2) recurrent substance use in situations in which it is physically hazardous (e.g., driving an automobile or operating a machine when impaired by substance use)

(3) recurrent substance-related legal problems (e.g., arrests for substance-related disorderly conduct)

(4) continued substance use despite having persistent or recurrent social or interpersonal problems caused or exacerbated by the effects of the substance (e.g., arguments with spouse about consequences of intoxication, physical fights)

B. The symptoms have never met the criteria for Substance Dependence for this class of substance.

Source: Reprinted with permission from the Diagnostic and Statistical Manual of Mental Disorders, Fourth Edition, Text Revision, (Copyright ©2000). American Psychiatric Association.

which is associated with acute health and social risks (Chassin, Presson, Rose, & Sherman, 2007). Adolescents' substance use also is strongly influenced by peers, their desire for autonomy and experimentation with adult "privileges," and the level of parental supervision they received (Branstetter, Low, & Furman, 2011). These influences affect the expression and features of the SUDs in ways that differ from adults.

Prevalence and Course

It should come as little surprise that alcohol remains the most prevalent substance used, and abused, by adolescents. As shown in ● Figure 12.1, two-thirds of high school seniors, over half of tenth graders, and a third of those in eighth grade report that they have used alcohol over the past year, based on 2010 survey data on over 46,000 students (Johnston, O'Malley, Bachman, & Schulenberg, 2011a). About one-quarter of these teens report a history of binge drinking, defined as episodic heavy drinking of five or more drinks in a row (inexplicably, recent rates of binge drinking in Canada fall closer to 50% [Young et al., 2011]).

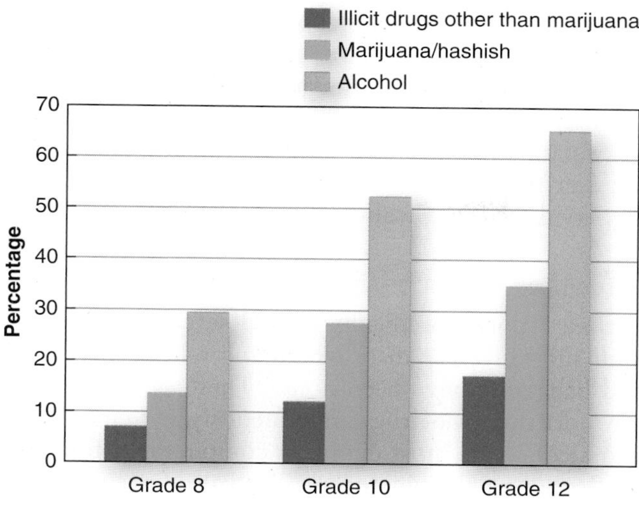

● **FIGURE 12.1** | Trends in annual prevalence of use of various drugs for eighth, tenth, and twelfth graders.
Data from *Monitoring the Future*, Johnston et al., 2011a.

Perhaps due to significant prevention efforts, adolescent cigarette smoking has been on the decline, with about one-fifth of high school seniors smoking cigarettes in the last month prior to the survey. However, marijuana use is common among these age groups, increasing from 14% in eighth grade to 35% in twelfth grade, its highest point in 30 years. Ironically, as daily cigarette smoking has decreased, daily marijuana use among adolescents appears to be increasing. One substance use problem of great concern regarding youths during the last decade is the increase in illicit drugs other than marijuana. The number of adolescents who have used MDMA (i.e., Ecstasy), opiates, cocaine, and crack has been increasing, although the number of adolescents using hallucinogens and inhalants has decreased somewhat (Johnston et al., 2011a).

Given the relatively high levels of substance use among adolescents, it is not surprising that a significant portion meet criteria for a substance abuse or dependence diagnosis. Community-based samples of youths estimate that about 12% of American adolescents met criteria for substance abuse or dependence (National Center on Addiction and Substance Abuse at Columbia University, 2011). Not surprisingly, much higher rates of these disorders (about one in three) are reported among youths with histories of other mental health problems, or with involvement in the child welfare or juvenile justice systems (Fidalgo, da Silveira, & da Silveira, 2008; Wilens, 2007).

Age of Onset

A certain amount of substance use during adolescence is normative behavior; therefore, researchers have looked at several factors that may differentiate trajectories of use that are relatively benign from those that have lasting significance. Age of first use is one of the most widely supported risk factors for the onset of substance use problems and subsequent disorders (Brown & Abrantes, 2006). The Canadian National Longitudinal Survey of Youth (NLSY), for example, found that the odds of developing alcohol dependence decreased by 9% for each year that the onset of drinking was delayed (Grant, Stinson, & Harford, 2001). In general, researchers find that alcohol use before age 14 is a strong predictor of subsequent alcohol abuse or dependence, especially when early drinking is followed by rapid escalation in the quantity of alcohol consumption (King & Chassin, 2007).

Sex and Ethnicity

Although past surveys have found that girls typically use fewer types of drugs and use them less often than boys, sex differences in the lifetime prevalence rates of substance use are converging, due mostly to increased substance use among girls. By 2005, girls caught up to boys by the 10th grade and have remained equivalent since. Similarly, rates of diagnoses for SUDs no longer differ significantly between boys and girls (Johnston et al., 2011a).

Notable ethnic differences in prevalence rates of substance use and abuse have been found, however. As shown in ● Figure 12.2, African American eighth, tenth, and twelfth grade students have substantially lower usage rates for most illicit drugs when compared to white students. Hispanics generally have rates of use for many drugs that tend to fall between usage rates for whites and African Americans. However, Hispanic seniors have the highest rate of lifetime usage for powder cocaine, crack cocaine, heroin with and without a

Rates of substance use among adolescent girls have increased over the last decade to a level similar to that of boys

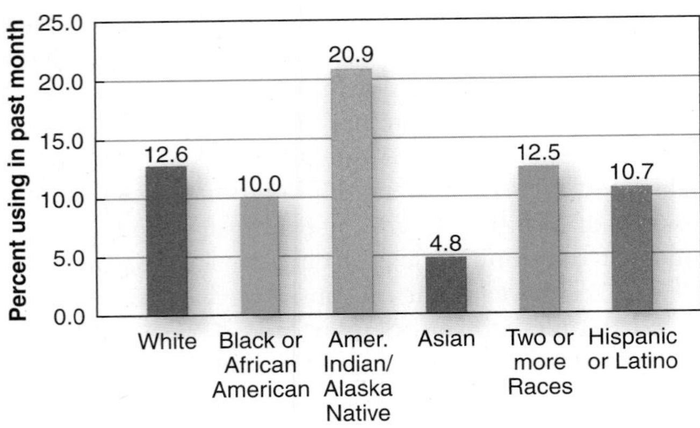

• **FIGURE 12.2** | Illicit drug use among persons aged 12 or older, by race/ethnicity: 2002.

Substance Abuse and Mental Health Services Administration (2003).

needle, methamphetamine, and crystal methamphetamine (Substance Abuse and Mental Health Services Administration [SAMHSA], 2003; Johnston et al., 2011b).

Course

Typically, rates of substance use peak around late adolescence and then begin to decline during young adulthood, in conjunction with adult roles of work, marriage, and parenthood (Brown & Abrantes, 2006). For some youths, however, a pronounced pattern of early-onset risk taking may signal a more troublesome course that can threaten their well-being in both the short and long term. As we note in Chapter 6 on conduct disorders, concern is particularly warranted when high-risk behaviors begin well before adolescence, are ongoing rather than occasional, and occur among a group of peers who engage in the same activities. Indeed, most adolescent risk and problem behaviors co-occur, so an indication of one problem is often a signal that others may be happening or on their way (Wolfe, Jaffe, & Crooks, 2006).

Although experimentation with substances is commonplace among teenagers, it is not harmless; substance use lowers inhibitions, reduces judgment, and increases the risk of physical harm and sexual assault (Thompson, Sims, Kingree, & Windle, 2008; Young, Grey, Abbey, Boyd, & McCabe, 2008). A survey of Canadian high school students found that alcohol use influenced the practice of, or involvement in, many other high-risk behaviors (Feldman, Harvey, Holowaty, & Shortt, 1999): most notably unsafe sexual activity, smoking, and drinking and driving. Moreover, girls who report dating aggression are 5 times more likely to use alcohol than girls in nonviolent relationships, whereas boys are 2.5 times more likely (Pepler, Craig, Connolly, & Henderson, 2002). Teens who use alcohol and drugs are more likely to have sexual intercourse at an earlier age, have more sexual partners, and have greater risk of sexually transmitted diseases (Connolly, Furman, & Konarski, 2000). Substance use is also a risk factor for unhealthy weight control (such as taking diet pills or laxatives), suicidality, and mood and anxiety disorders (Swahn, Bossarte, & Sullivent, 2008).

Associated Characteristics

Turning more specifically to adolescents diagnosed with substance use disorders, many related symptoms and behaviors have been noted. These youths tend to use more than one drug simultaneously, with marijuana and alcohol the most common combination, followed by alcohol and hallucinogens. They also have problems related to poor academic achievement, higher rates of academic failure, higher rates of delinquency, and more parental conflict (Chassin et al., 2007). Emerging research also suggests that heavy drinking may be physically more dangerous at 15 years of age than a few years later at age 20, because it may disrupt or disturb ongoing neurodevelopmental processes of myelination and synaptic pruning. When compared to teens with lower substance use levels, teens with long histories of heavy drinking performed poorly on tests of memory and attention, in addition to exhibiting other signs of abnormal neurological development (Clark, Thatcher, & Tapert, 2008). Given these characteristics associated with SUDs, it comes as no surprise that there is high comorbidity with many disorders covered in this textbook, especially ADHD and conduct problems (Brown & Abrantes, 2006).

Causes

Similar to conduct disorders, several pathways and various risk factors have been associated with problematic substance use in adolescents, including personality characteristics, family history, family functioning, and peer involvement.

Personality Characteristics

Personality characteristics that may predispose a teen to substance use stem from basic temperament characteristics, such as increased sensation seeking (Connell, Dishion, & Deater-Deckard, 2006). Sensation seeking has been described as a preference for novel, complex, and ambiguous stimuli, and has been linked to a range of high-risk behaviors including adolescent substance use (Martin, Storr, Alexandre, & Chilcoat, 2008). A longitudinal study looking at two samples of adolescents between grades 8 and 10 found sensation seeking had strong predictive value for both current and future marijuana and alcohol use (Crawford, Pentz,

Chou, Li, & Dwyer, 2003). The relationship between sensation seeking and substance use was strongest for predicting marijuana, followed by alcohol and, to a lesser extent, cigarette use. Furthermore, there were both sex and ethnicity differences in levels of sensation seeking—males tended to score higher than females, and white adolescents tended to score higher than adolescents with other ethnic backgrounds. One of the most important findings from this study indicated sensation seeking was not stable over time, suggesting that there may be a window of opportunity to intervene and prevent sensation seeking.

There are also many attitudes that predict substance use; some relate directly to substance use and others are more general attitudes. Having positive attitudes about substance use (i.e., high perceived benefit and acceptability, low perceived risk), and having friends who hold similar views, are attitudes and beliefs found to be associated with substance use (SAMSHA, 2003). Perceiving oneself to be physically older than same-age peers and striving for adult social roles are also risky attitudes. Finally, how highly positive adolescents feel about school—in particular, how connected they feel to their school community—predicts a lower risk for use of substances (Holmbeck, Friedman, Abad, & Jandasek, 2006). This concept of school connectedness is a nonspecific risk factor; that is, adolescents who feel engaged with and supported by their school tend to exhibit lower levels of risk behavior in a variety of domains (e.g., substance use, violence, sexual behavior, suicidality). In contrast, youths who are more alienated and not involved in school tend to report higher levels of these behaviors.

Family Functioning

The lack of parental involvement and parent–child affection, inconsistent parenting and poor monitoring, and negative parent–child and inter-parent interactions are all factors that increase the risk of substance use (Brown & Abrantes, 2006). An investigation of drinking initiation among sixth graders found that low parental expectations for abstaining from alcohol not only predicted earlier onset of drinking but also interacted with adolescents' own expectations. That is, if teens held positive expectancies about alcohol use and believed their parents did not hold strong expectations for them not to drink, they were much more likely to initiate alcohol use during grade 6. If they held positive expectancies about alcohol use, but thought that their parents had clear expectations for them not to use alcohol, they were not as likely to initiate (Simons-Morton & Chen, 2006). This finding was present for both males and females, and for both white and African American youths. It demonstrates that even at a time when youths are turning toward their peers for cues about acceptable behavior, parent attitudes and parental drinking patterns still play an important role (Latendresse et al., 2008).

Low parental monitoring, or the extent to which parents do not know "where their adolescents are and who they are with" has consistently emerged as a predictor of adolescent substance use (DiClemente, Marinilli, Singh, & Bellino, 2001). Interestingly, it seems to be the teens' perception of parental monitoring that is important. (Presumably there is a correlation between adolescent perceptions of parental monitoring and actual parental practices.) For example, research with six cross-sectional, culturally diverse data sets found a significant protective effect of perceived parental monitoring in predicting lower levels of substance use in each of the six cohorts (Rai et al., 2003).

Some researchers have found sex differences in the relationship between parental monitoring and substance use. For example, a study of 700 ninth and tenth graders found higher levels of parental monitoring were associated with less alcohol use in males, but had no effect on females' behavior (Borawski, Ievers-Landis, Lovegreen, & Trapl, 2003). In this same study, trust between adolescent females (but not males) and their parents was a strong deterrent for risk behaviors. Other family characteristics that have been linked to adolescent substance use include a parental history of substance abuse, poor parent–teen communication, and family conflict (Hussong, Bauer, & Chassin, 2008; Hussong, Flora, Curran, Chassin, & Zucker, 2008).

Associating with deviant and substance-using peers increases access to, and adoption of, beliefs supporting drug use

Peers and Culture

Given the importance that peer culture generally plays in adolescents' lives, it is not surprising that peer influences play a large role in determining substance use. The role of peers seems to operate in more than one way. For example, associating with deviant and substance-using peers causes youths to likely adopt beliefs supporting drug use (we tend to have beliefs similar to those of our friends). At the same time, affiliation with these peers also increases access to substances. In addition, the idea of a false consensus (i.e., the belief that everyone is doing it) exerts pressure on youths to engage in substance use. The extent to which individual teens think that their peer group is using substances is related to the individual's decision to use or not use substances (Branstetter et al., 2011). Peer culture also glamorizes substance use, encouraging teens to use alcohol and drugs as a way of "fitting in." About one-third of hit songs, including three-quarters of rap songs, have some form of explicit reference to drug, alcohol, or tobacco use (Primack, Dalton, Carroll, Agarwal, & Fine, 2008).

Treatment and Prevention

Treatment outcomes for adolescents with SUDs have been mixed. Approximately one-half of adolescents receiving treatment for substance use disorders (SUDs) relapse within the first 3 months following treatment, and only 20% to 30% remain abstinent at 1 year (Cornelius et al., 2003). Despite limitations, among the more promising treatments for adolescent substance abuse are those that involve the larger systems affecting the adolescent's behavior, such as peers, family, and school climate (Waldron & Turner, 2008). Other effective methods focus on personality factors linked to alcohol abuse, such as hopelessness, anxiety sensitivity, impulsivity, and sensation seeking (Conrod, Castellanos-Ryan, & Mackie, 2011).

Derived from interventions for conduct disorders, family-based approaches seek to modify negative interactions between family members, improve communication between members, and develop effective problem-solving skills to address areas of conflict (Anderson, Ramo, Schulte, Cummins, & Brown, 2007; Brown & Abrantes, 2006; Rowe & Liddle, 2006). Multisystemic Therapy (MST), for example, involves intensive intervention that targets family, peer, school, and community systems, and has been especially effective in the treatment of SUDs among delinquent adolescents (Henggeler et al., 2008).

The effectiveness of motivational interviewing (MI) with this population has also been supported (Jensen et al., 2011). Motivational interviewing uses a patient-centered and directive approach that addresses the ambivalence and discrepancies between a person's current values and behaviors and their future goals. In general, the type of treatment indicated depends on levels of use and the individual's home environment. Adolescents with low to moderate levels of substance abuse and a more stable home environment are reasonable candidates for outpatient treatment, whereas those with more severe levels of substance abuse, an unstable living situation, or comorbid psychopathology may require an inpatient or residential setting (Brown & Abrantes, 2006).

Because adolescence is a time of rapid, major transitions and changes in physical, emotional and social domains, prevention efforts related to substance use increasingly are being introduced at the elementary and secondary school levels. Facilitating successful transitions—for example, in the areas of romantic and peer relationships, sexual behavior, and healthy lifestyle choices—has the added major benefit of reducing multiple problematic outcomes in later life. Critical health-damaging behaviors that are preventable include substance use and abuse, unsafe sexual practices, and abusive behavior, which all have a common context of peer and dating relationships (Wolfe et al., 2006). These prevention efforts are being recognized as having important payoffs in terms of reductions in future health problems and enhancement of personal goals (Irwin, Burg, & Cart, 2002).

Effective approaches to adolescent substance abuse prevention have addressed multiple influences on the individual from peers, family, school, and community. Life Skills Training, a detailed and well-evaluated program, emphasizes building drug resistance skills, personal and social competence, and altering cognitive expectancies around substance use (Griffin & Botvin, 2010). Because adolescents must receive consistent messages and reinforcement regarding pressures to use alcohol and drugs, as well as develop effective refusal skills, societal messages about responsible use are emphasized to influence students' behavior. Prevention programs also target the social environment through community and school norms and their efficacy to enact change, and they often include some level of parent involvement and education to improve parent–child communication about substance use (Greenberg, Domitrovich, & Bumbarger, 2000; O'Leary-Barrett, Mackie, Castellanos-Ryan, Al-Khudhairy, & Conrod, 2010).

Study Resources

SECTION SUMMARIES

KEY TERMS

COURSEMATE

Access an interactive eBook and chapter-specific interactive learning tools, including flashcards, quizzes, videos, and more in your Psychology CourseMate, accessed through CengageBrain.com.

13

Eating Disorders and Related Conditions

I feel like I'm disappearing, getting smaller every day but I look in the mirror—I'm bigger in every way.

—Lyrics from "Tunic (Song for Karen)" by Sonic Youth, written in memory of singer Karen Carpenter, who died of anorexia

CHAPTER PREVIEW

ALTHOUGH SERIOUS EATING PROBLEMS have only recently been considered mental disorders, bizarre and unusual eating habits have been documented for many centuries. The ancient Egyptians believed that illness could be avoided through monthly purges. The ancient Romans built the aptly described "vomitorium," where men purged their stomachs after overindulging in a heavy banquet—before returning to eat more. For centuries, voluntary as well as forced starvation has had both saintly and evil guises, whether as religious fasting or as a way to put an end to individuals who seemed possessed and bewitched. Today, as always, overeating and starvation are connected to mental health problems and unusual cultural practices.

This chapter addresses several eating disorders and their related conditions that affect children and youths. We begin with a discussion of risk factors that affect eating habits among infants and children, followed by discussion of the developmental significance of childhood obesity. Obesity is not a psychiatric disorder, nor is it associated with greater psychopathology. However, children with obesity are at risk of establishing unhealthy dieting patterns, often caused by social discrimination, that sometimes lead to chronic health problems and eating disorders (Puhl & Latner, 2007; Puhl, Luedicke, & Heuer, 2011). We then turn our attention to feeding and eating disorders that occur during infancy or early childhood, such as pica and failure to thrive.

The last section of the chapter addresses the two major eating disorders of adolescence and young adulthood: anorexia nervosa and bulimia nervosa (shortened to "anorexia" and "bulimia" throughout the chapter). Anorexia emerges primarily among adolescent girls and may continue into young adulthood. It often is marked by an obsession with food and a drive for thinness that causes the person to lose sight of what is healthy. Bulimia is characterized by binge eating followed by an effort to compensate, usually through self-induced vomiting, but sometimes by fasting; by misusing laxatives, diuretics, or other medications; or by exercising excessively. Individuals with bulimia are also obsessed with food and with losing weight, but they do not experience the excessive weight loss associated with anorexia. Most persons with bulimia are within 10% of their normal weight, whereas individuals with anorexia refuse to maintain even a minimally normal weight.

Eating disorders have traditionally been only a medical concern. Studies of their etiology and treatment have focused on physiological mechanisms and the serious biological consequences associated with these disorders. Over the last quarter century, as mental health professionals began to study psychosocial factors—genetic makeup, cognitive and social development, and everyday experiences between infant and caregivers—they discovered that many of the same factors underlying other major childhood disorders significantly influence early feeding and eating disorders.

Unlike most disorders of childhood and adolescence described in this text, however, the causes of major eating disorders seem to be disproportionately related to sociocultural influences, rather than psychological and biological influences. What makes these disorders particularly unusual is that they are so closely linked to Western culture, where food is plentiful and a person's appearance, especially for young women, is so highly valued. The various types of eating disorders increasingly have become a problem for adolescents in Western society: collectively they are the third most common illness in adolescent females (Hudson, Hiripi, Pope, & Kessler, 2007).

How Eating Patterns Develop

Anyone who has ever watched a 2-year-old eat spaghetti knows that learning to feed oneself is not a simple process. In fact, feeding and eating problems are a normal part of development for most children as they learn through gradual approximations.

Normal Development

Troublesome eating habits and limited food preferences are among the most distinguishing characteristics of early childhood. Approximately one in four children (under age 12) are described as picky eaters by their parents (Mascola, Bryson, & Agras, 2010). Picky eating is more common among girls than boys (Rydell & Dahl, 2005), but its relationship to the emergence of eating disorders during adolescence or adulthood is unclear (Jacobi, Hayward, de Zwaan, Kraemer, & Agras, 2004). Beginning around age 9, girls are more anxious than boys about losing weight (Philipsen & Brooks-Gunn, 2008).

These typical developmental patterns are, in part, a function of societal norms and expectations—especially for girls—as portrayed through images of thinness and attractiveness in magazines, television, and movies (Bell & Dittmar, 2011; Nouri, Hill, & Orrell-Valente, 2011). In addition, normal concerns about weight and appearance can either be reduced or increased by the comments of parents, friends, and romantic partners. The effects of the early parent–child relationship on fundamental biological processes such as eating and growth patterns are of paramount importance (Corning, Gondoli, Bucchianeri, & Salafia, 2010). Entering school is the next significant developmental landmark because of increasing social pressure to conform to narrow perceptions of desirable body type.

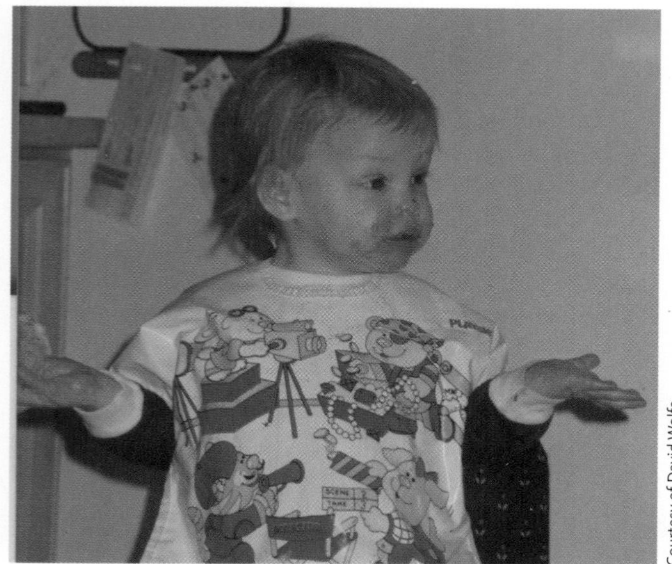

Eating disorders should not be confused with disorderly eating, a normal part of early development

Courtesy of David Wolfe

Significantly, the desire to achieve an ideal image can turn into an obsession during adolescence.

Developmental Risk Factors

A developmental perspective of eating problems and eating disorders raises the intriguing possibility of a continuum of "eating pathology" that ranges from dieting to clinical syndromes, across all developmental periods (Attie & Brooks-Gunn, 1995). ● Figure 13.1 illustrates how problem eating from a young age may contribute to being overweight or obese during childhood. Overweight children are often teased or rejected by their peers in elementary school, which in turn may cause a drive for thinness with the intention of improving their negative body image and acceptance (Lawler & Nixon, 2011; Puhl et al., 2011). **Drive for thinness** is a key motivational variable that underlies dieting and body image, among young females in particular, whereby the individual believes that losing more weight is the answer to overcoming her troubles and to achieving success (Philipsen & Brooks-Gunn, 2008). However, such behavior creates the negative side effects of weight preoccupation, concern with appearance, and restrained eating, which increase the risk of an eating disorder (Touyz, Polivy, & Hay, 2008).

Early Eating Habits, Attitudes, and Behaviors

Disturbed **eating attitudes** describe a person's belief that cultural standards for attractiveness, body image, and social acceptance are closely tied to one's ability to control diet and weight gain. Even among 7- to 10-year-olds, concerns about weight, dieting, and physique are common, suggesting that Western sociocultural values and preoccupation with body weight and dieting—factors that lead to eating disorders among vulnerable adolescents—may be internalized and expressed at a very early age (Thompson, Rafiroiu, & Sargent, 2003).

Researchers following sample groups of children and adolescents over several years have documented the continuity between eating problems during childhood (such as struggles at mealtime or disinterest in food) and the subsequent onset of a disorder. Examining patterns of eating problems over 8 years among normal adolescent girls, Graber, Brooks-Gunn, Paikoff, and Warren (1994) discovered that about 25% of them

Eating Problems

Problem eating

Early childhood

Teasing

Middle childhood

Drive for thinness,
Negative body image,
dieting, weight concerns

Adolescence

Developmental Periods

● **FIGURE 13.1** | A developmental continuum of eating habits and disorders.

Photo Credits (left to right): © iStockphoto.com/Frans Rombout; © 2012 BananaStock/Jupiterimages Corporation; © Elena Elisseeva/Dreamstime.com.

showed signs of a serious eating problem at each assessment. These teens had earlier pubertal maturation, higher percentages of body fat, concurrent psychological problems (especially depression), and poorer body image than teens without eating problems (Tyrka, Waldron, Graber, & Brooks-Gunn, 2003).

Weight concerns (such as fear of weight gain, worry over weight and body shape, diet history, and perceived fatness) and body image, in particular, appear to be significantly related to the onset of eating problems and eating disorders during adolescence (Juarascio et al., 2011). This constellation of physical and psychological factors, linked to early eating problems and distorted beliefs, signifies a considerable risk pattern for the development of persistent and possibly severe eating problems (Jacobi et al., 2004; Striegel-Moore & Bulik, 2007). The desire to appear thin may be responsible for the near-epidemic rates of referral of young people with eating disorders, especially bulimia, since the mid-1970s throughout Western society. In contrast, regular family meals may function as a protective factor for eating disorders (Bauer, Laska, Fulkerson, & Neumark-Sztainer, 2011).

Transition into Adolescence

Passage from childhood to early adolescence is full of unexpected challenges, not the least of which is undergoing the significant changes in body shape that require considerable adjustments in self-image. Research has consistently shown that anorexia and bulimia typically occur during adolescence and that onset thereafter is rare (Striegel-Moore et al., 2005). The timing of maturation also affects dieting behavior, because girls who mature early are likely to be heavier than their late-maturing peers (Derose, Shiyko, Foster, & Brooks-Gunn, 2011).

As we saw with younger children, girls report feeling worse about themselves than do boys, most likely because girls place greater emphasis on their self-perceptions of their physical appearance (Paxton, Eisenberg, & Neumark-Sztainer, 2006). Although they readily acknowledge their interpersonal and social abilities, many post-pubescent girls say they frequently feel fat and unattractive. In contrast, boys see themselves in a more positive light with respect to achievement, academic aspirations, self-assertion, and body image (O'Dea, 2006; 2008). Contradictory societal messages implying that women must be successful both in traditionally feminine and traditionally masculine roles place added pressure on young women to aspire to some elusive superwoman caricature (Cash & Smolak, 2011). Female adolescents who describe themselves in superwoman terms are more likely to associate thinness with autonomy, success, and recognition for their independent achievements; however, they also are significantly more at risk for eating disorders (Levine & Smolak, 2010).

The all-too-familiar interaction of pubertal weight gain, the beginning of social dating, and threats to achievement status often promote body dissatisfaction, distress, and perceived loss of control in young adolescents, especially because they occur cumulatively over a relatively short period (Philipsen & Brooks-Gunn, 2008). As you might expect, these changes also encourage smoking and other substance use among teenage girls, who feel that these activities protect them from the impulse to binge eat and the consequences of weight gain. The importance of one's perceived body image is discussed later in the sections on anorexia and bulimia.

Dieting and Weight Concerns

Restrictive dieting has become a North American pastime, especially among youths who choose to diet at very young ages. A large-scale survey of students in grades 5 through 8 found that approximately 60% had tried to lose weight in the past 7 days (Thompson et al., 2003), which is consistent with the notion that these concerns often begin as early as elementary school and increase steadily throughout adolescence (Neumark-Sztainer, Wall, Larson, Eisenberg, & Loth, 2011). A significant number of these students report feeling depressed after overeating and choosing strict dieting as a form of weight control (Stice, Marti, Spoor, Presnell, & Shaw, 2008).

Chronic dieting seems strongly related to both gender and developmental factors. By mid-adolescence, about two-thirds of girls report being on a diet during the previous year, which is a twofold increase over elementary school. Among those who diet, about 10% of girls are chronic dieters—that is, someone who continuously remains on a diet or who diets sporadically more than 10 times during the year (French, Story, Downes, Resnick, & Blum, 1995). In contrast, only 2% of boys are chronic dieters.

Why does dieting sometimes lead to overeating? Decreasing caloric intake reduces a person's metabolic rate, which allows fat to remain in the cells, so weight loss is in fact impeded. This failure to lose weight sets the stage for a vicious cycle of increased commitment to dieting and vulnerability to binge eating. Psychological consequences also contribute to this cycle by creating what some researchers call the "false hope syndrome"—an initial commitment to change one's appearance leads to short-term improvements in mood and self-image, but this hope declines as feelings of failure and loss of control increase (Polivy & Herman, 2005). Loss of control may lead to binge eating, and purging is seen as a way to counteract the perceived effects of binge eating on weight gain. **Purging** is the voluntary use of vomiting, laxatives, or other methods to rid the body of food. Invariably, purging is followed by disgust and self-recrimination, which prompts renewed

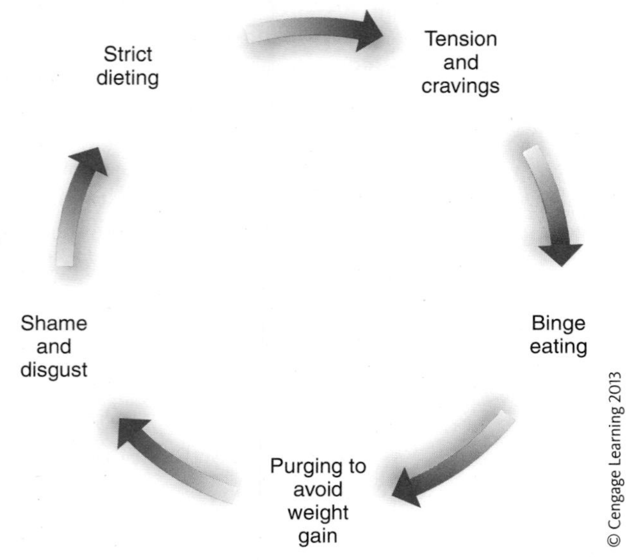

● **FIGURE 13.2** | The binge–purge cycle.

vows of abstinence and sets the stage for the whole cycle of dieting, overeating, dietary failure, and affective distress to begin again, as shown in ● Figure 13.2 (Polivy & Herman, 2005).

Although dieting is clearly a risk factor in relation to the onset of eating disorders, it should be viewed in perspective: Many young persons diet in order to influence body weight and shape, yet only a small minority develop eating disorders. Dieting can be harmful or beneficial, depending on the individual and the conditions. It is important to distinguish between dieting in individuals (especially children) who are not overweight, and dieting in individuals whose excess weight increases medical or psychological risk (Brownell & Rodin, 1994). There is a critical difference between watching your weight as part of a health-conscious lifestyle and chronic, unrealistic dieting that upsets your body's natural rhythm and balance.

A developmental approach to researching and treating eating disorders in youths is essential, yet few researchers have adopted a developmental perspective in their studies. While many of the symptoms exhibited are similar to adult symptoms, the effects of those symptoms may have lasting and significant effects on adolescents' growth and development. Adolescents with an eating disorder may be deprived of key social, emotional, and biological developmental processes that normally develop during this period.

Biological Regulators

How do we know when to eat and how much to eat? For most of us, eating, like sleeping, is a natural process, controlled by biorhythms that have adapted successfully over time to the stress and strain of our individual lives. However, normal patterns of eating and growth, as well as the disorders based on disturbances in these patterns, are influenced by physical and psychological processes that continuously interact. In essence, your particular growth and weight pattern is based on the relation between your genes and your constitution, which governs your ability from early infancy to self-regulate your sleep and elimination patterns, appetite, and past and current nutritional patterns.

Metabolic rate, or balance of energy expenditure, is established based on individual genetic and physiological makeup, as well as eating and exercise habits. Individual metabolism, in turn, serves to self-monitor and self-regulate behavior, which is why we may have trouble maintaining changes in weight or exercise. If you burn more energy than you take in, a state of chronic negative energy balance, or hypocaloric malnutrition, can occur. Malnutrition, even for brief periods of time, is followed by physical attempts to adapt that can produce significant biological, behavioral, and psychological effects, including loss of circadian rhythm; increase in the release of growth hormones; dermatological changes with the loss of fatty tissue or hair pigmentation; and emotional and behavioral changes such as lethargy, depression, and apathy (Woolston, 1991). These changes can have long-term consequences if they occur during crucial developmental stages, or during the acquisition of fundamental cognitive abilities. Feeding and eating disorders thus merit careful study, because these problems can be overlooked when they are accompanied by more pronounced emotional and behavioral problems.

Body Weight

Anyone who has tried dieting knows how hard it is to lose weight and keep it off. Weight loss is rapid for the first few weeks, but most of the lost weight returns with time. In fact, 90% to 95% of those who lose weight regain it within several years (Agras, 2010). Why is body weight so resistant to change? For years the blame was primarily placed on the dieter's weak resolve or lack of willpower, but today researchers place more credence in the view that each person is biologically and genetically programmed to weigh within a certain natural weight range. A person's natural weight is regulated around his or her own **set point**, which is a comfortable range of body weight that the body tries to "defend" and maintain (Levin, 2010).

In effect, people who gain or lose weight will experience metabolic changes that strive to bring the body back to its natural weight. If fat levels decrease below our body's normal range, the brain (specifically, the hypothalamus) compensates by slowing metabolism. We begin to feel lethargic, we increase our sleep, and our body temperature decreases slightly to conserve energy (which is why many persons with anorexia complain of being cold). In this state of relative deprivation, uncontrollable urges to binge are common because our bodies are telling us that they need more food than they are getting to function properly.

Similarly, the body fights against weight gain by increasing metabolism and raising body temperature in an effort to burn off extra calories. (Admittedly, this valiant effort is seldom enough to conquer the force of holidays and other feasts.) Because of its responsivity to change, researchers often compare the body's set point to the setting on a thermostat that regulates room temperature. When room temperature falls below a certain range, the thermostat automatically sends a signal to the heating system to increase the heat level until it again reaches the established temperature setting. Human bodies respond similarly to deviations in body weight by turning their metabolic "furnace" up or down (Wilkin, 2010).

Growth

Under normal conditions, the biological mechanisms of growth are like the well-orchestrated ecosystem of a forest or a lake—a system of feedback loops, messenger signals, and major organs that work together to maintain a healthy balance. For humans, the biology of growth fundamentally involves the manner in which circulating hormones interact with available nutritional resources to produce changes throughout the skeletal system. The most significant hormonal determinants of growth rate during childhood are the *growth hormone* (GH) and *thyroid hormone*, with additional gonadal steroids kicking in during adolescence to produce a further growth spurt and skeletal maturation. From 50% to 75% of growth hormone production occurs after the onset of deep sleep in children and young adults (Woolston, 1991), which may explain why eating and sleep disorders coexist in some younger children (Lyons-Ruth, Zeanah, & Benoit, 1996).

Individual growth depends on GH circulating throughout the body. The release of GH from the pituitary gland is determined by the hypothalamus and the higher brain structures that affect it (the limbic cortex and amygdala). These higher brain structures are involved in emotional sensation and response, which may account for the connection between eating and emotional disorders (discussed in the following section). Just as a thermostat determines the need to increase or decrease temperature, the hypothalamus senses the need to release more or less GH throughout the body. To accomplish this task, the hypothalamus releases two controlling hormones that exert opposite effects. The *growth hormone inhibiting factor* (i.e., somatostatin) essentially inhibits the GH response to internal signals of hunger, so we stop eating. In contrast, the *growth hormone releasing factor* has the specific function of telling our body when, how, and where to grow by releasing growth hormone from the pituitary.

Familiarity with these biological processes makes it easier to understand how the biological substrates of growth and metabolism can be thrown off balance by many factors that cause behavioral and physiological changes in children or young adults. Although we do not know if the majority of eating disorders are caused by biological abnormalities, or if the disorder itself creates a biological disruption, these underlying biological mechanisms influencing weight regulation are important to the understanding of eating disorders discussed in the remainder of this chapter.

SECTION SUMMARY

How Eating Patterns Develop

- Eating problems are common among children.
- Normal concerns about weight and appearance can be influenced unduly by parents and peers, sometimes resulting in eating disturbances.
- Early eating habits, attitudes, and behaviors that place undue concern on body image and a drive for thinness increase the risk of eating disorders.
- Increased dieting and weight concerns often accompany the transition into adolescence, especially for girls, which can lead to the emergence of unhealthy eating patterns.
- Attempts to reduce weight by dieting can lead to a vicious cycle of weight loss and weight gain. Chronic dieting is associated with the onset of adolescent eating disorders.
- Normal patterns of eating and growth, as well as the later emergence of eating disorders, are influenced by biological processes such as one's metabolic rate and set point.

Obesity

Approximately 1 in 6 children and adolescents (aged 2–19 years) in North America are obese (Centers for Disease Control and Prevention [CDC], 2011). **Childhood obesity** is considered to be a chronic medical condition similar to hypertension or diabetes, and is characterized by excessive body fat. Persons with obesity regulate their weight appropriately, but their set point is elevated. Obesity usually is defined in terms of a *body mass index* (BMI), essentially a height-to-weight ratio, which is above the 95th percentile, based on norms for the child's age and sex. A childhood BMI between the 85th and 95th percentiles is considered overweight.

● Figure 13.3 shows how the BMI is calculated and plotted. Note how the BMIs of overweight and

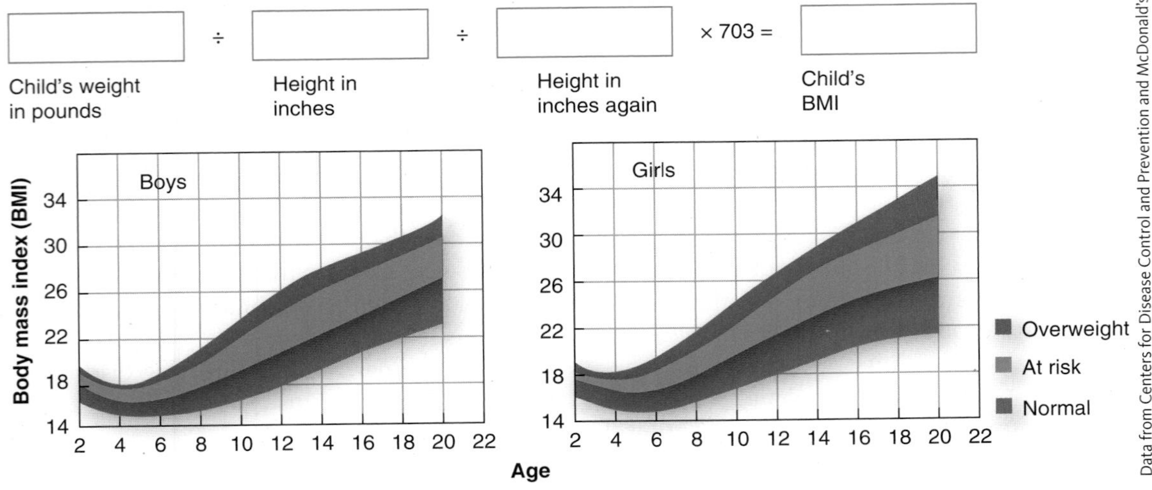

FIGURE 13.3 | How to calculate and plot a child's BMI by age and sex.

"at risk" children increase more rapidly than the normal BMIs for boys and girls, both of which increase with age, especially during adolescence. The exponential increase in fast-food restaurants and convenient junk foods can also contribute to the rise in obesity rates. On any given day, 30% of American children eat fast food (Bowman, Gortmaker, Ebbeling, Pereira, & Ludwig, 2004), and half of the caloric intake of youths in the United States comes from added sugar and fat (CDC, 2011). The size of meal portions makes a huge difference in caloric intake. For example, a traditional McDonald's burger with a 16-ounce Coke and a small order of fries carries 627 calories and 19 grams of fat. That same meal with cheese and "supersized" carries 1,805 calories and 84 grams of fat. These increases in caloric and fat intake may account for the jump in the percentages of boys and girls who are overweight.

As we have seen, more and more children and adolescents are caught up in a dieting cycle, and the reasons for wanting to lose weight are compelling. Obesity is severely stigmatized in North American society and carries many social and health hazards (Puhl & Latner, 2007). Herein lies a fundamental conflict: The mass media powerfully promote the thin ideal in a land where fast food is widely available and accessible. Although obesity clearly is not a mental disorder, it can affect a child's psychological and physical development significantly. Obese children and adolescents are five times more likely than healthy children to experience an impaired quality of life, similar to children with cancer (Schwimmer, Burwinkle, & Varni, 2003).

ELLEN

Self-Image and Self-Esteem

It does matter to me what people say and think about my size. I guess the whole self-esteem thing began when I was little and other kids made fun of me for being fat—which basically I feel has continued until about a year ago.

OK, fine, that is other people's rudeness and lack of sensitivity about someone's problem. Because of these a_holes, I have always had to try harder at everything to prove I wasn't just a fat blob—there was a person living, breathing, caring inside that has to be dealt with. . . .

. . . I fell into the trap from about age 5 of letting others' images of a fat me be my own self-image. I have now let myself get to the point of only accepting others' concept of my new getting-thin person and don't allow myself to think thin. There are times when I get what I need—either trying a smaller-sized outfit, having a total stranger compliment me or a friend tell me I'm looking nice that day—I get high on those compliments and I can be fueled on them for a day or so and then I'm back to square one—who is this person in the picture?

I am scared. All my life I have wanted to be thin. . . .

I know the day I weigh 170 . . . the number isn't going to make my mind snap into line and make me happy with my accomplishment.

The whole self-esteem thing seems as difficult if not more so than the actual weight loss. To lose weight you eat the right foods and exercise—the weight falls off—but to change how you feel about yourself is a whole different ball of wax. How do you change approximately 18 years of thinking about yourself one way when you are really no longer that person? How do I convince myself—do I write 500 times a day I am thin, worthwhile, nice, organized, good worker, pleasant personality, pretty, smart, logical mind, good advice giver? I know all these things about myself, but they are shadows of the tower of this whole f_ing weight thing. I need a bulldozer to knock over that tower. Where does the bulldozer come from—from inside? But where is it buried, where are the good feelings, the easiness with myself, the self-confidence that I do look nice and desirable? (From "Obesity," by J. P. Foreyt and J. H. Cousins, 1987, pp. 502–503. In M. Hersen and V. B. Van Hasselt (Eds.), *Behavior Therapy with Children and Adolescents*. Copyright © 1987 by John Wiley & Sons, Inc. Reprinted by permission of John Wiley & Sons, Inc.)

Ellen, an 18-year-old who first became aware of her obesity when she was 9, describes her thoughts and feelings with respect to her weight: Ellen's self-disclosure captures the social and emotional dilemma that overweight children and adolescents so often face, which she characterizes as "the self-esteem thing." Many obese children and adults suffer the consequences of Western cultural attitudes that equate attractiveness and competence with thinness. As early as first grade, children are less likely to befriend overweight peers, and these attitudes intensify during adolescence (Striegel-Moore & Bulik, 2007). Although her weight losses were slow, with the help of group and individual therapy, Ellen defeated the critical messages that had plagued her since childhood, allowing her to reach and maintain her realistic goal of 170 pounds.

Prevalence and Development

For the past three decades, alarm bells have been sounding over the fact that the number of children who are overweight or obese is increasing. As shown in ● Figure 13.4, obesity rates for all age groups of children and adolescents have increased from 5% to over 17% since the mid-1970s. In the U.S. and Canada, the obesity rate among boys age 7 to 13 nearly tripled between the early 1980s and the mid-2000s, while the prevalence of obesity among girls of the same age more than doubled (Ogden, Lamb, Carroll, & Flegal, 2010). This trend has emerged worldwide as well, although not to the same degree—the prevalence of childhood overweight and obesity has increased from 4.2% in 1990 to 6.7% in 2010 (de Onis, Blössner, & Borghi, 2010). Although there is recent evidence that this trend is stabilizing, rates of childhood obesity and overweight remain high and pose a significant public health issue worldwide (Olds et al., 2011).

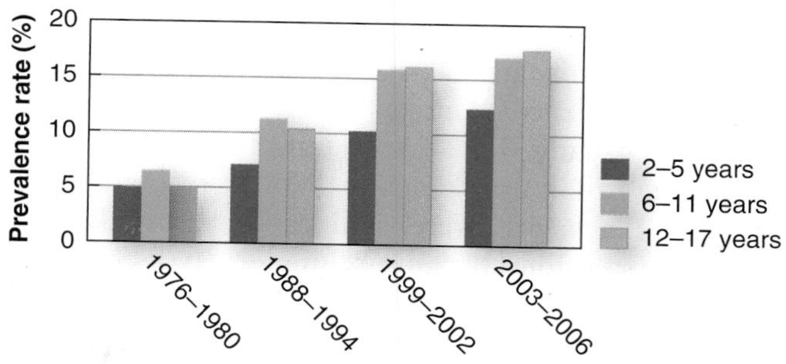

● **FIGURE 13.4** | Increasing prevalence of obese children and adolescents in the United States 1976–2006.
Ogden et al., 2002; Hedley et al., 2004; Ogden et al., 2008.

Although obesity during infancy and obesity during later childhood are not strongly related, *childhood-onset* obesity is more likely to persist into adolescence and adulthood (Wilkin, 2010). Even during their youth, individuals with obesity risk many health concerns, such as cardiovascular problems, diabetes, and elevated cholesterol and triglycerides (Power & Thomas, 2011; Wang, McPherson, Marsh, Gortmaker, & Brown, 2011). Obesity during childhood may have long-term effects in that many lifestyle and behavioral choices associated with obesity develop during the school-age years. In fact, obesity is a major factor in reducing life expectancy in North America (Katzmarzyk & Ardern, 2004; Preston & Stokes, 2011).

One troubling finding is that preadolescent obesity is a risk factor in the later emergence of eating disorders, especially for females, primarily due to the manner in which peers ignore or tease children who are obese. Obesity is strongly correlated with teasing by age-mates at an early age; teasing, in turn, predicts overall dissatisfaction with appearance and body image, and sets in motion a chain of restrictive and high-risk eating practices (Eisenberg, Neumark-Sztainer, & Story, 2003). Overweight children and adolescents may require assistance at an early age in developing a healthy, acceptable body image and eating patterns to resist the harmful and cruel pressures of early adolescence (Menzel et al., 2010; Mond, Van den Berg, Boutelle, Hannan, & Neumark-Sztainer, 2011).

Overweight students in middle and high schools use fewer healthy weight-control strategies (e.g., physical activity, healthier eating), and more unhealthy strategies (e.g., vomiting, diet pills, laxatives) than non-overweight students (Boutelle, Neumark-Sztainer, Story, & Resnick, 2002). Thus, a childhood pattern of being overweight may make it more difficult during adolescence and adulthood to achieve or maintain the culturally valued degree of thinness. The individual then may engage in the more extreme weight-control measures that may lead to an eating disorder.

Culture and SES

There are significant racial and ethnic disparities in obesity prevalence. Among U.S. children and adolescents, Hispanic boys are significantly more likely to be obese than non-Hispanic White boys, and non-Hispanic Black girls were significantly more likely to be obese than non-Hispanic White girls (CDC, 2011). Although reasons for such disparities are many, mothers identify pressures of familial and cultural influences favoring chubbier children (Lindsay, Sussner, Greaney, & Peterson, 2011; Ramirez, Chalela, Gallion, Green, & Ottoson, 2011). Researchers also point to the problem of "food deserts" that make healthier eating a challenge. In many inner cities and rural communities children and families are unable to access healthy, affordable food due to lack of transportation and the preponderance of cheap processed foods (Davis, Bennett, Befort, & Nollen, 2011; Schafft, Jensen, & Hinrichs, 2009).

Based on data from 15 industrialized countries, the United States holds the dubious distinction of having the highest percentage of overweight children, whether compared by age (13 vs. 15 years) or gender (Lissau et al., 2004). While the cultural factors that may account for this high rate are unclear, they seem to be transmittable: rates of obesity and eating disorders increase upon exposure to Western culture (Becker, Burwell, Herzog, Hamburg, & Gilman, 2002; O'Dea, 2008). It could be that the massive Western influence and globalization of the fast-food industries continue to fuel the rapid rise in obesity rates. Other countries, however, have obesity rates that are catching up. For example, there has been a dramatic increase in overweight Chinese children in recent years, believed to be due to an increased urban lifestyle (Lobstein, 2010).

Minorities make up a significant proportion of low-income populations in North America. Fast food and junk food tends to be relatively inexpensive and more available than healthy foods; thus rates of consumption of these foods are higher in low-income families (Davis et al., 2011; Swinburn et al., 2011). An additional problem for low-income families is that many of their neighborhoods are unsafe, and parents may keep their children at home out of safety concerns, which severely limits a child's opportunities for physical activities.

Causes

Body weight, like height and hair color, is to a large extent a function of pedigree. By age 17, a child of two obese parents has 3 times the chance of being obese as a child of lean parents; moreover, if one sibling is obese, there is a 40% chance that a second sibling also will be obese (Garn et al., 1976; Kral & Faith, 2009). Although heritability may account for a substantial proportion of the variance in obesity, other individual and family-related factors, such as dietary and lifestyle preferences, also play a role.

Leptin has been identified as a hormone that carries instructions to the brain to regulate energy and appetite (Kanoski et al., 2011). Leptin deficiencies have been found among children with severe obesity (Cole, 2007; Montague et al., 1997). Persons with obesity are somehow resistant to leptin's effect—a situation similar to adult diabetes, in which a person usually produces insulin but it fails to work properly, causing sugar levels to go out of control. Leptin levels decrease with dieting, so leptin is less likely to provide feedback to the hypothalamus. Paradoxically, this connection between dieting and lower leptin levels may explain why dieting increases hunger and slows metabolism, and results in gaining back the lost weight (Cornier, 2011; Moran & Ladenheim, 2011).

Despite strong biological forces, proper diet and exercise still play a critical role in determining a child's level of obesity. We not only inherit our biochemical makeup from our parents, we also look to them as routine instructors and role models as we develop our attitudes toward food and eating. Parents determine what food is available, and they model an approach to exercise and diet. However, inexperienced or highly pressured parents may respond to any sign of distress in the infant or toddler by attempts to feed, by neglect, or by both reactions. Moreover, parents of obese children sometimes have greater difficulty setting limits, which has obvious implications for the child's tendency to overeat (Schuetzmann, Richter-Appelt, Schulte-Markwort, & Schimmelman, 2008). Like many other childhood disorders, obesity and poor eating habits are related to the degree of family disorganization, ranging from poor communication and a lack of perceived family support, to sexual and physical abuse (Neumark-Sztainer, Eisenberg, Fulkerson, Story, & Larson, 2008).

Treatment

Because of the combination of health and social consequences, prevention or intervention of childhood obesity involves not only the individual's health but also the family's resources. Except when there are serious medical complications, pediatricians often recommend proper nutrition to arrest weight gain until the child's height and weight are proportional. Note, however, that this nutrition program does not involve putting the child on a diet, since energy-restricted or unbalanced diets can place a child in jeopardy of medical or learning problems.

Family functioning not only influences eating patterns and obesity, it also can be instrumental in its prevention and treatment. To no one's surprise, any decrease in physical activity relative to food intake, such as eating while viewing television, can result in increased weight. Thus, efforts to curb childhood obesity often focus on addressing parents' knowledge of nutrition and increasing children's physical activity (Kitzmann & Beech, 2011).

Treatment should instill active, less sedentary routines. Obese and overweight children need parental encouragement, so many effective weight-loss programs teach parents and children ways to be more active. Children who are taught to be active and reinforced for being less sedentary (such as playing outdoors rather than watching television) increase their liking for high-intensity activity, which in turn reduces weight (Kitzmann et al., 2010; Salvy, Kieffer, & Epstein, 2008). Similarly, pitfalls of weight-control plans must be anticipated and removed to allow the child's environment and daily routines to be altered. For example, parents may be advised not to bring high-calorie snack foods into the house and to monitor what they eat in front of their children, as obese children are highly sensitive to food cues in their environments (Temple, Giacomelli, Roemmich, & Epstein, 2008).

Other behavioral interventions focus on the goal of making the child's eating behaviors and physical activity patterns more adaptive and self-managed. Self-control procedures encourage children to set their own goals for diet, weight, and exercise, and teach them the necessary skills to achieve these goals with minimal outside directives from parents or therapists. For example, children may be taught to monitor the quantity and nature of their food, when they eat it, and who shared the meal; similar self-monitoring is encouraged for exercise goals (Wilfley et al., 2007). Even if some children are unable to reach or maintain their intended goal of weight loss, self-control training encourages a greater sense of perceived control among children with obesity (Munsch et al., 2008).

Lately, schools have begun to take a bigger role in helping young children develop a healthy body image and promote healthy eating habits. The increase in the involvement of educators was sparked by the alarming number of overweight children over the past decade, as well as by their concern that children may be inundated by cultural forces that place undue value on dieting and appearance. Given the greater awareness of the importance of early eating habits and the influence of cultural expectations, school-based programs now address children's and teens' desire for knowledge and support in developing a healthy body image and eating attitudes. As shown in Box 13.1, schools have been active in developing a range of educational strategies that involve the whole school environment, including classroom education, cafeteria and vending machine selections, and educating staff and parents to recognize signs of disordered eating and promote healthy eating attitudes and activities (Safron, Cislak, Gaspar, & Luszczynska, 2011).

BOX 13.1 A CLOSER LOOK

Junk Food Corporations in Schools

As education resources have decreased in recent years, schools boards have increasingly felt the need to seek funding elsewhere. Corporate sponsors have been quick to jump on board and sign contracts with school districts, allowing their products to be sold exclusively within the schools. In 2002, there were 240 U.S. school districts that had exclusive contracts with soft drink companies, and 60% of U.S. middle and high schools had soft-drink vending machines (Fried & Nestle, 2002). Junk food is readily available in most school cafeterias and vending machines, and is often cheaper than healthy foods.

The plethora of junk food and rising obesity rates have led to criticisms of corporate contracts, and some districts are starting to take action. For example, as of September 2011, students in Ontario, Canada, were no longer able to buy candy, chocolate, pop, fries, and energy drinks on school property. While certainly a step in the right direction, more needs to be done to reduce overweight and obesity among school children.

Source: Based on authors' case material.

SECTION SUMMARY

Obesity

- Childhood obesity is defined by a body mass index (BMI) above the 95th percentile for children of the same age and sex.
- Obesity is not a mental disorder, but it can affect a child's psychological and physical development in significant ways.
- Obesity poses a risk for unhealthy dieting patterns, chronic health problems, and later-onset eating disorders.
- Obesity rates have increased dramatically in the past few decades, with a steeper increase in U.S. minority populations.
- The causes of obesity include genetic predisposition as well as family and community influences, such as poor knowledge of nutrition, cultural patterns, and limited access to healthy food choices.
- Treatment and prevention efforts often are aimed at helping parents take an active role in children's proper nutrition and activity level. Schools contribute to this effort by educating children in nutrition, exercise, and awareness of healthy eating attitudes and body image.

FEEDING AND EATING DISORDERS

Feeding and eating disorders that occur during infancy or early childhood constitute a general diagnostic category that includes several different developmental and behavioral problems associated with eating and growth that are evident from a very young age.

Feeding Disorder of Infancy or Early Childhood

Feeding disorder of infancy or early childhood is characterized by a sudden or marked deceleration of weight gain in an infant or a young child (under age 6) and a slowing or disruption of emotional and social development. This disorder can lead to physical and mental retardation and even death.

Prevalence and Development

Feeding disorders and failure to gain weight are relatively common, affecting up to one-third of young children (Lyons-Ruth et al., 1996). If not identified early, feeding disorders are particularly troublesome because they can have lasting effects on growth and development. Feeding disorders are equally common among males and females.

There is no typical developmental outcome among children with feeding disorders, probably because many of the factors that initially led to the problem in the first place also affect the course of the illness. However, the onset of feeding disorder commonly occurs during the first 2 years of life, which can lead to malnutrition with serious developmental consequences. If there is no medical reason for the failure to gain weight, such early onset often is associated with poor caregiving that includes abuse and neglect (APA, 2000). Thus, feeding disorder can lead to, or be the result of, a failure to thrive (discussed in the following section). As expected, the factors that lead to more serious problems over time include the degree and chronicity of malnutrition, the degree and chronicity of developmental delay, and the severity and duration of the problems in the infant–caregiver relationship (Benoit, 2009; Blissett, Meyer, & Haycraft, 2007).

Causes and Treatment

The etiology of feeding disorder has been studied from both biological and psychosocial perspectives, and the best conclusion at present is that many interacting risk factors influence how a child adapts to a certain level of caloric intake, and influence whether the child shows normal or abnormal behavioral development. Because feeding disorder has long been associated with family disadvantage, poverty, unemployment, social isolation, and parental mental illness, considerable attention has been focused on those concerns.

Maternal eating disorders have been identified as a specific risk factor for an infant's eating or feeding disorder. A failure of children to thrive has been associated with mothers who have a history of disturbed eating habits and attitudes (Blissett et al., 2007). Because the mother–child relationship during the early stages of attachment is critical, eating disorders shown by infants and young children may be symptomatic of a fundamental problem in this relationship (Lyons-Ruth et al., 1996). Thus, treatment regimens involve a detailed assessment of feeding behavior and parent–child interactions, such as smiling, talking, and soothing, while allowing the parents to play a role in the infant's recovery (Linscheid, 2006).

Pica

Pica is the ingestion of inedible substances, such as hair, insects, or chips of paint, and primarily affects very young children and those with mental retardation. Infants and toddlers typically put things into their mouths, since taste and smell are their preferred ways of exploring the physical world. This disorder is one of the more common and usually less serious eating disorders found among very young children, yet an infant or young child who eats inedible, nonnutritive substances for a period of one month or longer may have a more serious problem (Bryant-Waugh, Markham, Kreipe, & Walsh, 2010).

Although children with pica also are interested in eating normal foods, they persist in consuming inedible items as well. In most reported cases, the disorder begins during infancy and lasts for several months, at which time it remits on its own or in conjunction with added infant stimulation and improved environmental conditions. For individuals with intellectual disability, however, pica may become more serious

Infants and toddlers with pica may develop the disorder as a result of poor stimulation and supervision. They are at considerable risk of lead poisoning or intestinal obstruction.

and life-threatening if it continues into adolescence (Matson, Belva, Hattier, & Matson, 2011).

Prevalence and Development

Pica is more prevalent among institutionalized children and adults, especially persons with more severe impairments and mental retardation (de Koning, Moreland, Valenti, & Dosen, 2007). Among children and adults with intellectual disabilities, the prevalence of pica ranges from 0.3% to 14.4% in the community, and 9% to 25% in institutions (Ali, 2001). The degree of severity often is related to the degree of environmental deprivation and mental retardation in individuals suffering from the more extreme forms of pica.

Causes and Treatment

Historically, pica was sometimes encouraged by fashions and social pressures that were similar to those affecting body image and appearance today. During the 18th and 19th centuries, for example, young girls sometimes ate lime, coal, vinegar, and chalk, because these substances were believed to produce a fashionably pale complexion (Parry-Jones & Parry-Jones, 1994).

Specific causes of pica have not been isolated. Pica may appear during the first and second years of life, even among otherwise normally developing infants and toddlers. The only distinguishing characteristic of these children is that they typically have poor stimulation in their home environment and may be poorly supervised. Because of the risk of lead poisoning or of obstruction in their intestine, pica can become a very serious and substantial problem for this group of infants or toddlers (Bryant-Waugh et al., 2010).

Researchers also have suspected, and in some cases discovered, vitamin or mineral deficiencies among persons with pica, although no specific biological abnormalities have shown a causal link to the disorder (de Koning et al., 2007). There is no evidence, except in cases of intellectual disability, that genetic factors play a role in the etiology of the disorder.

Because of the limited number of treatment studies, no conclusions can be drawn about the relative success of any treatment for pica. Most clinical interventions for children with pica emphasize operant conditioning procedures, in which caregivers are shown how to reinforce the child for desirable behaviors such as exploring the room or playing with objects. Positive forms of attention, including smiling, laughing, and tickling, provide additional stimulation and are especially beneficial, because the disorder often is related to inadequate interaction with caregivers (Linscheid, 2006). Caregivers are also taught to keep the child's environment tidy and to remove or safely store dangerous substances.

Failure to Thrive

Failure to thrive (FTT) is a growth disorder associated with early feeding disturbances, and it can have severe consequences for a child's physical and psychological development. Like feeding disorder, this associated disorder is embedded in social and economic disadvantage, and often is connected to inadequate or abusive caregiving that originates during early infancy. Failure to thrive is considered the final common pathway for multiple biological, psychological, and social factors that influence growth and viability of the infant or toddler (Benoit, 2009).

Prevalence

Failure to thrive is characterized by weight below the 5th percentile for age and/or a deceleration of at least 2 standard deviations in the rate of weight gain from birth to the present, using standard growth charts for comparison (Spencer, 2007). The eating and feeding disorders of early childhood previously described can lead to, coexist with, or be the result of failure to thrive.

Causes

A prominent controversy concerns the significance of emotional deprivation (lack of love) and malnutrition (lack of food). Investigators have argued that the infant with failure to thrive has been deprived of maternal stimulation and love, which results in emotional misery, developmental delays, and eventually, physiological changes. In one study, mothers of infants diagnosed with failure to thrive were found to be more insecurely attached than mothers of normal infants. These mothers also were more passive and confused, and either became intensely angry when discussing past and current attachment relationships or dismissed the attachments as unimportant and non-influential (Benoit, Zeanah, & Barton, 1989). Children who have suffered from failure

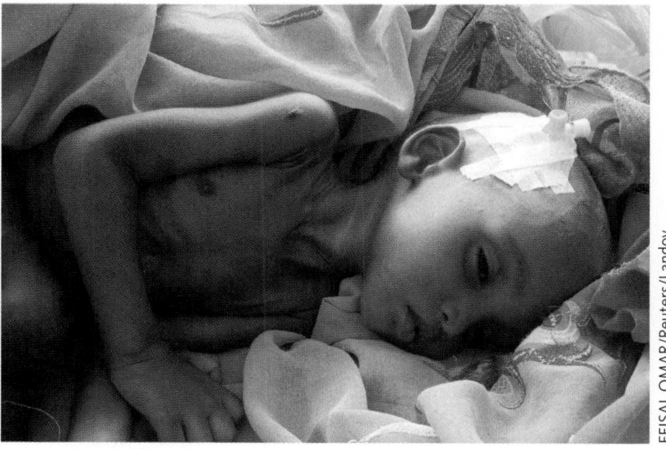

FEISAL OMAR/Reuters/Landov

This young child stopped gaining weight and developed failure to thrive to thrive as a result of early abuse exhibit poorer outcomes 20 years later than children whose failure to thrive resulted from neglect, lack of parenting, or feeding difficulties (Iwaniec, Sheddon, & Allen, 2003).

These findings support the notion that eating and growth disorders during early infancy are highly related to the poor quality of the caregiver–child attachment, which is likely to reflect the insensitive treatment the caregiver received as a child. Poverty, family disorganization, and limited social support contribute to the likelihood of malnutrition and growth failure, as do infants who are difficult to feed and nurture because of temperament and acute physical illnesses (Olsen et al., 2007). Hospitalization to achieve weight gain, without consideration of ways to improve the parent–child relationship, is often insufficient to protect the child from further harm (Black, Dubowitz, Krishnakumar, & Starr, 2007).

What is particularly striking about FTT is that a child's developmental outcome is highly related to the child's home environment. Significant changes in quality of care and in the emotional environment results in better adjustment 20 years later, even for children who failed to thrive because of abuse (Iwaniec et al., 2003). Moreover, early FTT may affect physical growth in childhood, but there is no evidence that it affects future cognitive functioning (Black et al., 2007). For these reasons, much of the etiology of FTT has focused on parental psychopathology that results in maltreatment of the child. In short, these associated feeding disorders may be a biological outcome of child abuse and neglect.

SECTION SUMMARY

Feeding and Eating Disorders

- Feeding disorder of infancy or early childhood is characterized by a sudden or rapid deceleration of weight gain and a disruption in major developmental milestones. The disorder can have serious consequences.
- Pica is the eating of inedible substances. It affects mostly infants, toddlers, and some children with mental retardation.
- Feeding disorder of early childhood can lead to or result from failure to thrive (FTT), characterized by weight below the fifth percentile for age.

EATING DISORDERS OF ADOLESCENCE

Eating disorders (EDs), as well as eating-related problems such as dieting and bingeing, are most likely to appear during two important periods of adolescent development: the early passage into adolescence and the movement from later adolescence to young adulthood (Herzog & Eddy, 2007; Touyz et al., 2008). Early- and middle-childhood risk factors, such as eating problems, dieting patterns, and negative body image, clash with the ongoing challenges that confront adolescents. This clash leads some teens, particularly girls, to exert excessive control over their eating in a misguided effort to manage stress and physical changes. In some instances this controlled pattern of eating, coupled with other ill-conceived efforts to overcompensate for eating and weight changes (such as excessive exercise), leads to major eating disorders such as anorexia nervosa and bulimia nervosa.

Anorexia nervosa gained medical attention in 1873, when two doctors first described the disorder. Sir William Gull, an English physician, named the malady and described it for the first time as a specific disease. About the same time, in Paris, psychiatrist Charles Lasègue described anorexia from a social and psychological standpoint. Both investigators observed that the disease was most prevalent in the wealthiest social classes, which prompted Lasègue to propose a connection between a lack of parental affection (believed to be relatively common among wealthy families) and a preoccupation with food. Conflict between parents and children could drive some teenage girls to refuse food as an expression of their feelings of rejection. Accordingly, by the turn of the century, the prescribed treatment for anorexia was a "parentectomy," the removal of the child from the family home, which was combined with force-feeding by any means necessary (Munn, Smeltzer, Smeltzer, & Westin, 2010).

References to the disorder we now refer to as bulimia date back to 6th-century descriptions of more than 40 individuals who displayed symptoms described as "insatiable voracity, morbid or canine appetite, with or without vomiting" (Parry-Jones & Parry-Jones, 1994, p. 288). Interestingly, almost all of these historical cases described males, perhaps because overeating was socially accepted as a sign of wealth or success, a reversal of the pattern today.

Ideal body sizes change with the times and with cultural preferences. Rubenesque figures were considered highly attractive and desirable until the late 19th century, when body image preferences were usurped by major cultural changes. During the Victorian period, refusing food was in keeping with prevailing social pressures. A hearty appetite was considered a wanton expression of sexuality and lack of self-restraint; women were expected to be passively uninterested in both sex and food. Thus, it became morally, spiritually, and socially desirable for women to refuse food, in response to shifting cultural norms for women's appearance and behavior (Brumberg, 1988).

According to physicians around the turn of the 20th century, anorexia nervosa was a symptom of inappropriate romantic choices, blocked educational or social opportunities, and conflicts with parents. Slimness symbolized asexuality and gentility, which implied a respectable amount of social distance from the working classes (Attie & Brooks-Gunn, 1995). Originating in the 1930s, today's attitudes and beliefs about women's ideal body size and appearance have been shaped by advertisers, film stars, clothing designers, and similar forces, resulting in a prevailing cultural preference for slimness.

The meaning of food and eating for female identity, the role of family and social class in determining body image and food choices, and the use of weight regulation as a substitute for self-regulation and control in adolescence remain salient causes of eating disorders to this day. Within the last quarter century, additional aspects of eating disorders, such as the chronic refusal of food, emphasis on overactivity, and bulimic symptoms of bingeing and purging, have gained recognition as significant and potentially dangerous complications (Tyrka et al., 2003).

Anorexia Nervosa

SOOKI

Obsessed with Food and Weight

Sooki is a 19-year old Asian-American College Student who is 5 feet 4 inches tall and weighs 90.3 pounds. Friends have not noticed that Sooki has lost so much weight over the last year (25 pounds!) because she wears baggy clothes. About a year ago, Sooki became extremely afraid of becoming fat. She was convinced that weight gain would be the worst thing possible and that her college life would be ruined. Sooki began skipping meals and, when she did eat once or twice a day, consumed only a "salad" of other small items. Her salad consists of four lettuce leaves, part of a carrot, an apple slice, and no dressing. Sooki is preoccupied with food and calories. Every bite of food she eats is carefully considered, and she carries charts that list calories per serving of many different foods. She drinks only water and diet soda.

Sooki is obsessed with how much she weighs and how she looks. She owns two scales: one is near her bed and one is in her bathroom. She weighs herself 10 or more times a day. Sooki has told others her butt is too big and her stomach is "poochy." Sooki is markedly underweight but frequently checks her body in the mirror to make sure she is not becoming fat. Her self-esteem depends heavily on her body weight. When Sooki weighs more than 90 pounds she feels bad about herself; when she weighs less than 90 pounds she is perkier. Sooki views weight loss as an impressive achievement in self-discipline. Family members have noticed her weight change and have told Sooki she is underweight. Sooki has not had her menstrual period for 6 months. Still, Sooki does not see her eating and low weight as a problem. She hopes to lose more weight by eliminating "fattening" foods from her diet such as apple slices and diet soda. Sooki has kept to herself recently and leaves her room only to attend class. (From Kearney/Trull. Cengage Advantage Books: Abnormal Psychology and Life, 1E. © 2012 Wadsworth, a part of Cengage Learning, Inc. Reproduced by permission. www.cengage.com/permissions)

Sooki is suffering from the *restricting* type of **anorexia nervosa**, an eating disorder characterized by:

- the refusal to maintain a minimally normal body weight.
- an intense fear of gaining weight.
- a significant disturbance in the individual's perception and experiences of his or her own size.

As Sooki's story shows, anorexia nervosa is a severe eating disorder with serious physical and mental health consequences if left untreated. One of the most

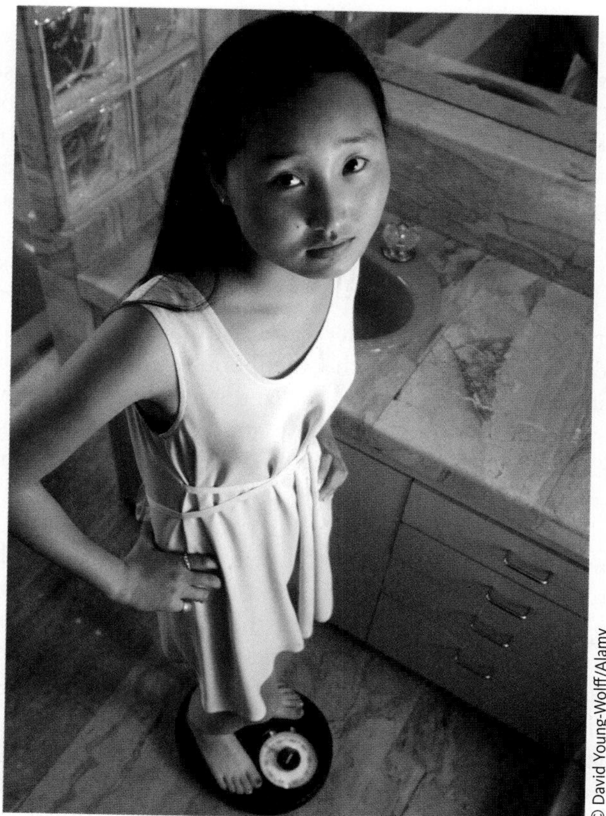

© David Young-Wolff/Alamy

19 year-old Sooki worries about being fat and weighs herself 10 or more times a day

TABLE 13.1 | **Diagnostic Criteria for Anorexia Nervosa**

DSM-IV-TR

A. Refusal to maintain body weight at or above a minimally normal weight for age and height.

B. Intense fear of gaining weight or becoming fat, even though underweight.

C. Disturbance in the way in which one's body weight or shape is experienced, undue influence of body weight or shape on self-evaluation, or denial of the seriousness of the current low body weight.

D. In postmenarcheal females, amenorrhea—that is, the absence of at least three consecutive menstrual cycles.

Specify type:

Restricting Type: During the current episode of anorexia nervosa, the person has not regularly engaged in binge-eating or purging behavior (i.e., self-induced vomiting or the misuse of laxatives, diuretics, or enemas).

Binge-Eating/Purging Type: During the current episode of anorexia nervosa, the person has regularly engaged in binge-eating or purging behavior (i.e., self-induced vomiting or the misuse of laxatives, diuretics, or enemas).

Source: Reprinted with permission from the Diagnostic and Statistical Manual of Mental Disorders, Fourth Edition, Text Revision, (Copyright © 2000). American Psychiatric Association.

notable features of the psychopathology of the disease is that persons who have it deny they are too thin or that they have a weight problem. As a result, friends or family members often must insist on taking them to see a physician. Diagnostic criteria for anorexia nervosa are shown in Table 13.1.

Although the word *anorexia* literally means "loss of appetite," that definition is misleading because the person with this disorder rarely suffers appetite loss. Weight loss is accomplished deliberately through a very restricted diet, purging, or exercise. Although many persons occasionally use these methods to lose weight, the individual with anorexia intensely fears obesity and pursues thinness relentlessly.

Young persons who suffer from anorexia show a major distortion in how they experience their weight and shape. They may become obsessed with measuring themselves to see whether the "fat" has been eliminated. Thus, how they see themselves and how they relate to others is often a function of their perceived shape and weight. To such an individual, weight loss is a triumph of self-discipline. But with anorexia there is never enough weight loss: The person always wants to lose more weight to be on the safe side, and if not enough weight is lost one day, the person may panic and work extra hard to lose weight the next day.

The DSM-IV-TR specifies two subtypes of anorexia based on the methods used to limit caloric intake. This distinction has to do with possible differences in etiology and treatment avenues. In the **restricting type**, individuals seek to lose weight primarily through diet, fasting, or excessive exercise; in the **binge-eating/purging type**, the individual regularly engages in episodes of binge eating or purging, or both. Compared with persons with bulimia, those with the binge-eating/purging type of anorexia eat relatively small amounts of food and commonly purge more consistently and thoroughly. Approximately one-half of the individuals meeting criteria for anorexia engage in binge-eating and purging behavior (APA, 2000).

While the two subtypes of anorexia may be useful for distinguishing different etiologies or treatment approaches in some cases, empirical support for the subtypes has been limited. Recent studies have failed to find significant evidence of the differences between the binge-purge and restricting subtypes of anorexia in comorbid psychopathology, recovery, relapse, or mortality rates (Eddy et al., 2009; Forbush et al., 2010). This lack of clarity has led some researchers to question the validity of the subtypes for anorexia (Wonderlich, Joiner, Keel, Williamson, & Crosby, 2007). The anorexia binge–purge subtype may represent a more severe form of anorexia rather than a distinct diagnostic subcategory (Eddy, Dorer, et al., 2008).

Bulimia Nervosa

PHILLIPA

A Well-Kept Secret

Phillipa developed bulimia nervosa at 18. Her strange eating behavior began when she started to diet. Phillipa began gaining weight because she was eating a lot at night. With the extra weight came self-loathing. "I felt like my body was in the way of me being successful at school, and getting dates. I looked in the mirror several times a day, thinking 'I don't even want to be in this body.' There wasn't a minute in my life that I didn't think about some aspect of how I looked."

Although Phillipa dieted and exercised to lose weight, she regularly ate huge amounts of food and maintained her normal weight by forcing herself to vomit. Phillipa often felt like an emotional powder keg—angry, frightened, and depressed. Unable to understand her own behavior, Phillipa thought no one else would either. She felt isolated and lonely. Typically, when things were not going well, she would be overcome with an uncontrollable desire for sweets. She would eat pounds of candy and cake at a time, and often not stop until she was exhausted or in severe pain. Then, overwhelmed with guilt and disgust, she would make herself vomit.

Her eating habits so embarrassed her that she kept them secret until, depressed by her mounting problems, she attempted suicide. Fortunately, she didn't succeed. While recuperating in the hospital, Phillipa was referred to an eating disorders clinic where she became involved in group therapy. There she received medications to treat the illness and the understanding and help she so desperately needed from others who had the same problem. With a smile, Phillipa explains: "It taught me that my self-worth is not absolutely correlated with my appearance or what others may think of me." (National Institute of Mental Health [NIMH], 1994b)

TABLE 13.2 | Diagnostic Criteria for Bulimia Nervosa

DSM-IV-TR

A. Recurrent episodes of binge eating. An episode of binge eating is characterized by both of the following:
   (1) Eating, in a discrete period of time (e.g., within any 2-hour period), an amount of food that is definitely larger than most people would eat during a similar period of time and under similar circumstances
   (2) A sense of lack of control over eating during the episode (e.g., a feeling that one cannot stop eating or control what or how much one is eating)

B. Recurrent inappropriate compensatory behavior in order to prevent weight gain, such as self-induced vomiting; the misuse of laxatives, diuretics or enemas, or other medications; fasting; or excessive exercise.

C. The binge eating and inappropriate compensatory behaviors both occur, on average, at least twice a week for 3 months.

D. Self-evaluation is unduly influenced by body shape and weight.

E. The disturbance does not occur exclusively during episodes of anorexia nervosa.

Specify type:

Purging Type: During the current episode of bulimia nervosa, the person has regularly engaged in self-induced vomiting or the misuse of laxatives, diuretics, or enemas.

Nonpurging Type: During the current episode of bulimia nervosa, the person has used other inappropriate compensatory behaviors, such as fasting or excessive exercise, but has not regularly engaged in self-induced vomiting or the misuse of laxatives, diuretics, or enemas.

Source: Reprinted with permission from the Diagnostic and Statistical Manual of Mental Disorders, Fourth Edition, Text Revision, (Copyright © 2000). American Psychiatric Association.

Of the two major forms of eating disorders afflicting adolescents and young adults, **bulimia nervosa** is far more common than anorexia. The DSM-IV-TR diagnostic criteria listed in Table 13.2 note that the primary hallmark of bulimia nervosa is binge eating. Because most of us overeat certain foods at certain times, you may ask "What exactly is a binge?" As noted in the criteria, a **binge** is an episode of overeating that must involve an objectively large amount of food (more than most people would eat under the circumstances), and lack of control.

No specific quantity of food constitutes a binge—it is the context of the behavior that must also be considered. Overeating at celebrations or holiday feasts, for example, is not considered bingeing. Although most binge eaters report overeating junk food rather than fresh fruits and vegetables, the amounts of food they consider a binge vary widely. On average, eaters consume roughly 1,500 calories during a binge, about 5 times more than they normally ate at one time (Rosen, Leitenberg, Fisher, & Khazam, 1986).

Persons with bulimia attempt to conceal binge eating out of shame. Although binges are not planned, a ritual may form wherein the person, sensing no one around, makes a split-second decision (on the way home from a late-night party, for example) to stop, purchase, and consume massive quantities of food. Typically, binge eating follows changes in mood or interpersonal stress, but it also may be related to intense hunger from dieting, or to feelings about personal appearance or body shape. Although these feelings may dissipate for awhile, the depressed mood and self-criticism usually return (Smyth et al., 2007).

The second important part of the diagnostic criteria involves the individual's attempts to compensate somehow for a binge. **Compensatory behaviors** are intended to prevent weight gain following a binge episode, and include self-induced vomiting, fasting, exercising, and the misuse of diuretics, laxatives, enemas, or diet pills. The criteria subdivide bulimia into *purging type*, in which there is regular self-induced vomiting or regular overuse of laxatives or diuretics to reduce fluids and solids, and *non-purging type*, in which the individual uses other forms of compensation, such as fasting or excessive exercise.

Approximately two-thirds of persons with bulimia engage in purging. By far the most common compensatory technique after an episode of binge eating is induced vomiting—stimulating the gag reflex with the fingers or another instrument—a method reported by 80% to 90% of individuals with bulimia who seek treatment. Vomiting produces immediate relief from physical discomfort and reduces fear of gaining weight.

A different pattern of compensatory behavior is reported among community samples of individuals who fit criteria for bulimia (i.e., individuals who have

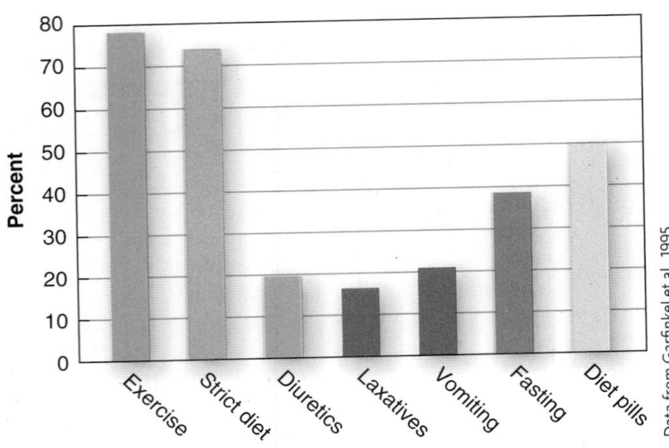

● **FIGURE 13.5** | Compensatory behaviors of full-syndrome bulimia nervosa among community samples.

not sought help but are identified through random interviews by phone or in person). ● Figure 13.5 shows the various compensatory behaviors of males and females who met all criteria for bulimia nervosa, based on their responses to part of the Ontario Health Survey, in which over 8,000 individuals were interviewed in person about their health habits. Among these non-referred subjects, vigorous exercise and strict diet are the preferred means of compensating for bingeing. In contrast to clinical samples, only 1 in 5 reported vomiting as a compensatory behavior (Garfinkel et al., 1995).

Research with community (nonclinical) samples has not identified any significant differences between persons with bulimia who purge and those who do not (Tanofsky-Kraff et al., 2007). Dietary symptoms (e.g., restraint, purging) are central features of bulimia, but only a subset of people with bulimia exhibit both dietary restraint and depressive affect. Young women who have the dietary-depressive subtype exhibit more eating pathology, social impairment, psychiatric comorbidity, and persistence of bulimic symptoms over 5 years than women with only the dietary subtype (Stice & Fairburn, 2003).

Like those with anorexia, adolescents and adults with bulimia often are described as rigid and absolutistic (displaying an all-or-nothing attitude) in their thinking (Joiner, Katz, & Heatherton, 2000; Thompson-Brenner, Eddy, Satir, Boisseau, & Westen, 2008). They see themselves as either completely in control or completely out of control, and view everyday events in extremes of either black or white. Phillipa expressed absolutistic thinking, attributing her woes to one thing and one thing only: "I felt like my body was in the way of me being successful at school, and getting dates." These beliefs relate to the DSM-IV-TR criteria, which stress the importance of body shape and weight to self-evaluation. Young women with bulimia, as well as those with anorexia, have greater dissatisfaction with their body proportions and distort their true body size, behaviors that are more strongly connected to cognitive factors, such as biases in attention and memory, and selective interpretation or judgment, than with any actual problem with perceptual ability (Striegel-Moore & Bulik, 2007).

The medical consequences of chronic bulimia can be significant, although they are not as severe as the consequences that result from anorexia. Common physical complaints include fatigue, headaches, and puffy cheeks (due to enlarged salivary glands). The permanent or significant loss of dental enamel, especially from the inside surface of the front teeth, is due to the contact of the acidic stomach contents with the teeth. Among females, menstrual irregularity or amenorrhea may occur, although it is not clear whether these disturbances are related to weight fluctuations, other nutritional deficiencies, or stress. Electrolyte imbalances due to purging behavior are sometimes severe enough to cause significant medical problems. Table 13.3 lists bulimia danger signals that point to the need for further assessment and intervention.

Binge eating disorder (BED) (APA, 2000) has become increasingly widespread during this age of abundant fast food and obesity. Although similar to the binge eating found in bulimia, BED is without the compensatory behaviors. It involves periods of eating more than other people would, accompanied by a feeling of a loss of control. Researchers differ on whether binge episodes are objective overeating (e.g., over 1,000 calories) or an individual, subjective feeling of losing control (e.g., eating two cookies on a strict diet).

TABLE 13.3 | **Bulimia Danger Signals**

- Regular bingeing (eating large amounts of food over a short period of time)
- Regular purging (by vomiting or using diuretics or laxatives), strict dieting, or excessive exercising
- Retaining or regaining weight despite frequent exercise and dieting
- Not gaining weight but eating enormous amounts of food at one sitting
- Disappearing into the bathroom for long periods of time to induce vomiting
- Abusing drugs or alcohol or stealing regularly
- Experiencing long periods of depression
- Having irregular menstrual periods
- Exhibiting dental problems, swollen cheek glands, bloating, or scars on the backs of the hands from forced vomiting

Youths define overeating in a variety of ways, including the amount and types of food eaten, emotional consequences after the binge (e.g., feeling guilty), and the individual's reasons for overeating (Neumark-Sztainer et al., 2006).

Although BED is more prevalent in young adulthood, it affects about 1.6% of adolescents (Swanson, Crow, Le Grange, Swendsen, & Merikangas, 2011). The mounting concern over BED is justified not only by the higher rates of obesity and weight loss attempts, but also by the negative mental health correlates. Youths with BED score lower on body satisfaction and self-esteem, score higher on depressive mood, and are more likely to report that weight and shape are very important to their overall feelings about themselves (Ackard, Neumark-Sztainer, Story, & Perry, 2003; Stice, Marti, Shaw, & Jaconis, 2009).

Prevalence and Development of Anorexia and Bulimia

Based on a large nationwide U.S. sample, lifetime prevalence of anorexia nervosa and bulimia among adolescents is 0.3% and 0.9%, respectively (Swanson et al., 2011). Distinguishing between the two major eating disorders of adolescents and young adults can be difficult, because anorexia and bulimia share many features. Members of both groups have distorted body images and nervous feelings after eating. However, persons with anorexia are 15% or more below normal weight, whereas persons with bulimia are within 10% of normal weight. Also, persons with anorexia engage in binge eating only occasionally and typically avoid forbidden food, whereas those with bulimia binge frequently on forbidden food, then purge to control their weight.

Eating disorders can overlap with other mental disorders, such as depression and schizophrenia, obscuring some features and leading to misdiagnosis (Herzog & Eddy, 2007). However, in terms of cognitive beliefs and self-image, only patients with anorexia show an intense drive for thinness and a disturbance in their perception of body image. As well, criteria for eating disorders defined by the DSM-IV-TR remain the subject of considerable debate. Recent data indicate that the majority (approximately 60%) of those with eating disorders do not meet the full DSM-IV-TR diagnostic criteria for either anorexia or bulimia (Eddy et al., 2009; Eddy, Doyle, Hoste, Herzog, & le Grange, 2008).

The diagnosis of eating disorders is especially difficult among youths, who are still maturing physically, cognitively, and emotionally. As a result, they are more likely to meet criteria for an **Eating Disorder, Not Otherwise Specified (EDNOS)**. Presently, EDNOS is a category of eating disorders used for individuals who are deemed to have a clinically significant eating disorder but who do not meet the full criteria for anorexia or bulimia. Within this broad category, binge-eating disorder is defined by significant binge eating and associated distress in the absence of any compensatory behaviors. The EDNOS category is less stringent than the DSM-IV-TR criteria for anorexia or bulimia, and therefore is sometimes more appropriate for adolescents (Keel, Gravener, Joiner, & Haedt, 2010; Lock & le Grange, 2006). Because the majority of adolescents with eating problems don't meet the diagnostic criteria for bulimia or anorexia, professional organizations such as the Society for Adolescent Medicine have advised clinicians to set lower thresholds for diagnosing adolescents with eating disorders (i.e., not requiring that they meet all the DSM criteria).

Eating Disorders Among Boys

There is increased recognition that eating disorders are more common among young men than originally believed. Males also are subjected to powerful media images, although not to the same extent as females. The increasingly muscular male body ideal may be contributing to body dissatisfaction, disordered eating, and harmful weight-control or body-building behaviors (Smolak, Murnen, & Thompson, 2005). Young men with eating disorders show some of the same clinical features as young women with eating disorders. However, young men show less of a preoccupation with food or a drive for thinness, and want to be more muscular than they actually are, and more muscular than the average male body (Olivardia, Pope, Borowiecki, & Cohane, 2004). Because eating disorders are considered a problem affecting primarily women, young men may be under diagnosed (Hudson et al., 2007).

Sexual Orientation and Eating Disorders

Since the early 1980s, the relationship between sexual orientation and eating disorders has attracted increasing attention from researchers. Gay men appear to be at greater risk for behavioral symptoms of eating disorders compared to heterosexual men (Jones & Morgan, 2010; Yelland & Tiggemann, 2003). Gay men also are more susceptible than heterosexual men to media images promoting thinness (Carper, Negy, & Tantleff-Dunn, 2010), and are more likely than heterosexual men to experience poor body image and body dissatisfaction and related eating disorders symptomatology (Martins, Tiggemann, & Kirkbride, 2007; Smith, Hawkeswood, Bodell, & Joiner, 2011).

While these studies suggest that gay men may be more susceptible to developing eating disorders and negative body image, the research examining the etiology of body dissatisfaction and eating problems in gay men is sparse. In a survey of 4,374 adolescent boys, those who described themselves as gay or bisexual reported making more efforts to look like boys or men in magazines than did heterosexual boys (Austin et al., 2004). While this study does not necessarily suggest a causal relationship to eating disorders, it does add to the body of literature suggesting homosexuality as a possible risk factor for the development of eating disorders in male adolescents. Further research into the risk factors that may influence the trajectory of eating problems in gay men will focus our clinical and intervention efforts more efficiently.

Ethnic, Cross-Cultural, and Socioeconomic Considerations

Anorexia has been observed in Western countries as well as every non-Western region of the world, suggesting that anorexia may not be a "culture-bound" syndrome as once believed (Sohl, Touyzl, & Surgenor, 2006). It is becoming increasingly clear that eating disorders do not always appear the same in different cultures. In Hong Kong, for example, studies suggest that anorexia may be divided into fat-phobic and non-fat-phobic subtypes, and that questionnaires used in Western countries to assess eating disorders may not be sufficiently sensitive to detect the Chinese non-fat-phobic subtype (Lee, Lee, & Leung, 1998).

However, the cross-cultural evidence for bulimia outside of a Western context tells a different story. Keel and Klump's (2003) review of culture and eating disorders found no studies reporting the presence of bulimia in individuals who have not been exposed to Western ideals. Epidemiological data for bulimia in non-Western nations suggest that bulimia has a lower prevalence than anorexia in these countries, and even when it is found in non-Western nations, it is not found in the absence of Western influence. A meta-analysis examining the role of ethnicity and culture in the development of eating disturbances found few differences across ethnic groups for bulimia (Wildes & Emery, 2001). These findings seem to suggest that bulimia is a culture-bound syndrome, arising predominately in Western regions of world or in places where individuals probably or definitely have been exposed to Western ideals and culture (Anderson-Fye, 2009).

Socioeconomic status (SES) has long been considered a risk factor for eating disorders among adults, with women of higher SES more likely to diet and have a lower body weight (Nevonen & Norring, 2004). It is plausible that as populations in non-Western nations become more affluent, the risk of developing an eating disorder will increase, regardless of culture or ethnicity. African American women from higher SES backgrounds reported levels of body dissatisfaction similar to those of North-European American women, suggesting that body dissatisfaction is associated more strongly with SES than with ethnicity (Polivy & Herman, 2002). But wealth itself does not automatically lead to an increased prevalence of eating disorders. Once a certain level of affluence has been achieved in a particular society, the association of high SES with eating disorders may no longer exist, owing to the globalization of the boundaries between the socioeconomic classes in modern times (Sohl et al., 2006).

The cross-cultural evidence for eating disorders is further complicated by what some researchers call a failure of a diagnostic system to adequately capture disorders of eating experienced by members of different ethnic and cultural groups (Wonderlich, Joiner, et al., 2007). This may have deleterious effects for these individuals who may be suffering from an eating disorder and not receiving the proper treatment.

Michael C. Gray/Shutterstock.com

Like African American women, Latinas were thought to possess a kind of cultural immunity to eating disorders, but current trends disprove that

Understanding the role that culture, ethnicity, and SES play in the etiology of eating disorders is challenging. Most of the studies on eating pathology and body image disturbances in non-Western subjects have been undertaken in Western nations rather than the country of origin. The question of whether or not exposure to Western culture induces eating pathology is complicated further by cultural differences in family environment and socioeconomic levels. Few studies have measured the degree to which an individual has retained his or her traditional cultural values or absorbed the mainstream values. Further complicating the study of ethnicity and eating disorders is that most of the cross-cultural research has focused on the disorders as they have been defined by the DSM-IV-TR. Thus, it is much more difficult to comment on the eating disorders such as binge-eating disorder outside of a Western context. Further scientific enquiry into all these areas hopefully will contribute to understanding and managing eating disorders, which now are increasingly recognized in individuals from all cultural or ethnic backgrounds.

Developmental Course

Anorexia nervosa usually strikes during adolescence, between the ages of 14 and 18, although it occasionally does affect older women, men, and prepubertal children. It often begins insidiously, with dieting that gradually leads to life-threatening starvation (Lock & le Grange, 2006). Sometimes the onset of this dieting and starvation pattern is linked to stressful events, such as being teased about weight, onset of menses, school transitions, and so forth.

Although the symptoms of anorexia are quite specific and well defined, its developmental course and outcome are highly variable. Findings averaged across 119 studies of persons with anorexia show that the rate of mortality is significant (5%); of the survivors, fewer than one-half show full recovery, one-third show fair improvement, and one-fifth continue on a chronic course (Steinhausen, 2009; Steinhausen, Grigoroiu-Serbanescu, Boyadjieva, Neumärker, & Winkler-Metzke, 2008).

Most common is a fluctuating pattern that involves a restoration of normal weight followed by relapse (Fichter, Quadflieg, & Hedlund, 2006). As the individual loses weight and becomes dangerously malnourished, she is hospitalized and begins to show signs of improvement. A significant number of patients—between 6% and 10%—die from medical complications or suicide (Arcelus, Mitchell, Wales, & Nielsen, 2011; Bulik et al., 2008). Features correlated with worse outcomes with anorexia are longer duration of illness, bingeing and purging, and comorbid affective or anxiety disorders (Steinhausen, 2009). Although the disorder itself is rare, it has the highest mortality rate of any psychiatric disorder and is a leading cause of death for females 15 to 24 years old in the general population (Preti, Rocchi, Sisti, Camboni, & Miotto, 2011; Striegel-Moore & Bulik, 2007).

Full-blown symptoms of bulimia usually emerge in late adolescence and young adulthood, although episodes of bingeing and purging and a preoccupation with weight begin much earlier (Lock & le Grange, 2006). A noteworthy aspect of bulimia is that binge eating often develops during or after a period of restrictive dieting (Treasure, Claudino, & Zucker, 2010). Because of the guilt and discomfort caused by binge eating, purging follows as compensation. Bulimia either can follow a chronic course or occur intermittently, with periods of remission alternating with binge eating and purging (Fairburn, Cooper, Doll, Norman, & O'Connor, 2000). However, it is not easy to reverse the developmental course. Because the habits and cultural influences that led to the disorder are so powerful, a chronic pattern of disturbed eating may be established, such as secretive bingeing at social gatherings, which in turn leads to further problems.

Follow-up studies of patients with bulimia indicate that they have a greater chance of recovery than patients with anorexia—between 50% and 75% show full recovery or significant improvement over several years (Chavez & Insel, 2007; Steinhausen & Weber, 2009). The best predictors of a more favorable outcome were younger age at onset and higher social class. Importantly, bulimia responds favorably to treatment that disrupts its cyclical course (Keel et al., 2010).

Similar to the study of long-term outcomes of persons with bulimia, studies of eating behaviors and attitudes among college student populations suggest that maturing into adulthood and getting away from powerful social pressures that emphasize thinness help many women escape from chronic dieting and abnormal eating. A 20-year follow-up study of body weight, dieting, and symptoms of eating disorders among male and female college students found both encouraging and discouraging results (Keel, Baxter, Heatherton, & Joiner, 2007). On a positive note, women reduced their eating disorder behaviors and increased their body satisfaction ratings. However, body dissatisfaction and desires to lose weight still remained relatively high. Men, on the other hand, were prone to weight gain after college, and many reported increased dieting or disordered eating in the 20 years following college. Although disordered eating tends to decline during the transition to early adulthood, body dissatisfaction remains an issue for many young adults (Keel et al., 2007).

cathy® **by Cathy Guisewite**

Causes

Why would people starve themselves to near emaciation or eat to the point of illness? The dramatic effects on physical and psychological well-being that can result from eating disorders have inspired many theories. No single factor has been isolated as the major cause of any type of eating disorder, and searching for causes is complicated by the "chicken and egg" problem of causation: Do neurobiological processes disrupt eating patterns, or do eating problems lead to changes in neurobiology?

The single best predictor or risk for developing an eating disorder is being female, and adolescence marks the period of the greatest risk for onset (Striegel-Moore & Bulik, 2007). But not all women or all adolescents develop eating disorders. Thus, explaining the gradual degenerative process of developing an eating disorder requires acknowledging the contribution of all three major etiological domains—biological, sociocultural (including family and peers), and psychological—which can operate singly or in combination to disturb self-regulation in any given individual. Too often, discussions of the etiology of eating disorders become polarized into "cultural" versus "biological" explanations that often ignore the fact that biological and environmental variables are inextricably linked (Striegel-Moore & Bulik, 2007). While the field has made great leaps in understanding the risk factors for the "prototypical" eating disorder case, which is often a young, white, middle- or upper-class North American woman, our knowledge about risk factors unique to diverse cultural populations remains incomplete.

The Biological Dimension

There is reasonable agreement that neurobiological factors play only a minor role in precipitating anorexia and bulimia. However, these factors may contribute to the maintenance of the disorder because of their effects on appetite, mood, perception, and energy regulation (Lock & le Grange, 2006).

It makes sense to suspect that biological mechanisms (a gene? a neurochemical process?) acting together or alone are responsible for corrupting normal regulatory functions. A slight twist of this scenario places the problem on the individual who disrupts his or her normal regulatory processes in an ill-conceived attempt to achieve weight or diet goals. This disruption may cause biological changes throughout the central nervous and neuroendocrine systems that, in turn, create more disruption. Thus, it also makes sense that success at controlling important bodily functions such as hunger or appetite may lead to unnatural eating habits, resulting in an abusive eating pattern.

Genetic and Constitutional Factors

Eating disorders tend to run in families. Research has found that relatives of patients with anorexia or bulimia, especially female relatives, are 4 to 5 times more likely than persons in the general population to develop an eating disorder (Strober, Freeman, Lampert, Diamond, & Kaye, 2000). A large-scale study of 31,406 Swedish twins born between 1935 and 1956 indicates that anorexia and bulimia moderately overlap in genetic and environmental contributors, with heritability playing the larger role in both disorders (Bulik et al., 2010). In this study, the contribution of the shared environment was found to be negligible, and the remaining variance was primarily attributable to unique environmental factors.

If bulimia and anorexia are connected to genetic factors, what exactly is inherited? Some people may have a biological vulnerability that interacts with social and psychological factors to increase their chances of developing an eating disorder (Bulik et al., 2006). For example, inherited personality traits, such as emotional instability and poor self-control, would predispose an individual to be emotionally reactive to stress, which, in turn, could lead to impulsive eating in an attempt to relieve the feelings associated with stress (Thompson-Brenner et al., 2008). Genome-wide association studies currently under way will likely identify genes and pathways involved in eating disorders in the near future (Scherag, Hebebrand, & Hinney, 2010).

Neurobiological Factors

Because serotonin regulates hunger and appetite, this neurotransmitter has been focused on as a possible cause of both anorexia and bulimia (Calati, De Ronch, Bellini, & Serretti, 2011). Essentially, the presence of serotonin leads to a feeling of fullness and a desire to decrease food intake, so a decrease in serotonin leads to continuous hunger and greater consumption of food at one time—the perfect condition for bingeing. This explanation stems from a gene–environment interaction: children having a genetic risk factor in a serotonin transporter gene are more susceptible to high parental control, which in turns interferes with the child's ability to regulate stress; by adolescence, life events could more easily trigger the onset of anorexia (Karwautz et al., 2011).

One of the strongest findings in support of the serotonin explanation for bulimia comes from studies investigating the relationship of diet to the availability in the brain of the serotonin precursor *tryptophan*. Meals that are rich in protein or low in carbohydrates decrease tryptophan; carbohydrate-rich meals increase it. Put another way, bingeing on sweet and starchy foods creates conditions in the brain that produce more serotonin, which, eventually, leads to a sense of fullness. Binge eating (which usually involves high-carbohydrate food), especially for women, may increase the availability of tryptophan, thereby temporarily increasing brain serotonin (Scherag et al., 2010). It is still not known, however, whether problems related to the availability of serotonin in the brain are due to dieting or are a pre-morbid characteristic (Jacobi et al., 2004).

In addition to connections between depression and eating disorders, scientists have found biochemical similarities between people with eating disorders and people with obsessive–compulsive disorder (OCD). Just as serotonin levels are known to be abnormal in people with depression and people with eating disorders, they also are abnormal in patients with OCD (Lock, Garrett, Beenhakker, & Reiss, 2011). Moreover, many persons with bulimia show obsessive–compulsive behavior as severe as that shown among patients diagnosed with OCD, and patients with OCD often have abnormal eating behaviors (Sallet et al., 2010).

In summary, neurobiological abnormalities are found among persons with eating disorders, although at present we cannot determine if these problems are the result, rather than the primary cause, of semi-starvation or the binge/purge cycle. Understanding how normal eating patterns may initially become disturbed requires a close look at the cultural and psychological components of eating disorders.

Social Dimension

The features of contemporary Western culture could be considered prerequisites for eating disorders. Personal freedom, an emphasis on instant gratification, the availability of food any time of night or day, lack of supervision, and the cultural ideal of diet and exercise for weight loss add up to powerful influences (Attie & Brooks-Gunn, 1995). These factors contribute to a drive for thinness and an emphasis on body image and appearance as the key to success. There is some evidence that bulimia, but not anorexia, is related primarily to Western culture. Examination of history and of other cultures reveals instances of anorexic behaviors for physical appearance or control issues; however, this is not the case for bulimia (Keel & Klump, 2003).

Sociocultural Factors

Adolescents' concerns about undereating and overeating are legendary, which causes us to question: What aspects of Western culture drive someone, most likely a young woman, to overcome the body's natural rhythm and force it into a punishing and dangerous routine of semistarvation or frequent purging?

It is well known that for most young white females in middle- and upper-class society, self-worth, happiness, and success are determined primarily by physical appearance, and most eating disorders represent an attempt to feel good with respect to personal appearance and self-control. In reality, body size itself has little or no long-term correlation with personal happiness and success; one's self-concept and self-efficacy are more important. However, a collision may be occurring between our culture and our physiological boundaries, because the average North American woman between the ages of 17 and 24 is heavier than 20 years ago by 5 to 6 pounds, and she is not satisfied with her body image (Andreyeva, Puhl, & Brownell, 2008; Brownell, 1991).

It appears that as fashion models and media images of women have gotten smaller, adolescent girls have become unhappier—only 15% of teenage girls feel happy "the way I am," compared to 29% in the mid-1990s (Clay, Vignoles, & Dittmar, 2005). The pursuit of the thin ideal is so pervasive that girls today consider weight loss and being skinny to be more important than sexual issues, alcohol and drug abuse, mental health, disease, and environmental issues (Clark & Tiggemann, 2007). Not surprisingly, some turn to the Internet to connect with others about their body image and receive group support for weight loss, resulting in the popularity of "pro–eating disorders" websites (Sharpe, Musiat, Knapton, & Schmidt, 2011) (see Box 13.2).

The influence of mass media on body dissatisfaction also affects younger children. Smolak (2004) pointed out that the observed gender, ethnic, cross-cultural, historical, and age differences in levels of body esteem all suggest that culture and society play a major role in the construction of body image in younger children, as they do in adults. While limited research exists on the influence of mass media on body dissatisfaction in children, sociocultural influences such as the media and peers are all potential contributors to children's body image.

For example, in 9- to 12-year-old girls, exposure to media did not predict body dissatisfaction directly but was predictive of conversations about appearance, which in turn predicted body dissatisfaction (Clark & Tiggemann, 2006). In accord with the sociocultural model, increased exposure to appearance media, such as television and magazines, and taking part in peer conversations about appearances were related to body dissatisfaction and dieting behaviors in young girls in grades 4 to 7 (Clark & Tiggemann, 2007). Although media exposure increases children's awareness that appearance is highly valued in our society, actual conversations about this among peers may be a better predictor of the importance a young girl places on this in her life. These findings may inform intervention or prevention efforts targeted at

BOX 13.2 A CLOSER LOOK

Pro–Eating Disorders Websites

The Internet can be a good source of information, but it also can help people who are isolated by a disorder to seek out similar others for mutual support, and not necessarily in healthy ways. With the advent of widespread Internet use has come a proliferation of pro-anorexia and pro-bulimia websites, or "pro-ana" and "pro-mia" as referred to on these sites. These websites recently have emerged as an online movement supporting the virtues of eating disorders. People on these sites reinforce each other's views, share tips on purging and fooling others, and defend their "lifestyle choice" (Haas, Irr, Jennings, & Wagner, 2011). However, some of these websites contain controversial and dangerous content, and unfortunately they are more numerous than pro-recovery or professional services websites (Chesley, Alberts, Klein, & Kreipe, 2003).

A "Letter from Ana" can be found on most personal websites: "I expect a lot from you. You are not allowed to eat much. I will expect you to drop your caloric intake and increase your exercise. I will push you to the limit. You must take it because you cannot defy me. Pretty soon, I am with you always."

Other excerpts from pro-ana websites:

"You'll be FAT if you eat today. Just put it off one more day.

Guys will want to get to know you, not laugh at you and walk away.

Starve off the parts you don't need. They're ugly and drag you down.

Nothing tastes as good as thin feels."

"What's the nutritional information for the chocolate laxatives? If anyone knows, please let me know. I can't believe I'm obsessing over the calorie and carb[ohydrate] content of a laxative."

Rob Wilson/Shutterstock.com

"That's the designer's dream size . . . On their sketches, the body is like a hanger. The smaller the sample, the better it drapes—the natural shape of the body distorts their clothing . . . It's almost like the body is not present." (*Cosmopolitan*, 2001)

preadolescent girls and the usefulness of media literacy, as well as targeting self and peer beliefs surrounding appearance.

Few would argue that eating disorders are more common in women because of sex-role identification. Images of women in the 21st century and assumptions about what it is to be feminine are based largely on the idea that girls must be pretty (i.e., not fat) to draw attention and praise from others, whereas boys are admired for their athletic or academic accomplishments. Body build and self-esteem are correlated for girls—but not for boys—by the time they reach the fourth grade (Striegel-Moore & Bulik, 2007). This finding endorses the view that the relationships on which young women's identity and self-worth depend are overly influenced by physical attractiveness and body image.

Sex-role identification is closely tied to cultural norms and expectations, so it is not surprising that women in different cultures do not share the same perception of ideal body weight. Cogan, Bhalla, Sefa-Dedeh, and Rothblum (1996) looked at cross-cultural trends in attitudes on obesity and thinness and how they affect dieting patterns in young women from the United States and Ghana. Ghanaian women, compared with American women, rated larger body sizes as ideal for both sexes. American women scored higher on measures of eating restraint and eating-disordered behavior, and perceived the experience of being overweight as interfering with social acceptance. A disturbing trend indicates that a greater drive for thinness is emerging among young African American girls in the United States in relation to increased peer criticism about weight and appearance (Gilbert, Crump, Madhere, & Schutz, 2009; Striegel-Moore, Leslie, Petrill, Garvin, & Rosenheck, 2000).

The forces of culture, combined with gender-based expectations, are powerful determinants of one's perception of ideal body size and associated eating and dieting patterns. Fortunately, these sociocultural patterns may be shifting gradually toward more healthy norms of eating behaviors and lifestyle choices. Eating disorder symptoms, dieting, and body dissatisfaction have been declining significantly on college campuses over the past 30 years (Keel, Heatherton, Dorer, Joiner, & Zalta, 2006; Keel et al., 2007). The increase in public health advertisements, talk shows, and television shows devoted to discussions of eating disorders and to healthy lifestyles may be responsible for raising awareness and prevention of these various disorders and dieting patterns. Perhaps as a further result of these awareness efforts, sociocultural messages about the importance of proper nutrition and body satisfaction are changing as well.

Family Influences

From the very start, researchers and clinicians have placed considerable importance on the role of the family, and parental psychopathology in particular, in considering causes of eating disorders. They have argued that alliances, conflicts, or interactional patterns within a family may play a causal role in the development of eating disorders among some individuals (Minuchin, Rosman, & Baker, 1978). Accordingly, a teen's eating disorder may be functional in that it directs attention away from basic conflicts in the family to the teen's more obvious (symptomatic) problem.

Because of the importance of the family in shaping a young adolescent's values, it is understandable that family processes may contribute to an overemphasis on weight and dietary control. For example, a mother who is critical of her daughter's weight, or who diets frequently herself and encourages her daughter to diet, may unintentionally become a co-conspirator in the development of an eating disorder. Similarly, parents who drink heavily or abuse drugs, or who often are absent, uninterested, demanding, or critical, may lay the groundwork for the emergence of bulimia and other disorders in their children. Young people recovering from an eating disorder also may face scrutiny and criticism by other family members, which can lead to poorer recovery (Munn et al., 2010).

Early clinical suspicions that child sexual abuse could be a risk factor for eating disorders have been supported by ongoing investigations of this important issue (Jacobi et al., 2004). For example, women with a history of one or more incidents of sexual abuse were three to five times more likely to have bulimia, compared to women without abuse histories (Sanci et al., 2008). Childhood sexual abuse may be more highly associated with symptoms of bulimia, such as binging or purging, because these behaviors can represent an attempt to regulate negative internal states, such as depression and anxiety, that can be the result of the earlier childhood abuse (Holzer, Uppala, Wonderlich, Crosby, & Simonich, 2008; Smolak, 2011).

Similar findings have been reported among population samples of school-aged youths, whereby youths at risk for disordered eating reported more negative perceptions of their families and parents, and more sexual or physical abuse experiences (Neumark-Sztainer, Story, Hannan, Beuhring, & Resnick, 2000). In addition, sexually abused children report many of the early risk signs of eating disorders, such as higher levels of weight dissatisfaction and purging and dieting behavior (Wonderlich, Rosenfeldt, et al., 2007). Recent studies have shown that the association between a history of child abuse and eating disorders also is evident among gay and bisexual men (Feldman & Meyer, 2007).

This connection between abuse and eating disorders should be tempered by the awareness that childhood sexual abuse is a general risk factor for psychopathology, rather than a specific risk factor for eating disorders. Such events are not uncommon in the backgrounds of individuals with eating disorders, as well as those with other psychiatric disorders. Presumably, childhood sexual abuse is associated with many undesirable adolescent and adult outcomes, of which eating disorders are prominent. (These issues are discussed further in Chapter 14.)

The importance of family factors has led to valuable treatment approaches, as we will see later in this chapter. Nonetheless, family factors must be considered in conjunction with individual and sociocultural factors to explain why the particular features of eating disorders emerge in some families with such dynamics, but not in others.

Psychological Dimension

Understanding the role of psychological processes in the expression of eating disorders requires keeping in mind the powerful social and cultural forces noted previously. External pressures to look thin and be in control of one's weight and appearance interact with certain psychological characteristics to increase the risk of an eating disorder, especially during important developmental transitions. This is a complex, interactive process embedded in multiple layers of biological, familial, personality, and environmental factors. Understandably, this complexity makes causal connections difficult to pinpoint.

Consideration of the psychological dimensions related to eating disorders grew out of the pioneering efforts of Hilda Bruch (1962, 1973), who was the first to propose that self-starvation among persons with anorexia was related to their struggle for autonomy, competence, control, and self-respect. She linked this struggle most closely to parental failure to recognize and confirm their child's emerging independent needs. This sets in motion further confusion that can lead to the principal symptoms of anorexia: disturbance in body image, the inability to recognize and respond to internal sensations or emotions, and the all-pervasive feelings of ineffectiveness and loss of self-control. Her early work set the stage for the cognitive–behavioral interventions used today. She proposed gradual but deliberate relabeling of misconceptions and errors in thinking resulting from faulty developmental experiences, and encouraged patients to learn healthy ways of expressing their thoughts and feelings in a genuine and more direct fashion (Silverman, 1997).

Arthur Crisp, another pioneer in the understanding and treatment of eating disorders, considers anorexia to be a type of phobic avoidance disorder in which the phobic objects are normal adult body weight and shape. He describes this fear metaphorically as a flight from growth (Crisp, 1997). As a result of family and cultural influences, a young female may begin to perceive herself as being fat as she reaches puberty and starts to change into a more adult size and weight. In response, she tries to pursue and maintain her prepubertal weight as a way to avoid the unwelcome aspects of her own growth. This pursuit becomes a vicious cycle, of course, because trying to maintain one's prepubertal body weight meets powerful biological resistance, so she continues her pursuit of weight loss as "insurance" against these unrelenting forces of nature. In effect, a person with anorexia fears loss of control over her attempts to avoid growth, which often translates into a fear of weight gain above 95 to 100 pounds. Like Hilda Bruch's insights, this explanation has led to important treatment efforts.

Adolescents with anorexia are described clinically as being obsessive and rigid, showing emotional restraint, preferring the familiar, having a high need for approval, and showing poor adaptability to change (Thompson-Brenner et al., 2008). These personality features render persons vulnerable to developmental events, such as puberty, that disrupt their carefully maintained sense of self. In a 10-year follow-up of anorexia patients, their obsessions, compulsions, and social interactions persisted even among those who had their weight restored, leading the researchers to conclude that these problems may be constitutional rather than a result of the disorder (Nilsson, Gillberg, Gillberg, & Rastam, 1999). Moreover, more than 4 out of 5 persons with adolescent-onset anorexia experienced at least one episode of major depression or dysthymia within 10 years after onset (Ivarsson, Rastam, Wentz, Gillberg, & Gillberg, 2000). The common association between anorexia and depression may be due to poor emotion regulation stemming from environmental or neurobiologic factors (Haynos & Fruzzetti, 2011), as well as the effect of malnutrition on mood regulation (Mischoulon et al., 2011).

Adolescents with bulimia exhibit somewhat different personality characteristics involving mood swings, poor impulse control, and obsessive–compulsive behaviors (Krug et al., 2011). In the study by Garfinkel et al. (1995), persons with bulimia had a threefold increase in the lifetime occurrence of major depression and at least a doubling of the rate for anxiety disorders. Specific phobias, agoraphobia, panic disorder, generalized anxiety disorder, and alcohol dependence were all more elevated among bulimic individuals than non-bulimic community members. Moreover, abuse of alcohol or stimulants to control appetite is also present in about one-third of the clinical samples of adolescents with bulimia (APA, 2000). Depression, in particular, may co-occur with bulimic symptoms in adolescent girls because they are reciprocally related—each one increases the risk for onset of the other disorder (Smyth et al., 2007; Stice, Burton, & Shaw, 2004). Finally, sex differences also emerge in relation to psychological factors. Females with chronic bulimic symptoms report more drive for thinness than do males with similar chronic symptoms, but these same males report more perfectionism and interpersonal distrust (Joiner et al., 2000; Keel et al., 2007).

Eating disorders almost always are accompanied by other disorders. Community samples in which adolescents are randomly selected and interviewed for psychiatric disorders reveal that almost 90% of persons fitting the criteria for an eating disorder also have other Axis I disorders—usually depression, anxiety, or OCD (Herzog & Eddy, 2007; Lewinsohn, Striegel-Moore, & Seeley, 2000). Although genetic links certainly play a role, researchers also have focused on personality characteristics such as perfectionism, rigidness, or neuroticism that may be a common link between these disorders (Thompson-Brenner et al., 2008). For example, persons who are high on the need for perfection and who also experience high levels of daily stress are more likely to exhibit symptoms of depression (Smyth et al., 2007). Similarly, individuals who score high on perfectionism and also perceive themselves as being overweight have a greater risk of bulimic symptoms (Tissot & Crowther, 2008). Simply stated, a discrepancy between one's actual self (in this case, perceived weight) and one's ideal self (striving toward perfection) increases the likelihood of eating problems, especially among women.

Let's look at a practical example of how the preceding information can be put into dynamic perspective. The adolescent with bulimia or anorexia feels her efforts to restrict her diet and lose weight are ways of gaining control over her life and of becoming a better person, beliefs that are formed during childhood and become operational when she faces the challenges of early adolescence. What develops into the rigidity of anorexia or the battle for control of bulimia may begin as a moderate diet. A teenager unwittingly may begin a dangerous eating pattern because of her dissatisfaction with body weight and shape, and her efforts initially are rewarded by weight loss and a sense of greater control and self-worth, such as former gymnast Erica Stokes describes in Box 13.3.

The transition from dieting to eating disorder may be prompted by the extra attention from peers for what appears to be dramatic willpower and weight loss. Therefore, powerful psychological needs may be at the root of the eating disorder, because the disorder itself is a way to cope with strong feelings that the person otherwise does not know how to express or resolve. This dynamic process accounting for the many determinants of eating disorders is depicted visually in ● Figure 13.6.

BOX 13.3 **A CLOSER LOOK**

Success—At What Price?

Former gymnast Erica Stokes clearly remembers the first time she threw up. The 14-year-old Olympic hopeful and National Team member had just eaten lunch and was feeling, as usual, fat. Living and training year-round at an elite gymnast camp in Houston, she was under constant pressure to maintain her tiny 4-foot 10-inch, 90-pound frame. Food was the enemy. And today, she decided on a solution to beat the foe. She marched into the bathroom and threw up. She didn't use her fingers—just her will and her strong stomach muscles to force out the food.

"My whole insides burned, it was the worst feeling," she remembers. "But afterwards, there was a sense of relief. I felt my stomach go down a little bit."

This started for Erica what was to be a vicious 2-year cycle of eating—sometimes bingeing—then vomiting. "It was my way of maintaining the weight," she reflected. It was also her way of succeeding—and surviving—in an obsessively weight-conscious sport where only the very few, and the very thin, have a shot at becoming a star.

Source: Dying to Win by Alison Bell, 1996, © Alison Bell.

Because of high-profile cases of gymnasts and other performers with eating disorders, the demands of competitive sports and performing arts have received much scrutiny. Both types of activities emphasize appearance or weight restriction, so involvement in them was cited early on as a risk factor for developing an eating disorder because of the pressure to be thin (Owens & Slade, 1987). Although elevated rates of subclinical symptoms of eating disorders have been found among female dancers and other athletes involved in weight-related sports, the relationship between participation in sports that emphasize thinness and eating disorders is a topic of considerable debate. In a meta-analysis of studies, researchers concluded that there are circumstances when sports participation constitutes a risk factor for eating disorders, as well as situations where it may be protective (Smolak, Murnen, & Ruble, 2000). That is, different combinations of body focus, sport type, performance level, age, and personality variables may influence risk (Krentz & Warschburger, 2011).

Sports participation has long been known to be associated with higher levels of self-esteem in boys and men and some research suggests the same is true

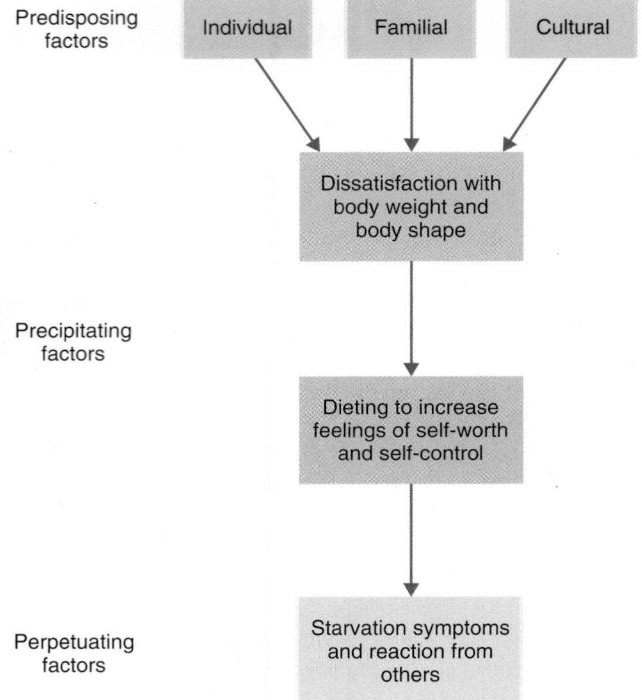

● **FIGURE 13.6** | A dynamic perspective on the determinants of eating disorders.

Reprinted from The Lancet, 341, D. M. Garner, Pathogenesis of Anorexia Nervosa, 1631–1635, Copyright 1993, with permission from Elsevier.

for girls and women (Schmalz, Deane, Birch, & Davison, 2007). Thus, sport participation might actually serve to help protect against the development of eating problems, given that high self-esteem generally is associated with lower psychopathology. On the other hand, personality characteristics such as perfectionism and a need for high achievement are found in both eating disorder patients and athletes (Sassaroli et al., 2008). The sporting environment, where an athlete's aim is often to improve performance rather than appearance, can lead to an unhealthy mix of pressure for some women (Hulley, Currie, Njenga, & Hill, 2007).

Treatment

Psychological interventions for eating disorders often include some form of individual and/or family-based psychotherapy, sometimes accompanied by medical interventions. However, the evidence base for the effectiveness of any form of intervention is still weak, especially for anorexia nervosa (Gowers & Bryant-Waugh, 2004). The discouraging news, based on a systematic review of treatment studies, is that very limited evidence exists to support specific interventions for anorexia at any age, especially for adolescents. The benefits of psychological treatments for bulimia, on the other hand, are more encouraging (Wilson, Grilo, & Vitousek, 2007). More than 30 controlled studies have supported the efficacy of cognitive–behavioral approaches that focus on modifying abnormal eating behaviors and related cognitions underlying bulimia and related conditions (Fairburn & Harrison, 2003). One of many challenges in community-based treatment delivery is that patients often seek (and receive) treatment for weight loss and disguise their eating disorder symptoms, thereby not receiving proper mental health assessment and treatment (Hart, Granillo, Jorm, & Paxton, 2011).

Most adolescents with anorexia, bulimia, and related eating disorders can be managed on an outpatient basis. Hospitalization usually is required only for a small percentage of adolescents with anorexia who have serious complications due to comorbid diagnoses, or are at high physical and/or psychiatric risk. Inpatient treatment is usually brief, as long as psychological counseling and outpatient psychotherapy are made available (Gowers & Bryant-Waugh, 2004). However, because psychological treatments are under pressure to show effectiveness in increasingly briefer periods of time, there is growing concern that high-risk patients are released too soon, before they reach their normal body weight, primarily to reduce costs (Pratt, Phillips, Greydanus, & Patel, 2003).

Pharmacological

Pharmacological treatments are gaining recognition for assistance in the management of eating disorders, although they are not considered to be the initial treatment of choice (Gowers & Bryant-Waugh, 2004). Because of the strong association between anorexia and bulimia and the affective disorders, serotonin-reuptake inhibitors (SSRIs) such as fluoxetine (Prozac) have been the most extensively studied and used medications to treat eating disorders, and are the only treatment approved by the U.S. Food and Drug Administration (Chavez & Insel, 2007). The weight-loss benefits of SSRIs were discovered serendipitously during clinical trials of their ability to regulate mood. Much the same way as bingeing elevates mood in some individuals by increasing carbohydrate levels (Haedt-Matt & Keel, 2011), a sense of well-being could be achieved artificially by regulating serotonin levels.

To date, however, no drug has proved useful or effective for treating symptoms of anorexia among adolescents, and none has improved long-term weight maintenance consistently, changed a distorted self-image, or prevented relapse (Lock & le Grange, 2006). In contrast, there is a consensus that antidepressants have a useful role in the treatment of bulimia, but probably not as the initial treatment of choice. Persons with bulimia may respond favorably to antidepressants and serotonin-reuptake inhibitors, as long as they are continued for 6 months or so and are accompanied by psychosocial treatments with proven effectiveness, as described in the next section (Touyz et al., 2008). Although drug therapy has its use, especially in cases that are not responding to psychological therapy, cognitive–behavior therapy (CBT) remains a more effective choice than medication alone (Gowers & Bryant-Waugh, 2004; Wilson et al., 2007).

Psychosocial

The presence of both emotional and physiological problems in eating disorders requires a comprehensive treatment plan, which ideally consists of a treatment team with an internist, a nutritionist, a psychotherapist, and a psychopharmacologist. Once an eating disorder has been diagnosed and any other illness has been medically ruled out, the clinician determines whether the individual can be treated as an outpatient. Family engagement then may become necessary, to assist family members in managing their fears and worries, as well as to enlist their cooperation. For younger patients, family involvement often is necessary and practical, since parents are responsible for their child's well-being and can offer important directives and guidance that increase successful treatment. In some cases, resolution of family problems—such as parental psychopathology, family isolation, and a poor parent–child relationship—are crucial to recovery from an eating disorder. Recovered patients consider the resolution of family and interpersonal problems as pivotal to their recovery (Lock & le Grange, 2006).

The etiology and course of anorexia result in a disorder that is less responsive to treatment than bulimia; nevertheless, inroads certainly are being made. The initial phase of treatment must involve the restoration of weight and the monitoring of any medical complications that might arise. However, restoring a patient's weight may be the easier part of the process. Many patients regain weight initially (especially if hospitalized), but the pattern of weight loss and distorted beliefs returns unless careful attention is paid to the family and individual factors that initially led to the overemphasis on control of eating.

The lack of empirical support for any treatment for anorexia is due partially to the difficulty of randomly assigning individuals with this life-threatening condition to a control group. Nonetheless, the "best practices" for treating this disorder have evolved based on existing clinical wisdom and modified research designs. One alternative is to assign patients to two different "known" treatment conditions to compare their relative effectiveness (without a no-treatment or placebo control group). Robin, Siegel, and Moye (1995), for example, compared behavioral family systems therapy (BFST) with ego-oriented individual therapy (EOIT) over a 16-month treatment regimen that involved 22 adolescents with anorexia. BFST emphasized parental control over eating, cognitive restructuring, and problem-solving communication training, whereas EOIT emphasized building ego strength, adolescent autonomy, and insight. Both treatments led to improvements in body mass and restoration of menstruation, and produced significant reductions in negative communication and parent–adolescent conflict. These changes were maintained 1 year later, which is a critical period for recovery, and were replicated in more recent work (Robin et al., 1999; Rutherford & Couturier, 2007).

As mentioned, family therapy is the initial treatment of choice for persons with anorexia who are younger and living at home. The facade of togetherness expressed by family members of girls with anorexia often is seen by clinicians as an attempt to disguise covert or overt aggression and avoid conflict. Family-based interventions, therefore, often are required to restore healthy communication patterns (Wilson et al., 2007). By involving the whole family, therapists can attend to the family's attitudes toward body shape and body image that, to an adolescent, can be perceived as subtle but critical judgments. Once weight is restored to within acceptable levels and family support becomes more available, cognitive–behavioral methods similar to the methods described previously can focus more specifically on the patient's rigid beliefs, self-esteem, and self-control processes.

Family therapy does not necessarily mean that all family members are seen at the same time (i.e., conjoint family therapy); in some cases seeing family members separately is the best approach. For instance, instead of challenging family members' negative interaction patterns, such as conflict avoidance and alliances (similar to the early work of Minuchin et al., 1978), therapists encourage parents to mobilize the family's resources to take control of their adolescent's eating patterns, raise parents' morale, and engage all members in further therapy. Focusing on the nature of the illness and its treatment helps to avoid both further criticism of the child and placing blame on family members. Working with parents separately from their teenage daughters (which of course makes it impossible to challenge interaction patterns and alliances) has been as effective as conjoint methods, and has been even more beneficial for families with high levels of criticism and hostility (Eisler et al., 2000; Lock et al., 2010).

As noted, the most effective current therapies for bulimia involve cognitive–behavioral treatment delivered individually or by involving the family unit (Rutherford & Couturier, 2007; Wilson et al., 2007). Cognitive–behavioral therapists change eating behaviors by rewarding or modeling appropriate behaviors, and by helping patients change distorted or rigid thinking patterns that may contribute to their obsession. CBT has become the standard treatment for bulimia nervosa, and forms the theoretical base for much of the treatment for anorexia (Chavez & Insel, 2007). This evidence-based method is the treatment that patients choose whose age does not mandate family therapy, and whose symptoms are moderate to severe.

The clinical application of CBT has been expanded to address specific cues that trigger the urge to binge or to vomit; it also addresses the underlying interpersonal issues that bother some patients, such as body dissatisfaction or distorted drive for thinness (Stice et al., 2008; Stice, Rohde, Shaw, & Gau, 2011). The goals of CBT are to modify abnormal cognitions on the importance of body shape and weight, and to replace efforts at dietary restraint and purging with more normal eating and activity patterns (Touyz et al., 2008). CBT for treatment of bulimia includes several components. Patients are taught at first to self-monitor their food intake and bingeing and purging episodes, as well as any thoughts and feelings that trigger these episodes. This is combined with regular weighing; specific recommendations on how to achieve desired goals, such as the introduction of avoided foods and meal planning, designed to normalize eating behavior and curb restrictive dieting; cognitive restructuring aimed at habitual reasoning errors and underlying assumptions relevant to the development and maintenance of the eating disorder; and regular review and revision of these procedures to prevent relapse.

Some evidence indicates that other psychotherapeutic approaches besides standard CBT also are effective for treating bulimia. One favored approach is to offer interpersonal therapy that addresses situational and personal issues contributing to the development and maintenance of the disorder (McIntosh, Bulik, McKenzie, Luty, & Jordan, 2000; McIntosh, Carter, Bulik, Frampton, & Joyce, 2011). The use of the Internet is also emerging as a practical strategy to reach more individuals before their symptoms become unmanageable. Individuals receive CBT lessons online, and may receive email or social networking support to meet their goals (Pretorius et al., 2009; Sanchez-Ortiz et al., 2011).

SECTION SUMMARY

Eating Disorders of Adolescence

- Anorexia nervosa is characterized by a refusal to maintain body weight, an intense fear of gaining weight or becoming fat, a distorted body image, and amenorrhea.
- Bulimia nervosa involves recurrent episodes of binge eating, followed by an effort to compensate by self-induced vomiting or other means of purging. Individuals with bulimia also are unduly influenced by body shape and weight, and are obsessed with food.
- Anorexia is less common than bulimia, and has an earlier onset (ages 14 to 18). Bulimia affects 1% to 3% of mostly older adolescents. These disorders are much more common in girls than boys, although the rate of EDs in males appears to be increasing.
- If untreated, both disorders can become chronic and pose serious threats to health; bulimia has a higher rate of recovery than anorexia.
- Biological factors likely do not precipitate eating disorders, but their effects on appetite, mood, perception, and energy regulation contribute to the maintenance of the disorder.
- Features of Western culture and family life play a significant causal role in eating disorders. Emphasis on dieting and physical appearance can lead to a drive for thinness.
- Eating disorders have one of the highest rates of comorbidity. The most common co-existing disorders are depression (including dysthymia) and anxiety (including OCD).
- Adolescents with anorexia are described clinically as being obsessive and rigid, preferring the familiar, having a high need for approval, and showing poor adaptability to change.
- Adolescents with bulimia are more likely to show mood swings, poor impulse control, and obsessive–compulsive behaviors.
- Psychosocial and pharmacological treatments for anorexia are limited, with no form of intervention particularly beneficial. Clinical approaches often emphasize the importance of changes in family communication patterns.
- Cognitive–behavioral treatments that focus on the attitudes, beliefs, and behaviors supporting dieting, binge eating, or purging are supported as the most effective psychosocial treatments for bulimia. Pharmacological intervention sometimes is used as a corollary treatment for comorbid disorders, such as depression.

Study Resources

SECTION SUMMARIES

KEY TERMS

anorexia nervosa 427
binge 429
binge eating disorder (BED) 430
binge-eating/purging type 428
bulimia nervosa 429
childhood obesity 419
compensatory behaviors 429
drive for thinness 416
eating attitudes 416
Eating Disorder, Not Otherwise Specified (EDNOS) 431
failure to thrive (FTT) 425
feeding disorder of infancy or early childhood 424
metabolic rate 418
pica 424
purging 417
restricting type 428
set point 418

COURSEMATE

Access an interactive eBook and chapter-specific interactive learning tools, including flashcards, quizzes, videos, and more in your Psychology CourseMate, accessed through CengageBrain.com.

14

Child Maltreatment and Non-Accidental Trauma

Peace in society depends upon peace in the family.

—Augustine

CHAPTER PREVIEW

MARY ELLEN

Her Legacy

She is a bright little girl, with features indicating unusual mental capacity, but with a careworn, stunted, and prematurely old look. Her apparent condition of health, as well as her scanty wardrobe, indicated that no change of custody or condition could be much for the worse.

. . . On her examination [in court] the child made a statement as follows: ". . . I don't know how old I am. . . . I have never had but one pair of shoes, but I cannot recollect when that was. I have had no shoes or stockings on this winter. . . . I am never allowed to play with any children, or to have any company whatever. Mamma has been in the habit of whipping and beating me almost every day. She used to whip me with a twisted whip—a raw hide. The whip always left a black and blue mark on my body. I have now the black and blue marks on my head which were made by mamma, and also a cut on the left side of my forehead which was made by a pair of scissors. She struck me with the scissors and cut me; I have no recollection of ever having been kissed by any one. . . . I have never been taken on my mamma's lap and caressed or petted. . . . I do not know for what I was whipped—mamma never said anything to me when she whipped me." (*New York Times*, April 10, 1874)

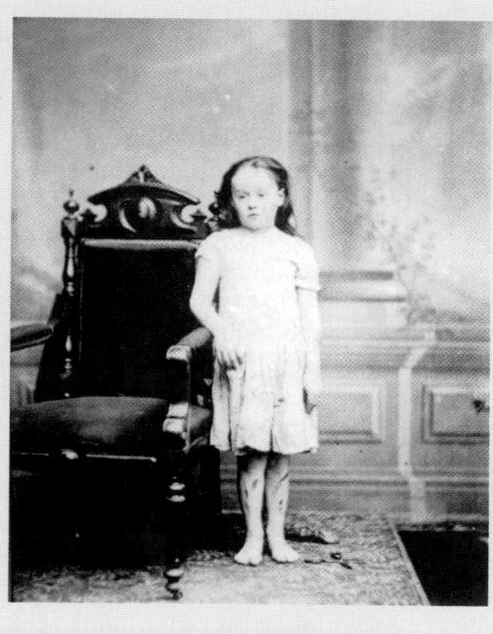

THIS HEARTBREAKING AND TRAGIC report of the abuse Mary Ellen experienced led to the formation in the winter of 1874 of the New York Society for the Prevention of Cruelty to Children, as citizens discovered that animals were protected from mistreatment, but children were not. Sadly, it took another 100 years before legislation was passed that clearly defined and mandated the reporting of child abuse and neglect, finally launching new efforts to identify and assist abused and neglected children in North America. Despite these efforts, child abuse and neglect remain one of the most common causes of non-accidental child deaths.

Since records of official reports began in the United States and many other countries in the early 1970s, child abuse and neglect has been recognized as a significant problem, and the fact that the lives of some children end tragically and without purpose has been revealed. Unfortunately, each day in the United States more than five children—most of whom are under four years old—die at the hands of their parents or caregivers (United States Government Accountability Office, 2011; U.S. Department of Health and Human Services, Administration on Children, Youth, and Families [USDHHS], 2010).

In North America, before they reach adulthood, one in ten children experience some form of sexual victimization by an adult or peer (Finkelhor, Turner, Ormrod, & Hamby, 2009). Each year, about 1 of every 10 children receives physical punishment by a parent or other caregiver harsh enough to put the child at risk of injury or harm (Straus & Stewart, 1999). Countless other children suffer the effects of emotional abuse and neglect, which, like the effects of physical and sexual abuse, can cause known harm to their psychological development.

For many generations, violence against children and other family members has been viewed as a private matter, and its significant negative effects continue to be poorly acknowledged. Until very recently, violence against members of one's family was considered, in the eyes of the law, to be less consequential, less damaging, and less worthy of society's serious attention than violence between strangers. Today we know better: Family violence occurs in numerous forms, from mild acts of frightening or yelling at children, to severe acts of assaulting them with fists and weapons. Moreover, violence and abuse wax and wane in a cyclical manner that creates tension, uncertainty, and fear in children, forcing them to cope with harsh realities and fearful demands (Wekerle, Miller, Wolfe, & Spindel, 2006).

We devote an entire chapter to maltreatment because severe disturbances in the parent–child relationship, the family, or the community are common causes of abnormal child development (Chapman, Dube, & Anda, 2007). This chapter departs from the traditional taxonomic approach to abnormal child psychology, and considers how disturbed child-rearing environments or unsafe communities play an important role in abnormal development during childhood and adolescence.

Child maltreatment is a generic term that refers to four primary acts: physical abuse, neglect, sexual abuse, and emotional abuse. Maltreatment can take many forms, including acts experienced by the majority of children, such as corporal punishment, sibling violence, and peer assault, as well as acts experienced by a significant minority, such as physical abuse (Centers for Disease Control [CDC], 2011). It cuts across all lines of gender, national origin, language, religion, age, ethnicity, disability, and sexual orientation. **Non-accidental trauma** refers to the wide-ranging effects of maltreatment on the child's ongoing physical and emotional development. Children, because of their social and psychological immaturity, are highly dependent on adults. This dependency makes them more vulnerable to different forms of **victimization**, which is defined as the abuse or mistreatment of someone whose ability to protect himself or herself is limited (Turner, Finkelhor, & Ormrod, 2010).

Child abuse and neglect have considerable psychological importance because they occur within ongoing relationships that are expected to be protective, supportive, and nurturing. Children from abusive and neglectful families grow up in environments that fail to provide consistent and appropriate opportunities to guide their development; instead, these children are placed in jeopardy of physical and emotional harm (Jaffe, Wolfe, & Campbell, 2011). Yet, their ties to their families—even to the abuser—are very important, so child victims may feel torn between a sense of belonging and a sense of fear and apprehension. A child victim of sexual abuse expressed it this way: "I was afraid. When it happened, [my father] behaved as if it never happened—he made me doubt myself. I was afraid that I would embarrass my father [the abuser] and be a shame to his family" (Sas, Hurley, Hatch, Malla, & Dick, 1993, p. 68). Because children are dependent on the people who harm or neglect them, they face other paradoxical dilemmas as well (American Psychological Association, 1996/2007):

- *The victim wants to stop the violence but also longs to belong to a family.* Loyalty and strong emotional ties to the abuser are powerful opponents to the victim's desire to be safe and protected.
- *Affection and attention may coexist with violence and abuse.* A recurring cycle may begin, whereby mounting tension, characterized by fear and anticipation, ultimately gives way to more abusive behavior. A period of reconciliation may follow, with increased affection and attention. Children are always hopeful that the abuse will not recur.
- *The intensity of the violence tends to increase over time, although in some cases physical violence may decrease or even stop altogether.* Abusive behavior may vary throughout the relationship, taking verbal, sexual, emotional, or physical forms, but the adult's abuse of power and control remains the central issue.

Many societies are struggling to balance parental rights (e.g., the right to discipline their children) and the rights of children to be safe and free of harm. Consequently, a significant shift is under way in how child maltreatment is defined and in how its effects are studied. In the past, abuse was defined primarily by visible physical injuries. However, today we recognize that physical injuries are only one of many consequences. Maltreatment also can damage an individual's developing relationships with others, and his or her fundamental sense of safety and self-esteem (United Nations Secretary-General's Study on Violence against Children [United Nations], 2006).

We begin our discussion of child abuse and neglect by considering the role of the family in children's healthy socialization, and the need for more clear and well-established boundaries between appropriate and inappropriate actions toward children.

History and Family Context

Society's view of child-rearing and intolerance of abuse and neglect has evolved over a relatively short period. Child maltreatment and non-accidental forms of trauma have always existed, and most likely were even more commonplace in previous generations (Radbill, 1987), but these acts were seldom identified as a problem or concern. For generations, children were viewed as the exclusive property and responsibility of their fathers, who had full discretion as to how punishment could be administered. This right was unchallenged by any countermovement to seek more humane treatment for children up until the recognition of the abuse Mary Ellen experienced, just over 100 years ago.

Ironically, the same legal system that was designed to support and assist the family has tolerated, and in some respects condoned, the abuse of family members, including children, women, and the elderly (Jaffe, Lemon, Sandler, & Wolfe, 1996). Two major cultural traditions have influenced this position until recently: absolute authority over the family by the husband, and the right to family privacy. The Roman Law of Chastisement (753 B.C.), for example, required that if a husband intended to beat his wife, he should use a stick no bigger around than his right thumb. This "rule of thumb" was later incorporated into Church doctrine, along with the adage "spare the rod and spoil the child" (Jaffe et al., 1996). Sadly, this view of children as personal property to be managed however the parent wishes is still adhered to throughout many developed and developing societies (Wolfe & Nayak, 2003).

Fortunately, over the last century and a half, particularly the last 30 years, the legal system's response has shifted to one of condemnation of such behavior throughout much of the Western world (albeit with considerable resistance). The Convention on the Rights of the Child (U.N. General Assembly, 1989) spurred efforts to value the rights and needs of children, and to recognize their exploitation and abuse in many developed countries. Today, 42 countries have established an official government policy regarding child abuse and neglect, and about one-third of the world's population is included in the various countries that conduct an annual count of child abuse and neglect cases (International Society for Prevention of Child Abuse and Neglect, 2010). These efforts provide the critical first steps to identifying the scope of the problem, and justify the implementation of important societal, community, and cultural changes to combat child abuse.

Healthy Families

It is difficult to talk about child abuse and neglect without talking about the importance of families. Family relations are the earliest and most enduring social relationships that significantly affect a child's competence, resilience, and sense of well-being. For most of us, family influences are positive and beneficial, offering a primary source of support and nurturance that sets the stage for lifetime patterns of secure relationships and well-being. For others, however, family events and experiences are profoundly negative and harmful, providing the context for some of the most severe violence in society (Straus, Gelles, & Steinmetz, 2003).

As parents, we recognize that children require considerable direction and control, and sometimes behave in ways that challenge our decisions and interfere with our plans. If you've not experienced this yourself, ask a parent you know if you can take their young child grocery shopping! Individuals who are ill-prepared for the vital and challenging role of being parents may rely heavily on child-rearing methods from their own childhood, without questioning or modifying those methods. Although this approach to parenting is natural and often appropriate, in some cases it can perpetuate undesirable child-rearing methods, such as physical coercion, verbal threats, and neglect of the child's needs (Gershoff, 2002; Wolfe, 1999).

Understanding the dire effects of abuse and neglect on the mental health of children and adults must begin with a discussion of what children should expect from a healthy family environment. For healthy development, children need a caregiving environment that balances their need for control and direction, or "demandingness," with their need for stimulation and sensitivity, or "responsiveness" (Maccoby & Martin, 1983). Determinants of healthy parent–child relationships and family roles derived from these two primary developmental needs include:

- Adequate knowledge of child development and expectations, including knowledge of children's normal sexual development and experimentation;
- Adequate skill in coping with stress related to caring for small children, and knowledge of ways to enhance child development through proper stimulation and attention;
- Opportunities to develop normal parent–child attachment and early patterns of communication;
- Adequate parental knowledge of home management, including basic financial planning, proper shelter, and meal planning;
- Opportunities and willingness to share the duties of child care between both parents, when applicable;
- Provision of necessary social and health services.

These healthy patterns depend not only on parental competence and developmental sensitivity, but also on family circumstances and the availability of community resources, such as education and child-rearing information, as well as social networks and supports. The family situation itself, including the parents' marital relationship and the child's characteristics, such as temperament, health, and developmental limitations, provides the basic context for child-rearing.

Although we would expect a considerable range in ability and resources among North American families, certain features of a child's environment should be fundamental and expectable. For infants, an **expectable environment** requires protective and nurturing adults, as well as opportunities for socialization within a culture. For older children, an expectable environment includes a supportive family, contact with peers, and ample opportunities to explore and master their environment (Cicchetti & Valentino, 2006). Moreover, responsible parenting involves a gradual shifting of control from the parent to the child and the community. Seldom is this process a smooth one, but healthy families learn to move gradually from nearly complete parental control, through shared control, to the child's growing self-control and eventual independence as an adult.

Family Stress and Disharmony

You know the only people who are always sure about the proper way to raise children? Those who've never had any.

—Bill Cosby

Children have an amazing ability to adapt to changing demands, an ability that is essential for healthy development. Nevertheless, they need a basic expectable environment to adapt successfully, or their development may be compromised. All children must cope with various degrees of stress, and these experiences can be strengthening if they do not exceed the child's coping ability (Masten & Wright, 2010). However, a child's method of adapting to immediate environmental demands (such as avoiding an abusive caregiver) may later compromise his or her ability to form relationships with others. A child's successful methods of adapting to outbursts of anger and aggression between family members are constantly challenged. Signs of stress appear, such as increased illness, symptoms of fear and anxiety, and problems with peers or school (El-Sheikh & Erath, 2011; Kim & Cicchetti, 2010).

Stressful events in the family affect each child in different and unique ways. However, certain situations trigger more intense stress reactions and consequences than others. (Consider, for example, the difference between the stress of moving to a new school and the stress of being bullied by an older child.) Child maltreatment is among the worst and most intrusive forms of stress. It impinges directly on the child's daily life, may be ongoing and unpredictable, and is often the result of actions or inactions of people the child is supposed to trust and depend on. Also keep in mind that even traumatic events such as abuse, neglect, and family violence do not affect each child in a predictable, characteristic fashion. Rather, their impact depends on the child's makeup and available supports (El-Sheikh & Erath, 2011).

A prime factor in how children respond to various forms of stress is the degree of support and assistance they receive from their parents to help them cope and adapt. Parents provide a model that teaches the child how to exert some control even in the midst of confusion and upheaval. Understandably, a warm relationship with an adult who provides a predictable routine and consistent, moderate discipline, and who buffers the child from unnecessary sources of stress, is a valuable asset. Maltreated children may have the hardest time adapting appropriately to any form of stress when they are deprived of positive adult relationships, effective models of problem solving, and a sense of personal control or predictability (Luthar, 2006).

Continuum of Care

Most of us agree that children who lack the basic necessities of life—food, affection, medical care, education, and intellectual and social stimulation—are placed in jeopardy, but different cultural values, community standards, and personal experiences make one person's abuse another person's discipline or education (Korbin, 2002).

● Figure 14.1 depicts a hypothetical range of child care, from healthy to abusive and neglectful, that provides some guidelines and boundaries for acceptable behavior between parents and children (Wolfe & McIsaac, 2011). At the positive end of this continuum we see appropriate and healthy forms of child-rearing actions that promote child development. Competent parents encourage their child's development in a variety of ways and match their demands and expectations to the child's needs and abilities. Of course, parents are human, and many on occasions will scold, criticize, or even show insensitivity to the child's state of need; in fact, discipline often requires such firm control, with accompanying verbal statements and affect.

Poor/dysfunctional actions, shown in the middle of the diagram, represent greater degrees of irresponsible and harmful child care. Parents who show any discernible degree of these actions toward their child often need instruction and assistance in effective child care methods. Finally, the far right of the diagram depicts parents who violate their child's basic needs and dependency status in a physically, sexually, or emotionally intrusive or abusive manner. Similarly, their failure to respond to a child's needs is the cornerstone of neglect.

SECTION SUMMARY

History and Family Context

- Child maltreatment refers to four primary acts: physical abuse, neglect, sexual abuse, and emotional abuse.
- Child abuse has always existed, but until fairly recently it was seldom identified as a problem or concern.
- Child maltreatment represents one of the greatest failures of the child's expectable environment. It is among the worst and most intrusive forms of stress, and often leads to poor adaptive outcomes.
- Maltreating families fail to provide many of the expected emotional and physical necessities for children, and offer few supports and opportunities for children to explore and master their environment.
- Child care can be described along a hypothetical continuum ranging from healthy to abusive and neglectful.
- Boundaries between appropriate and inappropriate behavior toward children are not always clear or well established, but an awareness of what is right and what is wrong can go a long way in preventing maltreatment.

Types of Maltreatment

Have you ever babysat a young child or been in charge of a group of children at a camp or school? If you saw bruises on a child, what would you do? First, you would consider that bruises on a child can be caused by any

MOST POSITIVE ⟷ MOST NEGATIVE		
Positive/Healthy Parenting Style	**Poor/Dysfunctional**	**Emotionally Abusive/Neglectful**
Stimulation and Emotional Expressions	***Stimulation and Emotional Expressions***	***Stimulation and Emotional Expressions***
Provides a variety of sensory stimulation and positive emotional expressions Expresses joy at child's efforts and accomplishments	Shows rigid emotional expression and inflexibility in responding to child Seems unconcerned with child's developmental/psychological needs	Expresses conditional love and ambivalent feelings toward child Shows little or no sensitivity to child's needs
Interactions	***Interactions***	***Interactions***
Engages in competent, child-centered interactions to encourage development Friendly, positive interactions that encourage independent exploration	Often insensitive to child's needs; unfriendly Poor balance between child independence and dependence on parent	Emotionally or physically rejects child's attention Takes advantage of child's dependency status through coercion, threats, or bribes
Consistency and Predictability	***Consistency and Predictability***	***Consistency and Predictability***
Demonstrates consistency and predictability to promote their relationship	Often responds unpredictably, sometimes with emotional discharge	Responds unpredictably, accompanied by emotional discharge
Rules and Limits	***Rules and Limits***	***Rules and Limits***
Makes rules for safety and health Appropriate safeguards for child's age	Unclear or inconsistent rules for safety and health	Sporadic, capricious Exploits or corrupts for parent's benefit
Disciplinary Practices	***Disciplinary Practices***	***Disciplinary Practices***
Occasionally scolds, criticizes, interrupts child activity Teaches child through behavioral rather than psychological control methods	Frequently uses coercive methods and minimizes child's competence Uses psychologically controlling methods that confuse, upset child	Uses cruel and harsh control methods that frighten child Violates minimal community standards on occasion
Emotional Delivery and Tone	***Emotional Delivery and Tone***	***Emotional Delivery and Tone***
Uses emotional delivery and tone that are firm but not frightening	Uses verbal and non-verbal pressure, often to achieve unrealistic expectations	Frightening, threatening, denigrating, insulting

● **FIGURE 14.1** | Continuum of parental emotional sensitivity and expression.

number of factors, so you would need to obtain more information, if possible, to see if the bruises were accidental or not. You should be aware that all states and provinces in North America have civil laws, or statutes, that obligate persons who come in contact with children as part of their job or volunteer work (bus drivers, day care workers, teachers, babysitters, and so forth) to report known or suspected cases of abuse to the police or child welfare authorities. These statutes also provide criteria for removing children from their homes if they are suspected of being maltreated. Criminal statutes further specify the forms of maltreatment that are criminally punishable. We all have a role to play in keeping children safe from harm that begins with being attentive to signs of possible abuse; professional or police involvement should be sought if you are concerned or uncertain.

A widely used definition of child maltreatment was established by the U.S. Child Abuse Prevention and Treatment Act (CAPTA):

> Any recent act or failure to act on the part of a parent or caretaker, which results in death, serious physical or emotional harm, sexual abuse, or exploitation, or an act or failure to act which presents an imminent risk of serious harm. (Child Welfare Information Gateway, 2011)

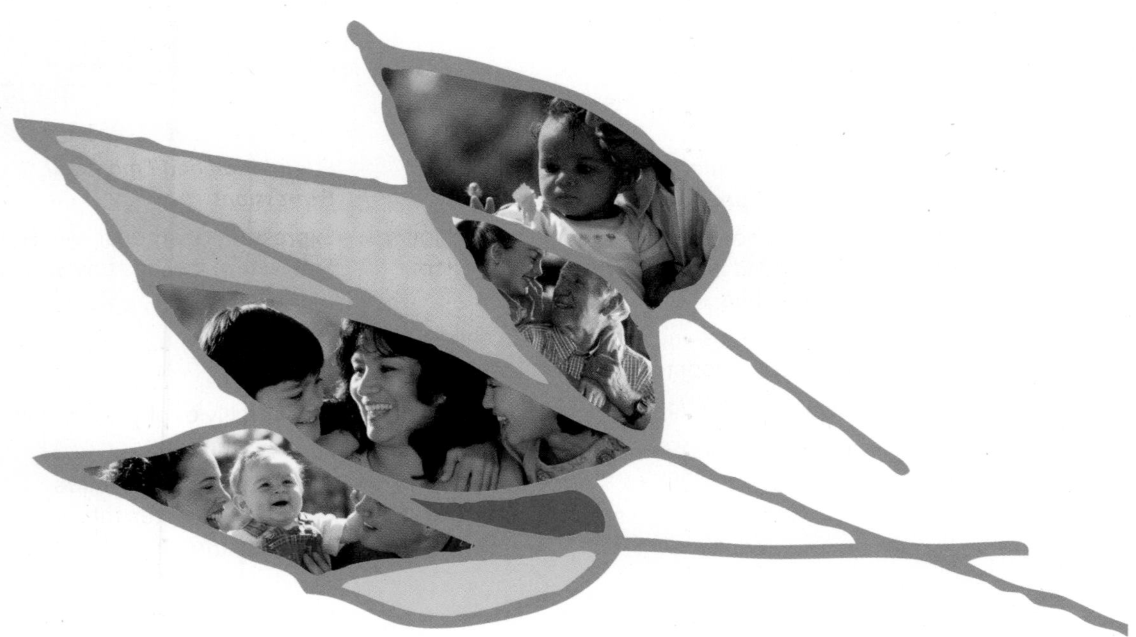

Promote Healthy Families in Your Community

What You Can Do

Protective factors increase the safety and well-being of children and families:

- Nurturing and Attachment—Encourage parents to play and talk with their children.
- Knowledge of Parenting and of Child and Youth Development—Talk about what parents can anticipate at different ages.
- Parental Resilience—Offer healthy ways to cope with stress.
- Social Connections—Connect caregivers with others for support.
- Concrete Supports—Help families access needed resources.

Protecting Children • Promoting Healthy Families • Preserving Communities

Find out more!
Visit the Prevention section of the Child Welfare Information Gateway website at
www.childwelfare.gov/preventing

FRIENDS National Resource Center for Community-Based Child Abuse Prevention
800 Eastowne Drive, Suite 105 Chapel Hill, NC 27514
919.490.5577
www.friendsnrc.org

A Service of the Children's Bureau/ACYF
1250 Maryland Avenue, SW Eighth Floor Washington, DC 20024
703.385.7565 or 800.394.3366 Email: info@childwelfare.gov
www.childwelfare.gov

U.S. Department of Health and Human Services
Administration for Children and Families
Administration on Children, Youth and Families
Children's Bureau
www.acf.hhs.gov/programs/cb

Courtesy of FRIENDS National Resource Center for Community-Based Child Abuse Prevention, U.S. Department of Health and Human Services, Administration for Children and Families, and the Children's Bureau.

Please note that incidents of maltreatment that affect children's health and well-being involve abuse and neglect by *adults*, and therefore are not forms of abnormal child behavior or psychological disorders. Thus, specific definitions of types of child maltreatment do not appear in DSM-IV-TR. Instead, DSM-IV-TR considers severe maltreatment (of an adult or a child) under the Axis I category "Other conditions that may be a focus of clinical attention." If a child who was abused is also suffering from a clinical disorder such as depression (Axis I), the maltreatment would be noted on Axis IV (psychosocial and environmental problems), because maltreatment may affect the diagnosis, treatment, and prognosis of the child's depression.

Physical Abuse

MILTON

Abused and Abusive

Four-year-old Milton's rambunctious nature and his mother's hair-trigger temper were an explosive mix. He was constantly in trouble at home and often was spanked, yelled at, and locked in his room. One evening his babysitter took him to the emergency department because she thought he had a bad cold. During the examination, the doctor discovered that Milton had a fracture to his left forearm that was a couple of weeks old. There was a goose egg on Milton's forehead and multiple bruises on his face at various stages of healing, as well as bruises on his back. Several people had noticed Milton's aggressive behavior—pushing other children or hitting them with something at preschool—but no one had realized that he was being abused. His preschool teacher told investigators, "I'm never sure from one minute to the next how Milton will react to the other children. He could be playing and suddenly become angry at something and start to destroy things or hit someone. I've also seen him become frightened—at what I don't know—and withdraw into a corner. I've tried several times to discuss these things with his mother, but she says he's just trying to get his way all the time." (Based on authors' material)

Milton has been physically abused. His behavior is indicative of growing up in an environment with punitive disciplinary methods that are the norm and are detrimental to child-centered stimulation and appropriate limit setting. **Physical abuse** is multiple acts of aggression that include punching, beating, kicking, biting, burning, shaking, or otherwise physically harming a child. In most cases, the injuries from physical abuse are not intentional, but they occur as a result of overdiscipline or severe physical punishment. The severity and nature of the injuries vary considerably, as shown by these sobering examples of physical abuse (Sedlak & Broadhurst, 1996:

- A 1-year-old child who died of a cerebral hemorrhage after being shaken by her father;
- A teen whose mother punched her and pulled out her hair;
- A child who sustained second- and third-degree "stocking" burns to the feet after being held in hot water.

As a result of their harsh and insensitive treatment, physically abused children like Milton often are described as more disruptive and aggressive than their age-mates, with disturbances that reach across a broad spectrum of emotional and cognitive functioning (Teisl & Cicchetti, 2008). Physical injuries may range from minor (bruises, lacerations), to moderate (scars, abrasions), to severe (burns, sprains, or broken bones). These physical signs represent only the visible injuries; we will see later in this chapter that the psychological development of physically abused children often is impaired in less visible—but very serious—ways as well. We ask you to keep Milton's case in mind, since we refer to him several times throughout the chapter.

Neglect

JANE AND MATT

Used to Neglect

Although Janet had worked for child protective services for over 10 years, she still cringed when she described the conditions of the home from which she had just removed two young siblings. "Neighbors and relatives have complained about the parents' never being around much, and how they often hear children crying," Janet explained during our interview. "I've been to the home before, and usually it stays clean for a few days after my visit. But this time the children were left with a teenaged babysitter, who went off to play in an arcade. They walked out of the home, and had to be returned by the police. What I saw this time was worse than before. Little Matt, who's almost 3 years old, was running around in soiled diapers, crawling across broken dishes and spilled food, putting things in his mouth. His sister Jane, who turns 6 next month, was dressed in dirty clothes and looked like she hadn't eaten in a week. The

(continues)

(*continued*)

odor from the house forced me to step outside for air. The children seemed used to it—they just moved things out of their way and didn't seem to care."

I met with both children once they were settled into a foster home, and offered ways for the foster parents to manage Jane's strong-willed behavior and Matt's delay in speech and toileting. The foster mother noted how both children seemed to need "constant attention and control," and how neither had knowledge of typical routines such as sitting down together for dinner, cleaning up, bed times, basic hygiene, and the need to wear clean clothing. (Based on authors' material)

These two children suffered the effects of physical and emotional neglect, characterized by a failure to provide for their basic physical, educational, and emotional needs. **Physical neglect** includes refusal or delay in seeking health care, expulsion from the home or refusal to allow a runaway to return home, abandonment, and inadequate supervision. **Educational neglect** involves actions such as allowing chronic truancy, failing to enroll in school a child who is of mandatory school age, and failing to attend to a child's special educational needs. **Emotional neglect**, one of the most difficult categories to define, includes actions such as marked inattention to the child's needs for affection, refusal or failure to provide needed psychological care, spousal abuse in the child's presence, and permission of drug or alcohol use by the child.

Estelle/Shutterstock.com

Child neglect, the most common form of maltreatment, is tied to poverty, substance abuse, and parental indifference

The determination of child neglect requires consideration of cultural values and standards of care, as well as recognition that the failure to provide the necessities of life may be related to poverty. The examples shown in Table 14.1 are actual cases of the three forms of neglect (Sedlak & Broadhurst, 1996).

Neglected children may suffer physical health problems, limited growth, and increased complications in other health conditions, such as diabetes, allergies, and failure-to-thrive (Lyons-Ruth, Zeanah, & Benoit, 2003; van Tilburg et al., 2010). They also may show behavior patterns that vacillate between undisciplined activity and extreme passivity (Hildyard & Wolfe, 2002), due to their ways of adapting to an unresponsive caregiver. As toddlers, they show little persistence and enthusiasm; as preschoolers, neglected children show poor impulse

TABLE 14.1 | The Three Forms of Child Neglect

Physical Neglect	Educational Neglect	Emotional Neglect
• A 2-year-old who was found wandering in the street late at night, naked and alone	• An 11-year-old and a 13-year-old who were chronically truant	• Siblings who were subjected to repeated incidents of family violence between their mother and father
• An infant who had to be hospitalized for near-drowning after being left alone in a bathtub	• A 12-year-old whose parents permitted him to decide whether to go to school, how long to stay there, and in which activities to participate	• A 12-year-old whose parents permitted him to drink and use drugs
• Children who were living in a home contaminated with animal feces and rotting food	• A special education student whose mother refused to believe he needed help in school	• A child whose mother helped him shoot out the windows of a neighbor's house

control and are highly dependent on teachers for support and nurturance (Erickson & Egeland, 2002).

Note that emotional neglect also includes children who witness parental or partner violence in the home. Child witnesses of abuse and violence are affected in much the same way as other victims of maltreatment (Jaffe et al., 2011; Wolfe, Crooks, Lee, McIntyre-Smith, & Jaffe, 2003). Younger abused children are fearful and often show regressive and somatic signs of distress, such as sleep problems, bed-wetting, headaches, stomachaches, diarrhea, ulcers, and enuresis. Older boys tend to be more aggressive with peers and dating partners; girls tend to be more passive, withdrawn, and low in self-esteem (Crooks & Wolfe, 2007). Based on a nationally representative sample of 1,615 dual-parent U.S. households, over 15 million American children live in families in which partner violence had occurred at least once in the previous year (McDonald, Jouriles, Ramisetty-Mikler, Caetano, & Green, 2006), which suggests that such events are significantly underreported to authorities.

Sexual Abuse

ROSITA

No Haven at Home

Rosita was not quite 4 years old when her family doctor suspected that something was going on that troubled her. He expressed his concerns to child welfare, and Rosita reenacted several sexual acts for them, using dolls depicting her father and herself. "Daddy said I can play a game, and it's OK 'cause grownups do it," she hesitantly explained. Rosita made the dolls kiss, then the male doll rubbed the female doll's vagina. "But he hurt me, and it made me scared. I didn't want to get in trouble." To make matters worse, her mother became furious with Rosita and the agency when she heard the accusations, and was unwilling to ensure her daughter's protection and safety at home. "Rosita just wants a lot of attention—she's said this stuff before and I don't believe her one minute," was her mother's only comment. (Based on authors' material)

Rosita was sexually abused by her father and disbelieved by her mother; as a result, she faces many ongoing psychological complications. Because Rosita was seen several times throughout the course of her childhood and adolescent development, her case is discussed further in a later section of this chapter on the course of development of children and adolescents who have been sexually abused.

Sexual abuse includes fondling a child's genitals, intercourse with the child, incest, rape, sodomy, exhibitionism, and commercial exploitation through prostitution or the production of pornographic materials. The actual number of sexual abuse cases may be underreported because of the secrecy or "conspiracy of silence" that so often characterizes these cases, making determination of abuse difficult (Mitchell, Wolak, & Finkelhor, 2007). The following are actual reported cases of sexual abuse (Sedlak & Broadhurst, 1996):

- A 10-year-old girl who was raped by her father;
- Two sisters and a brother who were sexually molested by their mother's live-in boyfriend;
- A 4-year-old who was fondled by his father during weekend visitations.

The behavior and development of sexually abused children may be affected significantly, especially in relation to the duration or frequency of abuse, the use of force, penetration, and a close relationship to the perpetrator (Berliner & Elliott, 2002). The physical health of these children may be compromised by urinary tract problems, gynecological problems, sexually transmitted diseases (including AIDS), and pregnancy (Maniglio, 2009).

About one-third of sexually abused children neither report nor exhibit visible symptoms, and about two-thirds of those who do show symptoms recover significantly during the first 12 to 18 months following the abuse (Kendall-Tackett, Williams, & Finkelhor, 2001). Nonetheless, the possibility of delayed emergence of symptoms is becoming more widely recognized (Trickett, Noll, & Putnam, 2011; L. M. Williams, 2003). Children's reports of sexual abuse and their reactions and recovery vary, depending on the nature of the sexual assault and the response of their important others, especially the mother (London, Bruck, Wright, & Ceci, 2008). Many acute symptoms of sexual abuse resemble children's common reactions to stress, such as fears, increased anger, anxiety, fatigue, depression, passivity, difficulties focusing and sustaining attention, and withdrawal from usual activities.

In reaction to an abusive incident, it is common for younger children to regress temporarily, such as by becoming enuretic or easily upset, or by having problems sleeping. In later childhood and early adolescence, these signs of distress may take the form of acting-out behaviors (such as delinquency, drug use, and promiscuity), or unhealthy relationships and self-destructive behavior (Trickett, Negriff, Ji, & Peckins, 2011). Some sexually abused children may exhibit sexualized behaviors with other children or toys that may include excessive masturbation, age-inappropriate knowledge of sexual activity, and/or pronounced seductive or promiscuous behavior. Any of these symptoms of distress may be associated with a decline or sudden change in school performance, behavior, and peer relations.

Unlike physical abuse and neglect, sexual abuse has no connection to child-rearing, discipline, or inattention to developmental needs. Rather, it constitutes a breach of trust, deception, intrusion, and exploitation of a child's innocence and status. Whereas all types of maltreatment share a common ground in relation to the abuse of power by an adult over a child, sexual abuse stands out from physical abuse and neglect in terms of these specific dynamics.

Emotional Abuse

EVAN

If This Is Love . . .

Evan described himself as "an eleven-year-old boy who can be good when he tries really hard, but most of the time he makes bad choices." One of these bad choices was to put paint in the teacher's coffee cup, leading to his suspension from school. Evan also started stealing and drinking beer. The school says he was threatening other kids, wanting their money. To document their plight, his parents volunteered to have a television documentary made about their "trouble with Evan," using motion-sensitive cameras in two rooms in their home. What emerged from the tapes, however, were repeated episodes of emotional abuse toward Evan by his stepfather and mother. Below are some illustrative conversations:

Evan's stepfather: "I would like to lock you up in a cage and let everybody look at you like you are an animal. I am fed up with this sh__. I can't put up with it no more and neither can your mother. And if you think I am talking to the wall, I am talking to you, beef head. If you'd of been me, you'd of been dead because my father would have killed you. Your insubordination is going to get you a hook on the side of your f__ing head. If you don't like it the door is right there."

Evan's parents were convinced that he was stealing money from them, and his mother's confrontation follows: "We already know that you are lying so you f__ing tell me the truth NOW! Everything. Go take a look in the mirror. Go take a look in the mirror and then come back here. You look guilty as sin. [Turns to husband] I am going to hit him. Now that is not how you normally look, is it? That is not a normal look for a child, is it? You have got great big letters written all over your face that spell guilty." Evan's mother then discovered she had miscounted the money. (Transcribed quote from "The Trouble with Evan," for the television program *The Fifth Estate*, executive producer, David Studer for the Canadian Broadcasting Corporation, originally aired on March 25, 1994)

Evan experienced very harsh, emotionally abusive threats and put-downs from his parents, which can be as harmful to a child's development as physical abuse or neglect. **Emotional abuse** includes repeated acts or omissions by the parents or caregivers that have caused, or could cause, serious behavioral, cognitive, emotional, or mental disorders. For example, the parents or caregivers may use extreme or bizarre forms of punishment, such as confinement of a child in a dark closet. Emotional abuse also includes verbal threats and put-downs like those Evan experienced, as well as habitual scapegoating, belittling, and name-calling. Emotional abuse exists, to some degree, in all forms of maltreatment, so the specific psychological consequences of this form of maltreatment are poorly understood (Glaser, 2011; Wolfe & McIsaac, 2011).

The following cases tend to be more severe forms of emotional abuse because of the definitional requirement that the acts have caused, or could cause, serious harm (Sedlak & Broadhurst, 1996):

- A young child strapped in a high chair all day while her parents went to work;
- A 4-year-old who was locked in a closet as a means of discipline;
- Children traumatized when their father took them to a store to buy a gun, with which he threatened to kill them and their mother.

Exploitation

Children also suffer trauma from commercial or other sexual exploitation, such as child labor and child prostitution. Globally, as many as 10 million children may be victims of child prostitution, the sex industry, sex tourism, and pornography, although accurate statistics are not available (United Nations, 2006). Sadly, many exploited children began as victims of abuse and rape in their homes, and are forced into commercial sexual activity at a young age (Cooper, Estes, Giardino, Kellogg, & Vieth, 2005). Rates of child prostitution tend to be higher in Asia and Latin America, but an alarming growth has been recorded in Africa, North America, and Europe (Wolfe & Nayak, 2003). Poverty is the greatest factor in the child prostitution explosion, as migration of families from the rural areas into cities creates unemployment, the breakdown of family structures, homelessness, and, inevitably, an increase in child prostitution.

SECTION SUMMARY

Types of Maltreatment

- Physical abuse includes acts of aggression such as punching, beating, kicking, biting, burning, shaking, or otherwise physically harming a child.

- Child neglect is a failure to provide for a child's basic physical, educational, or emotional needs.
- Sexual abuse ranges from sexual touching to exhibitionism, sexual intercourse, and commercial exploitation (pornography, prostitution).
- Emotional abuse includes acts or omissions that could cause serious behavioral, cognitive, emotional, or mental disorders.
- Exploitation of children includes child labor and child prostitution, which are recognized as a significant form of trauma to children and adolescents worldwide.

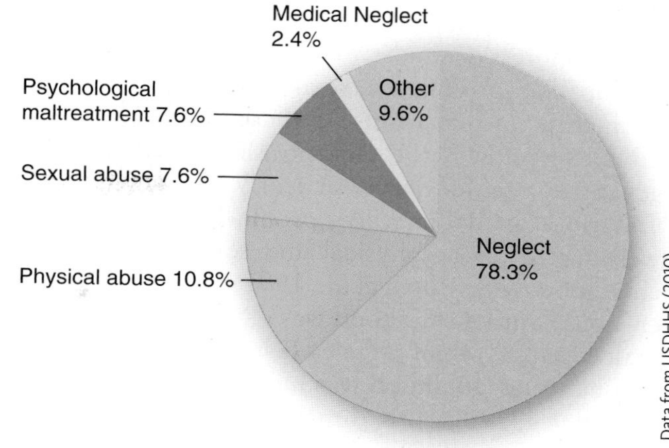

● **FIGURE 14.2** | Types of child maltreatment by percentage. "Other" forms of maltreatment include abandonment, threats of harm to the child, and congenital drug addiction. (Note that the percentages total more than 100% because children may have suffered from more than one type of maltreatment.)

Prevalence and Context

When the *battered child syndrome* (the early term for physical abuse) was first described in the early 1960s, it was believed that this phenomenon applied to fewer than 300 children in the United States (Kempe, Silverman, Steele, Droegenmueller, & Silver, 1962). Today, state child protective services agencies investigate close to 3.5 million suspected cases of child abuse and neglect each year, of which about one-third are confirmed (USDHHS, 2010).

Incidence of Abuse and Neglect in North America

Almost one million children in the United States are substantiated victims of child maltreatment each year, resulting in a rate of 10.1 per 1,000 children in the population (USDHHS, 2010). Incidence rates of maltreatment in Canada and the United Kingdom are somewhat higher than the U.S., about 14 per 1,000 children (Public Health Agency of Canada, 2010; National Society for the Prevention of Cruelty to Children, 2011). (Canada's and the United Kingdom's higher rates compared to the United States are likely due to differences in study procedures and definitions, and greater inclusion of exposure to domestic violence and emotional maltreatment in their incidence studies [N. Trocmé, personal communication, November 21, 2011].)

● Figure 14.2 shows the percentages of each subtype of abuse and neglect, based on U.S. data. As shown, child neglect (including medical neglect) continues to be a worrisome problem, accounting for four out of five documented cases of maltreatment in the United States. Physical abuse (11%), sexual abuse (7.6%), psychological maltreatment (7.6%), and other forms of maltreatment (e.g., abandonment or threats of harm, 9.6%) make up the remaining substantiated cases. In addition, about 1 in 4 of these children suffered more than one form of maltreatment.

Interestingly, both sexual abuse and physical abuse cases declined considerably since 1992 (Jones, Finkelhor, & Halter, 2006). Although no one knows for sure, this decline most likely stems from several factors occurring over the last 20 years. Economic improvement began in the early 1990s, along with more law enforcement and child protection resources and more aggressive prosecution and incarceration policies (however, the impact of subsequent economic decline in 2008 is not reflected in these numbers). North America also has seen more public awareness about abuse and neglect, and more forms of treatment have become available. Rates of child neglect, on the other hand, have remained fairly stable, perhaps because it has not received the same level of policy attention and public awareness as sexual and physical abuse (Finkelhor, 2008; Finkelhor & Jones, 2006).

Incidence of child maltreatment also can be estimated from large-scale community or nationwide surveys that represent societal views, and which avoid some factors that may inhibit children or adults from reporting maltreatment to officials. Consequently, asking representative samples of parents to respond anonymously about their various child-rearing methods results in much higher estimates of the number of children at risk of maltreatment each year than the estimates provided by official reports. Based on telephone interviews with over 3,500 families in the United States in both 1985 and 1995, about 10% of parents admitted using some method in the past year to control their child that amounted to a severe violent act, such as hitting with an object, pushing, or scalding their child (Straus & Gelles, 1986; Straus & Stewart, 1999).

Lifetime prevalence estimates of maltreatment are derived by asking adults if they experienced particular forms of maltreatment as children. These studies have been conducted almost exclusively on sexual abuse, perhaps because discrete sexual acts are more readily defined than other forms of abuse and neglect. A notable exception is the Ontario Health Supplement, a general population survey of nearly 10,000 residents of Ontario, Canada, in which people 15 years and older were asked about physical and sexual abuse during childhood (MacMillan et al., 1997). A history of physical abuse during childhood was reported more often by males (31.2%) than females (21.1%), whereas sexual abuse during childhood was more commonly reported by females (12.8%) than males (4.3%). Keep in mind that these figures are estimates only. Retrospective reports of childhood experiences are inexact, and it is rarely possible to corroborate episodes of maltreatment to get precise accounts. Nevertheless, these incidence and prevalence data indicate a substantial problem that, until quite recently, was disregarded.

Characteristics of Victimized Children

Improvements in data collection methods over the past decade indicate that child maltreatment affects more vulnerable or disadvantaged children disproportionately, as indicated by age, sex, and racial differences. Child maltreatment occurs at all ages, but there is correspondence between certain types of maltreatment and children's ages. Younger children, who have the greatest need for care and supervision, are the most common victims of abuse and neglect, which corresponds to the emergence of their greater independence and to parental conflict during this developmental period. Sexual abuse, in contrast, is more common among the older age groups (> age 12). Other than for sexual abuse, the rate of victimization is inversely related to the age of the child (USDHHS, 2010).

Child maltreatment affects boys and girls almost equally except for sexual abuse, where girls account for about 80% of the reported victims (USDHHS, 2010). Moreover, the dynamics of sexual abuse differ considerably for boys and girls. Although boys as well as girls are more likely to be abused by someone they know and trust than by a stranger, boys are more likely to be abused by male nonfamily members—camp staff, teachers, scout leaders—whereas girls are more likely to be sexually abused by male family members. This finding suggests different patterns of vulnerability for boys and girls, and has implications for safety and prevention (Wolfe, Jaffe, Jette, & Poisson, 2003).

In terms of racial characteristics, the majority of substantiated victims of maltreatment are white (44%), African American (22%), or Hispanic (21%). For all racial categories except Native Hawaiian and Pacific Islander, the largest percentage of victims suffered from neglect. African American children, American Indian or Alaska Native children, and children of multiple races had the highest rates of victimization at 15.1, 11.6, and 12.4 per 1,000 children (respectively) of the same race or ethnicity. White children and Hispanic children both had rates of approximately 8 per 1,000 children of the same race or ethnicity, whereas Asian American children had the lowest rate (2.0 per 1,000 children of the same race or ethnicity; USDHHS, 2010). These racial differences have been consistent over many years, and are believed to be a function of the disproportionate impact of poverty, stress, and disadvantage on minority children and their families (Jones et al., 2006).

Characteristics of Family and Perpetrator

Family characteristics remind us of the cultural and social forces that shape child-rearing methods. Most significant is the well-established finding that maltreatment is more common among the poor and disadvantaged (although it also occurs among higher-income families). This connection is not likely due to a reporting bias, because it has remained constant for the past 35 years, despite increased awareness and reporting (Wekerle et al., 2006). What it does imply, however, is that the economically based context of maltreatment—restricted child care opportunities, crowded and unsafe housing, and lack of health care, to name a few conditions—is a powerful backdrop to the high incidence rates.

Family structure also is connected to the probability of child maltreatment. Children living with a single parent with a live-in partner are at significantly greater risk of all types of maltreatment. Maltreatment—especially physical and educational neglect—is more common in larger families, where additional children in the household mean additional tasks, responsibilities, and demands.

Who commits these acts? It shouldn't surprise you that 80% of the victims are maltreated by one or both parents, across all forms of maltreatment. However, there are important exceptions, as well as key sex differences in the nature of abuse or neglect. Nearly 50% of sexually abused children are abused by persons other than parents or parent figures, compared with only a fraction in other categories. Child neglect is committed predominantly—about 90% of the time—by mothers, which fits with the fact that mothers and mother substitutes tend to be primary caregivers. In contrast, sexual abuse is committed more often—also about 90% of the time—by males, about 50% of whom are the child's father or father figure. While males are the dominant perpetrators in sexual abuse, for child maltreatment in general the most common perpetrator pattern overall is a female parent acting alone, who typically is younger than 30 years of age (USDHHS, 2010).

Cross-Cultural Comparisons

How do children fare in other Western countries and in other countries around the world? Although it is difficult to draw comparisons between countries because of the differences in defining and reporting cases of child maltreatment, what little is known about the prevalence of maltreatment in other countries suggests that physical and sexual abuse are at epidemic proportions in many societies worldwide.

International organizations estimate that 40 million children, by the age of 14, are victims of child abuse and neglect annually around the world (United Nations, 2006; World Health Organization, 2004), confirming suspicions that child abuse is found in all societies and is almost always a highly guarded secret. Studies in which children or young adults were interviewed about their childhood experiences further confirm that rates of child sexual abuse in other Western societies are comparable to those rates in North America, which cluster around 20% for females, and 8% for males (Finkelhor, 2008; Pereda, Guilera, Forns, & Gómez-Benito, 2009; Stoltenborgh, van IJzendoorn, Euser, & Bakermans-Kranenburg, 2011).

SECTION SUMMARY

Prevalence and Context

- Child abuse and neglect are at epidemic proportions in the United States, Canada, and many other countries worldwide.
- Physical neglect is most common among younger children.
- Physical and emotional abuse are most common among toddlers, preschoolers, and young adolescents.
- Sexual abuse affects children, mostly girls, from about age three on.
- Poverty and single parenthood are the most prominent demographic features of abuse and neglect.

Developmental Course and Psychopathology

The child trapped in an abusive environment is faced with formidable tasks of adaptation. She must find a way to preserve a sense of trust in people who are untrustworthy, safety in a situation that is unsafe, control in a situation that is terrifyingly unpredictable, power in a situation of helplessness.

—From Herman (1992)

This statement by prominent clinician and researcher Judith Herman captures the essence of the world of maltreated children and youth. Abuse and neglect are more than physical pain and transitory fear; to a child or adolescent, these events often represent threats to their emerging sense of self, their world, and their feelings of safety and well-being. We return to Rosita's case to illustrate this dramatic impact:

ROSITA

Feeling Trapped

At age 6, Rosita was brought to the hospital following two suicidal/self-harm gestures. While camping, she wrapped a rope that hung from a tree around her neck and her foster mother grabbed it and untangled it. She did not appear to be hurt, but she sat and cried for a long time while her foster mother cuddled her.

"Rosita is preoccupied with themes of death and self-harm, in her drawings, stories at school, and even with her classmates," her teacher explained. "She has problems making friends, because she acts silly when she tries to join their games. More than once she's asked other children to touch her vagina, and she has tried to put her finger in one girl's vagina. Needless to say, this has alarmed other parents and teachers. But she's such a needy child—she'll go from a temper tantrum to becoming clingy in a matter of seconds."

Rosita's life became more settled, and by age 9 her school performance had improved noticeably. However, at age 15, her psychological condition rapidly grew worse. She made suicide attempts and began cutting her arm with glass and other sharp objects. When I saw her following her release from the hospital, she was very distraught, and felt unloved and abandoned. Her feelings of depression and anxiety were evident: "I'll jump or get really scared, for no reason. I just want to go somewhere and hide, and get away from people," she explained. "I can't trust anybody except for my friend Mary—but even she thinks I'm weird when I get like this. It's like I'm trapped or caught, and can't get away." My interview went on to reveal Rosita's sleeping problems and her constant crying and sadness.

Rosita had never forgotten the abuse she experienced as a child, and sometimes had intrusive reminders of what happened. "I feel tied in a knot, and I feel like I'm going crazy or something. That's when I might start cutting on my arm or something, just to feel like I'm not dreaming, that I'm real." Sometimes she even blamed herself for losing her family years ago, explaining that "no matter how bad it was I wish no one had ever found out, because it wasn't worth all the pain I'm going through." (Based on authors' material)

Rosita lacks a sense of self-esteem and a sense of the future. She is very vulnerable to recurring victimization because she lacks self-awareness and has limited self-protection skills. She feels a terrible loss and ambivalence over her family, sometimes blaming herself for the abuse or wishing it had never been discovered. Although she is a verbal and insightful young woman, she often is overcome with worries, anxiety, fear, and emotional distress related to her current circumstances.

Resilience and Adaptation

What happens to the development of children who were abused or neglected during their important formative years? Normal development follows a predictable, organized course (see Chapter 1), beginning with the child's mastery of physiological regulation (eating, sleeping), and continuing throughout the development of higher skills, such as problem solving and peer relationships. However, under abnormal and unusual circumstances, especially abuse and neglect, predictability and organization are disrupted and thrown off course, which results in developmental failure and limited adaptation.

Maltreated children not only must face acute and unpredictable parental outbursts or betrayal, but also must adapt to environmental circumstances that pose developmental challenges. These influences include the more dramatic events, such as marital violence and separation of family members, as well as the mundane but important everyday activities that may be disturbing or upsetting, such as unfriendly interactions, few learning opportunities, and a chaotic lifestyle. Children who are sexually abused undergo pronounced interruptions in their developing view of themselves and the world that result in significant emotional and behavioral changes, indicative of their attempts to cope with such events. Because the source of stress and fear is centralized in their family, children who are maltreated are challenged regularly to find ways to adapt that pose the least risk, and offer maximum protection and opportunity for growth (Collishaw et al., 2007).

Child maltreatment, like other forms of adversity and trauma during childhood, does not affect each child in a predictable or consistent fashion. To the contrary, the impact of maltreatment depends not only on the severity and chronicity of the specific events, but also on how the events interact with the child's individual and family characteristics. Without proper support and assistance, young children who initially may have achieved normal developmental milestones can show a dramatic downturn in their developmental progress as a result of chronic or acute maltreatment and similar types of stress (Crooks & Wolfe, 2007). Consequently, their core developmental processes are impaired, which

© Donna Ferrato

Young Jason never goes unarmed. Grabbing his plastic gun and rubber knife, he tells his mother, "If daddy comes, I'll be able to stop him."

results in emotional and behavioral problems ranging from speech and language delays to criminal behavior.

Children may be protected, in part, from the effects of maltreatment or witnessing parental violence by a positive, supportive relationship with at least one important and consistent person in their lives who provides support and protection, such as other family members or peers (Haskett, Nears, Ward, & McPherson, 2006; Skopp, McDonald, Jouriles, & Rosenfield, 2007). Paradoxically, this person also could be a maltreating parent, a notion that at first may be hard to comprehend. However, many maltreated children do not think of their parents as abusive; rather, they adapt to their own experiences as best as possible. Loyalty to one's parents is a powerful emotional tie—so from the child's point of view, a parent who at times yells, hits, and castigates, may at other times be a source of connection, knowledge, or love (Wekerle & Wolfe, 2003). In addition to the importance of supportive relationships, personality characteristics such as positive self-esteem and sense of self also are related to fewer negative outcomes among maltreated children (Afifi & MacMillan, 2011).

Simply stated, if children are raised in environments where love and positive attention are expressed rarely or inconsistently, the children have no other standard of comparison. Their natural inclination is to distort their view of their parents as being more like other children's parents—positive, well-meaning, and all-important. It may be more adaptive for children to focus on what their parents provide, rather than what they don't provide, because this focus will allow them to seem normal and accepted themselves. This view has important implications for intervention efforts, because some interventions, such as removing children from their families, can become another source of stress and disruption, with undesired side effects (Wilson & Melton, 2002).

Developmental Consequences

Understanding the major consequences of the maltreatment of children requires consideration of the basic developmental processes that are impaired or delayed among this population. We begin by focusing on early attachment and affect regulation—the building blocks of the development of important self-regulatory and interpersonal competencies.

Early Attachment and Emotion Regulation

Episodes of child abuse and neglect, whether chronic or sporadic, can disrupt the important process of attachment, and can interfere with children's ability to seek comfort and to regulate their own physiological and emotional processes. As a result, maltreated children are more likely than other children to show an absence of an organized attachment strategy (Baer & Martinez, 2006).

Parent–child attachment and the home climate play a critical role in emotion regulation, another early developmental milestone. **Emotion regulation** refers to the ability to modulate or control the intensity and expression of feelings and impulses, especially intense ones, in an adaptive manner (Kim & Cicchetti, 2010). Without consistent stimulation, comfort, and routine to aid in the formation of secure attachment, maltreated infants and toddlers have considerable difficulty establishing a reciprocal, consistent pattern of interaction with their caregivers. Instead, they show a pattern described as *insecure–disorganized attachment*, characterized by a mixture of approach and avoidance, helplessness, apprehension, and a general disorientation (Barnett, Ganiban, & Cicchetti, 1999; Cyr, Euser, Bakermans-Kranenburg, & Van Ijzendoorn, 2010). The lack of a secure, consistent basis for relationships places maltreated children at greater risk of falling behind in their cognitive and social development, and can result in problems regulating their emotions and behavior with others. Emotions serve as important internal monitoring and guidance systems, designed to appraise events as beneficial or dangerous, and provide motivation for action.

Because emotions provide important signals about our internal and external worlds, children must learn to interpret and respond to them appropriately. Most children learn this naturally through the emotional expressions and explanations given by their caregivers. Maltreated children, on the other hand, live in a world of emotional turmoil and extremes, making it difficult for them to understand, label, and regulate their internal states (Shipman et al., 2007). Expressions of affect, such as crying or signals of distress, may trigger disapproval, avoidance, or abuse, so maltreated youngsters tend to inhibit their emotional expression and regulation, and remain more fearful and on alert. Similarly, they show increased attention to anger- and threat-related signals such as facial expressions, and less attention to other emotional expressions (Masten et al., 2008; Shackman, Shackman, & Pollak, 2007). When a new situation that involves a stranger or peer triggers emotional reactions, they do not have the benefit of a caring smile or words from a familiar adult to assure them that things are okay (El-Sheikh & Erath, 2011).

Difficulties modulating emotions can be expressed as depressive reactions as well as intense angry outbursts. Accordingly, as maltreated children grow older and face new situations involving peers and other adults, poor emotional regulation becomes more and more problematic, resulting in unusual and self-harmful behaviors, such as Rosita's attempts to cut herself (Mironova et al., 2011). Over time, this inability to regulate emotions is associated with internalizing disorders, such as depression and fearfulness, as well as externalizing disorders, such as hostility, aggression, and various forms of acting-out (Brensilver, Negriff, Mennen, & Trickett, 2011; Teisl & Cicchetti, 2008).

Neurobiological Development

Neuroscientists have connected the behavioral signs of poor emotion regulation among maltreated children to alterations in the developing brain, resulting in abnormalities in their ability to manage stress (Danese et al., 2011). Studies with maltreated children and adults with a history of childhood abuse show long-term alterations in the hypothalamic–pituitary–adrenal (HPA) axis and norepinephrine systems, which have a pronounced effect on one's responsiveness to stress (McCrory, De Brito, & Viding, 2010). Brain areas implicated in the stress response, which can lead to long-term mental health problems, include the hippocampus (involved in learning and memory), the prefrontal cortex, and the amygdala (Cicchetti, Rogosch, Howe, & Toth, 2010; Nunes, Watanabe, Morimoto, Moriya, & Reiche, 2010; Roth & Sweatt, 2011).

In effect, acute and chronic forms of stress associated with maltreatment may cause changes in brain development and structure from an early age (Danese et al., 2011). The neuroendocrine system is designed to handle sudden stressful events by releasing cortisol to produce a fight-or-flight response (see Chapter 2). However, after prolonged and unpredictable stressful episodes associated with all forms of child abuse and neglect, cortisol levels become depleted and the feedback systems that control hormone levels in the brain may not function correctly. Stress floods the brain with cortisol; the brain, in turn, resets the threshold at which cortisol is produced, so that ultimately it circulates at a dramatically low level. As a result, the neuroendocrine system becomes highly sensitive to stress (Davies, Sturge-Apple, Cicchetti, Manning, & Zale, 2009; Nunes et al., 2010). These neurobiological changes that occur in response to untoward early-life stress partially may account for the psychiatric problems that emerge throughout the lives of maltreated children, as described in the following section.

Emerging View of Self and Others

As normal development progresses, regulation of affect and behavior becomes less dependent on the caregiver and more and more autonomous (parents often use the vernacular expression, "terrible twos"). Toddlers' developing self-regulation is now applied to new situations, which further strengthens their emerging view of themselves and others. Importantly, children form complex mental representations of people, relationships, and the world during this developmental period. Their emerging view of themselves and their surroundings is fostered by healthy parental guidance and control that invoke concern for the welfare of others. Because these opportunities are seldom available to maltreated children, emotional and behavioral problems are more likely to appear as a result of their maladaptive view of themselves and others.

Representational models of oneself and others are significant because they contain experience, knowledge, and expectations that carry forward to new situations (Cicchetti & Lynch, 1995). For example, consider how a child's internalized belief that "my mother is usually there for me when I need her" or that "I am loved and worthy of love" shapes his basic beliefs about himself and others, and how these ideas reflect a sense of well-being and connection. Maltreated children, in contrast, often lack these core positive beliefs about themselves and their world. Instead, they may develop negative representational models of themselves and others based on a sense of inner "badness," self-blame, shame, or rage, all of which further impair their ability to regulate their affective responses (Simon, Feiring, & McElroy, 2010; Valentino, Cicchetti, Rogosch, & Toth, 2008). One male survivor of child sexual abuse explains this feeling of inferiority:

> I could not see anybody loving me. I could not see anybody liking me or wanting to be with me, I could not see myself as significant to the point where I would actually be in a relationship with someone else. (quoted in Lisak, 1994, p. 542)

Feelings of powerlessness and betrayal often are described by children and adults who have been victims of maltreatment—feelings that become salient components of their self-identity (van der Kolk, 2007; Wolfe et al., 2003). In a situation of powerlessness, the child's will, desire, and sense of self-efficacy are thwarted and rebuked, which is often linked to fears, worries, and depression. In the words of one survivor, "It's as if the world was evil, it's coming to get you, and you could do almost nothing to defend from it" (Lisak, 1994, p. 533). **Betrayal** involves the degree to which the child feels the perpetrator gained his confidence through manipulation and coercion, as well as the position of trust or authority held by the perpetrator. As a consequence, the child's emotional needs may be compromised by intense and contradictory feelings of the need for closeness and the fear of it.

One's sense of personal power or self-efficacy can be undermined by physical and verbal abuse, as well as by physical and emotional neglect; this maltreatment devalues the child as a person. Feelings of betrayal also can challenge an individual's sense of self, because the person the individual depended on violated that trust and confidence. Such feelings may not be identified until years later, once the individual reaches an age whereby he or she can recognize this betrayal dynamic as the source of feelings of self-blame, guilt, and powerlessness (Freyd, DePrince, & Gleaves, 2007; L. M. Williams, 2003).

The following are typical of children's and adolescents' descriptions of having their sense of safety and self-esteem undermined by the sexual abuser (Sas et al., 1993, p. 68):

> I was scared that if someone else found out, that my father would believe that we had told and that he would kill our mother.

> I was embarrassed, worried, especially as I was a boy, I was being molested by a man. I thought people might think I was gay or my parents might not believe me.

Emotional reactions elicited by harsh punishment or sexual exploitation require the child to search for an answer to a fundamental question concerning responsibility and blame: "Why did this happen to me?" The previous quotes about self-esteem illustrate how some sexually abused children feel responsible for failing to recognize the abuse, for participating in the abuse, for causing their families' reactions to disclosure, for failing to avoid or control the abuse, and for failing to protect themselves. Rather than acknowledge or believe that one's own parents or a trusted adult could be the person at fault, some maltreated children may ascribe non-malevolent intentions to the offender that can then be used to explain and justify to others their family problems and disruption. Shifting the blame to themselves or to situational factors that are less important than one's own parents provides a more acceptable explanation (McGee, Wolfe, & Olson, 2001). One male survivor describes this attribution of blame: "I had to make sense out of what was going on. And the sense I made out of this was that I'm not really a good person. There's something different about me and something wrong" (Lisak, 1994, p. 541).

Girls and boys tend to differ in the ways they process and express their turmoil. Maltreated girls tend to show more internalizing signs of distress, such as shame and self-blame; boys, on the other hand, tend to show heightened levels of physical and verbal aggression (Wekerle, MacMillan, Leung, & Jamieson, 2008).

Emotional and Behavioral Problems

It comes as no surprise that the relationships maltreated children have with their peers and teachers typically mirror the models of relationships they know best. Instead of a healthy sense of autonomy and self-respect, their models of relationships have elements of being a victim and a victimizer—those who rule and those who submit—and during interactions with peers, maltreated children may alternate between being the aggressor and being the victim (Dodge, Pettit, & Bates, 1994a). Their strategies for adaptation, such as hypervigilance and fear, evolve to become highly responsive to threatening or dangerous situations. These strategies conflict, however, with the new challenges of school and peer groups. As a result, some maltreated children, especially those with histories of physical abuse and neglect, may be more distracted by aggressive stimuli, and misread the intentions of their peers and teachers as being more hostile than they actually are (Dodge et al., 1994a).

The development of empathy and social sensitivity for others during the preschool years are prerequisites for the development of positive, reciprocal peer relationships. Physically abused and neglected children, however, show less skill at recognizing or responding to distress in others, since this has not been their experience (Smetana et al., 1999). Observational studies of the behavior of maltreated children and their nonmaltreated peers reveal that physically abused children engaged in more stealing behavior, and neglected children engaged in more cheating behavior and less rule-compatible behavior (Cicchetti & Valentino, 2006; Koenig, Cicchetti, & Rogosch, 2004).

This is how one 2-year-old boy, who had been physically abused by his parents, responded to a crying child:

> He then turned away from her to look at the ground and while looking at the ground began vocalizing "Cut it out! Cut it out!" with increasing agitation, each time speaking more loudly and more quickly. He patted the child on the back, but when this disturbed her he retreated from her, hissing and baring his teeth. He again began patting her on the back, but this time his patting turned into beating. He continued beating the little girl despite her screams. (Main & Goldwyn, 1984, p. 207)

Thomas, an abused 1-year-old, exhibits disturbing signs of fearful distress when he hears a child crying in the distance:

> Suddenly, Thomas becomes a statue. His smile fades and his face takes on a look of distress also. He sits very still, his hand frozen in the air. His back is straight, and he becomes more and more tense as the crying continues. . . . The (distant) crying diminishes. Suddenly Thomas is back to normal, calm, mumbling, and playing in the sand. (Main & George, 1985, p. 410)

These quotes illustrate a lack of social sensitivity as well as a disorganized, victim–victimizer reaction to peer distress. The non-abused children in these studies typically showed concern or attempted to provide comfort to the distressed child, but not one maltreated child exhibited a concerned response at witnessing the distress of another toddler. Maltreated children not only failed to show concern, but actively responded to distress in others with fear, physical attack, or anger. Can you see the continuity between their own experiences and their behavior with peers?

The general nature of maltreated children's peer relationships can be organized into two prominent themes (Cicchetti & Lynch, 1995). First, maltreated children, particularly physically abused children and those who witness violence between parents, are more physically and verbally aggressive toward their peers. They are more likely to respond with anger and aggression equally both to friendly overtures from peers and to signs of distress in other children (Shields & Cicchetti, 1998; Teisl & Cicchetti, 2008). As a result, they are less popular and have atypical social networks marked by aggression and negative attention-seeking.

Given their propensity to mistakenly attribute hostile intent to others and their lack of empathy and social skill, it is not surprising that abused and neglected children are rejected by their peers (Anthonysamy & Zimmer-Gembeck, 2007; Kim & Cicchetti, 2010).

The second theme is that maltreated children, especially neglected children, withdraw from and avoid peer interactions. Neglected preschool and school-age children tend to remain isolated and passive during opportunities for free play with other children, and seldom display overtures of affection or initiate play with their mothers or peers (Hildyard & Wolfe, 2002; McSherry, 2007).

Children with histories of physical abuse or neglect stand out as having the most severe and wide-ranging problems in school and interpersonal adjustment. They perform worse than other children on standardized tests of reading, language, and math (Mills et al., 2011). They are described by teachers unaware of their backgrounds as lacking maturity and academic readiness. These descriptions indicate problems completing schoolwork, lack of initiative, overreliance on teachers for help, and behavior that is both aggressive toward and withdrawn from their peers (Egeland, Yates, Appleyard, & van Dulmen, 2002). This pattern of poor adjustment often persists, contributing to higher rates of physical and mental health problems in later adolescence and adulthood (Clark, Thatcher, & Martin, 2010; Trickett, Negriff et al., 2011).

Longitudinal studies of girls who were sexually abused in childhood or early adolescence reveal deleterious effects across a host of biopsychosocial domains (the impact on boys has not been well established to date). The most illustrative of these studies followed a sample of sexually abused girls for 23 years, documenting problems and concerns at home, school, and with peers. The pattern and extent of harm to these girls was substantial: compared to a non-abused comparison group of girls, those with histories of sexual abuse had significant neurodevelopmental differences in their responses to stress; earlier onsets of puberty; greater cognitive deficits; more mental health problems (especially depression and PTSD); higher rates of obesity; and more major illnesses and healthcare utilization. They also had higher rates of dropping out of high school; self-mutilation; physical and sexual revictimization; teen motherhood; drug and alcohol abuse; and domestic violence in adulthood (Trickett, Noll et al., 2011). These findings, along with those pertaining to physical abuse and neglect, speak strongly to the need for greater prevention and early intervention, as we discuss at the end of this chapter.

As a useful summary of the preceding information, Table 14.2 shows the major dimensions of development that are affected by physical abuse, neglect, and sexual abuse.

Psychopathology and Adult Outcomes

The body mends soon enough. The broken spirit, however, takes the longest to heal.

—Adult survivor of sexual abuse (Transcribed from *The Nature of Things with David Suzuki*, executive producer, Michael Alder for the Canadian Broadcasting Corporation, originally aired on October 6, 1994)

TABLE 14.2 | Range of Child Characteristics Associated with Physical Abuse, Neglect, and Sexual Abuse

Dimension of Development	Physical Abuse	Neglect	Sexual Abuse
Physical	Minor: Bruises, lacerations, abrasions Major: Burns, brain damage, broken bones	Failure-to-thrive symptoms: Slowed growth, immature physical development	Physical symptoms: Headaches, stomachaches, appetite changes, vomiting; gynecological complaints
Cognitive	Mild delay in areas of cognitive and intellectual functioning; academic problems; difficulties in moral reasoning	Mild delay in areas of cognitive and intellectual functioning; academic problems; difficulties in moral reasoning	No evidence of cognitive impairment; self-blame; guilt
Behavioral	Aggression; peer problems; "compulsive compliance"	Passivity; "hyperactivity"	Fears, anxiety, PTSD-related symptoms; sleep problems
Socioemotional	Social incompetence; hostile intent attributions; difficulties in social sensitivity	Social incompetence; withdrawal, dependence; difficulties in social sensitivity	Symptoms of depression and low self-esteem; "sexualized" behavior; behaviors that accommodate to the abuse (e.g., passive compliance; no or delayed disclosure)

Source: From "Child Maltreatment" by C. Wekerle and D. A. Wolfe, in E. J. Mash and R. A. Barkley (Eds.), *Child Psychopathology, 2nd Edition*, p. 644. Copyright © 2003 Guilford Press. Reprinted with permission.

The developmental disruptions and impairments that accompany child abuse and neglect set in motion a series of events that increase the likelihood of failure and future maladaptations. As stated earlier, not all maltreated children who face these developmental challenges will develop psychopathology—let alone the same form of psychopathology—but they are at a much greater risk for significant emotional and adjustment problems.

In general terms, adolescents and adults with histories of physical abuse and exposure to violence between parents are at increased risk to develop interpersonal problems marked by their own acts of aggression and violence, or violent victimization by others (Berlin, Appleyard, & Dodge, 2011; El-Sheikh & Erath, 2011). This relationship between being abused as a child and becoming abusive toward others as an adult is known as the **cycle-of-violence hypothesis**. Although victims of violence have a greater chance of becoming perpetrators of violence, we caution that this relationship is not inevitable and can be attenuated through early intervention (Berlin et al., 2011).

Persons with histories of sexual abuse, on the other hand, are more likely (than non-victims) to develop chronic impairments in self-esteem, physical health problems, and emotional and behavioral self-regulation (Hillberg, Hamilton-Giachritsis, & Dixon, 2011; Irish, Kobayashi, & Delahanty, 2010). As adulthood approaches, developmental impairments that stem from child sexual abuse can lead to more pervasive and chronic psychiatric disorders and health problems, including anxiety and panic disorders, depression, eating disorders, sexual problems, and personality disturbances (Chapman et al., 2007; Maniglio, 2009; Paras et al., 2009). As we see below, one of the more significant impairments many sexual abuse victims suffer stems from post-traumatic stress disorder (PTSD) and chronic mood and affect regulatory problems (Campbell, Greeson, Bybee, & Raja, 2008).

In the following section, we examine four prominent developmental outcomes of maltreatment—mood and affect disturbances, post-traumatic stress-related problems, sexual adjustment, and criminal and antisocial behavior—and whenever appropriate note the similarities and differences in the outcomes according to particular forms of abuse.

Mood and Affect Disturbances

The following comment is from an adult survivor of sexual abuse:

> I trusted him so I think that it was confusing that he was doing this to me. I think that when I got older I was afraid more often than I was confused. I was really afraid. I really didn't want him to come near me. I'd try to avoid the situation and try to pretend that I was asleep so that he wouldn't come in to the room or anything like that, but it never worked. I felt helpless, which gradually turned into hopelessness and despair. ("The body mends soon enough. The broken spirit, however, takes the longest to heal"—Adult survivor of sexual abuse. Transcribed from *The Nature of Things with David Suzuki*, executive producer, Michael Alder for the Canadian Broadcasting Corporation, originally aired on October 6, 1994.)

Some say that child maltreatment affects children to their very soul, since it disrupts and impairs so many significant childhood memories and experiences. Perhaps this is why symptoms of depression, emotional distress, and suicidal ideation are common among children with histories of physical, emotional, and sexual abuse (Crooks & Wolfe, 2007). On a more positive note, the causes of these symptoms sometimes can be avoided if children are provided with available support from non-offending family members, and are given opportunities to develop healthy coping strategies and social supports. If symptoms of depression and mood disturbance go unrecognized, however, they are likely to increase during late adolescence and adulthood, and can lead to life-threatening suicide attempts and self-mutilating behavior, especially among those sexually or physically abused since childhood (Fitzgerald et al., 2008; Mironova et al., 2011).

Similarly, teens with histories of maltreatment have a much greater risk of substance abuse that, in turn, increases the risk of other adjustment problems (Clark et al., 2010; Lansford, Dodge, Pettit, & Bates, 2010). Perhaps as a result of their chronic emotional pain, some teens and adults attempt to cope with unpleasant memories and current stressors by abusing alcohol and drugs, in a futile effort to reduce or avoid their distress. Substance abuse may also temporarily bolster self-esteem and reduce feelings of isolation. As we note in Chapter 13, child sexual abuse also can lead to eating disorders, such as anorexia nervosa and bulimia nervosa (Murray, Macdonald, & Fox, 2008).

wrangler/Shutterstock.com

Many women, as well as men, with histories of child sexual abuse face lifelong struggles in establishing close and trusting relationships

CELIA

Walled Away

"What I would end up doing was separating from the physical feeling and couldn't comprehend the physical pain and emotional sensation. The only word I can use now—I didn't have the word when I was five—the word I use now is rape, and the only way I could deal with that was I would separate into the wallpaper and the wallpaper was all different ballerinas and different poses and what I could see from them was that they didn't move. They were always smiling or they always had this look on their face and they couldn't be touched. They just stood still. So I would become this ballerina and I couldn't be touched and whatever he did to me I couldn't feel it because I was in the wall." ("The body mends soon enough. The broken spirit, however, takes the longest to heal"—Adult survivor of sexual abuse. Transcribed from *The Nature of Things with David Suzuki*, executive producer, Michael Adler, for the Canadian Broadcasting Corporation, originally aired on October 6, 1994.)

Post-Traumatic Stress-Related Problems

A significant number of men and women who have been subjected to severe physical or sexual abuse during childhood suffer long-term stress-related disorders that we describe in Chapter 7. Like Rosita, these adults may be haunted by intrusive thoughts or feelings of being trapped or, like Celia, they may dissociate or become emotionally numb, as they had done originally to escape from the pain and fear.

As many as half of victims of maltreatment involving sexual abuse or combined sexual and physical abuse meet criteria for post-traumatic stress disorder (PTSD) during childhood or adolescence (Masho & Ahmed, 2007; Scott, Wolfe, & Wekerle, 2003). The prevalence of PTSD among adults is equally disturbing: About one-third of the childhood victims of sexual abuse, physical abuse, or neglect meet criteria for lifetime PTSD (Koenen & Widom, 2009; Widom, 1999). The course of this disorder may begin during childhood with abuse-specific fears, such as fear of being alone and fear of men, as well as idiosyncratic fears related to specific events of abuse, such as fear of sleeping (van der Kolk, 2007). PTSD-related symptoms also are more likely to occur if the abuse was chronic and the perpetrator relied on a method of coercion or trickery to force compliance (L. Williams, 2003).

In reaction to emotional and physical pain from abusive experiences, children voluntarily or involuntarily may induce an altered state of consciousness known as **dissociation**, which can be adaptive when neither resistance nor escape are possible (Valentino et al., 2008). The process allows the victim to feel detached from the body or self, as if what is happening is not happening to him or her. Almost all people dissociate in minor ways, such as daydreaming, but abuse victims may rely on this form of psychological escape to the extent that profound disruptions to self and memory can occur (Macfie, Cicchetti, & Toth, 2001). Over time, this fragmentation of experience and affect can progress into borderline disorder, multiple personality disorder, or chronic pain (Briere, Hodges, & Godbout, 2010; Raphael & Widom, 2011; Widom, Czaja, & Paris, 2009).

Sexual Adjustment

As we noted earlier, sexual abuse also can lead to **traumatic sexualization**, in which a child's sexual knowledge and behavior are shaped in developmentally inappropriate ways. About 35% of preschoolers who have been sexually abused show age-inappropriate sexual behaviors, such as French-kissing, open masturbation, and genital exposure (Friedrich & Trane, 2002).

For some children, the offenders' means of enticement—gifts, privileges, affection, and special attention—teaches them that their own sexual behavior is a means to an end. Thus, the abused child may attempt to sexualize interpersonal relationships by indiscriminately hugging and kissing strange adults and children, something that is relatively uncommon among non-sexually abused children (Cosentino, Meyer-Bahlburg, Alpert, Weinberg, & Gaines, 1995). For others, however, sexual behavior is associated with strong emotions, such as fear, disgust, shame, and confusion. These feelings may translate into distorted views about the body and sexuality, in some cases leading to weight problems, eating disorders, poor physical health care, and physically self-destructive behaviors (Trickett, Noll et al., 2011).

Although sexualized behaviors are more common among younger abused children, they sometimes re-emerge during adolescence or young adulthood in the guise of promiscuity, prostitution, sexual aggression, and victimization of others (Tricket, Noll et al., 2011; Wilson & Widom, 2011). In fact, a history of any type of maltreatment among males is a significant risk factor for inappropriate sexual behaviors, alienation, and social incompetence during adolescence (Salter et al., 2003; Tewksbury, 2007). Women with childhood histories of sexual abuse, in particular, are more likely to report difficulties during adulthood related to sexual adjustment that range from low sexual arousal to intrusive flashbacks, disturbing sensations, and feelings of guilt, anxiety, and low self-esteem concerning their sexuality (Merrill, Guimond, Thomsen, & Milner, 2003).

Because their normal development of self-awareness and self-protection was severely compromised, adult survivors of child sexual abuse may become less capable of identifying risk situations or persons, or knowing how to respond to unwanted sexual or physical attention. Consequently, both men and women who were sexually abused as children are more likely to fall victim to further trauma and violence during adulthood, such as rape or domestic violence (McIntyre & Spatz Widom, 2011; Widom, Czaja, & Dutton, 2008; Wolfe, Francis, & Straatman, 2006).

Criminal and Antisocial Behavior

Does violence beget violence, as predicted by the cycle-of-violence hypothesis mentioned earlier? Although many persons convicted of heinous crimes and child abuse report significant histories of child abuse and neglect, most abused children do not go on to commit crimes. How do we reconcile this obvious, but complicated, connection between victim and victimizer roles?

Consider the developmental importance of adolescence. This developmental stage may represent a critical transition between being a victim of child maltreatment and the future likelihood of becoming abusive or being abused as an adult (Scott et al., 2003). Social dating, a favorite—and significant—adolescent pastime, can be a testing ground whereby one's knowledge and expectations about relationships are played out. Youths who have learned to adapt to violence and intimidation as a way of life, and who lack suitable alternative role models or experiences, are more likely to enter the social dating arena with inappropriate expectations about relationships.

Indeed, youths (girls as well as boys) who grew up in violent homes report more violence—especially verbal abuse and threats—toward their dating partners and toward themselves (Wolfe, Wekerle, Scott, Straatman, & Grasley, 2004). Dating violence that occurs during adolescence, when combined with a past history of violence in their own family, is a strong pre-relationship predictor of intimate violence during early adulthood and marriage (White & Widom, 2003). Thus, adolescence may be the middle stage, or initiation period, in the formation of a violent dynamic in intimate partnerships.

As we said, most children with maltreatment histories do not become violent offenders or child abusers as young adults. Nonetheless, there is a significant connection between these events and subsequent arrests as a juvenile or an adult, even among girls, or engaging in sexual and physical violence as a young adult, especially for males (Campbell et al., 2008; Lansford et al., 2007). A history of maltreatment is associated with an earlier mean age at first offense and a higher frequency of offenses, as well as a higher proportion of chronic offenders (Widom, 1989). A history of child physical abuse (but not neglect) was also associated with physical abuse of their offspring for about one in five mothers (Berlin et al., 2011).

Growing up with power-based, authoritarian methods—even if they don't result in physical injuries or identified maltreatment—can be toxic to relationship and social patterns. Many investigators believe that the prolonged and significant harm created by acts of child maltreatment by caregivers stems from emotional and psychological damages implicit in such acts. In other words, child maltreatment involves more than physical harm to a child. Such acts by caregivers undermine the child's basic sense of trust and safety, leading to lifelong struggles in their interpersonal relationships and sense of well-being (Wekerle, 2011; Wolfe & McIsaac, 2011). Even the amount of routine violence—frequently being hit with objects or physically punished—that one experiences as a child is significantly associated with violent delinquent behavior later in life (Straus, 2001). Box 14.1 describes a study that links childhood violence and adult violence.

SECTION SUMMARY

Developmental Course and Psychopathology

- Child maltreatment disrupts the normal course of development; therefore, maltreated children show a wide range of developmental problems.
- Children may be protected, in part, from the effects of maltreatment by a positive relationship with at least one important and consistent person who provides support and protection in their lives.
- Early child maltreatment can disrupt caregiver–infant attachment, thus interfering with the child's ability to seek comfort and to regulate his or her emotions and behavior.
- Emotion regulation refers to the ability to modulate or control the intensity and expression of feelings and impulses.
- By early childhood, maltreated children show deficits in sensitivity to others, including problems with empathy, interpersonal trust, and mood.
- Impairments in cognitive and moral development often lead to problems in social judgment, communication, and school performance, as well as problems in self-control and aggression toward peers.
- Child maltreatment can result in significant negative repercussions that persist into adulthood, including mood disturbances, PTSD, difficulties in sexual adjustment, and criminal and antisocial behavior.

Causes of Child Maltreatment

My father was frightened of his mother. I was frightened of my father and I am damn well going to see to it that my children are frightened of me.

—George V, King of England (1865–1936)

Why do some family relationships give rise to pain and conflict instead of support and harmony? There is no simple answer to this question, so we must rely on a combination of theory, clinical observations, and empirical findings. For physical abuse and neglect, an important consideration is that they are **relational disorders.** These forms of maltreatment occur most often during

BOX 14.1 A CLOSER LOOK

What Are the Long-Term Criminal Consequences of Child Maltreatment?

This important question has plagued the general public and the field, from therapists and educators to policy makers and criminal justice officials. Cathy Widom (1996) addressed this question by examining the criminal records of over 900 individuals subjected as children to physical or sexual abuse or neglect prior to age 12, along with a matched cohort of non-maltreated children. Both groups were followed into adolescence and early adulthood to determine whether they engaged in criminal or delinquent behavior as adolescents or adults.

The results are telling: Of the people who experienced any type of child maltreatment (physical abuse, sexual abuse, or neglect), 27% were arrested as juveniles, compared with 17% of their non-abused counterparts. The same pattern continued into adulthood: 42% of the abused/neglected group, compared with 33% of the controls, had arrest records as adults. Consistent with the cycle-of-violence hypothesis, those with histories of physical abuse (21%), neglect (20%), or both (16%) were particularly likely to be arrested for a violent crime (Maxfield & Widom, 1996).

One disturbing result is that women with histories of physical abuse and neglect were significantly more likely than non-maltreated women to be arrested for a violent act (7% vs. 4%, respectively), whereas this relationship was barely significant for men (26% vs. 22%, respectively). Notably, persons with histories of sexual abuse were no different from the other maltreated children in their rates of criminal offenses.

But what about sex crimes? Are persons who were sexually abused during childhood more likely to commit sexual offenses, as suggested by the backgrounds of the known sexual offenders? If all types of abuse and neglect are combined, the odds of being arrested for a sex crime were 2 times greater for maltreatment victims than for non-victims. However, if maltreatment backgrounds were broken down by type, only those with physical abuse and neglect backgrounds were associated with increased arrest for sex crimes; those with sexual abuse backgrounds were not (this finding remained when only male subjects were compared). Children who were sexually abused were about as likely as the controls to be arrested later for any sex crime, and less likely than victims of physical abuse and neglect (see the accompanying figure).

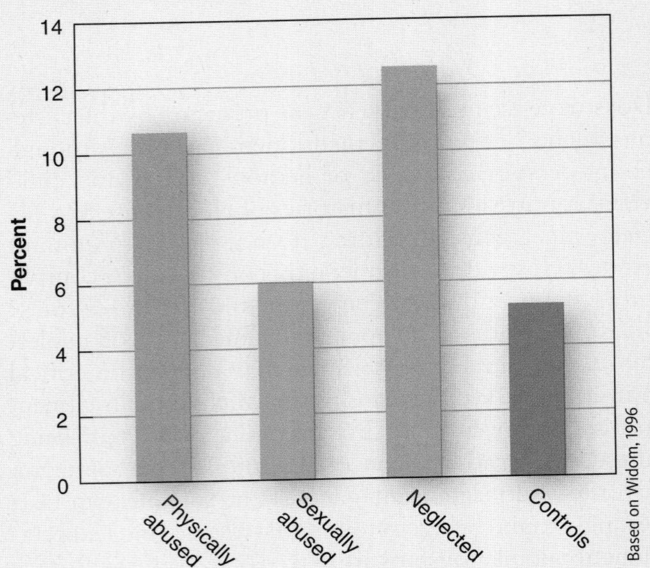

Sex crimes and maltreatment backgrounds

Thus, although any type of maltreatment puts victims at higher risk for criminal behavior, persons who were sexually abused in childhood are less likely than victims of physical abuse or neglect to commit a sex crime, and no more likely than demographically similar individuals.

periods of stressful role transitions for parents, such as the postnatal attachment period, the early childhood and early adolescence "oppositional" periods of testing limits, and the times of family instability and disruption (Wolfe, 1999). The caregivers' failure to provide nurturant, sensitive, available, and supportive care, especially during critical periods, is a fundamental feature of maltreatment.

Notwithstanding the critical role of the adult offender, abuse and neglect are rarely caused by a single risk factor. In addition, even though the risk signs and indicators are present, it is still very difficult to predict who will become abusive and who will not. Remember that child maltreatment is an event, not a uniform disorder; therefore, it is necessary to consider multiple causes that interact unpredictably. Like a tornado that arises from just the right conditions of heavy wind, atmospheric pressure, and open terrain, child maltreatment may emerge in any given family if the "right" conditions exist. These causal conditions stem largely from the interaction of child, familial, and cultural influences, but it is not possible to predict with precision where and when they will detonate (Cicchetti & Valentino, 2006).

Stress is one of those forces of nature and humankind that can convert static, stable conditions into dynamic, chaotic patterns. For example, physical abuse and neglect occur most often in the context of social and economic family deprivation, which can transform any predisposed, high-risk parents into abusive or neglectful ones. A greater degree of stress experienced by the abusive parent in the social environment will increase the probability that violence will surface as an attempt to gain control or cope with irritating, stressful events. In the case of neglect, stress may be so severe that parents withdraw from their childcare responsibilities.

Sexual abuse also is influenced by cultural and familial practices, as well as the dynamic forces of stress. However, unlike physical abuse and neglect, sexual abuse is primarily a premeditated act, during which the adult offender plays a purposeful and intentional role. The abuser plans ways to circumvent the child's natural resistance and self-protection, and controls the situation to avoid detection. In the following sections, we address these important causal issues in relation to psychological, social, and cultural dimensions. Maltreatment seldom is caused by severe forms of adult psychopathology (Wolfe, 1999). Fewer than 10% of maltreating parents have a primary psychiatric illness, such as paranoid schizophrenia or Factitious disorder by proxy (formerly Munchausen by proxy; see Box 14.2), that might cause them to harm a child. However, these parents with primary psychiatric illnesses are likely to have a history of learning and intellectual deficits and personality disorders that impede their day-to-day abilities to cope successfully with child-related and other stressors (Haskett, Smith Scott, & Sabourin Ward, 2004). Similarly, child sexual abuse perpetrators often show various personality disorders related to immaturity and interpersonal adjustment, but these disorders do not fit a homogeneous pattern (Fagan, Wise, Schmidt, & Berlin, 2002).

Physical Abuse and Neglect

BRENDA

Unhappy Childhood, Unhappy Motherhood

Milton's mother, Brenda, described her childhood as one of harsh discipline and physical abuse. "My father was an alcoholic, and when he was drunk he'd start picking on one of us—me, my older brother, or my mom," Brenda explained. "After being pushed around and beaten for so long, I took off and left home as soon as I was able to, when I was 15. I lived with friends until I was old enough to get welfare; then I hooked up with Milton's father. He was good to me at first, but it wasn't long until he started hitting me, just like my dad had done." In recounting her background, Brenda would sometimes grow quiet and sad, but this soon was overpowered by her efforts to force herself back to her complaints about her son. Her affect changed rapidly to one of hostility and annoyance, which spilled over into her actions with Milton. (Based on authors' material)

To many parents like Brenda, child-rearing is a difficult and aversive event that can escalate unpredictably into a sudden abusive incident, or more gradually turn into avoidance and neglect. Lacking experience and guidance in child-rearing and facing overwhelming stress, these parents cannot think of ways to best handle the situation. Instead, they succumb to the irritation of the moment—the child—and respond emotionally, without thinking.

Brenda's history and situation are very typical: How would she know how to raise her child, given her own childhood experiences? Many abusive and neglectful parents had little past or present exposure to positive

BOX 14.2 A CLOSER LOOK

Factitious Disorder by Proxy—The Deadly Game

After 22 months of unsuccessful diagnostic procedures in a hospital setting in England to determine the cause of a baby's breathing problem, staff concealed a video camera in the baby's hospital room, and a policewoman and a nurse jointly monitored the scene. The following events occurred:

Sixteen hours after the onset of video monitoring, the child was asleep in his cubicle with only his mother in attendance. She moved the chair away from the cot and lowered the cot sides. She then placed a soft garment (a T-shirt) on the bedding close to the child's face. Five minutes later she placed the garment over his nose and mouth and forced his head onto the mattress. He awoke immediately and struggled violently. After ten seconds the officer alerted the nurses who went into the cubicle. . . . In this first episode the police officer had intervened prematurely [by legal standards] because of her own distress at what she had seen. She decided to continue surveillance. Twenty minutes later, when the child was asleep on his side and the mother was again alone in the cubicle, she placed him in a supine position with his face upright and tucked his arms under the bedding. Ten minutes later she again applied the garment to his nose and mouth and forced his head onto the mattress. The child struggled violently. Forty-two seconds later the nursing staff was alerted by the police and went into the cubicle. . . . The mother claimed that he had woken screaming and that she was comforting him. (Schreier & Libow, 1993, p. 40)

Munchausen is the name of an 18th-century military mercenary who became famous for his wartime tales, suspected to be fabrications. As an adult disorder, Munchausen syndrome (now called Factitious disorder) refers to an intentional fabrication of illness. As a form of child abuse, it refers to physical and psychological harm either through direct attack by the parent (which can be life-threatening) or as a function of being subjected to painful and numerous medical assessment procedures. Although the disorder is more likely to involve the mother, the father may be a passive colluder and an uninvolved or absent parent. Little is known of this form of abuse, other than over 95% of known cases are perpetrated by women (Schreier, 2002).

Source: Schreier & Libow, 1993.

parental models and supports. Their own childhoods often were full of difficult, sometimes very traumatic, episodes of family violence, alcoholism, and harsh family circumstances related to frequent moves, unemployment, and poverty (Wolfe, 1999). As adults, they find daily living stressful and irritating, and prefer to avoid potential sources of support because it takes additional energy to maintain social relationships. Chronic physical ailments and a pervasive mood of discontent are common complaints, which are understandable in light of the circumstances and limited coping resources.

Offender Characteristics

Maltreatment doesn't happen accidentally, but it rarely is a planned or intentional act. One parent described it this way:

> I felt I was spinning out of control. Everywhere I went, things just built up and tension mounted. When I tried to quiet my kids down, I would start shouting. When I tried to run away, everything followed me like a trail of debris. I just wanted the craziness to stop.

Like a chain reaction, a tragic combination of events can cause some predisposed individuals to maltreat a child in their care. Most of these events have one factor in common: They pose added stress for an individual who has already reached his or her limit.

Because abuse and neglect usually occur in relation to child-rearing demands, it is not surprising that both neglectful and abusive parents interact with their children less often than other parents during everyday activities involving their children. In general, neglectful parents actively avoid interacting with their children, even when the child appropriately seeks attention, most likely because social interaction is unfamiliar and even unpleasant. Physically abusive parents, in contrast, tend to deliver a lot of threats or angry commands that exceed the demands of the situation when interacting with their children, rather than offer their children positive forms of guidance and praise (Azar & Wolfe, 2006; Wolfe, 1985).

Let's return to Brenda's situation and consider how her learning history, combined with her situational events, became a recipe for disaster. When her son misbehaved, she responded with a harsh combination of emotional and physical threats—the methods most familiar to her. At first, the physical punishment would stop Milton's misbehavior, but over time it led to a standoff, forcing her to increase the severity of her punishment, and the child to escalate his aversiveness to the punishment.

Her cognitive perceptions and distortion of events also played a significant role in this coercive process. The effect of **information-processing disturbances** causes maltreating parents to misperceive or mislabel typical child behavior in ways that lead to inappropriate responses and increased aggression (Berlin et al., 2011; Francis & Wolfe, 2008). They are unfamiliar with their roles as parents and with what is developmentally appropriate behavior for a child at a given age. Brenda believed not only that her son was able to understand—at age 4—what she was thinking and feeling, but also that he was able to put her needs ahead of his own.

Over time, Brenda thought Milton was misbehaving intentionally, presumably because, in her mind, he should have known better. ("I can never get him to listen—he's a troublemaker, and he knows how to push my buttons.") Some parents apply the same faulty reasoning to their own behavior as well, which results in lowered self-efficacy. ("I'm not a good mother; other mothers can get their children to do these things.") These unrealistic expectations and negative intent attributions can lead to greater punishment for child misbehavior, and less reliance on explanation and positive teaching methods (Azar & Wolfe, 2006). Children are seen as deserving of harsh punishment, and its use is rationalized as a way to maintain control. By now you can see where this process might end up.

Neglectful parents have received far less research attention than physically abusive ones, perhaps because omissions of proper caretaking behaviors are more difficult to describe and detect than commissions (Dubowitz & Bennett, 2007). As groups, the personality characteristics and lifestyle choices of abusive and neglectful parents overlap considerably. However, neglectful parents have more striking personality disorders and inadequate knowledge of children's needs, and they suffer more chronic patterns of social isolation than both abusive and non-maltreating parents. Furthermore, neglectful caregivers typically disengage when they are under stress, whereas abusive parents become emotionally and behaviorally reactive. Neglectful parents try to cope with the stress of child-rearing and related family matters through escape and avoidance, which can lead to severe consequences for the child and to higher risk of substance abuse and similar coping failures for the parents (Hildyard & Wolfe, 2007).

Like a tropical storm with an unpredictable course, a conflict between the parent and child suddenly can increase in intensity and turn into a damaging hurricane, or it simply can blow over. Negative arousal and emotions are highly "conditionable," so that salient events later can trigger the same feelings. This conditioning may occur gradually and build into uncontrollable outbursts, or occur suddenly during highly stressful, provocative episodes of conflict (Averill, 2001).

To illustrate, picture yourself trying to get your child ready for school each day, and going through the same frustrating chain of events: You're late for work and under pressure to get to a meeting, when your preschooler starts to fuss about wearing his boots or combing her hair. For all but a hearty few, this combination of stress and all-too-familiar child demands spells anger and frustration. While most of us manage to control our emotions to deal with the situation in the best possible way, parents who have deficits in child-rearing and information-processing skills may see the child as intentionally causing them to be late. Anger and arousal are powerful emotions, so rational problem solving quickly can give way to emotional and reflexive reactions.

Anger and rage are highly dependent on situational cues that usually stem from prior emotionally arousing events. In Brenda's case, certain "looks" that her son gave led her to believe that he wasn't going to comply. We discovered this interaction by videotaping the two of them playing together, and then having Brenda ask Milton to straighten up the room. We played the tape back and asked Brenda to tell us whenever she felt that Milton was doing something that bothered her. She stopped the tape at several different points, telling us that "he's giving me that look," or "I know what he's thinking—why should I have to do what she says?" At this point, Brenda's tone of voice would become more tense and frustrated, and her instructions to Milton more forceful and abrupt.

Although Brenda could acknowledge she was getting very angry, at first she was not able to interrupt this process and calm herself down. This demonstrates how parental arousal can be triggered by events, including past memories and current emotional tension, that may be highly specific to a particular parent–child relationship. This may lead, of course, to an overgeneralized—more angry, more aggressive—parental response, because the parent is responding impulsively to cues that previously have been associated with frustration and anger.

Child and Family Influences

Do certain child characteristics or behaviors increase the likelihood of abusive or neglectful care? Children have an uncanny ability to figure out what their parents are going to do before they actually do it, and they become amazingly accomplished at weighing the odds for desired outcomes. However, even though children might do things that are annoying, adults are fully responsible for abuse and neglect. No child—no matter how difficult to manage or how challenging to teach—ever deserves to be mistreated. Children's behavior or developmental limitations may increase the potential for abuse, but only if accompanied by the other critical factors noted previously.

With the important exception of girls being sexually abused more often than boys, no child characteristic, such as conduct problems, has been associated with the risk of maltreatment, once environmental and adult factors are controlled (USDHHS, 2010). Unintentionally, however, the child may still play a role in the continuation or escalation of abusive or neglectful relationships. For example, children with disabilities such as mental retardation or physical impairments are more likely to be abused than are their nondisabled peers (Hershkowitz & Lamb, 2007; Sullivan & Knutson, 2000).

The kind of coercive family interactions that we discuss in Chapter 6, with regard to aggressive children, frequently occur in abusive families (Stith et al., 2009; Wolfe, 1999). Physically abused or neglected children, for example, may learn from an early age that misbehaving often elicits a predictable parent reaction—even though it's negative—which gives the child some sense of control. If crying and clinging are the only ways to get a parent's attention, these behaviors may escalate in intensity over time, especially if the parent fails to provide appropriate child stimulation and control.

This type of coercive interaction explains why abusive incidents occur most often during difficult—but not uncommon—episodes of child behavior such as disobedience, fighting and arguing, accidents, and dangerous behavior, which may produce anger and tension in some adults. In contrast, circumstances surrounding incidents of neglect relate more to chronic adult inadequacy that spills over into daily family functioning (Stith et al., 2009). Neglected children's early feeding problems or irritability may place an increased strain on the parents' limited child-care abilities, again setting in motion an escalation in the child's dependency needs and demands, accompanied by further parental withdrawal (Drotar, 1999).

Family circumstances, most notably conflict and marital violence, also have a causal connection to child maltreatment. In about one-half of the families in which adult partners are violent toward one another, one or both parents also have been violent toward a child at some point during the previous year (Edleson, 1999). Domestic conflicts and violence against women most often arise during disagreements over child-rearing, discipline, and each partner's responsibilities in child care (Gewirtz & Edleson, 2007). Children may be caught in the cross fire between angry adults, or in some cases they may instigate a marital conflict by misbehaving or demanding attention. In either case, an escalating cycle of family turmoil and violence begins, whereby children's behavioral and emotional reactions to the violence create additional stress on the marital relationship, further aggravating an already volatile situation.

The physical and psychological consequences of violence, moreover, cause abused women to be less capable of responding to their children's needs, which again increases pressure on the family system. Tragically, not only do marital violence and family turmoil frighten and disturb children in a direct manner, but the resulting fallout from these events—ranging from changes in financial status and living quarters to loss of family unity and safety—prolongs the stress and thus the harmful impact on children's development (Jaffe et al., 2011).

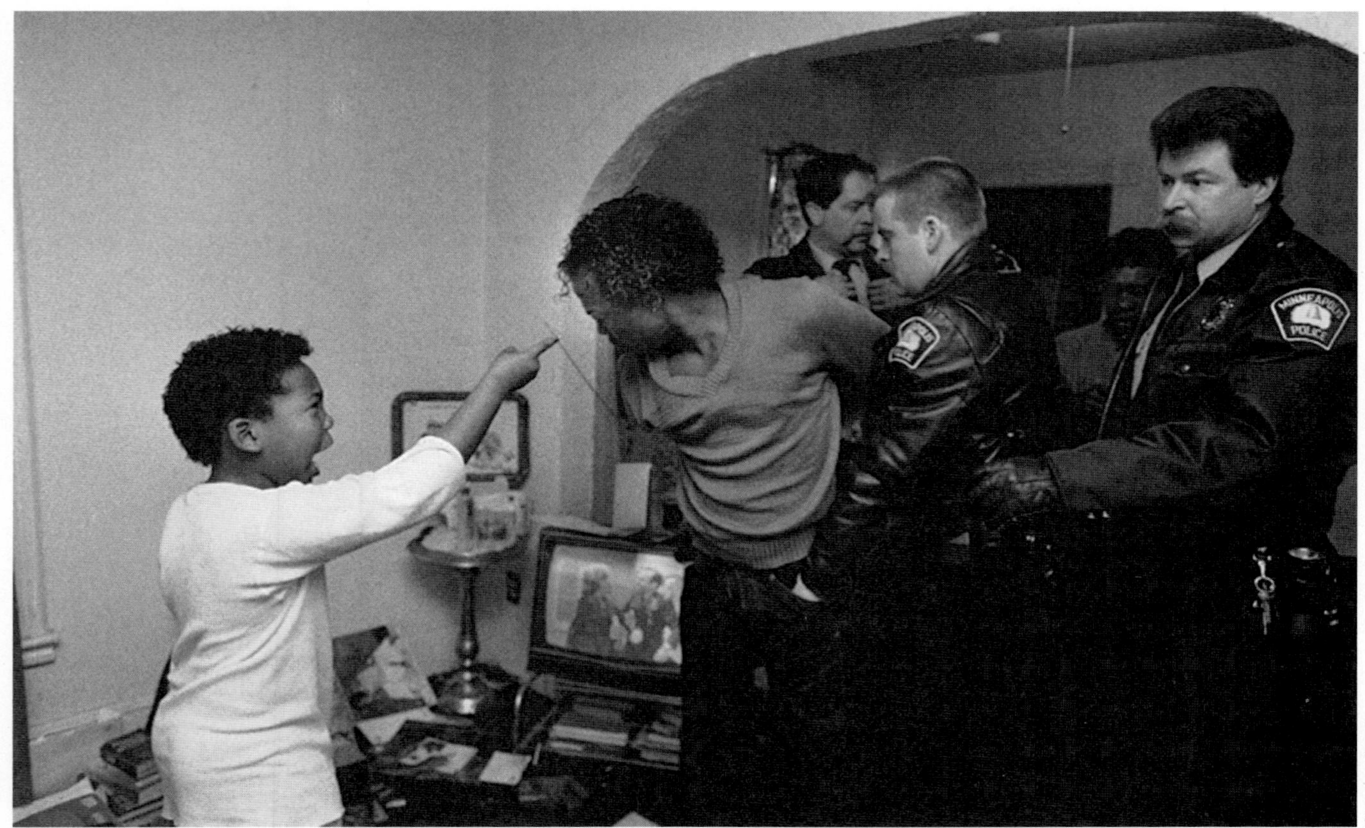

"I hate you! Never come back to my house," screamed an 8-year-old at his father as police arrested the man for attacking his wife.

An Integrated Model

In a dynamic process, parental and situational factors interact over time either to increase or decrease the risk of physical abuse or neglect (MacKenzie, Kotch, & Lee, 2011). ● Figure 14.3 depicts this dynamic process in relation to three hypothetical transitional stages. These stages suggest that maladaptive interaction patterns, like adaptive ones, do not develop simply because of the predilections of the parent or child. To the contrary, these patterns are the result of complex interactions between child characteristics, parental personality and style, the history of the parent–child relationship, and the supportive or non-supportive nature of the broader social context within which the family is embedded (Wolfe, 1999). This process, moreover, includes both destabilizing and compensatory factors that can influence the likelihood of abuse or neglect in a negative or positive fashion, respectively.

Sexual Abuse

Those seeking explanations for child sexual abuse have looked for evidence of deviant sexual histories of the adult offender, as well as environmental and cultural risk factors that play a role in the sexual exploitation of children. Yet, similar to physical abusers of children, sexual abusers are a very mixed group who defy all personality labels or psychiatric descriptors. Some are described as timid and unassertive, whereas others show a pattern of poor impulse control and domineering interpersonal style. Their common ground is a preference for sexual exploitation of children and adolescents who, because of their age and innocence, cannot consent to the activities or easily disclose the abuse to someone.

Offender Characteristics

Sexual abusers of children come from many walks of life, and they are seldom discernible based on personality traits, occupation, or age (other than the conclusion that the vast majority of offenders are male). As a group, these offenders are more likely to have significant social and relationship deficits, including social isolation; difficulty forming emotionally close, trusting relationships; and low self-esteem (Marshall, Serran, Marshall, & O'Brien, 2008). Comorbid psychiatric disorders and substance abuse also emerge as proximate risk factors for sexual abuse of children (Fagan et al., 2002).

Sexual offenders of children usually meet DSM-IV-TR criteria for **pedophilia**, defined as sexual activity or sexually arousing fantasies involving a prepubescent child (generally age 13 years or younger), by someone

Stage 1: Reduced tolerance for stress and disinhibition of aggression

Destabilizing factors	Compensatory factors
• Poor child-rearing preparation • Low sense of control and predictability • Stressful life events	• Supportive spouse • Socioeconomic stability • Success at work and school • Social supports and healthy models

Stage 2: Poor management of acute crises and provocation

Destabilizing factors	Compensatory factors
• Conditioned emotional arousal to child behavior • Multiple sources of anger and aggression • Belief that child's behavior is threatening or harmful to parent	• Improvement in child behavior • Community programs for parents • Coping resources

Stage 3: Habitual patterns of arousal and aggression with family members

Destabilizing factors	Compensatory factors
• Child habituates to physical punishment • Parent is reinforced for using strict control techniques • Child increases problem behavior	• Parental dissatisfaction with physical punishment • Child responds favorably to non-coercive methods • Community restraints/services

Wolfe, 1999

● **FIGURE 14.3** | An integrated model of physical child abuse.

who is at least 16 years old and at least 5 years older than the child. Some persons with pedophilia are sexually attracted only to children (exclusive type), whereas others also are attracted to adults (nonexclusive type). Sexual offenses against children occur most often during two life stages: adolescence, when delinquent behavior generally increases, and the thirties, when access to children again becomes more common (Finkelhor, 2009).

Persons who commit pedophilia may limit their activities to incest that involves their own children, stepchildren, or other relatives, or they may victimize children outside their families (APA, 2000; Marshall et al., 2008). Significantly, over 50% of individuals who are pedophiles report an awareness of their pedophilic interests before they turn 17 years old (63% of those who target male children and 50% of those who target female children), which they begin to act out on average by their late teens or early twenties (Abel, Osborn, & Twigg, 1993; Seto, 2008a). There is emerging evidence of deficiencies in cerebral white matter in cortical regions of the brain that respond to sexual cues, suggesting that pedophilia may result from early neurodevelopmental problems resulting in a partial disconnection within that network (Cantor et al., 2008; Kruger & Schiffer, 2011).

Those who victimize children develop complicated techniques to gain access and compliance from the child, which emphasizes the sexually opportunistic and predatory nature of this behavior. Pedophiles may win the trust of the child's mother or marry a woman with an attractive child. They may use methods to lower a child's resistance such as initiating a friendship, playing games or giving presents, having hobbies or interests that appeal to the child, and using peer pressure (Wekerle et al., 2006; Wolak, Finkelhor, Mitchell, & Ybarra, 2008).

Sexual offenders seldom resort to violence or force to gain the child's compliance; rather, they are attentive to the child's needs in order to gain the child's affection, interest, and loyalty as well as to reduce the chances that the child will report the sexual activity. Typically, sexual behavior takes place only after a period of "grooming," with a gradual indoctrination into sexual activity, underscoring how sex offenders of children are "sophisticated, calculating, and patient" (Singer, Hussey, & Strom, 1992, p. 884). As one offender asserted, "You can spot the child who is unsure of himself and target him with compliments and positive attention" (Elliott, Browne, & Kilcoyne, 1995, p. 584).

A perpetrator's efforts to establish a relationship with the child or youth, such as spending time alone or singling the child out as favored or special, also may reduce the child's internal inhibition by distorting the roles of the relationship and blurring interpersonal boundaries. His special status as a teacher, religious figure, or scout leader may cover his intentions with a sense of entitlement or privilege with a child, distorting his role into one that is a central part of the child's life

BOX 14.3 A CLOSER LOOK

Abuse in the Catholic Church

AP Photo/Michael Dwyer, Pool

John Geoghan stands out as one of the worst serial molesters in the recent history of the Catholic Church in America. For three decades, Geoghan preyed on young boys in a half-dozen parishes in the Boston area while church leaders looked the other way. Despite his disturbing pattern of abusive behavior, Geoghan was transferred from parish to parish for many years before the church finally defrocked him in 1998

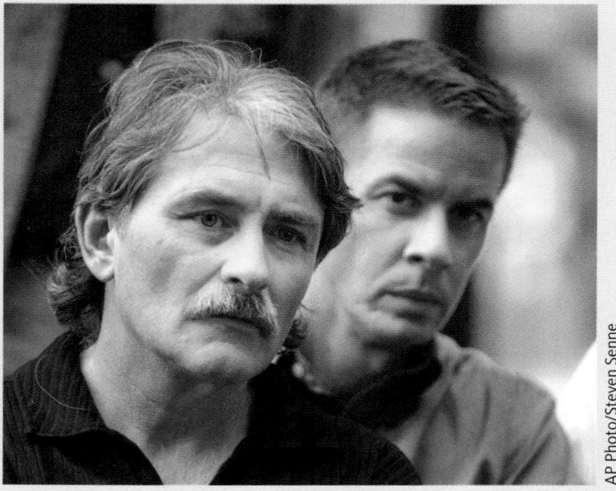

AP Photo/Steven Senne

Bernie McDaid and Gary Bergeron, right, say they were molested by Rev. Joseph Birmingham in the 1960s

(Wolfe, Jaffe, et al., 2003). Sadly, children made more than 11,000 allegations of sexual abuse by over 4,000 priests between 1950 and 2002, which represents about 4% of the 110,000 priests who served during the 52 years covered by the study (U.S. Conference of Catholic Bishops, 2004) (see Box 14.3).

Two recent meta-analyses comparing thousands of child sex offenders and non-offenders confirm a link between offenders and a history of having been sexually abused during their own childhood (Jespersen, Lalumière, & Seto, 2009; Seto & Lalumière, 2010). One possibility is that negative childhood experiences—sexual abuse, as well as other forms of maltreatment—set in motion a cautious, distrustful approach to intimate relationships. A history of child sexual abuse or exposure to other forms of violence or trauma may lead to atypical sexual interests in early adolescence for some male victims. In turn, deviant sexual fantasies provide a way of temporarily avoiding, interrupting, or reducing painful abuse-related mental states and psychiatric symptoms (Maniglio, 2011).

For example, an adolescent male with a history of unhealthy or exploitative relationships may justify using coercive and abusive actions toward others who are smaller or weaker because his other attempts at closeness have failed (Ward & Beech, 2008). His sexual interests and arousal become fused with his need for emotional closeness, which can lead to sexual preoccupation, promiscuity, and the possibility of increasing sexual deviancy as his attempts to gain intimacy escalate through sexual contact (Seto, 2008a).

Family and Situational Influences

Families in which incest has occurred often are isolated from other families and community activities as an attempt by the offender to maintain control and domination of other family members. He may restrict what other family members are allowed to do, and/

or enforce strict moral and religious views in a veiled attempt to protect the "family secret" (Seto, 2008b). Not surprisingly, marital couples report significant levels of relationship distress and dissatisfaction, including sexual discontentment (Berliner & Elliott, 2002). As in other types of maltreating families, these characteristics reflect a climate of domination and abuse of power, in which children are powerless at controlling unpleasant, unwanted, or abusive events toward themselves or others.

Certain situational factors increase children's vulnerability to sexual abuse, a fact that offenders exploit to their advantage. Offenders see children as more vulnerable if they have family problems, spend a lot of time alone, and seem unsure of themselves; they also admit to preferring victims who are attractive, trusting, and young (Elliott et al., 1995). To gain access to the child, offenders look for circumstances that create lax supervision or opportunities for them to become involved, such as parental unavailability, illness, stress, spousal abuse, or lack of emotional closeness to the child.

Social and Cultural Dimensions

What role does our culture play in the abuse and neglect of children? Intuitively, a primary focus on individual factors as causes of child abuse and neglect is very limiting, since we live in a society that not only condones violence but also glorifies it directly and indirectly.

Consider how the entertainment industry, including many aspects of the media and professional sports, earns billions of dollars in profits from exploiting our interests in violence in all of its forms. Equally disturbing is the portrayal of sex roles by society's envoys in the media and the entertainment industry: Females are stereotypically presented as relatively powerless and passive, and men as vested with power; women are encouraged to defer to the benevolence of powerful men, and men are encouraged to challenge the autonomy of powerful and assertive women (Hedley, 2002). These cultural phenomena are ingrained through years of repeated imagery, and are presumed to be the basis for the motivation of some men to maintain control and power in a relationship (Williams, 2003).

At the family level, we have noted that child maltreatment usually occurs in the context of homes and neighborhoods with multiple problems, where poverty, social isolation, and wide acceptance of corporal punishment significantly influence child development. These factors stem from racism and inequality, which are arguably the major sociocultural factors contributing to abuse and neglect—not only of children, but of many adults and members of minority groups. The extent to which a society deems any particular group as being less worthy of recognition and economic or political support represents the level of vulnerability for that group to violence and a host of other indignities.

Poverty and Social Isolation

Although child maltreatment certainly is not limited by the boundaries of socioeconomic status, the problem must be considered in the context of poverty and environmental stress. Poverty is associated with severe restrictions within the child's expectable environment—lack of adequate day care, safety, and housing—that often impair or impede the development of healthy parent–child relationships. In addition, adults who exist below poverty level suffer more individual and family problems, such as substance abuse and emotional disorders. This is reflected by the fact that, on average, 40% of substantiated child maltreatment cases involve substance abuse (Wekerle & Wall, 2002).

Although the relationship between poverty and child maltreatment is a fact, this explanation is not sufficient. To explain this connection more fully requires consideration of the psychological dimensions noted previously. Social and cultural disadvantage amounts to an extra burden of stress and confusion, and a limited number of alternatives. The coping abilities of family members are impaired by their circumstances and further constrained by their lack of resources.

Perhaps as a result of cultural and social factors, maltreating families often lack significant social connections to others within their extended families, neighborhoods, and communities, as well as to social assistance agencies (Coulton, Crampton, Irwin, Spilsbury, & Korbin, 2007). Unfortunately, maintaining family privacy and isolation may result in restricted access to healthier child-rearing models and social supports. Neglectful families especially are prone to isolation and insularity, which may be related directly to the parents' significant interpersonal problems (Gaudin, Polansky, Kilpatrick, & Shilton, 1996).

Child-Rearing Practices and Family Privacy

Child-rearing practices have been changing dramatically over the past 50 years or so. Today's parents are expected to appreciate their child's developmental strengths and limitations, and to move away from total reliance on disciplinary control methods toward methods that encourage the child's emerging independence and self-control. However, hypocrisy emerges when attempting to differentiate child abuse from child discipline, because cultural norms in many countries have long accepted corporal punishment as a primary, even necessary, component of discipline. As a result, four out of five 3-year-old children in the United States are physically punished by their parents during any given year, and about one in ten receive discipline so severe that they are at considerable risk of physical and emotional harm (Straus & Stewart, 1999).

Whether it is acceptable to spank children has become very controversial among lay and professional audiences in recent years (Benjet & Kazdin, 2003; Gershoff, 2002). Does corporal punishment, however, influence the likelihood of child abuse? The tentative answer is yes, but only indirectly. Most parents who use physical discipline are not abusing their children in either the physical or psychological sense. However, a change in circumstances—increased stress, more difficult child behavior—can up the ante quite suddenly.

Acceptance of corporal punishment leaves it up to local standards and parental judgment to define what is reasonable punishment, because no universal standard exists. Cultural values, historical precedent, and community standards, therefore, may set the stage for one person's abuse as being another person's discipline. Thus, child maltreatment occurs to a certain extent because of limited cultural opportunities to learn about appropriate child-rearing and receive necessary education and supports, as well as because of long-held social customs that endorse the use of physical force to resolve child conflicts. Given increasing evidence that corporal punishment of children is harmful (Gershoff & Bitensky, 2007), a growing number of countries are choosing to abolish the practice. Thirty-one countries have passed legislative bans on corporal punishment since the passage of the Convention on the Rights of the Child in 1989 (Zolotor & Puzia, 2010) (see Box 14.4).

Cultural norms and practices influence the prevalence of sexual abuse as well. The erotic portrayal of children—not only in pornography but also in mainstream advertising—raises many concerns about personal boundaries and appropriate messages. There is also grave concern stemming from the quantity of child pornography circulating on the Internet, where sexual abusers of children share information, exchange pornography, and make contact with potential child victims. Children exposed to pornography, directly or through the Internet, may be desensitized and socialized into believing that the activity is normal (Wolak et al., 2008). Children used in the production of pornography show psychological symptoms such as emotional withdrawal, antisocial behavior, mood swings, depression, fear and anxiety, and disorders such as PTSD (Cooper et al., 2005).

BOX 14.4 A CLOSER LOOK

Mounting Evidence Against Corporal Punishment of Children

A meta-analysis examined the long-range effects (positive as well as negative) of parental corporal punishment on key aspects of development and behavior. Negative or undesirable outcomes were found in terms of:

- decreased moral internalization;
- increased child aggression;
- increased child delinquent and antisocial behavior;
- decreased quality of relationship between parent and child;
- decreased child mental health;
- increased risk of being a victim of physical abuse;
- increased aggression as an adult;
- increased criminal and antisocial behavior as an adult;
- decreased mental health as an adult;
- increased risk as an adult of abusing their own child or spouse.

Corporal punishment was associated with only one desirable behavior: increased immediate compliance on the part of the child (which is often why parents say they rely on this method). Although causal relationships cannot be firmly established by these results, the findings make it fairly evident that the use of corporal punishment is a risk factor for a number of undesired outcomes in childhood and adulthood.

Source: Gershoff, 2002.

Given the accumulating evidence, many countries have abolished the use of corporal punishment of children by parents or other caregivers (dates of abolition in parentheses):

Austria (1989)
Bulgaria (2000)
Costa Rica (2008)
Croatia (1999)
Cyprus (1994)
Denmark (1997)
Finland (1983)
Germany (2000)
Greece (2006)
Hungary (2005)
Iceland (2003)
Israel (2000)
Kenya (2010)
Latvia (1998)
Liechtenstein (2008)
Luxembourg (2008)
Netherlands (2007)
New Zealand (2007)
Norway (1987)
Poland (2010)
Portugal (2007)
Romania (2004)
Rep. of Moldova (2008)
South Sudan (2011)
Spain (2007)
Sweden (1979)
Togo (2007)
Tunisia (2010)
Ukraine (2004)
Uruguay (2007)
Venezuela (2007)

Source: Global Initiative to End All Corporal Punishment of Children (2012).

SECTION SUMMARY

Causes of Child Maltreatment

- Abusive and neglectful parents often have had little past or present exposure to positive parental models and supports.
- Parental lack of knowledge of child-rearing and ways of coping with anger and arousal play prominent roles in physical abuse and neglect.
- Mental disorders seldom are responsible for child abuse and neglect; however, stress-filled environments contribute to poor coping and social isolation.
- A sexual offender's preference for sexual exploitation of children and adolescents is a primary cause of sexual abuse.
- Sexual offenders of children usually meet DSM-IV-TR criteria for pedophilia, defined as sexual activity or sexually arousing fantasies involving a child.
- Child maltreatment also stems from poverty and inequality, social isolation, and unhealthy cultural norms concerning child-rearing practices and family privacy.

PREVENTION AND TREATMENT

Violence against children is never justifiable. Nor is it inevitable. If its underlying causes are identified and addressed, violence against children is entirely preventable.

—Kofi Annan

It should come as no surprise that child maltreatment exacts an enormous toll on society, both in terms of human suffering as well as economic loss. The total lifetime economic costs of medical, legal, educational, and child welfare services related to maltreatment are estimated to be a staggering $124 billion a year in the United States (Fang, Brown, Florence, & Mercy, 2012). Accordingly, there is a sense of urgency in addressing this issue at all levels of prevention and intervention (Wekerle, 2011).

Consider these obstacles to intervention and prevention services for maltreating families: (1) Those most in need are least likely to seek help on their own; (2) they are brought to the attention of professionals as a result of someone else's concern, usually after they have violated expected norms or laws; and (3) parents do not want to admit to problems because they fear losing their children or being charged with a crime (fears that are, of course, realistic).

Many children and adults who seek treatment related to child abuse and neglect are under some form of legal constraint. Similar to other psychological interventions, child abuse treatments are based on the principle of beneficial assistance—but who wants assistance for something they won't admit to being a problem? As a result, treatments for child abuse and neglect have languished because of this basic dilemma: Access to treatment and prevention depends on admitting to or recognizing one's own culpability (Azar & Wolfe, 2006).

Despite these obstacles, children and youths who have grown up with violence can make major shifts through treatment in how they relate to others, especially if treatment is begun early. Seeing their strengths and abilities, rather than their deficits, is a plausible approach to preventing physical abuse, neglect, and related social problems. Fifteen years after receiving pre- and postnatal home-visitation services to establish resource linkages and learn about their child's developmental needs, first-time parents—who were initially at risk of maltreating their child based on either low socioeconomic status, young age (under 19 years), or unmarried status—gained controls on important dimensions such as better family planning concerning number and spacing of children, less need for welfare, less child maltreatment, and fewer arrests of their children during adolescence (Eckenrode et al., 2010; Kitzman et al., 2010; Olds et al., 1997). As a result of intensive research, home-visitation programs to prevent child abuse and neglect have become widespread in many parts of North America (MacMillan et al., 2009).

Clearly, efforts to enhance positive experiences at an early stage in the development of the parent–child relationship hold considerable promise for prevention of child maltreatment and the reduction of its consequences. As shown in ● Figure 14.4, child abuse interventions include efforts to prevent such acts altogether (i.e., universal and targeted prevention), as well as efforts to prevent recurrence or significant impairments.

Similarly, programs that instruct children and their parents on how to avoid and report sexual abuse will improve children's responses to victimization, especially programs that encourage children to participate actively in prevention activities (Finkelhor, 2009). Formal treatment efforts also increase the chances of overcoming the harmful effects of abuse and neglect. We discuss treatments for physical abuse and neglect in the same section because of their close connection to child-rearing disturbances. Treatment of child sexual abuse is presented separately because of its unique nature and course.

Physical Abuse and Neglect

Treatment of child abuse and neglect can be delivered in many ways: to individual parents, to children, to parents and children together, or to the entire family. Although most interventions emphasize desired changes in parental behavior, such changes can have a pronounced effect on their children's development as well.

Interventions for physical abuse usually involve ways to change how parents teach, discipline, and attend to their children, most often by training parents in basic child-rearing skills, accompanied by

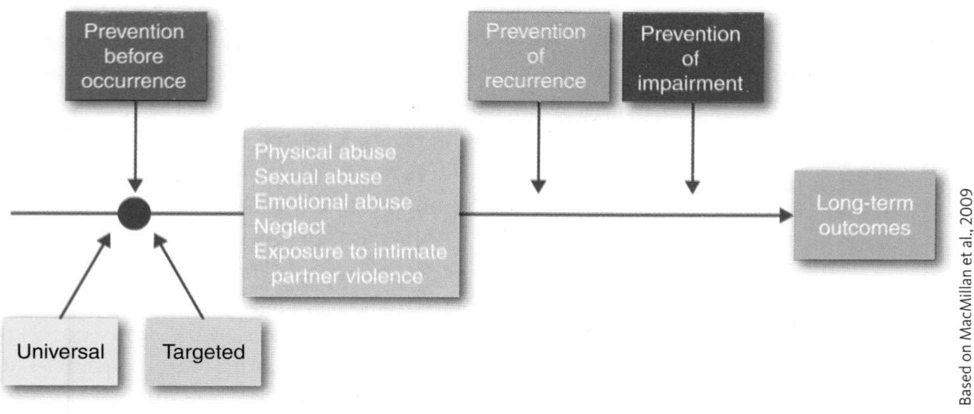

● FIGURE 14.4 | A continuum depicting opportunities for preventing child abuse or its long-term outcomes.

cognitive–behavioral methods that target specific anger patterns or distorted beliefs. Treatment for child neglect also focuses on parenting skills and expectations, coupled with teaching parents how to improve their skills in organizing important family needs, such as home safety, finances, and medical needs, among others, as well as drug and alcohol counseling (Azar & Wolfe, 2006). Similarly, children who have witnessed violence in the home benefit from interventions that address their needs in the context of their family circumstances. For example, their non-offending mothers may attend treatment with them, so that mothers learn ways to deal with problem child behavior while providing appropriate maternal support (Graham-Bermann, Lynch, Banyard, DeVoe, & Halabu, 2007; Jaffe et al., 2011).

Because maltreating parents place too much emphasis on control and discipline, or ways to avoid contact and responsibilities, they seldom know how to enjoy their child's company. Treatment, therefore, often begins with efforts designed to increase positive parent–child interactions and pleasant experiences. Parents are shown, through modeling, role playing, and feedback, how to engage with their children in daily activities that serve to strengthen the child's areas of deficiency, and to promote adaptive functioning (Wolfe, 1991). Activities are selected to maximize the child's attention and provide ample opportunity for pleasant interchanges. Milton's treatment plan illustrates this important initial step:

MILTON'S TREATMENT

Session 1

It didn't take long to see what Brenda faced at home. Partway through our first session, Milton (age 4) wanted his mother's attention and became quite angry when she was asked to leave the room for a few minutes. During this outburst, he pushed an easy chair over and tried to hit Brenda with a rolled-up poster. She happily left for the observation room, leaving him and me together for the first time. I found a game and some puppets that he liked, and began the process of establishing a relationship. As soon as Milton started to lose interest, I switched to a new activity. I modeled for Brenda some ways simply to observe Milton's behavior and express my interest:

"Milton likes to explore everything! Look! I have a talking doll! Can you make him say something? Excellent—he spoke to you!" (Milton starts to go for the toy chest). "Look, Milton! I have a puppet. Would you like to hold him? Good, you're coming back to play with me. After we play with the puppet, mommy will come in and play too! When we're all done, we'll go get a drink. Can you stack these blocks? Oops, you knocked them down; that looked like fun. Let's try again; only this time, you put one on here for me." I closely guided Milton to new activities to reduce his distractibility, all the time talking aloud so that his mother could hear in the adjoining room where she was observing the interaction. (Based on authors' material)

Once parents learn a more flexible, adaptive teaching style that suits their child's development, efforts are begun to strengthen the child's compliance and self-control. Parents observe while the therapist models positive ways to encourage the child's attention and appropriate behavior, followed by practice and feedback. Therapists model for the parent how to express positive affect—with smiles, hugs, physical affection, and praise—and how to show dismay or concern when necessary with appropriate facial expression, firmer voice tone, and similar cues that express disapproval.

Parent training seldom goes smoothly, especially with multiproblem families. What do you do when a child just "acts himself" and doesn't follow your directions, while his parent watches? These situations often are valuable for helping a parent apply the new skills under naturalistic, this-is-what-it's-really-like conditions. Serendipitously, the value of modeling how to handle such a challenge was discovered a few sessions later:

MILTON'S TREATMENT

Session 4

Milton was tired of following my directions. Unaware that his mother was watching, he seized the opportunity to have some fun. He picked up toys and tossed them, and turned the light switch off and on. I thought I could simply get Milton to settle down by taking him down from his chair (which he was using to reach the light switch) and bringing him back to the couch. I was wrong. He started throwing a tantrum and screaming violently. With no other choice (child psychologists know when they're licked), I decided to talk above the noise so that his mother could hear how I was feeling and what I thought I might do: "I'm not sure just what to do yet. Milton seems to be uninterested in listening at the moment. Rather than getting angry, I think I'll wait a minute or two and try again. I've seen my 3-year-old do this, and I know you can't always expect kids to listen."

Brenda, familiar with this behavior at home, thought the situation was priceless—"Now you know what I have to deal with!" In lighthearted defense, I explained how there may not be an easy solution for these situations, which is why it is so important to maintain your composure and not expect or demand cooperation from Milton immediately. Tongue-in-cheek, I reminded her of Murphy's law of child behavior—"Anything that can go wrong, will"—and its corollary, "Just because it worked last time doesn't mean it will work every time!" (Based on authors' material)

From this and similar misadventures, we discovered how familiar problems that emerge during treatment delivery will add authenticity for parents (and conveniently happen whether or not we plan them!). These situations, as well as less stressful ones, also are used to teach parents how to manage themselves calmly, yet firmly. Therapists model how parents can express frustration and annoyance without becoming abusive and harsh, and parents then are encouraged to discuss and rehearse how they can handle the situation. Gradually, they learn to replace physical punishment or apathy with more positive approaches. This process takes time, and parental frustration and impatience are to be anticipated.

On the whole, evaluations of interventions for physical abuse and neglect indicate that for several valid reasons, cognitive–behavioral approaches are the most widely supported methods for assisting maltreating parents (Saunders et al., 2004). Most significantly, these methods are effective (relative to standard protective-service interventions that involve brief counseling and monitoring) in modifying parental behaviors most relevant to child maltreatment, such as appropriate child-rearing and self-control skills. Techniques such as relaxation and self-management skills training, cognitive restructuring (viewing child behavior more appropriately), problem-solving training, and stress and anger management training often are combined with structured training in basic child-rearing skills. These methods, either alone or in combination, have been successful at teaching coping and problem-solving skills to abusive and neglectful parents as well as parents at-risk for maltreating their children (MacMillan et al., 2009; Mikton & Butchart, 2009; Moss et al., 2011; Thomas & Zimmer-Gembeck, 2011).

In addition to learning new ways to stimulate child development and structure child activities, neglectful parents often require very basic education and assistance in managing everyday demands, such as financial planning and home cleanliness (Allin, Wathen, & MacMillan, 2005). Programs like Project SafeCare provide multi-component interventions, such as marital counseling, financial planning, and lessons on cleanliness and similar concerns, that address the various needs of neglectful and multi-problem families (Gershater-Molko, Lutzker, & Wesch, 2003). Treatment services for abused or neglected children are less common than parent-oriented interventions, largely because parental behavior is often the primary concern. We have seen, however, that maltreated children often lag in important developmental competencies, which is a strong rationale for focusing additional attention on these areas.

The programmatic efforts of John Fantuzzo and his colleagues provide an excellent example of a developmentally focused intervention for maltreated children. Day care activities are coupled with resilient peer treatment (RPT), a peer-mediated classroom intervention that involves pairing withdrawn children (some with maltreatment histories) with resilient peers who are exceptionally strong at positive play activities (Bulotsky-Shearer, Fantuzzo, & McDermott, 2008; Fantuzzo, Manz, Atkins, & Meyers, 2005). Play activities are specifically targeted in this program, because play is a primary means for younger children to develop peer relationship skills. Competent "players" are encouraged to interact with less competent children in special play areas where adults participate in a minimal role. As a result, withdrawn children have the uncommon experience of being the center of another child's attention, and of experiencing a resilient child's repertoire of tactics for creating play and getting along with others. Relative to controls, withdrawn children with histories of abuse or neglect show improvement in social behavior, cognitive development, and self-concept, and reduction in aggressive and coercive behaviors.

The wave of the future in preventing child abuse and neglect is likely to involve public health approaches that offer comprehensive assistance to parents and families based on their level of need and proper timing of assistance. For example, the well-supported Triple P program offers five tiers of assistance to best meet the needs of all parents in a community, from brief sessions to intense training and one-on-one assistance (Prinz, Sanders, Shapiro, Whitaker, & Lutzker, 2009). Similarly, information and guidance for parents of younger children can be readily provided by pediatric primary care providers as part of regular health visits (Dubowitz, Feigelman, Lane, & Kim, 2009).

Sexual Abuse

What allowed this to happen was that so many people were silent about it.

—Adult sexually abused as a child

Sexually abused children have experienced a world of secrecy, silence, and isolation. After they break that silence by disclosing the abuse, or the abuse is discovered by accident, the path toward healing can be difficult. They must access not only unpleasant memories, but also buried feelings of guilt, confusion, fear, and low self-worth.

Despite advances in understanding the prevalence and impact of sexual abuse of children, children's treatment programs are only beginning. Like physical abuse and neglect, sexual abuse carries a special treatment challenge: Sexually abusive experiences affect each child unpredictably, which leads to diverse short- and long-range outcomes. As a result, treatments must match the needs of a wide age range of children who may show all kinds of symptoms or no symptoms at all.

Moreover, sexual abuse, like many other problems of childhood, occurs in the context of other individual, family, and community problems that affect its impact and treatment. Elements of family functioning, especially maternal support and help-seeking in response to the crisis, are known to affect children's levels of distress and aid in their recovery, so treatment often must address these situational issues as well.

Treatment programs for children who have been sexually abused usually provide several crucial elements to restore the child's sense of trust, safety, and guiltlessness (Cohen, Mannarino, & Murray, 2011; Johnson, 2008). One major element of treatment involves education and support to help these children understand why this happened to them, and how they can learn to feel safe once again. Information and education about the nature of sexual abuse helps clarify false beliefs that might lead to self-blame, and children's feelings of stigma and isolation often are addressed through reassurance or group therapy that involves other child victims. Animated films and videos offer ways for child victims to acknowledge and validate their feelings, and to help them talk about their feelings, allowing these children to move toward the future with a sense of hope and empowerment. Children also are taught ways to prevent sexual abuse and restore their sense of personal power and safety. Through the use of animated films and behavioral rehearsal, children learn how to distinguish appropriate from inappropriate touches.

Cognitive–behavioral methods are particularly valuable in achieving these goals (Cohen, Mannarino, Murray, & Igelman, 2006). Preferably, education and support are provided not only to the child victim, but to (non-offending) parents as well. The secretive betrayal that underlies the nature of sexual abuse causes some parents to feel ambivalent about whether to believe their child or how they feel about the alleged perpetrator, whom they may have trusted. Parents may need advice on ways to understand and manage their child's behavior, which due to the abuse may involve regressive or sexual behaviors. Parents often experience their own fears and worries as a result of the disclosure, and discussion with other parents and therapists can provide valuable support.

In conjunction with education and support, sexually abused children must express their feelings about the abuse and its aftermath—anger, ambivalence, fear—within a safe and supportive context. Younger children, for example, often cannot report their psychological reactions to the trauma unless they are asked specifically about the aspects of the trauma (Wolfe et al., 1994). Sexual abuse elicits attempts by children to cope with powerful and confusing feelings, and it is understandable that some will use every method possible to avoid these feelings. However, attempts to escape or avoid internal states of fear and anxiety, paradoxically, can make them worse.

For these reasons, controlled-exposure techniques, similar to those used for treatment of anxiety disorders (see Chapter 7), have been adapted for child sexual abuse victims. The child is asked to recall gradually her memories of events, often to the point of feeling distressed, to allow the powerful emotions to be extinguished with repeated exposure. In addition, she learns to cope with negative thoughts and feelings about the abuse by using positive statements and imagery. Overall, gradual exposure, modeling, education, coping, and prevention-skills training have shown positive effects in the treatment of PTSD and other common outcomes of sexual abuse (Harvey & Taylor, 2010; Trask, Walsh, & DiLillo, 2011).

There is strong agreement that successful interventions for sexually abused children should result in several important outcomes (Berliner & Elliott, 2002). Treatment services should help children understand that what happened to them was abuse, that it was wrong, and that it may have caused them some temporary problems. Emotional and behavioral problems that may have arisen from the abuse should subside, and children should have the personal resources to handle future problems. Importantly, they should have supportive relationships in place, especially with parents and other caregivers who have received adequate knowledge and assistance to understand the possible impact the abuse may have on their children's behavior and adjustment. Finally, successful treatment results in children's regaining their normal rate of development.

Twenty years ago, psychology textbooks never discussed these issues. We had little knowledge of the devastating developmental, mental health, and societal consequences of abuse and neglect, and very few treatments were available. Since that time, considerable progress has been made in understanding and helping children who have been abused and neglected and their families. Most importantly, broader efforts at prevention and family support may help reduce or eliminate the likelihood of such unnecessary and harmful mistreatment of children and youths.

SECTION SUMMARY

Prevention and Treatment

- Treatment services for maltreating families have been limited, in part due to the difficulty of parents' acknowledging their own weaknesses and seeking help without coercion.
- Prevention of maltreatment holds considerable promise, especially if begun early in the formation of the parent–child relationship.
- Interventions for physical abuse and neglect emphasize parent- and family-focused training in child-rearing and stress management. This method also benefits the child as a result of improved parental care.
- Treatment of physical abuse involves training parents in more positive child-rearing skills, accompanied by cognitive–behavioral methods to target specific anger patterns or distorted beliefs.
- Treatment for child neglect focuses on parenting skills and expectations, coupled with training in social competence and household management.
- Interventions for children who have been sexually abused emphasize the children's needs for safety, understanding, and expression of emotional consequences.
- Cognitive–behavioral methods have shown value in working with sexually abused children, especially when accompanied as well by education and support for non-offending, supportive caregivers.

Study Resources

SECTION SUMMARIES

KEY TERMS

COURSEMATE

Access an interactive eBook and chapter-specific interactive learning tools, including flashcards, quizzes, videos, and more in your Psychology CourseMate, accessed through CengageBrain.com.

Courtesy of David Wolfe

Annie, age 3

Annie

I feel peaceful and safe

I feel Peaceful and
Safe in my house. I
feel Peaceful and
Safe in my cotteg.
I feel peaceful and
Safe with my moma
and my DaDa. I feel
peaceful and safe with
my sister and my
brother. I feel peaceful and
safe in my bed. I
feel peaceful and safe
with my teddy bear.

I feel peaceful and
Safe with my friends.
I feel peaceful and
Safe when the
Sun is up. I
feel peaceful and
Safe when it is
Quiet: I feel peaceful
and Safe when I
am working. I feel
peaceful and safe
when I am whering
SOft slipers. I feel
peaceful and safe when I am
with my family.

Courtesy of David Wolfe

Annie, age 7

Glossary

A-B-A-B reversal design A type of single-case experimental design in which a baseline of behavior is first taken (A), followed by an intervention phase (B), then a return to baseline phase where the intervention is removed (A), and a final phase in which the intervention is reintroduced (B). When changes in behavior occur only during the intervention phases, this provides evidence that changes in behavior are due to the intervention.

acute stress disorder A form of anxiety disorder characterized by the development of anxiety, dissociation, and other symptoms following exposure to an extremely traumatic stressor. These symptoms last for at least two days but do not persist for more than a month.

adaptational failure Failure to master or progress in accomplishing developmental milestones.

adaptive functioning The ability to cope effectively with ordinary life demands, to live independently, and to abide by community standards. Adaptive functioning is a necessary component for defining levels of intellectual disability.

ADHD: combined type (ADHD-C) A subtype of attention-deficit/hyperactivity disorder characterized by a combination of inattentive symptoms and hyperactive–impulsive symptoms. (Also see *attention-deficit/hyperactivity disorder.*)

ADHD: predominantly hyperactive–impulsive type (ADHD-HI) A subtype of attention-deficit/hyperactivity disorder characterized by predominantly hyperactive–impulsive symptoms. (Also see *attention-deficit/hyperactivity disorder.*)

ADHD: predominantly inattentive type (ADHD-PI) A subtype of attention-deficit/hyperactivity disorder characterized by predominantly inattentive symptoms. (Also see *attention-deficit/hyperactivity disorder.*)

adolescent-limited (AL) path A developmental pathway to antisocial behavior whereby the child's antisocial behavior begins around puberty, continues into adolescence, and later desists in young adulthood.

adolescent-onset conduct disorder A specific type of conduct disorder for which the characteristics are not exhibited prior to 10 years of age.

agoraphobia A form of anxiety characterized by a fear of being alone in, and avoiding, certain places or situations from which escape may be difficult or embarrassing, or in which help may be unavailable in the event of a panic attack.

alerting Refers to an initial reaction to a stimulus, and involves the ability to prepare for what is about to happen.

amplifier hypothesis The premise that stress may serve to amplify the maladaptive predispositions of parents, thereby disrupting family management practices and compromising the parents' ability to be supportive of their children.

analogue research Research that evaluates a specific variable of interest under conditions that only resemble or approximate the situation to which one wishes to generalize.

Angelman syndrome A genetic disorder associated with an abnormality of chromosome 15. Children with Angelman syndrome typically suffer from moderate to severe mental retardation, ataxia (awkward gait), jerky movements, hand flapping, seizures, the absence of speech, and distinctive facial features such as a large jaw and open-mouthed expression.

anhedonia A negative mood state characterized by a lack of enjoyment in anything one does and a loss of interest in nearly all activities.

anorexia nervosa A severe eating disorder characterized by the refusal to maintain a minimally normal body weight, an intense fear of gaining weight, and a significant disturbance in the individual's perception and experiences of his or her own size.

antisocial behavior See *conduct problems.*

antisocial personality disorder (APD) An adult disorder characterized by a pervasive pattern of disregard for, and violation of, the rights of others, as well as engagement in multiple illegal behaviors.

anxiety A mood state characterized by strong negative affect, bodily symptoms of tension, and apprehensive anticipation of future danger or misfortune.

anxiety disorder A disorder in which the child experiences excessive and debilitating anxiety.

Asperger's disorder (AD) A pervasive developmental disorder characterized by major difficulties in social interaction and unusual patterns of interest and behavior in children with relatively intact cognitive and communication skills.

assent Evidence of some form of agreement on the part of a child to participate in a research study without the child's having the full understanding of the research that would be needed to give informed consent.

attachment The process of establishing and maintaining an emotional bond with parents or other significant caregivers. This process is ongoing, typically beginning between 6 and 12 months of age, and provides infants with a secure, consistent base from which to explore and learn about their worlds.

attentional capacity The amount of information in short-term memory to which one can attend.

attention-deficit/hyperactivity disorder (ADHD) A disorder in which the individual consistently and repeatedly shows age-inappropriate behaviors in the two general categories of inattention and hyperactivity–impulsivity, resulting in significant impairment in life functioning.

autism A pervasive developmental disorder characterized by abnormalities in social functioning and in language and communication, and by unusual interests and behaviors. More specifically, autism affects every aspect of the child's interaction with his or her world, involves many parts of the brain, and undermines the very traits that make us human—our social responsiveness, ability to communicate, and feelings for other people.

autism spectrum disorders Autism spectrum disorders include several pervasive developmental disorders (PDDs), all characterized by significant impairments in social and communication skills, and stereotyped patterns of interests and behaviors. These include autistic disorder, Asperger's disorder, and Pervasive Developmental Disorder, Not Otherwise Specified (PDD-NOS).

autistic disorder DSM-IV-TR diagnostic category used to describe children with autism.

behavior analysis or functional analysis of behavior An effort to identify as many factors as possible that could be contributing to a child's problem behavior, thoughts, and feelings, and to develop hypotheses about which ones are the most important and/or most easily changed.

behavior lens principle A principle that states that child psychopathology reflects a mixture of actual child behavior and the lens through which it is viewed by others in a child's culture.

behavioral activation system (BAS) A subsystem of the brain that activates behavior in response to cues of reward or nonpunishment.

behavioral assessment The evaluation of the child's thoughts, feelings, and behaviors in specific settings, based on which hypotheses are formulated about the nature of the problem and what can be done about it.

behavioral genetics A branch of genetics that investigates possible connections between a genetic predisposition and observed behavior.

behavioral inhibition (BI) The ability to delay one's initial reactions to events or to stop behavior once it has begun.

behavioral inhibition system (BIS) A subsystem of the brain that produces anxiety and inhibits ongoing behavior in the presence of novel events, innate fear stimuli, and signals of nonreward or punishment.

best practice guidelines Systematically developed statements to assist practitioners and patients with decisions regarding appropriate treatment(s) for specific clinical conditions.

betrayal The degree to which a child feels a perpetrator gained his or her confidence through manipulation and coercion, as well as by the position of trust or authority held by the perpetrator. As a consequence, the child's emotional needs may be compromised by intense and contradictory feelings of the need for closeness and the fear of it.

binge Episode of overeating that involves both excessive amounts of food and a lack of control.

binge eating disorder (BED) A disorder that involves periods of excessive eating with a feeling of a loss of control. It is similar to binge eating but without the compensatory behaviors and has become increasingly widespread during this age of abundant fast food and obesity.

binge eating/purging type A type of anorexia whereby the individual regularly engages in episodes of binge eating or purging, or both.

bipolar disorder (BP) A type of mood disorder characterized by an ongoing combination of extreme highs and extreme lows. An episode of mania is an abnormally elevated or expansive mood, and feelings of euphoria are an exaggerated sense of well-being. The highs may alternate with lows, or both extremes may be felt at about the same time.

brain circuits Paths made up of clustered neurons that connect one part of the brain to another.

bulimia nervosa An eating disorder that involves recurrent episodes of binge eating, followed by an effort to compensate by self-induced vomiting or other means of purging. Individuals with bulimia are also unduly influenced by body shape and weight, and are obsessed with food.

bullying When one or more children expose another child, repeatedly and over time, to negative actions, such as physical contact, words, making faces or dirty gestures, and intentional exclusion from a group.

callous and unemotional interpersonal style A mode of social interaction that is characterized by such traits as the absence of feelings of guilt, not showing empathy, and not showing emotions.

case study An intensive and usually anecdotal observation and analysis of an individual subject.

categorical classification The diagnostic systems that are primarily based on informed professional consensus, which is an approach that has dominated and continues to dominate the field of child (and adult) psychopathology.

central coherence The strong tendency of humans to interpret stimuli in a relatively global way that takes the broader context into account.

child maltreatment The abuse and neglect of children by parents or by others responsible for their welfare. Child maltreatment is a generic term used to refer to the four primary acts of physical abuse, neglect, sexual abuse, and emotional abuse of persons less than 18 years of age.

childhood disintegrative disorder (CDD) A pervasive developmental disorder characterized by a significant loss of previously acquired skills, as well as the presence of abnormalities in two of the following three areas of functioning: social interaction, communication, and patterns of behavior, interests, and activities.

childhood obesity A chronic medical condition characterized by an excessive accumulation of body fat relative to gender- and age-based norms.

childhood-onset conduct disorder A specific type of conduct disorder whereby the child displays at least one characteristic of the disorder prior to 10 years of age.

chronic illness An illness that is long lasting and often irreversible.

classification A system for representing the major categories or dimensions of child psychopathology and the boundaries and relations among them. One definition of diagnosis is the assignment of cases to categories of the classification system.

clinical assessment A process of differentiating, defining, and measuring the behaviors, cognitions, and emotions that are of concern, as well as the environmental circumstances that may be contributing to these problems.

clinical description A summary of unique behaviors, thoughts, and feelings that together make up the features of a given psychological disorder.

coercion theory A developmental theory proposing that coercive parent-child interactions serve as the training ground for the development of antisocial behavior. Specifically, it is proposed that through a four-step escape-conditioning sequence, the child learns how to use increasingly intense forms of noxious behavior to escape and avoid unwanted parental demands.

cohort A group of individuals who are followed over time and who experience the same cultural or historical events during the same time period.

combined type (ADHD-C) See under *ADHD*.

communication deviance A measure of interpersonal attentional and thought disturbance observed in families of children with schizophrenia or schizotypal personality disorder. Children from families with high communication deviance show the most severe impairment and the poorest attentional functioning.

communication disorders A diagnostic term that refers to difficulty producing speech sounds (phonological disorder) or with speech fluency (stuttering); difficulty using spoken language to communicate (expressive language disorder); or difficulty understanding what other people say (mixed expressive-receptive language disorder).

comorbidity The overlapping of two or more disorders at a rate that is greater than would be expected by chance alone.

compensatory behavior Behavior shown by persons suffering from bulimia nervosa to prevent weight gain following a binge episode. Compensatory behaviors include self-induced vomiting, fasting, exercising, and the misuse of diuretics, laxatives, enemas, or diet pills. (Also see *purging*.)

competence The ability to adapt to one's environment. Children's competence involves their performance relative to their same-age peers as well as their individual course of development.

compulsions Repetitive, purposeful, and intentional behaviors or mental acts that are performed in response to an obsession.

conduct disorder (CD) A form of disruptive behavior disorder in which the child exhibits an early, persistent, and extreme pattern of aggressive and antisocial acts that involve the infliction of pain on others or interference with others' rights through physical and verbal aggression, stealing, vandalism, truancy, or running away.

conduct problems (antisocial behavior) Age-inappropriate actions and attitudes that violate family expectations, societal norms, and the personal or property rights of others.

continuity of development A theoretical position for explaining development which proposes that normal and abnormal developmental changes are gradual and quantitative. Continuity theorists argue that development is an additive process that is ongoing rather than occurring in distinct stages.

correlation coefficient A number that describes the degree of association between two variables of interest.

cortisol A stress hormone produced by the adrenal glands.

co-rumination A negative form of self-disclosure and discussion between peers focused narrowly on problems or emotions to the exclusion of other activities or dialogue.

cross-sectional research A method of research whereby different individuals at different ages/stages of development are studied at the same point in time.

cultural compatibility hypothesis The hypothesis that treatment is likely to be more effective when compatible with the cultural patterns of the child and family.

cultural-familial group Intellectual disability (ID) in which there is no evidence of organic brain damage (usually associated with mild ID).

culture-bound syndromes Recurrent patterns of maladaptive behaviors and/or troubling experiences specifically associated with different cultures or localities. These syndromes rarely fit neatly into one Western diagnostic category.

cycle-of-violence hypothesis The repetition of patterns of violent behavior across generations. For example, persons who are abused as children are more likely to be abusive toward others as adults.

decoding A skill necessary for reading that involves breaking words down into parts.

delusions Disturbances in thinking involving disordered thought content and strong beliefs that are misrepresentations of reality.

depressogenic cognitions The negative perceptual and attributional styles and beliefs associated with depressive symptoms.

destructive-nondestructive dimension An independent dimension of antisocial behavior consisting of a continuum ranging from acts such as cruelty to animals or destruction of property at one end, to nondestructive behaviors such as arguing or irritability at the other.

developmental coordination disorder A disorder characterized by marked motor incoordination (e.g., clumsiness and delays in achieving motor milestones).

developmental history or family history Information obtained from the parents about potentially significant historical milestones and events that might have a bearing on the child's current difficulties.

developmental pathway A concept to describe the sequence and timing of particular behaviors, and to highlight the known and suspected relationships of behaviors over time.

developmental psychopathology An approach to describing and studying disorders of childhood and adolescence in a manner that emphasizes the importance of developmental processes and tasks. This approach uses abnormal development to inform normal development and vice versa.

developmental tasks Psychosocial tasks of childhood that reflect broad domains of competence and tell us how children typically progress within each of these domains as they grow.

developmental tests Tests used to assess infants and young children that are generally carried out for the purposes of screening, diagnosis, and evaluation of early development.

developmental-versus-difference controversy A debate regarding the developmental progression of children with mental impairments. The developmental position argues that all children, regardless of intellectual impairments, progress through the same developmental stages in the same sequence, but at different rates. The difference position argues that the development of children with mental impairments proceeds in a different, less sequential, and less organized fashion than that of children without impairments.

diagnosis The identification of a disorder from an examination of the symptoms.

diathesis–stress model of depression A theory of depression proposing that the impact of stress is moderated by individual risk factors and that the occurrence of depression depends on the interaction between the subject's personal vulnerability and life stress.

difference viewpoint The view that cognitive development of children with intellectual disability differs from that of normally developing children in more ways than merely differences in developmental rate and upper limit.

dimensional classification An empirically based approach to the diagnosis and classification of child psychopathology that assumes that there are a number of independent dimensions or traits of behavior and that all children possess these to varying degrees.

direct instruction An approach to teaching children with learning disorders based on the premise that to improve a skill the instructional activities have to approximate those of the skill being taught.

discontinuity of development A theoretical position for explaining development proposing that normal and abnormal developmental changes are abrupt and qualitative. Discontinuity theorists, such as Piaget and Erikson, argue that children pass through developmental stages that are qualitatively different from each other.

discrete trial training A method of teaching readiness skills or other desired behaviors that involves a step-by-step approach of presenting a stimulus and requiring a specific response.

disruptive behavior disorders A DSM-IV-TR category for persistent patterns of antisocial behavior that includes oppositional defiant disorder and conduct disorder.

dissociation An altered state of consciousness in which the individual feels detached from the body or self. This process may be voluntary or involuntary, and can be adaptive when resistance or escape from a life-threatening situation is not possible.

distractibility A term used to describe deficits in selective attention.

double depression An instance in which a major depressive episode is superimposed on the subject's previous dysthymic disorder.

Down syndrome A chromosomal abnormality in which there are three 21st chromosomes rather than the normal two. Children with Down syndrome typically function at the moderate level of intellectual disability, have an increased likelihood of medical problems, and have unusual physical features. This syndrome is also called trisomy 21.

drive for thinness A motivational variable underlying dieting and body image, among young females in particular, whereby the individual believes that losing more weight is the answer to overcoming her troubles and achieving success.

dyslexia Disorder of reading not due to low intelligence.

dysphoria A negative mood state characterized by prolonged bouts of sadness.

dyssomnias A category of sleep disorders involving difficulties initiating or maintaining sleep. Such disorders are often characterized by problems with getting enough sleep, not sleeping when one wants to, and not feeling refreshed after sleeping.

dysthymic disorder (DD) or dysthymia A form of depressive disorder characterized by at least 1 year (2 years in adults) of depressed mood for more days than not, accompanied by additional depressive symptoms that do not meet criteria for a major depressive episode. In comparison to major depressive disorder, dysthymia is milder, but more long-term.

eating attitudes A person's belief that cultural standards for attractiveness, body image, and social acceptance are closely tied to the ability to control one's diet and weight gain.

eating disorders, not otherwise specified (EDNOS) A category of eating disorders that includes problems that do not quite fulfill criteria for anorexia nervosa or bulimia nervosa. The EDNOS category is less stringent than DSM-IV-TR criteria for anorexia nervosa or bulimia nervosa, and therefore is sometimes more appropriate for adolescents.

echolalia A child's immediate or delayed parrot-like repetition of words or word combinations.

educational neglect Failure to provide for a child's basic educational needs, including allowing chronic truancy, failing to enroll a child of mandatory school age in school, and failing to attend to a special educational need.

electroencephalogram (EEG) An electrophysiological measure of brain functioning whereby electrodes are taped to the surface of the subject's scalp to record the electrical activity of the brain. EEG recordings are sensitive to changes in state and emotionality, thereby making them particularly useful for studying social and emotional processes.

emotion reactivity A dimension of emotional processes associated with individual differences in the threshold and intensity of emotional experience.

emotion regulation The processes by which emotional arousal is redirected, controlled, or modified to facilitate adaptive functioning.

emotional abuse Abusive behavior that involves acts or omissions by parents or caregivers that cause, or could cause, serious behavioral, cognitive, emotional, or mental disorders.

emotional neglect Failure to provide for a child's basic emotional needs, including marked inattention to the child's needs for affection, refusal of or failure to provide needed psychological care, spousal abuse in the child's presence, and permission of drug or alcohol use by the child.

encopresis The passage of feces into inappropriate places, such as clothing, whether involuntary or intentional.

enuresis Involuntary discharge of urine occurring in persons over 5 years of age or the developmental equivalent.

epidemiological research The study of the incidence, prevalence, and co-occurrence of childhood disorders and competencies in clinic-referred and community samples.

epigenetic The underlying biological changes to genetic structure resulting from environmental factors, such as toxins, diet, stress, and many others.

epinephrine A hormone produced by the adrenal glands that is released into the bloodstream in response to stress in order to energize and prepare the body for a possible threat. This hormone is also known as adrenaline.

equifinality The concept that similar outcomes may stem from different early experiences.

etiology The study of the causes of disorders. With respect to childhood disorders, etiology considers how biological, psychological, and environmental processes interact.

eugenics First defined by Sir Francis Galton in 1883 as "the science which deals with all influences that improve the inborn qualities of a race." In the early 1900s, public and professional emphasis shifted away from the needs of persons with intellectual disability toward a consideration of the needs of society; society was to be protected from the presumable harm done by the presence of these persons in the community. This misdirected view provided justification for restricting the rights of individuals with intellectual disability and their opportunities for advancement.

euphoria An exaggerated sense of well-being.

executive functions Higher-order mental processes that enable a child to maintain a problem-solving orientation in order to attain a future goal. Examples of executive functions include working memory, mental computation, flexibility of thinking, internalization of speech, response inhibition, motor coordination, self-regulation of arousal level, and mature moral reasoning, among others.

expectable environment External conditions or surroundings that are considered to be fundamental and necessary for healthy development. The expectable environment for infants includes protective and nurturant adults and opportunities for socialization; for older children it includes a supportive family, contact with peers, and ample opportunities to explore and master the environment.

exposure A behavior therapy technique for treating anxiety disorders that exposes the subject to the source of his or her fear while providing appropriate and effective ways of coping with the fear (other than through escape and avoidance).

expressive language disorder A form of communication disorder characterized by deficits in expression despite normal comprehension of speech.

external validity The degree to which findings can be generalized or extended to people, settings, times, measures, and characteristics other than the ones in the original study.

externalizing behavior A continuous dimension of behavior that includes a mixture of impulsive, overactive, aggressive, and delinquent acts.

externalizing problems Problem behaviors that begin during childhood and encompass acting-out behaviors such as aggression and delinquent behavior.

failure to thrive (FTT) Characterized by weight below the fifth percentile for age, and/or deceleration in the rate of weight gain from birth to the present of at least 2 standard deviations, using standard growth charts for comparison.

family history Using a background questionnaire or interview, information is obtained from the parents regarding potentially significant developmental milestones and historical events that might have a bearing on the child's current difficulties.

family systems Theory that the behavior of an individual can be most accurately understood in the context of the dynamics of his or her family.

fear An alarm reaction to current danger or life-threatening emergencies; marked by strong escape-oriented tendencies and a surge in the sympathetic nervous system.

feeding disorder of infancy or early childhood A disorder characterized by a sudden or marked deceleration of weight gain in an infant or a young child (under age 6) and a slowing or disruption of emotional and social development.

fetal alcohol syndrome A disorder stemming from extensive prenatal exposure to alcohol. Children with this disorder typically suffer from problems in intellectual functioning, central nervous system dysfunction, cranial feature defects, behavior problems, growth retardation, and physical abnormalities of the face.

fight/flight response The immediate reaction to perceived danger or threat whereby efforts are directed toward protecting against potential harm, either by confronting the source of danger (fight), or by escaping from the situation (flight).

flooding A procedure for treating anxiety that involves prolonged and repeated exposure to the anxiety-provoking situation until the subject's level of anxiety has diminished.

fragile-X syndrome A chromosomal abnormality in which one area on the X chromosome is pinched. Children with fragile-X syndrome typically suffer from moderate intellectual disability.

frontal lobe Area of the brain located at the front of each cerebral hemisphere; responsible for the functions underlying much of our thinking and reasoning abilities, including memory.

frontostriatal circuitry of the brain A structure of the brain consisting of the prefrontal cortex and the basal ganglia; associated with attention, executive functions, delayed response, and response organization. Abnormalities within this structure have been linked to ADHD.

functional analysis of behavior (See *behavior analysis*.)

Gene–environment interactions (G×E) Complex interplay of nature and nurture to account for genetic and environmental influences and their timing.

general intellectual functioning One's general level of intellectual ability, defined by an intelligence quotient (IQ or equivalent) derived from an assessment with one or more of the standardized, individually administered intelligence tests.

generalized anxiety disorder (GAD) A form of anxiety disorder in which the subject experiences chronic or exaggerated worry and tension, almost always anticipating disaster, even in the absence of an obvious reason to do so. The worrying is often accompanied by physical symptoms such as trembling, muscle tension, headache, and nausea.

generalized social phobia A severe form of social phobia in which the subject fears most social situations, is afraid to meet or talk with new people, avoids contact with anyone outside his or her family, and finds it extremely difficult to attend school, participate in recreational activities, or socialize at all.

genotype An individual's specific genetic makeup.

goodness of fit The extent to which two things are suited. For instance, with respect to child psychopathology, one might use the term to refer to the extent to which the child's early temperament and the parent's style of interaction are suited to each other.

graded exposure Gradual exposure of a subject to a feared situation.

hallucinations Disturbances in perception in which things are seen, heard, or otherwise sensed even though they are not real or present.

health promotion An approach to the prevention of disease that involves education, public policy, and similar actions to promote health.

heritability The proportion of the variance of a trait that is attributable to genetic influences.

hopelessness theory The view that depression-prone individuals make internal, stable, and global attributions to explain the causes of negative events, and external, unstable, and specific attributions about positive events. This attributional style results in the individual taking personal blame for negative events in his or her life and leads to helplessness, avoidance, and hopelessness about the future, which promotes further depression.

hostile attributional bias The tendency of aggressive children to attribute negative intent to others, especially when the intentions of another child are unclear (e.g., when a child accidentally bumps into them, they are likely to think the other child did it on purpose).

hyperactive Displaying an unusually high level of energy and an inability to remain still or quiet.

hypothalamic-pituitary-adrenal (HPA) axis A regulatory system of the brain made up of the hypothalamus control center and the pituitary and adrenal glands; it influences a person's response to stress and his or her ability to regulate emotions.

idiographic case formulation An approach to case formulation or assessment that emphasizes the detailed representation of the individual child or family as a unique entity. This approach is in contrast to the nomothetic approach, which instead emphasizes the general laws that apply to all individuals.

impulsive Prone to acting with little or no consideration of possible consequences. This term is frequently used to describe children who suffer from attention-deficit/hyperactivity disorder.

inattentive Lacking the ability to focus or sustain one's attention. Children who are inattentive find it difficult to sustain mental effort during work or play and behave carelessly, as if they are not listening.

incidence rate The rate at which new cases of a disorder appear over a specified period of time.

incidental training A method of teaching readiness skills or other desired behaviors that works to strengthen the behavior by capitalizing on naturally occurring opportunities.

inclusion The education strategies that are based on the premise that the abilities of children with special needs will improve from associating with normally developing peers and being spared the effects of labeling and special placements.

inclusion movement The integration of individuals with disabilities into regular classroom settings, regardless of the severity of the disability. The school curriculum must be adaptable to meet the individual needs and abilities of these children.

information-processing disturbances Cognitive misperceptions and distortions in the way events are perceived and interpreted.

informed consent An individual's expressed willingness to participate in a research study, based on his or her understanding of the nature of the research, the potential risks and benefits involved, the expected outcomes, and possible alternatives.

insulin-dependent diabetes mellitus A lifelong metabolic disorder in which the body is unable to metabolize carbohydrates due to inadequate pancreatic release of insulin.

interdependent Applies to the assumption that abnormal child behavior is determined by both the child and his or her environment, and that these two factors are interconnected. (Also see *transaction*.)

internal validity The extent to which an intended manipulation of a variable, rather than extraneous influences, accounts for observed results, changes, or group differences.

internalizing problems Problem behaviors that begin during childhood and include anxiety, depression, somatic complaints, and withdrawn behavior.

intervention A broad concept that encompasses many different theories and methods with a range of problem-solving strategies directed at helping the child and family adapt more effectively to their current and future circumstances.

irritability A common symptom of depression characterized by easy annoyance and touchiness, an angry mood, and temper outbursts.

joint attention The ability to coordinate one's focus of attention on another person and an object of mutual interest.

juvenile delinquency A broad term used to describe children who have broken a law, anything from sneaking into a movie without a ticket to homicide.

learning disabilities A general term that refers to significant problems in mastering one or more of the following skills: listening, speaking, reading, writing, reasoning, and mathematics.

learning disorders A diagnostic term that refers to specific problems in reading (disorder of reading), math (disorder of mathematics), or writing ability (disorder of written expression) as determined by achievement test results that are substantially below what would be expected for the child's age, schooling, and intellectual ability.

life-course-persistent (LCP) path A developmental pathway to antisocial behavior in which the child engages in antisocial behavior at an early age and continues to do so into adulthood.

longitudinal research A method of research whereby the same individuals are studied at different ages/stages of development.

maintenance Efforts to increase adherence to treatment over time in order to prevent a relapse or recurrence of a problem.

major depressive disorder (MDD) A form of depressive disorder characterized by one or more major depressive episodes that last for at least 2 weeks and are accompanied by additional symptoms such as sleep disturbances or thoughts of suicide.

mania An abnormally elevated or expansive mood.

mediator variables The process, mechanism, or means through which a variable produces a specific outcome.

mentalization Awareness of other people's and one's own mental states. Also referred to as *theory of mind*.

metabolic control The degree to which an individual's glucose level is maintained within the normal range (in reference to diabetes mellitus).

metabolic rate The body's balance of energy expenditure. Metabolic rate is determined by genetic and physiological makeup, along with eating and exercise habits.

metacognitive training Instruction in techniques that help to improve memory and learning, including how to coordinate learned skills across learning situations.

methylphenidate The stimulant medication most commonly used in treating children with attention-deficit/hyperactivity disorder. It is sold under the name Ritalin.

mild mental retardation An IQ level in the range of 50–55 to approximately 70.

mixed receptive–expressive language disorder A form of communication disorder characterized by deficits in expressive language coupled with a difficulty in understanding some aspects of speech (i.e., deficits in receptive language).

moderate mental retardation An IQ level in the range of 35–40 to 50–55.

moderator variables A factor that influences the direction or strength of a relationship between variables.

molecular genetics The methods of genetics that directly assess the association between variations in DNA sequences and variations in particular traits. More than an association, variations in genetic sequences are thought to cause the variations in the trait(s). These methods offer more direct support for genetic influences on child psychopathology.

mood disorder A disorder in which the subject suffers from extreme, persistent, or poorly regulated emotional states. DSM-IV-TR mood disorders include major depressive disorder, dysthymia, and bipolar disorder.

morbidity The various forms of physical and functional consequences and limitations that result from an illness.

multiaxial system A classification system consisting of several different domains (axes) of information about the subject that may assist a clinician in planning the treatment of a disorder. The DSM-IV-TR is an example of a multiaxial classification system.

multifinality The concept that various outcomes may stem from similar beginnings.

multimethod assessment approach A clinical assessment that emphasizes the importance of obtaining information from different informants, in a variety of settings, using a variety of procedures that include interviews, observations, questionnaires, and tests.

multiple-baseline design A single-case experimental design in which the effect of a treatment is shown by demonstrating that behaviors in more than one baseline change as a result of the institution of a treatment.

multisystemic treatment (MST) An approach to treatment that attempts to address the multiple determinants of problematic behavior by involving family members, school personnel, peers, juvenile justice staff, and others in the child's life, and by drawing on multiple techniques such as parent management training, cognitive problem-solving skills training, and marital therapy, as well as specialized interventions such as special education placements, referral to substance abuse treatment programs, or referral to legal services.

natural experiment An experiment in which comparisons are made between preexisting conditions or treatments (i.e., random assignment is not used).

naturalistic observation The unstructured observation of a child in his or her natural environment.

negative affectivity A persistent negative mood evidenced by nervousness, sadness, anger, and guilt.

negative cognitive schemata Stable structures in memory, including self-critical beliefs and attitudes, that guide information processing in a way that is consistent with the negative self-image of the subject. These cognitive schemata are rigid and resistant to change even in the face of contradictory evidence.

negative cognitive triad Negative views about oneself, the world, and the future that are characteristic of youngsters with depression. These views maintain feelings of helplessness, undermine the child's mood and energy level, and are related to the severity of depression.

neural plasticity The malleable nature of the brain, evidenced throughout the course of development (use-dependent). Although infants are born with basic brain processes, experience leads to anatomical differentiation. That is, certain synapses of the brain are strengthened and stabilized, while others regress and disappear.

neurodevelopmental model of schizophrenia This model proposes that genetic vulnerability and early neurodevelopmental insults result in impaired connections among many brain regions. This defective neural circuitry is then vulnerable to dysfunction and ultimately revealed by developmental processes and events during puberty and by exposure to stress. The neurodevelopmental model is consistent with findings that infants and children who later develop schizophrenia often display developmental impairments in motor, language, cognitive, and social functioning well before the onset of their psychotic symptoms.

neuroimaging A method of examining the structure and/or function of the brain. Neuroimaging procedures include magnetic resonance imaging (MRI), coaxial tomographic scan (CT), positron emission tomography (PET), functional magnetic resonance imaging (fMRI), and diffusion MRI (dMRI).

neuropsychological assessment A form of assessment that attempts to link brain functioning with objective measures of behavior known to depend on an intact central nervous system.

neurotic paradox The pattern of self-perpetuating behavior in which children who are overly anxious in various situations, even while being aware that the anxiety may be unnecessary or excessive, find themselves unable to abandon their self-defeating behaviors.

nightmares A form of parasomnia that occurs during REM sleep and is characterized by repeated awakenings with detailed recall of extended and extremely frightening dreams, usually involving threats to survival, security, or self-esteem.

nomothetic formulation An approach to case formulation or assessment that emphasizes general principles that apply to all people. This approach contrasts with the idiographic approach, which instead emphasizes a detailed representation of the individual or family as a unique entity.

non-accidental trauma The wide-ranging effects of maltreatment on the child's ongoing physical and emotional development.

nondisjunction The failure of the 21st pair of the mother's chromosomes to separate during meiosis. In most Down syndrome cases, the extra chromosome results from this failure of the chromosomes to separate.

nonshared environment A subtype of environmental influences that refers to the environmental factors that produce behavioral differences among siblings living in the same household. Nonshared environmental influence can be estimated and is calculated by subtracting the MZ twin correlation from 1.0.

nonverbal learning disabilities (NLD) Learning disabilities characterized by deficits related to right-hemisphere brain functioning, such as problems in social skills, spatial orientation, and problem solving.

nosologies Efforts to classify psychiatric disorders into descriptive categories.

obsessions Persistent, intrusive, and irrational thoughts, ideas, impulses, or images that focus on improbable or unrealistic events or on real-life events that are greatly exaggerated.

obsessive–compulsive disorder (OCD) A form of anxiety disorder in which the subject experiences repeated, intrusive, and unwanted thoughts that cause anxiety and often engages in ritualized behavior to relieve this anxiety.

operant speech training A strategy used to help children use language more appropriately. It involves a step-by-step approach that successively increases the child's vocalizations; teaches the child to imitate sounds and words; teaches the meanings of words; and teaches the child to use language expressively to label objects, make verbal requests, and express desires. This training is often employed for children with autism.

oppositional defiant disorder (ODD) The least severe form of disruptive behavior disorder, in which children show an age-inappropriate and persistent pattern of irritable, hostile, oppositional, and defiant behavior.

organic group intellectual disability stemming from clear organic (physical) causes such as brain damage or improper CNS development.

organization of development The assumption that early patterns of adaptation evolve over time and transform into higher-order functions in a structured manner. For instance, infant eye contact and speech sounds evolve and transform into speech and language.

overt–covert dimension An independent dimension consisting of a continuum of antisocial behavior ranging from overt forms such as physical aggression at one end, to covert forms (i.e., hidden or sneaky acts) at the other. The overt forms of antisocial behavior correspond roughly to those on the aggressive subdimension of the externalizing dimension, whereas the covert behaviors correspond roughly to those on the delinquent subdimension of the externalizing dimension.

panic A group of unexpected physical symptoms of the fight/flight response that occur in the absence of any obvious threat or danger.

panic attack A sudden and overwhelming period of intense fear or discomfort accompanied by four or more physical and cognitive symptoms characteristic of the fight/flight response.

panic disorder (PD) A form of anxiety disorder characterized by panic attacks and sudden feelings of terror that strike repeatedly and without warning. Physical symptoms include chest pain, heart palpitations, shortness of breath, dizziness, and abdominal stress. There is also persistent concern about having another attack and the possible implications and consequences it would bring.

parasomnias A category of sleep disorders in which behavioral or physiological events intrude on ongoing sleep. Persons suffering from parasomnias often complain of unusual behaviors during sleep such as sleepwalking and nightmares.

parent management training (PMT) A program aimed at teaching parents to cope effectively with their child's difficult behavior and their own reactions to it.

pedophilia Sexual activity or sexually arousing fantasies involving a prepubescent child by someone who is at least 16 years old and at least 5 years older than the child.

pervasive developmental disorder, not otherwise specified (PDD-NOS) A disorder in which the child displays social, communication, and behavioral impairments associated with PDD, but does not meet the criteria for PDD, schizophrenia, or other disorders.

pervasive developmental disorders (PDDs) A category of disorders characterized by severe and extensive impairments in social interaction and communication skills, along with stereotyped patterns of behaviors, interests, and activities.

phenotype An individual's observable characteristics or behavior (the expression of one's genotype in the environment).

phobia Fear that occurs at an inappropriate age, persists, is irrational or exaggerated, leads to avoidance of the object or event, and causes impairment in normal routines.

phonemes The basic sounds that make up language.

phonological awareness A broad construct that includes recognition of the relationship that exists between sounds and letters, detection of rhyme and alliteration, and awareness that sounds can be manipulated within syllables in words.

phonological disorder A form of communication disorder characterized by difficulties in articulation or sound production, but not necessarily in word expression.

phonology The ability to learn and store phonemes as well as the rules for combining the sounds into meaningful units or words. Deficits in phonology are a chief reason that most children and adults with communication and learning disorders have problems in language-based activities such as learning to read and spell.

physical abuse The infliction or risk of physical injury as a result of punching, beating, kicking, biting, burning, shaking, or otherwise intentionally harming a child.

physical neglect Failure to provide for a child's basic physical needs, including refusal of or delay in seeking health care, inadequate provision of food, abandonment, expulsion from the home or refusal to allow a runaway to return home, inadequate supervision, and inadequate provision of clean clothes.

pica A form of eating disorder in which the infant or toddler persists in eating inedible, nonnutritive substances. This disorder is one of the more common and usually less serious eating disorders found among very young children.

positive affectivity A persistent positive mood as reflected in states such as joy, enthusiasm, and energy.

positive illusory bias A person's report of higher self-esteem than is warranted by his or her behavior. This exaggeration of one's competence may, for example, cause a child with ADHD to perceive their relationships with their parents no differently than do control children, even though their parents see things in a more negative light.

post-traumatic stress disorder (PTSD) A form of anxiety disorder whereby the child displays persistent anxiety following exposure to or witnessing of an overwhelming traumatic event that is outside the range of usual human experience.

Prader-Willi syndrome A complex genetic disorder associated with an abnormality of chromosome 15. Children with Prader-Willi syndrome typically suffer from short stature, intellectual disability or learning disabilities, incomplete sexual development, certain behavior problems, low muscle tone, and an involuntary urge to eat constantly.

pragmatics The aspect of language that focuses on its appropriate use in social and communicative contexts.

predominantly hyperactive–impulsive type (ADHD-HI) See under *ADHD*.

predominantly inattentive type (ADHD-PI) See under *ADHD*.

preservation of sameness A characteristic of children with autistic disorder who show an anxious and obsessive insistence on the maintenance of sameness that no one but the child may disrupt. Changes in daily routine, arrangement of objects, or the wording of requests, or the sight of anything broken or incomplete will produce tantrums or despair.

prevalence rates The number of cases of a disorder, whether new or previously existing, that are observed during a specified period of time.

prevention Activities directed at decreasing the chances that undesired future outcomes will occur.

problem-solving skills training (PSST) Instruction aimed at targeting the cognitive deficiencies and distortions displayed by children and adolescents who experience conduct problems in interpersonal situations, particularly those children who are aggressive.

profound mental retardation An IQ level below 20 or 25.

prognosis The prediction of the course or outcome of a disorder.

projective test A form of assessment that presents the child with ambiguous stimuli, such as inkblots or pictures of people. The hypothesis is that the child will "project" his or her own personality on the ambiguous stimuli of other people and things. Without being aware, the child discloses his or her unconscious thoughts and feelings to the clinician.

pronoun reversal The repetition of personal pronouns exactly as heard, without changing them according to the person being referred to. For example, if asked "Are you hungry?" one might reply "You are hungry," rather than "I am hungry."

protective factor A variable that precedes a negative outcome of interest and decreases the chances that the outcome will occur.

protodeclarative gestures Gestures or vocalizations that direct the visual attention of other people to objects of shared interest, such as pointing to a dog; done with the prime purpose of engaging another person in interaction.

protoimperative gestures Gestures or vocalizations used to express needs, such as pointing to an object that one desires but cannot reach.

psychological disorder A pattern of behavioral, cognitive, or physical symptoms that includes one or more of the following prominent features: (a) some degree of distress in the subject; (b) behavior indicating some degree of disability; and (c) an increased risk of suffering, death, pain, disability, or an important loss of freedom.

psychological factors affecting physical condition Psychological disorders or conditions that are presumed to cause or exacerbate a physical condition.

psychopathy A pattern of deceitful, callous, manipulative, and remorseless behavior.

purging Behavior aimed at ridding the body of consumed food, including self-induced vomiting and the misuse of laxatives, diuretics, or enemas. (Also see *compensatory behavior.*)

qualitative research Research for which the purpose is to describe, interpret, and understand the phenomenon of interest in the context in which it is experienced.

quality of life A person's subjective perception of their position in life as evidenced by their physical, psychological, and social functioning.

random assignment The assignment of research participants to treatment conditions whereby each participant has an equal chance of being assigned to each condition. Random assignment increases the likelihood that characteristics other than the independent variable will be equally distributed across treatment groups.

randomized controlled trials (RCT) A design used to evaluate treatment outcomes in which children with a particular problem are randomly assigned to various treatment and control conditions.

real-time prospective design A research design in which the research sample is identified and then followed longitudinally over time, with data collected at specified time intervals.

reciprocal influence The theory that the child's behavior is both influenced by and itself influences the behavior of other family members.

relational disorders Disorders that occur in the context of relationships, such as child abuse and neglect. Relational disorders signify the connection between children's behavior patterns and the availability of a suitable childrearing environment.

reliability The extent to which the result of an experiment is consistent or repeatable.

research Generally viewed as a systematic way of finding answers to questions—a method of inquiry that follows certain rules.

research designs Research designs are the strategies used to examine questions of interest. They detail the ways in which a researcher arranges conditions to draw valid inferences about the variables of interest.

residential care A living arrangement in which a child whose family or school cannot adequately provide for him or her is cared for in a specialized out-of-home setting.

resilience The ability to avoid negative outcomes despite being at risk for psychopathology.

response prevention A procedure used in the treatment of anxiety that prevents the child from engaging in escape or avoidance behaviors. This procedure is usually used in conjunction with flooding.

response-cost procedure A technique for managing a subject's behavior that involves the loss of reinforcers such as privileges, activities, points, or tokens in response to inappropriate behavior.

restricting type A type of anorexia where the individual uses dieting, fasting, or excessive exercise to lose or avoid gaining weight. During the current episode of anorexia, the person has not engaged in binge-eating or purging behavior.

retrospective design A research design in which the research sample is asked to provide information relating to an earlier time period.

Rett's disorder A pervasive developmental disorder characterized by a deceleration of head growth in the early years, a loss of previously acquired purposeful hand skills with subsequent development of stereotyped hand movements, a loss of social engagement, poorly coordinated gait or trunk movements, severe impairments in expressive and receptive language development, and severe psychomotor retardation.

risk factor A variable that precedes a negative outcome of interest and increases the chances that the outcome will occur.

schizophrenia A form of psychotic disorder that involves characteristic disturbances in thinking (delusions), perception (hallucinations), speech, emotions, and behavior.

school refusal behavior A form of anxious behavior in which the child refuses to attend classes or has difficulty remaining in school for an entire day.

screening Identification of subjects at risk for a specific negative outcome.

selective attention The ability to concentrate exclusively on relevant stimuli and to avoid distraction by irrelevant stimuli in the environment.

selective mutism The inability or refusal to talk in social situations, despite the fact that the subject may talk at home or in other settings.

self-injurious behavior (SIB) Severe and sometimes life-threatening acts that cause damage to the subject's own body, such as head banging, eye gouging, severe scratching, rumination, some types of pica, and inserting objects under the skin.

self-instructional training Teaching children to use verbal cues to process information, which are initially taught by the therapist or teacher, to keep themselves on task.

self-stimulatory behaviors Repetitive body movements or movements of objects, such as hand flapping or spinning a pencil.

semistructured interviews Interviews that include specific questions designed to elicit information in a relatively consistent manner regardless of who is doing the interview. The interview format usually ensures that the most important aspects of a particular disorder are covered.

sensitive periods Windows of time during which environmental influences on development (both good and bad) are heightened, thus providing enhanced opportunities to learn.

separation anxiety disorder (SAD) A form of anxiety disorder in which the subject displays age-inappropriate, excessive, and disabling anxiety about being apart from his or her parents or away from home.

set point A comfortable range of body weight that the body tries to "defend" and maintain.

severe mental retardation An IQ level in the range of 20–25 to 35–40.

sexual abuse Abusive acts that are sexual in nature, including fondling a child's genitals, intercourse, incest, rape, sodomy, exhibitionism, and commercial exploitation through prostitution or the production of pornographic materials.

shared environment A subtype of environmental influences that refers to the environmental factors that produce similarities in developmental outcomes among siblings living in the same household. If siblings are more similar than expected from only their shared genetics, this implies an effect of the environment both siblings share, such as being exposed to marital conflict or poverty, or being parented in a similar manner.

single-case experimental design A type of research design most frequently used to evaluate the impact of a clinical treatment on a subject's problem. Single-case experimental designs involve repeated assessment of behavior over time, the replication of treatment effects on the same subject over time, and the subject serving as his or her own control by experiencing all treatment conditions.

sleep terrors A form of parasomnia that occurs during deep sleep and is characterized by abrupt awakening, accompanied by autonomic arousal but no recall.

sleepwalking A form of parasomnia that occurs during deep sleep, in which the individual gets out of bed and walks around but has no recall of such activity upon awakening.

social anxiety See *social phobia*.

social cognition A construct to describe how people think about themselves in relation to others, and how they interpret ambiguous events and solve problems.

social–cognitive abilities The skills involved in attending to, interpreting, and responding to social cues.

social learning A theoretical approach to the study of behavior that is interested in both overt behaviors and the role of possible cognitive mediators that may influence such behaviors directly or indirectly.

social phobia A marked and persistent fear of social or performance situations in which the subject is exposed to possible scrutiny and embarrassment.

social selection hypothesis The premise that people tend to select environments in which there are other people similar to themselves.

somatoform disorders A group of related problems involving physical symptoms that resemble or suggest a medical condition, but lack organic or physiological evidence: somatization (i.e., expression of feelings through physical symptoms), hypochondriasis (i.e., preoccupation with real or fancied ailments), and pain disorders (e.g., recurring stomach pains).

specific phobia A marked and persistent fear of clearly discernible, circumscribed objects or situations.

standardization The process by which a set of standards or norms is specified for a measurement procedure so that it can be used consistently across different assessments.

stigma A cluster of negative attitudes and beliefs that motivates fear, rejection, avoidance, and discrimination against people with mental illnesses.

stimulant medications Drugs that alter the activity in the frontostriatal region of the brain by impacting three or more neurotransmitters important to the functioning of this region—dopamine, norepinephrine, and epinephrine, and possibly serotonin.

structured observation Observation of a subject, usually occurring in a clinic or laboratory, in which the subject is given specific tasks or instructions to carry out, and researchers look for specific information.

subclinical levels of symptoms Troubling symptoms too few in number to qualify for a categorical diagnosis.

substance abuse In contrast to substance dependence, this diagnosis involves one or more harmful and repeated negative consequences of substance use over the last 12 months. Because substance dependence is the more serious diagnosis, a diagnosis of substance abuse is not given if an individual meets criteria for substance dependence.

substance dependence A diagnosis of an adolescent (or adult) who must show a maladaptive pattern of substance use for at least 12 months, accompanied by three or more significant clinical signs of distress: tolerance (the need for increased amounts to achieve intoxication), withdrawal (cognitive and physiological changes upon discontinuation of the drug), and other indices of compulsive use. Substance dependence is also characterized as with or without physiological dependence (i.e., with or without evidence of tolerance or withdrawal).

substance use disorders (SUDs) Disorders that occur during adolescence and include substance dependence and substance abuse that result from the self-administration of any substance that alters mood, perception, or brain functioning.

subtype A group of people with a specific disorder who have something in common, such as symptoms, etiology, problem severity, or likely outcome, that makes them distinct from people with other subtypes of the same disorder.

sustained attention The ability to maintain a persistent focus of attention over time or when fatigued.

systematic desensitization A three-step behavior therapy technique for treating anxiety whereby (1) the child is taught to relax, (2) an anxiety hierarchy is constructed, and (3) the anxiety-provoking stimuli are presented sequentially while the child remains relaxed.

target behaviors Behaviors that are the primary problems of concern.

temperament The child's innate reactivity and self-regulation with respect to the domains of emotions, activity level, and attention; the child's organized style of behavior that appears early in development, such as fussiness or fearfulness, that shapes the child's approach to his or her environment and vice versa.

test A task or set of tasks given under standard conditions with the purpose of assessing some aspect of the subject's knowledge, skill, personality, or condition.

theory of mind (ToM) The cognition and understanding of mental states that cannot be observed directly, such as beliefs and desires, both in one's self and in others. Also referred to as *mentalization*.

tic disorders Disorders characterized by sudden, repetitive, nonrhythmic motor movements or phonic productions, such as eye blinking, facial grimacing, throat clearing, and grunting or other sounds.

transaction The process by which the subject and environment interact in a dynamic fashion to contribute to the expression of a disorder. (Also see *interdependent*.)

traumatic sexualization One possible outcome of child sexual abuse, whereby the child's sexual knowledge and behavior are shaped in developmentally inappropriate ways.

treatment Corrective actions that will permit successful adaptation by eliminating or reducing the impact of an undesired outcome that has already occurred.

treatment effectiveness The degree to which a treatment can be shown to work in actual clinical practice, as opposed to controlled laboratory conditions.

treatment efficacy The degree to which a treatment can produce changes under well-controlled conditions that depart from those typically used in clinical practice.

treatment planning and evaluation The process of using assessment information to generate a treatment plan and evaluate its effectiveness.

true experiment An experiment in which the researcher has maximum control over the independent variable or conditions of interest, and in which the researcher can use random assignment of subjects to groups, can include needed control conditions, and can control possible sources of bias.

two-factor theory Theory used to explain the learning and maintenance of fears through a combination of classical and operant conditioning.

unexpected discrepancy A basic premise of definitions of learning disorders that denotes a disparity or discrepancy between an individual's measured ability and actual performance.

validity The extent to which a measure actually assesses the dimension or construct that the researcher sets out to measure.

victimization Abuse or mistreatment of someone whose ability to protect himself or herself is limited (e.g., the mistreatment of a child by his or her parents).

References

AAIDD Ad Hoc Committee on Terminology and Classification. (2010). *Intellectual disability: Definition, classification, and systems of supports* (11th ed. of AAIDD definition manual). Washington, DC, US: American Association on Intellectual and Developmental Disabilities.

Aase, H., & Sagvolden, T. (2006). Infrequent, but not frequent, reinforcers produce more variable responding and deficient sustained attention in young children with attention-deficit/hyperactivity disorder. *Journal of Child Psychology and Psychiatry, 47*, 457–471. doi:10.1111/j.1469-7610.2005.01468.x

Abel, C. G., Osborn, C. A., & Twigg, D. A. (1993). Sexual assault through the life span: Adult offenders with juvenile histories. In H. E. Barbaree, W. L. Marshall, & S. M. Husdon (Eds.), *The juvenile sex offender* (pp. 104–117). New York: Guilford Press.

Abel, K. M., Drake, R., & Goldstein, J. M. (2010). Sex differences in schizophrenia. *International Review of Psychiatry, 22*, 417–428. doi:10.3109/09540261.2010.515205

Abela, J. R. Z., & Hankin, B. J. (2008a). Cognitive vulnerability in children and adolescents. In J. R. Z. Abela & B. J. Hankin (Eds.), *Handbook of depression in children and adolescents* (pp. 35–78). New York: Guilford Press.

Abela, J. R. Z., & Hankin, B. J. (Eds.). (2008b). *Handbook of depression in children and adolescents*. New York: Guilford Press.

Abela, J. R. Z., & Hankin, B. L. (2011). Rumination as a vulnerability factor to depression during the transition from early to middle adolescence: A multiwave longitudinal study. *Journal of Abnormal Psychology, 120*, 259–271. doi:10.1037/a0022796

Aber, J. L., Jones, S. M., & Raver, C. C. (2007). Poverty and child development: New perspectives on a defining issue. In J. L. Aber, S. J. Bishop-Josef, S. M. Jones, K. T. McLearn, & D. A. Phillips (Eds.), *Child development and social policy: Knowledge for action* (pp. 149–166). Washington, DC: American Psychological Association.

Abikoff, H. (2009). ADHD psychosocial treatments: Generalization reconsidered. *Journal of Attention Disorders, 13*, 207–210. doi:10.1177/1087054709333385

Abikoff, H., Courtney, M., Pelham, W., & Koplewicz, H. (1993). Teachers' ratings of disruptive behaviors: The influence of halo effects. *Journal of Abnormal Child Psychology, 21*, 519–533. doi:10.1007/BF00916317

Abramowitz, J. S., & Braddock, A. E. (2011). *Hypochondriasis and health anxiety.* Cambridge, MA: Hogrefe Publishing.

Abrams, E. Z., & Goodman, J. F. (1998). Diagnosing developmental problems in children: Parents and professionals negotiate bad news. *Journal of Pediatric Psychology, 23*, 87–98. doi:10.1093/jpepsy/23.2.87

Abramson, L. Y., Metalsky, G. I., & Alloy, L. B. (1989). Hopelessness depression: A theory-based subtype of depression. *Psychological Review, 96*, 358–372. doi:10.1037/0033-295X.96.2.358

Abramson, L. Y., Seligman, M. E., & Teasdale, J. D. (1978). Learned helplessness in humans: Critique and reformulation. *Journal of Abnormal Psychology, 37*, 49–74. doi:10.1037/0021-843X.87.1.49

Acebo, C., Sadeh, A., Seifer, R., Tzischinsky, O., Hafer, A., & Carskadon, M. A. (2005). Sleep/wake patterns derived from activity monitoring and maternal report for healthy 1- to 5-year-old children. *Sleep, 28*, 1568–1577. Retrieved from http://www.journalsleep.org

Achenbach, T. M. (1982). *Developmental psychopathology* (2nd ed.). New York: Wiley.

Achenbach, T. M. (1985). *Assessment and taxonomy of child and adolescent psychopathology.* Beverly Hills, CA: Sage.

Achenbach, T. M. (1991a). *Manual for the Child Behavior Checklist/4-18 and 1991 Profile.* Burlington: University of Vermont, Department of Psychiatry.

Achenbach, T. M. (1991b). *Manual for the Youth Self-Report and 1991 Profile.* Burlington: University of Vermont, Department of Psychiatry.

Achenbach, T. M. (2010). Multicultural evidence-based assessment of child and adolescent psychopathology. *Transcultural Psychiatry, 47*, 707–726. doi:10.1177/1363461510382590

Achenbach, T. M., Becker, A., Dopfner, M., Heiervang, E., Roessner, V., Steinhausen, H., . . . Rothenberger, A. (2008). Multicultural assessment of child and adolescent psychopathology with ASEBA and SDQ instruments: Research findings, applications, and future directions. *Journal of Child Psychology and Psychiatry, 49*, 251–275. doi:10.1111/j.1469-7610.2007.01867.x

Achenbach, T. M., McConaughy, S., Ivanova, M. Y., & Rescorla, L. A. (2011). *Brief Problem Monitor: For normed multi-informant assessment of children's functioning & responses to interventions (RTIs).* Burlington, VT: University of Vermont, Research Center for Children, Youth, & Families.

Achenbach, T. M., & Rescorla, L. A. (2001). *Manual for the ASEBA school-age forms & profiles.* Burlington: University of Vermont, Research Center for Children, Youth, and Families.

Achenbach, T. M., & Rescorla, L. A. (2006). *Developmental issues in assessment, taxonomy, and diagnosis of psychopathology: Life span and multicultural perspectives.* Hoboken, NJ: Wiley.

Achenbach, T. M., & Rescorla, L. A. (2007). *Multicultural understanding of child and adolescent psychopathology: Implications for mental health assessment.* New York: Guilford Press.

Ackard, D. M., Neumark-Sztainer, D., Story, M., & Perry, C. (2003). Overeating among adolescents: Prevalence and associations with weight-related characteristics and psychological health. *Pediatrics, 111*, 67–74. doi:10.1542/peds.111.1.67

Adams, D., & Oliver, C. (2011). The expression and assessment of emotions and internal states in individuals with severe or profound intellectual disabilities. *Clinical Psychology Review, 31*, 293–306. doi:10.1016/j.cpr.2011.01.003

Addington, J., Piskulic, D., & Marshall, C. (2010). Psychosocial treatments for schizophrenia. *Current Directions in Psychological Science, 19*, 260–263. doi:10.1177/0963721410377743

Afifi, T. O., & MacMillan, H. L. (2011). Resilience following child maltreatment: A review of protective factors. *The Canadian Journal of Psychiatry / La Revue Canadienne De Psychiatrie, 56*(5), 266–272.

Agency for Healthcare Research and Quality. (2011). *Minority Health: Recent Findings.* AHRQ Publication No. 00-PO41. Rockville, MD: Author. Retrieved from http://www.ahrq.gov/research/minorfind3.htm#health

Agras, W. S. (2010). *The Oxford handbook of eating disorders.* New York: Oxford University Press.

Ainsworth, M. D. S., Blehar, M. C., Waters, E., & Wall, S. (1978). *Patterns of attachment: A psychological study of the strange situation.* Hillsdale, NJ: Erlbaum.

Ajdacic-Gross, V., Vetter, S., Müller, M., Kawohl, W., Frey, F., Lupi, G., . . . Rössler, W. (2010). Risk factors for stuttering: A secondary analysis of a large data base. *European Archives of Psychiatry and Clinical Neuroscience, 260*, 279–286. doi:10.1007/s00406-009-0075-4

Akinbami, L. J., Moorman, J. E., & Liu, X. (2011). Asthma prevalence, health care use, and mortality: United States, 2005–2009. *National health statistics reports* (32). Hyattsville, MD: National Center for Health Statistics.

Alarcón, R. D. (2009). Culture, cultural factors and psychiatric diagnosis: Review and projections. *World Psychiatry, 8*, 131–139. Retrieved from http://www.wpanet.org/detail.php?section_id=10&content_id=421

Albano, A. M. (1995). Treatment of social anxiety in adolescents. *Cognitive and Behavioral Practice, 2*, 271–298. doi:10.1016/S1077-7229(95)80014-X

Albano, A. M. (2003). Treatment of social anxiety disorder. In M. A. Reinecke & F. M. Dattilio (Eds.), *Cognitive therapy with children and adolescents: A* casebook for clinical practice* (2nd ed., pp. 128–161). New York: Guilford Press.

Albano, A. M., Chorpita, B. F., & Barlow, D. H. (2003). Childhood anxiety disorders. In E. J. Mash & R. A. Barkley (Eds.), *Child psychopathology* (2nd ed., pp. 279–329). New York: Guilford Press.

Albano, A. M., Detweiler, M. F., & Logsdon-Conradsen, S. (1999). Cognitive-behavioral interventions with socially phobic children. In S. W. Russ & T. H. Ollendick (Eds.), *Handbook of psychotherapies with children and families* (pp. 255–280). New York: Plenum Press.

Albano, A. M., & DiBartolo, P. M. (2007). *Cognitive-behavioral therapy for social phobia in adolescents: Stand up, speak out* [Therapist guide]. New York: Oxford University Press.

Albano, A. M., Knox, L. S., & Barlow, D. H. (1995). Obsessive-compulsive disorder. In A. R. Eisen, C. A. Kearney, & C. A. Schaefer (Eds.), *Clinical handbook of anxiety disorders in children and adolescents* (pp. 282–316). Northvale, NJ: Aronson.

Albano, A. M., Miller, P. P., Zarate, R., Côté, G., & Barlow, D. H. (1997). Behavioral assessment and treatment of PTSD in prepubertal children: Attention to developmental factors and innovative strategies in the case study of a family. *Cognitive and Behavioral Practice, 4*, 245–262. doi:10.1016/S1077-7229%2897%2980003-X

Albaugh, M. D., Harder, V. S., Althoff, R. R., Rettew, D.C., Ehli, E. A., Lengyel-Nelson, T., . . . Hudziak, J. J. (2010). COMT Val158Met genotype as a risk factor for problem behaviors in youth. *Journal of the American Academy of Child & Adolescent Psychiatry, 49*, 841–849. doi:10.1016/j.jaoc.2010.05.015

Alegria, M., Vallas, M., & Pumariega, A. J. (2010). Racial and ethnic disparities in pediatric mental health. *Child and Adolescent Psychiatric Clinics of North America, 19*(4), 759–774. doi:10.1016/j.chc.2010.07.001

Alfano, C. A., Beidel, D. C., & Turner, S. M. (2002). Cognition in childhood anxiety: Conceptual, methodological, and developmental issues. *Clinical Psychology Review, 22*, 1209–1238. doi:10.1016/S0272-7358(02)00205-2

Alfano, C. A., Beidel, D. C., Turner, S. M., & Lewin, D. S. (2006). Preliminary evidence for sleep complaints among children referred for anxiety. *Sleep Medicine, 7*, 467–473. doi:10.1016/j.sleep.2006.05.002

Alfano, C. A., Ginsburg, G. S., & Kingery, J. N. (2007). Sleep-related problems among children and adolescents with anxiety disorders. *Journal of the American Academy of Child & Adolescent Psychiatry, 46*, 224–232. doi:10.1097/01.chi.0000242233.06011.8e

Ali, Z. (2001). Pica in people with intellectual disability: A literature review of aetiology, epidemiology and complications. *Journal of Intellectual & Developmental Disability, 26*, 205–215. doi:10.1080/13668250020054486

Allin, H., Wathen, C. N., & MacMillan, H. (2005). Treatment of child neglect: A systematic review. *The Canadian Journal of Psychiatry / La Revue Canadienne De Psychiatrie, 50*(8), 497–504.

Alriksson-Schmidt, A. I., Wallander, J., & Biasini, F. (2007). Quality of life and resilience in adolescents with a mobility disability. *Journal of Pediatric Psychology, 32*, 370–379. doi:10.1093/jpepsy/jsl002

Alsabban, S., Rivers, M., & McGuffin, P. (2011). Genome-wide searches for bipolar disorder genes. *Current Psychiatry Reports*. Advance on publication. doi:10.1007/s11920-011-0226-y

Alwell, M., & Cobb, B. (2009). Social and communicative interventions and transition outcomes for youth with disabilities: A systematic review. *Career Development for Exceptional Individuals, 32*, 94–107. doi:10.1177/0885728809336657

Amaya-Jackson, L., & March, J. S. (1995). Posttraumatic stress disorder. In J. S. March (Ed.), *Anxiety disorders in children and adolescents* (pp. 276–300). New York: Guilford Press.

Amendah, D. D., Grosse, S. D., & Bertrand, J. (2011). Medical expenditures of children in the United States with fetal alcohol syndrome. *Neurotoxicology and Teratology, 33*, 322–324. doi:10.1016/j.ntt.2010.10.008

Amendah, D. D., Mvundura, M., Kavanagh, P. L., Sprinz, P. G., & Grosse, S. D. (2010). Sickle cell disease–related pediatric medical expenditures in the U.S. *American Journal of Preventive Medicine, 38*, S550–S556. doi:10.1016/j.amepre.2010.01.004

American Academy of Child and Adolescent Psychiatry (1980/1995). *Code of ethics*. Retrieved from http://www.aacap.org/galleries/AboutUs/CodeOfEthics.PDF

American Academy of Child and Adolescent Psychiatry (2004). *Psychiatric medication for children and adolescents. II: Types of medications*. Retrieved from http://www.aacap.org/publications/factsfam/29.htm

American Academy of Child and Adolescent Psychiatry (AACAP). (2001). Practice parameter for the assessment and treatment of children and adolescents with suicidal behavior. *Journal of the American Academy of Child & Adolescent Psychiatry, 40*(Suppl.), 24S–51S. doi:10.1097/00004583-200107001-00003

American Academy of Child and Adolescent Psychiatry (AACAP). (2007a). AACAP official action: Practice parameter on child and adolescent mental health care in community systems of care. *Journal of the American Academy of Child & Adolescent Psychiatry, 46*, 284–299. doi:10.1097/01.chi.0000246061.70330.b8

American Academy of Child and Adolescent Psychiatry (AACAP). (2007b). Practice parameter for the assessment and treatment of children and adolescents with anxiety disorders. *Journal of the American Academy of Child & Adolescent Psychiatry, 46*, 267–283. doi:10.1097/01.chi.0000246070.23695.06

American Academy of Child and Adolescent Psychiatry (AACAP). (2007c). AACAP official action: Practice parameter for the assessment and treatment of children and adolescents with bipolar disorder. *Journal of the American Academy of Child & Adolescent Psychiatry, 46*, 107–125. doi:10.1097/01.chi.0000242240.69678.c4

American Academy of Child and Adolescent Psychiatry (AACAP). (2007d). AACAP official action: Practice parameter for the assessment and treatment of children and adolescents with depressive disorders. *Journal of the American Academy of Child & Adolescent Psychiatry, 46*, 1503–1526. doi:10.1097/chi.0b013e318145ae1c

American Academy of Child and Adolescent Psychiatry (AACAP). (2010). Practice parameter for the assessment and treatment of children and adolescents with posttraumatic stress disorder. *Journal of the American Academy of Child & Adolescent Psychiatry, 49*, 414–430. doi:10.1016/j.jaac.2009.12.020

American Psychiatric Association. (1952). *Diagnostic and statistical manual of mental disorders*. Washington, DC: Author.

American Psychiatric Association. (1968). *Diagnostic and statistical manual of mental disorders* (2nd ed.). Washington, DC: Author.

American Psychiatric Association. (1980). *Diagnostic and statistical manual of mental disorders* (3rd ed.). Washington, DC: Author.

American Psychiatric Association. (1987). *Diagnostic and statistical manual of mental disorders* (3rd ed., rev.). Washington, DC: Author.

American Psychiatric Association. (1994). *Diagnostic and statistical manual of mental disorders* (4th ed.). Washington, DC: Author.

American Psychiatric Association. (2000). *Diagnostic and statistical manual of mental disorders DSM-IV-TR* (text revision). Washington, DC: Author.

American Psychiatric Association. (2010). *Issues pertinent to a developmental approach to bipolar disorder in DSM-5*. Washington, DC: American Psychiatric Association. Retrieved from http://www.dsm5.org/ProposedRevision/Pages/proposedrevision.aspx?rid=524#

American Psychiatric Association (2010). *Proposed draft revisions to DSM disorders and criteria*. Retrieved from http://www.dsm5.org/ProposedRevisions/

American Psychological Association (2002). Ethical principles of psychologists and code of conduct. *American Psychologist, 57*, 1060–1073. doi:10.1037/0003-066X.57.12.1060

American Psychological Association. (2010). *Ethical principles of psychologists and code of conduct: 2010 Amendments*. Retrieved from http://www.apa.org/ethics/code/index.aspx

American Psychological Association. (1996/2007). Violence and the family. *Report of the American Psychological Association Presidential Task Force on Violence and the Family*. Washington, DC: Author. Available: http://www.apa.org/pi/viol&fam.html. Accessed May 1, 2008.

American Speech-Language-Hearing Association (ASHA). (2008). Incidence and prevalence of communication disorders and hearing loss in children—2008 edition. Retrieved from http://www.asha.org/members/research/reports/children.htm

Anders, T. F., & Eiben, L. A. (1997). Pediatric sleep disorders: A review of the past 10 years. *Journal of the American Academy of Child & Adolescent Psychiatry, 36*, 9–20. doi:10.1097/00004583-199701000-00012

Anders, T., Goodlin-Jones, B., & Sadeh, A. (2000). Sleep disorders. In C. H. Zeanah Jr. (Ed.), *Handbook of infant mental health* (2nd ed., pp. 326–338). New York: Guilford Press.

Anderson, C. A., & Bushman, B. J. (2002). The effects of media violence on society. *Science, 295*, 2377–2379. doi:10.1126/science.1070765

Anderson, E. (1994, May). The code of the streets. *Atlantic Monthly, 273*, 81–94. Retrieved from http://www.theatlantic.com/magazine/archive/1994/05/the-code-of-the-streets/6601/

Anderson, E. R., & Hope, D. A. (2008). A review of the tripartite model for understanding the link between anxiety and depression in youth. *Clinical Psychology Review, 28*, 275–287. doi:10.1016/j.cpr.2007.05.004

Anderson, E. R., & Mayes, L. C. (2009). Race/ethnicity and internalizing disorders in youth: A review. *Clinical Psychology Review, 30*, 338–348. doi:10.1016/j.cpr.2009.12.008

Anderson, E. R., & Mayes, L. C. (2010). Race/ethnicity and internalizing disorders in youth: A review. *Clinical Psychology Review, 30*, 338–348. doi:10.1016/j.cpr.2009.12.008

Anderson, J. S., Druzgal, T. J., Froehlich, A., BuBray, M. B., Lange, N., Alexander., A. L., . . . Lainhart, J. E. (2011). Decreased interhemispheric functional connectivity in autism. *Cerebral Cortex, 21*, 1134–1146. doi:10.1093/cercor/bhq190

Anderson, K. E., Lytton, H., & Romney, D. M. (1986). Mothers' interactions with normal and conduct-disordered boys: Who affects whom? *Developmental Psychology, 22*, 604–609. doi:10.1037/0012-1649.22.5.604

Anderson, K. G., Ramo, D. E., Schulte, M. T., Cummins, K., & Brown, S. A. (2007). Substance use treatment outcomes for youth: Integrating personal and environmental predictors. *Drug and Alcohol Dependence, 88*, 42–48. doi:10.1016/j.drugalcdep.2006.09.014

Anderson, S. E., Murray, D. M., Johnson, C. C., Elder, J. P., Lyttle, L. A., Jobe, J. B., . . . Stevens, J. (2011). Obesity and depressed mood associations differ by race/ethnicity in adolescent girls. *International Journal of Pediatric Obesity, 6*, 69–78. doi:10.3109/17477161003728477

Anderson-Fye, E. (2009). Cross-cultural issues in body image among children and adolescents. In L. Smolak, & J. K. Thompson (Eds.), *Body image, eating disorders, and obesity in youth: Assessment, prevention, and treatment.* (2nd ed., pp. 113–133). Washington, DC: American Psychological Association.

Andersson, U. (2010). Skill development in different components of arithmetic and basic cognitive functions: Findings from a 3-year longitudinal study of children with different types of learning difficulties. *Journal of Educational Psychology, 102*, 115–134. doi:10.1037/a0016838

Andrade, A. R., Lambert, E. W., & Bickman, L. (2000). Dose effect in child psychotherapy: Outcomes associated with negligible treatment. *Journal of the American Academy of Child & Adolescent Psychiatry, 39*, 161–168. doi:10.1097/00004583-200002000-00014

Andrews, B., Brewin, C. R., Philpott, R., & Stewart, L. (2007). Delayed-onset posttraumatic stress disorder: A systematic review of the evidence. *American Journal of Psychiatry, 164*, 1319–1326. doi:10.1176/appi.ajp.2007.06091491

Andrews, G., Hobbs, M. J., Borkovec, T. D., Beesdo, K., Craske, M. G., Heimberg, R. G., . . . & Stanley, M. A. (2010). Generalized worry disorder: A review of DSM-IV generalized anxiety disorder and options for DSM-V. *Depression and Anxiety, 27*, 134–147. doi:10.1002/da.20658

Andreyeva, T., Puhl, R. M., & Brownell, K. D. (2008). Changes in perceived weight discrimination among Americans, 1995–1996 through 2004–2006. *Obesity, 6*, 1129–1134. doi:10.1038/oby.2008.35

Angold, A., Costello, E. J., Burns, B. J., Erkanli, A., & Farmer, E. M. Z. (2000). Effectiveness of nonresidential specialty mental health services for children and adolescents in the "real world." *Journal of the American Academy of Child & Adolescent Psychiatry, 39*, 154–160. doi:10.1097/00004583-200002000-00013

Angold, A., Erkanli, A., Egger, H., & Costello, E. J. (2000). Stimulant treatment for children: A community perspective. *Journal of the American Academy of Child & Adolescent Psychiatry, 39*, 975–984. doi:10.1097/00004583-200008000-00009

Angold, A., Worthman, C., & Costello, E. J. (2003). Puberty and depression. In C. Hayward (Ed.), *Gender differences at puberty* (pp. 137–164). New York: Cambridge University Press.

Annin, P. (1996, January 22). Superpredators arrive. *Newsweek, 127*, 57. Retrieved from http://www.newsweek.com/1996/01/21/superpredators-arrive.html

Anthony, J. L., Lonigan, C. J., & Hecht, S. A. (1999). Dimensionality of posttraumatic stress disorder symptoms in children exposed to disaster: Results from confirmatory factor analyses. *Journal of Abnormal Psychology, 108*, 326–336. doi:10.1037/0021-843X.108.2.326

Anthonysamy, A., & Zimmer-Gembeck, M. J. (2007). Peer status and behaviors of maltreated children and their classmates in the early years of school. *Child Abuse & Neglect, 31*, 971–991.

Antrop, I., Roeyers, H., Van Oost, P., & Buysse, A. (2000). Stimulation seeking and hyperactivity in children with ADHD. *Journal of Child Psychology and Psychiatry, 41*, 225–231. doi:10.1111/1469-7610.00603

Antshel, K. M., & Arnold, G. (2007). Inborn errors of metabolism. In M. M. Mazzocco & J. L. Ross (Eds.), *Neurogenetic developmental disorders: Variation of manifestation in childhood* (pp. 297–334). Cambridge, MA: MIT Press.

Antshel, K. M., & Barkley, R. (2008). Psychosocial interventions in attention deficit hyperactivity disorder. *Child and Adolescent Psychiatric Clinics of North America, 17*, 421–437. doi:10.1016/j.chc.2007.11.005

Antshel, K. M., & Barkley, R. (2009). Developmental and behavioral disorders grown up: Attention deficit hyperactivity disorder. *Journal of Developmental and Behavioral Pediatrics, 30*, 81–90. doi:10.1097/DBP.0b013e31819359ea

Antshel, K. M., Faraone, S. V., Maglione, K., Doyle, A., Fried, R., Seidman, L., & Biederman, J. (2008). Temporal stability of ADHD in the high-IQ population: Results from the MGH longitudinal family studies of ADHD. *Journal of the American Academy of Child & Adolescent Psychiatry, 47*, 817–825. doi:10.1097/CHI.0b013e318172eecf

Antshel, K. M., Phillips, M. H., Gordon, M., Barkley, R., & Faraone, S. V. (2006). Is ADHD a valid disorder in children with intellectual delays? *Clinical Psychology Review, 26*, 555–572. doi:10.1016/j.cpr.2006.03.002

Applegate, B., Lahey, B. B., Hart, E. L., Biederman, J., Hynd, G. W., Barkley, R. A., . . . Shaffer, D. (1997). Validity of the age-of-onset criterion for ADHD: A report from the DSM-IV field trials. *Journal of the American Academy of Child & Adolescent Psychiatry, 36*, 1211–1221. doi:10.1097/00004583-199709000-00013

Arcelus, J., Mitchell, A. J., Wales, J., & Nielsen, S. (2011). Mortality rates in patients with anorexia nervosa and other eating disorders: A meta-analysis of 36 studies. *Archives of General Psychiatry, 68*, 274–731. doi:10.1001/archgenpsychiatry.2011.74

Aries, P. (1962). *Centuries of childhood.* New York: Vintage.

Armenteros, J. L., & Davies, M. (2006). Antipsychotics in early onset schizophrenia: Systematic review and meta-analysis. *European Child and Adolescent Psychiatry, 15*, 141–148. doi:10.1007/s00787-005-0515-2

Arnold, L. E., & DiSilvestro, R. A. (2005). Zinc in attention-deficit/hyperactivity disorder. *Journal of Child and Adolescent Psychopharmacology, 15*, 619–627. doi:10.1089/cap.2005.15.619

Arseneault, L., Cannon, M., Fisher, H. L., Polanczyk, G., & Moffitt, T. E. (2011). Childhood trauma and children's emerging psychotic symptoms: A genetically sensitive longitudinal cohort study. *American Journal of Psychiatry, 168*, 65–72. doi:10.1176/appi.ajp.2010.10040567

Arsenio, W. F., & Lemerise, E. A. (Eds.). (2010). *Emotions, aggression, and morality in children: Bridging development and psychopathology.* Washington, DC: American Psychological Association. doi:10.1037/12129-000

Asarnow, J. R., & Asarnow, R. F. (2003). Childhood-onset schizophrenia. In E. J. Mash & R. A. Barkley (Eds.), *Child psychopathology* (2nd ed., pp. 455–485). New York: Guilford Press.

Asarnow, J. R., Goldstein, M. J., & Ben-Meir, S. (1988). Parental communication deviance in childhood-onset schizophrenia spectrum and depressive disorders. *Journal of Child Psychology and Psychiatry, 29*, 825–838. doi:10.1111/j.1469-7610.1988.tb00756.x

Asarnow, J. R., Tompson, M. C., & McGrath, E. P. (2004). Childhood-onset schizophrenia: Clinical and treatment issues. *Journal of Child Psychology and Psychiatry, 45*, 180–194. doi:10.1111/j.1469-7610.2004.00213.x

Asarnow, R. F., & Asarnow, J. R. (1994). Childhood-onset schizophrenia. *Schizophrenia Bulletin, 20*, 591–598. doi:10.1111/j.1469-7610.1994.tb01280.x

Asarnow, R. F., & Kernan, C. L. (2008). Childhood schizophrenia. In T. P. Beauchaine & S. P. Hinshaw (Eds.), *Child and adolescent psychopathology* (pp. 614–642). New York: Wiley.

Asarnow, R. F., Nuechterlein, K. H., Fogelson, D., Subotnik, K. L., Payne, D. A., Russell, A. T., . . . Kendler, K. S. (2001). Schizophrenia and schizophrenia-spectrum personality disorders in the first-degree relatives of children with schizophrenia: The UCLA family study. *Archives of General Psychiatry, 58*, 581–588. Retrieved from http://archpsyc.ama-assn.org

Aschenbrand, S. G., Kendall, P. C., Webb, A., Safford, S. M., & Flannery-Schroeder, E. (2003). Is childhood separation anxiety disorder a predictor of adult panic disorder and agoraphobia? A seven-year longitudinal study. *Journal of the American Academy of Child & Adolescent Psychiatry, 42*, 1478–1485. doi:10.1097/00004583-200312000-00015

Asperger, H. (1944). Die autistischen Psychopathen im Kindesalter [The autistic psychopathy of childhood], *Archiv für Psychiatrie und Nervenkrankheiten, 117*, 76–136. doi:10.1007/BF01837709

Atkins, M. S., Hoagwood, K. E., Kutash, K., & Seidman, E. (2010). Toward the integration of education and mental health in schools. *Administration and Policy in Mental Health and Mental Health Services Research, 37*, 40–47. doi:10.1007/s10488-010-0299-7

Atkinson, A. P. (2009). Impaired recognition of emotions from body movements is associated with elevated motion coherence thresholds in autism spectrum disorders. *Neuropsychologia, 47*, 3023–3029. doi:10.1016/j.neuropsychologia.2009.05.019

Attie, I., & Brooks-Gunn, J. (1995). The development of eating regulation across the life span. In D. Cicchetti & D. J. Cohen (Eds.), *Developmental psychopathology: Vol. 2. Risk, disorder, and adaptation* (pp. 332–368). New York: Wiley.

Austin, S. B., Ziyadeh, N., Kahn, J. A., Camargo, C. A., Jr., Colditz, G. A., & Field, A. E. (2004). Sexual orientation, weight concerns, and eating-disordered behaviors in adolescent girls and boys. *Journal of the American Academy of Child & Adolescent Psychiatry, 43*, 1115–1123. doi:10.1097/01.chi.0000131139.93862.10

Avenevoli, S., Knight, E., Kessler, R. C., & Merikangas, K. R. (2008). Epidemiology of depression in children and adolescents. In J. R. Z. Abela & B. L. Hankin (Eds.), *Handbook of depression in children and adolescents* (pp. 6–32). New York: Guilford Press.

Averill, J. R. (2001). Studies on anger and aggression: Implications for theories of emotion. In W. Parrott (Ed.), *Emotions in social psychology: Essential readings* (pp. 337–352). Philadelphia, PA: Psychology Press.

Axelson, D., Birmaher, B., Strober, M., Gill, M. K., Valeria, S., Chiappetta, L., . . . Keller, M. (2006). Phenomenology of children and adolescents with bipolar spectrum disorders. *Archives of General Psychiatry, 63*, 1139–1148. doi:10.1001/archpsyc.63.10.1139

Axline, V. M. (1947). *Play therapy: The inner dynamics of childhood*. Boston: Houghton Mifflin.

Azar, S., & Wolfe, D. (2006). Child physical abuse and neglect. In E. J. Mash & R. A. Barkley (Eds.), *Treatment of childhood disorders* (3rd ed., pp. 595–646). New York: Guilford.

Bédard, A. C., Schulz, K. P., Cook, Jr., E. H., Fan, J., Clerkin, S. M., Ivanov, I., . . . Newcorn, J. H. (2010). Dopamine transporter gene variation modulates activation of striatum in youth with ADHD. *Neuroimage, 53*, 935–942. doi:10.1016/j.neuroimage.2009.12.041

Bögels, S. M., Alden, L., Beidel, D. C., Clark, L. A., Pine, D. S., Stein, M. B., & Voncken, M. (2010). Social anxiety disorder: Questions and answers for the DSM-V. *Depression and Anxiety, 27*, 168–189. doi:10.1002/da.20670

Bögels, S. M., & Brechman-Toussaint, M. L. (2006). Family issues in child anxiety: Attachment, family functioning, parental rearing and beliefs. *Clinical Psychology Review, 26*, 834–856. doi:10.1016/j.cpr.2005.08.001

Bögels, S. M., & Phares, V. (2008). Fathers' role in the etiology, prevention and treatment of child anxiety: A review and new model. *Clinical Psychology Review, 28*, 539–558. doi:10.1016/j.cpr.2007.07.011

Babinski, D. E., Pelham, W. E., Molina, B. S. G., Gnagy, E. M., Waschbusch, D. A., Yu, J., . . . Karch, K. M. (2010). Late adolescent and young adult outcomes of girls diagnosed with ADHD in childhood: An exploratory investigation. *Journal of Attention Disorders, 15*, 204–214. doi:10.1177/1087054710361586

Baer, J. C., & Martinez, C. D. (2006). Child maltreatment and insecure attachment: A meta-analysis. *Journal of Reproductive and Infant Psychology, 24*, 187–197.

Bagner, D. M., & Eyberg, S. M. (2007). Parent-child interaction therapy for disruptive behavior in children with mental retardation: A randomized controlled trial. *Journal of Clinical Child and Adolescent Psychology, 36*, 418–429. doi:10.1080/15374410701448448

Bagner, D. M., Pettit, J. W., Lewinsohn, P. M., & Seeley, J. R. (2011). Effect of maternal depression on child behavior: A sensitive period? *Journal of the American Academy of Child and Adolescent Psychiatry, 49*, 699–707. doi:10.1016/j.jaac.2010.03.012

Bailey, A., Phillips, W., & Rutter, M. (1996). Autism: Towards an integration of clinical, genetic, neuropsychological, and neurobiological perspectives. *Journal of Child Psychology and Psychiatry, 37*, 89–126. doi:10.1111/j.1469-7610.1996.tb01381.x

Baird, G., Charman, T., Pickles, A., Chandler, S., Loucas, T., Meldrum, D., . . . Simonoff, E. (2008). Regression, developmental trajectory and association problems in disorders in the autism spectrum: The SNAP study. *Journal of Autism and Developmental Disorders, 38*, 1827–1836. doi:10.1007/s10803-008-0571-9

Baker, L. A., Jacobson, K. C., Raine, A., Lozano, D. I., & Bezdjian, S. (2007). Genetic and environmental bases of childhood antisocial behavior: A multi-informant twin study. *Journal of Abnormal Psychology, 116*, 219–235. doi:10.1037/0021-843X.116.2.219

Bakermans-Kranenburg, M. J., & Van Ijzendoorn, M. H. (2011). Differential susceptibility to rearing environment depending on dopamine-related genes: New evidence and a meta-analysis. *Development and Psychopathology, 23*, 39–52. doi:10.1017/S0954579410000635

Bakwin, H. (1973). The genetics of enuresis. In I. Kolvin, R. C. MacKeith, & R. Meadow (Eds.), *Bladder control and enuresis* (pp. 73–77). Philadelphia: Lippincott.

Baldwin, W. K. (1958). The social position of mentally handicapped children in the regular class in the public schools. *Exceptional Children, 25*, 106–108. Retrieved from http://www.cec.sped.org

Ball, L. K., Ball, R., & Pratt, D. (2001). An assessment of thimerosal use in childhood vaccines. *Pediatrics, 107*, 1147–1154. doi:10.1542/peds.107.5.1147

Banaschewski, T., Becker, K., Scherag, S., Franke, B., & Coghill, D. (2010). Molecular genetics of attention-deficit/hyperactivity disorder: An overview. *European Child & Adolescent Psychiatry, 19*, 237–257. doi:10.1007/s00787-010-0090-z

Banaschewski, T., Hollis, C., Oosterlaan, J., Roeyers, H., Rubia, K., Willcutt, E., & Taylor, E. (2005). Towards an understanding of unique and shared pathways in the psychopathophysiology of ADHD. *Developmental Science, 8*, 132–140. doi:10.1111/j.1467-7687.2005.00400.x

Bandura, A. (1977). *Social learning theory*. Englewood Cliffs, NJ: Prentice Hall.

Bandura, A. (1986). *Social foundations of thought and action: A social cognitive theory*. Englewood Cliffs, NJ: Prentice Hall.

Bandura, A., & Walters, R. H. (1963). *Social learning and personality development*. New York: Holt, Rinehart, & Winston.

Banerjee, T. D., Middleton, F., Faraone, S. V. (2007). Environmental risk factors for attention-deficit hyperactivity disorder. *Acta Paediatrica, 96*, 1269–1274. doi:10.1111/j.1651-2227.2007.00430.x

Barenbaum, J., Ruchkin, V., & Schwab-Stone, M. (2004). The psychosocial aspects of children exposed to war: Practice and policy initiatives. *Journal of Child Psychology and Psychiatry, 45*, 41–62. doi:10.1046/j.0021-9630.2003.00304.x

Bar-Haim, Y., Henkin, Y., Ari-Even-Roth, D., Tetin-Schneider, S., Hildesheimer, M., & Muchnik, C. (2004). Reduced auditory efferent activity in childhood selective mutism. *Biological Psychiatry, 55*, 1061–1068. doi:10.1016/j.biopsych.2004.02.021

Bar-Haim, Y., Lamy, D., Pergamin, L., Bakersman-Kranenburg, M. J., & van IJzendoorn, M. H. (2007). Threat-related attentional bias in anxious and non-anxious individuals: A meta-analytic study. *Psychological Bulletin, 133*, 1–24. doi:10.1037/0033-2909.133.1.1

Barker, E. D., Tremblay, R. E., van Lier, P. A. C., Vitaro, F., Nagin, D. S., Assaad, J. M., & Seguin, J. R. (2011). The neurocognition of conduct disorder behaviors: Specificity to physical aggression and theft after controlling for ADHD symptoms. *Aggressive Behavior, 37*, 63–72. doi:10.1002/ab.20373

Barkley, R. A. (1988). The effects of methylphenidate on the interactions of preschool ADHD children with their mothers. *Journal of the American Academy of Child & Adolescent Psychiatry, 26*, 336–341. doi:10.1097/00004583-198805000-00012

Barkley, R. A. (1995). *Taking charge of ADHD: The complete, authoritative guide for parents*. New York: Guilford Press.

Barkley, R. A. (1997a). *ADHD and the nature of self-control*. New York: Guilford Press.

Barkley, R. A. (1997b). *Defiant children: A clinician's manual for assessment and parent training* (2nd ed.). New York: Guilford Press.

Barkley, R. A. (2000). *Taking charge of ADHD: The complete, authoritative guide for parents* (Rev. ed.). New York: Guilford Press.

Barkley, R. A. (2003). Attention-deficit/hyperactivity disorder. In E. J. Mash & R. A. Barkley (Eds.), *Child psychopathology* (pp. 75–143). New York: Guilford Press.

Barkley, R. A. (2006a). *Attention-deficit hyperactivity disorder: A handbook for diagnosis and treatment* (3rd ed.). New York: Guilford Press.

Barkley, R. A. (2006b). Attention-deficit/hyperactivity disorder in adolescents. In D. A. Wolfe & E. J. Mash (Eds.), *Behavioral and emotional disorders in adolescents* (pp. 91–152). New York: Guilford Press.

Barkley, R. A. (2010). Against the status quo: Revising the diagnostic criteria for ADHD. *Journal of the American Academy of Child & Adolescent Psychiatry, 49*, 205–207. doi:10.1016/j.jaac.2009.12.005

Barkley, R. A., & Biederman, J. (1997). Toward a broader definition of the age-of-onset criterion for attention-deficit hyperactivity disorder. *Journal of the American Academy of Child & Adolescent Psychiatry, 36*, 1204–1210. doi:10.1097/00004583-199709000-00012

Barkley, R. A., & Fischer, M. (2010) The unique contribution of emotional impulsiveness to impairment in major life activities in hyperactive children as adults. *Journal of the American Academy of Child & Adolescent Psychiatry, 49*, 503–513. doi:10.1016/j.jaac.2010.01.019

Barkley, R. A., Fischer, M., Smallish, L., & Fletcher, K. (2002). The persistence of attention-deficit/hyperactivity disorder into young adulthood as a function of reporting source and definition of disorder. *Journal of Abnormal Psychology, 111*, 279–289. doi:10.1037/0021-843X.111.2.279

Barkley, R. A., Murphy, K. R., & Fischer, M. (2008). *ADHD in adults: What the science says*. New York: Guilford Press.

Barkley, R. A., & Pfiffner, L. J. (1995). Off to school on the right foot: Managing your child's education. In R. A. Barkley, *Taking charge of ADHD: The complete, authoritative guide for parents* (pp. 206–221). New York: Guilford Press.

Barkley, R. A., Shelton, T. L., Crosswait, C., Moorehouse, M., Fletcher, K., Barrett, S., . . . Metevia, L. (2002). Preschool children with high levels of disruptive behavior: Three-year outcomes as a function of adaptive disability. *Development and Psychopathology, 14*, 45–68. doi:10.1017/S0954579402001037

Barlow, D. H. (2002). *Anxiety and its disorders: The nature and treatment of anxiety and panic* (2nd ed.). New York: Guilford Press.

Barlow, D. H., Nock, M. K., & Hersen, M. (2009). *Single case experimental designs: Strategies for studying behavior change*. Boston: Allyn & Bacon.

Barnea-Goraly, N., Lotspeich, L. J., & Reiss A. L. (2010). Similar white matter aberrations in children with autism and their unaffected siblings: A diffusion tensor imaging study using tract-based spatial statistics. *Archives of General Psychiatry, 67*, 1052–1060. doi:10.1001/archgenpsychiatry.2010.123

Barnett, D., Ganiban, J., & Cicchetti, D. (1999). Maltreatment, negative expressivity, and the development of Type D attachments from 12 to 24 months of age. *Monographs of the Society for Research in Child Development, 64*, 97–118.

Baron-Cohen, S. (1995). *Mindblindness: An essay on autism and theory of mind*. Cambridge, MA: MIT Press.

Baron-Cohen, S. (2002). The extreme male brain theory of autism. *Trends in Cognitive Sciences, 6*, 248–254. doi:10.1016/S1364-6613(02)01904-6

Baron-Cohen, S., & Bolton, P. (1993). *Autism: The facts*. Oxford, England: Oxford University Press.

Baron-Cohen, S., Richler, J., Bisarya, D., Gurunathan, N., & Wheelright, S. (2003). The systemizing quotient: An investigation of adults with Asperger syndrome or high-functioning autism, and normal sex differences. *Philosophical Transactions of the Royal Society: Biological Sciences, 358*, 361–374. doi:10.1098/rstb.2002.1206

Baron-Cohen, S., Tager-Flusberg, H., & Cohen, D. (2000). *Understanding other minds: Perspectives from developmental cognitive neuroscience*. Oxford, England: Oxford University Press.

Barrera, A. Z., Torres, L. D., & Munoz, R. F. (2007). Prevention of depression: The state of the science at the beginning of the 21st century. *International Review of Psychiatry, 19*, 655–670. doi:10.1080/09540260701797894

Barrett, J., & Fleming, A. S. (2011). All mothers are not created equal: Neural and psychobiological perspectives on mothering and the importance of individual differences. *Journal of Child Psychology and Psychiatry, 52*, 368–397. doi:10.1111/j.1469-7610.2010.02306.x

Barrett, P. M., Dadds, M. R., & Rapee, R. M. (1996). Family treatment of childhood anxiety: A controlled trial. *Journal of Consulting and Clinical Psychology, 64*, 333–342. doi:10.1037/0022-006X.64.2.333

Barrett, P. M., Farrell, L. J., Ollendick, T. H., & Dadds, M. (2006). Long-term outcomes of an Australian universal prevention trial of anxiety and depression symptoms in children and youth: An evaluation of the Friends program. *Journal of Clinical Child and Adolescent Psychology, 35*, 403–411. doi:10.1207/s15374424jccp3503_5

Barrett, P. M., Farrell, L., Pina, A. A., Peris, T. A., & Piacentini, J. (2008). Evidence-based psychosocial treatments for child and adolescent obsessive-compulsive disorder. *Journal of Clinical Child and Adolescent Psychology, 37*, 131–155. doi:10.1080/15374410701817956

Barrett, P. M., Rapee, R. M., Dadds, M. M., & Ryan, S. M. (1996). Family enhancement of cognitive style in anxious and aggressive children. *Journal of Abnormal Child Psychology, 24*, 187–203. doi:10.1007/BF01441484

Barrios, B. A., & Hartmann, D. P. (1997). Fears and anxieties. In E. J. Mash & L. G. Terdal (Eds.), *Assessment of childhood disorders* (3rd ed., pp. 230–327). New York: Guilford Press.

Barry, M. M. (2009). Addressing the determinants of positive mental health: Concepts, evidence and practice. *The International Journal of Mental Health Promotion, 11*, 4–17.

Barter, C., & Renold, E. (2000). "I wanna tell you a story": Exploring the application of vignettes in qualitative research with children and young people. *International Journal of Social Research Methodology: Theory & Practice, 3*, 307–323. doi:10.1080/13645570050178594

Barth, C., Fein, D., & Waterhouse, L. (1995). Delayed match-to-sample performance in autistic children. *Developmental Neuropsychology, 11*, 53–69. doi:10.1080/87565649509540603

Barton, M., & Volkmar, F. (1998). How commonly are known medical conditions associated with autism? *Journal of Autism and Developmental Disorders, 28*, 273–278. doi:10.1023/A:1026052417561

Bate, K. S., Malouff, J. M., Thorsteinsson, E. T., & Bhullar, N. (2011). The efficacy of habit reversal therapy for tics, habit disorders, and stuttering: A meta-analytic review. *Clinical Psychology Review, 31*, 865–871. doi:10.1016/j.cpr.2011.03.013

Batsche, G. M., Kavale, K. A., & Kovaleski, J. F. (2006). Competing views: A dialogue on response to intervention. *Assessment for Effective Intervention [Special issue: Using response to intervention to assess learning disabilities], 32*, 6–19. doi:10.1177/15345084060320010301

Bauer, K. W., Laska, M. N., Fulkerson, J. A., & Neumark-Sztainer, D. (2011). Longitudinal and secular trends in parental encouragement for healthy eating, physical activity, and dieting throughout the adolescent years. *Journal of Adolescent Health, 49*, 306–311. doi:10.1016/j.jadohealth.2010.12.023

Bauermeister, J. J., Canino, G. Polanczyk, G., & Rohde, L. A. (2010). ADHD across cultures: Is there evidence for a bidimensional organization of symptoms? *Journal of Clinical Child and Adolescent Psychology, 39*, 362–372. doi:10.1080/15374411003691743

Baughman, F. (2006). *The ADHD fraud: How psychiatry makes "patients" out of normal children*. Oxford, England: Trafford.

Bauman, M. L. (1996). Neuroanatomic observations of the brain in pervasive developmental disorders. *Journal of Autism and Developmental Disorders, 26*, 199–203. doi:10.1007/BF02172012

Bauman, M. L., & Kemper, T. L. (2005). Structural brain anatomy in autism: What is the evidence? In M. L. Bauman & T. L. Kemper (Eds.), *The neurobiology of autism* (2nd ed., pp. 121–135). Baltimore: Johns Hopkins University Press.

Baumeister, R. F., Bushman, B. J., & Campbell, W. K. (2000). Self-esteem, narcissism, and aggression: Does violence result from low self-esteem or from threatened egotism? *Current Directions in Psychological Science, 9*, 26–29. doi:10.1111/1467-8721.00053

Beardon, C. E., Soares, J. C., Klunder, A. D., Nicoletti, M., Dierschke, N., Hayashi, K. M., . . . Thompson, P. M. (2007). Three-dimensional mapping of hippocampal anatomy in adolescents with bipolar disorder. *Journal of the American Academy of Child & Adolescent Psychiatry, 47*, 515–525. doi:10.1097/CHI.0b013e31816765ab

Beardslee, W. R., Chien, P. L., & Bell, C. C. (2011). Prevention of mental disorders, substance abuse, and problem behaviors: A developmental perspective. *Psychiatric Services, 62*, 247–254. doi:10.1176/appi.ps.62.3.247

Bearman, S. K., & Weisz, J. R. (2009). Primary and secondary control enhancement training (PASCET): Applying the deployment-focused model of treatment development and testing. In C. A. Essau (Ed.), *Treatments for adolescent depression: Theory and practice* (pp. 97–121). New York: Oxford University Press.

Beauchaine, T. P. (2003). Taxometrics and developmental psychopathology. *Development and Psychopathology, 15*, 501–527. doi:10.1017/S0954579403000270

Beauchaine, T. P., Hinshaw, S. P., & Pang, K. L. (2010). Comorbidity of attention-deficit/hyperactivity disorder and early-onset conduct disorder: Biological, environmental, and developmental mechanisms. *Clinical Psychology: Science and Practice, 17*, 327–336. doi:10.1111/j.1468-2850.2010.01224.x

Beauchaine, T. P., Katkin, E. S., Strassberg, Z., & Snarr, J. (2001). Disinhibitory psychopathology in male adolescents: Discriminating conduct disorder from attention-deficit/hyperactivity disorder through concurrent assessment of multiple autonomic states. *Journal of Abnormal Psychology, 110*, 610–624. doi:10.1037/0021-843X.110.4.610

Bebko, J. M., & Weiss, J. A. (2006). Mental retardation. In R. T. Ammerman (Ed.), *Comprehensive handbook of personality and psychopathology* (Vol. 3, pp. 233–253). Hoboken, NJ: Wiley.

Beck, A. T. (1967). *Depression: Clinical, experimental, and theoretical aspects*. Philadelphia: University of Pennsylvania Press.

Beck, H. P., Levinson, S., & Irons, G. (2009). Finding Little Albert: A journey to John B. Watson's infant laboratory. *American Psychologist, 64*(7), 605–614. doi:10.1037/a0017234

Beck, S. J., Hanson, C. A., Puffenberger, S. S., Benninger, K. L., & Benninger, W. B. (2010). A controlled trial of working memory training for children and adolescents with ADHD. *Journal of Clinical Child and Adolescent Psychology, 39*, 825–836. doi:10.1080/15374416.2010.517162

Becker, A. E., Burwell, R. A., Herzog, D. B., Hamburg, P., & Gilman, S. E. (2002). Eating behaviours and attitudes following prolonged exposure to television among ethnic Fijian adolescent girls. *British Journal of Psychiatry, 180*, 509–514. doi:10.1192/bjp.180.6.509

Becker, K. D., Chorpita, B. F., & Daleiden, E. L. (2011). Improvement in symptoms versus functioning: How do our best treatments measure up? *Administration and Policy in Mental Health and Mental Health Services Research, 38*, 440–458. doi:10.1007/s10488-010-0332-x

Becker-Blease, K. A., Turner, H. A., & Finkelhor, D. (2010). Disasters, victimization, and children's mental health. *Child Development, 81*, 1040–1052. doi:10.1111/j.1467-8624.2010.01453.x

Beesdo, K., Knappe, S., & Pine, D. S. (2009). Anxiety and anxiety disorders in children and adolescents: Developmental issues and implications for DSM-V. *Psychiatric Clinics of North America, 32*, 483–524. doi:10.1016/j.psc.2009.06.002

Beesdo, K., Pine, D. S., Lieb, R., & Wittchen, H.U. (2010). Incidence and risk patterns of anxiety and depressive disorders and categorization of generalized anxiety disorder. *Archives of General Psychiatry, 67*, 47–57. doi:10.1001/archgenpsychiatry.2009.177

Beidel, D. C., & Turner, S. M. (1997). At risk for anxiety: I. Psychopathology in the offspring of anxious parents. *Journal of the American Academy of Child & Adolescent Psychiatry, 36*, 918–924. doi:10.1097/00004583-199707000-00013

Beidel, D. C., & Turner, S. M. (1998). *Shy children, phobic adults: Nature and treatment of social phobia*. Washington, DC: American Psychological Association.

Beidel, D. C., & Turner, S. M. (2007). *Clinical presentation of social anxiety disorder in children and adolescents*. Washington, DC: American Psychological Association.

Beidel, D. C., Turner, S. M., & Morris, T. L. (1999). Psychopathology of childhood social phobia. *Journal of the American Academy of Child & Adolescent Psychiatry, 38*, 643–650. doi:10.1097/00004583-199906000-00010

Belfer, M. L. (2008). Child and adolescent mental disorders: The magnitude of the problem across the globe. *Journal of Child Psychology and Psychiatry, 49*, 226–236. doi:10.1111/j.1469-7610.2007.01855.x

Belitz, J., & Bailey, R. A. (2009). Clinical ethics for the treatment of children and adolescents: A guide for general psychiatrists. *Psychiatric Clinics of North America, 32*, 243–257. doi:10.1016/j.psc.2009.02.001

Bell, A. (1996, March). Dying to win: The shocking stories of eating disorders and female athletes. *Teen*, 34–41.

Bell, A. S. (2011). A critical review of ADHD diagnostic criteria: What to address in the DSM-V. *Journal of Attention Disorders, 15*, 3–10. doi:10.1177/1087054710365982

Bell, B. T., & Dittmar, H. (2011). Does media type matter? The role of identification in adolescent girls' media consumption and the impact of different thin-ideal media on body image. *Sex Roles, 65*, 478–490. doi:10.1007/s11199-011-9964-x

Bell, D. J., Foster, S. L., & Mash, E. J. (Eds.). (2005). *Handbook of behavioral and emotional problems in girls*. New York: Kluwer.

Bell-Dolan, D. J., Last, C. G., & Strauss, C. C. (1990). Symptoms of anxiety disorders in normal children. *Journal of the American Academy of Child & Adolescent Psychiatry, 29*, 759–765. doi:10.1097/00004583-199009000-00014

Bellamy, C. (2002). *The state of the world's children 2002: Leadership*. New York: United Nations Children's Fund.

Bellin, M. H., & Kovacs, P. J. (2006). Fostering resilience in siblings of youths with a chronic health condition: A review of the literature. *Health & Social Work, 31*, 209–216. Retrieved from http://www.naswpress.org/publications/journals/hsw.html

Belmonte, M. K., Gomot, M., & Baron-Cohen, S. (2010). Visual attention in autism families: 'unaffected' sibs share atypical frontal activation. *Journal of Child Psychology and Psychiatry, 51*, 259–276. doi:10.1111/j.1469-7610.2009.02153.x

Belsky, J., & de Haan, M. (2011). Parenting and children's brain development: The end of the beginning. *Journal of Child Psychology and Psychiatry, 52*, 409–428. doi:10.1111/j.1469-7610.2010.02281.x

Bemporad, J. R. (1979). Adult recollections of a formerly autistic child. *Journal of Autism and Developmental Disorders, 9*, 179–197. doi:10.1007/BF01531533

Bemporad, J. R. (1994). Dynamic and interpersonal theories of depression. In W. M. Reynolds & H. F. Johnston (Eds.), *Handbook of depression in children and adolescents* (pp. 81–95). New York: Plenum Press.

Ben-Zeev, D., Young, M. A., Corrigan, P. W. (2010). DSM-V and the stigma of mental illness. *Journal of Mental Health, 19*, 318–327. doi:10.3109/09638237.2010.492484

Benasich, A. A., Curtiss, S., & Tallal, P. (1993). Language, learning, and behavioral disturbances in childhood: A longitudinal perspective. *Journal of the American Academy of Child & Adolescent Psychiatry, 32*, 585–594.

Benassi, M., Simonelli, L., Giovagnoli, S., & Bolzani, R. (2010). Coherence motion perception in developmental dyslexia: A meta-analysis of behavioral studies. *Dyslexia: An International Journal of Research and Practice, 16*, 341–357. doi:10.1002/dys.412

Benes, F. M. (2006). The development of the prefrontal cortex: The maturation of neurotransmitter systems and their interactions. In D. Cicchetti & D. J. Cohen (Eds.), *Developmental psychopathology: Vol. 2. Developmental neuroscience* (2nd ed., pp. 216–258). Hoboken, NJ: Wiley.

Benjamin, L. T., Jr., & Shields, S. A. (1990). Leta Stetter Hollingworth (1886–1939). In A. N. O' Connell & N. F. Russo (Eds.), *Women in psychology: A bio-biographic sourcebook* (pp. 173–183). Westport, CT: Greenwood.

Benjamin, L. T., Jr., Whitaker, J. L., Ramsey, R. M., & Zeve, D. R. (2007). John B. Watson's alleged sex research: An appraisal of the evidence. *American Psychologist, 62*, 131–139. doi:10.1037/0003-066X.62.2.131

Benjet, C., & Kazdin, A. E. (2003). Spanking children: The controversies, findings and new directions. *Clinical Psychology Review. 23*, 197–224. doi:10.1016/S0272-7358%2802%2900206-4

Bennett, T., Szatmari, P., Bryson, S., Volden, J., Zwaigenbaum, L., Vaccarella, L., . . . Boyle, M. (2008). Differentiating autism and Asperger syndrome on the basis of language delay or impairment. *Journal of Autism and Developmental Disorders, 38*, 616–625. doi:10.1007/s10803-007-0428-7

Bennett-Gates, D., & Zigler, E. (1998). Resolving the developmental-difference debate: An evaluation of the triarchic and systems theory models. In J. A. Burack, R. M. Hodapp, & E. Zigler (Eds.), *Handbook of mental retardation and development* (pp. 115–131). New York: Cambridge University Press.

Benoit, D. (2009). Feeding disorders, failure to thrive, and obesity. In C. H. Zeanah (Ed.), *Handbook of infant mental health* (3rd ed., pp. 377–391). New York: Guilford Press.

Benoit, D., Zeanah, C. H., & Barton, L. M. (1989). Maternal attachment disturbances in failure to thrive. *Infant Mental Health Journal, 10*, 185–202. doi:10.1002/1097-0355(198923)10:3<185::AID-IMHJ2280100306>3.0.CO;2-0

Berger, A., & Berger, A. (2011). Individual differences in self-regulation. In A. Berger (Ed.), *Self-regulation: Brain, cognition, and development.* (pp. 61–90). Washington, DC: American Psychological Association. doi:10.1037/12327-004

Bergman, R. L., Piacentini, J., & McKracken, J. T. (2002). Prevalence and description of selective mutism in a school-based sample. *Journal of the American Academy of Child & Adolescent Psychiatry, 41*, 938–946. doi:10.1097/00004583-200208000-00012

Berlin, L. J., Appleyard, K., & Dodge, K. A. (2011). Intergenerational continuity in child maltreatment: Mediating mechanisms and implications for prevention. *Child Development, 82*(1), 162–176. doi:10.1111/j.1467–8624.2010.01547.x

Berliner, L., & Elliot, D. (2002). Sexual abuse of children. In J. E. B. Myers, L. Berliner, J. Briere, C. T. Hendrix, C. Jenny, & T. A. Reid (Eds.), *The APSAC handbook on child maltreatment* (2nd Ed., pp. 55–78). Thousand Oaks, CA: Sage.

Berman, A. L., & Jobes, D. A. (1991). *Adolescent suicide: Assessment and intervention.* Washington, DC: American Psychological Association.

Bernard-Brak, L., Sulak, T. N., & Fearon, D. D. (2010). Coexisting disorders and academic achievement among children with ADHD. *Journal of Attention Disorders.* doi:10.1177/1087054710369667

Bernstein, G. A., & Victor, A. M. (2010). Separation anxiety disorder and school refusal.

Bernstein, G. A., Borchardt, C. M., & Perwien, A. R. (1996). Anxiety disorders in children and adolescents: A review of the past 10 years. *Journal of the American Academy of Child & Adolescent Psychiatry, 35*, 1110–1119. doi:10.1097/00004583-199609000-00008

Best, J. R., & Miller, P. H. (2010). A developmental perspective on executive function. *Child Development, 81*, 1641–1660. doi:0009-3920/2010/8106-0002

Bettelheim, B. (1967). *The empty fortress: Infantile autism and the birth of the self.* New York: Free Press.

Biederman, J., Faraone, S. V., Mick, E., Spencer, T., Wilens, T., Kiely, K., . . . Warburton, R. (1995). High risk for attention deficit hyperactivity disorder among children of parents with childhood onset of the disorder: A pilot study. *American Journal of Psychiatry, 152*, 431–435. Retrieved from http://ajp.psychiatryonline.org/index.dtl

Biederman, J., Mick, E., & Faraone, S. V. (1998). Depression in attention deficit hyperactivity disorder (ADHD) children: "True" depression or demoralization? *Journal of Affective Disorders, 47*, 113–122. doi:10.1016/S0165-0327(97)00127-4

Biederman, J., Monuteaux, M. C., Mick, E., Spencer, T., Wilens, T. E., Klein, K. L., . . . Faraone, S. V. (2006). Psychopathology in females with attention-deficit/hyperactivity disorder: A controlled five-year prospective study. *Biological Psychiatry, 60*, 1098–1105. doi:10.1016/j.biopsych.2006.02.031

Biederman, J., Petty, C. R., Monuteaux, M. C., Fried, R., Byrne, D., Mirto, T., . . . Faraone, S. V. (2010). Adult psychiatric outcomes of girls with attention deficit hyperactivity disorder: 11-year follow-up in a longitudinal case-control study. *American Journal of Psychiatry, 167*, 409–417. doi:10.1176/appi.ajp.2009.09050736

Bierman, K. L., Coie, J. D., Dodge, K. A., Greenberg, M. T., Lochman, J. E., McMahon, R. J., . . . Conduct Problems Prevention Research Group. (2010). The effects of a multiyear universal social–emotional learning program: The role of student and school characteristics. *Journal of Consulting and Clinical Psychology, 78*, 156–168. doi:10.1037/a0018607

Biklen, D. (1990). Communication unbound: Autism and praxis. *Harvard Educational Review, 60*, 291–314. Retrieved from http://www.hepg.org/main/her/Index.html

Biklen, D., & Cardinal, D. N. (Eds.). (1997). *Contested words, contested science: Unraveling the facilitated communication controversy.* New York: Teachers College Press.

Bird, H. R., Canino, G. J., Davies, M., Zhang, H., Ramirez, R., & Lahey, B. B. (2001). Prevalence and correlates of antisocial behaviors among three ethnic groups. *Journal of Abnormal Child Psychology, 29*, 465–478. doi:10.1023/A:1012279707372

Birmaher, B., Arbelaez, C., & Brent, D. A. (2002). Course and outcome of child and adolescent major depressive disorder. *Child and Adolescent Psychiatric Clinics of North America, 11*, 619–637. doi:10.1016/S1056-4993(02)00011-1

Birmaher, B., Axelson, D., Strober, M., Gill, M. K., Valeri, S., Chiappetta, L., . . . Keller, M. (2006). Clinical course of children and adolescents with bipolar spectrum disorders. *Archives of General Psychiatry, 63*, 175–183. doi:10.1001/archpsyc.63.2.175

Birmaher, B., Ryan, N. D., Williamson, D. E., Brent, D. A., Kaufman, J., Dahl, R. E., . . . Nelson, B. (1996). Childhood and adolescent depression: A review of the past 10 years: Part I. *Journal of the American Academy of Child & Adolescent Psychiatry, 35*, 1427–1439. doi:10.1097/00004583-199611000-00011

Birmaher, B., Williamson, D. E., Dahl, R. E., Axelson, D. A., Kaufman, J., Dorn, L. D., & Ryan, N. D. (2004). Clinical presentation and course of depression in youth: Does onset in childhood differ from onset in adolescence? *Journal of the American Academy of Child & Adolescent Psychiatry, 43*, 63–70. doi:10.1097/00004583-200401000-00015

Bishop, D. V. M., Bishop, S. J., Bright, P., James, C., Delaney, T., & Tallal, P. (1999). Different origin of auditory and phonological processing problems in children with language impairment: Evidence from a twin study. *Journal of Speech, Language, & Hearing Research, 42*, 155–168. Retrieved from http://www.jslhr.asha.org

Bishop, V. M. (2006). Developmental cognitive genetics: How psychology can inform genetics and vice versa. *Quarterly Journal of Experimental Psychology, 59*, 1153–1168. doi:10.1080/17470210500489372

Bittner, A., Egger, H. L., Erkanli, A., Costello, J., Foley, D. L., & Angold, A. (2007). What do childhood anxiety disorders predict? *Journal of Child Psychology and Psychiatry, 48*, 1174–1183. doi:10.1111/j.1469-7610.2007.01812.x

Black, M. M., Dubowitz, H., Krishnakumar, A., & Starr, R. H., Jr. (2007). Early intervention and recovery among children with failure to thrive: Follow-up at age 8. *Pediatrics, 120*, 59–69. doi:10.1542/peds.2006-1657

Blair, R. J. R. (2010). Empathy, moral development, and aggression: A cognitive neuroscience perspective. In W. F. Arsenio & E. A. Lemerise (Eds.), *Emotions aggression, and morality in children: Bridging development and psychopathology* (pp. 97–114). Washington, DC: American Psychological Association.

Blair, R. J. R. (2011). Commentary: Are callous unemotional traits all in the eyes? Examining eye contact in youth with conduct problems and callous-unemotional traits-reflections on Dadds et al. (2011). *Journal of Child Psychology and Psychiatry, 52*, 246–247. doi:10.1111/j.1469-7610.2010.02364.x

Blair, R. J. R., Peschardt, K. S., Budhani, S., Mitchell, D. G. V., & Pine, D. S. (2006). The development of psychopathy. *Journal of Child Psychology and Psychiatry, 47*, 262–275. doi:10.1111/j.1469-7610.2006.01596.x

Blazei, R. W., Iacono, W. G., & Krueger, R. F. (2006). Intergenerational transmission of antisocial behavior: How do kids become antisocial adults? *Applied and Preventive Psychology, 11*, 230–253. doi:10.1016/j.appsy.2006.07.001

Blissett, J., Meyer, C., & Haycraft, E. (2007). Maternal mental health and child feeding problems in a non-clinical group. *Eating Behaviors, 8*, 311–318. doi:10.1016/j.eatbeh.2006.11.007

Block, J., Block, J. H., & Gjerde, P. F. (1986). The personality of children prior to divorce: A prospective study. *Child Development, 57*, 827–840. doi:10.1111/1467-8624.ep7250240

Bloom, B., Cohen, R. C., & Freeman, G. (2011). Summary Health Statistics for U.S. Children: National Health Interview Survey, 2010. *Vital and Health Statistics Series 10* (250). DHHS Publication No. (PHS)-2012-1578. Hyattsville, MD: U.S. Department of Health and Human Services, Centers for Disease Control and Prevention, National Center for Health Statistics.

Blumberg, H. P., Kaufman, J., Martin, A., Whiteman, R., Zhang, J. H., Gore, J. C., . . . Peterson, B. S. (2003). Amygdala and hippocampal volumes in adolescents and adults with bipolar disorder. *Archives of General Psychiatry, 60*, 1201–1208. doi:10.1001/archpsyc.60.12.1201

Boada, R., & Pennington, B. F. (2006). Deficient implicit phonological representations in children with dyslexia. *Journal of Experimental Child Psychology, 95*, 153–193. doi:10.1016/j.jecp.2006.04.003

Bodden, D. H. M., Dirksen, C. D., & Bögels, S. M. (2008). Societal burden of clinically anxious youth referred for treatment: A cost-of-illness study. *Journal of Abnormal Child Psychology, 36*, 487–497. doi:10.1007/s10802-007-9194-4

Boden, J. M., Fergusson, D. M., & Horwood, L. J. (2011). Age of menarche and psychosocial outcomes in a New Zealand birth cohort. *Journal of the American Academy of Child & Adolescent Psychiatry, 50*, 132–140. doi:10.1016/j.jaac.2010.11.007

Bodfish, J. W. (2007). Stereotypy, self-injury, and related abnormal repetitive behaviors. In J. W. Jacobson, J. A. Mulick, & J. Rojahn (Eds.), *Handbook of intellectual and developmental disabilities: Issues in clinical child psychology* (pp. 481–505). New York: Springer.

Boetsch, E. A., Green, P. A., & Pennington, B. F. (1996). Psychosocial correlates of dyslexia across the life span. *Development and Psychopathology, 8*, 539–562. doi:10.1017/S0954579400007264

Bogdan, R., & Taylor, S. J. (1982). *Inside out: The social meaning of mental retardation*. Toronto, Ontario, Canada: University of Toronto Press.

Bolton, D., Eley, T. C., O'Connor, T. G., Perrin, S., Rabe-Hesketh, S., Rijsdijk, F., & Smith, P. (2006). Prevalence and genetic and environmental influences on anxiety disorders in 6-year-old twins. *Psychological Medicine, 36*, 335–344. doi:10.1017/S0033291705006537

Bolton, P., MacDonald, H., Pickles, A., Rios, P., Goode, S., Crowson, M., . . . Rutter, M. (1994). A case-control family history study of autism. *Journal of Child Psychology and Psychiatry, 35*, 877–900. doi:10.1111/j.1469-7610.1994.tb02300.x

Bongers, I. L., Koot, H. M., van der Ende, J., & Verhulst, F. C. (2003). The normative development of child and adolescent problem behavior. *Journal of Abnormal Psychology, 112*, 179–192. doi:10.1037/0021-843X.112.2.179

Booth, C. M., Li, G., Jina Zhang-Salomons, J., & Mackillop, W. J. (2010). The impact of socioeconomic status on stage of cancer at diagnosis and survival: A population-based study in Ontario, Canada. *Cancer, 116*, 4160–4167. doi:10.1002/cncr.25427

Bootzin, R. R., & Chambers, M. J. (1990). Childhood sleep disorders. In A. M. Gross & R. S. Drabman (Eds.), *Handbook of clinical behavioral pediatrics* (pp. 205–227). New York: Plenum Press.

Boraston, Z. L., Corden, B., Miles, L. K., Skuse, D. H., & Blakemore, S. J. (2008). Brief report: Perception of genuine and posed smiles by individuals with autism. *Journal of Autism and Developmental Disorders, 38*, 574–580. doi:10.1007/s10803-007-0421-1

Borawski, E. A., Ievers-Landis, C. E., Lovegreen, L. D., & Trapl, E. S. (2003). Parental monitoring, negotiated unsupervised time, and parental trust: The role of perceived parenting practices in adolescent health risk behaviors. *Journal of Adolescent Health, 33*, 60–70. doi:10.1016/S1054-139X(03)00100-9

Borkovec, T. D. (1994). The nature, functions, and origins of worry. In G. C. L. Davey & F. Tallis (Eds.), *Worrying: Perspectives on theory, assessment and treatment* (pp. 5–33). Chichester, England: Wiley.

Borkovec, T. D., Ray, W. J., & Stoeber, J. (1998). Worry: A cognitive phenomenon intimately linked to affective, physiological, and interpersonal behavioral processes. *Cognitive Therapy and Research, 22*, 561–576. doi:10.1023/A:1018790003416

Bornovalova, M. A., Hicks, B. M., Iacono, W. G., & McGue, M. (2010). Familial transmission and heritability of childhood disruptive disorders. *American Journal of Psychiatry, 167*, 1066–1074. doi:10.1176/appi.ajp.2010.09091272

Borowsky, I. W., Ireland, M., & Resnick, M. D. (2001). Adolescent suicide attempts: Risks and protectors. *Pediatrics, 107*, 485–493. doi:10.1542/peds.107.3.485

Borstelmann, L. J. (1983). Children before psychology: Ideas about children from antiquity to the late 1800s. In W. Kessen (Vol. Ed.), *Handbook of child psychology: Vol. 1. History, theory, and methods* (4th ed., pp. 1–40). New York: Wiley.

Bothe, A. K., Davidow, J. H., Bramlett, R. E., & Ingham, R. J. (2006). Stuttering treatment research 1970–2005: I. Systematic review incorporating trial quality assessment of behavioral, cognitive, and related approaches. *American Journal of Speech-Language Pathology, 15*, 321–341. doi:10.1044/1058-0360(2006/031)

Bouras, N., & Holt, G. (2007). *Psychiatric and behavioural disorders in intellectual and developmental disabilities* (2nd ed.). New York: Cambridge University Press.

Boutelle, K., Neumark-Sztainer, D., Story, M., & Resnick, M. (2002). Weight control behaviors among obese, overweight, and nonoverweight adolescents. *Journal of Pediatric Psychology, 27*, 531–540. doi:10.1093/jpepsy/27.6.531

Bowlby, J. (1950, March 11) Research into the origins of delinquent behavior. *British Medical Journal* 1 (4653): 570–573. doi:10.1136/bmj.1.4653.570

Bowlby, J. (1961). The Adolf Meyer lecture: Childhood mourning and its implications for psychiatry. *American Journal of Psychiatry, 118*, 481–498. doi:10.1176/appi.ajp.118.6.481

Bowlby, J. (1973). *Attachment and loss: Vol. 2. Separation: Anxiety and anger.* New York: Basic Books.

Bowlby, J. A. (1988). *A secure base: Parent–child attachment and healthy human development.* New York: Basic Books.

Bowler, P. J. (1989). Holding your head up high: Degeneration and orthogenesis in theories of human evolution. In J. R. Moore (Ed.), *History, humanity, and evolution: Essays for John C. Greene* (pp. 329–353). Cambridge, England: Cambridge University Press.

Bowman, S. A., Gortmaker, S. L., Ebbeling, C. B., Pereira, M. A., & Ludwig, D. S. (2004). Effects of fast-food consumption on energy intake and diet quality among children in a national household survey. *Pediatrics, 113*, 112–118. Retrieved from http://pediatrics.aappublications.org

Boyle, C. A., Boulet, S., Schieve, L. A., Cohen, R. A., Blumberg, S. J., Yeargin-Allsopp, M., . . . Kogan, M. D. (2011). Trends in the prevalence of developmental disabilities in US children, 1997–2008. *Pediatrics, 127*, 1034–1042. doi:10.1542/peds.2010-2989

Bradley, R. G., Binder, E. B., Epstein, M. P., Tang, Y., Nair, H. P., Liu, W., . . . Ressler, K. J. (2008). Influence of child abuse on adult depression: Moderation by the corticotropin-releasing hormone receptor gene. *Archives of General Psychiatry, 65*, 190–200. doi:10.1001/archgenpsychiatry.2007.26

Brame, B., Nagin, D. S., & Tremblay, R. E. (2001). Developmental trajectories of physical aggression from school entry to late adolescence. *Journal of Child Psychology and Psychiatry, 42*, 503–512. doi:10.1017/S0021963001007120

Branstetter, S. A., Low, S., & Furman, W. (2011). The influence of parents and friends on adolescent substance use: A multidimensional approach. *Journal of Substance Use, 16*, 150–160. doi:10.3109/14659891.2010.519421

Braun, J. M., Kahn, R. S., Froehlich, T., Auinger, P., & Lamphear, P. (2006). Exposures to environmental toxicants and Attention Deficit Hyperactivity Disorder in U. S. children. *Environmental Health Perspectives, 114*, 1904–1909. doi:10.1289/ehp.9478

Brazoria County Sheriff's Department, Narcotic Division. Retrieved http://www.brazoria-county.com/sheriff/narc/quiz.htm

Brecht, B. (1980). *The life of Galileo/BerthOlt Brecht* (1980 translation by H. Brenton). London: Eyre Methuen.

Breggin, P. (2001). *Talking back to Ritalin: What doctors aren't telling you about stimulants for children* (Rev. ed.). Cambridge, MA: Perseus Books.

Brehaut, J. C., Miller, A., Raina, P., & McGrail, K. M. (2003). Childhood behavior disorders and injuries among children and youth. *Pediatrics, 111*, 262–269. doi:10.1542/peds.111.2.262

Bremner, J. D. (2007). Does stress damage the brain? In L. J. Kirmayer, R. Lemelson, & M. Barad (Eds.), *Understanding trauma: Integrating biological, clinical, and cultural perspectives* (pp. 118–141). New York: Cambridge University Press.

Brennan, P. A., Grekin, E. R., & Mednick, S. (2003). Prenatal and perinatal influences on conduct disorder and serious delinquency. In B. B. Lahey, T. E. Moffitt, & A. Caspi (Eds.), *Causes of conduct disorder and serious delinquency* (pp. 319–344). New York: Guilford Press.

Brennan, P. A., Hall, J., Bor, W., Najman, J. M., & Williams, G. (2003). Integrating biological and social processes in relation to early-onset persistent aggression in boys and girls. *Developmental Psychology, 39*, 309–323. doi:10.1037/0012-1649.39.2.309

Brensilver, M., Negriff, S., Mennen, F. E., & Trickett, P. K. (2011). Longitudinal relations between depressive symptoms and externalizing behavior in adolescence: Moderating effects of maltreatment experience and gender. *Journal of Clinical Child and Adolescent Psychology, 40*, 607–617. doi:10.1080/15374416.2011.581618

Brent, D. A., & Maalouf, F. T. (2009). Pediatric depression: Is there evidence to improve evidence-based treatments? *Journal of Child Psychology and Psychiatry, 50*, 143–152. doi:10.1111/j.1469-7610.2008.02037.x

Brent, D. A., Perper, J. A., Goldstein, C. E., Kolko, D. J., Allan, M. J., Allman, C. J., & Zelenak, J. P. (1988). Risk factors for adolescent suicide: A comparison of adolescent suicide victims with suicidal inpatients. *Archives of General Psychiatry, 45*, 581–588. Retrieved from http://archpsyc.ama-assn.org/

Brent, D. A., Perper, J. A., Moritz, G., Allman, C., Friend, A., Roth, C., . . . Baugher, M. (1993). Psychiatric risk factors for adolescent suicide: A case control study. *Journal of the American Academy of Child & Adolescent Psychiatry, 32*, 521–529. doi:10.1097/00004583-199305000-00006

Brent, D. A., Perper, J. A., Moritz, G., Allman, C., Friend, A., Schweers, J., . . . Harrington, K. (1992). Psychiatric effects of exposure to suicide among the friends and acquaintances of adolescent suicide victims. *Journal of the American Academy of Child & Adolescent Psychiatry, 31*, 629–640. doi:10.1097/00004583-199207000-00009

Brent, D. A., Poling, K. D., Goldstein, T. R. (2011). *Treating depressed and suicidal adolescents: A clinician's guide*. New York: Guilford Press.

Bretherton, I., & Munholland, K. A. (2008). Internal working models in attachment relationships: Elaborating a central construct in attachment theory. In J. Cassidy & P. R. Shaver (Eds.), *Handbook of attachment: Theory, research, and clinical applications* (2nd ed.). (pp. 102–127). New York: Guilford Press.

Bridge, J. A., Iyengar, S., Salary, C. B., Barbe, R. P., Birmaher, B., Pincus, H. A., . . . Brent, D. A. (2007). Clinical response and risk for reported suicidal ideation and suicide attempts in pediatric antidepressant medication: A meta-analysis of randomized controlled trials. *JAMA: Journal of the American Medical Association, 297*, 1683–1696. doi:10.1001/jama.297.15.1683

Briere, J., Hodges, M., & Godbout, N. (2010). Traumatic stress, affect dysregulation, and dysfunctional avoidance: A structural equation model. *Journal of Traumatic Stress, 23*, 767–774. doi:10.1002/jts.20578

Briggs-Gowan, M. J., Carter, A. S., Clark, R., Augustyn, M., McCarthy, K. J., & Ford, J. D. (2010). Exposure to potentially traumatic events in early childhood: Differential links to emergent psychopathology. *Journal of Child Psychology and Psychiatry, 51*, 1132–1140. doi:10.1111/j.1469-7610.2010.02256.x

Brinkmeyer, M. Y., & Eyberg, S. M. (2003). Parent-child interaction therapy for oppositional children. In A. E. Kazdin & J. R. Weisz (Eds.), *Evidence-based psychotherapies for children and adolescents* (pp. 204–223). New York: Guilford Press.

Britton, J. C., Lissek, S., Grillon, C., Norcross, M. A., & Pine, D. S. (2011). Development of anxiety: The role of threat appraisal and fear learning. *Depression and Anxiety, 28*, 5–17. doi:10.1002/da.20733

Broidy, L. M., Nagin, D. S., Tremblay, R. E., Bates, J. E., Brame, B., Dodge, K. A., . . . Vitaro, F. (2003). Developmental trajectories of childhood disruptive behaviors and adolescent delinquency: A six-site, cross-national study. *Developmental Psychology, 39*, 222–245. doi:10.1037//0012-1649.39.2.222

Bromberg, M. H., Gil, K. M., & Schanberg, L. E. (2011). Daily sleep quality and mood as predictors of pain in children with juvenile polyarticular arthritis. *Health Psychology*, doi:10.1037/a0025075

Bromet, E. J., & Fennig, S. (1999). Epidemiology and natural history of schizophrenia. *Biological Psychiatry, 46*, 871–881. doi:10.1016/S0006-3223(99)00153-5

Bronfenbrenner, U. (1977). Toward an experimental ecology of human development. *American Psychologist, 52*, 513–531. doi:10.1037/0003-066X.32.7.513

Brooks-Gunn, J., Klebanov, P. K., Smith, J., Duncan, G. J., & Lee, K. (2003). The Black-White test score gap in young children: Contributions of test and family characteristics. *Applied Developmental Science, 7*, 239–252. doi:10.1207/S1532480XADS0704_3

Brotman, M. A., Rich, B. A., Guyer, A. E., Lunsford, J. R., Horsey, S. E., Reising, M. M., . . . Leibenluft, E. (2010). Amygdala activation during emotion processing of neutral faces in children with severe mood dysregulation versus ADHD or bipolar disorder. *American Journal of Psychiatry, 167*, 61–69. doi:10.1176/appi.ajp.2009.09010043

Brown, E. (2011, March 10). *Obama at White House Bullying conference: I wasn't immune*. Retrieved from http://articles.latimes.com/2011/mar/10/news/la-heb-obama-bullying-conference-20110310

Brown, J. S., Meadows, S. O., & Elder, G. H., Jr. (2007). Race-ethnic inequality and psychological distress: Depressive symptoms from adolescence to young adulthood. *Developmental Psychology, 43*, 1295–1311. doi:10.1037/0012-1649.43.6.1295

Brown, M. L., Pope, A. W., & Brown, E. J. (2011). Treatment of primary nocturnal enuresis in children: A review. *Child: Care, Health and Development, 37*, 153–160. doi:10.1111/j.1365-2214.2010.01146.x

Brown, R. T., Antonuccio, D. O., DuPaul, G. J., Fristad, M. A., King, C. A., Leslie, L. K., . . . Vitiello, B. (2008). Elimination disorders. In R. T. Brown, D. O. Antonuccio, G. J. DuPaul, M. A. Fristad, C. A. King, L. K. Leslie . . . B. Vitiello. (Eds.), *Childhood mental health disorders: Evidence base and contextual factors for psychosocial, psychopharmacological, and combined interventions* (pp. 121–127). Washington, DC: American Psychological Association.

Brown, R. T., Daly, B. P., & Rickel, A. U. (2007). *Chronic illness in children and adolescents. Advances in psychotherapy: Evidence-based practice*. Ashland, OH: Hogrefe & Huber.

Brown, S. A., & Abrantes, A. M. (2006). Substance use disorders. In E. J. Mash & D. A. Wolfe (Eds.), *Behavioral and emotional disorders in adolescence* (pp. 226–256). New York: Guilford Press.

Brown, T. E. (2000). Emerging understandings of attention-deficit disorders and comorbidities. In T. E. Brown (Ed.), *Attention-deficit disorders and comorbidities in children, adolescents, and adults* (pp. 3–55). Washington, DC: American Psychiatric Press.

Brownell, K. D. (1991). Dieting and the search for the perfect body: Where physiology and culture collide. *Behavior Therapy, 22*, 1–12. doi:10.1016/S0005-7894(05)80239-4

Brownell, K. D., & Rodin, J. (1994). The dieting maelstrom: Is it possible and advisable to lose weight? *American Psychologist, 49*, 781–791. doi:10.1037/0003-066X.49.9.781

Brownlie, E. B., Jabbar, A., Beitchman, J., Vida, R., & Atkinson, L. (2007). Language impairment and sexual assault of girls and women: Findings from a community sample. *Journal of Abnormal Child Psychology, 35*, 618–626. doi:10.1007/s10802-007-9117-4

Bruch, H. (1962). Perceptual and conceptual disturbances in anorexia nervosa. *Psychosomatic Medicine, 24*, 187–194. Retrieved from http://www.psychosomaticmedicine.org

Bruch, H. (1973). *Eating disorders: Obesity, anorexia nervosa and the person within*. New York: Basic Books.

Brumariu, L. E., & Kerns, K. A. (2010). Parent-child attachment and internalizing symptoms in childhood and adolescence: A review of empirical findings and future directions. *Developmental Psychopathology, 22*, 177–203. doi:10.1017/S0954579409990344

Brumberg, J. J. (1988). *Fasting girls: The emergence of anorexia nervosa as a modern disease*. Cambridge, MA: Harvard University Press.

Bryant-Waugh, R., Markham, L., Kreipe, R. E., & Walsh, B. T. (2010). Feeding and eating disorders in childhood. *International Journal of Eating Disorders, 43*, 98–111. doi:10.1002/eat.20795

Bryson, S. E., Rogers, S. J., & Fombonne, E. (2003). Autism spectrum disorders: Early detection, intervention, education, and psychopharmacological management. *Canadian Journal of Psychiatry, 48*, 506–515. Retrieved from http://www.cpa-apc.org/

Bryson, S. E., Zwaigenbaum, L., McDermott, C., Rombough, V., & Brian, J. (2008). The Autism Observation Scale for Infants: Scale development and reliability data. *Journal of Autism and Developmental Disorders, 38*, 731–738. doi:10.1007/s10803-007-0440-y

Buckholtz, J. W., & Meyer-Lindenberg, A. (2008). MAOA and the neurogenetic architecture of human aggression. *Trends in Neurosciences, 31*, 120–129. doi:10.1016/j.tins.2007.12.006

Buitelaar, J. K., Barton, J., Danckaerts, M., Friedrichs, E. Gillberg, C., & Hazell, P. L., Hellmans, H., . . . Zuddas, A. (2006). A comparison of North American and non-North American ADHD study populations. *European Child & Adolescent Psychiatry, 15*, 177–181. doi:10.1007/s00787-005-0523-2

Bulik, C. M., Sullivan, P. F., Tozzi, F., Furberg, H., Lichtenstein, P., & Pedersen, N. L. (2006). Prevalence, heritability, and prospective risk factors for anorexia nervosa. *Archives of General Psychiatry, 63*, 305–312. Retrieved from http://archpsyc.ama-assn.org/

Bulik, C. M., Thornton, L., Pinheiro, A. P., Plotnicov, K., Klump, K. L., Brandt, H., . . . Kaye, W. H. (2008). Suicide attempts in anorexia nervosa. *Psychosomatic Medicine, 70*, 378–383. doi:10.1097/PSY.0b013e3181646765

Bulik, C. M., Thornton, L. M., Root, T. L., Pisetsky, E. M., Lichtenstein, P., & Pedersen, N. L. (2010). Understanding the relation between anorexia nervosa and bulimia nervosa in a Swedish national twin sample. *Biological Psychiatry, 67*, 71–77. doi:10.1016/j.biopsych.2009.08.010

Bulotsky-Shearer, R. J., Fantuzzo, J. W., & McDermott, P. A. (2008). An investigation of classroom situational dimensions of emotional and behavioral adjustment and cognitive and social outcomes for head start children. *Developmental Psychology, 44*, 139–154.

Burke, J. D., Hipwell, A. E., & Loeber, R. (2010). Dimensions of oppositional defiant disorder as predictors of depression and conduct disorder in preadolescent girls. *Journal of the American Academy of Child & Adolescent Psychiatry, 49*, 484–492. doi:10.1016/j.jaac.2010.11.007

Burke, J. D., & Loeber, R. (2010). Oppositional defiant disorder and the explanation of the comorbidity between behavioral disorders and depression. *Clinical Psychology: Science and Practice, 17*, 319–326. doi:10.1111/j.1468-2850.2010.01223.x

Burke, J. D., Waldman, I., & Lahey, B. B. (2010). Predictive validity of childhood oppositional defiant disorder and conduct disorder: Implications for the *DSM–V*. *Journal of Abnormal Psychology, 119*, 739–751. doi:10.1037/a0019708

Burket, R. C., Cox, D. J., Tam, A. P., Ritterband, L., Borowitz, S., Sutphen, J., . . . Kovatchev, B. (2006). Does "stubbornness" have a role in pediatric constipation? *Journal of Developmental & Behavioral Pediatrics, 27*, 106–111. doi:10.1097/00004703-200604000-00004

Burns, G. L., Walsh, J. A., Patterson, D. R., Holte, C. S., Somers-Flanagan, R., & Parker, C. M. (1997). Internal validity of the disruptive behavior disorder symptoms: Implications from parent ratings for a dimensional approach to symptom validity. *Journal of Abnormal Child Psychology, 25*, 307–319. doi:10.1023/A:1025764403506

Burt, S. A., Krueger, R. F., McGue, M., & Iacono, W. G. (2001). Sources of covariation among attention-deficit hyperactivity disorder, oppositional defiant disorder, and conduct disorder: The importance of shared environment. *Journal of Abnormal Psychology, 110*, 516–525. doi:10.1037//0021-843X.110.4.516

Burt, S. A., McGue, M., DeMarte, J. A., Krueger, R. F., & Iacono, W. G. (2006). Timing of menarche and the origins of conduct disorder. *Archives of General Psychiatry, 63*, 890–896. doi:10.1001/archpsyc.63.8.890

Burt, S. A., & Neiderhiser, J. M. (2009). Aggressive versus nonaggressive antisocial behavior: Distinctive etiological moderation by age. *Developmental Psychology, 45*, 1164–1176. doi:10.1037/a0016130

Bush, G. (2008). Neuroimaging of attention deficit hyperactivity disorder: Can new imaging findings be integrated into clinic practice? *Child and Adolescent Psychiatric Clinics of North America, 17*, 385–404. doi:10.1016/j.chc.2007.11.002

Bussing, R., Zima, B. T., Gary, F. A., Mason, D. M., Leon, C. E., Sinha, K., & Garvan, C. W. (2003). Social networks, caregiver strain, and utilization of mental health services among elementary school students at high risk for ADHD. *Journal of the American Academy of Child & Adolescent Psychiatry, 42*, 842–850. doi:10.1097/01.CHI.0000046876.27264.BF

Butcher, J. N., Williams, C. L., Graham, J. R., Archer, J. P., Tellegen, A., Ben-Porath, Y. S., & Kaemmer, B. (2006). *Minnesota Multiphasic Personality Inventory-Adolescent (MMPI-A)*. Minneapolis: University of Minnesota Press

Button, T. M. M., Corley, R. P., Rhee, S. H., Hewitt, J. K., Young, S. E., & Stallings, M. C. (2007). Delinquent peer affiliation and conduct problems: A twin study. *Journal of Abnormal Psychology, 116*, 554–564. doi:10.1037/0021-843X.116.3.554

Cadman, D., Boyle, M., Szatmari, P., & Offord, D. R. (1987). Chronic illness, disability, and mental and social well-being: Findings of the Ontario Child Health Study. *Pediatrics, 79*, 805–813. Retrieved from http://pediatrics.aappublications.org/

Calati, R., De Ronch, D., Bellini, M., & Serretti, A. (2011). The 5-HTTLPR polymorphism and eating disorders: A meta-analysis. *International Journal of Eating Disorders, 44*, 191–199. doi:10.1002/eat.20811

Calder, J. (1980). *RLS: A life study*. London: Hamish Hamilton.

Calkins, S. D., & Keane, S. P. (2009). Developmental origins of early antisocial behavior. *Development and Psychopathology, 21*, 1095–1109. doi:10.1017/S095457940999006X

Camp OOCHIGEAS (2006). A camp for children with cancer. Retrieved http://www.ooch.org/page.aspx?pid=221

Campbell, F. A., & Ramey, C. T. (2010). Carolina Abecedarian Project. In A. J. Reynolds, A. J. Rolnick, M. M. Englund, & J. A. Temple (Eds.), *Childhood programs and practices in the first decade of life: A human capital integration* (pp. 76–98). New York: Cambridge University Press.

Campbell, F. A., Ramey, C. T., Pungello, E., Sparling, J., & Miller-Johnson, S. (2002). Early childhood education: Young adult outcomes from the Abecedarian Project. *Applied Developmental Science, 6*, 42–57. doi:10.1016/j.ecresq.2008.03.003

Campbell, L. K., Cox, D. J., & Borowitz, S. M. (2009). Elimination disorders: Enuresis and encopresis. In M. C. Roberts & R. G. Steele (Eds.), *Handbook of pediatric psychology* (4th ed., pp. 481–490). New York: Guilford Press.

Campbell, R., Greeson, M. R., Bybee, D., & Raja, S. (2008). The co-occurrence of childhood sexual abuse, adult sexual assault, intimate partner violence, and sexual harassment: A mediational model of posttraumatic stress disorder and physical health outcomes. *Journal of Consulting and Clinical Psychology, 76*, 194–207.

Campbell, S. B. (2002). *Behavior problems in preschool children: Clinical and developmental issues* (2nd ed.). New York: Guilford Press.

Campbell, S. B., Shaw, D. S., & Gilliom, M. (2000). Early externalizing behavior problems: Toddlers and preschoolers at risk for later maladjustment. *Development and Psychopathology, 12*, 467–488. Retrieved from http://journals.cambridge.org/action/displayJournal?jid=DPP

Campbell, S. B., Spieker, S., Vandergrift, N., Belsky, J., Burchinal, M., & The NICHD Early Child Care Research Network (2010). Predictors and sequelae of trajectories of physical aggression in school-age boys and girls. *Development and Psychopathology, 22*, 133–150. doi:10.1017/S0954579409990319

Campbell, S. B., & von Stauffenberg, C. (2009). Delay and inhibition as early predictors of ADHD in third grade. *Journal of Abnormal Child Psychology, 37*, 1–15. doi:10.1007/s10802-008-9270-4

Canadian Diabetes Association. (2008). *The prevalence and costs of diabetes*. Retrieved from http://www.diabetes.ca/Section_About/prevalence.asp

Canino, G., & Alegria, M. (2008). Psychiatric diagnosis—Is it universal or relative to culture? *Journal of Child Psychology and Psychiatry, 49*, 237–250. doi:10.1111/j.1469-7610.2007.01854.x

Canino, G., Polanczck, G., Bauermeister, J. J., Rohde, L. A., & Frick, P. J. (2010). Does the prevalence of CD and ODD vary across cultures? *Social Psychiatry and Psychiatric Epidemiology, 45*, 695–704. doi:10.1007/s00127-010-0242-y

Cannon, T. D., Cadenhead, K., Cornblatt, B., Woods, S. W., Addington, J., Walker, E., . . . Heinssen, R. (2008). Prediction of psychosis in youth at high clinical risk. *Archives of General Psychiatry, 65*, 28–37. doi:10.1001/archgenpsychiatry.2007.3

Cantor, J. M., Kabani, N., Christensen, B. K., Zipursky, R. B., Barbaree, H. E., Dickey, R., . . . Blanchard, R. (2008). Cerebral white matter deficiencies in pedophilic men. *Journal of Psychiatric Research, 42*, 167–183.

Cantrell, M. A. (2011). A narrative review summarizing the state of the evidence on the health-related quality of life among childhood cancer survivors. *Journal of Pediatric Oncology Nursing, 28*, 75–82. doi:10.1177/1043454210377901

Cantwell, D. P. (1990). Depression across the early life span. In M. Lewis & S. M. Miller (Eds.), *Handbook of developmental psychopathology* (pp. 293–309). New York: Plenum Press.

Capaldi, D. M., & Patterson, G. R. (1994). Interrelated influences of contextual factors on antisocial behavior in childhood and adolescence. In D. Fowles, P. Sutker, & S. Goodman (Eds.), *Psychopathy and antisocial personality: A developmental perspective* (pp. 165–198). New York: Springer.

Caplan, R. (1994). Communication deficits in childhood schizophrenia spectrum disorders. *Schizophrenia Bulletin, 20*, 671–684. doi:10.1093/schbul/20.4.671

Caplan, R., Guthrie, D., Tang, B., Komo, S., & Asarnow, R. F. (2000). Thought disorder in childhood schizophrenia: Replication and update of concept. *Journal of the American Academy of Child & Adolescent Psychiatry, 39*, 771–778. doi:10.1097/00004583-200006000-00016

Capps, L., Sigman, M., Sena, R., & Henker, B. (1996). Fear, anxiety and perceived control in children of agoraphobic parents. *Journal of Child Psychology & Psychiatry, 37*, 445–452. doi:10.1111/j.1469-7610.1996.tb01425.x

Carballo, J. J., Baca-Garcia, E., Blanco, C., Perez-Rodriguez, M. M., Arriero, M. A. J., Group for the Study of Evolution of Diagnosis (SED), & Oquendo, M. A. (2010). Stability of childhood anxiety disorder diagnoses: A follow-up naturalistic study in psychiatric care. *European Child and Adolescent Psychiatry, 19*, 395–403. doi:10.1007/s00787-009-0064-1

Carlson, E. A., Jacobvitz, D., & Sroufe, L. A. (1995). A developmental investigation of inattentiveness and hyperactivity. *Child Development, 66*, 37–54. doi:10.1111/j.1467-8624.1995.tb00854.x

Carlson, E. A., & Sroufe, L. A. (1995). Contribution of attachment theory to developmental psychopathology. In D. Cicchetti & D. J. Cohen (Eds.), *Developmental psychopathology: Vol. 1. Theory and methods* (pp. 581–617). New York: Wiley.

Carlson, G. A. (1994). Adolescent bipolar disorder: Phenomenology and treatment implications. In W. M. Reynolds & H. F. Johnston (Eds.), *Handbook of depression in children and adolescents* (pp. 41–60). New York: Plenum Press.

Carlson, G. A. (2002). Bipolar disorder in children and adolescents: A critical review. In D. Shaffer & B. Waslick (Eds.), *The many faces of depression in children and adolescents* (pp. 105–128). Washington, DC: American Psychiatric Press.

Carlson, G. A. (2011). Will the child with mania please stand up? *The British Journal of Psychiatry, 198*, 171–172. doi:10.1192/bjp.bp.110.084517

Carlson, G. A., Pine, D. S., Nottelmann, E., & Leibenluft, E. (2004). Defining subtypes of childhood bipolar illness: Response and commentary. *Journal of the American Academy of Child & Adolescent Psychiatry, 43*, 3–4. doi:10.1097/00004583-200401000-00003

Carmichael, M. (2008, May 16). Welcome to Max's world. *Newsweek*, 33–38. Retrieved from http://www.newsweek.com/2008/05/17/welcome-to-max-s-world.html

Carpenter, D. O., & Nevin, R. (2010). Environmental causes of violence. *Physiology & Behavior, 99*, 260–268. doi:10.1016/j.physbeh.2009.09.001

Carper, T. L. M., Negy, C., & Tantleff-Dunn, S. (2010). Relations among media influence, body image, eating concerns, and sexual orientation in men: A preliminary investigation. *Body Image, 7*, 301–309. doi:10.1016/j.bodyim.2010.07.002

Carr, E. G. (1977). The motivation of self-injurious behavior: A review of some hypotheses. *PsychologicalBulletin, 84*, 800–811. doi:10.1037/0033-2909.84.4.800

Carr, J. (2005). Stability and change in cognitive ability over the life span: A comparison of populations with and without Down's syndrome. *Journal of Intellectual Disability Research, 49*, 915–928. doi:10.1111/j.1365-2788.2005.00735.x

Carretti, B., Borella, E., Cornoldi, C., & De Beni, R. (2009). Role of working memory in explaining the performance of individuals with specific reading comprehension difficulties: A meta-analysis. *Learning and Individual Differences, 19*, 245–251. doi:10.1016/j.lindif.2008.10.002

Carter, A. S., Black, D. O., Tewani, S., Connoly, C. E., Kadlec, M. B., & Tager-Flusberg, H. (2007). Sex differences in toddlers with autism spectrum disorders. *Journal of Autism and Developmental Disorders, 37*, 86–97. doi:10.1007/s10803-006-0331-7

Cartwright-Hatton, S., McNally, D., Field, A. P., Rust, S., Laskey, B., Dison, C., & Woodham, A. (2011). A new parenting-based group intervention for young anxious children: Results of a randomized controlled trial. *Journal of the American Academy of Child & Adolescent Psychiatry, 50*, 242–241. doi:10.1016/j.jaac2010.12.015

Cartwright-Hatton, S., McNicol, K., & Doubleday, E. (2006). Anxiety in a neglected population: Prevalence of anxiety disorders in pre-adolescent children. *Clinical Psychology Review, 26*, 817–833. doi:10.1016/j.cpr.2005.12.002

Casey, B. J., Nigg, J. T., & Durston, S. (2007). New potential leads in the biology and treatment of attention deficit-hyperactivity disorder. *Current Opinion in Neurology, 20*, 119–124. doi:10.1097/WCO.0b013e3280a02f78

Cash, T. F., & Smolak, L. (2011). Understanding body images: Historical and contemporary perspectives. In T. F. Cash & L. Smolak (Eds.), *Body image: A handbook of science, practice, and prevention.* (2nd ed., pp. 3–11). New York: Guilford Press.

Cashel, M. L. (2002). Child and adolescent psychological assessment: Current clinical practices and the impact of managed care. *Professional Psychology: Research and Practice, 33*, 446–453. doi:10.1037//0735-7028.33.5.446

Caspi, A., Harrington, H., Milne, B., Amell, J. W., Theodore, R. F., & Moffitt, T E. (2003). Children's behavioral styles at age 3 are linked to their adult personality traits at age 26. *Journal of Personality, 71*, 495–513. doi:10.1111/1467-6494.7104001

Caspi, A., Langley, K., Milne, B., Moffitt, T. E., O'Donovan, M., Owen, M. J., . . . Thapar, A. (2008). A replicated molecular genetic basis for subtyping antisocial behavior in children with attention-deficit/hyperactivity disorder. *Archives of General Psychiatry, 65*, 203–210. doi:10.1001/archgenpsychiatry.2007.24

Caspi, A., McClay, J., Moffitt, T. E., Mill, J., Martin, J., Craig, I. W., . . . Poulton, R. (2002). Role of genotype in the cycle of violence in maltreated children. *Science, 297*, 851–854. doi:10.1126/science.1072290

Caspi, A., & Moffitt, T. E. (1995). The continuity of maladaptive behavior: From description to understanding in the study of antisocial behavior. In D. Cicchetti & D. J. Cohen (Eds.), *Developmental psychopathology: Vol. 2. Risk, disorder, and adaptation* (pp. 472–511). New York: Wiley.

Cassano, M., Adrian, M., Veits, G., & Zeman, J. (2006). The inclusion of fathers in the empirical investigation of child psychopathology: An update. *Journal of Clinical Child and Adolescent Psychology, 35*, 583–589. doi:10.1207/s15374424jccp3504_10

Castellanos, F. X., Sharp, W. S., Gottesman, R. F., Greenstein, D. K., Giedd, J. N., & Rapoport, J. L. (2003). Anatomic brain abnormalities in monozygotic twins discordant for attention deficit hyperactivity disorder. *American Journal of Psychiatry, 160*, 1693–1696. doi:10.1176/appi.ajp.160.9.1693

Caylak, E. (2011). The auditory temporal processing deficit theory in children with developmental dyslexia. *Journal of Pediatric Neurology, 9*, 151–168. Retrieved from http://search.proquest.com/docview/885703117?accountid=15115

Cederlund, M., Hagberg, B., Billstedt, E., Gillberg, I. C., & Gillberg, C. (2008). Asperger syndrome and autism: A comparative longitudinal follow-up study more than 5 years after original diagnosis. *Journal of Autism and Developmental Disorders, 38*, 72–85. doi:10.1007/s10803-007-0364-6

Centers for Disease Control (CDC). (2007, February 9). Prevalence of autism spectrum disorders: Autism and developmental disabilities monitoring network, six sites, United States, 2000. *Surveillance Summaries, 56*(SS-1), 1–11. Retrieved from http://www.cdc.gov/mmwr/preview/mmwrhtml/ss5601a1.htm

Centers for Disease Control. (2010). *"Healthy Youth!" Health Topics*. Retrieved June 24, 2011, from http://www.cdc.gov/HealthyYouth/healthtopics/index.htm

Centers for Disease Control (CDC). (2011). *Understanding child maltreatment factsheet 2010*. Atlanta, GA: Author. Available: www.cdc.gov/violenceprevention/pdf/CM-FactSheet-a.pdf.

Centers for Disease Control and Prevention. (2002). *Centers for Disease Control and Prevention Web-based Injury Statistics Query and Reporting System* (WISQARS). Retrieved from http://www.cdc.gov/ncipc/WISQARS/

Centers for Disease Control and Prevention (CDC). (2007). Trends in childhood cancer mortality—United States, 1990–2004. *MMWR, 56*, 1257–1261.

Centers for Disease Control and Prevention (CDC), Autism and Developmental Disabilities Monitoring Network Surveillance Year 2006 Principal Investigators. (2009, December). Prevalence of autism spectrum disorders—Autism and Developmental Disabilities Monitoring Network, United States, 2006. *MMWR Surveillance Summary, 18; 58*(10), 1–20.

Centers for Disease Control and Prevention (CDC). (2010). *Autism Spectrum Disorders (ASDs)*. Retrieved from http://www.cdc.gov/ncbddd/autism/index.html

Centers for Disease Control and Prevention (CDC). (2011) *Children and diabetes*. Retrieved from http://www.cdc.gov/diabetes/projects/diab_children.htm#1

Centers for Disease Control and Prevention (CDC). (2011). *Childhood overweight and obesity*. Available: http://www.cdc.gov/obesity/childhood/index.html

Centers for Disease Control and Prevention (2011). *Tracking Fetal Alcohol Syndrome (FAS)*. Retrieved July 20, 2011 from http://www.cdc.gov/ncbddd/fasd/research-tracking.html

Cerel, J., Fristad, M. A., Verducci, J., Weller, R. A., & Weller, E. B. (2006). Childhood bereavement: Psychopathology in the 2 years postparental death. *Journal of the American Academy of Child & Adolescent Psychiatry, 45*, 681–690. doi:10.1097/01.chi.0000215327.58799.05

Challman, T. D., Barbaresi, W. J., Katusic, S. K., & Weaver, A. (2003). The yield of the medical evaluation of children with pervasive developmental disorders. *Journal of Autism and Developmental Disorders, 33*, 187–192. doi:10.1023/A:1022995611730

Chan, E., Zhan, C., & Homer, C. J. (2002). Health care use and costs for children with attention-deficit/hyperactivity disorder: National estimates from the medical expenditure panel study. *Archives of Pediatrics and Adolescent Medicine, 156*, 504–512. Retrieved from http://archpedi.ama-assn.org/

Chansky, T. E., & Kendall, P. C. (1997). Social expectancies and self-perceptions in anxiety-disordered children. *Journal of Anxiety Disorders, 11*, 347–363. doi:10.1016/S0887-6185(97)00015-7

Chapman, D. A., Scott, K. G., & Stanton-Chapman, T. L. (2008). Public health approach to the study of mental retardation. *American Journal on Mental Retardation, 113*, 102–116. doi:10.1352/0895-8017(2008)113[102:PHATTS]2.0.CO;2

Chapman, D. P., Dube, S. R., & Anda, R. F. (2007). Adverse childhood events as risk factors for negative mental health outcomes. *Psychiatric Annals, 37*, 359–364. Retrieved from http://www.psychiatricannalsonline.com/

Charach, A., Yeung, E., Climans, T., & Lillie, E. (2011). Childhood attention deficit/hyperactivity disorder and future substance use disorders: Comparative meta-analyses. *Journal of the American Academy of Child & Adolescent Psychiatry, 50*, 9–21. doi:10.1106/J4aac.2010.09.201

Charman, T. (2003). Why is joint attention a pivotal skill in autism? *Philosophical Transactions of the Royal Society: Biological Sciences, 358*, 315–324. doi:10.1098/rstb.2002.1199

Charman, T. (2011). Commentary: Glass half full or half empty? Testing social communication interventions for young children with autism – reflections on Landa, Holman, O'Neill, and Stuart (2011). *Journal of Child Psychology and Psychiatry, 52*, 22–23. doi:10.1111/j.1469-7610.2010.02359.x

Chassin, L., Presson, C. C., Rose, J., & Sherman, S. J. (2007). What is addiction? Age-related differences in the meaning of addiction. *Drug and Alcohol Dependence, 87*, 30–38. doi:10.1016/j.drugalcdep.2006.07.006

Chavez, M., & Insel, T. R. (2007). Eating disorders: National Institute of Mental Health's perspective. *American Psychologist [Special issue: Eating disorders], 62*, 159–166. doi:10.1037/0003-066X.62.3.159

Chavira, D. A., Shipon-Blum, E., Hitchcock, C., Cohan, S., & Stein, M. B. (2007). Selective mutism and social anxiety disorder: All in the family? *Journal of the American Academy of Child & Adolescent Psychiatry, 46*, 1464–1472. doi:10.1097/chi.0b013e318149366a

Chen, M., & Johnston, C. (2007). Maternal inattention and impulsivity and parenting behaviors. *Journal of Clinical Child and Adolescent Psychology, 36*, 455–468. doi:10.1080/15374410701448570

Chen, X., Rubin, K. H., & Li, Z. Y. (1995). Social functioning and adjustment in Chinese children: A longitudinal study. *Developmental Psychology, 31*, 531–539. doi:10.1037/0012-1649.31.4.531

Chen, X., Rubin, K. H., Li, B., & Li, D. (1999). Adolescent outcomes of social functioning in Chinese children. *International Journal of Behavioral Development, 23*, 199–223. doi:10.1080/016502599384071

Chesley, E. B., Alberts, J .D., Klein, J. D., & Kreipe, R. E. (2003). Pro or con? Anorexia nervosa and the Internet. *Journal of Adolescent Health, 32*, 123–124. doi:10.1016/S1054-139X(02)00615-8

Chess, S. (1960). Diagnosis and treatment of the hyperactive child. *New York State Journal of Medicine, 60*, 2379–2385. Retrieved from http://www.mssny.org/index.cfm

Chess, S., & Thomas, A. (1984). *Origins and evolution of behavior disorders*. New York: Brunner/Mazel.

Chethik, M. (2000). *Techniques of child therapy: Psychodynamic strategies* (2nd ed.). New York: Guilford Press.

Cheung, A. H., Zuckerbrot, R. A., Jensen, P. S., Ghalib, K., Laraque, D., Stein, R. E. K., & GLAD-PC Steering Group. (2007). Guidelines for adolescent depression in primary care (GLAD-PC): II. Treatment and ongoing management. *Pediatrics, 120*, e1313–e1326. doi:10.1542/peds.2006-1395

Chiang, H.-M., & Carter, M. (2008). Spontaneity of communication in individuals with autism. *Journal of Autism and Developmental Disorders, 38*, 693–705. doi:10.1007/s10803-007-0436-7

Child Medication Safety Act. (2003). *Child medication safety act of 2007*. 110th U.S. Congress, 1st Session, S 891 IS 1170 (Report No. 108–121, Union Calendar No. 62). Introduced March 15, 2007.

Child Welfare Information Gateway. (2011). *Definitions of child abuse and neglect in federal law*. Available: http://www.childwelfare.gov/can/defining/federal.cfm

Children's Defense Fund (2007). *America's cradle to prison pipeline: A report of the Children's Defense Fund*. Washington, DC:

Author. Retrieved May 27, 2011 from: www.childrensdefense.org/child-research-data-publications/data/cradle-prison-pipeline-report-2007-full-highres.html

Chorney, D. B., Detweiler, M. F., Morris, T. L., & Kuhn, B. R. (2008). The interplay of sleep disturbance, anxiety, and depression in children. *Journal of Pediatric Psychology, 33*, 339–348. doi:10.1093/jpepsy/jsm105

Chorpita, B., Daleiden, E. L., Ebesutani, C., Young, J., Becker, K. D., Nakamura, B. J., . . . Starace, N. (2011). Evidence-based treatments for children and adolescents: An updated review of indicators of efficacy and effectiveness. *Clinical Psychology: Science and Practice, 18*, 152–172. doi:10.1111/j.1468-2850.2011.01247.x

Chorpita, B. F. (2002). The tripartite model and dimensions of anxiety and depression: An examination of structure in a large school sample. *Journal of Abnormal Child Psychology, 30*, 177–190. doi:10.1023/A:1014709417132

Chorpita, B. F. (2007). *Modular cognitive-behavioral therapy for childhood anxiety disorders*. New York: Guilford Press.

Chorpita, B. F., Albano, A. M., & Barlow, D. H. (1996). Cognitive processing in children: Relation to anxiety and family in influences. *Journal of Clinical Child Psychology, 25*, 170–176. doi:10.1207/s15374424jccp2502_5

Chorpita, B. F., Daleiden, E. L., Ebesutani, C., Young, J., Becker, K. D., Nakamura, B. J., & Storace, N. (2011). Evidence-based treatments for children and adolescents: An updated review of indicators of efficacy and effectiveness. *Clinical Psychology: Science and Practice, 18*, 154–172. doi:10.1111/j.1468-2850.2011.01247.x

Chorpita, B. F., Reise S., Weisz, J. R., Grubbs, K., Becker, K. D., Krull, J. L., & The Research Network on Youth Mental Health. (2010). Evaluation of the Brief Problem Checklist and caregiver interviews to measure clinical progress. *Journal of Consulting and Clinical Psychology, 78*, 4, 526–536. doi:10.1037/a0019602

Chorpita, B. F., & Southam-Gerow, M. A. (2006). Fears and anxieties. In E. J. Mash & R. A. Barkley (Eds.), *Treatment of childhood disorders* (3rd ed., pp. 271–335). New York: Guilford Press.

Chorpita, B. F., Tracey, S. A., Brown, T. A., Collica, T. J., & Barlow, D. H. (1997). Assessment of worry in children and adolescents: An adaptation of the Penn State Worry Questionnaire. *Behaviour Research and Therapy, 35*, 569–581. doi:10.1016/S0005-7967(96)00116-7

Christian, R. E., Frick, P. J., Hill, N. L., Tyler, L., & Frazer, D. R. (1997). Psychopathy and conduct problems in children: II. Implications for subtyping children with conduct problems. *Journal of the American Academy of Child & Adolescent Psychiatry, 36*, 233–241. doi:10.1097/00004583-199702000-00014

Christophersen, E. R., & Friman, P. C. (2010). *Elimination disorders in children and adolescents*. Cambridge, MA: Hogrefe Publishing.

Chronis, A. M., Chacko, A., Fabiano, G. A., Wymbs, B. T., & Pelham, W. E., Jr. (2004a). Enhancements to the behavioral parent training paradigm for families of children with ADHD: Review and future directions. *Clinical Child and Family Psychology Review, 7*, 1–27. doi:10.1023/B:CCFP.0000020190.60808.a4

Chronis, A. M., Fabiano, G. A., Gnagy, E. M., Onyango, A. N., Pelham, W. E., Lopez-Williams, A., . . . Seymour, K. E. (2004b). An evaluation of the summer treatment program for children with ADHD using a treatment withdrawal design. *Behavior Therapy, 35*, 561–585. doi:10.1016/S0005-7894(04)80032-7

Chronis, A. M., Jones, H. A., & Raggi, V. L. (2006). Evidence-based psychosocial treatments for children and adolescents with attention-deficit/hyperactivity disorder. *Clinical Psychology Review, 26*, 486–502. doi:10.1016/j.cpr.2006.01.002

Chronis-Tuscano, A., Degnan, K.A., Pine, D. S., Perez-Edgar, K., Henderson, H. A., Diaz, Y., & Fox, N. A. (2009). *Journal of the American Academy of Child & Adolescent Psychiatry, 48*, 928–935. doi:10.1097/CHI.0b013e3181ae09df

Chronis-Tuscano, A., Molina, B. S. G., Pelham, W. E., Applegate, B., Dahlke, A., Overmyer, M., & Lahey, B. B. (2010). Very early predictors of adolescent depression and suicide attempts in children with attention-deficit/hyperactivity disorder. *Archives of General Psychiatry, 67*, 1044–1051. doi:10.1001/archgenpsychiatry.2010.127

Chronis-Tuscano, A., Raggi, V. L., Clarke, T. L., Rooney, M. E., Diaz, Y., & Pian, J. (2008). Associations between maternal attention-deficit/hyperactivity disorder symptoms and parenting. *Journal of Abnormal Child Psychology, 36*, 1237–1250. doi:10.1007/s10802008-9246-4

Chronis-Tuscano, A., Rooney, M., Seymour, K. E., Lavin, H. J., & Pian, J. (2010). Effects of maternal stimulant medication on observed parenting in mother-child dyads with attention-deficit hyperactivity disorder. *Journal of Abnormal Child Psychology, 39*, 581–587. doi:10.1080/15374416.2010.486326

Cicchetti, D. (2006). Development and psychopathology. In D. Cicchetti & D. J. Cohen (Eds.), *Developmental psychopathology: Vol. 1. Theory and method* (2nd ed., pp. 1–23). Hoboken, NJ: Wiley.

Cicchetti, D., & Cannon, T. D. (1999). Neurodevelopmental processes in the ontogenesis and epigenesis of psychopathology. *Development and Psychopathology, 11*, 375–393. Retrieved from http://journals.cambridge.org/action/displayJournal?jid=DPP

Cicchetti, D., & Curtis, W. J. (2006). The developing brain and neural plasticity: Implications for normality, psychopathology, and resilience. In D. Cicchetti & D. J. Cohen (Eds.), *Developmental psychopathology: Vol. 2. Developmental neuroscience* (pp. 1–64). Hoboken, NJ: Wiley.

Cicchetti, D., & Hinshaw, S. P. (2003). Conceptual, methodological, and statistical issues in developmental psychopathology. *Development and Psychopathology, 15*(Whole No. 3). doi:10.1017/S0954579403000269

Cicchetti, D., & Lynch, M. (1995). Failures in the expectable environment and their impact on individual development: The case of child maltreatment. In D. Cicchetti & D. J. Cohen (Eds.), *Developmental psychopathology: Vol. 2. Risk, disorder, and adaptation* (pp. 32–71). New York: Wiley.

Cicchetti, D., & Rogosch, R. A. (2002). A developmental psychopathology perspective on adolescence. *Journal of Consulting & Clinical Psychology, 70*, 6–20. doi:10.1037/0022-006X.70.1.6

Cicchetti, D., Rogosch, F. A., Gunnar, M. R., & Toth, S. L. (2010). The differential impacts of early physical and sexual abuse and internalizing problems on daytime cortisol rhythm in school-aged children. *Child Development, 81*, 252–269. doi:10.1111/j.1467-8624.2009.01393.x

Cicchetti, D., Rogosch, F. A., Howe, M. L., & Toth, S. L. (2010). The effects of maltreatment and neuroendocrine regulation on memory performance. *Child Development, 81*(5), 1504–1519. doi:10.1111/j.1467-8624.2010.01488.x

Cicchetti, D., & Valentino, K. (2006). An ecological-transactional perspective on child maltreatment: Failure of the average expectable environment and its influence on child development. In D. Cicchetti & D. J. Cohen (Eds.), *Developmental psychopathology, Vol 3: Risk, disorder, and adaptation* (2nd ed.). (pp. 129–201). Hoboken, NJ: John Wiley & Sons.

Clark, D. B., Thatcher, D. L., & Martin, C. S. (2010). Child abuse and other traumatic experiences, alcohol use disorders, and health problems in adolescence and young adulthood. *Journal of Pediatric Psychology, 35*, 499–510. doi:10.1093/jpepsy/jsp117

Clark, D. B., Thatcher, D. L., & Tapert, S. F. (2008). Alcohol, psychological dysregulation, and adolescent brain development. *Alcohol, Clinical and Experimental Research, 32*, 375–385. doi:10.1111/j.1530-0277.2007.00601.x

Clark, L. S., & Tiggemann, M. (2006). Appearance culture in 9- to 12-year-old girls: Media and peer influences on body dissatisfaction. *Social Development, 15*, 628–643. doi:10.1111/j.1467-9507.2006.00361.x

Clark, L. S., & Tiggemann, M. (2007). Sociocultural influences and body image in 9- to 12-year-old girls: The role of appearance schemas. *Journal of Clinical Child and Adolescent Psychology, 36*, 76–86. doi:10.1080/15374410709336570

Clark, R. W. (1971). *Einstein: The life and times*. New York: World.

Clarke, G. N., & DeBar, L. L. (2010). Group cognitive-behavioral treatment for adolescent depression. In J. R. Weisz & A. E. Kazdin (Eds.), *Evidence-based psychotherapies for children and adolescents* (2nd ed., pp. 110–125). New York: Guilford Press.

Clarke, G. N., Lewinsohn, P. M., & Hops, H. (2001). *Instructor's manual for adolescent coping with depression course*. Retrieved from http://www.kpchr.org/public/acwd/acwd.html

Clay, D., Vignoles, V. L., & Dittmar, H. (2005). Body image and self-esteem among adolescent girls: Testing the influence of sociocultural factors. *Journal of Research on Adolescence 15*, 451–477.

doi:10.1111/j.1532-7795.2005.00107.x

Clay, D. L., Mordhorst, M. J., & Lend, L. (2002). Empirically supported treatments in pediatric psychology: Where is the diversity? *Journal of Pediatric Psychology, 27*, 325–337. doi:10.1093/jpepsy/27.4.325

Clifford, S. M., & Dissanayake, C. (2008). The early development of joint attention in infants with autistic disorder using home video observations and parental interview. *Journal of Autism and Developmental Disorders, 38*, 791–805. doi:10.1007/s10803-007-0444-7

Cobb, B., Sample, P. L., Alwell, M., & Johns, N. R. (2006). Cognitive-behavioral interventions, dropout, and youth with disabilities: A systematic review. *Remedial and Special Education, 27*, 259–275. doi:10.1177/07419325060270050201

Coccaro, E. F., Sripada, C. S., Yanowitch, R. N., & Phan, K. L. (2011). Corticolimbic function in impulsive aggressive behavior. *Biological Psychiatry, 69*, 1153–1159. doi:10.1016/j.biopsych.2011.02.032

Cogan, J. C., Bhalla, S. K., Sefa-Dedeh, A., & Rothblum, E. D. (1996). A comparison study of United States and African students on perceptions of obesity and thinness. *Journal of Cross Cultural Psychology, 27*, 98–113. doi:10.1177/0022022196271007

Coghill, D., Nigg, J., Rothenberger, A., Sonuga-Barke, E., & Tannock, R. (2005). Whither causal models in the neuroscience of ADHD? *Developmental Science, 8*, 105–114. doi:10.1111/j.1467-7687.2005.00397.x

Cohan, S. L., & Chavira, D. A. (2008). Refining the classification of children with selective mutism: A latent profile analysis. *Journal of Clinical Child and Adolescent Psychology, 37*, 770–784. doi:10.1080/15374410802359759

Cohan, S. L., Chavira, D. A., & Stein, M. B. (2006). Practitioner review: Psychosocial interventions for children with selective mutism: A critical evaluation of the literature from 1990–2005. *Journal of Child Psychology and Psychiatry, 47*, 1085–1097. doi:10.1111/j.1469-7610.2006.01662.x

Cohen, J. A., Mannarino, A. P., Murray, L. K., & Igelman, R. (2006). Psychosocial interventions for maltreated and violence-exposed children. *Journal of Social Issues, 62*, 737–766.

Cohen, J., Mannarino, A., & Murray, L. (2011). Trauma-focused CBT for youth who experience ongoing traumas. *Child Abuse and Neglect, 35*, 637–646. doi:10.1016/j.chiabu.2011.05.002

Cohen, M.A. (2005). *The costs of crime and justice*. New York: Routledge.

Cohen, P (2008). Child development and personality disorder. *Psychiatric Clinics of North America, 31*, 477–493. doi:10.1016/j.psc.2008.03.005

Cohen, P., Cohen, J., & Brook, J. S. (1993). An epidemiological study of disorders in late childhood and adolescence: II. Persistence of disorders. *Journal of Child Psychology and Psychiatry, 34*, 869–877. doi:10.1111/j.1469-7610.1993.tb01095.x

Coker, T. R., Austin, S. B., & Schuster, M. A. (2010). The health and health care of lesbian, gay, and bisexual adolescents. *Annual Review of Public Health, 31*, 457–477. doi:10.1146/annurev.publhealth.012809.103636

Colapinto, J. (1993, November). The trouble with Nick. *Redbook*, 121–123, 145, 151–153.

Colder, C. R., Lochman, J. E., & Wells, K. C. (1997). The moderating effects of children's fear and activity level on relations between parenting practices and childhood symptomatology. *Journal of Abnormal Child Psychology, 25*, 251–263. doi:10.1023/A:1025704217619

Cole, D. A. (1990). The relation of social and academic competence to depressive symptoms in childhood. *Journal of Abnormal Psychology, 99*, 422–429. doi:10.1037/0021-843X.99.4.422

Cole, D. A., Ciesla, J. A., Dallaire, H., Jacquez, F. M., Pineda, A. Q., Lagrange, B., . . . Felton, J. W. (2008). Emergence of attributional style and its relation to depressive symptoms. *Journal of Abnormal Psychology, 117*, 16–31. doi:10.1037/0021-843X.117.1.16

Cole, D. A., Martin, J. M., Peeke, L., Henderson, A., & Harwell, J. (1998). Validation of depression and anxiety measures in White and Black youths: Multitrait-multimethod analyses. *Psychological Assessment, 10*, 261–276. doi:10.1037/1040-3590.10.3.261

Cole, D. A., Truglio, R., & Peeke, L. (1997). Relation between symptoms of anxiety and depression in children: A multitrait-multimethod-multigroup assessment. *Journal of Consulting and Clinical Psychology, 65*, 110–119. doi:10.1037/0022-006X.65.1.110

Cole, P. M., & Hall, S. E. (2008). Emotion dysregulation as a risk factor for psychopathology. In T. P. Beauchaine & S. P. Hinshaw (Eds.), *Child and adolescent psychopathology* (pp. 265–298). Hoboken, NJ: Wiley.

Cole, T. J. (2007). Early causes of child obesity and implications for prevention. *Acta Paediatrica, 96*(Suppl. 454), 2–4. doi:10.1111/j.1651-2227.2007.00162.x

Coll, C. G., Akerman, A., & Cicchetti, D. (2000). Cultural influences on developmental processes and outcomes: Implications for the study of development and psychopathology. *Development and Psychopathology* [Special issue: Reflecting on the past and planning for the future of developmental psychopathology], *12*, 333–356. doi:10.1017/S0954579400003059

Collins, D. W., & Rourke, B. P. (2003). Learning-disabled brains: A review of the literature. *Journal of Clinical & Experimental Neuropsychology, 25*, 1011–1034. doi:10.1076/jcen.25.7.1011.16487

Collishaw, S., Maughan, B., Goodman, R., & Pickles, A. (2004). Time trends in adolescent mental health. *Journal of Child Psychology and Psychiatry, 45*, 1350–1362. doi:10.1111/j.1469-7610.2004.00335.x

Collishaw, S., Pickles, A., Messer, J., Rutter, M., Shearer, C., & Maughan, B. (2007). Resilience to adult psychopathology following childhood maltreatment: Evidence from a community sample. *Child Abuse & Neglect, 31*, 211–229.

Comer, J. S., & Kendall, P. C. (2007). Terrorism: The psychological impact on youth. *Clinical Psychology: Science and Practice, 14*, 179–212. doi:10.1111/j.1468-2850.2007.00078.x

Comer, J. S., Olfson, M., & Mojtabai, R. (2010). National trends in child and adolescent psychotropic polypharmacy in office-based practice, 1996–2007. *Journal of the American Academy of Child & Adolescent Psychiatry, 49*, 1001–1010. doi:10.1016/j.jaac.2010.07.007

Compas, B. E., Connor-Smith, J. K., Saltzman, H., Thomsen, A. H., & Wadsworth, M. E. (2001). Coping with stress during childhood and adolescence: Problems, progress, and potential in theory and research. *Psychological Bulletin, 127*, 87–127. doi:10.1037/0033-2909.127.1.87

Compas, B. E., Forehand, R., Thigpen, J. C., Keller, G., Hardcastle, E. J., Cole, D. A., . . . Roberts, L. (2011). Family group cognitive–behavioral preventive intervention for families of depressed parents: 18- and 24-month outcomes. *Journal of Consulting and Clinical Psychology, 79*, 488–499. doi:10.1037/a0024254

Compas, B. E., & Hammen, C. L. (1994). Child and adolescent depression: Covariation and comorbidity in development. In R. J. Haggerty, L. R. Sherrod, N. Garmezy, & M. Rutter (Eds.), *Stress, risk, and resilience in children and adolescents: Processes, mechanisms, and interventions* (pp. 225–267). New York: Cambridge University Press.

Compton, S. N., Nelson, A. H., & March, J. S. (2000). Social phobia and separation anxiety symptoms in community and clinical samples of children and adolescents. *Journal of the American Academy of Child & Adolescent Psychiatry, 39*, 1040–1046. doi:10.1097/00004583-200008000-00020

Conduct Problems Prevention Research Group. (2007). Fast track randomized controlled trial to prevent externalizing psychiatric disorders: Findings from grades 3 to 9. *Journal of the American Academy of Child & Adolescent Psychiatry, 46*, 1250–1262. doi:10.1097/chi.0b013e31813e5d39

Conduct Problems Prevention Research Group. (2011). The effects of the Fast Track preventive intervention on the development of conduct disorder across childhood. *Child Development, 82*, 331–345. doi:10.1111/j.1467-8624.2010.01558.x

Conger, R. D., Ge, X., Elder, G. H., Lorenz, F. O., & Simons, R. L. (1994). Economic stress, coercive family process, and developmental problems of adolescents. *Child Development, 65*, 541–561. doi:10.1111/j.1467-8624.1994.tb00768.x

Connell, A. M., & Goodman, S. H. (2002). The association between psychopathology in fathers versus mothers and children's internalizing and externalizing behavior problems: A meta-analysis. *Psychological Bulletin, 128*, 746–773. doi:10.1037/0033-2909.128.5.746

Connell, A. M., Dishion, T. J., & Deater-Deckard, K. (2006). Variable- and person-centered approaches to the analysis of early adolescent substance use: Linking peer, family, and intervention effects with developmental trajectories. *Merrill-Palmer Quarterly, 52*, 421–448. doi:10.1353/mpq.2006.0025

Conner, B. T., & Lochman, J. E. (2010). Comorbid conduct disorder and substance use disorders. *Clinical Psychology: Science and Practice, 17*, 337–349. doi:10.1111/j.1468-2850.2010.01225.x

Connell, A. M., Hughes-Scalise, A., Klostermann, S., & Azem, T. (2011). Maternal depression and the heart of parenting: Respiratory sinus arrhythmia and affective dynamics during parent-adolescent interactions. *Journal of Family Psychology, 25*, 653–662. doi:10.1037/a0025225

Conners, K., Epstein, J., March, J., Angold, A., Wells, K. C., Klaric, J., . . . Wigal, T. (2001). Multimodal treatment of ADHD in the MTA: An alternative outcome analysis. *Journal of the American Academy of Child & Adolescent Psychiatry, 40*, 168–179. doi:10.1097/00004583-200102000-00010

Connolly, J., Furman, W., & Konarski, R. (2000). The role of peers in the emergence of heterosexual romantic relationships in adolescence. *Child Development, 71*, 1395–1408. doi:10.1111/1467-8624.00235

Conrod, P. J., Castellanos-Ryan, N., & Mackie, C. (2011). Long-term effects of a personality-targeted intervention to reduce alcohol use in adolescents. *Journal of Consulting and Clinical Psychology, 79*, 296–306. doi:10.1037/a0022997

Constantine, M. G., & Sue, D. W. (2006). Factors contributing to optimal human functioning in people of color in the United States. *Counseling Psychologist, 34*, 228–244. doi:10.1177/0011000005281318

Constantino J. N., Zhang, Y., Frazier, T., Abbacchi, A.M., & Law, P. (2010). Sibling recurrence and the genetic epidemiology of autism. *American Journal of Psychiatry, 167*, 1349–1356. doi:10.1176/appi.ajp.2010.09101470

Cook, F., & Oliver, C. (2011). A review of defining and measuring sociability in children with intellectual disabilities. *Research in Developmental Disabilities, 32*, 11–24. doi:10.1016/j.ridd.2010.09.021

Coolidge, F. L., Thede, L. L., & Young, S. E. (2000). Heritability and the comorbidity of attention deficit hyperactivity disorder with behavioral disorders and executive function deficits: A preliminary investigation. *Developmental Neuropsychology, 17*, 273–287. doi:10.1207/S15326942DN1703_1

Cooper, P. J., Fearn, V., Willets, L., Seabrook, H., & Parkinson, M. (2006). Affective disorders in the parents of a clinical sample of children with anxiety disorders. *Journal of Affective Disorders, 93*, 205–212. doi:10.1016/j.jad.2006.03.017

Cooper, S. W., Estes, R. J., Giardino, A. P., Kellogg, N. D., & Vieth, V. I. (2005). Medical, legal, & social science aspects of child sexual exploitation: A comprehensive review of pornography, prostitution, and internet crimes, Vol 1. St. Louis, MO: GW Medical Publishing.

Copeland, W. E., Keeler, G., Angold, A., & Costello, E. J. (2007). Traumatic events and posttraumatic stress in childhood. *Archives of General Psychiatry, 64*, 577–584. Retrieved from http://archpsyc.ama-assn.org/

Copeland, W. E., Keeler, G., Angold, A., & Costello, E. J. (2010). Posttraumatic stress without trauma in children. *American Journal of Psychiatry, 167*, 1059–1065. doi:10.1176/appi.ajp.2010.09020178

Copeland, W., Shanahan, L., Costello, E. J., & Angold, A. (2011). Cumulative prevalence of psychiatric disorders by young adulthood: A prospective cohort analysis from the great smoky mountains study. *Journal of the American Academy of Child & Adolescent Psychiatry, 50*, 252–261. doi:10.1016/j.jaac.2010.12.014

Corbett, B. A., Constantine, L. J., Hendren, R., Rocke, D., & Ozonoff, S. (2009). Examining executive functioning in children with autism spectrum disorder, attention deficit hyperactivity disorder and typical development. *Psychiatry Research, 166*, 210–222. doi:10.1016/j.psychres.2008.02.005

Cornelius, J. R., Maisto, S. A., Pollock, N. K., Martin, C. S., Salloum, I. M., Lynch, K. G., & Clark, D. B. (2003). Rapid relapse generally follows treatment for substance use disorders among adolescents. *Addictive Behaviors, 28*, 381–386. doi:10.1016/S0306-4603(01)00247-7

Cornier, M. (2011). Is your brain to blame for weight regain? *Physiology & Behavior, 104*, 608–612. doi:10.1016/j.physbeh.2011.04.003

Corning, A. F., Gondoli, D. M., Bucchianeri, M. M., & Salafia, E. H. B. (2010). Preventing the development of body issues in adolescent girls through intervention with their mothers. *Body Image, 7*, 289–295. doi:10.1016/j.bodyim.2010.08.001

Cornish, K. M., Levitas, A., & Sudhalter, V. (2007). Fragile X syndrome: The journey from genes to behavior. In M. M. Mazzocco & J. L. Ross (Eds.), *Neurogenetic developmental disorders: Variation of manifestation in childhood* (pp. 73–103). Cambridge, MA: MIT Press.

Corrigan, P. W. (2000). Mental health stigma as social attribution: Implications for research methods and attitude change. *Clinical Psychology: Science and Practice, 7*, 48–67. doi:10.1093/clipsy.7.1.48

Cortese, S., Faraone, S. V., Konofal, E., & Lecendreux, M. (2009). Sleep in children with attention-deficit/ hyperactivity disorder: Meta-analysis of subjective and objective studies. *Journal of the American Academy of Child & Adolescent Psychiatry, 48*, 894–908. doi:10.1097/CHI.0b013e3181ae09c9

Cosmopolitan. (2001, August). "Why models got so skinny." Retrieved from http://www.highbeam.com/doc/1G1-76667021.html

Cosentino, C. E., Meyer-Bahlburg, H. F., Alpert, J., Weinberg, S. L., & Gaines, R. (1995). Sexual behavior problems and psychopathology symptoms in sexually abused girls. *Journal of the American Academy of Child and Adolescent Psychiatry, 34*, 1033–1042.

Costello, E. J., & Angold, A. (2006). Developmental epidemiology. In D. Cicchetti & D. J. Cohen (Eds.), *Developmental psychopathology: Vol. 1. Theory and method* (2nd ed., pp. 41–75). Hoboken, NJ: Wiley.

Costello, E. J., Egger, H., & Angold, A. (2005a). 10-year research update review: The epidemiology of child and adolescent psychiatric disorders: I. Methods and public health burden. *Journal of the American Academy of Child & Adolescent Psychiatry, 44*, 972–986. doi:10.1097/01.chi.0000172552.41596.6f

Costello, E. J., Egger, H., & Angold, A. (2005b). The developmental epidemiology of anxiety disorders: Phenomenology, prevalence, and comorbidity. *Child and Adolescent Psychiatric Clinics of North America, 14*, 631–648. doi:10.1016/j.chc.2005.06.003

Costello, E. J., Erkanli, A., & Angold, A. (2006). Is there an epidemic of child or adolescent depression? *Journal of Child Psychology and Psychiatry, 47*, 1263–1271. doi:10.1111/j.1469-7610.2006.01682.x

Costello, E. J., Farmer, E. M. Z., Angold, A., Burns, B. J., & Erkanli, A. (1997). Psychiatric disorders among American Indian and white youth in Appalachia: The Great Smoky Mountains Study. *American Journal of Public Health, 87*, 827–832. doi:10.2105/AJPH.87.5.827

Costello, E. J., Pine, D. S., Hammen, C., March, J. S., Plotsky, P. M., Weissman, M. M., . . . Leckman, J. F. (2002). Development and natural history of mood disorders. *Biological Psychiatry, 52*, 529–542. doi:10.1016/S0006-3223(02)01372-0

Costello, E. J., Worthman, C., Erkanli, A., & Angold, A. (2007). Prediction from low birth weight to female adolescent depression. *Archives of General Psychiatry, 64*, 338–344. doi:10.1001/archpsyc.64.3.338

Cote, S. M., Vaillancourt, T., Barker, E. D., Nagin, D., & Tremblay, R. E. (2007). The joint development of physical and indirect aggression: Predictors of continuity and change during childhood. *Development and Psychopathology, 19*, 37–55. doi:10.1017/S0954579407070034

Coulton, C. J., Crampton, D. S., Irwin, M., Spilsbury, J. C., & Korbin, J. E. (2007). How neighborhoods influence child maltreatment: A review of the literature and alternative pathways. *Child Abuse & Neglect, 31*, 1117–1142.

Courchesne, E., Carper, R., & Akshoomoff, N. (2003). Evidence of brain overgrowth in the first year of life in autism. *JAMA: Journal of the American Medical Association, 290*, 337–344. doi:10.1001/jama.290.3.337

Courchesne, E., Pierce, K., Schumann, C. M., Redcay, E., Buckwalter, J. A., Kennedy, D. P., . . . Morgan, J. (2007). Mapping early brain development in autism. *Neuron, 56*, 399–413. doi:10.1016/j.neuron.2007.10.016

Cowan, P. A., & Cowan, C. P. (2006). Developmental psychopathology from family systems and family risk factors perspectives: Implications for family research, practice, and policy. In D. Cicchetti & D. Cohen (Eds.), *Developmental psychopathology: Vol. 1. Theory and method* (2nd ed., pp. 530–587). Hoboken, NJ: Wiley.

Cowan, P. A., Cowan, C. P., & Knox, V. (2010). Marriage and fatherhood programs. *The Future of Children, 20*, 205–230. doi:10.1353/foc.2010.0000

Cox, D. J., Madaan, V., & Cox, B. S. (2011, July). Adult attention-deficit/hyperactivity disorder and driving: Why and how to manage it. *Current Psychiatry Reports, 13,* 345–350. doi:10.1007/s11920-011-0216-0

Cox, M. J., Mills-Koonce, R., Propper, C., & Gariépy, J. (2010). Systems theory and cascades in developmental psychopathology. *Development and Psychopathology. Special Issue: Developmental Cascades: Part 1, 22,* 497–506. doi:10.1017/S0954579410000234

Coyne, J. C., Downey, G., & Boergers, J. (1992). Depression in families: A systems perspective. In D. Cicchetti & S. L. Toth (Eds.), *Rochester symposium on developmental psychopathology: Vol. 4. Developmental perspectives on depression* (pp. 211–249). New York: University of Rochester Press.

Craig, A., Hancock, K., Tran, Y., Craig, M., & Peters, K. (2002). Epidemiology of stuttering in the community across the entire life span. *Journal of Speech, Language, & Hearing Research, 45,* 1097–1105. doi:10.1044/1092-4388(2002/088)

Craig, T. K., Cox, A. D., & Klein, K. (2002). Intergenerational transmission of somatization behaviour: A study of chronic somatizers and their children. *Psychological Medicine, 32,* 805–816. doi:10.1017/S0033291702005846

Craske, M. G., Kircanski, K., Epstein, A., Wittchen, H-U., Pine, D. S., Lewis-Fernández, R., . . . Posttraumatic and Dissociative Disorder Work Group. (2010). Panic disorder: A review of DSM-IV panic disorder and proposals for DSM-V. *Depression and Anxiety, 27,* 93–112. doi:10.1002/da.20654

Craske, M. G., & Rowe, M. K. (1997). Nocturnal panic. *Clinical Psychology: Science and Practice, 4,* 153–174. doi:10.1111/j.1468-2850.1997.tb00107.x

Crawford, A. M., Pentz, M. A., Chou, C., Li, C., & Dwyer, J. H. (2003). Parallel developmental trajectories of sensation seeking and regular substance use in adolescents. *Psychology of Addictive Behaviors, 17,* 179–192. doi:10.1037/0893-164X.17.3.179

Creswell, C., & Cartwright-Hatton, S. (2007). Family treatment of child anxiety: Outcomes, limitations and future directions. *Clinical Child and Family Psychology Review, 10,* 232–252. doi:10.1007/s10567-007-0019-3

Crick, N. R. (1995). Relational aggression: The role of intent attributions, feelings of distress, and provocation type. *Development and Psychopathology, 7,* 313–322. doi:10.1017/S0954579400006520

Crick, N. R. (1997). Engagement in gender normative versus nonnormative forms of aggression: Links to social-psychological adjustment. *Developmental Psychology, 33,* 610–617. doi:10.1037/0012-1649.33.4.610

Crick, N. R., Bigbee, M. A., & Howes, C. (1996). Gender differences in children's normative beliefs about aggression: How do I hurt thee? Let me count the ways. *Child Development, 67,* 1003–1014. doi:10.1111/j.1467-8624.1996.tb01779.x

Crick, N. R., & Dodge, K. A. (1994). A review and reformulation of social-information-processing mechanisms in children's social adjustment. *Psychological Bulletin, 115,* 74–101. doi:10.1037/0033-2909.115.1.74

Crick, N. R., & Dodge, K. A. (1996). Social information-processing mechanisms on reactive and proactive aggression. *Child Development, 67,* 993–1002. doi:10.1111/j.1467-8624.1996.tb01778.x

Crick, N. R., & Nelson, D. A. (2002). Relational and physical victimization within friendships: Nobody told me there'd be friends like these. *Journal of Abnormal Child Psychology, 30,* 599–607. doi:10.1023/A:1020811714064

Crick, N. R., Nelson, D. A., Morales, J. R., Cullerton-Sen, C., Casas, J. F., & Hickman, S. E. (2001). Relational victimization in childhood and adolescence: I hurt you through the grapevine. In J. Juvonen & S. Graham (Eds.), *Peer harassment in school: The plight of the vulnerable and victimized* (pp. 196–214). New York: Guilford Press.

Crick, N. R., Ostrov, J. M., & Werner, N. E. (2006). A longitudinal study of relational aggression, physical aggression, and children's social-psychological adjustment. *Journal of Abnormal Child Psychology, 34,* 131–142. doi:10.1007/s10802-005-9009-4

Crick, N. R., & Rose, A. J. (2000). Toward a gender-balanced approach to the study of social-emotional development: A look at relational aggression. In P. H. Miller & E. K. Scholnick (Eds.), *Toward a feminist developmental psychology* (pp. 153–168). Florence, KY: Taylor & Francis/Routledge.

Crijnen, A. A. M., Achenbach, T. M., & Verhulst, F. C. (1997). Comparisons of problems reported by parents of children in 12 cultures: Total problems, externalizing, and internalizing. *Journal of the American Academy of Child & Adolescent Psychiatry, 36,* 1269–1277. doi:10.1097/00004583-199709000-00021

Crisp, A. H. (1997). Anorexia nervosa as flight from growth: Assessment and treatment based on the model. In D. M. Garner & P. E. Garfinkel (Eds.), *Handbook of treatment for eating disorders* (2nd ed., pp. 248–277). New York: Guilford Press.

Crisp, R. J., & Turner, R. N. (2011). Cognitive adaptation to the experience of social and cultural diversity. *Psychological Bulletin, 137,* 242–266. doi:10.1037/a0021840

Croen, L. A., Grether, J. K. Yoshida, C. K., Odouli, R., & Hendrick, V. (2011, July). Antidepressant use during pregnancy and childhood spectrum disorders. *Archives of General Psychiatry*. Advance online publication. doi:10.1001/archgenpsychiatry.2011.73

Crooks, C. V., & Wolfe, D. A. (2007). Child abuse and neglect. In E. J. Mash & R. A. Barkley (Eds.), *Assessment of childhood disorders* (Fourth Edition, pp. 639–684). New York: Guilford.

Cuéllar, I. (2000). Acculturation as a moderator of personality and psychological assessment. In R. H. Dana (Ed.), *Handbook of cross-cultural and multicultural personality assessment* (pp. 113–129). Mahwah, NJ: Erlbaum.

Cuccaro, M. L., Brinkley, J., Abramson, R. K., Hall, A., Wright, H. H., Hussman, J. P., . . . Pericak-Vance, M. A. (2007). Autism in African American families: Clinical-phenotypic findings. *American Journal of Medical Genetics Part B: Neuropsychiatric Genetics, 144,* 1022–1026. doi:10.1002/ajmg.b.30535

Cuffe, S. P., Moore, C. G., & McKeown, R. E. (2005). Prevalence and correlates of ADHD symptoms in the National Health Interview Survey. *Journal of Attention Disorders, 9,* 392–401. doi:10.1177/1087054705280413

Cuijpers, P., Muñoz, R. F., Clarke, G. N., & Lewinsohn, P. M. (2010). Psychoeducational treatment and prevention of depression: The "coping with depression" course thirty years later. *Clinical Psychology Review, 29,* 449–458. doi:10.1016/j.cpr.2009.04.005

Culbertson, F. M. (1997). Depression and gender: An international review. *American Psychologist, 52,* 25–31. doi:10.1037/0003-066X.52.1.25

Cummings, E. M., & Davies, P. T. (2002). Effects of marital conflict on children: Recent advances and emerging themes in process-oriented research. *Journal of Child Psychology, 43,* 31–63. doi:10.1111/1469-7610.00003

Cummings, J., & Druss, B. (2011). Racial/ethnic differences in mental health service use among adolescents with major depression. *Journal of the American Academy of Child & Adolescent Psychiatry, 50,* 160–170. doi:10.1016/j.jaac.2010.11.004

Cummings, J. R., & Druss, B. G. (2011). Racial/ethnic differences in mental health service use among adolescents with major depression. *Journal of the American Academy of Child & Adolescent Psychiatry, 50,* 160–170. doi:10.1016/j.jaac.2010.11.004

Cunningham, P. B., Henggeler, S. W., Brondino, M., & Pickrel, S. G. (1999). Testing underlying assumptions of the family empowerment perspective. *Journal of Child and Family Studies, 8,* 437–449. doi:10.1023/A:1021951720298

Curry, J., Silva, S., Rohde, P., Ginsburg, G., Kratochvil, C., Simons, A., . . . March, J. (2011). Recovery and recurrence following treatment for adolescent major depression. *Archives of General Psychiatry, 68,* 263–270. doi:10.1001/archgenpsychiatry.2010.150

Cuthburt, B. (2010). Editorial: Early prevention in childhood anxiety disorders. *American Journal of Psychiatry, 167,* 1428–1430. doi:10.1176/appi.ajp.2010.10091316

Cyr, C., Euser, E. M., Bakermans-Kranenburg, M., & Van Ijzendoorn, M. H. (2010). Attachment security and disorganization in maltreating and high-risk families: A series of meta-analyses. *Development and Psychopathology, 22,* 87–108. doi:10.1017/S0954579409990289

Cytryn, L., & McKnew, D. H. (1974). Factors influencing the changing clinical expression of the depressive process in children. *American Journal of Psychiatry, 131,* 879–881. doi:10.1176/appi.ajp.131.8.879

Cytryn, L., & McKnew, D. H. (1996). *Growing up sad: Childhood depression and its treatment.* New York: Norton.

D'Augelli, A. R. (2006). Developmental and contextual factors and mental health among lesbian, gay, and bisexual youths. In A. M. Omoto & H. S. Kurtzman (Eds.), *Sexual orientation and mental health: Examining identity and development in lesbian, gay, and bisexual people. Contemporary perspectives on lesbian, gay, and bisexual psychology* (pp. 37–53). Washington, DC: American Psychological Association.

D'Onofrio, B. M., Goodnight, J. A., Van Hulle, C. A., Rodgers, J. L., Rathouz, P. J., Waldman, I. D., & Lahey, B. B. (2009). Maternal age at childbirth and offspring disruptive behaviors: Testing the causal hypothesis. *Journal of Child Psychology and Psychiatry, 50,* 1018–1028. doi:10.1111/j.1469-7610.2009.02068.x

D'Onofrio, B. M., Singh. A. L., Iliadou, A., Lambe, M., Hultman, C. M., Grann, M., . . . Lichtenstein, P. (2010). Familial confounding of the association between maternal smoking during pregnancy and offspring criminality: A population-based study in Sweden. *Archives of General Psychiatry, 67,* 529–538. doi:10.1001/archgenpsychiatry.2010.33

D'Onofrio, B. M., Singh, A. L., Iliadou, A., Lambe, M., Hultman, C. M., Neiderhiser, J. M., . . . Lichtenstein, P. (2010). A quasi-experimental study of maternal smoking during pregnancy and offspring academic achievement. *Child Development, 81,* 80–100. doi:10.1111/j.1467-8624.2009.01382.x

D'Onofrio, B. M., Van Hulle, C. A., Waldman, I. D., Rodgers, J. L., Harden, K. P., Rathouz, P. J., & Lahey, B. B. (2008). Smoking during pregnancy and offspring externalizing problems: An exploration of genetic and environmental confounds. *Development and Psychopathology, 20,* 139–164. doi:10.1017/S0954579408000072

D'Onofrio, B. M., Van Hulle, C. A., Waldman, I. D., Rodgers, J. L., Rathouz, P. J., & Lahey, B. B. (2007). Causal inferences regarding prenatal alcohol exposure and childhood externalizing problems. *Archives of General Psychiatry, 64,* 1296–1304. doi:10.1001/archpsyc.64.11.1296

Dadds, M. R. (2002). Learning and intimacy in the families of anxious children. In R. J. McMahon & R. DeV. Peters (Eds.), *The effects of parental dysfunction on children* (pp. 87–94). New York: Kluwer/Plenum.

Dadds, M. R., Jambrak, J., Pasalich, D., Hawes, D. H., & Brennan, J. (2011). Impaired attention to the eyes of attachment figures and the developmental origins of psychopathy. *Journal of Child Psychology and Psychiatry, 52,* 238–245. doi:10.1111/j.1469-7610.2010.02323.x

Dagne, G. A., & Snyder, J. (2011). Relationship of maternal negative moods to child emotion regulation during family interaction. *Development and Psychopathology, 23,* 211–223. doi:10.1017/S095457941000074X

Dahl, R. E. (1996). The regulation of sleep and arousal: Development and psychopathology. *Development and Psychopathology, 8,* 3–27. doi:10.1017/S0954579400006945

Dahl, R. E. (2006). Sleeplessness and aggression in youth. *Journal of Adolescent Health, 38,* 641–642. doi:10.1016/j.jadohealth.2006.03.013

Dahl, R. E. (2007). Sleep and the developing brain. *Sleep, 30,* 1079–1080. Retrieved from http://www.journalsleep.org/

Dahl, R. E., & El-Sheikh, M. (2007). Considering sleep in a family context: Introduction to the special issue. *Journal of Family Psychology [Special issue: Carpe noctem: Sleep and family processes], 21,* 1–3. doi:10.1037/0893-3200.21.1.1

Dahlquist, L. M. (1999). *Pediatric pain management.* New York: Plenum Press.

Dahlquist, L. M., & Nagel, M. S. (2009). *Chronic and recurrent pain.* New York: Guilford Press.

Daley, S. E., Hammen, C., Burge, D., Davila, J., Paley, B., Lindberg, N., & Herzberg, D. S. (1999). Depression and Axis II symptomatology in an adolescent community sample: Concurrent and longitudinal associations. *Journal of Personality Disorders, 13,* 47–59. doi:10.1521/pedi.1999.13.1.47

Daley, S. E., Hammen, C., & Rao, U. (2000). Predictors of first onset and recurrence of major depression in young women during the 5 years following high school graduation. *Journal of Abnormal Psychology, 109,* 525–533. doi:10.1037/0021-843X.109.3.525

Dalton, K. M., Nacewicz, B. M., Johnstone, T., Schaefer, H. S., Gernsbacher, M. A., Goldsmith, H. H., . . . Davidson, R. J. (2005). Gaze fixation and the neural circuitry of face processing in autism. *Nature Neuroscience, 8,* 519–526. doi:10.1038/nn1421

Damasio, H., Tranel, D., Grabowskia, T., Adolphs, R., & Damasio, A. (2004). Neural systems behind word and concept retrieval. *Cognition [Special issue: Towards a new functions anatomy of language], 92,* 179–229. doi:10.1016/j.cognition.2002.07.001

Danckaerts, M., Sonuga-Barke, E. J. S., Banaschewski, T., Buitelaar, J., Dopfner, M., Hollis, C., . . . Coghill, D. (2010). The quality of life of children with attention deficit/hyperactivity disorder: A systematic review. *European Child & Adolescent Psychiatry, 19,* 83–105. doi:10.1007/s00787-009-0046-3

Dandreaux, D. M., & Frick, P. J. (2009). Developmental pathways to conduct problems: A further test of the childhood and adolescent-onset distinction. *Journal of Abnormal Child Psychology, 37,* 375–385. doi:10.1007/s10802-008-9261-5

Danese, A., Caspi, A., Williams, B., Ambler, A., Sugden, K., Mika, J., . . . Arseneault, L. (2011). Biological embedding of stress through inflammation processes in childhood. *Molecular Psychiatry, 16,* 244–246. doi:10.1038/mp.2010.5

Danner, S., Fristad, M. A., Arnold, L. E., Youngstrom, E. A., Birmaher, B., Horwitz, S. M., . . . The LAMS Group. (2009). Early-onset bipolar spectrum disorders: Diagnostic issues. *Clinical Child and Family Psychology Review, 12,* 271–293. doi:10.1007/s10567-009-0055-2

Dardennes, R. M., Al Anbar, N. N., Prado-Netto, A., Kaye, K., Contejean, Y., & Al Anbar, N. N. (2011). Treating the cause of the illness rather than the symptoms: Parental causal beliefs and treatment choices in autism spectrum disorder. *Research in Developmental Disabilities, 32,* 1137–1146. doi:10.1016/j.ridd.2011.01.010

Daughton, J. M., & Kratochvil, C. J. (2009). Review of ADHD pharmacotherapies: Advantages, disadvantages, and clinical pearls. *Journal of the American Academy of Child & Adolescent Psychiatry, 48,* 240–248. doi:10.1097/CHI.0b013e318197748f

David, C. F., & Kistner, J. A. (2000). Do positive self-perceptions have a "dark side"? Examination of the link between perceptual bias and aggression. *Journal of Abnormal Child Psychology, 28,* 327–337. doi:10.1023/A:1005164925300

David-Ferdon, C., & Kaslow, N. J. (2008). Evidence-based psychosocial treatments for child and adolescent depression. *Journal of Clinical Child and Adolescent Psychology, 37,* 62–104. doi:10.1080/15374410701817865

Davidson, R. J., Pizzagalli, D., & Nitschke, J. (2002). The representation and regulation of emotion in depression: Perspectives from affective neuroscience. In I. H. Gotlib & C. L. Hammen (Eds.), *Handbook of depression* (pp. 219–244). New York: Guilford Press.

Davies, P. T., Sturge-Apple, M., Cicchetti, D., Manning, L. G., & Zale, E. (2009). Children's patterns of emotional reactivity to conflict as explanatory mechanisms in links between interpartner aggression and child physiological functioning. *Journal of Child Psychology and Psychiatry, 50*(11), 1384–1391. doi:10.1111/j.1469-7610.2009.02154.x

Davis, A. M., Bennett, K. J., Befort, C., & Nollen, N. (2011). Obesity and related health behaviors among urban and rural children in the United States: Data from the national health and nutrition examination survey 2003–2004 and 2005–2006. *Journal of Pediatric Psychology, 36,* 669–676. doi:10.1093/jpepsy/jsq117

Davis, E. P., Glynn, L. M., Waffarn, F., & Sandman, C. A. (2011). Prenatal maternal stress programs infant stress regulation. *Journal of Child Psychology and Psychiatry, 52,* 119–129. doi:10.1111/j.1469-7610.2010.02314.x

Davis, L., & Siegel, L. J. (2000). Posttraumatic stress disorder in children and adolescents: A review and analysis. *Clinical Child and Family Psychology Review, 3,* 135–154. doi:10.1023/A:1009564724720

Davis, N., Barquero, L., Compton, D. L., Fuchs, L. S., Fuchs, D., Gore, J. C., & Anderson, A. W. (2011). Functional correlates of children's responsiveness to intervention. *Developmental Neuropsychology, 36,* 288–301. doi:10.1080/87565641.2010.549875

Davis, O. S. P., Arden, R., & Plomin, R. (2008). g in middle childhood: Moderate genetic and shared environmental influence using diverse measures of general cognitive ability at 7, 9 and 10 years in a large population sample of twins. *Intelligence, 36*, 68–80. doi:10.1016/j.intell.2007.01.006

Dawson, D. (2010). *Autism Treatment Network: Improving the quality of medical care for children with ASD*. Presentation to the IACC on the Autism Treatment Network (ATN), April 30, 2010, Washington, DC. Retrieved from: http://iacc.hhs.gov/events/2010/full-committee-mtg-minutes-april30.shtml#geraldine-dawson

Dawson, G. (1996). Neuropsychology of autism: A report on the state of the science. *Journal of Autism and Developmental Disorders, 2*, 179–181. doi:10.1007/BF02172008

Dawson, G. (2008). Early behavioral intervention, brain plasticity, and the prevention of autism spectrum disorder. *Development and Psychopathology, 20*, 775–803. doi:10.1017/S0954579408000370

Dawson, G., & Faja, S. (2008). Autism spectrum disorders: A developmental perspective. In T. P. Beauchaine & S. P. Hinshaw (Eds.), *Child and adolescent psychopathology* (pp. 575–613). New York: Wiley.

Dawson, G., Frey, K., Panagiotides, H., Osterling, J., & Hessl, D. (1997). Infants of depressed mothers exhibit atypical frontal brain activity: A replication and extension of previous findings. *Journal of Child Psychology and Psychiatry, 38*, 179–186. doi:10.1111/j.1469-7610.1997.tb01852.x

Dawson, G., Munson, J., Webb, S. J., Nalty, T., Abbott, R., & Toth, K. (2007). Rate of head growth decelerates and symptoms worsen in the second year of life in autism. *Biological Psychiatry, 15*, 458–464. doi:10.1016/j.biopsych.2006.07.016

Dawson, G., Rogers, S., Munson, J., Smith, M., Winter, J., Greenson J., . . . Varley, J. (2010). Randomized, controlled trial of an intervention for toddlers with autism: The Early Start Denver Model. *Pediatrics, 125*, e17–e23. doi:10.1542/peds.2009-0958

Dawson, G., & Toth, K. (2006). Autism spectrum disorders. In D. Cicchetti & D. J. Cohen (Eds.), *Developmental psychopathology: Vol. 3. Risk, disorder, and adaptation* (2nd ed., pp. 317–357). Hoboken, NJ: Wiley.

Dawson, G., Webb, S. J., & McPartland, J. (2005). Understanding the nature of face processing impairment in autism: Insights from behavioral and electrophysiological studies. *Developmental Neuropsychology, 27*, 403–424. doi:10.1207/s15326942dn2703_6

Dawson, G., Webb, S., Schellenberg, G. D., Dager, S., Friedman, S., Aylward, E., & Richards, T. (2002). Defining the broader phenotype of autism: Genetic, brain, and behavioral perspectives. *Development and Psychopathology, 14*, 581–611. doi:10.1017/S0954579402003103

Dawson, M., Soulieres, I., Gernsbacher, M. A., & Mottron, L. (2007). The level and nature of autistic intelligence. *Psychological Science, 18*, 657–662. doi:10.1111/j.1467-9280.2007.01954.x

Day, N. L., Leech, S. L., Richardson, G. A., Cornelius, M. D., Robles, N., & Larkby, C. (2002). Prenatal alcohol exposure predicts continued deficits in offspring size at 14 years of age. *Alcoholism: Clinical and Experimental Research, 26*, 1584–1591. doi:10.1111/j.1530-0277.2002.tb02459.x

De Bellis, M. D., Keshavan, M. S., Frustaci, K., Shifflett, H., Iyengar, S., Beers, S. R., & Hall, J. (2002). Superior temporal gyrus volumes in maltreated children and adolescents with PTSD. *Biological Psychiatry, 51*, 544–552. doi:10.1016/S0006-3223(01)01374-9

De Bellis, M. D., Keshavan, M. S., Shifflett, H., Iyengar, S., Dahl, R. E., Axelson, D. A., & Ryan, N. D. (2002). Superior temporal gyrus volumes in pediatric generalized anxiety disorder. *Biological Psychiatry, 51*, 553–562. doi:10.1016/S0006-3223(01)01375-0

de Koning, N. D., Moreland, F., Valenti, R. J., & Dosen, A. (2007). Feeding and eating disorders. In R. Fletcher, E. Loschen, C. Stavrakaki, & M. First (Eds.), *Diagnostic manual—intellectual disability: A textbook of diagnosis of mental disorders in persons with intellectual disability* (pp. 145–155). Kingston, NY: National Association for the Dually Diagnosed.

De Los Reyes, A., & Kazdin, A. E. (2005). Informant discrepancies in the assessment of childhood psychopathology: A critical review, theoretical framework, and recommendations for further study. *Psychological Bulletin, 131*, 483–509. doi:10.1037/0033-2909.131.4.483

de Onis, M., Blössner, M., & Borghi, E. (2010). Global prevalence and trends of overweight and obesity among preschool children. *American Journal of Clinical Nutrition, 92*, 1257–1264. doi:10.3945/ajcn.2010.29786

de Ruiter, K. P., Dekker, M. C., Douma, J. C. H., Verhulst, F. C., & Koot, H. M. (2008). Development of parent- and teacher-reported emotional and behavioural problems in young people with intellectual disabilities: Does level of intellectual disability matter? *Journal of Applied Research in Intellectual Disabilities, 21*, 70–80. doi:10.1111/j.1468-3148.2007.00370.x

de Ruiter, K. P., Dekker, M. C., Verhulst, F. C., & Koot, H. M. (2007). Developmental course of psychopathology in youths with and without intellectual disabilities. *Journal of Child Psychology and Psychiatry, 48*, 498–507. doi:10.1111/j.1469-7610.2006.01712.x

Dean, K. L., Langley, A. K., Kataoka, S. H., Jaycox, L. H., Wong, M., & Stein, B. D. (2008). School-based disaster mental health services: Clinical, policy, and community challenges. *Professional Psychology: Research and Practice, 39*, 52–57. doi:10.1037/0735-7028.39.1.52

Dean, R. R., Kelsey, J. E., Heller, M. R., & Ciaranello, R. D. (1993). Structural foundations of illness and treatment: Receptors. In D. L. Dunner (Ed.), *Current psychiatric therapy.* Philadelphia: Saunders.

Deater-Deckard, K., & Dodge, K. A. (1997). Externalizing behavior problems and discipline revisited: Nonlinear effects and variation by culture, context, and gender. *Psychological Inquiry, 8*, 161–175. doi:10.1207/s15327965pli0803_1

Deater-Deckard, K., Mullineaux, P. Y., Beekman, C., Petrill, S. A., Schatschneider, C., & Thompson, L. A. (2009). Conduct problems, IQ, and household chaos: A longitudinal multi-informant study. *Journal of Child Psychology and Psychiatry, 50*, 1301–1308. doi:10.1111/j.1469-7610.2009.02108.x

DeGrandpre, R. J. (2000). A science of meaning: Can behaviorism bring meaning to psychological science? *American Psychologist, 55*, 721–739. doi:10.1037/0003-066X.55.7.721

Del'Homme, M., Kim, T. S., Loo, S. K., Yang, M. H., & Smalley, S. L. (2007). Familial association and frequency of learning disabilities in ADHD sibling pair families. *Journal of Abnormal Child Psychology, 35*, 55–62. doi:10.1007/s10802-006-9080-5

DelBello, M. P., Carlson, G. A., Tohen, M., Bromet, E. J., Schwiers, M., & Strakowski, S. M. (2003). Rates and predictors of developing a manic or hypomanic episode 1 to 2 years following a first hospitalization for major depression with psychotic features. *Journal of Child and Adolescent Psychopharmacology, 13*, 173–185. doi:10.1089/104454603322163899

DelBello, M. P., Hanseman, D., Adler, C. M., Fleck, D. E., & Strakowski, S. M. (2007). Twelve-month outcome of adolescents with bipolar disorder following first hospitalization for a manic or mixed episode. *American Journal of Psychiatry, 164*, 582–590. doi:10.1176/appi.ajp.164.4.582

DelCarmen-Wiggens, R., & Carter, A. (Eds.). (2004). *Handbook of infant, toddler, and preschool mental health assessment*. New York: Oxford University Press.

Denzin, N. K., & Lincoln, Y. S. (Eds.). (2011). *The Sage handbook of qualitative research* (4th ed.). Thousand Oaks, CA: Sage Publications, Inc.

Deren, D. M. (1996). *A childhood without laughter*. Retrieved from Internet website "A childhood without laughter," by D. M. Deren.

Derose, L. M., Shiyko, M. P., Foster, H., & Brooks-Gunn, J. (2011). Associations between menarcheal timing and behavioral developmental trajectories for girls from age 6 to age 15. *Journal of Youth and Adolescence, 40*, 1329–1342. doi:10.1007/s10964-010-9625-3

Derosier, M. E., Swick, D. C., Davis, N. O., McMillen, J. S., & Matthews, R. (2010). The efficacy of a social skills group intervention for improving social behaviors in children with high functioning autism spectrum disorders. *Journal of Autism and Developmental Disorders, 41*, 1033–1043. doi:10.1007/s10803-010-1128-2

Dervic, K., Brent, D. A., & Oquendo, M. A. (2008) Completed suicide in childhood. *Psychiatric Clinics of North America, 31*, 271–291. doi:10.1016/j.psc.2008.01.006

Desmond, A. J., & Moore, J. (1991). *Darwin.* New York: Warner Books.

Despert, J. L. (1955). Differential diagnosis between obsessive-compulsive neurosis and schizophrenia in children. In P. Hoch & J. Zubins (Eds.), *Psychopathology of childhood* (pp. 241–253). New York: Grune & Stratton.

Devlin, B., Daniels, M., & Roeder, K. (1997). The heritability of IQ. *Nature, 388*, 468–471. doi:10.1038/388468a0

Di Nuovo, S. F., & Buono, S. (2007). Psychiatric syndromes comorbid with mental retardation: Differences in cognitive and adaptive skills. *Journal of Psychiatric Research, 41*, 795–800. doi:10.1016/j.jpsychires.2006.02.011

Diamantopoulou, S., Verhulst, F. C., & van der Ende, J. (2011). Gender differences in the development and adult outcome of co-occurring depression and delinquency in adolescence. *Journal of Abnormal Psychology, 120*, 644–655. doi:10.1037/a0023669

Dick, D. (2007). Identification of genes influencing a spectrum of externalizing psychopathology. *Current Directions in Psychological Science, 16*, 331–335. doi:10.1111/j.1467-8721.2007.00530.x

Dickens, W. T., & Flynn, J. R. (2006). Black Americans reduce the racial IQ gap: Evidence from standardization samples. *Psychological Science, 17*, 913–920. doi:10.1111/j.1467-9280.2006.01802.x

DiClemente, C. C., Marinilli, A. S., Singh, M., & Bellino, L. E. (2001). The role of feedback in the process of health behavior change. *American Journal of Health Behavior, 25*, 217–227. Retrieved from http://www.ajhb.org/

Didden, R., Sigafoos, J., Korzilius, H., Baas, A., Lancioni, G. E., O'Reilly, M. F., & Curfs, L. M. G. (2009). Form and function of communicative behaviours in individuals with Angelman syndrome. *Journal of Applied Research in Intellectual Disabilities, 22*, 526–537. doi:10.1111/j.1468-3148.2009.00520.x

Dillon, K. M. (1993). Facilitated communication, autism, and Ouija. *Skeptical Inquirer, 17*, 281–287. Retrieved from http://www.csicop.org/si/

Dishion, T. J., & Andrews, D. W. (1995). Preventing escalation in problem behaviors with high-risk young adolescents: Immediate and 1-year outcomes. *Journal of Consulting and Clinical Psychology, 63*, 538–548. doi:10.1037/0022-006X.63.4.538

Dishion, T. J., Bullock, B. M., & Granic, I. (2002). Pragmatism in modeling peer influence: Dynamics, outcomes and change processes. *Development and Psychopathology, 14*, 969–981. doi:10.1017/S0954579402004169

Dishion, T. J., & Dodge, K. A. (2005). Peer contagion in interventions for children and adolescents: Moving toward an understanding of the ecology and dynamics of change. *Journal of Abnormal Child Psychology, 33*, 395–400. doi:10.1007/s10802-005-3579-z

Dishion, T. J., & Granic, I. (2004). Naturalistic observation of relationship processes. In S. N. Haynes & E. M. Heiby (Eds.), *Comprehensive handbook of psychological assessment: Vol. 3. Behavioral assessment* (pp. 143–161). New York: Wiley.

Dishion, T. J., & Kavanagh, K. (2003). *Intervening in adolescent problem behavior: A family-centered approach.* New York: Guilford Press.

Dishion, T. J., & Patterson, G. R. (1992). Age effects in parent training outcome. *Behavior Therapy, 23*, 719–729. doi:10.1016/S0005-7894(05)80231-X

Dishion, T. J., & Patterson, G. R. (2006). The development and ecology of antisocial behavior in children and adolescents. In D. Cicchetti & D. J. Cohen (Eds.), *Developmental psychopathology: Vol. 3. Risk, disorder, and adaptation* (2nd ed., pp. 503–541). New York: Wiley.

Dishion, T. J., & Stormshak, E. (2007b). Intervening in children's lives: An ecological, family-centered approach to mental health care. Washington, DC: APA Books.

Dishion, T. J., & Stormshak, E. A. (2007a). Ethical and professional standards in child and family interventions. In T. J. Dishion & E. A. Stormshak, *Intervening in children's lives: An ecological, family-centered approach to mental health care* (pp. 241–264). Washington, DC: APA Books.

Dissanayake, C., & Sigman, M. (2000). Attachment and emotional responsiveness in children with autism. *International Review of Research in Mental Retardation, 23*, 239–266. doi:10.1016/S0074-7750(00)80013-0

Dodge, K. A. (2009). Mechanisms of gene-environment interaction effects in the development of conduct disorder. *Perspectives on Psychological Science, 4*, 408–414. doi:10.1111/j.1745-6924.2009.01147.x

Dodge, K. A. (2011). Context matters in child and family policy. *Child Development, 82*, 433–442. doi:10.1111/j.1467-8624.2010.01565.x

Dodge, K. A., Coie, J. D., & Lynam, D. (2006). Aggression and antisocial behavior in youth. In N. Eisenberg, W. Damon, & R. M. Lerner (Eds.), *Handbook of child psychology: Vol. 3. Social emotional and personality development* (6th ed., pp. 719–788). Hoboken, NJ: Wiley.

Dodge, K. A., & McCourt, S. N. (2010). Translating models of antisocial behavioral development into efficacious intervention policy to prevent adolescent violence. *Developmental Psychobiology, 52*, 277–285. doi:10.1002/dev.20440

Dodge, K. A., & Pettit, G. S. (2003). A biopsychosocial model of the development of chronic conduct problems in adolescence. *Developmental Psychology, 39*, 349–371. doi:10.1037//0012-1649.39.2.349

Dodge, K. A., Pettit, G. S., & Bates, J. E. (1994a). Effects of physical maltreatment on the development of peer relations. *Development and Psychopathology, 6*, 43–55. doi:10.1017/S0954579400005873

Dodge, K. A., Pettit, G. S., & Bates, J. E. (1994b). Socialization mediators of the relation between socioeconomic status and child conduct problems. *Child Development, 65*, 649–665. doi:10.1111/j.1467-8624.1994.tb00774.x

Doerfler, L. A., Connor, D. F., Volungis, A. M., & Toscano, P. F. (2007). Panic disorder in clinically referred children and adolescents. *Child Psychiatry and Human Development, 38*, 57–71. doi:10.1007/s10578-006-0042-5

Dong, Q., Yang, B., & Ollendick, T. H. (1994). Fears in Chinese children and adolescents and their relations to anxiety and depression. *Journal of Child Psychology and Psychiatry, 35*, 351–363. doi:10.1111/j.1469-7610.1994.tb01167.x

Donnellan, A. M. (1988, February). Our old ways just aren't working. *Dialect* [Newsletter of the Saskatchewan Association for the Mentally Retarded]. Available from Saskatchewan Association for Community Living, 3031 Louise Street, Saskatoon, SK S7J 3L1.

Donohue, B., Hersen, M., & Ammerman, R. T. (2000). Historical overview. In M. Hersen & R. Ammerman (Eds.), *Abnormal child psychology* (2nd ed., pp. 3–14). Mahwah, NJ: Erlbaum.

Douglas, V. I. (1972). Stop, look, and listen: The problem of sustained attention and impulse control in hyperactive and normal children. *Canadian Journal of Behavioural Science, 4*, 259–282. doi:10.1037/h0082313

Douglas, V. I. (1999). Cognitive control processes in attention deficit/hyperactivity disorder. In H. C. Quay & A. E. Hogan (Eds.), *Handbook of disruptive behavior disorders* (pp. 105–138). New York: Kluwer/Plenum Press.

Dowell, K. A., & Ogles, B. M. (2010). The effects of parent participation on child psychotherapy outcome: A meta-analytic review. *Journal of Clinical Child and Adolescent Psychology, 39*, 151–162. doi:10.1080/15374410903532585

Dowling, C. (1992, January 20). *Rescuing your child from depression.* New York, 45–51.

Dowling, C. G., & Hollister, A. (1997, May). An epidemic of sneezing and wheezing. *Life Magazine,* 79.

Down, J. L. H. (1866). Observations on an ethnic classification of idiots. *Clinical Lectures and Reports (London Hospital), 3*, 259–262.

Dozois, D. J. A.(1997). *A developmental cognitive model of unipolar major depression.* Unpublished manuscript, Department of Psychology, University of Calgary, Calgary, Alberta T2N 1N4.

Drabick, D. A. G., & Kendall, P. C. (2010). Developmental psychopathology and the diagnosis of mental health problems among youth. *Clinical Psychology: Science and Practice, 17*, 272–280. doi:10.1111/j.1468-2850.2010.01219.x

Drabick, D. A. G., Ollendick, T. H., & Bubier, J. L. (2010). Co-occurrence of ODD and anxiety: Shared risk processes and evidence for a dual pathway model. *Clinical Psychology: Science and Practice, 17*, 307–318. 10.1111/j.1468-2850.2010.01222.x

Drotar, D. (1999). Child neglect in the family context: Challenges and opportunities for management in pediatric settings. *Children's Health Care, 28*, 109–121.

Drotar, D. (2006). *Psychological interventions in childhood chronic illness.* Washington, DC: American Psychological Association.

Drotar, D., & Bonner, M. S. (2009). Influences on adherence to pediatric asthma treatment: A review of correlates and predictors. *Journal of Developmental and Behavioral Pediatrics, 30*, 574. doi:10.1097/DBP.0b013e3181c3c3bb

Drummond, C. R., Ahmad, S. A., & Rourke, B. (2005). Rules for the classification of younger children with nonverbal learning disabilities and basic phonological processing disabilities. *Archives of Clinical Neuropsychology, 20*, 171–182. doi:10.1016/j.acn.2004.05.001

Drury, S. S., Theall, K. P., Smyke, A. T., Keats, B. J. B. Keats, Egger, H. L., . . . Zeanah, C. H. (2010). Modification of depression by COMT val158met polymorphism in children exposed to early severe psychosocial deprivation. *Child Abuse & Neglect, 34*, 387–395. doi:10.1016/j.chiabu.2009.09.021

Du Rocher Schudlich, T. D., Youngstrom, E. A., Calabrese, J. R., Findling, R. L. (2008). The role of family functioning in bipolar disorder in families. *Journal of Abnormal Child Psychology, 36*, 849–863. doi:10.1007/s10802-008-9217-9

Duax, J. M., Youngstrom, E. A., Calabrese, E. A., & Findling, R. L. (2007). Sex differences in pediatric bipolar disorder. *Journal of Clinical Psychiatry, 68*, 1565–1573. Retrieved from http://www.psychiatrist.com/

Dubowitz, H., & Bennett, S. (2007). Physical abuse and neglect of children. *Lancet, 369*(9576), 1891–1899.

Dubowitz, H., Feigelman, S., Lane, W., & Kim, J. (2009). Pediatric primary care to help prevent child maltreatment: The Safe Environment for Every Kid (SEEK) model. *Pediatrics, 123*, 858–86.

Duel, B. P., Steinberg-Epstein, R., Hill, M., & Lerner, M. (2003). A survey of voiding dysfunction in children with attention deficit-hyperactivity disorder. *Journal of Urology, 170*, 1521–1524. doi:10.1097/01.ju.0000091219.46560.7b

Duff, F. J., & Clarke, P. J. (2011). Practitioner review: Reading disorders: What are the effective interventions and how should they be implemented and evaluated? *Journal of Child Psychology and Psychiatry, 52*, 3–12. doi:10.1111/j.1469-7610.2010.02310.x

Dummit, E. S., Klein, R. G., Tancer, N. K., Asche, B., Martin, J., & Fairbanks, J. A. (1997). Systematic assessment of 50 children with selective mutism. *Journal of the American Academy of Child & Adolescent Psychiatry, 36*, 653–660. doi:10.1097/00004583-199705000-00016

Duncan, P. M., & Millard, W. (1866). *A manual for the classification, training, and education of the feeble-minded, imbecile, and idiot.* London: Longmans, Green.

Dunlap, K. (1932). *Habits: Their making and unmaking.* New York: Liveright.

DuPaul, G. J. (2007). School-based interventions for students with attention deficit hyperactivity disorder: Current status and future directions. *School Psychology Review, 36*, 183–194. Retrieved from http://www.nasponline.org/index.aspx

DuPaul, G. J., & Eckert, T. L. (1997). The effects of school-based interventions for attention deficit hyperactivity disorder: A meta-analysis. *School Psychology Digest, 26*, 5–27. Retrieved from http://www.researchgate.net/journal/0160-5569_The_School_psychology_digest

DuPaul, G. J., & Stoner, G. (2003). *ADHD in the schools* (2nd ed.). New York: Guilford Press.

Durbin, C. E., & Shafir, D. M. (2008). Emotion regulation and risk for depression. In J. R. Z. Abela & B. L. Hankin (Eds.), *Handbook of depression in children and adolescents* (pp. 149–176). New York: Guilford Press.

Durkin, K., & Conti-Ramsden, G. (2010). Young people with specific language impairment: A review of social and emotional functioning in adolescence. *Child Language Teaching and Therapy, 26*, 105–121. doi:10.1177/0265659010368750

Durlak, J. A., Weissberg, R. P., Dymnicki, A. B., Taylor, R. D., & Schellinger, K. B. (2011). The impact of enhancing students' social and emotional learning: A meta-analysis of school-based universal interventions. *Child Development, 82*, 405–432. doi:10.1111/j.1467-8624.2010.01564.x

Dworzynski, K., Remington, A., Rijsdijk, F., Howell, P., & Plomin, R. (2007). Genetic etiology in cases of recovered and persistent stuttering in an unselected longitudinal sample of young twins. *American Journal of Speech-Language Pathology, 16*, 169–178.

Dykens, E. M., Cassidy, S. B., & DeVries, M. L. (2011). *Prader-Willi syndrome.* New York: Guilford Press.

Dykens, E. M., Hodapp, R. M., & Evans, D. W. (2006). Profiles and development of adaptive behavior in children with Down syndrome. *Down Syndrome: Research & Practice, 9*, 45–50. doi:10.3104/reprints.293

Dykens, E. M., & Volkmar, F. (1997). Medical conditions associated with autism. In D. J. Cohen & F. R. Volkmar (Eds.), *Handbook of autism and pervasive developmental disorders* (pp. 388–410). New York: Wiley.

Earleywine, M. (2009). *Substance use problems.* Ashland, OH: Hogrefe & Huber Publishers.

Eaton, D. K., Kann, L., Kinchen, S., Shanklin, S., Ross, J., Hawkins, J., & Wechsler, H. (2010, June 4). Youth risk behavior surveillance – United States, 2009. *MMWR: Morbidity and Mortality Weekly Report, 59 (No. SS-5)*, 1–142. Department of Health and Humans Services, Centers for Disease Control and Prevention.

Eaves, L. C., & Ho, H. H. (2008). Young adult outcome of autism spectrum disorders. *Journal of Autism and Developmental Disorders, 38*, 739–747. doi:10.1007/s10803-007-0441-x

Eaves, L., Silberg, J., & Erkanli, A. (2003). Resolving multiple epigenetic pathways to adolescent depression. *Journal of Child Psychology and Psychiatry, 44*, 1006–1014. doi:10.1111/1469-7610.00185

Ebesutani, C., Bernstein, A., Chorpita, B. F., & Weisz, J. R. (2012). A transportable assessment protocol for prescribing youth psychosocial treatments in real-world settings: Reducing assessment burden via self-report scales. Reducing assessment burden via self-report scales. *Psychological Assessmen*t, 24, 141–155. Advance online publication. doi:10.1037/a0025176

Ebstein, R. P., Novick, O., Umansky, R., Priel, B., Osher, Y., Blaine, D., . . . Belmaker, R. H. (1996). Dopamine D4 receptor (D4DR) exon III polymorphism associated with the human personality trait of novelty seeking. *Nature Genetics, 12*, 78–80. doi:10.1038/ng0196-78

Eckenrode, J., Campa, M., Luckey, D., Henderson, C., Cole, R., Kitzman, H., . . . Olds, D. (2010). Long-term effects of prenatal and infancy nurse home visitation on the life course of youths: 19-year follow-up of a randomized trial. *Archives of Pediatrics & Adolescent Medicine, 164*(1), 9.

Eddy, K. T., Crosby, R. D., Keel, P. K., Wonderlich, S. A., le Grange, D., Hill, L., . . . Mitchell, J. E. (2009). Empirical identification and validation of eating disorder phenotypes in a multisite clinical sample. *Journal of Nervous and Mental Disease, 197*, 41–49. doi:10.1097/NMD.0b013e3181927389

Eddy, K. T., Dorer, D. J., Franko, D. L., Tahilani, K., Thompson-Brenner, H., & Herzog, D. B. (2008). Diagnostic crossover in anorexia nervosa and bulimia nervosa: Implications for DSM-V. *American Journal of Psychiatry, 165*, 245–250. doi:10.1176/appi.ajp.2007.07060951

Eddy, K. T., Doyle, A. C., Hoste, R. R., Herzog, D. B., & le Grange, D. (2008). Eating disorder not otherwise specified in adolescents. *Journal of the American Academy of Child & Adolescent Psychiatry, 47*, 156–164. doi:10.1097/chi.0b013e31815cd9cf

Edelbrock, C., Crnic, K., & Bohnert, A. (1999). Interviewing as communication: An alternative way of administering the Diagnostic Interview Schedule for Children. *Journal of Abnormal Child Psychology, 27*, 447–453. doi:10.1023/A:1021979925865

Eden, G. F., & Moats, L. (2002). The role of neuroscience in the remediation of students with dyslexia. *Nature Neuroscience [Special issue: Beyond the bench: The practical promise of neuroscience], 5*, 1080–1084. doi:10.1038/nn946

Eden, G. F., VanMeter, J. W., Rumsey, J. M., Maisog, J. M., Woods, R. P., & Zeffiro, T. A. (1996). Abnormal processing of visual motion in dyslexia revealed by functional brain imaging. *Nature, 382*, 66–69. doi:10.1038/382066a0

Edleson, J. L. (1999). The overlap between child maltreatment and woman battering. *Violence Against Women, 5*, 134–154.

Education for All Handicapped Children Act. (1975). *Public law 94–142.* Washington, DC: U.S. Government Printing Office.

Edwards, A. C., Dodge, K. A., Latendresse, S. J., Lansford, J. E., Bates, J. E., Pettit, G. S., Dick, D. M. (2010). MAOA-uVNTR and early physical discipline interact to influence delinquent behavior. *Journal of Child Psychology and Psychiatry, 51*, 679–687. doi:10.1111/j.1469-7610.2009.02196.x

Edwards, S. L., Rapee, R. M., & Kennedy, S. (2010). Prediction of anxiety symptoms in preschool-aged children: Examination of maternal and paternal perspectives. *Journal of Child Psychology and Psychiatry, 51*, 313–321. doi:10.1111/j.1469-7610.2009.02160.x

Egeland, B., Yates, T., Appleyard, K., & van Dulmen, M. (2002). The long-term consequences of maltreatment in the early years: A developmental pathway model to antisocial behavior. *Children's Services:*

Social Policy, Research, & Practice, 5, 249–260.

Egger, H. L., & Angold A. (2006). Common emotional and behavioral disorders in preschool children: Presentation, nosology, and epidemiology. *Journal of Child Psychology and Psychiatry, 47,* 313–337. doi:10.1111/j.1469-7610.2006.01618.x

Egger, H. L., Costello, E. J., Erkanli, A., & Angold, A. (1999). Somatic complaints and psychopathology in children and adolescents: Stomach aches, musculoskeletal pains, and headaches. *Journal of the American Academy of Child & Adolescent Psychiatry, 38,* 852–860. doi:10.1097/00004583-199907000-00015

Egger, H. L., & Emde, R. D. (2011). Developmentally sensitive diagnostic criteria for mental health disorders in early childhood: The Diagnostic and Statistical Manual of Mental Disorders-IV, the Research Diagnostic Criteria-Preschool Age, and the Diagnostic Classification of Mental Health and Developmental Disorders of Infancy and Early Childhood-Revised. *American Psychologist, 66,* 95–106. doi:10.1037/a0021026

Egley, Jr., A., & O'Donnell, C. E. (2009). Highlights of the 2007 National Youth Gang Survey. *OJJDP Fact Sheet* (April). Washington, DC: U.S. Department of Justice, Office of Juvenile Justice and Delinquency Prevention. Retrieved from http://www.ncjrs.gov/pdffiles1/ojjdp/225185.pdf

Ehntholt, K. A., & Yule, W. (2006). Practitioner review: Assessment and treatment of refugee children and adolescents who have experienced war-related trauma. *Journal of Child Psychology and Psychiatry, 47,* 1197–1210. doi:10.1111/j.1469-7610.2006.01638.x

Ehringer, M. A., Rhee, S. H., Young, S., Corley, R., & Hewitt, J. K. (2006). Genetic and environmental contributions to common psychopathologies of childhood and adolescence: A study of twins and their siblings. *Journal of Abnormal Child Psychology, 34,* 1–17. doi:10.1007/s10802-005-9000-0

Ehrmantrout, N., Allen, N. B., Leve, C., Davis, B., & Sheeber, L. (2011). Adolescent recognition of parental affect: Influence of depressive symptoms. *Journal of Abnormal Psychology, 120,* 628–634. doi:10.1037/a0022500

Eikeseth, S., Smith, T., Jahr, E., & Eldevik, S. (2007). Outcome for children with autism who began behavioral treatment between ages 4 and 7: A comparison controlled study. *Behavior Modification, 31,* 264–278. doi:10.1177/0145445506291396

Einfeld, S. L. (2005). Behaviour problems in children with genetic disorders causing intellectual disability. *Educational Psychology, 25,* 341–346. doi:10.1080/0144341042000301256

Einfeld, S. L., Gray, K. M., Ellis, L. A., Taffe, J., Emerson, E., Tonge, B. J., & Horstead, S. K. (2010). Intellectual disability modifies gender effects on disruptive behaviors. *Journal of Mental Health Research in Intellectual Disabilities, 3,* 177–189. doi:10.1080/19315864.2010.519098

Einfeld, S. L., Piccinin, A. M., Mackinnon, A., Hofer, S. M., Taffe, J., Gray, K. M. . . . Tonge, B. J. (2006). Psychopathology in young people with intellectual disability. *JAMA: Journal of the American Medical Association, 296,* 1981–1989. doi:10.1001/jama.296.16.1981

Eisen, A. R., & Engler, L. B. (1995). Chronic anxiety. In A. R. Eisen, C. A. Kearney, & C. A. Schaefer (Eds.), *Clinical handbook of anxiety disorders in children and adolescents* (pp. 223–250). Northvale, NJ: Aronson.

Eisenberg, L. (2007). Commentary with a historical perspective by a child psychiatrist: When "ADHD" was the "brain-damaged child." *Journal of Child and Adolescent Psychopharmacology, 17,* 279–283. doi:10.1089/cap.2006.0139

Eisenberg, M., Neumark-Sztainer, D., & Story, M. (2003). Associations of weight-based teasing and emotional well-being among adolescents. *Archives of Pediatric and Adolescent Medicine, 157,* 733–738. Retrieved from http://archpedi.ama-assn.org/

Eisenberg, N., Smith, C. L., & Spinrad, T. L. (2011). *Effortful control: Relations with emotion regulation, adjustment, and socialization in childhood.* New York: Guilford Press.

Eiser, C. (2007). Beyond survival: Quality of life and follow-up after childhood cancer. *Journal of Pediatric Psychology [Special issue: A tribute to the life of Raymond K. Mulhern], 32,* 1140–1150. doi:10.1093/jpepsy/jsm052

Eisler, I., Dare, C., Hodes, M., Russell, G., Dodge, E., & Le Grange, D. (2000). Family therapy for adolescent anorexia nervosa: The results of a controlled comparison of two family interventions. *Journal of Child Psychology and Psychiatry and Allied Disciplines, 41,* 727–736. doi:10.1111/1469-7610.00660

El-Fishawy, P., & State, M. W. (2010). The genetics of autism: Key issues, recent findings, and clinical implications. *Psychiatric Clinics of North America, 33,* 83–105. doi:10.1016/j.psc.2009.12.002

El-Sheikh, M., & Erath, S. A. (2011). Family conflict, autonomic nervous system functioning, and child adaptation: State of the science and future directions. *Development and Psychopathology, 23,* 703–721. doi:10.1017/S0954579411000034

Eley, T. C. (1999). Behavioral genetics as a tool for developmental psychology: Anxiety and depression in children and adolescents. *Clinical Child and Family Psychology Review, 2,* 21–36. doi:10.1023/A:1021863324202

Eley, T. C., & Lau, J. Y. F. (2005). Genetics and the family environment. In J. L. Hudson & R. M. Rapee (Eds.), *Psychopathology and the family* (pp. 3–19). New York: Elsevier.

Eley, T. C., Lichenstein, P., & Moffitt, T. E. (2003). A longitudinal behavioral genetic analysis of the etiology of aggressive and nonaggressive antisocial behavior. *Development and Psychopathology, 15,* 383–402. doi:10.1017/S095457940300021X

Eley, T. C., Napolitano, M., Lau, J. Y. F., & Gregory, A. M. (2010). Does childhood anxiety evoke maternal control? A genetically informed study. *Journal of Child Psychology and Psychiatry, 51,* 772–779. doi:10.1111/j.1469-7610.2010.02227.x

Eley, T. C., & Stevenson, J. (2000). Specific life events and chronic experiences differentially associated with depression and anxiety in young twins. *Journal of Abnormal Child Psychology, 28,* 383–394. doi:10.1023/A:1005173127117

Elkin, T. D., & Stoppelbein, L. (2008). Evidence-based treatments for children with chronic illnesses. In R. G. Steele, T. D. Elkin, & M. C. Roberts (Eds.), *Handbook of evidence-based therapies for children and adolescents: Bridging science and practice. Issues in clinical child psychology* (pp. 297–309). New York: Springer.

Elliott, D. S., Huizinga, D., & Ageton, S. S. (1985). *Explaining delinquency and drug use.* Beverly Hills, CA: Sage.

Elliott, D. S., Huizinga, D., & Menard, S. (1989). *Multiple problem youth: Delinquency, substance use, and mental health problems.* New York: Springer.

Elliott, M., Browne, K., & Kilcoyne, J. (1995). Child sexual abuse prevention: What offenders tell us. *Child Abuse and Neglect, 19,* 579–594.

Ellis, B. J., & Boyce, W. T. (2011). Special section editorial: Differential susceptibility to the environment: Toward an understanding of sensitivity to developmental experiences and context. *Development and Psychopathology, 23,* 1–5. doi:10.1017/S095457941000060X

Ellis, B. J., Boyce, W. T., Belsky, J., Bakermans-Kranenburg, M. J., & Van Ijzendoorn, M. H. (2011). Differential susceptibility to the environment: An evolutionary–neurodevelopmental theory. *Development and Psychopathology, 23,* 7–28. doi:10.1017/S0954579410000611

Ellis, D. A., Templin, T., Naar-King, S., Frey, M. A., Cunningham, P. B., Podolski, C., & Cakan, N. (2007). Multisystemic therapy for adolescents with poorly controlled type I diabetes: Stability of treatment effects in a randomized controlled trial. *Journal of Consulting and Clinical Psychology, 75,* 168–174. doi:10.1037/0022-006X.75.1.168

Ember, C. R., & Ember, M. (1994). War, socialization, and interpersonal violence: A cross-cultural study. *Journal of Conflict Resolution, 38,* 620–646. doi:10.1177/0022002794038004002

Eme, R. F. (2007). Sex differences in child-onset, life-course persistent conduct disorder: A review of biological influences. *Clinical Psychology Review, 27,* 607–627. doi:10.1016/j.cpr.2007.02.001

Emerson, E. (2003). Prevalence of psychiatric disorders in children and adolescents with and without intellectual disability. *Journal of Intellectual Disability Research, 47,* 51–58. doi:10.1046/j.1365-2788.2003.00464.x

Emerson, E., Einfeld, S., & Stancliffe, R. J. (2010). The mental health of young children with intellectual disabilities or borderline intellectual functioning. *Social Psychiatry and Psychiatric Epidemiology, 45,* 579–587. doi:10.1007/s00127-009-0100-y

Emery, R. E. (1999). Postdivorce family life for children: An overview of research and some implications for policy. In R. A. Thompson

& P. R. Amato (Eds.), *The postdivorce family: Children, parenting, and society* (pp. 3–27). Thousand Oaks, CA: Sage.

Eminson, D. M. (2007). Medically unexplained symptoms in children and adolescents. *Clinical Psychology Review, 27*, 855–871. doi:10.1016/j.cpr.2007.07.007

Ensor, R., Marks, A., Jacobs, L., & Hughes, C. (2010). Trajectories of antisocial behavior towards siblings predict antisocial behavior towards peers. *Journal of Child Psychology and Psychiatry, 51*, 1208–1216. doi:10.1111/j.1469-7610.2010.02276.x

Erhardt, D., & Hinshaw, S. P. (1994). Initial sociometric impressions of attention-deficit hyperactivity disorder and comparison boys: Predictions from social behaviors and from nonbehavioral variables. *Journal of Consulting and Clinical Psychology, 62*, 833–842. doi:10.1037/0022-006X.62.4.833

Erickson, M. R., & Egeland, B. (2002). Child neglect. In John E.B. Myers, L. Berliner, J. Briere, C. T. Hendrix, C. Jenny, & T.A. Reid (Eds.), *The APSAC handbook on child maltreatment* (pp. 3–20). Thousand Oaks, CA: Sage.

Essau, C. A. (2007). Course and outcome of somatoform disorders in non-referred adolescents. *Psychosomatics, 48*, 502–509. doi:10.1176/appi.psy.48.6.502

Essau, C. A., Conradt, J., & Petermann, F. (1999). Frequency and comorbidity of social phobia and social fears in adolescents. *Behaviour Research and Therapy, 37*, 831–843. doi:10.1016/S0005-7967(98)00179-X

Essex, M. J., Klein, M.H., Slattery, M. J., Goldsmith, H. H., & Kalin, N. H. (2010). Early risk factors and developmental pathways to chronic high inhibition and social anxiety disorder in adolescence. *American Journal of Psychiatry, 167*, 40–46. doi:10.1176/appi.ajp.2009.07010051

Essex, M. J., Kraemer, H. C., Slattery, M. J., Burk, L. R., Boyce, W. T., Woodward, H. R., & Kupfer, D. J. (2009). Screening for childhood mental health problems: Outcomes and early identification. *Journal of Child Psychology and Psychiatry, 50*, 562–570. doi:10.1111/j.1469-7610.2008.02015.x

Evans, D. W., Gray, F. L., & Leckman, J. F. (1999). The rituals, fears and phobias of young children: Insights from development, psychopathology and neurobiology. *Child Psychiatry and Human Development, 29*, 261–276. doi:10.1023/A:1021392931450

Evans, D. W., & Leckman, J. F. (2006). Origins of obsessive-compulsive disorder: Developmental and evolutionary perspectives. In D. Cicchetti & D. J. Cohen (Eds.), *Developmental psychopathology: Vol. 3. Risk, disorder, and adaptation* (2nd ed., pp. 404–435). New York: Wiley.

Evans, D. W., Leckman, J. F., Carter, A., Reznick, J. S., Henshaw, D., King, R. A., & Pauls, D. (1997). Ritual, habit, and perfectionism: The prevalence and development of compulsive-like behavior in normal young children. *Child Development, 68*, 58–68. doi:10.1111/j.1467-8624.1997.tb01925.x

Eyberg, S. M., Nelson, M. M., & Boggs, S. R. (2008). Evidence-based psychosocial treatments for children and adolescents with disruptive behavior. *Journal of Clinical Child and Adolescent Psychology, 37*, 215–237. doi:10.1080/15374410701820117

Fabiano, G. A., Pelham, W. E., Coles, E. K., Gnagy, E. M., Chronis-Tuscano, A., & O'Connor, B. B. (2009). A meta-analysis of behavioral treatments for attention deficit/ hyperactivity disorder. *Clinical Psychology Review, 29*, 129–140. doi:10.1016/j.cpr.2008.11.001

Fabricius, W. V., & Luecken, L. J. (2007). Postdivorce living arrangements, parent conflict, and long-term physical health correlates for children of divorce. *Journal of Family Psychology, 21*, 195–205. doi:10.1037/0893-3200.21.2.195

Fagan, P. J., Wise, T. N., Schmidt, C. W., Jr., & Berlin, F. S. (2002). Pedophilia. *JAMA: Journal of the American Medical Association, 288*, 2458–2465.

Fair, D. A., Posner, J., Nagel, B. J., Bathula, D., Costa Dias, T. G., Mills, K. L., . . . Nigg, J. T. (2010). Atypical default network connectivity in youth with attention-deficit/hyperactivity disorders. *Biological Psychiatry, 68*, 1084–1091. doi:10.1016/j.biopsych.2010.07.003

Fairburn, C. G., Cooper, Z., Doll, H., Norman, P., & O'Connor, M. (2000). The natural course of bulimia nervosa and binge eating disorder in young women. *Archives of General Psychiatry, 57*, 659–665. Retrieved from http://archpsyc.ama-assn.org/

Fairburn, C. G., & Harrison, P. J. (2003). Eating disorders. *Lancet, 361*, 407–416. doi:10.1016/S0140-6736(03)12378-1

Fairchild, G., Passamonti, L., Hurford, G., Hagan, C. C., von dem Hagen, E. A. H., van Goozen, S. H. M., . . . Calder, A. J. (2011). Brain structural abnormalities in early-onset and adolescent-onset conduct disorder. *American Journal of Psychiatry, 168*, 624–633. doi:10.1176/appi.ajp.2010.10081184

Fairchild, G., Van Goozen, S. H. M., Calder, A. J., Stollery, S. K., & Goodyer, I. M. (2009). Deficits in facial expression recognition in male adolescents with early-onset or adolescence-onset conduct disorder. *Journal of Child Psychology and Psychiatry, 50*, 627–636. doi:10.1111/j.1469-7610.2008.02020.x

Fairchild, S. R. (2002). Women with disabilities: The long road to equality. *Journal of Human Behavior in the Social Environment, 6*, 13–28. doi:10.1300/J137v06n02_02

Falicov, C. J. (2003). Culture, society and gender in depression. *Journal of Family Therapy, 25*, 371–387. doi:10.1111/1467-6427.00256

Fallucca, E., MacMaster, F. P., Haddad, J., Easter, P., Dick, R., May, G., . . . Rosenberg, D. R. (2011). Distinguishing between major depressive disorder and obsessive-compulsive disorder in children by measuring regional cortical thickness. *Archives of General Psychiatry, 68*, 527–533. doi:10.1001/archgenpsychiatry.2011.36

Famularo, R., Fenton, T., Kinscherff, R., & Augustyn, M. (1996). Psychiatric comorbidity in childhood posttraumatic stress disorder. *Child Abuse and Neglect, 20*, 953–961. doi:10.1016/0145-2134(96)00084-1

Fang, X., Brown, D. S., Florence, C., & Mercy, J. (2012). The economic burden of child maltreatment in the United States and implications for prevention. *Child Abuse & Neglect*, 36, 156–165. doi:10.1016/j.chiabu.2011.10.006

Fantuzzo, J., Manz, P., Atkins, M., & Meyers, R. (2005). Peer-mediated treatment of socially withdrawn maltreated preschool children: Cultivating natural community resources. *Journal of Clinical Child and Adolescent Psychology, 34*, 320–325.

Farah, M. J., Shera, D. M., Savage, J. H., Betancourt, L., Giannetta, J. M., Brodsky, N. L., . . . Hurt, H. (2006). Childhood poverty: Specific associations with neurocognitive development. *Brain Research, 1110*, 166–174. doi:10.1016/j.brainres.2006.06.072

Faraone, S. V., Biederman, J., & Mick, E. (2006). The age-dependent decline of attention deficit hyperactivity disorder: A meta-analysis of follow-up studies. *Psychological Medicine, 36*, 159–165. doi:10.1017/S003329170500471X

Faraone, S. V., & Buitelaar, J. (2010). Comparing the efficacy of stimulants for ADHD in children and adolescents using meta-analysis. *European Child & Adolescent Psychiatry, 19*, 353–364. doi:10.1007/s00787-009-0054-3

Faraone, S. V., & Mick, E. (2010). Molecular genetics of attention deficit hyperactivity disorder. *Psychiatric Clinics of North America, 33*, 159–180. doi:10.1016/j.psc.2009.12.004

Faraone, S. V., Sergeant, J., Gillberg, C., & Biederman, J. (2003). The worldwide prevalence of ADHD: Is it an American condition? *World Psychiatry, 2*, 104–112. Retrieved from http://www.wpanet.org/v1/publications/journal.shtml

Farmer, J. E., & Muhlenbruck, L. (2000). Pediatric neuropsychology. In R. G. Frank & T. R. Elliott (Eds.), *Handbook of rehabilitation psychology* (pp. 377–397). Washington, DC: American Psychological Association.

Farrell, L. J., & Barrett, P. M., (2007). Prevention of childhood emotional disorders: Reducing the burden of suffering associated with anxiety and depression. *Child and Adolescent Mental Health, 12*, 58–65. doi:10.1111/j.1475-3588.2006.00430.x

Farrington, D. P. (1986). Age and crime. In M. Tonry & N. Morris (Eds.), *Crime and justice: An annual review of research* (Vol. 7, pp. 189–250). Chicago: University of Chicago Press.

Farrington, D. P. (1991). Childhood aggression and adult violence: Early precursors and later life outcomes. In D. J. Pepler & K. H. Rubin (Eds.), *The development and treatment of childhood aggression* (pp. 5–29). Hillsdale, NJ: Erlbaum.

Fasmer, O. B., Riise, T., Eagan, T. M., Lund, A., Dilsaver, S. C. Hundal, Ø., & Oedegaard, K. J. (2011). Comorbidity of asthma with ADHD. *Journal of Attention Disorders, 15*, 564–571. doi:10.1177/1087054710372493

Fatemi, S. H., & Folsom, T. D. (2011). The role of fragile X mental retardation protein in major mental disorders. *Neuropharmacology, 60*, 1221–1226. doi:10.1016/j.neuropharm.2010.11.011

Feinberg, M. E., Button, T. M. M., Neiderhiser, J. M., Reiss, D., & Hetherington, E. M. (2007). Parenting and adolescent antisocial behavior and depression. *Archives of General Psychiatry, 64*, 457–465. doi:10.1001/archpsyc.64.4.457

Feldman, L., Harvey, B., Holowaty, P., & Shortt, L. (1999). Alcohol use beliefs and behaviors among high school students. *Journal of Adolescent Health, 24*, 48–58. doi:10.1016/S1054-139X(98)00026-3

Feldman, M. B., & Meyer, I. H. (2007). Childhood abuse and eating disorders in gay and bisexual men. *International Journal of Eating Disorders, 40*, 418–423. doi:10.1002/eat

Felton, R. H. (1993). Effects of instruction on the decoding skills of children with phonological-processing problems. *Journal of Learning Disabilities, 26*, 583–589. doi:10.1177/002221949302600904

Fergusson, D. M., Boden, J. M., & Horwood, J. (2007). Recurrence of major depression in adolescence and early adulthood, and later mental health, educational, and economic outcomes. *British Journal of Psychiatry, 191*, 335–342. doi:10.1192/bjp.bp.107.036079

Fergusson, D. M., Boden, J. M., & Horwood, L. J. (2010). Classification of behavior disorders in adolescence: Scaling methods, predictive validity, and gender differences. *Journal of Abnormal Psychology, 119*, 699–712. doi:10.1037/a0018610

Fergusson, D. M., & Horwood, L. J. (2002). Male and female offending trajectories. *Development and Psychopathology, 14*, 159–177. doi:10.1017/S0954579402001098

Fergusson, D. M., Horwood, L. J., & Lynskey, M. T. (1993). Early dentine lead levels and subsequent cognitive and behavioural development. *Journal of Child Psychology and Psychiatry, 34*, 215–227. doi:10.1111/j.1469-7610.1993.tb00980.x

Fergusson, D. M., Horwood, L. J., Miller, A. L., & Kennedy, M. A. (2011). Life stress, 5-HTTLPR and mental disorder: Findings from a 30-year longitudinal study. *The British Journal of Psychiatry, 198*, 129–135. doi:10.1192/bjp.bp.110.085993

Fergusson, D. M., Horwood, L. J., & Ridder, E. M. (2005). Show me the child at seven: The consequences of conduct problems in childhood for psychosocial functioning in adulthood. *Journal of Child Psychology and Psychiatry, 46*, 837–849. doi:10.1111/j.1469-7610.2004.00387.x

Fergusson, D. M., Horwood, L. J., & Ridder, E. M. (2007). Conduct and attentional problems in childhood and adolescence and later substance use, abuse, and dependence: Results of a 25-year longitudinal study. *Drug and Alcohol Dependence, 88*, S14–S26. doi:10.1016/j.drugalcdep.2006.12.011

Fernandez-Ballesteros, R. (2004). Self-report questionnaires. In S. N. Haynes & E. M. Heiby (Eds.), *Comprehensive handbook of psychologica3l assessment: Vol. 3. Behavioral assessment* (pp. 194–221). New York: Wiley.

Ferrer, E., Shaywitz, B. A., Holahan, J. M., Marchione, K., & Shaywitz, S. E. (2010). Uncoupling of reading and IQ over time: Empirical evidence for a definition of dyslexia. *Psychological Science, 21*, 93–101. doi:10.1177/0956797609354084

Ferris, T. (1998, July 20). Not rocket science. *The New Yorker*, 74(20), 4–5.

Fichman, L., Koestner, R., & Zuroff, D. C. (1996). Dependency, self-criticism, and perceptions of inferiority at summer camp: I'm even worse than you think. *Journal of Youth and Adolescence, 25*, 113–126. doi:10.1007/BF01537383

Fichter, M. M., Quadflieg, N., & Hedlund, S. (2006). Twelve year course and outcome predictors of anorexia nervosa. *International Journal of Eating Disorders, 39*, 87–100. doi:10.1002/eat.20215

Fidalgo, T. M., da Silveira, E. D., & da Silveira, D. X. (2008). Psychiatric comorbidity related to alcohol use among adolescents. *American Journal of Drug and Alcohol Abuse, 34*, 83–89. doi:10.1080/00952990701764664

Field, A. P. (2006). The behavioral inhibition system and the verbal information pathway to children's fears. *Journal of Abnormal Psychology, 115*, 742–752. doi:10.1037/0021-843X.115.4.742

Fielding, D. M., & Doleys, D. M. (1988). Elimination problems: Enuresis and encopresis. In E. J. Mash & L. G. Terdal (Eds.), *Behavioral assessment of childhood disorders* (2nd ed., pp. 586–623). New York: Guilford Press.

Fiese, B. H., & Bickham, N. L. (1998). Qualitative inquiry: An overview for pediatric psychology. *Journal of Pediatric Psychology, 23*, 79–86. doi:10.1093/jpepsy/23.2.79

Filipek, P. A., Semrud-Clikeman, M., Steingard, R. J., Renshaw, P. F., Kennedy, D. N., & Beiderman, J. (1997). Volumetric MRI analysis comparing subjects having attention-deficit hyperactivity disorder with controls. *Neurology, 48*, 589–601. Retrieved from http://www.neurology.org/

Findling, R. L., Connor, D. F., Wigal, T., Eagan, C., & Onofrey, M. N. (2009). A linguistic analysis of in-office dialogue among psychiatrists, parents, and child and adolescent patients with ADHD. *Journal of Attention Disorders, 13*, 78–86. doi:10.1177/1087054708323002

Finger, E. C., Marsh, A. A., Blair, K. S., Reid, M. E., Sims, C., Ng, P., . . . Blair, R. J. R. (2011). Disrupted reinforcement signaling in the orbitofrontal cortex and caudate in youths with conduct disorder or oppositional defiant disorder and a high level of psychopathic traits. *American Journal of Psychiatry, 168*, 152–162. doi:10.1176/appi.ajp.2010.10010129

Finkelhor, D. (2008). *Child victimization: Violence, crime, and abuse in the lives of young people.* New York: Oxford University Press.

Finkelhor, D. (2009). The prevention of childhood sexual abuse. *The Future of Children, 19*, 169–194. doi:10.1353/foc.0.0035

Finkelhor, D. (2011). Prevalence of child victimization, abuse, crime, and violence exposure. In J. W. White, M. P. Koss, & A. E. Kazdin (Eds.), *Violence against women and children, Vol. 1: Mapping the terrain.* (pp. 9–29). Washington, DC, US: American Psychological Association. doi:10.1037/12307-001

Finkelhor, D., & Jones, L. (2006). Why have child maltreatment and child victimization declined? *Journal of Social Issues, 62*, 685–716. doi:10.1111/j.1540-4560.2006.00483.x

Finkelhor, D., Turner, H., Ormrod, R., & Hamby, S. L. (2009). Violence, abuse, and crime exposure in a national sample of children and youth. *Pediatrics, 124*, 1411–1423. doi:10.1542/peds.2009-0467

Finn, P., Bothe, A. K., & Bramlett, R. E. (2005). Science and pseudoscience in communication disorders: Criteria and applications. *American Journal of Speech-Language Pathology, 14*, 172–186. doi:10.1044/1058-0360(2005/018)

Fischer, M. H. (1879–1962). *Fischerisms, being a sheaf of sundry and diverse utterances from the lectures of Martin H. Fisher (3rd ed.*, edited by H. Fabing & R. Marr, 1944). Springfield, IL: Charles C. Thomas.

Fischer, M., Barkley, R. A., Smallish, L., & Fletcher, K. (2002). Young adult follow-up of hyperactive children: Self-reported psychiatric disorders, comorbidity, and the role of childhood conduct problems and teen CD. *Journal of Abnormal Child Psychology, 30*, 463–476. doi:10.1023/A:1019864813776

Fitzgerald, D. A., Angstadt, M., Jelsone, L. M., Nathan, P. J., & Phan, K. L. (2006). Beyond threat. *Neuroimage, 30*, 1441–1448. doi:10.1016/j.neuroimage.2005.11.003

Fitzgerald, M. M., Schneider, R. A., Salstrom, S., Zinzow, H. M., Jackson, J., & Fossel, R. V. (2008). Child sexual abuse, early family risk, and childhood parentification: Pathways to current psychosocial adjustment. *Journal of Family Psychology, 22*, 320–324.

Flax, J. F., Realpe-Bonilla, T., Hirsch, L. S., Brzustowicz, L. M., Bartlett, C. W., & Tallal, P. (2003). Specific language impairment in families: Evidence for co-occurrence with reading impairments. *Journal of Speech, Language, & Hearing Research, 46*, 530–543. doi:10.1044/1092-4388(2003/043)

Fletcher, J. M., Shaywitz, S. E., & Shaywitz, B. A. (1999). Comorbidity of learning and attention disorders: Separate but equal. *Pediatric Clinics of North America, 46*, 885–897. doi:10.1016/S0031-3955(05)70161-9

Fletcher, K. E. (2003). Childhood posttraumatic stress disorder. In E. J. Mash & R. A. Barkley (Eds.), *Child psychopathology* (2nd ed., pp. 330–371). New York: Guilford Press.

Fletcher, K. E. (2007). Posttraumatic stress disorder. In E. J. Mash & R. A. Barkley (Eds.), *Assessment of childhood disorders* (4th ed., pp. 398–483). New York: Guilford Press.

Fliers, E. A., Franke, B., Lambregts-Rommelse, N. N. J., Altink, M. E., Buschgens, C. J. M., Nijhuis-van der Sanden, M W. G., . . . Buitelaar, J. K. (2010). *Child and*

Adolescent Mental Health, 15, 85–90. doi:10.1111/j.1475-3588.2009.00538.x
Flynn, J. R. (2007). *What is intelligence? Beyond the Flynn effect.* Cambridge, England: Cambridge University Press.
Fombonne, E. (2003). Epidemiological surveys of autism and other pervasive developmental disorders: An update. *Journal of Autism and Developmental Disorders, 33*, 365–382. doi:10.1023/A:1025054610557
Fombonne, E. (2008). Thimerosal disappears but autism remains. *Archives of General Psychiatry, 65*, 15–16. doi:10.1001/archgenpsychiatry.2007.2
Fombonne, E., Simmons, H., Ford, T., Meltzer, H., & Goodman, R. (2003). Prevalence of pervasive developmental disorders in the British nationwide survey of child mental health. *International Review of Psychiatry, 15*, 158–165. doi:10.1097/00004583-200107000-00017
Fombonne, E., Wostear, G., Cooper, V., Harrington, R., & Rutter, M. (2001a). The Maudsley long-term follow-up of child and adolescent depression: 1. Psychiatric outcomes in adulthood. *British Journal of Psychiatry, 179*, 210–217. doi:10.1192/bjp.179.3.210
Fombonne, E., Wostear, G., Cooper, V., Harrington, R., & Rutter, M. (2001b). The Maudsley long-term follow-up of child and adolescent depression: 2. Suicidality, criminality and social dysfunction in adulthood. *British Journal of Psychiatry, 179*, 218–223. doi:10.1192/bjp.179.3.218
Fombonne, E., Zakarian, R., Bennett, A., Meng, L., & McLean-Heywood, D. (2006). Pervasive developmental disorder in Montreal, Quebec, Canada: Prevalence and links with immunizations. *Pediatrics, 118*, e139–e150. doi:10.1542/peds.2005-2993
Fombonne, E., & Zinck, S. (2008). Psychopharmacological treatment of depression in children and adolescents. In J. R. Z. Abela & B. L. Hankin (Eds.), *Handbook of depression in children and adolescents* (pp. 207–223). New York: Guilford Press.
Fonagy, P., Target, M., & Gergely, G. (2006). Psychoanalytic perspectives on developmental psychopathology. In D. Cicchetti & D. J. Cohen (Eds.), *Developmental psychopathology: Vol. 1. Theory and method* (2nd ed., pp. 701–749). Hoboken, NJ: Wiley.
Fontaine, N. M. G., McCrory, E. J. P., Boivin, M., Moffitt, T. E., & Viding, E. (2011, February 21). Predictors and outcomes of joint trajectories of callous-unemotional traits and conduct problems in childhood. *Journal of Abnormal Psychology, 120*, 730–742. doi:10.1037/a0022620
Fontaine, R. G., Tanha, M., Yang, C., Dodge, K. A., Bates, J. E., & Pettit, G. S. (2010). Does response evaluation and decision (RED) mediate the relation between hostile attributional style and antisocial behavior in adolescence. *Journal of Abnormal Child Psychology, 38*, 615–626. doi:10.1007/s10802-010-9397-y
Forbes, E. E., Bertocci, M. A., Gregory, A. M., Ryan, N. D., Axelson, D. A., Birmaher, B., & Dahl, R. E. (2008). Objective sleep in pediatric anxiety disorders and major depressive disorder. *Journal of the American Academy of Child & Adolescent Psychiatry, 47*, 148–155. doi:10.1097/chi.0b013e31815cd9bc
Forbes, E. E., May, C., Siegle, G. J., Ladouceur, C. D., Ryan, N. D., Carter, C. S., . . . Dahl, R. E. (2006). Reward-related decision-making in pediatric major depressive disorder: An fMRI study. *Journal of Child Psychology and Psychiatry, 47*, 1031–1040. doi:10.1111/j.1469-7610.2006.01673.x
Forbes, E. E., Shaw, D. S., Silk, J. S., Feng, X., Cohn, J., Fox, N. A., & Kovacs, M. (2008). Children's affect expression and frontal EEG asymmetry: Transactional associations with mothers' depressive symptoms. *Journal of Abnormal Child Psychology, 36*, 207–221. doi:10.1007/s10802-007-9171-y
Forbush, K. T., South, S. C., Krueger, R. F., Iacono, W. G., Clark, L. A., Keel, P. K., . . . Watson, D. (2010). Locating eating pathology within an empirical diagnostic taxonomy: Evidence from a community-based sample. *Journal of Abnormal Psychology, 119*, 282–292. doi:10.1037/a0019189
Forehand, R. L., & Kotchik, B. A. (1996). Cultural diversity: A wake-up call for parent training. *Behavior Therapy, 27*, 187–206. doi:10.1016/S0005-7894(96)80014-1
Foreyt, J. P., & Cousins, J. H. (1987). Obesity. In M. Hersen & V. B. Van Hasselt (Eds.), *Behavior therapy with children and adolescents: A clinical approach* (pp. 485–511). New York: Wiley.
Foster, E. M., Jones, D. E., and The Conduct Problems Prevention Research Group. (2005). The high costs of aggression: Public expenditures resulting from conduct disorder. *American Journal of Public Health, 95*, 1767–1772. doi:10.2105/AJPH.2004.061424
Foster, S. L. (2005). Aggression and antisocial behavior in girls. In D. J. Bell, S. L. Foster, & E. J. Mash (Eds.), *Handbook of behavioral and emotional problems in girls* (pp. 149–180). New York: Kluwer/Plenum Press.
Fowles, D. C. (2001). Biological variables in psychopathology: A psychobiological perspective. In P. Sutker & H. E. Adams (Eds.), *Comprehensive handbook of psychopathology* (3rd ed., pp. 85–104). New York: Kluwer/Plenum Press.
Fox, S. E., Levitt, P., & Nelson, C. A. (2010). How the timing and quality of early experiences influence the development of brain architecture. *Child Development, 81*, 28–40. doi:10.1111/j.1467-8624.2009.01380.x
Fox, T. L., Barrett, P. M., & Shortt, A. L. (2002). Sibling relationships of anxious children: A preliminary investigation. *Journal of Clinical Child and Adolescent Psychology, 31*, 375–383. doi:10.1207/S15374424JCCP3103_09
Francis, K. J., & Wolfe, D. A. (2008). Cognitive and emotional differences between abusive and non-abusive fathers. *Child Abuse & Neglect, 32*, 1127–1137.
Francis, S. E., & Chorpita, B. F. (2004). Behavioral assessment of children in outpatient settings. In S. N. Haynes & E. M. Heiby (Eds.), *Comprehensive handbook of psychological assessment: Vol. 3. Behavioral assessment* (pp. 291–319). New York: Wiley.
Franco, O. H., Steyerberg, E. W., Hu, F. B., Mackenbach, J., & Nusselder, W. (2007). Associations of diabetes mellitus with total life expectancy and life expectancy with and without cardiovascular disease. *Archives of Internal Medicine, 167*, 1145–1151. Retrieved from http://archinte.ama-assn.org/
Franic, S., Middeldorp, C. M., Dolan, C. V., Ligthart, L., & Boomsma, D. I. (2010). Childhood and adolescent anxiety and depression: Beyond heritability. *American Journal of Child & Adolescent Psychiatry, 49*, 820–829. doi:10.1016/i.laac.2010.05.013
Frankel, F., Myatt, R., Sugar, C., Whitham, C., Gorospe, C. M., & Laugeson, E. A. (2010). A randomized controlled study of parent-assisted Children's Friendship Training with children having autism spectrum disorders. *Journal of Autism and Developmental Disorders, 40*, 827–842. doi:10.1007/s10803-009-0932-z
Frazier, T. W., Demaree, H. A., & Youngstrom, E. (2004). Meta-analysis of intellectual and neuropsychological test performance in attention-deficit/hyperactivity disorder. *Neuropsychology, 18*, 543–555. doi:10.1037/0894-4105.18.3.543
Frazier, T. W., & Hardan, A. Y. (2009). A meta-analysis of the corpus callosum in autism. *Biological Psychiatry, 66*, 935–941. doi:10.1016/j.biopsych.2009.07.022
Frazier, T. W., Youngstrom, E. A., Haycook, T., Sinoff, A., Dimitriou, F., Knapp, J., & Sinclair, L. (2010). Effectiveness of medication combined with intensive behavioral intervention for reducing aggression in youth with autism spectrum disorder. *Journal of Child and Adolescent Psychopharmacology, 20*, 167–177. doi:10.1089/cap.2009.0048
Freeman, J. B., Garcia, A. M., Coyne, L., Ale, C., Przeworski, A., Himle, M., . . . Leonard, H. L. (2008). Early childhood OCD: Preliminary findings from a family-based cognitive-behavioral approach. *Journal of the American Academy of Child & Adolescent Psychiatry, 47*, 593–602. doi:10.1097/CHI.0b013e31816765f9
Freitag, C. M., Staal, W., Klauck, S. M., Duketis, E., & Waltes, R. (2010). Genetics of autistic disorders: Review and clinical implications. *European Child and Adolescent Psychiatry, 19*, 169–178. doi:10.1007/s00787-009-0076-x
French, D. C., & Dishion, T. (2003). Predictors of early initiation of sexual intercourse among high-risk adolescents. *Journal of Early Adolescence, 23*, 295–315. doi:10.1177/0272431603254171
French, S. A., Story, M., Downes, B., Resnick, M. D., & Blum, R. W. (1995). Frequent dieting among adolescents: Psychosocial and health behavior correlates. *American Journal of Public Health, 85*, 695–710. doi:10.2105/AJPH.85.5.695
French, V. (1977). History of the child's influence: Ancient Mediterranean civilizations. In R. Q. Bell & L. V. Harper (Eds.), *Child effects on adults* (pp. 3–29). Hillsdale, NJ: Erlbaum.

Freud, S. (1909/1953). Analysis of a phobia in a five-year-old boy. In J. Strachey (Ed.), *The standard edition of the complete psychological works of Sigmund Freud* (Vol. 10, pp. 3–149). London: Hogarth Press.

Freyd, J. J., DePrince, A. P., & Gleaves, D. H. (2007). The state of betrayal trauma theory: Reply to McNally—conceptual issues and future directions. *Memory, 15*, 295–311.

Frick, P. J. (2000). A comprehensive and individualized treatment approach for children and adolescents with conduct disorders. *Cognitive and Behavioral Practice, 7*, 30–37. doi:10.1016/S1077-7229(00)80005-X

Frick, P. J., Cornell, A. H., Bodin, S. D., Dane, H. E., Barry, C. T., & Loney, B. R. (2003). Callous–unemotional traits and developmental pathways to severe conduct problems. *Developmental Psychology, 39*, 246–260. doi:10.1037/0012-1649.39.2.246

Frick, P. J., Lahey, B. B., Loeber, R., Tannenbaum, L., Van Horn, Y., Christ, M. A. G., . . . Hanson, K. (1993). Oppositional defiant disorder and conduct disorder: A meta-analytic review of factor analyses and cross-validation in a clinic sample. *Clinical Psychology Review, 13*, 319–340. doi:10.1016/0272-7358(93)90016-F

Frick, P. J., Lilienfeld, S. O., Ellis, M., Loney, B., & Silverthorn, P. (1999). The association between anxiety and psychopathy dimensions in children. *Journal of Abnormal Child Psychology, 27*, 383–392. doi:10.1023/A:1021928018403

Frick, P. J., & Moffitt, T. E. (2010). *A proposal to the DSM-V childhood disorder and the ADHD and disruptive behavior disorders work groups to include a specifier to the diagnosis of conduct disorder based on the presence of callous-unemotional traits*. Washington, DC: American Psychiatric Association. Retrieved July 2, 2011 from www.dsm5.org/ProposedRevision/Pages/proposedrevision.aspx?rid=424#

Frick, P. J., & Viding, E. (2009). Antisocial behavior from a developmental psychopathology perspective. *Development and Psychopathology, 21*, 111–1131. doi:10.1017/S0954579409990071

Frick, P. J., & White, S. F. (2008). Research review: The importance of callous-unemotional traits for developmental models of aggressive and antisocial behavior. *Journal of Child Psychology and Psychiatry, 49*, 359–375. doi:10.1111/j.1469-7610.2007.01862.x

Fried, E. J., & Nestle, M. (2002). The growing political movement against soft drinks in schools. *JAMA: Journal of the American Medical Association, 288*, 2181. doi:10.1001/jama.288.17.2181

Friedlander, L., & Desrocher, M. (2006). Neuroimaging studies of obsessive-compulsive disorder in adults and children. *Clinical Psychology Review, 26*, 32–49. doi:10.1016/j.cpr.2005.06.010

Friedman, A. G., Latham, S. A., & Dahlquist, L. M. (1998). Childhood cancer. In T. H. Ollendick & M. Hersen (Eds.), *Handbook of child psychopathology* (3rd ed., pp. 435–461). New York: Plenum Press.

Friedman, H. S., Tucker, J. S., Schwartz, J. E., Tomlinson-Keasey, C., Martin, L. R., Wingard, D. L., & Criqui, M. H. (1995). Psychosocial and behavioral predictors of longevity: The aging and death of the "termites." *American Psychologist, 50*, 69–78. doi:10.1037/0003-066X.50.2.69

Friedrich, W. N., & Trane, S. T. (2002). Sexual behavior in children across multiple settings. *Child Abuse & Neglect, 26*, 243–245.

Friman, P. C. (2008). Evidence-based therapies for enuresis and encopresis. In R. G. Steele, T. D. Elkin, & M. C. Roberts (Eds.), *Handbook of evidence-based therapies for children and adolescents: Bridging science and practice. Issues in clinical child psychology* (pp. 311–333). New York: Springer.

Fristad, M. A., & Goldberg Arnold, J. S. (2004). *Raising a moody child: How to cope with depression and bipolar disorder.* New York: Guilford Press.

Fristad, M. A., Verducci, J. S., Walters, K., & Young, M. E. (2009). Impact of multifamily psychoeducational psychotherapy in treating children aged 8 to 12 years with mood disorders. *Archives of General Psychiatry, 66*, 1013–1021. doi:10.1001/archgenpsychiatry.2009.112

Frith, U. (1989). *Autism: Explaining the enigma*. Oxford, England: Blackwell.

Frith, U. (1993, June). Autism. *Scientific American*, 108–114. doi:10.1038/scientificamerican0693-108

Frith, U. (1997). Autism [Special issue]. *Scientific American*, 92–98. Retrieved from http://www.scientificamerican.com/

Frith, U. (2003). *Autism: Explaining the enigma* (2nd ed.). Oxford, England: Blackwell.

Frith, U. (2004). Confusions and controversies about Asperger syndrome. *Journal of Child Psychology and Psychiatry, 45*, 672–686. doi:10.1111/j.1469-7610.2004.00262.x

Frith, U., & Happé, F. (1994). Autism: Beyond "theory of mind." *Cognition, 50*, 115–132. doi:10.1016/0010-0277(94)90024-8

Fritz, G., Rockney, R., and the Work Group on Quality Issues. (2004). Summary of the practice parameter for the assessment and treatment of children and adolescents with enuresis. *Journal of the American Academy of Child & Adolescent Psychiatry, 43*, 123–125. doi:10.1097/00004583-200401000-00029

Froehlich, T. E., Anixt, J. S., Loe, I. M., Chirdkiatgumchai, V., Kuan, L., & Gilman, R. C. (2011). Update on environmental risk factors for attention-deficit/hyperactivity disorder. *Current Psychiatry Reports, 13*, 333–344. doi:10.1007/s11920-011-0221-3

Froehlich, T. E., Lanphear, B. P., Auinger, P., Hornung, R., Epstein, J. N., Braun, J., & Kahn, R. (2009). Association of tobacco and lead exposures with attention-deficit/hyperactivity disorder. *Pediatrics, 124*, 1054–1063. doi:10.1289/ehp.9478

Froelich, W. (2011). Making a case to continue considering treatment with selective serotonin reuptake inhibitors for children with autism spectrum disorders. *Current Psychiatric Reports, 13*, 170–173. doi:10.1007/s11920-011-0196-0

Furr, J. M., Comer, J. S., Edmunds, J. M., & Kendall, P. C. (2010). Disasters and youth: A meta-analytic examination of posttraumatic stress. *Journal of Consulting and Clinical Psychology, 78*, 765–780. doi:10.1037/a0021482

Gaab, N., Gabrieli, J. D. E., Deutsch, G. K., Tallal, P., & Temple, E. (2007). Neural correlates of rapid auditory processing are disrupted in children with developmental dyslexia and ameliorated with training: An fMRI study. *Restorative Neurology and Neuroscience, 25*, 295–310. Retrieved from http://www.iospress.nl/

Gadow, K. D., & Nolan, E. E. (2002). Differences between preschool children with ODD, ADHD and ODDADHD symptoms. *Journal of Child Psychology and Psychiatry, 43*, 191–201. doi:10.1111/1469-7610.00012

Gadow, K. D., & Sprafkin, J. (1993). Television "violence" and children with emotional and behavioral disorders. *Journal of Emotional and Behavioral Disorders, 1*, 54–63. doi:10.1177/106342669300100108

Gaffrey, M. S., Luby, J. L., Beldon, A. C., Hirshberg, J. S., Volsche, J., & Barch, D. M. (2011). Association between depression severity and amygdala reactivity during sad face viewing in depressed preschoolers: An fMRI study. *Journal of Affective Disorders, 129*, 364–370. doi:10.1016/j.jad.2010.08.031

Galaburda, A. M., Sherman, G. F., Rosen, G. D., & Geschwind, A. F. (1985). Developmental dyslexia: Four consecutive patients with cortical anomalies. *Annals of Neurology, 18*, 222–223. doi:10.1002/ana.410180210

Galatzer-Levy, R. M., Bachrach, H., Skolnikoff, A., & Waldron, S. (2000). *Does psychoanalysis work?* New Haven, CT: Yale University Press.

Gallagher, H. L., & Frith, C. C. (2003). Functional imaging of "theory of mind." *Trends in Cognitive Sciences, 7*, 77–83. doi:10.1016/S1364-6613(02)00025-6

Gallerini, C. M., Garber, J., & Martin, N. C. (2010). The temporal relation between depression and comorbid psychopathology in adolescents at varied risk for depression. *Journal of Child Psychology and Psychiatry, 51*, 242–249. doi:10.1111/j.1469-7610.2009.02155.x

Galway, T. M., & Metsala, J. L. (2011). Social cognition and its relation to psychosocial adjustment in children with nonverbal learning disabilities. *Journal of Learning Disabilities, 44*, 33–49. doi:10.1177/0022219410371680

Ganz, M. L. (2007). The lifetime distribution of the incremental societal costs of autism. *Archives of Pediatric Adolescent Medicine, 161*, 343–349. doi:17404130

Gao, T., Raine, A., Venables, P. H., Dawson, M. E., & Mednick, S. A. (2010). Association of poor childhood fear conditioning and crime. *American Journal of Psychiatry, 167*, 56–60. doi:10.1176/appi.ajp.2009.09040499

Garber, J., & Cole, D. A. (2010). Intergenerational transmission of depression: A launch and grow model of change across adolescence. *Development and Psychopathology, 22*, 819–830. doi:10.1017/S0954579410000489

Garber, J., & Flynn, C. (2001). Vulnerability to depression in childhood and adolescence. In R. E. Ingram & J. M. Price (Eds.), *Vulnerability to psychopathology: Risk across the lifespan* (pp. 175–225). New York: Guilford Press.

Garber, J., & Horowitz, J. L. (2002). Depression in children. In I. H. Gotlib & C. Hammen (Eds.), *Handbook of depression* (pp. 510–540). New York: Guilford Press.

Garber, J., & Kaminsky, K. M. (2000). Laboratory and performance-based measures of depression in children and adolescents. *Journal of Clinical Child Psychology, 29*, 509–525. doi:10.1207/S15374424JCCP2904_5

Garber, J., & Weersing, V. R. (2010). Comorbidity of anxiety and depression in youth: Implications for treatment and prevention. *Clinical Psychology: Science and Practice, 17*, 293–306. doi:10.1111/j.1468-2850.2010.01221.x

Garcia, A. M., Sapyta, J. J., Moore, P. S., Freeman, J. B., Franklin, M. E., March, J. S., & Foa, E. B. (2010). Outcome in the pediatric obsessive compulsive treatment study (POTS I). *Journal of the American Academy of Child and Adolescent Psychiatry, 49*, 1024–1033. doi:10.1016/j.jaac.2010.06.013

Garcia-Perez, R. M., Hobson, R. P., & Lee, A. (2008). Narrative role taking in autism. *Journal of Autism and Developmental Disorders, 38*, 156–168. doi:10.1007/s10803-007-0379-z

Gardener, H., Spiegelman, D., & Buka, S. L. (2009). Prenatal risk factors for autism: Comprehensive meta-analysis. *British Journal of Psychiatry, 195*, 7–14. doi:10.1192/bjp.bp.108.051672

Gardner, H. (2006). *The development and education of the mind: The selected works of Howard Gardner (World Library of Educationalists Series)*. New York: Routledge/Taylor & Francis.

Gardner, W. I., Graeber-Whalen, J. L., & Ford, D. R. (2001). Behavioral therapies: Individualizing interventions through treatment formulations. In A. Dosen & K. Day (Eds.), *Treating mental illness and behavior disorders in children and adults with mental retardation* (pp. 69–100). Washington, DC: American Psychiatric Press.

Garfinkel, P. E., Lin, E., Goergin, P., Spegg, C., Goldbloom, D. S., Kennedy, S., . . . Woodside, D. B. (1995). Bulimia nervosa in a Canadian community sample: Prevalence and comparison of subgroups. *American Journal of Psychiatry, 152*, 1052–1058. Retrieved from http://ajp.psychiatryonline.org/

Garn, S. M., Clark, D. C., Lowe, C. U., Forbes, G., Garn, S., Owen, G. M., . . . Rowe, N. (1976). Trends in fatness and the origins of obesity: Ad hoc committee to review the ten-state nutrition survey. *Pediatrics, 57*, 443–456. Retrieved from http://pediatrics.aappublications.org/

Garner, D. M. (1993). Pathogenesis of anorexia nervosa. *Lancet, 341*, 1631–1635. doi:10.1016/0140-6736(93)90768-C

Garrett, A., & Chang, K. (2008). The role of the amygdala in bipolar disorder development. *Development and Psychopathology, 20*, 1285–1296. doi:10.1017/S0954579408000618

Garrison, W. T., & McQuiston, S. (1989). *Chronic illness during childhood and adolescence: Psychological aspects*. Newbury Park, CA: Sage.

Garvie, P. A., Lawford, J., Banet, M. S., & West, R. L. (2009). Quality of life measurement in paediatric and adolescent populations with HIV: A review of the literature. *Child Care, Health and Development, 35*, 440. doi:10.1111/j.1365-2214.2009.00985.x

Gathje, R. A., Lewandowski, L. J., & Gordon, M. (2008). The role of impairment in the diagnosis of ADHD. *Journal of Attention Disorders, 11*, 529–537. doi:10.1177/1087054707314028

Gatt, J. M., Nemeroff, C. B., Schofield, P. R., Paul, R. H., Clark, C. R., Gordon, E., & Williams, L. M. (2010). Early life stress combined with serotonin 3A receptor and brain-derived neurotrophic factor valine 66 to methionine genotypes impacts emotional brain and arousal correlates of risk for depression. *Biological Psychiatry, 68*, 818–824. doi:10.1016/j.biopsych.2010.06.025

Gatzke-Kopp, L. M., & Beauchaine, T. P. (2007). Direct and passive prenatal nicotine exposure and the development of externalizing psychopathology. *Child Psychiatry and Human Development, 38*, 255–269. doi:10.1007/s10578-007-0059-4

Gaudin, J. M., Polansky, N.A., Kilpatrick, A.C., & Shilton, P. (1996). Family functioning in neglectful families. *Child Abuse & Neglect, 20*, 363–377.

Gaysina, D., Maughan, B., & Richards, M. (2010). Association of reading problems with speech and motor development: Results from a British 1946 birth cohort. *Developmental Medicine & Child Neurology, 52*, 680–681. doi:10.1111/j.1469-8749.2010.03649.x

Gejman, P. V., Sanders, A. R., & Duan, J. (2010). The role of genetics in the etiology of schizophrenia. *Psychiatric Clinics of North America, 33*, 35–66. doi:10.1016/j.psc.2009.12.003

Gelb, S. A. (1995). The beast in man: Degenerationism and mental retardation, 1900–1920. *Intellectual and Developmental Disabilities, 33*, 1–9. Retrieved from http://www.aaiddjournals.org/loi/mere.1

Geller, B., & DelBello, M. P. (2008). *Treatment of bipolar disorder in children and adolescents*. New York: Guilford Press.

Geller, B., & DelBello, M. P. (Eds.). (2003). *Bipolar disorder in childhood and early adolescence*. New York: Guilford Press.

Geller, B., & Luby, J. (1997). Child and adolescent bipolar disorder: A review of the past 10 years. *Journal of the American Academy of Child & Adolescent Psychiatry, 36*, 1168–1176. doi:10.1097/00004583-199709000-00008

Geller, B., Sun, K., Zimerman, B., Luby, J., Frazier, J., & Williams, M. (1995). Complex and rapid cycling in bipolar children and adolescents. *Journal of Affective Disorders, 34*, 259–268. doi:10.1016/0165-0327(95)00023-G

Geller, B., Tillman, R., Bolhofner, K., Zimerman, B., Strauss, N. A., & Kaufmann, P. (2006). Controlled, blindly rated, direct-interview family study of a prepubertal and early-adolescent bipolar I disorder phenotype: Morbid risk, age at onset, and comorbidity. *Archives of General Psychiatry, 63*, 1130–1138. doi:10.1001/archpsyc.63.10.1130

Geller, D. A., Biederman, J., Jones, J., Park, K., Schwartz, S., Shapiro, S., & Coffey, B. (1998). Is juvenile obsessive–compulsive disorder a developmental subtype of the disorder? A review of the pediatric literature. *Journal of the American Academy of Child & Adolescent Psychiatry, 37*, 420–427. doi:10.1097/00004583-199804000-00020

George, M. S., Ketter, T. A., Parekh, P. I., Herscovitch, P., & Post, R. M. (1996). Gender differences in regional cerebral blood flow during transient self-induced sadness or happiness. *Biological Psychiatry, 40*, 859–871. doi:10.1016/0006-3223(95)00572-2

Gerdes, A. C., Hoza, B., & Pelham, W. E. (2003). Attention-deficit/hyperactivity disordered boy's relationships with their mothers and fathers: Child, mother, and father perceptions. *Development and Psychopathology, 15*, 363–382. doi:10.1017/S0954579403000208

Gerenser, J., & Forman, B. (2007). Speech and language deficits in children with developmental disabilities. In J. W. Jacobson, J. A. Mulick, & J. Rojahn (Eds.), *Handbook of intellectual and developmental disabilities. Issues in clinical child psychology* (pp. 563–579). New York: Springer.

Gernsbacher, M. A., Sauer, E. A., Geye, H. M., Schweigert, E. K., & Goldsmith, H. H. (2008). Infant and toddler oral- and manual-motor skills predict later speech fluency in autism. *Journal of Child Psychology and Psychiatry, 49*, 43–50. doi:10.1111/j.1469-7610.2007.01820.x

Gershater-Molko, R. M., Lutzker, J. R., & Wesch, D. (2003). Project SafeCare: Improving health, safety, and parenting skills in families reported for, and at-risk for child maltreatment. *Journal of Family Violence, 18*, 377–386.

Gershoff, E. T. (2002). Corporal punishment by parents and associated child behaviors and experiences: A meta-analytic and theoretical review. *Psychological Bulletin, 128*, 539–579.

Gershoff, E. T., & Bitensky, S. H. (2007). The case against corporal punishment of children: Converging evidence from social science research and international human rights law and implications for U.S. public policy. *Psychology, Public Policy, and Law, 13*, 231–272.

Gerstein, E. D., Crnic, K. A., Blacher, J., & Baker, B. L. (2009). Resilience and the course of daily parenting stress in families of young children with intellectual disabilities. *Journal of Intellectual Disability Research, 53*, 981–997. doi:10.1111/j.1365-2788.2009.01220.x

Gewirtz, A. H., & Edleson, J. L. (2007). Young children's exposure to intimate partner violence: Towards a developmental risk and resilience framework for research and intervention. *Journal of Family Violence, 22*, 151–163.

Ghaemi, S. N., & Martin, A. (2007). Defining the boundaries of childhood bipolar disorder. *American Journal of Psychiatry, 164*, 185–188. doi:10.1176/appi.ajp.164.2.185

Ghaziuddin, M. (2008). Defining the behavioral phenotype of Asperger syndrome. *Journal of Autism and Developmental Disorders, 38*, 138–142. doi:10.1007/s10803-007-0371-7

Ghezzi, P. M. (2007). Discrete trials teaching. *Psychology in the Schools, 44*, 667–679. doi:10.1002/pits.20256

Ghidoni, B. B. Z. (2007). Rett syndrome. *Child and Adolescent Psychiatric Clinics of North America, 16*, 723–743. doi:10.1016/j.chc.2007.03.004

Ghuman, J. K., Aman, M. G., Lecavalier, L., Riddle, M. A., Gelenberg, A., Wright, R., . . . Fort, C. (2009). Randomized, placebo-controlled, crossover study of methylphenidate for attention-deficit/hyperactivity disorder symptoms in preschoolers with developmental disorders. *Journal of Child and Adolescent Psychopharmacology, 19*, 329–339. doi:10.1089/cap.2008.0137

Giarelli, E., Wiggins, L. D., Rice, C. E., Levy, S. E., Kirby, R. S., Pinto-Martin, J., & Mandell, D. (2010). Sex differences in the evaluation and diagnosis of autism spectrum disorders among children. *Disability and Health Journal, 3*, 107–116. doi:10.1016/j.dhjo.2009.07.001

Gibbons, R. D., Brown, C. H., Hur, K., Marcus, S. M., Bhaumik, D. K., Erkens, J. A., . . . Mann, J. J. (2007). Early evidence on the effects of regulators' suicidality warnings on SSRI prescriptions and suicide in children and adolescents. *American Journal of Psychiatry, 164*, 1356–1363. doi:10.1176/appi.ajp.2007.07030454

Gibbons, R. D., Brown, H., Hur, K., Davis, J. M., & Mann, J. J. (2012, February 6). Suicidal thoughts and behavior with antidepressant treatment: Reanalysis of the randomized placebo-controlled studies of fluoxetine and venlafaxine. Advance online publication. *Archives of General Psychiatry*. doi:10.1001/archgenpsychiatry.2011.2048

Gibbons, R. D., Hur, K., Bhaumik, D. L., & Mann, J. J. (2006). The relationship between antidepressant prescription rates and rate of early adolescent suicide. *American Journal of Psychiatry, 163*, 1898–1904. doi:10.1176/appi.ajp.163.11.1898

Gil, K. M., Anthony, K. K., & Carson, J. (2001). Daily coping practice predicts treatment effects in children with sickle cell disease. *Journal of Pediatric Psychology, 26*, 163–173. doi:10.1093/jpepsy/26.3.163

Gilbert, A. R., Akkal, D., Almeida, J. R.C., Mataix-Cols, D., Kalas, C., Devlin, B., . . . Phillips, M. L. (2009). Neural correlates of symptom dimension in pediatric obsessive-compulsive disorder: A functional magnetic resonance imaging study. *Journal of the American Academy of Child & Adolescent Psychiatry, 48*, 936–944. doi:10.1097/CHI.0b013e3181b2163c

Gilbert, S. C., Crump, S., Madhere, S., & Schutz, W. (2009). Internalization of the thin ideal as a predictor of body dissatisfaction and disordered eating in African, African-American, and Afro-Caribbean female college students. *Journal of College Student Psychotherapy, 23*, 196–211. doi:10.1080/87568220902794093

Gillberg, C. (2002). *A guide to Asperger syndrome*. New York: Cambridge University Press.

Gillberg, C., & de Souza, L. (2002). Head circumference in autism, Asperger syndrome, and ADHD: A comparative study. *Developmental Medicine & Child Neurology, 44*, 296–300. doi:10.1017/S0012162201002110

Gillham, J. E., & Reivich, K. J. (1999). Prevention of depressive symptoms in school children: A research update. *Psychological Science, 10*, 461–462. doi:10.1111/1467-9280.00188

Gilman, S. E., Kawachi, I., Fitzmaurice, G. M., & Buka, S. (2003). Family disruption in childhood and risk of adult depression. *American Journal of Psychiatry, 160*, 939–946. doi:10.1176/appi.ajp.160.5.939

Gilvarry, E. (2000). Substance abuse in young people. *Journal of Child Psychology and Psychiatry, 41*, 55–80. doi:10.1111/1469-7610.00549

Ginsburg, G. S., & Silverman, W. (1996). Phobic and anxiety disorders in Hispanic and Caucasian youth. *Journal of Anxiety Disorders, 10*, 517–528. doi:10.1016/S0887-6185(96)00027-8

Ginsburg, G. S., & Silverman, W. K. (2000). Gender role orientation and fearfulness in children with anxiety disorders. *Journal of Anxiety Disorders, 14*, 57–67. doi:10.1016/S0887-6185(99)00033-X

Glaser, D. (2011). How to deal with emotional abuse and neglect—further development of a conceptual framework (FRAMEA). *Child Abuse & Neglect, 35*, 866.

Glass, K., Flory, K., & Hankin, B. L. (2010). Symptoms of ADHD and close friendships in adolescence. *Journal of Attention Disorders*. Advance online publication. doi:10.1177/1087054710390865

Gleason, M. M., Egger, H. L., Emslie, G. J., Greenhill, L. L., Kowatch, R. A., Lieberman, A. F., . . . Zeanah, C. H. (2007). Psychopharmacological treatment for very young children: Contexts and guidelines. *Journal of the American Academy of Child & Adolescent Psychiatry, 46*, 1532–1572. doi:10.1097/chi.0b013e3181570d9e

Gleason, M. M., Fox, N. A., Drury, S., Smyke, A., Egger, H. L., Nelson, C. A., . . . Zeanah, C. H. (2011). Validity of evidence-derived criteria for reactive attachment disorder: Indiscriminately social/disinhibited and emotionally withdrawn/inhibited types. *Journal of the American Academy of Child & Adolescent Psychiatry, 50*, 216–231. doi:10.1016/j.jaac.2010.12.012

Glicklich, L. B. (1951). An historical account of enuresis. *Pediatrics, 8*, 859–876. Retrieved from http://pediatrics.aappublications.org/

Global Initiative to End All Corporal Punishment of Children. (2012). States with full abolition. Available: http://www.endcorporalpunishment.org/pages/progress/prohib_states.html.

Glover, S. H., & Pumariega, A. J. (1998). The importance of children's mental health epidemiological research with culturally diverse populations. In M. Hernandez & M. R. Isaacs (Eds.), *Promoting cultural competence in children's mental health services* (pp. 271–303). Baltimore: Brookes.

Glover, V. (2011). Prenatal stress and the origins of psychopathology: An evolutionary perspective. *Journal of Child Psychology and Psychiatry, 52*, 356–367. doi:10.1111/j.1469-7610.2011.02371.x

Goddard, H. H. (1912). *The kallikak family: A study in the heredity of feeble-mindedness*. New York: MacMillan Co. doi:10.1037/10949-000

Gogtay, N., Ordonez, A., Herman, D. H., Hayashi, K. M., Greenstein, D., Vaituzis, C., . . . Rapoport, J. L. (2007). Dynamic mapping of cortical development before and after the onset of pediatric bipolar illness. *Journal of Child Psychology and Psychiatry, 48*, 852–862. doi:10.1111/j.1469-7610.2007.01747.x

Goin-Kochel, R. P., Myers, B. J., & Mackintosh, V. H. (2007). Parental reports on the use of treatments and therapies for children with autism spectrum disorders. *Research in Autism Spectrum Disorders, 1*, 195–209. doi:10.1016/j.rasd.2006.08.006

Goldentyer, T. (1994). *Gangs*. Austin, TX: Steck-Vaughn.

Goldstein, T. R., Axelson, D. A., Birmaher, B., & Brent, D. A. (2007). Dialectical behavior therapy for adolescents with bipolar disorder: A 1-year open trial. *Journal of the American Academy of Child & Adolescent Psychiatry, 46*, 820–830. doi:10.1097/chi.0b013e31805c1613

Goldstein, T. R., Bridge, J. A., & Brent, D. A. (2008). Sleep disturbance preceding completed suicide in adolescents. *Journal of Consulting and Clinical Psychology, 76*, 84–91. doi:10.1037/0022-006X.76.1.84

Goldston, D. B., & Compton, J. S. (2007). Adolescent suicidal and nonsuicidal self-harm behaviors and risk. In E. J. Mash & R. A. Barkley (Eds.), *Assessment of childhood disorders* (4th ed., pp. 305–343). New York: Guilford Press.

Goldston, D. B., Daniel, S. S., & Arnold, E. M. (2006). Suicidal and non-suicidal self-harm behaviors. In D. A. Wolfe & E. J. Mash (Eds.), *Behavioral and emotional disorders in adolescents: Nature, assessment, and treatment* (pp. 343–380). New York: Guilford Press.

Goldston, D. B., Molock, S. D., Whitbeck, L. B., Murakami, J. L., Zayas, L. H., & Hall, G. C. N. (2008). Cultural considerations in adolescent suicide: Prevention and psychosocial treatment. *American Psychologist, 63*, 14–31. doi:10.1037/0003-066X.63.1.14

Goldston, D. B., Walsh, A., Arnold, E. M., Reboussin, B., Daniel, S. S., Erkanli, A., . . . Wood, F. B. (2007). Reading problems, psychiatric disorders, and functional impairment from mid- to late adolescence. *Journal of the American Academy of Child & Adolescent Psychiatry, 46*, 25–32. doi:10.1097/01.chi.0000242241.77302.f4

Golombek, A. A., & King, B. (2010). Pharmacotherapy. In R. C. Dryden-Edwards & L. Combrinck-Graham (Eds.), *Developmental disabilities from childhood to adulthood: What works for psychiatrists in community and institutional settings* (pp. 271–295). Baltimore, MD: Johns Hopkins University Press.

Gooch, D., Snowling, M., & Hulme, C. (2011). Time perception, phonological skills and executive function in children with dyslexia and/or ADHD symptoms. *Journal of Child Psychology and Psychiatry, 52*, 195–203. doi:10.1111/j.14697610.2010.02312.x

Goodkind, J. R., NaNoue, M. D., & Milford, J. (2010). Adaptation and implementation of cognitive behavioral intervention for trauma in schools with American Indian youth. *Journal of Clinical Child and Adolescent Psychology, 39*, 858–873. doi:10.1080/15374416.2010.517166

Goodlin-Jones, B., Schwichtenberg, A. J., Iosif, A., Tang, K., Liu, J., & Anders, T. F. (2009). Six-month persistence of sleep problems in young children with autism, developmental delay, and typical development. *Journal of the American Academy of Child & Adolescent Psychiatry, 48*, 247–254. doi:10.1097/CHI.0b013e3181a8135a

Goodman, S. H. (2007). Depression in mothers. *Annual Review of Clinical Psychology, 3*, 107–135. doi:10.1146/annurev.clinpsy.3.022806.091401

Goodman, S. H., & Brand, S. R. (2009). Infants of depressed mothers: Vulnerabilities, risk factors, and protective factors for the later development of psychopathology. In C. H. Zeanah, Jr. (Ed.), *Handbook of infant mental health* (3rd ed., pp. 153–170). New York: Guilford Press.

Goodman, S. H., Rouse, M. H., Connell, A. M., Broth, M. R., Hall, C. M., & Heyward, D. (2011). Maternal depression and child psychopathology: A meta-analytic review. *Clinical Child and Family Psychology Review, 14*, 1–27. doi:10.1007/s10567-010-0080-1

Goodman, S. H., Schwab-Stone, M., Lahey, B., Shaffer, D., & Jensen, P. (2000). Major depression and dysthymia in children and adolescents: Discriminant validity and differential consequences in a community sample. *Journal of the American Academy of Child & Adolescent Psychiatry, 39*, 761–770. doi:10.1097/00004583-200006000-00015

Goodman, S. H., & Tully, E. (2008). Children of depressed mothers: Implications for etiology, treatment, and prevention of depression in children and adolescents. In J. R. Z. Abela & B. L. Hankin (Eds.), *Handbook of depression in children and adolescents* (pp. 415–440). New York: Guilford Press.

Goodwin, R. D., & Gotlib, I. H. (2004). Panic attacks and psychopathology among youth. *Acta Psychiatrica Scandinavica, 109*, 216–221. doi:10.1046/j.1600-0447.2003.00255.x

Goodyer, I. M. (1999). The influence of recent life events on the onset and outcome of major depression in young people. In C. Essau & F. Petermann (Eds.), *Depressive disorders in children and adolescents: Epidemiology, risk factors, and treatment* (pp. 237–260). Northvale, NJ: Aronson.

Goodyer, I. M. (2008). Emanuel Miller Lecture: Early onset depressions—meanings, mechanisms and processes. *Journal of Child Psychology and Psychiatry, 49*, 1239–1256. doi:10.1111/j.1469-7610.2008.01964.x

Goodyer, I. M., & Cooper, P. (1993). A community study of depression in adolescent girls: II. The clinical features of identified disorder. *British Journal of Psychiatry, 163*, 374–380. doi:10.1192/bjp.163.3.374

Goodyer, I. M., Dubicka, B., Wilkinson, P., Kelvin, R., Roberts, C., Byford, S., . . . Harrington, R. (2007). Selective serotonin reuptake inhibitors (SSRIs) and routine specialist care with and without cognitive behaviour therapy in adolescents with major depressive disorder: Randomized controlled trial. *British Medical Journal, 335*, 142–146. doi:10.1136/bmj.39224.494340.55

Goodyer, I. M., Herbert, J., Tamplin, A., Secher, S. M., & Pearson, J. (1997). Short-term outcome of major depression: II. Life events, family dysfunction, and friendship difficulties as predictors of persistent disorder. *Journal of the American Academy of Child & Adolescent Psychiatry, 36*, 474–480. doi:10.1097/00004583-199704000-00009

Gotlib, I. H., & Hammen, C. L. (Eds.). (1992). *Psychological aspects of depression: Toward a cognitive-interpersonal integration*. London: Wiley.

Gotlib, I. H., Lewinsohn, P. M., & Seeley, J. R. (1995). Symptoms versus a diagnosis of depression: Differences in psychosocial functioning. *Journal of Consulting and Clinical Psychology, 63*, 90–100. doi:10.1037/0022-006X.63.1.90

Gotlib, I. H., Lewinsohn, P. M., & Seeley, J. R. (1998). Consequences of depression during adolescence: Marital status and marital functioning in early adulthood. *Journal of Abnormal Psychology, 107*, 686–690. doi:10.1037/0021-843X.107.4.686

Gottfredson, D. C., Gottfredson, G. D., & Hybel, L. G. (1993). Managing adolescent behavior: A multi-year, multi-school study. *American Educational Research Journal, 30*, 179–215. doi:10.3102/00028312030001179

Gowers, S., & Bryant-Waugh, R. (2004). Management of child and adolescent eating disorders: The current evidence base and future directions. *Journal of Child Psychology and Psychiatry 45*, 63–83. doi:10.1046/j.0021-9630.2003.00309.x

Graber, J. A., Brooks-Gunn, J., Paikoff, R. L., & Warren, M. P. (1994). Prediction of eating problems: An 8-year study of adolescent girls. *Developmental Psychology, 30*, 823–834. doi:10.1037/0012-1649.30.6.823

Gracious, B. L., Findling, R. L., Seman, C., Youngstrom, E. A., Demeter, C. A., & Calabrese, J. R. (2004). Elevated thyrotropin in bipolar youths prescribed both lithium and divalproex sodium. *Journal of the American Academy of Child & Adolescent Psychiatry, 43*, 215–220. doi:10.1097/00004583-200402000-00018

Graeff-Martins, A. S., Flament, M. F., Fayyad, J., Tyano, S., Jensen, P., & Rohde, L. A. (2008). Diffusion of efficacious interventions for children and adolescents with mental health problems. *Journal of Child Psychology and Psychiatry, 49*, 335–352. doi:10.1111/j.1469-7610.2007.01827.x

Grafodatskaya, D., Chung, B., Szatmari, P., & Weksberg, R. (2010). Autism spectrum disorders and epigenetics. *Journal of the American Academy of Child & Adolescent Psychiatry, 49*, 794–809. doi:10.1016/j.jaac.201 0.05.005

Graham, J., Banaschewski, T., Buitelaar, J., Coghill, D., Danckaerts, M., Dittmann, R. W., . . . Taylor, E. (for the European Guidelines Group). (2011). European guidelines on managing adverse effects of medication for ADHD. *European Child & Adolescent Psychiatry, 20*, 17–37. doi:10.1007/s00787-010-0140-6

Graham, S., MacArthur, C., Schwartz, S., & Voth, T. (1992). Improving LD student's compositions using a strategy involving product and process goal-setting. *Exceptional Children, 58*, 322–334.

Graham-Bermann, S. A., Lynch, S., Banyard, V., DeVoe, E. R., & Halabu, H. (2007). Community-based intervention for children exposed to intimate partner violence: An efficacy trial. *Journal of Consulting and Clinical Psychology, 75*, 199–209.

Granic, I., & Patterson, G. R. (2006). Toward a comprehensive model of antisocial development: A dynamic systems approach. *Psychological Review, 113*, 101–131. doi:10.1037/0033-295X.113.1.101

Grant, B. F., Stinson, F. S., & Harford, T. C. (2001). Age of onset of alcohol use and DSM-IV alcohol abuse and dependence: A 12-year follow-up. *Journal of Substance Abuse, 13*, 493–504. doi:10.1016/S0899-3289(01)00096-7

Grant, G., Ramcharan, P., & Flynn, M. (2007). Resilience in families with children and adult members with intellectual disabilities: Tracing elements of a psychosocial model. *Journal of Applied Research in Intellectual Disabilities, 20*, 563–575. doi:10.1111/j.1468-3148.2007.00407.x

Gray, J. A. (1987). *The psychology of fear and stress* (2nd ed.). New York: Cambridge University Press.

Gray, K. M., Piccinin, A. M., Hofer, S. M., Mackinnon, A., Bontempo, D. E., Einfeld, S. L., . . . Tonge, B. J. (2011). The longitudinal relationship between behavior and emotional disturbance in young people with intellectual disability and maternal mental health. *Research in Developmental Disabilities, 32*, 1194–1204. doi:10.1016/j.ridd.2010.12.044

Greenberg, H., Raymond, S. U., & Leeder, S. R. (2011). The prevention of global chronic disease: Academic public health's new frontier. *American Journal of Public Health, 101*, 1386–1391. doi:10.2105/AJPH.2011.300147

Greenberg, M. T., Domitrovich, C., & Bumbarger, B. (2001). The prevention of mental disorders in school-aged children: Current state of the field. *Prevention & Treatment, 4*. doi:10.1037/1522-3736.4.1.41a

Greene, R. W., & Doyle, A. E. (1999). Toward a transactional conceptualization of oppositional defiant disorder: Implications for assessment and treatment. *Clinical Child and Family Psychology Review, 2*, 129–148. doi:10.1023/A:1021850921476

Greene, R. W., Biederman, J., Faraone, S. V., Ouellette, C. A., Courtney, P., & Griffin, S. M. (1996). Toward a new psychometric definition of social disability in children with attention-deficit hyperactivity disorder. *Journal of the American Academy of Child & Adolescent Psychiatry,*

35, 571–578. doi:10.1097/00004583-199605000-00011

Greenhill, L. L., Posner, K., Vaughan, B. S., & Kratochvil, C. J. (2008). Attention deficit hyperactivity disorder in preschool children. *Child and Adolescent Psychiatric Clinics of North American, 17*, 347–366. doi:10.1016/j.chc.2007.11.004

Greenspan, S. I., & Wieder, S. (2006). *Engaging autism: Using the floortime approach to help children relate, communicate, and think*. Cambridge, MA: Da Capo Lifelong Books.

Greey, M. (1995, November). Special families, special needs: The rigours and rewards of raising children with disabilities. *Today's Parent, 97*.

Gregg, N. (2011). Adults with learning disabilities: Barriers and progress. In S. Goldstein, J. A. Naglieri & M. DeVries (Eds.), *Learning and attention disorders in adolescence and adulthood: Assessment and treatment (2nd ed.)* (pp. 87–111). Hoboken, NJ: John Wiley & Sons Inc.

Gregory, A. M., Caspi, A., Moffitt, T. E., Koenen, K. Eley, T. C., & Poulton, R. (2007). Juvenile mental health histories of adults with anxiety disorders. *American Journal of Psychiatry, 164*, 301–308. doi:10.1176/appi.ajp.164.2.301

Gregory, A. M., & Eley, T. C. (2007). Genetic influences on anxiety in children: What we've learned and where we're heading. *Clinical Child and Family Psychology Review, 10*, 199–212. doi:10.1007/s10567-007-0022-8

Gregory, A. M., Van der Ende, J., Willis, T. A., & Verhulst, F. C. (2008). Parent-reported sleep problems during development and self-reported anxiety/depression, attention problems, and aggressive behavior later in life. *Archives of Pediatric and Adolescent Medicine, 162*, 330–335. Retrieved from http://archpedi.ama-assn.org/

Gresham, F. M., & MacMillan, D. L. (1997). Autistic recovery? An analysis and critique of the empirical evidence. *Behavioral Disorders, 22*, 185–201. Retrieved from http://www.ccbd.net/

Grether, J. K., Anderson, M. C., Croen, L. A., Smith, D., & Windham, G. C. (2009). Risk of autism and increasing maternal and paternal age in a large North American population. *American Journal of Epidemiology, 170*, 1118–1126. doi:10.1093/aje/kwp247

Griffin, K. W., & Botvin, G. J. (2010). Evidence-based interventions for preventing substance use disorders in adolescents. *Child and Adolescent Psychiatric Clinics of North America, 19*, 505–526. doi:10.1016/j.chc.2010.03.005

Griffith, E. M., Pennington, B. F., Wehner, E. A., & Rogers, S. J. (1999). Executive functions in young children with autism. *Child Development, 70*, 817–832. doi:10.1111/1467-8624.00059

Grigorenko, E. L. (2007). Triangulating developmental dyslexia: Behavior, brain, and genes. In D. Coch, G. Dawson, & K. W. Fischer (Eds.), *Human behavior, learning, and the developing brain: Atypical development* (pp. 117–144). New York: Guilford Press.

Grigorenko, E. L., Geiser, C., Slobodskaya, H. R., & Francis, D. J. (2010). Cross informant symptoms from CBCL, TRF, and YSR: Trait and method variance in a normative sample of Russian youths. *Psychological Assessment, 22*, 893–911. doi:10.1037/a0020703

Grinker, R. R. (2007). *Unstrange minds: Remapping the world of autism*. New York: Basic Books.

Grizenko, N., Paci, M., & Joober, R. (2010). Is the inattentive subtype of ADHD different from the combined/hyperactive subtype? *Journal of Attention Disorders, 13*, 649–657. doi:10.1177/1087054709347200

Groen, W., Teluij, M., Buitelaar, J., & Tendolkar, I. (2010). Amygdala and hippocampus enlargement during adolescence in autism. *Journal of the American Academy of Child & Adolescent Psychiatry, 49*, 552–560. doi:10.1016/j.jaac.2009.12.023

Gross, M. D. (1995). Origin of stimulant use for treatment of attention deficit disorder. *American Journal of Psychiatry, 152*, 298–299. Retrieved from http://ajp.psychiatryonline.org/

Gruber, R. (2009). Sleep characteristics of children and adolescents with attention deficit-hyperactivity disorder. *Child and Adolescent Psychiatric Clinics of North America, 18*, 863–876. doi:10.1016/j.chc.2009.04.011

Gruber, R., Sadeh, A., & Raviv, A. (2000). Instability of sleep patterns in children with attention-deficit/hyperactivity disorder. *Journal of the American Academy of Child & Adolescent Psychiatry, 39*, 495–501. doi:10.1097/00004583-200004000-00019

Guedeney, A. (2007). Withdrawal behavior and depression in infancy. *Infant Mental Health Journal, 28*, 393–408. doi:10.1002/imhj.20143

Guerra, N. G., Williams, K. R., & Sadek, S. (2011). Understanding bullying and victimization during childhood and adolescence: A mixed methods study. *Child Development, 82*, 295–310. doi:10.1111/j.1467-8624.2010.01556.x

Guerrero, A. P. S., Hishinuma, E. S., Andrade, N. N., Bell, C. K., Kurahara, D. K., Lee, T. G., . . . Stokes, A. J. (2003). Demographic and clinical characteristics of adolescents in Hawaii with obsessive-compulsive disorder. *Archives of Pediatric Adolescent Medicine, 157*, 665–670. Retrieved from http://archpedi.ama-assn.org/

Guimarães, A. P., Schmitz, M., Polanczyk, G. V., Zeni, C., Genro, J. Roman, T., . . . Hutz, M. H. (2009). Further evidence for the association between attention deficit/hyperactivity disorder and the serotonin receptor 1B gene. *Journal of Neural Transmission, 116*, 1675–1680. doi:10.1007/s00702-009-0305-y

Guite, J. W., Lobato, D. J., Shalon, L., Plante, W., & Kao, B. T. (2007). Pain, disability, and symptoms among siblings of children with functional abdominal pain. *Journal of Developmental & Behavioral Pediatrics, 28*, 2–8. doi:10.1097/DBP.0b013e3180307c26

Gullone, E. (1999). The assessment of normal fear in children and adolescents. *Clinical Child and Family Psychology Review, 2*, 91–106. doi:10.1023/A:1021895630678

Guralnick, M. J., Neville, B., Hammond, M. A., & Connor, R. T. (2007). The friendships of young children with developmental delays: A longitudinal analysis. *Journal of Applied Developmental Psychology, 28*, 64–79. doi:10.1016/j.appdev.2006.10.004

Guralnick, M. J., Neville, B., Hammond, M. A., & Connor, R. T. (2008). Continuity and change from full-inclusion early childhood programs through the early elementary period. *Journal of Early Intervention, 30*, 237–250. doi:10.1177/1053815108317962

Gurley, D., Cohen, P., Pine, D. S., & Brook, J. (1996). Discriminating depression and anxiety in youth: A role for diagnostic criteria. *Journal of Affective Disorders, 39*, 191–200. doi:10.1016/0165-0327(96)00020-1

Gustafson, K. E., Bonner, M. J., Hardy, K. K., & Thompson, R. J., Jr. (2006). Biopsychosocial and developmental issues in sickle cell disease. In R. T. Brown (Ed.), *Comprehensive handbook of childhood cancer and sickle cell disease: A biopsychosocial approach* (pp. 431–448). New York: Oxford University Press.

Guttmann-Steinmetz, S., Gadow, K. D., & DeVincent, C. J. (2009). Oppositional defiant and conduct disorders in boys with autism spectrum disorder with and without attention-deficit hyperactivity disorder versus several comparison samples. *Journal of Autism and Developmental Disorders, 39*, 976–985. doi:10.1007/s10803-009-0706-7

Guyer, A. E., Chaote, V. R., Grimm, K. J., Pine, D. S., & Keenan, K. (2011). Emerging depression is associated with face memory deficits in adolescent girls. *Journal of the American Academy of Child and Adolescent Psychiatry, 50*, 180–190. doi:10.1016/j.jaac.2010.11.008

Guyer, A. E., McClure-Tone, E., Shiffrin, N. D., Pine, D. S., & Nelson, E. E. (2009). Probing the neural correlates of anticipated peer evaluation in adolescence. *Child Development, 80*, 1000–1015. doi.10.1111/j.1467-8624.2009.01313.x

Gzowski, P. (1993, April). Gzowski's Canada: Extraordinary guests. *Canadian Living*, 91.

Häfner, H., an der Heiden, W., Behrens, S., Gattaz, W. F., Hambrecht, M., Löffler, W., . . . Stein, A. (1998). Causes and consequences of the gender difference in age of onset of schizophrenia. *Schizophrenia Bulletin, 24*, 99–113. Retrieved from http://schizophreniabulletin.oxfordjournals.org/

Haager, D., Klingner, J., & Vaughn, S. (Eds.). (2007). *Evidence-based reading practices for response to intervention.* New York: Brookes.

Haas, S. M., Irr, M. E., Jennings, N. A., & Wagner, L. M. (2011). Communicating thin: A grounded model of online negative enabling support groups in the pro-anorexia movement. *New Media & Society, 13*, 40–57. doi:10.1177/1461444810363910

Hadwin, J. A., Garner, M., & Perez-Olivas, G. (2006). The development of information processing biases in childhood anxiety: A review and exploration of its origins in

parenting. *Clinical Psychology Review, 26*, 876–894. doi:10.1016/j.cpr.2005.09.004
Haedt-Matt, A. A., & Keel, P. K. (2011). Revisiting the affect regulation model of binge eating: A meta-analysis of studies using ecological momentary assessment. *Psychological Bulletin, 137*, 660–681. doi:10.1037/a0023660
Hagberg, B. (1995). Clinical delineation of Rett syndrome variants. *Neuropediatrics, 26*, 62. doi:10.1055/s-2007-979723
Hagerman, R. J. (2011). *Fragile X syndrome and fragile X-associated disorders*. New York: Guilford Press.
Hajcak, G., Franklin, M. E., Foa, E. B., & Simons, R. F. (2008). Increased error-related brain activity in pediatric obsessive-compulsive disorder before and after treatment. *American Journal of Psychiatry, 165*, 116–123. doi:10.1176/appi.ajp.2007.07010143
Hale, W. M., Raaijmakers, Q., Muris, P., van Hoof, A., & Meeus, W. (2008). Developmental trajectories of adolescent anxiety disorder symptoms: A 5-year prospective community study. *Journal of the American Academy of Child & Adolescent Psychiatry, 47*, 556–564. doi:10.1097/CHI.0b013e3181676583
Haller, M., Handley, E., Chassin, L., & Bountress, K. (2010). Developmental cascades: Linking adolescent substance use, affiliation with substance use promoting peers, and academic achievement to adult substance use disorders. *Development and Psychopathology, 22*, 899–916. doi:10.1017/S0954579410000532
Halliday-Boykins, C. A., Schoenwald, S. K., & Letourneau, E. J. (2005). Caregiver-therapist ethnic similarity predicts youth outcomes from an empirically based treatment. *Journal of Consulting and Clinical Psychology, 73*, 808–818. doi:10.1037/0022-006X.73.5.808
Hallmayer. J., Cleveland, S., Torres, A., Phillips, J., Cohen, B., Torigoe, T., . . . Risch N. (2011). Genetic heritability and shared environmental factors among twin pairs with autism. *Archives of General Psychiatry, 68*, 1095–1102. doi:10.1001/archgenpsychiatry.2011.76
Hallowell, E. M., & Ratey, J. J. (1994). *Answers to distraction*. New York: Pantheon Books.
Halmøy, A., Johansson, S., Winge, I., McKinney, J. A., Knappskog, P. M., & Haavik, J. (2010). Attention-deficit/hyperactivity disorder symptoms in offspring of mothers with impaired serotonin production. *Archives of General Psychiatry, 67*, 1033–1043. doi:10.1001/archgenpsychiatry.2010.124
Hamalainen, M., & Pulkkinen, L. (1996). Problem behavior as a precursor of male criminality. *Development and Psychopathology, 8*, 443–455. doi:10.1017/S0954579400007185
Hammad, T. A., Laughren, T., & Racoosin, J. (2006). Suicidality in pediatric patients treated with antidepressant drugs. *Archives of General Psychiatry, 63*, 323–329. doi:10.1001/archpsyc.63.3.332
Hammen, C. (1999). The emergence of an interpersonal approach to depression. In T. Joiner & J. Coyne (Eds.), *The interactional nature of depression: Advances in interpersonal approaches* (pp. 22–36). Washington, DC: American Psychological Association.
Hammen, C. (2002). Context of stress in families of children with depressed parents. In S. H. Goodman & I. H. Gotlib (Eds.), *Children of depressed parents: Mechanisms of risk and implications for treatment* (pp. 175–202). Washington, DC: American Psychological Association.
Hammen, C., Brennan, P. A., Keenan-Miller, D., & Herr, N. R. (2008). Early onset recurrent subtype of adolescent depression: Clinical and psychosocial correlates. *Journal of Child Psychology and Psychiatry, 49*, 433–440. doi:10.1111/j.1469-7610.2007.01850.x
Hammen, C., Brennan, P. A., & Le Brocque, R. (2011). Youth depression and early childrearing: Stress generation and intergenerational transmission of depression. *Journal of Consulting and Clinical Psychology, 79*, 353–363. doi:10.1037/a0023536
Hammen, C., & Rudolph, K. D. (2003). Childhood mood disorders. In E. J. Mash & R. A. Barkley (Eds.), *Child psychopathology* (2nd ed., pp. 233–278). New York: Guilford Press.
Hammerness, P., Geller, D., Petty, C., Lamb, A., Bristol, E., & Biederman, J. (2010). Does ADHD moderate the manifestation of anxiety disorders in children? *European Child & Adolescent Psychiatry, 19*, 107–112. doi:10.1007/s00787-009-0041-8
Hammill, D. D. (1993). A brief look at the learning disabilities movement in the United States. *Journal of Learning Disabilities, 26*, 295–310. doi:10.1177/002221949302600502
Hammill, D. D., Mather, N., Allen, E. A., & Roberts, R. (2002). Using semantics, grammar, phonology, and rapid naming tasks to predict word identification. *Journal of Learning Disabilities, 35*, 121–136. doi:10.1177/002221940203500204
Hampton, T. (2007). Reports help identify and manage autism. *JAMA: Journal of the American Medical Association, 298*, 2610. doi:10.1001/jama.298.22.2610
Handen, B. L. (2007). Intellectual disability (mental retardation). In E. J. Mash & R. A. Barkley (Eds.), *Assessment of childhood disorders* (4th ed., pp. 551–597). New York: Guilford Press.
Handen, B. L., McAuliffe, S., Janosky, J., Feldman, H., & Breaux, A. M. (1998). A playroom observation procedure to assess children with mental retardation and ADHD. *Journal of Abnormal Child Psychology, 26*, 269–277. doi:10.1023/A:1022654417460
Hankin, B. L., & Abramson, L. Y. (2001). Development of gender differences in depression: An elaborated cognitive vulnerability-transactional stress theory. *Psychological Bulletin, 127*, 773–796. doi:10.1037/0033-2909.127.6.773
Hankin, B. L., Gibb, B. E., Abela, J. R. Z., & Flory, K. (2010). Selective attention to affective stimuli and clinical depression among youths: Role of anxiety and specificity of emotion. *Journal of Abnormal Psychology, 119*, 491–501. doi:10.1037/a0019609
Hankin, B. L., Jenness, J., Abela, J. R. Z., & Smolen, A. (2011). Interaction of 5-HTTLPR and idiographic stressors predicts prospective depressive symptoms specifically among youth in a multiwave design. *Journal of Clinical Child and Adolescent Psychology, 40*, 572–585. doi:10.1080/15374416.2011.581613
Hankin, B. L., Wetter, E., & Cheely, C. (2008). Sex differences in child and adolescent depression. In J. R. Z. Abela & B. L. Hankin (Eds.), *Handbook of depression in children and adolescents* (pp. 377–414). New York: Guilford Press.
Hanley, G. P., Iwata, B. A., & McCord, B. E. (2003). Functional analysis of problem behavior: A review. *Journal of Applied Behavior Analysis, 36*, 147–185. doi:10.1901/jaba.2003.36-147
Hanna, G. (1995). Demographic and clinical features of obsessive-compulsive disorder in children and adolescents. *Journal of the American Academy of Child & Adolescent Psychiatry, 34*, 19–27. doi:10.1097/00004583-199501000-00009
Hannesdottir, D. K., & Ollendick, T. H. (2007). The role of emotion regulation in the treatment of child anxiety disorders. *Clinical Child and Family Psychology Review, 10*, 275–293. doi:10.1007/s10567-007-0024-6
Happé, F. G. E. (1994a). Current psychological theories of autism: The "theory of mind" account and rival theories. *Journal of Child Psychology and Psychiatry, 35*, 215–230. doi:10.1111/j.1469-7610.1994.tb01159.x
Happé, F. G. E. (1994b). Wechsler IQ profile and theory of mind in autism: A research note. *Journal of Child Psychology and Psychiatry, 35*, 1461–1471. doi:10.1111/j.1469-7610.1994.tb01287.x
Happé, F. G. E. (1995a). The role of age and verbal ability in the theory of mind task performance of subjects with autism. *Child Development, 66*, 843–855. doi:10.1111/j.1467-8624.1995.tb00909.x
Happé, F. G. E. (1995b, March). *Wechsler IQ profile and theory of mind in autism*. Paper presented at the biennial meeting of the Society for Research in Child Development, Indianapolis, IN.
Happé, F .G. E., & Frith, U. (1996). The neuropsychology of autism. *Brain, 119*, 1377–1400. doi:10.1093/brain/119.4.1377
Harden, K. P., D'Onofrio, B. M., Van Hulle, C., Turkheimer, E., Rodgers, J. L., Waldman, I. D., & Lahey, B. B. (2009). Population density and youth antisocial behavior. *Journal of Child Psychology and Psychiatry, 50*, 999–1009. doi:10.1111/j.1469-7610.2009.02044.x
Harden, K. P., & Mendle, J. (2012). Gene-environment interplay in the association between pubertal timing and delinquency in adolescent girls. *Journal of Abnormal Psychology, 121*, 73–87. doi:10.1037/a0024160
Hare, R. D. (1993). *Without conscience: The disturbing world of the psychopaths among us*. New York: Pocketbooks.
Harkness, K. L., Lumley, M. N., & Truss, A. E. (2008). Stress generation in adolescent depression: The moderating role of child abuse and neglect. *Journal of Abnormal Child Psychology, 36*, 421–432. doi:10.1007/s10802-007-9188-2

Harmon, H., Langley, A., & Ginsburg, G. S. (2006). The role of gender and culture in treating youth with anxiety disorders. *Journal of Cognitive Psychotherapy, 20*, 301–310. doi:10.1891/088983906780644000

Harrington, J. A., Rosen, L., Garneco, A., & Patrick, P. A. (2006). Parental perceptions and use of complementary and alternative medicine practices for children with autistic spectrum disorders in private practice. *Journal of Developmental and Behavioral Pediatrics, 27*(Suppl.), S156–S161. doi:10.1097/00004703-200604002-00014

Harris, J. C. (2006). *Intellectual disability: Understanding its development, causes, classification, evaluation, and treatment.* Oxford, England: Oxford University Press.

Harris, S. L., Handleman, J. S., & Jennett, H. K. (2005). Models of educational intervention for students with autism: Home, center, and school based programming. In F. R. Volkmar, R. Paul, A. Klin, & D. Cohen (Eds.), *Handbook of autism and pervasive developmental disorders: Vol. 2. Assessment, interventions, and policy* (3rd ed., pp. 1043–1054). Hoboken, NJ: Wiley.

Hart, L. M., Granillo, M. T., Jorm, A. F., & Paxton, S. J. (2011). Unmet need for treatment in the eating disorders: A systematic review of eating disorder specific treatment seeking among community cases. *Clinical Psychology Review, 31*, 727–735. doi:10.1016/j.cpr.2011.03.004

Hart, S., Jones, N. A., & Field, T. (2003). Atypical expressions of jealousy in infants of intrusive- and withdrawn-depressed mothers. *Child Psychiatry and Human Development, 33*, 193–207. doi:10.1023/A:1021452529762

Hartmann, D. P., Pelzel, K. E., & Abbott, C. B. (2011). Design, measurement, and analysis in developmental research. In M. H. Bornstein & M. E. Lamb (Eds.), *Cognitive development: An advanced textbook* (pp. 125–213). New York: Psychology Press.

Hartmann, T. (1993). *Attention deficit disorder: A different perception.* Lancaster, PA: Underwood-Miller.

Hartung, C. M., & Widiger, T. A. (1998). Gender differences in the diagnosis of mental disorders. Conclusions and controversies of DSM-IV. *Psychological Bulletin, 123*, 260–278. doi:10.1037/0033-2909.123.3.260

Hartup, W. W. (1996). The company they keep: Friendships and their developmental significance. *Child Development, 67*, 1–13. doi:10.1111/j.1467-8624.1996.tb01714.x

Harvey, S. T., & Taylor, J. E. (2010). A meta-analysis of the effects of psychotherapy with sexually abused children and adolescents. *Clinical Psychology Review, 30*, 517–535. doi:10.1016/j.cpr.2010.03.006

Haskett, M. E., Nears, K., Ward, C. S., & McPherson, A. V. (2006). Diversity in adjustment of maltreated children: Factors associated with resilient functioning. *Clinical Psychology Review, 26*, 796–812.

Haskett, M. E., Smith Scott, S., & Sabourin Ward, C. (2004). Subgroups of physically abusive parents based on cluster analysis of parenting behavior and affect. *American Journal of Orthopsychiatry, 74*, 436–447.

Hassan, A., Agha, S. S., Langley, K., & Thapar, A. (2011). Prevalence of bipolar disorder in children and adolescents with attention-deficit hyperactivity disorder. *The British Journal of Psychiatry, 198*, 195–198. doi:10.1192/bjp.bp.110.078741

Hastings, P. D., Zahn-Waxler, C., Robinson, J., Usher, B., & Bridges, D. (2000). The development of concern for others in children with behavior problems. *Developmental Psychology, 36*, 531–546. doi:10.1037/0012-1649.36.5.531

Hastings, P. D., Zahn-Waxler, C., & Usher, B. A. (2007). Cardiovascular and affective responses to social stress in adolescents with internalizing and externalizing problems. *International Journal of Behavioral Development, 31*, 77–87. doi:10.1177/0165025407073575

Hatch, M. L., Friedman, S., & Paradis, C. M. (1996). Behavioral treatment of obsessive-compulsive disorder in African Americans. *Cognitive and Behavioral Practice, 3*, 303–315. doi:10.1016/S1077-7229(96)80020-4

Hatch, S. L., Harvey, S. B., & Maughan, B. (2010). A developmental-contextual approach to understanding mental health and well-being in early adulthood. *Social Science & Medicine, 70*, 261–268. doi:10.1016/j.socscimed.2009.10.005

Hatcher, P. J., Hulme, C., Miles, J. N. V., Carroll, J. M., Hatcher, J., Gibbs, S., . . . Snowling, M. J. (2006). Efficacy of small group reading intervention for beginning readers with reading-delay: A randomised controlled trial. *Journal of Child Psychology and Psychiatry, 47*, 820–827. doi:10.1111/j.1469-7610.2005.01559.x

Havermans, T., Wuytack, L., Deboel, J., Tijtgat, A., Malfroot, A., De Boeck, C., & Proesmans, M. (2011). Siblings of children with cystic fibrosis: Quality of life and the impact of illness. *Child: Care, Health and Development, 37*, 252–260. doi:10.1111/j.1365-2214.2010.01165.x

Hawke, J. L., Olson, R. K., Willcut, E. G., Wadsworth, S. J., & DeFries, J. C. (2009). Gender ratios for reading difficulties. *Dyslexia: An International Journal of Research and Practice, 15*, 239–242. doi:10.1002/dys.v15:310.1002/dys.389

Hay, I., Elias, G., Fielding-Barnsley, R., Homel, R., & Freiberg, K. (2007). Language delays, reading delays, and learning difficulties: Interactive elements requiring multidimensional programming. *Journal of Learning Disabilities, 40*, 400–409. doi:10.1177/00222194070400050301

Haynes, S. N., & Heiby, E. M. (Eds.). (2004). *Comprehensive handbook of psychological assessment: Vol. 3. Behavioral assessment.* New York: Wiley.

Haynes, S. N., Mumma, G. H., & Pinson, C. (2009). Idiographic assessment: Conceptual and psychometric foundations of individualized behavioral assessment. *Clinical Psychology Review, 29*, 179–191. doi:10.1016/j.cpr.2008.12.003

Haynes, S. N., Smith, G. T., & Hunsley, J. (2011). *Scientific foundations of clinical assessment.* New York: Routledge, Taylor, & Francis.

Haynos, A. F., & Fruzzetti, A. E. (2011). Anorexia nervosa as a disorder of emotional dysregulation: Evidence and treatment implications. *Clinical Psychology: Science and Practice, 18*, 183–202. doi:10.1111/j.1468-2850.2011.01250.x

Hayward, C., Gotlib, I. H., Schraedley, P. K., & Litt, I. F. (1999). Ethnic differences in the association between pubertal status and symptoms of depression in adolescent girls. *Journal of Adolescent Health, 25*, 143–149. doi:10.1016/S1054-139X(99)00048-8

Hayward, C., Killen, J. D., Hammer, L. D., Litt, I. F., Wilson, D. M., Simmonds, B., & Taylor, C. B. (1992). Pubertal stage and panic attack history in sixth-and seventh-grade girls. *American Journal of Psychiatry, 149*, 1239–1243. Retrieved from http://ajp.psychiatryonline.org/index.dtl

Hayward, C., Killen, J. D., Wilson, D. M., & Hammer, L. D. (1997). Psychiatric risk associated with early puberty in adolescent girls. *Journal of the American Academy of Child & Adolescent Psychiatry, 36*, 255–262. doi:10.1097/00004583-199702000-00017

Hazlett, H. C., Hammer, J., Hooper, S. R., & Kamphaus, R. W. (2011). *Down syndrome.* New York: Guilford Press.

Health Resources and Services Administration. (2010). *Health professional shortage areas: Mental health designated populations. Rural Assistance Center.* Retrieved June 16, 2011 from www.raconline.org/maps/mapfiles/hpsa_mental.png

Hebebrand, J., Schrag, A., Schimmelmann, B. G., & Hinney, A. (2010). Child and adolescent psychiatric genetics. *European Child Adolescent Psychiatry, 19*, 259–279. doi:10.1007/s00787-010-0091-y

Hechtman, L. (2006). Long-term treatment of children and adolescents with attention-deficit/hyperactivity disorder (ADHD). *Current Psychiatry Reports, 8*, 398–408. doi:10.1007/s11920-006-0043-x

Hedley, A. A., Ogden, C. L., Johnson, C. L., Carroll, M. D., Curtin, L. R., Flegal, K. M. (2004). Prevalence of overweight and obesity among US children, adolescents, and adults, 1999-2002. *JAMA: Journal of the American Medical Association, 291*, 2847–2850. doi:10.1001/jama.291.23.2847

Hedley, M. (2002). The geometry of gendered conflict in popular film: 1986–2000. *Sex Roles, 47*(5–6), 201–217.

Heflinger, C. A., & Hinshaw, S. P. (2010). Stigma in child and adolescent mental health services research: Understanding professional and institutional stigmatization of youth with mental health problems and their families. *Administration and Policy in Mental Health and Mental Health Services Research, 37*(1-2), 61–70. doi:10.1007/s10488-010-0294-z

Heim, C., & Nemeroff, C. B. (2001). The role of childhood trauma in the neurobiology of mood and anxiety disorders: Preclinical and clinical studies. *Biological Psychiatry, 49*, 1023–1039. doi:10.1016/S0006-3223(01)01157-X

Heim, C., Shugart, M., Craighead, W. E., & Nemeroff, C. B. (2010). Neurobiological and psychiatric consequences of child abuse and neglect.

Developmental Psychobiology, 52, 671–690. doi.10.1002/dev.20494

Heim, S., & Benasich, A. A. (2006). Developmental disorders of language. In D. Cicchetti & D. J. Cohen (Eds.), *Developmental psychopathology, Vol. 3. Risk, disorder, and adaptation* (2nd ed., pp. 268–316). Hoboken, NJ: Wiley.

Helland, W. A., Biringer, E., Helland, T., & Heimann, M. (2012). Exploring language profiles for children with ADHD and children with Asperger Syndrome. *Journal of Attention Disorders, 16*, 34–43. doi:10.1177/1087054710378233

Henderson, H. A., & Wachs, T. D. (2007). Temperament theory and the study of cognition-emotion interactions across development. *Developmental Review, 27*, 396–427. doi:10.1016/j.dr.2007.06.004

Hendren, R. L., De Backer, I., & Pandina, G. J. (2000). Review of neuroimaging studies of child and adolescent psychiatric disorders from the past 10 years. *Journal of the American Academy of Child & Adolescent Psychiatry, 39*, 815–828. doi:10.1097/00004583-200007000-00010

Hendry, C. N. (2000). Childhood disintegrative disorder: Should it be considered a distinct diagnosis? *Clinical Psychology Review, 20*, 77–90. doi:10.1016/S0272-7358(98)00094-4

Henggeler, S. W. (1996). Treatment of violent juvenile offenders—We have the knowledge: Comment on Gorman-Smith et al. (1996). *Journal of Family Psychology, 10*, 137–141. doi:10.1037/0893-3200.10.2.137

Henggeler, S. W., Chapman, J. E., Rowland, M. D., Halliday-Boykins, C. A., Randall, J., Shackelford, J., & Schoenwald, S. K. (2008). Statewide adoption and initial implementation of contingency management for substance-abusing adolescents. *Journal of Consulting and Clinical Psychology, 76*, 556–567. doi:10.1037/0022-006X.76.4.556

Henggeler, S. W., Melton, G. B., & Smith, L. A. (1992). Family preservation using multisystemic therapy: An effective alternative to incarcerating serious juvenile offenders. *Journal of Consulting and Clinical Psychology, 60*, 953–961. doi:10.1037/0022-006X.60.6.953

Henggeler, S. W., & Santos, A. B. (Eds.). (1997). *Innovative approaches for difficult-to-treat populations*. Washington, DC: American Psychiatric Press.

Henggeler, S. W., & Schaeffer, C. (2010). Treating serious antisocial behavior using multisystemic therapy. In J. R. Weisz & A. E. Kazdin (Eds.), *Evidence-based psychotherapies for children and adolescents* (2nd ed., pp. 259–276). New York: Guilford.

Henggeler, S. W., Schoenwald, S. K., Borduin, C. M., Rowland, M. D., & Cunningham, P. B. (2009). *Multisystemic therapy for antisocial behavior in children and adolescents* (2nd ed.). New York: Guilford Press.

Herba, C. M., Roza, S. J., Govaert, P., van Rossum, J., Hofman, A., Jaddoe, V.,. . . Tiemeier, H. (2010). Infant brain development and vulnerability to later internalizing difficulties: The Generation R Study. *Journal of the American Academy of Child & Adolescent Psychiatry, 49*, 1053–1063. doi:10.1016/j.jaac.2010.07.003

Herman, J. L. (1992). *Trauma and recovery: The aftermath of violence—from domestic abuse to political terror*. New York: Basic Books.

Hermann, C. (2011). Psychological interventions for chronic pediatric pain: State of the art, current developments and open questions. *Pain Management, 1*, 473–483. doi:10.2217/pmt.11.48

Herndon, R. W., & Iacono, W. G. (2005). Psychiatric disorder in the children of antisocial parents. *Psychological Medicine, 35*, 1815–1824. doi:10.1017/S0033291705005635

Herrenkohl, R. C., Herrenkohl, E. C., & Egolf, B. P. (1983). Circumstances surrounding the occurrence of child maltreatment. *Journal of Consulting and Clinical Psychology, 51*, 424–431. doi:10.1037/0022-006X.51.3.424

Herrmann, E., Call, J., Hernández-Lloreda, M. V., Hare, B., & Tomasello, M. (2007). Humans have evolved specialized skills of social cognition: The cultural intelligence hypothesis. *Science, 317*, 1360–1366. doi:10.1126/science.1146282

Hershkowitz, I., & Lamb, M. (2007). Victimization of children with disabilities. *American Journal of Orthopsychiatry, 77*, No. 4, 629–635.

Herzog, D. B., & Eddy, K. T. (2007). Diagnosis, epidemiology, and clinical course of eating disorders. In J. Yager & P. Powers (Eds.), *Clinical manual of eating disorders* (pp. 1–29). Washington, DC: American Psychiatric Press.

Hetherington, E. M., Bridges, M., & Insabella, G. M. (1998). What matters? What does not? Five perspectives on the association between marital transitions and children's adjustment. *American Psychologist, 53*, 167–184. doi:10.1037/0003-066X.53.2.167

Hetrick, S. E., McKenzie, J. E., & Merry, S. N. (2010). The use of SSRIs in children and adolescents. *Current Opinion in Psychiatry, 23*, 53–57. doi:10.1097/YCO.0b013e328334bc92

Hildyard, K., & Wolfe, D. A. (2002). Child neglect: Developmental issues and outcomes. *Child Abuse & Neglect, 26*, 679–695.

Hildyard, K., & Wolfe, D. A. (2007). Understanding child neglect: Cognitive processes underlying neglectful parenting. *Child Abuse & Neglect, 31*, 895–907.

Hill, E. L. (2004). Executive dysfunction in autism. *Trends in Cognitive Sciences, 8*, 26–32. doi:10.1016/j.tics.2003.11.003

Hillberg, T., Hamilton-Giachritsis, C., & Dixon, L. (2011). Review of meta-analyses on the association between child sexual abuse and adult mental health difficulties: A systematic approach. *Trauma, Violence, & Abuse, 12*, 38–49. doi:10.1177/1524838010386812

Hinshaw, S. P. (1992). Externalizing behavior problems and academic underachievement in childhood and adolescence: Causal relationships and underlying mechanisms. *Psychological Bulletin, 111*, 127–155. doi:10.1037/0033-2909.111.1.127

Hinshaw, S. P. (2007). Moderators and mediators of treatment outcome for youth with ADHD: Understanding for whom and how treatments work. *Ambulatory Pediatrics, 7*(Suppl. 1), 91–100. doi:10.1093/jpepsy/jsl055

Hinshaw, S. P. (2007a). *The mark of shame: Stigma of mental illness and an agenda for change*. New York: Oxford University Press.

Hinshaw, S. P. (2008). Lessons from research on the developmental psychopathology of girls and women. *Journal of the American Academy of Child & Adolescent Psychiatry, 47*, 359–361. doi:10.1097/CHI.0b013e3181647ba0

Hinshaw, S. P., & Blachman, D. R. (2005). Attention-deficit/hyperactivity disorder in girls. In D. Bell, S. L. Foster, & E. J. Mash (Eds.), *Handbook of behavioral and emotional problems in girls* (pp. 117–147). New York: Kluwer.

Hinshaw, S. P., Carte, E. T., Fan, C., Jassy, S., & Owens, E. B. (2007). Neuropsychological functioning of girls with attention-deficit/ hyperactivity disorder: Evidence for continuing deficits? *Neuropsychology, 21*, 263–273. doi:10.1037/0894-4105.21.2.263

Hinshaw, S. P., & Lee, S. S. (2003). Conduct and oppositional defiant disorders. In E. J. Mash & R. A. Barkley (Eds.), *Child psychopathology* (2nd. ed., pp. 144–198). New York: Guilford Press.

Hinshaw, S. P., Owens, E. B., Sami, N., & Fargeon, S. (2006). Prospective follow-up of girls with attention-deficit/hyperactivity disorder into adolescence: Evidence for continuing cross-domain impairment. *Journal of Consulting and Clinical Psychology, 74*, 489–499. doi:10.1037/0022-006X.74.3.489

Hinshaw, S. P., & Stier, A. (2008). Stigma as related to mental disorders. *Annual Review of Clinical Psychology, 4*, 367–393. doi:10.1146/annurev.clinpsy.4.022007.141245

Hinton, E. C., Isles, A. R., Williams, N. M., & Parkinson, J. A. (2010). Excessive appetitive arousal in Prader–Willi syndrome. *Appetite, 54*, 225–228. doi:10.1016/j.appet.2009.12.002

Hirschi, T., & Gottfredson, M. (1983). Age and the explanation of crime. *American Journal of Sociology, 89*, 552–583. doi:10.1086/227905

Hirshfeld, D. R., Biederman, J., & Rosenbaum, J. F. (1997). Expressed emotion toward children with behavioral inhibition: Associations with maternal anxiety disorder. *Journal of the American Academy of Child & Adolescent Psychiatry, 36*, 910–919. doi:10.1097/00004583-199707000-00012

Hirshfeld-Becker, D. R., Masek, B., Henin, A., Blakely, L. R., Pollock-Wurman, R. A., McQuade, J., …Biederman, J. (2010). Cognitive behavior therapy for 4- to 7-year-old children with anxiety disorders: A randomized clinical trial. *Journal of Consulting and Clinical Psychology, 78*, 498–510. doi:10.1037/a0019055

Ho, H. Y., Cheung, M. C., & Chan, A. S. (2003). Music training improves verbal but not visual memory: Cross-sectional and longitudinal explorations in children. *Neuropsychology, 17*, 439–450. doi:10.1037/0894-4105.17.3.439

Hoagwood, K. E., & Cavaleri, M. A. (2010). Ethical issues in child and adolescent psychosocial treatment research. In J. R.

Weisz & A. E. Kazdin (Eds.), *Evidence-based psychotherapy for children and adolescents* (2nd ed., 10–27). New York: Guilford Press.

Hobson, R. P. (2002/2004). *The cradle of thought*. London/New York: Macmillan/Oxford University Press.

Hodapp, R. M. (2007). Families of persons with Down syndrome: New perspectives, findings, and research and service needs. *Mental Retardation and Developmental Disabilities Research Reviews [Special issue: Down syndrome], 13*, 279–287. doi:10.1002/mrdd.20160

Hodapp, R. M., & Burack, J. A. (2006). Developmental approaches to children with mental retardation: A second generation? In D. Cicchetti & D. J. Cohen (Eds.), *Developmental psychopathology, Vol. 3: Risk, disorder, and adaptation* (2nd ed., pp. 235–267). Hoboken, NJ: Wiley.

Hodapp, R. M., & Dykens, E. M. (2003). Mental retardation (intellectual disabilities). In E. J. Mash & R. A. Barkley (Eds.), *Child psychopathology* (2nd ed., pp. 486–519). New York: Guilford Press.

Hodapp, R. M., & Dykens, E. M. (2009). Intellectual disabilities and child psychiatry: Looking to the future. *Journal of Child Psychology and Psychiatry, 50*, 99–107. doi:10.1111/j.1469-7610.2008.02038.x

Hodapp, R. M., Kazemi, E., Rosner, B. A., & Dykens, E. M. (2006). Mental retardation. In D. A. Wolfe & E. J. Mash (Eds.), *Behavioral and emotional disorders in adolescents: Nature, assessment, and treatment* (pp. 383–409). New York: Guilford Press.

Hodapp, R. M., Thornton-Wells, T. A., & Dykens, E. M. (2009). Intellectual disabilities. In C. H. Zeanah Jr. (Ed.), *Handbook of infant mental health* (3rd ed., pp. 332–344). New York: Guilford Press.

Hodge, S. M., Makris, N., Kennedy, D. N., Caviness Jr., V. S., Howard, J., McGrath, L., . . . Harris, G. J. (2010). Cerebellum, language and cognition in autism and specific language impairment. *Journal of Autism and Developmental Disorders, 40*, 300–316. doi:10.1007/s10803-009-0872-7

Hodgins, S., Faucher, B., Zarac, A., & Ellenbogen, M. (2002). Children of parents with bipolar disorder: A population at high risk for major affective disorders. *Child and Adolescent Psychiatric Clinics of North America, 11*, 533–553. doi:10.1016/S1056-4993(02)00002-0

Hodgins, S., Kratzer, L., & McNeil, T. F. (2001). Obstetrical complications, parenting, and risk of criminal behavior. *Archives of General Psychiatry, 58*, 746–752. doi:10.1001/archpsyc.58.8.746

Hoeve, M., Blokland, A., Dubas, J. S., Loeber, R., Gerris, J. R. M., & van der Laan, P. H. (2008). Trajectories of delinquency and parenting styles. *Journal of Abnormal Child Psychology, 36*, 223–235. doi:10.1007/s10802-007-9172-x

Hoffman, E. C., & Mattis, S. G. (2000). A developmental adaptation of panic control treatment for panic disorder in adolescence. *Cognitive and Behavioral Practice, 7*, 253–261. doi:10.1016/S1077-7229(00)80081-4

Hoffmann, H. (1845). *Struwwelpeter.* London: Blackie.

Hofmann, S., Albano, A. M., Heimberg, R. G., Tracey, S., Chorpita, B. F., & Barlow, D. H. (1999). Subtypes of social phobia in adolescents. *Depression and Anxiety, 9*, 15–18. doi:10.1002/(SICI)1520-6394(1999)9:1<15::AID-DA2>3.0.CO;2-6

Hollway, J. A., & Anan, M. G. (2011). Sleep correlates of pervasive developmental disorders: A review of the literature. *Research in Developmental Disabilities, 32*, 1399–1421. doi:10.1016/j.ridd.2011.04.001

Holmans, P., Weissman, M. M., Zubenko, G. S., Scheftner, W. A., Crowe, R. R., Depaulo, J. R., Jr., . . . Levinson, D. F. (2007). Genetics of early-onset major depression (GenRED): Final genome scan report. *American Journal of Psychiatry, 164*, 248–258. doi:10.1176/appi.ajp.164.2.248

Holmbeck, G. N., Friedman, D., Abad, M., & Jandasek, B. (2006). Development and psychopathology in adolescence. In D. A. Wolfe & E. J. Mash (Eds.), *Behavioral and emotional disorders in adolescents: Nature, assessment, and treatment* (pp. 21–55). New York: Guilford Press.

Holmes, F. B. (1936). An experimental investigation of a method of overcoming children's fears. *Child Development, 7*, 6–30. doi:10.2307/1125540

Holmes, J., Gathercole, S. E., Place, M., Alloway, T. P., Elliott, J. G., & Hilton, K. A. (2010). The diagnostic utility of executive function assessments in the identification of ADHD in children. *Child and Adolescent Mental Health, 15*, 37–43. doi:10.1111/j.1475-3588.2009.00536.x

Holzer, S. R., Uppala, S., Wonderlich, S. A., Crosby, R. D., & Simonich, H. (2008). Mediational significance of PTSD in the relationship of sexual trauma and eating disorders. *Child Abuse & Neglect, 32*, 561–566. doi:10.1016/j.chiabu.2007.07.011

Honey, E., McConachie, H., Randle, V., Shearer, H., & Le Couteur, A. S. (2008). One-year change in repetitive behaviours in young children with communication disorders including autism. *Journal of Autism and Developmental Disorders, 38*, 1439–1450. doi:10.1007/s10803-006-0191-1

Hooper, S. R., Costa, L., McBee, M., Anderson, K. L., Yerby, D. C., Knuth, S. B., & Childress, A. (2011). Concurrent and longitudinal neuropsychological contributors to written language expression in first and second grade students. *Reading and Writing, 24*, 221–252. doi:10.1007/s11145-010-9263-x

Hoover, D. W., & Milich, R. (1994). Effects of sugar ingestion expectancies on mother-child interactions. *Journal of Abnormal Child Psychology, 22*, 501–514. doi:10.1007/BF02168088

Horowitz, J. L., & Garber, J. (2006). The prevention of depressive symptoms in children and adolescents: A meta-analytic review. *Journal of Consulting and Clinical Psychology, 74*, 401–415. doi:10.1037/0022-006X.74.3.401

Horst, R. (2009). Diagnostic issues in childhood bipolar disorder. *Psychiatric Clinics of North America, 32*, 71–80. doi:10.1016/j.psc.2008.11.005

Houts, A. C. (2010). Behavioral treatment for enuresis. In J. R. Weisz & A. E. Kazdin (Eds.), *Evidence-based psychotherapies for children and adolescents* (2nd ed., pp. 359–374). New York: Guilford Press.

Howard, A. L., Robinson, M., Smith, G. J., Ambrosini, G. L., Piek, J. P., & Oddy, W. H. (2011). ADHD is associated with a "Western" dietary pattern in adolescents. *Journal of Attention Disorders, 15*, 403–411. doi:10.1177/1087054710365990

Howard, J. S., Sparkman, C. R., Cohen, H. G., Green, G., & Stanislaw, H. (2005). A comparison of intensive behavior analytic and eclectic treatment for young children with autism. *Research in Developmental Disabilities, 26*, 359–383. doi:10.1016/j.ridd.2004.09.005

Howell, P. (2011). *Recovery from stuttering*. New York: Psychology Press.

Howell, P., & Davis, S. (2011). Predicting persistence of and recovery from stuttering by the teenage years based on information gathered at age 8 years. *Journal of Developmental and Behavioral Pediatrics, 32*, 196–205. doi:10.1097/DBP.0b013e31820fd4a9

Howes, O. D., & Falkenberg, I. (2011). Early detection and intervention in bipolar affective disorder: Targeting the development of the disorder. *Current Psychiatry Reports*. Advance online publication. doi:10.1007/s11920-011-0229-8

Howland, L. C., Storm, D. S., Crawford, S. L., Ma, Y., Gortmaker, S. L., & Oleske, J. M. (2007). Negative life events: Risk to health-related quality of life in children and youth with HIV infection. *JANAC: Journal of the Association of Nurses in AIDS Care, 18*, 3–11. doi:10.1016/j.jana.2006.11.008

Howlin, P., Goode, S., Hutton, J., & Rutter, M. (2004). Adult outcome for children with autism. *Journal of Child Psychology and Psychiatry, 45*, 212–229. doi:10.1111/j.1469-7610.2004.00215.x

Hoza, B. (2007). Peer functioning in children with ADHD. *Journal of Pediatric Psychology, 32*, 655–663. doi:10.1093/jpepsy/jsm024

Hoza, B., Mrug, S., Gerdes, A. C., Hinshaw, S. P., Bukowski, W. M., Gold, J. A., . . . Arnold, L. E. (2005). What aspects of peer relationships are impaired in children with attention-deficit/hyperactivity disorder? *Journal of Consulting and Clinical Psychology, 73*, 411–423. doi:10.1037/0022-006X.73.3.411

Hoza, B., Murray-Close, D., Arnold, L. E., Hinshaw, S. P., Hechtman, L., and the MTA Cooperative Group (2010). Time-dependent changes in positively biased self-perceptions of children with attention-deficit/hyperactivity disorder: A developmental psychopathology perspective. *Development and Psychopathology, 22*, 375–390. doi:10.1017/S095457941000012X

Hoza, B., Waschbusch, D. A., Pelham, W. E., Molina, B. S. G., & Milich, R. (2000). Attention-deficit/hyperactivity disordered and control boys' responses to social success and failure. *Child Development, 71*, 432–446. doi:10.1111/1467-8624.00155

Huck, S., Kemp, C., & Carter, M. (2010). Self-concept of children with intellectual disability in mainstream settings. *Journal of Intellectual and Developmental Disability, 35*, 141–154. doi:10.3109/13668250.2010.489226

Hudson, J. I., Hiripi, E., Pope, H. G., & Kessler, R. C. (2007). The prevalence and correlates of eating disorders in the National Comorbidity Survey Replication. *Biological Psychiatry, 61*, 348–358. doi:10.1016/j.biopsych.2006.03.040

Huebner, T., Vloet, T. D., Marx, I., Konrad, K., Fink, G. R., Herpertz, S. C., & Herpertz-Dahlmann, B. (2008). Morphometric brain abnormalities in boys with conduct disorder. *Journal of the American Academy of Child & Adolescent Psychiatry, 47*, 540–547. doi:10.1097/CHI.0b013e3181676545

Huemer, J., Erhart, F., & Steiner, H. (2010). Posttraumatic stress disorder in children and adolescents: A review of psychopharmacological treatment. *Child Psychiatry and Human Development, 41*, 624–640. doi:10.1007/s10578-010-0192-3

Huesmann, L. R., Eron, L. D., Lefkowitz, M. M., & Walder, L. O. (1984). Stability of aggression over time and generations. *Developmental Psychology, 20*, 1120–1134. doi:10.1037/0012-1649.20.6.1120

Huesmann, L. R., Moise-Titus, J., Podolski, C., & Eron, L. D. (2003). Longitudinal relations between children's exposure to TV violence and their aggressive and violent behavior in young adulthood: 1977–1992. *Developmental Psychology, 39*, 201–221. doi:10.1037/0012-1649.39.2.201

Huey, S. J., & Polo, A. J. (2008). Evidence-based treatment for minority youth: A review and meta-analysis. *Journal of Clinical Child and Adolescent Psychology, 37*, 262–301. doi:10.1080/15374410701820174

Huizink, A. C., Mulder, E. J. H., & Buitelaar, J. K (2004). Prenatal stress and risk for psychopathology: Specific effects or induction of general susceptibility. *Psychological Bulletin, 130*, 115–142. doi:10.1037/0033-2909.130.1.115

Hulley, A., Currie, A., Njenga, F., & Hill, A. (2007). Eating disorders in elite female distance runners: Effects of nationality and running environment. *Psychology of Sport and Exercise, 8*, 521–533. doi:10.1016/j.psychsport.2006.07.001

Hunsley, J., & Mash, E. J. (Eds.). (2008). *A guide to assessments that work*. New York: Oxford University Press.

Hunt, P., & McDonnell, J. (2007). Inclusive education. In S. L. Odom, R. H. Horner, M. E. Snell, & J. Blacher (Eds.), *Handbook of developmental disabilities* (pp. 269–291). New York: Guilford Press.

Huppke, P., Held, M., Laccone, F., & Hanefeld, F. (2003). The spectrum of phenotypes in females with Rett syndrome. *Brain & Development, 25*, 346–351. doi:10.1016/S0387-7604(03)00018-4

Hurlbert, R. T., Happé, F., & Frith, U. (1994). Sampling the form of inner experience in three adults with Asperger syndrome. *Psychological Medicine, 24*, 385–395. doi:10.1017/S0033291700027367

Hurt, E. A., Arnold, L. E., & Lofthouse, N. (2011). Dietary and nutritional treatments for attention-deficit/hyperactivity disorder: Current research support and recommendations for practitioners. *Current Psychiatry Reports, 13*, 323–332. doi:10.1007/s11920-011-0217-z

Huss, M., Verney, J. P., Fosker, T., Mead, N., & Goswami, U. (2011). Music, rhythm, rise time perception and developmental dyslexia: Perception of musical meter predicts reading and phonology. *Cortex: A Journal Devoted to the Study of the Nervous System and Behavior, 47*, 674–689. doi:10.1016/j.cortex.2010.07.010

Hussong, A., Bauer, D., & Chassin, L. (2008). Telescoped trajectories from alcohol initiation to disorder in children of alcoholic parents. *Journal of Abnormal Psychology, 117*, 63–78. doi:10.1037/0021-843X.117.1.63

Hussong, A. M., Flora, D. B., Curran, P. J., Chassin, L. A., & Zucker, R. A. (2008). Defining risk heterogeneity for internalizing symptoms among children of alcoholic parents. *Development and Psychopathology, 20*, 165–193. doi:10.1017/S0954579408000084

Hysing, M., Elgen, I., Gillberg, C., & Lundervold, A. J. (2009). Emotional and behavioural problems in subgroups of children with chronic illness: Results from a large-scale population study. *Child: Care, Health and Development, 35*, 527–533. doi:10.1111/j.1365-2214.2009.00967.x

Ialongo, N., Edelsohn, G., Werthamer-Larsson, L., Crockett, L., & Kellam, S. (1995). The significance of self-reported anxious symptoms in first grade children: Prediction to anxious symptoms and adaptive functioning in fifth grade. *Journal of Child Psychology and Psychiatry, 36*, 427–437. doi:10.1111/j.1469-7610.1995.tb01300.x

Ialongo, N. S., Rogosch, F. A., Cicchetti, D., Toth, S. L., Buckley, L., Petras, H., & Neiderhiser, J. (2006). A developmental psychopathology approach to the prevention of mental health disorders. In D. Cicchetti & D. J. Cohen (Eds.), *Developmental psychopathology: Vol. 1. Theory and method* (2nd ed., pp. 968–1018). New York: Wiley.

Illick, J. E. (1974). Childrearing in seventeenth century England and America. In L. deMause (Ed.), *The history of childhood* (pp. 303–350). New York: Psychohistory Press.

Ilott, N., Saudino, K. J., Wood, A., & Asherson, P. (2010). A genetic study of ADHD and activity level in infancy. *Genes, Brain, and Behavior, 9*, 296–304. doi:10.1111/j.1601-183X.2009.00560.x

In M. Dulcan (Ed.), *Dulcan's textbook of child and adolescent psychiatry* (pp. 325–338). Arlington, VA: American Psychiatric Publishing, Inc.

Inderbitzen-Nolan, H. M., & Walters, K. S. (2000). Social anxiety scale for adolescents: Normative data and further evidence of construct validity. *Journal of Clinical Child Psychology, 29*, 360–371. doi:10.1207/S15374424JCCP2903_7

Individuals with Disabilities Education Improvement Act. (2004). *Public Law No. 108–446*. Washington, DC: U.S. Government Printing Office.

Individuals with Disabilities Education Improvement Act (IDEA). (2004). *Public Law No. 104–446*. Retrieved from http://idea.ed.gov/explore/view/p/%2Croot%2Cstatute%2CJ

Ingman, K. A., Ollendick, T. H., & Akande, A. (1999). Cross-cultural aspects of fears in African children and adolescents. *Behaviour Research and Therapy, 37*, 337–345. doi:10.1016/S0005-7967(98)00108-9

Innocenti, G. M. (1982). Development of interhemispheric cortical connections. *Neurosciences Research Program Bulletin, 20*, 532–540. Retrieved from http://www.nsi.edu/

Insel, T. (2010, October 7). *Brain scans: Not quite ready for prime time*. NIMH, Director's Blog. Retrieved from http://www.nimh.nih.gov/about/director/2010/brain-scans-not-quite-ready-for-prime-time.shtml

Institute of Education Sciences. (2010, August). Early childhood education intervention for children with disabilities: Lovaas Model of Applied Behavior Analysis. *WWC Intervention Report*, pp. 1–10, U.S. Department of Education. Retrieved from http://ies.ed.gov/ncee/wwc/reports/ece_cd/lovaas_model/effectiveness.asp

Institute of Medicine. (2004). *Immunization safety review: Vaccines and autism*. Washington, DC: Author.

Interactive Autism Network. (2011, September). *Interactive Autism Network (IAN): Linking the autism community and researchers*. Retrieved from: http://www.ianproject.org/

Interagency Autism Coordinating Committee (IACC). (2011, January). *2011 IACC Strategic Plan for Autism Spectrum Disorder Research*. Retrieved from http://iacc.hhs.gov/strategic-plan/2011/index.shtml

International Human Genome Sequencing Consortium. (2004). Finishing the euchromatic sequence of the human genome. *Nature, 431*, 931–945. doi:10.1038/nature03001

International Society for Prevention of Child Abuse and Neglect. (2010). *World Perspectives on Child Abuse: Ninth Edition*. Aurora, CO: Author.

Ireland, J. L., & Culpin, V. (2006). The relationship between sleeping problems and aggression, anger, and impulsivity in a population of juvenile and young offenders. *Journal of Adolescent Health, 38*, 649–655. doi:10.1016/j.jadohealth.2005.05.027

Irish, L., Kobayashi, I., & Delahanty, D. L. (2010). Long-term physical health consequences of childhood sexual abuse: A meta-analytic review. *Journal of Pediatric Psychology, 35*, 450–461. doi:10.1093/jpepsy/jsp118

Irwin, C. E. Jr., Burg, S. J., & Cart, C. U. (2002). America's adolescents: Where have we been, where are we going? *Journal of Adolescent Health, 31*, 91–121. doi:10.1016/S1054-139X(02)00489-5

Ivanov, I., Bansal, R., Hao, X., Zhu, H., Kellendonk, C., Miller, L., . . . Peterson,

B. S. (2010). Morphological abnormalities of the thalamus in youths with attention deficit hyperactivity disorder. *American Journal of Psychiatry, 167*, 397–408. doi:10.1176/appi.ajp.2009.09030398

Ivarsson, T., Granqvist, P., Gillberg, C., & Broberg, A. G. (2010). Attachment states of mind in adolescent with obsessive compulsive disorder and/ or depressive disorders: A controlled study. *European Child and Adolescent Psychiatry, 19*, 845–853. doi:10.1007/s00787-010-0120-x

Ivarsson, T., Rastam, M., Wentz, E., Gillberg, I. C., & Gillberg, C. (2000). Depressive disorders in teenage-onset anorexia nervosa: A controlled longitudinal, partly community-based study. *Comprehensive Psychiatry, 41*, 398–403. doi:10.1053/comp.2000.9001

Iwaniec, D., Sheddon, H., & Allen, S. (2003). The outcomes of a longitudinal study of non-organic failure-to-thrive. *Child Abuse Review, 12*, 216–226. doi:10.1002/car.805

Izard, C. E., Youngstrom, E. A., Fine, S. E., Mostow, A. J., & Trentacosta, C. J. (2006). Emotions and developmental psychopathology. In D. Cicchetti & D. J. Cohen (Eds.), *Developmental psychopathology: Vol. 1. Theory and method* (2nd ed., pp. 244–292). Hoboken, NJ: Wiley.

Jaaniste, T., Hayes, B., & von Baeyer, C. L. (2007). Providing children with information about forthcoming medical procedures: A review and synthesis. *Clinical Psychology: Science and Practice, 14*, 124–143. doi:10.1111/j.1468-2850.2007.00072.x

Jackson, Y., Alberts, F. L., & Roberts, M. C. (2010). Clinical child psychology: A practice specialty serving children, adolescents, and their families. *Professional Psychology: Research and Practice, 41*, 75–81. doi:10.1037/a0016156

Jacobi, C., Hayward, C., de Zwaan, M., Kraemer, H. C., & Agras, S. (2004). Coming to terms with risk factors for eating disorders: Application of risk terminology and suggestions for a general taxonomy. *Psychological Bulletin, 130*, 19–65. doi:10.1037/0033-2909.130.1.19

Jacobson, J. W., Mulick, J. A., & Schwartz, A. A. (1995). A history of facilitated communication: Science, pseudoscience, and antiscience. *American Psychologist, 50*, 750–765. doi:10.1037/0003-066X.50.9.750

Jaffe, P., Lemon, N., Sandler, J., & Wolfe, D. (1996). *Working together to end domestic violence*. Tampa, FL: Mancorp.

Jaffe, P., Wolfe, D. A., & Campbell, M. (2011). *Growing up with domestic violence: Assessment, intervention & prevention strategies for children & adolescents*. Cambridge. MA: Hogrefe & Huber.

Jaffee, S. R., Moffitt, T. E., Caspi, A., & Taylor, A. (2003). Life with (or without) father: The benefits of living with two biological parents depend on the father's antisocial behavior. *Child Development, 74*, 109–126. doi:10.1111/1467-8624.t01-1-00524

Jaffee, W. B., & D'Zurilla, T. J. (2003). Adolescent problem solving, parent problem solving, and externalizing behavior in adolescents. *Behavior Therapy, 34*, 295–311. doi:10.1016/S0005-7894(03)80002-3

Jakobson, A., & Kikas, E. (2007). Cognitive functioning in children with and without attention-deficit/hyperactivity disorder with and without comorbid learning disabilities. *Journal of Learning Disabilities, 40*, 194–202. doi:10.1177/00222194070400030101

Jamison, K. R. (1997, January). Manic-depressive illness and creativity. *Scientific American, 7*, 44–49. Retrieved from http://www.sciamdigital.com/index.cfm?fa=Main.ViewMain

Jaser, S. S., & White, L. E. (2011). Coping and resilience in adolescents with type 1 diabetes. *Child: Care, Health and Development, 37*, 335–342. doi:10.1111/j.1365-2214.2010.01184.x

Jaycox, L. H., Stein, B. D., Paddock, S., Miles, J. N. V., Chandra, A., & Burnam, M. A. (2009). Impact of teen depression on academic, social, and physical functioning. *Pediatrics, 125*, e596–e605. doi:10.1542/peds.2008-3348

Jellesma, F. C. (2008). Health in young people: Social inhibition and negative affect and their relationship with self-reported somatic complaints. *Journal of Development and Behavioral Pediatrics, 29*, 94–100. doi:10.1097/DBP.0b013e31815f24e1

Jellesma, F. C., Rieffe, C., & Terwogt, M. M. (2008). My peers, my friend, and I: Peer interactions and somatic complaints in boys and girls. *Social Science and Medicine, 66*, 2195–2205. doi:10.1016/j.socscimed.2008.01.029

Jellesma, F. C., Rieffe, C., Terwogt, M. M., & Westenberg, P. M. (2008). Do parents reinforce somatic complaints in their children? *Health Psychology, 27*, 280–285. doi:10.1037/0278-6133.27.2.280

Jemal, A., Siegel, R., Ward, E., Hao, Y., Xu, J., & Thun, M.J. (2009). Cancer statistics, 2009. *CA: A Cancer Journal for Clinicians, 59*, 225–249. doi:10.3322/caac.20006

Jencks, C., & Phillips, M. (1998). *The Black–White test score gap*. Washington, DC: Brookings Institution Press.

Jenkins, M. M., Youngstrom, E. A., Washburn, J. J., & Youngstrom, J. K. (2010). Evidence-based strategies improve assessment of pediatric bipolar disorder by community practitioners. *Professional Psychology: Research and Practice, 42*, 121–129. doi:10.1037/a0022506

Jensen, C. D., Cushing, C. C., Aylward, B. S., Craig, J. T., Sorell, D. M., & Steele, R. G. (2011). Effectiveness of motivational interviewing interventions for adolescent substance use behavior change: A meta-analytic review. *Journal of Consulting and Clinical Psychology, 79*, 433–440. doi:10.1037/a0023992

Jensen, P. S. (2000). Commentary. *Journal of the American Academy of Child & Adolescent Psychiatry, 39*, 984–987. doi:10.1097/00004583-200008000-00010

Jensen, P. S., Arnold, L. E., Swanson, J. M., Vitiello, B., Abikoff, H. B., Greenhill, L. L., . . . Hur, K. (2007). 3-year follow-up of the NIMH MTA Study. *Journal of the American Academy of Child & Adolescent Psychiatry, 46*, 989–1002. doi:10.1097/CHI.0b013e3180686d48

Jensen, P. S., Goldman, E., Offord, D., Costello, E. J., Friedman, R., Huff, B., . . . Roberts, R. (2011). Overlooked and underserved: "Action signs" for identifying children with unmet mental health needs. *Pediatrics, 128*, 970–979. doi:10.1542/peds.2009-0367

Jensen, P. S., Hoagwood, K., & Petti, T. (1996). Outcomes of mental health care for children and adolescents: II. Literature review and application of a comprehensive model. *Journal of the American Academy of Child & Adolescent Psychiatry, 35*, 1064–1077. doi:10.1097/00004583-199608000-00018

Jensen, P. S., Kettle, L., Roper, R. S., Sloan, M. T., Dulcan, M. K., Hoven, C., . . . Payne, J. D. (1999). Are stimulants overprescribed? Treatment of ADHD in four U.S. communities. *Journal of the American Academy of Child & Adolescent Psychiatry, 38*, 797–804. doi:10.1097/00004583-199907000-00008

Jepsen, J. R. M., Fagerlund, B., & Mortensen, E. L. (2009). Do attention deficits influence IQ assessment in children and adolescents with ADHD? *Journal of Attention Disorders, 12*, 551–562. doi:10.1177/1087054708322996

Jespersen, A. F., Lalumière, M. L., & Seto, M. C. (2009). Sexual abuse history among adult sex offenders and non-sex offenders: A meta-analysis. *Child Abuse & Neglect, 33*, 179–192. doi:10.1016/j.chiabu.2008.07.004

Johansson, B. B. (2006). Cultural and linguistic influence on brain organization for language and possible consequences for dyslexia: A review. *Annals of Dyslexia, 56*, 13–50. doi:10.1007/s11881-006-0002-6

Johnson, C. J., & Beitchman, J. H. (2006). Specific developmental disorders of speech and language. In C. Gillberg, R. Harrington, & H. Steinhausen (Eds.), *A clinician's handbook of child & adolescent psychiatry* (pp. 388–416). New York: Cambridge University Press.

Johnson, C. J., Beitchman, J. H., & Brownlie, E. B. (2010). Twenty-year follow-up of children with and without speech-language impairments: Family, educational, occupational, and quality of life outcomes. *American Journal of Speech-Language Pathology, 19*, 51–65. doi:10.1044/1058-0360(2009/08-0083)

Johnson, C. P., Myers, S. M., & the Council on Children with Disabilities. (2007). Identification and evaluation of children with autism spectrum disorders. *Pediatrics, 120*, 1183–1215. doi:10.1542/peds.2007-2361

Johnson, J. G., Cohen, P., Smailes, E. M., Kasen, S., & Brook, J. S. (2002). Television viewing and aggressive behavior during adolescence and adulthood. *Science, 295*, 2468–2471. doi:10.1126/science.1062929

Johnson, M. H., & de Haan, M. (2006). Typical and atypical human functional brain development. In D. Cicchetti & D. J. Cohen (Eds.), *Developmental psychopathology: Vol. 2. Developmental neuroscience* (2nd ed., pp. 197–215). Hoboken, NJ: Wiley.

Johnson, R. J. (2008). Advances in understanding and treating childhood sexual abuse: Implications for research and policy. *Family & Community Health. Special Issue: Advancing Adolescent Health, 31*(Suppl 1), S24–S34.

Johnson, S., Hollis, C., Kochhar, P., Hennessey, E., Wolke, D., & Marlow, N. (2010). Autism spectrum disorders in extremely preterm children. *Journal of Pediatrics, 156*, 525–531. doi:10.1016/j.jpeds.2009.10.041

Johnston, C., & Freeman, W. (1998). Parent training interventions for sibling conflict. In J. Briesmeister & C. E. Schaefer (Eds.), *Handbook of parent training: Parents as co-therapists for children's behavior problems* (2nd ed., pp. 153–176). New York: Wiley.

Johnston, C., Hommersen, P., & Seipp, C. M. (2009). Maternal attributions and child oppositional behavior: A longitudinal study of boys with and without attention-deficit/hyperactivity disorder. *Journal of Consulting and Clinical Psychology, 77*, 189–195. doi:10.1037/a0014065

Johnston, C., & Leung, D. W. (2001). Effects of medication, behavioral, and combined treatments on parents' and children's attributions for the behavior of children with attention-deficit hyperactivity disorder. *Journal of Consulting and Clinical Psychology, 69*, 67–76. doi:10.1037//0022-006X.69.1.67

Johnston, C., & Mah, J. W. T. (2008). Child attention-deficit/hyperactivity disorder. In J. Hunsley & E. J. Mash (Eds.), *A guide to assessments that work* (pp. 17–40). New York: Oxford University Press.

Johnston, C., & Mash, E. J. (2001). Families of children with attention-deficit hyperactivity disorder: A review and recommendations for future research. *Clinical Child and Family Psychology Review, 4*, 183–207. doi:10.1023/A:1017592030434

Johnston, L. D., O'Malley, P. M., & Bachman, J., & Schulenberg, J. E. (2008). *Monitoring the future: National results on adolescent drug use: Overview of key findings, 2007* (NIH Publication No. 08-6418). Bethesda, MD: National Institute on Drug Abuse. Retrieved from www.monitoringthefuture.org

Johnston, L. D., O'Malley, P. M., Bachman, J. G., & Schulenberg, J. E. (2011a). *Monitoring the Future: National results on adolescent drug use: Overview of key findings, 2010.* Ann Arbor: Institute for Social Research, The University of Michigan.

Johnston, L. D., O'Malley, P. M., Bachman, J. G., & Schulenberg, J. E. (2011b). *Demographic subgroup trends for various licit and illicit drugs, 1975–2010* (Monitoring the Future Occasional Paper No. 74). Ann Arbor, MI: Institute for Social Research.

Joiner, T. E., Jr. (1999). A test of interpersonal theory of depression in youth psychiatric inpatients. *Journal of Abnormal Child Psychology, 27*, 77–85. doi:10.1023/A:1022666424731

Joiner, T. E., Katz, J., & Heatherton, T. (2000). Personality features differentiate late adolescent females and males with chronic bulimic symptoms. *International Journal of Eating Disorders, 27*, 191–197. doi:10.1002/(SICI)1098-108X(200003)27:2<191::AID-EAT7>3.0.CO;2-S

Joinson, C., Heron, J., Emond, A., & Butler, R. (2007). Psychological problems in children with bedwetting and combined (day and night) wetting: A UK population-based study. *Journal of Pediatric Psychology, 32*, 605–616. doi:10.1093/jpepsy/jsl039

Joint Committee on Testing Practices. (2004). *Code of fair testing practices in education.* Washington, DC: Author.

Jolliffe, T., & Baron-Cohen, S. (1997). Are people with autism and Asperger syndrome faster than normal on the embedded figures test? *Journal of Child Psychology and Psychiatry, 38*, 527–534. doi:10.1111/j.1469-7610.1997.tb01539.x

Jones, H. A., Epstein, J. N., Hinshaw, S. P., Owens, E. B., Chi, T. C., Arnold, L. E., . . . Wells, K. C. (2010). Ethnicity as a moderator of treatment effects on parent-child interaction for children with ADHD. *Journal of Attention Disorders, 13*, 592–600. doi:10.1177/1087054709332158

Jones, L. M., Finkelhor, D., & Halter, S. (2006). Child maltreatment trends in the 1990's: Why does neglect differ from sexual and physical abuse? *Child Maltreatment, 11*, 107–120

Jones, M. C. (1924). The elimination of children's fears. *Journal of Experimental Psychology, 1*, 383–390. doi:10.1037/h0072283

Jones, W. R., & Morgan, J. F. (2010). Eating disorders in men: A review of the literature. *Journal of Public Mental Health, 9*, 23–31. doi:10.5042/jpmh.2010.0326

Jones, W., & Klin, A. (2009). Heterogeneity and homogeneity across the autism spectrum: The role of development. *Journal of the American Academy of Child and Adolescent Psychiatry, 48*, 471–473. doi:10.1097/CHI.0b013e31819f6c0d

Jordan, A. E., & Cole, D. A. (1996). Relation of depressive symptoms to the structure of self-knowledge in childhood. *Journal of Abnormal Psychology, 105*, 530–540. doi:10.1037/0021-843X.105.4.530

Joseph, R. M., & Tanaka, J. (2003). Holistic and part-based face recognition in children with autism. *Journal of Child Psychology and Psychiatry, 44*, 529–542. doi:10.1111/1469-7610.00142

Juarascio, A. S., Forman, E. M., Timko, C. A., Herbert, J. D., Butryn, M., & Lowe, M. (2011). Implicit internalization of the thin ideal as a predictor of increases in weight, body dissatisfaction, and disordered eating. *Eating Behaviors, 12*, 207–213. doi:10.1016/j.eatbeh.2011.04.004

Juffer, F., & van IJzendoorn, M. H. (2007). Adoptees do not lack self-esteem: A meta-analysis of studies on self-esteem of transracial, international, and domestic adoptees. *Psychological Bulletin, 133*, 1067–1083. doi:10.1037/0033-2909.133.6.1067

Jung, C. G. (1939). *The integration of the personality* (p. 285). New York: Farrar & Rinehart, Inc. (translation by S. M. Dell).

Kagan, J. (2008). Behavioral inhibition as a risk factor for psychopathology. In T. P. Beauchaine & S. P. Hinshaw (Eds.), *Child and adolescent psychopathology* (pp. 157–179). Hoboken, NJ: Wiley.

Kagan, J., & Snidman, N. (1999). Early child predictors of adult anxiety disorders. *Biological Psychiatry, 46*, 1536–1541. doi:10.1016/S0006-3223(99)00137-7

Kagan, J., Snidman, N., & Arcus, D. M. (1992). Initial reactions to unfamiliarity. *Current Directions in Psychological Science, 1*, 171–174. doi:10.1111/1467-9566.ep10770010

Kahn, C. A., Kelly, P. C., & Walker, W. O. (1995). Lead screening in children with attention deficit hyperactivity disorder and developmental delay. *Clinical Pediatrics, 34*, 498–501. doi:10.1177/000992289503400909

Kaiser, N. M., McBurnett, K., & Pfiffner, L. J. (2011). Child ADHD severity and positive and negative parenting as predictors of child social functioning: Evaluation of three theoretical models. *Journal of Attention Disorders, 15*, 193–203. doi:10.1177/1087054709356171

Kaiser, N. M., & Pfiffner, L. J. (2011). Evidence-based psychosocial treatments for childhood ADHD. *Psychiatric Annals, 41*, 9–15. doi:10.3928/00485713-20101221-03

Kallman, F. J., & Roth, B. (1956). Genetic aspects of preadolescent schizophrenia. *American Journal of Psychiatry, 112*, 599–606. doi:10.1176/appi.ajp.112.8.599

Kaminski, K. M., & Garber, J. (2002). Depressive spectrum disorders in high-risk adolescents: Episode duration and predictors of time to recovery. *Journal of the American Academy of Child & Adolescent Psychiatry, 41*, 410–418. doi:10.1097/00004583-200204000-00013

Kamp-Becker, I., Smidt, J., Ghahreman, M., Heinzel-Gutenbrunner, M., Becker, K., & Remschmidt, H. (2010). Categorical and dimensional structure of autism spectrum disorders: The nosologic validity of Asperger Syndrome. *Journal of Autism and Developmental Disorders, 40*, 921–929. doi:10.1007/s10803-010-0939-5

Kanaya, T., Scullin, M. H., & Ceci, S. J. (2003). The Flynn effect and U.S. policies: The impact of rising IQ scores on American society via mental retardation diagnoses. *American Psychologist, 58*, 778–790. doi:10.1037/0003-066X.58.10.778

Kane, P., & Garber, J. (2004). The relations among depression in fathers, children's psychopathology, and father-child conflict: A meta-analysis. *Clinical Psychology Review, 24*, 339–360. doi:10.1016/j.cpr.2004.03.004

Kanner, L. (1943). Autistic disturbances of affective contact. *Nervous Child, 2*, 217–250.

Kanner, L. (1944). Early infantile autism. *Journal of Pediatrics, 25*, 211–217. doi:10.1016/S0022-3476(44)80156-1

Kanner, L. (1962). Emotionally disturbed children: A historical review. *Child Development, 33*, 97–102. Retrieved from http://www.jstor.org/stable/1126636

Kanner, L. (1964). *A history of the care and study of the mentally retarded.* Springfield, IL: Thomas.

Kanoski, S. E., Hayes, M. R., Greenwald, H. S., Fortin, S. M., Gianessi, C. A., Gilbert, J. R., & Grill, H. J. (2011). Hippocampal leptin signaling reduces food intake and modulates food-related memory processing. *Neuropsychopharmacology, 36*, 1859–1870. doi:10.1038/npp.2011.70

Kaplan, R. M. (2000). Two pathways to prevention. *American Psychologist, 55*, 382–396. doi:10.1037/0003-066X.55.4.382

Kaplow, J. B., Saunders, J., Angold, A., & Costello, E. J. (2010). Psychiatric symptoms in bereaved versus nonbereaved youth and young adults. A longitudinal epidemiological study. *American Journal of Child and Adolescent Psychiatry, 49*, 1145–1154. doi:10.1016/j.jaac.2010.08.004

Kapp, S. K. (2011). Navajo and autism: The beauty of harmony. *Disability & Society, 26*, 583–595. doi.org/10.1080/09687599.2011.589192

Karg, K., Burmeister, M., Shedden. K., & Sen, S. (2011). The serotonin transporter promoter variant (5-HTTLPR), stress, and depression meta-analysis revisited: evidence of genetic moderation. *Archives of General Psychiatry, 68*, 444–454. doi:10.1001/archgenpsychiatry.2010.189

Karier, C. J. (1986). *Scientists of the mind: Intellectual founders of modern psychology*. Urbana, IL: University of Illinois Press.

Karlsgodt, K. H., Sun, D., Jimenez, A. M., Lutzenhoff, E. S., Willhite, R., van Erp, T. G. M., & Cannon, T. D. (2008). Developmental disruptions in neural connectivity in the pathophysiology of schizophrenia. *Development and Psychopathology, 20*, 1297–1327. doi:10.1017/S095457940800062X

Karna, A., Voeten, M., Little, T. D., Poskiparta, E., Kaljonen, A., & Salmivalli, C. (2011). A large-scale evaluation of the KiVa Antibullying Program: Grades 4–6. *Child Development, 82*, 311–330. doi:10.1111/j.1467-8624.2010.01557.x

Karwautz, A. F. K., Wagner, G., Waldherr, K., Nader, I. W., Fernandez-Aranda, F., Estivill, X., . . . Treasure, J. L. (2011). Gene-environment interaction in anorexia nervosa: Relevance of non-shared environment and the serotonin transporter gene. *Molecular Psychiatry, 16*, 590–592. doi:10.1038/mp.2010.125

Kasen, S., Cohen, P., Brook, J. S., & Hartmark, C. (1996). A multiple-risk interaction model: Effects of temperament and divorce on psychiatric disorders in children. *Journal of Abnormal Child Psychology, 24*, 121–150. doi:10.1007/BF01441481

Kashani, J. H., Allan, W. D., Dahlmeier, J. M., Rezvani, M., & Reid, J. C. (1995). An examination of family functioning utilizing the circumplex model in psychiatrically hospitalized children with depression. *Journal of Affective Disorders, 35*, 65–73. doi:10.1016/0165-0327(95)00042-L

Kates, W. R. (2007). Editorial: Inroads to mechanisms of disease in child psychiatric disorders. *American Journal of Psychiatry, 164*, 547–551. doi:10.1176/appi.ajp.164.4.547

Kats-Gold, I., Besser, A., & Priel, B. (2007). The role of simple emotion recognition skills among school aged boys at risk of ADHD. *Journal of Abnormal Child Psychology, 35*, 363–378. doi:10.1007/s10802-006-9096-x

Katzmarzyk, P. T., & Ardern, C. I. (2004). Overweight and obesity mortality trends in Canada, 1985–2000. *Canadian Journal of Public Health, 95*, 16–20. Retrieved from http://journal.cpha.ca/index.php/cjph

Kaufman, A. S., & Kaufman, N. L. (2004). *KABC-II: Kaufman assessment battery for children* (2nd ed.). Circle Pines, MN: AGS.

Kaufman, J., Martin, A., King, R. A., & Charney, D. (2001). Are child-, adolescent-, and adult-onset depression one and the same disorder? *Biological Psychiatry, 49*, 980–1001. doi:10.1016/S0006-3223(01)01127-1

Kaufman, J., Yang, B.Z., Douglas-Palumberi, H., Grasso, D., Lipschitz, D., Houshyar, S., . . . Gelernter, J. (2006). Brain-derived neurotrophic factor-5-HTTLPR gene interactions and environmental modifiers of depression in children. *Biological Psychiatry, 59*, 673–680. doi:10.1016/j.biopsych.2005.10.026

Kavale, K. A., & Flanagan, D. P. (2007). Ability-achievement discrepancy, response to intervention, and assessment of cognitive abilities/processes in specific learning disability identification: Toward a contemporary operational definition. In S. R. Jimerson, M. K. Burns, & A. M. VanDerHeyden (Eds.), *Handbook of response to intervention: The science and practice of assessment and intervention* (pp. 130–147). New York: Springer.

Kavale, K. A., & Forness, S. R. (1983). Hyperactivity and diet treatment: A meta-analysis of the Feingold hypothesis. *Journal of Learning Disabilities, 16*, 324–330. doi:10.1177/002221948301600604

Kazak, A. E., Alderfer, M., Rourke, M. T., Simms, S., Streisand, R., & Grossman, J. R. (2004). Posttraumatic stress disorder (PTSD) and posttraumatic stress symptoms (PTSS) in families of adolescent childhood cancer survivors. *Journal of Pediatric Psychology, 29*, 211–219. doi:10.1093/jpepsy/jsh022

Kazak, A. E., & Bart, C. (2007). Families of infants and young children with cancer: A post-traumatic stress framework. *Pediatric Blood Cancer, 49*, 1109–1113. doi:10.1002/pbc.21345

Kazak, A. E., Hoagwood, K., Weisz, J. R., Hood, K., Kratochwill, T. R., Vargas, L. A., & Banez, G. A. (2010). A meta-systems approach to evidence-based practice for children and adolescents. *American Psychologist, 65*, 85–97. doi:10.1037/a0017784

Kazdin, A. E. (1992). Overt and covert antisocial behavior: Child and family characteristics among psychiatric inpatient children. *Journal of Child and Family Studies, 1*, 3–20. doi:10.1007/BF01321339

Kazdin, A. E. (1995). *Conduct disorders in childhood and adolescence* (2nd ed.). Thousand Oaks, CA: Sage.

Kazdin, A. E. (1996). Combined and multimodal treatments in child and adolescent psychotherapy: Issues, challenges, and research directions. *Clinical Psychology: Science and Practice, 3*, 69–100. doi:10.1111/j.1468-2850.1996.tb00059.x

Kazdin, A. E. (1996). Problem solving and parent management training in treating aggressive and antisocial behavior. In E. D. Hibbs & P. S. Jensen (Eds.), *Psychosocial treatments for child and adolescent disorders: Empirically based strategies for clinical practice* (pp. 377–408). Washington, DC: American Psychological Association.

Kazdin, A. E. (1997). A model for developing effective treatments: Progression and interplay of theory, research, and practice. *Journal of Clinical Child Psychology, 26*, 114–129. doi:10.1207/s15374424jccp2602_1

Kazdin, A. E. (2000). *Psychotherapy for children and adolescents: Directions for research and practice.* New York: Oxford University Press.

Kazdin, A. E. (2005). *Parent management training: Treating for oppositional, aggressive, and antisocial behavior in children and adolescents.* New York: Oxford University Press.

Kazdin, A. E. (2007). Psychosocial treatments for conduct disorder in children and adolescents. In P. E. Nathan & J. M. Gorman (Eds.), *A guide to treatments that work* (3rd ed., pp. 71–104). New York: Oxford University Press.

Kazdin, A. E. (2010). Problem-solving skills training and parent management training for oppositional defiant disorder and conduct disorder. In J. R. Weisz & A. E. Kazdin (Eds.), *Evidence-based psychotherapies for children and adolescents* (2nd ed., pp. 211–226). New York: Guilford.

Kazdin, A. E. (2011). *Single case research designs: Methods for clinical and applied settings* (2nd ed.). New York: Oxford University Press.

Kazdin, A. E., & Blase, S. L. (2011). Rebooting psychotherapy research and practice to reduce the burden of mental illness. *Perspectives on Psychological Science, 6*, 21–37. doi:10.1177/1745691610393527

Kazdin, A. E., & Wassell, G. (1999). Barriers to treatment participation and therapeutic change among children referred for conduct disorder. *Journal of Clinical Child Psychology, 28*, 160–172. doi:10.1207/s15374424jccp2802_4

Kazdin, A. E., & Whitley, M. K. (2006). Comorbidity, case complexity, and effects of evidence-based treatment for children referred for disruptive behavior. *Journal of Consulting and Clinical Psychology, 74*, 455–467. doi:10.1037/0022-006X.74.3.455

Kearney, C. A. (1995). School refusal behavior. In A. R. Eisen, C. A. Kearney, & C. A. Schaefer (Eds.), *Clinical handbook of anxiety disorders in children and adolescents* (pp. 19–52). Northvale, NJ: Aronson.

Kearney, C. A. (2007). Forms and functions of school refusal behavior in youth: An empirical analysis of absenteeism severity. *Journal of Child Psychology and Psychiatry, 48*, 53–61. doi:10.1111/j.1469-7610.2006.01634.x

Kearney, C. A., & Albano, A. M. (2004). The functional profiles of school refusal behavior: Diagnostic aspects.

Behavior Modification, 28, 147–161. doi:10.1177/0145445503259263
Kearney, C. A., & Albano, A. M. (2007). *When children refuse school: A cognitive-behavioral therapy approach, therapist guide* (2nd ed.). New York: Oxford University Press.
Kearney, C. A., & Silverman, W. K. (1996). The evolution and reconciliation of taxonomic strategies for school refusal behavior. *Clinical Psychology: Science and Practice, 3*, 339–354. doi:10.1111/j.1468-2850.1996.tb00087.x
Keehn, B., Lincoln, A. J., Muller, R.-A., & Townsend, J. (2010). Attentional networks in children and adolescents with autism spectrum disorder. *Journal of Child Psychology and Psychiatry, 51*, 1251–1259. doi:10.1111/j.1469-7610.2010.02257.x
Keel, P. K., Baxter, M. G., Heatherton, T. F., & Joiner, T. E. (2007). A 20-year longitudinal study of body weight, dieting, and eating disorder symptoms. *Journal of Abnormal Psychology, 116*, 422–432. doi:10.1037/0021-843X.116.2.422
Keel, P. K., & Klump, K. L. (2003). Are eating disorders culture-bound syndromes? Implications for conceptualizing their etiology. *Psychological Bulletin, 129*, 747–769. doi:10.1037/0033-2909.129.5.747
Keel, P. K., Gravener, J. A., Joiner, T. E., & Haedt, A. A. (2010). Twenty-year follow-up of bulimia nervosa and related eating disorders not otherwise specified. *International Journal of Eating Disorders, 43*, 492–497. doi:10.1002/eat.20743
Keenan, K. (2000). Emotion dysregulation as a risk factor for child psychopathology. *Clinical Psychology: Science and Practice, 7*, 418–434. doi:10.1093/clipsy.7.4.418
Keenan, K. (2011, June). Mind the gap: Assessing impairment among children affected by proposed revisions to the diagnostic criteria for oppositional defiant disorder. *Journal of Abnormal Psychology*. Advance online publication. doi:10.1037/a0024340
Keenan, K., Boeldt, D. Chen, D., Coyne, C., Donald, R., Duax, J., . . . Humphries, M. (2011). Predictive validity of DSM-IV oppositional defiant and conduct disorders in clinically referred preschoolers. *Journal of Child Psychology and Psychiatry, 52*, 47–55. doi:10.1111/j.1469-7610.2010.02290.x
Keenan, K., & Shaw, D. (1997). Developmental and social influences on young girls' early problem behavior. *Psychological Bulletin, 121*, 95–113. doi:10.1037/0033-2909.121.1.95
Keenan, K., Wroblewski, K., Hipwell, A., Loeber, R., & Stouthamer-Loeber, M. (2010). Age of onset, symptom threshold, and expansion of the nosology of conduct disorder in girls. *Journal of Abnormal Psychology, 119*, 689–698. doi:10.1037/a0019346
Keenan-Miller, D., Hammen, C. L., & Brennan, P. A. (2007). Health outcomes related to early adolescent depression. *Journal of Adolescent Health, 41*, 256–262. doi:10.1016/j.jadohealth.2007.03.015
Kell, C. A., Neumann, K., von Kriegstein, K., Posenenske, C., von Gudenberg, A. W., Euler, H., & Giraud, A. (2009). How the brain repairs stuttering. *Brain: A Journal of Neurology, 132*, 2747–2760. doi:10.1093/brain/awp185
Keller, M., Lavori, P., Wunder, J., Beardslee, W., Schwartz, C., & Roth, J. (1992). Chronic course of anxiety disorders in children and adolescents. *Journal of the American Academy of Child & Adolescent Psychiatry, 31*, 595–599. doi:10.1097/00004583-199207000-00003
Kelly, A. M. C., Margulies, D. S., & Castellanos, F. X. (2007). Recent advances in structural and functional brain imaging studies of attention-deficit/hyperactivity disorder. *Current Psychiatry Reports, 9*, 401–407. doi:10.1007/s11920-007-0052-4
Kelly, R. J., & El-Sheikh, M. (2011). Marital conflict and children's sleep: Reciprocal relations and socioeconomic effects. *Journal of Family Psychology, 25*, 412–422. doi:10.1037/a0023789
Kemp, C., & Carter, M. (2002). The social skills and social status of mainstreamed students with intellectual disabilities. *Educational Psychology, 22*, 391–411. doi:10.1080/0144341022000003097
Kempe, C. H., Silverman, F. N., Steele, B. F., Droegenmueller, W., & Silver, H. K. (1962). The battered child syndrome. *Journal of the American Medical Association, 181*, 17–24.
Kendall, J. (1999). Sibling accounts of attention deficit hyperactivity disorder (ADHD). *Family Process, 38*, 117–136. doi:10.1111/j.1545-5300.1999.00117.x
Kendall, P. C. (Ed.). (2011a). *Child and adolescent therapy: Cognitive-behavioral procedures* (4th ed.). New York: Guilford Press.
Kendall, P. C. (2011b). Guiding theory for therapy with children and adolescents. In P. C. Kendall (Ed.), *Child and adolescent therapy: Cognitive behavioral procedures* (4th ed., pp. 3–24). New York: Guilford Press.
Kendall, P. C., & Flannery-Schroeder, E. C. (1998). Methodological issues in treatment research for anxiety disorders in youth. *Journal of Abnormal Child Psychology, 26*, 27–38. doi:10.1023/A:1022630706189
Kendall, P. C., Furr, J. M., & Podell, J. L. (2010). Child focused treatment of anxiety. In J. R. Weisz & A. E. Kazdin (Eds.), *Evidence-based therapies for children and adolescents* (2nd ed., pp. 45–60). New York: Guilford.
Kendall, P. C., Panichelli-Mindel, S. M., Sugarman, A., & Callahan, S. A. (1997). Exposure to child anxiety: Theory, research, and practice. *Clinical Psychology: Science and Practice, 4*, 29–39. doi:10.1111/j.1468-2850.1997.tb00096.x
Kendall, P. C., Safford, S., Flannery-Schroeder, E., & Webb, A. (2004). Child anxiety treatment: Outcomes in adolescence and impact on substance use and depression at 7.4-year follow-up. *Journal of Consulting and Clinical Psychology, 72*, 276–287. doi:10.1037/0022-006X.72.2.276
Kendall, P. C., & Suveg, C. (2006). Treating anxiety disorders in youth. In P. C. Kendall (Ed.), *Child and adolescent therapy: Cognitive-behavioral procedures* (3rd ed., pp. 243–294). New York: Guilford Press.
Kendall-Tackett, K. A., Williams, L. M., & Finkelhor, D. (2001). Impact of sexual abuse on children: A review and synthesis of recent empirical studies. In R. Bull (Ed.), *Children and the law: The essential readings. Essential readings in developmental psychology* (pp. 31–76). Malden, MA: Blackwell Publishing.
Kennedy, E. E. (2008). Media representations of attention deficit disorder: Portrayals of cultural skepticism in popular media. *Journal of Popular Culture, 41*, 91–117. doi:10.1111/j.1540-5931.2008.00494.x
Kennedy, P., Terdal, L., & Fusetti, L. (1993). *The hyperactive child book*. New York: St. Martin's Press.
Kessler, R. C., Adler, L. A., Barkley, R., Biederman, J., Conners, K., Faraone, S. V., . . . Zaslavsky, A. M. (2005). Patterns and predictors of attention-deficit/hyperactivity disorder persistence into adulthood: Results from the National Comorbidity Survey replication. *Biological Psychiatry, 57*, 1442–1451. doi:10.1016/j.biopsych.2005.04.001
Kessler, R. C., Aguilar-Gaxiola, S., Alonso, J., Chatterji, S., Lee, S., Ormel, J., et al. (2009). The global burden of mental disorders: An update from the WHO World Mental Health (WMH) Surveys. *Epidemiologia e Psichiatria Sociale, 18*, 23–33.
Kessler, R. C., Cox, B. J., Green, J. G., Ormel, J., McLaughlin, K. A., Merikangas, K. R., . . . Zaslavsky, A. M. (2011). The effects of latent variables in the development of comorbidity among common mental disorders. *Depression and Anxiety, 28*, 29–39. doi:10.1002/da.20760
Kessler, R. C., Merikangas, K. R., & Wang, P. S. (2007). Prevalence, comorbidity, and service utilization for mood disorders in the United States at the beginning of the twenty-first century. *Annual Review of Clinical Psychology, 3*, 137–158. doi:10.1146/annurev.clinpsy.3.022806.091444
Khanna, M. S., & Kendall, P. C. (2010). Computer-assisted cognitive behavioral therapy for child anxiety: Results of a randomized clinical trial. *Journal of Consulting and Clinical Psychology, 78*, 737–745. doi:10.1037/a0019739
Kieling, C., Gonclaves, R. R. F., Tannock, R., & Castellanos, F. X. (2008). Neurobiology of attention deficit hyperactivity disorder. *Child and Adolescent Psychiatric Clinics of North America, 17*, 285–307. doi:10.1016/j.chc.2007.11.012
Kieling, C., Kieling, R. A., Rohde, L. A., Frick, P. J., Moffitt, T., Nigg, J. T., . . . Castellanos, F. X. (2010). Commentary: Age of onset of attention deficit hyperactivity disorder. *American Journal of Psychiatry, 167*, 14–16. doi:10.1176/appi.ajp.2009.09060796
Kilgus, M. D., Pumariega, A. J., & Cuffe, S. P. (1995). Influence of race on diagnosis in adolescent psychiatric inpatients. *Journal of the American Academy of Child & Adolescent Psychiatry, 34*, 67–72. doi:10.1097/00004583-199501000-00016
Kilpatrick, D. G., Ruggiero, K. J., Acierno, R., Saunders, B. E., Resnick, H. S., & Best, C. L. (2003). Violence and risk of PTSD, major depression, substance abuse/dependence, and comorbidity: Results from the National Survey of Adolescents. *Journal of*

Consulting & Clinical Psychology, 71, 692–700. doi:10.1037/0022-006X.71.4.692

Kim, E. Y., & Miklowitz, D. J. (2002). Childhood mania, attention deficit hyperactivity disorder and conduct disorder: A critical review of diagnostic dilemmas. *Bipolar Disorder, 4*, 215–225. doi:10.1034/j.1399-5618.2002.01191.x

Kim, J., & Cicchetti, D. (2010). Longitudinal pathways linking child maltreatment, emotion regulation, peer relations, and psychopathology. *Journal of Child Psychology and Psychiatry, 51*, 706–716. doi:10.1111/j.1469–7610.2009.02202.x

Kim-Cohen, J., Caspi, A., Taylor, A., Williams, B., Newcombe, R., Craig, I. W., & Moffitt, T. E. (2006). MAOA, maltreatment, and gene-environment interaction predicting children's mental health: New evidence and a meta-analysis. *Molecular Psychiatry, 11*, 903–913. doi:10.1038/sj.mp.4001851

Kim-Cohen, J., & Gold, A. L. (2009). Measured gene-environment interactions and mechanisms promoting resilient development. *Current Directions in Psychological Science, 18*, 138–142. doi:10.1111/j.1467-8721.2009.01624.x

King, B. H., & Lord, C. (2011). Is schizophrenia on the autism spectrum? *Brain Research, 1380*, 34–41. doi:10.1016/j.brainres.2010.11.031

King, K. M., & Chassin, L. (2007). A prospective study of the effects of age of initiation of alcohol and drug use on young adult substance dependence. *Journal of Studies on Alcohol and Drugs, 68*, 256–265. Retrieved from http://www.jsad.com/

King, M., & Bearman, P. (2009). Diagnostic change and the increased prevalence of autism. *International Journal of Epidemiology, 38*, 1224–1234. doi:10.1093/ije/dyp261

King, N. J., Ollendick, T. H., & Mattis, S. G. (1994). Panic in children and adolescents: Normative and clinical studies. *Australian Psychologist, 29*, 89–93. doi:10.1080/00050069408257329

King, S., St-Hilaire, A., & Heidkamp, D. (2010). Prenatal factors in schizophrenia. *Current Directions in Psychological Science, 19*, 209–213. doi:10.1177/0963721410378360

Kirby, M. J. L., & Keon, W. J. (2006). *Out of the shadows at last: Transforming mental health, mental illness and addiction services in Canada*. Ottawa, Ontario, Canada: Standing Senate Committee on Social Affairs, Science and Technology. Retrieved from www.parl.gc.ca/39/1/parlbus/commbus/sen ate/com-e/soci-e/rep-e/rep02may06-e.htm

Kirchhoff, A. C., Leisenring, W., Krull, K. R., Ness, K. K., Friedman, D. L., Armstrong, G. T., . . . Wickizer, T. (2010). Unemployment among adult survivors of childhood cancer: A report from the childhood cancer survivor study. *Medical Care, 48*, 1015–1025. doi:10.1097/MLR.0b013e3181eaf880

Kirmayer, L. J., Dandeneau, S., Marshall, E., Phillips, M. K., & Williamson, K. J. (2011). Rethinking resilience from indigenous perspectives. *The Canadian Journal of Psychiatry / La Revue Canadienne De Psychiatrie, 56*(2), 84–91.

Kirsch, V., Wilhelm, F. H., & Goldbeck, L. (2011). Psychophysiological characteristics of PTSD in children and adolescents: A review of the literature. *Journal of Traumatic Stress, 24*, 146–154. doi:10.1002/jts.20620

Kiser, L. J. (2007). Protecting children from the dangers of urban poverty. *Clinical Psychology Review, 27*, 211–225. doi:10.1016/j.cpr.2006.07.004

Kishiyama, M. M., Boyce, W. T., Jimenez, A. M., Perry, L. M., & Knight, R. T. (2009). Socioeconomic disparities affect prefrontal function in children. *Journal of Cognitive Neuroscience, 21*, 1106–1115. doi:10.1162/jocn.2009.21101

Kitzman, H., Olds, D., Cole, R., Hanks, C., Anson, E., Arcoleo, K., . . . Holmberg, J. (2010). Enduring effects of prenatal and infancy home visiting by nurses on children: Follow-up of a randomized trial among children at age 12 years. *Archives of Pediatrics & Adolescent Medicine, 164*, 412.

Kitzmann, K. M., & Beech, B. M. (2011). Family-based interventions for pediatric obesity: Methodological and conceptual challenges from family psychology. *Couple and Family Psychology: Research and Practice, 1*, 45–62. doi:10.1037/2160-4096.1.S.45

Kitzmann, K. M., Dalton, W. T., Stanley, C. M., Beech, B. M., Reeves, T. P., Buscemi, J., . . . Midgett, E. L. (2010). Lifestyle interventions for youth who are overweight: A meta-analytic review. *Health Psychology, 29*, 91–101. doi:10.1037/a0017437

Kiuru, N., Leskinen, E., Nurmi, J.-E., & Salmela-Aro, K. (2011). Depressive symptoms during adolescence: Do learning difficulties matter? *International Journal of Behavioral Development, 35*, 298–306. doi:10.1177/0165025410396764

Klahr, A. M., McGue, M., Iacono, W. G., & Burt, S. A. (2011). The association between parent-child conflict and adolescent conduct problems over time: Results from a longitudinal adoption study. *Journal of Abnormal Psychology, 120*, 46–56. doi:10.1037/a0021350

Klein, D. N., Lewinsohn, P. M., & Seeley, J. R. (1997). Psychosocial characteristics of adolescents with a past history of dysthymic disorder: Comparison with adolescents with past histories of major depressive and non-affective disorders, and never mentally ill controls. *Journal of Affective Disorders, 42*, 127–135. doi:10.1016/S0165-0327(96)01403-6

Kleinman, J. M., Ventola, P. E., Pandey, J., Verbalis, A. D., Barton, M., Hodgson, S., . . . Fein, D. (2008). Diagnostic stability in very young children with autism spectrum disorders. *Journal of Autism and Developmental Disorders, 38*, 606–615. doi:10.1007/s10803-007-0427-8

Klietz, S. J., Borduin, C. M., & Schaeffer, C. M. (2010). Cost–benefit analysis of multisystemic therapy with serious and violent juvenile offenders. *Journal of Family Psychology, 24*, 657–666. doi:10.1037/a0020838

Klin, A., Lin, D. J., Gorrindo, P., Ramsay, G., & Jones, W. (2009). Two-year olds with autism orient to non-social contingencies rather than biological motion. *Nature, 459*, 257–261. doi:10.1038/nature07868

Klin, A., Volkmar, F. R., & Sparrow, S. S. (Eds.). (2000). *Asperger syndrome*. New York: Guilford Press.

Klinger, L. G., Dawson, G., & Renner, P. (2003). Autistic disorder. In E. J. Mash & R. A. Barkley (Eds.), *Child psychopathology* (2nd ed., pp. 409–454). New York: Guilford Press.

Klintwall, L., Holm, A., Erikkson, Carlsson, L. H., Olsson, B., Hedvall, A., . . . & Fernell, E. (2011). Sensory abnormalities in autism: A brief report. *Research in Developmental Disabilities, 32*, 795–800. doi:10.1016/j.ridd.2010.10.021

Knapp, M., Romeo, R., & Beechum, J. (2009). Economic cost of autism in the UK. *Autism, 13*, 317–336. doi:10.1177/1362361309104246

Knappe, S., Beesdo-Baum, K., Fehm, L., Stein, M. B., Lieb, R., & Wittchen, H.-U. (2011). Social fear and social phobia types among community youth: Differential clinical features and vulnerability factors. *Journal of Psychiatric Research, 45*, 111–120. doi:10.1016/j.jpsychires.2010.05.002

Knappe, S., Beesdo-Baum, K., Wittchen, H.-U. (2010). Familial factors in social anxiety disorder: Calling for a family-oriented approach for targeted prevention and early intervention. *European Child and Adolescent Psychiatry, 19*, 857–871. doi:10.1007/s00787-010-0138-0

Knickmeyer, R. C., Wheelwright, S., & Baron-Cohen, S. B. (2008). Sex-typical play: Masculinization/defeminization in girls with an autism spectrum condition. *Journal of Autism and Developmental Disorders, 38*, 1028–1035. doi:10.1007/s10803-007-0475-0

Kochanska, G., De Vet, K., Goldman, M., Murray, K., & Putnam, S. P. (1994). Maternal reports of conscience development and temperament in young children. *Child Development, 65*, 852–868. doi:10.1111/j.1467-8624.1994.tb00788.x

Koenen, K. C., & Widom, C. S. (2009). A prospective study of sex differences in the lifetime risk of posttraumatic stress disorder among abused and neglected children grown up. *Journal of Traumatic Stress, 22*, 566–574.

Koenig, A. L., Cicchetti, D., & Rogosch, F. A. (2004). Moral development: The association between maltreatment and young children's prosocial behaviors and moral transgressions. *Social Development, 13*, 97–106.

Koenig, K., & Tsatsanis, K. D. (2005). Pervasive developmental disorders in girls. In D. Bell, S. L. Foster, & E. J. Mash (Eds.), *Handbook of behavioral and emotional problems in girls* (pp. 211–237). New York: Kluwer.

Kofler, M. J., McCart, M. R., Zajac, K., Ruggiero, K J., Saunders, B. E., & Kilpatrick, D. G. (2011). Depression and delinquency covariation in an accelerated longitudinal sample of adolescents. *Journal of Consulting and Clinical Psychology, 79*, 458–469. doi:10.1037/a0024108

Kofler, M. J., Rapport, M. D., & Alderson, R. M. (2008). Quantifying ADHD classroom inattentiveness, its moderators, and variability: A meta-analytic review. *Journal of Child Psychology and Psychiatry, 49*, 59–69. doi:10.1111/j.1469-7610.2007.01809.x

Kohler, F. W., Strain, P. S., & Goldstein, H. (2005). Learning experiences . . . An alternative program for preschoolers and parents: Peer-mediated interventions for young children with autism. In E. D. Hibbs & P. S. Jensen (Eds.), *Psychosocial treatments for child and adolescent disorders: Empirically based strategies for clinical practice* (2nd ed., pp. 659–687). Washington, DC: American Psychological Association.

Kokko, K., & Pulkkinen, L. (2000). Aggression in childhood and long-term unemployment in adulthood: A cycle of maladaptation and some protective factors. *Developmental Psychology, 36*, 463–472. doi:10.1037/0012-1649.36.4.463

Kolko, D. J. (1987). Depression. In M. Hersen & V. B. Van Hasselt (Eds.), *Behavior therapy with children and adolescents: A clinical approach* (pp. 159–164). New York: John Wiley and Sons.

Korbin, J. E. (2002). Culture and child maltreatment: Cultural competence and beyond. *Child Abuse & Neglect, 26*, 637–644.

Kortlander, E., Kendall, P. C., & Panichelli-Mindel, S. M. (1997). Maternal expectations and attributions about coping in anxious children. *Journal of Anxiety Disorders, 11*, 297–315. doi:10.1016/S0887-6185(97)00012-1

Kosciw, J. G., Greytak, E. A., & Diaz, E. M. (2009). Who, what, where, when, and why: Demographic and ecological factors contributing to hostile school climate for lesbian, gay, bisexual, and transgender youth. *Journal of Youth and Adolescence, 38*, 976–988. doi:10.1007/s10964-009-9412-1

Kotsopoulos, S. (1986). Aretaeus the Cappadocian on mental illness. *Comprehensive Psychiatry, 27*, 171–179. doi:10.1016/0010-440X(86)90026-X

Kovacs, M. (1996). Presentation and course of major depressive disorder during childhood and later years of the life span. *Journal of the American Academy of Child & Adolescent Psychiatry, 35*, 705–715. doi:10.1097/00004583-199606000-00010

Kovacs, M. (1997). Depressive disorders in childhood: An impressionistic landscape. *Journal of Child Psychology and Psychiatry, 38*, 287–298. doi:10.1111/j.1469-7610.1997.tb01513.x

Kovacs, M., Akiskal, H. S., Gatsonis, C., & Parrone, P. L. (1994). Childhood-onset dysthymic disorder: Clinical features and prospective naturalistic outcome. *Archives of General Psychiatry, 51*, 365–374. Retrieved from http://archpsyc.ama-assn.org/

Kovacs, M., & Goldston, D. (1991). Cognitive and social cognitive development of depressed children and adolescents. *Journal of the American Academy of Child & Adolescent Psychiatry, 30*, 388–392. doi:10.1097/00004583-199105000-00006

Kovacs, M., Obrosky, D. S., Gatsonis, C., & Richards, C. (1997). First-episode major depressive and dysthymic disorder in childhood: Clinical and sociodemographic factors in recovery. *Journal of the American Academy of Child & Adolescent Psychiatry, 36*, 777–784. doi:10.1097/00004583-199706000-00014

Kowatch, R. A., Fristad, M., Birmaher, B., Wagner, K. D., Findling, R. L., & Hellander, M. (2005). Treatment guidelines for children and adolescents with bipolar disorder. *Journal of the American Academy of Child & Adolescent Psychiatry, 44*, 213–235. doi:10.1097/00004583-200503000-00006

Kröner-Herwig, B., Gassmann, J., van Gessel, H., & Vath, N. (2011). Multiple pains in children and adolescents: A risk factor analysis in a longitudinal study. *Journal of Pediatric Psychology, 36*, 420–432. doi:10.1093/jpepsy/jsq099

Krain, A. L., & Castellanos, F. X. (2006). Brain development and ADHD. *Clinical Psychology Review, 26*, 433–444. doi:10.1016/j.cpr.2006.01.005

Krain, A. L., Hefton, S., Pine, D. S., Ernst, M., Castellanos, F. X., Klein, R. G., & Milham, M. P. (2006). An fMRI examination of developmental differences in the neural correlates of uncertainty and decision making. *Journal of Child Psychology and Psychiatry, 47*, 1023–1030. doi:10.1111/j.1469-7610.2006.01677.x

Krain, A. L., & Kendall, P. C. (2000). The role of parental emotional distress in parent report of child anxiety. *Journal of Clinical Child Psychology, 29*, 328–335. doi:10.1207/S15374424JCCP2903_4

Kral, T. V. E., & Faith, M. S. (2009). Influences on child eating and weight development from a behavioral genetics perspective. *Journal of Pediatric Psychology, 34*, 596–605. doi:10.1093/jpepsy/jsn037

Kratzer, L., & Hodgins, S. (1997). Adult outcomes of child conduct problems: A cohort study. *Journal of Abnormal Child Psychology, 25*, 65–81. doi:10.1023/A:1025711525255

Krentz, E. M., & Warschburger, P. (2011). Sports-related correlates of disordered eating in aesthetic sports. *Psychology of Sport and Exercise, 12*, 375–382. doi:10.1016/j.psychsport.2011.03.004

Krijn, M., Emmelkamp, P. M. G., Olafsson, R. P., & Biemond, R. (2004). Virtual reality exposure therapy of anxiety disorders: A review. *Clinical Psychology Review, 24*, 259–281. doi:10.1016/j.cpr.2004.04.001

Kroneman, L. M., Hipwell, A. E., Loeber, R., Koot, H. M., & Pardini, D. A. (2011). Contextual risk factors as predictors of disruptive behavior disorder trajectories in girls: The moderating effect of callous-unemotional features. *Journal of Child Psychology and Psychiatry, 52*, 167–175. doi:10.1111/j.1469-7610.2010.02300.x

Krug, I., Root, T., Bulik, C., Granero, R., Penelo, E., Jiménez-Murcia, S., & Fernández-Aranda, F. (2011). Redefining phenotypes in eating disorders based on personality: A latent profile analysis. *Psychiatry Research, 188*, 439–445. doi:10.1016/j.psychres.2011.05.026

Kruger, T. H. C., & Schiffer, B. (2011). Neurocognitive and personality factors in homo- and heterosexual pedophiles and controls. *Journal of Sexual Medicine, 8*, 1650–1659. doi:10.1111/j.1743–6109.2009.01564.x

Krull, K. R., Huang, S., Gurney, J. G., Klosky, J. L., Leisenring, W., Termuhlen, A., . . . Hudson, M. M. (2010). Adolescent behavior and adult health status in childhood cancer survivors. *Journal of Cancer Survivorship, 4*, 210–217. doi:10.1007/s11764-010-0123-0

Kuhl, E. S., Hoodin, F., Rice, J., Felt, B. T., Rausch, J. R., & Patton, S. R. (2010). Increasing daily water intake and fluid adherence in children receiving treatment for retentive encopresis. *Journal of Pediatric Psychology, 35*, 1144–1151. doi:10.1093/jpepsy/jsq033

Kuhl, P. K., Stevens, E., Hayashi, A., Deguchi, T., Kiritani, S., & Iverson, P. (2006). Infants show a facilitation effect for native language phonetic perception between 6 and 12 months. *Developmental Science, 9*, F13–F21. doi:10.1111/j.1467-7687.2006.00468.x

Kumar, A., Sundaram, S. K., Sivaswamy, L., Behen, M. E., Makki, M. I., Ager J., . . . Chugani, D. C. (2010). Alterations in frontal lobe tracts and corpus callosum in young children with autism spectrum disorder. *Cerebral Cortex, 20*, 2103–2013. doi:10.1093/cercor/bhp278

Kumpfer, K. L., Alvarado, R., Smith, P., & Bellamy, N. (2002). Cultural sensitivity and adaptation in family-based prevention interventions. *Prevention Science, 3*, 241–246. doi:10.1023/A:1019902902119

Kutcher, S., Aman, M., Brooks, S. J., Buitelaar, J., van Daalen, E., Fegert, J., . . . Tyano, S. (2004). International consensus statement on attention-deficit/hyperactivity disorder (ADHD) and disruptive behaviour disorders (DBDs): Clinical implications and treatment practice suggestions. *European Neuropsychopharmacology, 14*, 11–28. doi:10.1016/S0924-977X(03)00045-2

Kuusikko, S., Pollock-Wurman, R., Jussila, K., Carter, A. S., Mattila, M. L., Ebeling, H., . . . Moilanen, I. (2008). Social anxiety and high-functioning children and adolescents with autism and Asperger syndrome. *Journal of Autism and Developmental Disorders, 38*, 1697–1709. doi:10.1007/s10803-008-0555-9

Kyriakopoulos, M., & Frangou, S. (2007). Pathophysiology of early onset schizophrenia. *International Review of Psychiatry, 19*, 315–324. doi:10.1080/09540260701486258

La Greca, A. M., Bearman, K. J., & Moore, H. (2002). Peer relations of youth with pediatric conditions and health risks: Promoting social support and healthy lifestyles. *Journal of Developmental & Behavioral Pediatrics, 23*, 271–280. Retrieved from http://www.sdbp.org/journal.cfm

La Greca, A. M., & Lopez, N. (1998). Social anxiety among adolescents: Linkages with peer relations and friendships. *Journal of Abnormal Child Psychology, 26*, 83–94. doi:10.1023/A:1022684520514

La Greca, A. M., Silverman, W., Vernberg, E., & Roberts, M. C. (Eds.). (2002). *Helping children copy with disasters and terrorism*. Washington, DC: APA Books.

Lachar, D. (1999). Personality Inventory for Children, Second Edition (PIC-2), Personality Inventory for Youth (PIY), and Student Behavior Survey (SBS). In M. E. Maruish (Ed.), *The use of psychological testing for treatment planning and outcomes assessment* (2nd ed., pp. 399–427). Mahwah, NJ: Erlbaum.

LaFreniere, P. J. (2000). *Emotional development: A biosocial perspective.* Belmont, CA: Wadsworth.

LaGrange, B., Cole, D. A., Dallaire, D. H., Ciesla, J. A., Pineda, A. Q., Truss, A. E., & Follmer, A. (2008). Developmental changes in depressive cognitions: A longitudinal evaluation of the cognitive triad inventory for children. *Psychological Assessment, 20,* 217–226. doi:10.1037/1040-3590.20.3.217

Lahey, B. B. (2008). Oppositional defiant disorder, conduct disorder, and juvenile delinquency. In T. P. Beauchaine & S. P. Hinshaw (Eds.), *Child and adolescent psychopathology* (pp. 335–369). Hoboken, NJ: Wiley.

Lahey, B. B., Goodman, S. H., Waldman, I. D., Bird, H., Canino, G., Jensen, P., . . . Applegate, B. (1999). Relation of age of onset to type and severity of child and adolescent conduct problems. *Journal of Abnormal Child Psychology, 27,* 247–260. doi:10.1023/A:1022661224769

Lahey, B. B., Loeber, R., Burke, J. D., & Applegate, B. (2005). Predicting future antisocial personality disorder in males from a clinical assessment in childhood. *Journal of Consulting and Clinical Psychology, 73,* 389–399. doi:10.1037/0022-006X.73.3.389

Lahey, B. B., Loeber, R., Burke, J., & Rathouz, P. J. (2002). Adolescent outcomes of childhood conduct disorder among clinic-referred boys: Predictors of improvement. *Journal of Abnormal Child Psychology, 30,* 333–348. doi:10.1023/A:1015761723226

Lahey, B. B., Loeber, R., Hart, E. L., Frick, P. J., Applegate, B., Zhang, Q., . . .Russo, M. F. (1995). Four-year longitudinal study of conduct disorder in boys: Patterns and predictors of persistence. *Journal of Abnormal Psychology, 104,* 83–93. doi:10.1037/0021-843X.104.1.83

Lahey, B. B., Loeber, R., Quay, H. C., Frick, P. J., & Grimm, S. (1992). Oppositional defiant and conduct disorders: Issues to be resolved for DSM-IV. *Journal of the American Academy of Child & Adolescent Psychiatry, 31,* 539–546. doi:10.1097/00004583-199205000-00023

Lahey, B. B., Miller, T. L., Gordon, R. A., & Riley, A. W. (1999). Developmental epidemiology of the disruptive behavior disorders. In H. C. Quay & A. E. Hogan (Eds.), *Handbook of disruptive behavior disorders* (pp. 23–48). New York: Kluwer/Plenum Press.

Lahey, B. B., Rathouz, P. J., Lee, S. S., Chronis-Tuscano, A., Pelham, W. E., Waldman, I. E., & Cook, E. H. (2011). Interactions between early parenting and a polymorphism of the child's dopamine transporter gene in predicting future child conduct disorder symptoms. *Journal of Abnormal Psychology, 120,* 33–45. doi:10.1037/a0021133

Lahey, B. B., Van Hulle, C. A., D'Onofrio, B. M., Rodgers, J. L., & Waldman, I. D. (2008). Is parental knowledge of their adolescent offspring's whereabouts and peer associations spuriously associated with offspring delinquency? *Journal of Abnormal Child Psychology, 36,* 807–823. doi:10.1007/s10802-008-9214-z

Lahey, B. B., Van Hulle, C. A., Keenan, K., Rathouz, P. J., D'Onofrio, B. M., Rodgers, J. L., & Waldman, I. D. (2008). Temperament and parenting during the first year of life predict future child conduct problems. *Journal of Abnormal Child Psychology, 36,* 1139–1158. doi:10.1007/s10802-008-9247-3

Lahey, B. B., Van Hulle, C. A., Waldman, L. C., Rodgers, J. L., D'Onofrio, B. M., Pedlow, S., . . . Keenan, K. (2006). Testing descriptive hypotheses regarding sex differences in the development of conduct problems and delinquency. *Journal of Abnormal Child Psychology, 34,* 737–755. doi:10.1007/s10802-006-9064-5

Lahey, B. B., & Waldman, I. D. (2003). A developmental propensity model of the origins of conduct problems during childhood and adolescence. In B. B. Lahey, T. E. Moffitt, & A. Caspi (Eds.), *Causes of conduct disorder and juvenile delinquency* (pp. 76–117). New York: Guilford Press.

Lahey, B. B., & Willcutt, E. G. (2010). Predictive validity of a continuous alternative to nominal subtypes of attention-deficit/hyperactivity disorder for DSM-V. *Journal of Clinical Child and Adolescent Psychology, 39,* 761–775. doi:10.1080/15374416.2010.517173

Lahti, J., Raikkonen, K., Sovio, U., Miettunen, J., Hartikainen, A-L., Pouta, A., . . . Veijola, J. (2009). Early-life origins of schizotypal traits in adulthood. *British Journal of Psychiatry, 195,* 132–137. doi:10.1192/bjp.bp.108.054387

Laird, R. D., Jordan, K., Dodge, K. A., Pettit, G. S., & Bates, J. E. (2001). Peer rejection in childhood, involvement with antisocial peers in early adolescence, and the development of externalizing problems. *Development and Psychopathology, 13,* 337–354. doi:10.1017/S0954579401002085

Laird, R. D., Pettit, G. S., Dodge, K. A., & Bates, J. E. (2005). Peer relationship antecedents of delinquent behavior in late adolescence: Is there evidence of demographic group differences in developmental processes? *Development & Psychopathology, 17,* 127–144. doi:10.1017/S0954579405050078

Lakdawalla, Z., Hankin, B. L., & Mermelstein, R. (2007). Cognitive theories of depression in children and adolescents: A conceptual and quantitative review. *Clinical Child and Family Psychology Review, 10,* 1–24. doi:10.1007/s10567-006-0013-1

Lambek, R., Tannock, R., Dalsgaard, S., Trillingsgaard, A., Damm, D., & Thomsen, P. H. (2010). ADHD: How do children with and without an executive function deficit differ? *Journal of Child Psychology and Psychiatry, 51,* 895–904. doi:10.1111/j.1469-7610.2010.02248.x

Lambek, R., Tannock, R., Dalsgaard, S., Trillingsgaard, A., Damm, D., & Thomsen, P. H. (2011). Executive dysfunction in school-age children with ADHD. *Journal of Attention Disorders, 15,* 646–655. doi:10.1177/1087054710370935

Lancioni, G. E., Singh, N. N., O'Reilly, M. F., & Sigafoos, J. (2009). Intellectual disability and adaptive-social skills. In J. L. Matson (Ed.), *Social behavior and skills in children* (pp. 141–157). New York: Springer Science + Business Media.

Landa, R. J., Holman, K. C., O'Neill, A. H., & Stuart, E. A. (2011). Synchronous engagement in toddlers with autism spectrum disorder: A randomized controlled trial. *Journal of Child Psychology and Psychiatry, 52,* 13–21. doi:10.1111/j.1469-7610.2010.02288.x

Landau, S., & Milich, R. (1988). Social communication patterns of attention-deficit-disordered boys. *Journal of Abnormal Child Psychology, 16,* 69–81. doi:10.1007/BF00910501

Landerl, K., & Moll, K. (2010). Comorbidity of learning disorders: Prevalence and familial transmission. *Journal of Child Psychology and Psychiatry, 51,* 287–294. doi:10.1111/j.1469-7610.2009.02164.x

Lang, A. R., Pelham, W. E., Johnston, C., & Gelernter, S. (1989). Levels of adult alcohol consumption induced by interactions with child confederates exhibiting normal versus externalizing behaviors. *Journal of Abnormal Psychology, 98,* 294–299. doi:10.1037/0021-843X.98.3.294

Lansford, J. E., Criss, M. M., Laird, R. D., Shaw, D. S., Pettit, G. S., Bates, J. E., & Dodge, K. A. (2011). Reciprocal relations between parents' physical discipline and children's externalizing behavior during middle childhood and adolescence. *Development and Psychopathology, 23,* 225–238. doi:10.1017/S0954579410000751

Lansford, J. E., Dodge, K. A., Pettit, G. S., & Bates, J. E. (2010). Does physical abuse in early childhood predict substance use in adolescence and early adulthood? *Child Maltreatment, 15,* 190–194. doi:10.1177/1077559509352359

Lansford, J. E., Malone, P. S., Dodge, K. A., Pettit, G. S., & Bates, J. E. (2010). Developmental cascades of peer rejection, social information processing biases, and aggression during middle childhood. *Development and Psychopathology. Special Issue: Developmental Cascades: Part 1, 22,* 593–602. doi:10.1017/S0954579410000301

Lansford, J. E., Miller-Johnson, S., Berlin, L. J., Dodge, K. A., Bates, J. E., & Pettit, G. S. (2007). Early physical abuse and later violent delinquency: A prospective longitudinal study. *Child Maltreatment, 12,* 233–245.

Larkby, C. A., Goldschmidt, Hanusa, B. H., & Day, N. L. (2011). Prenatal alcohol exposure is associated with conduct disorder in adolescence: Findings from a birth cohort. *Journal of the American Academy of Child & Adolescent Psychiatry, 50,* 262–271. doi:10.1016/joac.2010.12.004

Larkin, R. F., & Snowling, M. J. (2008). Comparing phonological skills and spelling abilities in children with reading and language impairments. *International Journal of Language & Communication Disorders, 43,* 111–124. doi:10.1080/13682820601178584

Larsson, H., Viding, E., Rijsdijk, F. V., & Plomin, R. (2008). Relationships between parental negativity and childhood antisocial behavior over time: A bidirectional effects model in a longitudinal genetically informative design. *Journal of Abnormal Child Psychology, 36*, 633–645. doi:10.1007/s10802-007-9151-2

Last, C. G. (1988). Separation anxiety. In M. Hersen & C. G. Last (Eds.), *Child behavior therapy casebook* (pp. 11–17). New York: Plenum Press.

Last, C. G., & Perrin, S. (1993). Anxiety disorders in African-American and white children. *Journal of Abnormal Child Psychology, 21*, 153–164. doi:10.1007/BF00911313

Last, C. G., Perrin, S., Hersen, M., & Kazdin, A. E. (1996). A prospective study of childhood anxiety disorders. *Journal of the American Academy of Child & Adolescent Psychiatry, 35*, 1502–1510. doi:10.1097/00004583-199611000-00019

Last, C. G., & Strauss, C. C. (1989). Panic disorder in children and adolescents. *Journal of Anxiety Disorders, 3*, 87–95. doi:10.1016/0887-6185(89)90003-0

Latendresse, S. J., Rose, R. J., Viken, R. J., Pulkkinen, L., Kaprio, J., & Dick, D. M. (2008). Parenting mechanisms in links between parents' and adolescents' alcohol use behaviors. *Alcoholism: Clinical and Experimental Research, 32*, 322–330. doi:10.1111/j.1530-0277.2007.00583.x

Lau, J. Y., Britton, J. C., Nelson, E. E., Angold, A., Ernst, M., Goldwin, M., . . . Pine, D. S. (2011). Distinct neural signatures of threat learning in adolescents and adults. *PNAS, 108*, 4500–4505. doi:10.1073/pnas.1005494108

Lau, J. Y. F., Goldman, D., Buzas, B., Fromm, S. J., Guyer, A. E., Hodgkinson, C., . . . Ernst, M. (2009). Amygdala function and 5-HTT gene variants in adolescent anxiety and major depressive disorder. *Biological Psychiatry, 65*, 349–355. doi:10.1016/j.biopsych.2008.08.037

Lau, J. Y. F., & Pine, D. S. (2008). Elucidating risk mechanisms of gene-environment interactions on pediatric anxiety: Integrating findings from neuroscience. *European Archives of Psychiatry and Clinical Neurosciences, 258*, 97–206. doi:10.1007/s00406-007-0788-1

Laucht, M., Skowronek, M. H., Becker, K., Schmidt, M. H., Esser, G., Schulze, T. G., . . . Rietschel, M. (2007). Interacting effects of the transporter gene and psychosocial adversity on the attention-deficit/hyperactivity disorder symptoms among 15-year-olds from a high-risk community sample. *Archives of General Psychiatry, 64*, 585–590. Retrieved from http://archpsyc.ama-assn.org/

Laufer, M., Denhoff, E., & Solomons, G. (1957). Hyperkinetic impulse disorder in children's behavior problems. *Psychosomatic Medicine, 19*, 38–49. Retrieved from http://www.psychosomaticmedicine.org/

Lavigne, J. V., & Faier-Routman, J. (1993). Correlates of psychological adjustment to pediatric physical disorders: A meta-analytic review and comparison with existing models. *Journal of Developmental and Behavioral Pediatrics, 14*, 117–123. doi:10.1097/00004703-199304000-00007

Law, J., Garrett, Z., & Nye, C. (2004). The efficacy of treatment for children with developmental speech and language delay/disorder: A meta-analysis. *Journal of Speech, Language, and Hearing Research, 47*, 924–943. doi:10.1044/1092-4388(2004/069)

Lawler, M., & Nixon, E. (2011). Body dissatisfaction among adolescent boys and girls: The effects of body mass, peer appearance culture and internalization of appearance ideals. *Journal of Youth and Adolescence, 40*, 59–71. doi:10.1007/s10964-009-9500-2

LeBeau, R. T., Glenn, D., Liao, B., Wittchen, H.-U., Bessdo-Baum, K., Ollendick, T., & Craske, M. G. (2010). Specific phobia: A review of DSM-IV specific phobia and preliminary recommendations for DSM-V. *Depression and Anxiety, 27*, 148–167. doi:10.1002/da.20655

Leckman, J. F., Denys, D., Simpson, H. B., Mataix-Cols, D., Hollander, E., Saxena, S., . . . Stein, D. J. (2010). Obsessive-compulsive disorder: A review of the diagnostic criteria and possible subtypes and dimensional specifiers for DSM-V. *Depression and Anxiety, 27*, 507–527. doi:10.1002/da.20669

Lee, S. S., Chronis-Tuscano, A., Keenan, K., Pelham, W. E., Loney, J., Van Hulle, C. A., . . . Lahey, B. B. (2010). Association of maternal dopamine transporter genotype with negative parenting: Evidence for a gene-environment interaction with child disruptive behavior. *Molecular Psychiatry, 15*, 548–558. doi:10.1038/mp.2008.102

Lee, S. S., Humphreys, K. L., Flory, K., Liu, R., & Glass, K. (2011). Prospective association of childhood attention-deficit/hyperactivity disorder (ADHD) and substance use and abuse/dependence: A meta-analytic review. *Clinical Psychology Review, 31*, 328–341. doi:10.1016/j.cpr.2011.01.006

Lee, S. S., Lahey, B. B., Owens, E. B., & Hinshaw, S. P. (2008). Few preschool boys and girls with ADHD are well-adjusted during adolescence. *Journal of Abnormal Child Psychology, 36*, 373–383. doi:10.1007/s10802-007-9184-6

Lee, S., Lee, A. M., & Leung, T. (1998). Cross-cultural validity of the eating disorder inventory: A study of Chinese patients with eating disorders in Hong Kong. *International Journal of Eating Disorders, 23*, 177–188. doi:10.1002/(SICI)1098-108X(199803)23:2<177::AID-EAT8>3.0.CO;2-H

Lee, W. E., Wadsworth, M. E. J., & Hotopf, M. (2006). The protective role of trait anxiety: A longitudinal study. *Psychological Medicine, 36*, 345–351. doi:10.1017/S0033291705006847

Leekam, S. R., Nieto, C., Libby, S. J., Wing, L., & Gould, J. (2007). Describing the sensory abnormalities of children and adults with autism. *Journal of Autism and Developmental Disorders, 37*, 894–910. doi:10.1007/s10803-006-0218-7

Leekam, S. R., Prior, M. R., Uljarevic, M. (2011). Restricted and repetitive behaviors in autism spectrum disorders: A review of research in the last decade. *Psychological Bulletin, 137*, 562–593. doi:10.1037/a0023341

Leffert, J. S., Siperstein, G. N., & Widaman, K. F. (2010). Social perception in children with intellectual disabilities: The interpretation of benign and hostile intentions. *Journal of Intellectual Disability Research, 54*, 168–180. doi:10.1111/j.1365-2788.2009.01240.x

Legerstee, J. S., Garnefski, N., Jellesma, F. C., Verhulst, F. C., & Utens, E. M. W. J. (2010). Cognitive coping and childhood anxiety disorders. *European Child and Adolescent Psychiatry, 19*, 143–150. doi:10.1007/s00787-009-0051-6

Leibenluft, E., & Rich, B. A. (2008). Pediatric bipolar disorder. *Annual Review of Clinical Psychology, 4*, 163–187. doi:10.1146/annurev.clinpsy.4.022007.141216

Leibson, C. L., Katusic, S., Barbaresi, W. J., Ransom, J., & O'Brien, P. C. (2001). Use and costs of medical care for children and adolescents with and without attention-deficit/hyperactivity disorder. *JAMA: Journal of the American Medical Association, 285*, 60–66. doi:10.1001/jama.285.1.60

Leichtman, M. (2004). Projective tests: The nature of the task. In M. J. Hilsenroth & D. L. Segal (Eds.), *Comprehensive handbook of psychological assessment: Vol. 2. Personality assessment* (pp. 297–314). New York: Wiley.

Leland, J. (1995, December 11). Violence, reel to real. *Newsweek*, 46–48. Retrieved from http://www.newsweek.com/1995/12/10/violence-reel-to-real.html

Lemery, K. S., & Doelger, K. S. (2005). Genetic vulnerabilities to the development of psychopathology. In B. L. Hankin & J. R. Z. Abela (Eds.), *Development of psychopathology: A vulnerability-stress perspective* (pp. 161–198). Thousand Oaks, CA: Sage Publications.

Lenroot, R. K., & Giedd, J. N. (2011). Annual research review: Developmental considerations of gene by environment interactions. *Journal of Child Psychology and Psychiatry, 52*, 429–441. doi:10.1111/j.1469-7610.2011.02381.x

Lenze, S. N., Pautsch, J., & Luby, J. (2011). Parent-child interaction therapy emotion development: A novel treatment for depression in preschool children. *Depression and Anxiety, 28*, 153–159. doi:10.1002/da.20770

Leonard, H., Silberstein, J., Falk, R., Houwink-Manville, I., Ellaway, C., Raffaele, L. S., . . . Schanen, C. (2001). Occurrence of Rett syndrome in boys. *Journal of Child Neurology, 16*, 333–338. doi:10.1177/088307380101600505

Leonard, H. L., & Dow, S. (1995). Selective mutism. In J. S. March (Ed.), *Anxiety disorders in children and adolescents* (pp. 235–250). New York: Guilford Press.

Lesch, K. P., Bengel, D., Heils, A., Sabol, S. Z., Greenberg, B. D., Petri, S., & Murphy, D. L. (1996). Association of anxiety-related traits with a polymorphism in the serotonin transporter gene regulatory region. *Science, 274*, 1527–1531. doi:10.1126/science.274.5292.1527

Lesser, S. T. (1972). Psychoanalysis with children. In B. B. Wolman (Ed.), *Manual of child psychopathology* (pp. 847–864). New York: McGraw-Hill.

Leventhal, T., & Brooks-Gunn, J. (2000). The neighborhoods they live in: The effects of neighborhood residence on child and adolescent outcomes.

Psychological Bulletin, 126, 309–337. doi:10.1037/0033-2909.126.2.309

Levin, B. E. (2010). Developmental gene × environment interactions affecting systems regulating energy homeostasis and obesity. *Frontiers in Neuroendocrinology, 31*, 270–283. doi:10.1016/j.yfrne.2010.02.005

Levine, K. (1995, October). Childhood depression. *Parents*, 42–45.

Levine, M., & Levine, A. (1992). *Helping children: A social history*. New York: Oxford University Press.

Levine, M. P., & Smolak, L. (2010). Cultural influences on body image and the eating disorders. In W. S. Agras (Ed.), *The Oxford handbook of eating disorders*. (pp. 223–246). New York: Oxford University Press.

Levinson, D. F. (2006). The genetics of depression: A review. *Biological Psychiatry, 60*, 84–92. doi:10.1016/j.biopsych.2005.08.024

Levitt, E. E., & French, J. (1992). Projective testing of children. In C. E. Walker & M. C. Roberts (Eds.), *Handbook of clinical child psychology* (2nd ed., pp. 149–162). New York: Wiley.

Levitt, S. D., & Fryer, R. G. (2004). Falling behind: New evidence on the Black-White achievement gap. *Education Next, 4*, 64–71. Retrieved from http://educationnext.org/

Levy, F., & Hay, D. (2001). *Attention, genes, and ADHD*. Philadelphia: Brunner-Routledge.

Lewandowski, A., & Drotar, D. (2007). The relationship between parent-reported social support and adherence to medical treatment in families of adolescents with type 1 diabetes. *Journal of Pediatric Psychology, 32*, 427–436. doi:10.1093/jpepsy/jsl037

Lewin-Bizan, S., Bowers, E. P., & Lerner, R. M. (2010). One good thing leads to another: Cascades of positive youth development among American adolescents. *Development and Psychopathology. Special Issue: Developmental Cascades: Part 2, 22*, 759–770. doi:10.1017/S0954579410000441

Lewinsohn, P. M. (1974). A behavioral approach to depression. In R. Friedman & M. Katz (Eds.), *The psychology of depression: Contemporary theory and research* (pp. 157–185). Washington, DC: Winston-Wiley.

Lewinsohn, P. M., & Essau, C. A. (2002). Depression in adolescents. In I. H. Gotlib & C. L. Hammen (Eds.), *Handbook of depression* (pp. 541–559). New York: Guilford Press.

Lewinsohn, P. M., Gotlib, I. H., Lewinsohn, M., Seeley, J. R., & Allen, N. B. (1998). Gender differences in anxiety disorders and anxiety symptoms in adolescents. *Journal of Abnormal Psychology, 107*, 109–117. doi:10.1037/0021-843X.107.1.109

Lewinsohn, P. M., Gotlib, I. H., & Seeley, J. R. (1997). Depression-related psychosocial variables: Are they specific to depression in adolescents? *Journal of Abnormal Psychology, 106*, 365–375. doi:10.1037/0021-843X.106.3.365

Lewinsohn, P. M., Holm-Denoma, J. M., Small, J. W., Seeley, J. R., & Joiner, T. E. (2008). Separation anxiety disorder in childhood as a risk factor for future mental illness. *Journal of the American Academy of Child & Adolescent Psychiatry, 47*, 548–555. doi:10.1097/CHI.0b013e31816765e7

Lewinsohn, P. M., Hops, H., Roberts, R. E., Seeley, J. R., & Andrews, J. A. (1993). Adolescent psychopathology: I. Prevalence and incidence of depression and other DSM-III-R disorders in high school students. *Journal of Abnormal Psychology, 102*, 133–144. doi:10.1037/0021-843X.102.1.133

Lewinsohn, P. M., Klein, D., & Seeley, J. R. (1995). Bipolar disorders in a community sample of older adolescents: Prevalence, phenomenology, comorbidity, and course. *Journal of the American Academy of Child & Adolescent Psychiatry, 34*, 454–463. doi:10.1097/00004583-199504000-00012

Lewinsohn, P. M., Klein, D. N., & Seeley, J. (2000). Bipolar disorder during adolescence and young adulthood in a community sample. *Bipolar Disorder, 2*, 281–293. doi:10.1034/j.1399-5618.2000.20309.x

Lewinsohn, P. M., Pettit, J. W., Joiner, T. E., & Seeley, J. R. (2003). The symptomatic expression of major depressive disorder in adolescents and young adults. *Journal of Abnormal Psychology, 112*, 244–252. doi:10.1037/0021-843X.112.2.244

Lewinsohn, P. M., Roberts, R. E., Seeley, J. R., Rohde, P., Gotlib, I. H., & Hops, H. (1994). Adolescent psychopathology: II. Psychosocial risk factors for depression. *Journal of Abnormal Psychology, 103*, 302–315. doi:10.1037/0021-843X.103.2.302

Lewinsohn, P. M., Seeley, J. R., Buckley, M. E., & Klein, D. N. (2002). Bipolar disorder in adolescence and young adulthood. *Child and Adolescent Psychiatric Clinics of North America, 11*, 461–476. doi:10.1016/S1056-4993(02)00005-6

Lewinsohn, P. M., Striegel-Moore, R., & Seeley, J. (2000). Epidemiology and natural course of eating disorders in young women from adolescence to young adulthood. *Journal of the American Academy of Child & Adolescent Psychiatry, 39*, 1284–1292. doi:10.1097/00004583-200010000-00016

Lewis, D. A., & Lieberman, J. A. (2000). Catching up on schizophrenia: Natural history and neurobiology. *Neuron, 28*, 325–334. doi:10.1016/S0896-6273(00)00111-2

Lewis, J. D., & Elman, J. L. (2008). Growth-related neural organization and the autism phenotype: A test of the hypothesis that altered brain growth leads to altered connectivity. *Developmental Science, 11*, 135–155. doi:10.1111/j.1467-7687.2007.00634.x

Lewis-Fernández, R., Hinton, D. E., Laria, A. J., Patterson, E. H., Hofmann, S. G., Craske, M. G., . . . Liao, B. (2010). Culture and anxiety disorders: Recommendations for DSM-V. *Depression and Anxiety, 27*, 212–229. doi:10.1002/da.20647

Li, D., Sham, P. C., Owen, M. J., & He, L. (2006). Meta-analysis shows significant association between dopamine system genes and attention deficit hyperactivity disorder (ADHD). *Human Molecular Genetics, 15*, 2276–2284. doi:10.1093/hmg/ddl152

Libby, A. M., Brent, D. A., Morrato, E. H., Orton, H. D., Allen, R., & Valuck, R. J. (2007). Decline in treatment of pediatric depression after FDA advisory on risk of suicidality with SSRIs. *American Journal of Psychiatry, 164*, 884–891. doi:10.1176/appi.ajp.164.6.884

Liberman, I. Y., & Shankweiler, D. (1991). Phonology and beginning reading: A tutorial. In L. Rieben & C. A. Perfetti (Eds.), *Learning to read: Basic research and its implications* (pp. 46–73). Hillsdale, NJ: Erlbaum.

Lichtenstein, P., Carlström, E., Råstam, M., Gillberg, C., & Anckarsäter H. (2010). The genetics of autism spectrum disorders and related neuropsychiatric disorders in childhood. *American Journal of Psychiatry, 167*, 1357–1363. doi:10.1176/appi.ajp.2010.10020223

Lilienfeld, S. O. (2007). Psychological treatments that cause harm. *Perspectives on Psychological Science, 2*, 53–70. doi:10.1111/j.1745-6916.2007.00029.x

Lilienfeld, S. O., Lynn, S., J., & Lohr, J. M. (Eds.). (2003). *Science and pseudoscience in clinical psychology*. New York: Guilford Press.

Lilienfeld, S. O., Wood, J. M., & Garb, H. N. (2006). Why questionable psychological tests remain popular. *Scientific Review of Alternative Medicine, 10*, 6–15. Retrieved from http://www.sram.org/

Linares, L. O. (2006). An understudied form of intra-family violence: Sibling-to-sibling aggression among foster children. *Aggression and Violent Behavior, 11*, 95–109. doi:10.1016/j.avb.2005.07.001

Lindsay, A. C., Sussner, K. M., Greaney, M. L., & Peterson, K. E. (2011). Latina mothers' beliefs and practices related to weight status, feeding, and the development of child overweight. *Public Health Nursing, 28*, 107. doi:10.1111/j.1525-1446.2010.00906.x

Lindström, K., Lindblad, F., & Hjern, A. (2011). Preterm birth and attention-deficit/hyperactivity disorder in school children. *Pediatrics, 127*, 858–865. doi:10.1542/peds.2010-1279

Linnet, K. M., Dalsgaard, S., Obel, C., Wisborg, K., Henriksen, T. B., Rodriguez, A., . . . Jarvelin, M. (2003). Maternal lifestyle factors in pregnancy risk of attention deficit hyperactivity disorder and associated behaviors: Review of the current evidence. *American Journal of Psychiatry, 160*, 1028–1040. Retrieved from http://ajp.psychiatryonline.org/

Linscheid, T. R. (2006). Behavioral treatments for pediatric feeding disorders. *Behavior Modification, 30*, 6–23. doi:10.1177/0145445505282165

Lipka, O., & Siegel, L. S. (2006). Learning disabilities. In D. A. Wolfe & E. J. Mash (Eds.), *Behavioral and emotional disorders in adolescents: Nature, assessment, and treatment* (pp. 410–443). New York: Guilford Press.

Lipsey, M. W. (1995). What do we learn from 400 research studies on the effectiveness of treatment with juvenile delinquents? In J. McGuire (Ed.), *What works: Reducing reoffending: Guidelines from research and practice* (pp. 63–78). Chichester, England: Wiley.

Lisak, D. (1994). The psychological impact of sexual abuse: Content analysis of interviews with male survivors. *Journal of Traumatic Stress, 7*, 525–548.

Lissau, I., Overpeck, M. D., Ruan, W. J., Due, P., Holstein, B. E., Hediger, M. L., & the Health Behaviour in School-aged Children Obesity Working Group. (2004). Body mass index and overweight in adolescents in 13 European countries, Israel, and the United States. *Archives of Pediatrics and Adolescent Medicine, 158*, 27–33. Retrieved from http://archpedi.ama-assn.org/

Liston, C., Cohen, M. M., Teslovich, T., Levenson, D., & Casey, B. J. (2011). Atypical prefrontal connectivity in attention-deficit/hyperactivity disorder: Pathway to disease or pathological end point? *Biological Psychiatry, 69*, 1168–1177. doi:10.1016/j.biopsych.2011.03.022

Little, S. G., Akin-Little, A., & Newman-Eig, L. M. (2010). Effects on homework completion and accuracy of varied and constant reinforcement within an interdependent group contingency system. *Journal of Applied School Psychology, 26*, 115–131. doi:10.1080/15377900903471989

Lobato, D., Kao, B., Plante, W., Seifer, R., Grullon, E., Cheas, L., & Canino, G. (2011). Psychological and school functioning of Latino siblings of children with intellectual disability. *Journal of Child Psychology and Psychiatry, 52*, 696–703. doi:10.1111/j.1469-7610.2010.02357.x

Lobstein, T. (2010). China joins the fatter nations. *International Journal of Pediatric Obesity, 5*, 362–364. doi:10.3109/17477166.2010.510563

Lochman, J. E., Powell, N. P., Boxmeyer, C. L., & Jimenez-Camargo, L. (2011). Cognitive behavioral therapy for externalizing disorders in children and adolescents. *Child and Adolescent Psychiatric Clinic of North America, 20*, 305–318. doi:10.1016/j.chc.2011.01.005

Lock, J., Garrett, A., Beenhakker, J., & Reiss, A. L. (2011). Aberrant brain activation during a response inhibition task in adolescent eating disorder subtypes. *The American Journal of Psychiatry, 168*, 55–64. doi:10.1176/appi.ajp.2010.10010056

Lock, J., & Le Grange, D. (2006). Eating disorders in adolescence. In D. A. Wolfe & E. J. Mash (Eds.), *Behavioral and emotional disorders in adolescents: Nature, assessment, and treatment* (pp. 485–504). New York: Guilford Press.

Lock, J., Le Grange, D., Agras, W. S., Moye, A., Bryson, S. W., & Jo, B. (2010). Randomized clinical trial comparing family-based treatment with adolescent-focused individual therapy for adolescents with anorexia nervosa. *Archives of General Psychiatry, 67*, 1025–1032. doi:10.1001/archgenpsychiatry.2010.128

Loe, I. M., & Feldman, H. M. (2007). Academic and educational outcomes of children with ADHD. *Journal of Pediatric Psychology, 32*, 643–654. doi:10.1093/jpepsy/jsl054

Loeber, R., Burke, J. D., & Pardini, D. A. (2009a). Development and etiology of disruptive and delinquent behavior. *Annual Review of Clinical Psychology, 5*, 291–310. doi:10.1146/annurev.clinpsy.032408.153631

Loeber, R., Burke, J. D., & Pardini, D. A. (2009b). Perspectives on oppositional defiant disorder, conduct disorder, and psychopathic features. *Journal of Child Psychology and Psychiatry, 50*, 133–142. doi:10.1111/j.1469-7610.2008.02011.x

Loeber, R., Burke, J. D., Lahey, B. B., Winters, A., & Zera, M. (2000). Oppositional defiant and conduct disorder: A review of the past 10 years, Part 1. *Journal of the American Academy of Child & Adolescent Psychiatry, 39*, 1468–1484. doi:10.1097/00004583-200012000-00007

Loeber, R., & Farrington, D. P. (2000). Young children who commit crime: Epidemiology, developmental origins, risk factors, early interventions, and policy implications. *Development and Psychopathology, 12*, 737–762. doi:10.1017/S0954579400004107

Loeber, R., Green, S. M., Lahey, B. B., & Kalb, L. (2000). Physical fighting in childhood as a risk factor for later mental health problems. *Journal of the American Academy of Child & Adolescent Psychiatry, 39*, 421–428. doi:10.1097/00004583-200004000-00010

Loeber, R., Lahey, B. B., & Thomas, C. (1991). Diagnostic conundrum of oppositional defiant disorder and conduct disorder. *Journal of Abnormal Psychology, 100*, 379–390. doi:10.1037/0021-843X.100.3.379

Lofthouse, N., McBurnett, K., Arnold, L. E., & Hurt, E. (2011). Biofeedback and Neurofeedback treatment for ADHD. *Psychiatric Annals, 41*, 42–48. doi:10.3928/00485713-20101221-07

London, K., Bruck, M., Wright, D. B., & Ceci, S. J. (2008). Review of the contemporary literature on how children report sexual abuse to others: Findings, methodological issues, and implications for forensic interviewers. *Memory. Special Issue: New Insights in Trauma and Memory, 16*, 29–47.

Long, K. A., & Marsland, A. L. (2011). Family adjustment to childhood cancer: A systematic review. *Clinical Child and Family Psychology Review, 14*, 57–88. doi:10.1007/s10567-010-0082-z

Lonigan, C. J., Phillips, B. M., & Hooe, E. S. (2003). Relations of positive and negative affectivity to anxiety and depression in children: Evidence from a latent variable longitudinal study. *Journal of Consulting and Clinical Psychology, 71*, 465–481. doi:10.1037/0022-006X.71.3.465

Lonigan, C. J., Vasey, M. W., Phillips, B. M., & Hazen, R. A. (2004). Temperament, anxiety, and the processing of threat-relevant stimuli. *Journal of Clinical Child and Adolescent Psychology, 33*, 8–20. doi:10.1207/S15374424JCCP3301_2

Loo, J. H. Y., Bamiou, D., Campbell, N., & Luxon, L. M. (2010). Computer-based auditory training (CBAT): Benefits for children with language- and reading-related learning difficulties. *Developmental Medicine & Child Neurology, 52*, 708–717. doi:10.1111/j.1469-8749.2010.03654.x

Looby, A. (2008). Childhood attention deficit hyperactivity disorder and the development of substance use disorders: Valid concern or exaggeration? *Addictive Behaviors, 33*, 451–463. doi:10.1016/j.addbeh.2007.10.006

Lopez-Duran, N. L., Kovacs, M., & George, C. J. (2009). Hypothalamic-pituitary-adrenal axis dysregulation in depressed children and adolescents: A meta-analysis. *Psychoendocrinology, 34*, 1272–1283. doi:10.1016/j.psyneuen.2009.03.016

Lorber, M. (2004). Psychophysiology of aggression, psychopathy, and conduct problems. *Psychological Bulletin, 130*, 531–552. doi:10.1037/0033-2909.130.4.531

Lord, C., Cook, E. H., Leventhal, B. L., & Amaral, D. G. (2000). Autism spectrum disorders. *Neuron, 28*, 355–363. doi:10.1016/S0896-6273(00)00115-X

Loth, E., Gomez, J. C., & Happé, F. (2008). Event schemas in autism spectrum disorders: The role of theory of mind and weak central coherence. *Journal of Autism and Developmental Disorders, 38*, 449–463. doi:10.1007/s10803-007-0412-2

Lotter, V. (1978). Follow-up studies. In M, Rutter & E. Schopler (Eds.), *Autism: A reappraisal of concepts and treatment* (pp. 475–495). New York: Plenum Press.

Lovaas, O. I. (2003). *Teaching individuals with developmental delays*. Austin, TX: Pro-Ed.

Lovaas, O. I., & Smith, T. (2003). Early and intensive behavioral intervention in autism. In A. E. Kazdin & J. R. Weisz (Eds.), *Evidence-based psychotherapies for children and adolescents* (pp. 325–340). New York: Guilford Press.

Loveland, K. A., Tunali-Kotoski, B., Pearson, D. A., Brelsford, K. A., Ortegon, J., & Chen, R. (1994). Imitation and expression of facial affect in autism. *Development and Psychopathology, 6*, 433–444. doi:10.1017/S0954579400006039

Lovett, B. J., & Sheffield, R. A. (2007). Affective empathy deficits in aggressive children and adolescents: A critical review. *Clinical Psychology Review, 27*, 1–13. doi:10.1016/j.cpr.2006.03.003

Lowe, J. (1998). *Oprah Winfrey speaks: Insight from the world's most influential voice*. New York: Wiley.

Luby, J. A., Belden, A., Sullivan, J., Hayen, R., McCadney, A., & Spitznagel, E. (2009). Shame and guilt in preschool depression: Evidence for elevations in self-conscious emotions in depression as early as age 3. *Journal of Child Psychology and Psychiatry, 50*, 1156–1166. doi:10.1111/j.1469-7610.2009.02077.x

Luby, J., & Belden, A. (2006). Defining and validating bipolar disorder in the preschool period. *Development and Psychopathology, 18*, 971–988. doi:10.1017/S0954579406060482

Luby, J. L., Belden, A., Sullivan, J., & Spitznagel, E. (2007). Preschoolers' contribution to their diagnosis of depression and anxiety: Uses and limitations of young child self-report of symptoms. *Child Psychiatry & Human Development, 38*, 321–338. doi:10.1007/s10578-007-0063-8

Luby, J. L., Essex, M. J., Armstrong, J. M., Klein, M. H., Zahn-Waxler, C., Sullivan, J. P., & Goldsmith, H. H. (2009). Gender differences in emotional reactivity of depressed and at-risk preschoolers: Implications for gender specific manifestations of preschool depression. *Journal of Clinical Child and Adolescent Psychology, 38*, 525–537. doi:10.1080/15374410902976312

Luby, J. L., Heffelfinger, A., Mrakotsky, C., Brown, K., Hessler, M., & Spitznagel, E. (2003). Alterations in stress cortisol reactivity in depressed preschoolers relative to psychiatric and no-disorder comparison groups. *Archives of General Psychiatry, 60*, 1248–1255. doi:10.1001/archpsyc.60.12.1248

Luby, J. L., & Navsaria, N. (2010). Pediatric bipolar disorder: Evidence for prodromal states and early markers. *Journal of Child Psychology and Psychiatry, 51*, 459–471. doi:10.1111/j.1469-7610.2010.02210.x

Luby, J. L., Si, X., Belden, A. C., Tandon, M., & Spitznagel, E. (2009). Preschool depression: Homotypic continuity and course over 24 months. *Archives of General Psychiatry, 66*, 897–905. doi:10.1001/archgenpsychiatry.2009.97

Luby, J. L., Tandon, M., & Belden, A. (2009). Preschool bipolar disorder. *Child and Adolescent Psychiatric Clinics of North America, 18*, 391–403. doi:10.1016/j.chc.2008.11.007

Lundahl, B., Risser, H. J., & Lovejoy, M. C. (2006). A meta-analysis of parent training: Moderators and follow-up effects. *Clinical Psychology Review, 26*, 86–104. doi:10.1016/j.cpr.2005.07.004

Luthar, S. S. (2006). Resilience in development: A synthesis of research across five decades. In D. Cicchetti & D. J. Cohen (Eds.), *Developmental psychopathology: Vol. 3. Risk, disorder, and adaptation* (2nd ed., pp. 739–795). Hoboken, NJ: Wiley.

Luyster, R. J., Kadlec, M. B., Carter, A., & Tager-Flusberg, H. (2008). Language assessment and development in toddlers with autism spectrum disorders. *Journal of Autism and Developmental Disorders, 38*, 1426–1438. doi:10.1007/s10803-007-0510-1

Lynam, D. R., Caspi, A., Moffitt, T. E., Loeber, R., & Stouthamer-Loeber, M. (2007). Longitudinal evidence that psychopathy scores in early adolescence predict adult psychopathy. *Journal of Abnormal Psychology, 116*, 155–165. doi:10.1037/0021-843X.116.1.155

Lynam, D. R., Charnigo, R., Moffitt, T. E., Raine, A., Loeber, R., & Stouthamer-Loeber, M. (2009). The stability of psychopathy across adolescence. *Development and Psychopathology. Special Issue: Precursors and Diverse Pathways to Personality Disorder in Children and Adolescents: Part 2, 21*, 1133–1153. doi:10.1017/S0954579409990083

Lynam, D., Moffitt, T. E., & Stouthamer-Loeber, M. (1993). Explaining the relation between IQ and delinquency: Race, class, test motivation, school failure, or self-control. *Journal of Abnormal Psychology, 102*, 187–196. doi:10.1037/0021-843X.102.2.187

Lyon, G. R., & Cutting, L. (1998). Treatment of learning disabilities. In E. J. Mash & L. C. Terdal (Eds.), *Treatment of childhood disorders* (2nd ed.). New York: Guilford Press.

Lyon, G. R., Fletcher, J. M., & Barnes, M. C. (2003). Learning disabilities. In E. J. Mash & R. A. Barkley (Eds.), *Child psychopathology* (2nd ed., pp. 520–586). New York: Guilford Press.

Lyon, G. R. Fletcher, J. M., Fuchs, L. S., & Chhabra, V. (2006). Learning disabilities. In E. J. Mash & R. A. Barkley (Eds.), *Treatment of childhood disorders* (3rd ed., pp. 512–591). New York: Guilford Press.

Lyons, E., & Coyle, A. (Eds.). (2007). *Analysing qualitative data in psychology*. Thousand Oaks, CA: Sage.

Lyons, V., & Fitzgerald, M. (2007). Did Hans Asperger (1906–1980) have Asperger syndrome? *Journal of Autism and Developmental Disorders, 37*, 2020–2021. doi:10.1007/s10803-007-0382-4

Lyons-Ruth, K., Zeanah, C. H., & Benoit, D. (1996). Disorder and risk for disorder during infancy and toddlerhood. In E. J. Mash & R. A. Barkley (Eds.), *Child psychopathology* (pp. 457–491). New York: Guilford Press.

Lyons-Ruth, K., Zeanah, C. H., & Benoit, D. (2003). Disorder and risk for disorder during infancy and toddlerhood. In E. J. Mash & R. A. Barkley (Eds.), Child psychopathology (2nd ed., pp. 589–631). New York: Guilford Press.

MacBrayer, E. K., Milich, R., & Hundley, M. (2003). Attributional biases in aggressive children and their mothers. *Journal of Abnormal Psychology, 112*, 698–708. doi:10.1037/0021-843X.112.4.598

Maccoby, E. E., & Martin, J. A. (1983). Socialization in the context of the family: Parent-child interaction. In P. H. Mussen (Ed.), *Handbook of child psychology: Vol. IV. Socialization, personality, and social development* (4th ed., pp. 1–101). New York: Wiley.

Macfie, J., Cicchetti, D., & Toth, S. L. (2001). The development of dissociation in maltreated preschool-aged children. *Development and Psychopathology, 13*, 233–254.

Machel, G. (2001). *The impact of war on children*. London: Hurst.

Macintosh, K. E., & Dissanayake, C. (2004). Annotation: The similarities and differences between autistic disorder and Asperger's disorder: A review of the empirical evidence. *Journal of Child Psychology and Psychiatry, 45*, 421–434. doi:10.1111/j.1469-7610.2004.00234.x

MacKenzie, M. J., Kotch, J. B., & Lee, L. (2011). Toward a cumulative ecological risk model for the etiology of child maltreatment. *Children and Youth Services Review, 33*, 1638–1647. doi:10.1016/j.childyouth.2011.04.018

Mackie, S., Shaw, P., Lenroot, R., Pierson, R., Greenstein, D. K., Nugent, T. F., . . . Rapoport, J. L. (2007). Cerebellar development and clinical outcome in attention deficit hyperactivity disorder. *American Journal of Psychiatry, 164*, 647–655. doi:10.1176/appi.ajp.164.4.647

MacMillan, H. L., Fleming, J. E., Trocme, N., Boyle, M. H., Wong, M., Racine, Y. A., Beardslee, W. R., & Offord, D. R. (1997). Prevalence of child physical and sexual abuse in the community: Results from the Ontario Health Supplement. *Journal of the American Medical Association, 278*, 131–135.

MacMillan, H. L., Wathen, C. N., Barlow, J., Fergusson, D. M., Leventhal, J. M., & Taussig, H. N. (2009). Interventions to prevent child maltreatment and associated impairment. *The Lancet, 373*(9659), 250–266. doi:10.1016/S0140–6736(08)61708–0

Maedgen, J. W., & Carlson, C. L. (2000). Social functioning and emotional regulation in the attention deficit hyperactivity disorder subtypes. *Journal of Clinical Child Psychology, 29*, 30–42. doi:10.1207/S15374424jccp2901_4

Maehler, C., & Schuchardt, K. (2011). Working memory in children with learning disabilities: Rethinking the criterion of discrepancy. *International Journal of Disability, Development and Education, 58*, 5–17. doi:10.1080/1034912X.2011.547335

Magiati, I., Charman, T., & Howlin, P. (2007). A two-year prospective follow-up study of community-based early intensive behavioural intervention and specialist nursery provision for children with autism spectrum disorders. *Journal of Child Psychology and Psychiatry, 48*, 803–812. doi:10.1111/j.1469-7610.2007.01756.x

Magnuson, K. M., & Constantino, J. N. (2011). Characterization of depression in children with autism spectrum disorders. *Journal of Developmental & Behavioral Pediatrics, 32*, 332–340. doi:10.1097/DBP.0b013e318213f56c

Main, M., & George, C. (1985). Responses of abused and disadvantaged toddlers to distress in agemates: A study in the daycare setting. *Developmental Psychology, 21*, 407–412.

Main, M., & Goldwyn, R. (1984). Predicting rejecting of her infant from mother's representation of her own experience: Implications for the abused-abusing intergenerational cycle. *Child Abuse and Neglect, 8*, 203–217.

Makari, G. J. (1993). Educated insane: A nineteenth-century psychiatric paradigm. *Journal of the History of the Behavioral Sciences, 29*, 8–21. doi:10.1002/1520-6696(199301)29:1<8::AID-JHBS2300290103>3.0.CO;2-E

Maki, P., Riekki, T., Miettunen, J., Isohanni, M., Jones, P. B., Murray, G., . . . Veijola, J. (2010). Schizophrenia in the offspring of antenatally depressed mothers in the northern Finland 1966 birth cohort: Relationship to family history of psychosis. *American Journal of Psychiatry, 167*, 70–77. doi:10.1176/appi.ajp.2009.09010133

Malgady, R. G. (2010). Treating Hispanic children and adolescents using Narrative Therapy. In J. R. Weisz & A. E. Kazdin (Eds.), *Evidence-based psychotherapies for children and adolescents* (2nd ed., pp. 391–400). New York: Guilford Press.

Malhotra, S., & Gupta, N. (1999). Childhood disintegrative disorder. *Journal of Autism and Developmental Disorders, 29*, 491–498. doi:10.1023/A:1022247903401

Malhotra, S., & Gupta, N. (2002). Childhood disintegrative disorder: Reexamination of the current concept. *European Child and Adolescent Psychiatry, 11*, 108–114. doi:10.1007/s00787-002-0270-6

Manassis, K. (2007). When attention-deficit/hyperactivity disorder co-occurs with anxiety disorders: Effects on treatment. *Expert Review of Neurotherapeutics, 7*, 981–988. doi:10.1586/14737175.7.8.981

Manassis, K., Bradley, S., Goldberg, S., Hood, J., & Swinson, R. P. (1994). Attachment in mothers with anxiety disorders and their children. *Journal of the American Academy of Child & Adolescent Psychiatry, 33*, 1106–1113. doi:10.1097/00004583-199410000-00006

Manassis, K., Tannock, R., Young, A, & Francis, J. S. (2007). Cognition in anxious children with attention deficit hyperactivity disorder: A comparison with clinical and normal children. *Behavioral and Brain Functions, 3*, 4. doi:10.1186/1744-9081-3-4

Mancini, C., van Ameringen, M., Szatmari, P., Fugere, C., & Boyle, M. (1996). A high-risk pilot study of the children of adults with social phobia. *Journal of the American Academy of Child & Adolescent Psychiatry, 35*, 1511–1517. doi:10.1097/00004583-199611000-00020

Mandell, D. S., Ittenbach, R. F., Levy, S. E., & Pinto-Martin, J. A. (2007). Disparities in diagnoses received prior to a diagnosis of autism spectrum disorder. *Journal of Autism and Developmental Disorders, 37*, 1795–1802. doi:10.1007/s10803-006-0314-8

Mandell, D. S., Morales, K. H., Marcus, S. C., Stahmer, A. C., Doshi, J., & Polsky, D. E. (2008). Psychotropic medication use among Medicaid-enrolled children with autism spectrum disorders. *Pediatrics, 121*, e441–e448. doi:10.1542/peds.2007-0984

Maniglio, R. (2009). The impact of child sexual abuse on health: A systematic review of reviews. *Clinical Psychology Review, 29*, 647–657. doi:10.1016/j.cpr.2009.08.003

Maniglio, R. (2011). The role of childhood trauma, psychological problems, and coping in the development of deviant sexual fantasies in sexual offenders. *Clinical Psychology Review, 31*(5), 748–756. doi:10.1016/j.cpr.2011.03.003

Manning, M. A., & Hoyme, H. E. (2007). Fetal alcohol spectrum disorders: A practical clinical approach to diagnosis. *Neuroscience & Biobehavioral Reviews, 31*, 230–238. doi:10.1016/j.neubiorev.2006.06.016

Mans, L., Cicchetti, D., & Sroufe, L. A. (1978). Mirror reactions of Down's syndrome infants and toddlers: Cognitive underpinnings of self-recognition. *Child Development, 49*, 1247–1250. doi:10.2307/1128771

March, J. S. (2010). Commentary on 'Forum: Use of antidepressants in children and adolescents.' *Current Opinion in Psychiatry, 23*, 63–65. doi:10.1097/YCO.0b013e328334bd2c

March, J. S., & Mulle, K. (1998). *OCD in children and adolescents: A cognitive-behavioral treatment manual*. New York: Guilford Press.

March, J. S., Stzatmari, P., Bukstein, O., Chrisman, A., Kondo, D., Hamilton, J. D., . . . Kratochvil, C. J. (2007). AACAP 2005 research forum: Speeding the adoption of evidence-based practice in pediatric psychiatry. *Journal of the American Academy of Child & Adolescent Psychiatry, 46*, 1098–1110. doi:10.1097/chi.0b013e318074eb48

March, J. S., & Vitiello, B. (2009). Clinical messages from the Treatment for Adolescents with Depression Study (TADS). *American Journal of Psychiatry, 166*, 1118–1123. doi:10.1176/appi.ajp.2009.08101606

Marchand-Martella N., Martella, R., & Ausdemore, K. (2005). An Overview of Direct Instruction. Retrieved from: http://education.jhu.edu/newhorizons/Special%20Needs/Inclusion/Teaching%20and%20Learning

Marchetto, M. C. N., Carromeu, C., Acab, A., Yu, D., Yeo, G. W., Mu, Y., . . . Muotri, A. R. (2010). A model for neural development and treatment of Rett syndrome using human induced pluripotent stem cells. *Cell, 143*, 527–539. doi:10.1016/j.cell.2010.10.016

Marciano, P. L., & Kazdin, A. E. (1994). Self-esteem, depression, hopelessness, and suicidal intent among psychiatrically disturbed inpatient adolescents. *Journal of Clinical Child Psychology, 23*, 151–160. doi:10.1207/s15374424jccp2302_5

Marcus, D. K., & Barry, T. D. (2011). Does Attention-Deficit/Hyperactivity Disorder have a dimensional latent structure? A taxometric analysis. *Journal of Abnormal Psychology, 120*, 427–442. doi:10.1037/a0021405

Marenco, S., & Weinberger, D. R. (2000). The neurodevelopmental hypothesis of schizophrenia: Following a trail of evidence from cradle to grave. *Development and Psychopathology, 12*, 501–527. doi:10.1017/S0954579400003138

Margallo-Lana, M. L., Moore, P. B., Kay, D. W. K., Perry, R. H., Reid, B. E., Berney, T. P., & Tyrer, S. P. (2007). Fifteen-year follow-up of 92 hospitalized adults with Down's syndrome: Incidence of cognitive decline, its relationship to age and neuropathology. *Journal of Intellectual Disability Research, 51*, 463–477. doi:10.1111/j.1365-2788.2006.00902.x

Mark, T. L., Harwood, H. J., McKusick, D. C., King, E. C., Vandivort-Warren, R., & Buck, J. A. (2008). Mental health and substance abuse spending by age, 2003. *The Journal of Behavioral Health Services & Research, 35*, 279–289. doi:10.1007/s11414-008-9118-2

Marks, A. K., Patton, F., & Coll, C. G. (2011). Being bicultural: A mixed-methods study of adolescents' implicitly and explicitly measured multiethnic identities. *Developmental Psychology, 47*, 270–288. doi:10.1037/a0020730

Marshall, T., Jones, D. P., Ramchandani, P. G., Stein, A., & Bass, C. (2007). Intergenerational transmission of health beliefs in somatoform disorders: An exploratory study. *British Journal of Psychiatry, 191*, 449–450. doi:10.1192/bjp.bp.107.035261

Marshall, W. L., Serran, G. A., Marshall, L. E., & O'Brien, M. D. (2008). Sexual deviation. In M. Hersen & J. Rosqvist (Eds.). *Handbook of psychological assessment, case conceptualization, and treatment, Vol 1: Adults.* (pp. 590–615). Hoboken, NJ: John Wiley & Sons Inc.

Martel, M. M. (2009). Research review: A new perspective on attention deficit/hyperactivity disorder: Emotion dysregulation and trait models. *Journal of Child Psychology and Psychiatry, 50*, 1042–1051. doi:10.1111/j.1469-7610.2009.02105.x

Martel, M. M., Goth-Owens, T., Martinez-Torteya, C., & Nigg, J. T. (2010). A person-centered personality approach to heterogeneity in attention-deficit/hyperactivity disorder (ADHD). *Journal of Abnormal Psychology, 119*, 186–196. doi:10.1037/a0017511

Martel, M. M., Lucia, V. C., Nigg, J. T., & Breslau, N. (2007). Sex differences in the pathway from low birth weight to inattention/hyperactivity. *Journal of Abnormal Child Psychology, 35*, 87–96. doi:10.1007/s10802-006-9089-9

Martel, M. M., Nikolas, M., Jernigan, K., Friderici, K., Waldman, I., & Nigg, J. T. (2011). The dopamine receptor D4 gene (*DRD4*) moderates family environmental effects on ADHD. *Journal of Abnormal Child Psychology, 39*, 1–10. doi:10.1007/s10802-010-9439-5

Marten, P. A., Albano, A. M., & Holt, C. S. (1991, January). *Cognitive-behavioral group treatment of adolescent social phobia with parent participation.* Unpublished manuscript, University of Louisville, Department of Psychology, Louisville, KY.

Martin, J. F. (1995, Fall/Winter). Life with Karl. *Entourage, 10*.

Martin, S. S., Storr, C. L., Alexandre, P. K., & Chilcoat, H. D. (2008). Adolescent ecstasy and other drug use in the National Survey of Parents and Youth: The role of sensation-seeking, parental monitoring and peer's drug use. *Addictive Behaviors, 33*, 919–933. doi:10.1016/j.addbeh.2008.02.010

Martins, Y., Tiggemann, M., & Kirkbride, A. (2007). Those speedos become them: The role of self-objectification in gay and heterosexual men's body image. *Personality and Social Psychology Bulletin, 33*, 634–647. doi:10.1177/0146167206297403

Mascola, A. J., Bryson, S. W., & Agras, W. S. (2010). Picky eating during childhood: A longitudinal study to age 11 years. *Eating Behaviors, 11*, 253–257. doi:10.1016/j.eatbeh.2010.05.006

Mash, E. J. (2006). Treatment of child and family disturbance: A cognitive-behavioral systems perspective. In E. J. Mash & R. A. Barkley (Eds.), *Treatment of childhood disorders* (3rd ed., pp. 3–62). New York: Guilford Press.

Mash, E. J., & Barkley, R. A. (Eds.). (2007). *Assessment of childhood disorders* (4th ed.). New York: Guilford Press.

Mash, E. J., & Dozois, D. J. A. (2003). Child psychopathology: A developmental-systems perspective. In E. J. Mash & R. A. Barkley (Eds.), *Child psychopathology* (2nd ed., pp. 3–71). New York: Guilford Press.

Mash, E. J., & Foster, S. L. (2001). Exporting analogue behavioral observation from research to clinical practice: Useful or cost-defective? *Psychological Assessment, 13*, 86–98. doi:10.1037/1040-3590.13.1.86

Mash, E. J., & Hunsley, J. (2005). Evidence-based assessment of child and adolescent disorders: Issues and challenges. *Journal of Clinical Child and Adolescent Psychology, 34*, 362–379. doi:10.1207/s15374424jccp3403_1

Mash, E. J., & Hunsley, J. (2007). Assessment of child and family disturbance: A developmental-systems approach. In E. J. Mash & R. A. Barkley (Eds.),

Assessment of childhood disorders (4th ed., pp. 3–50). New York: Guilford Press.
Mash, E. J., & Johnston, C. (1990). Determinants of parenting stress: Illustrations from families of hyperactive children and families of physically abused children. *Journal of Clinical Child Psychology, 19*, 313–328. doi:10.1207/s15374424jccp1904_3
Mash, E. J., & Johnston, C. (2005). Attention-deficit/hyperactivity disorder (ADHD) and the family: A developmental psychopathology perspective. In J. Hudson & R. Rapee (Eds.), *Current thinking on psychopathology and the family* (pp. 95–126). New York: Elsevier.
Masho, S. W., & Ahmed, G. (2007). Age at sexual assault and posttraumatic stress disorder among women: Prevalence, correlates, and implications for prevention. *Journal of Women's Health, 16*(2), 262–271.
Masi, G., Millepiedi, S., Mucci, M., Pascale, R. P., Perugi, G., & Akiskal, H. S. (2003). Phenomenology and comorbidity of dysthymic disorder in 100 consecutively referred children and adolescents: Beyond DSM-IV. *Canadian Journal of Psychiatry, 48*, 99–105. Retrieved from http://publications.cpa-apc.org/browse/sections/0
Mason, A. (2003). Melanie Klein, 1882–1960. *American Journal of Psychiatry, 160*, 241. doi:10.1111/j.1469-7610.1961.tb02006.x
Massetti, G. M., Lahey, B. B., Pelham, W. E., Loney, J., Ehrhardt, A., Lee, S. S., & Kipp, H. (2008). Academic achievement over 8 years among children who met modified criteria for attention-deficit/hyperactivity disorder at 4–6 years of age. *Journal of Abnormal Child Psychology, 36*, 399–410. doi:10.1007/s10802-007-9186-4
Masten, A. S. (2011). Resilience in children threatened by extreme adversity: Frameworks for research, practice, and translational synergy. *Development and Psychopathology, 23*, 493–506. doi:10.1017/S0954579411000198
Masten, A. S., & Cicchetti, D. (2010). Developmental cascades. *Development and Psychopathology. Special Issue: Developmental Cascades: Part 1, 22*, 491–495. doi:10.1017/S0954579410000222
Masten, A. S., & Coatsworth, J. D. (1998). The development of competence in favorable and unfavorable environments: Lessons from research on successful children. *American Psychologist, 53*, 205–220. doi:10.1037/0003-066X.53.2.205
Masten, A. S., Roisman, G. I., Long, J. D., Burt, K. B., Obradovic, J., Riley, J. R., Boelcke-Stennes, K., & Tellegen, A. (2005). Developmental cascades: Linking academic achievement and externalizing and internalizing symptoms over 20 years. *Developmental Psychology, 41*, 733–746. doi:10.1037/0012-1649.41.5.733
Masten, A. S., & Wright, M. O. (2010). *Resilience over the lifespan: Developmental perspectives on resistance, recovery, and transformation.* New York: Guilford Press.
Masten, C. L., Eisenberger, N. I., Borofsky, L. A., McNealy, K., Pfeifer, J. H., & Dapretto, M. (2011). Subgenual anterior cingulate responses to peer rejection: A marker of adolescents' risk for depression. *Development and Psychopathology, 23*, 283–292. doi:10.1017/S0954579410000799
Masten, C. L., Guyer, A. E., Hodgdon, H. B., McClure, E. B., Charney, D. S., Ernst, M., . . . Monk, C. S. (2008). Recognition of facial emotions among maltreated children with high rates of post-traumatic stress disorder. *Child Abuse & Neglect, 32*, 139–153.
Mathers, M. E. (2006). Aspects of language in children with ADHD: Applying functional analyses to explore language use. *Journal of Attention Disorders, 9*, 523–533. doi:10.1177/1087054705282437
Matson, J. L., Belva, B., Hattier, M. A., & Matson, M. L. (2011). Pica in persons with developmental disabilities: Characteristics, diagnosis, and assessment. *Research in Autism Spectrum Disorders, 5*, 1459–1464. doi:10.1016/j.rasd.2011.02.006
Matson, J. L., Matson, M. L., & Rivet, T. T. (2007). Social-skills treatments for children with autism spectrum disorders: An overview. *Behavior Modification, 31*, 682–707. doi:10.1177/0145445507301650
Matsuishi, T., Yamashita, Y., Takahashi, T., & Nagamitsu, S. (2011). Rett syndrome: The state of clinical and basic research, and future perspectives. *Brain & Development, 33*, 627–631. doi:10.1016/j.braindev.2010.12.007
Mattis, S. G., & Ollendick, T. H. (1997). Children's cognitive responses to the somatic symptoms of panic. *Journal of Abnormal Child Psychology, 25*, 47–57. doi:10.1023/A:1025707424347
Mattis, S. G., & Ollendick, T. H. (2002). Nonclinical panic attacks in late adolescence: Prevalence and associated psychopathology. *Journal of Anxiety Disorders, 16*, 321–367. doi:10.1016/S0887-6185(01)00085-8
Maughan, A., Cicchetti, D., Toth, S. L., & Rogosch, F. A. (2007). Early occurring maternal depression and maternal negativity in predicting young children's emotion regulation and socioemotional difficulties. *Journal of Abnormal Child Psychology, 35*, 685–703. doi:10.1007/s10802-007-9129-0
Maughan, B., Gray, G., & Rutter, M. (1985). Reading retardation and antisocial behavior: A follow-up into employment. *Journal of Child Psychology and Psychiatry, 26*, 741–758. doi:10.1111/j.1469-7610.1985.tb00588.x
Maughan, B., Rowe, R., Loeber, R., & Stouthamer-Loeber, M. (2003). Reading problems and depressed mood. *Journal of Abnormal Child Psychology, 31*, 219–229. doi:10.1023/A:1022534527021
Maughan, B., & Rutter, M. (2001). Antisocial children grown up. In J. Hill & B. Maughan (Eds.), *Conduct disorders in childhood and adolescence* (pp. 507–552). London: Cambridge University Press.
Maulik, P. K., Mascarenhas, M. N., Mathers, C. D., Dua, T., & Saxena, S. (2011). Prevalence of intellectual disability: A meta-analysis of population-based studies. *Research in Developmental Disabilities, 32*, 419–436. doi:10.1016/j.ridd.2010.12.018
Maurice, C. (1993a, June). Rescuing my daughter. *McCall's, 75*, 76, 78, 84, 156.
Maurice, C. (1993b). *Let me hear your voice: A family's triumph over autism.* New York: Fawcett Columbine.
Maxfield, M. G., & Widom, C. S. (1996). The cycle of violence: Revisited 6 years later. *Archives of Pediatric and Adolescent Medicine, 150*, 390–395.
Mayes, R., & Rafalovich, A. (2007). Suffer the restless children: The evolution of ADHD and paediatric stimulant use, 1900-80. *History of Psychiatry, 18*, 435–457. doi:10.1177/0957154X06075782
Mayes, S. D., & Calhoun, S. L. (2008). WISC-IV and WIAT-II profiles in children with high-functioning autism. *Journal of Autism and Developmental Disorders, 38*, 428–439. doi:10.1007/s10803-007-0410-4
Mayes, S. D., & Calhoun, S. L. (2011). Impact of IQ, age, SES, gender, and race on autistic symptoms. *Research in Autism Spectrum Disorders, 5*, 749–757. doi:10.1016/j.rasd.2010.09.002
McAlonan, G. M., Suckling, J., Wong, N, Cheung, V., Lienenkaemper, N., Cheung, C., & Chua, S. E. (2008). Distinct patterns of grey matter abnormality in high-functioning autism and Asperger's syndrome. *Journal of Child Psychology and Psychiatry, 49*, 1287–1295. doi:10.1111/j.1469-7610.2008.01933.x
McAlpine, L., & McGrath, P. J. (1999). Chronic and recurrent pain in children. In A. R. Block, E. F. Kremer, et al. (Eds.), *Handbook of pain syndromes: Biopsychosocial perspectives* (pp. 529–549). Mahwah, NJ: Erlbaum.
McBurnett, K., Lahey, B. B., Frick, P. J., Risch, C., Loeber, R., Hart, E. L., . . . Hanson, K. S. (1991). Anxiety, inhibition, and conduct disorders in children, II. Relation to salivary cortisol. *Journal of the American Academy of Child & Adolescent Psychiatry, 30*, 192–196. doi:10.1097/00004583-199103000-00005
McBurnett, K., Lahey, B. B., Rathouz, P. J., & Loeber, R. (2000). Low salivary cortisol and persistent aggression in boys referred for disruptive behavior. *Archives of General Psychiatry, 57*, 38–43. doi:10.1001/archpsyc.57.1.38
McBurnett, K., Pfiffner, L. J., & Frick, P. J. (2001). Symptom properties as a function of ADHD type: An argument for continued study of sluggish cognitive tempo. *Journal of Abnormal Child Psychology, 29*, 207–213. doi:10.1023/A:1010377530749
McCabe, D. P., & Castel, A. D. (2008). Seeing is believing: The effect of brain images on judgments of scientific reasoning. *Cognition, 107*, 343–352. doi:10.1016/j.cognition.2007.07.017
McCabe, M. A. (1996). Involving children and adolescents in medical decision making: Developmental and clinical considerations. *Journal of Pediatric Psychology, 21*, 505–516. doi:10.1093/jpepsy/21.4.505
McCann, D., Barrett, A., Cooper, A., Crumpler, D., Dalen, L., Grimshaw, K., . . . Stevenson, J. (2007). Food additives and hyperactive behaviour in 3-year-old and 8/9-year-old children in the community: A randomised,

double-blinded, placebo-controlled trial. *Lancet, 370*, 1560–1567. doi:10.1016/S0140-6736(07)61306-3

McCauley, E., Myers, K., Mitchell, J., Calderon, R., Scholoredt, K., & Treder, R. (1993). Depression in young people: Initial presentation and clinical course. *Journal of the American Academy of Child & Adolescent Psychiatry, 32*, 714–722. doi:10.1097/00004583-199307000-00003

McCauley, E., Schloredt, K., Gudmundsen, G., Martell, C., & Dimidjian, S. (2011). Expanding behavioral activation to depressed adolescents: Lessons learned in treatment development. *Cognitive and Behavioral Practice, 18*, 371–383. doi:10.1016/j.cbpra.2010.07.006

McClellan, J., Breiger, D., McCurry, C., & Hlastala, S. A. (2003). Premorbid functioning in early-onset psychotic disorders. *Journal of the American Academy of Child & Adolescent Psychiatry, 42*, 666–672. doi:10.1097/01.CHI.0000046844.56865.6B

McClellan, J. M., Sikich, L., Findling, R. L., Frazier, J. A., Vitiello, B., Hlastala, S. A., . . . Lieberman, J. A. (2007). Treatment of early-onset schizophrenia spectrum disorders (TEOSS): Rationale, design, and methods. *Journal of the American Academy of Child & Adolescent Psychiatry, 46*, 969–978. doi:10.1097/CHI.0b013e3180691779

McClure, E. B., Adler, A., Monk, C. S., Cameron, J., Smith, S., Nelson, E. E., . . . Pine, D. S. (2007a). fMRI predictors of treatment outcome in pediatric anxiety disorders. *Psychopharmacology, 191*, 97–105. doi:10.1007/s00213-006-0542-9

McClure, E. B., Monk, C. S., Nelson, E. E., Parrish, J. M., Adler, A., Blair, R. J. R., . . . Pine, D. S. (2007b). Abnormal attention modulation of fear circuit activation in pediatric generalized anxiety disorder. *Archives of General Psychiatry, 64*, 97–106. doi:10.1001/archpsyc.64.1.97

McClure, E. B., & Pine, D. S. (2006). Social anxiety and emotional regulation: A model for developmental psychopathology perspectives on anxiety disorders. In D. Cicchetti & D. J. Cohen (Eds.), *Developmental psychopathology: Vol. 3. Risk, disorder, and adaptation* (2nd ed., pp. 470–502). Hoboken, NJ: Wiley.

McCluskey, K. K., & McCluskey, A. (2000). Excerpts from Butterfly Kisses: Amber's journey through hyperactivity. *The Canadian, 6*, 11–15.

McConkey, R., Truesdale-Kennedy, M., & Cassidy, A. (2009). Mothers' recollections of early features of autism spectrum disorders. *Child and Adolescent Mental Health, 14*, 31–36. doi:10.1111/j.1475-3588.2008.00495.x

McCrory, E., De Brito, S. A., & Viding, E. (2010). Research review: The neurobiology and genetics of maltreatment and adversity. *Journal of Child Psychology and Psychiatry, 51*, 1079–1095. doi:10.1111/j.1469–7610.2010.02271.x

McCullough, J. P., Klein, D. N., Borian, F. E., Howland, R. H., Riso, L. P., Keller, M. B., Banks, P. L. C. (2003). Group comparisons of DSM-IV subtypes of chronic depression: Validity of the distinctions, Part 2. *Journal of Abnormal Psychology, 112*, 614–622. doi:10.1037/0021-843X.112.4.614

McDermott, P. A. (1996). A nationwide study of developmental and gender prevalence for psychopathology in childhood and adolescence. *Journal of Abnormal Child Psychology, 24*, 53–66. doi:10.1007/BF01448373

McDermott, S., Durkin, M. S., Schupf, N., & Stein, Z. A. (2007). Epidemiology and etiology of mental retardation. In J. W. Jacobson, J. A. Mulick, & J. Rojahn (Eds.), *Handbook of intellectual and developmental disabilities: Issues in clinical child psychology* (pp. 3–40). New York: Springer.

McDermott, S., Zhou, L., & Mann, J. (2008). Injury treatment among children with autism or pervasive developmental disorder. *Journal of Autism and Developmental Disorders, 38*, 626–633. doi:10.1007/s10803-007-0426-9

McDonald, R., Jouriles, E. N., Ramisetty-Mikler, S., Caetano, R., & Green, C. E. (2006). Estimating the number of American children living in partner-violent families. *Journal of Family Psychology, 20*, 137–142.

McDonnell, M. G., & Dyck, D. G. (2004). Multiple family group treatment as an effective intervention for children suffering from psychological disorders. *Clinical Psychology Review, 24*, 685–706. doi:10.1016/j.cpr.2004.02.004

McDonnell, M. G., & McClellan, J. M. (2007). Early-onset schizophrenia. In E. J. Mash & R. A. Barkley (Eds.), *Assessment of childhood disorders* (4th ed., pp. 526–550). New York: Guilford Press.

McDougle, C. J., Scahill, L., Aman, M. G., McCracken, J. T., Tierney, E., Davies, M., . . . Vitiello, B. (2005). Risperidone for the core symptom domains of autism: Results from the study by the autism network of the research units on pediatric psychopharmacology. *American Journal of Psychiatry, 162*, 1142–1148. doi:10.1176/appi.ajp.162.6.1142

McEwan, K., Waddell, C., & Barker, J. (2007). Bringing children's mental health "out of the shadows." *Canadian Medical Association Journal, 176*, 471–472. doi:10.1503/cmaj.061028.

McGee, R., Stanton, W. R., & Sears, M. R. (1993). Allergic disorders and attention deficit disorder in children. *Journal of Abnormal Child Psychology, 21*, 79–88. doi:10.1007/BF00910490

McGee, R., Wolfe, D. A., & Olson, J. (2001). Multiple maltreatment, attribution of blame, and adjustment among adolescents. *Development and Psychopathology, 13*, 827–846.

McGee, R. A., Wolfe, D. A., & Wilson, S. K. (1997). Multiple maltreatment experiences and adolescent behavior problems: Adolescents' perspectives. *Development and Psychopathology, 9*, 131–149. doi:10.1017/S0954579497001107

McGrath, L. M., Hutaff-Lee, C., Scott, A., Boada, R., Shriberg, L. D., & Pennington, B. F. (2008). Children with comorbid speech sound disorder and specific language impairment are at increased risk for attention-deficit/hyperactivity disorder. *Journal of Abnormal Child Psychology, 36*, 151–163. doi:10.1007/s10802-007-9166-8

McGrath, L. M., Pennington, B. F., Shanahan, M. A., Santerre-Lemmon, L. E., Barnard, H. F., Willcutt, E. G., . . . & Olson, R. K. (2011). A multiple deficit model of reading disability and attention-deficit/hyperactivity disorder: Searching for shared cognitive deficits. *Journal of Child Psychology and Psychiatry, 52*, 547–557. doi:10.1111/j.1469-7610.2010.02346.x

McGrath, L. M., Pennington, B. F., Willcutt, E. G., Boada, R., Shriberg, L. D., & Smith, S. D. (2007). Gene × environment interactions in speech sound disorder predict language and preliteracy outcomes. *Development and Psychopathology [Special issue: Gene–environment interaction], 19*, 1047–1072. doi:10.1017/S0954579407000533

McInnes, A., Humphries, T., Hogg-Johnson, S., & Tannock, R. (2003). Listening comprehension and working memory are impaired in attention-deficit hyperactivity disorder irrespective of language impairment. *Journal of Abnormal Child Psychology, 31*, 427–443. doi:10.1023/A:1023895602957

McIntosh, V. V., Bulik, C. M., McKenzie, J. M., Luty, S. E., & Jordan, J. (2000). Interpersonal psychotherapy for anorexia nervosa. *International Journal of Eating Disorders, 27*, 125–139. doi:10.1002/(SICI)1098-108X(200003)27:2<125::AID-EAT1>3.0.CO;2-4

McIntosh, V. V. W., Carter, F. A., Bulik, C. M., Frampton, C. M. A., & Joyce, P. R. (2011). Five-year outcome of cognitive behavioral therapy and exposure with response prevention for bulimia nervosa. *Psychological Medicine: A Journal of Research in Psychiatry and the Allied Sciences, 41*, 1061–1071. doi:10.1017/S0033291710001583

McIntyre, J. K., & Spatz Widom, C. (2011). Childhood victimization and crime victimization. *Journal of Interpersonal Violence, 26*, 640–663. doi:10.1177/0886260510365868

McKnew, D. H., Jr., Cytryn, L., & Yahraes, H. (1983). *Why isn't Johnny crying? Coping with depression in children.* New York: Norton.

McLaughlin, K. A., Fairbank, J. A., Bruber, M. J., Jones, R. T., Osofsky, J. D., Pfefferbaum, B., . . . Kessler, R. C. (2010). Trends in serious emotional disturbance among youths exposed to Hurricane Katrina. *Journal of the American Academy of Child & Adolescent Psychiatry, 49*, 990–1000. doi:10.1016/j.jaac.2010.06.012

McLaughlin, K. A., Hilt, L. M., & Nolen-Hoeksema, S. (2007). Racial/ethnic differences in internalizing and externalizing symptoms in adolescents. *Journal of Abnormal Child Psychology, 35*, 801–816. doi:10.1007/s10802-007-9128-1

McLean, C. P., & Anderson, E. R. (2009). Brave men and timid women? A review of gender differences in fear and anxiety. *Clinical Psychology Review, 29*, 496–505. doi:10.1016/j.cpr.2009.05.003

McLearn, K. T., Knitzer, J., & Carter, A. S. (2007). Mental health: A neglected partner in the healthy development of young children. In J. L. Aber, S. J. Bishop

Josef, S. M. Jones, K. T. McLearn, & D. A. Phillips (Eds.), *Child development and social policy: Knowledge for action* (pp. 233–248). Washington, DC: American Psychological Association.

McLeod, B. D., Wood, J. J., & Weisz, J. R. (2007). Examining the association between parenting and childhood anxiety: A meta-analysis. *Clinical Psychology Review, 27*, 155–172. doi:10.1016/j.cpr.2006.09.002

McLeod, J. D., Fettes, D. L., Jensen, P. S., Pescosolido, B. A., & Martin, J. K. (2007). Public knowledge, beliefs, and treatment preferences concerning attention-deficit hyperactivity disorder. *Psychiatric Services, 58*, 626–631. doi:10.1176/appi.ps.58.5.626

McMahon, R. J., & Forehand, R. L. (2003). *Helping the noncompliant child: Family-based treatment for oppositional behavior* (2nd ed.). New York: Guilford Press.

McMahon, R. J., Wells, K. C., & Kotler, J. S. (2006). Conduct problems. In E. J. Mash & R. A. Barkley (Eds.), *Treatment of childhood disorders* (3rd ed., pp. 137–268). New York: Guilford Press.

McMahon, R. J., Witkiewitz, K., Kotler, J. S., & The Conduct Problems Prevention Research Group. (2010). Predictive validity of callous–unemotional traits measured in early adolescence with respect to multiple antisocial outcomes. *Journal of Abnormal Psychology, 119*, 752–763. doi:10.1037/a0020796

McMahon, T. J., & Luthar, S. S. (2007). Defining characteristics and potential consequences of caretaking burden among children living in urban poverty. *American Journal of Orthopsychiatry, 77*, 267–281. doi:10.1037/0002-9432.77.2.267

McManis, M. H., Kagan, J., Snidman, N. C., & Woodward, S. A. (2002). EEG asymmetry, power, and temperament in children. *Developmental Psychobiology, 41*, 169–177. doi:10.1002/dev.10053

McNamara, N. K., & Findling, R. L. (2008). Guns, adolescents, and mental illness. *American Journal of Psychiatry, 165*, 190–194. doi:10.1176/appi.ajp.2007.07071096

McPheeters, M. L., Warren, Z., Sathe, N., Bruzek, J. L., Krishnaswami. R. N., & Veenstra-Vanderweele, J. and J. (2011). A systematic review of medical treatments for children with autism spectrum disorders. *Pediatrics, 127*, e1312–e1321. doi:10.1542/peds.2011-0427

McSherry, D. (2007). Understanding and addressing the "neglect of neglect": Why are we making a mole-hill out of a mountain? *Child Abuse & Neglect, 31*(6), 607–614.

Mead, M. A., Hohenshil, T. H., & Singh, K. (1997). How the DSM system is used by clinical counselors: A national study. *Journal of Mental Health Counseling, 19*, 383–401. Retrieved from http://www.amhca.org/news/journal.aspx

Meaux, J. B., & Bell, P. L. (2001). Balancing recruitment and protection: Children as research subjects. *Issues in Comprehensive Pediatric Nursing, 24*, 241–251. doi:10.1080/014608601753260335

Medvescek, C. R. (1997, April). Special kids. *Parents*, 67–70.

Meichenbaum, D. (1977). *Cognitive-behavior modification: An integrative approach*. New York: Plenum Press.

Meier, M. H., Slutske, W. S., Heath, A. C., & Martin, N. G. (2011). Sex differences in the genetic and environmental influences on childhood conduct disorder and adult antisocial behavior. *Journal of Abnormal Psychology, 120*, 377–388. doi:10.1037/a0022303

Meijer, S. A., Sinnema, G., Bijstra, J. O., Mellenbergh, G. J., & Wolters, W. H. G. (2002). Coping styles and locus of control as predictors for psychological adjustment of adolescents with a chronic illness. *Social Science & Medicine, 54*, 1453–1461. doi:10.1016/S0277-9536(01)00127-7

Meiser-Stedman, R., Dalgleish, T., Smith, P., Yule, W., & Glucksman, E. (2007). Diagnostic, demographic, memory quality, and cognitive variables associated with acute stress disorder in children and adolescents. *Journal of Abnormal Psychology, 116*, 65–79. doi:10.1037/0021-843X.116.1.65

Mellin, E. A. (2010). Children of families affected by a parental mental illness. In M. H. Guindon (Ed.), *Self-esteem across the lifespan: Issues and interventions* (pp. 79–90). New York: Routledge/Taylor & Francis Group.

Mellon, M. W., & Houts, A. C. (2006). Nocturnal enuresis. In J. E. Fisher & W. T. O'Donohue (Eds.), *Practitioner's guide to evidence-based psychotherapy* (pp. 432–441). New York: Springer.

Melnick, S. M., & Hinshaw, S. P. (1996). What they want and what they get: The social goals of boys with ADHD and comparison boys. *Journal of Abnormal Child Psychology, 24*, 169–185. doi:10.1007/BF01441483

Melton, G. B. (2000). Privacy issues in child mental health services. In J. J. Gates & B. S. Arons (Eds.), *Privacy and confidentiality in mental health care* (pp. 47–70). Baltimore: Brookes.

Meltzer, L. J., & Mindell, J. A. (2007). Relationship between child sleep disturbances and maternal sleep, mood, and parenting stress: A pilot study. *Journal of Family Psychology, 21*, 67–73. doi:10.1037/0893-3200.21.1.67

Menon, M., Tobin, D. D., Corby, B. C., Menon, M., Hodges, E. V. E., & Perry, D. G. (2007). The developmental costs of high self-esteem for antisocial children. *Child Development, 78*, 1627–1639. doi:10.1111/j.1467-8624.2007.01089.x

Menting, B., van Lier, P. A. C., & Koot, H. M. (2011). Language skills, peer rejection, and the development of externalizing behavior from kindergarten to fourth grade. *Journal of Child Psychology and Psychiatry, 52*, 72–79. doi:10.1111/j.1469-7610.2010.02279.x

Menzel, J. E., Schaefer, L. M., Burke, N. L., Mayhew, L. L., Brannick, M. T., & Thompson, J. K. (2010). Appearance-related teasing, body dissatisfaction, and disordered eating: A meta-analysis. *Body Image, 7*, 261–270. doi:10.1016/j.bodyim.2010.05.004

Merikangas, K. R., Akiskal, H. S., Angst, J., Greenberg, P. E., Hirschfeld, R. M. A., Petukhova, M., & Kessler, R. C. (2007). Lifetime and 12-month prevalence of bipolar spectrum disorder in the National Comorbidity Survey Replication. *Archives of General Psychiatry, 64*, 543–552. doi:10.1001/archpsyc.64.5.543

Merikangas, K. R., Avenevoli, S., Dierker, L., & Grillon, C. (1999). Vulnerability factors among children at risk for anxiety disorders. *Biological Psychiatry, 46*, 1523–1535. doi:10.1016/j.chc.2005.06.005

Merikangas, K. R., He, J. P., Burstein, M., Swanson, S. A., Avenevoli, S., Cui, L. . . . Swendsen, J. (2010). Lifetime prevalence of mental disorders in U.S. adolescents: Results from the National Comorbidity Survey Replication-Adolescent Supplement (NCS-A). *Journal of the American Academy of Child & Adolescent Psychiatry, 49*, 980–989. doi:10.1016/j.jaac.2010.05.017

Merikangas, K. R., He, J., Burstein, M., Swanson, S. A., Avenevoli, S., Cui. L., . . . & Swendsen, J. (2010). Lifetime prevalence of mental disorders in U.S. adolescents: Results from the National Comorbidity Survey Replication-Adolescent Supplement (NCS-A). *Journal of the American Academy of Child & Adolescent Psychiatry, 49*, 980–989. doi:10.1016/j.jaac.2010.05.017

Merikangas, K. R., He, J. P., Burstein, M., Swendsen, J., Avenevoli, S., Base, B., . . . Olfson, M. (2011). Service utilization for lifetime mental disorders in U.S. adolescents: Results of the National Comorbidity Survey-Adolescent Supplement (NCS-A). *Journal of the American Academy of Child & Adolescent Psychiatry, 50*, 32–45. doi:10.1016/j.jaac.2010.10.006

Merrill, L. L., Guimond, J. M., Thomsen, C. J., & Milner, J. S. (2003). Child sexual abuse and number of sexual partners in young women: The role of abuse severity, coping style, and sexual functioning. *Journal of Consulting and Clinical Psychology, 71*, 987–996.

Mervielde, I., & Fruyt, F. D. (2002). Assessing children's traits with the hierarchical personality inventory for children. In B. de Raad (Ed.), *Big five assessment* (pp. 129–142). Ashland, OH: Hogrefe & Huber.

Mesibov, G. B., Shea, V., & Schopler, E. (2005). *The TEACCH approach to autism spectrum disorders*. New York: Kluwer/Plenum Press.

Messer, J., Goodman, R., Rowe, R., Meltzer, H., & Maughan, B. (2006). Preadolescent conduct problems in girls and boys. *Journal of the American Academy of Child & Adolescent Psychiatry, 45*, 184–191. doi:10.1097/01.chi.0000186403.13088.d8

Messer, S. C., & Gross, A. M. (1995). Childhood depression and family interaction: A naturalistic observation study. *Journal of Clinical Child Psychology, 24*, 77–88. doi:10.1207/s15374424jccp2401_10

Meyer, K., & Damasio, A. (2009). Convergence and divergence in a neural architecture for recognition and memory. *Trends in Neurosciences, 32*, 376–382. doi:10.1016/j.tins.2009.04.002

Micco, J., Henin, A., Mick, E., Kim, S., Hopkins, C., Biederman, J., & Hirshfeld-Becker, D. (2009). Anxiety and depressive disorders in offspring at high risk for anxiety: A meta-analysis. *Journal* of Anxiety Disorders, 23,* 1158–1164. doi:10.1016/j.janxdis.2009.07.021

Mick, E., Biederman, J., Faraone, S. V., Sayer, J., & Kleinman, S. (2002). Case-control study of attention-deficit hyperactivity disorder and maternal smoking, alcohol use, and drug use during pregnancy. *Journal of the American Academy of Child & Adolescent Psychiatry, 41,* 378–385. doi:10.1097/00004583-200204000-00009

Mick, E., Biederman, J., Jetton, J., & Faraone, S. V. (2000). Sleep disturbances associated with attention deficit hyperactivity disorder: The impact of psychiatric comorbidity and pharmacotherapy. *Journal of Child and Adolescent Psychopharmacology, 10,* 223–231. doi:10.1089/10445460050167331

Mick, E., Byrne, D., Fried, R., Monuteaux, M., Faraone, S. V., & Biederman, J. (2011). Predictors of ADHD persistence in girls at 5-year follow-up. *Journal of Attention Disorders, 15,* 183–192. doi:10.1177/1087054710362217

Mick, E., & Faraone, S. V. (2008). Genetics of attention deficit hyperactivity disorder. *Child and Adolescent Psychiatric Clinics of North America, 17,* 261–284. doi:10.1016/j.chc.2007.11.011

Mick, E., Santangelo, S. L., Wypij, D., & Biederman, J. (2000). Impact of maternal depression on ratings of comorbid depression in adolescents with attention-deficit/hyperactivity disorder. *Journal of the American Academy of Child & Adolescent Psychiatry, 39,* 314–319. doi:10.1097/00004583-200003000-00013

Mick, E., Todorov, A., Smalley, S., Hu, X., Loo, S., Todd, R. D., . . . Faraone, S. V. (2010). Family based genome-wide association scan of attention-deficit/hyperactivity disorder. *Journal of the American Academy of Child & Adolescent Psychiatry, 49,* 898–905. doi:10.1016/j.jaac.2010.02.014

Mikami, A. Y., Hinshaw, S. P., Patterson, K. A., & Lee, J. C. (2008). Eating pathology among adolescent girls with attention-deficit/hyperactivity disorder. *Journal of Abnormal Psychology, 117,* 225–235. doi:10.1037/0021-843X.117.1.225

Mikami, A. Y., & Pfiffner, L. J. (2008). Sibling relationships among children with ADHD. *Journal of Attention Disorders, 11,* 482–492.doi:10.1177/1087054706295670

Mikkelsen, E. J. (2010). Elimination disorders. In M. K. Dulcan (Ed.), *Dulcan's textbook of child and adolescent psychiatry* (pp. 435–447). Arlington, VA: American Psychiatric Publishing, Inc.

Miklowitz, D. J. (2011). Functional impairment, stress, and psychosocial intervention in bipolar disorder. *Current Psychiatry Reports.* Advance online publication. doi:10.1007/s11920-011-0227-x

Miklowitz, D. J., Chang, K. D., Taylor, D.O., George, E.L., Singh, M. K., Schneck, C. D., . . . Garber, J. (2011). Early psychosocial intervention for youth at risk for bipolar I or II disorder: A 1-year treatment development trial. *Bipolar Disorders, 13,* 67–75. doi:10.1111/j.1399-5618.2011.00890.x

Mikton, C., & Butchart, A. (2009). Child maltreatment prevention: A systematic review of reviews. *Bulletin of the World Health Organization,* 87, 353–361.

Miles, M. B., & Huberman, A. M. (1994). *Qualitative data analysis: An expanded sourcebook* (2nd ed.). Thousand Oaks, CA: Sage.

Milich, R., Balentine, A. C., & Lynam, D. R. (2001). ADHD combined type and ADHD predominantly inattentive type are distinct and unrelated disorders. *Clinical Psychology: Science and Practice, 8,* 463–488. doi:10.1093/clipsy.8.4.463

Milich, R., & Lorch, E. P. (1994). Television viewing methodology to understand cognitive processing of ADHD children. In T. H. Ollendick & R. J. Prinz (Eds.), *Advances in clinical child psychology* (Vol. 16, pp. 177–202). New York: Plenum Press.

Milich, R., Wolraich, M. C., & Lindgren, S. (1986). Sugar and hyperactivity: A critical review of empirical findings. *Clinical Psychology Review, 6,* 493–513. doi:10.1016/0272-7358(86)90034-6

Miller, A. (2007). Social neuroscience of child and adolescent depression. *Brain and Cognition, 65,* 47–68. doi:10.1016/j.bandc.2006.02.008

Miller, A. L., & Olson, S. L. (2000). Emotional expressiveness during peer conflicts: A predictor of social maladjustment among high-risk preschoolers. *Journal of Abnormal Child Psychology, 28,* 339–352. doi:10.1023/A:1005117009370

Miller, K. B., & La Greca, A. M. (2005). Adjustment to chronic illness in girls. In D. J. Bell, S. L. Foster, & E. J. Mash (Eds.), *Handbook of behavioral and emotional problems in girls. Issues in clinical child psychology* (pp. 489–522). New York: Kluwer/Plenum Press.

Miller, T. W., Nigg, J. T., & Miller, R. L. (2009). Attention deficit disorder in African American children: What can be concluded from the past 10 years. *Annual Review of Clinical Psychology, 29,* 77–86. doi:10.1016/j.cpr.2008.10.001

Mills, R., Alati, R., O'Callaghan, M., Najman, J. M., Williams, G. M., Bor, W., & Strathearn, L. (2011). Child abuse and neglect and cognitive function at 14 years of age: Findings from a birth cohort. *Pediatrics, 127,* 4–10. doi:10.1542/peds.2009–3479

Milne, A. A. (1926). *Winnie-the-pooh.* London: Methuen.

Minshew, N. J., Johnson, C., & Luna, B. (2000). The cognitive and neural basis of autism: A disorder of complex information processing and dysfunction of neocortical systems. *International Review of Research in Mental Retardation, 23,* 112–140. doi:10.1016/S0074-7750(00)80008-7

Minuchin, S., Rosman, B. L., & Baker, L. (1978). *Psychosomatic families: Anorexia nervosa in context.* Cambridge, MA: Harvard University Press.

Mironova, P., Rhodes, A. E., Bethell, J. M., Tonmyr, L., Boyle, M. H., Wekerle, C., . . . Leslie, B. (2011). Childhood physical abuse and suicide-related behavior: A systematic review. *Vulnerable Children and Youth Studies, 6,* 1–7. doi:10.1080/17450128.2010.542301

Mischoulon, D., Eddy, K. T., Keshaviah, A., Dinescu, D., Ross, S. L., Kass, A. E., . . . Herzog, D. B. (2011). Depression and eating disorders: Treatment and course. *Journal of Affective Disorders, 130,* 470–477. doi:10.1016/j.jad.2010.10.043

Mitchell, K. J., Wolak, J., & Finkelhor, D. (2007). Trends in youth reports of sexual solicitations, harassment and unwanted exposure to pornography on the internet. *Journal of Adolescent Health, 40,* 116–126.

Mitchell, S., Brian, J., Zwaigenbaum, L., Roberts, W., Szatmari, P., Smith, I., & Bryson, S. (2006). Early language and communication development of infants later diagnosed with autism spectrum disorder. *Journal of Developmental and Behavioral Pediatrics, 27*(Suppl.), S69–S78. doi:10.1097/00004703-200604002-00004

Mittal, V. A., & Walker, E. F. (2007). Movement abnormalities predict conversion to axis I psychosis among prodromal adolescents. *Journal of Abnormal Psychology, 116,* 796–803. doi:10.1037/0021-843X.116.4.796

MMWR. (2002, May 24). Fetal alcohol syndrome—Alaska, Arizona, Colorado, and New York, 1995–1997. *MMWR: Morbidity and Mortality Weekly Report, 51,* 433–435. doi:10.1001/jama.288.1.38

Moffitt, T. E. (1990). Juvenile delinquency and attention deficit disorder in boys' developmental trajectories from age 3 to age 15. *Child Development, 61,* 893–910. doi:10.1111/j.1467-8624.1990.tb02830.x

Moffitt, T. E. (1993). Adolescence-limited and life-course-persistent antisocial behavior: A developmental taxonomy. *Psychological Review, 100,* 674–701. doi:10.1037/0033-295X.100.4.674

Moffitt, T. E. (2006). Life-course-persistent versus adolescence-limited antisocial behavior. In D. Cicchetti & D. J. Cohen (Eds.), *Developmental psychopathology: Vol. 3. Risk, disorder, and adaptation* (2nd ed., pp. 570–598). New York: Wiley.

Moffitt, T. E., Arseneault, L., Belsky, D., Dickson, N., Hancox, R. J., Harrington, H., . . . Caspi, A. (2011). A gradient of childhood self-control predicts health, wealth, and public safety. *PNAS Proceedings of the National Academy of Sciences of the United States of America, 108,* 2693–2698. doi:10.1073/pnas.1010076108

Moffitt, T. E., Arseneault, L., Jaffee, S. R., Kim-Cohen, L., Koenen, K. C., Odgers, C. L., . . . Viding, E. (2008). Research review: DSM-V conduct disorder: Research needs for an evidence base. *Journal of Child Psychology and Psychiatry, 49,* 3–33. doi:10.1111/j.1469-7610.2007.01823.x

Moffitt, T. E., Caspi, A., Belsky, J., & Silva, P. A. (1992). Childhood experience and the onset of menarche: A test of a sociobiological model. *Child Development, 63,* 47–58. doi:10.1111/j.1467-8624.1992.tb03594.x

Moffitt, T. E., Caspi, A., Dickson, N., Silva, P., & Stanton, W. (1996). Childhood-onset versus adolescent-onset antisocial conduct problems in males: Natural history from ages 3 to 18 years. *Development and Psychopathology, 8,* 399–424. doi:10.1017/S0954579400007161

Moffitt, T. E., Caspi, A., Harrington, H. L., & Milne, B. J. (2002). Males on the life-course persistent and adolescence-limited antisocial pathways: Follow-up at age 26. *Development and Psychopathology, 14*, 179–207. doi:10.1017/S0954579402001104

Moffitt, T. E., Caspi, A., Rutter, M., & Silva, P. A. (2001). *Sex differences in antisocial behaviour: Conduct disorder, delinquency and violence in the Dunedin Longitudinal Study*. Cambridge, England: Cambridge University Press.

Moffitt, T. E., Caspi, A., Taylor, A., Kokaua, J., Milne, B. J., Polanczyk, G., & Poulton, R. (2010). Evidence that lifetime prevalence rates are doubled by prospective versus retrospective ascertainment. *Psychological Medicine, 40*, 899–909. doi:10.1017/S0033291709991036

Moffitt, T. E., Lynam, D., & Silva, P. A. (1994). Neuropsychological tests predict persistent male delinquency. *Criminology, 32*, 101–124. doi:10.1111/j.1745-9125.1994.tb01155.x

Moffitt, T. E., & Melchior, M. (2007). Editorial: Why does the worldwide prevalence of childhood attention deficit disorder matter? *American Journal of Psychiatry, 164*, 856–858. doi:10.1176/appi.ajp.164.6.856

Molina, B. S. G., Flory, K., Hinshaw, S. P., Greiner, A. R., Arnold, L. E., Swanson, J. M., . . . Wigal, T. (2007). Delinquent behavior and emerging substance abuse in the MTA at 36 months: Prevalence, course, and treatment effects. *Journal of the American Academy of Child & Adolescent Psychiatry, 46*, 1028–1040. doi:10.1097/chi.0b013e3180686d96

Molina, B. S. G., Hinshaw, S. P., Swanson, J. M. Arnold, L. E., Vitiello, B., Jensen, P. S., . . . & The MTA Cooperative Group. (2009). The MTA at 8 years: Prospective follow-up of children treated for combined-type ADHD in a multisite study. *Journal of the American Academy of Child & Adolescent Psychiatry, 48*, 484–500. doi:10.1097/CHI.0b013e31819c23d0

Monastra, V. J., Lubar, J. F., & Linden, M. (2001). The development of a quantitative electroencephalographic scanning process for attention deficit-hyperactivity disorder: Reliability and validity studies. *Neuropsychology, 15*, 136–144. doi:10.1037/0894-4105.15.1.136

Mond, J., Van den Berg, P., Boutelle, K., Hannan, P., & Neumark-Sztainer, D. (2011). Obesity, body dissatisfaction, and emotional well-being in early and late adolescence: Findings from the project EAT study. *Journal of Adolescent Health, 48*, 373–378. doi:10.1016/j.jadohealth.2010.07.022

Monk, C. S. (2008). The development of emotion-related neural circuitry in health and psychopathology. *Development and Psychopathology, 20*, 1231–1250. doi:10.1017/S095457940800059X

Monk, S., Klein, R. G., Telzer, E. H., Schroth, E. A., Mannuzza, S., Moulton, J. L., . . . Ernst, M. (2008). Amygdala and nucleus accumbens activation to emotional facial expressions in children and adolescents at risk for major depression. *American Journal of Psychiatry, 165*, 90–98. doi:10.1176/appi.ajp.2007.06111917

Monroe, S. M., Rohde, P., Seeley, J. R., & Lewinsohn, P. M. (1999). Life events and depression in adolescence: Relationship loss as a prospective risk factor for first onset of major depressive disorder. *Journal of Abnormal Psychology, 108*, 606–614. doi:10.1037/0021-843X.108.4.606

Montague, C. T., Farooqi, I. S., Whitehead, J. P., Soos, M. A., Rau, H., Wareham, N. J., . . . O'Rahilly, S. (1997). Congenital leptin deficiency is associated with severe early-onset obesity in humans. *Nature, 387*, 903–907. Retrieved from http://www.nature.com/nature/index.html

Monuteaux, M. C., Mick, E., Faraone, S. V., & Biederman, J. (2010). The influence of sex on the course and psychiatric correlates of ADHD from childhood to adolescence: A longitudinal study. *Journal of Child Psychology and Psychiatry, 51*, 233–241. doi:10.1111/j.1469-7610.2009.02152.x

Moran, T. H., & Ladenheim, E. E. (2011). Adiposity signaling and meal size control. *Physiology & Behavior, 103*, 21–24. doi:10.1016/j.physbeh.2010.11.013

Moreno, C., Arango, C., Parellada, M., Shaffer, D., & Bird, H. (2007a). Antidepressants in child and adolescent depression: Where are the bugs? *Acta Psychiatrica Scandinavica, 115*, 184–195. doi:10.1111/j.1600-0447.2006.00951.x

Moreno, C., Laje, G., Blanco, C., Jiang, H., Schmidt, A. B., & Olfson, M. (2007b). National trends in the outpatient diagnosis and treatment of bipolar disorder in youth. *Archives of General Psychiatry, 64*, 1032–1039. doi:10.1001/archpsyc.64.9.1032

Morgan, R. K. (1999). *Case studies in child and adolescent psychopathology*. Upper Saddle River, NJ: Prentice Hall.

Morgan, W. P. (1896). A case of congenital word-blindness. *British Medical Journal, 2*, 1543–1544. doi:10.1136/bmj.2.1871.1378

Morris, A. S., Silk, J. S., Morris, M. D. S., Steinberg, L., Aucoin, K. J., & Keyes, A. W. (2011). The influence of mother–child emotion regulation strategies on children's expression of anger and sadness. *Developmental Psychology, 47*, 213–225. doi:10.1037/a0021021

Morris, J. K., Wald, N. J., Mutton, D. E., & Alberman, E. (2003). Comparison of models of maternal age-specific risk for Down syndrome live births. *Prenatal Diagnosis, 23*, 252–258. doi:10.1002/pd.568

Morris, R. J., & Kratochwill, T. R. (Eds.). (2007). *The practice of child therapy* (4th ed.). Needham Heights, MA: Allyn & Bacon.

Morrisey-Kane, E., & Prinz, R. J. (1999). Engagement in child and adolescent treatment: The role of parental cognitions and attributions. *Clinical Child and Family Psychology Review, 2*, 183–198. doi:10.1023/A:1021807106455

Mortensen, E. L., Andresen, J., Kruuse, E., Sanders, S. A., & Reinisch, J. M. (2003). IQ stability: The relation between child and young adult intelligence test scores in low-birthweight samples. *Scandinavian Journal of Psychology, 44*, 395–398. doi:10.1111/1467-9450.00359

Moss, E., Dubois-Comtois, K., Cyr, C., Tarabulsy, G. M., St-Laurent, D., & Bernier, A. (2011). Efficacy of a home-visiting intervention aimed at improving maternal sensitivity, child attachment, and behavioral outcomes for maltreated children: A randomized control trial. *Development and Psychopathology, 23*, 195–210. doi:10.1017/S0954579410000738

Mostert, M. P. (2001). Facilitated communication since 1995: A review of published studies. *Journal of Autism and Developmental Disorders, 31*, 287–313. doi:10.1023/A:1010795219886

Mostert, M. P. (2010). Facilitated communication and its legitimacy—twenty-first century developments. *Exceptionality, 18*, 31–41. doi:10.1080/09362830903462524

Motlagh, M. G., Katsovich, L., Thompson, N., Lin, H., Young-Shin, K., Scahill, L., . . . Leckman, J. F. (2010). Severe psychosocial stress and heavy cigarette smoking during pregnancy: An examination of the pre- and perinatal risk factors associated with ADHD and Tourette syndrome. *European Child & Adolescent Psychiatry, 19*, 755–764. doi:10.1007/s00787-010-0115-7

Mouridsen, S. E. (2003). Childhood disintegrative disorder. *Brain & Development, 25*, 225–228. doi:10.1016/s0387-7604(02)00228-0

Mouridsen, S. E., Rich, B., & Isager, T. (2011). A longitudinal study of epilepsy and other central nervous system diseases in individuals with and without a history of infantile autism. *Brain & Development, 33*, 361–366. doi:10.1016/j.braindev.2010.07.002

Mowrer, O. H. (1947). On the dual nature of learning: A reinterpretation of "conditioning" and "problem solving." *Harvard Educational Review, 17*, 102–148. Retrieved from http://www.hepg.org/main/her/Index.html

Mowrer, O. H. (1950). *Learning theory and the personality dynamics*. New York: Arnold Press.

Mowrer, O. H., & Mowrer, W. M. (1938). Enuresis: A method for its study and treatment. *American Journal of Orthopsychiatry, 8*, 436–459. doi:10.1111/j.1939-0025.1938.tb06395.x

MTA Cooperative Group. (1999a). Fourteen-month randomized clinical trial of treatment strategies for attention-deficit hyperactivity disorder. *Archives of General Psychiatry, 56*, 1073–1086. Retrieved from http://archpsyc.ama-assn.org/

MTA Cooperative Group. (1999b). Moderators and mediators of treatment response for children with ADHD: The MTA Study. *Archives of General Psychiatry, 56*, 1088–1096. Retrieved from http://archpsyc.ama-assn.org/

MTA Cooperative Group. (2004a). National Institute of Mental Health Multimodal Treatment Study of ADHD follow-up: 24-month outcomes of treatment strategies for attention-deficit/hyperactivity disorder. *Pediatrics, 113*, 754–761. Retrieved from http://pediatrics.aappublications.org/

MTA Cooperative Group. (2004b). National Institute of Mental Health Multimodal

Treatment Study of ADHD follow-up: Changes in effectiveness and growth after the end of treatment. *Pediatrics, 113*, 762–769. Retrieved from http://pediatrics.aappublications.org/

Muehlenkamp, J. J., Ertelt, T. W., Miller, A. L., & Claes, L. (2011). Borderline personality symptoms differentiate non-suicidal and suicidal self-injury in ethnically diverse outpatients. *Journal of Child Psychology and Psychiatry, 52*, 148–155. doi:10.1111/j.1469-7610.2010.02305.x

Mueller, C. E., & Prout, H. T. (2009). Psychosocial adjustment of adolescents and young adults with intellectual disabilities. *Journal of Mental Health Research in Intellectual Disabilities, 2*, 294–311. doi:10.1080/19315860903308572

Mufson, L. (2010). Interpersonal psychotherapy for depressed adolescents (IPT-A): Extending the reach from academic to community settings. *Child and Adolescent Mental Health, 15*, 66–72. doi:10.1111/j.1475-3588.2009.00556.x

Mufson, L., Dorta, K. P., Moreau, D., & Weissman, M. M. (2004). *Interpersonal psychotherapy for depressed adolescents* (2nd ed.). New York: Guilford Press.

Mufson, L. H., Dorta, K. P., Wickramaratne, P., Momura, Y., Olfson, M., & Weissman, M. M. (2004). A randomized effectiveness trial of interpersonal psychotherapy for depressed adolescents. *Archives of General Psychiatry, 61*, 577–584. doi:10.1001/archpsyc.61.6.577

Mulhern, R. K., Merchant, T. E., Gajjar, A., Reddick, W. E., & Kun, L. E. (2004). Late neurocognitive sequelae in survivors of brain tumours in childhood. *Lancet Oncology, 5*, 399–408. doi:10.1016/S1470-2045(04)01507-4

Mullane, J. C., Corkum, P. V., Klein, R. M., McLaughlin, E. N., & Lawrence, M. A. (2011). Alerting, orienting, and executive attention in children with ADHD. *Journal of Attention Disorders, 15*, 310–320. doi:10.1177/1087054710366384

Mullins, L. L., Wolfe-Christensen, C., Pai, A. L. H., Carpentier, M. Y., Gillaspy, S., Cheek, J., & Page, M. (2007). The relationship of parental overprotection, perceived child vulnerability, and parenting stress to uncertainty in youth with chronic illness. *Journal of Pediatric Psychology, 32*, 973–982. doi:10.1093/jpepsy/jsm044

Mundy, P., & Neal, A. R. (2001). Neural plasticity, joint attention, and a transactional social-orienting model of autism. In L. M. Glidden (Ed.), *International review of research in mental retardation: Autism* (Vol. 23, pp. 139–168). San Diego, CA: Academic Press.

Mundy, P., & Newell, L. (2007). Attention, joint attention, and social cognition. *Current Directions in Psychological Science, 16*, 269–274. doi:10.1111/j.1467-8721.2007.00518.x

Munn, R., Smeltzer, D., Smeltzer, T., & Westin, K. (2010). The most painful gaps: Family perspectives on the treatment of eating disorders. In M. Maine, H. McGilley, & D. Bunnell (Eds.), *Treatment of eating disorders: Bridging the research–practice gap* (pp. 349–364). San Diego, CA: Elsevier Academic Press.

Munsch, S., Roth, B., Michael, T., Meyer, A. H., Biedert, E., Roth, S., . . . Margraf, J. (2008). Randomized controlled comparison of two cognitive behavioral therapies for obese children: Mother versus mother-child cognitive behavioral therapy. *Psychotherapy and Psychosomatics, 77*, 235–246. doi:10.1159/000129659

Muratori, F., Picchi, L., Bruni, G., Patarnello, M., & Romagnoli, G. (2003). A two-year follow-up of psychodynamic psychotherapy for internalizing disorders in children. *Journal of the American Academy of Child & Adolescent Psychiatry, 42*, 331–339. doi:10.1097/00004583-200303000-00014

Muris, P. (2007). *Normal and abnormal fear in children and adolescents*. Burlington, MA: Elsevier.

Muris, P., & Meesters, C. (2002). Attachment, behavioral inhibition, and anxiety disorders symptoms in normal adolescents. *Journal of Psychopathology and Behavioral Assessment, 24*, 97–106. doi:10.1023/A:1015388724539

Muris, P., & Merckelbach, H. (2001). The etiology of childhood specific phobia: A multifactorial model. In M. W. Vasey & M. M. Dadds (Eds.), *The developmental psychopathology of anxiety* (pp. 355–385). New York: Oxford University Press.

Muris, P., Rapee, R., Meesters, C., Schouten, E., & Geers, M. (2003). Threat perception abnormalities in children: The role of anxiety disorders symptoms, chronic anxiety, and state anxiety. *Journal of Anxiety Disorders, 17*, 271–287. doi:10.1016/S0887-6185(02)00199-8

Murphy, W. P., Yaruss, J. S., & Quesal, R. W. (2007). Enhancing treatment for school-age children who stutter: I. Reducing negative reactions through desensitization and cognitive restructuring. *Journal of Fluency Disorders, 32*, 121–138. doi:10.1016/j.jfludis.2007.02.002

Murray, C., & Johnston, C. (2006). Parenting in mothers with and without attention-deficit/hyperactivity disorder. *Journal of Abnormal Psychology, 115*, 52–61. doi:10.1037/0021-843X.115.1.52

Murray, C. D., Macdonald S., Fox, J. (2008) Body satisfaction, eating disorders and suicide ideation in an Internet sample of self-harmers reporting and not reporting childhood sexual abuse. *Psychology, Health and Medicine, 13*, 29–42.

Murray, J., Irving, B., Farrington, D. P., Colman, I., & Bloxsom, C. A. J. (2010). Very early predictors of conduct problems and crime: Results from a national cohort study. *Journal of Child Psychology and Psychiatry, 51*, 1198–1207. doi:10.1111/j.1469-7610.2010.02287.x

Murray-Close, D., Hoza, B., Hinshaw, S. P., Arnold, L. E., Swanson, J., Jenson, P. S., . . . Wells, K. (2010). Developmental processes in peer problems of children with attention-deficit/hyperactivity disorder in The Multimodal Treatment Study of Children with ADHD: Developmental cascades and vicious cycles. *Development and Psychopathology, 22*, 785–802. doi:10.1017/S0954579410000465

Myers, N. L. (2011). Update: Schizophrenia across cultures. *Current Psychiatry Reports, 13*, 305–311. doi:10.1007/s11920-011-0208-0

Myers, S. M., Johnson, C. P., and the Council on Children with Disabilities. (2007). Management of children with autism spectrum disorders. *Pediatrics, 120*, 1162–1182. doi:10.1542/peds.2007-2362

Naber, F. B. A., Bakersman-Kranenburg, M. J., van IJzendoorn, M. H., Swinkels, S. H. N., Buitelaar, J. K., Dietz, C., . . . van Engeland, H. (2008). Play behavior and attachment in toddlers with autism. *Journal of Autism and Developmental Disorders, 38*, 857–866. doi:10.1007/s10803-007-0454-5

Naber, F. B. A., Swinkels, S. H. N., Buitelaar, J. K., Dietz, C., Van Daalen, E., Dietz, C., . . . van Engeland, H. (2007). Attachment in toddlers with autism and other developmental disorders. *Journal of Autism and Developmental Disorders, 37*, 1123–1138. doi:10.1007/s10803-006-0255-2

Nadeau, K., Littman, E. B., & Quinn, P. O. (1999). *Understanding girls with AD/HD*. Silver Spring, MD: Advantage Books.

Nagel, B. J., Bathula, D., Herting, M., Schmitt, C., Kroenke, C. D., Fair, D., & Nigg, J. T. (2011). Altered white matter microstructure in children with attention-deficit/hyperactivity disorder. *Journal of the American Academy of Child & Adolescent Psychiatry, 50*, 283–292. doi:10.1016/j.jaac.201012.003

Nagin, D. S., & Tremblay, R. F. (2001). Parental and early childhood predictors of persistent physical aggression in boys from kindergarten to high school. *Archives of General Psychiatry, 58*, 389–394. doi:10.1001/archpsyc.58.4.389

Narusyte, J., Neiderhiser, J. M., Andershed, A.-K., D'Onofrio, B. M., Reiss, D., Spotts, E., . . . Lichtenstein, P. (2011). Parental criticism and externalizing behavior problems in adolescents: The role of environment and genotype-environment correlation. *Journal of Abnormal Psychology, 120*, 365–376. doi:10.1037/a0021815

Nation, K., Snowling, M. J., & Clarke, P. (2007). Dissecting the relationship between language skills and learning to read: Semantic and phonological contributions to new vocabulary learning in children with poor reading comprehension. *Advances in Speech Language Pathology, 9*(2), 131–139.

National Center for Learning Disabilities (NCLD). (2007). *Rewards & roadblocks: How special education students are faring under No Child Left Behind.* New York: Author.

National Center on Addiction and Substance Abuse at Columbia University. (2011). *Adolescent substance use: America's #1 public health problem*. Retrieved from http://www.casacolumbia.org/templates/publications_reports.aspx

National Childhood Cancer Foundation. (2008). Childhood cancer 101. Retrieved from http://www.curesearch.org/our_research/index_sub.aspx?id=1475

National Institute of Justice. (1996). *Victim costs and consequences: A new look.* Washington, DC: Author.

National Institute of Mental Health. (1994a). *Attention deficit hyperactivity disorder:*

Decade of the brain (NIMH Publication No. 94-3572). Washington, DC: Author.

National Institute of Mental Health. (1994b). *Eating disorders (DHHS Publication No. NIMH 94-3477)*. Washington, DC: U.S. Government Printing Office.

National Institute of Mental Health (NIMH). (2003). *Breaking ground, breaking through: The strategic plan for mood disorders research of the National Institute of Mental Health*. Washington, DC: U.S. Department of Health and Human Services.

National Institutes of Health. (2007). *Fact sheet: Reading difficulty and disability*. Washington, DC: Author.

National Society for the Prevention of Cruelty to Children (NSPCC) (2011). *Child abuse and neglect in the UK today*. London, UK: Author. Available: http://www.nspcc.org.uk/Inform/research/findings/child_abuse_neglect_research_wda84173.html

Neal, J., & Edelmann, R. J. (2003). The etiology of social phobia: Toward a developmental profile. *Clinical Psychology Review, 23*, 761–786. doi:10.1016/S0272-7358(03)00076-X

Neale, B. M., Medland, S., Ripke, S., Anney, R. J. L., Asherson, P., Buitelaar, J., Franke, B., ...Biederman, J. for the IMAGE II Consortium. (2010). Case-control genomewide association study of attention-deficit/hyperactivity disorder. *Journal of the American Academy of Child & Adolescent Psychiatry, 49*, 906–920. doi:10.1016/j.jaac.2010.06.007

Neece, C. L., Blacher, J., & Baker, B. L. (2010). Impact on siblings of children with intellectual disability: The role of child behavior problems. *American Journal on Intellectual and Developmental Disabilities, 115*, 291–306. doi:10.1352/1944-7558-115.4.291

Negriff, S., Ji, J., & Trickett, P. K. (2011). Exposure to peer delinquency as a mediator between self-report pubertal timing and delinquency: A longitudinal study of mediation. *Development and Psychopathology, 23*, 293–304. doi:10.1017/S0954579410000805

Neisser, U., Boodoo, G., Bouchard, T. J., Jr., Boykin, A. W., Brody, N., Ceci, S. J., . . . Urbina, S. (1996). Intelligence: Knowns and unknowns. *American Psychologist, 51*, 77–101. doi:10.1037/0003-066X.51.2.77

Nelles, W. B., & Barlow, D. H. (1988). Do children panic? *Clinical Psychology Review, 8*, 359–372. doi:10.1016/0272-7358(88)90064-5

Nelson, C. A. (2011). Neural development and lifelong plasticity. In D. P. Keating (Ed.), *Nature and nurture in early child development.* (pp. 45–69). New York: Cambridge University Press.

Nelson, J. M., & Harwood, H. (2011). Learning disabilities and anxiety: A meta-analysis. *Journal of Learning Disabilities, 44*, 3–17. doi:10.1177/0022219409359939

Nemeth, M. (1994, April 4). Altered states. *Maclean's*, 48–49.

Neuhaus, E., Beauchaine, T. P., & Bernier, R. (2010). Neurobiological correlates of social functioning in autism. *Clinical Psychology Review, 30*, 733–748. doi:10.1016/j.cpr.2010.05.007

Neuman, R. J., Lobos, E., Reich, W., Henderson, C. A., Sun, L. W., & Todd, R. D. (2007). Prenatal smoking exposure and dopaminergic genotypes interact to cause a severe ADHD subtype. *Biological Psychiatry, 61*, 1320–1328. doi:10.1016/j.biopsych.2006.08.049

Neumark-Sztainer, D., Eisenberg, M. E., Fulkerson, J. A., Story, M., & Larson, N. I. (2008). Family meals and disordered eating in adolescents: Longitudinal findings from project EAT. *Archives of Pediatric & Adolescent Medicine, 162*, 17–22. Retrieved from http://archpedi.ama-assn.org/

Neumark-Sztainer, D., Story, M., Hannan, P., Beuhring, T., & Resnick, M. (2000). Disordered eating among adolescents: Associations with sexual/physical abuse and other familial/psychosocial factors. *International Journal of Eating Disorders, 28*, 249–258. doi:10.1002/1098-108X(200011)28:3<249::AID-EAT1>3.0.CO;2-H

Neumark-Sztainer, D., Wall, M., Guo, J., Story, M., Haines, J., & Eisenberg, M. (2006). Obesity, disordered eating, and eating disorders in a longitudinal study of adolescents: How do dieters fare 5 years later? *Journal of the American Dietetic Association, 106*, 559–568. doi:10.1016/j.jada.2006.01.003

Neumark-Sztainer, D., Wall, M., Larson, N. I., Eisenberg, M. E., & Loth, K. (2011). Dieting and disordered eating behaviors from adolescence to young adulthood: Findings from a 10-year longitudinal study. *American Dietetic Association Journal of the American Dietetic Association, 111*, 1004. doi:10.1016/j.jada.2011.04.012

Nevonen, L., & Norring, C. (2004). Socioeconomic variables and eating disorders: A comparison between patients and normal controls. *Eating and Weight Disorders, 9*, 279–284. Retrieved from http://www.kurtis.it/ewd/it/

Nevsimalova, S. (2009). Narcolepsy in childhood. *Sleep Medicine Reviews, 13*, 169–180. doi:10.1016/j.smrv.2008.04.007

Newbury, D. F., Paracchini, S., Scerri, T. S., Winchester, L., Addis, L., Richardson, A. J., . . . Monaco, A. P. (2011). Investigation of dyslexia and SLI risk variants in reading- and language-impaired subjects. *Behavior Genetics, 41*, 90–104. doi:10.1007/s10519-010-9424-3

Newsom, C., & Hovanitz, C. A. (2006). Autistic spectrum disorders. In E. J. Mash & R. A. Barkley (Eds.), *Treatment of childhood disorders* (3rd ed., pp. 455–511). New York: Guilford Press.

Nguyen, L., Huang, L. N., Arganza, G. F., & Liao, Q. (2007). The influence of race and ethnicity on psychiatric diagnoses and clinical characteristics of children and adolescents in children's services. *Cultural Diversity & Ethnic Minority Psychology, 13*, 18–25. doi:10.1037/1099-9809.13.1.18

Niccols, A. (2007). Fetal alcohol syndrome and the developing socio-emotional brain. *Brain and Cognition, 65*, 135–142. doi:10.1016/j.bandc.2007.02.009

Nichols, M. (1995, January 30). Schizophrenia: Hidden torment. *Maclean's*, 70–74.

Nicolson, R., Lenane, M., Singaracharlu, S., Malaspina, D., Giedd, J. N., Hamburger, S. D., . . . Rapoport, J. L. (2000). Premorbid speech and language impairments in childhood-onset schizophrenia: Association with risk factors. *American Journal of Psychiatry, 157*, 794–800. doi:10.1016/S0920-9964(00)90420-1

Nicolson, R., & Rapoport, J. L. (1999). Childhood-onset schizophrenia: Rare but worth studying. *Biological Psychiatry, 46*, 1418–1428. doi:10.1016/S0006-3223(99)00231-0

Nigg, J. T. (2005). Neuropsychologic theory and findings in attention-deficit/hyperactivity disorder: The state of the field and salient challenges for the coming decade. *Biological Psychiatry, 57*, 1424–1435. doi:10.1016/j.biopsych.2004.11.011

Nigg, J. T. (2006). Temperament and developmental psychopathology. *Journal of Child Psychology and Psychiatry, 47*, 395–422. doi:10.1111/j.1469-7610.2006.01612.x

Nigg, J. T., & Breslau, N. (2007). Prenatal smoking exposure, low birth weight, and disruptive behavior disorders. *Journal of the American Academy of Child & Adolescent Psychiatry, 46*, 362–369. doi:10.1097/01.chi.0000246054.76167.44

Nigg, J. T., Hinshaw, S. P., & Huang-Pollack, C. (2006). Disorders of attention and impulse regulation. In D. Cicchetti & D. J. Cohen (Eds.), *Developmental psychopathology: Vol. 3. Risk, disorder, and adaptation* (2nd ed., pp. 358–403). New York: Wiley.

Nigg, J. T., Nikolas, M., Knottnerus, M., Cavanagh, K., & Frederici, K. (2010). Confirmation and extension of association of blood lead with attention-deficit/hyperactivity disorders (ADHD) and ADHD symptom domains at population-typical exposure levels. *Journal of Child Psychology and Psychiatry, 51*, 58–65. doi:10.1111/j.1469-7610.2009.02135.x

Nigg, J. T., Tannock, R., & Rohde, L. A. (2010). What is to be the fate of ADHD subtypes? An introduction to the Special Section on research on the ADHD subtypes and implications for the DSM-V. *Journal of Clinical Child Psychology, 39*, 723–725. doi:10.1080/15374416.2010.517171

Nijmeijer, J. S., Minderaa, R. B., Buitelaar, J. K., Mulligan, A., Hartman, C. A., & Hoekstra, P. J. (2008). Attention-deficit/hyperactivity disorder and social dysfunctioning. *Clinical Psychology Review, 28*, 692–708. doi:10.1016/j.cpr.2007.10.003

Nikapota, A. (2009). Cultural issues in child assessment. *Child and Adolescent Mental Health, 14*, 200–206. doi:10.1111/j.1475-3588.2009.00537.x

Nikolas, M., Friderici, K., Waldman, I., Jernigan, K., & Nigg, J. T. (2010). Gene × environment interactions for ADHD: Synergistic effect of 5HTTLPR genotype and youth appraisals of inter-parental conflict. *Behavioral and Brain Functions, 6*, 1–15. doi:10.1186/1744-9081-6-23

Nikolas, M. A., & Burt, S. A. (2010). Genetic and environmental influences on ADHD symptom dimensions of inattention and hyperactivity: A meta-analysis. *Journal of Abnormal Psychology, 119*, 1–17. doi:10.1037/a0018010

Nilsson, E. W., Gillberg, C., Gillberg, I. C., & Rastam, M. (1999). Ten-year follow-up of adolescent-onset anorexia nervosa: Personality disorders. *Journal of the American Academy of Child & Adolescent Psychiatry, 38*, 1389–1395. doi:10.1097/00004583-199911000-00013

Nisbett, R. E. (2009). *Intelligence and how to get it: Why schools and cultures count.* New York: W. W. Norton & Co.

Nock, M. K., Borges, G., Bromet, E. J., Alonso, J., Angermeyer, M., Beautrais, A., . . . Williams, D. (2008). Cross-national prevalence and risk factors for suicidal ideation, plans, and attempts. *British Journal of Psychiatry, 192*, 98–105. doi:10.1192/bjp.bp.107.040113

Nock, M. K., Kazdin, A. E., Hiripi, E., & Kessler, R. C. (2007). Lifetime prevalence, correlates and persistence of oppositional defiant disorder: Results from the National Comorbidity Survey Replication. *Journal of Child Psychology and Psychiatry, 48*, 703–713. doi:10.1111/j.1469-7610.2007.01733.x

Nolen-Hoeksema, S., Girgus, J. S., & Seligman, M. E. P. (1992). Predictors and consequences of childhood depressive symptoms: A 5-year longitudinal study. *Journal of Abnormal Psychology, 101*, 405–422. doi:10.1037/0021-843X.101.3.405

Noll, R. B., LeRoy, S., Bukowski, W. M., Rogosch, F. A., & Kulkarni, R. (1991). Peer relationships and adjustment in children with cancer. *Journal of Pediatric Psychology, 16*, 307–326. doi:10.1093/jpepsy/16.3.307

Norgaard, J. P., Pederson, E. B., & Djurhuus, J. C. (1985). Diurnal antidiuretic hormone levels in enuretics. *Journal of Urology, 134*, 1029–1031.

Nottelman, E. D., & Jensen, P. S. (1995). Comorbidity of disorders in children and adolescents: Developmental perspectives. In T. H. Ollendick & R. J. Prinz (Eds.), *Advances in clinical child psychology* (Vol. 17, pp. 109–155). New York: Plenum Press.

Nouri, M., Hill, L. G., & Orrell-Valente, J. K. (2011). Media exposure, internalization of the thin ideal, and body dissatisfaction: Comparing Asian American and European American college females. *Body Image, 8*, 366–372. doi:10.1016/j.bodyim.2011.05.008

Nunes, S. O. V., Watanabe, M. A. E., Morimoto, H. K., Moriya, R., & Reiche, E. M. V. (2010). The impact of childhood sexual abuse on activation of immunological and neuroendocrine response. *Aggression and Violent Behavior, 15*, 440–445. doi:10.1016/j.avb.2010.07.006

Nusslock, R., Shackman, A. J., Harmon-Jones, E., Alloy, L. B., Coan, J. A., & Abramson, L. Y. (2011). Cognitive vulnerability and frontal lobe asymmetry: Common predictors of first prospective depression episode. *Journal of Abnormal Psychology, 120*, 497–503. doi:10.1037/a0022940

O'Connor, T. G. (2006). The persisting effects of early experiences on psychological development. In D. Cicchetti & D. J. Cohen (Eds.), *Developmental psychopathology: Vol. 3. Risk, disorder, and adaptation* (2nd ed., pp. 202–234). Hoboken, NJ: Wiley.

O'Dea, J. A. (2006). Self-concept, self-esteem and body weight in adolescent females: A three-year longitudinal study. *Journal of Health Psychology, 11*, 599–611. doi:10.1177/1359105306065020

O'Dea, J. A. (2008). Gender, ethnicity, culture and social class influences on childhood obesity among Australian schoolchildren: Implications for treatment, prevention and community education. *Health and Social Care in the Community, 16*, 282–290. doi:10.1111/j.1365-2524.2008.00768.x

O'Hearn, K., Asato, M., Ordaz, S., & Luna, B. (2008). Neurodevelopment and executive function in autism. *Development and Psychopathology, 20*, 1103–1132. doi:10.1017/S0954579408000527

O'Leary-Barrett, M., Mackie, C. J., Castellanos-Ryan, N., Al-Khudhairy, N., & Conrod, P. J. (2010). Personality-targeted interventions delay uptake of drinking and decrease risk of alcohol-related problems when delivered by teachers. *Journal of the American Academy of Child & Adolescent Psychiatry, 49*, 954–963. doi:10.1016/j.jaac.2010.04.011

Obel, C., Olsen, J., Henriksen, T. B., Rodriguez, A., Jarvelin, M. R., Moilanen, I., . . . Gissler, M. (2011). Is maternal smoking during pregnancy a risk factor for hyperkinetic disorder?—Findings from a sibling design. *International Journal of Epidemiology, 40*, 338–345. doi:10.1093/ije/dyq185

Obradovic, J., Burt, K. B., & Masten, A. S. (2010). Testing a dual cascade model linking competence and symptoms over 20 years from childhood to adulthood. *Journal of Clinical Child and Adolescent Psychology, 39*, 90–102. doi:10.1080/15374410903401120

Obradovic, J., Bush, N. R., Stamperdahl, J., Adler, N. E., & Boyce, W. T. (2010). Biological sensitivity to context: The interactive effects of stress reactivity and family adversity on socioemotional behavior and school readiness. *Child Development, 81*, 270–289. doi:10.1111/j.1467-8624.2009.01394.x

Odgers, C. L., Caspi, A., Broadbent, J. M., Dickson, N., Hancox, R. J., Harrington, H., . . . Moffitt, T. E. (2007a). Prediction of differential adult health burden by conduct problem subtypes in males. *Archives of General Psychiatry, 64*, 476–484. doi:10.1001/archpsyc.64.4.476

Odgers, C. L., Milne, B. J., Caspi, A., Crump, R., Poulton, R., & Moffitt, T. E. (2007b). Predicting prognosis for the conduct-problem boy: Can family history help? *Journal of the American Academy of Child & Adolescent Psychiatry, 46*, 1240–1249. doi:10.1097/chi.0b013e31813c6c8d

Odgers, C. L., & Moretti, M. M. (2002). Aggressive and antisocial girls: Research update and challenges. *International Journal of Forensic Mental Health Services, 1*, 103–119. Retrieved from http://www.iafmhs.org/iafmhs.asp?pg=journal

Oeseburg, B., Dijkstra, G. J., Groothoff, J. W., Reijneveld, S. A., & Jansen, D. E. M. C. (2011). Prevalence of chronic health conditions in children with intellectual disability: A systematic literature review. *Intellectual and Developmental Disabilities, 49*, 59–85. doi:10.1352/1934-9556-49.2.59

Offord, D. R., Alder, R. J., & Boyle, M. H. (1986). Prevalence and sociodemographic correlates of conduct disorder. *American Journal of Social Psychiatry, 4*, 272–278. Retrieved from http://www.offordcentre.com/about/offordpapers.html

Ogden, C. L., Carroll, M. D., & Flegal, K. M. (2008). High body mass index for age among US children and adolescents, 2003-2006. *JAMA: Journal of the American Medical Association, 299*, 2401–2405. doi:10.1001/jama.299.20.240

Ogden, C. L., Flegal, K. M., Carroll, M. D., & Johnson, C. L. (2002). Prevalence and trends in overweight among US children and adolescents, 1999-2000. *JAMA: Journal of the American Medical Association, 288*, 1728–1732. doi:10.1001/jama.288.14.1728

Ohan, J. L., & Johnston, C. (2002). Are the performance overestimates given by boys with ADHD self-protective? *Journal of Clinical Child Psychology, 31*, 230–241. doi:10.1207/S15374424JCCP3102_08

Ohan, J. L., & Johnston, C. (2005). Gender appropriateness of symptom criteria for attention-deficit/hyperactivity disorder, oppositional-defiant disorder, and conduct disorder. *Child Psychiatry and Human Development, 35*, 359–381. doi:10.1007/s10578-005-2694-y

Ogden, C. L., Lamb, M. M., Carroll, M. D., & Flegal, K. M. (2010). Obesity and socioeconomic status in children and adolescents: United States, 2005–2008. *NCHS Data Brief,* (51), 1–8.

Ohan, J. L., & Visser, T. A. W. (2009). Why is there a gender gap in children presenting for attention deficit/hyperactivity disorder services? *Journal of Clinical Child and Adolescent Psychology, 38*, 650–660. doi:10.1080/15374410903103627

Ojemann, G. A. (1991). Cortical organization of language. *Journal of Neuroscience, 11*, 2281–2287. Retrieved from http://www.jneurosci.org/

Olds, D., Eckenrode, J., Henderson, C. R., Kitzman, H., Powers, J., Cole, R., . . . Pettit, L. M. (1997). Long-term effects of home visitation on maternal life course and child abuse and neglect: Fifteen-year follow-up of a randomized trial. *Journal of the American Medical Association, 278*, 637–643.

Olds, T., Maher, C., Zumin, S., Péneau, S., Lioret, S., Castetbon, K., . . . Summerbell, C. (2011). Evidence that the prevalence of childhood overweight is plateauing: Data from nine countries. *International Journal of Pediatric Obesity, 6*, 342–360. doi:10.3109/17477166.2011.605895

Olfson, M., Gameroff, M. J., Marcus, S. C., Jensen, P. S. (2003). National trends in the treatment of attention deficit hyperactivity disorder. *American Journal of Psychiatry, 160*, 1071–1077. doi:10.1176/appi.ajp.160.6.1071

Olfson, M., Gameroff, M. J., Marcus, S. C., & Waslick, B. D. (2003). Outpatient treatment of child and adolescent depression in the United States. *Archives of General Psychiatry, 60*, 1236–1242. doi:10.1001/archpsyc.60.12.1236

Olfson, M., Marcus, S. C., Weissman, M. M., & Jensen, P. S. (2002). National trends in the use of psychotropic medications by children. *Journal of the American Academy of Child & Adolescent Psychiatry, 41*, 514–521. doi:10.1097/00004583-200205000-00008

Olino, T. M., Lopez-Duran, N. L., Kovacs, M., George, C. J., Gentzler, & Shaw, D. S. (2011). Developmental trajectories of positive and negative affect in children at high and low familial risk for depressive disorder. *Journal of Child Psychology and Psychiatry, 52*, 792–799. doi:10.1111/j.1469-7610.2010.02331.x

Olivardia, R., Pope, H. G., Borowiecki, J. J., & Cohane, G. C. (2004). Biceps and body image: The relationship between muscularity and self-esteem, depression and eating disorder symptoms. *Psychology of Men and Masculinity, 5*, 112–120. doi:10.1037/1524-9220.5.2.112

Oliver, B. R., Barker, E. D., Mandy, W. P. L., Skuse, D. H., & Maughan, B. (2011). Social cognition and conduct problems: A developmental approach. *Journal of the American Academy of Child & Adolescent Psychiatry, 40*, 385–394. doi:10.1016/i.jaac.2011.01.006

Ollendick, T. H., & King, N. J. (1994). Fears and their level of interference in adolescents. *Behaviour Research and Therapy, 32*, 635–638. doi:10.1016/0005-7967(94)90018-3

Ollendick, T. H., King, N. J., & Chorpita, B. F. (2006). *Empirically supported treatments for children and adolescents.* New York: Guilford Press.

Ollendick, T. H., Seligman, L. D., Goza, A. B., Byrd, D. A., & Singh, K. (2003). Anxiety and depression in children and adolescents: A factor-analytic examination of the tripartite model. *Journal of Child and Family Studies, 12*, 157–170. doi:10.1023/A:1022806731527

Ollendick, T. H., Yang, B., King, N., J., Dong, Q., & Akande, A. (1996). Fears in American, Australian, Chinese, and Nigerian children and adolescents: A cross-cultural study. *Journal of Child Psychology and Psychiatry, 37*, 213–220. doi:10.1111/j.1469-7610.1996.tb01393.x

Olsen, E. M., Petersen, J., Skovgaard, A. M., Weile, B., Jørgensen, T., & Wright, C. M. (2007). Failure to thrive: The prevalence and concurrence of anthropometric criteria in a general infant population. *Archives of Disease in Childhood, 92*, 109–114. doi:10.1136/adc.2005.080333

Olson, S. L., Bates, J. E., Sandy, J. M., & Lanthier, R. (2000). Early developmental precursors of externalizing behavior in middle childhood and adolescence. *Journal of Abnormal Child Psychology, 28*, 119–133. doi:10.1023/A:1005166629744

Olson, S. L., Lopez-Duran, N., Lunkenheimer, E. S., Chang, H., & Sameroff, A. J. (2011). Individual differences in the development of early peer aggression: Integrating contributions of self-regulation, theory of mind, and parenting. *Development and Psychopathology, 23*, 253–266. doi:10.1017/S0954579410000775

Olweus, D. (1995). Bullying or peer abuse at school: Facts and intervention. *Current Directions in Psychological Science, 4*, 196–200. doi:10.1111/1467-8721.ep10772640

Omdal, H. (2007). Can adults who have recovered from selective mutism in childhood and adolescence tell us anything about the nature of the condition and/or recovery from it? *European Journal of Special Needs Education, 22*, 237–253. doi:10.1080/08856250701430323

Oosterling, I. J., Wensing, M., Swinkels, S. H., van der Gaag, R. J., Visser, J. C., Woudenberg, T., . . . Buitelaar, J. K. (2010). Advancing early detection of autism spectrum disorder by applying an integrated two-stage approach. *Journal of Child Psychology and Psychiatry, 51*, 250–258. doi:10.1111/j.1469-7610.2009.02150.x

Oppenheimer, C. W., & Hankin, B. L. (2011). Relationship quality and depressive symptoms among adolescents: A short-term multiwave investigation of longitudinal, reciprocal associations. *Journal of Clinical Child and Adolescent Psychology, 40*, 486–493. doi:10.1080/15374416.2011.563462

Ornitz, E. M., Russell, A. T., Hanna, G. L., Gabikian, P., Gehricke, J. G., Song, D., & Guthrie, D. (1999). Prepulse inhibition of startle and the neurobiology of primary nocturnal enuresis. *Biological Psychiatry, 45*, 1455–1466. doi:10.1016/S0006-3223(98)00205-4

Orobio de Castro, B., Brendgen, M., Van Boxtel, H., Vitaro, F., & Schaepers, L. (2007). "Accept me, or else . . .": Disputed overestimation of social competence predicts increases in proactive aggression. *Journal of Abnormal Child Psychology, 35*, 165–178. doi:10.1007/s10802-006-9063-6

Oster, G. D., & Montgomery, S. S. (1995). *Helping your depressed teenager: A guide for parents and caregivers.* New York: Wiley.

Oswald, D. P., & Sonenklar, N. A. (2007). Medication use among children with autism-spectrum disorders. *Journal of Child and Adolescent Psychopharmacology, 17*, 348–355. doi:10.1089/cap.2006.17303

Owen, B. (1993, May 18). *Kids in the dumps.* Winnipeg Free Press, p. C1.

Owen, M. J., O'Donovan, M. C., Thapar, A., & Craddock, N. (2011). Neurodevelopmental hypothesis of schizophrenia. *The British Journal of Psychiatry, 198*, 173–175. doi:10.1192/bjp.bp.110.084384

Owens, J. A., Palermo, T. M., & Rosen, C. L. (2002). Overview of current management of sleep disturbances in children: II–behavioral interventions. *Current Therapeutic Research, 63*, B38–B52. doi:10.1016/S0011-393X(02)80102-3

Owens, J. S., Goldfine, M. E., Evangelista, N. M., Hoza, B., & Kaiser, N. M. (2007). A critical review of self-perceptions and the positive illusory bias in children with ADHD. *Clinical Child and Family Psychology Review, 10*, 335–351. doi:10.1007/s10567-007-0027-3

Owens, R. G., & Slade, P. D. (1987). Running and anorexia nervosa: An empirical study. *International Journal of Eating Disorders, 6*, 771–775. doi:10.1002/1098-108X(198711)6:6<771::AID-EAT2260060612>3.0.CO;2-V

Ozgen, H. M., Hop, J. W., Hox, J. J., Beemer, F. A., & van Engeland, H. (2010). Minor physical anomalies in autism: A meta-analysis. *Molecular Psychiatry, 15*, 300–307. doi:10.1038/mp.2008.75

Ozonoff, S., & South, M. (2001). Early social development in young children with autism: Theoretical and clinical implications. In G. Bremner & A. Fogel (Eds.), *Blackwell handbook of infant development* (pp. 565–588). Malden, MA: Blackwell.

Ozonoff, S., Iosif, A. M., Baguio, F., Cook, I. C., Hill, M. M., Hutman, T., . . . Young, G. S. (2010). A prospective study of the emergence of early behavioral signs of autism. *Journal of the American Academy of Child & Adolescent Psychiatry, 49*, 256–266. doi:10.1097/00004583-201003000-00009

Ozonoff, S., Pennington, B. F., & Solomon, M. (2006). *Neuropsychological perspectives on developmental psychopathology.* Hoboken, NJ: Wiley.

Ozonoff, S., Young, G. S., Carter, A., Messinger, D., Yirmiya N., Zwaigenbaum, L., . . . Stone, W. L. (2011, August 15). Recurrence risk for autism spectrum disorders: A baby siblings research consortium study. *Pediatrics, 128*, e488–e495. doi:10.1542/peds.2010-2825

Ozonoff, S., Young, G. S., Steinfeld, M. B., Hill, M. M., Cook, I., Hutman, T., . . . Sigman, M. (2009). How early do parent concerns predict later autism diagnosis? *Journal of Developmental and Behavioral Pediatrics, 30*, 367–375. doi:10.1097/DBP.0b013e3181ba0fcf

Paavonen, E. J., Vehkalahti, K., Vanhala, R., von Wendt, L., Nieminen-von Wendt, T., & Aronen, E. T. (2008). Sleep in children with Asperger syndrome. *Journal of Autism and Developmental Disorders, 38*, 41–51. doi:10.1007/s10803-007-0360-x

Packman, A., Code, C., & Onslow, M. (2007). On the cause of stuttering: Integrating theory with brain and behavioral research. *Journal of Neurolinguistics, 20*, 353–362. doi:10.1016/j.jneuroling.2006.11.001

Pagani, L., Boulerice, B., Vitaro, F., & Tremblay, R. E. (1999). Effects of poverty on academic failure and delinquency in boys: A change and process model approach. *Journal of Child Psychology and Psychiatry, 40*, 1209–1219. doi:10.1111/1469-7610.00537

Pagani, L. S., Japel, C., Vaillancourt, T., Cote, S., & Tremblay, R. E. (2008). Links between life course trajectories of family dysfunction and anxiety during middle childhood. *Journal of Abnormal Child Psychology, 36*, 41–53. doi:10.1007/s10802-007-9158-8

Pai, A. L. H., Drotar, D., Zebracki, K., Moore, M., & Youngstrom, E. (2006). A meta-analysis of the effects of psychological interventions in pediatric oncology on outcomes of psychological distress and adjustment. *Journal of Pediatric Psychology, 31*, 978–988. doi:10.1093/jpepsy/jsj109

Pai, A. L. H., Greenley, R. N., Lewandowski, A., Drotar, D., Youngstrom, E., & Peterson, C. C. (2007). A meta-analytic review of the influence of pediatric cancer on parent and family functioning. *Journal of Family Psychology, 21*, 407–415. doi:10.1037/0893-3200.21.3.407

Pajer, K., Chung, J., Leininger, L., Wei Wang, M. A. S., Gardner, W., & Yeates, K. (2008). Neuropsychological function in adolescent girls with conduct disorder. *Journal of the American Academy of Child & Adolescent Psychiatry, 47*, 416–425. doi:10.1097/CHI.0b013e3181640828

Palermo, S. D., Bloch, M. H., Craiglow, B., Landeros-Weisenberger, A., Dombrowski, P. A., Panza, K., . . . Leckman, J. F. (2011). Predictors of early adulthood quality of life in children with obsessive-compulsive disorder. *Social Psychiatry and Psychiatric Epidemiology, 46*, 291–297. doi:10.1007/s00127-010-0194-2

Palmer, E. D., and Finger, S. (2001). An early description of ADHD (Inattentive Subtype): Dr. Alexander Crichton and "Mental Restlessness" (1798). *Child Psychology and Psychiatry Review, 6*, 66–73. doi:10.1111/1475-3588.00324

Palmer, R., Enderby, P., & Hawley, M. (2007). Addressing the needs of speakers with longstanding dysarthria: Computerized and traditional therapy compared. *International Journal of Language & Communication Disorders, 42(Suppl. 1)*, 61–79. doi:10.1080/13682820601173296

Palomo, R., Thompson, M., Colombi, C., Cook, I., Goldring, S., Young, G. S., & Ozonoff, S. (2008). A case study of childhood disintegrative disorder using systematic analysis of family home movies. *Journal of Autism and Developmental Disorders, 38*, 1853–1858. doi:10.1007/s10803-008-0579-1

Pao, M., & Bosk, A. (2011). Anxiety in medically ill children/adolescents. *Depression and Anxiety, 28*, 40–49. doi:10.1002/da.20727

Papanikolaou, K., Richardson, C., Pehlivanidis, A., & Papadopoulou-Daifoti, Z. (2006). Efficacy of antidepressants in child and adolescent depression: A meta-analytic study. *Journal of Neural Transmission, 113*, 399–415. doi:10.1007/s00702-005-0340-2

Paras, M. L., Murad, M. H., Chen, L. P., Goranson, E. N., Sattler, A. L., Colbenson, K. M., . . . Zirakzadeh, A. (2009). Sexual abuse and lifetime diagnosis of somatic disorders: A systematic review and meta-analysis. *JAMA: Journal of the American Medical Association, 302*, 550–561. doi:10.1001/jama.2009.1091

Pardini, D. A. (2011). Perceptions of social conflicts among incarcerated adolescents with callous-unemotional traits: 'You're going to pay. It's going to hurt, but I don't care.' *Journal of Child Psychology and Psychiatry, 52*, 248–255. doi:10.1111/j.1469-7610.2010.02336.x

Pardini. D. A., & Loeber, R. (2008). Interpersonal callousness trajectories across adolescence: Early social influences and adult outcomes. *Criminal Justice and Behavior, 3*, 173–96. doi:10.1177/0093854807310157

Parry-Jones, W. L., & Parry-Jones, B. (1994). Implications of historical evidence for the classification of eating disorders: A dimension overlooked in DSM-III-R and ICD-10. *British Journal of Psychiatry, 165*, 287–292. doi:10.1192/bjp.165.3.287

Pasco Fearon, R., Bakersmans-Kranenburg, M. J., van IJzendoorn, M. H., Lapsley, A.M., & Roisman, G. I. (2010). The significance of insecure attachment and disorganization in the development of children's externalizing behavior: A meta-analytic study. *Child Development, 81*, 435–436. doi:0009-3920/2010/8102-0002

Passamonti, L., Fairchild, G., Goodyer, I. M., Hurford, G., Hagan, C., Rowe, J. B., & Calder, A. J. (2010). Neural abnormalities in early-onset and adolescence-onset conduct disorder. *Archives of General Psychiatry, 67*, 729–738. doi:10.1001/archgenpsychiatry.2010.75

Patterson, G. R. (1996). Some characteristics of a developmental theory for early-onset delinquency. In M. F. Lenzenweger & J. J. Haugaard (Eds.), *Frontiers of developmental psychopathology* (pp. 81–124). New York: Oxford University Press.

Patterson, G. R., Reid, J. B., & Dishion, T. J. (1992). *Antisocial boys*. Eugene, OR: Castalia.

Patton, M. Q. (2002). *Qualitative research and evaluation methods* (3rd ed.). Beverly Hills, CA: Sage.

Paul, R., Fuerst, Y., Ramsay, G., Chawarska, K., & Klin, A. (2011). Out of the mouths of babes: Vocal production in infant siblings of children with ASD. *Journal of Child Psychology and Psychiatry, 52*, 588–598. doi:10.1111/j.1469-7610.2010.02332.x

Paxton, S. J., Eisenberg, M. E., & Neumark-Sztainer, D. (2006). Prospective predictors of body dissatisfaction in adolescent girls and boys: A five year longitudinal study. *Developmental Psychology, 42*, 888–899. doi:10.1037/0012-1649.42.5.888

Pearsall-Jones, J. G., Piek, J. P., & Levy, F. (2010). Etiological pathways for developmental coordination disorder and attention-deficit/hyperactivity disorder: Shared or discrete? *Expert Review of Neurotherapeutics, 10*, 491–494. doi:10.1586/ERN.10.20

Peleg-Popko, O., & Dar, R. (2003). Ritual behavior in children and mothers' perceptions of family patterns. *Journal of Anxiety Disorders, 17*, 667–681. doi:10.1016/S0887-6185(02)00235-9

Pelham, W. E., Foster, E. M., & Robb, J. A. (2007). The economic impact of attention-deficit/hyperactivity disorder in children and adolescents. *Journal of Pediatric Psychology, 32*, 711–727. doi:10.1093/jpepsy/jsm022

Pelham, W. E., Gnagy, E. M., Greiner, A. R., Hoza, B., Hinshaw, S. P., Swanson, J. M., . . . Baron-Myak, C. (2000). Behavioral versus behavioral and pharmacological treatment in ADHD children attending a summer treatment program. *Journal of Abnormal Child Psychology, 28*, 507–525. doi:10.1023/A:1005127030251

Pelham, W. E., Gnagy, E. M., Greiner, A. R., Waschbusch, D. A., Fabiano, G. A., & Burrows-Maclean, L. (2010). Summer treatment programs for attention-deficit/hyperactivity disorder. In J. R. Weisz & A. E. Kazdin (Eds.), *Evidence-based psychotherapies for children and adolescents* (2nd ed., pp. 277–292). New York: Guilford Press.

Pelham, W. E., Jr., & Fabiano, G. A. (2008). Evidence-based psychosocial treatments for attention-deficit/hyperactivity disorder. *Journal of Clinical Child and Adolescent Psychology, 37*, 184–214. doi:10.1080/15374410701818681

Pelham, W. E., Jr., & Lang, A. R. (1999). Can your children drive you to drink?: Stress and parenting in adults interacting with children with ADHD. *Alcohol Research and Health, 23*, 292–298. Retrieved from http://www.niaaa.nih.gov/Pages/default.aspx

Pelham, W. E., Waxmonsky, J. G., Schentag, J., Ballow, C. H., Panahon, C. J., Gnagy, E. M., . . . González, M. A. (2011). Efficacy of a methylphenidate transdermal system versus t.i.d. methylphenidate in a laboratory setting. *Journal of Attention Disorders, 15*, 28–35. doi:10.1177/1087054709359163

Pelphrey, K. A., Shultz, S., Hudac, C. M., & Vander Wyk, B. C. (2011). Constraining heterogeneity: The social brain and its development in autism spectrum disorder. *Journal of Child Psychology and Psychiatry, 52*, 631–644. doi:10.1111/j.1469-7610.2010.02349.x

Pennington, B. F. (2006). From single to multiple deficit models of developmental disorders. *Cognition, 101*, 385–413. doi:10.1016/j.cognition.2006.04.008

Pennington, B. F., & Ozonoff, S. (1996). Executive functions and developmental psychopathology. *Journal of Child Psychology and Psychiatry, 37*, 51–87. doi:10.1111/j.1469-7610.1996.tb01380.x

Pennington, B. F., Moon, J., Edgin, J., Stedron, J., & Nadel, L. (2003). The neuropsychology of Down syndrome: Evidence for hippocampal dysfunction. *Child Development, 74*, 75–93. doi:10.1111/1467-8624.00522

Pennington, B. P. (2009). How neuropsychology informs our understanding of developmental disorders. *Child Psychology and Psychiatry, 50*, 72–78. doi:10.1111/j.1469-7610.2008.01977.x

Pepler, D. J., Craig, W. M., Connolly, J., & Henderson, K. (2002). Bullying, sexual harassment, dating violence, and substance use among adolescents. In C. Wekerle & A. Wall (Eds.), *The violence and addiction equation: Theoretical and clinical issues in substance abuse and relationship violence* (pp. 153–168). New York: Brunner-Routledge.

Peppe, S., McCann, J., Gibbon, F., O'Hare, A., & Rutherford, M. (2007). Receptive and expressive prosodic ability in children with high-functioning autism. *Journal of Speech, Language, and Hearing Research, 50*, 1015–1028. doi:10.1044/1092-4388(2007/071)

Pereda, N., Guilera, G., Forns, M., & Gómez-Benito, J. (2009). The prevalence of child sexual abuse in community and student samples: A meta-analysis. *Clinical Psychology Review, 29*, 328–338. doi:10.1016/j.cpr.2009.02.007

Perez-Edgar, K., Bar-Haim, Y., McDermott, J. M., Chronis-Tuscano, A., Pine, D. S., & Fox, N. A. (2010). Attention biases to threat and behavioral inhibition in early childhood shape adolescent social withdrawal. *Emotion, 10*, 349–357. doi:10.1037/a0018486

Perlman, S. B., & Pelphrey, K. A. (2010). Regulatory brain development: Balancing emotion and cognition. *Social Neuroscience, 5*, 533–542. doi:10.1080/17470911003683219

Perlman, S. B., & Pelphrey, K. A. (2011). Developing connections for affective regulation: Age-related changes in emotional brain connectivity. *Journal of Experimental Child Psychology, 108*, 607–620. doi:10.1016/j.jecp.2010.08.006

Perrin, S., Smith, P., & Yule, W. (2000). Practitioner review: The assessment and treatment of post-traumatic stress disorder in children and adolescents. *Journal of Child Psychology and Psychiatry, 41*, 277–289. doi:10.1111/1469-7610.00612

Peterson, B. S. (2003). Conceptual, methodological, and statistical challenges in brain imaging studies of developmentally based psychopathologies. *Development and Psychopathology, 15*, 811–832. doi:10.1017/S0954579403000385

Peterson, B. S., Pine, D. S., Cohen, P., & Brook, J. S. (2001). Prospective, longitudinal study of tic, obsessive-compulsive, and attention-deficit/hyperactivity disorders in an epidemiological sample. *Journal of the American Academy of Child & Adolescent Psychiatry, 40*, 685–695. doi:10.1097/00004583-200106000-00014

Peterson, B. S., Warner, V., Bansal, R., Zhu, H., Hao, X., Liu, J., . . . Weissman, M. M. (2009). Cortical thinning in persons at increased familial risk for major depression. *PNAS, 106*, 6273–6278. doi:10.1073_pnas.0805311106

Peterson, C. C., & Drotar, D. (2006). Family impact of neurodevelopmental late effects in survivors of pediatric cancer: Review of research, clinical evidence, and future directions. *Clinical Child Psychology and Psychiatry, 11*, 349–366. doi:10.1177/1359104506064980

Peterson, L., Reach, K., & Grube, S. (2003). Health-related disorders. In E. J. Mash & R. A. Barkley (Eds.), *Child psychopathology* (2nd ed., pp. 716–749). New York: Guilford Press.

Peterson, R. L., & Pennington, B. F. (2010). *Reading disability*. New York: Guilford Press.

Pfiffner, L. J., Barkley, R. A., & DuPaul, G. J. (2006). Treatment of ADHD in school settings. In R. A. Barkley, *Attention deficit hyperactivity disorder: A handbook for diagnosis and treatment* (3rd ed., pp. 547–589). New York: Guilford Press.

Pfiffner, L. J., Mikami, A. Y., Huang-Pollack, C., Easterlin, B., Zalecki, C., & McBurnett, K. (2007). A randomized, controlled trial of integrated home-school behavioral treatment for ADHD, predominately inattentive type. *Journal of the American Academy of Child & Adolescent Psychiatry, 46*, 1041–1050. doi:10.1097/chi.0b013e318064675f

Phelan, K., Khoury, J., Atherton, H., & Kahn, R. S. (2008). Maternal depression, child behavior and injury. *Injury Prevention, 13*, 403–408. doi:10.1136/ip.2006.014571

Philipsen, N., & Brooks-Gunn, J. (2008). Overweight and obesity in childhood. In T. P. Gullotta & G. M. Blau (Eds.), *Handbook of childhood behavioral issues: Evidence-based approaches to prevention and treatment* (pp. 125–146). New York: Routledge/Taylor & Francis.

Phillips, W., Gomez, J. C., Baron-Cohen, S., Laa, V., & Riviere, A. (1995). Treating people as objects, agents, or "subjects": How young children with and without autism make requests. *Journal of Child Psychology and Psychiatry, 36*, 1383–1398. doi:10.1111/j.1469-7610.1995.tb01670.x

Piacentini, J. (1997). *Cognitive-behavioral treatment of OCD in children and adolescents*. Unpublished manuscript, UCLA, Childhood OCD and Related Disorders Program.

Piacentini, J., & Graae, F. (1997). Childhood OCD. In E. Hollander & D. Stein (Eds.), *Obsessive-compulsive disorders: Diagnosis, etiology, treatment* (pp. 23–46). New York: Dekker.

Piacentini, J., Jacobs, C., & Maidment, K. (1997). *Behavioral family treatment for families of children and adolescents with obsessive-compulsive disorder: Preliminary treatment manual outline*. Unpublished manuscript, UCLA, Childhood OCD and Related Disorders Program.

Pickles, A., & Angold, A. (2003). Natural categories or fundamental dimensions: On carving nature at the joints and the rearticulation of psychopathology. *Development and Psychopathology, 15*, 529–551. doi:10.1017/S0954579403000282

Pickles, A., & Hill, J. (2006). Developmental pathways. In D. Cicchetti & D. J. Cohen (Eds.), *Developmental psychopathology: Vol. 1. Theory and methods* (2nd ed., pp. 211–243). Hoboken, NJ: Wiley.

Piehler, T. F., & Dishion, T. J. (2007). Interpersonal dynamics within adolescent friendships: Dyadic mutuality, deviant talk, and patterns of antisocial behavior. *Child Development, 78*, 1611–1624. doi:10.1111/j.1467-8624.2007.01086.x

Pierce, K., Carter, C., Weinfeld, M., Desmond, J., Hazin, R., Bjork, R., & Gallagher N. (2011). Detecting, studying, and treating autism early: The one-year well-baby check-up approach. *Journal of Pediatrics, 159*, 458–465. doi:10.1016/j.jpeds.2011.02.036

Pietrefesa, A. S., & Evans, D. W. (2007). Affective and neuropsychological correlates of children's rituals and compulsive-behaviors: Continuities and discontinuities with obsessive-compulsive disorder. *Brain and Cognition, 65*, 36–46. doi:10.1016/j.bandc.2006.02.007

Pike, A., & Kretschmer, T. (2009). Shared versus nonshared effects: Parenting and children's adjustment. *European Journal of Developmental Science, 3*, 115–130.

Pike, A., & Plomin, R. (1996). Importance of nonshared environmental factors for childhood and adolescent psychopathology. *Journal of the American Academy of Child & Adolescent Psychiatry, 35*, 560–570. doi:10.1097/00004583-199605000-00010

Pinborough-Zimmerman, J., Satterfield, R., Miller, J., Bilder, D., Hossain, S., & McMahon, W. (2007). Communication disorders: Prevalence and comorbid intellectual disability, autism, and emotional/behavioral disorders. *American Journal of Speech-Language Pathology, 16*, 359–367. doi:10.1044/1058-0360(2007/039)

Pine, D. S. (2003). Developmental psychobiology and response to threats: Relevance to trauma in children and adolescents. *Biological Psychiatry, 53*, 796–808. doi:10.1016/S0006-3223(03)00112-4

Pine, D. S. (2007). Research review: A neuroscience framework for pediatric anxiety disorders. *Journal of Child Psychology and Psychiatry, 48*, 631–648. doi:10.1111/j.1469-7610.2007.01751.x

Pine, D. S., Cohen, E., Cohen, P., & Brook, J. S. (2000). Social phobia and the persistence of conduct problems. *Journal of Child Psychology and Psychiatry, 41*, 657–665. doi:10.1111/1469-7610.00652

Pine, D. S., Costello, E. J., Dahl, R., James, R., Leckman, J. F., Leibenluft, E., . . . Zeanah, C. H. (2011). Increasing the developmental focus in DSM-5: Broad issues and specific potential applications in anxiety. In D. A. Regier, W. E. Narrow, E. A. Kuhl, & D. J. Kupfer (Eds.), *The conceptual evolution of DSM-5* (pp. 305–321). Washington, DC: American Psychiatric Publishing, Inc.

Pine, D. S., & Grun, J. (1999). Childhood anxiety: Integrating developmental psychopathology and affective neuroscience. *Journal of Child & Adolescent Psychopharmacology, 9*, 1–12. doi:10.1089/cap.1999.9.1

Pinquart, M., & Shen, Y. (2011). Depressive symptoms in children and adolescents with chronic physical illness: An updated meta-analysis. *Journal of Pediatric Psychology, 36*, 375–384. doi:10.1093/jpepsy/jsq104

Piven, J. (1999). Genetic liability for autism: The behavioural expression in relatives. *International Review of Psychiatry, 11*, 299–308. doi:10.1080/09540269974186

Pliszka, S. R. (2000). Patterns of psychiatric comorbidity with attention-deficit/hyperactivity disorder. *Child and Adolescent Psychiatric Clinics of North America, 9*, 525–540. Retrieved from http://www.childpsych.theclinics.com/

Pliszka, S. R., Liotti, M., & Woldorff, M. G. (2000). Inhibitory control in children with attention-deficit/hyperactivity disorder: Event-related potentials identify the processing component and timing of an impaired right-frontal response-inhibition mechanism. *Biological Psychiatry, 48*, 238–246. doi:10.1016/S0006-3223(00)00890-8

Plomin, R., Haworth, C. M. A., & Davis, O. S. P. (2010). Genetics of learning abilities and disabilities: Recent developments from the UK and possible directions for research in China. *Behavior Genetics, 40*, 297–305. doi:10.1007/s10519-010-9355-z

Poelmans, G., Pauls, D. L., Buitelaar, J. K., & Franke, B. (2011). Integrated genome-wide association study findings: Identification of a neurodevelopmental network for attention deficit hyperactivity disorder. *American Journal of Psychiatry, 168*, 365–377. doi:10.1176/appi.ajp.2010.10070948

Pogue-Geile, M. F>, & Yokley, J. L. (2010). Current research on the genetic contributors to schizophrenia. *Current Directions in Psychological Science, 19*, 214–219. doi:10.1177/0963721410378490

Polanczyk, G., Caspi, A., Houts, R., Kollins, S. H., Rohde, L. A., & Moffitt, T. E. (2010). Implications of extending the ADHD age-of-onset criterion to age 12: Results from a prospectively studied birth cohort. *Journal of the American Academy of Child & Adolescent Psychiatry, 49*, 210–216. doi:10.1016/j.jaac.2009.12.014

Polanczyk, G., & Jensen, P. (2008). Epidemiologic considerations in attention deficit hyperactivity disorder: A review and update. *Child and Adolescent Psychiatric Clinics of North America, 17*, 245–260. doi:10.1016/j.chc.2007.11.006

Polanczyk, G., Moffitt, T. E., Arseneault, L., Cannon, M., Ambler, A., Keefe, R. S. E., . . . Caspi, A. (2010). Etiological and clinical features of childhood psychotic symptoms: Results from a birth cohort. *Archives of General Psychiatry, 67*, 328–338. doi:10.1001/archgenpsychiatry.2010.14

Polanczyk, G., Silva de Lima, M. S., Horta, B. L., Biederman, J., & Rohde, L. A. (2007). The worldwide prevalence of ADHD: A systematic review and metaregression analysis. *American Journal of Psychiatry, 164*, 942–948. doi:10.1176/appi.ajp.164.6.942

Polivy, J., & Herman, C. P. (2002). Causes of eating disorders. *Annual Review of Psychology, 53*, 187–213. doi:10.1146/annurev.psych.53.100901.135103

Polivy, J., & Herman, C. P. (2005). Mental health and eating behaviours: A bi-directional relation. *Canadian Journal of Public Health, 96*(Suppl. 3), S43–46, S49–53. Retrieved from http://www.cpha.ca/en/cjph.aspx

Pollak, S. D., Nelson, C. A., Schlaak, M. F., Roeber, B. J., Wewerka, S. S., Wiik, K. L., . . . Gunnar, M. R. (2010). Neurodevelopmental effects of early deprivation in postinstitutionalized children. *Child Development, 81*, 224–236. doi:10.1111/j.1467-8624.2009.01391.x

Pollock, L. (1987). *A lasting relationship: Parents and children over three centuries*. Hanover: University of New Hampshire Press.

Polloway, E. A., Schewel, R., & Patton, J. R. (1992). Learning disabilities in adulthood: Personal perspectives. *Journal of Learning Disabilities, 25*, 520–522. doi:10.1177/002221949202500805

Post, R. M., Luckenbaugh, D. A., Leverich, G. S., Altshuler, L. L., Frye, M. A., Suppes, T., . . . Walden, J. (2008). Incidence of childhood-onset bipolar illness in the USA and Europe. *British Journal of Psychiatry, 192*, 150–151. doi:10.1192/bjp.bp.107.037820

Post, R. M., & Weiss, S. B. (1998). Sensitization and kindling phenomena in mood, anxiety, and obsessive-compulsive disorders: The role of serotonergic mechanisms in illness progression. *Biological Psychiatry, 44*, 193–206. doi:10.1016/S0006-3223(98)00144-9

Post, R. M., Weiss, S. B., Leverich, G. S., George, M. S., Frye, M., & Ketter, T. A. (1996). Developmental psychobiology of cyclic affective illness: Implications for early intervention. *Development and Psychopathology, 8*, 273–305. doi:10.1017/S0954579400007082

Powell, N. R., Lochman, J. E., & Boxmeyer, C. L. (2007). The prevention of conduct problems. *International Review of Psychiatry, 19*, 597–605. doi:10.1080/09540260701797738

Power, C., & Thomas, C. (2011). Changes in BMI, duration of overweight and obesity, and glucose metabolism: 45 years of follow-up of a birth cohort. *Diabetes Care, 34*, 1986–1991. doi:10.2337/dc10-1482

Poznanski, E. O. (1979). Childhood depression: A psychodynamic approach to the etiology of depression in children. In A. French & I. Berlin (Eds.), *Depression in children and adolescents* (pp. 46–68). New York: Human Sciences Press.

Pratt, H. D., Phillips, E. L., Greydanus, D. E., & Patel, D. R. (2003). Eating disorders in the adolescent population: Future directions. *Journal of Adolescent Research, 18*, 297–317. doi:10.1177/0743558403018003007

President's New Freedom Commission on Mental Health. (2003). *Achieving the promise: Transforming mental health care in America*. Retrieved from http://www.mentalhealthcommission.gov

Preston, S. H., & Stokes, A. (2011). Contribution of obesity to international differences in life expectancy. *American Journal of Public Health, 101*, 2137–2143. doi:10.2105/AJPH.2011.300219

Preti, A., Rocchi, M. B. L., Sisti, D., Camboni, M. V., & Miotto, P. (2011). A comprehensive meta-analysis of the risk of suicide in eating disorders. *Acta Psychiatrica Scandinavica, 124*, 6–17. doi:10.1111/j.1600-0447.2010.01641.x

Pretorius, N., Arcelus, J., Beecham, J., Dawson, H., Doherty, F., Eisler, I., . . . Schmidt, U. (2009). Cognitive-behavioural therapy for adolescents with bulimic symptomatology: The acceptability and effectiveness of internet-based delivery. *Behaviour Research and Therapy, 47*, 729–736. doi:10.1016/j.brat.2009.05.006

Prevent Child Abuse America. (2008). *Total estimated cost of child abuse and neglect in the united states.* Retrieved June, 6, 2011, from http://www.preventchildabuse.org/about_us/media_releases/national_press_release_final.pdf

Prifitera, A., Saklofske, D. H., & Weiss, L. G. (2005). *WISC-IV clinical use and interpretation: Scientist-practitioner perspectives*. San Diego, CA: Elsevier.

Primack, B. A., Dalton, M. A., Carroll, M. V., Agarwal, A. A., & Fine, M. J. (2008). Content analysis of tobacco, alcohol, and other drugs in popular music. *Archives of Pediatric and Adolescent Medicine, 162*, 169–175. Retrieved from http://archpedi.ama-assn.org/

Pring, L., Hermelin, B., & Heavey, L. (1995). Savants, segments, art and autism. *Journal of Child Psychology and Psychiatry, 36*, 1065–1076. doi:10.1111/j.1469-7610.1995.tb01351.x

Prinstein, M. J., & Roberts, M. C. (2006). The professional adolescence of clinical child and adolescent psychology and pediatric psychology: Grown up and striving for autonomy. *Clinical Psychology: Science and Practice, 13*, 263–268. doi:10.1111/j.1468-2850.2006.00035.x

Prinz, R. J., & Sanders, M. R. (2007). Adopting a population-level approach to parenting and family support interventions. *Clinical Psychology Review, 27*, 739–749. doi:10.1016/j.cpr.2007.01.005

Prinz, R. J., Sanders, M. R., Shapiro, C. J., Whitaker, D. J., & Lutzker, J. R. (2009). Population-based prevention of child maltreatment: The U.S. Triple P system population trial. *Prevention Science, 10*(1), 1–12.

Prior, M., Smart, D., Sanson, A., & Oberklaid, F. (2000). Does shy-inhibited temperament in childhood lead to anxiety problems in adolescence? *Journal of the American Academy of Child & Adolescent Psychiatry, 39*, 461–468. doi:10.1097/00004583-200004000-00015

Pritchard, J. C. (1837). *A treatise on insanity and other disorders affecting the mind.* Philadelphia: Haswell, Barrington, & Haswell.

Prizant, B. (1996). Communication, language, social, and emotional development. *Journal of Autism and Developmental Disorders, 26*, 173–178. doi:10.1007/BF02172007

Prizant, B., & Wetherby, A. (1989). Enhancing language and communication in autism: From theory to practice. In G. Dawson (Ed.), *Autism: Nature, diagnosis, and treatment* (pp. 282–309). New York: Guilford Press.

Prout, S. M., & Prout, H. T. (2007). Ethical and legal issues in psychological interventions with children and adolescents. In H. T. Prout & D. T. Brown (Eds.), *Counseling and psychotherapy with children and adolescents: Theory and practice for school and clinical settings* (4th ed., pp. 32–63). Hoboken, NJ: Wiley.

Public Health Agency of Canada. (2010). Canadian incidence study of reported child abuse and neglect – 2008: Major findings. Ottawa, Ontario: Author. Available: http://www.phac-aspc.gc.ca/cm-vee/public-eng.php

Puhl, R. M., & Latner, J. D. (2007). Stigma, obesity, and the health of the nation's children. *Psychological Bulletin, 133*,557–580. doi:10.1037/0033-2909.133.4.557

Puhl, R. M., Luedicke, J., & Heuer, C. (2011). Weight-based victimization toward overweight adolescents: Observations and reactions of peers. *The Journal of School Health, 81*, 696. doi:10.1111/j.1746-1561.2011.00646.x

Pumariega, A. J., Rothe, E. M., Song, S., & Lu, F. G. (2010). Culturally informed child psychiatric practice. *Child and Adolescent Psychiatric Clinics of North America, 19*, 739–757. doi:10.1016/j.chc.2010.07.004

Pungello, E. P., Kainz, K., Burchinal, M., Wasik, B. H., Sparling, J. J., Ramey, C. T., & Campbell, F. A. (2010). Early educational intervention, early cumulative risk, and the early home environment as predictors of young adult outcomes within a high-risk sample. *Child Development, 81*, 410–426. doi:10.1111/j.1467-8624.2009.01403.x

Pynoos, R. S., Frederick, C., Nader, K., Arroyo, W., Steinberg, A., Eth, S., . . . Fairbanks, L. (1987). Life threat and posttraumatic stress in school-age children. *Archives of General Psychiatry, 44*, 1057–1063. Retrieved from http://archpsyc.ama-assn.org/

Pynoos, R. S., Steinberg, A. M., Layne, C. M., Briggs, E. C., Ostrowski, S. A., & Fairbank, J. A. (2009). DSM-V PTSD diagnostic criteria for children and adolescents: A developmental perspective and recommendations. *Journal of Traumatic Stress, 22*, 391–398. doi:10.1002/jts.20450

Qualter, P., Brown, S. L., Munn, P., Rotenberg, K. J. (2010). Childhood loneliness as a predictor of adolescent depressive symptoms. *European Child and Adolescent Psychiatry, 19*, 493–501. doi:10.1007/s00787-009-0059-y

Röpcke, B., & Eggers, C. (2005). Early-onset schizophrenia: A 15-year follow-up. *European Child and Adolescent Psychiatry, 14*, 341–350. doi:10.1007/s00787-005-0483-6

Rabiner, D., Coie, J. D., and the Conduct Problems Prevention Research Group. (2000). Early attention problems and children's reading achievement: A longitudinal investigation. *Journal of the American Academy of Child & Adolescent Psychiatry, 39*, 859–867. doi:10.1097/00004583-200007000-00014

Rabiner, D. L., Murray, D. W., Skinner, A. T., & Malone, P. S. (2010). A randomized trial of two promising computer-based interventions for students with attention difficulties. *Journal of Abnormal Child Psychology, 38*, 131–142. doi:10.1007/s10802-009-9353-x

Radbill, S. X. (1968). A history of child abuse and infanticide. In R. E. Helfer & C. H. Kempe (Eds.), *The battered child* (pp. 3–17). Chicago: University of Chicago Press.

Radbill, S. X. (1987). Children in a world of violence: A history of child abuse. In R. E. Helfer & R. S. Kempe (Eds.), *The battered child* (4th rev. & exp. ed., pp. 3–22). Chicago: University of Chicago Press.

Radke-Yarrow, M., & Zahn-Waxler, C. (1990). Research on children of affectively ill parents: Some considerations for theory and research on normal development. *Development and Psychopathology, 2*, 349–366. doi:10.1017/S0954579400005770

Rai, A. A., Stanton, B., Wu, Y., Li, X., Galbraith, J., Cottrell, L., . . . Burns, J. (2003). Relative influences of perceived parental monitoring and perceived peer involvement on adolescent risk behaviors: An analysis of six cross-sectional data sets. *Journal of Adolescent Health, 33*, 108–118. doi:10.1016/S1054-139X(03)00179-4

Raine, A. (2002). The role of prefrontal deficits, low autonomic arousal and early health factors in the development of antisocial and aggressive behavior in children. *Journal of Child Psychology and Psychiatry, 43*, 417–434. doi:10.1111/1469-7610.00034

Raine, A., Moffitt, T. R., Caspi, A., Loeber, R., Stouthamer-Loeber, M., & Lynam, D. (2005). Neurocognitive impairments in boys on the life-course persistent antisocial path. *Journal of Abnormal Psychology, 114*, 38–49. doi:10.1037/0021-843X.114.1.38

Ramey, C. T., Campbell, F. A., Burchinal, M., Skinner, M. L., Gardner, D. M., & Ramey, S. L. (2000). Persistent effects of early childhood education on high-risk children and their mothers. *Applied Developmental Science, 4*, 2–14. doi:10.1207/S1532480XADS0401_1

Ramey, C. T., Campbell, F. A., & Ramey, S. L. (1999). Early intervention: Successful pathways to improving intellectual development. *Developmental Neuropsychology, 16*, 385–392. doi:10.1207/S15326942DN1603_22

Ramey, C. T., & Ramey, S. L. (1992). Effective early intervention. *Mental Retardation, 6*, 337–345. Retrieved from http://www.aaiddjournals.org/loi/mere.1

Ramey, S. L., Ramey, C. T., & Lanzi, R. G. (2007). Early intervention: Background, research findings, and future directions. In J. W. Jacobson, J. A. Mulick, & J. Rojahn (Eds.), *Handbook of intellectual and developmental disabilities: Issues in clinical child psychology* (pp. 445–463). New York: Springer.

Ramirez, A. G., Chalela, P., Gallion, K. J., Green, L. W., & Ottoson, J. (2011). "Salud America!" developing a national Latino childhood obesity research agenda. *Health Education & Behavior, 38*, 251–260. doi:10.1177/1090198110372333

Ramrakha, S., Bell, M. L., Paul, C., Dickson, N., Moffitt, T. E., & Caspi, A. (2007). Childhood behavior problems linked to sexual risk taking in young adulthood. *Journal of the American Academy of Child & Adolescent Psychiatry, 46*, 1272–1279. doi:10.1097/chi.0b013e3180f6340e

Rapee, R. M. (2002). The development and modification of temperamental risk for anxiety disorders: Prevention of a lifetime of anxiety? *Biological Psychiatry, 52*, 947–957. doi:10.1016/S0006-3223(02)01572-X

Rapee, R. M., Kennedy, S. J., Ingram, M., Edwards, S. L., & Sweeney, L. (2010). Altering the trajectory of anxiety in at-risk young children. *American Journal of Psychiatry, 167*, 1518–1525. doi:10.1176/appi.ajp.2010.09111619

Rapee, R. M., Schneiring, C. A., & Hudson, J. L. (2009). Anxiety disorders during childhood and adolescence. *Annual Review of Clinical Psychology, 5*, 311–341. doi:10.1146/annurev.clinpsy.032408.153628

Raphael, K. G., & Widom, C. S. (2011). Post-traumatic stress disorder moderates the relation between documented childhood victimization and pain 30 years later. *Pain, 152*(1), 163–169. doi:10.1016/j.pain.2010.10.014

Rapoport, J. C., Addington, A. M., & Frangou, S. (2005). The neurodevelopmental model of schizophrenia: Update 2005. *Molecular Psychiatry, 10*, 434–449. doi:10.1038/sj.mp.4001642

Rapoport, J. L., & Gogtay, N. (2011). Child onset schizophrenia: Support for a progressive neurodevelopmental disorder. *International Journal of Developmental Neuroscience, 29*, 251–258. doi:10.1016/j.ijdevneu.2010.10.003

Rapoport, J. L., Inoff-Germain, G., Weissman, M. M., Greenwald, S., Jensen, P. S., Lahey, B. B., . . . Canino, G. (2000). Childhood obsessive-compulsive disorder in the NIMH MECA study: Parent versus child identification of cases. *Journal of Anxiety Disorders, 14*, 535–548. doi:10.1016/S0887-6185(00)00048-7

Rapoport, J., Chavez, A., Greenstein, D., Addington, A., & Gogtay, N. (2009). Autism spectrum disorders and childhood-onset schizophrenia: Clinical and biological contributions to a relation revisited. *Journal of the American Academy of Child and Adolescent Psychiatry, 48*, 10–18. doi:10.1097/CHI.0b013e31818b1c63

Rappaport, L. (1993). The treatment of nocturnal enuresis: Where are we now? Pediatrics, 92, 465–466. Retrieved from http://pediatrics.aappublications.org/

Raschle, N. M., Chang, M., & Gaab, N. (2011). Structural brain alterations associated with dyslexia predate reading onset. *NeuroImage, 57*, 742–749. doi:10.1016/j.neuroimage.2010.09.055

Raskauskas, J., & Stoltz, A. D. (2007). Involvement in traditional and electronic bullying among adolescents. *Developmental Psychology, 43*, 564–575. doi:10.1037/0012-1649.43.3.564

Rasmussen, B., Ward, G., Jenkins, A., King, S. J., & Dunning, T. (2011). Young adults' management of type 1 diabetes during life transitions. *Journal of Clinical Nursing, 20*, 1981–1992. doi:10.1111/j.1365-2702.2010.03657.x

Razza, R. A., Martin, A., & Brooks-Gunn, J. (2010). Associations among family environment, sustained attention, and school readiness for low-income children. *Developmental Psychology, 46*, 1528–1542. doi:10.1037/a0020389

Reardon, L. E., Leen-Feldner, E. W., & Hayward, C. (2009). A critical review of the literature on the relation between anxiety and puberty. *Clinical Psychology Review, 29*, 1–23. doi:10.1016/j.cpr.2008.09.005

Redcay, E., & Courchesne, E. (2005). When is the brain enlarged in autism? A meta-analysis of all brain size reports. *Biological Psychiatry, 58*, 1–9. doi:10.1016/j.biopsych.2005.03.026

Reeb, B. C., Fox, N. A., Nelson, C. A., & Zeanah, C. H. (2009). The effects of early institutionalization on social behavior and underlying neural correlates. In M. de Haan, & M. R. Gunnar (Eds.), *Handbook of developmental social neuroscience.* (pp. 477–496). New York: Guilford Press.

Reef, J., van Meurs, I., Verhulst, F. C., & van der Ende, J. (2010). Children's problems predict adults' DSM-IV disorders across 24 years. *Journal of the American Academy of Child & Adolescent Psychiatry, 49*, 1117–1124. doi:10.1016/j.jaac.2010.08.002

Reef, J., van Meurs, I., Verhulst, F. C., & van der Ende, J. (2010). Children's problems predict adults' *DSM-IV* disorders across 24 years. *Journal of the American*

Academy of Child & Adolescent Psychiatry, 49, 1117–1124. doi:10.1097/00004583-201011000-00005

Reeves, C. B., Palmer, S. L., Reddick, W. E., Merchant, T. E., Buchanan, G. M., Gajjar, A., & Mulhern, R. K. (2006). Attention and memory functioning among pediatric patients with medulloblastoma. *Journal of Pediatric Psychology, 31*, 272–280. doi:10.1093/jpepsy/jsj019

Regier, D. A., Narrow, W. E., Kuhl, E. A., & Kupfer, D. J. (Eds.). (2011). *The conceptual evolution of DSM-5*. Washington, DC: American Psychiatric Publishing, Inc.

Rehm, L. P., & Sharp, R. N. (1996). Strategies for childhood depression. In M. A. Reineke, F. M. Dattilio, & A. Freeman (Eds.), *Cognitive therapy with children and adolescents: A casebook for clinical practice* (pp. 103–123). New York: Guilford Press.

Reichenberg, A., Caspi, A., Harrington, H., Houts, R., Keefe, R. S. E., Murray, R. M., . . . Moffitt, T. E. (2010). Static and dynamic cognitive deficits in childhood preceding adult schizophrenia: A 30-year study. *American Journal of Psychiatry, 167*, 160–169. doi:10.1176/appi.ajp.2009.09040574

Reichow, B., & Wolery, M. (2009). Comprehensive synthesis of early intensive behavioral interventions for young children with autism based on the UCLA Young Autism Project model. *Journal of Autism and Developmental Disorders, 39*, 23–41. doi:10.1007/s10803-008-0596-0

Reid, G. J., Huntley, E. D., & Lewin, D. S. (2009). Insomnias of childhood and adolescence. *Child and Adolescent Psychiatric Clinics of North America, 18*, 979–1000. doi:10.1016/j.chc.2009.06.002

Reinblatt, S. P., & Riddle, M. A. (2007). The pharmacological management of childhood anxiety disorders: A review. *Psychopharmacology, 191*, 67–86. doi:10.1007/s00213-006-0644-4

Reiss, A. L., & Hall, S. S. (2007). Fragile X syndrome: Assessment and treatment implications. *Child and Adolescent Psychiatric Clinics of North America, 16*, 663–675. doi:10.1016/j.chc.2007.03.001

Remschmidt, H., Martin, M., Fleischhaker, C., Theisen, F. M., Hennighausen, K., Gutenbrunner, C., & Schulz, E. (2007). Forty-two years later: The outcome of childhood-onset schizophrenia. *Journal of Neural Transmission, 114*, 505–512. doi:10.1007/s00702-006-0553-z

Renaud, J., Brent, D. A., Birmaher, B., Chiappetta, L., & Bridge, J. (1999). Suicide in adolescents with disruptive behavior disorders. *Journal of the American Academy of Child & Adolescent Psychiatry, 38*, 846–851. doi:10.1097/00004583-199907000-00014

Rende, R., & Waldman, I. (2006). Behavioral and molecular genetics and developmental psychopathology. In D. Cicchetti & D. J. Cohen (Eds.), *Developmental psychopathology: Vol. 2. Developmental neuroscience* (2nd ed., pp. 427–464). Hoboken, NJ: Wiley.

Rende, R., Birmaher, B., Axelson, D., Strober, M., Gill, M. K., Valeri, S., . . . Keller, M. (2007). Childhood-onset bipolar disorder: Evidence for increased familial loading of psychiatric illness. *Journal of the American Academy of Child & Adolescent Psychiatry, 46*, 197–204. doi:10.1097/01.chi.0000246069.85577.9e

Renouf, A. G., & Kovacs, M. (1995). Dysthymic disorder during childhood and adolescence. In J. H. Kocsis & D. N. Klein (Eds.), *Diagnosis and treatment of chronic depression* (pp. 20–40). New York: Guilford Press.

Rescorla, L.A., Achenbach, T.M., Ivanova, M.Y., Harder, V.S., et al. (2011). International comparisons of behavioral and emotional problems in preschool children: Parents' reports from 24 societies. *Journal of Clinical Child & Adolescent Psychology, 40*, 456–467. doi:10.1080/15374416.2011.563472

Restifo, K., & Bögels, S. (2009). Family processes in the development of youth depression: Translating the evidence to treatment. *Clinical Psychology Review, 29*, 294–316. doi:10.1016/j.cpr.2009.02.005

Rett, A. (1966). On an unusual brain atrophy syndrome in hyperammonemia in childhood. *Wiener Medizinische Wochenschrift, 116*, 723–726.

Reynolds, C. R., Kamphaus. R. W. (2004). *Behavior Assessment System for Children – Second Edition* (BASC-2). Bloomington, MN: Pearson.

Reynolds, S., & Lane, S. J. (2008). Diagnostic validity of sensory over-responsivity: A review of the literature and case reports. *Journal of Autism and Developmental Disorders, 38*, 516–529. doi:10.1007/s10803-007-0418-9

Rhee, S. H., Willcutt, E. G., Hartman, C. A., Pennington, B. F., & DeFries, J. C. (2008). Test of alternative hypotheses explaining the comorbidity between attention-deficit/hyperactivity disorder and conduct disorder. *Journal of Abnormal Child Psychology, 36*, 29–40. doi:10.1007/s10802-007-9157-9

Riccio, C. A., Sullivan, J. R., & Cohen, M. J. (2010). *Neuropsychological assessment and intervention for childhood and adolescent disorders.* New York: Wiley.

Rice, F., Harold, G. T., Shelton, K. H., & Thapar, A. (2006). Family conflict interacts with genetic liability in predicting childhood and adolescent depression. *Journal of the American Academy of Child & Adolescent Psychiatry, 45*, 841–848. doi:10.1097/01.chi.0000219834.08602.44

Rice, F., Harold, G., & Thapar, A. (2003). Negative life events as an account of age-related differences in the genetic aetiology of depression in childhood and adolescence. *Journal of Child Psychology and Psychiatry, 44*, 977–987. doi:10.1111/1469-7610.00182

Rice, F., Lifford, K. J., Thomas, H. V., & Thapar, A. (2007). Mental health and functional outcomes of maternal and adolescent reports of adolescent depressive symptoms. *Journal of the American Academy of Child & Adolescent Psychiatry, 46*, 1162–1170. doi:10.1097/chi.0b013e3180cc255f

Rice, M. L. (2007). Children with specific language impairment: Bridging the genetic and developmental perspectives. In E. Hoff & M. Shatz (Eds.), *Blackwell handbook of language development* (pp. 411–431). Malden, MA: Blackwell.

Rich, B. A., Fromm, S. J., Berghorst, L. H., Dickstein, D. P., Brotman, M. A., Pine, D. S., & Leibenluft, E. (2008). Neural connectivity in children with bipolar disorder: Impairment in the face emotion processing circuit. *Journal of Child Psychology and Psychiatry, 49*, 88–96. doi:10.1111/j.1469-7610.2007.01819.x

Richlan, F., Kronbichler, M., & Wimmer, H. (2009). Functional abnormalities in the dyslexic brain: A quantitative meta-analysis of neuroimaging studies. *Human Brain Mapping, 30*, 3299-3308. doi:10.1002/hbm.20752

Richlan, F., Kronbichler, M., & Wimmer, H. (2011). Meta-analyzing brain dysfunctions in dyslexic children and adults. *NeuroImage, 56*, 1735–1742. doi:10.1016/j.neuroimage.2011.02.040

Richler, J., Bishop, S. L., Kleinke, J. R., & Lord, C. (2007). Restricted and repetitive behaviors in young children with autism spectrum disorders. *Journal of Autism and Developmental Disorders, 37*, 73–85. doi:10.1007/s10803-006-0332-6

Richler, J., Huerta, M., Bishop, S. L., & Lord, C. (2010). Developmental trajectories of restricted and repetitive behaviors and interests in children with autism spectrum disorders. *Development and Psychopathology, 22*, 55–69. doi:10.1017/S0954579409990265

Riddle, M. A. (2004). Paroxetine and the FDA. *Journal of the American Academy of Child & Adolescent Psychiatry, 43*, 128–130. doi:10.1097/00004583-200402000-00001

Rie, H. E. (1971). Historical perspective of concepts of child psychopathology. In H. E. Rie (Ed.), *Perspectives in child psychopathology* (pp. 3–50). Chicago: Aldine-Atherton.

Rie, H. E. (1980). Definitional problems. In H. E. Rie & E. D. Rie (Eds.), *Handbook of minimal brain dysfunctions: A critical review* (pp. 3–17). New York: Wiley.

Riley, E. P., Infante, M. A., & Warren, K. R. (2011). Fetal alcohol spectrum disorders: An overview. *Neuropsychology Review, 21*, 73–80. doi:10.1007/s11065-011-9166-x

Rilling, M. (2000). John Watson's paradoxical struggle to explain Freud. *American Psychologist, 55*, 301–312. doi:10.1037/0003-066X.55.3.301

Risch, N., Herrell, R., Lehner, T., Liang, K. Y., Eaves, L., Hoh, J., . . . Merikangas, K. R. (2009). Interaction between the serotonin transporter gene (5-HTTLPR), stressful life events, and risk of depression: A meta-analysis. *JAMA, 301*, 2462-2471. doi.10.1001/jama.2009.878

Rivett, M. (2008). Towards a metamorphosis: Current developments in the theory and practice of family therapy. *Child and Adolescent Mental Health, 13*, 102–106. doi:10.1111/j.1475-3588.2008.00491.x

Robers, S., Zhang, J., & Truman, J. (2010). *Indicators of school crime and safety: 2010* (NCES 2011-002/NCJ 230812).

National Center for Education Statistics, U.S. Department of Education, and Bureau of Justice Statistics, Office of Justice Programs, U.S. Department of Justice. Washington, DC.

Roberts, B. W., & DelVecchio, W. F. (2000). The rank-order consistency of personality traits from childhood to old age: A quantitative review of longitudinal studies. *Psychological Bulletin, 126*, 3–25. doi:10.1037//0033-2909.126.1.3

Roberts, J. E., Price, J., & Malkin, C. (2007). Language and communication development in Down syndrome. *Mental Retardation and Developmental Disabilities Research Reviews [Special issue: Language and communication], 13*, 26–35. doi:10.1002/mrdd.20136

Roberts, M. C., & Steele, R. G. (Eds.). (2009). *Handbook of pediatric psychology* (4th ed.). New York: Guilford Press.

Roberts, M. W., & Hope, D. A. (2001). Clinic observations of structured parent-child interaction designed to evaluate externalizing disorders. *Psychological Assessment, 13*, 46–58. doi:10.1037/1040-3590.13.1.46

Roberts, R. E., & Gotlib, I. H. (1997). Temporal variability in global self-esteem and specific self-evaluation as prospective predictors of emotional distress: Specificity in predictors and outcomes. *Journal of Abnormal Psychology, 106*, 521–529. doi:10.1037/0021-843X.106.4.521

Roberts, R. E., Roberts, C. R., & Chen, Y. R. (1997). Ethnocultural differences in prevalence of adolescent depression. *American Journal of Community Psychology, 25*, 95–110. doi:10.1023/A:1024649925737

Roberts, R. E., Roberts, C. R., & Xing, Y. (2006). Prevalence of youth-reported DSM-IV psychiatric disorders among African, European, and Mexican American adolescents. *Journal of the American Academy of Child & Adolescent Psychiatry, 45*, 1329–1337. doi:10.1097/01.chi.0000235076.25038.81

Roberts, R. E., Roberts, C. R., & Xing, Y. (2011). Restricted sleep among adolescents: Prevalence, incidence, persistence, and associated factors. *Behavioral Sleep Medicine, 9*, 18–30. doi:10.1080/15402002.2011.533991

Robin, A. L., Siegel, P. T., & Moye, A. (1995). Family versus individual therapy for anorexia: Impact on family conflict. *International Journal of Eating Disorders, 17*, 313–322. doi:10.1002/1098-108X(199505)17:4<313::AID-EAT2260170402>3.0.CO;2-8

Robin, A. L., Siegel, P. T., Moye, A. W., Gilroy, M., Dennis, A. B., & Sikand, A. (1999). A controlled comparison of family versus individual therapy for adolescents with anorexia nervosa. *Journal of the American Academy of Child & Adolescent Psychiatry, 38*, 1482–1489. doi:10.1097/00004583-199912000-00008

Robinson, K. E., Gerhardt, C. A., Vannatta, K., & Noll, R. B. (2007). Parent and family factors associated with child adjustment to pediatric cancer. *Journal of Pediatric Psychology, 32*, 400–410. doi:10.1093/jpepsy/jsl038

Robison, L. M., Skaer, T. L., Sclar, D. A., & Galin, R. S. (2002). Is attention deficit hyperactivity disorder increasing among girls in the US? Trends in diagnosis and the prescribing of stimulants. *CNS Drugs, 16*, 129–137. doi:10.2165/00023210-200216020-00

Rochlin, G. (1959). The loss complex. *Journal of the American Psychoanalytic Association, 7*, 299–316. doi:10.1177/000306515900700207

Rockhill, C. M., Fan, M. Y., Katon, W. J., McCauley, E., Crick, N. R., & Pleck, J. H. (2007). Friendship interactions in children with and without depressive symptoms: Observation of emotion during game-playing interactions and post-game evaluations. *Journal of Abnormal Child Psychology, 35*, 429–441. doi:10.1007/s10802-007-9101-z

Rodkin, P. C., Farmer, T. W., Van Acker, R. P., & Van Acker, R. (2000). Heterogeneity of popular boys: Antisocial and prosocial configurations. *Developmental Psychology, 36*, 14–24. doi:10.1037/0012-1649.36.1.14

Rodrigues, N., & Patterson, J. M. (2007). Impact of severity of a child's chronic condition on the functioning of two-parent families. *Journal of Pediatric Psychology, 32*, 417–426. doi:10.1093/jpepsy/jsl031

Roeser, R. W., & Eccles, J. S. (2000). Schooling and mental health. In A. J. Sameroff, M. Lewis, & S. M. Miller (Eds.), *Handbook of developmental psychopathology* (2nd ed., pp. 135–156). New York: Kluwer/Plenum Press.

Rogers, S. J., & Ozonoff, S. (2005). Annotation: What do we know about sensory dysfunction in autism? A critical review of the empirical evidence. *Journal of Child Psychology and Psychiatry, 46*, 1255–1268. doi:10.1111/j.1469-7610.2005.01431.x

Rogers, S. J., Ozonoff, S., & Maslin-Cole, C. (1993). Developmental aspects of attachment behavior in young children with pervasive developmental disorders. *Journal of the American Academy of Child & Adolescent Psychiatry, 32*, 1274–1282. doi:10.1097/00004583-199311000-00023

Rogers, S. J., & Vismara, L. A. (2008). Evidence-based comprehensive treatments for early autism. *Journal of Clinical Child and Adolescent Psychology, 37*, 8–38. doi:10.1080/15374410701817808

Rohde, L. A. (2008). Is there a need to reformulate attention deficit hyperactivity disorder in future nosologic classifications? *Child and Adolescent Psychiatric Clinics of North America, 17*, 405–420. doi:10.1016/j.chc.2007.11.007

Roid, G. H. (2003). *Stanford-Binet intelligence scales* (5th ed.). Itasca, IL: Riverside.

Roisman, G. I., Monahan, K. C., Campbell, S. B., Steinberg, L., Cauffman, E., & The National Institute of Child Health and Human Development Early Child Care Research Network (2010). Is adolescence-onset antisocial behavior developmentally normative? *Developmental Psychopathology, 22*, 295–311. doi:10.1017/S0954579410000076

Roizen, N. J. (2007). Down syndrome. In M. L. Batshaw, L. Pellegrino, & N. J. Roizen (Eds.), *Children with disabilities* (6th ed., pp. 263–273). Baltimore, MD: Paul H Brookes Publishing.

Roizen, N. J., & Patterson, D. (2003). Down's syndrome. *Lancet, 361*, 1281–1289.

Rommelse, N. N. J., Guerts, H. M., Franke, B., Buitelaar, J. K., & Hartman, C. A. (2011). A review on cognitive and brain endophenotypes that may be common in autism spectrum disorder and attention-deficit/hyperactivity disorder and facilitate the search for pleiotropic genes. *Neuroscience and Biobehavioral Reviews, 35*, 1363–1396. doi:10.1016/j.neubiorev.2011.02.015

Rommelse, N. N. J., Peters, C. T. R., Oosterling, I. J., Visser, J. C., Bons, D., van Steijn, D. J., . . . Buitelaar, J. K. (2011). A pilot study of abnormal growth in autism spectrum disorders and other psychiatric disorders. *Journal of Autism and Developmental Disorders, 41*, 44–54. doi:10.1007/s10803-010-1026-7

Ronald, A., Happé, F., Dworzynski, K., Bolton, P., & Plomin, R. (2010). Exploring the relation between prenatal and neonatal complications and later autistic-like features in a representative community sample of twins. *Child Development, 81*, 166–182. doi:10.1111/j.1467-8624.2009.01387.x

Rose, A. J., & Rudolph, K. D. (2006). A review of sex differences in peer relationship processes: Potential tradeoffs for the emotional and behavioral development of girls and boys. *Psychological Bulletin, 132*, 98–131. doi:10.1037/0033-2909.132.1.98

Rosen, J. C., Leitenberg, H., Fisher, C., & Khazam, C. (1986). Binge-eating episodes in bulimia nervosa: The amount and type of food consumed. *International Journal of Eating Disorders, 5*, 255–267. doi:10.1002/1098-108X(198602)5:2<255::AID-EAT2260050206>3.0.CO;2-D

Ross, D. M., & Ross, S. A. (1982). *Hyperactivity: Current issues, research, and theory* (2nd ed.). New York: Wiley.

Ross, D. M., & Ross, S. A. (1984). Childhood pain: The school-aged child's viewpoint. *Pain, 20*, 179–191. doi:10.1016/0304-3959(84)90099-X

Roth, T. L., & Sweatt, J. D. (2011a). Annual research review: Epigenetic mechanisms and environmental shaping of the brain during sensitive periods of development. *Journal of Child Psychology and Psychiatry, 52*, 398–408. doi:10.1111/j.1469-7610.2010.02282.x

Roth, T. L., & Sweatt, J. D. (2011b). Epigenetic mechanisms and environmental shaping of the brain during sensitive periods of development. *Journal of Child Psychology and Psychiatry, 52*, 398–408. doi:10.1111/j.1469-7610.2010.02282.x

Rothbart, M. K., & Posner, M. (2006). Temperament, attention, and developmental psychopathology. In D. Cicchetti & D. J. Cohen (Eds.), *Developmental psychopathology: Vol. 2. Developmental neuroscience* (2nd ed., pp. 465–501). Hoboken, NJ: Wiley.

Rothenberger, A. (2009). Brain oscillations forever—Neurophysiology in future research of child psychiatric problems. *Journal of Child Psychology and Psychiatry, 50*, 79–86. doi:10.1111/j.1469-7610.2008.01994.x

Rousseau, I., Packman, A., Onslow, M., Harrison, E., & Jones, M. (2007). An investigation of language and phonological development and the responsiveness of preschool age children to the lidcombe program. *Journal of Communication Disorders, 40*, 382–397.

Rowe, C. L., & Liddle, H. A. (2006). Family-based treatment development for adolescent alcohol abuse. *International Journal of Adolescent Medicine and Health, 18*, 43–51.

Rowe, R., Costello, E. J., Angold, A., Copeland, W. E., & Maughan, B. (2010). Developmental pathways in oppositional defiant disorder and conduct disorder. *Journal of Abnormal Psychology, 119*, 726–738. doi:10.1037/a0020798

Roza, S. J., Hofstra, M. B., van der Ende, J., & Verhulst, F. C. (2003). Stable prediction of mood and anxiety disorders based on behavioral and emotional problems in childhood: A 14-year follow-up during childhood, adolescence, and young adulthood. *American Journal of Psychiatry, 160*, 2116-2121. doi:10.1176/appi.ajp.160.12.2116

Rubia, K. (2010). "Cool" inferior frontostriatal dysfunction in attention/deficit disorders versus "hot" ventromedial orbitofrontal-limbic dysfunction in conduct disorder: A review. *Biological Psychiatry, 69*, e69–e87. doi:10.1016/j.biopsych.2010.09.023

Rubin, K. H., Hemphill, S. A., Chen, X., Hastings, P., Sanson, A., Coco, A. L., . . . Cui, L. (2006). A cross-cultural study of behavioral inhibition in toddlers: East-west-north-south. *International Journal of Behavioral Development, 30*, 219–226. doi:10.1177/0165025406066723

Rucklidge, J. J. (2008). Gender differences in ADHD: Implications for psychosocial treatments. *Expert Review of Neurotherapeutics, 8*, 643–655. doi:10.1586/14737175.8.4.643

Rucklidge, J. J., & Tannock, R. (2001). Psychiatric, psychosocial, and cognitive functioning of female adolescents with ADHD. *Journal of the American Academy of Child & Adolescent Psychiatry, 40*, 530–540. doi:10.1097/00004583-200105000-00012

Rudolph, K. D., & Flynn, M. (2007). Child adversity and youth depression: Influence of gender and pubertal status. *Development and Psychopathology, 19*, 497–521. doi:10.1017/S0954579407070241

Rudolph, K. D., Flynn, M., & Abaied, J. L. (2008). A developmental perspective on interpersonal theories of youth depression. In J. R. Z. Abela & B. L. Hankin (Eds.), *Handbook of depression in children and adolescents* (pp. 79–102). New York: Guilford Press.

Rudolph, K. D., Hammen, C., & Burge, D. (1997). A cognitive-interpersonal approach to depressive symptoms in preadolescent children. *Journal of Abnormal Child Psychology, 25*, 33–45. doi:10.1023/A:1025755307508

Rudolph, K. D., Hammen, C., & Daley, S. E. (2006). Adolescent mood disorders. In D. A. Wolfe & E. J. Mash (Eds.), *Behavioral and emotional disorders in adolescents: Nature, assessment, and treatment* (pp. 300–342). New York: Guilford Press.

Rudolph, K. D., & Lambert, S. F. (2007). Child and adolescent depression. In E. J. Mash & R. A. Barkley (Eds.), *Assessment of childhood disorders* (4th ed., pp. 213–252). New York: Guilford Press.

Rushton, J. L., Forcier, M., & Schectman, R. M. (2002). Epidemiology of depressive symptoms in the National Longitudinal Study of Adolescent Health. *Journal of the Academy of Child & Adolescent Psychiatry, 41*, 199–205. doi:10.1097/00004583-200202000-00014

Rushton, J. P., & Jensen, A. R. (2006). The totality of available evidence shows the race IQ gap still remains. *Psychological Science, 17*, 921–922. doi:10.1111/j.1467-9280.2006.01803.x

Russell, A. T. (1994). The clinical presentation of childhood-onset schizophrenia. *Schizophrenia Bulletin, 20*, 631–646. doi:10.1093/schbul/20.4.631

Russell, A. T., Bott, L., & Sammons, C. (1989). The phenomenology of schizophrenia occurring in childhood. *Journal of the American Academy of Child & Adolescent Psychiatry, 28*, 399–407. doi:10.1097/00004583-198905000-00017

Russell, G., Kelly, S., & Golding, J. (2009). A qualitative analysis of lay beliefs about the aetiology and prevalence of autistic spectrum disorders. *Child: Care, Health, and Development, 36*, 431–436. doi:10.1111/j.1365-2214.2009.00994.x

Russell, J. (Ed.). (1997). *Autism as an executive disorder*. New York: Oxford University Press.

Russo, N., Flanagan, T., Iarocci, G., Berringer, D., Zelazo, P. D., & Burack, J. A. (2007). Deconstructing executive deficits among persons with autism: Implications for cognitive neuroscience. *Brain and Cognition, 65*, 77–86. doi:10.1016/j.bandc.2006.04.007

Rutherford, L., & Couturier, J. (2007). A review of psychotherapeutic interventions for children and adolescents with eating disorders. *Journal of the Canadian Academy of Child and Adolescent Psychiatry, 16*, 153–157. Retrieved from http://cacap-acpea.org/en/cacap/Journal_p828.html

Rutter, M. (1972). Childhood schizophrenia reconsidered. *Journal of Autism and Childhood Schizophrenia, 2*, 315–337. doi:10.1007/BF01537622

Rutter, M. (1989). Pathways from childhood to adult life. *Journal of Child Psychology and Psychiatry, 30*, 23–51. doi:10.1111/j.1469-7610.1989.tb00768.x

Rutter, M. (1999). Psychosocial adversity and child psychopathology. *British Journal of Psychiatry, 174*, 480–493. doi:10.1192/bjp.174.6.480

Rutter, M. (2000). Genetic studies of autism: From the 1970s into the millennium. *Journal of Abnormal Child Psychology, 28*, 3–14. doi:10.1023/A:1005113900068

Rutter, M. (2003a). Poverty and child mental health: Natural experiments and social causation. *JAMA: Journal of the American Medical Association, 290*, 2063–2064. doi:10.1001/jama.290.15.2063

Rutter, M. (2003b). Commentary: Causal processes leading to antisocial behavior. *Developmental Psychology, 39*, 372–378. doi:10.1037/0012-1649.39.2.372

Rutter, M. (2005). Genetic influences and autism. In F. R. Volkmar, R. Paul, A. Klin, & D. Cohen (Eds.), *Handbook of autism and pervasive developmental disorders* (3rd ed., pp. 425–452). Hoboken, NJ: Wiley.

Rutter, M. (2006a). *Genes and behavior: Nature-nurture interplay explained*. Malden, MA: Blackwell.

Rutter, M. (2006b). Autism: Its recognition, early diagnosis, and service implications. *Journal of Developmental and Behavioral Pediatrics, 27*(Suppl.), S54-S58. doi:10.1097/00004703-200604002-00002

Rutter, M. (2007a). Resilience, competence, and coping. *Child Abuse & Neglect, 31*, 205–209. doi:10.1016/j.chiabu.2007.02.001

Rutter, M. (2007b). Proceeding from observed correlation to causal inference: The use of natural experiments. *Perspectives on Psychological Science, 2*, 377–395. doi:10.1111/j.1745-6916.2007.00050.x

Rutter, M. (2010). Child and adolescent psychiatry: Past scientific achievements and challenges for the future. *European Child and Adolescent Psychiatry, 19*, 689–703. doi:10.1007/s00787-010-0111-y

Rutter, M. (2011). Biological and experiential influences on psychological development. In D. P. Keating (Ed.), *Nature and nurture in early child development.* (pp. 7–44). New York: Cambridge University Press.

Rutter, M. (2011). Research Review: Child psychiatric diagnosis and classification: Concepts, findings, challenges, and potential. *Journal of Child Psychology and Psychiatry, 52*, 647–660. doi:10.1111/j.1469-7610.2011.02367.x

Rutter, M., Caspi, A., Fergusson, D., Horwood, L. J., Goodman, R., Maughan, B., . . . Carroll, J. (2004). Sex differences in developmental reading disability: New findings from 4 epidemiological studies. *JAMA: Journal of the American Medical Association, 291*, 2007–2012. doi:10.1001/jama.291.16.2007

Rutter, M., Caspi, A., & Moffitt, T. E. (2003). Using sex differences in psychopathology to study causal mechanisms: Unifying issues and research strategies. *Journal of Child Psychology and Psychiatry, 44*, 1092–1115. doi:10.1111/1469-7610.00194

Rutter, M., & Dodge, K. A. (2011). Gene-environment interactions: State of the science. In K. A. Dodge & M. Rutter (Eds.), *Gene-environment interactions in developmental psychopathology* (pp. 87–101). New York: Guilford Press.

Rutter, M., Giller, H., & Hagell, A. (1998). *Antisocial behavior by young people.* New York: Cambridge University Press.

Rutter, M., Kim-Cohen, J., & Maughan, B. (2006). Continuities and discontinuities in psychopathology between childhood and adult life. *Journal of Child Psychology and Psychiatry, 47*, 276–295. doi:10.1111/j.1469-7610.2006.01614.x

Rutter, M., Kreppner, J., & Sonuga-Barke, E. (2009). Attachment insecurity, disinhibited attachment, and attachment disorders: Where do research findings leave the concepts? *Journal of Child Psychology and Psychiatry, 50*, 529–543. doi:10.1111/j.1469-7610.2009.02042.x

Rutter, M., & Smith, D. J. (Eds.). (1995). *Psychosocial disorders in young people: Time trends and their causes*. Chichester, England: Wiley.

Rutter, M., & Sroufe, L. A. (2000). Developmental psychopathology: Concepts and challenges. *Development and Psychopathology, 12*, 265–296. doi:10.1017/S0954579400003023

Rutter, M., Tizard, J., Yule, W., Graham, P., & Whitmore, K. (1976). Research report: Isle of Wight studies, 1964–1974. *Psychological Medicine, 6*, 313–332. doi:10.1017/S003329170001388X

Rvachew, S. (2007). Phonological processing and reading in children with speech sound disorders. *American Journal of Speech-Language Pathology, 16*, 260–270. doi:10.1044/1058-0360(2007/030)

Rydell, A. M., & Dahl, M. (2005). Children with early refusal to eat: Follow-up in adolescence. *Acta Paediatrica, 94*, 1186–1191. doi:10.1111/j.1651-2227.2005.tb02072.x

Saavedra, L. M., Silverman, W. K., Morgan-Lopez, A. A., & Kurtines, W. M. (2010). Cognitive behavioral treatment for childhood anxiety disorders: Long-term effects on anxiety and secondary disorders young adulthood. *Journal of Child Psychology and Psychiatry, 51*, 924–934. doi:10.1111/j.1469-7610.2010.02242.x

Sabb, F. W., van Erp, T. G. M., Hardt, M. E., Dapretto, M., Caplan, R., Cannon, T. D., & Bearden, C. E. (2010). Language network dysfunction as a predictor of outcome in youth at high-risk for psychosis. *Schizophrenia Research, 116*, 173–183. doi:10.1016/j.schres.2009.09.042

Sackett, D. L., Straus, S. E., Richardson, W. S., Rosenberg, W., & Haynes, R. B. (2000). *Evidence-based medicine: How to practice and teach EBM* (2nd ed.). London: Churchill Livingstone.

Safron, M., Cislak, A., Gaspar, T., & Luszczynska, A. (2011). Effects of school-based interventions targeting obesity-related behaviors and body weight change: A systematic umbrella review. *Behavioral Medicine, 37*, 15–25. doi:10.1080/08964289.2010.543194

Sala, R., Axelson, D. A., Castro-Fornieles, J., Goldstein, T. R., Ha, W., Liao, F., . . . Birmaher, B. (2010). Comorbid anxiety in children and adolescents with bipolar spectrum disorders. *Journal of Clinical Psychiatry, 71*, 1344–1350. doi:10.4088/JCP.09m05845gre

Sallee, R., & Greenawald, J. (1995). Neurobiology. In J. S. March (Ed.), *Anxiety disorders in children and adolescents* (pp. 3–34). New York: Guilford Press.

Sallet, P. C., de Alvarenga, P. G., Ferrão, Y., de Mathis, M. A., Torres, A. R., Marques, A., . . . Fleitlich-Bilyk, B. (2010). Eating disorders in patients with obsessive-compulsive disorder: Prevalence and clinical correlates. *International Journal of Eating Disorders, 43*, 315–325. doi:10.1002/eat.20697

Salter, D., McMillan, D., Richards, M., Talbot, T., Hodges, J., Bentovim, A., Hastings, R., Stevenson, J., & Skuse, D. (2003). Development of sexually abusive behaviour in sexually victimised males: A longitudinal study. *Lancet, 361*, 471–476.

Salvy, S., Kieffer, E., & Epstein, L. H. (2008). Effects of social context on overweight and normal-weight children's food selection. *Eating Behaviors, 9*, 190–196. doi:10.1016/j.eatbeh.2007.08.001

Sameroff, A. (2010). A unified theory of development: A dialectic integration of nature and nurture. *Child Development, 81*, 6–22. doi:10.1111/j.1467-8624.2009.01378.x

Sameroff, A. J., & MacKenzie, M. J. (2003). Research strategies for capturing transactional models of development: The limits of the possible. *Development and Psychopathology, 15*, 613–640. doi:10.1017/S0954579403000312

Sameroff, A. J., Peck, S. C., & Eccles, J. S. (2004). Changing ecological determinants of conduct problems from early adolescence to early adulthood. *Development and Psychopathology, 16*, 873–896. doi:10.1017/S0954579404040052

Sampson, R. J. (1992). Family management and child development: Insights from social disorganization theory. In J. McCord (Ed.), *Advances in criminological theory: Facts, frameworks, and forecasts* (Vol. 3, pp. 63–91). New Brunswick, NJ: Transaction.

Sampson, R. J., & Groves, W. B. (1989). Community structure and crime: Testing social-disorganization theory. *American Journal of Sociology, 94*, 774–802. doi:10.1086/229068

Sampson, R. J., & Laub, J. H. (1994). Urban poverty and the family context of delinquency: A new look at structure and process in a classic study. *Child Development, 65*, 523–540. doi:10.1111/j.1467-8624.1994.tb00767.x

Sampson, R. J., Raudenbush, S. W., & Earls, F. (1997). Neighborhoods and violent crime: A multilevel study of collective efficacy. *Science, 277*, 918–924. doi:10.1126/science.277.5328.918

Sanchez, M., & Soares, J. C. (2011). New drugs for bipolar disorder. *Current Psychiatry Reports*. Advance online publication. doi:10.1007/s11920-011-0231-1

Sanchez-Ortiz, V. C., Munro, C., Stahl, D., House, J., Startup, H., Treasure, J., . . . Schmidt, U. (2011). A randomized controlled trial of internet-based cognitive-behavioural therapy for bulimia nervosa or related disorders in a student population. *Psychological Medicine: A Journal of Research in Psychiatry and the Allied Sciences, 41*, 407–417. doi:10.1017/S0033291710000711

Sanci, L., Coffey, C., Olsson, C., Reid, S., Carlin, J. B., & Patton, G. (2008). Childhood sexual abuse and eating disorders in females: Findings from the Victorian Adolescent Health Cohort Study. *Archives of Pediatric Adolescent Medicine, 162*, 261–267. Retrieved from http://archpedi.ama-assn.org/

Sanders, M. R., & Dadds, M. R. (1992). Children's and parents' cognitions about family interaction: An evaluation of video-mediated recall and thought listing procedures in the assessment of conduct-disordered children. *Journal of Clinical Child Psychology, 21*, 371–379. doi:10.1207/s15374424jccp2104_7

Sapolsky, R. (1997, October). A gene for nothing. *Discover*, 40–46. Retrieved from http://discovermagazine.com/1997/oct/agenefornothing1242

Sas, L., Hurley, P., Hatch, A., Malla, S., & Dick, T. (1993). *Three years after the verdict: A longitudinal study of the social and psychological adjustment of child witnesses referred to the child witness project* (FVDS No. 4887–06–91–026). Health and Welfare Canada, Family Violence Prevention Division.

Sassaroli, S., Romero Lauro, L. J., Maria Ruggiero, G., Mauri, M. C., Vinai, P., & Frost, R. (2008). Perfectionism in depression, obsessive-compulsive disorder and eating disorders. *Behavior Research Therapy, 46*, 757–765. doi:10.1016/j.brat.2008.02.007

Sattler, J. M. (1998). *Clinical and forensic interviewing of children and families: Guidelines for the mental health, education, pediatric, and child maltreatment fields*. San Diego, CA: Sattler.

Sattler, J. M. (2006). *Assessment of children: Behavioral, social, and clinical foundations* (5th ed.). La Mesa, CA: Sattler.

Sattler, J. M. (2008). *Assessment of children: Cognitive foundations* (5th ed.). La Mesa, CA: Sattler.

Sattler, J. M., & Dumont, R. (2004). *Assessment of children: WISC-IV and WPPSI-III Supplement*, Exhibit 1-1. La Mesa, CA: Jerome M. Sattler, Publisher, Inc.

Sattler, J. M., & Hoge, R. D. (2006). *Assessment of children: Behavioral, social, and clinical foundations* (5th ed.). La Mesa, CA: Sattler.

Sattler, J. M., & Mash, E. J. (1998). Introduction to clinical assessment interviewing. In J. M. Sattler, *Clinical and forensic interviewing of children and families: Guidelines for the mental health, education, pediatric, and child maltreatment fields* (pp. 2–44). San Diego, CA: Sattler.

Saunders, B. E., Berliner, L., & Hanson, R. F. (Eds.). (2004). *Child physical and sexual abuse: Guidelines for treatment* [revised report]. Charleston, SC: National Crime Victims Research and Treatment Center. Retrieved from http://www.musc.edu/cvc/

Sawyer, M. G., Pfeiffer, S., Spence, S. H., Bond, L., Graetz, B., Kay, D., . . . Sheffield, J. (2010). School-based prevention of depression: A randomised controlled study of the *beyond blue* schools research initiative. *Journal of Child Psychology and Psychiatry, 51*, 199–209. doi:10.1111/j.1469-7610.2009.02136.x

Scerri, T. S., & Schulte-Körne, G. (2010). Genetics of developmental dyslexia. *European Child & Adolescent Psychiatry, 19*, 179–197. doi:10.1007/s00787-009-0081-0

Schafft, K. A., Jensen, E. B., & Hinrichs, C. C. (2009). Food deserts and overweight schoolchildren: Evidence from Pennsylvania. *Rural Sociology, 74*, 153–177. doi:10.1111/j.1549-0831.2009.tb00387.x

Schalock, R. L., Luckasson, R. A., Shogren, K. A., Borthwick-Duffy, S., Bradley, V., Buntinx, W. H. E., . . . Yeager, M. H. (2007). The renaming of mental retardation: Understanding the change to the term intellectual disability. *Intellectual and Developmental Disabilities, 45*, 116–124. doi:10.1352/1934-9556(2007)45[116:TROMRU]2.0.CO;2

Scheepers, F. E., Buitelaar, J, K., & Mathyss, W. (2011). Conduct disorder and the specifier callous and unemotional traits in DSM-5. *European Child and Adolescent Psychiatry, 20*, 89–93. doi:10.1007/s00787-010-0149-x

Scheeringa, M. S., Zeanah, C. H., & Cohen, J. A. (2010). PTSD in children and adolescents: Toward an empirically based algorithm. *Depression and Anxiety, 28*, 770–782. doi:10.1002/da.20736

Scheeringa, M. S., Zeanah, C. H., Myers, L., & Putnam, F. W. (2005). Predictive validity in a prospective follow-up of PTSD in preschool children. *Journal of the American Academy of Child & Adolescent Psychiatry, 44*, 899–906. doi:10.1097/01.chi.0000169013.81536.71

Scheffler, R. M., Hinshaw, S. P., Modrek, S., & Levine, P. (2007). TRENDS: The global market for ADHD medications. *Health Affairs, 26*, 450–457. doi:10.1377/hlthaff.26.2.450

Scherag, S., Hebebrand, J., & Hinney, A. (2010). Eating disorders: The current status of molecular genetic research. *European Child & Adolescent Psychiatry, 19*, 211–226. doi:10.1007/s00787-009-0085-9

Schmalz, D. L., Deane, G. D., Birch, L. L., & Davison, K. K. (2007). A longitudinal assessment of the links between physical activity and self-esteem in early adolescent non-Hispanic females. *Journal of Adolescent Health, 41*, 559–565. doi:10.1016/j.jadohealth.2007.07.001

Schniering, C. A., & Rapee, R. M. (2004). The structure of negative self-statements in children and adolescent: A confirmatory factor-analytic approach. *Journal of Abnormal Child Psychology, 32*, 95–109. doi:10.1023/B:JACP.0000007583.90038.7a

Schonberg, M. A., & Shaw, D. S. (2007). Risk factors for boys' conduct problems in poor and low-middle-class neighborhoods. *Journal of Abnormal Child Psychology, 35*, 759–772. doi:10.1007/s10802-007-9125-4

Schredl, M., & Reinhard, I. (2011). Gender differences in nightmare frequency: A meta-analysis. *Sleep Medicine Reviews, 15*, 115–121. doi:10.1016/j.smrv.2010.06.002

Schreier, H. (2002). On the importance of motivation in Munchausen by Proxy: The case of Kathy Bush. *Child Abuse & Neglect, 26*, 537–549.

Schreier, H. A., & Libow, J. A. (1993). *Hurting for love: Munchausen by proxy syndrome*. New York: Guilford Press.

Schuchardt, K., Gebhardt, M., & Mäehler, C. (2010). Working memory functions in children with different degrees of intellectual disability. *Journal of Intellectual Disability Research, 54*, 346–353. doi:10.1111/j.1365-2788.2010.01265.x

Schuele, C. M., & Boudreau, D. (2008). Phonological awareness intervention: Beyond the basics. *Language, Speech, and Hearing Services in Schools, 39*, 3–20. doi:10.1044/0161-1461(2008/002)

Schuetzmann, M., Richter-Appelt, H., Schulte-Markwort, M., & Schimmelman, B. G. (2008). Associations among the perceived parent-child relationship, eating behavior, and body weight in preadolescents: Results from a community-based sample. *Journal of Pediatric Psychology, 33*, 772–782. doi:10.1093/jpepsy/jsn002

Schulenberg, J. E., Sameroff, A. J., & Cicchetti, D. (2006). The transition to adulthood as a critical juncture in the course of psychopathology and mental health. *Development and Psychopathology [Special issue: Transition from adolescence to adulthood], 16*, 799–806. doi:10.1017/S0954579404040015

Schulkin, J. (2007). Autism and the amygdala: An endocrine hypothesis. *Brain and Cognition, 65*, 87–99. doi:10.1016/j.bandc.2006.02.009

Schumann, C. M., & Amaral, D. G. (2009). The human amygdala in autism. In P. J. Whalen & E. A. Phelps (Eds.), *The human amygdala* (pp. 362–381). New York: Guilford Press.

Schumann, C. M., Barnes, C. C., Lord, C., & Courchesne, E. (2009). Amygdala enlargement in toddlers with autism related to severity of social and communication impairments. *Biological Psychiatry, 66*, 942–949. doi:10.1016/j.biopsych.2009.07.007

Schumann, C. M., Bloss, C. S., Barnes, C. C., Wideman. G. M., Carper, R. A., Akshoomoff, N., . . . Courchesne E. (2010). Longitudinal magnetic resonance imaging study of cortical development through early childhood in autism. *Journal of Neuroscience, 30*, 4419–4427. doi:10.1523/JNEUROSCI.5714-09.2010

Schwartz, C. E., Wright, C. I., Shin, L. M., Kagan, J., & Rauch, S. L. (2003). Inhibited and uninhibited infants "grown up": Adult amygdalar response to novelty. *Science, 300*, 1952–1953. doi:10.1126/science.1083703

Schwartz, D. D., Axelrad, M. E., Cline, V. D., & Anderson, B. J. (2011). A model psychosocial screening program for children and youth with newly diagnosed type 1 diabetes: Implications for psychologists across contexts of care. *Professional Psychology: Research and Practice, 42*, 324–330. doi:10.1037/a0023836

Schwartz, L., & Drotar, D. (2006). Posttraumatic stress and related impairment in survivors of childhood cancer in early adulthood compared to healthy peers. *Journal of Pediatric Psychology [Special issue: Posttraumatic stress related to pediatric illness and injury], 31*, 356–366. doi:10.1093/jpepsy/jsj018

Schwartz, S. J., Unger, J. B., Zamboanga, B. L., & Szapocznik, J. (2010). Rethinking the concept of acculturation: Implications for theory and research. *American Psychologist, 65*, 237–251. doi:10.1037/a0019330

Schwimmer, J. B., Burwinkle, T. M., & Varni, J. W. (2003). Health-related quality of life of severely obese children and adolescents. *JAMA: Journal of the American Medical Association, 289*, 1813–1819. doi:10.1001/jama.289.14.1813

Schwoeri, L. D., Sholevar, G. P., & Combs, M. P. (2003). Impact of culture and ethnicity on family interventions. In G. P. Sholevar (Ed.), *Textbook of family and couples therapy: Clinical applications* (pp. 725–745). Washington, DC: American Psychiatric Press.

Scott, J. A., Schumann, C. M., Goodlin-Jones, B. L., & Amaral, D. G. (2009). A comprehensive volumetric analysis of the cerebellum in children and adolescents with autism spectrum disorder. *Autism Research, 2*, 246–257. doi:10.1002/aur.97

Scott, K. L., Wolfe, D. A., & Wekerle, C. (2003). Maltreatment and trauma: Tracking the connections in adolescence. *Child and Adolescent Psychiatric Clinics of North America, 12*, 211–230.

Scott, M., Wilcox, H., Huo, Y., Turne, J. B., Fisher, P., & Shaffer, D. (2010). *American Journal of Public Health, 100*, 1648–1652. doi:10.2105/AJPH.2009.175224

Scott, S., O'Connor, T. G., Futh, A., Matias, C., Price, J., & Doolan, M. (2010). Impact of a parenting program in a high-risk multi-ethnic community: The PALS trial. *Journal of Child Psychology and Psychiatry, 51*, 1331–1341. doi:10.1111/j.1469-7610.2010.02302.x

Scourfield, J., Rice, F., Thapar, A., Harold, G. T., Martin, N., & McGuffin, P. (2003). Depressive symptoms in children and adolescents: Changing aetiological influences with development. *Journal of Child Psychology and Psychiatry, 44*, 968–976. doi:10.1111/1469-7610.00181

Sedlak, A. J., & Broadhurst, D. D. (1996, September). *Third national incidence study of child abuse and neglect: Final report*. Washington, DC: U.S. Department of Health and Human Services.

Seiverling, L., Williams, K., & Sturmey, P. (2010). Assessment of feeding problems in children with autism spectrum disorders. *Journal of Developmental and Physical Disabilities, 22*, 401–413. doi:10.1007/s10882-010-9206-0

Seligman, M. E. P. (1971). Phobias and preparedness. *Behavior Therapy, 2*, 307–320. doi:10.1016/S0005-7894(71)80064-3

Semenak, S. (1996, November 21). Coping with autism is a full-time job. *Montreal Gazette*, pp. A1, A15.

Semrud-Clikeman, M., Walkowiak, J., Wilkinson, A., & Minne, E. P. (2010). Direct and indirect measures of social perception, behavior, and emotional functioning in children with Asperger's disorder, nonverbal learning disability, or ADHD. *Journal of Abnormal Child Psychology: An Official Publication of the International Society for Research in Child and Adolescent Psychopathology, 38*, 509–519. doi:10.1007/s10802-009-9380-7

Serafica, F. C., & Vargas, L. A. (2006). Cultural diversity in the development of child psychopathology. In D. Cicchetti & D. J. Cohen (Eds.), *Developmental psychopathology: Vol. 1. Theory and method* (2nd ed., pp. 588–626). New York: Wiley.

Serketich, W. J., & Dumas, J. E. (1996). The effectiveness of behavioral parent training to modify antisocial behavior in children: A meta-analysis. *Behavior Therapy, 27*, 171–186. doi:10.1016/S0005-7894(96)80013-X

Seroczynski, A. D., Cole, D. A., & Maxwell, S. E. (1997). Cumulative and compensatory effects of competence and incompetence on depressive symptoms in children. *Journal of Abnormal Psychology, 106*, 586–597. doi:10.1037/0021-843X.106.4.586

Sethi, S., Bhargava, S., & Phil, S. M. (2005). Nocturnal enuresis: A review. *Journal of Pediatric Neurology, 3*, 11–18.

Seto, M. C. (2008a). Etiology of pedophilia. In M. C. Seto (Ed.), *Pedophilia and sexual offending against children: Theory, assessment, and intervention* (pp. 101–122). Washington, DC: American Psychological Association.

Seto, M. C. (2008b). Incest. In M. C. Seto (Ed.), *Pedophilia and sexual offending against children: Theory, assessment, and intervention* (pp. 123–140). Washington, DC: American Psychological Association.

Seto, M. C., & Lalumière, M. L. (2010). What is so special about male adolescent sexual offending? A review and test of explanations through meta-analysis. *Psychological Bulletin, 136*, 526–575. doi:10.1037/a0019700

Sexton, J. (1996, September 5). For dead child's family, long history of troubles. *New York Times*, p. B3.

Shackman, J. E., Shackman, A. J., & Pollak, S. D. (2007). Physical abuse amplifies attention to threat and increases anxiety in children. *Emotion, 7*, 838–852.

Shafer, V. L., & Garrido-Nag, K. (2007). *The neurodevelopmental bases of language*. Malden, MA: Blackwell.

Shaffer, D., Gould, M., Fisher, P., Trautman, P., Moreau, D., Kleinman, M., & Flory, M. (1996). Psychiatric diagnosis in child and adolescent suicide. *Archives of General Psychiatry, 53*, 339–348. Retrieved from http://archpsyc.ama-assn.org/

Shaffer, D., Scott, M., Wilcox, H., Maslow, C., Hicks, R., Lucas, C., . . . Greenwald, S. (2004). The Columbia Suicide Screen: Validity and reliability of a screen for youth suicide and depression. *Journal of the American Academy of Child & Adolescent Psychiatry, 43*, 71–79. doi:10.1097/00004583-200401000-00016

Shalev, R. S. (2007). Prevalence of developmental dyscalculia. In D. B. Berch & M. M. Mazzocco (Eds.), *Why is math so hard for some children? The nature and origins of mathematical learning difficulties and disabilities* (pp. 49–60). Baltimore: Brookes.

Shankman, S. A., Klein, D. N., Torpey, D. C., Olino, T. M., Dyson, M. W., Kim, J., . . . Tenke, C. E. (2011). Do positive and negative temperament traits interact in predicting risk for depression? A resting EEG study of 329 preschoolers. *Development and Psychopathology, 23*, 551–562. doi:10.1017/S0954579411000022

Sharpe, D., & Rossiter, L. (2002). Siblings of children with a chronic illness: A meta-analysis. *Journal of Pediatric Psychology, 27*, 699–710. doi:10.1093/jpepsy/27.8.699

Sharpe, H., Musiat, P., Knapton, O., & Schmidt, U. (2011). Pro-eating disorder websites: Facts, fictions and fixes. *Journal of Public Mental Health, 10*, 34–44. doi:10.1108/17465721111134538

Shaw, D. S., & Bell, R. Q. (1993). Developmental theories of parental contributors to antisocial behavior. *Journal of Abnormal Child Psychology, 21*, 493–518. doi:10.1007/BF00916316

Shaw, P., Eckstrand, K., Sharp, W., Blumenthal, Lerch, J. P., Greenstein, D., . . . Rapoport, J. L. (2007). Attention-deficit/hyperactivity disorder is characterized by a delay in cortical maturation. *Proceedings of the National Academy of Sciences, 104*, 19649–19654. doi:10.1073/pnas.0707741104

Shaw, P., Gilliam, M., Liverpool, M., Weddle, C., Malek, M., Sharp, W., . . . Giedd, J. (2011). Children with symptoms of hyperactivity and impulsivity: Support for a dimensional view of attention deficit hyperactivity disorder. *American Journal of Psychiatry, 168*, 143–151. doi:10.1176/appi.ajp.2010.10030385

Shaw, P., & Rapoport, J. L (2006). Decision making about children with psychotic symptoms: Using the best evidence in choosing a treatment. *Journal of the American Academy of Child & Adolescent Psychiatry, 45*, 1381–1386. doi:10.1097/01.chi.0000251618.25248.00

Shaywitz, B. A., Shaywitz, S. E., Pugh, K. R., Mencl, W. E., Fulbright, R. K., Skudlarski, P., . . . Gore, J. C. (2002). Disruption of posterior brain systems for reading in children with developmental dyslexia. *Biological psychiatry, 52*, 101–110. doi:10.1016/S0006-3223(02)01365-3

Shaywitz, S. E. (1998). Current concepts: Dyslexia. *New England Journal of Medicine, 338*, 307–312. doi:10.1056/NEJM199801293380507

Shaywitz, S. E., & Shaywitz, B. A. (2008). Paying attention to reading: The neurobiology of reading and dyslexia. *Development and Psychopathology, 20*, 1329–1349. doi:10.1017/S0954579408000631

Shaywitz, S. E., Escobar, M. D., Shaywitz, B. A., Fletcher, J. M., & Makuch, R. (1992). Evidence that dyslexia may represent the lower tail of a normal distribution of reading ability. *The New England Journal of Medicine, 326*, 145–150. Retrieved from http://www.nejm.org/

Shaywitz, S. E., Gruen, J. R., Mody, M., & Shaywitz, B. A. (2009). Dyslexia. In R. G. Schwartz (Ed.), *Handbook of child language disorders* (pp. 115–139). New York: Psychology Press.

Shaywitz, S. E., Mody, M., & Shaywitz, B. A. (2006). Neural mechanisms in dyslexia. *Current Directions in Psychological Science, 15*, 278–281. doi:10.1111/j.1467-8721.2006.00452.x

Shaywitz, S. E., Morris, R., & Shaywitz, B. A. (2008). The education of dyslexic children from childhood to young adulthood. *Annual Review of Psychology, 59*, 451–475. doi:10.1146/annurev.psych.59.103006.093633

Shear, K., Jin, R., Ruscio, A. M., Walters, E. E., & Kessler, R. C. (2006). Prevalence and correlates of estimated DSM-IV child and adult separation anxiety disorder in the National Comorbidity Survey Replication. *Archives of General Psychiatry, 163*, 1074–1083. doi:10.1176/appi.ajp.163.6.1074

Sheeber, L. B., Allen, N., Davis, B., & Sorensen, E. (2000). Regulation of negative affect during mother-child problem-solving interactions: Adolescent depressive status and family processes. *Journal of Abnormal Child Psychology, 28*, 467–479. doi:10.1023/A:1005135706799

Sheeber, L. B., Davis, B., Leve, C., Hops, H., & Tildesley, E. (2007). Adolescents' relationships with their mothers and fathers: Associations with depressive disorder and subdiagnostic symptomatology. *Journal of Abnormal Psychology, 116*, 144–154. doi:10.1037/0021-843X.116.1.144

Sheeber, L., Hops, H., Alpert, A., Davis, B., & Andrews, J. (1997). Family support and conflict: Prospective relations to adolescent depression. *Journal of Abnormal Child Psychology, 25*, 333–344. doi:10.1023/A:1025768504415

Sheffer, R. E., & Linden, S. (2007). Concurrent medical conditions with pediatric bipolar disorder. *Current Opinion in Psychiatry, 20*, 398–401. doi:10.1097/YCO.0b013e3281a305c3

Sheridan, M. A., Hinshaw, S. P., & D'Esposito, M. D. (2010). Stimulant medication and prefrontal functional connectivity during working memory in ADHD: A preliminary report. *Journal of Attention Disorders, 14*, 69–78. doi:10.1177/1087054709347444

Shic, F., Bradshaw, J., Klin, A., Scassellati, B., & Chawarska, K. (2011). Limited activity monitoring in toddlers with autism spectrum disorder. *Brain Research, 1380*, 246–254. doi:10.1016/j.brainres.2010.11.074

Shields, A., & Cicchetti, D. (1998). Reactive aggression among maltreated children: The contributions of attention and emotion dysregulation. *Journal of Clinical Child Psychology, 27*, 381–395.

Shiels, K., & Hawk, Jr., L. W. (2010). Self-regulation in ADHD: The role of error processing. *Clinical Psychology Review, 30*, 951–961. doi:10.1016/j.cpr.2010.06.010

Shin-ichi, I., Okajima, I., Matsuoka, H., & Sakano, Y. (2007). Cognitive behavioural therapy for anxiety disorders in children and adolescents: A meta-analysis. *Child and Adolescent Mental Health, 12*, 164–172. doi:10.1111/j.1475-3588.2006.00433.x

Shiner, R. (2007). Personality disorders. In E. J. Mash & R. A. Barkley (Eds.), *Assessment of childhood disorders* (4th ed., pp. 781–816). New York: Guilford Press.

Shipman, K. L., Schneider, R., Fitzgerald, M. M., Sims, C., Swisher, L., & Edwards, A. (2007). Maternal emotion socialization in maltreating and non-maltreating families: Implications for children's emotion regulation. *Social Development, 16*, 268–285.

Shochet, I. M., Dadds, M. R., Holland, D., Whitefield, K., Harnett, P. H., & Osgarby, S. M. (2001). The efficacy of a universal school-based program to prevent adolescent depression. *Journal of Clinical Child Psychology, 30*, 303–315. doi:10.1207/S15374424JCCP3003_3

Shonkoff, J. P. (2010). Building a new biodevelopmental framework to guide the future of early childhood policy. *Child Development, 81*, 357–367. doi:10.1111/j.1467-8624.2009.01399.x

Shonkoff, J. P., & Bales, S. N. (2011). Science does not speak for itself: Translating child development research for the public and its policymakers. *Child Development, 82*, 17–32. doi:10.1111/j.1467-8624.2010.01538.x

Short, E. J., Fairchild, L., Findling, R. L., & Manos, M. J. (2007). Developmental and subtype differences in behavioral assets and problems in children diagnosed with ADHD. *Journal of Attention Disorders, 11*, 28–36. doi:10.1177/1087054707299370

Shukla, D. K., Keehn, B., & Muller, R.-A. (2011). Tract-specific analyses of diffusion tensor imaging show widespread white matter compromise in autism spectrum disorder. *Journal of Child Psychology and Psychiatry, 52*, 286–295. doi:10.1111/j.1469-7610.2010.02342.x

Siegel, L. J. (2008). Children medically at risk. In R. J. Morris & T. R. Kratochwill (Eds.), *The practice of child therapy* (4th ed., pp. 363–409). Mahwah, NJ: Erlbaum.

Siegel, L. J., Smith, K. E., & Wood, T. A. (1991). Children medically at risk. In T. R. Kratochwill & R. J. Harris (Eds.), *The practice of child therapy* (2nd ed., pp. 328–363). Toronto, Ontario, Canada: Pergamon Press.

Sigman, M., & Mundy, P. (1989). Social attachments in autistic children. *Journal of the American Academy of Child & Adolescent Psychiatry, 28*, 74–81. doi:10.1097/00004583-198901000-00014

Sigman, M., Spence, S. J., & Wang, A. T. (2006). Autism from developmental and neuropsychological perspectives. *Annual Review of Clinical Psychology, 2*, 327–355. doi:10.1146/annurev.clinpsy.2.022305.095210

Silk, J., Shaw, D. S., Prout, J. T., O'Rourke, F., Lane, T. J., & Kovacs, M. (2011). Socialization of emotion and offspring internalizing symptoms in mothers with childhood-onset depression. *Journal of Applied Developmental Psychology, 32*, 127–136. doi:10.1016/j.appdev.2011.02.001

Sills, M. R., Shetterly, S., Xu, S., Magid, D., & Kempe, A. (2007). Association between parental depression and children's health care use. *Pediatrics, 119*, e829–e836. doi:10.1542/peds.2006-2399

Silverman, J. A. (1997). Anorexia nervosa: Historical perspective on treatment. In D. M. Garner & P. E. Garfinkel (Eds.), *Handbook of treatment for eating disorders* (2nd ed., pp. 3–10). New York: Guilford Press.

Silverman, W. K., & Ginsburg, C. S. (1995). Specific phobia and generalized anxiety disorder. In J. S. March (Ed.), *Anxiety disorders in children and adolescents* (pp. 151–180). New York: Guilford Press.

Silverman, W. K., & Hinshaw, S. P. (Eds.). (2008). Evidence-based psychosocial treatments for children and adolescents: A ten-year update [Special issue]. *Journal of Clinical Child and Adolescent Psychology, 37*, 1–7. doi:10.1080/15374410701817725

Silverman, W. K., La Greca, A. M., & Wasserstein, S. (1995). What do children worry about? Worries and their relation to anxiety. *Child Development, 66*, 671–686. doi:10.2307/1131942

Silverman, W. K., Ortiz, C. D., Viswesvaran, C., Burns, B. J., Kolko, D. J., Putnam, F. W., & Amaya-Jackson, L. (2008). Evidence-based psychosocial treatments for children and adolescents exposed to traumatic events. *Journal of Clinical Child and Adolescent Psychology, 37*, 184–214. doi:10.1080/15374410701818293

Silverman, W. K., Pina, A. A., & Viswesvaran, C. (2008). Evidence-based psychosocial treatments for phobic and anxiety disorders in children and adolescents. *Journal of Clinical Child and Adolescent Psychology, 37*, 105–130. doi:10.1080/15374410701817907

Silverthorn, P., Frick, P. J., Kuper, K., & Ott, J. (1996). Attention deficit hyperactivity disorder and sex: A test of two etiological models to explain the male predominance. *Journal of Clinical Child Psychology, 25*, 52–59. doi:10.1207/s15374424jccp2501_6

Simard, V., Nielsen, T. A., Tremblay, R. E., Boivin, M., & Montplaisir, J. Y. (2008). Longitudinal study of preschool sleep disturbance: The predictive role of maladaptive parental behaviors, early sleep problems, and child/mother psychological factors. *Archives of Pediatric and Adolescent Medicine, 162*, 360–367. Retrieved from http://archpedi.ama-assn.org/

Simmons, D. R., Robertson, A. E., McKay, L. S., Toal, E., McAleer, P., & Pollick, F. E. (2009). Vision in autism spectrum disorders. *Vision Research, 49*, 2705–2739. doi:10.1016/j.visres.2009.08.005

Simmons, R. R. (2002). *Odd girl out: The hidden culture of aggression in girls.* New York: Harcourt.

Simon, T. R., Dent, C. W., & Sussman, S. (1997). Vulnerability to victimization, concurrent problem behaviors, and peer influence as predictors of in-school weapon carrying among high school students. *Violence and Victims, 12*, 277–289. Retrieved from http://www.springerpub.com/product/08866708

Simon, V. A., Feiring, C., & McElroy, S. K. (2010). Making meaning of traumatic events: Youths' strategies for processing childhood sexual abuse are associated with psychosocial adjustment. *Child Maltreatment, 15*(3), 229–241. doi:10.1177/1077559510370365

Simonoff, E., Bolton, P., & Rutter, M. (1996). Mental retardation: Genetic findings, clinical implications and research agenda. *Journal of Child Psychology and Psychiatry, 37*, 259–280. doi:10.1111/j.1469-7610.1996.tb01404.x

Simonoff, E., Pickles, A., Meyer, J. M., Silberg, J. L., Maes, H. H., Loeber, R., . . . Eaves, L. J. (1997). The Virginia Twin Study of adolescent behavioral development: Influences of age, sex, and impairment on rates of disorder. *Archives of General Psychiatry, 54*, 801–808. Retrieved from http://archpsyc.ama-assn.org/

Simons-Morton, B. G., & Chen, R. (2006). Over time relationships between early adolescent and peer substance use. *Addictive Behavior, 31*, 1211–1223. doi:10.1016/j.addbeh.2005.09.006

Simpson, H. A., Jung, L., & Murphy, T. K. (2011). Update on attention-deficit/hyperactivity disorder and tic disorders: A review of the current literature. *Current Psychiatry Reports, 13*, 351–356. doi:10.1007/s11920-011-0223-1

Singer, M. I., Hussey, D. L., & Strom, K. J. (1992). Grooming the victim: An analysis of a perpetrator's seduction letter. *Child Abuse and Neglect, 16*, 877–886.

Singh, I., Kendall, T., Taylor, C., Mears, A., Hollis, C., Batty, M., & Keenan, S. (2010). Young people's experience of ADHD and stimulant medication. A qualitative study for the NICE guideline. *Child and Adolescent Mental Health, 15*, 186–192. doi:10.1111/j.1475-3588.2010.00565.x

Singh, M. K., DelBello, M. P., Stanford, K. E., Soutullo, C., McDonough-Ryan, P., McElroy, S. L., & Strakowski, S. M. (2007). Psychopathology in children of bipolar parents. *Journal of Affective Disorders, 102*, 131–136. doi:10.1016/j.jad.2007.01.004

Siperstein, G. N., Glick, G. C., & Parker, R. C. (2009). Social inclusion of children with intellectual disabilities in a recreational setting. *Intellectual and Developmental Disabilities, 47*, 97–107. doi:10.1352/1934-9556-47.2.97

Siqueland, L., Kendall, P. C., & Steinberg, L. (1996). Perceived family environment and observed family interaction styles. *Journal of Clinical Child Psychology, 25*, 225–237. doi:10.1207/s15374424jccp2502_12

Sites, P. (1967). Lee Harvey Oswald and the American dream. New York: Pageant.

Skiba, R. J., Knesting, K., & Bush, L. D. (2002). Culturally competent assessment: More than nonbiased tests. *Journal of Child and Family Studies, 11*, 61–78. doi:10.1023/A:1014767511894

Skopp, N. A., McDonald, R., Jouriles, E. N., & Rosenfield, D. (2007). Partner aggression and children's externalizing problems: Maternal and partner warmth as protective factors. *Journal of Family Psychology, 21*, 459–467.

Skottun, B. C., & Skoyles, J. R. (2008). Coherent motion, magnocellular sensitivity and the causation of dyslexia. *International Journal of Neuroscience, 118*, 185–190. doi:10.1080/00207450601041872

Skovgaard, A. M., Houmann, T., Christiansen, E., Landorph, S., Jorgensen, T., Olsen, E. M., . . . Lichtenberg, A. (2007). The prevalence of mental health problems in children 1 1/2 years of age—the Copenhagen child cohort 2000. *Journal of Child Psychology and Psychiatry, 48*, 62–70. doi:10.1111/j.1469-7610.2006.01659.x

Slavin, L. A., & Rainer, K. (1990). Gender differences in emotional support and depressive symptoms among adolescents: A prospective analysis. *American Journal of Community Psychology, 18*, 407–421. doi:10.1007/BF00938115

Slough, N. M., McMahon, R. J., & The Conduct Problems Prevention Research Group. (2008). Preventing serious conduct problems in school-age youth: The Fast Track program. *Cognitive and Behavioral Practice, 15*, 3–17. doi:10.1016/j.cbpra.2007.04.002

Smalley, S. L., McGough, J. J., Del'Homme, M., NewDelman, J., Gordon, E., Kim, T., . . . McCracken, J. T. (2000). Familial clustering of symptoms and disruptive behaviors in multiplex families with attention-deficit/hyperactivity disorder. *Journal of the American Academy of Child & Adolescent Psychiatry, 39*, 1135–1143. doi:10.1097/00004583-200009000-00013

Smarty, S., & Findling, R. L. (2007). Psychopharmacology of pediatric bipolar disorder: A review. *Psychopharmacology, 191*, 39–54. doi:10.1007/s00213-006-0569-y

Smetana, J. G., Daddis, C., Toth, S. L., Cicchetti, D., Bruce, J., & Kane, P. (1999). Effects of provocation on maltreated and nonmaltreated preschoolers' understanding of moral transgressions. *Social Development, 8*, 335–348.

Smith, A. R., Hawkeswood, S. E., Bodell, L. P., & Joiner, T. E. (2011). Muscularity versus leanness: An examination of body ideals and predictors of disordered eating in heterosexual and gay college students. *Body Image, 8*, 232–236. doi:10.1016/j.bodyim.2011.03.005

Smith, B. H., Barkley, R. A., & Shapiro, C. J. (2006). Attention-deficit/hyperactivity disorder. In E. J. Mash & R. A. Barkley (Eds.), *Treatment of childhood disorders* (4th ed., pp. 65–136). New York: Guilford Press.

Smith, B. H., Barkley, R. A., & Shapiro, C. J. (2007). Attention-deficit/hyperactivity disorder. In E. J. Mash & R. A. Barkley (Eds.), *Assessment of childhood disorders* (4th ed., pp. 53–131). New York: Guilford Press.

Smith, T., & Lovaas, O. I. (1997). The UCLA Young Autism Project: A reply to Gresham and Macmillan. *Behavioral Disorders, 22*, 202–218. Retrieved from http://www.ccbd.net/

Smolak, L. (2004). Body image in children and adolescents: Where do we go from here? *Body Image, 1*, 15–28. doi:10.1016/S1740-1445(03)00008-1

Smolak, L. (2011). Sexual abuse and body image. In T. F. Cash & L. Smolak (Eds.), *Body image: A handbook of science, practice, and prevention* (2nd ed., pp. 119–126). New York: Guilford Press.

Smolak, L., Murnen, S. K., & Ruble, A. E. (2000). Female athletes and eating problems: A meta-analysis. *International Journal of Eating Disorders, 27*, 371–380. doi:10.1002/(SICI)1098-108X(200005)27:4<371::AID-EAT1>3.0.CO;2-Y

Smolak, L., Murnen, S. K., & Thompson, J. K. (2005). Sociocultural influences and muscle building in adolescent boys. *Psychology of Men & Masculinity, 6*, 227–239. doi:10.1037/1524-9220.6.4.227

Smoller, J. W., Rosenbaum, J. F., Biederman, J., Kennedy, J., Dai, D., Racette, S. R., . . . Slaugenhaupt, S. A. (2003). Association of a genetic marker at the corticotropin-releasing hormone locus with behavioral inhibition. *Biological Psychiatry, 54*, 1376–1381. doi:10.1016/S0006-3223(03)00598-5

Smyth, J. M., Wonderlich, S. A., Heron, K. E., Sliwinski, M. J., Crosby, R. D., Mitchell, J. E., & Engel, S. G. (2007). Daily and momentary mood and stress are associated with binge eating and vomiting in bulimia nervosa patients in the natural environment. *Journal of Consulting and Clinical Psychology, 75*, 629–638. doi:10.1037/0022-006X.75.4.629

Snowling, M. J. (2008). Specific disorders and broader phenotypes: The case of dyslexia. *The Quarterly Journal of Experimental Psychology, 61*, 142–156. doi:10.1080/17470210701508830

Snowling, M. J., Gallagher, A., & Frith, U. (2003). Family risk of dyslexia is continuous: Individual differences in the precursors of reading skill. *Child development, 74*, 358–373. doi:10.1111/1467-8624.7402003

Snyder, H. N., & Sickmund, M. (2006). *Juvenile offenders and victims: 2006 national report*. Washington, DC: U.S. Department of Justice, Office of Justice Programs, Office of Juvenile Justice and Delinquency Prevention.

Snyder, J. (1991). Discipline as a mediator of the impact of maternal stress and mood on child conduct problems. *Development and Psychopathology, 3*, 263–276. doi:10.1017/S0954579400005307

Sobel, L. J., Banshal, R., Maia, T. V., Sanchez, J., Mazzone, L., Durkin, K., . . . Peterson, B. S. (2010). Basal ganglia surface morphology and the effects of stimulant medications in youth with attention deficit hyperactivity disorder. *American Journal of Psychiatry, 167*, 977–986. doi:10.1176/appi.ajp.2010.09091259

Soderstrom, H., Rastam, M., & Gillberg, C. (2002). Temperament and character in adults with Asperger syndrome. *Autism, 6*, 287–297. doi:10.1177/1362361302006003006

Sohl, N. L., Touyz, S. W., & Surgenor, L. J. (2006). Eating and body image disturbances across cultures: A review. *European Eating Disorders Review, 14*, 54–65. doi:10.1002/erv.678

Solanto, M. V., & Alvir, J. (2009). Reliability of DSM-IV symptom ratings of ADHD: Implications for DSM-V. *Journal of Attention Disorders, 13*, 107–116. doi:10.1177/1087054708322994

Solanto, M. V., Gilbert, S. N., Raj, A., Zhu, J., Pope-Boyd, S., Stepak, B., . . . Newcorn, J. H. (2007). Neurocognitive functioning in AD/HD, predominantly inattentive and combined subtypes. *Journal of Abnormal Child Psychology, 35*, 729–744. doi:10.1007/s10802-008-9276-y

Solanto, M. V., Pope-Boyd, S. A., Tryon, W. W., & Stepak, B. (2009). *Journal of Attention Disorders, 13*, 27–35. doi:10.1177/1087054708320403

Solin, S. (1995, April 1). I did not want to live. *Seventeen*, 154–156, 176.

Son, M., Kim, J., Oh, J., & Kawachi, I. (2011). Inequalities in childhood cancer mortality according to parental socioeconomic position: A birth cohort study in South Korea. *Social Science & Medicine, 72*, 108–115. doi:10.1016/j.socscimed.2010.10.007

Sondheimer, D. L., Schoenwald, S. K., & Rowland, M. D. (1994). Alternatives to the hospitalization of youth with a serious emotional disturbance. *Journal of Clinical Child Psychology, 23*, 7–12. Retrieved from http://www.clinicalchildpsychology.org/journal/

Sonuga-Barke, E. J. (2011). Editorial: The elephant in the laboratory – on the influence of non-scientific assumptions on research in child psychology and psychiatry. *Journal of Child Psychology and Psychiatry, 52*, 1–2. doi:10.1111/j.1469-7610.2010.02358.x

Sonuga-Barke, E. J. S., Auerbach, J., Campbell, S. B., Daley, D., & Thompson, M. (2005). Varieties of preschool hyperactivity: Multiple pathways from risk to disorder. *Developmental Science, 8*, 141–150. doi:10.1111/j.1467-7687.2005.00401.x

Sonuga-Barke, E. J. S., Daley, D., & Thompson, M. (2002). Does maternal ADHD reduce the effectiveness of parent training for preschool children's ADHD? *Journal of the American Academy of Child & Adolescent Psychiatry, 41*, 696–702. doi:10.1097/00004583-200206000-00009

Sonuga-Barke, E. J. S., Koerting, J., Smith, E., McCann, D. C., & Thompson, M. (2011). Early detection and intervention for attention-deficit hyperactivity disorder. *Expert Review of Neurotherapeutics, 11*, 557–563. doi:10.1586/ern.11.39

Sonuga-Barke, E. J. S., Kumsta, R., Schlotz, W., Lasky-Su, Marco, R., Miranda, A., . . . Faraone, S. V. (2011). A functional variant of the serotonin transporter gene (SLC6A4) moderates impulsive choice in attention deficit/hyperactivity disorder boys and siblings. *Biological Psychiatry, 70*, 230–236. doi:10.1016/j.biopsych.2011.01.040

Sonuga-Barke, E. J. S., Sergeant, J. A., Nigg, J., & Willcutt, E. (2008). Executive dysfunction and delay aversion in attention deficit hyperactivity disorder: Nosologic and diagnostic implications. *Child and Adolescent Psychiatric Clinics of North America, 17*, 367–384. doi:10.1016/j.chc.2007.11.008

Sonuga-Barke, E. J. S., Thompson, M., Abikoff, H., Klein, R., & Brotman, L. M. (2006). Nonpharmacological Interventions for preschoolers with ADHD: The case for specialized parent training. *Infants and Young Children, 19*, 142–153. doi:10.1097/00001163-200604000-00007

Sourander, A., Jensen, P., Davies, M., Niemela, S., Elonheimo, H., Ristkari, T.,. . . Almqvist, F. (2007). Who is at the greatest risk of adverse long-term outcomes? The Finnish From a Boy to a Man Study. *Journal of the American Academy of Child & Adolescent Psychiatry, 46*, 1148–1161. doi:10.1097/chi.0b013e31809861e9

Southam-Gerow, M. A., & Kendall, P. C. (2000). A preliminary study of the emotion understanding of youths referred for treatment of anxiety disorders. *Journal of Clinical Child Psychology, 29*, 319–327. doi:10.1207/S15374424JCCP2903_3

Southam-Gerow, M. A., & Kendall, P. C. (2002). Emotion regulation and understanding: Implications for child psychopathology and therapy. *Clinical Psychology Review, 22*, 189–222. doi:10.1016/S0272-7358(01)00087-3

Southam-Gerow, M. A., Kendall, P. C., & Weersing, R. V. (2001). Examining outcome variability: Correlates of treatment response in a child and adolescent anxiety clinic. *Journal of Clinical Child Psychology, 30*, 422–436. doi:10.1207/S15374424JCCP3003_13

Special Olympics. (2007). *Impact of Special Olympics programming*. Retrieved July 20, 2011from http://www.specialolympics.org/research_studies.aspx

Spector, S. G., & Volkmar, F. R. (2006). Autism spectrum disorders. In D. A. Wolfe & E. J. Mash (Eds.), *Behavioral and emotional disorders in adolescents: Nature, assessment, and treatment* (pp. 444–460). New York: Guilford Press.

Speier, P. L., Sherak, D. L., Hirsch, S., & Cantwell, D. P. (1995). Depression in children and adolescents. In E. E. Beckham & W. R. Leber (Eds.), *Handbook of depression* (2nd ed., pp. 467–493). New York: Guilford Press.

Spence, S. H., Donovan, C. L., March, S., Gamble, A., Anderson, R. E., Prosser, S., & Kenardy, J. (2011). A randomized controlled trial of online versus clinic-based CBT for adolescent anxiety. *Journal of Consulting and Clinical Psychology, 79*, 629–642. doi:10.1037/a0024512

Spencer, N. J. (2007). Failure to think about failure to thrive. *Archives of Disease in Childhood, 92*, 95–96. doi:10.1136/adc.2006.098624

Spencer, T. J., Biederman, J., & Mick, E. (2007). Attention-deficit/hyperactivity disorder: Diagnosis, lifespan, comorbidities, and neurobiology. *Journal of Pediatric Psychology, 32*, 631–642. doi:10.1093/jpepsy/jsm005

Spencer, T. J., Biederman, J., & Wilens, T. (2000). Pharmacotherapy of attention deficit hyperactivity disorder. *Child and Adolescent Psychiatric Clinics of North America, 9*, 77–97. Retrieved from http://www.childpsych.theclinics.com/

Spencer, T. J., Wilens, T., Biederman, J., Wozniak, J., & Harding-Crawford, M. (2000). Attention-deficit/hyperactivity disorder with mood disorders. In T. E. Brown (Ed.), *Attention-deficit disorders and comorbidities in children, adolescents, and adults* (pp. 79–124). Washington, DC: American Psychiatric Press.

Spicer, P., & Sarche, M. C. (2006). Responding to the crisis in American Indian and Alaska Native children's mental health. In H. E. Fitzgerald, B. M. Lester, & B. Zuckerman (Eds.), *The crisis in youth mental health: Critical issues and effective programs: Vol. 1. Childhood disorders. Child psychology and mental health* (pp. 257–275). Westport, CT: Praeger/Greenwood.

Spiker, D., Lotspeich, L. J., Dimiceli, S., Myers, R. M., & Rische, N. (2002). Behavioral phenotypic variation in autism multiplex families: Evidence for a continuous severity gradient. *American Journal of Medical Genetics, 114*, 129–136. doi:10.1002/ajmg.10188

Spitz, R. (1945). Hospitalism: An inquiry into the genesis of psychiatric conditions in early childhood. *Psychoanalytic Study of the Child, 1*, 53–74. Retrieved from http://yalepress.yale.edu/yupbooks/SeriesPage.asp?Series=75

Spitz, R. A., & Wolf, M. (1946). Anaclitic depression: An enquiry into the genesis of psychiatric conditions in early childhood: II. *Psychoanalytic Study of the Child, 2*, 342–363. Retrieved from http://yalepress.yale.edu/yupbooks/SeriesPage.asp?Series=75

Spock, B. (1945). *Baby and child care*. London: Bodley Head.

Sprich, S., Biederman, J., Crawford, M. H., Mundy, E., & Faraone, S. V. (2000). Adoptive and biological families of children and adolescents with ADHD. *Journal of the American Academy of Child & Adolescent Psychiatry, 39*, 1432–1437. doi:10.1097/00004583-200011000-00018

Sprung, M. (2010). Clinically relevant measures of children's theory of mind and knowledge about thinking: Non-standard and advanced measures. *Child and Adolescent Mental Health, 15*, 204–216. doi:10.1111/j.1475-3588.2010.00568.x

Spruyt, K., & Gozal, D. (2011). Sleep disturbances in children with attention-deficit/hyperactivity disorder. *Expert Review of Neurotherapeutics, 11*, 565–577. doi:10.1586/ern.11.7

Sroufe, A. L. (2005). Attachment and development: A prospective, longitudinal study from birth to adulthood. *Attachment & Human Development, 7*, 349–367. doi:10.1080/14616730500365928

Sroufe, L. A., Carlson, E. A., Levy, A. K., & Egeland, B. (1999). Implications of attachment theory for developmental psychopathology. *Development and Psychopathology, 11*, 1–13. doi:10.1017/S0954579499001923

Sroufe, L. A., Coffino, B., & Carlson, E. A. (2010). Conceptualizing the role of early experience: Lessons from the Minnesota longitudinal study. *Developmental Review, 30*, 36–51. doi:10.1016/j.dr.2009.12.002

St Clair, M. C., Pickles, A., Durkin, K., & Conti-Ramsden, G. (2011). A longitudinal study of behavioral, emotional and social difficulties in individuals with a history of specific language impairment (SLI). *Journal of Communication Disorders, 44*, 186–199. doi:10.1016/j.jcomdis.2010.09.004

St. James-Roberts, I., & Alston, E. (2006). Attention development in 10-month-old infants selected by the WILSTAAR screen for pre-language difficulties. *Journal of Child Psychology and Psychiatry, 47*, 63–68. doi:10.1111/j.1469-7610.2005.01449.x

Stanley, G. C., & Konstantareas, M. M. (2007). Symbolic play in children with autism spectrum disorder. *Journal of Autism and Developmental Disorders, 37*, 1215–1223. doi:10.1007/s10803-006-0263-2

Stanley-Cary, C., Rinehart, N., Tonge, B., White, O., & Fielding, J. (2011). Greater disruption to control of voluntary saccades in autistic disorder than Asperger's Disorder: Evidence for greater cerebellar involvement in autism? *Cerebellum, 10*, 70–80. doi:10.1007/s12311-010-0229-y

Stark, K. D., Hargrave, J., Hersh, B., Greenberg, M., Herren, J., & Fisher, M. (2008). Treatment of childhood depression: The ACTION treatment program. In J. R. Z. Abela & B. L. Hankin (Eds.), *Handbook of depression in children and adolescents* (pp. 224–249). New York: Guilford Press.

Stark, K. D., & Kendall, P. C. (1996). *Treating depressed children: Therapist manual for "Taking ACTION."* Ardmore, PA: Workbook.

Stark, K. D., Sander, J., Hauser, M., Simpson, J., Schnoebelen, S., Glenn, R., & Moiner, J. (2006). Depressive disorders during childhood and adolescence. In E. J. Mash & R. A. Barkley (Eds.), *Treatment of childhood disorders* (3rd ed., pp. 336–407). New York: Guilford Press.

Stark, K. D., Schmidt, K. L., & Joiner, T. E., Jr. (1996). Cognitive triad: Relationship to depressive symptoms, parents' cognitive triad, and perceived parental messages. *Journal of Abnormal Child Psychology, 24*, 615–631. doi:10.1007/BF01670103

Stark, K. D., Streusand, W., Krumholz, L. S., & Patel, P. (2010). Cognitive-behavioral therapy for depression: The ACTION treatment program for girls. In J. R. Weisz & A. E. Kazdin (Eds.), *Evidence-based psychotherapies for children and adolescents* (2nd ed., pp. 93–109). New York: Guilford Press.

Statistics Canada. (2011). *Persons in low income before tax 2009* (No. 75-202-XIE). Ottawa, Ontario, Canada: Author.

Staton, D., Volness, L. J., & Beatty, W. B. (2008). Diagnosis and classification of pediatric bipolar disorder. *Journal of Affective Disorders, 105*, 205–212. doi:10.1016/j.jad.2007.05.015

Steege, M. W., Wacker, D. P., Cigrand, K. C., Berg, W. K., Novak, C. G., . . . & DeRaad, A. (1990). Use of negative reinforcement in the treatment of self-injurious behavior. *Journal of Applied Behavior Analysis*, 23, 459–467.

Stefanatos, G. A., & Baron, I. S. (2011). The ontogenesis of language impairment in autism: A neuropsychological perspective. *Neuropsychological Review, 21*, 252–270. doi:10.1007/s11065-011-9178-6

Stein, D., Williamson, D. E., Birmaher, B., Brent, D. A., Kaufman, J., Dahl, R. E., . . . Ryan, N. D. (2000). Parent-child bonding and family functioning in depressed children and children at high risk and low risk for future depression. *Journal of the American Academy of Child & Adolescent Psychiatry, 39*, 1387–1395. doi:10.1097/00004583-200011000-00013

Stein, M. A., Szumoski, E., Blondis, T. A., & Roizen, N. J. (1995). Adaptive skills dysfunction in ADD and ADHD children. *Journal of Child Psychology and Psychiatry, 36*, 663–670. doi:10.1111/j.1469-7610.1995.tb02320.x

Steinberg, L. (2009). Adolescent development and juvenile justice. *Annual Review of Clinical Psychology, 5*, 459–485. doi:10.1146/annurev.clinpsy.032408.153603

Steinhausen, H. (2009). Outcome of eating disorders. *Child and Adolescent Psychiatric Clinics of North America, 18*,

225–242. doi:10.1016/j.chc.2008.07.013

Steinhausen, H., & Weber, S. (2009). The outcome of bulimia nervosa: Findings from one-quarter century of research. *The American Journal of Psychiatry, 166*, 1331–1341. doi:10.1176/appi.ajp.2009.09040582

Steinhausen, H. C., Grigoroiu-Serbanescu, M., Boyadjieva, S., Neumärker, K. J., & Winkler-Metzke, C. (2008). Course and predictors of rehospitalization in adolescent anorexia nervosa in a multisite study. *International Journal of Eating Disorders, 41*, 29–36. doi:10.1002/eat.20414

Sternberg, E. M., & Gold, P. W. (1997). The mind body interaction in disease. *Scientific American, 7*, 8–15. Retrieved from http://www.scientificamerican.com/

Sternberg, R. J. (2010). The Flynn effect: So what? *Journal of Psychoeducational Assessment, 28*, 434–440. doi:10.1177/0734282910373349

Sternberg, R. J., Grigorenko, E. L., & Kidd, K. K. (2005). Intelligence, race, and genetics. *American Psychologist, 60*, 46–59. doi:10.1037/0003-066X.60.1.46

Stevens, L., Zhang, W., Peck, L., Kuczek, T., Grevstad, N., Mahon, A., . . . Burgess, J. R. (2003). EFA supplementation in children with inattention, hyperactivity, and other disruptive behavior disorders. *Lipids, 38*, 1007–1021. doi:10.1007/s11745-006-1155-0

Stevenson, J. (2010). Recent research on food additives: Implications for CAMH. *Child and Adolescent Mental Health, 15*, 130–133. doi:10.1111/j.1475-3588.2010.00563.x

Stevenson, J., Sonuga-Barke, E., McCann, D., Grimshaw, K., Parker, K. M., Rose-Zerilli, M. J., . . . Warner, J. O. (2010). The role of histamine degradation gene polymorphisms in moderating the effects of food additive on ADHD symptoms. *American Journal of Psychiatry, 167*, 1108–1115. doi:10.1176/appi.ajp.2010.09101529

Stice, E., & Fairburn, C. G. (2003). Dietary and dietary-depressive subtypes of bulimia nervosa show differential symptom presentation, social impairment, comorbidity, and course of illness. *Journal of Consulting and Clinical Psychology, 71*, 1090–1094. doi:10.1037/0022-006X.71.6.1090

Stice, E., Burton, E. M., & Shaw, H. (2004). Prospective relations between bulimic pathology, depression, and substance abuse: Unpacking comorbidity in adolescent girls. *Journal of Consulting and Clinical Psychology, 72*, 62–71. doi:10.1037/0022-006X.72.1.62

Stice, E., Marti, C. N., Shaw, H., & Jaconis, M. (2009). An 8-year longitudinal study of the natural history of threshold, subthreshold, and partial eating disorders from a community sample of adolescents. *Journal of Abnormal Psychology, 118*, 587–597. doi:10.1037/a0016481

Stice, E., Marti, C. N., Spoor, S., Presnell, K., & Shaw, H. (2008). Dissonance and healthy weight eating disorder prevention programs: Long-term effects from a randomized efficacy trial. *Journal of Consulting and Clinical Psychology, 76*, 329–340. doi:10.1037/0022-006X.76.2.329

Stice, E., Rohde, P., Gau, J. M., & Wade, E. (2010). Efficacy trial of a brief cognitive behavioral depression prevention program for high-risk adolescents: Effects at 1- and 2-year follow-up. *Journal of Consulting and Clinical Psychology, 78*, 856–867. doi:10.1037/a0020544

Stice, E., Rohde, P., Shaw, H., & Gau, J. (2011). An effectiveness trial of a selected dissonance-based eating disorder prevention program for female high school students: Long-term effects. *Journal of Consulting and Clinical Psychology, 79*, 500–508. doi:10.1037/a0024351

Stice, E., Shaw, H., Bohon, C., Marti, C. N., & Rohde, P. (2009). A meta-analytic review of depression prevention programs for children and adolescents: Factors that predict magnitude of intervention effects. *Journal of Consulting and Clinical Psychology, 77*, 486–503. doi:10.1037/a0015168

Stigler, K. A., McDonald, B. C., Anand, A., Saykin, A. J., & McDougle, C. J. (2011). Structural and functional magnetic imaging of autism spectrum disorders. *Brain Research, 1380*, 146–161. doi:10.1016/j.brainres.2010.11.076

Stigler, K. A., Sweeten, T. L., Posey, D. J., & McDougle, C. J. (2009). Autism and immune factors: A comprehensive review. *Research in Autism Spectrum Disorders, 3*, 840–860. doi:10.1016/j.rasd.2009.01.007

Stith, S. M., Liu, T., Davies, L. C., Boykin, E. L., Alder, M. C., Harris, J. M., . . . Dees, J. E. M. E. G. (2009). Risk factors in child maltreatment: A meta-analytic review of the literature. *Aggression and Violent Behavior, 14*(1),13–29. doi:10.1016/j.avb.2006.03.006

Stoltenborgh, M., van IJzendoorn, M. H., Euser, E. M., & Bakermans-Kranenburg, M. (2011). A global perspective on child sexual abuse: Meta-analysis of prevalence around the world. *Child Maltreatment, 16*, 79–101. doi:10.1177/1077559511403920

Stone, L. B., Hankin, B. L., Gibb, B. E., & Abela, J. R. Z. (2011). Co-rumination predicts the onset of depressive disorders during adolescence. *Journal of Abnormal Psychology, 120*, 752–757. doi:10.1037/a0023384

Stoppelbein, L., & Greening, L. (2007). Brief report: The risk of posttraumatic stress disorder in mothers of children diagnosed with pediatric cancer and type I diabetes. *Journal of Pediatric Psychology, 32*, 223–229. doi:10.1093/jpepsy/jsj120

Straus, M. (2001). Beating the devil out of them: Corporal punishment in American families and its effects on children. New Brunswick, NJ: Transaction.

Straus, M. A., & Gelles, R. J. (1986). Societal change and change in family violence from 1975 to 1985 as revealed by two national surveys. *Journal of Marriage and the Family, 48*, 465–479.

Straus, M. A., Gelles, R. J., & Steinmetz, S.K. (2003). The marriage license as a hitting license. In: M. Silberman (Ed.), *Violence and society: A reader* (pp. 125–135). Upper Saddle River, NJ: Prentice Hall.

Straus, M. A., & Stewart, J. H. (1999). Corporal punishment by American parents: National data on prevalence, chronicity, severity, and duration, in relation to child and family characteristics. *Clinical Child and Family Psychology Review, 2*, 55–70.

Strauss, A. A., & Lehtinen, L. E. (1947). *Psychopathology and education of the brain-injured child*. New York: Grune & Stratton.

Strauss, A. A., & Werner, H. (1943). Comparative psychopathology of the brain-injured child and the traumatic brain-injured adult. *American Journal of Psychiatry, 99*, 835–838. doi:10.1176/appi.ajp.99.6.835

Strauss, C. C., Lease, C. A., Last, C. G., & Francis, G. (1988). Overanxious disorder: An examination of developmental differences. *Journal of Abnormal Child Psychology, 16*, 433–443. doi:10.1007/BF00914173

Streissguth, A. (2007). Offspring effects of prenatal alcohol exposure from birth to 25 years: The Seattle prospective longitudinal study. *Journal of Clinical Psychology in Medical Settings, 14*, 81–101. doi:10.1007/s10880-007-9067-6

Striegel-Moore, R. H., & Bulik, C. M. (2007). Risk factors for eating disorders. *American Psychologist, 62*, 181–198. doi:10.1037/0003-066X.62.3.181

Striegel-Moore, R. H., Franko, D. L., Thompson, D., Barton, B., Schreiber, G. B., & Daniels, S. R. (2005). An empirical study of the typology of bulimia nervosa and its spectrum variants. *Psychological Medicine, 35*, 1563–1572. doi:10.1017/S0033291705006057

Striegel-Moore, R. H., Leslie, D., Petrill, S. A., Garvin, V., & Rosenheck, R. A. (2000). One-year use and cost of inpatient and outpatient services among female and male patients with an eating disorder: Evidence from a national database of health insurance claims. *International Journal of Eating Disorders, 27*, 381–389. doi:10.1002/(SICI)1098-108X(200005)27:4<381::AID-EAT2>3.0.CO;2-U

Stright, A. D., Gallagher, K. C., & Kelley, K. (2008). Infant temperament moderates relations between maternal parenting in early childhood and children's adjustment in first grade. *Child Development, 79*, 186–200. doi:10.1111/j.1467-8624.2007.01119.x

Stringaris, A. (2011). Irritability in children and adolescents: A challenge for DSM-5. *European Child and Adolescent Psychiatry, 20*, 61–66. doi:10.1007/s00787-010-0150-4

Stringaris, A., Cohen, P., Pine, D. S., & Leibenluft, E. (2009). Adult outcomes of youth irritability: A 20-year prospective community-based study. *American Journal of Psychiatry, 166*, 1048–1054. doi:10.1176/appi.ajp.2009.08121849

Stringaris, A., & Goodman, R. (2009). Longitudinal outcome of youth oppositionality: Irritable, headstrong, and hurtful behaviors have distinctive predictions. *Journal of the American Academy of Child & Adolescent Psychiatry, 48*, 404–412. doi:10.1097/CHI.0b013e3181984f30

Stringaris, A., Maughan, B., & Goodman, R. (2010). Oppositional defiant disorder:

Findings from the Avon Longitudinal Study. *Journal of the American Academy of Child & Adolescent Psychiatry, 49*, 474–483. doi:10.1016/j.jaac.2010.01.021

Stringaris, A., Santosh, P., Leibenluft, E., & Goodman, R. (2010). Youth meeting symptom and impairment criteria for manic-like episodes lasting less than four days: An epidemiological enquiry. *Journal of Child Psychology and Psychiatry, 51*, 31–38. doi:10.1111/j.1469-7610.2009.02129.x

Stringhini, S., Sabia, S., Shipley, M., Brunner, E., Nabi, H., Kivimaki, M., & Singh-Manoux, A. (2010). Association of socioeconomic position with health behaviors and mortality. *JAMA: Journal of the American Medical Association, 303*, 1159–1166. doi:10.1001/jama.2010.297

Strober, M., Freeman, R., Lampert, C., Diamond, J., & Kaye, W. (2000). Controlled family study of anorexia nervosa and bulimia nervosa: Evidence of shared liability and transmission of partial syndromes. *American Journal of Psychiatry, 157*, 393–401. doi:10.1176/appi.ajp.157.3.393

Strober, M., Schmidt-Lackner, S., Freeman, R., Bower, S., Lampert, C., & DeAntonio, M. (1995). Recovery and relapse in adolescents with bipolar affective illness: A five-year naturalistic, prospective follow-up. *Journal of the American Academy of Child & Adolescent Psychiatry, 34*, 724–731. doi:10.1097/00004583-199506000-00012

Stroud, C. B., Davila, J., Hammen, C., & Vrshek-Shallhorn, S. (2011). Severe and nonsevere events in first onsets versus recurrences of depression: Evidence for stress sensitization. *Journal of Abnormal Psychology, 120*, 142–154. doi:10.1037/a0021659

Stuber, M. L., Meeske, K. A., Leisenring, W., Stratton, K., Zeltzer, L. K., Dawson, K., . . . Krull, K. R. (2011). Defining medical posttraumatic stress among young adult survivors in the childhood cancer survivor study. *General Hospital Psychiatry, 33*, 347–353. doi:10.1016/j.genhosppsych.2011.03.015

Stuber, M. L., & Shemesh, E. (2006). Post-traumatic stress response to life-threatening illnesses in children and their parents. *Child and Adolescent Psychiatric Clinics of North America, 15*, 597–609. doi:10.1016/j.chc.2006.02.006

Su, M. S., Li, A. M., So, H. K., Au, C. T., Ho, C., & Wing, Y. K. (2011). Nocturnal enuresis in children: Prevalence, correlates, and relationship with obstructive sleep apnea. *The Journal of Pediatrics, 159*, 238–242. doi:10.1016/j.jpeds.2011.01.03

Substance Abuse and Mental Health Services Administration (SAMHSA). (2003). *Results from the 2002 National Survey on Drug Use and Health: National findings* (Office of Applied Studies, NHSDA Series H-22, DHHS Publication No. SMA 03–3836). Rockville, MD: Author.

Substance Abuse and Mental Health Services Administration (SAMHSA; 2011). *Leading Change: A Plan for SAMHSA's Roles and Actions 2011–2014*. HHS Publication No. (SMA) 11-4629. Rockv'lle, MD: Author.

Sugden, K., Arseneault, L., Harrington, H., Moffitt, T. E., Williams, B., & Caspi, A. (2010). Serotonin transporter gene moderates the development of emotional problems among children following bullying victimization. *Journal of the American Academy of Child & Adolescent Psychiatry, 49*, 830–840. doi:10.1016/i.jacc.2010.01.024

Sullivan, P. M., & Knutson, J. F. (2000). Maltreatment and disabilities: A population-based epidemiological study. *Child Abuse and Neglect, 24*, 1257–1273.

Sund, A. M., Larrson, B., & Wichstrom, L. (2003). Psychosocial correlates of depressive symptoms among 12–14-year-old Norwegian adolescents. *Journal of Child Psychology and Psychiatry, 44*, 588–597. doi:10.1111/1469-7610.00147

Suveg, C., Roblek, T. L., Robin, J., Krain, A., Aschenbrand, S., & Ginsburg, G. S. (2006). Parental involvement when conducting cognitive-behavioral therapy for children with anxiety disorders. *Journal of Cognitive Psychotherapy, 20*, 287–299. doi:10.1891/088983906780644019

Suzuki, D. (1994, October 6). *The nature of things with David Suzuki: Easy targets*. Ottawa: Canadian Broadcasting Corporation.

Swackhamer, K. (1993). Believer. *JAMA: Journal of the American Medical Association, 270*, 312. doi:10.1001/jama.1993.03510030036015

Swahn, M. H., Bossarte, R. M., & Sullivent, E. E. (2008). Age of alcohol use initiation, suicidal behavior, and peer and dating violence victimization and perpetration among high-risk, seventh-grade adolescents. *Pediatrics, 121*, 297–305. doi:10.1542/peds.2006-2348

Swanson, H. L., Zheng, X., & Jerman, O. (2009). Working memory, short-term memory, and reading disabilities: A selective meta-analysis of the literature. *Journal of Learning Disabilities, 42*, 260–287. doi:10.1177/0022219409331958

Swanson, J. M., Kraemer, H. C., Hinshaw, S. P., Arnold, L. E., Conners, C. K., Abikoff, H. B., . . . Wu, M. (2001). Clinical relevance of the primary findings of the MTA: Success rates based on severity of ADHD and ODD symptoms at the end of treatment. *Journal of the American Academy of Child & Adolescent Psychiatry, 40*, 168–179. doi:10.1097/00004583-200102000-00011

Swanson, J. M., McBurnett, K., Christian, D. L., & Wigal, T. (1995). Stimulant medications and the treatment of children with ADHD. *Advances in Clinical Child Psychology, 17*, 265–322.

Swanson, J. M., & Volkow, N. D. (2009). Psychopharmacology: Concepts and opinions about the use of stimulant medications. *Journal of Child Psychology and Psychiatry, 50*, 180–193. doi:10.1111/j.1469-7610.2008.02062.x

Swanson, S. A., Crow, S. J., Le Grange, D., Swendsen, J., & Merikangas, K. R. (2011). Prevalence and correlates of eating disorders in adolescents: Results from the national comorbidity survey replication adolescent supplement. *Archives of General Psychiatry, 68*, 714–723. doi:10.1001/archgenpsychiatry.2011.22

Sweeney, G. M. (2007). Why childhood attachment matters: Implications for personal happiness, families, and public policy. In A. S. Loveless & T. B. Holman (Eds.), *The family in the new millennium: World voices supporting the "natural" clan: Vol. 1. The place of family in human society* (pp. 332–346). Westport, CT: Praeger/Greenwood.

Swinburn, B. A., Sacks, G., Hall, K. D., McPherson, K., Finegood, D. T., Moodie, M. L., & Gortmaker, S. L. (2011). Obesity 1: The global obesity pandemic: Shaped by global drivers and local environments. *The Lancet, 378*, 804–814. doi:10.1016/S0140-6736(11)60813-1

Swinkels, S. H. N., Dietz, C., Van Daalen, E., Kerkhof, I., Van Engeland, H., & Buitelaar, J. K. (2006). Screening for autism spectrum disorders in children aged 14–15 months. 1. The development of the early screening for autistic traits questionnaire. *Journal of Autism and Developmental Disorders, 36*, 723–732. doi:10.1007/s10803-006-0115-0

Szasz, T. S. (1970). *The manufacture of madness*. New York: Dell.

Szatmari, P. (2011). Editorial: Is autism, at least in part, a disorder in fetal programming? *Archives of General Psychiatry, 68*, 1091–1092. doi:10.1001/archgenpsychiatry.2011.99

Szatmari, P., Offord, D. R., & Boyle, M. H. (1989). Correlates, associated impairments, and patterns of service utilization of children with attention deficit disorders: Findings from the Ontario Child Health Study. *Journal of Child Psychology and Psychiatry, 30*, 205–217. doi:10.1111/j.1469-7610.1989.tb00235.x

Szobot, C. M., & Bukstein, O. (2008). Attention deficit hyperactivity disorder and substance use disorders. *Child and Adolescent Psychiatric Clinics of North America, 17*, 309–323. doi:10.1176/appi.ajp.163.12.2059

TADS Team (2009). The treatment for adolescents with depression study (TADS): Outcomes over one year of naturalistic follow-up. *American Journal of Psychiatry, 166*, 1141–1149. doi:10.1176/appi.ajp.2009.08111620

Tager-Flusberg, H. (1993). What language reveals about the understanding of minds in children with autism. In S. Baron-Cohen, H. Tager-Flusberg, & D. J. Cohen (Eds.), *Understanding other minds: Perspectives from autism* (pp. 138–157). Oxford, England: Oxford University Press.

Tager-Flusberg, H. (2007). Evaluating the theory-of-mind hypothesis of autism. *Current Directions in Psychological Science, 16*, 311–315. doi:10.1111/j.1467-8721.2007.00527.x

Tager-Flusberg, H., Paul, R., & Lord, C. (2005). Language and communication in autism. In F. R. Volkmar, R. Paul, A. Klin, & D. Cohen (Eds.), *Handbook of autism and pervasive developmental disorders: Vol. 1. Diagnosis, development, neurobiology, and behavior* (3rd ed., pp. 335–364). Hoboken, NJ: Wiley.

Talbot, L. S., McGlinchey, E. L., Kaplan, K. A., Dahl, R. E., & Harvey, A. G. (2010). Sleep deprivation in adolescents and adults: Changes in affect. *Emotion, 10*, 831–841. doi:10.1037/a0020138

Tallal, P. (2003). Language learning disabilities: Integrating research approaches. *Current Directions in Psychological Science, 12*, 206–211. doi:10.1046/j.0963-7214.2003.01263.x

Tallal, P., & Benasich, A. A. (2002). Developmental language learning impairments. *Development and Psychopathology, 14*, 559–579. doi:10.1017/S0954579402003097

Tanguay, P. E. (2000). Pervasive developmental disorders: A 10-year review. *Journal of the American Academy of Child & Adolescent Psychiatry, 39*, 1079–1095. doi:10.1097/00004583-200009000-00007

Tannock, R. (2000). Language, reading, and motor control problems in ADHD: A potential behavioral phenotype. In L. L. Greenhill (Ed.), *Learning disabilities: Implications for psychiatric treatment* (pp. 129–167). Washington, DC: American Psychiatric Press.

Tannock, R., Fine, J., Heintz, T., & Schachar, R. J. A. (1995). A linguistic approach detects stimulant effects in two children with attention-deficit hyperactivity disorder. *Journal of Child and Adolescent Psychopharmacology, 5*, 177–189. doi:10.1089/cap.1995.5.177

Tanofsky-Kraff, M., Yanovski, S. Z., Wilfley, D. E., Marmarosh, C., Morgan, C. M., & Yanovski, J. A. (2004). Eating-disordered behaviors, body fat, and psychopathology in overweight and normal-weight children. *Journal of Consulting and Clinical Psychology, 72*, 53–61. doi:10.1037/0022-006X.72.1.53

Tapscott, M., Frick, P. J., Wootton, J., & Kruh, I. (1996). The intergenerational link to antisocial behavior: Effects of paternal contact. *Journal of Child and Family Studies, 5*, 229–240. doi:10.1007/BF02237945

Tarullo, A. R., Obradovic, J., & Gunnar, M. R. (2009). Self-control and the developing brain. *Zero to Three, 29*, 31–37. doi:10.1016/j.dr.2009.12.002

Tate, D. C., Reppucci, N. D., & Mulvey, E. P. (1995). Violent juvenile delinquents: Treatment effectiveness and implications for action. *American Psychologist, 50*, 777–781. doi:10.1037/0003-066X.50.9.777

Taylor, E. (1995). Dysfunctions of attention. In D. Cicchetti & D. J. Cohen (Eds.), *Developmental psychopathology: Risk disorder, and adaptation* (Vol. 2, pp. 243–273). New York: Wiley.

Taylor, E. (2009). Developing ADHD. *Journal of Child Psychology and Psychiatry, 50*. 126–132. doi:10.1111/j.1469-7610.2008.01999.x

Taylor, E. (2011). Commentary: Reading and attention problems—how are they connected? Reflection on reading McGrath et al. (2011). *Journal of Child Psychology and Psychiatry, 52*, 558–559. doi:10.1111/j.1469-7610.2011.02403.x

Taylor, E. (2011). How to classify? *Journal of the American Academy of Child & Adolescent Psychiatry, 50*, 3–5. doi:10.1016/j.jaac.2010.06.017

Taylor, L., Oliver, C., & Murphy, G. (2011). The chronicity of self-injurious behaviour: A long-term follow-up of a total population study. *Journal of Applied Research in Intellectual Disabilities, 24*, 105–117. doi:10.1111/j.1468-3148.2010.00579.x

Taylor, S., & Jang, K. L. (2011). Biopsychosocial etiology of obsessions and compulsions: An integrated behavioral-genetic and cognitive behavioral analysis. *Journal of Abnormal Psychology, 120*, 174–186. doi:10.1037/a0021403

Taylor, S., Jang, K. L., & Asmundson, G. J. G. (2010). Etiology of obsessions and compulsions: A behavioral-genetic analysis. *Journal of Abnormal Psychology, 119*, 672–682. doi:10.1037/a0021132

Taylor, S. E., Way, B. M., & Seeman, T. E. (2011). Early adversity and health outcomes. *Development and Psychopathology, 23*, 939–954. doi:10.1017/S0954579411000411

Teachman, B. A., & Allen, J. P. (2007). Development of social anxiety: Social interaction predictors of implicit and explicit fear of negative evaluation. *Journal of Abnormal Child Psychology, 35*, 63–78. doi:10.1007/s10802-006-9084-1

Teicher, M. H., Ito, Y., Glod, C. A., & Barber, N. I. (1996). Objective measurement of hyperactivity and attentional problems in ADHD. *Journal of the American Academy of Child & Adolescent Psychiatry, 35*, 334–342. doi:10.1097/00004583-199603000-00015

Teisl, M., & Cicchetti, D. (2008). Physical abuse, cognitive and emotional processes, and aggressive/disruptive behavior problems. *Social Development, 17*, 1–23.

Temple, J. L., Giacomelli, A. M., Roemmich, J. N., & Epstein, L. H. (2008). Dietary variety impairs habituation in children. *Health Psychology, 27*(1, Suppl), S10–S19. doi:10.1037/0278-6133.27.1.S10

Tewksbury, R. (2007). Effects of sexual assaults on men: Physical, mental and sexual consequences. *International Journal of Men's Health, 6*, 22–35.

Thapar, A., Rice, F., Hay, D., Boivin, J., Langley, K., van den Bree, M., . . . Harold, G. (2009). Prenatal smoking might not cause attention-deficit/hyperactivity disorder: Evidence from a novel design. *Biological Psychiatry, 66*, 722–727. doi:10.1016/j.biopsych.2009.05.032

Thapar, A., van den Bree, M., Fowler, T., Langley, K., & Whittinger, N. (2006). Predictors of antisocial behaviour in children with attention-deficit/hyperactivity disorder. *European Child & Adolescent Psychiatry, 15*, 118–125. doi:10.1007/s00787-006-0511-1

The Editors of The Lancet (February, 2010). Retraction—Ileal-lymphoid-nodular hyperplasia, non-specific colitis, and pervasive developmental disorder in children. *Lancet, 375*, 445. doi:10.1016/S0140-6736(10)60175-4

Theodora, M. F., Talebizadeh, Z., & Butler, M. G. (2006). Body composition and fatness patterns in Prader-Willi syndrome: Comparison with simple obesity. *Obesity, 14*, 1685–1690. doi:10.1038/oby.2006.193

Time. (1994, July 18). "Hail to the Hyperactive Hunter."

Thomas, A., & Chess, S. (1977). *Temperament and development*. New York: Brunner/Mazel.

Thomas, R., & Zimmer-Gembeck, M. J. (2011). Accumulating evidence for parent–child interaction therapy in the prevention of child maltreatment. *Child Development, 82*, 177–192. doi:10.1111/j.1467–8624.2010.01548.x

Thompson, C. L., & Reid, A. (2002). Behavioural symptoms among people with severe and profound intellectual disabilities: A 26-year follow-up study. *British Journal of Psychiatry, 181*, 67–71. doi:10.1192/bjp.181.1.67

Thompson, M. P., & Light, L. S. (2010). Examining gender differences in risk factors for suicide attempts made 1 and 7 years later in a nationally representative sample. *Journal of Adolescent Health, 48*, 391–397. doi:10.1016/j.jadohealth.2010.07.018

Thompson, M. P., Sims, L., Kingree, J. B., & Windle, M. (2008). Longitudinal associations between problem alcohol use and violent victimization in a national sample of adolescents. *Journal of Adolescent Health, 42*, 21–27. doi:10.1016/j.jadohealth.2007.07.003

Thompson, R. A., & Meyer, S. (2007). *Socialization of emotion regulation in the family*. New York: Guilford Press.

Thompson, R. J., Jr., & Gustafson, K. E. (1996). *Adaptation to chronic childhood illness*. Washington, DC: American Psychological Association.

Thompson, R. J., Jr., Gustafson, K. E., George, L. K., & Spock, A. (1994). Change over a 12-month period in the psychological adjustment of children and adolescents with cystic fibrosis. *Journal of Pediatric Psychology, 19*, 189–203. doi:10.1093/jpepsy/19.2.189

Thompson, S. H., Rafiroiu, A. C., & Sargent, R. G. (2003). Examining gender, racial, and age differences in weight concern among third, fifth, eighth, and eleventh graders. *Eating Behaviors, 3*, 307–323. doi:10.1016/S1471-0153(02)00093-4

Thompson-Brenner, H., Eddy, K. T., Satir, D. A., Boisseau, C. L., & Westen, D. (2008). Personality subtypes in adolescents with eating disorders: Validation of a classification approach. *Journal of Child Psychology and Psychiatry, 49*, 170–180. doi:10.1111/j.1469-7610.2007.01825.x

Tiffin, P. A. (2007). Managing psychotic illness in young people: A practical overview. *Child and Adolescent Mental Health, 12*, 173–186. doi:10.1111/j.1475-3588.2006.00418.x

Tissot, A. M., & Crowther, J. H. (2008). Self-oriented and socially prescribed perfectionism: Risk factors within an integrative model for bulimic symptomatology. *Journal of Social and Clinical Psychology, 27*, 734–755. doi:10.1521/jscp.2008.27.7.734

Tolan, P. H., Gorman-Smith, D., & Henry, D. B. (2003). The developmental ecology of urban males' youth violence. *Developmental Psychology, 39*, 274–291. doi:10.1037/0012-1649.39.2.274

Tomlinson, D., Wilkinson, H., & Wilkinson, P. (2009). Diet and mental health in children. *Child and Adolescent Mental Health, 14*, 148–155. doi:10.1111/j.1475-3588.2008.00520.x

Torgesen, J. K., Wagner, R. K., Rashotte, C. A., Herron, J., & Lindamood, P. (2010). Computer-assisted instruction to prevent early reading difficulties in students at risk for dyslexia: Outcomes from two instructional approaches. *Annals of Dyslexia, 60*, 40–56. doi:10.1007/s11881-009-0032-y

Torr, J., Strydom, A., Patti, P., & Jokinen, N. (2010). Aging in Down syndrome: Morbidity and mortality. *Journal of Policy and Practice in Intellectual Disabilities, 7*, 70–81. doi:10.1111/j.1741-1130.2010.00249.x

Toth, K., & King, B. H. (2010). *Intellectual disability (mental retardation)*. Arlington, VA: American Psychiatric Publishing, Inc.

Toth, S. L., & Cicchetti, D. (1996). Patterns of relatedness, depressive symptomatology, and perceived competence in maltreated children. *Journal of Consulting and Clinical Psychology*, *64*, 32–41. doi:10.1037/0012-1649.35.1.269

Touyz, S. W., Polivy, J., & Hay, P. (2008). Eating disorders. In D. Wedding (Series Ed.), *Advances in psychotherapy: Evidence-based practice (Vol. 13)*. Cambridge, MA: Hogrefe & Huber.

Trask, E. V., Walsh, K., & DiLillo, D. (2011). Treatment effects for common outcomes of child sexual abuse: A current meta-analysis. *Aggression and Violent Behavior, 16*(1), 6–19. doi:10.1016/j.avb.2010.10.001

Treasure, J., Claudino, A. M., & Zucker, N. (2010). Eating disorders. *The Lancet, 375*, 583–593. doi:10.1016/S0140-6736(09)61748-7

Treatment for Adolescents with Depression Study (TADS) Team. (2004). Fluoxetine, cognitive behavioral therapy, and their combination for adolescents with depression: Treatment for Adolescents with Depression Study (TADS) randomized controlled trial. *JAMA: Journal of the American Medical Association, 292*, 807–820. doi:10.1001/jama.292.7.807

Treatment for Adolescents with Depression Study (TADS) Team. (2007). The Treatment for Adolescents with Depression Study (TADS): Long-term effectiveness and safety outcomes. *Archives of General Psychiatry*, *64,* 1132–1144. doi:10.1001/archpsyc.64.10.1132

Treffers, P. D. A., & Silverman, W. K. (2001). Anxiety and its disorders in children and adolescents before the twentieth century. In W. K. Silverman & P. D. A. Treffers (Eds.), *Anxiety disorders in children and adolescents: Research, assessment, and intervention* (pp. 1–22). New York: Cambridge University Press.

Tremblay, R. E. (2000). The development of aggressive behaviour during childhood: What have we learned in the past century? *International Journal of Behavioral Development, 24*, 129–141. doi:10.1080/016502500383232

Tremblay, R. E. (2003). Why socialization fails: The case of chronic physical aggression. In B. B. Lahey, T. E. Moffitt, & A. Caspi (Eds.), *Causes of conduct disorder and juvenile delinquency* (pp. 182–226). New York: Guilford Press.

Trentacosta, C. J., & Shaw, D. S. (2008). Maternal predictors of rejecting parenting and early antisocial behavior. *Journal of Abnormal Child Psychology, 36*, 247–259. doi:10.1007/s10802-007-9174-8

Treuting, J. J., & Hinshaw, S. P. (2001). Depression and self-esteem in boys with attention-deficit/hyperactivity disorder: Associations with comorbid aggression and explanatory attributional mechanisms. *Journal of Abnormal Child Psychology, 29*, 23–39. doi:10.1023/A:1005247412221

Trickett, P. K., Negriff, S., Ji, J., & Peckins, M. (2011). Child maltreatment and adolescent development. *Journal of Research on Adolescence, 21*, 3–20. doi:10.1111/j.1532–7795.2010.00711.x

Trickett, P. K., Noll, J. G., & Putnam, F. W. (2011). The impact of sexual abuse on female development: Lessons from a multigenerational, longitudinal research study. *Development and Psychopathology, 23*, 453–476. doi:10.1017/S0954579411000174

Tully, E. C., & Goodman, S. H. (2007). Early developmental processes inform the study of mental disorders. In S. O. Lilienfeld & W. T. O'Donohue (Eds.), *The great ideas of clinical science: 17 principles that every mental health professional should understand* (pp. 313–328). New York: Routledge/Taylor & Francis.

Turk, J., & Graham, P. (1997). Fragile X syndrome, autism and autistic features. *Autism, 1*, 175–197. doi:10.1177/1362361397012005

Turkheimer, E., Haley, A., Waldron, M., D'Onofrio, B., & Gottesman, I. I. (2003). Socioeconomic status modifies heritability of IQ in young children. *Psychological Science, 14*, 623–628. doi:10.1046/j.0956-7976.2003.psci_1475.x

Turner, H. A., Finkelhor, D., & Ormrod, R. (2010). Poly-victimization in a national sample of children and youth. *American Journal of Preventive Medicine, 38*, 323–330. doi:10.1016/j.amepre.2009.11.012

Turner, M. (1999). Repetitive behaviour in autism: A review of psychological research. *Journal of Child Psychology and Psychiatry, 40*, 839–849. doi:10.1111/1469-7610.00502

Twisk, M., Haadsma, M., van der Veen, F., Repping, S., Mastenbroek, S., Heineman, M., . . . Korevaar, J. C. (2007). Preimplantation genetic screening as an alternative to prenatal testing for Down syndrome: Preferences of women undergoing in vitro fertilization/intracytoplasmic sperm injection treatment. *Fertility and Sterility, 88*, 804–810. doi:10.1016/j.fertnstert.2006.12.033

Tyrer, F., Smith, L. K., & McGrother, C. W. (2007). Mortality in adults with moderate to profound intellectual disability: A population-based study. *Journal of Intellectual Disability Research, 51*, 520–527. doi:10.1111/j.1365-2788.2006.00918.x

Tyrka, A. R., Waldron, I., Graber, J. A., & Brooks-Gunn, J. (2003). Prospective predictors of the onset of anorexic and bulimic syndromes. *International Journal of Eating Disorders, 32*, 282–290. doi:10.1002/eat.10094

U.N. Convention on the Rights of the Child. (1989). *UN General Assembly Document* A/RES/44/25. Retrieved June 24, 2011, from http://www.un.org/documents/ga/res/44/a44r025.htm

U.S. Census Bureau (2011a). *Small area income and poverty estimates: Estimates for the United States, 2009*. Retrieved June 24, 2011 from http://www.census.gov/cgi-bin/saipe/national.cgi#SA51

U.S. Census Bureau (2011b). *Population: An Older and More Diverse Nation by Midcentury.* Retrieved June 24, 2011, from http://www.census.gov/newsroom/releases/archives/population/cb08-123.html

U.S. Conference of Catholic Bishops. (2004). http://edition.cnn.com/2004/US/02/16/church.abuse/. Tuesday, February 17, 2004 Posted: 1354 GMT (9:54 PM HKT).

U.S. Department of Health and Human Services (2001). *Youth violence: A report of the Surgeon General*. Washington, DC: Author.

U.S. Department of Health and Human Services, Administration for Children and Families, Administration on Children, Youth and Families, Children's Bureau. (2010). *Child Maltreatment 2009*. Retrieved June 24, 2011, from http://www.acf.hhs.gov/programs/cb/stats_research/index.htm#can

U. S. Department of Health and Human Services, Administration on Children, Youth, and Families [USDHHS]. (2010). *Child Maltreatment 2009*. Washington, DC: U. S. Government Printing Office. Available: http://www.acf.hhs.gov/programs/cb/pubs/cm09/index.htm.

U.S. Department of Health and Human Services. (2011). *Your guide to healthy sleep* (NIH Publication No. 11-5271). Retrieved from http://www.nhlbi.nih.gov/health/public/sleep/healthy_sleep.htm

U. S. Dept. of Special Education Programs (2010). *Individuals with Disabilities Education Act Data. Part B Child Count* (2010). Retrieved from https://www.ideadata.org/arc_toc12.asp#partbCC

Umbarger, G. T., III. (2007). State of the evidence regarding complementary and alternative medical treatments for autism spectrum disorders. *Education and Training in Developmental Disabilities, 42*, 437–447. Retrieved from http://www.dddcec.org/publications.htm#ETDD

Ungar, M. (2010). What is resilience across cultures and contexts? Advances to the theory of positive development among individuals and families under stress. *Journal of Family Psychotherapy, 21*, 1–16. doi:10.1080/08975351003618494

United Nations Secretary-General's Study on Violence against Children [United Nations] (2006). *World Report on Violence against Children.* Geneva: Author. Available: http://www.violencestudy.org/a553. Accessed May 1, 2008.

United States Government Accountability Office (2011). *Child maltreatment: strengthening national data on child fatalities could aid in prevention* (GAO-11–599). Retrieved from http://www.gao.gov/new.items/d11599.pdf

Valentino, K., Cicchetti, D., Rogosch, F. A., & Toth, S. L. (2008). True and false recall and dissociation among maltreated children: The role of self-schema. *Development and Psychopathology, 20*, 213–232.

Valera, E. M., Faraone, S. V., Murray, K. E., & Seidman, L. J. (2007). Meta-analysis of structural imaging findings in attention-deficit/hyperactivity disorder. *Biological Psychiatry, 61*, 1361–1369. doi:10.1016/j.biopsych.2006.06.011

Valo, S., & Tannock, R. (2010). Diagnostic instability of DSM-IV ADHD subtypes: Effects of informant source, instrumentation, and methods for combining symptom reports. *Journal of Clinical Child and Adolescent Psychology, 39*, 749–760. doi:10.1080/15374416.2010.517172.

Van Ameringen, M., Mancini, C., & Farvolden, P. (2003). The impact of anxiety disorders on educational achievement. *Journal of Anxiety Disorders, 17*, 561–571. doi:10.1016/S0887-6185(02)00228-1

Van Cleave, J., Gortmaker, S. L., & Perrin, J. M. (2010). Dynamics of obesity and chronic health conditions among children and youth. *JAMA: Journal of the American Medical Association, 303*, 623–630. doi:10.1001/jama.2010.104

van Daal, J., Verhoeven, L., & van Balkom, H. (2007). Behaviour problems in children with language impairment. *Journal of Child Psychology and Psychiatry, 48*, 1139–1147. doi:10.1111/j.1469-7610.2007.01790.x

van der Kolk, B. A. (2007). *The developmental impact of childhood trauma*. In L. J. Kirmayer, R. Lemelson, & M. Barad (Eds.). *Understanding trauma: Integrating biological, clinical, and cultural perspectives* (pp. 224–241). New York: Cambridge University Press.

van der Schuit, M., Segers, E., van Balkom, H., & Verhoeven, L. (2011). Early language intervention for children with intellectual disabilities: A neurocognitive perspective. *Research in Developmental Disabilities, 32*, 705–712. doi:10.1016/j.ridd.2010.11.010

van der Vegt, E. J. M, van der Ende, J., Huizink, A. C., Verhulst, F. C., & Tiemeier, H. (2010). Childhood adversity modifies the relationship between anxiety disorders and cortisol secretion. *Biological Psychiatry, 68*, 1048–1054. doi:10.1016/j.biopsych.2010.07.027

van Geijlswijk, I. M., Korzilius, H. P. L. M., & Smits, M. G. (2010). The use of exogenous melatonin in delayed sleep phase disorder: A meta-analysis. *Sleep: Journal of Sleep and Sleep Disorders Research, 33*, 1605–1614.

van Goozen, S. H. M., Fairchild, G., Snoek, H., & Harold, G. T. (2007). The evidence for a neurobiological model of childhood antisocial behavior. *Psychological Bulletin, 133*, 149–182. doi:10.1037/0033-2909.133.1.149

Van Hoecke, E., De Fruyt, F., De Clercq, B., Hoebeke, P., & Walle, J. V. (2006). Internalizing and externalizing problem behavior in children with nocturnal and diurnal enuresis: A five-factor model perspective. *Journal of Pediatric Psychology, 31*, 460–468. doi:10.1093/jpepsy/jsj037

Van Houten, R., Axelrod, S., Bailey, J. S., Favell, J. E., Foxx, R. M., Iwata, B. A., & Lovaas, O. I. (1988). The right to effective behavioral treatment. *The Behavior Analyst, 11*, 111–114. doi:10.1901/jaba.1988.21-381

Van IJzendoorn, M. H., & Juffer, F. (2005). Adoption is a successful natural intervention enhancing adopted children's IQ and school performance. *Current Directions in Psychological Science, 14*, 326–330. doi:10.1111/j.0963-7214.2005.00391.x

van Ijzendoorn, M. H., Schuengel, C., & Bakermans-Kranenburg, M. J. (1999). Disorganized attachment in early childhood: Meta-analysis of precursors, concomitants, and sequelae. *Development and Psychopathology, 11*, 225–249. doi:10.1017/S0954579499002035

Van Lieshout, R. J., & Boylan, K. (2010). Increased depressive symptoms in female but not male adolescents born a low birth weight in the offspring of a national cohort. *Canadian Journal of Psychiatry, 55*, 422–430. Retrieved from http://publications.cpa-apc.org/browse/sections/0

van Tilburg, Miranda A. L., Runyan, D. K., Zolotor, A. J., Graham, J. C., Dubowitz, H., Litrownik, A. J., . . . Whitehead, W. E. (2010). Unexplained gastrointestinal symptoms after abuse in a prospective study of children at risk for abuse and neglect. *Annals of Family Medicine, 8*(2), 134–140. doi:10.1370/afm.1053

Van Voorhees, B. W., Fogel, J., Reinecke, M. A., Gladstone, T., Stuart, S., Gollan, J., . . . Bell, C. (2009). Randomized clinical trial of an Internet-based depression prevention program for adolescents: 12-week outcomes. *Journal of Developmental and Behavioral Pediatrics, 30*, 23–27. doi:10.1097/DBP.0b013e3181966c2a

Vaness, C., Prior, M. R., Bavin, E., Eadie, P., Cini, E., & Reilly, S. (2011, July). Early indicators of autism spectrum disorders at 12 and 24 months of age: A prospective, longitudinal comparative study. *Autism*. Advance online publication. doi:10.1177/1362361311399936

Varnhagen, C. (2006). Children and the Internet. In J. Gackenbach (Ed.), *Psychology and the Internet: Intrapersonal, interpersonal, and transpersonal implications* (2nd ed., pp. 37–54). New York: Elsevier.

Vaughn, B. E., Contreras, J., & Seifer, R. (1994). Short-term longitudinal study of maternal ratings of temperament in samples of children with Down syndrome and children who are developing normally. *American Journal on Mental Retardation, 98*, 607–618. Retrieved from http://www.aaiddjournals.org/loi/ajmr.1

Vellutino, F. R., Fletcher, J. M., Snowling, M. J., & Scanlon, D. M. (2004). Specific reading disability (dyslexia): What have we learned in the past four decades? *Journal of Child Psychology & Psychiatry & Allied Disciplines, 45*, 2–40. doi:10.1046/j.0021-9630.2003.00305.x

Vellutino, F. R., Tunmer, W. E., Jaccard, J. J., & Chen, R. (2007). Components of reading ability: Multivariate evidence for a convergent skill model of reading development. *Scientific Studies of Reading, 11*, 3–32. doi:10.1080/10888430709336632

Verduin, T. L., & Kendall, P. C. (2008). Peer perceptions and liking of children with anxiety disorders. *Journal of Abnormal Child Psychology, 36*, 459–469. doi:10.1007/s10802-007-9192-6

Verma, S. K. (2000). Some popular misconceptions about inkblot techniques. *Journal of Projective Psychology and Mental Health, 7*, 79–81. Retrieved from http://www.somaticinkblots.com/SISJournal/tabid/61/Default.aspx

Via, E., Radua, J., Cardona, N., Happé, F., & Mataix-Cols, D. (2011). Meta-analysis of gray matter abnormalities in autism spectrum disorder: Should Asperger Disorder be subsumed under a broader umbrella of autistic spectrum disorder? *Archives of General Psychiatry, 68*, 409–418. doi:10.1001/archgenpsychiatry.2011.27

Viana, A. G., Beidel, D. C., & Rabian, B. (2009). Selective mutism: A review and integration of the last 15 years. *Clinical Psychology Review, 29*, 57–67. doi:10.1016/j.cpr.2008.09.009

Vidal, C. N., Rapoport, J. L., Hayashi, K. M., Geaga, J. A., Sui, Y., McLemore, L. E., . . . Thompson, P. M. (2006). Dynamically spreading frontal and cingulated deficits mapped in adolescents with schizophrenia. *Archives of General Psychiatry, 63*, 25–34. doi:10.1001/archpsyc.63.1.25

Viding, E., & Jones, A. P. (2008). Cognition to genes via the brain in the study of conduct disorder. *Quarterly Journal of Experimental Psychology, 61*, 171–181. doi:10.1080/17470210701508889

Viding, E., Jones, A. P., Frick, P. J., Moffitt, T. E., & Plomin, R. (2008). Heritability of antisocial behavior at age 9: Do callous-unemotional traits matter? *Developmental Science, 11*, 17–22. doi:10.1111/j.1467-7687.2007.00648.x

Virués-Ortega, J. (2010). Applied behavior analytic intervention for autism in early childhood: Meta-analysis, meta-regression and dose-response meta-analysis of multiple outcomes. *Clinical Psychology Review, 30*, 387–399. doi:10.1016/j.cpr.2010.01.008

Vismara, L. A., & Rogers, S. J. (2010). Behavioral treatments in autism spectrum disorder: What do we know? *Annual Review of Clinical Psychology, 27*, 447–468. doi:10.1146/annurev.clinpsy.121208.131151

Vitiello, B. (2007). Research in child and adolescent psychopharmacology: Recent accomplishments and new challenges. *Psychopharmacology [Special issue: Pediatric psychopharmacology: Mood, anxiety and disruptive behavior/pervasive developmental disorders], 191*, 5–13. doi:10.1007/s00213-006-0414-3

Vitiello, B., Zuvekas, S. H., & Norquist, G. S. (2006). National estimates of antidepressant medication use among U.S. children, 1997–2002. *Journal of the American Academy of Child & Adolescent Psychiatry, 45*, 271–279. doi:10.1097/01.chi.0000192249.61271.81

Volkmar, F. R., Klin, A., & Pauls, D. (1998). Nosological and genetic aspects of Asperger syndrome. *Journal of Autism and Developmental Disorders, 28*, 457–463. doi:10.1023/A:1026012707581

Volkmar, F. R., Klin, A., Schultz, R., Bronen, R., Marans, W. D., Sparrow, S., & Cohen, D. J. (1996). Grand rounds: Asperger's syndrome. *Journal of the American*

Academy of Child & Adolescent Psychiatry, 35, 118–123. doi:10.1097/00004583-199601000-00020

Volkmar, F., Shaffer, D., & First, M. (2000). Letter to the editor: PDDNOS in DSM-IV. *Journal of Autism and Developmental Disorders, 30*, 74–75. doi:10.1023/A:1017203929453

Volkow, N. D., Wang, G. J., Wang, Kollins, S. H., Wigal, T. L., Newcorn, J. H., . . . Swanson, J. M. (2009). Evaluating dopamine reward pathway in ADHD: Clinical implications. *JAMA, 302*, 1084–1091. doi:10.1001/jama.2009.1308

Vukovic, R. K., & Siegel, L. S. (2010). Academic and cognitive characteristics of persistent mathematics difficulty from first through fourth grade. *Learning Disabilities Research & Practice, 25*, 25–38. doi:10.1111/j.1540-5826.2009.00298.x

Wachs, T. D., Black, M. M., & Engle, P. L. (2009). Maternal depression: A global threat to children's health, development, and behavior and to human rights. *Child Development Perspectives, 3*, 51–59. doi:10.1111/j.1750-8606.2008.00077.x

Wade, T. J., Cairney, J., & Pevalin, D. J. (2002). Emergence of gender differences in depression during adolescence: National panel results from three countries. *Journal of the Academy of Child & Adolescent Psychiatry*, *41*, 190–198. doi:10.1097/00004583-200202000-00013

Wagner, E. F., Swenson, C. C., & Henggeler, S. W. (2000). Practical and methodological challenges in validating community-based interventions. *Children's Services: Social Policy, Research, and Practice, 3*, 211–231. doi:10.1207/S15326918CS0304_2

Wahlberg, K.-E., Wynne, L. C., Hakko, H., Laksy, K., & Moring, J. (2004). Interaction of genetic risk and adoptive parent communication deviance: Longitudinal prediction of adoptee psychiatric disorders. *Psychological Medicine, 34*, 1531–1541. doi:10.1017/S0033291704002661

Waisbren, S. E. (2011). Phenylketonuria. In S. Goldstein & C. R. Reynolds (Eds.), *Handbook of neurodevelopmental and genetic disorders in children* (2nd ed.). (pp. 398–424). New York: Guilford Press.

Waite, R., & Ramsay, J. R. (2010) Cultural proficiency: A Hispanic woman with ADHD—A case example. *Journal of Attention Disorders, 13*, 424–432. doi:10.1177/1087054709332393

Wakefield, A. J., Murch, S. H, Anthony, A., Linnell, J., Casson, D.M., Malik, M., . . . Walker-Smith J. A. (1998). Ileal-lymphoid-nodular hyperplasia, non-specific colitis, and pervasive developmental disorder in children. *Lancet, 351*, 637–641. doi:10.1016/S0140-6736(97)11096-0

Wakely, M. B., Hooper, S. R., de Kruif, R. E. L., & Swartz, C. (2006). Subtypes of written expression in elementary school children: A linguistic-based model. *Developmental Neuropsychology [Special issue: Writing], 29*, 125–159. doi:10.1207/s15326942dn2901_7

Waldman, I. D., & Lilienfeld, S. O. (1995). Diagnosis and classification. In M. Hersen & R. T. Ammerman (Eds.), *Advanced abnormal child psychology* (pp. 21–36). Hillsdale, NJ: Erlbaum.

Waldman, I. D., Tackett, J., Van Hulle, C. A., Applegate, B., Pardini, D., Frick, P. J., & Lahey, B. B. (2011). Child and adolescent conduct disorder substantially shares genetic influences with three socioemotional dispositions. *Journal of Abnormal Psychology, 120*, 57–70. doi:10.1037/a0021351

Waldron, H. B., & Turner, C. W. (2008). Evidence-based psychosocial treatments for adolescent substance abuse. *Journal of Clinical Child & Adolescent Psychology, 37*, 238–261. doi:10.1080/15374410701820133

Walitza, S., Wendland, J. R., Gruenblatt, E., Warnke, A., Sontag, T. A., Tucha, O., & Lange, K. W. (2010). Genetics of early-onset obsessive-compulsive-disorder. *European Child and Adolescent Psychiatry, 19*, 227–235. doi:10.1007/s00787-010-0087-7

Walker, E., Shapiro, D., Esterberg, M., & Trotman, H. (2010). Neurodevelopment and schizophrenia: Broadening the focus. *Current Directions in Clinical Science, 19*, 204–208. doi:10.1177/0963721410377744

Walker, L. S., Smith, C. A., Garber, J., & Claar, R. L. (2007). Appraisal and coping with daily stressors by pediatric patients with chronic abdominal pain. *Journal of Pediatric Psychology, 32*, 206–216. doi:10.1093/jpepsy/jsj124

Wallace, K. S., & Rogers, S. J. (2010). Intervening in infancy: Implications for autism spectrum disorders. *Journal of Child Psychology and Psychiatry, 51*, 1300–1320. doi:10.1111/j.1469-7610.2010.02308.x

Wang, Y., & Ollendick, T. H. (2001). A cross-cultural and developmental analysis of self-esteem in Chinese and Western children. *Clinical Child and Family Psychology Review, 4*, 253–271. doi:10.1023/A:1017551215413

Wang, Y. C., McPherson, K., Marsh, T., Gortmaker, S. L., & Brown, M. (2011). Obesity 2: Health and economic burden of the projected obesity trends in the USA and the UK. *The Lancet, 378*, 815–825. doi:10.1016/S0140-6736(11)60814-3

Ward, T., & Beech, A. R. (2008). *An integrated theory of sexual offending*. In D. Laws & W. T. O'Donohue (Eds.). *Sexual deviance: Theory, assessment, and treatment* (2nd ed.). (pp. 21–36). New York: Guilford Press.

Ware, J., & Raval, H. (2007). A qualitative investigation of fathers' experiences of looking after a child with a life-limiting illness, in process and in retrospect. *Clinical Child Psychology and Psychiatry, 12*, 549–565. doi:10.1177/1359104507080981

Warner, C. M., Fisher, P. H., Shrout, P. E., Rathor, S., & Klein, R. G. (2007). Treating adolescents with social anxiety disorder in school: An attention control trial. *Journal of Child Psychology and Psychiatry, 48*, 676–686. doi:10.1111/j.1469-7610.2007.01737.x

Warren, Z., McPheeters, M. L., Sathe, N., Foss-Feig, J. H., Glasser, A., & Veenstra-VanderWeele, J. (2011). A systematic review of early intensive intervention for autism spectrum disorders. *Pediatrics, 127*, e1303–e1311. doi:10.1542/peds.2011-0426

Waschbusch, D. (2002). A meta-analytic examination of comorbid hyperactive-impulsive-attention problems and conduct problems. *Psychological Bulletin, 128*, 118–150. doi:10.1037/0033-2909.128.1.118

Waschbusch, D. A., & Hill, G. P. (2003). Empirically supported, promising, and unsupported treatments for children with attention-deficit/hyperactivity disorder. In S. O. Lilienfeld, S. J. Lynn, & J. M. Lohr (Eds.), *Science and pseudoscience in clinical psychology* (pp. 333–362). New York: Guilford Press.

Waschbusch, D. A., Pelham, W. E., & Massetti, G. (2005). The behavior education support and treatment (BEST) school intervention program: Pilot project data examining schoolwide, targeted-school, and targeted-home approaches. *Journal of Attention Disorders, 9*, 313–322. doi:10.1177/1087054705279999

Wassenberg, R., Hendriksen, J. G. M., Hurks, P. P. M., Feron, F. J. M., Vles, J. S. H., & Jolles, J. (2010). Speed of language comprehension is impaired in ADHD. *Journal of Attention Disorders, 13*, 374–385. doi:10.1177/1087054708326111

Watanabe, N., Hunot, V., Omori, I. M., Churchill, R., & Furukawa, T. A. (2007). Psychotherapy for depression among children and adolescents: A systematic review. *Acta Psychiatrica Scandinavica, 116*, 84–95. doi:10.1111/j.1600-0447.2007.01018.x

Waters, A. M., Henry, J., Mogg, K., Bradley, B. P., & Pine, D. S. (2010). Attentional bias towards angry faces in childhood anxiety disorders. *Journal of Behavior Therapy and Experimental Psychiatry, 41*, 158–164. doi:10.1016/j.jbtep.2009.12.001

Waters, T. L., & Barrett, P. M. (2000). The role of the family in childhood obsessive-compulsive disorder. *Clinical Child and Family Psychology Review, 3*, 173–184. doi:10.1023/A:1009551325629

Watkins, M. W. (2010). Structure of the Wechsler Intelligence Scale for Children—Fourth Edition among a national sample of referred students. *Psychological Assessment, 22*, 782–787. doi:10.1037/a0020043

Watson, D. (2009). Differentiating the mood and anxiety disorders: A quadripartite model. *Annual Review of Clinical Psychology, 5*, 221–247. doi:10.1146/annurev.clinpsy.032408.153510

Watson, E., Finkelstein, N., Gurewich, D., & Morse, B. (2011). The feasibility of screening for fetal alcohol spectrum disorders risk in early intervention settings: A pilot study of systems change. *Infants & Young Children, 24*, 193–206. doi:10.1097/IYC.0b013e31820d97c9

Watson, J. B. (1925). *Behaviorism.* New York: People's Institute.

Watson, J. B., & Rayner, R. R. (1920). Conditioned emotional reactions. *Journal of Experimental Psychology, 3*, 1–14. doi:10.1037/h0069608

Watson, R. R. (1930/1996, August). I am the mother of a behaviorist's sons. *Parent's Magazine, 50*. (Original article published August 1930).

Wazana, A., Besnahan, M., & Kline, J. (2007). The autism epidemic: Fact or artifact? *Journal of the American Academy of Child & Adolescent Psychiatry, 46*, 721–730. doi:10.1097/chi.0b013e31804a7f3b

Webster-Stratton, C. (1996). Early-onset conduct problems: Does gender make a difference? *Journal of Consulting and Clinical Psychology, 64*, 540–551. doi:10.1037//0022-006X.64.3.540

Webster-Stratton, C., & Herbert, M. (1994). *Troubled families—Problem children: Working with parents: A collaborative process*. New York: Wiley.

Webster-Stratton, C., Reid, M., & Hammond, M. (2004). Treating children with early-onset conduct problems: Intervention outcomes for parent, child, and teacher training. *Journal of Clinical Child and Adolescent Psychology, 33*, 105–124. doi:10.1207/S15374424JCCP3301_11

Webster-Stratton, C., & Reid, M. J. (2010). The Incredible Years parents, teachers, and children training series: A multifaceted treatment approach for young children with conduct disorders. In J. R. Weisz & A. E. Kazdin (Eds.), *Evidence-based psychotherapies for children and adolescents* (2nd ed., pp. 194–210). New York: Guilford.

Webster-Stratton, C., Rinaldi, J., & Reid, J. M. (2010). Long-term outcomes of Incredible Years Parenting Progam: Predictors of adolescent adjustment. *Child and Adolescent Mental Health, 16*, 38–46. doi:10.1111/j.1475-3588.2010.00576.x

Webster-Stratton, C. H., Reid, M. J., & Beauchaine, T. (2011). Combining parent and child training for young children with ADHD. *Journal of Clinical Child and Adolescent Psychology, 40*, 191–203. doi:10.1080/15374416.2011.546044

Wechlser, D. (2002). *WPPSI-III: Administration and scoring manual*. San Antonio, TX: Psychological Corporation.

Wechsler, D. (1974). *Manual for the Wechsler Intelligence Scale for Children—Revised (WISC-R)*. New York: Psychological Corporation.

Wechsler, D. (2003). *Wechsler Intelligence Scale for Children: Fourth edition (WISC-IV)*. San Antonio, Texas: Psychological Corporation.

Weeks, S. J., & Hobson, R. P. (1987). The salience of facial expression for autistic children. *Journal of Child Psychology and Psychiatry, 28*, 137–152. doi:10.1111/j.1469-7610.1987.tb00658.x

Weems, C., & Silverman, W. (2008). Anxiety disorders. In T. P. Beauchaine & S. P. Hinshaw (Eds.), *Child and adolescent psychopathology* (pp. 447–476). Hoboken, NJ: Wiley.

Weems, C. F., Pina, A. A., Costa, N. M., Watts, S. E., Taylor, L. K., & Cannon, M. F. (2007). Predisaster trait anxiety and negative affect predict posttraumatic stress in youths after Hurricane Katrina. *Journal of Consulting and Clinical Psychology, 75*, 154–159. doi:10.1037/0022-006X.75.1.154

Weems, C. F., Silverman, W. K., & La Greca, A. M. (2000). What do youth referred for anxiety problems worry about? Worry and its relation to anxiety and anxiety disorders in children and adolescents. *Journal of Abnormal Child Psychology, 28*, 63–72. doi:10.1023/A:1005122101885

Weiss, B., Catron, T., & Harris, V. (2000). A 2-year follow-up of the effectiveness of traditional child psychotherapy. *Journal of Consulting and Clinical Psychology, 68*, 1094–1101. doi:10.1037/0022-006X.68.6.1094

Weiss, B., & Garber, J. (2003). Developmental differences in the phenomenology of depression. *Development and Psychopathology, 15*, 403–430. doi:10.1017/S0954579403000221

Weiss, B., Weisz, J. R., & Bromfield, R. (1986). Performance of retarded and nonretarded persons on information-processing tasks: Further tests of the similar structure hypothesis. *Psychological Bulletin, 100*, 157–175. doi:10.1037/0033-2909.100.2.157

Weiss, L. (1992). *Attention deficit disorder in adults*. Dallas, TX: Taylor.

Weissman, M. M., McAvay, G., Goldstein, R. B., Nunes, E. V., Verdeli, H., & Wickramaratne, P. J. (1999). Risk/protective factors among addicted mothers' offspring: A replication study. *American Journal of Drug and Alcohol Abuse, 25*, 661–679. doi:10.1081/ADA-100101885

Weissman, M. M., Warner, V., Wickramaratne, P., Moreau, D., & Olfson, M. (1997). Offspring of depressed parents: 10 years later. *Archives of General Psychiatry, 54*, 932–940. Retrieved from http://archpsyc.ama-assn.org/

Weissman, M. M., Warner, V., Wickramaratne, P., & Prusoff, B. A. (1988). Early-onset major depression in parents and their children. *Journal of Affective Disorders, 15*, 269–277. doi:10.1016/0165-0327(88)90024-9

Weissman, M. M., Wickramaratne, P., Nomura, Y., Warner, V., Pilowsky, D. J., & Verdeli, H. (2006). Offspring of depressed parents: 20 years later. *American Journal of Psychiatry, 163*, 1001–1008. doi:10.1176/appi.ajp.163.6.1001

Weissman, M. M., Wickramaratne, P., Nomura, Y., Warner, V., Verdeli, H., Pilowsky, D. J., . . . Weissman, M. M. (2005). Families at high and low risk for depression: A 3-generation study. *Archives of General Psychiatry, 62*, 29–36. doi:10.1016/j.biopsych.2005.01.045

Weisz, J. R. (1998). Empirically supported treatments for children and adolescents: Efficacy, problems, and prospects. In K. S. Dobson & K. D. Craig (Eds.), *Empirically supported therapies: Best practice in professional psychology* (pp. 66–92). Newbury Park, CA: Sage.

Weisz, J. R. (1999). Cognitive performance and learned helplessness in mentally retarded persons. In E. Zigler & D. Bennett-Gates (Eds.), *Personality development in individuals with mental retardation* (pp. 17–46). New York: Cambridge University Press.

Weisz, J. R., Chayaisit, W., Weiss, B., Eastman, K. L., & Jackson, E. W. (1995). A multimethod study of problem behavior among Thai and American children in school: Teacher reports versus direct observations. *Child Development, 66*, 402–415. doi:10.1111/j.1467-8624.1995.tb00879.x

Weisz, J. R., Chorpita, B. F., Frye, A., Ng, M. Y., Lau, N., Bearman, S. K., . . . Hoagwood, K. E. (2011). Youth top problems: Using idiographic, consumer-guided assessment to identify treatment needs and to track change during psychotherapy. *Journal of Consulting and Clinical Psychology, 79*, 369–380. doi:10.1037/a0023307

Weisz, J. R., Donenberg, G. R., Han, S. S., & Weiss, B. (1995). Bridging the gap between laboratory and clinic in child and adolescent psychotherapy. *Journal of Consulting and Clinical Psychology, 63*, 688–701. doi:10.1037/0022-006X.63.5.688

Weisz, J. R., Jensen-Doss, A., & Hawley, K. M. (2006). Evidence-based youth psychotherapies versus usual clinical care: A meta-analysis of direct comparisons. *American Psychologist, 61*, 671–689. doi:10.1037/0003-066X.61.7.671

Weisz, J. R., & Kazdin, A. E. (Eds.). (2010). *Evidence-based psychotherapies for children and adolescents* (2nd ed.). New York: Guilford Press.

Weisz, J. R., McCarty, C. A., & Valeri, S.M. (2006). Effects of psychotherapy for depression in children and adolescents: A meta-analysis. *Psychological Bulletin, 132*, 132–149. doi:10.1037/0033-2909.132.1.132

Weisz, J. R., Sandler, I. N., Durlak, J. A., & Anton, B. S. (2005). Promoting and protecting youth mental health through evidence-based prevention and treatment. *American Psychologist, 60*, 628–648. doi:10.1037/0003-066X.60.6.628

Weisz, J. R., Southam-Gerow, M. A., Gordis, E. B., & Connor-Smith, J. (2003). Primary and secondary control enhancement training for youth depression: Applying the deployment-focused model of treatment development and testing. In A. E. Kazdin & J. R. Weisz (Eds.), *Evidence-based psychotherapies for children and adolescents* (pp. 165–183). New York: Guilford Press.

Weisz, J. R., & Weiss, B. (1993). *Effects of psychotherapy with children and adolescents*. Newbury Park, CA: Sage.

Weisz, J. R., Weiss, B., Suwanlert, S., & Chaiyasit, W. (2003). Syndromal structure of psychopathology in children in Thailand and the United States. *Journal of Consulting and Clinical Psychology, 71*, 375–385. doi:10.1037/0022-006X.71.2.375

Weisz, J. R., Weiss, B., Suwanlert, S., & Chaiyasit, W. (2006). Culture and youth psychopathology: Testing the syndromal sensitivity model in Thai and American adolescents. *Journal of Consulting and Clinical Psychology, 74*, 1098–1107. doi:10.1037/0022-006X.74.6.1098

Wekerle, C. (2011). Emotionally maltreated: The under-current of impairment? *Child Abuse & Neglect, 35*, 899–903.

Wekerle, C. (2011). The dollars and senselessness in failing to prioritize childhood maltreatment prevention. *Child Abuse & Neglect, 35*, 159–161.

Wekerle, C., MacMillan, H. L., Leung, E., & Jamieson, E. (2008). Child maltreatment.

In M. Hersen & A. M. Gross (Eds.), *Handbook of clinical psychology, Vol 2: Children and adolescents* (pp. 856–903). Hoboken, NJ: John Wiley & Sons Inc.

Wekerle, C., Miller, A., Wolfe, D. A., & Spindel, C. B. (2006). Childhood maltreatment. In D. Wedding (Series Ed.), *Advances in psychotherapy: Evidence-based practice.* Cambridge, MA: Hogrefe & Huber.

Wekerle, C., Miller, A., Wolfe, D. A., & Spindel, C. B. (2006a). *Childhood maltreatment.* Cambridge, MA: Hogrefe & Huber.

Wekerle, C., & Wall, A-M. (2002). The overlap between intimate violence and substance abuse. In C. Wekerle & A-M. Wall (Eds.), *The violence and addiction equation: Theoretical and clinical issues in substance abuse and relationship violence* (pp. 1–21). New York: Brunner-Routledge.

Wekerle, C., & Wolfe, D. A. (2003). Child maltreatment. In E. J. Mash & R. A. Barkley (Eds.), *Child psychopathology* (2nd ed., pp. 632–684). New York: Guilford Press.

Wells, C., Adhyaru, J., Cannon, J., Lamond, M., & Baruch, G. (2010). Multisystemic Therapy (MST) for youth offending, psychiatric disorder and substance abuse: Case examples from a UK MST team. *Child and Adolescent Mental Health, 15*, 142–149. doi:10.1111/j.1475-3588.2009.00555.x

Welsh, B. C., Loeber, R., Stevens, B. R., Stouthamer-Loeber, M., Cohen, M. A., & Farrington, D. P. (2008). Costs of juvenile crime in urban areas: A longitudinal perspective. *Youth Violence and Juvenile Justice, 6*, 3–27. doi:10.1177/1541204007308427

Wermter, A., Laucht, M., Schimmelmann, B. G., Banaschweski, T., Sonuga-Barke, E. J. S., Rietschel, M., & Becker, K. (2010). From nature versus nurture, via nature and nurture, to gene × environment interaction in mental disorders. *European Child & Adolescent Psychiatry, 19*, 199–210. doi:10.1007/s00787-009-0082-z

Werner, E. E. (1993). Risk and resilience in individuals with learning disabilities: Lessons learned from the Kauai Longitudinal Study. *Learning Disabilities Research and Practice, 8*, 28–34. Retrieved from http://www.blackwellpublishing.com/journal.asp?ref=0938-8982

Werner, E. E. (2005). Resilience research: Past, present, and future. In R. DeV. Peters, B. Leadbeater, & R. J. McMahon (Eds.), *Resilience in children, families, and communities: Linking context to practice and policy* (pp. 3–11). New York: Kluwer/Plenum Press.

Whalen, C. K., & Henker, B. (1992). The social profile of attention-deficit hyperactivity disorder: Five fundamental facets. In G. Weiss (Ed.), *Child and adolescent psychiatric clinics of North America: Attention-deficit hyperactivity disorder* (pp. 395–410). Philadelphia: Saunders.

Whalen, C. K., Odgers, C. L., Reed, P. L., & Henker, B. (2011). Dissecting daily distress in mothers of children with ADHD: An electronic diary study. *Journal of Family Psychology, 25*, 402–411. doi:10.1037/a0023473

Whaley, S. E., Pinto, A., & Sigman, M. (1999). Characterizing interactions between anxious mothers and their children. *Journal of Consulting and Clinical Psychology, 67*, 826–836. doi:10.1037/0022-006X.67.6.826

Wheeler, D. L., Jacobson, J. W., Paglieri, R. A., & Schwartz, A. A. (1993). An experimental assessment of facilitated communication. *Mental Retardation, 31*, 49–60. Retrieved from http://www.aaiddjournals.org/loi/ajmr

Whitaker, S. (2008). The stability of IQ in people with low intellectual ability: An analysis of the literature. *Intellectual and Developmental Disabilities, 46*, 120–128. doi:10.1352/0047-6765(2008)46[120:TSOIIP]2.0.CO;2

White, H. R., & Widom, C. S. (2003). Intimate partner violence among abused and neglected children in young adulthood: The mediating effects of early aggression, antisocial personality, hostility and alcohol problems. *Aggressive Behavior, 29*, 332–345.

White, L. K., McDermott, J. M., Degnan, K. A., Henderson, H. A., & Fox, N. A. (2011). Behavioral inhibition and anxiety: The moderating roles of inhibitory control and attention shifting. *Journal of Abnormal Child Psychology: An Official Publication of the International Society for Research in Child and Adolescent Psychopathology, 39*, 735–747. doi:10.1007/s10802-011-9490-x

White, S. W., Keonig, K., & Scahill, L. (2007). Social skills development in children with autism spectrum disorders: A review of the intervention research. *Journal of Autism and Developmental Disorders, 37*, 1858–1868. doi:10.1007/s10803-006-0320-x

White, S. W., Oswald, D., Ollendick, T., & Scahill, L. (2009). Anxiety in children and adolescents with autism spectrum disorders. *Clinical Psychology Review, 29*, 216–229. doi:10.1016/j.cpr.2009.01.003

White, T., & Hilgetag, C. C. (2011). Gyrification and neural connectivity in schizophrenia. *Developmental Psychopathology, 23*, 339–352. doi:10.1017/S0954579410000842

Whitehouse, A. J. O., Bishop, D. V. M., Ang, Q. W., Pennell, C. E., & Fisher, S. E. (2011). CNTNAP2 variants affect early language development in the general population. *Genes, Brain & Behavior, 10*, 451–456. doi:10.1111/j.1601-183X.2011.00684.x

Whitehurst, G. J., & Lonigan, C. J. (1998). Child development and emergent literacy. *Child Development, 69*, 848–872. doi:10.1111/j.1467-8624.1998.tb06247.x

Whittle, S., Yap, M. B. H., Sheeber, L., Dudgeon, P., Yucel, M., Pantelis, C., . . . Allen, N. B. (2011). Hippocampal volume and sensitivity to maternal aggressive behavior: A prospective study of adolescent depressive symptoms. *Development and Psychopathology, 23*, 115–129. doi:10.1017/S0954579410000684

Wich, L. G., Ma, M. W., Price, L. S., Sidash, S., Berman, R. S., Pavlick, A. C., . . . Osman, I. (2011). Impact of socioeconomic status and sociodemographic factors on melanoma presentation among ethnic minorities. *Journal of Community Health: The Publication for Health Promotion and Disease Prevention, 36*, 461–468. doi:10.1007/s10900-010-9328-4

Wickramaratne, P., Gameroff, M. J., Pilowsky, D. J., Hughes, C. W., Garber, J., Malloy, E., . . . & Fava, M. (2011). Children of depressed mothers 1 year after remission of maternal depression: Findings from the STAR*D-Child study. *American Journal of Psychiatry, 168*, 593–602. doi:10.1176/appi.ajp.2010.10010032

Wickramaratne, P. J., Greenwald, S., & Weissman, M. M. (2000). Psychiatric disorders in the relatives of probands with prepubertal-onset or adolescent-onset major depression. *Journal of the American Academy of Child & Adolescent Psychiatry, 39*, 1396–1405. doi:10.1097/00004583-200011000-00014

Widiger, T. A. (1993). The DSM-III-R categorical personality disorder diagnoses: A critique and alternative. *Psychological Inquiry, 4*, 75–90. doi:10.1207/s15327965pli0402_1

Widom, C. S. (1989). Does violence beget violence? A critical examination of the literature. *Psychological Bulletin, 106*, 3–28.

Widom, C. S. (1996, May/June). Childhood sexual abuse and its criminal consequences. *Society*, pp. 47–53.

Widom, C. S. (1999). Posttraumatic stress disorder in abused and neglected children grown up. *American Journal of Psychiatry, 156*, 1223–1229.

Widom, C. S., Czaja, S. J., & Dutton, M. A. (2008). Childhood victimization and lifetime revictimization. *Child Abuse & Neglect, 32*, 785–796. doi:10.1016/j.chiabu.2007.12.006

Widom, C. S., Czaja, S. J., & Paris, J. (2009). A prospective investigation of borderline personality disorder in abused and neglected children followed up into adulthood. *Journal of Personality Disorders, 23*, 433–446. doi:10.1521/pedi.2009.23.5.433

Wildes, J. E., & Emery, R. E. (2001). The roles of ethnicity and culture in the development of eating disturbance and body dissatisfaction: A meta-analytic review. *Clinical Psychology Review, 21*, 521–551. doi:10.1016/S0272-7358(99)00071-9

Wilens, T. E. (2007). The nature of the relationship between attention-deficit/hyperactivity disorder and substance use. *Journal of Clinical Psychiatry, 68(Suppl. 11)*, 4–8. Retrieved from http://www.psychiatrist.com/

Wilens, T. E. (2011). A sobering fact: ADHD leads to substance abuse. *Journal of the American Academy of Child & Adolescent Psychiatry, 50*, 6–8. doi:10.1016/j.Jaac.2010.10.002

Wilfley, D. E., Stein, R. I., Saelens, B. E., Mockus, D. S., Matt, G. E., Hayden-Wade, H. A., . . . Epstein, L. H. (2007). Efficacy of maintenance treatment approaches for childhood overweight: A randomized controlled trial. *JAMA: Journal of the American Medical Association, 298*, 1661–1673. doi:10.1001/jama.298.14.1661

Wilkin, T. (2010). Preventing obesity and metabolic disease: Pointers from the

earlybird study. *International Journal of Pediatric Obesity, 5*(Suppl 1), 43–44.
Wilkins, J., & Matson, J. L. (2009). History of treatment in children with developmental disabilities and psychopathology. In J. L. Matson, F. Andrasik, & M. L. Matson (Eds.), *Treating childhood psychopathology and developmental disabilities* (pp. 3–28). New York: Springer Science + Business Media. doi:10.1007/978-0-387-09530-1_1
Wilkinson, P. O., & Goodyer, I. M. (2006). Attention difficulties and mood-related ruminative response style in adolescents with unipolar depression. *Journal of Child Psychology and Psychiatry, 47*, 1284–1291. doi:10.1111/j.1469-7610.2006.01660.x
Willcutt, E. G., Betjemann, R. S., Pennington, B. F., Olson, R. K., DeFries, J. C., & Wadsworth, S. J. (2007). Longitudinal study of reading disability and attention-deficit/hyperactivity disorder: Implications for education. *Mind, Brain, and Education, 1*, 181–192. doi:10.1111/j.1751-228X.2007.00019.x
Williams, D. L. (2010). *Developmental language disorders: Learning, language, and the brain.* San Diego, CA: Plural Publishing.
Williams, D. L., & Minshew, N. J. (2007). Understanding autism and related disorders: What has imaging taught us? *Neuroimaging Clinics of North America, 17*, 495–509. doi:10.1016/j.nic.2007.07.007
Williams, L. M. (2003). Understanding child abuse and violence against women: A life course perspective. *Journal of Interpersonal Violence Special Issue: Children and domestic violence, 18*, 441–451.
Williams, L. R., & Steinberg, L. (2011). Reciprocal relations between parenting and adjustment in a sample of juvenile offenders. *Child Development, 82*, 633–645. doi:10.1111/j.1467-8624.2010.01523.x
Williams, P. G., Holmbeck, G. N., & Greenley, R. N. (2002). Adolescent health psychology. *Journal of Consulting and Clinical Psychology, 70*, 828–842. doi:10.1037/0022-006X.70.3.828
Williams, S. E., Blount, R. L., & Walker, L. S. (2011). Children's pain threat appraisal and catastrophizing moderate the impact of parent verbal behavior on children's symptom complaints. *Journal of Pediatric Psychology, 36*, 55–63. doi:10.1093/jpepsy/jsq043
Willoughby, M. T., Curran, P. J., Costello, E. J., & Angold, A. (2000). Implications of early versus late onset of attention-deficit/hyperactivity disorder symptoms. *Journal of the American Academy of Child & Adolescent Psychiatry, 39*, 1512–1519. doi:10.1097/00004583-200012000-00013
Wilson, G. T., Grilo, C. M., & Vitousek, K. M. (2007). Psychological treatment of eating disorders. *American Psychologist, 62*, 199–216. doi:10.1037/0003-066X.62.3.199
Wilson, H. W., & Widom, C. S. (2011). Pathways from childhood abuse and neglect to HIV-risk sexual behavior in middle adulthood. *Journal of Consulting and Clinical Psychology, 79*(2), 236–246. doi:10.1037/a0022915
Wilson, K. K., & Melton, G. B. (2002). Exemplary neighborhood-based programs for child protection. In G. B. Melton, R. A. Thompson, & M. A. Small (Eds.), *Toward a child-centered, neighborhood-based child protection system: A report of the consortium on children, families, and the law* (pp. 197–213). Westport, CT: Praeger Publishers/Greenwood Publishing Group.
Wilson, S., & Durbin, C. E. (2010). Effects of paternal depression on fathers' parenting behaviors: A meta-analytic review. *Clinical Psychology Review, 30*, 167–180. doi:10.1016/j.cpr.2009.10.007
Wilson, S. J., & Lipsey, M. W. (2007). School-based interventions for aggressive and disruptive behavior: Update of a meta-analysis. *American Journal of Preventive Medicine, 33*(2S), S130–S143. doi:10.1016/j.amepre.2007.04.011
Wing, L., Gould, J., & Gillberg, C. (2011). Autism spectrum disorders in the DSM-V: Better or worse than the DSM-IV? *Research in Developmental Disabilities, 32*, 768–773. doi:10.1016/j.ridd.2010.11.003
Wing, L., & Potter, D. (2002). The epidemiology of autistic spectrum disorders: Is the prevalence rising? *Mental Retardation and Developmental Disabilities Research Reviews, 8*, 151–161. doi:10.1177/14690047030073006
Winskel, H. (2006). The effects of an early history of otitis media on children's language and literacy skill development. *British Journal of Educational Psychology, 76*, 727–744. doi:10.1348/000709905X68312
Winstanley, C. A., Eagle, D. M., & Robbins, T. W. (2006). Behavioral models of impulsivity in relation to ADHD: Translation between clinical and preclinical studies. *Clinical Psychology Review, 26*, 379–395. doi:10.1016/j.cpr.2006.01.001
Witkin, P. K., Oltman, E., Raskin, E., & Karp, S. A. (1971). *A manual for the Embedded Figures Test (pp. 21–26).* Palo Alto, CA. Consulting Psychologists Press, Inc.
Witt, W. P., Riley, A. W., & Coiro, M. J. (2003). Childhood functional status, family stressors, and psychological adjustment among school-aged children with disabilities in the United States. *Archives of Pediatric and Adolescent Medicine, 157*, 687–695. Retrieved from http://archpedi.ama-assn.org/
Wittchen, H.-U., Gloster, A. T., Beesdo-Baum, K., Fava, G. A., & Craske, M. G. (2010). Agoraphobia: A review of the diagnostic classificatory position and criteria. *Depression and Anxiety, 27*, 113–133. doi:10.1002/da.20646
Wittchen, H., Stein, M., & Kessler, R. (1999). Social fears and social phobias in a community sample of adolescents and young adults: Prevalence, risk factors, and comorbidity. *Psychological Medicine, 29*, 309–323. doi:10.1017/S0033291798008174
Witwer, A. N., & Lecavalier, L. (2008). Examining the validity of autism spectrum disorder subtypes. *Journal of Autism and Developmental Disorders, 38*, 1611–1624. doi:10.1007/s10803-008-0541-2
Wolak, J., Finkelhor, D., Mitchell, K. J., & Ybarra, M. L. (2008). Online "predators" and their victims: Myths, realities, and implications for prevention and treatment. *American Psychologist, 63*(2), 111–128.
Wolfe, D., & McIsaac, C. (2011). Distinguishing between poor/dysfunctional parenting and child emotional maltreatment. *Child Abuse & Neglect, 35*, 802–813.
Wolfe, D. A. (1985). Child abusive parents: An empirical review and analysis. *Psychological Bulletin, 97*, 462–482.
Wolfe, D. A. (1991). *Preventing physical and emotional abuse of children.* New York: Guilford Press.
Wolfe, D. A. (1999). *Child abuse: Implications for child development and psychopathology* (2nd Edition). Thousand Oaks, CA: Sage.
Wolfe, D. A., Crooks, C. V., Lee, V., McIntyre-Smith, A., & Jaffe, P. G. (2003). The effects of exposure to domestic violence on children: A meta-analysis and critique. *Clinical Child and Family Psychology Review, 6*, 171–187.
Wolfe, D. A., Francis, K. J., & Straatman, A. (2006). Child abuse in religiously-affiliated institutions: Long–term impact on men's mental health. *Child Abuse & Neglect, 30, 205–212.*
Wolfe, D. A., Jaffe, P., Jette, J., & Poisson, S. (2003). The impact of child abuse in community institutions and organizations: Advancing professional and scientific understanding. *Clinical Psychology: Science and Practice, 10*, 179–191.
Wolfe, D. A., Jaffe, P. G., & Crooks, C. V. (2006). *Adolescent risk behaviors: Why teens experiment and strategies to keep them safe.* New Haven, CT: Yale University Press.
Wolfe, D. A., & Nayak., M. B. (2003). Child abuse in peacetime. In B. L. Green, M. J. Friedman, J. de Jong, S. D. Solomon, T. M. Keane, J. A. Fairbank, B. Donelan, & E. Frey-Wouters (Eds.), *Trauma interventions in war and peace: Prevention, practice, and policy* (pp. 75–104). Kluwer Academic / Plenum.
Wolfe, D. A., & Mash, E. J. (Eds.). (2006). *Behavioral and emotional disorders in adolescents: Nature, assessment, and treatment.* New York: Guilford Press.
Wolfe, D. A., & McIsaac, C. (2011). Distinguishing between poor/dysfunctional parenting and child emotional maltreatment. *Child Abuse & Neglect, 35*, 802–813.
Wolfe, D. A. Wekerle, C., Scott, K., Straatman, A., & Grasley, C. (2004). Predicting abuse in adolescent dating relationships over one year: The role of child maltreatment and trauma. *Journal of Abnormal Psychology, 113*, 406–415.
Wolff, J. C., & Ollendick, T. H. (2006). The comorbidity of conduct problems and depression in childhood and adolescence. *Clinical Child and Family Psychology Review, 9*, 201–220. doi:10.1007/s10567-006-0011-3
Wolke, D., Rizzo, P., & Woods, S. (2002). Persistent infant crying and hyperactivity problems in middle childhood. *Pediatrics, 109*, 154–160. doi:10.1542/peds.109.6.1054
Wonderlich, S. A., Joiner, T. E., Jr., Keel, P. K., Williamson, D. A., & Crosby, R. D.

(2007). Eating disorder diagnoses: Empirical approaches to classification. *American Psychologist [Special issue: Eating disorders], 62,* 167–180. doi:10.1037/0003-066X.62.3.167
Wonderlich, S. A., Rosenfeldt, S., Crosby, R. D., Mitchell, J. E., Engel, S. G., Smyth, J., & Miltenberger, R. (2007). The effects of childhood trauma on daily mood lability and comorbid psychopathology in bulimia nervosa. *Journal of Traumatic Stress, 20,* 77–87. doi:10.1002/jts.20184
Wong, D. F., Grunder, G., & Brasic, J. R. (2007). Brain imaging research: Does the science serve clinical practice? *International Review of Psychiatry, 19,* 541–558. doi:10.1080/09540260701564849
Wood, F. B., Felton, R. H., Flowers, L., & Naylor, C. (1991). Neurobehavioral definition of dyslexia. In D. D. Duane & D. B. Gray (Eds.), *The reading brain: The biological basis of dyslexia* (pp. 1–26). Parkton, MD: York Press.
Wood, J. M., Lilienfeld, S. O., Garb, H. N., & Nezworski, M. T. (2000). The Rorschach test in clinical diagnosis: A critical review, with a backward look at Garfield (1947). *Journal of Clinical Psychology, 56,* 395–430. doi:10.1002/(SICI)1097-4679(200003)56:3<395::AID-JCLP15>3.0.CO;2-O
Woodward, L. J., & Fergusson, D. M. (2001). Life course outcomes of young people with anxiety disorders in adolescence. *Journal of the American Academy of Child & Adolescent Psychiatry, 40,* 1086–1093. doi:10.1097/00004583-200109000-00018
Woolston, J. L. (1991). *Eating and growth disorders in infants and children.* Newbury Park, CA: Sage.
Wootton, J. M., Frick, P. J., Shelton, K. K., & Silverthorn, P. (1997). Ineffective parenting and childhood conduct problems: The moderating role of callous-unemotional traits. *Journal of Consulting and Clinical Psychology, 65,* 292–300. doi:10.1037/0022-006X.65.2.292.b
World Health Organization. (2004). *Prevention of mental disorders: Effective interventions and policy options. Summary report.* Geneva, Switzerland: WHO.
World Health Organization. (2004). *Preventing violence: A guide to implementing the recommendations of the World Report on Violence and Health.* Geneva: Author.
World Health Organization. (2007). *Child and adolescent mental health initiatives of the Department of Mental Health and Substance Abuse.* Retrieved from http://www.who.int/mental_health/prevention/childado/en/
World Health Organization. (2010). *Child maltreatment Fact sheet N°150.* Retrieved June 24, 2011, from http://www.who.int/mediacentre/factsheets/fs150/en/
Wren, F. J., Berg, E. A., Heiden, L. A., Kinnamon, C. J., Ohlson, L. A., Bridge, J. A., . . . Bernal, M. (2007). Childhood anxiety in a diverse primary care population: Parent-child reports, ethnicity and SCARED factor structure. *Journal of the American Academy of Child & Adolescent Psychiatry, 46,* 332–340. doi:10.1097/chi.0b013e31802f1267
Wright, J., & Jacobs, B. (2003). Teaching phonological awareness and metacognitive strategies to children with reading difficulties: A comparison of the two instructional methods. *Educational Psychology, 23,* 17–45. doi:10.1080/01443410303217
Wynne, L. C., Tienari, P., Nieminen, P., Sorri, A., Lahti, I., Moring, J., . . . Miettunen, J. (2006). Genotype-environment interaction in the schizophrenia spectrum: Genetic liability and global family ratings in the Finnish Adoption Study. *Family Process, 45,* 419–434. doi:10.1111/j.1545-5300.2006.00180.x
Wysocki, T., Harris, M. A., Buckloh, L. M., Mertlich, D., Lochrie, A. S., Taylor, A., . . . White, N. H. (2008). Randomized, controlled trial of behavioral family systems therapy for diabetes: Maintenance and generalization of effects on parent-adolescent communication. *Behavior Therapy, 39,* 33–46. doi:10.1016/j.beth.2007.04.001
Yaganeh, R., Beidel, D. C., & Turner, S. (2006). Selective mutism: More than social anxiety? *Depression and Anxiety, 23,* 117–123. doi:10.1002/da.20139
Yao, S., Zou, T., Zhu, X., Abela, J. R. Z., Auerbach, R. P., & Tong, X. (2007). Reliability and validity of the Chinese version of the Multidimensional Anxiety Scale for Children among Chinese secondary school students. *Child Psychiatry and Human Development, 38,* 1–16. doi:10.1007/s10578-006-0039-0
Yap, M. B. H., Allen, N. B., O'Shea, M., Di Parsia, P., Simmons, J. G., & Sheeber, L. (2011). Early adolescents' temperament, emotion regulation during mother-child interactions, and depressive symptomatology. *Development and Psychopathology, 23,* 267–282. doi:10.1017/S0954579410000787
Yasui, M., & Dishion, T. J. (2007). The ethnic context of child and adolescent problem behavior: Implications for child and family interventions. *Clinical Child and Family Psychology Review, 10,* 137–179. doi:10.1007/s10567-007-0021-9
Yeh, M., McCabe, K., Hough, R. L., Lau, A., Fakhty, F., & Garland, A. (2005). Why bother with beliefs? Examining relationships between race/ethnicity, parental beliefs about causes of child problems, and mental health service use. *Journal of Consulting and Clinical Psychology, 73,* 800–807. doi:10.1037/0022-006X.73.5.800
Yelland, C., & Tiggemann, M. (2003). Muscularity and the gay ideal: Body dissatisfaction and disordered eating in homosexual men. *Eating Behaviors, 4,* 107–116. doi:10.1016/S1471-0153(03)00014-X
Yirmiya, N., & Charman, T. (2010). The prodrome of autism: Early behavioral and biological signs, regression, peri- and post-natal development and genetics. *Journal of Child Psychology and Psychiatry, 51,* 432–458. doi:10.1111/j.1469-7610.2010.02214.x
Yoritomo-Tashi. (1916). *Timidity: How to overcome it (M.W. Artois, Trans.).* New York: Funk & Wagnalls.
Young, A. R., Beitchman, J. H., Johnson, C., Douglas, L., Atkinson, L., Escobar, M., & Wilson, B. (2002). Young adult academic outcomes in a longitudinal sample of early identified language impaired and control children. *Journal of Child Psychology & Psychiatry & Allied Disciplines, 43,* 635–645. doi:10.1111/1469-7610.00052
Young, A., Grey, M., Abbey, A., Boyd, C. J., & McCabe, S. E. (2008). Alcohol-related sexual assault victimization among adolescents: Prevalence, characteristics, and correlates. *Journal on Studies of Alcohol and Drugs, 69,* 39–48. Retrieved from http://www.jsad.com/
Young, J., Corea, C., Kimani, J., & Mandell, D. (2010, March). *Autism Spectrum Disorders (ASDs) Services: Final Report on Environmental Scan.* Prepared for the Centers for Medicare & Medicaid Services. Retrieved from http://www.impaqint.com/files/4-content/1-6-publications/1-6-2-project-reports/finalasdreport.pdf
Young, J. F., & Mufson, L. (2008). Interpersonal psychotherapy for treatment and prevention of adolescent depression. In J. R. Z. Abela & B. L. Hankin (Eds.), *Handbook of depression in children and adolescents* (pp. 288–306). New York: Guilford Press.
Young, J. F., Mufson, L., & Davies, M. (2006). Efficacy of interpersonal psychotherapy adolescent skills training: An indicated preventive intervention for depression. *Journal of Child Psychology and Psychiatry, 47,* 1254–1262. doi:10.1111/j.1469-7610.2006.01667.x
Young, M. M., Saewyc, E., Boak, A., Jahrig, J., Anderson, B., Doiron, Y., Taylor, S., Pica, L., Laprise, P., and Clark, H. (Student Drug Use Surveys Working Group) (2011). *Cross-Canada report on student alcohol and drug use: Technical report.* Ottawa: Canadian Centre on Substance Abuse.
Young, S., Bramham, J., Gray, K., & Rose, E. (2008). The experience of receiving a diagnosis and treatment of ADHD in adulthood: A qualitative study of clinically referred patients using interpretive phenomenological analysis. *Journal of Attention Disorders, 11,* 493–503. doi:10.1177/1087054707305172
Youngstrom, E. A. (2007). Pediatric bipolar disorder. In E. J. Mash & R. A. Barkley (Eds.), *Assessment of childhood disorders* (4th ed., pp. 253–403). New York: Guilford Press.
Youngstrom, E. A., Arnold, L. E., & Frazier, T. W. (2010). Bipolar and ADHD comorbidity: Both artifact and outgrowth of shared mechanisms. *Clinical Psychology: Science and Practice, 17,* 350–359. doi:10.1111/j.1468-2850.2010.01226.x
Youngstrom, E. A., Findling, R. L., Youngstrom, J. K., & Calabrese, J. R. (2005). Toward an evidence-based assessment of pediatric bipolar disorder. *Journal of Clinical Child and Adolescent Psychology, 34,* 433–448. doi:10.1207/s15374424jccp3403_4
Yurgelun-Todd, D. A., Sava, S., & Dahlgren, M. K. (2007). Mood disorders. *Neuroimaging Clinics of North America, 17,* 511–521. doi:10.1016/j.nic.2007.08.001
Zachar, P., & Kendler, K. S. (2007). Psychiatric disorders: A conceptual taxonomy. *American Journal of Psychiatry,*

164, 557–565. doi:10.1176/appi.ajp.164.4.557

Zadeh, Z. Y., Im-Bolter, N., & Cohen, N. J. (2007). Social cognition and externalizing psychopathology: An investigation of the mediating role of language. *Journal of Abnormal Child Psychology, 35*, 141–152. doi:10.1007/s10802-006-9052-9

Zahn, M. A., Brumbaugh, S., Steffensmeier, D., Feld, B. C., Morash, M., Chesney-Lind, M., & Kruttschnitt, C. (2008, May). *Violence by teenage girls: Trends and Context* (pp. 1–21). Office of Juvenile Justice and Delinquency Prevention, Office of Justice Programs, U.S. Department of Justice. Washington, DC. Retrieved from http://www.ojp.usdoj.gov/ojjdp

Zahn-Waxler, C., Crick, N. R., Shirtcliff, E. A., & Woods, K. E. (2006). The origins and development of psychopathology in females and males. In D. Cicchetti & D. J. Cohen (Eds.), *Developmental psychopathology: Vol. 1. Theory and methods* (2nd ed., pp. 76–138). Hoboken, NJ: Wiley.

Zahn-Waxler, C., Race, E., & Duggal, S. (2005). Mood disorders and symptoms in girls. In D. J. Bell, S. L. Foster, & E. J. Mash (Eds.), *Handbook of behavioral and emotional problems in girls* (pp. 25–77). New York: Kluwer/Plenum.

Zebrack, B. J., Zeltzer, L. K., Whitton, J., Mertens, A. C., Odom, L., Berkow, R., . . . Robison, L. L. (2002). Psychological outcomes in long-term survivors of childhood leukemia, Hodgkin's disease, and non-Hodgkin's lymphoma: A report from the Childhood Cancer Survivor Study. *Pediatrics, 110*, 42–52. Retrieved from http://pediatrics.aappublications.org/

Zelizer, V. A. (1994). *Pricing the priceless child: The changing social value of children*. Princeton, NJ: Princeton University Press.

Zentall, S. S. (1985). A context for hyperactivity. In K. Gadow & I. Bialer (Eds.), *Advances in learning and behavioral disabilities* (Vol. 4, pp. 273–343). Greenwich, CT: JAI Press.

Zigler, E., & Hodapp, R. (1986). *Understanding mental retardation*. New York: Cambridge University Press.

Zikopoulos. B., & Barbas, H. (2010). Changes in prefrontal axons may disrupt the network in autism. *Journal of Neuroscience,* 30, 14595–14609. doi:10.1523/JNEUROSCI.2257-10.2010

Zilbovicius, M. Garreau, B., Samson, Y., Remy, P., Barthelemy, C., Syrota, A., & Lelord, G. (1995). Delayed maturation of the frontal cortex in childhood autism. *American Journal of Psychiatry, 152*, 248–252. Retrieved from http://ajp.psychiatryonline.org

Zima, B. T., Bussing, R., Tang, L., Zhang, L., Ettner, S., Belin, T. R., & Wells, K. B. (2010). Quality of care for childhood attention-deficit/hyperactivity disorder in a managed care Medicaid program. *Journal of the American Academy of Child & Adolescent Psychiatry, 49*, 1225–1237. doi:10.1016/jaac.2010.08.012

Zimmerman, F. J. (2005). Social and economic determinants of disparities in professional help-seeking for child mental health problems: Evidence from a national sample. *Health Research and Educational Trust, 40*, 1514–1533. doi:10.1111/j.1475-6773.2005.00411.x

Zimmerman, M. A., & Arunkumar, R. (1994). Resiliency research: Implications for schools and policy. *Social Policy Report, 8*, 1–17. Retrieved from http://www.srcd.org

Zoccolillo, M. (1993). Gender and the development of conduct disorder. *Development and Psychopathology, 5*, 65–78. doi:10.1017/S0954579400004260

Zoccolillo, M., Pickles, A., Quinton, D., & Rutter, M. (1992). The outcome of conduct disorder: Implications for defining adult personality disorder and conduct disorder. *Psychological Medicine, 22*, 971–986. doi:10.1017/S003329170003854X

Zoccolillo, M., & Rogers, K. (1991). Characteristics and outcome of hospitalized adolescent girls with conduct disorder. *Journal of the American Academy of Child & Adolescent Psychiatry, 30*, 973–981. doi:10.1097/00004583-199111000-00016

Zoccolillo, M., & Rogers, K. (1992). Characteristics and outcome of hospitalized adolescent girls with conduct disorder: Erratum. *Journal of the American Academy of Child & Adolescent Psychiatry, 31*, 561. doi:10.1097/00004583-199203000-00038

Zohar, A. H. (1999). The epidemiology of obsessive-compulsive disorder in children and adolescents. *Child and Adolescent Psychiatric Clinics of North America, 8*, 445–460.

Zolotor, A. J., & Puzia, M. E. (2010). Bans against corporal punishment: A systematic review of the laws, changes in attitudes and behaviours. *Child Abuse Review, 19*, 229–247. doi:10.1002/car.1131

Zuvekas, S. H., Vitiello, B., & Norquist, G. S. (2006). Recent trends in stimulant medication use among U.S. children. *American Journal of Psychiatry, 163*, 579–585. doi:10.1176/appi.ajp.163.4.579

Zwaigenbaum, L., Bryson, S., Lord, C., Rogers, S., Carter, A., Carver, L., . . . Yirmiya, N. (2009). Clinical assessment and management of toddlers with suspected autism spectrum disorder: Insights from studies of high-risk infants. *Pediatrics, 123*, 1383–1391. doi:10.1542/peds.2008-1606

Name Index

Subject Index

Note to the reader: Numerals followed by "f" refer to figures and illustrations; numerals followed by "t" refer to tables; numerals followed by "b" refer to boxed information.

DSM-IV-TR Classification: Axes I and II

AXIS I

Disorders Usually First Diagnosed in Infancy, Childhood, or Adolescence

Learning Disorders (Academic Skills Disorders)
Reading Disorder/Mathematics Disorder/Disorder of Written Expression
Motor Skills Disorder
Developmental Coordination Disorder
Communication Disorders
Expressive Language Disorder/Mixed Receptive/Expressive Language Disorder/Phonological Disorder/Stuttering
Pervasive Developmental Disorders
Autistic Disorder /Rett's Disorder/Childhood Disintegrative Disorder/ Asperger's Disorder/PDD Not Otherwise Specified (Including Atypical Autism)
Attention-Deficit and Disruptive Behavior Disorders
Attention-Deficit/Hyperactivity Disorder/Oppositional Defiant Disorder/Conduct Disorder
Feeding and Eating Disorders of Infancy or Early Childhood
Pica/Rumination Disorder/Feeding Disorder of Infancy or Early Childhood
Tic Disorders
Tourette's Disorder/Chronic Motor or Vocal Tic Disorder/Transient Tic Disorder
Elimination Disorders
Encopresis/Enuresis (Not Due to a Medical Condition)
Other Disorders of Infancy, Childhood, or Adolescence
Separation Anxiety Disorder/Selective Mutism (Elective Mutism) / Reactive Attachment Disorder of Infancy or Early Childhood/ Stereotypic Movement Disorder (Stereotypy/Habit Disorder)

Delirium, Dementia, Amnestic and Other Cognitive Disorders

Deliria
Delirium Due to a General Medical Condition/Substance-Induced Delirium/Delirium Due to Multiple Etiologies
Dementias
Dementia of the Alzheimer's Type; With Early Onset: if onset at age 65 or below; With Late Onset; if onset after age 65/Vascular Dementia/Dementias Due to Other General Medical Conditions/ Substance-Induced Persisting Dementia/Dementia Due to Multiple Etiologies
Amnestic Disorders
Amnestic Disorder Due to a General Medical Condition/Substance-Induced Persisting Amnestic Disorder (refer to specific Substance for code)

Substance-Related Disorders

Alcohol Use Disorders
Amphetamine (or Related Substance) Use Disorders
Caffeine Use Disorders
Cannabis Use Disorders
Cocaine Use Disorders
Hallucinogen Use Disorders
Inhalant Use Disorders
Nicotine Use Disorders
Opioid Use Disorders
Phencyclidine (or Related Substance) Use Disorders
Sedative, Hypnotic, or Anxiolytic Substance Use Disorders
Polysubstance Use Disorder

Schizophrenia and Other Psychotic Disorders

Schizophrenia
Paranoid Type/Disorganized Type/Catatonic Type/Undifferentiated Type/Residual Type
Schizophreniform Disorder
Schizoaffective Disorder
Delusional Disorder
Brief Psychotic Disorder
Shared Psychotic Disorder (Folie à Deux)
Psychotic Disorder Due to a General Medical Condition
With Delusions/With Hallucinations/Substance-Induced Psychotic Disorder
Psychotic Disorder Not Otherwise Specified

Mood Disorders

Depressive Disorders
Major Depressive Disorder/Dysthymic Disorder/Depressive Disorder Not Otherwise Specified
Bipolar Disorders
Bipolar I Disorder/Bipolar II Disorder (Recurrent Major Depressive Episodes with Hypomania)/Cyclothymic Disorder/Bipolar Disorder Not Otherwise Specified/
Mood Disorder Due to a General Medical Condition
Substance-Induced Mood Disorder
Mood Disorder Not Otherwise Specified

Anxiety Disorders

Panic Disorder
Without Agoraphobia/With Agoraphobia
Agoraphobia without History of Panic Disorder
Specific Phobia (Simple Phobia)
Social Phobia (Social Anxiety Disorder)
Obsessive-Compulsive Disorder
Posttraumatic Stress Disorder
Acute Stress Disorder
Generalized Anxiety Disorder (Includes Overanxious Disorder of Childhood)
Anxiety Disorder Due to a General Medical Condition
Substance-Induced Anxiety Disorder
Anxiety Disorder Not Otherwise Specified

CONTINUED

DSM-IV-TR Classification CONTINUED

Somatoform Disorders
Somatization Disorder
Conversion Disorder
Hypochondriasis
Body Dysmorphic Disorder
Pain Disorder
Somatoform Disorder Not Otherwise Specified
Undifferentiated Somatoform Disorder

Factitious Disorders
Factitious Disorder
Factitious Disorder Not Otherwise Specified

Dissociative Disorders
Dissociative Amnesia
Dissociative Fugue
Dissociative Identity Disorder (Multiple Personality Disorder)
Depersonalization Disorder
Dissociative Disorder Not Otherwise Specified

Sexual and Gender Identity Disorders
Sexual Dysfunctions
Sexual Desire Disorders: Hypoactive Sexual Desire Disorder; Sexual Aversion Disorder/Sexual Arousal Disorders: Female Sexual Arousal Disorder; Male Erectile Disorder/Orgasm Disorders: Female Orgasmic Disorder (Inhibited Female Orgasm); Male Orgasmic Disorder (Inhibited Male Orgasm); Premature Ejaculation/Sexual Pain Disorders: Dyspareunia; Vaginismus/Sexual Dysfunctions Due to a General Medical Condition/Substance-Induced Sexual Dysfunction
Paraphilias
Exhibitionism /Fetishism/Frotteurism /Pedophilia/Sexual Masochism/Sexual Sadism/Voyeurism/Transvestic Fetishism
Gender Identity Disorders
Gender Identity Disorder: in Children/in Adolescents and Adults (Transsexualism)

Eating Disorders
Anorexia Nervosa
Bulimia Nervosa
Eating Disorder Not Otherwise Specified

Sleep Disorders
Primary Sleep Disorders
Dyssomnias: Primary Insomnia; Primary Hypersomnia; Narcolepsy; Breathing-Related Sleep Disorder; Circadian Rhythm Sleep Disorder (Sleep-Wake Schedule Disorder) /Parasomnias; Nightmare Disorder (Dream Anxiety Disorder); Sleep Terror Disorder; Sleepwalking Disorder/Sleep Disorders Related to Another Mental Disorder
Sleep Disorder Due to a General Medical Condition
Substance-Induced Sleep Disorder
Impulse Control Disorders Not Elsewhere Classified
Intermittent Explosive Disorder
Kleptomania
Pyromania
Pathological Gambling
Trichotillomania
Impulse-Control Disorder Not Otherwise Specified

Adjustment Disorder
Adjustment Disorder
With Anxiety
With Depressed Mood
With Disturbance of Conduct
With Mixed Disturbance of Emotions and Conduct
With Mixed Anxiety and Depressed Mood
Unspecified

Other Conditions That May Be a Focus of Clinical Attention
Psychological Factors Affecting Medical Condition
Medication-Induced Movement Disorders
Relational Problems
Relational Problem Related to a Mental Disorder or General Medical Condition/Parent-Child Relational Problem/Partner Relational Problem/Sibling Relational Problem
Problems Related to Abuse or Neglect
Physical Abuse of Child/Sexual Abuse of Child/Neglect of Child/ Physical Abuse of Adult/Sexual Abuse of Adult
Additional Conditions That May Be a Focus of Clinical Attention
Bereavement/Borderline Intellectual Functioning/Academic Problem/Occupational Problem/Childhood or Adolescent Antisocial Behavior/Adult Antisocial Behavior/Malingering Phase of Life Problem/Noncompliance With Treatment for a Mental Disorder/Identity Problem/Religious or Spiritual Problem/ Acculturation Problem/Age-Associated Memory Decline

AXIS II

Personality Disorders
Paranoid Personality Disorder
Schizoid Personality Disorder
Schizotypal Personality Disorder
Antisocial Personality Disorder
Borderline Personality Disorder
Histrionic Personality Disorder
Narcissistic Personality Disorder
Avoidant Personality Disorder
Dependent Personality Disorder
Obsessive-Compulsive Personality Disorder

Mental Retardation
Mild Mental Retardation/Moderate Mental Retardation/Severe Mental Retardation/Profound Mental Retardation